1 MONTH OF
FREE
READING

at

www.ForgottenBooks.com

By purchasing this book you are eligible for one month membership to ForgottenBooks.com, giving you unlimited access to our entire collection of over 1,000,000 titles via our web site and mobile apps.

To claim your free month visit:

ISBN 978-0-260-69938-1
PIBN 10964952

SESSIONAL PAPERS.

VOL. XLIV.—PART XIII.

FIRST SESSION

OF THE

THIRTEENTH LEGISLATURE

OF THE

PROVINCE OF ONTARIO.

SESSION 1912.

TORONTO:
Printed and[Published by L. K. CAMERON, Printer to the King's Most Excellent Majesty
1912

Printed by
WILLIAM BRIGGS,
29-37 Richmond Street West,
TORONTO

LIST OF SESSIONAL PAPERS

TITLE.	No.	REMARKS.
English-French Schools, Merchant's Report	62	*Printed for Distribution.*
Entomological Society, Report	36	*Printed.*
Estimates	2	"
Factories, Report	45	*Printed.*
Farmers' Institutes, Report	40	"
Feeble-Minded, Report	23	"
Fruit Branch, Report	33	
Fruit-Growers' Report	32	
Game and Fisheries, Report	13	*Printed.*
Game and Fisheries Commission, Report	52	"
Government Employees, Interference in Elections	72	*Not Printed.*
Hardy, Judge, Commutation	63	*Not Printed.*
Health, Report	20	*Printed.*
Highways, Permanent, Correspondence *re* Construction	74	*Not Printed.*
Highways, Improvement, Report	14	*Printed.*
Horticultural Societies, Report	42	"
Hospitals and Charities, Report	24	"
Hydro-Electric Power Commission, Report	47	"
Idiots and Epileptics, Report	22	*Printed.*
Industries Report	44	"
Infant Mortality, Report	60	"
Insane Hospitals, Report	21	"
Insurance, Report	10	
James Bay Surveys, Report	70	*Printed for Distribution.*
Judicature Act, Commutation	63	*Not Printed.*
Labour, Report	15	*Printed.*
Lands, Forests and Mines, Report	3	"
Legal Offices, Report	6	"
Library, Report	51	*Not Printed.*
Liquor License Acts, Report	27	*Printed.*
Liquor, Illegal Sale of, Prosecutions for	55	*Not Printed.*
Live Stock Associations, Report	39	*Printed.*
Loan Corporations, Statements	11	"
Mines, Report	4	*Printed.*
Municipal Auditor, Provincial, Report	8	"

TITLE.	No.	REMARKS.
Ne Temere Decree, Questions	58	Not Printed.
Northern Ontario, Prosecutions in	55	"
Ontario and Manitoba Boundary, Order-in-Council	59	Not Printed. .
Ontario and Manitoba Boundary, Correspondence	54	Printed.
Ontario Railway and Municipal Board, Report	48	"
Political Contests, Official Interference in	72	Not Printed.
Provincial Municipal Auditor, Report	8	Printed.
Printing Paper Agreements	66 67 68	..
Prisons and Reformatories, Report	25	"
Psychiatry in Ontario, Bulletin	69	Printed for Distribution.
Public Accounts	1	Printed.
Public Works, Report	12	"
Queen Victoria Niagara Falls Park, Report	9	Printed.
Railway and Municipal Board, Report	48	Printed.
Registrar-General, Report	19	"
Registry Offices, Report	7	"
Sarnia, Typhoid Fever in, Cause of	71	Printed.
Secretary and Registrar, Report	18	"
Springer Township, Teaching French in, etc.	78	Not Printed.
Statutes, Distribution of	73	"
Statute Revision, Payments made	77	"
Subject, Charles, Correspondence	61	"
Surrogate Court, Orders-in-Council	56	
Temiskaming and N. O. Railway, Report	46	Printed.
Temiskaming and N. O. Railway, Running Rights over, etc.	64	Not Printed.
Temiskaming and N. O. Railway, Elk Lake Branch	76	"
Timber Limits, Number of Sales of, since 1905	79	"
Toronto University, Report	17	Printed.
Typhoid Fever in Sarnia	71	"
Vegetable Growers' Association, Report	34	Printed.
Veterinary College, Report	30	"
Women's Institutes, Report	41	Printed.

LIST OF SESSIONAL PAPERS

Arranged in Numerical Order with their Titles at full
length ; the dates when presented to the Legislature ;
the name of the Member who moved the same,
and whether ordered to be Printed or not.

CONTENTS OF PART IV.

No. 11   Financial Statements made by Loan Corporations, Building Societies, Loaning Land Companies and Trust Companies, for the year 1911. Presented to the Legislature, 1st March, 1912. *Printed.*

No. 12   Report of the Minister of Public Works of the Province, for the year 1911. Presented to the Legislature, 1st March, 1912. *Printed.*

No. 13   Report of the Game and Fisheries Department, for the year 1911. Presented to the Legislature, 1st March, 1912. *Printed.*

CONTENTS OF PART V.

No. 14   Report on Highway Improvement in the Province, for the year 1911. Presented to the Legislature, 3rd April, 1912. *Printed.*

No. 15   Report of the Bureau of Labour, for the year 1911. Presented to the Legislature, 11th April, 1912. *Printed.*

CONTENTS OF PART VI.

No. 16   Report of the Minister of Education, for the year 1911. Presented to the Legislature, 1st March, 1912. *Printed.*

No. 17   Report of the Board of Governors of the University of Toronto, for the year ending 30th June, 1911. Presented to the Legislature, 22nd February, 1912. *Printed.*

CONTENTS OF PART VII.

No. 18   Report of the Secretary and Registrar of the Province, for the year 1911. Presented to the Legislature, 2nd April, 1912. *Printed.*

No. 19   Report upon the Registration of Births, Marriages and Deaths, for the year 1910-11. Presented to the Legislature, 1st March, 1912. *Printed.*

No. 20   Report of the Provincial Board of Health, for the year 1911. Presented to the Legislature, 1st March, 1912. *Printed.*

No. 21   Report on the Hospitals for the Insane, for the year 1911. Presented to the Legislature, 18th March, 1912. *Printed.*

No. 22   Report on the Hospitals for Idiots and Epileptics, for the year 1911. Presented to the Legislature, 18th March, 1912. *Printed.*

CONTENTS OF PART VIII.

CONTENTS OF PART IX.

CONTENTS OF PART X.

CONTENTS OF PART XI.

CONTENTS OF PART XII.

CONTENTS OF PART XIII.

No. 50 | Report of the Archivist of Ontario. Presented to the Legislature, 3rd April, 1912. *Printed.*

No. 51 | Report on the State of the Legislative Library. Presented to the Legislature, 8th February, 1912. *Not Printed.*

No. 52 | Report of the Game and Fisheries Commission, for 1909-11. Presented to the Legislature, 2nd April, 1912. *Printed.*

CONTENTS OF PART XIV.

No. 53 | Statements of Provincial Auditor under Audit Acts. Presented to the Legislature, 26th March, 1912. *Printed.*

No. 54 | Return to an Address to His Honour the Lieutenant-Governor of the Fourteenth day of February, 1912, praying that he will cause to be laid before this House a Return of copies of—

1. All correspondence which has passed since the 1st day of August, 1908, between the Government of the Province of Ontario or any member thereof or any person on its behalf, and the Government of the Dominion of Canada, or any member thereof or any person on its behalf, in reference to the Boundary between the Provinces of Ontario and Manitoba, through the territory now known as the District of Keewatin.

2. All correspondence which has passed since the 1st day of August, 1908, between the Government of the Province of Ontario or any member thereof or any person on its behalf, and the Government of the Province of Manitoba or any member thereof or any person on its behalf, in reference to the boundary between the Province of Ontario and Manitoba through the territory now known as the District of Keewatin.

3. All other papers in the possession of the Government in reference to the said boundary, including all reports in the possession of the Government in reference to the character and resources of the territory now known as the District of Keewatin. Presented to the Legislature, 20th February, 1912. *Mr. Rowell. Printed for Distribution.*

No. 55 | Return to an Order of the House of the Fourteenth day of February, 1912, shewing—

1. What prosecutions have been instituted against parties in Northern Ontario for the illegal sale of liquor in Northern Ontario during the calendar year 1911.

2. The result of such prosecutions.

3. What amount the Government has received during the calendar year 1911 by way of fines imposed for the illegal sale of liquor in Northern Ontario. Presented to the Legislature, 20th February, 1912. *Mr. McDonald. Not Printed.*

No. 56   Copies of Orders-in-Council in accordance with the provisions of s-s. 6 of s. 78 of the Surrogate Courts Act. Presented to the Legislature, 22nd February, 1912. *Not Printed.*

No. 57   Copies of Orders-in-Council and Regulations required by section 27 of the Department of Education Act. Presented to the Legislature, 22nd February, 1912. *Not Printed.*

No. 58   Copy of Questions submitted to the Supreme Court, by the Government of Canada, relative to the *Ne Temere* decree and an Act to amend the Marriage Act. Presented to the Legislature, 27th February, 1912. *Not Printed.*

No. 59   Copy of an Order-in-Council of the Government of Canada, respecting the Boundary Line between Ontario and Manitoba. Presented to the Legislature, 27th February, 1912. *Not Printed.*

No. 60   Report upon Infant Mortality in the Province. (*Not Presented.*)

No. 61   Return to an Order of the House of the 23rd of February, 1912, for a Return of all correspondence from August, 1st, 1911, to date, between the Attorney-General or any official of his Department and any person or persons of the Town of Chesley or elsewhere, respecting the prosecution, conviction and fining of one Charles Subject by Magistrate Montgomery for an infringement of the provisions of the Liquor License Act. Presented to the Legislature, 1st March, 1912. *Mr. McDonald. Not Printed.*

No. 62   Merchant's report on the condition of English-French Schools in the Province. Presented to the Legislature, 6th March, 1912. *Printed for Distribution.*

No. 63   Copy of an Order-in-Council increasing the commutation paid to His Honour A. D. Hardy, Judge of the County Court of Brant. Presented to the Legislature, 13th March, 1912. *Not Printed.*

No. 64   Return to an Order of the House of the Twenty-sixth day of February, 1912, for a Return of copies of: 1. All correspondence between the Government or any member or official thereof or the Temiskaming and Northern Ontario Railway Commission or any member or official thereof and the Grand Trunk Pacific Railway Company or the Grand Trunk Railway or any official of either of them with respect to.

(a) The acquisition of running rights over the Temiskaming and Northern Ontario Railway;

(b) The leasing, running, or operating of dining, cafe, or buffet cars on the tracks of the Temiskaming and Northern Ontario Railway.

2. All agreements between the Government of Ontario or any department thereof or the Temiskaming and Northern Ontario Railway Commission and any other person or corporation with respect to:

(a) The acquisition of running rights over the Temiskaming and Northern Ontario Railway;

(b) The leasing, running, or operating of dining, cafe, or buffet cars on the tracks of the Temiskaming and Northern Ontario Railway. Presented to the Legislature, 19th March, 1912. *Mr. Rowell. Not Printed.*

No. 65   Interim Report on Laws, relating to the liability of employers to make compensation to their employees for injuries received in the course of their employment which are in force in other countries and as to how far such laws are found to work satisfactorily. Presented to the Legislature, 29th March, 1912. *Printed.*

No. 66   Agreement made by and between the Kinleith Paper Company, Limited, of the first part, and His Majesty the King, represented by the Honourable the Treasurer, of the second part, conditioned for the supply of printing paper for the use of the Province. Presented to the Legislature, 20th of March, 1912. *Printed.*

No. 67   Agreement made by and between the Montrose Paper Mills, Limited, of the first part and His Majesty the King, represented by the Honourable the Treasurer, of the second part, conditioned for the supply of printing paper for the use of the Province. Presented to the Legislature, 20th March, 1912. *Printed.*

No. 68   Agreement made by and between the Georgetown Coated Paper Mills, Limited, of the first part, and His Majesty the King, represented by the Honourable the Treasurer, of the second part, conditioned for the supply of printing paper for the use of the Province. Presented to the Legislature, 20th March, 1912. *Printed.*

No. 69   Bulletin of the Ontario Hospitals for the Insane in the interests of Psychiatry. Presented to the Legislature, 21st March, 1912. *Printed for Distribution.*

No. 70   Report on James Bay Survey Explorations, Cochrane to James Bay, June 9th to September 12th, 1911. Presented to the Legislature, 21st March, 1912. *Printed for Distribution.*

No. 71   Report of special investigation into the cause of Typhoid Fever in the Town of Sarnia. Presented to the Legislature, 21st March, 1912. *Printed.*

No. 72   A Return to an Order of the House of the 14th February, 1912, for a Return shewing: 1. All complaints received by the Government since the first day of January, 1911, in reference to the participation of any officers, officials or employees of the Government in political contests or taking part in political matters in this Province.

2. All correspondence arising out of or incidental to such complaints.

3. All correspondence passing between the Government or any Department or Member thereof and any officer, officials, or employees of the Government with reference to the participation of such officers, officials or employees in political contests or taking part in political matters in this Province since the first day of January, 1911. Presented to the Legislature, 22nd March, 1912. *Mr. Mageau. Not Printed.*

No. 73   Statement of the distribution of Revised and Sessional Statutes. Presented to the Legislature, 25th March, 1912. *Not Printed.*

No. 74   Return to an Address to His Honour the Lieutenant-Governor of the 14th February, 1912, praying that he will cause to be laid before this House a Return of copies of all correspondence between the Government of the Province of Ontario or any member thereof, or any person on its behalf, and the Government of the Dominion of Canada, or any member thereof, or any person on its behalf, with reference to the construction of permanent highways in the Province or grants to aid in such construction. Presented to the Legislature, 26th March, 1912. *Mr. Ferguson (Kent). Not Printed.*

No. 75   Return to an Order of the House of the 27th February, 1912, showing:—1. How many barrels of apples were produced in each year in each of the 45 Demonstration Orchards instituted by the Government. 2. What was the sale price *per* barrel of the apples from each of the said Demonstration Orchards. 3. What are the names and qualifications of the several orchard demonstrators now in the employ of the Government. Presented to the Legislature, 26th March, 1912. *Mr. Anderson (Bruce). Not Printed.*

No. 76   Return to an Order of the House of the 8th March, 1912, for a Return of copies of all correspondence between any person and the Government or any member thereof with respect to the construction of a Branch of the Temiskaming and Northern Ontario Railway to Elk Lake or further, with memorandum of dates upon which delegations waited upon the Government or any member thereof in support of the construction of the said Branch; also all surveyors' or other reports received by the Government with respect to the feasibility and cost of construction of the said Branch and all other papers or documents bearing upon the question of the construction of the said Branch. Presented to the Legislature, 27th March, 1912. *Mr. Mageau.* *Not Printed.*

No. 77   Return to an Order of the House of the 23rd February, 1912, for a Return shewing: The names of all persons to whom payments have been made in connection with the present Revision of the Statutes, and the total amount paid to each, and the services or other matter in respect of which such payments were made. Presented to the Legislature, 29th March, 1912. *Mr. Proudfoot.* *Not Printed.*

No. 78   Return to an Order of the House of the 15th March, 1912, for a Return of copies of all correspondence since the first day of January, 1911, between the Minister of Education, the Deputy-Minister of Education or any Official of the Department of Education and any School Trustee, Board of Trustees, or any person in the Township of Springer, with respect to the character of teaching in the Schools of the said Township, with respect to the teaching of French in the said Schools, with respect to the employment of teachers in the said Schools, or with respect to the giving or withholding of grants from the said Schools or any of them. Presented to the Legislature, 1st April, 1912. *Mr. Marshall.* *Not Printed.*

No. 79   Return to an Order of the House of the 28th day of February, 1911, for a Return shewing: (a) The number of sales of timber limits which have taken place in each year since 1905; (b) The location and acreage of each limit sold; and (c) The name of the purchaser in each case; (d) The price paid per acre, or otherwise, in each case; (e) The berth, or area of each berth, which had been under permit previous to the sale, with the original date of the permit; (f) The area of each berth damaged by fire previous to the sale; (g) The berth, or berths, which were virgin territory; (h) The reasons which caused each timber sale to be held from 1905 down to date; (i) The number of permits to cut timber current in the season of 1904-5; the number of permits to cut timber current in the season of 1910-11. Presented to the Legislature, 3rd April, 1912. *Mr. MacKay.* *Not Printed.*

No. 80   Report of Proceedings of the Twelfth Canadian Conference of Charities and Correction. Presented to the Legislature, 10th April, 1912. *Printed for Distribution.*

No. 81   Report of the Sixth Annual Meeting of the Canadian Hospital Association. Presented to the Legislature, 10th April, 1912. *Printed for Distribution.*

No. 82   Return to an Order of the House of the 14th February, 1912, for a Return of copies of all correspondence passing in the years 1905 and 1906 between the Attorney-General or any officer or official of his Department and Mr. J. W. Curry, K.C., Crown Attorney of the City of Toronto, or his successor, with reference to the prosecution of any alleged combines and all briefs, statements or other documents furnished by Mr. Curry to the Attorney-General or any officer or official of his Department with reference to any of the said alleged combines. Presented to the Legislature, 10th April, 1912. *Mr. Elliott. Not Printed.*

No. 83   Return to an Order of the House of the 9th April, 1912, for a Return of copies of (1) All correspondence between the Government or any Minister or Officer thereof and any person, association, board or organization whatsoever, between the 1st day of July, 1911, and the present date; and also (2) All protests, resolutions, objections or written statements of any kind whatsoever received by the Government or any Minister or Officer thereof, between the said dates with respect to: (*a*) The conduct of one S. J. Dempsey, in his official capacity as Police Magistrate or as Crown Lands Agent; (*b*) The participation of the said S. J. Dempsey in the Federal Election contest in South Renfrew; (*c*) The participation of the said S. J. Dempsey in the Provincial Election contests held in December, 1911. Presented to the Legislature, 12th April, 1912. *Mr. McQueen. Not Printed.*

⁻ RETURN FROM THE RECORDS

OF THE

GENERAL ELECTION

TO THE

LEGISLATIVE ASSEMBLY IN 1911

HELD ON 4th AND 11th DECEMBER

SHEWING:

(1) The number of Votes Polled for each Candidate in each Electoral District in which there was a contest;
(2) The majority whereby each successful Candidate was returned;
(3) The total number of Votes Polled;
(4) The number of Votes remaining Unpolled;
(5) The number of names on the Polling Lists;
(6) The number of Ballot Papers sent out to each Polling Place;
(7) The Used Ballot Papers;
(8) The Unused Ballot Papers;
(9) The Rejected Ballot Papers;
(10) The Cancelled Ballot Papers;
(11) The Declined Ballot Papers; and
(12) The Ballot Papers taken from Polling Places.

PRINTED BY ORDER OF

THE LEGISLATIVE ASSEMBLY OF ONTARIO

TORONTO:

Printed and Published by L. K. CAMERON, Printer to the King's Most Excellent Majesty

1912.

LIST OF RETURNING OFFICERS AT GENERAL ELECTION, 1911.

Constituency.	Returning Officer.	Post Office.
1. Addington	Alfred M. Bell	Moscow.
2. Algoma	William Boyd	Thessalon.
3. Brant, North	John Jefferson	Paris.
4. Brant, South	Thomas Simpson Wade	Brantford.
5. Brockville	William Richardson	Brockville.
6. Bruce, Centre	Thomas E. Morgan	Ripley.
7. Bruce, North	John Kennedy Davidson	Allenford.
8. Bruce, South	James Andrew Lamb	Walkerton.
9. Carleton	Alexander Murphy	Antrim.
10. Dufferin	Robert Gallaugher	Perm.
11. Dundas	Robert H. Hogaboam	Cass Bridge.
12. Durham, East	Hugh Walker	Port Hope.
13. Durham, West	Joseph Pattinson	Bowmanville.
14. Elgin, East	Henry T. Godwin	Bayham.
15. Elgin, West	Leonard E. Gillett	St. Thomas.
16. Essex, North	Maxfield Sheppard	Windsor.
17. Essex, South	Walter H. Noble	Cottam.
18. Fort William	George H. Adair	Fort William.
19. Frontenac	George V. Stuart	Eric.
20. Glengarry	Alexander R. McDougall	Glen Norman.
21. Grenville	John Johnston	Merrickville.
22. Grey, Centre	Thomas Scott	McIntyre.
23. Grey, North	Allan Cameron Maitland	Owen Sound.
24. Grey, South	William B. Vollett	Durham.
25. Haldimand	Henry B. Sawle	Caledonia.
26. Halton	John M. Bastedo	Milton.
27. Hamilton, East	Ernest Edward Linger	Hamilton.
28. Hamilton, West	William Henry Childs	Hamilton.
29. Hastings, East	Good McKinney Campbell	Corbyville.
30. Hastings, North	William J. Douglas	Greenview.
31. Hastings, West	William Parker Hudson	Belleville.
32. Huron, Centre	Michael Broderick	Seaforth.
33. Huron, North	Peter W. Scott	Belgrave.
34. Huron, South	Thomas B. Carling	Exeter.
35. Kenora	Charles Wiggins Belyea	Kenora.
36. Kent, East	William Edmund Bottoms	Ridgetown.
37. Kent, West	John R. Gemmill	Chatham.
38. Kingston	J. B. Walkem	Kingston.
39. Lambton, East	William English	Inwood.
40. Lambton, West	James Flintoft	Sarnia.
41. Lanark, North	James Wesley Wilson	Carleton Place.
42. Lanark, South	William James Pink	Perth.
43. Leeds	Joseph De Wolfe	Gananoque.
44. Lennox	James Reid	Napanee.
45. Lincoln	Henry O'Loughlin	St. Catharines.
46. London	Edward Herbert Johnston	London.
47. Manitoulin	Albert E. Graham	Gore Bay.
48. Middlesex, East	William E. Wright	Glanworth.
49. Middlesex, North	Walter Bolton	Crathie.
50. Middlesex, West	David James Donaldson	Strathroy.
51. Monck	Jacob Fretz	South Pelham.
52. Muskoka	William Mayhew	Huntsville.
53. Nipissing	William Martin, the younger	North Bay.
54. Norfolk, North	Frederick Samuel Snider	Simcoe.
55. Norfolk, South	Samuel H. Harding	Port Rowan.
56. Northumberland, East	Albert Lyman Boyce	Dartford.
57. Northumberland, West	John Grandy Nicholls	Coburg.
58. Ontario, North	John Blanchard	Leaskdale.
59. Ontario, South	William Morcomb Real	Greenbank.
60. Ottawa, East	C. S. O. Boudreault	Ottawa.
61. Ottawa, West	Charles L. Bray	Ottawa.

LIST OF RETURNING OFFICERS AT GENERAL ELECTION, 1911.—Continued.

Constituency.	Returning Officer.	Post Office.
62. Oxford, North	Wesley S. West	Woodstock.
63. Oxford, South	Thomas Wells	Ingersoll.
64. Parry Sound	Alexander Logan	Parry Sound.
65. Peel	Thomas H. Goodison	Streetsville.
66. Perth, North	Thomas Magwood	Stratford.
67. Perth, South	H. Fred. Sharpe	St. Mary's.
68. Peterborough, East	S. P. Ford	Norwood.
69. Peterborough, West	James Albro Hall	Peterborough.
70. Porth Arthur	James Hartley Woodside	Port Arthur.
71. Prescott	Eden Abbot Johnson	L'Orignal.
72. Prince Edward	Charles Ferguson Vandusen	Picton.
73. Rainy River	Walter John Keating	Fort Frances.
74. Renfrew, North	Andrew Johnson	Pembroke.
75. Renfrew, South	George Eady	Renfrew.
76. Russell	J. L. Rolston	Metcalfe.
77. Sault Ste. Marie	Henry James Moorhouse	Sault Ste. Marie.
78. Simcoe, Centre	John Switzer	New Lowell.
79. Simcoe, East	John Hugh Hammond	Orillia.
80. Simcoe, South	Richard J. Hill	Thornton.
81. Simcoe, West	William Matthew Lockhart	Alliston.
82. Stormont	Albert Sheek Hodgins	Osnabruck, Centre.
83. Sturgeon Falls	Jules Albert Phillion	Sturgeon Falls.
84. Sudbury	Alexander Irving	Sudbury.
85. Temiskaming	C. W. Hæntschel	Haileybury.
86. Toronto, E., Seat "A"	}William Temple Stewart	Toronto.
87. Toronto, E., Seat "B"		
88. Toronto, N., Seat "A"	}William Richard Cavell	Toronto.
89. Toronto, N., Seat "B"		
90. Toronto, S., Seat "A"	}W. H. Smith	Toronto.
91. Toronto, S., Seat "B"		
92. Toronto, W., Seat "A"	}Thomas Hurst	Toronto.
93. Toronto, W., Seat "B"		
94. Victoria, East	Isaac Naylor	Islay.
95. Victoria, West	John Jackson	Lindsay.
96. Waterloo, North	George Davidson	Berlin.
97. Waterloo, South	William R. Plum	New Hamburg.
98. Welland	Menno House	Bridgeburg.
99. Wellington, East	Sem Wissler	Elora.
100. Wellington, South	William Wallace White	Guelph.
101. Wellington, West	George M. Fox	Drayton.
102. Wentworth, North	William McDonald	Rockton.
103. Wentworth, South	Robert H. Lewis	Hamilton.
104. York, East	Thomas Gordon Paterson	Coleman.
105. York, North	William James Stevenson	Aurora.
106. York, West	Samuel Ryding	West Toronto.

STATEMENT of Votes Polled, Number of Polling Booths, and Number of Votes on Voters'
Lists at General Election held on 4th and 11th days of December, 1911.

Legislature d ssolved on Monday, November 13th, 1911.

Constituency.	No. of Polling Booths.	No. of Votes Polled.	No. of Voters on Polling Lists
1. Addington	*By Acclama tion		
2. Algoma	54	2,785	5,638
3. Brant, North	31	3,268	4,765
4. Brant, South	35	6,018	7,899
5. Brockville	35	3,972	5,430
6. Bruce, Centre	30	3,350	4,255
7. Bruce, North	51	3,973	5,474
8. Bruce, South	37	3,483	4,578
9. Carleton	40	2,240	2,550
10. Dufferin	41	3,484	5,633
11. Dundas	35	3,564	5,215
12. Durham, East	*By Acclama tion		
13. Durham, West	28	2,880	3,518
14. Elgin, East	29	3,673	5,343
15. Elgin, West	44	5,108	8,585
16. Essex, North	64	6,091	11,268
17. Essex, South	48	5,200	6,965
18. Fort William	62	3,151	6,111
19. Frontenac	58	2,661	4,510
20. Glengarry	33	3,712	5,496
21. Grenville	†40	3,823	5,633
22. Grey, Centre	53	3,286	6,051
23. Grey, North	69	6,529	9,141
24. Grey, South	41	4,199	6,035
25. Haldimand	35	3,423	4,414
26. Halton	35	4,438	6,333
27. Hamilton, East	49	6,363	10,170
28. Hamilton, West	39	3,743	7,688
29. Hastings, East	†38	3,564	5,269
30. Hastings, North	†42	3,401	5,878
31. Hastings, West	†26	3,591	5,060
32. Huron, Centre	41	4,080	5,301
33. Huron, North	41	4,153	5,143
34. Huron, South	44	4,243	5,140
35. Kenora	45	1,912	4,168
36. Kent, East	49	4,692	6,682
37. Kent, West	67	5,345	9,630
38. Kingston	†26	4,066	4,819
39. Lambton, East	50	4,276	5,461
40. Lambton, West	82	6,908	10,178
41. Lanark, North	†33	3,563	4,530
42. Lanark, South	*By Acclama tion		
43. Leeds	37	3,828	5,338
44. Lennox	25	2,821	3,710
45. Lincoln	†48	5,814	8,028
46. London	†51	8,765	11,806
47. Manitoulin	31	1,679	4,348
48. Middlesex, East	45	4,053	5,881
49. Middlesex, North	40	3,947	5,255
50. Middlesex, West	33	2,952	4,051
51. Monck	38	3,637	4,795
52. Muskoka	58	2,530	5,561
53. Nipissing	56	2,792	5,623
54. Norfolk, North	29	3,185	4,272
55. Norfolk, South	27	2,497	3,753
56. Northumberland, East	39	3,622	5,861
57. Northumberland, West	30	2,997	3,778

* No figures available. Acclamation in 1908 as well.
† These figures are for 1908. By acclamation in 1911.

STATEMENT of Votes Polled, Number of Polling Booths, and Number of Votes on Voters' Lists at General Election held on 4th and 11th days of December 1911.—*Continued.*

Constituency.	No.of Polling Booths.	No. of Votes Polled.	No. of Voters on Polling Lists
58. Ontario, North.	46	3,445	4,700
59. Ontario, South	49	4,930	6,705
60. Ottawa, East.	36	4,409	7,357
61. Ottawa, West.	76	6,694	13,915
62. Oxford, North.	49	4,742	7.008
63. Oxford, South.	41	4,742	6,468
64. Parry Sound	74	3,361	9.447
65. Peel.	40	4,728	6,702
66. Perth, North.	57	6,674	8,684
67. Perth, South.	40	4,703	5,862
68. Peterborough, East.	39	2,775	4,485
69. Peterborough, West.	51	2,867	7,597
70. Port Arthur	59	2,088	4,968
71. Prescott.	40	3,668	6,168
72. Prince Edward.	38	3,985	5,278
73. Rainy River.	47	1,974	3,685
74. Renfrew, North.	†33	4,350	5,616
75. Renfrew, South.	†48	5,007	7,047
76. Russell.	60	4.740	8,690
77. Sault Ste Marie.	†33	2,571	4,771
78. Simcoe, Centre.	36	3,487	5,289
79. Simcoe, East.	55	5,877	9,062
80. Simcoe, South	*By Acclamation....		
81. Simcoe, West	†38	2,938	5,942
82. Stormont.	45	4,273	6,774
83. Sturgeon Falls.	30	1,623	2,452
84. Sudbury.	74	3,688	12,841
85. Temiskaming	87	4,542	11,307
86. Toronto, East—Seat "A".	89	4,236	13,208
87. Toronto, East—Seat "B".	89	4,338	13,208
88. Toronto, North—Seat "A".	103	6,478	14,421
89. Toronto, North—Seat "B"	103	7,118	14,421
90. Toronto, South—Seat "A"	97	3,364	11,465
91. Toronto, South—Seat "B"	97	3,356	11,465
92. Toronto, West—Seat "A"	165	7,203	23,572
93. Toronto, West—Seat "B"	165	6,974	23,572
94. Victoria, East.	*By Acclamation....		
94½. Victoria, East, By-Election.	‡49	1,874	5,383
95. Victoria, West.	32	3 662	5,405
96. Waterloo, North.	49	6,414	9,220
97. Waterloo, South.	42	5,125	8,638
98. Welland.	62	6.217	10,173
99. Wellington, East	37	3,527	4.888
100. Wellington, South.	42	5,374	7,452
101. Wellington, North.	31	3,431	4,460
102. Wentworth, North.	28	3,441	4,210
103. Wentworth, South.	32	3,134	4.978
104. York, East.	64	3,892	9,396
105. York, North.	40	5,553	6,226
106. York, West.	72	4,369	11,106

* No figures available. Acclamation in 1908 as well.
† These figures are for 1908. Acclamation in 1911.   ‡ In May 1909.

CONSTITUENCIES IN WHICH REGISTRATION WAS HELD IN 1908.

City or Town.	Vote Registered.	Chairman of Board.
1. Belleville	678	Judge Fralick.
2. Berlin	752	Judge Chisholm.
3. Brantford	1,671	Pol. Mag. Livingstone.
4. Chatham	836	Judge Bell.
5. Fort William	966	Pol. Mag. Palling.
6. Guelph	1,435	Judge Chadwick.
7. Hamilton	6,050	Judge Snider.
8. Kingston	1,537	Judge Price.
9. London	2,625	Judge Macbeth.
10. Niagara Falls	627	Pol. Mag. Cruickshank.
11. Ottawa	5,679	Judge MacTavish.
12. Peterborough	1,320	Judge Weller.
13. Port Arthur	1,164	Judge O'Leary.
14. St. Catharines	834	Judge Carman.
15. St. Thomas	1,030	Judge Ermatinger.
16. Stratford	970	Judge Barron.
17. Toronto	16,034	Judge Morson.
18. Toronto, West	556	Judge Morgan.
19. Windsor	629	Judge McHugh.
20. Woodstock	554	Judge Finkle.
Total	44,947	

CONSTITUENCIES IN WHICH REGISTRATION WAS HELD IN 1911.

City or Town.	Vote Registered.	Chairman of Board.
1. Belleville	384	Judge Fralick.
2. Berlin	839	Judge Chisholm.
3. Brantford	2,226	Pol. Mag. Livingstone
4. Brockville	619	Judge McDonald.
5. Chatham	486	Judge Dowlin.
6. Fort William	1,172	Pol. Mag. Palling.
7. Guelph	1,516	Judge Chadwick.
8. Hamilton	4,863	Judge Snider.
9. Kingston	1,233	Judge Price.
10. London	1,066	Judge Macbeth.
11. Niagara Falls	664	Pol. Mag. Fraser.
12. Ottawa	4,508	Judge MacTavish.
13. Owen Sound	577	Pol. Mag. Creasor.
14. Peterborough	1,443	Judge Huycke.
15. Port Arthur	710	Judge O'Leary.
16. St. Catharines	157	Judge Carman.
17. St. Thomas	733	Judge Ermatinger.
18. Sarnia	924	Judge MacWatt.
19. Sault Ste. Marie	429	Judge Stone.
20. Stratford	950	Judge Steele.
21. Toronto	12,458	Judge Morson.
22. Windsor	873	Judge McHugh.
23. Woodstock	584	Judge Finkle.
Total	39,414	

ARTHUR H. SYDERE,
Clerk of the Crown in Chancery.

SUMMARY OF VOTES CAST AT THE GENERAL ELECTION, HELD ON THE FOURTH
AND ELEVENTH DAYS OF DECEMBER, 1911.
Shewing the number of votes polled for each Candidate and the majority accorded to the one
elected in each Constituency in which there was a contest;

Constituency.	Candidates.	Votes counted.	Remarks.
1. Addington..	William David Black........	By acclamation.	
2. Algoma..............	Albert Grigg...............	1,723	
	Thomas G. Wigg......... ...	1,062	
	Majority for Grigg........	661	
3. Brant, North........	John Wesley Westbrook	1,722	
	James Rufus Layton........	1,546	
	Majority or Westbrook ...	176	
4. Brant, South	Willoughby Staples Brewster	3,201	
	Morgan E. Harris	2,817	
	Majority for Brewster	384	
5. Brockville	Albert Edward Donovan	2,090	
	George Edwin Smart........	1,641	
	Byron Wing...............	213	
	Majority for Donovan......	449	
6. Bruce, Centre........	William MacDonald........	1,727	
	William H. McFarline	1,623	
	Majority for MacDonald....	104	
7. Bruce, North........	Charles Martin Bowman.....	2,182	
	Harold Alva Vandusen.......	1,791	
	Majority for Bowman	391	
8. Bruce, South	John George Anderson.......	1,894	
	Robert Edwin Clapp........	1,589	
	Majority for Anderson.....	305	
9. Carleton	Robert Herbert McElroy	1,347	
	Clarke Craig...............	893	
	Majority for McElroy......	454	

SUMMARY OF RECAPITULATION.—*Continued.*

Constituency.	Candidates.	Votes counted.	Remarks.
10. Dufferin	Charles Robert McKeown.... Robert John Woods..........	1,880 1,604	
	Majority for McKeown	276	
11. Dundas	Hon. Sir James P. Whitney.. Robert Stewart Muir........	2,239 1,318	
	Majority for Whitney......	921	
12. Durham, East	Josiah Johnston Preston......	By acclamation.	
13. Durham, West......	John Henry Devitt .... Arthur Austin Powers.......	1,553 1,327	
	Majority for Devitt........	226	
14. Elgin, East	Charles Andrew Brower ..... Daniel McIntyre.............	2,127 1,546	
	· Majority for Brower	581	
15. Elgin, West	Finlay George Macdiarmid... Henry Stafford McDiarmid...	3,188 1,920	
	Majority for Macdiarmid ..	1,268	
16. Essex, North	Hon. Joseph Octave Reaume.. Severin Ducharme ....'...... John Robert Mason..........	2,586 2,533 972	
	Majority for Reaume......	53	On recount.
17. Essex, South	Charles N. Anderson........ Richard Ruddy Brett........	2,665 2,535	
	Majority for Anderson.....	130	
18. Fort William........	Charles W. Jarvis........... James Tonkin.............. Joseph Martin..............	1,363 1,109 659	
	Majority for Jarvis........	254	

SUMMARY OF RECAPITULATION.—*Continued.*

Constituency.	Candidates.	Votes counted.	Remarks.
19. Frontenac..........	Anthony McGuin Rankin .... J. P. MacInnes	1,641 1,020	
	Majority for Rankin.......	621	
20. Glengarry...........	Hugh Munro................ Donald M. Robertson.........	1,988 1.724	
	Majority for Munro	264	
21. Grenville...........	George Howard Ferguson....	By acclama- tion	
22. Grey, Centre	Hon. Isaac Benson Lucas..... Patrick McCullough	2,223 1,051	
	Majority for Lucas........	1.172	
23. Grey, North..........	Hon. Alex. Grant MacKay.... George Milward Boyd.........	3,635 2,894	
	Majority for MacKay......	741	
24. Grey, South..........	David Jamieson.............. William Calder.............	2,281 1,918	
	Majority for Jamieson......	363	
25. Haldimand..........	Christian Kohler............ William Jacques............	1,924 1,499	
	Majority for Kohler........	425	
26. Halton	Alfred Westland Nixon...... Robert Donald Warrin........	2,385 2,053	
	Majority for Nixon........	332	
27. Hamilton, East......	Allan Studholme............ William Henry Cooper.......	3,521 2,842	
	Majority for Studholme....	679	
28. Hamilton, West......	Hon. John Strathearn Hendrie James Russell..............	2,594 1,149	
	Majority for Hendrie......	1.445	
29. Hastings. East	Sandy Grant................	By acclama- tion.	

SUMMARY OF RECAPITULATION.—*Continued.*

Con tituency.	Candidates.	Votes counted.	Remarks.
30. Hastings, North......	Robert John Cook............	By acclamation.	
31. Hastings, West......	John Wesley Johnson........	By acclamation.	
32. Huron, Centre........	William Proudfoot..........	2,148	
	Joseph Elliott...............	1,932	
	Majority for Proudfoot....	216	
33. Huron, North........	Armstrong H. Musgrove......	2,210	
	William Henry Kerr.........	1.943	
	Majority for Musgrove.....	267	
34. Huron, South........	Henry Eilber.................	681	
	Edmund Zellar..............	402	
	Majority for Eilber........	279	
35. Kenora...............	HaroldArthur Clement Machin	1,179	
	John Thomas Brett..........	733	
	Majority for Machin.......	446	
36. Kent, East..........	Walter Renwick Ferguson....	2.452	
	Philip Henry Bowyer........	2.240	
	Majority for Ferguson......	212	
37. Kent, West..........	George William Sulman	3,106	
	Edwin Hea..................	2,239	
	Majority for Sulman.......	867	
38. Kingston.............	Arthur Edward Ross........	By acclamation.	
39. Lambton, East.......	Robert John McCormick......	2,170	
	J. B. Martyn...............	2,081	
	Majority for McCormick....	89	
40. Lambton, West......	Hon. William John Hanna....	3,969	
	William Anderson Henderson.	2,908	
	Majority for Hanna.........	1,061	
41. Lanark, North.......	Richard Franklin Preston.....	By acclamation.	

SUMMARY OF RECAPITULATIONN.—*Continued.*

Constituency.	Candidates.	Votes counted.	Remarks.
42. Lanark, South........	Hon. Arthur James Matheson.	By acclamation.	
43. Leeds	John Robertson Dargavel	1,995	
	William J. Wilson..........	1,833	
	Majority for Dargavel	162	
44. Lennox	Thomas George Carscallen...	1,450	
	Marshall Seymour Madole...	1,371	
	Majority for Carscallen ...	79	
45. Lincoln.............	Elisha Jessop	By acclamation.	
46. London	Hon. Adam Beck	By acclamation.	
47. Manitoulin..........	Robert Roswell Gamey	1,254	
	Robert Tilson..............	425	
	Majority for Gamey	829	
48. Middlesex. East.....	Robert Sutherland	2,039	
	George W. Neely	2,014	
	Majority for Sutherland...	25	
49. Middlesex, North....	Duncan MacArthur..........	1,991	
	John Grieve...............	1,956	
	Majority for MacArthur ...	35	
50. Middlesex, West	John Campbell Elliott	1,767	
	Neil A. Galbraith	1,185	
	Majority for Elliott.......	582	
51. Monck..............	Thomas Marshall	1,875	
	James Alway Ross	1,721	
	Majority for Marshall.....	154	

SUMMARY OF RECAPITULATIⁱᴼN.—*Continued.*

Constituency.	Candidates.	Votes counted.	Remarks.
52. Muskoka	Arthur Arnold Mahaffy...... John Galbraith.............	1,970 560	
	Majority for Mahaffy	1,410	
53. Nipissing	Henry Morel................ Robert Rankin.............	1,800 992	
	Majority for Morel........	808	
54. Norfolk, North......	Thomas Robert Atkinson .... William Murray McGuire....	1,740 1,412	
	Majority for Atkinson	328	
55. Norfolk, South......	Arthur Clarence Pratt ...... George Hammond .... Freeman Arthur Ravin......	1,423 1,046 28	Cornelius S. Killmaster nominated, but re-signed before ballots printed.
	Majority for Pratt	377	
56. Northumberland, E.	Samuel Greerson Murray Nesbitt................ Thomas James Atkinson.....	2,311 1,288	
	Majority for Nesbitt	1,023	
57. Northumberland, W.	Samuel Clarke.............. Hugh McCullough...........	1,615 1,382	
	Majority for Clarke	233	
58. Ontario, North......	William Henry Hoyle........ Peter McMillan............	1,971 1,474	
	Majority for Hoyle........	497	
59. Ontario, South	William Edmund Newton Sinclair .... Charles Calder.............	2,577 2,330	
	Majority for Sinclair......	247	

SUMMARY OF RECAPITULATION.—*Continued.*

Constituency.	Candidates.	Votes counted.	Remarks.
60. Ottawa, East........	Napoleon Champagne........ Louis J. Kehoe.............	2,842 1,567	
	Majority for Champagne...	1,275	
61. Ottawa, West........	James Albert Ellis......... Gordon Smith Henderson.....	4,398 2,296	
	Majority for Ellis........	2,102	
62. Oxford, North.......	Newton Wesley Rowell...... Robert Lockhart............	2,651 2,091	
	Majority for Rowell.......	560	
63. Oxford, South.......	Thomas Richard Mayberry... William McGhee............	2,457 2,254	
	Majority for Mayberry.....	203	
64. Parry Sound........	John Galna................. Albert E. Bradwin..........	2,218 1,143	
	Majority for Galna........	1,075	
65. Peel	Samuel Charters............ Robert Smith...............	2,705 1,989	
	Majority for Charters......	716	
66. Perth, North........	James Torrance............. John Brown.................	3,523 3,151	
	Majority for Torrance.....	372	
67. Perth, South........	John Bennewies............. Valentin Stock.............	2,388 2,315	
	Majority for Bennewies...	73	
68. Peterborough, East..	James Thompson............ Edward Hawthorne.......... David Andrews.............	1,579 1,076 120	
	Majority for Thompson....	503	

SUMMARY OF RECAPITULATION.—*Continued.*

Constituency.	Candidates.	Votes counted.	Remarks.
69. Peterborough, West..	Edward Armour Peck....... Robert Richard Hall........	2,674 2,056	
	Majority for Peck........	618	
70. Port Arthur.........	Donald MacDonald Hogarth.. Frederick Urry............	1,515 573	
	Majority for Hogarth......	942	
71. Prescott.............	Gustave Evanturel......... George Hector Pharand......	1,976 1,692	
	Majority for Evanturel....	284	
72. Prince Edward......	Robert Addison Norman..... Stewart Edgar Mathie.......	2,286 1,699	
	Majority for Norman......	587	
73. Rainy River.........	James Arthur Mathieu....... William Alfred Preston.....	1,130 844	
	Majority for Mathieu......	286	
74. Renfrew, North......	Edward Arunah Dunlop......	By acclamation.	
75. Renfrew, South......	Thomas William McGarry...	By acclamation.	
76. Russell.............	Damase Racine............. W. J. W. Lowrie............	3,041 1,699	
	Majority for Racine.......	1,342	
77. Sault Ste. Marie	Hon. William Howard Hearst.	By acclamation.	
78. Simcoe, Centre	Alfred Burke Thompson..... Hampton E. Jory............	1,791 1,696	
	ajority for Thompson....	95	

SUMMARY ᵒF RECAPITULATIᵒN.—*Continued.*

Co ituency.	Candidates.	Votes counted.	Remarks.
79. Simcoe, East	James Irwin Hartt	3,103	
	Erastus Long................	2,774	
	Majority for Hartt	329	
80. Simcoe, South.........	Alexander Ferguson..........	By acclama- tion	.
81. Simcoe, West........	Hon. James Stoddart Duff....	By acclama- tion.	
82. Stormont............	John Colborne Milligan.......	2,249	
	Ambrose Fitzgerald Mulhern.	2,024	
	Majority for Milligan......	225	
83. Sturgeon Falls.......	Zotique Mageau..............	885	
	Adulpheᵢ Azaire Aubin........	738	
	Majority for Mageau	147	
84. Sudbury	Charles McCrea..............	2,541	
	Frank Herbert Sangster.....	1,147	
	Majority for McCrea........	1,394	
85. Temiskaming........	Robert Taylor Shillington.....	2,403	
	Arthur Wentworth Roebuck..	2,139	
	Majority for Shillington....	264	
86. Toronto, East—Seat	Hon Robert Allan Pyne	3,299	
"A"...............	David Bulloch..............	922	
	Majority for Pyne	2,377	
87. Toronto. East—Seat	Thomas Richard Whitesides..	2,767	
"B"...............	John B. Reid..............	1,060	
	James Stevenson...........	512	
	Majority for Whitesides....	1,707	
88. Toronto, North—Seat	W. Kirkpatrick McNaught....	5,165	
"A".............	William Stephenson.........	1,313	
	Majority for McNaught....	3,852	
89. Toronto, North—Seat	Hon. James Joseph Foy	3,824	
"B".............	Joseph Oliver	3,116	
	James Richards.............	178	
	Majority for Foy.........	708	

SUMMARY OF RECAPITULATION.—*Continued.*

Constituency.	Candidates.	Votes counted.	Remarks.
90. Toronto, South—Seat "A"	Edward William James Owens W. R. James	2,594 770	
	Majority for Owens	1.824	
91. Toronto, South—Seat "B"................	George Horace Gooderham.... E. Fielding...................	2.647 709	
	Majority for Gooderham	1.938	
92. Toronto, West—Seat "A"	Hon. Thomas Crawford...... John Hunter................ Robert Buist Noble	5,469 1,519 215	
	Majority for Crawford......	3,950	
93. Toronto, West—Seat "B"................	William David McPherson.... James Watt	5,225 1,749	
	Majority for McPherson....	3.476	
94. Victoria, East........	Robert Mercer Mason........	By acclamation.	
95. Victoria, West.......	Adam Edward Vrooman...,. Charles Edgar Weeks........ Edward John Johnson........	1,836 1,732 94	
	Majority for Vrooman......	104	
96. Waterloo, North.....	Henry George Lackner....... William D. Euler...........: Hilkiah Martin.............	3,059 2,866 454	
	Majority for Lackner......	193	
97. Waterloo, South......	George Pattinson........... John Taylor, the younger .... James P. Maguire..........	2,770 1,773 582	
	Majority for Pattinson.....	997	
98. Welland.............	Evan Eugene Fraser........ Carlton F. Monroe..........	3,511 2,706	
	Majority for Fraser.......	805	

SUMMARY OF RECAPITULATION.—*Concluded.*

Constituency.	Candidates.	Votes counted.	Remarks.
99. Wellington, East.....	Udney Richardson...........	1,932	
	James J. Craig.............	1,595	
	Majority for Richardson....	337	
100. Wellington, South...	Henry Chadwick Schofield....	2,912	
	James Innes McIntosh.......	2,462	
	Majority for Schofield.....	450	
101. Wellington, West...	William Clark Chambers....	1,778	
	James McEwing.............	1,653	
	Majority for Chambers.....	125	
102. Wentworth, North..	James McQueen.............	1,723	
	William Lawson............	1,694	
	Majority for McQueen.....	29	
103. Wentworth, South..	James Thos. Hammill Regan.	1,496	
	Daniel Reed................	1,391	
	William Barrett............	209	
	Majority for Regan.......	105	
104. York, East.........	Alexander McCowan........	2,337	
	William D. Annis...........	1,555	
	Majority for McCowan.....	782	
105. York, North........	Thomas Herbert Lennox.....	3,023	
	Jesse M. Walton............	2.530	
	Majority for Lennox.......	493	
106. York, West.........	Forbes Godfrey.............	2,847	
	George William Verral......	1,522	
	Majority for Godfrey......	1.325	

ARTHUR H. SYDERE,
Clerk of the Crown in Chancery for Ontario.

2 R.E.

RETURN from the Records of the GENERAL ELECTION to the Legislative Assembly at the Election held on the Fourth and Eleventh Days of December, 1911.

Addington.—William David Black, by Acclamation.

Algoma.—ALFRED MAXWELL BELL, Returning Officer.

Electoral District	Numbers of Polling Places	Names of Candidates and No. of Votes Polled for each		Total No. of Votes Polled	No. of Votes remaining Unpolled	No. of Names on the Polling Lists	No. of Ballot Papers sent out to each Polling Place	Used Ballot Papers	Unused Ballot Papers	Rejected Ballot Papers	Cancelled Ballot Papers	Declined Ballot Papers	Ballot Papers taken from Polling Places
		Griggs.	Wigg.										
Algoma	Webbwood	57	24	81	71	152	150	81	69				
	Hallam Tp.	29	12	41	37	78	75	41	34				
	McKinnon, Shakespeare and Gough	25	00	25	80	105	100	25	75				
	Massey	66	39	105	75	180	175	105	70				
	Salter-May Tps.	92	23	115	107	222	225	116	109	1			
	Broken Front, Salter, etc	17	8	25	67	92	100	25	75				
	Walford	55	14	69	40	109	100	69	31				1
	Spanish	29	18	47	31	78	100	47	53				
	Aird Island	5	7	12	80	92	100	12	88				
	Cutler	18	9	27	80	107	100	27	73				
	John's Island	6	5	11	19	30	25	11	14				
	Spragge	21	11	32	95	127	125	32	93				
	Alma Mills	12	4	16	25	41	50	16	34				
	Striker & Eden	11	15	26	34	60	60	26	34				
	Blind River No. 1	48	84	132	398	530	500	134	366			1	
	do " 2	24	47	71	105	176	175	73	102			1	
	do " 3	35	45	80	233	313	300	82	218				
	Thompson Tp.	30	13	43	17	60	60	44	16			1	1
	Patton Tp.	17	19	36	19	55	60	37	23				1
	Galstone Tp.	33	10	43	41	84	85	43	42				
	Bright Tp.	13	4	17	4	21	25	17	8				
	Parkinson, Finder's School	12	14	26	25	51	50	26	24				
	Parkinson and Grassette	7	8	15	10	25	25	15	10				

Municipality											
Day and Bright Tps	27	18	45	23	68	75	45	32	30		
Wells and Gould	17	15	32	22	54	50	32	15	18		
Thessalon Town	46	78	124	117	241	225	124	101			
do	32	83	115	105	220	225	115	110			
Allen Tp. No. 1	28	44	70	34	104	125	70	55			
" No. 2	26	19	45	22	67	100	45	15			
Kirkwood and Lefroy No. 1	26	9	35	16	51	50	35	15			
Kirkwood and Lefroy No. 2	37	50	88	86	173	175	87	87		1	
Bruce Mines	19	6	26	13	38	50	25	24			
Plummer Additional	85	26	111	82	193	200	111	89			
Tiler and Rose (Rydal Bank)	57	16	73	77	150	150	73	77			
Allen Tp. (Fraser's)	82	26	108	36	144	150	108	42		1	
Galbraith and Houghton	17	9	26	17	43	50	26	24			
Allen Tp. (Poplardale)	22	9	31	9	40	45	31	14			
do	17	2	19	5	24	25	19	6			
Johnston, Tar and Tarbutt Add'l No. 1	16	8	24	10	34	35	24	11			
do do	29	15	44	18	62	60	44	16			
do do	30	23	54	28	81	85	53	31		1	
Laird Tp.	61	27	88	32	120	125	88	37			
McDonald, Meredith & Aberdeen No. 1	36	18	54	76	130	125	54	71			
do do	40	19	59	68	127	120	59	61			
do do	21	14	35	31	66	60	35	90			
St. Joseph Tp. No. 1	20	11	31	29	60	175	31	29			
do	80	44	124	47	171	85	124	50			
Hilton Tp.	51	6	57	34	91	70	57	28			
do	24	9	33	32	65	60	33	37			
Jocelyn Tp. No. 1	32	9	41	30	71	70	41	29			
do No. 2	21	4	25	37	62	35	25	35			
do No. 3	20	5	25	9	34	35	25	10			
	23	2	26	9	34	35	26	10			
	21	5		6	32			9			
Totals	**1,723**	**1,062**	**2,785**	**2,853**	**5,638**	**5,760**	**2,798**	**2,962**		7	4	2
Majority for Grigg	661										

	Layton.	Westbrook.							
South Dumfries Tp. No. 1	40	24	64	28	92	125	64	61	
do	47	35	82	44	126	150	82	68	
do	63	15	78	49	127	150	78	72	
do	48	43	91	41	132	150	91	59	
do	63	63	126	32	158	175	126	49	
do	50	35	79	31	110	125	79	46	
Brant, North	26	20	46	25	71	100	46	54	

RETURN from the Records of the GENERAL ELECTION to the Legislative Assembly, 1911.—*Continued.*

Electoral District	Numbers of Polling Places	No.	Westbrook	Layton	Total No. of Votes Polled	No. of Votes remaining Unpolled	No. of Names on the Polling Lists	No. of Ballot Papers sent out to each Polling Place	Used Ballot Papers	Unused Ballot Papers	Rejected Ballot Papers	Cancelled Ballot Papers	Declined Ballot Papers	Ballot Papers taken from Polling Places
Brant, North—Con.	Paris Town	1	66	71	137	55	192	225	138	87	1			
	do	2	86	68	154	72	226	249	154	95				
	do	3	73	71	144	49	193	225	146	79	2			
	do	4	63	53	116	29	145	175	116	59	1	1		
	do	5	74	43	117	35	152	175	120	77				
	do	6	106	66	172	54	226	250	173	85		5		
	Brantford Tp	7	26	38	64	55	119	250	65	88				
	do	8	93	68	161	66	227	200	162	116				
	do	9	41	43	84	84	168	375	84	187	1		1	
	do	10	121	65	186	153	339		188	91				
	do	11	87	92	179	67	246	275	184	61	2			
	do	12	10	29	39	12	51	100	39	44				
	do	13	56	49	105	12	117	150	106	80				
	Burford Tp	1	55	39	94	46	140	175	95	42			1	
	do	2	54	52	106	30	136	150	108	55				
	do	3	45	62	94	25	119	150	95	54	1			
	do	4	34	51	96	31	127	150	96	100		1		
	do	5	49	48	86	45	145	200	87	113				
	do	6	38	26	86	62	148	200	86	114				
	do	7	60	26	87	55	141	151	87	64				
	do	8	61	29	73	36	123	150	73	77				
	Onondaga Tp	1	44	35	100	38	132	200	100	100				
	do	2	65	36	122	59	159	200	122	78				
			86			56	178							
	Totals		**1,722**	**1,546**	**3,268**	**1,497**	**4,765**	**5,700**	**3,290**	**2,410**	**11**	**9**		
	Majority for Westbrook		**176**											

JOHN JEFFERSON, Returning Officer.

Brant, South

THOMAS S. WADE, Returning Officer.

Municipality	No.	Brewster	Harris										
Brantford City	1	98	77	175	39	214	216	176	40				1
do	2	96	83	179	52	231	234	183	51				
do	3	89	68	157	54	211	212	159	53			1	
do	4	73	85	158	43	201	202	159	43	1			
do	5	89	74	163	39	202	203	166	37	3			
do	6	74	92	166	57	223	224	168	56	2			
do	7	130	91	221	70	291	294	226	68	2	1	1	
do	8	112	79	191	52	261	265	196	69	2			
do	9	100	95	195	59	247	248	202	46	2			
do	10	86	79	165	39	224	224	168	56	6			
do	11	124	102	226	48	265	266	228	38	3			
do	12	75	53	128	50	170	170	128	42	1		1	
do	13	85	46	131	59	179	180	135	45				
do	14	135	99	234	59	284	284	240	44	5	1	1	
do	15	117	105	222	63	281	282	223	59	1			
do	16	104	93	197	62	256	256	201	55	4			
do	17	116	80	196	70	259	260	200	60	3			
do	18	94	86	180	43	242	242	183	59	3			
do	19	124	93	217	69	287	288	218	70	1			
do	20	96	87	183	50	226	226	183	43		2	2	
do	21	157	70	227	82	296	296	229	67	2	1	1	
do	22	94	79	173	84	223	224	177	47	1			
do	23	142	107	249	78	331	331	251	80	4			
do	24	140	111	251	80	335	336	255	81	3			
do	25	112	84	196	83	274	274	200	74	2			
do	26	135	108	243	33	324	324	247	77	2	1		
do	27	159	139	298	16	381	382	301	81	1			
Brantford Tp.	1	26	68	94	43	127	128	94	34				
do	2	15	33	48	29	64	64	48	16				
do	3	24	48	72	19	115	116	72	44				
do	4	62	70	132	81	161	162	133	29				
do	5	23	53	76	29	95	96	76	20				
do	6	37	63	100	81	181	182	101	81				
Oakland Tp.	1	31	57	88	29	117	118	89	29				
do	2	27	60	87	35	122	122	87	35				
Totals		**3,201**	**2,817**	**6,018**	**1,881**	**7,899**	**7,931**	**6,102**	**1,829**	**59**	**7**	**7**	**1**
Majority for Brewster		384											

RETURN from the Records of the GENERAL ELECTION to the Legislative Assembly, 1911.—*Continued.*

Electoral District	Numbers of Polling Places	Donovan	Smart	Wing	Total No. of Votes Polled	No. of Votes remaining Unpolled	No. of Names on the Polling Lists	No. of Ballot Papers sent out to each Polling Place	Used Ballot Papers	Unused Ballot Papers	Rejected Ballot Papers	Cancelled Ballot Papers	Declined Ballot Papers	Ballot Papers taken from Polling Places
Brockville	South Ward ..... No. 1	85	68	18	173	71	244	250	173	77	2			
	do ..... No. 2	44	72	3	123	68	191	200	123	77	4			
	Nth Ward ..... No. 1	63	62	14	139	76	215	225	139	86				
	do 2	60	47	8	117	64	181	200	117	83	2			
	do 3	60	37	7	105	37	142	100	165	45	1			
	Centre Ward ..... No. 1	66	72	18	157	74	231	250	157	93	1			
	do 2	38	45	10	94	56	150	150	94	56				
	do 3	55	59	6	120	64	184	200	120	80	3		4	
	East Ward ..... No. 1	126	99	27	255	71	326	350	255	95				
	do 2	95	136	18	250	47	297	300	250	50	3			
	West Ward ..... No. 1	81	60	22	166	65	231	250	166	84				
	do 2	77	65	17	159	58	217	225	159	66	1			
	do 3	88	114	2	218	66	284	300	222	78				
	E...... No. 1	56	39	5	102	51	153	175	102	73	1			
	do	37	61	1	82	39	121	125	82	43				
	do	23	50	2	85	13	98	100	85	15				
	do	36	44	1	88	20	108	125	88	37				
	do	63	11		108	15	123	125	108	17	1			
	do	48	27		65	17	82	100	65	35				
	do	67	51		81	8	89	100	81	19	1			
	do	58	6	2	86	15	101	125	86	39				
	do	91	35	1	144	17	161	175	144	31	1			
	do	39	9	1	45	13	58	75	45	30				
	Kitley	25	24		60	22	82	100	60	40				
	do	75			84	88	172	175	84	91				
		66		2	92	60	152	175	92	83				

WILLIAM RICHARDSON,
Returning Officer

do	3	53	45	1	99	31	130	150	99	51	1	
do	4	66	6		73	25	98	100	73	27	2	
Rear of Yonge and Escott	1	56	41	4	103	9	112	125	103	22	1	
do	2	53	40	1	94	24	118	125	94	31		1
do	3	50	29	2	82	18	100	125	83	42	1	
South Elmsley	1	50	19	2	71	82	153	175	71	104	1	
do	2	23	12	1	36	46	82	100	36	64		
Athens	1	49	54	1	105	17	122	125	105	20	1	1
do	2	68	41	1	111	11	122	122	112	13		
Totals		2,090	1,641	213	3,972	1,458	5,430	5,875	3,978	1,897	28	6
Majority for Donovan		449										

Bruce Centre

		MacDonald	McFarlane								
Township of Elderslie	1	97	50	147	21	168	175	147	28		
do	2	41	70	111	21	132	150	111	39		
do	3	72	61	133	26	139	175	133	42		
do	4	88	56	144	22	166	175	144	31		
Township of Huron	2	53	57	110	23	133	150	110	39	1	
do	3	35	80	115	29	144	150	115	35		
do	4	39	78	117	22	139	150	117	33		
do	5	66	44	110	24	134	150	110	40		
do	6	73	48	121	49	170	175	121	54	2	
Township of Kincardine	1	81	32	113	41	154	150	113	62		
do	2	57	61	118	26	144	175	118	32		
do	3	46	103	149	35	184	150	149	58		
do	4	49	45	94	23	117	209	94	30		
do	5	64	15	89	25	114	125	89	36		
Township of	2	71	25	86	15	101	125	86	39		
do	3	39	27	66	19	85	125	66	34	1	1
do	4	21	32	53	19	72	100	53	21		
do	5	33	108	141	72	213	75	141	84		
do	6	51	52	103	18	121	225	103	20	2	
do	7	44	57	101	19	120	225	101	24		
Town of Kincardine	1	28	12	40	10	50	125	40	10		3
do	2	13	18	31	7	38	125	31	19		
do	3	73	76	149	66	215	50	149	72	1	
do	4	63	58	121	44	165	50	121	52	2	
Village of Paisley	1	49	63	112	65	177	225	112	88		
do	2	39	54	93	55	148	175	93	57		
do		66	56	123	13	135	200	122	27	1	1
do		44	41	85	7	92	150	85	15		

THOMAS E. MORGAN,
Returning Officer.

RETURN from the Records of the GENERAL ELECTION to the Legislative Assembly, 1911.—*Continued.*

Electoral District	Numbers of Polling Places	Names of Candidates and No. of Votes Polled for each		Total No. of Votes Polled	No. of Votes Remaining Unpolled	No. of Names on the Polling Lists	No. of Ballot Papers sent out to each Polling Place	Used Ballot Papers	Unused Ballot Papers	Rejected Ballot Papers	Cancelled Ballot Papers	Declined Ballot Papers	Ballot Papers taken from Polling Places
		MacDonald.	McFarlane.										
Bruce Centre—Con. Town of Chesley	No. 1	99	62	161	36	197	200	162	38	1			
do	No. 2	133	82	215	53	268	276	216	60	1	7	1	
Totals		1,727	1,623	3,350	905	4,255	4,584	3,365	1,219				
Majority for MacDonald		104											
		Bowman.	Vandusen.										
Bruce, North. St. Edmunds	No. 1	4	26	30	9	39	50	30	20				
do	No. 2	7	3	10	14	24	50	10	40				
do	No. 3	16	42	58	38	96	100	58	42				
Lindsay	No. 1	34	20	54	29	83	100	54	46	1			
do	No. 2	5	6	11	12	23	50	11	39				
do	No. 3	21	15	36	13	49	75	36	39				
do	No. 4	7	10	17	8	25	50	17	33	1			
Eastnor	No. 1	57	86	143	49	192	200	144	56				
do	No. 2	23	50	73	30	103	125	73	52				
do	No. 3	9	38	47	12	59	75	47	28	1			
do	No. 4	29	22	51	13	64	50	52	21				
do	No. 5	9	14	23	20	43	75	23	21				
Albemarle	No. 1	7	22	29	5	34	50	29	25				
do	No. 2	24	26	50	14	64	75	50	53				
do	No. 3	26	44	70	31	101	124	71	32	1			
do	No. 4	13	29	42	25	67	75	43	75				
do	No. 5	25	39	64	12	76	100	64	35	1			1

JOHN K. DAVIDSON, Returning Officer.

Arran	No. 1	34	25	59	15	74	100	59	41			
do	2	60	46	106	30	136	151	107	44	1		
do	3	27	27	54	16	70	75	55	20	1		
do	4	42	35	77	80	157	175	77	98			
do	5	32	54	86	50	136	150	86	64	1		
do	6	16	24	40	27	67	75	40	35			
Saugeen	No. 1	76	39	115	24	139	151	116	33		1	
do	2	16	121	137	20	157	175	137	38			
do	3	28	68	96	25	121	127	97	30			
do	4	28	43	71	11	82	100	71	29			
Bruce	No. 1	37	40	77	30	107	125	77	48			
do	2	53	37	90	9	99	126	90	36	1		
do	3	48	18	66	12	78	100	66	34			
do	4	50	17	67	13	80	100	67	33			
do	5	48	13	61	10	71	77	61	16			
do	6	40	17	57	13	70	80	57	23			
afa	No. 1	57	14	71	38	109	125	71	54	1		
Tiverton	2	76	31	107	49	156	175	108	67			
Hepworth	3	60	36	96	59	155	175	96	79	1		
do	4	83	18	101	70	171	175	102	73	1		
Wiarton	No. 1	56	19	75	43	118	126	76	50		1	
do	2	90	13	103	72	175	200	104	96	2	1	
do	3	44	94	138	31	169	175	138	37	1		
Southampton	No. 1	46	21	67	44	111	128	67	61		1	
do	2	40	35	75	15	90	100	76	24	1	1	
do	3	43	60	103	53	156	175	104	71	2		
do		51	55	106	50	156	175	109	66	1		
Port Elgin	No. 1	48	55	103	54	157	175	104	71			
do	2	48	69	117	46	163	175	117	58			
		149	35	184	45	229	256	185	71	1	1	
		99	17	116	36	152	101	118	57			
		47	16	63	21	84	175	63	38			
		81	47	128	26	154	175	128	46			1
		113	40	153	30	183	200	154	46	1		
Totals		2,182	1,791	3,973	1,501	5,474	6,297	3,995	2,302	18	4	2

Majority for Bowman 391

RETURN from the Records of the GENERAL ELECTION to the Legislative Assembly, 1911.—*Continued.*

Electoral District	Numbers of Polling Places	Names of Candidates and No. of Votes Polled for each		Total No. of Votes Polled	No. of Votes Remaining Unpolled	No. of Names on the Polling Lists	No. of Ballot Papers sent out to each Polling Place	Used Ballot Papers	Unused Ballot Papers	Rejected Ballot Papers	Cancelled Ballot Papers	Declined Ballot Papers	Ballot Papers taken from Polling Places
Bruce, South	Township of Brant......... No. 1	50	App.	94	65	159	175	96	79	1		1	
	do 2	60	44	106	31	137	150	106	44				
	do 3	56	46	99	65	164	175	99	76				
	do 4	32	43	108	17	126	150	108	42				
	do 5	44	76	82	44	127	150	82	68				
	do 6	60	38	101	26	113	150	101	49		1		
	do 7	63	41	91	22	119	125	92	33				1
	do 8	51	28	79	40	112	125	79	46				
	Township of Carrick...... No. 1	27	28	101	11	186	201	102	23	1		1	
	do 2	36	74	165	21	148	175	169	32				
	do 3	40	129	108	40	114	125	108	67				
	do 4	50	68	89	25	122	150	89	36				
	do 5	40	39	98	24	116	150	98	52	1		1	
	do 6	37	58	89	27	125	150	98	52				
	do 7	36	52	97	28	69	75	59	16				
	do 8	43	61	59	10	57	125	39	36	1		1	
	Township of Culross...... No. 1	26	16	39	19	106	150	63	62				
	do 2	46	13	63	43	124	150	90	60				
	do 3	65	17	90	34	128	150	79	71		3		
	do 4	61	25	79	49	130	150	89	63				
	do 5	61	18	87	43	128	100	87	50	1		1	1
	do 6	29	26	87	41	79	75	50	22				
	do 7	34	58	50	29	64	100	53	40				
	Township of Kinloss...... No. 1	30	16	53	11	72		60	50	1			
	do 2	25	23	60	12	136	150	53	40			1	
	do 3	67	35	111	25			111	39				

JAMES ANDREW LAMB,
Returning Officer.

					1	3	4							
do	4			1				3	32	118	150	133	15	118	20	98
do	5								32	68	100	79	11	68	20	48
do	6								45	55	100	69	14	55	21	34
Village of Teeswater	No. 1			1					44	81	125	106	25	81	26	55
do "	2			3				3	32	118	150	144	28	116	50	66
Village of Lucknow, North	No. 1								34	141	150	156	18	138	40	98
S uth o	2								37	88	175	97	18	88	25	63
Twn of Walkerton, East	3								50	150	125	186	9	150	64	86
do West	4								84	150	200	244	36	188	105	83
do South									76	191	275	174	56	124	64	60
									53	124	200	104	50	72	38	34
										72	125		32			
Totals					1	3	4	11	1,774	3,502	5,276	4,578	1,095	3,483	1,589	1,894
Majority for Anderson																305

Carleton																M
Fitzroy	No. 1					1			162	38	200	136	98	38	18	20
do	2						2		163	62	225	207	146	61	13	48
do	3								129	71	200	175	104	71	1	60
do	4					1			153	47	200	120	73	47	6	46
Tarbolton	No. 1								97	28	125	115	87	28	7	22
do	2					1		1	156	44	200	173	129	44	9	37
Huntley	No. 1								126	74	200	120	46	74	13	65
do	2								39	87	226	259	74	185	21	172
do	3							1	127	23	150	71	48	23	22	7
March	No. 1								145	30	175	83	54	29	13	58
do	2								79	71	150	149	78	71	17	34
Nepean	No. 1								99	51	150	135	84	51	12	26
do	2								86	39	125	117	79	38	4	11
do	3								34	16	50	37	22	15	19	36
do	4								70	55	125	110	55	55	21	13
do	5								93	57	125	110	53	57	10	21
do	6							1	100	25	150	90	67	23	25	36
do	7 A								14	46	150	129	83	46	5	41
do	7 B								109	41	150	108	67	41	2	22
do	8								106	44	200	94	51	43	4	54
do	9 A								99	26	125	118	92	26	13	4
do	9								133	67	150	189	91	67	85	12
do	10								111	89	200	180	82	89	14	34
Goulborn	No. 1								98	27	125	108	51	28	4	44
do	2							1	112	38	150	119	45	38	13	23
do	3								68	57	125	102	78	57	13	
									114	36	150	114		36		

RETURN from the Records of the GENERAL ELECTION to the Legislative Assembly, 1911.—*Continued.*

Electoral District	Numbers of Polling Places	Names of Candidates and No. of Votes Polled for each.		Total No. of Votes Polled.	No. of Votes remaining Unpolled.	No. of Names on the Polling Lists.	No. of Ballot Papers sent out to each Polling Place.	Used Ballot Papers.	Unused Ballot Papers.	Rejected Ballot Papers.	Cancelled Ballot Papers.	Declined Ballot Papers.	Ballot Papers taken from Polling Places.
		McElroy.	Craig.										
Carleton.—Con...	No. 4 torn	39	17	56	42	98	125	57	68				1
	do 5	40	36	76	63	139	175	77	98	1			
	No. 6 Richmond	29	19	48	25	73	100	48	52				
	No. 1 Marlboro	50	18	68	41	79	200	68	132				
	do 2	8	73	81	33	114	150	81	69				
	do 3	25	21	46	63	109	200	46	154	1			
	No. 1	12	55	67	29	96	150	67	83				
	do 2	4	12	16	33	49	75	16	59		1		
	do 3	29	120	149	40	189	224	150	74	1			
	do 4	42	26	68	52	120	150	69	81				
	do 5	58	20	78	39	117	150	78	72	1			
	do	12	58	70	13	83	100	70	30				
	do	15	23	38	18	56	75	39	36	1			
		1,347	893	2,240	2,550	4,790	6,175	2,255	3,920	8	5		2
	Majority for	454											
		McKeown	W										
Dufferin	Amaranth	33	32	65	46	111	111	66	45	1			
	do	46	54	100	63	163	166	100	66				
	do	23	29	52	59	111	111	52	59				
	do	19	44	63	69	132	132	64	68	1			
	do	27	66	93	62	155	157	93	64				
	do	26	38	64	37	101	103	65	38	1			

Polling Division	No.								
East Garafraxa	1	42	31	73	72	42	30	19	11
do	2	28	38	66	66	28	38	10	28
do	3	35	37	72	72	35	37	24	13
do	4	56	73	129	128	56	72	29	43
East Luther	1	65	71	136	136	65	71	20	51
do	2	62	39	101	101	62	39	15	24
do	3	80	75	155	153	78	75	50	25
Mono	1	70	91	161	159	70	89	45	44
do	2	29	78	107	104	26	78	19	59
do	3	43	82	125	121	41	80	08	72
do	4	45	66	111	103	37	66	33	33
do	5	67	65	132	128	64	64	17	47
do	6	37	88	125	121	33	88	39	49
do	7	55	110	165	165	55	110	48	62
Melancthon	1	65	93	158	153	61	92	52	40
do	2	44	143	187	187	44	143	72	71
do	3	36	29	65	64	35	29	23	06
do	4	31	56	87	86	31	55	40	15
do	5	53	99	152	150	51	99	66	53
do	6	48	133	181	179	46	133	102	31
do	7	41	91	132	131	40	91	72	19
Mulmur	1	28	65	93	92	27	65	48	17
do	2	70	138	208	205	67	138	24	114
do	3	16	47	63	62	15	47	16	31
do	4	67	111	178	176	66	110	29	81
Orangeville, North Ward	1	50	52	102	101	49	52	11	41
do East Ward	2	74	86	160	158	72	86	40	46
do South Ward	3	70	91	161	159	68	91	47	44
do West Ward	4	86	120	206	204	84	120	41	79
Shelburne, North Ward	1	72	130	202	199	69	130	36	94
do South Ward	2	116	150	266	262	113	149	34	115
Grand Valley	1	55	104	159	157	55	102	38	64
Totals		2,208	3,501	5,709	5,633	2,149	3,484	1,604	1,880
Majority for McKeown									276

ROBERT GALLAUGHER,
Returning Officer.

RETURNS from the Records of the GENERAL ELECTION to the Legislative Assembly, 1911.—*Continued.*

Electoral District	Numbers of Polling Places	No.	Names of Candidates and No. of Votes Polled for each		Voters at each Polling Place			Ballot Papers sent out and how disposed of in each Polling Place						
			Whitney	Muir	Total No. of Votes Polled	No. of Votes remaining Unpolled	No. of Names on the Polling Lists	No. of Ballot Papers sent out to each Polling Place	Used Ballot Papers	Unused Ballot Papers	Rejected Ballot Papers	Cancelled Ballot Papers	Declined Ballot Papers	Ballot Papers taken from Polling Places
Dundas	Winchester, Village	1	65	37	102	22	124	150	102	48				
	do	2	78	49	127	32	159	175	127	48				
	Winchester, Twp.	1	41	31	72	25	97	100	72	28		1		
	do	2	91	32	123	42	165	175	123	52				
	do	3	40	28	68	20	88	100	68	32				
	do	4	29	38	67	50	107	125	67	58	1			
	do	5	25	44	69	27	96	125	69	56				
	do	6	109	44	153	63	216	225	153	72	1			
	do	7	58	35	93	38	131	150	93	57				
	Chesterville	1	108	73	181	38	219	250	181	69				
	Mountain	2	99	36	135	58	193	200	135	65	1			
	do	3	96	30	126	57	183	200	126	74				
	do	4	52	19	71	35	106	150	71	79	1		1	
	do	5	90	19	109	51	160	175	109	66	1			
	do	6	94	33	128	49	177	200	128	72				
	Matilda	1	23	9	32	17	49	75	32	43				
	do	2	62	51	113	74	187	250	113	112				
	do	3	102	16	119	94	213	250	119	131				
	do	4	75	48	123	85	208	225	123	102				
	do	5	63	35	99	73	172	200	99	101				
	do	6	90	21	104	98	209	225	104	114				
	Williamsburg	1	93	11	97	87	191	175	97	121				
	do	2	43	54	101	75	172	125	101	78				
	do	3	29	71	97	28	129	150	97	24				
	do	4	48	49	141	49	190	200	141	59				

ROBERT H. HOGABOAM,
Returning Officer.

Dundas (continued)

	No.										
do	5	40	51	91	59	150	150	91	59		
do	6	63	45	108	29	137	150	109	41		
do	7	22	44	66	39	105	125	66	59		
do	8	5	37	42	10	52	75	42	33		
Morrisburg		41	73	114	39	153	175	114	61		1
do	1	56	58	114	56	170	175	114	61		
do	2	39	52	91	52	143	150	91	59		
Iroquois	1	45	52	97	36	133	150	97	53		
do	2	25	54	79	25	105	125	80	45		
Totals		**1,318**	**2,239**	**3,564**	**1,651**	**5,215**	**5,850**	**3,565**	**2,285**	**1**	**2**
Majority for Whitney			921								

Durham East—Josiah Johnston Preston—by Acclamation—HUGH WALKER, Returning Officer.

Durham West

	No.	Devitt	Powers										
Bowmanville Town—	1	34	51	85	16	101	125	88	37				3
West Ward	2	54	32	86	18	104	125	86	39				
North Ward	1	72	57	129	32	161	175	129	46		1		
do	2	80	64	144	44	188	200	147	53				1
South Ward	1	64	49	113	18	81	150	114	36			2	
do	2	52	24	76	19	95	125	77	48			1	
Darlington Tp	1	35	99	134	36	170	200	134	66				
do	2	71	80	151	19	170	200	151	49			1	
do	3	41	58	99	28	127	150	100	50			1	
do	4	66	68	134	31	165	175	135	40				
do	5	60	70	130	23	153	175	131	44				1
do	6	59	57	116	52	168	200	116	84				
do	7	52	84	136	46	182	125	137	63				
Cartwright Tp	1	80	16	96	14	110	125	96	29				
do	2	90	7	97	8	105	175	97	28				
do	3	106	36	142	21	163	125	143	32		1		
do	4	60	26	86	10	102	150	86	39				
Clark Tp	1	53	40	93	29	122	160	94	56				
do	2	40	34	74	12	86	100	74	26				
do	3	25	2	69	15	84	150	70	30				
do	4	64	67	106	22	128	150	108	33				
do	5	46	46	113	13	137	150	117	40		1		
do	6	39	18	85	8	98	100	85	30			1	
do	7	52	40	70	24	78	125	70	44			1	3
do	8	38	75	78	21	102	150	81	29			1	2
do	9	44		119		140		121					

RETURNS from the Records of the GENERAL ELECTION to the Legislative Assembly, 1911.—*Continued.*

Electoral District	Numbers of Polling Places	Names of Candidates and No. of Votes Polled for each		Total No. of Votes Polled	No. of Votes remaining Unpolled	No. of Names on the Polling Lists	No. of Ballot Papers sent out to each Polling Place	Used Ballot Papers	Unused Ballot Papers	Rejected Ballot Papers	Cancelled Ballot Papers	Declined Ballot Papers	Ballot Papers taken from Polling Places
		Devitt	Powers										
Durham West—Con.	Newcastle Village No. 1	36	20	56	56	15	100	57	43			1	1
	do No. 2	40	23	63	63	14	100	64	36				
	Totals	1,553	1,327	2,880	2,889	668	3,518	2,908	1,192	16	6	6	6
	Majority for Devitt	226											
		Brower	Powers										
Elgin East	Bayham No. 1	115	66	181	96	277	300	190	110	9			
	do 2	41	29	70	91	161	171	70	111				
	do 3	56	16	72	54	126	150	72	78				
	do 4	108	41	149	53	202	225	151	74	2			
	do 5	75	40	115	53	168	201	115	86				
	do 6	49	36	85	75	160	175	85	90				
	Yarmouth No. 1	79	87	166	50	216	225	167	58	1			4
	do 2	78	78	156	76	232	250	159	91	3			1
	do 3	74	52	126	37	163	175	126	49				1
	do 4	58	41	99	43	142	150	99	51				
	do 5	127	77	204	120	324	351	208	143	4			
	do 6	49	34	83	25	108	125	84	41	1			
	do 7	91	66	157	56	213	226	158	68	1			
	do 8	14	37	51	24	75	100	51	49				
	do 9	27	60	87	35	122	150	87	63				
	Malahide No. 1	70	62	132	61	193	225	132	93				
	do 2	76	83	159	79	238	250	159	91				

HENRY T. GODWIN, Returning Officer.

	No.										
do	3	80	62	142	67	209	225	143	82		
do	4	86	59	145	37	182	200	145	55		
do	5	106	47	153	60	213	225	153	72		
South Dorchester	1	42	68	110	35	182	175	111	64		
do	2	83	51	134	48	182	200	134	66		
do	3	47	51	98	52	150	175	98	77		
do		89	80	169	81	250	275	171	104		
...er	1	121	67	188	89	277	300	190	110		
do	2	74	50	124	56	180	200	126	74		
do	3	104	33	137	59	196	225	137	88		
Port Stanley	1	37	23	60	27	87	100	60	40		
...		71	50	121	31	152	175	121	54		
Springfield										29	
		2,127	1,546	3,673	1,670	5,343	5,924	3,702	2,222		
Majority for Brower		581									

	No.	Macdi...	McDiarmid.							
Aldborough	1	58	49	107	95	202	225	109	116	2
do	2	52	38	90	67	157	175	91	84	1
do	3	60	20	80	47	127	150	80	70	
do	4	83	28	121	36	157	175	121	54	
do	5	54	37	91	35	126	150	92	58	1
do	6	34	24	58	28	86	100	58	42	
do	7	37	33	70	46	116	125	71	54	
do	8	16	33	49	35	84	100	49	51	1
Rodney	1	46	34	80	40	120	125	91	45	
do	2	42	45	87	33	120	150	87	38	
West Lorne	1	70	37	107	27	134	125	108	42	1
do	2	53	25	78	19	97	200	79	46	
Dunwich	1	76	62	138	52	190	175	138	62	
do	2	57	43	100	68	168	125	100	75	
do	3	19	36	55	57	112	150	55	58	
do	4	20	47	67	36	103	125	67	70	
do	5	16	64	80	50	130	150	80	41	
do	6	12	70	82	23	105	125	82	59	
do	7	50	41	91	48	140	125	91	43	1
do	8	44	38	82	18	100	250	82	47	
...ton	1	105	95	200	41	211	125	203	18	3
Southwold	1	46	61	107	58	165	125	107	52	
do	2	38	35	73	41	114	150	73	35	
do	3	40	58	115	27	142	175	115	60	
do	4	57	32	73	38	153	125	115	52	
do	5	41		73	23	96		73		

3 R.E.

RETURN from the Records of the GENERAL ELECTION to the Legislative Assembly, 1911.—*Continued.*

Electoral District	Numbers of Polling Places	No.	Names of Candidates and No. of Votes Polled for each — Macdiarmid	McDiarmid	Total No. of Votes Polled	No. of Votes remaining Unpolled	No. of Names on the Polling Lists	No. of Ballot Papers sent out to each Polling Place	Used Ballot Papers	Unused Ballot Papers	Rejected Ballot Papers	Cancelled Ballot Papers	Declined Ballot Papers	Ballot Papers taken from Polling Places
Elgin, West—Con..	Southwold	6	111	32	143	74	217	225	143	82				
	do	7	59	39	98	65	163	175	98	77				
	do	8	39	34	73	82	155	175	74	101				
	St. Th mas	1	81	31	112	68	180	200	112	88			1	
	do	2	179	61	240	43	283	300	241	59				
	do	3	122	54	176	114	290	325	178	147				
	do	4	198	71	269	163	432	450	272	178	1	1		
	do	5	117	33	150	168	318	350	150	200	3			
	do	6	125	37	162	201	363	375	162	213				
	do	7	106	28	134	123	257	275	134	141				
	do	8	101	44	145	115	260	275	145	130				
	do	9	57	42	99	136	235	250	99	151				
	do	10	168	40	208	200	408	425	225	200				
	do	11	91	57	148	189	337	375	149	226				
	do	12	95	40	135	115	250	275	135	140	1			
	do	13	148	45	193	290	483	500	194	306				
	do	14	138	49	187	207	394	425	187	238				
	do	15	27	13	40	41	81	100	40	60				
	Totals		3,188	190	5,108	3,477	8,585	9,325	5,146	4,179	15	2	1	1
	Majority for Macdiarmid		1,268											

Ward No. 1			
Sub-division	No. 1		
do	2		
do	3		
do	4		1
Ward No. 2			
Sub-division	No. 1		
do	2		
do	3		
do	4		2
do	5		
do	6 A		1
do	6 B		2
Ward No. 3			
Sub-division	No. 1		
do	2		
do	3		
do	4		
Ward No. 4			
Sub-division	No. 1		
do	2		
do	3 A		
do	3 B		
do	4		2
do	5		
Town of Walkerville—			
Sub-division	No. 1		
do	2		
do	3		
do	4 A		
do	4 B		
Village of Belleriver—			
Sub-division	No. 1		
Town of Sandwich—			
Sub-division	No. 1	2	99
do	2		05
Totals		2	513 / 27
Majority for		4	

MAXFIELD SHEPPARD,
Returning Officer.

RETURN from the Records of the GENERAL ELECTION to the Legislative Assembly, 1911.—*Continued.*

Electoral District: North Essex

Numbers of Polling Places	No.	Names of Candidates and No. of Votes Polled for each — Ducharme	Mason	Resaume	Total No. of Votes Polled	No. of Votes remaining Unpolled	No. of Names on the Polling Lists	No. of Ballot Papers sent out to each Polling Place	Used Ballot Papers	Unused Ballot Papers	Rejected Ballot Papers	Cancelled Ballot Papers	Declined Ballot Papers	Ballot Papers taken from Polling Places
Tp. of ...ton	1	18	3	37	58	80	138	150	58	92				
do	2	17	1	22	40	22	62	75	40	35				
do	3	23	1	66	90	56	146	150	90	60				
do	4	38	5	31	70	59	129	150	70	80				
Tp. of Sandwich West	1	23	5	28	56	78	134	150	56	94				
do	2	53	12	52	110	29	139	150	110	40				
do	3	41	6	51	104	68	172	175	104	71				
do	4	44	7	20	70	65	135	150	71	79	1			
do	5	86		56	149	79	228	250	150	100				
do	6	33	3	15	48	12	60	75	48	27				
Tp. of Sandwich East	1	35	5	29	67	51	118	125	68	57				1
do	2	37	5	41	83	36	119	125	84	41	2			
do	3	69	2	69	143	40	183	200	165	35				
do	4	14	3	29	45	101	101	250	46	204				
do	5	11	8	60	74	27	240	100	74	26				
do	6	58	4	48	114	126	100	250	114	136				
do	7	49	2	28	51	49	123	125	53	72	1			
Tp. of Sandwich South	1	34	14	33	84	39	120	125	85	40				
do	2	25	6	27	75	45	95	100	76	49	2			
do	3	22	3	24	55	40	112	125	55	45				
do	4	43	6	52	77	35	197	200	77	48				
Tp. of Maidstone	1	49	5	50	99	98	170	175	99	101	1			
do	2	39	11	32	86	84	172	175	87	88	2			
do	3	27	15	30	80	92	176	200	82	93	1			
do	4	31	23	19	73	103	175	200	73	127				
do	5				73	102			74	126				

Returning Officer: MAXFIELD SHEPPARD.

Essex, South — **WALTER H. NOBLE, Returning Officer.**

		Anderson	Brett						
Tp. of Rochester	No. 1	50	11	61	58	119	125	62	63
do	2	23	32	76	50	126	150	76	74
do	3	61	16	112	55	167	175	113	62
do	4	86	23	111	33	144	150	111	39
Tp. of Tilbury North	No. 1	75	48	124	21	58	150	124	26
do	2	36	4	40	18	145	75	41	34
do	3	39	15	56	62	58	125	56	69
do	4	40	8	48	60	108	125	48	77
do	5	36	10	46	28	74	75	46	29
Totals		2,533	2,586	6,091	5,177	11,268	12,240	6,188	6,052
Majority for Reaume			53						

		Anderson	Brett						
Amherstburg	No. 1	83	76	159	67	226	250	159	91
do	2	72	78	150	91	251	275	156	119
do	3	55	86	141	90	231	250	142	108
Colchester	No. 1	76	87	163	109	272	300	163	137
do	2	30	46	76	60	136	150	78	72
do	3	26	42	68	49	117	150	68	57
do South	1	69	109	178	35	213	225	178	47
do	2	75	60	135	50	185	200	135	65
do	3	71	98	169	70	239	250	169	81
do	4	49	84	133	75	208	225	134	91
Essex	1	32	48	80	18	98	125	89	45
do	2	45	62	107	19	126	150	107	43
do	3	61	53	114	23	137	150	115	35
field, North	1	75	65	140	50	190	200	140	60
do	2	90	57	147	29	176	200	147	53
do	3	62	45	107	54	161	75	108	67
do	4	24	28	52	09	61	100	52	23
do South	1	30	28	58	12	70	200	58	42
do	2	70	74	144	42	186	150	146	54
do	3	71	50	121	15	136	125	122	28
do	4	39	48	87	18	105	125	87	38
Kingsville	1	37	34	71	25	96	150	71	54
do	2	59	59	118	12	130	175	118	38
do	3	84	52	136	25	161	175	137	24
Leamington	1	59	42	101	14	93	100	101	12
do	2	45	42	87	06	175	200	88	51
do	3	90	59	149	26	170	175	136	39
do	4	45	44	89	14	103	125	89	36

Return from the Records of the General Election to the Legislative Assembly, 1911.—Continued.

Electoral District	Numbers of Polling Places	Names of Candidates and No. of Votes Polled for each — Brett	Anderson	Total No. of Votes Polled	No. of Votes Remaining Unpolled	No. of Names on the Polling Lists	No. of Ballot Papers sent out to each Polling Place	Used Ballot Papers	Unused Ballot Papers	Rejected Ballot Papers	Cancelled Ballot Papers	Declined Ballot Papers	Ballot Papers taken from Polling Places
Essex, South—Con.	Leamington No. 5	83	94	117	38	215	225	181	44		3	1	
	Malden No. 1	64	38	102	40	142	150	102	48		1		
	do 2	35	54	89	29	118	125	90	35				
	do 3	48	24	72	44	116	125	72	53			1	
	Mersea No. 1	80	79	159	78	237	250	161	89	1			
	do 2	26	20	46	24	70	100	47	53	1			
	do 3	15	42	57	21	78	100	57	43				
	do 4	78	51	129	22	151	175	129	46			1	
	do 5	18	61	79	14	93	100	80	20				
	do 6	33	63	96	27	123	150	96	54				
	do 7	26	64	90	26	116	150	90	60				
	do 8	74	81	155	49	204	225	155	70	1			
	do 9	21	24	45	26	71	100	45	55				
	Pelee Island No. 1	73	82	155	54	209	225	155	70				
	Tilbury West No. 1	88	97	185	39	224	250	186	64	1			
	do 2	12	22	34	11	45	50	34	16				
	do 3	15	13	28	12	40	50	28	22				
	do 4	20	35	55	45	100	125	56	69	1	1	1	
	do 5	23	08	31	15	46	50	32	18				
	Totals	2,535	2,665	5,200	1,765	6,965	7,800	5,229	2,571	10	10	9	
	Majority for Anderson		130										

Fort William

No.	Jarvis.									
1	53	46	50	149	81	230	325	154	171	
2	57	35	33	125	103	228	350	128	222	
3A	54	104	38	196	162	358	250	201	49	
3B	26	58	15	99	76	175	250	100	150	
4A	36	41	34	111	93	204	250	93	157	
4B	9	30	14	53	65	118	250	53	197	
5A	73	35	54	162	109	271	250	168	82	
5B	24	12	21	57	55	112	250	58	192	
6	69	15	74	158	113	271	300	161	89	
7A	94	28	80	202	109	311	300	205	70	
7B	43	7	52	102	49	151	275	104	171	
8A	84	67	77	228	168	396	275	228	222	
8B	45	25	49	119	68	187	450	123	151	
9	44	16	63	123	53	176	274	124	176	
10	49	11	37	97	91	188	300	98	202	
11A	46	36	44	126	115	241	300	127	198	
11B	23	21	13	57	75	132	325	60	215	
12A	31	19	68	118	109	227	275	119	206	
12B	14	8	22	44	50	94	325	44	256	
13	4		13	17	34	51	300	17	58	
14A	27	2	54	83	103	186	200	88	112	
14B	14	2	11	27	159	186	75	27	48	
15A	42	8	32	82	101	183	200	83	117	
15B	13		7	20	163	183	75	20	55	
16	40		24	64	75	139	175	65	110	
17	3	2	1	4	1	5	25	4	21	
18	20		6	8	4	12	25	9	16	
19	21		2	12	37	49	75	12	63	
20	31	1	6	27	39	66	100	28	72	
21	8	1	27	60	31	91	100	62	33	
22	13		9	10	20	30	50	11	39	
23	2	3	6	22	5	27	25	23	27	
24	21	1		8		8	50	8	17	
25	29		5	22	16	38	25	22	28	
26	14	2	2	35	14	49	50	37	38	
27	29	1	1	16	20	36	75	17	33	
28	15	3	4	33	53	86	50	33	67	
29	4	1	1	20	16	36	100	22	28	
30	2		2	5		5	50	5	20	
31	3	2		5		5	25	3	22	
32	3			3		7	25	6	44	
33	6	1		6	8	11	25	7	43	
34				7	10	16	50	7	43	
35	1			2	11	18	50	2	23	

Fort William ......

do. (repeated for each poll)

GEORGE H. ADAIR,
Returning Officer.

RETURN from the Records of the GENERAL ELECTION to the Legislative Assembly, 1911.—*Continued.*

Electoral District	Numbers of Polling Places	No.	Jarvis	Martin	Tonkin	Total No. of Votes Polled	No. of Votes remaining Unpolled	No. of Names on the Polling Lists	No. of Ballot Papers sent out to each Polling Place	Used Ballot Papers	Unused Ballot Papers	Rejected Ballot Papers	Cancelled Ballot Papers	Declined Ballot Papers	Ballot Papers taken from Polling Places
Fort William—Con.	Fort William	36	3	3	6	6	15	7	25	6	19				
	do	37	1	5	18	12	30	27	50	12	38				
	do	38	8	1	7	27	5	57	75	28	47				
	do	39	2	21	3	4	36	9	25	4	21				
	do	40	15	21	1	7	7	33	50	7	43			1	
	do	41	1	4		8	17	15	25	8	17	1			
	do	42	4		2	4	20	5	25	4	21				
	do	43	3		7	4	18	21	50	4	46	1			
	do	44	16		6	26	18	43	75	24	51				
	do	45	6	2	2	6	19	24	50	6	44				
	do	46	6			6	56	24	80	7	43	1			
	do	47	5			14	25	33	50	14	36				
	do	48	11			21	7	77	100	21	79				
	do	49	17			31		54	75	31	44				
	do	50	21			10	6	17	50	10	40	1			
	do	51	4	1	2	9	14	15	25	6	15				
	do	52	6			6		20	50	6	44				
	do	53	6			9	43	52	75	9	66				
	Totals		1,363	659	1,109	3,131	2,992	6,123	8,274	3,175	5,099	44	13	5	
	Majority for Jarvis		254												

	No.	McInnes	Rankin								
Tp. of Bedford	1	41	63	104	80	184	200	105	95		
do	2	2	32	34	26	60	75	34	41	1	
do	3	3	27	30	15	45	75	31	44		
do	4	34	11	45	43	88	100	45	55		
Tp. of Longhboro	1	68	91	159	86	245	275	161	114		
do	2	13	28	41	37	78	100	43	57		
do	3	34	21	55	32	87	100	56	44		
do	4	24	52	76	71	147	175	77	98		
do	5	2	18	20	19	39	50	20	30		1
Tp. of Portland	1	30	36	66	28	94	125	66	59		
do	2	25	92	117	53	170	200	118	82		
do	3	16	64	80	41	121	150	81	69		
do	4	16	31	47	20	67	75	48	27		
do	5	28	79	107	71	178	200	107	93		
do	6	22	23	45	44	89	100	45	55		
Tp. of Storrington	1	56	74	130	49	179	200	131	69		
do	2	62	95	157	60	217	225	157	68		
do	3	51	72	123	80	203	225	124	101	2	
do	4	4	5	9	19	28	50	9	41	1	
Tp. of Kingston	1	21	79	100	68	168	175	100	75		
do	2	53	87	140	96	236	250	140	110		
do	3	50	64	114	50	164	200	116	84		
do	4	26	48	74	44	118	150	75	75		
do	5	52	45	97	72	169	200	98	102		
do	6	20	17	37	42	79	100	38	63		
do	7	9	9	18	13	31	50	18	32		
Tp. of Pittsburgh	1	19	56	75	57	132	150	86	74		
do	2	31	34	65	49	114	125	65	60		
do	3	22	46	68	52	120	150	68	82	1	
do	4	26	43	69	54	123	175	70	105		
do	5	25	39	64	97	161	175	64	111		
Tp. of Wolfe Island	1	29	26	55	45	100	175	55	70		
do	2	38	31	69	78	147	125	69	106	1	
do	3	13	24	37	51	88	175	38	87		
do	4	8	8	16	27	43	75	17	58		
do	5	12	15	27	30	57	75	27	48		
Tp. of Garden Isd		3	41	44	11	55	75	44	31	1	
Tp. of Howe Isd		32	15	47	39	86	100	47	53		
Totals		1,020	1,641	2,661	1,849	4,510	5,350	2,682	2,668	13	8
Majority for Rankin			621								

Frontenac.

GEORGE V. STUART, Returning Officer.

RETURN from the Records of the GENERAL ELECTION to the Legislative Assembly, 1911.—Continued.

Electoral District	Numbers of Polling Places	No.	Munro	Robertson	Total No. of Votes Polled	No. of Votes Remaining Unpolled	No. of Names on the Polling Lists	No. of Ballot Papers sent out to each Polling Place	Used Ballot Papers	Unused Ballot Papers	Rejected Ballot Papers	Cancelled Ballot Papers	Declined Ballot Papers	Ballot Papers taken from Polling Places
Glengarry	Charl tsh	No. 1	50	80	130	77	207	225	130	95				
	do	2	31	113	144	73	217	250	144	106	1			
	do	3	33	34	67	60	127	150	67	83				
	do	4	37	62	99	83	182	225	100	125				
	do	5	28	31	59	64	123	150	60	90				
	do	6	33	50	83	41	124	150	83	67				
	do	7	44	73	117	63	180	200	117	60	1			
	do	8	56	55	96	68	164	200	96	83				
	Lancaster	1	73	65	121	65	201	200	121	104	3			
	do	2	41	44	138	63	112	150	138	79	1		1	
	do	3	58	34	85	27	154	175	87	63				
	do	4	38	47	92	62	117	150	92	83	1		1	1
	do	5	43	35	79	38	150	175	80	70				
	Kenyon	1	80	57	90	60	171	200	90	85				
	do	2	63	65	115	56	214	250	116	84				
	do	3	75	18	120	94	187	225	120	130				
	do	4	34	54	140	47	78	125	143	82				
	do	5	52	28	52	26	159	175	52	73	1			
	do	6	47	61	106	53	111	150	107	68				
	do	7	67	16	75	36	187	200	76	74		1		
	Lochiel	1	24	51	128	59	70	100	128	72				
	do	2	80	20	40	30	197	225	41	59	1		1	
	do	3	96	59	131	66	182	225	132	93	1			
	do	4	78	88	116	66	197	250	138	109	1			
			69		157	62	219		157	87				

Polling place	No.										
Locheil	No. 5				73	152	225	199	47	152	54	98
do	No. 6				66	134	200	179	45	134	50	84
Alexandria Town	No. 1	2	28	172	200	196	27	169	54	115
do do	No. 2	1	36	164	200	186	24	162	46	116
do do	No. 3		55	120	175	149	29	120	37	83
Lancaster Village	No. 1		86	114	200	176	62	114	65	49
Maxville Village	No. 1	1	81	144	225	195	51	144	72	72
Totals	5	3	11	2,669	3,731	6,400	5,496	1,784	3,712	1,724	1,988
Majority for Munro											264

Grenville: George Howard Ferguson, by Acclamation.   JOHN JOHNSTON, Returning Officer.

Grey, Centre.....

Polling subdivision	No.							McCullough	Lucas
Artemesia Tp.	No. 1	28	54	82	82	28	54	13	40
do	No. 2	85	99	184	184	85	99	47	51
do	No. 3	30	51	81	81	30	51	7	44
do	No. 4	47	75	122	122	46	76	33	2
do	No. 5	73	75	148	148	73	75	46	29
do	No. 6	20	49	69	69	20	49	21	28
do	No. 7	59	91	150	50	59	91	27	62
do	No. 8	39	44	83	83	39	44	3	41
Sullivan Tp.	No. 1	75	80	155	104	74	80	27	53
do	No. 2	106	69	175	175	106	69	33	36
do	No. 3	63	106	169	169	63	106	35	71
do	No. 4	92	88	180	180	92	88	49	39
do	No. 5	80	135	215	213	78	135	38	96
Euphrasia Tp.	No. 1	53	31	84	84	53	31	4	27
do	No. 2	62	63	125	122	59	63	19	44
do	No. 3	23	33	56	56	23	33	6	27
do	No. 4	69	77	146	46	69	77	28	49
do	No. 5	58	83	141	141	58	83	2	71
do	No. 6	30	50	80	80	30	50	13	37
do	No. 7	78	58	136	135	77	58	27	31
do	No. 8	84	71	155	155	84	71	19	52
do	No. 9	37	53	90	90	37	53	32	21
Osprey Tp.	No. 1	40	35	75	76	41	35	9	26
do	No. 2	99	76	175	173	97	76	15	61
do	No. 3	109	71	180	178	107	71	16	55
do	No. 4	80	45	125	125	80	45	7	38
do	No. 5	47	48	95	92	44	48	25	22
do	No. 6	43	42	85	84	42	42	13	29

THOMAS SCOTT, Returning Officer.

RETURN from the Records of the GENERAL ELECTION to the Legislative Assembly, 1911.—Continued.

Electoral District	Numbers of Polling Places	Names of Candidates and No. of Votes Polled for each		Voters at each Polling Place			Ballot Papers sent out and how disposed of in each Polling Place						
		Lucas.	McCullough.	Total No. of Votes Polled.	No. of Votes remaining Unpolled.	No. of Names on the Polling Lists.	No. of Ballot Papers sent out to each Polling Place.	Used Ballot Papers.	Unused Ballot Papers.	Rejected Ballot Papers.	Cancelled Ballot Papers.	Declined Ballot Papers.	Ballot Papers taken from Polling Places.
Grey, Centre—Con. Osprey Tp.	No. 7	36	17	54	67	121	125	55	71			1	1
do	No. 8	34	4	34	25	59	60	34	26				
Collingwood Tp.	No. 1	6	4	11	17	28	30	11	19				
do	2	10	5	14	40	54	55	14	41				
do	3	10	10	15	23	38	39	15	24	1			
do	4	13	18	23	57	80	80	23	57				
do	5	27	24	45	22	67	70	45	24				
do	6	40	13	32	57	121	125	65	60				
do	7	19	15	61	26	58	60	22	28				
do	8	36	12	51	40	91	91	51	40	1			
do	9	40	43	52	58	110	110	52	58				
do	10	70	7	113	75	188	188	113	75	1			
do	11	15	2	22	13	35	35	22	13				
do	12	10	19	12	18	31	32	12	18				
Holland Tp.	No. 1	20	30	39	79	118	118	39	79				
do	2	100	28	129	101	151	150	80	70	1			
do	3	39	33	72	84	230	225	129	96				
do	4	74	19	93	27	156	156	72	84	1			
do	5	42	16	58	34	120	129	93	36				
do	6	16	8	24	6	92	84	58	26				
Thornbury Town	No. 1	50	18	68	27	30	30	21	6				
do	2	47	21	68	20	95	95	68	27	1			
do	3					88	91	68	23				
Markdale Village	No. 1	150	40	191	44	235	275	191	84	1			
Chatsworth Village	No. 1	47	21	68	40	108	110	68	42				
Totals		2,223	1,611	3,286	2,765	6,051	6,124	3,287	2,837	11		1	1

North Grey.

Polling Place	No.							MacKay	Boyd	
St. Vincent	No. 1			64	61	125	101	40	61	28	39
do	2			55	70	125	101	31	70	36	34
do	3		3	54	96	150	133	40	93	40	53
do	4			56	119	175	164	45	119	84	35
do	5	1		50	75	125	101	26	75	44	31
do	6			31	69	100	94	26	68	31	37
do	7			57	68	125	121	53	68	36	32
do	8			33	42	75	67	25	42	17	25
do	9	1		44	56	100	84	28	56	28	28
Sydenham	No. 1	1		35	90	150	100	10	90	55	35
do	2	2		45	105	150	128	23	105	60	45
do	3	1		36	64	100	79	16	63	36	27
do	4			18	57	75	64	7	57	36	21
do	5			26	74	140	86	12	74	53	21
do	6			51	124	175	162	39	123	86	37
do	7	1		24	76	100	95	21	74	60	14
do	8			27	98	125	107	10	97	83	14
do	9			9	41	50	46	7	39	22	17
do	10		1	24	51	75	68	17	51	28	23
Derby	No. 1			28	97	125	112	15	97	37	60
do	2	1	2	42	133	175	152	20	132	77	55
do	3		1	45	105	150	122	18	104	67	37
Keppel	No. 1			35	115	150	129	15	114	57	57
do	2			12	63	75	68	5	63	32	31
do	3	1		41	84	125	103	19	84	58	26
do	4		1	35	65	100	84	20	64	24	40
do	5	1		44	81	125	118	37	81	27	54
do	6			19	81	100	95	15	80	40	40
do	7			44	99	150	136	31	105	63	42
do	8			26	77	125	118	19	99	54	45
Sarawak	Nos. 1 and 2			48	59	125	105	29	76	59	17
do	3		1	41	77	100	77	19	58	33	25
do	4			24	59	75	61	10	51	29	22
...rd	No. 1	1		20	51	75	66	11	55	15	40
do	2			23	55	100	100	24	76	42	34
do	3		3	50	77	100	208	41	167	87	80
do	4	3	2	50	175	225	179	60	119	73	46
do	5			65	120	200	141	41	100	56	44
do	6			69	100	150	163	53	110	72	38
Shallow Lake	No. 1		2	53	106	175	158	51	103	56	47
Owen Sound A to L		2		73	122	175	173	51	122	52	70
do M to Z			2	89	127	200	195	70	125	55	53
do A to L			3	86	111	200	176	67	109	56	57
					139	225	209	78	136	79	57

ALLAN CAMERON MAITLAND, Returning Officer.

RETURN from the Records of the GENERAL ELECTION to the Legislative Assembly, 1911.—*Continued.*

Electoral District.	Numbers of Polling Places.	No.	Names of Candidates and No. of Votes Polled for each.		Voters at each Polling Place.			Ballot Papers sent out and how disposed of in each Polling Place.							
			Boyd.	May.	Total No. of Votes Polled.	No. of Votes remaining Unpolled.	No. of Names on the Polling Lists.	No. of Ballot Papers sent out to each Polling Place.	Used Ballot Papers.	Unused Ballot Papers.	Rejected Ballot Papers.	Cancelled Ballot Papers.	Declined Ballot Papers.	Ballot Papers taken from Polling Places.
Grey, North—Con., Owen Sound	M to Z	2	55	77	132	63	195	200	134	66	1	1		
do	A to L	3	42	69	111	66	177	200	112	88				
do	M to Z	3	25	57	92	71	163	175	92	83	1			
do	A to L	4	57	72	129	57	186	200	130	70				
do	M to Z	4	39	53	92	30	122	125	92	33	1			
do	A to L	5	66	69	135	33	168	175	138	37				
do	M to Z	5	50	52	102	26	128	150	102	48				
do	A to L	6	79	67	146	51	197	200	146	56				
do	M to Z	7	62	59	121	40	161	175	121	53	3			
do	A to L	7	64	79	143	58	201	225	143	82				
do	M to Z	7	63	63	142	61	203	225	146	79	1			
do	A A to L	8	70	47	133	54	187	200	133	67				
do	A A to L	8	50	24	97	78	161	175	99	76	3			
do	M to Z	9	18	36	42	74	120	125	44	81				
do	A to L	9	18	67	54	67	128	150	55	95				
do	M to Z	10	67	56	134	55	201	225	137	88	4	2		
do	A to L	10	42	49	98	59	153	175	98	77				
do	M to Z	11	26	42	75	29	104	125	75	50	1			
do	A to L	12	34	68	76	25	101	125	76	49				
do	M to Z	12	54	61	122	57	179	200	123	77				
do	A to L	13	33	67	94	71	165	175	94	81				
do	M to Z	13	51	71	118	64	182	200	119	81				
do	A to L	13	51	52	122	45	167	175	126	49				
po	A to L		43	42	95	44	139	150	95	55				
do	M to Z		27		69	35	104	125	70	55				7
	Totals		**2,894**	**3,635**	**6,529**	**2,612**	**9,141**	**10,150**	**6,593**	**3,557**	**39**	**18**	**7**	

Municipality	Poll						
Grey, South	Neu statt		73	36		175	110	65
	Tp. Proton	No. 1	52	92		200	144	56
	do	2	18	37		125	56	69
	do	3	74	34		175	109	66
	do	4	45	50		175	95	80
	do	5	43	33		125	76	49
	do	6	10	43		100	53	47
	do	7	36	18		100	54	46
	do	8	24	28		125	53	72
	Normanby	No. 1	5	31		75	36	39
	do	2	44	58		200	102	98
	do	3	44	131		275	178	97
	do	4	39	35		150	74	76
	do	5	41	45		125	86	39
	do	6	27	46		125	73	52
	do	7	21	23		75	44	31
	Egremont	No. 1	23	52		150	75	75
	do	2	20	76		150	100	50
	do	3	54	55		175	109	66
	do	4	99	57		200	156	44
	do	5	60	45		150	107	43
	do	6	63	31		175	94	81
	Gl nelg	No. 1	55	34		150	90	60
	do	2	42	85		175	129	46
	do	3	62	43		150	105	45
	do	4	41	38		150	80	70
	Bentinck	No. 1	32	50		125	82	43
	do	2	45	65		175	111	64
	do	3	23	32		100	56	44
	do	4	41	40		125	82	43
	do	5	16	47		125	63	62
	do	6	42	83		200	126	74
	do	7	14	44		125	60	65
	do	8	52	67		200	119	81
	Hanover	No. 1	37	59		175	97	78
	do	2	55	25		125	80	45
	do	3	100	82		300	184	116
	do	4	107	62		300	171	129
	do	5	95	114		300	209	91
	do	6	98	55		125	98	27
	do	7	42	70		150	118	32
	do	8	56	130		225	186	39
	Totals		1,918	2,281		6,825	4,230	2,595
	Majority for Jamieson			363				

RETURN from the Records of the GENERAL ELECTION to the Legislative Assembly, 1911.—*Continued.*

Electoral District	Numbers of Polling Places		Names of Candidates and No. of Votes Polled for each		Total No. of Votes Polled	No. of Votes remaining Unpolled	No. of Names on the Polling Lists	No. of Ballot Papers sent out to each Polling Place	Used Ballot Papers	Unused Ballot Papers	Rejected Ballot Papers	Cancelled Ballot Papers	Declined Ballot Papers	Ballot Papers taken from Polling Places
			Jacques	K										
Haldimand	Monia	No. 1	74	44	118	32	150	175	118	57	1			
	do	No. 2	58	42	100	27	127	150	102	48		1		
	Cayuga	No. 1	40	108	148	48	196	200	148	52	1	1	1	
	Hagersville	No. 1	66	91	157	25	182	200	159	41				
	do	No. 2	46	44	90	20	110	175	90	35				
	Innis	No. 1	75	49	124	39	163	134	130	45			1	1
	Seneca	No. 1	29	54	83	41	124	60	47	51	6			
	do	No. 2	3	43	46	10	56	139		13	1			
	do	No. 3	57	43	100	29	129	125	101	38	1			
	do	No. 4	47	47	85	29	114	125	111	40				
	do	No. 5	63	38	110	38	133	158	105	47				
	Dunn	No. 1	73	32	105	28	99	200	73	95				
	do	No. 2	43	30	73	26	200	111	149	38			1	1
	South Cayuga	No. 1	44	104	148	52	160	210	132	61	1		1	1
	Rainham	No. 2	49	82	131	29	191	175	159	43	1			
	do	No. 3	71	80	151	40	179	200	147	47				
	Oneida	No. 1	40	106	146	33	73	190	84	43				
	do	No. 2	26	58	84	32	95	125	51	41				
	do	No. 3	30	20	50	23	112	75	68	24				
	do	No. 4	20	48	68	27	47	105	72	37				
	do	No. 5	54	18	72	40	110	125	38	53			1	1
	North Cayuga	No. 1	14	25	38	11	74	50	96	12				
	do	No. 2	13	82	96	14	59	125	62	29				
	do	No. 3	10	49	62	12	113	80	41	18		1	1	
	do	No. 4	42	31	41	18		69	95	28				3
				50	92	21		125		30				

HENRY B. SAWLE, Returning Officer.

Walpole (Majority for Kohler)

Poll	No.							Nixon	Warren
Walpole	5	19	96	115	105	9	96	34	62
do	1	34	111	145	139	30	109	57	52
do	2	36	131	167	157	31	126	45	81
do	3	30	100	130	120	21	99	44	55
do	4	53	115	168	158	43	115	57	58
do	5	17	58	75	64	6	58	27	31
do	6	42	108	150	142	36	106	50	56
do	7	61	106	167	157	53	104	65	39
do	8	32	93	125	112	20	92	20	72
Totals		1,396	3,423	4,854	4,414	991	3,423	1,499	1,924
Majority for Kohler									425

Halton. — JOHN M. BASTEDO, Returning Officer.

Township	No.						Nixon	Warren
Esquesing	1	79	121	200	186	66	50	70
do	2	79	146	225	207	62	69	76
do	3	39	136	175	170	34	76	60
do	4	68	107	175	153	46	38	69
do	5	60	115	175	166	51	85	30
do	6	60	165	225	213	52	113	48
Trafalgar	1	75	150	225	209	61	58	90
do	2	67	133	200	195	62	79	54
do	3	51	74	125	107	34	27	46
do	4	63	112	175	168	57	52	59
do	5	41	109	150	139	30	58	51
do	6	88	137	225	211	74	89	48
do	7	41	84	125	120	36	28	56
Nelson	1	84	91	175	161	70	34	57
do	2	68	107	150	173	66	53	54
do	3	55	95	150	136	43	44	49
do	4	62	88	100	132	45	50	37
do	5	45	55	200	90	35	27	28
do	6	68	132	275	181	49	84	48
Nassagaweya	1	98	177	200	262	86	85	91
do	2	75	125	200	196	72	58	66
do	3	74	120	125	183	59	31	93
Mton E. Ward		39	86	150	108	22	55	31
do N. do		43	107	200	143	36	64	43
do S. do		74	126	200	180	55	60	65
Oakville	1	60	140	225	191	53	84	54
do	2	77	200	300	205	57	98	50
do	3	94	200	250	284	80	104	100
Burlington	1	124	126	250	243	117	84	42

RETURN from the Records of the General Election to the Legislative Assembly, 1911.—*Continued.*

Halton—Con.

Polling Place	No.	Nixon	Warren	Total No. of Votes Polled	No. of Votes Remaining Unpolled	No. of Names on the Polling Lists	No. of Ballot Papers sent out	Used Ballot Papers	Unused Ballot Papers	Rejected Ballot Papers	Cancelled Ballot Papers	Declined Ballot Papers	Ballot Papers taken from Polling Places
Burlington	2	105	52	157	86	243	250	158	92	1			
do	3	43	32	75	27	102	125	75	50				
Georgetown	1	104	83	187	28	215	225	187	38	2	1		
do	2	121	73	194	40	234	250	197	53	1	1		
Acton	1	77	69	146	28	174	200	148	52				
do	2	98	79	177	76	253	275	180	95	3		7	
Totals		**2,385**	**2,053**	**4,438**	**1,895**	**6,333**	**6,800**	**4,469**	**2,331**	**21**	**3**	**7**	

Majority for Nixon 332

Hamilton, East.

Polling Place	No.	Cooper	Studholm.	Total No. of Votes Polled	No. of Votes Remaining Unpolled	No. of Names on the Polling Lists	No. of Ballot Papers sent out	Used Ballot Papers	Unused Ballot Papers	Rejected Ballot Papers	Cancelled Ballot Papers	Declined Ballot Papers	Ballot Papers taken from Polling Places
Division	3	73	57	130	58	188	200	130	70				
do	4	51	36	87	39	126	150	88	62				
do	5	94	76	170	105	275	275	175	100	1	5		
do	6	78	46	124	62	186	200	126	74	2			
do	7	54	36	90	49	139	150	93	57	3			
do	8	65	77	142	97	239	250	150	100	8			
do	9	73	51	124	69	193	200	150	71	5			
do	10	53	63	116	85	201	225	116	109				
do	11	53	78	131	67	198	200	132	68	1			
do	12	65	57	122	59	181	200	123	77				1
do	13	43	56	99	74	173	200	100	100	1			
do	14	59	80	139	89	228	250	140	110	1			
do	7	0	63	123	83	206	225	132	93	8	1	1	

16	do		1	3 1		58	117	175	168	55	118	44	69
55	do				5	35	65	100	92	28	64	14	50
56	do				1	100	150	250	248	104	144	90	54
57	do				2	94	156	250	237	82	155	92	63
58	do				1	106	169	275	271	104	167	100	67
59	do				1	88	137	225	202	66	136	77	59
60	do				1	110	115	225	206	92	114	68	46
61	do		1		2	105	120	225	203	84	119	81	38
62	do		7		4	102	173	225	257	88	169	98	71
63	do					49	76	125	118	44	74	41	33
64	do				9	101	149	250	239	94	145	91	54
65	do		1		1	79	146	225	213	68	145	99	46
66	do			2	4	89	161	250	240	86	154	101	53
67	do				5	89	111	200	179	77	102	53	49
68	do					82	93	175	158	66	92	65	27
69	do			2	1	101	174	275	259	89	170	90	80
70	do		2	1	2	76	149	225	214	72	142	77	65
71	do		1	1		98	177	275	276	100	176	112	64
72	do					85	165	250	250	86	164	83	81
73	do				5	96	179	275	262	85	177	101	76
74	do					76	174	225	248	76	172	79	93
75	do					93	132	225	202	70	132	71	61
76	do A to L			2	1	115	185	300	276	93	183	104	79
77	do M to Z	1	1	1		75	125	200	188	64	124	74	50
78	do A to L					64	136	200	195	64	131	77	54
79	do M to Z					67	83	150	135	55	80	42	38
80	do A to L	2		1	2	117	183	300	284	102	182	112	70
81	do M to Z	1		1	1	77	123	200	195	72	123	65	58
82	do					79	96	175	173	78	95	58	37
83	do A to L					124	176	300	288	113	175	98	77
87	do M to Z	2		1		89	136	225	209	77	132	70	62
88	do A to L				2	59	91	150	146	56	90	56	34
	do M to Z				1	109	141	250	245	106	139	89	50
	do			1	4	99	101	200	176	79	97	61	36
	do					137	138	275	258	122	136	86	50
	do					93	57	150	127	74	53	26	27
Totals		20	20	90	4,307	6,493	10,800	10,170	3,807	6,363	3,521	2,842
Majority for Studholme											679	

ERNEST E. LINGER, Returning Officer.

RETURNS from the Records of the GENERAL ELECTION to the Legislative Assembly, 1911.—*Continued.*

Electoral District	Numbers of Polling Places		Names of Candidates and No. of Votes Polled for each.		Total No. of Votes Polled.	No. of Votes remaining Unpolled.	No. of Names on the Polling Lists.	No. of Ballot Papers sent out to each Polling Place.	Used Ballot Papers.	Unused Ballot Papers.	Rejected Ballot Papers.	Cancelled Ballot Papers.	Declined Ballot Papers.	Ballot Papers taken from Polling Places.
			Russell.	Hen. rie.										
Hamilton, West...	Division	No.	17											
	do	17	16	17	33	35	68	75	33	42	3			
	do	18	44	79	123	97	220	225	126	99	2			
	do	19	50	92	142	73	215	225	144	81	2	1		
	do	20	35	72	107	54	161	175	107	68	1			
	do	21	48	93	141	90	231	250	144	106		1		
	do	22	21	62	83	77	160	175	85	90	1			2
	do	23	21	80	101	75	176	175	102	73	3			
	do	24	35	60	95	67	162	175	95	80				
	do	25	34	83	117	109	226	225	118	107				
	do	26	32	79	111	125	236	250	111	139	2			
	do	27	38	83	121	119	240	250	124	126				
	do	28	59	103	162	111	273	275	164	111		2		4
	do	29	24	55	79	85	164	200	79	121				
	do	30	16	46	62	90	152	175	62	113				
	do	31	13	41	54	99	153	250	56	119				
	do	32	23	74	97	136	233	150	99	151				
	do	33	25	66	91	125	216	275	62	130	4			
	do	34	20	42	62	84	146	175	135	88	2		2	
	do	35	43	88	131	129	260	225	77	140	1			
	do	36	15	60	75	100	175	225	114	161	4			
	do	37	29	84	113	155	268	150	124	101				
	do	38	46	74	120	106	226	275	74	76				
	do	39	19	55	74	59	133	250	127	148			4	2
	do	40	30	82	125	150	275	250	126	124				
	do	41	29	97	122	106	228	250	127	123	1			
							253							

WILLIAM HENRY CHILDS,
Returning Officer.

Hastings, East (continued)

No.									Rejected			
do 42	63	38	101	115	216	225	102	123				
do 43	43	19	62	98	160	175	64	111			2	
do 44	76	24	100	150	250	250	102	148	2			1
do 45	68	23	91	130	221	225	92	133	1			
do 46	51	18	69	56	125	125	70	55	1	1		
do 47	29	17	46	67	113	125	47	78	1		1	
do 48	64	31	95	121	216	225	97	128	1	2	1	
do 49	46	21	67	108	175	175	69	106	2			
do 50	74	24	98	104	202	225	100	125	2	1	1	
do 51	53	26	79	73	152	175	83	92	1	2		
do 52	55	36	89	130	219	225	90	135		2		
do 53	55	35	89	77	167	175	91	84		1		
do 54	57	32	89	133	222	225	90	135			1	
Totals	2,594	1,149	3,743	3,945	7,688	8,075	3,807	4,268	38	14	11	1
Majority for Hendrie	1,445											

Hastings, East: Sandy Grant, by Acclamation. GOOD MCKINNEY CAMPBELL, Returning Officer.

Hastings, North: Robert John Cook, by Acclamation. WILLIAM J. DOUGLAS, Returning Officer.

Hastings, West: John Wesley Johnson, by Acclamation. WILLIAM PARKER HYDSON, Returning Officer.

Huron, Centre

	No.	Proudfoot	Elliott										
Grey	1	42	47	89	30	119	150	89	61				
do	2	50	25	75	21	96	125	75	50				
do	3	55	21	76	22	98	125	77	48				
do	4	63	32	95	36	131	150	95	55				
do	5	60	55	115	46	161	150	116	59				
do	6	40	33	73	46	119	150	74	76			1	
do	7	64	27	91	28	119	175	91	59				
McKillop	1	85	47	112	43	155	175	112	63				
do	2	85	83	132	9	141	200	132	43				
do	3	56	59	139	31	170	175	139	61				
do	4	58	28	117	29	146	75	117	58				
Brussels	1	31	31	59	7	66	100	59	16		1		
do	2	37	29	68	16	84	100	69	31				
do	3	35	62	64	16	80	225	64	36				
Seaforth	1	98	35	160	31	191	125	160	65				
do	2	53	37	88	20	108	125	88	37				
do	3	17	37	54	20	74	100	54	46				

RETURN from the Records of the GENERAL ELECTION to the Legislative Assembly, 1911.—Continued.

Electoral District	Numbers of Polling Places	Proudfoot	Elliott	Total No. of Votes Polled	No. of Votes remaining Unpolled	No. of Names on the Polling Lists	No. of Ballot Papers sent out to each Polling Place	Used Ballot Papers	Unused Ballot Papers	Rejected Ballot Papers	Cancelled Ballot Papers	Declined Ballot Papers	Ballot Papers taken from Polling Places
Huron, Centre - Con.	Seaforth No. 4	17	30	47	9	56	75	47	28				
	do No. 5	42	51	93	22	115	150	93	57				
	Hullet do 1	51	53	104	29	124	150	104	46		1		
	do 2	63	52	115	25	140	175	115	60				
	do 3	28	29	57	25	82	100	57	43				
	do 4	68	46	114	26	140	175	114	61				
	do 5	28	28	56	18	74	100	56	44				
	do 6	45	21	66	27	93	150	66	44				
	do 7	43	31	74	16	90	125	75	59				
	Colborne do 1	78	44	122	26	148	175	123	50	2			
	do 2	24	43	67	14	81	100	67	52				
	do 3	58	80	138	30	168	175	138	36				
	do 4	47	26	73	16	89	100	73	37				
	Clinton do 1	56	62	118	19	137	150	120	27				
	d o 2	66	80	146	31	177	200	146	30				
	do 3	48	71	119	37	156	175	120	54				
	do 4	47	60	107	24	131	150	107	43			1	
	Goderich do 1	56	84	140	47	187	200	141	59		1	1	
	do 2	67	74	141	91	232	250	142	108				
	do 3	73	55	128	64	192	250	129	96	1			
	do 4	66	56	122	59	125	200	123	77				
	do 5	42	48	90	35	125	125	90	35				
	do 6	61	86	147	62	209	225	148	77			1	1
	do 7	45	44	89	26	115	150	90	60				
Totals		2,148	1,932	4,080	1,221	5,301	6,250	4,095	2,155	5	5	5	5
Majority for Proudfoot	216												

Huron, North

					Kerr.	Move.
Tp. of Ashfield	No. 1	45	108	153	132	24	108	72	36
do	2	49	101	150	132	31	101	63	38
do	3	38	88	126	115	27	88	49	39
do	4	36	90	126	112	22	90	62	28
do	5	42	84	126	120	37	83	27	56
do	6	42	83	125	114	31	83	29	64
do	7	46	79	125	100	21	79	17	62
Village of Blth	No. 1	29	96	125	115	20	95	45	50
do	2	20	80	100	94	15	79	36	43
Tp. of Wawanash, East	No. 1	38	64	100	71	7	64	26	38
do	2	38	116	154	135	19	116	63	53
do	3	29	96	125	103	7	96	42	54
do	4	24	76	100	88	12	76	27	49
do West	1	42	58	100	74	16	58	20	38
do	2	45	106	151	133	28	105	57	48
do	3	36	89	125	113	24	89	56	33
Tp. of Howick	No. 1	36	64	100	88	24	64	39	25
do	2	39	88	127	105	17	88	37	51
do	3	22	78	100	91	13	78	27	51
do	4	41	135	176	160	25	135	86	49
do	5	56	119	175	164	45	119	85	34
Tp. of Morris	No. 1	42	160	202	198	38	160	115	45
do	2	64	165	229	202	37	165	102	63
do	3	67	133	200	172	39	133	61	72
do	4	31	119	150	149	30	119	69	50
do	5	37	86	123	106	21	85	26	59
do	6	54	97	151	122	25	97	44	53
Tp. of Turnberry	No. 1	40	86	126	99	14	85	47	38
do	2	33	94	127	104	10	94	45	48
do	3	43	111	154	123	12	111	59	52
do	4	32	118	150	133	15	118	61	57
Town of Wingham	No. 1	55	140	175	162	26	136	88	48
do	2	15	135	150	139	4	135	72	63
do	3	22	102	124	113	11	102	54	48
do	4	54	96	150	113	29	96	44	52
Tp. of Wingham	do	23	95	118	108	14	94	59	35
do		27	99	126	111	14	97	59	38
do		48	133	181	161	29	132	79	53
Village of Moxeter		55	145	200	174	30	144	86	58
do		129	71	200	185	114	71	54	17
do		14	86	100	98	13	85	31	54
Totals		**1,656**	**4,169**	**5,825**	**5,143**	**990**	**4,153**	**2,210**	**1,943**
Majority for Musgrove								**267**	

RETURN from the Records of the GENERAL ELECTION to the Legislative Assembly, 1911.—*Continued.*

Electoral District	Numbers of Polling Places	Names of Candidates and No. of Votes Polled for each — Eilber.	Zellar.	Total No. of Votes Polled.	No. of Votes Remaining Unpolled.	No. of Names on the Polling Lists.	No. of Ballot Papers sent out to each Polling Place.	Used Ballot Papers.	Unused Ballot Papers.	Rejected Ballot Papers.	Cancelled Ballot Papers.	Declined Ballot Papers.	Ballot Papers taken from Polling Places.
Huron, South	Exeter ... No. 1	87	32	119	26	145	161	121	40				
	do ... 2	85	54	139	34	173	192	139	53				
	do ... 3	52	43	95	28	123	135	95	40		1		
	do ... 4	33	20	53	17	70	79	53	26	1			
	Hensall ... No. 1	105	81	186	29	215	235	186	49				
	Bayfield ... 2	93	25	118	37	155	170	118	52				
	Tp. of Stephen ... 3	66	21	87	23	110	120	87	33				
	do ... 1	45	15	60	17	77	85	60	25	1			
	do ... 2	80	31	111	10	121	132	111	21				
	do ... 3	87	45	132	19	151	168	132	36	1			
	do ... 4	41	42	83	13	96	106	83	23				
	do ... 5	74	51	125	13	138	153	125	28				
	do ... 6	33	57	90	15	105	116	90	26				
	do ... 7	58	20	78	20	98	108	78	30				
	Tp. of Tuckersmith ... No. 1	63	43	106	22	128	138	106	32				
	do ... 2	30	67	97	27	124	167	98	69	1			
	do ... 3	38	49	87	26	113	114	87	27				
	do ... 4	14	47	61	24	85	93	61	32				
	do ... 5	20	64	84	19	103	116	84	32				
	do ... 6	32	67	99	21	120	135	99	36	1			
	Tp. of Goderich ... No. 1	26	61	87	22	109	120	87	33				
	do ... 2	64	30	94	43	137	152	94	58				
	do ... 3	55	26	81	20	101	112	82	30				
	do ... 4	65	38	103	16	119	133	104	29				
	do ... 5	56	11	67	13	80	88	67	21				
	do ... 6	50	34	84	25	109	120	84	36	1			
	do ...	34	21	55	17	72	87	55	32				

THOMAS B. CARLING,
Returning Officer.

Tp. of Stanley	No. 1	..	..	..	36	71	107	99	28	71	48	23	
do	2	..	..	..	34	78	112	104	26	78	50	28	
do	3	..	..	..	35	115	150	139	24	115	26	89	
do	4	..	..	..	16	65	81	75	10	65	18	47	
do	5	..	..	..	34	106	140	130	24	106	73	33	
Tp. of Hay	No. 1	..	..	..	19	65	84	78	13	65	41	24	
do	2	..	..	..	18	65	83	76	11	65	45	20	
do	3	1	..	..	31	169	200	177	9	168	109	59	
do	4	..	..	..	25	126	151	139	13	126	91	35	
do	5	..	..	..	25	72	97	88	16	72	46	26	
do	6	..	..	..	32	111	143	121	10	111	56	55	
do	7	..	1	..	9	56	65	59	3	56	29	27	
do	8	..	..	..	25	60	85	78	18	60	48	12	
Tp. of Usborne	No. 1	..	..	..	36	136	172	154	19	135	44	91	
do	2	..	..	1	29	117	146	134	17	117	63	54	
do	3	1	..	1	33	135	168	166	32	134	31	103	
do	4	..	..	..	42	119	161	148	28	118	69	49	
Totals		2	2	6	1,428	4,252	5,680	5,140	897	4,243	1,982	2,261	
Majority for Eilber												279	

	Brett.								adn.				
Ingolf	..	..	..	..	19	6	25	11	5	6	4	2	min.
Ostersund	..	..	..	..	33	17	50	38	21	17	3	14	
Keewatin (outside)	..	..	..	1	73	7	75	6	4	7	2	1	
Wak Lake	..	..	..	..	18	2	25	13	6	2	6	11	
Waldof	..	..	..	..	8	7	24	24	8	7	5	20	
afit	..	..	..	..	44	16	100	90	34	16	36	4	
rihrogia	..	..	..	1	49	56	75	71	45	56	22	..	
Van Horne (outside)	..	..	..	..	20	26	25	10	15	26	5	1	
Bedworth	..	..	..	..	35	5	50	30	22	5	14	3	
Wabigoon	..	..	..	..	28	15	50	46	7	15	21	2	
Dinorwic	..	..	..	..	13	24	25	18	2	24	9	..	
Dyment	..	..	..	..	21	12	25	6	1	4	4	2	
lan	..	..	..	1	10	4	25	16	1	15	15	3	
Bonheur	..	..	..	..	20	15	50	6	2	5	3	6	
Ouok	..	..	..	..	33	17	25	28	1	17	14	2	
Corkscrew Isbd	..	..	..	..	16	9	25	10	1	8	2	7	
wia Mine	..	..	..	1	17	8	50	8	2	8	6	9	
Regina Me	..	..	..	..	15	9	25	26	16	10	3	1	
French Portage (L of W.)	..	..	..	..	40	8	25	18	8	9	1	4	
Malachi (T.N.R.)	..	..	..	..	16	10	50	12	3	10	8		
M naki (T.N.R.)	..	..	..	..	10	9	25	19	4	15	11		

Kenora

CHARLES WIGGINS BELYEA,
Returning Officer.

Return from the Records of the General Election to the Legislative Assembly, 1911.—Continued.

Electoral District	Numbers of Polling Places	Names of Candidates and No. of Votes Polled for each — Brett.	— Machin.	Total No. of Votes Polled	No. of Votes remaining Unpolled	No. of Names on the Polling Lists	No. of Ballot Papers sent out to each Polling Place	Used Ballot Papers	Unused Ballot Papers	Rejected Ballot Papers	Cancelled Ballot Papers	Declined Ballot Papers	Ballot Papers taken from Polling Places
Kenora—Con.	Redditt (T.N.R.)	12	36	48	36	84	100	49	51	1			
	Quitell	4	8	12	11	23	25	12	13				
	Richan	1	17	18	15	33	50	18	32				
	Pyrites	6	13	19	10	29	50	19	31	3			
	Graham	24	106	130	127	257	175	133	42				
	Superior	11	16	27	64	91	100	27	73	3			
	Wako		4	4	20	24	25	4	21	4			
	Keewatin No. 1	28	43	71	48	119	125	74	51	1			
	do	30	53	83	48	131	150	87	63				
	do	36	60	96	67	163	175	97	78		1		
	Kenora	23	35	58	66	124	125	58	67				
	do	41	62	103	13	116	200	103	97	1			
	do	45	71	131	363	494	250	132	118	2			
	do	37	80	108	386	494	225	113	112	2			
	do	59	76	139	145	284	250	142	108		2	2	
	do	50	59	126	120	246	250	126	124			1	
	Norman (Pt. Kenora) No. 7	81	23	140	105	245	200	142	58				
	Jaffray & Melick	51	12	74	83	157	150	74	76				
	Machin (Pt.) No. 1	33	29	45	124	169	175	45	130			2	
	do No. 2	9		38	48	86	100	38	62				
	Van Horne	16	7	3	12	15	25	3	22				
	Dryden	31	66	23	4	27	50	23	27				
	Ignace	13	20	97	74	171	175	97	78				
				33	47	80	100	33	67				
	Totals	733	1,179	1,912	2,256	4,168	4,074	1,937	2,137	17	3	5	5
	Majority for Machin		446										

Kent, East

Township	No.							Ferguson	Bowyer
Harwich	1	64	61	125	112	52	60	32	28
do	2	38	87	125	120	33	87	46	41
do	3	96	79	175	163	85	78	25	53
do	4	45	105	150	146	42	74	43	61
do	5	70	105	175	168	64	104	55	49
do	6	70	105	175	161	56	105	65	40
do	7	63	87	150	135	49	86	40	46
do	8	57	118	175	161	43	118	62	56
do	9	70	105	175	153	48	105	53	52
do	10	53	122	175	156	34	122	63	59
do	11	41	109	150	135	48	108	76	32
Orford	1	18	57	75	72	27	57	27	30
do	2	33	92	125	114	15	91	61	30
do	3	39	86	125	106	23	86	55	31
do	4	35	90	225	121	20	90	58	32
do	5	45	180	125	204	31	80	108	72
do	6	27	98	75	122	24	97	57	40
do	7	22	53	100	64	25	53	39	14
Howard	1	37	63	100	93	11	62	30	32
do	2	22	78	200	98	31	78	50	28
do	3	90	110	199	191	20	108	63	45
do	4	75	124	175	183	83	124	69	55
do	5	68	107	250	152	59	107	60	47
do	6	74	176	150	237	45	176	84	92
Camden	1	45	105	175	146	61	104	27	77
do	2	60	115	175	164	42	115	70	45
do	3	84	91	100	110	49	91	46	28
do	4	43	57	100	77	69	56	28	19
do	5	31	69	150	92	21	69	50	39
Zone	1	64	86	100	126	23	86	47	34
do	2	26	74	150	132	40	74	42	51
do	3	57	95	125	117	19	93	42	34
Bothwell	1	39	85	100	88	39	86	52	31
do	2	44	77	125	105	31	56	25	42
Dresden	1	48	61	100	93	32	74	35	40
do	2	39	6	125	16	28	77	21	4
do	3	19	124	175	169	20	61	2	55
Blenheim	1	51	86	150	145	10	6	67	50
do	2	64	151	199	196	47	122	33	80
do	3	48	122	151	144	62	83	69	69
do	4	29	76	100	94	47	149	53	36

RETURN from the Records of the GENERAL ELECTION to the Legislative Assembly, 1911.—*Continued.*

Electoral District.	Numbers of Polling Places.	Names of Candidates and No. of Votes Polled for each.		Total No. of Votes Polled.	No. of Votes remaining Unpolled.	No. of Names on the Polling Lists.	No. of Ballot Papers sent out to each Polling Place.	Used Ballot Papers.	Unused Ballot Papers.	Rejected Ballot Papers.	Cancelled Ballot Papers.	Declined Ballot Papers.	Ballot Papers taken from Polling Places.
		Bowyer.	Ferguson.										
Kent East—Con... Ridgetown	No. 1	63	26	89	77	166	175	90	85		1	1	
do	2	64	37	101	82	183	199	102	97		1		
do	3	63	65	128	72	200	200	130	70	2	3		
do	4	67	63	130	77	207	225	133	92		1		
Thamesville	No. 1	69	121	190	37	227	250	191	59			1	
Totals		2,240	2,452	4,692	1,990	6,682	7,248	4,720	2,528	17	11		
Majority for Ferguson			212										
		Hea.	Sulman.										
Kent, West...... City of Chm	No. 1	36	47	83	66	149	150	83	67			1	
do	1 A	63	75	138	63	201	225	138	87	2			
do	2	63	94	157	68	225	225	157	68	1			
do	3	55	96	151	76	227	250	153	97				
do	4	44	83	127	52	179	200	129	71	2	2		
do	5	14	69	83	38	121	125	83	42	1			
do	6	17	85	102	40	142	150	104	46	2			
do	7	31	57	88	38	126	150	84	66	1	2		
do	8	34	74	108	49	168	175	109	66	2	1		
do	9	48	82	130	64	179	200	133	67				
do	10	60	79	140	58	204	225	142	83			1	
do	11	54	59	133	62	191	200	133	67				
do	12 A	41	59	100	62	62	175	100	75				
do	12 B	40	59	99	46	145	150	99	51				

RETURN from the Records of the GENERAL ELECTION to the Legislative Assembly, 1911 —*Continued.*

Electoral District	Numbers of Polling Places	Names of Candidates and No. of Votes Polled for each		Total No. of Votes Polled	No. of Votes Remaining Unpolled	No. of Names on the Polling Lists	No. of Ballot Papers sent out to each Polling Place	Used Ballot Papers	Unused Ballot Papers	Rejected Ballot Papers	Cancelled Ballot Papers	Declined Ballot Papers	Ballot Papers taken from Polling Places
		Hea.	Sulman.										
Kent, West—Con...	Township of East Tilbury.. No. 7	3	19	22	29	51	75	23	52	1			
	do No. 8	29	21	50	39	89	100	50	50				
	Town of Tilbury No. 1	28	44	72	68	140	150	73	77		1		
	do No. 2	41	65	106	91	197	200	106	94	1	1	1	
	Town of Wallaceburg No. 1	45	61	106	158	264	300	108	192				
	do 2 A	33	29	62	104	166	150	63	112	1			
	do 2 B	29	29	58	85	143	150	59	91	1			1
	do 3	37	66	103	116	219	200	104	96				
	Totals	2,239	3,106	5,345	4,285	9,630	10,425	5,372	5,053	21	8	4	
	Majority for Sulman		67										

Kingston—Arthur Edward Ross—by Acclamation.—J. B. WALKEM. Returning Officer.

Electoral District	Numbers of Polling Places	Martyn.	McCormick.	Total No. of Votes Polled	No. of Votes Remaining Unpolled	No. of Names on the Polling Lists	No. of Ballot Papers sent out	Used Ballot Papers	Unused Ballot Papers	Rejected	Cancelled	Declined	Taken
Lambton, East....	Alvinston. No. 1	54	20	70	13	89	100	70	24	2			
	do 2	83	46	129	28	159	175	129	44	2			
	Arkona No. 1	43	55	98	30	129	150	98	51		3		
	Br ke 2	34	29	63	11	74	75	63	12				
	do 3	37	34	71	14	85	100	71	29				
	do 4	96	74	170	28	201	225	170	52				
	do 5	64	45	109	36	145	150	109	41				
	*	36	34	70	12	82	100	70	30				

Dawn	No. 6				14	36	50	38	2	36	22	14
do	7				21	54	75	64	10	54	21	33
do	8				13	37	50	44	7	37	25	12
do	9			3	22	53	75	70	17	53	15	38
do	10				25	50	75	69	19	50	13	37
do	11				14	61	75	67	6	61	21	40
Bosanquet	No. 1		1		46	104	150	144	40	103	57	46
do	2				42	133	175	172	39	130	49	81
do	3				30	95	125	114	19	95	34	61
do	4		2		39	70	100	94	24	70	40	30
do	5				38	61	100	79	18	61	41	20
do	6				26	62	50	92	31	61	46	15
do	7				43	24	150	40	16	24	18	11
Euphemia	No. 1				51	107	100	131	24	105	56	49
do	2				26	49	125	88	39	48	21	27
do	3		2		30	99	100	124	25	99	62	37
do	4				42	70	100	90	20	70	37	33
do	5				20	58	75	81	23	58	22	36
Plympton	No. 1				44	55	125	62	7	53	24	29
do	2		1		20	81	175	107	26	81	48	33
do	3		2		44	116	125	154	38	116	55	31
do	4				59	88	175	115	27	88	57	47
do	5				37	138	202	159	21	137	90	45
do	6				55	147	50	188	41	145	100	14
Warwick	No. 1				15	35	125	47	12	35	21	34
do	2		1		35	90	150	110	20	90	56	29
do	3		1		39	61	100	87	26	61	32	48
do	4				32	101	150	133	32	101	53	47
do	5				36	93	175	115	22	92	45	60
Forest	No. 1				38	139	127	162	23	138	78	37
do	2				83	87	100	125	38	87	50	15
do	3				32	84	125	101	17	84	69	22
Thedford	No. 1		1		76	77	175	97	29	77	46	36
Wyoming	No. 1				78	92	175	102	25	91	41	39
do	2				50	99	175	128	36	99	52	56
Watford	do				54	125	175	144	47	125	59	75
do					30	71	150	93	22	71	28	43
do					43	70	100	84	14	70	31	39
do					34	132	175	153	21	81	60	71
do			1		63	116	150	139	23	115	52	63
Totals		11	14		1,902	4,277	6,179	5,461	1,185	4,276	2,170	2,081
Majority for McCormick											89	

RETURN from the Records of the GENERAL ELECTION to the Legislative Assembly, 1911.—*Continued.*

Electoral District	Numbers of Polling Places		Names of Candidates and No. of Votes Polled for each.		Total No. of Votes Polled.	No. of Votes remaining Unpolled.	No. of Names on the Polling Lists.	No. of Ballot Papers sent out to each Polling Place.	Used Ballot Papers.	Unused Ballot Papers.	Rejected Ballot Papers.	Cancelled Ballot Papers.	Declined Ballot Papers.	Ballot Papers taken from Polling Places.
			dn.	Henderson.										
Lambton West....	Sarnia Town. Ward 1	Div. No. 1	92	102	194	114	308	325	194	131	1			
	1	2	66	60	126	74	201	225	127	98	1			
	2	1	68	57	125	66	191	225	125	100				
	2	2	69	90	159	69	229	250	160	90	2			
	3	2	75	43	118	126	246	275	118	57	2			
	3	3	112	82	194	116	312	325	148	129				
	3	4	73	73	146	70	218	250	158	102	3			
	4	2	85	59	158	98	256	300	167	142	1			
	4	3	105	76	164	182	269	300	171	133				
	4	4	70	55	109	71	170	250	70	103				
	5	5	54	55	123	59	210	200	125	89	3			
	5	5	68	41	79	87	143	225	163	102				
	5	5	38	37	126	64	241	175	127	96				
	6		89	55	160	115	276	275		49	3			
	6		105	43	127	113	281	300		137				
	Petrolia Town Ward 1	Div. No. 1	84	26	84	154	123	150	84	173				
	1		58	16	79	39	169	125	79	66				
	2	2	63	13	39	30	61	75	39	46				
	2		26	41	156	22	202	225	156	36				
	3		115	37	135	45	190	125	135	69				
	4		98	33	85	55	105	125	85	90				
	4		52	16	74	20	106	125	74	40				
			58	16	43	32	58	75	43	51				
			27	19	50	15	64	75	51	32				
			31			13				24	1			

JAMES FLINTOFT,
Returning Officer.

No.	Locality									maj.
	Oil Springs Village.									
26	Sub-division No. 1	43	82	125	97	15	82	30	52	
27	Sub-division No. 2	25	50	75	61	11	50	19	31	
	Point Edward Village.									
28	Sub-division No. 1	82	118	200	164	46	117	45	72	1
29	Sub-division No. 2	66	84	150	130	46	83	32	51	1
	Courtright Village.									
30	Sub-division No. 1	63	62	125	104	42	61	21	40	1
	Sarnia Township.									
31	Sub-division No. 1	44	81	125	104	23	81	46	35	
32	Sub-division No. 2	62	113	175	147	34	112	51	61	1
33	Sub-division No. 3	31	94	125	108	14	94	33	61	
34	Sub-division No. 4	49	76	125	98	22	76	16	60	1
35	Sub-division No. 5	33	42	75	60	18	41	14	27	
36	Sub-division No. 6	58	92	150	119	27	92	42	50	
	Enniskillen Tp.									
37	Sub-division No. 1	44	31	75	44	13	31	13	18	1
38	Sub-division No. 2	36	39	75	54	15	38	15	23	
39	Sub-division No. 3	27	48	75	67	19	48	24	24	
40	Sub-division No. 4	44	31	75	42	11	31	20	11	
41	Sub-division No. 5	53	72	125	105	33	72	28	44	
42	Sub-division No. 6	25	50	75	68	18	50	25	25	
43	Sub-division No. 7	30	45	75	66	21	45	15	30	
44	Sub-division No. 8	48	52	100	67	15	52	19	33	
45	Sub-division No. 9	47	28	75	38	10	28	10	18	
46	Sub-division No. 10	38	37	75	47	14	37	18	19	
47	Sub-division No. 11	44	31	75	45	7	31	16	15	
48	Sub-division No. 12	22	28	50	35	25	28	3	25	
49	Sub-division No. 13	36	39	75	64	21	39	8	31	
50	Sub-division No. 14	46	54	100	75	38	54	17	37	
51	Sub-division No. 15	70	80	150	118	23	80	22	58	
52	Sub-division No. 16	53	47	100	70	10	47	18	29	
53	Sub-division No. 17	44	56	100	66		56	25	31	
	Dawn Tp.									
54	Sub-division No. 1	45	55	100	78	23	55	25	30	2
55	Sub-division No. 2	47	53	100	81	28	51	19	32	1
56	Sub-division No. 3	50	75	125	98	23	75	42	33	
57	Sub-division No. 4	51	49	100	70	21	48	12	36	
58	Sub-division No. 5	48	52	100	82	30	52	20	32	
59	Sub-division No. 6	47	53	100	76	23	53	22	31	
60	Sub-division No. 7	58	42	100	69	27	42	15	27	
61	Sub-division No. 8	52	48	100	74	26	48	21	27	
62	Sub-division No. 9	59	66	100	102	36	66	30	36	
63	Sub-division No. 10	25	60	125	61	11	49	23	26	
64	Sub-division No. 11	50	50	100	69	19	50	24	26	1

RETURN from the Records of the GENERAL ELECTION to the Legislative Assembly, 1911.—Continued.

Electoral District	Numbers of Polling Places	Names of Candidates and No. of Votes Polled for each		Voters at each Polling Place			Ballot Papers sent out and how disposed of in each Polling Place						
		Hanna	Henderson	Total No. of Votes Polled	No. of Votes remaining Unpolled	No. of Names on the Polling Lists	No. of Ballot Papers sent out to each Polling Place	Used Ballot Papers	Unused Ballot Papers	Rejected Ballot Papers	Cancelled Ballot Papers	Declined Ballot Papers	Ballot Papers taken from Polling Places
Lambton, W.—Con.													
	Sombra Tp. Sub-division No. 1 65	41	71	112	66	178	200	112	88				
	2 66	83	42	125	45	171	200	126	74	1			
	3 67	65	55	120	66	186	200	121	79	1			
	4 68	60	42	102	84	186	200	102	98				
	5 69	34	34	68	36	104	125	68	57				
	6 70	55	16	71	57	108	125	71	54				
	7 71	33	14	47	36	83	100	47	53				
	8 72	17	29	46	19	65	100	46	54				
	9 73	26	23	49	13	62	100	49	51				
	Moore Tp. Sub-division No. 1 74	29	16	45	37	82	100	45	55				
	2 75	19	12	31	5	36	50	31	19				
	3 76	53	74	127	36	164	200	128	72	1			
	4 77	51	90	141	48	189	200	141	59				
	5 78	35	71	106	13	119	150	106	44				
	6 79	58	28	86	22	108	125	86	39				
	7 80	104	94	198	36	235	250	199	51	1			
	8 81	30	56	86	14	101	125	87	38	1			
	9 82	48	25	73	18	91	125	73	52				
	Totals	3,969	2,908	6,877	3,270	10,178	12,125	6,908	5,217	27	1	2	1
	Majority for Hanna	1,061											

Lanark, North: Richard Franklin Preston, by Acclamation. JAMES WESLEY WILSON, Returning Officer.

Lanark, South: The Honourable Arthur James Matheson, by Acclamation. WILLIAM JAMES PINK, Returning Officer.

Leeds.....

JOSEPH DE WOLFE, Returning Officer.

Polling Division	Dargavel	Wilson									
Front Leeds and Lansdowne....No. 1	45	35	80	64	144	150	80	70	1		
do " 2	21	24	45	32	77	100	47	53		1	
do " 3	58	56	114	49	163	150	114	36	1		
do " 4	26	42	68	36	104	150	70	80		1	2
do " 5	39	34	73	36	109	150	77	73			
do " 6	118	49	167	25	192	200	167	33			
do " 7	50	29	79	45	124	150	79	69			
Crosby, South......No. 1	90	43	133	69	202	200	133	67	1		
do " 2	78	81	159	52	211	250	160	89	2		
do " 3	44	24	68	37	105	107	70	35	1		
Yonge Front....No. 1	51	99	150	29	179	200	151	48	1	1	
do " 2	32	37	78	32	110	150	79	70	2		
do " 3	47	46	95	25	120	150	98	49	1		
Westp rto....No. 1	48	48	132	56	188	200	133	68			
Newboro....No. 1	59	84	91	24	115	150	92	57	1		
Bastard and Burgess....No. 1	99	32	142	88	230	250	142	106			
do " 2	57	43	101	57	158	150	101	49			
do " 3	30	44	92	38	130	150	92	58	1		
do " 4	57	62	118	60	178	200	119	80	1		
do " 5	49	61	140	46	186	200	141	58	1		
Escott, Front....No. 1	39	91	85	39	124	150	87	61			
do " 2	49	46	83	25	108	150	84	65	1		
do " 3	45	34	72	9	81	100	73	26	1		
Crosby, orth....No. 1	48	27	77	31	108	100	77	23	1		
do " 2	16	29	67	40	107	100	68	31	1		
do " 3	32	51	57	36	93	100	58	41	2		
Gananoque....No. 1	57	25	103	25	128	150	104	45			
do " 2	86	46	149	60	209	150	151	72	2		
do " 3	60	63	145	70	215	235	146	78	2	2	
do " 4	92	85	171	67	238	225	173	50	1		
do " 5	37	79	67	10	77	100	69	29	1		
do " 6	73	30	165	79	244	225	167	56			
Rear leis and Lansdowne....No. 1	66	92	136	20	156	150	138	14		1	
do " 2	44	70	69	36	105	150	70	77			
do " 3	52	25	112	29	141	150	112	36		2	
do " 4	64	18	82	21	103	150	82	68		1	
do " 5	37	26	63	13	76	100	63	37			
Totals....	1,995	1,833	3,828	1,510	5,338	5,957	3,828	2,067	26	9	2
Majority for Dargavel....	162										

Returns from the Records of the General Election to the Legislative Assembly, 1911.—Continued.

Electoral District	Numbers of Polling Places	Carscallen	Madole	Total No. of Votes Polled	No. of Votes remaining Unpolled	No. of Names on the Polling Lists	No. of Ballot Papers sent out to each Polling Place	Used Ballot Papers	Unused Ballot Papers	Rejected Ballot Papers	Cancelled Ballot Papers	Declined Ballot Papers	Ballot Papers taken from Polling Places
Lennox	Amherst Island......No. 1	48	63	111	42	153	175	111	64				
	do 2	35	38	73	15	88	100	73	27				
	Bath ......No. 1	38	47	85	18	103	125	86	39		1		
	Adolphustown......No. 1	69	49	118	22	140	150	118	32				
	Fredericksburgh, South..No. 2	11	18	29	8	37	50	29	21				
	do North	83	51	134	30	164	175	135	40	1			
	do	69	49	118	24	142	151	120	31	2		1	
	do	46	45	91	25	116	125	92	33	1			
	Richmond Tp......No. 1	64	59	123	34	157	175	123	52	1			
	do 2	67	79	146	44	190	200	147	53	1		1	
	do 3	75	103	178	47	225	225	179	46	1			
	do 4	65	85	150	25	175	175	151	24				
	Ernesttown Tp......No. 1	54	36	90	15	105	125	90	35				
	do 2	73	43	118	42	160	200	120	55	1			
	do 3	46	61	89	33	122	150	89	36				
	do 4	78	58	139	23	177	150	140	60				
	do 5	58	55	116	31	139	225	117	33		1		
	do 6	42	65	97	43	128	176	97	53	3			
	Napanee Town—	96	44	161	33	204		164	61				
	East Ward......No. 1	73		117		150		117	59				
	Centre Ward	49	52	101	71	172	175	105	70	3		1	
	do	54	57	111	90	201	225	116	109	2			
	do	48	61	109	34	146	150	114	36	5	3		

JAMES REID, Returning Officer.

West Ward ..... " 1 54
do .... " 2 55

Totals 1,450

Majority for Carscallen 79

Lincoln—Elisha Jessop—by Acclamation.—HENRY O'LAUGHLIN, Returning Officer.

London—The Honourable Adam Beck—by Acclamation.—EDWARD HERBERT JOHNSTON, Returning Officer.

Column totals (upper riding): 1,202 | 2,850 | 4,052 | 3,710 | 889 | 2,821 | 1,371 | 1,450

Header poll figures: 72/61 | 103/114 | 175/175 | 151/165 | 48/51 | 103/114 | 49/59 | 54/55

Manitoulin — ALBERT E. GRAHAM, Returning Officer.

No.	Gamey	Thi.						
1	37	6	43	48	91	99	43	56
2	42	16	58	36	94	100	59	41
3	115	16	131	55	86	150	133	17
4	90	10	100	82	182	200	100	100
5	46	4	50	15	65	100	52	48
6	40	6	46	22	68	74	46	28
7	37	15	52	71	123	150	54	96
8	71	16	87	37	124	125	87	38
9	24	6	30	205	235	100	31	69
10	116	37	153	131	284	300	159	141
11	24	3	27	208	235	100	27	73
12	62	24	86	149	235	200	88	112
13	56	23	79	131	210	200	79	121
14	27	30	57	153	210	101	57	143
15	9	8	17	59	76	100	17	84
16	3	7	10	66	76	100	10	90
17	21	12	33	43	132	151	33	67
18	54	31	85	47	286	50	85	66
19	23	6	29	257	104	275	29	21
20	79	60	139	147	93	125	139	136
21	37	4	41	63	80	100	41	84
22	38	18	56	37	52	66	56	44
23	38	6	44	36	130	150	45	55
24	24	9	33	19	68	75	33	33
25	22	13	35	95	67	75	36	114
26	8	3	11	57	27	50	11	64
27	6	1	7	60			7	68
28	8	1	9	18			9	41

RETURN from the Records of the GENERAL ELECTION to the Legislative Assembly, 1911.—*Continued.*

Electoral District	Numbers of Polling Places	Names of Candidates and No. of Votes Polled for each	Total No. of Votes Polled	No. of Votes Remaining Unpolled	No. of Names on the Polling Lists	No. of Ballot Papers sent out to each Polling Place	Used Ballot Papers	Unused Ballot Papers	Rejected Ballot Papers	Cancelled Ballot Papers	Declined Ballot Papers	Ballot Papers taken from Polling Places
Manitoulin	No. 29	Tilson 19 / Gamey 65	84	126	210	200	84	116				
	" 30	Gamey 18	18	15	33	50	18	32				
	" 31	Tilson 15 / Gamey 14	29	181	210	100	29	71				
	Totals	Tilson 425 / Gamey 1,254	1,679	2,669	4,348	3,966	1,697	2,269	10	8		
	Majority for Gamey	829										
Middlesex, East	London Tp. No. 1	Neely 38 / Sutherland 20	58	94	152	175	58	117				1
	do " 2	Neely 64 / Sutherland 30	94	45	139	150	94	56				
	do " 3	Neely 52 / Sutherland 20	72	29	101	125	75	51				
	do " 4	Neely 53 / Sutherland 104	157	32	189	200	157	43				
	do " 5	Neely 61 / Sutherland 48	109	28	137	150	109	41				
	do " 6A	Neely 63 / Sutherland 37	100	100	200	200	100	100				
	do " 6B	Neely 58 / Sutherland 32	90	73	163	175	91	84	1			
	do " 7	Neely 105 / Sutherland 49	154	107	261	275	154	121			1	
	do " 8	Neely 41 / Sutherland 41	82	114	196	200	83	117				
	do " 9	Neely 60 / Sutherland 22	82	32	114	125	88	42	1			
	do " 10	Neely 52 / Sutherland 36	88	41	129	150	78	62			1	
	do " 11	Neely 54 / Sutherland 23	77	29	106	125	69	47			1	
	do " 12	Neely 56 / Sutherland 13	69	36	105	125	86	56			1	
	do " 13	Neely 43 / Sutherland 42	85	53	138	150	93	57				
	do " 14	Neely 50 / Sutherland 43	93	47	140	150	93	57			1	
	do " 15	Neely 39 / Sutherland 20	59	33	92	100	60	40				1

Polling Place	No.									
do	16	30	47	77	34	111	125	80	45	
do	17	23	21	44	24	68	75	44	31	
West Nissouri Tp	1	54	35	89	17	106	125	90	35	1
do	2	90	42	132	33	165	175	133	42	1
do	3	57	39	96	21	117	125	98	27	
do	4	36	27	63	20	83	100	63	38	1
do	5	13	53	66	4	70	75	66	9	2
do	6	17	22	39	50	89	100	39	61	
do	7	32	24	56	48	104	125	57	49	1
do	8	36	39	75	29	153	125	75	59	2
North Dorchester Tp	1	49	72	121	32	147	150	123	52	
do	2	59	71	130	17	107	125	130	20	
do	3	41	46	87	20	117	125	103	37	1
do	4	55	46	101	16	87	100	71	22	1
do	5	18	53	71	16	143	150	119	29	
do	6	62	57	119	24	120	125	90	31	
do	7	50	40	90	30	128	150	91	59	
North Dorchester Tp	8	46	45	91	37	122	175	94	31	1
Westminster Tp	1	22	71	93	29	157	100	115	60	
do	2	25	89	114	43	91	125	76	24	
do	3	20	56	76	15	103	100	80	45	
do	4	12	68	80	23	81	200	51	49	
do	5	10	41	51	30	179	175	122	78	
do	6	59	62	121	58	171	175	115	60	1
do	7	42	73	115	56	152	175	113	62	
do	8	55	58	113	39	163	175	113	62	
do	9	48	65	113	50	172	175	84	91	
do	10	20	64	84	88	109	125	77	47	
do	11	44	33	77	32					
Totals		2,014	2,039	4,053	1,828	5,881	6,475	4,053	2,422	18
Majority for Sutherland......			25							

Polling Place	No.								
Strathy	1	65	68	133	45	178	180	135	45
do	2	47	26	73	41	114	115	74	41
do	3	66	74	140	113	253	275	140	135
do	4	63	51	114	37	151	175	114	61
do	5	39	53	92	46	138	155	93	62
Adelaide......	1	51	82	133	42	175	200	133	64
do	2	55	37	97	39	136	100	97	53
do	3	27	78	64	36	100	100	64	36
do	4	65	43	143	50	193	209	143	66
		86		129	49	178	200	129	71

Middlesex, North..

RETURN from the Records of the GENERAL ELECTION to the Legislative Assembly, 1911.—*Continued.*

Electoral District: **Middlesex, North —Con.**
Returning Officer: **WALTER BOLTON.**

Polling Place	No.	G— wis	MacArthur	Total No. of Votes Polled	No. of Votes Remaining Unpolled	No. of Names on the Polling Lists	No. of Ballot Papers sent out to each Polling Place	Used Ballot Papers	Unused Ballot Papers	Rejected Ballot Papers	Cancelled Ballot Papers	Declined Ballot Papers	Ballot Papers taken from Polling Places
Adelaide	No. 5	25	18	43	14	57	75	43	32				
Metcalfe	No. 1	25	41	66	21	87	100	66	34				
do	2	12	42	54	21	75	100	54	46				
do	3	26	45	71	16	87	100	74	26	3			
do	4	40	37	77	24	101	115	77	38				
Biddulph	5	41	27	68	29	97	110	68	42				
do	No. 1	29	68	97	24	121	135	98	37	1			
do	2	32	58	90	25	115	125	90	35				
do	3	13	47	60	18	78	100	60	40				
McGillivray	4	68	40	108	33	141	160	108	52				
do	5	32	115	147	38	185	200	147	53				
do	No. 1	33	59	92	33	125	140	92	48				
do	2	47	46	93	29	122	135	94	41	1			
do	3	48	59	107	35	142	154	108	46	1			
do	4	52	28	80	20	100	115	80	35				
do	5	57	56	113	47	160	175	113	62				
East Williams	6	52	40	92	17	109	125	92	33				
do	7	57	46	103	17	120	135	103	32				
do	No. 1	61	36	97	31	128	150	97	53				
West Williams	2	75	28	103	44	147	170	103	67				
do	3	59	59	118	38	156	180	118	62				
do	No. 1	64	46	110	39	149	165	110	55				
Ailsa Craig	2	66	27	93	31	124	150	94	56	1			
do	3	57	43	100	27	127	150	101	49	1			
do	No. 1	76	72	148	16	164	180	149	31	1			
Lucan		22	66	88	22	110	125	88	37				

Top section

Poll		1	2	3	4	5	6	7	8	9	10	11
do	No. 1	33	63	96	27	123	145	98	47			
Parkhill	No. 2	54	37	91	24	115	135	92	42	2		2
do	No. 3	62	34	96	19	115	135	96	39	1		
do		74	54	128	31	159	175	131	44			
Totals		1,956	991	3,947	1,308	5,255	5,918	3,970	1,948		1	1
Majority for MacArthur			35						14	5		2

Middlesex, West. — DAVID JAMES DONALDSON, Returning Officer.

Township	Poll	Elliott	Galbraith							
Caradoc	No. 1	64	58	731	381	1,112	190	734		
do	No. 2	48	52				150			
do	No. 3	90	73				200			
do	No. 4	88	27				175			
do	No. 5	61	20				134			
do	No. 6	55	21				130			
do	No. 7	52	22				130			
Delaware	No. 1	56	24	325	102	427	120	325		
do	No. 2	49	68				150			
do	No. 3	37	37				100			
do	No. 4	24	30				75			
Lobo	No. 1	58	31	559	179	738	140	560		
do	No. 2	60	78				155			
do	No. 3	79	25				145			
do	No. 4	97	19				160			
do	No. 5	72	40				145			
Ekfrid	No. 1	39	34	577	161	738	90	580		
do	No. 2	38	37				135			
do	No. 3	64	37				100			
do	No. 4	30	39				100			
do	No. 5	33	34				150			
do	No. 6	58	57				90			
do	No. 7	48	29				118			
Mosa	No. 1	56	19	418	172	590	73	420		
do	No. 2	35	11				91			
do	No. 3	39	26				162			
do	No. 4	63	57				87			
do	No. 5	39	57				89			
Glencoe	No. 1	37	16	205	45	250	131	205		
do	No. 2	51	54				129			
Wardsville		60	40	60	40	100	109	60		
Newbury		37	23	77	19	96	100	77		
		50	27							
Totals		1,767	, 85	2,952	1,099	4,051	4,153	2,961	1,192	9
Majority for Elliott		582								

*No details given by Returning Officer.

RETURN from the Records of the GENERAL ELECTION to the Legislative Assembly, 1911.—*Continued.*

Electoral District	Numbers of Polling Places	No.	Names of Candidates and No. of Votes Polled for each		Voters at each Polling Place			Ballot Papers sent out and how disposed of in each Polling Place						
			Ross.	Marshall.	Total No. of Votes Polled.	No. of Votes Remaining Unpolled.	No. of Names on the Polling Lists.	No. of Ballot Papers sent out to each Polling Place.	Used Ballot Papers.	Unused Ballot Papers.	Rejected Ballot Papers.	Cancelled Ballot Papers.	Declined Ballot Papers.	Ballot Papers taken from Polling Places.
Monck	Dunville	No. 1	140	71	211	38	251	273	213	60	2	2		
	do	2	114	73	187	41	230	225	192	33	2			1
	do	3	131	68	199	29	229	225	200	25	1			
	do	4	96	62	158	13	114	122	161	64	3			
	Sherbrooke	No. 1	56	23	79	32	124	125	79	43				
	Canboro	2	48	50	98	19	124	125	105	20	7		1	1
	do	3	18	54	72	17	89	100	72	28				
	Pelham	No. 1	23	39	62	20	82	100	62	38	2			
	do	2	35	41	74	32	108	150	76	49				
	do	3	49	60	95	47	142	150	95	55		1		
	do	4	13	63	112	39	151	125	113	37				
	do	5	17	63	76	26	102	75	76	49	1			1
	do	6	34	20	37	13	51	175	38	37				
	do	7	31	90	124	39	163	150	125	50				
	Gainsboro	No. 1	66	85	119	30	146	150	116	34				
	do	2	22	53	88	18	137	125	119	31		1		
	do	3	18	66	63	12	100	100	88	37			1	1
	do	4	47	45	97	12	76	123	64	36				
	do	5	31	50	67	10	110	100	101	22	1			
	do	6	26	36	59	11	79	125	68	32				
	do	7	33	33	84	17	77	123	60	40	3		1	1
	ben	No. 1	37	51	75	34	100	200	86	39				
	do	2	60	38	112	60	109	75	75	48				
	do	3	29	52	38	26	172	150	112	88				
	do	4	47	9	110	28	64		38	37	2		1	
				63			136		110	40				

JACOB FRETZ,
Returning Officer.

Municipality	No.								
do	5	53	72	125	102	31	71	36	35
Wainfleet	1	94	106	200	171	65	106	75	31
do	2	41	84	125	121	37	81	33	48
do	3	59	116	175	164	48	114	52	62
do	4	70	130	200	191	61	126	63	49
do	5	97	103	200	197	94	103	54	21
do	6	30	45	75	65	20	40	19	35
Caistor	1	94	56	150	84	28	56	21	54
do	2	95	80	175	110	30	80	26	30
do	3	104	71	175	115	44	70	40	41
do	4	95	80	175	99	19	80	39	48
do	5	43	57	100	63	6	57	9	48
Totals		**1,947**	**3,644**	**5,591**	**4,735**	**58**	**3,596**	**1,721**	**1,875**
Majority for Marshall									**154**

No.	Municipality	Galbraith	Mahaffy
1	Brunel Tp.	6	75
2	Bracebridge	33	73
3	do	34	82
4	do	25	75
5	do	23	73
6	Cardwell Tp.	6	24
7	do	5	9
8	Chaffey Tp.	9	63
9	do	5	17
10	Draper Tp.	13	25
11	do	7	47
12	Ferst	42	92
13	do	16	63
14	do	2	21
15	Huntsville	41	32
16	do	14	79
17	do	33	26
18	Medora and Wood		7
19	do	9	12
20	do	12	21
21	do	1	9
22	do	1	28
23	do	1	12
24	do	3	11
25	do	6	47
26	Morrison Tp.		

Muskoka ......

RETURN from the Records of the GENERAL ELECTION to the Legislative Assembly, 1911.—*Continued.*

Electoral District	Numbers of Polling Places		Mahaffy	Galbraith	Total No. of Votes Polled	No. of Votes Remaining Unpolled	No. of Names on the Polling Lists	No. of Ballot Papers sent out to each Polling Place	Used Ballot Papers	Unused Ballot Papers	Rejected Ballot Papers	Cancelled Ballot Papers	Declined Ballot Papers	Ballot Papers taken from Polling Places
Muskoka—Con.	27	Morrison Tp	No. 2	55	6	61	47	108	100	61	39				
	28	do	No. 1	25	10	35	43	78	75	35	40				
	29	do	No. 2	22	6	28	79	107	100	28	47				
	30	do	No. 3	48	16	64	39	103	100	65	35				
	31	do	No. 2	27	6	33	79	112	100	33	67				
	32	Macauley Tp	No. 1	12	3	15	51	66	50	15	34				
	33	do	No. 2	45	8	53	66	119	100	53	47				
	34	McLean Tp	No. 1	20	3	23	14	37	50	23	27				
	35	Oakley Tp	No. 1	59	16	75	48	123	100	75	26				
	36	do	No. 2	13	2	15	12	27	50	15	10				
	37	Port do	No. 1	31	7	38	17	55	101	38	12				
	38	Ryde Village	No. 2	54	9	63	41	104	100	63	27	1			
	39	Tp	No. 1	42	6	48	50	98	75	48	26				
	40	do	No. 2	23	4	27	22	49	50	28	22				
	41	Ridout do	No. 1	10	5	15	20	38	50	15	35				
	42	do	No. 2	12	5	17	21	104	75	17	33				
	43	Stisted do	No. 1	22	9	31	73	104	50	31	44		2		
	44	do	No. 2	4	2	6	64	70	150	6	44		1		
	45	Stephenson	No. 1	72	22	94	92	186	75	96	54	1			
	46	do	No. 2	26	16	42	39	81	100	43	32				
	47	Mct	No. 2	47	2	49	53	102	99	49	51				
	48	do	No. 3	25	11	36	54	90	50	36	63				1
	49	do	No. 1	6	4	10	15	25	99	11	39				
	50	Baxter	No. 2	17	7	24	47	71	75	25	50		1		
	51	do	No. 1	14	1	15	28	43	50	15	15				
	52	Franklin	No. 1	36	5	41	17	58	50	9	41				

Nipissing.

No.	Place	Morel	Rankin												
1	Nipissing	52	32	84	84	176	334	136				52			1
2	do	42	32	74	74			125			1	52		1	
3	do	40	48	88	88	234	396	125				35		1	
4	do	45	29	74	74			125		2		50		1	
5	do	49	47	96	96	204	374	125				29			
6	do	36	38	74	74			175				49			
7	do	73	39	112	112	284	712	175				63			
8	do	85	38	123	123			75				50			
9	do	23	19	42	42	18	49	75				33			
10	do	76	75	151	151	69	131	50		2		24			
11	do	13	18	31	31	13	34	100				19			
12	do	21	41	62	62	37	58	39			1	38			
13	do	10	11	21	21			75				18			
14	do	14	7	21	21	69	220	50				54			
15	do	11	16	27	27			75				23			
16	do	39	13	52	53	88	145	100				22			
17	do	37	35	72	72			100				28			
18	do	39	18	57	57	129	278	50				43			
19	do	18	9	27	27			150				23			
20	do	56	18	74	74	61	137	150				51			
21	do	30	18	48	48	55	101	125				102			
22	do	57	19	76	76	87	168	200				74			
23	do	35	11	46	46	84	155	175				79			
24	do	64	17	81	84	66	148	175				116		1	
25	do	61	10	71	72	37	78	100				103		1	
26	do	72	10	82	83	26	52	75				92			
27	do	29	12	41	41		100	75				59			
28	do	19	7	26	26	47		75				49			
29	do	23	2	25	25		42	50				50			
30	do	11	6	17	17	11						58			
31	do	10	1	11	11							64			
32	do	21	10	31	31							19			

No.										
53		20	55	75	96	41	55	42	13	
54	Freeman	69	29	100	126	97	29	27	2	No.1
55	Gibson	23	27	50	48	22	26	24	2	No.2
56		25	16	50	10	20	16	11	5	No.2
57	Sinclair	34	4	50	51	35	4	11		No.1
58		21		25	17	13	4	4		No.2

Totals	2,075	2,550	4,625	5,561	3,031	2,530	1,970	560
Majority for Mahaffy							1,410	

Nipissing.

RETURN from the Records of the GENERAL ELECTION to the Legislative Assembly, 1911.—*Continued.*

Electoral District	Numbers of Polling Places	No.	Morel	Rankin	Total No. of Votes Polled	No. of Votes Remaining Unpolled	No. of Names on the Polling Lists	No. of Ballot Papers sent out to each Polling Place	Used Ballot Papers	Unused Ballot Papers	Rejected Ballot Papers	Cancelled Ballot Papers	Declined Ballot Papers	Ballot Papers taken from Polling Places
Nipissing—Con.	Nipissing	33	4	3	4	20	24	50	4	46		1		
	do	34	27		30	11	41	50	31	19	1			
	do	35	42	9	51	65	116	150	140	98	1			
	do	36	76	61	137	111	248	300	4	160	2		1	
	do	37	4		4	3	7	25	9	21				
	do	38	4	5	9	43	15	25	21	16				
	do	39	19	1	20	42	63	75	55	54	2			
	do	40	18	35	53	75	95	100	64	45	1			
	do	41	23	40	63	48	138	100	50	86	1			
	do	42	17	18	35	51	83	125	7	64	2			
	do	43	43	5	48	16	99	50	7	75				
	do	44	2	1	7	11	23	25	37	43	1			
	do	45	6	12	7	16	18	75	5	18				
	do	46	24	3	36	39	52	50	70	38	2			
	do	47	2	29	5	110	44	150	74	45	1			
	do	*48	37	13	66	114	190	200	23	80	2	2		
	do	49	58	9	71	59	185	100	56	126	1	2		
	do	50	12		21	38	80	100	44	77				
	do	51	55	1	55	88	93	100	30	44	2			
	do	52	15	7	16		124	75	14	84	1			
	do	53	35	3	42			75	55	90	2			
	do	54	27	4	30	88	88	150		45	1	4		
	do	*55	10	22	14	122	173	200		136	2			
	do	56	29		51					145				3
	Totals		1,800	992	2,792	2,831	5,623	6,050	2,883	3,217	26	14	3	3
	Majority for Morel		808											

*Polling Places Nos. 48 and 55 are both included in the same Voters' List.

Norfolk, North — FREDERICK SAMUEL SNIDER, Returning Officer.

Poll									McGuire.	Atkinson.
Simcoe Town No. 1		3	84	141	225	212	71	138	67	71
do No. 2			65	135	200	190	55	135	70	65
do No. 3		2 1	55	95	150	124	29	89	47	46
do No. 4			73	127	200	184	58	125	38	87
do No. 5		3 1 1	46	104	150	123	19	104	45	59
Townsend Tp No. 1			45	105	150	142	37	102	25	57
do No. 2			56	119	175	152	33	118	39	93
do No. 3		4	50	75	125	112	37	74	38	35
do No. 4			56	94	150	124	30	93	14	55
do No. 5		3 2 2	35	90	125	109	34	89	39	75
do No. 6		2 2	51	99	150	133	39	95	30	56
do No. 7			61	114	175	153	32	114	35	84
do No. 8			54	96	150	128	18	96	20	61
do No. 9		1	40	85	125	103	30	85	65	65
Waterford Village No. 1			41	134	175	164	25	131	64	66
do No. 2			50	150	200	175	36	148	116	84
Delhi Village No. 1		1	46	179	225	215	56	177	46	61
Middleton Tp No. 1			82	93	175	149	40	93	63	47
do No. 2		2	54	96	150	136	39	94	74	31
do No. 3		1 1	82	118	200	177	39	116	30	42
do No. 4			61	89	150	128	20	89	38	59
do No. 5			44	80	124	100	46	79	48	41
Windham Tp No. 1			71	104	175	150	58	104	56	56
do No. 2			77	98	175	155	32	96	79	40
do No. 3			47	128	175	160	36	128	45	49
do No. 4			61	114	175	150	27	112	53	67
do No. 5			64	111	175	138	45	110	35	57
do No. 6			70	105	150	150	26	104	48	69
do No. 7			40	110	150	136		110		62
Totals		33	1,661	3,188	4,849	4,272	1,087	3,152	1,412	1,740
Majority for Atkinson										328

Norfolk, South

Poll							Ravin.	Pratt.	Hammond.
Charlotteville No. 1		3	43	107	150	134	1	62	43
do No. 2			45	80	125	117	0	51	29
do No. 3		1	60	115	175	156	0	77	38
do No. 4			80	45	125	106	0	28	16
do No. 5		1	63	87	150	128	1	56	29
do No. 6		1	85	90	175	161	0	52	37
do No. 7		1	51	74	125	120	0	40	34
Houghton No. 1			47	78	125	126	0	47	31

RETURN from the Records of the GENERAL ELECTION to the Legislative Assembly, 1911.—*Continued.*

Electoral District	Numbers of Polling Places	No.	Names of Candidates and No. of Votes Polled for each — Hammond	Pratt.	Ravin.	Total No. of Votes Polled.	No. of Votes remaining Unpolled.	No. of Names on the Polling Lists.	No. of Ballot Papers sent out to each Polling Place.	Used Ballot Papers.	Unused Ballot Papers.	Rejected Ballot Papers.	Cancelled Ballot Papers.	Declined Ballot Papers.	Ballot Papers taken from Polling Places.
Norfolk, South —Con.	Houghton	2	22	31	5	58	65	123	125	59	66	1			
	do	3	23	57	1	81	71	152	150	82	68	1			
	do	4	31	45	6	82	51	133	150	83	67	1	1		
	Walsing hm, South	1	73	19	0	92	20	112	125	93	32		2		
	do	2	64	56	0	120	22	142	150	121	29	1	1		
	do	3	34	51	2	87	36	123	150	91	59	2			
	Walsingham, North	4	40	61	2	103	34	137	150	104	46	1			
	do	1	18	45	2	65	48	113	125	66	59				
	do	2	29	44	0	80	42	122	125	80	45				
	do	3	21	48	0	65	49	114	100	65	60				
	do	4	16	48	0	64	36	100	125	64	36	2			
	Woodhouse	5	44	45	0	92	29	122	125	94	31				
	do	1	62	50	0	107	47	154	175	107	68	1	1		
	do	2	46	47	0	96	68	157	200	97	78	1			
	do	3	54	69	1	102	55	190	200	104	71	1			
	Port Dover	4	51	70	2	122	68	141	200	125	71	1			1
	do	2	38	86	0	108	33	200	240	110	90		5	5	
	Port Ro wan	1	52	87	4	139	61	206	240	139	61	1			
			71			162	44			162	38				
	Totals		**1,046**	**1,423**	**28**	**2,497**	**1,256**	**3,753**	**4,075**	**2,520**	**1,555**	**17**	**5**	**5**	**1**
	Majority for Pratt			**377**											

SAMUEL H. HARDING,
Returning Officer.

Place	No.	Nesbitt								
Township of Percy	1	67	..	151	195	44	200	151	49	
do	2	94	84	164	237	70	250	167	83	3
do	3	92	70	138	181	42	200	139	61	1
do	4	25	46	37	88	51	101	37	64	
do	5	48	12	88	155	67	175	88	87	1
do	6	23	40	46	63	16	77	47	30	1
Village of Hastings	1	53	23	105	185	79	200	106	94	2
Town of Campbellford	1	25	52	38	53	15	75	38	37	
do	2	85	13	129	210	79	226	131	95	2
do	3	63	44	96	155	59	175	96	79	
do	4	98	33	141	200	57	226	143	83	1
Brighton Village	1	84	34	118	175	57	200	118	82	
do	2	88	28	116	190	74	225	116	109	2
Village of Colborne	1	64	17	81	135	53	150	82	68	
Township of Seymour	1	55	19	74	125	51	154	74	80	
do	2	87	58	145	208	63	200	145	80	
do	3	36	21	57	86	27	100	59	41	
do	4	47	23	70	130	60	150	70	80	
do	5	50	17	67	100	33	125	67	58	
do	6	59	40	99	165	66	200	99	101	2
do	7	38	30	68	140	72	175	68	107	
do	8	27	14	41	120	79	150	41	109	
Township of Murray	1	24	6	30	77	47	100	30	70	
do	2	30	13	43	65	22	75	43	32	
do	3	37	10	47	64	17	75	47	28	
do	4	72	30	102	201	97	225	104	121	
Township of Brighton	1	66	28	89	167	78	302	89	213	
do	2	85	43	128	182	54	250	128	170	2
do	3	70	44	114	227	111	250	116	134	
do	4	34	22	56	110	54	225	56	69	
do	5	67	46	113	205	92	225	113	112	
Township of	1	75	41	116	200	84	225	116	109	
do	2	65	35	100	140	40	175	100	70	
do	3	71	37	108	205	97	226	108	75	
do	4	50	16	66	120	54	150	66	118	4
Township of	1	70	7	77	128	51	150	77	84	2
do	2	68	31	99	144	45	175	99	73	
do	3	60	54	114	150	32	175	118	76	
do	4	59	69	128	180	50	200	130	57/70	
Totals		2,311	1,288	3,599	5,861	2,239	6,910	3,622	3,288	23
Majority for Nesbitt		1,023								

Northumberland, East

ALBERT LYMAN BOYCE,
Returning Officer.

6 R.E.

RETURN from the Records of the GENERAL ELECTION to the Legislative Assembly, 1911.—*Continued.*

Electoral District	Numbers of Polling Places		Names of Candidates and No. of Votes Polled for each		Voters at each Polling Place			Ballot Papers sent out and how disposed of in each Polling Place						
			Clarke	McCullough	Total No. of Votes Polled	No. of Votes remaining Unpolled	No. of Names on the Polling Lists	No. of Ballot Papers sent out to each Polling Place	Used Ballot Papers	Unused Ballot Papers	Rejected Ballot Papers	Cancelled Ballot Papers	Declined Ballot Papers	Ballot Papers taken from Polling Places
Northumberland, West	No. 1	do	80	59	139	44	183	195	141	54	1	1		
	2	do	60	97	157	50	207	210	157	53				
	3	do	63	55	118	31	149	159	118	41	4			
	4	do	82	97	179	45	224	240	183	57	5			
	5	do	112	68	180	44	224	249	181	68	1	1		
	6	Haldimand	103	76	179	56	235	250	185	65		2		
	1	do	22	42	64	33	97	105	65	40				
	2	do	90	33	73	20	93	100	73	27				
	3	do	44	34	124	36	160	169	124	45	1			
	4	do	84	14	58	24	82	90	59	31				
	5	do	66	21	105	50	155	159	108	51	1			
	6	do	44	29	95	25	120	130	95	35				
	7	do	41	46	90	15	105	110	91	19				
	8	do	46	26	70	26	96	100	70	30				
	9	do	30	22	63	15	78	85	63	22				
	10	Hamilton	38	16	62	16	78	100	62	23				
	1	do	40	32	66	22	77	85	66	38				
	2	do	42	28	82	11	99	1	82	19				
	3	do	27	42	61	17	126	130	92	29				
	4	do	60	50	124	34	68	80	61	38				
	5	do	23	34	43	7	139	150	124	19				
	6	do	33	64	69	15	45	50	43	26				
	7	do	42	21	100	20	89	60	69	7				
	8	do	63	36	133	4	104	100	100	31				
	9	do		58		19	152	110		10				
	10	do		70				160	133	27				

Alnwick	No. 1				46	149	195	186	37	149	72	77
do	No. 2		1		10	50	60	55	6	49	25	24
South Monaghan	No. 1			1	29	111	140	131	20	111	58	53
do	No. 2	1			44	101	145	137	37	100	57	43
Totals		1	5	15	1,034	3,018	4,052	3,778	781	2,997	1,382	1,615
Majority for Clarke												233

Ontario, North

		Hoyle	McMillan
Cannington	No. 1	80	41
do	No. 2	52	31
Beaverton	No. 1	84	44
do	No. 2	45	23
Thorah Tp	No. 1	21	15
do	No. 2	28	28
do	No. 3	28	26
do	No. 4	27	9
do	No. 5	52	35
Brock Tp	No. 1	28	44
do	No. 2	156	20
do	No. 3	81	19
do	No. 4	69	51
do	No. 5	45	21
do	No. 6	57	11
do	No. 7	34	4
Scott Tp	No. 1	22	39
do	No. 2	40	25
do	No. 3	30	59
do	No. 4	50	26
do	No. 5	38	12
Uxbridge Tp	No. 1	85	77
do	No. 2	55	57
do	No. 3	32	22
do	No. 4	69	48
do	No. 5	46	50
do	No. 6	19	20
Uxbridge Tn	No. 1	27	33
do	No. 2	41	63
do	No. 3	37	18
Mara Tp	No. 1	56	37
		36	49
		63	52
		52	47

Return from the Records of the General Election to the Legislative Assembly, 1911.—*Continued.*

Electoral District.	Numbers of Polling Places.	Names of Candidates and No. of Votes Polled for each.		Total No. of Votes Polled.	No. of Votes remaining Unpolled.	No. of Names on the Polling Lists.	No. of Ballot Papers sent out to each Polling Place.	Used Ballot Papers.	Unused Ballot Papers.	Rejected Ballot Papers.	Cancelled Ballot Papers.	Declined Ballot Papers.	Ballot Papers taken from Polling Places.
Ontario, North—Con.	Mara Tp. No. 2	Hoyle. 32	McMillan. 69	101	47	148	150	101	49				
	do 3	28	37	65	46	111	200	65	135				
	do 4	19	15	34	34	68	75	34	41			3	
	do 5	23	36	59	23	83	100	60	40				
	do 6	42	64	106	32	141	100	109	41		·	1	
	do 7	23	20		40	43	100	43	57				
	Rama Tp. No. 1	7	10	17	26	43	49	40	32	17			
	do 2	13	27	34	29	49	75	35	15				5
	do 3	12	22	33	15	55	50	33	42				
	do 4	29	4	16	22	91	75	16	35				
	do 5	16		56	17		51	56	44				
	do 6	42	14		35		100						
	Totals	1,971	1,474	3,445	1,230	4,700	5,470	3,471	990	17	3	5	
	Majority for Hoyle	497											
Ontario, South	Pickering No. 1	Calder. 30	Sinclair. 37	67	53	120	150	67	83				
	do 2	54	113	167	61	228	250	167	83				
	do 3	23	53	76	66	144	175	78	47	2			
	do 4	9	19	28	21	49	75	28	97				
	do 5	30	29	59	32	91	129	59	70			1	
	do 6	37	29	66	36	104	125	68	57			1	
	do 7	83	56	139	53	192	228	139	89	1	1		
	do 8	61	41	102	46	149	202	103	99	1		1	

Place	No.											
do	9	49	27	76	28	104	150	76	74			
do	10	61	81	142	53	196	199	143	56			
do	11	29	56	85	41	126	150	85	65	1		
Oshawa ...No.	1	51	55	106	53	159	200	106	94			
A to L	2	68	57	125	38	163	200	125	75	1		
M to L	3	47	42	89	39	129	150	90	60	2	1	
A to L	3	47	96	143	56	200	226	144	82	2		
M to Z	4	43	55	98	40	140	150	100	50	1		
A to L	4	86	59	145	30	177	275	147	128			
M to Z	5	59	46	105	95	202	226	105	121			
A to L	5	42	63	105	38	143	176	106	70			
M to Z	6	43	56	99	12	111	150	99	51			
do	7	44	91	135	45	180	200	135	65			
Whitby Town ...	1	66	112	178	46	225	250	179	71			
do	2	50	49	94	24	118	150	94	41			
do	3	49	32	98	26	124	150	98	52		1	
do	4	29	48	61	23	84	110	61	49	1		
Whitby Tp ...	1	48	30	96	26	122	150	96	54	1		
do	2	53	60	83	17	101	128	83	44			
do	3	47	53	107	42	150	176	107	68	1		
do	4	61	40	114	25	140	150	114	35			
East Whitby Tp ...	1	94	59	134	24	158	175	134	41	1		
do	2	61	61	120	24	145	165	121	44	1		
do	3	38	89	127	52	179	201	127	74	1		
do	4	42	89	131	95	226	250	131	119			
do	5	30	68	98	63	161	202	98	104			
Scugog ...No.	1	48	66	114	34	148	175	114	61			
Port Perry ...No.	2	44	30	74	38	112	150	74	76	1		
do	3	50	52	102	27	130	175	103	72	1		
Reach ...No.	1	41	58	99	22	121	135	99	36	1		
do	2	74	41	115	18	134	150	116	34	1		
do	3	47	42	88	17	105	135	88	47			
do	4	44	52	86	39	126	148	88	60	1		
do	5	55	14	107	23	131	150	108	42			
do	6	34	60	48	19	67	86	48	38			
do	7	39	47	99	20	119	149	99	50			
do	8	36	30	83	18	101	126	83	43			
do	9	66	19	96	18	114	125	96	29			
do		27	59	46	19	65	85	46	39			
do		38	59	97	29	126	150	97	53			
do		23	32	55	11	66	100	55	45			
Totals		**2,330**	**2,577**	**4,907**	**1,775**	**6,705**	**8,067**	**4,930**	**3,137**	**19**	**2**	**2**
Majority for Sinclair			**247**									

RETURN from the Records of the GENERAL ELECTION to the Legislative Assembly, 1911.—*Continued.*

Electoral District	Numbers of Polling Places		Names of Candidates and No. of Votes Polled for each		Voters at each Polling Place			No. of Ballot Papers	Ballot Papers sent out and how disposed of in each Polling Place						
	Polling	Subdivision No.	Champagne	Kehoe	Total No. of Votes Polled	No. of Votes Remaining Unpolled	No. of Names on the Polling Lists	No. of Ballot Papers sent out to each Polling Place	Used Ballot Papers	Unused Ballot Papers	Rejected Ballot Papers	Cancelled Ballot Papers	Declined Ballot Papers	Ballot Papers taken from Polling Places	
East Ottawa	Polling	53	83	45	128	125	253	300	129	171		1			
	do	54	85	81	166	94	260	300	172	128	6				
	do	55	83	99	182	98	280	325	187	138	5				
	do	55A	35	23	58	33	91	150	58	92					
	do	56	79	65	144	89	233	275	144	131					
	do	57	69	56	125	97	222	275	127	148	2				
	do	58	113	57	170	122	292	350	171	179	1	1			
	do	59	69	56	125	86	211	300	126	174					
	do	60	71	51	122	133	255	300	135	178	1				
	do	61	68	66	134	76	210	300	135	115	1				
	do	62	81	52	133	116	249	300	135	165	2	1			
	do	62A	37	11	48	28	76	125	49	76	1				
	do	63	68	27	95	138	233	300	95	205	1				
	do	64	84	60	144	125	269	300	145	155	2				
	do	65	79	41	120	81	201	250	124	126	1				
	do	65A	37	11	48	28	76	125	49	76					
	do	66	113	31	144	83	227	320	146	174	2				1
	do	67	124	56	180	95	275	325	180	140	1	1			
	do	67A	30	19	49	33	82	125	49	76					
	do	68	95	56	151	123	274	325	156	169	1	2			1
	do	69	80	47	127	120	247	300	129	171	2				2
	do	70	92	46	138	73	211	250	141	109	3	1			2
	do	71	144	47	191	66	257	300	198	102	7				1
	do	72	90	50	140	47	187	225	142	83	2	4			1
	do	72A	35	19	54	35	89	150	55	95	1				1
	do	73	107	45	152	45	197	250	154	96	1	1			1

C. S. O. BOUDREAULT,
Returning Officer.

		Ellis	Henderson											
Ottawa, West	do "73A	48	15	63	130	193	225	64	161					
	do "74	83	40	123	91	214	275	123	152					1
	do "74A	52	29	81	22	103	250	82	168					
	do "75	56	44	100	74	174	225	104	121			3		
	do "76	123	57	180	105	285	325	182	143		1	2	4	
	do "77	1	60	161	53	214	275	165	110					
	do "77A	46	26	72	31	103	150	73	77			1		
	do "78	97	50	147	88	235	275	148	127			1		
	do "79	109	29	138	112	250	300	138	162					
	do "79A	66	10	76	53	129	175	76	99					
	Totals	2,842	,567	4,409	2,948	7,357	9,220	4,473	4,747		1	17	47	
	Majority for Champagne	1,275												

		Ellis	Henderson											
Victoria Ward	do No. 1	50	27	77	142	275	200	77	123					
	do 1 A	25	20	45	127	241	100	46	54					
	do 2	76	38	114	113	187	250	121	129		1			
	do 3	55	19	74	81	144	200	77	123			7		
	do 4	38	25	63	184	201	200	64	136			3		
	do 5	8	9	17			100	17	83			1		
	do 6	42	52	94	148	261	175	96	79			1	1	
	do 6 A	26	28	54			100	58	42			3		
	do 7	59	68	127	179	351	175	128	147			1		
	do 7 A	25	27	52			125	52	73					
	do 8	77	28	105	149	303	225	106	119			1		
	do 8 A	29	15	44	98	200	100	45	55					
	do 9	49	53	102	237	511	200	104	96		1	1	2	
Dalhousie Ward	do 10	104	49	153			350	154	196			1	1	
	do 10 A	67	17	84	175	340	175	85	90					
	do 11	64	59	123	144	298	225	123	102		1	1		
	do 11 A	26	26	52			125	54	71			1		
	do 12	49	57	106	160	298	200	106	94					
	do 12 A	60	18	38			300	39	61					
	do 13	104	34	138	150	268	200	138	162					
	do 14	60	18	106			100	106	94			1		
	do 14 A	26	46	44	183	378	300	45	55			1		
	do 15	53	18	125			125	126	174					
	do 15 A	25	72	58	227	421	300	58	67			1		
	do 16	99	33	157			100	158	142			1		
	do 16 A	41	58	70	169	327	150	73	77			1	3	
	do 17	78	29	118			250	119	131		1			
	do 17A	35	16	51			100	51	49					

Returns from the Records of the GENERAL ELECTION to the Legislative Assembly, 1911.—Continued.

Electoral District	Numbers of Polling Places	Ellis	Henderson	Total No. of Votes Polled	No. of Votes remaining Unpolled	No. of Names on the Polling Lists	No. of Ballot Papers sent out to each Polling Place	Used Ballot Papers	Unused Ballot Papers	Rejected Ballot Papers	Cancelled Ballot Papers	Declined Ballot Papers	Ballot Papers taken from Polling Places
Ottawa West—Con. Dalhousie Ward	No. 18	86	44	130	188	344	250	132	118	2			
do	18 A	41	17	58	147	246	100	58	42				
Wellington Ward	No. 19	73	26	99	114	228	250	100	150		1		
do	20	93	21	114	133	242	225	114	1	3	3		
do	21	78	31	109	145	288	250	115	135				
do	22	59	43	102	108	213	200	102	98				
do	22 A	24	19	43	77	181	100	44	56				
do	23	66	39	105	88	196	225	108	117	1			
do	24	67	37	104	100	225	225	104	121	3			
do	25	62	46	108	79	240	200	109	91	1			
do	26	84	56	140	80	195	250	141	109				
do	27	76	40	116	102	219	200	116	84	1			
do	28	73	27	100			200	100	100				
do	29	85	32	117	145	309	225	118	107				
do	30 A	89	22	111			200	111	89				
do	31	29	5	34			100	34	66	1			
do	31 A	80	23	103			225	103	122				
do	32	34	11	45	148	312	100	45	55				
Central Ward	No. 33	64	23	87	127	214	225	87	138				
do	34	33	16	49	174	223	175	136	49	1			
do	35 A	60	42	102	134	236	250	103	147				
do	35	85	48	133	187	343	250	133	117				
do	36 A	36	18	54	118	237	125	54	71	1			
do	36	52	30	82			175	82	93				
do	37	25	11	36			175	36	139				
do	37 A	59	33	92	138	287	225	93	132				
		28	18	46			100	46	54				

Oxford, North

	Lockhart	Rowell										
38 do	73	34	107	120	227	225	107	118				
39 do	88	36	119	106	225	225	119	106				
40 do	89	37	126	109	235	250	128	122				
41 do	48	36	84	90	174	200	84	106			2	
42 do	61	24	85			200	85	115				
42 A do	26	11	37	122	287	100	39	61		1		
43 do	61	33	94	130	272	200	94	106				
43 A do	21	15	36	78	149	150	37	63				
44 do	46	25	71	127	377	100	72	78				
45 Capital Ward	51	37	88			275	88	187				
45 A do	27	12	39	166	348	150	39	111		1		
46 do	94	24	118			250	118	132		1		
46 A do	34	14	48	166	336	125	49	76				
47 do	82	30	112	120	231	250	113	137		1		
47 A do	46	8	54	104	203	100	54	46				
48 do	89	22	111	113	236	250	112	138				
49 do	71	28	99	134	249	225	99	126				
50 do	93	30	123			250	124	126				
51 do	79	36	115	218	429	200	115	85				
52 do	1	36	147			300	148	152				
52 A do	62	9	71			150	71	79				
Totals	4,398	2,296	6,694	7,221	13,915	4,650	6,845	7,805	42	16	2	1
Majority for Ellis	2,102											

Blandford

	Lockhart	Rowell		
No. 1	49	22	71	78
2 do	20	25	45	67
3 do	26	35	61	84
4 do	27	26	53	75
5 do	30	35	65	89
Bl...dim No. 1	58	60	118	167
2 do	33	40	73	133
3 do	41	52	93	133
4 do	23	34	57	92
5 do	87	65	155	204
6 do	5	50	61	98
7 do	13	63	76	102
8 do	46	82	128	169
East Nissouri No. 1	38	51	89	110
2 do	41	48	89	140
3 do	36	67	103	157
do	9	54	63	72

RETURN from the Records of the GENERAL ELECTION to the Legislative Assembly, 1911.—*Continued.*

Electoral District	Numbers of Polling Places	Names of Candidates and No. of Votes Polled for each		Total No. of Votes Polled	No. of Votes remaining Unpolled	No. of Names on the Polling Lists	No. of Ballot Papers sent out to each Polling Place	Used Ballot Papers	Unused Ballot Papers	Rejected Ballot Papers	Cancelled Ballot Papers	Declined Ballot Papers	Ballot Papers taken from Polling Places
		Lockhart	Rowell										
Oxford, North —Con. East Nissouri	No. 4	2	39	41	14	55	75	42	33	1			
do	5	24	33	57	25	82	100	57	43				
do	6	13	26	39	41	80	100	39	61				
do	7	29	25	54	43	97	125	54	71			1	
do	8	15	21	36	43	79	100	36	64				
East Zorra	1	68	70	138	98	236	250	139	111	1			
do	2	40	87	127	40	167	175	127	48				
do	3	48	78	126	64	190	200	127	73	1		1	
do	4	11	48	59	53	112	125	59	66				
do	5	25	60	85	68	153	175	86	89	1			
do	6	23	27	50	101	151	175	51	124	1			
West Zorra	1	15	55	70	48	118	125	70	55				
do	2	20	46	66	69	135	150	66	84				
do	3	7	84	91	58	149	175	91	84				
do	4	18	72	90	68	158	175	91	84	1			
do	5	37	66	103	105	208	225	103	122				
Woodstock, City	1	60	55	115	57	172	200	116	84	1			
do	2	71	52	123	54	177	200	125	75	2			
do	3	33	36	69	29	98	175	69	56				
do	4	73	55	128	32	160	275	128	47				
do	5	99	94	193	54	247	175	196	79	2			
do	6	84	79	163	52	215	175	162	63		2		2
do	7	66	59	125	37	162	200	127	48	2		2	
do	8	77	79	120	46	166	175	148	52	1			
do	9	67	43	146	44	190	200	127	52	1		1	
do	10	102	95	197	70	267	225	198	27	1		1	

Oxford, South

Polling											Rowell	Mayberry
do					129	121	250	227	108	119	44	75
do			2		47	153	200	188	36	152	69	83
do			1		48	102	150	134	32	102	60	42
do					56	169	225	219	52	167	56	1
Embro			1		45	105	150	131	27	104	64	40
Tavistock			1		28	97	125	115	19	96	65	31
Totals	6	5	24		2,988	4,787	7,775	7,008	2,266	4,742	2,651	2,091
Majority for Rowell											560	

Polling											Rowell	Mayberry
Ingersoll No. 1					48	177	225	249	72	176	95	81
do No. 2					83	117	200	166	49	117	68	49
do No. 3					49	151	200	207	57	150	72	78
do No. 4					56	169	225	217	48	169	87	82
do No. 5					79	221	300	308	87	218	92	126
do No. 6					57	118	175	158	42	116	50	66
Dereham No. 1					72	103	175	159	56	103	26	77
do No. 2					73	127	200	175	48	127	64	63
do No. 3					59	141	200	179	38	141	75	66
do No. 4					77	123	200	181	58	123	70	53
do No. 5			2		110	118	225	207	89	118	81	37
do No. 6			1		99	126	225	181	55	126	64	62
Ti... No. 1	4		1		79	221	300	285	64	216	115	101
do No. 2	1				62	188	350	254	66	185	119	66
do No. 3		1			113	237	350	329	92	235	149	86
Norwich No. 1					12	88	100	100	12	88	33	55
do No. 2			2		32	93	125	114	21	93	46	47
do No. 3	1		1		34	91	125	119	24	88	46	42
South Norwich do					45	80	150	144	39	79	22	57
do			3		66	86	150	169	58	84	47	37
do					64	136	200	134	33	136	73	63
do		1			41	109	150	144	25	108	58	50
North Norwich do			1		82	93	175	176	51	93	48	45
do					77	123	200	194	53	123	54	69
do					89	136	225	165	58	134	60	74
do	1		1		63	112	175	128	40	1	59	53
East ...rd					38	88	150	116	29	88	35	53
do					113	87	125	124	41	85	21	64
do					43	82	125	108	21	81	44	37
do			1		45	79	200	94	15	87	32	55
do					46	*104	150	126	23	103	37	66

THOMAS WELLS,
Returning Officer.

* One unused ballot not accounted for.

Returns from the Records of the General Election to the Legislative Assembly, 1911.—*Continued.*

Electoral District	Numbers of Polling Places	Names of Candidates and No. of Votes Polled for each		Total No. of Votes Polled	No. of Votes remaining Unpolled	No. of Names on the Polling Lists	No. of Ballot Papers sent out to each Polling Place	Used Ballot Papers	Unused Ballot Papers	Rejected Ballot Papers	Cancelled Ballot Papers	Declined Ballot Papers	Ballot Papers taken from Polling Places
		Mayberry.	Me										
Oxford, South —Con. West Oxford	No. 1	53	26	79	23	102	125	79	46				1
do	2	71	54	125	35	160	175	136	49				
do	3	78	31	109	26	135	150	109	41				
do	4	88	27	115	28	144	150	115	59	1	1	1	
North Oxford	No. 1	10	10	20	12	95	50	21	29				
do	2	23	43	66	30	72	125	67	58				
do	3	32	24	56	16	106	100	56	44	1			
do	4	48	35	83	22	94	125	84	4				
do	5	31	47	78	16		125	78	47	1			
Totals		2,457	2,254	4,711	1,726	6,468	7,227	4,745	2,482	18	7	8	1
Majority for Mayberry		203											
		Bradwin.	Galna.										
Parry Sound	Armour	10	53	63	128	191	190	63	127				
do	:	8	35	43	53	96	100	43	57				
Burk's Falls	No. 1	44	122	166	88	254	250	169	81	2		1	
do	:	34	45	79	94	173	175	79	96				
Christie	No. 1	5	11	16	18	40	40	16	24				
do	:	8	45	53	149	202	200	54	146				
Carling	No. 1	13	6	19	183	202	200	19	181		1		
Foley	No. 1	7	24	31	63	94	100	31	69	1			
do	:	18	50	68	93	161	175	68	107			1	
Himsworth	No. 1	41	65	96	244	340	200	96	104				

Place	No.								
do				62	62	53	177	175	124
do				37	61	100	198	200	98
do		2		20	29	91	140	150	50
Humphrey	No.	3		33	38	69	140	150	71
do		4		6	5	24	35	40	11
Hagerman	No.	1		24	48	78	150	160	72
Joly	No.	2		3	13	109	115	120	6
do	No.	1		1	11	81	95	100	14
Har		2		6	20	83	100	100	17
do		3		2	4	49	75	75	26
do		1	E.	15	13	34	40	40	6
McMurrich	No.	2	W.	31	37	62	90	100	28
do			W.	15	50	57	125	125	68
McDougall	No.	1	C.		33	80	145	145	65
McKellar	No.	2		13	44	67	100	100	33
do				11	44	33	90	100	57
Ng				12	41	95	150	165	55
do	No.	1		40	69	127	250	250	23
Parry S uth		2		28	101	141	250	250	111
do		3		45	104	121	275	275	130
do				36	104	126	260	260	151
do	No.	1		10	54	120	150	150	142
Perry		2		11	54	86	180	180	65
do		3		2	14	115	40	40	66
do	No.	1		9	17	24	124	125	16
Ryerson		2		8	13	98	43	50	26
do				22	64	22	168	170	21
S uthoRi er		1		21	39	82	207	200	86
Strong	No.	2		8	13	147	207	210	60
do				13	55	186	133	135	21
Sundridge		1		1	11	65	45	50	68
Ardbeg					14	33	36	40	12
Burpee		1		7	10	21	88	90	15
Bethune		2		4	11	71	88	90	17
do					8	73	95	100	15
Conger		1			36	85	95	100	11
do (Cowper)		2		3	9	84	86	90	41
Croft		1		5	6	45	29	30	10
do		2		1	4	19	29	30	13
do		3				16	191	195	95
Depot Harbour				31	64	96	26	30	5
Perrie		1		3	2	21	44	45	18
Ferguson		2		8	14	27	108	110	32
Gurd				15	17	76	76	80	28
do	No.			18	9	49			

ALEXANDER LOGAN,
Returning Officer.

RETURN from the Records of the GENERAL ELECTION to the Legislative Assembly, 1911.—*Continued.*

Electoral District	Numbers of Polling Places	Bradwin	Galna	Total No. of Votes Polled	No. of Votes remaining Unpolled	No. of Names on the Polling Lists	No. of Ballot Papers sent out to each Polling Place	Used Ballot Papers	Unused Ballot Papers	Rejected Ballot Papers	Cancelled Ballot Papers	Declined Ballot Papers	Ballot Papers taken from Polling Places
Parry Sound—Con.	...rd No. 3	3	3	6	30	36	40	6	34				
	...ier No. 1	8	10	18	91	109	110	18	92				
	do 2		8	8	101	109	110	8	102				
	Lount	7	13	20	51	71	75	21	54				
	French R'	2	15	17	53	70	70	17	53			1	
	Jarlsburg	1	16	17	49	66	70	17	53				
	Seguin Falls	3	22	25	20	45	45	25	20				
	Loring	18	28	46	90	136	140	46	94				
	...ain	3	10	13	38	51	55	13	42				
	...ale	6	5	11	88	99	100	11	89				
	Pringle	10	17	27	53	80	80	27	53				
	Proudfoot	2	17	19	90	109	110	19	91				
	Shawanaga No. 1	13	8	21	35	56	60	21	39				
	Spence	3	19	22	44	66	75	22	53				
	do	2	17	19	39	58	60	19	41				
	Wallbridge No. 1	14	12	26	23	49	50	26	24				
	do 2	125	54	179	305	484	250	181	69		2		
	Kearney	66		90	394	484	250	90	160				4
		20	26	46	38	84	90	46	44				
	Totals	1,143	2,218	3,361	6,086	9,447	9,055	3,381	5,674	16			
	Majority for Galna		1,075										

Peel

Division	No.									Smith.	Charters.
Albion	1			69	81	150	141	60	81	30	51
do	2			44	56	100	89	33	56	24	32
do	3			52	58	125	121	48	73	34	39
do	4		4	85	115	200	177	62	115	17	98
do	5		4	51	49	100	78	29	49	18	31
do	6		5	62	88	150	141	53	88	31	57
do	7			34	41	75	64	23	41	6	35
Brampton, S. Ward			1	100	200	300	269	73	192	84	108
do W. Ward			3	135	215	350	279	69	215	84	121
do E. Ward			2	97	203	300	284	81	203	78	125
do N. Ward				125	200	325	273	73	195	79	116
Bolton Village	1		2	66	156	250	198	42	155	94	61
Caledon	1			38	112	150	139	27	109	67	42
do	2			41	134	175	161	27	133	71	62
do	3		1	66	109	175	162	53	109	42	67
do	4		1	59	66	200	181	38	65	13	52
do	5			70	141	200	175	40	138	56	82
do	6		1	59	130	125	102	45	128	54	74
do	7			67	58	125	105	44	58	29	29
do	8			42	83	150	140	22	81	25	56
Chinguacousy	1			44	106	175	147	34	106	43	63
do	2			69	106	250	197	41	124	49	57
do	3			126	124	175	148	73	124	61	63
do	4			50	125	175	125	23	103	26	98
do	5		1	46	104	150	167	21	127	67	36
do	6		1	48	127	175	141	40	103	71	56
do	7			46	104	175	163	37	118	57	46
do	8			57	118	175	153	45	111	69	49
Streetsville Village			1	64	181	300	299	42	181	39	72
Toronto Tp	1		1	119	111	225	167	118	118	48	133
do	2			50	181	250	220	42	181	48	77
do	3			82	125	175	242	77	125	42	101
do	4			89	143	150	173	81	143	74	87
do	5			53	161	200	172	51	161	31	90
do	6			42	122	175	130	39	121	71	60
do	7			48	133	175	184	28	131	44	58
do	8		2	85	102	200	206	69	102	56	59
do	9			130	115	150	130	61	115	57	87
Toronto Gore	1		1	74	145	175	184	54	144	55	21
do	2			76	99	175	155	56	99	45	54
Totals			34	2,760	4,740	7,500	6,702	1,974	4,694	1,989	2,705
Majority for Charters											716

THOMAS H. GOODISON,
Returning Officer.

RETURN from the Records of the GENERAL ELECTION to the Legislative Assembly, 1911.—*Continued.*

Electoral District	Numbers of Polling Places		Names of Candidates and No. of Votes Polled for each.		Voters at each Polling Place.			Ballot Papers sent out and how disposed of in each Polling Place.						
			Brown.	Torrance.	Total No. of Votes Polled.	No. of Votes remaining Unpolled.	No. of Names on the Polling Lists.	No. of Ballot Papers sent out to each Polling Place.	Used Ballot Papers.	Unused Ballot Papers.	Rejected Ballot Papers.	Cancelled Ballot Papers.	Declined Ballot Papers.	Ballot Papers taken from Polling Places.
Perth, North	Stratford— Avon Ward	No. 1	60	68	128	33	161	175	128	47				
	do	2	79	59	138	30	168	175	140	35	2			
	do	3	68	70	138	40	178	175	138	37				
	Falstaff Ward	No. 1	97	108	205	43	248	225	206	19	1			
	do	2	68	80	148	41	189	200	149	51	1			
	Hamlet Ward	No. 1	72	66	138	38	176	200	138	62				
	do	2	74	114	188	43	231	225	188	37				
	Romeo Ward	No. 1	82	69	151	*		250	153	97	2			
	do	2	58	98	156	53	209	225	158	67	2			
	do	3	62	82	144	64	208	225	146	79	2			
	do	4	71	94	165	63	228	225	165	60				
	do	5	50	75	125	43	168	225	125	100				
	do	6	38	75	113	79	192	175	114	61	1			
	do	7	57	59	116	50	166	175	117	58	1			
	Shakespeare Ward	No. 1	47	67	114	39	153	200	114	86				
	do	2	85	76	161	49	210	275	162	113	1			
	do	3	45	66	111	55	166	225	116	109	5			
	do	4	52	66	118	57	175	150	118	32				
	do	5	49	74	123	44	167	175	124	51	1			
	North Easthope	No. 1	71	7	78	28	106	125	80	45	2			
	do	2	105	15	120	41	161	175	120	55				
	do	3	65	31	96	33	129	150	96	54				
	do	4	77	17	94	59	153	175	94	81				
	do	5	41	18	59	21	80	100	59	41				
	Ellice	No. 1	44	42	86	47	133	150	86	64				
	do	2	27	65	92	23	115	150	92	58				

Perth, North ...... Returning Officer, THOMAS MAGWOOD.

* No details furnished.

Place	No.	Bennewies	Stock						
do	3	23	35	58	22	80	100	58	42
do	4	65	103	168	47	215	225	168	57
do	5	84	48	132	53	185	200	132	68
do	6	29	42	71	35	106	125	71	54
Wallace	7	46	42	88	33	121	125	88	37
do	1	34	76	110	18	128	150	110	40
do	2	62	60	122	34	156	200	122	78
do	3	59	69	129	39	167	200	129	71
do	4	25	33	58	22	80	100	58	42
do	5	13	20	33	9	42	75	33	42
do	6	64	64	129	16	144	175	129	46
Listowel—									
Bismark Ward	1	37	75	112	30	142	175	112	63
Gladstone Ward	2	44	72	116	34	150	175	117	58
Victoria Ward	3	33	52	85	25	110	125	85	40
Dufferin Ward	4	58	55	113	22	135	175	113	62
do	5	37	47	84	14	98	125	86	38
Elma	1	38	78	116	30	146	175	116	58
do	2	48	35	83	23	106	150	84	59
do	3	38	57	95	18	113	150	95	66
do	4	41	89	130	33	163	200	131	55
do	5	53	82	135	22	157	200	135	69
do	6	54	75	129	40	169	200	131	65
do	7	18	29	47	17	64	75	47	69
do	8	100	56	156	42	198	225	159	28
Mornington	1	48	52	100	19	119	150	100	66
do	2	62	38	100	42	142	175	100	50
do	3	43	80	123	18	141	175	123	75
do	4	38	77	115	13	128	150	115	52
do	5	75	29	104	26	130	175	104	60
do	6	62	63	125	23	148	150	125	46
Milverton	1	76	129	205	19	224	275	205	50
Totals		3,151	3,523	6,674	2,010	8,684	10,075	6,708	3,367
Majority for Torrance			372						

Place	No.	Bennewies	Stock						
St. Marys	1	38	28	66	15	81	100	66	34
do	2	46	52	98	19	117	150	98	52
do	3	55	57	112	39	151	174	112	62
do	4	118	104	222	61	283	300	222	78
do	5	118	61	179	70	249	250	181	69
do	6	78	44	122	37	159	200	125	75
Blanshard	1	46	36	82	19	101	150	82	68

Perth, South

Taken from the Records of the General Election to the Legislative Assembly, 1911.—Continued.

Electoral District	Numbers of Polling Places	Bennewies	Stock	Total No. of Votes Polled	No. of Votes remaining Unpolled	No. of Names on the Polling Lists	No. of Ballot Papers sent out to each Polling Place	Used Ballot Papers	Unused Ballot Papers	Rejected Ballot Papers	Cancelled Ballot Papers	Decline Ballot Papers	Ballot Papers taken from Polling Places
Perth, South—Con. B	Bard. No.	49	40	89	21	110	150	89	61				
	do 2	55	24	79	46	125	150	79	71	1			
	do 3	70	54	124	20	144	175	125	50				
	do 4	31	46	77	57	134	150	77	98				
	Fullarton 5	70	28	98	19	117	150	98	52				
	do 6	22	49	71	19	90	125	71	54				
	do 1	45	24	69	11	80	125	69	56				
	do 2	24	47	71	25	96	125	72	53	1			
	do 3	96	43	139	14	153	200	139	61	1	1		
	Do mie 4	32	49	81	10	91	125	81	44			1	1
	do 5	54	36	90	70	160	150	91	59				
	do 6	62	91	153	46	199	225	154	71				1
	Hibbert 1	32	120	152	32	184	175	152	73				
	do 2	29	84	113	37	150	200	114	61	1			
	Logan 3	48	64	112	48	160	225	112	88				
	do 4	110	49	159	17	176	200	160	65				1
	do 1	79	65	144	25	169	201	145	55				
	do 2	55	72	127	28	155	200	127	74			1	
	Mitchell 3	77	65	142	17	159	200	142	58	1			
	do 4	44	90	134	18	152	200	134	66				
	do 5	71	25	96	25	121	150	96	54				
	do 1	80	42	122	24	146	200	124	76			1	
	do 2	82	57	139	35	174	226	140	60				
	do 3	81	62	143	47	190	225	143	83			1	1
	Mitchell	135	42	177	25	202	200	177	48				1
		84	35	119	12	131		119	81				

Municipality	No.										Hawthorne	Andrews
do				1		61	139	200	153	15	138	63	75	7	4
do	No.					72	178	250	201	24	177	70	107	20	
South Easthope				1		78	122	200	166	44	122	103	19	1	
do						51	74	125	87	14	88	68	5	41	3
do						36	64	100	76	12	53	51	13	31	21
do						61	66	127	88	22	110	55	11	30	7
Tavistock	No.				1	63	162	225	182	20	162	120	42	26	
Totals	4	4	10	**2,532**	**4,721**	**7,253**	**5,862**	**1,159**	**4,703**	**2,3 5**	**2,388**	12	2
City for Bennewies													73	14	3

Peterborough, East	No.	Hawthorne	Andrews							
Burleigh and Anstruther	No. 1	24		32	32	75	64	33	31	
do	2	29	4	22	53	75	78	25	53	
do	3	11		38	12	50	24	12	12	1
Asphodel	No. 1	44	3	37	88	125	126	38	88	
do	2	49	21	47	53	100	85	32	53	
do	3	59	7	89	1	200	194	84	110	
do	4	28		88	62	125	85	65	61	1
Belmont and Methuen	No. 1	26	2	28	52	75	70	18	52	
do	2	87	1	27	101	125	128	27	101	
do	3	24	3	48	27	75	54	27	27	
do	4	69	1	64	86	150	145	69	86	1
do	5	19		26	24	50	30	37	23	
do	6	29		32	43	75	80	12	43	
Chandos	No. 1	11	1	12	13	25	25	62	13	
do	2	25		82	43	50	102	35	40	
do	3	20		62	39	150	73	12	38	
Douro	No. 1	31		11	80	100	51	70	39	1
do	2	40	17	70	84	150	150	57	80	
do	3	17	7	66	65	200	200	135	83	
do	4	22	3	135	59	125	125	66	61	
Emer	No. 1	39	2	66	82	100	130	48	60	
do	2	52	4	39	61	50	95	35	137	
do	3	33		63	137	100	185	25	50	
do	4	48	1	50	50	50	75	11	34	1
do	5	22		16	34	100	45	18	82	
Otonabee	No. 1	27		68	57	50	75	78	126	
do	2	41	16	24	82	150	160	14	80	
do	3	34	47	19	126	150	140	20	78	3
do	4	62	64	72	81	100	100	88		
do	5	42	38							
		38	37							

RETURN from the Records of the GENERAL ELECTION to the Legislative Assembly, 1911.—Continued.

Electoral District.	Numbers of Polling Places.	Names of Candidates and No. of Votes Polled for each.			Total No. of Votes Polled.	No. of Votes remaining Unpolled.	No. of Names on the Polling Lists.	No. of Ballot Papers sent out to each Polling Place.	Used Ballot Papers.	Unused Ballot Papers.	Rejected Ballot Papers.	Cancelled Ballot Papers.	Declined Ballot Papers.	Ballot Papers taken from Polling Places.
		Thompson.	Hawthorne.	Andrews.										
Peterborough, East —Con. Otonabee	No. 6	25	48	—	73	67	140	150	73	77				
do	7	32	43	4	76	124	200	200	76	124				
Havelock	1	134	20	3	158	91	250	250	159	91			1	
do	2	81	33	3	117	58	175	175	117	58				
Lakefield	No. 1	65	36	3	104	81	185	200	105	95		1		
do	2	96	40	3	139	61	200	200	139	61				
Norwood	No. 1	34	42	15	91	24	115	150	91	59				
do	2	40	27	7	74	11	85	100	74	26				
Totals		1,579	1,076	120	2,775	1,710	4,485	4,910	2,787	2,123				
Majority for Thompson		503												
		Hall.	Peck.											
Peterborough, West Peterborough City	No. 1	35	59		94	79	173	200	94	106				
do	2 A	39	46		85	46	131	150	85	65				
do	2	54	83		137	105	242	250	137	113				
do	3	66	82		148	100	248	275	148	127				
do	4	44	72		116	92	208	225	116	109				
do	4 A	31	51		82	52	134	150	82	68				
do	5 A	24	79		103	44	147	150	103	47				
do	6	32	59		91	45	136	150	91	59				
do	7	53	82		135	55	190	200	135	65				
do	7 A	35	80		115	69	184	200	115	85				
do		26	61		87	54	141	150	87	63				

Polling Subdivision									
Galway Tp 8 A	27	30	57	108	165	175	57	118	
do 8 A	22	23	45	80	125	150	45	105	
do 9	51	72	123	78	201	225	125	100	
do 10	32	63	95	58	153	175	96	79	2
do 10 A	37	46	83	53	136	150	83	67	1
do 11	45	66	111	41	152	175	111	64	
do 11 A	52	52	84	47	131	150	84	66	
do 12	28	65	93	60	153	175	93	82	1
do 12 A	36	55	91	34	125	150	91	59	
do 13	74	79	153	108	261	275	154	121	
do 14	65	62	127	81	208	225	127	98	3
do 15	48	54	102	81	145	150	102	48	1
do 15 A	34	52	86	43	124	160	86	64	3
do 16	51	102	153	38	216	225	156	69	
do 71	38	59	97	63	140	150	98	52	
do 7 A	42	57	99	43	125	150	99	51	
do 18	36	79	115	26	176	150	118	82	1
do 19	44	61	105	61	105	125	105	45	1
do 19 A	33	38	71	41	213	225	71	54	
do 20	65	87	152	34	226	250	152	73	
do 21	69	111	180	61	172	200	172	78	3
do 22	54	66	120	46	120	150	121	79	
do 22 A	37	48	85	52	14	25	86	64	
Bush Tp No. 1	2	4	6	35	60	75	6	19	
do 2	24	13	37	8	88	100	37	38	
Harvey Tp No. 1	40	6	46	23	13	25	46	54	
do 2	1	4	5	42	24	25	5	20	
do 3	3	6	9	8	97	100	9	16	
Ennismore Tp No. 1	53	25	78	15	110	125	78	22	
do 2	23	37	60	19	101	100	60	65	
Smith Tp No. 1	26	26	52	50	175	175	52	48	
do 2	86	34	120	49	80	100	120	55	
do 3	38	13	51	55	194	200	54	46	
do 4	53	38	91	29	186	200	91	109	1
do 5	72	55	127	103	137	150	132	68	
North Monaghan Tp No. 1	38	41	67	67	103	100	79	121	
do 2	30	37	71	107	272	275	67	83	
do	32	39	156	70	97	100	71	29	
do	72	84	55	32			156	119	
do	24	31		116			55	45	
Totals	2,056	2,674	4,730	2,867	7,597	8,325	4,743	3,582	17
Majority for Peck	618								

JAMES A. HALL, Returning Officer.

RETURN from the Records of the GENERAL ELECTION to the Legislative Assembly, 1911.—*Continued.*

Electoral District: Port Arthur

No. (Polling Place)	Numbers of Polling Places	Names of Candidates and No. of Votes Polled — Urry	Names of Candidates and No. of Votes Polled — Hogarth	Total No. of Votes Polled	No. of Votes remaining Unpolled	No. of Names on the Polling Lists	No. of Ballot Papers sent out to each Polling Place	Used Ballot Papers	Unused Ballot Papers	Rejected Ballot Papers	Cancelled Ballot Papers	Declined Ballot Papers	Ballot Papers taken from Polling Places
1	Port [Arthur]		15	15	7	22	30	15	15				
2	do	3	8	11	21	32	40	13	27	2			
3	do	3	11	14	22	36	40	14	26				
4	do	1	4	5	17	22	30	5	25				
5	do		7	7	25	32	40	7	33				
6	do		3	3	10	13	20	3	17				
7	do	1	19	20	21	41	50	22	28	2			
8	do	3	12	15	47	62	75	15	60				
9	do	1	4	5	10	15	20	5	15				
10	do				10	10	15		15				
11	do		8	8	22	30	30	8	22				
12	do		3	3	11	14	20	3	17				
13	do	3	16	19	41	60	75	19	56				
14	do	11	25	36	42	78	90	36	54				
15	do	2	18	20	70	90	100	20	80				
16	do	2	16	18	29	47	50	18	32				
17	do	1	5	6	20	26	40	6	34				
18	do	5	6	11	19	30	40	11	29				
19, 20	do	3	4	7	61	68	85	7	78				
21	do	1	7	8	26	34	50	8	42				
22	do	3	12	15	3	18	25	15	10				
23	do	2	5	7	24	31	40	7	33				
24	do		9	9	6	15	25	9	16				
25	do		12	12	1	13	20	12	8				
26	do	4	13	17	7	24	40	17	23				
26 A	do	9	20	29	3	32	50	30	20	1			

JAMES HARTLEY WOODSIDE,
Returning Officer.

Subdivision	No.											
do	27	10					29	39	50	10	40	
do	28	1					8	9	15	1	14	
do	29	6					28	34	50	6	44	
do	30	8					11	21	40	10	30	
do	31	16			2		21	31	50	18	31	
do	32	1			2		30	31	40	1	39	
do	33	7					29	36	40	7	33	
do	34	7	1				28	36	50	7	42	
do	35	15					49	67	100	8	82	
do	36	5					6	12	20	18	14	
do	37	5					4	8	15	6	11	
do	38	4			3		3	25	40	4	18	
do	39	18			5		35	48	60	22	47	
do	40	9			3		24	28	45	13	41	
City of Port Arthur	No. 1	2			6		93	233	250	4	107	
do A to M	2	112	1		2		131	261	275	140	140	
do N to Z	3	106	3		1		53	115	125	130	60	
do A to M	4	49	1	4	2		180	357	250	62	73	
do N to Z	5	129		1	1		85	166	175	171	91	
do A to M	6	61		4			135	254	275	81	156	
do N to Z	7	65	2	1			291	305	320	119	203	
do A to M	8	59	1	2	2		80	136	150	114	92	
do N to Z	9	21	2	1			29	59	70	56	38	
do	10	18	1		1		143	326	350	30	165	
Nepigon Tp	No. 11	129					65	135	150	183	75	
Schreiber Tp	12	50					41	109	125	70	56	
Mre Tp., No. 3 School	13	33					177	300	325	68	201	
No. 2	14	94					97	172	175	123	96	
do		44			2		93	142	200	75	150	
		47			1		123	253	250	49	119	
		94					39	56	150	130	53	
		17			1		145	167	170	22	147	
Totals		1,515	11	5	33		2,880	4,968	5,460	2,088	3,323	

Majority for Hogarth 942

	No.	Evanturel	Pharand						
Prescott .... Alfred Tp	1	110	64	174	35	209	225	178	47
do	2	48	21	69	9	78	75	71	4
do	3	65	31	96	24	120	125	96	29
do	4	94	71	165	44	209	225	167	58
do	5	54	18	72	16	88	100	73	27
Caledonia Tp	1	41	14	55	38	93	100	56	44
do	2	39	36	75	74	149	150	75	75

RETURN from the Records of the GENERAL ELECTION to the Legislative Assembly, 1911.—*Continued.*

Electoral District	Numbers of Polling Places		Names of Candidates and No. of Votes Polled for each.		Voters at each Polling Place.			Ballot Papers sent out and how disposed of in each Polling Place.						
			Evanturel.	Pharand.	Total No. of Votes Polled.	No. of Votes remaining Unpolled.	No. of Names on the Polling Lists.	No. of Ballot Papers sent out to each Polling Place.	Used Ballot Papers.	Unused Ballot Papers.	Rejected Ballot Papers.	Cancelled Ballot Papers.	Declined Ballot Papers.	Ballot Papers taken from Polling Places.
Prescott—Con.	Cal[edoni]a Tp	3	43	50	93	55	148	150	95	55	2			
	do	4	35	13	48	25	73	75	48	27	1			
	East H[awkes]bury Tp	1	27	10	37	95	132	150	38	112				
	do	2	12	11	23	57	80	100	23	77				
	do	3	102	56	158	64	222	225	158	67	1			
	do	3	15	43	58	120	178	175	58	117				
	West [Hawkes]bury Tp	4	87	85	172	84	256	275	173	102	1			
	do	5	51	44	95	68	163	175	96	79				
	do	6	30	39	94	63	157	175	94	81				
	Longueuil Tp	1	24	64	63	104	167	175	64	111				
	do	2	6	22	28	90	118	100	28	97	2			
	North [Plantagen]et Tp	3	38	25	63	22	85	150	63	37	1			
	do	1	45	57	102	47	149	150	103	47				
	do	2	42	30	72	58	130		73	77		1		
	do	1	86	66	152	142	294	300	152	148				
	South Plantagenet Tp	2	57	57	114	69	183	150	114	86				
	do	3	18	39	57	73	130	200	57	93				
	do	4	68	42	110	75	185	150	110	90				
	do	5	38	82	120	43	163	175	121	54		1		
	Hawkesbury Town	1	37	33	70	110	180	200	72	128				
	do	2	24	37	61	93	154	150	61	89			1	
	do	3	95	12	107	27	134	150	108	42	2			
	do	4	82	34	116	51	167	250	116	59	1	1		
	do	5	110	34	144	92	236	175	145	105				
	do	1	58	28	86	80	166	225	87	88				
	do	2	68	62	130	77	207		137	88	3	4		4

EDEN ABBOTT JOHNSON,
Returning Officer.

Left section:

	No.										
do	4	78	97	175	166	70	96	26	70		1
do	5	62	88	150	138	50	88	47	41		
L'Orignal Village	1	59	116	175	173	57	116	98	18		
do	2	35	115	150	133	35	115	89	26		
Isle Hill Town	1	90	60	150	133	73	60	40	20		
do	2	160	65	225	114	49	65	35	30		
do	3	51	49	100	91	42	49	27	22		
Totals		2,975	3,700	6,675	6,168	2,500	3,668	,692	1,976		
Majority for Evanturel								284			

Right section — Prince Edward:

Norman.

	No.	Min.	Norman.								
Picton	1	54	119	173	155	37	118	46	72		
do	2	59	119	178	168	49	119	43	76		
do	3	70	132	202	187	58	129	58	71	1	
do	4	55	95	150	133	18	95	35	'60		
do	5	51	69	120	97	29	68	18	50		
do	6	64	86	150	126	42	84	29	55		
do	7	84	163	247	228	67	161	36	125	2	
Amelliasburgh	1	57	119	176	159	41	118	46	72		
do	2	75	119	226	191	40	151	42	109		
do	3	86	151	200	172	60	112	39	73	1	
do	4	52	114	151	128	29	99	34	65		
do	5	42	99	124	154	23	131	58	73		
Hillier	1	58	66	151	97	31	66	30	36		
do	2	50	101	125	132	31	101	36	65	2	
do	3	28	97	124	120	24	96	26	70		
Athol	1	36	88	199	106	21	85	51	34		
do	2	67	132	101	168	36	132	60	72		
do	3	45	80	125	97	18	79	38	41		
Wellington	1	27	107	150	137	21	107	29	49	2	
do	2	43	98	125	116	30	98	48	59		
Bloomfield	1	27	166	200	193	18	165	51	47		
South Marysburgh	1	34	99	125	120	28	99	77	88		
do	2	26	95	151	116	14	95	41	58		
North Marysburgh	1	53	103	126	125	25	103	45	50		
do	2	50	98	151	115	13	97	38	65		
do	3	51	76	126	103	28	76	49	48		
Sophiasburgh	1	57	72	123	162	39	72	33	43	1	
do	2	50	117	174	188	31	117	39	33		
do	3	79	148	198	151	45	146	74	78		
						42	56	95	42	53	

Prince Edward....

RETURN from the Records of the GENERAL ELECTION to the Legislative Assembly, 1911.—*Continued.*

Electoral District	Numbers of Polling Places	Names of Candidates and No. of Votes Polled for each		Total No. of Votes Polled	No. of Votes remaining Unpolled	No. of Names on the Polling Lists	No. of Ballot Papers sent out to each Polling Place	Used Ballot Papers	Unused Ballot Papers	Rejected Ballot Papers	Cancelled Ballot Papers	Declined Ballot Papers	Ballot Papers taken from Polling Places
		Mastin	**Norman**										
Prince Edward —Con.	Sophiasburgh ..... No. 4	69	27	96	33	139	150	96	54				
	Hallowell .... No. 1	60	41	101	47	148	175	101	74				
	do 2	28	25	53	8	61	101	53	48		1		
	do 3	64	53	117	16	133	150	118	32	1			
	do 4	52	77	129	49	178	200	130	70				
	do 5	26	40	66	26	92	100	66	34				
	do 6	70	61	131	42	173	200	131	69				
	Totals	1,699	2,286	3,985	1,293	5,278	5,995	4,011	1,984	18	4	4	
	Majority for Norman ...		587										
		Preston	**Mathien**										
Rainy River	Fort Frances ...... No. 1	28	104	132	144	276	200	134	66	1	2	2	
	do .... " 2	24	69	93	135	228	200	96	104				
	McIrvine .... No. 1		3	3	3	6	5	3	2				
	Alberton .... " 2	11	23	34	13	47	50	34	16				
	do	5	19	24	12	36	50	24	26				
	Big Fork	17	9	26	4	30	35	26	9				
	Devlin	22	18	40	11	51	55	40	15				
	LaVallee	21	16	38	13	51	55	38	17				
	Burriss, West	21	16	37	23	60	65	37	28				
	do East		5	26	12	38	45	26	19				
	Emo	75	63	138	53	191	200	140	60			1	
	Carpenter, North..	9	4	13	19	32	35	13	22				

	No.										
Aylesworth		5	30	35	33	3	30	9	21		
Dilke		26	54	80	76	23	53	25	28		
Worthington		66	59	125	113	57	56	25	31		
Morley		34	116	150	149	33	116	45	71		
Rainy River, A—L		30	35	65	59	24	35	11	24		
do M—Z		127	148	275	276	129	147	67	80		
Chapple No. 1	1	89	136	225	222	92	130	47	83		
do " 2	2	22	63	85	83	20	63	26	37		
do " 3	3	13	22	35	31	9	22	13	9		
do " 4	4	19	31	50	45	14	31	12	19		
do " 5	5	30	10	40	33	23	10	3	7		
do " 6	6	32	18	50	44	26	18	4	14		
Budros		17	33	50	50	17	33	14	19		
Grassy River		25	35	60	55	21	34	9	30		
Pratt		19	31	50	45	15	30	7	21		
Nelles and Sherland		8	7	15	10	3	7	13			
Shin and Nelles		9	16	25	20	4	16	11	3		
Potts		11	24	35	29	5	24	6	13		
Richardson		19	11	30	25	14	11	4	5		
Kingsford		25	10	35	30	21	9	11	5		
all		14	21	30	33	12	21	4	10		
Miscampbell		16	14	25	26	21	14	11	3		
Fort Frances		12	13	65	19	6	13	17	9		
Ash Bay		17	48	60	67	20	47	33	30		
Cascades		21	39	57	55	16	39	7	6		
Rocky		21	36	50	55	19	36	21	29		
Bear's Pass		23	27	15	46	19	27	2	6		
Lile Turtle		10	5	70	10	5	5	19	3		
Os Mine		27	43	10	65	22	43	3	24		
Min		5	5	237	10	1	5	4	2		
Banning		150	87	105	237	152	85	13	81		
Gin		76	29	210	101	74	27	37	14		
Rain		160	50	120	206	156	50	22	13		
Steep lock		67	53	69	117	67	50	30	28		
		36	33		68	35	33		3		
Totals		1,665	2,003	3,668	3,685	1,711	1,974	844	1,130		
Majority for Mathieu									286		

RETURN from the Records of the GENERAL ELECTION to the Legislative Assembly, 1911.—*Continued.*

Renfrew, North: Edward Arunah Dunlop, by Acclamation—ANDREW JOHNSTONE, Returning Officer.

Renfrew, South: Thomas William McGarry, by Acclamation—GEORGE EADY, Returning Officer.

Electoral District	Numbers of Polling Places	Names of Candidates and No. of Votes Polled for each		Total No. of Votes Polled	No. of Votes Remaining Unpolled	No. of Names on the Polling Lists	No. of Ballot Papers sent out to each Polling Place	Used Ballot Papers	Unused Ballot Papers	Rejected Ballot Papers	Cancelled Ballot Papers	Declined Ballot Papers	Ballot Papers taken from Polling Places
		Racine	Lowrie										
Russell	No. 1 Gloucester	64	14	78	25	103	200	78	122				
	2 do	10	17	27	92	119	100	27	73				
	3 do	8	7	15	39	54	50	15	35				
	4 do	11	45	56	54	110	100	56	44				
	5 do	26	33	59	55	114	100	59	41				
	6 do	22	32	54	61	115	100	54	46				
	7 do	13	24	37	63	100	100	37	63				
	8 do	9	39	48	61	109	100	48	52				
	9 do	30	22	52	57	109	100	52	48				
	10 do	42	21	63	173	236	225	63	162				
	11 do	13	32	45	79	124	125	45	80				
	12 do	42	31	73	85	158	150	73	77				
	13 do	24	10	34	31	65	75	34	41				
	14 do	31	40	72	176	248	250	75	175	3			
	Eastview No. 1	44	25	69	151	220	225	70	155	1			
	2 do	32	24	56	116	172	175	57	118	1			
	3 do	17	20	37	54	91	75	37	38				
	Osgoode No. 1	54	10	64	41	105	100	64	36				
	2 do	15	71	86	125	211	200	87	113	1			
	3 do	18	26	44	49	93	125	44	81				
	4 do	19	39	58	83	141	150	59	91	1			

J. L. ROLSTON,
Returning Officer.

Place	No.				4,034	4,766	8,800	8,690	3,950	4,740	1,699	3,041
do	6				48	52	100	73	21	52	21	31
do	7				57	43	100	68	25	43	31	12
do	8				113	87	200	142	55	87	61	26
do	9				64	86	150	122	36	86	48	38
do	10				52	73	125	127	54	73	32	41
do	11			2	29	96	125	138	42	96	52	44
do	12				64	61	125	91	30	61	46	15
Russell	No. 1				61	64	125	101	38	63	29	34
do	2			1	120	155	275	244	89	155	129	26
do	3				34	66	100	96	30	66	56	10
do	4		2	1	45	80	125	112	32	80	12	68
do	5				34	91	125	161	70	91	16	75
do	6				93	157	250	251	99	152	8	144
Cumberland	No. 1				42	33	75	67	34	33	1	32
do	2				80	95	175	177	82	95	42	53
do	3		3		2	148	150	170	22	148	57	91
do	4				32	118	150	147	29	118	77	41
Rockland	No. 1			1 2 1	59	91	150	163	72	91	57	34
do	2		1		51	74	125	138	64	74	19	55
...bridge	No. 1	3			130	245	375	390	146	244	42	202
do	2				127	223	350	353	132	221	46	175
do	3				63	137	200	197	61	136	21	115
do	4				53	197	250	243	49	194	11	183
do	5				32	110	175	188	45	143	39	104
do	6			1	90	78	200	212	102	110	17	93
Clarence	No. 1				72	57	150	158	80	78	8	70
do	2				43	55	100	94	37	57	11	46
do	3		1 3		20	132	75	74	20	54	3	51
do	4				118	99	250	247	116	131	32	99
do	5				76	43	175	189	93	96	10	86
do	6			1	57	56	100	109	66	43	16	27
do	7				44	61	100	112	56	56	2	54
do	8			1	39	73	100	118	59	60	18	42
do	9				27	41	100	117	44	73	6	67
do	10				34	49	75	64	23	41	4	37
do	11				51	22	100	99	50	49	7	42
do	12				53	46	75	66	44	22	7	15
do					54	50	100	89	43	46	10	36
do					50	50	100	101	51	50	5	45
do					30	45	75	84	39	45	7	38
Totals		**3**	**9**	**14**	**4,034**	**4,766**	**8,800**	**8,690**	**3,950**	**4,740**	**1,699**	**3,041**
Majority for Racine												**1,342**

RETURNS from the Records of the GENERAL ELECTION to the Legislative Assembly, 1911.—*Continued.*

Sault Ste. Marie—The Honourable William Howard Hearst—by Acclamation—HENRY JAMES MOORHOUSE, Returning Officer.

Electoral District	Numbers of Polling Places	Jorey	Thompson	Total No. of Votes Polled	No. of Votes remaining Unpolled	No. of Names on the Polling Lists	No. of Ballot Papers sent out to each Polling Place	Used Ballot Papers	Unused Ballot Papers	Rejected Ballot Papers	Cancelled Ballot Papers	Declined Ballot Papers	Ballot Papers taken from Polling Places
Simcoe, Centre....	Barrie .... No. 1	69	73	142	58	200	250	142	108				
	do .... 2 A	84	61	145	67	212	250	145	105				
	do .... 2 B	37	33	70	25	95	125	70	55				
	do .... 3 A	39	57	96	44	140	175	96	75				
	do .... 3 B	31	43	74	24	98	125	74	51				
	do .... 4 A	83	101	184	98	282	325	185	140	1			
	do .... 4 B	39	39	78	41	119	150	78	72				
	do .... 5 A	54	71	125	137	262	300	127	173	2			
	do .... 6 A	20	39	59			150	59	91				
	do .... 6 B	26	98	124	124	248	275	125	150	4			
	Tiny Township No. 1	27	46	70	57	127	150	74	76		1		
	do 2	70	51	95	61	156	200	95	105				
	do 3	109	68	121	40	161	275	121	79				
	do 4	49	65	174	65	239	200	174	101			1	
	do 5	64	76	125	53	178	200	126	74				
	do 6	11	51	115	63	178	75	115	85				
	Flos Township No. 1	52	25	36	10	46	150	36	39				
	do 2	47	40	92	34	126	175	92	58				
	do 3	75	49	96	38	134	200	96	79				
	do 4	73	24	99	25	181	175	99	76	1			
	do 5	59	83	156	48	146	175	157	43				
	do 6	50	39	98	38	142	175	98	77				
	do 7	35	54	104	38	124		104	71				
			51	86				86	89				

JOHN SWITZER,
Returning Officer.

Vespra Township

No.											
1			1	78	72	150	131	59	72	26	46
2				70	80	150	121	41	80	36	44
3			1	93	82	175	154	73	81	44	37
4				82	118	200	150	33	117	55	62
5		1		91	72	163	150	68	72	27	45
6				50	25	75	37	12	25	12	13
7			1	144	31	175	57	26	31	12	19

Sunnidale Township

No.											
1				108	67	175	107	40	67	39	28
2				101	124	225	192	68	124	62	62
3				63	112	175	145	33	112	61	51
4				66	109	175	148	40	108	51	57
5				66	34	100	65	31	34	29	5

| Totals | 1 | 2 | 12 | 3,088 | 3,500 | 6,588 | 5,289 | 1,802 | 3,487 | 1,791 | 1,696 |
| Majority for Thompson | | | | | | | | | | 95 | |

Simcoe, East. JOHN HUGH HAMMOND, Returning Officer.

No.								Long.	Hartt.
1	Mer				64	1	44	1	45	66
2	Nash		1	65	85	84	46	7	77
3	Me			72	103	103	49	54	49
4	do			31	69	69	26	57	12
5	do		1	43	82	82	31	42	40
6	do		4	45	105	105	35	50	55
7	do		4	68	107	107	44	72	35
8	Mi Ind		4	49	76	75	42	28	47
9	do			85	95	95	64	21	74
10	do	1	1	153	193	189	156	70	119
11	do	7		113	237	232	116	97	135
12	do		2	139	242	230	132	95	135
13A	do			110	190	190	96	70	120
13B	do	1		48	77	76	48	29	47
14	Orillia Tp.			46	79	78	38	50	28
15	do	1		42	58	58	15	28	30
16	do			47	53	53	34	17	36
17	d4			38	62	61	22	25	67
18	do			81	94	94	59	27	47
19	do			29	71	69	28	22	38
20	do			45	46	46	19	8	41
21	do			26	55	55	37	14	30
22	do			67	49	49	6	19	34
23	do			78	83	83	44	49	80
24	Orillia Town			113	147	146	63	66	87
25A	do		5		162	157	98	70	

RETURN from the Records of the GENERAL ELECTION to the Legislative Assembly, 1911.—*Continued.*

Electoral District	Numbers of Polling Places	Candidate No.	Long.	Hart.	Total No. of Votes Polled	No. of Votes remaining Unpolled	No. of Names on the Polling Lists	No. of Ballot Papers sent out to each Polling Place	Used Ballot Papers	Unused Ballot Papers	Rejected Ballot Papers	Cancelled Ballot Papers	Declined Ballot Papers	Ballot Papers taken from Polling Places
Simcoe, East—Con.	25B Orillia Town	2B	32	39	71	44	115	125	72	53				
	26 do	3	118	79	197	70	267	275	198	77	1		1	
	27 do	4	103	104	207	83	290	250	207	43				
	28A do	5A	88	66	154	35	189	200	155	45	3			
	28B do	5B	38	44	82	30	112	125	82	43				
	29A do	6A	106	76	182	60	242	250	185	65	7		2	
	29B do	6B	55	46	101	59	160	200	110	90	1			
	30 do	7	65	80	145	85	230	250	146	104	2			
	31 Oro Tp.	No. 1	64	38	102	49	151	175	105	70				
	32 do	2	49	32	81	49	130	150	81	69				
	33 do	3	76	21	97	29	126	150	97	53				
	34 do	4	61	40	101	82	183	200	101	99	1		1	
	35 do	5	88	46	134	31	165	175	134	41				
	36 do	6	46	27	73	25	98	100	74	26				
	37 do	7	38	62	100	43	143	150	100	50				
	38 Tay Tp.	No. 1	53	90	143	121	264	275	144	131	2			
	39 do	2	8	52	60	47	107	125	60	65				
	40 do	3	9	45	54	65	119	125	54	71				
	41A do	4A	78	80	158	148	306	250	161	89	1		1	
	41B do	4B	43	41	84	44	128	225	84	141		1		
	42 do	5	73	73	146	108	254	275	146	129				
	43 do	6	18	39	57	64	121	125	58	67	1			
	44 do	7	9	22	31	24	55	75	31	44				
	45 do	8	17	38	55	31	86	100	55	45				
	47 Penetanguishene Twn	No. 1A	94	66	160	105	265	275	160	115			2	
	47B do	1B	36	28	64	22	86	100	66	34	2			

48A	do	do	" 2A	74	116	190	103	293	300	191	160		
48B	do	do	" 2B	33	41	74	93	167	175	76	99		1
49	do	do	" 3	57	20	77	44	121	125	77	48		
Totals				3,103	2,774	5,877	3,185	9,062	9,780	5,953	3,847	9	6
Majority for Hartt				329									

Simcoe, South: Alexander Ferguson, by Acclamation. RICHARD J. HILL, Returning Officer.

Simcoe, West: The Honourable James Stoddart Duff, by Acclamation. WILLIAM MATHEW LOCKHART, Returning Officer.

Stormont.

	Milligan.	Mulhern.							
Cornwall Town...No. 1	34	61	95	51	146	150	96	54	
do No. 2	37	51	88	31	119	125	88	37	
do No. 3	50	51	71	48	119	125	72	53	
do No. 4	56	21	86	35	121	125	86	39	
do No. 5	57	30	85	58	143	150	86	64	1
do No. 6	53	28	92	58	142	150	93	57	
do No. 7	55	39	87	50	137	150	88	62	1
do No. 8	40	32	61	49	110	125	61	64	1
do No. 9	46	21	85	68	153	175	85	90	
do No. 10	67	39	105	64	169	175	105	70	
do No. 11	44	38	92	42	134	150	92	58	1
... Tp...No. 1	85	48	172	67	239	250	173	77	
do No. 2	39	87	74	52	126	150	75	50	
do No. 3	36	35	76	53	129	125	76	74	
do No. 4	56	40	62	61	123	150	62	63	
do No. 5	43	6	71	57	128	175	71	79	1
do No. 6	58	28	99	74	173	175	100	75	
do No. 7	35	41	104	93	197	200	104	96	
do No. 8	56	84	140	78	218	225	142	83	2
do No. 9	100	51	151	56	207	225	153	72	2
do No. 10	83	17	100	48	148	150	100	50	
Finch Tp...No. 1	30	44	74	39	113	125	74	51	1
do No. 2	30	18	48	39	87	100	48	51	
do No. 3	36	37	73	46	119	125	73	52	
do No. 4	29	60	89	88	177	175	90	110	1
do No. 5	38	58	94	72	166	200	95	80	1
do No. 6	7	75	113	71	184	100	115	85	2
do No. 7	30	54	61	27	88	100	63	37	2
do No. 8	30	10	40	37	77	100	40	60	

ALBERT SHEER HODGINS, Returning Officer.

8 R.E.

RETURN from the Records of the GENERAL ELECTION to the Legislative Assembly, 1911.—*Continued.*

Electoral District	Numbers of Polling Places	Names of Candidates and No. of Votes Polled for each		Total No. of Votes Polled	No. of Votes Remaining Unpolled	No. of Names on the Polling Lists	No. of Ballot Papers sent out to each Polling Place	Used Ballot Papers	Unused Ballot Papers	Rejected Ballot Papers	Cancelled Ballot Papers	Declined Ballot Papers	Ballot Papers taken from Polling Places
		Milligan	Mulhern										
Stormont—Con....	Osnabruck Tp. No. 1	88	50	138	41	179	200	139	61			1	
	do 2	47	45	92	60	152	175	93	82			1	
	do 3	61	60	121	31	152	175	122	53	1			
	do 4	78	49	127	43	170	175	127	48	1	1		
	do 5	47	48	95	58	153	175	97	78	1			
	do 6	36	30	66	39	105	125	66	59				
	do 7	96	47	143	77	220	225	144	81		2		
	do 8	40	37	77	80	157	175	77	98	1			
	Roxborough Tp. No. 1	95	56	151	97	248	250	153	97	1			
	do 2	53	18	71	38	109	135	71	64				
	do 3	20	43	63	49	112	125	63	62	1			
	do 4	82	75	157	48	205	225	158	67				
	do 5	13	53	66	48	114	200	66	59				
	do 6	32	85	117	63	180	225	117	83	2			
	do 7	49	73	122	95	217	225	124	101	2		1	
	Finch Village	46	33	79	30	109	125	80	45				
	Totals........	2,249	2,024	4,273	2,501	6,774	7,335	4,304	3,031	23	6	2	
	Majority for Milligan......	225											
		Aubin	Mageau										
Sturgeon Falls....	Polling Sub-division...... No. 1	24	63	87	98	185	162	90	72				
	do 2	43	25	68	71	139	135	68	67	2		1	
	do 3	31	22	53	65	118	110	53	57			1	
	do 4	41	40	81	95	176	200	82	118	1			
	do 5	84	35	119	180	299	225	120	105	1			

Left table

Poll	Mazeau	Sangster
7	23	39
8	4	14
9	70	107
10	60	60
11	10	30
12	38	37
13	22	60
14	6	7
15	12	13
16	21	17
17	13	20
18	24	11
19	18	18
20	16	20
21	9	29
22	15	25
23	11	1
24	6	12
25	29	32
26	23	10
27	3	13
28	22	50
29	3	1
30	13	12
Totals	738	885
Majority for Mazeau		147

JULES ALBERT PHILION, Returning Officer.

Sudbury.

Right table

	Sangster	Na.						
Sudbury, Town ...... A to K No. 1	7	103	110	132	242	250	110	140
do ...... L to J No. 1	8	93	101	135	236	250	101	145
do ...... A to K No. 2	3	74	77	126	205	200	78	122
do ...... K to Z No. 2	4	61	65	123	188	150	66	84
do ...... A to K No. 3	18	81	99	153	252	250	102	148
do ...... L to Z No. 3	13	88	101	141	242	250	103	147
Coppercliff	3	7	10	25	35	50	10	40
do	17	53	70	80	150	150	71	79
do	10	65	75	72	147	150	75	75
Township of Neelon	21	70	91	156	241	250	93	157
Garson		8	8	233	161	200	8	192
do	5	50	55	106		150	58	92
do Hanmer	3	107	110	78	188	275	110	165

*No details furnished by R.O.

RETURN from the Records of the GENERAL ELECTION to the Legislative Assembly, 1911.—*Continued.*

Electoral District	Numbers of Polling Places	Names of Candidates and No. of Votes Polled for each		Voters at each Polling Place			Ballot Papers sent out and how disposed of in each Polling Place						
		Sangster	McCrea	Total No. of Votes Polled	No. of Votes Remaining Unpolled	No. of Names on the Polling Lists	No. of Ballot Papers sent out to each Polling Place	Used Ballot Papers	Unused Ballot Papers	Rejected Ballot Papers	Cancelled Ballot Papers	Declined Ballot Papers	Ballot Papers taken from Polling Places
Sudbury—Con.	Township of Blezard	2	47	49	58	107	100	49	51				
	do McKim		20	20	40	60	75	20	55				
	do Waters	7	19	26	23	49	50	26	24				
	Tps. Drury, Dennison and Graham ... No. 1		8	8	68	76	75	8	67				
	do Worthington ... No. 2	3	14	17	37	54	74	17	57	1			
	do Whitefish ... 3	6	38	44	421	465	300	45	255	1			
	do Mine ... 4	33	20	53	95	148	150	56	94		2		
	do Mine	10	71	81	100	181	175	82	93	1	1		
	do Rayside	6	43	49	70	119	125	50	75				
	do Balfour	13	47	60	84	144	175	60	115	1			
	Tps.	1	56	57	85	142	125	57	68				
	Tps. Carey, Street & Hawley	1	9	10	41	51	50	10	40				
	Hobon		2	2	31	33	50	2	48				
	Missanabie		8	8	148	156	150	9	141				
	Windemere Lake	3	9	9	27	36	50	9	41				
	Pine	5	36	39	96	135	150	39	1				
	Biscotasing		50	55	365	420	400	58	342	3			
	Buei	5	11	11	151	162	150	11	164				
	Poole		16	17	64	81	100	17	83	1			
	Sellwood Junct		27	32	102	134	150	32	118				
	Sellwood	3	2	2	114	116	50	2	98				
	Gowganda Junct	2	8	11	24	35	25	12	38				
	on	11	14	16	10	26		16	9				
	Tp. of Lumsden		50	61	101	162	175	61	114				
	Tp. of Capreol		8	8	57	65	74	8	66				
	Washagaming												

ALEXANDER IRVING, Returning Officer.

Polling place											
Wahnapitae Sch'b House	17	40	21	30	51	50	21	29			
Wahnapitae Lake	5	6	5	9	14	25	6	19			
Wilson & Snider	40	3	80	30	110	150	82	68			
Baxter & Dill	34	2	40	49	89	100	40	69			
Good	27	20	30	80	110	100	32	68			
Cartier	42		44	38	82	200	44	56			
Windy Lake	56		76	135	211	50	82	118	1		
Bannerman Siding	11	89	11	29	40		11	39	1		
Cam B, S. R. P. and P. Co.	15	9	82	241	345	350	106	244			
Chapleau	82	3	34	205	296	275	92	183			
do	34	87	104	102	149	250	38	212			
Tp 14. Moor & Co.	106	43	91	307	500	500	193	307			
Glen City	23	44	37	258	354	350	66	284	3		
do	37	45	66	296	377	375	81	294	1		
do	47	34	81	251	343	350	93	257			
do	42	71	92	209	285	350	77	273	3		
Pottsville	37	49	108	292	400	400	112	288			
South Porcupine	42	49	91	257	348	325	93	232	1		
do	56	44	105	279	384	350	106	244	2		
do	30	18	74	242	316	275	77	198	2		
do	40	14	58	134	192	425	62	363	2		
Lakeview	38	15	52	180	232	250	53	197	1		
Dome Mine	15	17	30	196	226	275	32	243	3		
do	20	56	37	250	287	250	39	211			
Aurora Lake	8	73	64	218	282	250	66	184			
do	19	48	92	192	284	250	93	157			
do	10	13	58	174	232	200	61	139			
Sandy Falls	2	3	15	167	182		15	185			
Quartz Mine	1	5	4	4	8	25	4	21			
Tp. of Kite	6	1	11	25	36	50	11	39			
Ground Hog River	12	1	12	19	31	50	12	38			
Kapuskasing	6		7	23	30	50	7	43			
Missanabie River	16		17	13	30	50	17	33			
Grant	18	15	19	12	31	50	19	31			
Residency	44		59	217	276	300	59	241			
Residency	10		11	18	29	100	13	87	1		
Totals	2,541	1,147	3,688	9,153	12,841	3,398	3,756	9,642	48	11	9
Majority for McCrea	1,394										

RETURN from the Record of the GENERAL ELECTION to the Legislative Assembly, 1911.—*Continued.*

Electoral District: Temiskaming — Returning Officer: C. W. HÆNTSCHEL.

No. of Polling Place	Shillington	Roebuck	Total No. of Votes Polled	No. of Votes Remaining Unpolled	No. of Names on the Polling Lists	No. of Ballot Papers sent out to each Polling Place	Used Ballot Papers	Unused Ballot Papers	Rejected Ballot Papers	Cancelled Ballot Papers	Declined Ballot Papers	Ballot Papers taken from Polling Places
1	71	19	90	154	244	250	90	160		1		
2	33	19	52	116	168	175	55	120	2		3	
3	90	27	117	60	177	175	121	54			1	
4	40	13	53	79	132	150	55	95		2		
5	48	68	116	70	186	200	120	80	2	1		
6	55	76	131	60	191	200	134	66	3			
7	53	76	129	50	179	175	129	46				
8	21	11	32	293	325	200	33	167				
9	12	12	24	236	260	200	24	176	1			
10	19	9	28	189	217	200	28	172	1			
11	23	5	28	60	88	100	28	72				
12	83	60	143	82	225	225	144	81	1			
13	30	34	64	33	97	100	65	35				
14	52	16	68	40	108	125	68	57				
15	46	56	102	54	156	150	103	47				
16	32	69	101	47	148	150	102	48	2			
17	17	26	43	69	112	125	44	81		1		
18	39	22	61	29	90	100	63	37				
19	46	68	114	69	183	200	117	83				
20	32	23	55	123	178	175	57	118				
21	29	28	57	125	182	175	57	118	1	2	3	
22 A	30	60	90	413	503	400	91	309				
22 B	27	32	59	301	360	250	62	188				
23	14	45	59	89	148	150	60	90		1		
24	8	2	10	18	28	50	10	40	1			
25	12	11	23	30	53	50	24	26			1	

No.											
26	2	10	12	44	56	75	12	63			
27	133	14	147	120	267	300	150	150	3	3	
28	72	21	93	120	213	225	97	128	3	3	1
29	48	31	79	103	182	200	82	118	3		
30	65	43	108	143	251	275	109	166	1		4
31 A	42	46	88	92	180	200	92	108	3		
31 B	27	35	62	88	150	149	65	84			
32	64	52	116	177	293	301	119	182			
33	12	58	70	87	157	150	70	80			
34	22	56	78	85	163	176	78	98			
35	32	42	74	60	134	150	74	76			
36	37	56	93	133	226	225	93	132		1	
37	28	23	51	81	132	125	51	74			
38	34	27	61	81	142	151	51	90			
39	19	30	49	65	114	125	49	76			1
40	29	58	87	120	207	200	87	113			
41	1	14	15	14	29	51	15	36			
42	119	10	11	12	23	25	12	13			
43	4	15	134	66	200	200	138	62	3		
44	2	6	10	14	24	25	10	15			
45	10	31	35	25	60	75	35	40			
46	25	33	35	17	52	75	36	39			
47	5	8	18	50	68	75	18	57	5		
48	16	14	39	106	145	150	42	108			
49	28	12	17	8	25	50	17	33			
50	34	12	28	41	69	74	28	46			
51 A	9	27	55	115	170	175	55	120			
51 B	4	29	63	102	165	175	68	107			
5?	29	6	15	31	46	50	15	35			
53		3	7	19	26	50	7	43			
54		8		21	29	50	8	42			
55	1	118	147	306	453	400	148	252	1	1	
56	9	8	8	60	68	100	8	92			
57	11	18	19	38	57	75	19	56			
58	12	12	21	7	28	50	21	29			
59	5	11	22	19	41	50	23	27			
60	11	17	29	19	48	50	29	21			
61	1	5	10	8	18	25	10	15			
62	4	7	18	6	24	50	18	32			
63	46	19	20	8	28	50	20	30			
64	1	31	35	10	45	75	35	40			
65	5	51	97	41	138	150	98	52			
66	11	1	8	3	11	25	9	16	1		
67		15	6	12	18	25	7	18	1	1	
68			26	33	59	74	28	46	1	1	1

RETURN from the Records of the GENERAL ELECTION to the Legislative Assembly, 1911.—*Continued.*

Electoral District	Numbers of Polling Places	Names of Candidates and No. of Votes Polled for each		Total No. of Votes Polled	No. of Votes Remaining Unpolled	No. of Names on the Polling Lists	No. of Ballot Papers sent out to each Polling Place	Used Ballot Papers	Unused Ballot Papers	Rejected Ballot Papers	Cancelled Ballot Papers	Declined Ballot Papers	Ballot Papers taken from Polling Places
		Shillington	Roebuck										
Temiskaming—Con.	No. 69	13	2	15	17	32	50	15	35				
	70 A	16	28	44	34	278	250	45	205				
	70 B	8	18	26	25	271	225	26	99				
	70 C	7	9	16	28	194	175	16	159				
	71	12	11	23	34	57	75	23	52				
	72	12	4	16	43	59	75	16	59	1			
	73	18	9	21	35	56	75	21	54				
	74	14	6	24	39	63	75	25	50		1		
	75	27	11	25	36	61	100	25	55	1			
	76	34	16	43	40	83	75	45	12	1			
	77	10	6	40	35	75	25	40	84	1		1	
	78	73	3	13	1	14	200	13	49				
	79	1	42	115	90	205	50	116	43		1		1
	80	24	7	31	23	24	75	1	9				
	81				30	61	75	32					
	82	10	6	16	6	22	25	16					
	Totals..........	2,403	2,139	4,542	6,765	11,307	11,602	4,623	6,979	43	23	15	4
	Majority for Shillington......	84											
		Bulloch	Pyne										
Toronto, East—Seat " A "..	Ward 1..........No. 1	3	16	19	91	110	125	19	106	4			4
	do " 2	2	18	20	70	90	100	24	76	2			
	do " 3	11	41	52	108	160	175	54	121				
	do " 4	6	28	34	71	105	125	38	87				

No.														
5				2		1	2	141	59	200	171	112	59	9
6		7		9				121	54	175	160	114	46	10
7			2	1				149	51	200	184	133	61	10
8								124	51	175	160	111	49	4
9			2	1				112	63	175	171	117	54	13
10			5	1	3			125	50	200	169	121	48	3
11								156	44	175	177	134	43	11
12				1				132	43	125	161	118	43	4
13		1		2	1			101	24	200	102	78	24	17
14				1				147	53	150	179	126	53	13
15			4	6				108	42	200	153	114	39	12
16				1				142	58	174	181	129	52	6
17				2				128	46	150	167	121	46	9
18		4		1				96	54	150	146	94	52	8
19				2				107	43	200	122	80	42	8
20			4	4				132	68	100	176	112	64	8
21				3				59	41	150	95	55	40	3
22		2		1				107	43	150	127	90	37	6
23								88	37	125	100	64	36	14
24				1				88	38	126	123	78	45	11
25		1						130	70	200	182	117	65	5
26				1				124	51	175	154	105	49	9
27		4		5				139	61	200	174	117	57	13
28				3				79	46	125	125	82	43	19
29			2					102	48	150	128	85	43	10
30		1		1	5			109	66	175	170	105	65	5
31				6				95	55	150	138	89	49	14
32		4		8				83	42	125	110	71	39	16
33			1	4				131	69	200	189	122	67	15
34				7				117	58	175	174	121	53	14
35				3				110	65	225	169	108	61	17
36		3		2				152	73	300	221	157	64	37
37		3		7				186	114	250	271	161	110	12
38		3		4				177	73	250	220	151	69	13
39				5				174	76	175	230	161	69	16
40								113	62	200	166	108	58	18
41			1					151	49	200	150	103	47	20
42				2				118	82	175	191	116	75	15
43								103	72	175	166	98	68	5
44								106	69	150	153	89	64	4
45								115	60	175	155	98	57	15
46		3						107	43	150	140	97	43	11
47		3		1				98	52	175	125	77	48	
48								109	66	225	155	92	63	
49			1					146	79		204	128	76	
50	do.													

RETURN from the Records of the GENERAL ELECTION to the Legislative Assembly, 1911.—*Continued.*

Electoral District	Numbers of Polling Places	Names of Candidates and No. of Votes Polled for each — Pyne	Names of Candidates and No. of Votes Polled for each — Bulloch	Total No. of Votes Polled	Voters at each Polling Place — No. of Votes Remaining Unpolled	Voters at each Polling Place — No. of Names on the Polling Lists	Ballot Papers sent out and how disposed of in each Polling Place — No. of Ballot Papers sent out to each Polling Place	Used Ballot Papers	Unused Ballot Papers	Rejected Ballot Papers	Cancelled Ballot Papers	Declined Ballot Papers	Ballot Papers taken from Polling Places
Toronto, East— Seat "A"—Con.	Ward 1 No. 51	48	24	72	129	201	225	73	152	1			
do	52	45	7	52	131	183	200	54	146	1			
do	53	21	6	27	61	88	100	27	63				
do	54	52	14	66	146	212	225	66	159			5	
do	55	39	18	57	136	193	200	62	138				
do	56	39	17	56	116	172	174	58	116				
do	57	37	21	58	112	170	175	61	114	2	5	1	
do	58	23	16	39	91	130	150	39	1			5	
do	59	23	16	39	139	178	200	41	159	2			
do	Ward 2 No. 2	19	2	21	91	112	125	25	100		5		
do	3	22	9	31	108	139	150	36	114	2			
do	6	16	1	17	72	89	100	19	81	2			1
do	7	23	6	29	80	109	125	31	94				
do	8	14	2	16	97	113	125	19	106				
do	9	29	9	38	87	125	150	41	109			2	
do	10	24	11	35	120	155	175	41	135			4	
do	11	22	15	37	117	154	150	59	134	2			
do	14	44	10	54	92	146	150	39	91	4		1	
do	15	25	11	36	101	137	175	39	1	5			5
do	16	22	12	34	118	152	200	44	136	2			2
do	17	32	8	40	87	127	125	28	156			6	
do	18	16	11	27	97	124	150	57	97	4		2	
do	19	48	4	52	90	142	225	49	93	1			
do	20	30	15	45	158	203	175	67	176	5		8	
do	21	46	14	60	98	158	175	67	108	2		6	2
do	22	22	9	31	115	146	175	33	142	6		2	1

Toronto, East— Seat "A"

do	26		66	82	148	175	68	107	2	
do	27		55	80	135	150	57	93		
do	28		60	88	148	150	62	88		1
do	29		39	108	147	175	39	136	6	
do	30		47	103	150	175	54	121	2	2
do	31		45	83	128	150	47	103	5	
do	32		58	89	147	150	63	87		1
do	33		62	80	142	150	63	82	2	
do	34		55	84	139	150	57	93		
do	35		54	108	162	175	61	114	1	6
Ward 4	No. 1 and 2		15	3	18	25	16	9		1
Totals		922	4,236	8,972	13,208	14,599	4,494	10,105	169	37	65
Majority for Pyne		2,377								

Toronto, East— Seat "B"

Ward 1	No.	Whiteside	Reid	Stevenson							
Ward 1	1	15	3	1	19	91	110	125	19	106	
do	2	16	4	1	21	75	96	100	24	76	
do	3	33	11	8	52	108	160	175	54	121	3
do	4	25	9	2	36	69	105	125	39	86	2
do	5	40	12	8	60	1	171	200	63	137	
do	6	26	14	6	46	114	160	175	54	121	3
do	7	32	17	6	55	129	184	200	56	144	5
do	8	35	11	5	51	109	160	175	51	124	1
do	9	44	11	5	60	1	171	175	63	112	
do	10	27	12	8	47	122	169	200	50	125	3
do	11	36	8		44	133	177	175	44	156	3
do	12	30	5	1	43	118	161	125	43	132	
do	13	18	5		24	78	102	200	24	101	
do	14	31	22	11	56	123	179	150	56	144	
do	15	21	8	7	40	103	143	174	43	107	
do	16	31	15	5	53	128	181	150	58	142	1
do	17	35	8	6	48	119	167	200	50	124	2
do	18	36	11	6	53	93	146	100	54	96	1
do	19	31	5	6	42	80	122	150	43	107	
do	20	44	11	7	61	135	196	125	68	132	5
do	21	31	4	5	42	82	95	200	47	53	1
do	22	22	15	3	42	67	124	150	43	107	4
do	23	25	5	6	33	86	100	125	37	88	
do	24	28	3	8	37	114	123	126	38	88	1
do	25	33	27	7	68	107	182	200	70	130	3
do	26				47		154	175	49	126	1
do	27	32	8		47	107	154	175	49	126	2

Toronto, East—
Seat "B"

RETURN from the Records of the GENERAL ELECTION to the Legislative Assembly, 1911.—*Continued.*

Electoral District	Numbers of Polling Places	Names of Candidates and No. of Votes Polled for each.			Total No. of Votes Polled.	No. of Votes Remaining Unpolled.	No. of Names on the Polling Lists.	No. of Ballot Papers sent out to each Polling Place.	Used Ballot Papers.	Unused Ballot Papers.	Rejected Ballot Papers.	Cancelled Ballot Papers.	Declined Ballot Papers.	Ballot Papers taken from Polling Places.
		Wae.	Reid.	Stevenson.										
Toronto, East—Seat "B"—Con. Ward 1	" 28	38	13	5	56	118	174	200	61	139	5			
do	" 29	32	8	4	44	81	125	125	46	79	1	1		
do	" 30	27	10	10	47	81	128	150	48	102				
do	" 31	42	12	12	66	104	170	175	66	109		1	1	
do	" 32	32	13	4	49	89	138	150	55	95				
do	" 33	29	8	2	39	71	110	125	42	83				
do	" 34	40	19	9	68	121	189	200	59	131	5		1	
do	" 35	26	24	9	59	115	174	175	59	116	3			
do	" 36	37	18	8	63	106	169	175	68	107				
do	" 37	35	25	7	67	154	221	225	67	158				
do	" 38	72	23	15	110	161	271	300	119	181	3	1	1	
do	" 39	38	21	13	72	148	220	250	73	177				
do	" 40	25	40	11	76	154	230	250	76	174	8		1	
do	" 41	39	6	11	56	110	166	175	62	113				
do	" 42	31	10	7	48	102	150	200	49	151				
do	" 43	47	23	8	78	113	191	200	82	118	5	1	2	1
do	" 44	39	25	7	71	95	166	175	72	103	1		1	
do	" 45	40	23	4	67	86	153	175	69	106	4	1		
do	" 46	39	17	4	60	95	155	175	60	115	1			
do	" 47	35	8	2	45	95	140	150	47	103	2	1		
do	" 48	39	8	3	49	76	125	150	52	98				
do	" 49	42	20	3	65	90	155	175	66	109				
do	" 50	56	15	10	74	130	204	225	78	147	4	1		
do	" 51	32	29	2	71	130	201	225	73	152	2			
do	" 52	41	10	5	53	130	183	200	54	146			1	
do	" 53	14	8		27	61	88	100	27	73				

No.								22	32
54	do	45	13	8	66	146			
55	do	30	23	8	61	132			3
56	do	32	13	11	56	116			
57	do	32	9	7	58	112			1
58	Ward 2	19	13	7	39	91	3		
59	do	21	9	10	39	138			
2	do	16	4		40	92			
3	do	19	8	6	20	106			
6	do	11	4	2	33	42			
7	do	22	4	3	17	80			
8	do	12	4	3	29	94			
9	do	29	5	6	19	85			2
10	do	23	6	10	40	116			
11	do	19	10	11	39	115			
14	do	36	19	2	39	89			1
15	do	21	11	5	57	100			
16	do	17	12	10	37	113			
17	do	30	10	3	39	84			
18	do	12	6	9	43	97			
19	do	42	9	2	27	89			
20	do	22	15	11	53	155			
21	do	44	10	10	48	94	2		2
22	do	22	5	3	64	116			
25	do	42	10	2	30	83			
26	do	45	15	6	54	82			
27	do	44	7	5	66	79			
28	do	47	8	5	56	88			
29	do	25	10	3	60	09			
30	do	36	10	3	38	01			
31	do	30	14	3	49	81	1	1	
32	do	34	20	7	47	86			
33	do	51	13	2	61	76			
34	do	40	11	5	66	83			2
35	do	40	10	6	56	106			
Nos. 1 and 2	Ward 4	13		2	15	3			
Totals		2,767	1,060	512	4,338	8,853			
Majority for Whiteside		1,707							

RETURN from the Records of the GENERAL ELECTION to the Legislative Assembly, 1911.—*Continued.*

Electoral District	No. of Polling Place	McNaught	Si—	Total No. of Votes Polled	No. of Votes Remaining Unpolled	No. of Names on the Polling Lists	No. of Ballot Papers sent out to each Polling Place	Used Ballot Papers	Unused Ballot Papers	Rejected Ballot Papers	Cancelled Ballot Papers	Declined Ballot Papers	Ballot Papers taken from Polling Places
Ward 2	36	74	14	88	61	149	150	100	50	11	1		
do	37	44	10	54	66	120	125	57	68	3			
do	38	42	9	51	76	127	125	77	48	26			
do	39	78	13	91	74	165	175	91	84				
do	40	49	9	58	55	113	125	61	64	3			
do	41	54	12	66	90	156	175	77	98	11		8	
do	42	51	9	70	100	170	175	75	100	5			
do	43	44	13	57	85	142	150	64	86	7		6	
do	44	70	5	75	55	130	150	81	69	6			
do	45	52	19	71	109	180	200	79	121			7	
do	46	48	11	59	87	146	150	62	88	3		1	
do	47	50	10	60	65	125	125	66	59	6			
do	48	39	9	48	98	146	150	54	96				
do	49	44	16	60	120	180	200	60	140	10			
do	50	48	10	58	61	119	100	66	59	8			
do	51	51	13	64	57	121	125	70	55	6	7		
do	52	58	18	76	100	176	200	84	116				
do	53	39	10	49	46	95	150	58	42	9			
do	54	53	7	60	73	133	125	63	87	2			
do	55	56	11	67	54	121	150	76	49	9			
do	56	54	13	67	72	139	150	73	77	6			
do	57	37	17	54	79	133	150	59	91	5		2	2
do	58	49	8	57	76	133	150	64	86	7		11	11
do	59	76	8	84	96	180	200	96	104	12			
do	60	29	14	43	70	113	125	48	77	3			
do	61	53	19	72	61	133	150	83	67				

Toronto, North— Seat A.

WILLIAM RICHARD CAVELL, Returning Officer.

								No.	Ed
72	78	150	86	71	65	12	53	58	Ed 3
83	117	200	190	85	105	16	89	59	do
106	69	175	159	90	69	19	50	60	do
98	102	200	183	90	93	16	77	61	do
100	100	200	193	108	85	14	81	62	do
70	105	175	174	83	91	15	76	63	do
80	70	150	141	84	57	15	42	64	do
67	83	150	147	72	75	12	63	65	do
65	85	150	126	66	60	10	50	66	do
53	72	150	122	60	62	9	53	67	do
82	68	150	145	87	58	4	54	68	do
66	84	150	135	56	79	18	61	69	do
81	69	175	131	73	58	13	45	70	do
87	88	150	160	82	78	18	60	71	do
69	81	175	152	79	73	26	47	72	do
75	100	200	169	86	83	23	60	73	do
83	117	200	182	83	99	25	74	74	do
106	94	200	179	94	85	28	57	75	do
87	93	175	180	99	81	18	53	76	do
91	88	160	173	104	69	16	53	77	do
57	59	125	142	92	50	8	35	78	do
92	68	175	123	61	62	20	54	79	do
110	83	175	168	91	77	17	57	80	do
89	65	150	157	99	58	16	41	81	do
114	61	200	149	91	58	17	42	82	do
54	86	125	202	132	70	6	53	83	do
31	71	75	121	62	59	7	43	84	do
14	44	25	75	32	43	2	36	85	do
31	11	100	16	5	11	23	9	86	do
74	69	175	93	33	60	14	37	47	Ed 4
107	101	200	162	74	88	11	74	48	do
94	93	175	177	91	86	10	75	49	do
82	81	125	160	84	76	8	66	50	do
86	43	125	116	76	40	13	32	51	do
83	64	150	136	81	55	12	42	52	do
61	67	125	127	70	57	12	45	53	do
67	64	150	120	64	56	7	44	54	do
98	58	125	122	67	55	8	48	55	do
68	52	100	137	85	52	5	44	56	do
75	52	125	92	62	30	9	25	57	do
86	50	125	110	64	46	6	37	58	do
66	39	100	113	81	32	6	26	59	do
74	34	125	90	60	30	10	24	60	d.
57	51	125	103	57	46	15	36	61	do
	68	125	123	63	60	17	45	62	do

RETURN from the Records of the GENERAL ELECTION to the Legislative Assembly, 1911.—*Continued.*

Electoral District	Numbers of Polling Places	No.	McNaught	Stephenson	Total No. of Votes Polled	No. of Votes Remaining Unpolled	No. of Names on the Polling Lists	No. of Ballot Papers sent out to each Polling Place	Used Ballot Papers	Unused Ballot Papers	Rejected Ballot Papers	Cancelled Ballot Papers	Declined Ballot Papers	Ballot Papers taken from Polling Places
Toronto, North— Seat "A."—Con.	Ward 4	63	49	8	57	61	118	125	62	63	3	5		
	do	64	31	8	39	80	119	125	42	83				
	do	65	35	6	41	79	120	125	45	80	4			
	do	66	28	11	39	72	115	125	41	84	2			
	do	67	42	5	47	68	126	125	50	75			3	
	do	68	48	12	76	50	118	125	84	41	8	5	8	
	do	69	64	14	62	56	182	200	70	55	10		5	1
	do	70	51	25	76	106	175	175	87	113	10		3	
	do	71	72	16	88	87	131	150	103	72	2			
	do	72	49	10	59	72	129	150	66	84	15			7
	do	73	38	5	43	86	148	200	46	104	1			4
	do	74	47	16	63	85	179	150	78	72				
	do	75	66	13	79	100	132	150	90	110		9	10	
	do	76	44	14	58	74	129	200	65	85				8
	do	77	53	10	63	66	178	125	83	86				6
	do	78	73	10	83	95	159	150	87	117	10		1	5
	do	79	74	9	83	76	122	200	71	88				
	do	80	54	8	73	60	148	175	68	54	1			
	do	81	42	16	71	90	187	150	81	82			7	
	do	82	53	20	62	14	116	175	80	119	2			4
	do	83	58	13	65	95	147	125	68	95	4	9		3
	do	84	54	8	50	85	169	175	72	82	5			6
	do	85	50	15	61	104	114	175	54	103	8			5
	do	86	41	9	61	64	125	125	67	71				1
	do	87	51	10	61	64	161	175	83	58				
	Ward 5	46	61	14	75	89	164			92				

Toronto, North — Seat B.

Left block (summary / totals)

do	57	68	125	117	55	62	11	51	47		
do	71	54	125	106	58	48	15	33	48		
do	35	40	75	73	37	36	9	27	49		
do	113	62	175	176	117	59	13	46	70		
do	101	49	150	128	88	40	10	30	71		
do	119	56	175	164	115	49	9	40	72		
Totals	8,243	7,257	15,500	14,421	7,943	6,478	1,313	5,165			

Majority for McNaught …… 3,852

Ward 2 / Ward 3

No.	F G.	Oliver	Richards
36	48	47	3
37	33	24	3
38	33	29	1
39	57	38	2
40	36	23	1
41	39	29	4
42	36	31	4
43	33	28	1
44	49	32	
45	45	22	7
46	53	31	3
47	42	17	
48	30	21	2
49	33	30	1
50	36	27	1
51	57	37	
52	41	45	
53	28	30	2
54	32	31	
55	26	48	1
56	35	36	
57	33	27	
58	38	28	2
59	60	36	5
60	21	19	2
61	38	43	
Ward 3			
do	37	36	5
do	68	46	2
do	40	31	2
do	56	42	2
do	59	38	

RETURN from the Records of the GENERAL ELECTION to the Legislative Assembly, 1911.—*Continued.*

Electoral District.	Numbers of Polling Places.	Ry.	Ol.	Richards.	Total No. of Votes Polled.	No. of Votes remaining Unpolled.	No. of Names on the Polling Lists.	No. of Ballot Papers sent out to each Polling Place.	Used Ballot Papers.	Unused Ballot Papers.	Rejected Ballot Papers.	Cancelled Ballot Papers.	Declined Ballot Papers.	Ballot Papers taken from Polling Places.
Toronto, North—Seat B—Con. Ward 3	64	26	34	2	62	79	141	150	63	87	1			
do	65	42	40	1	83	64	147	150	83	67				
do	66	32	34	2	68	58	126	150	72	78		4		6
do	67	52	18	3	73	49	122	125	79	46	1			
do	68	45	21	1	67	78	145	150	68	82				
do	69	45	33	2	80	55	135	150	80	70		1		2
do	70	36	28	3	67	64	135	150	69	81	1	7		
do	71	44	39	3	86	74	160	150	88	87				
do	72	39	34	7	85	67	152	150	93	57	1	1	5	
do	73	47	56	7	88	81	169	200	99	76				
do	74	53	32	10	116	66	182	200	117	83	10	4		
do	75	46	33	8	88	91	179	200	94	106		4		3
do	76	45	32	1	86	94	180	175	92	108	2			2
do	77	42	31	4	75	98	173	150	75	100		1		
do	78	20	24		55	87	142	125	59	91				
do	79	42	38		66	57	123	175	66	59				
do	80	44	30		83	85	168	175	83	92				
do	81	25	28	1	62	95	157	150	65	110	4	4		
do	82	36	48	7	85	84	149	200	69	81	2	2		
do	83	34	53	1	82	120	202	175	87	113	1	1		
do	84	17	22		70	51	121	125	71	54	1			
do	85	21	4		43	32	75	75	44	31				
do	86	7			11	5	16	25	11	14				
Ward 4	47	26	40	1	67	26	93	100	67	33				
do	48	69	29		98	64	162	175	100	75	1	1		
do	49	56	34	1	91	86	177	200	93	107		2		

No.											
do	51				82	43	125	116	74	42	7
do	52				86	64	150	136	75	61	1
do	53	1		3	81	69	150	127	60	67	1
do	54	3	2	1	61	64	125	120	60	60	1
do	55	1		1	67	58	125	122	65	57	3
do	56			2	91	59	150	137	80	57	
do	57	2		1	62	38	100	92	57	35	2
do	58		2	1	75	50	125	110	63	47	1
do	59			3	86	39	125	113	77	36	2
do	60	1		4	62	38	100	90	56	34	1
do	61				74	51	125	103	53	50	1
do	62			1	57	68	125	123	55	68	2
do	63		2	3	62	63	125	118	57	61	3
do	64				83	42	125	119	78	41	3
do	65				80	45	125	120	78	42	
do	66	1			84	41	125	111	70	41	2
do	67				75	50	125	115	67	48	
do	68				41	84	200	126	63	83	
do	69	3	2	2	55	70	175	118	43	69	2
No.	70	1		2	13	87	150	182	49	87	
do	71		1	2	72	03	150	175	95	98	
do	72			1	79	71	200	131	77	68	
do	73			1	03	47	150	129	63	45	
do	74	13			72	78	150	148	84	76	2
do	75	2	1		10	90	200	179	72	88	
do	76				85	65	150	132	91	63	
do	77	2		2	86	64	150	129	69	64	3
do	78			2	93	07	200	178	65	94	
do	79	5	2 1	1	82	93	150	159	84	89	
do	80			1	51	74	175	122	70	74	1
do	81				82	68	125	148	48	68	2
do	82				18	82	150	187	80	78	1
do	83				95	80	200	166	09	79	
do	84	1			82	68	175	147	87	68	
do	85	1	1		95	80	175	169	79	73	
do	86			2	71	55	125	114	96	52	
do	87			1	58	67	125	125	62	64	
do	46			1	91	84	125	164	61	82	3
do	47		2 1	2	57	54	175	117	82	66	3
do	48	1		1	71	68	150	106	51	53	1
do	49	1		1	33	42	75	73	53	41	
do	70				113	62	175	176	32	60	
do	71		3	2	91	59	150	128	116	57	
do	72				119	56	175	164	71	53	
Totals		70	56	123	8,133	7,367	15,500	14,421	7,503	7,118	178

RETURN from the Records of the GENERAL ELECTION to the Legislative Assembly, 1911.—*Continued.*

Electoral District	Numbers of Polling Places	Jas.	James.	Total No. of Votes Polled	No. of Votes remaining Unpolled	No. of Names on the Polling Lists	No. of Ballot Papers sent out to each Polling Place	Used Ballot Papers	Unused Ballot Papers	Rejected Ballot Papers	Cancelled Ballot Papers	Declined Ballot Papers	Ballot Papers taken from Polling Places
Toronto South Seat A	Ward 2 ....Sub-div. No. 1	36	7	43	72	115	125	43	82				
	do 4	20	11	31	58	89	125	33	92	2			
	do 5	32	5	37	77	114	125	42	83	2			
	do 12	59	18	77	132	209	225	78	147	1			6
	do 13	52	15	67	136	203	225	70	155				
	do 23	32	5	37	70	107	125	40	85	3		2	
	do 24	29	20	49	72	121	125	51	74	2		3	
	Ward 3 ....Sub-div. No. 1, 3	11	3	14	14	28	50	15	35	1			
	do 5, 6, 7, 8	5	2	7	21	28	50	8	42				
	do ....Sub-div. No. 9, 10, 11, 12	9		5	11	16	25	12	13	3			
	do ....Sub-div. No. 13, 14	6	2	11	14	25	50	11	39	2		2	
	do 15	14		6	34	20	25	7	18	1		1	1
	do 16	15	2	16	54	50	75	16	59				
	do 17	16	5	20	93	74	75	22	53				
	do 18, 19	8	5	21	22	114	125	21	104	2		2	
	do 20	10	1	9	22	31	50	10	40	1			
	do ....Sub-div. No. 21, 22, 23	25	1	11	14	33	50	11	39	2		1	
	do ....Sub-div. No. 25, 26	4	1	26	4	40	50	29	21				
	do ....Sub-div. No. 27, 28	7		4	7	8	25	4	21				
	do 29, 30, 31	7		7	19	14	25	7	18				
	do 32	6	3	10	25	29	50	10	40	1			
	do 33	7	3	9	31	34	50	10	40		1		1
	do 34, 35	14	1	8	60	39	75	8	42	1			
	do 36	17		14	28	74	50	14	61				
	do 37	46	2	19	74	47	75	21	29	1		2	
	do 38	52	7	53	138	127	125	56	69			3	
			7	59		197	225	63	162		1		

														4	1																														
											1		3		2	1		1		1		1				4		5	3		4			2		2							
4	1		3	1													2			3	1		1			2		2		2							4						
5	1		3	4		3	6	1		1		5		4		2	4		2	5	4		2		2	1																		
195	102	109	96	143	103	121	30	129	130	76	74	135	69	86	112	116	84	135	93	106	56	72	115	54	86	131	50	120	44	107	96	100	123	156	146	107	109	106	113	132	108	94	94	113
30	23	41	54	32	47	54	20	46	45	24	51	40	31	39	63	59	41	90	32	19	44	28	35	21	39	44	75	30	31	18	29	25	27	69	54	43	66	44	37	43	42	31	31	37
225	125	150	150	175	150	175	150	175	175	100	125	175	175	125	225	125	125	100	100	150	75	125	175	125	175	125	125	150	225	200	150	175	150	150	175	125	125	150						
177	106	138	136	151	164	187	113	135	137	100	125	146	82	119	162	128	96	191	117	90	109	78	132	69	100	148	152	129	143	121	100	100	128	208	172	152	187	124	132	160	139	106	125	137
152	84	101	83	122	121	136	94	92	98	77	74	106	52	184	101	74	58	105	87	72	67	52	102	48	62	106	85	101	106	104	73	79	101	148	122	111	125	82	95	119	97	77	98	100
25	22	37	53	29	43	51	19	43	39	23	51	40	30	35	61	54	38	86	30	18	42	26	30	21	38	42	67	28	37	17	27	21	27	60	50	41	62	42	37	41	42	29	27	37
7	5	8	6	7	8	7	2	12	14	3	10	11	8	11	13	17	4	31	6	6	8	3	6	6	11	16	9	4	12	5	6	5	10	12	16	8	12	6	6	10	12	7	6	9
18	17	29	47	22	35	44	17	31	25	20	41	29	22	24	48	37	34	55	24	12	34	23	24	15	27	26	58	24	25	12	21	16	17	48	34	33	50	36	27	31	30	22	21	28

Sub-div. No. ... 39 40 41 42 43 44 45 46 47 48 49 50 51 52 53 54 55 56 57 | 3 4 5 6 7 8 9 10 11 12 13 14 15 16 17 18 19 20 21 22 23 24 25 26 27 28

W'd 4 ... do do to do do do to do do do do do to do do do do do do / do do do do do do do to do do do do do to do do do do do do

RETURN from the Records of the GENERAL ELECTION to the Legislative Assembly, 1911.—*Continued.*

Electoral District	Numbers of Polling Places	Names of Candidates and No. of Votes Polled for each		Total No. of Votes Polled	No. of Votes Remaining Unpolled	No. of Names on the Polling Lists	No. of Ballot Papers sent out to each Polling Place	Used Ballot Papers	Unused Ballot Papers	Rejected Ballot Papers	Cancelled Ballot Papers	Declined Ballot Papers	Ballot Papers taken from Polling Places
		James.	Owens.										
Toronto. South— Seat "A"—Con.	Ward 4......Sub-Div. No. 29	1	2	30	102	132	150	31	119	1			
	do 30	16	37	53	114	167	175	56	119			3	
	do 31	16	16	32	94	126	150	32	118	5			
	do 32	10	28	38	81	119	150	43	107	4		3	
	do 33	27	45	72	136	208	225	80	145	2	1	1	
	do 34	11	43	54	102	156	150	57	93	1			
	do 35	5	24	29	103	132	150	30	120			4	
	do 36	16	33	49	94	143	150	53	97	3			
	do 37	6	37	43	78	121	150	43	107	6	2	1	
	do 38	11	40	51	111	162	175	54	121	3		1	
	do 39	6	21	27	101	128	221	35	186			2	
	do 40	2	18	20	124	144	200	54	128				
	do 41	15	36	51	121	172	150	22	146	2		1	
	do 42	9	30	39	104	143	150	54	110	2			
	do 43	8	34	42	82	124	125	40	106	4		2	
	do 44	2	25	27	76	103	175	44	98				
	do 45	11	17	28	80	108	125	27	96	1		1	
	do 46	8	44	52	111	163	150	29	121	3			
	Ward 5......Sub-div. No. 1	13	23	36	117	153	150	54	113	4	2		
	do 4	7	18	25	110	136	125	37	96				
	do 11	9	28	37	85	147	150	29	112	1		2	
	do 14	8	25	33	124	118	125	38	91				
	do 15	8	23	31	80	165	149	34	116	3		4	
	do 30	7	34	41	111	121	150	33	78				
	do 31	7	29	36		147		48	110				
	Totals......	770	2,594	3,364	8,101	11,465	12,971	3,579	9,392	16	31	67	11
	Majority for Owens......		1,824										

Toronto, South—Seat "B"

Ward 2	No.	Gooderham	Fielding						
Ward 2	No. 1	41	4	45	70	115	125	45	80
do.	No. 4	22	8	30	59	89	125	33	92
do.	No. 5	34	5	39	75	114	125	41	84
do.	No. 8	65	12	77	132	209	225	80	145
do.	No. 13	52	15	67	136	203	125	69	156
do.	No. 23	32	6	38	69	107	125	40	85
do.	No. 24	27	21	48	73	121	125	51	74
do.	Nos. 1, 2	12	4	16	21	28	50	18	32
do.	3, 4	6	1	7	12	28	50	7	43
do.	5, 8	5		5	11	16	25	12	13
do.	Nos. 9, 10, 11, 12	9	2	11	14	25	50	11	39
do.	Nos. 13, 14	7	1	8	12	20	50	9	16
do.	No. 15	14	2	16	34	50	75	17	58
do.	16	15	5	20	54	74	75	22	53
do.	17	16	5	21	93	114	125	21	104
do.	Nos. 18, 19	9		9	22	31	50	10	40
do.	No. 20	11	2	11	22	33	50	11	39
do.	Nos. 21, 22, 23, 24	25	1	27	23	40	50	30	20
do.	Nos. 25, 26	3		4	4	8	25	4	21
do.	No. 27	7	4	7	7	14	25	7	18
do.	Nos. 29, 30, 31	6	3	10	19	29	50	10	40
do.	No. 32	8	1	11	23	34	50	12	63
do.	33	7	1	8	31	39	75	8	42
do.	Nos. 34, 35	15	2	16	30	47	50	26	49
do.	No. 36	15	8	17	77	127	75	17	33
do.	37	42	8	50	135	197	150	52	98
do.	38	54	10	62	151	177	225	63	162
do.	39	16	5	26	84	106	175	28	147
do.	40	17	6	22	102	138	150	23	102
do.	41	30	4	36	83	136	150	39	11
do.	42	49	9	53	120	151	175	53	97
do.	43	22	7	31	118	164	170	32	143
do.	44	39	7	46	137	187	200	47	103
do.	45	43	4	50	95	119	150	52	148
do.	46	14	11	18	94	135	175	18	132
do.	47	30	8	41	108	137	175	46	129
do.	48	21		29	78	120	100	35	140
do.	49	22	9	22	74	125	125	23	77
do.	50	41	9	51	107	146	175	51	74
do.	51	30	9	39	53	82	100	40	135
do.	52	20	10	29	83	119	125	30	70
do.	53	26	14	36	99	162	175	41	84
do.	54	49	15	63	99	162	175	64	11
do.	55	38		53	75	128	175	57	118

W. H. SMITH,
Returning Officer.

RETURN from the Records of the GENERAL ELECTION to the Legislative Assembly, 1911.—*Continued.*

Electoral District	Numbers of Polling Places	No.	Names of Candidates and No. of Votes Polled for each — Gooderham	Field...idg.	Total No. of Votes Polled	No. of Votes remaining Unpolled	No. of Names on the Polling Lists	No. of Ballot Papers sent out to each Polling Place	Used Ballot Papers	Unused Ballot Papers	Rejected Ballot Papers	Cancelled Ballot Papers	Declined Ballot Papers	Ballot Papers taken from Polling Places
Toronto, South— Seat "B".—Con.	Ward 3	56	30	7	37	59	96	125	39	86	4			2
	do	57	54	29	83	18		225	87	137				
	Ward 4	3	26	6	32	85	101	125	32	93		3		1
	do	4	16	4	20	70	117	125	21	104		2		
	do	5	38	5	43	66	90	100	46	54	1			4
	do	6	24	3	27	51	109	150	29	71	1	1		
	do	7	25	4	29	103	78	150	34	116	1		3	1
	do	8	17	4	21	48	132	75	21	54	5		1	
	do	9	30	7	37	63	69	125	40	85	3			
	do	10	27	16	43	105	100	175	44	131	1			2
	do	11	62	7	69	83	148	125	77	48				3
	do	12	24	5	29	100	152	150	30	120				
	do	13	30	10	40	103	129	175	44	131	2	4		
	do	14	13	4	17	104	143	125	18	107	3	3		
	do	15	22	4	26	74	121	150	28	122	1	2		
	do	16	14	5	19	81	100	125	19	106		1		
	do	17	19	8	27	101	128	225	27	123				
	do	18	51	10	61	147	208	200	69	156	2	4		2
	do	19	33	15	48	124	172	150	54	146	3	3		3
	do	20	35	6	41	11	182	175	43	107	1	2		
	do	21	51	14	65	122	187	150	66	109		1		2
	do	22	39	5	44	80	124	150	47	103				1
	do	23	26	8	34	98	132	150	37	113				
	do	24	32	10	42	118	160	175	43	132				
	do	25	32	11	43	96	139	150	44	106	1	3		

No.											Noble	
27 do					95	30	125	125	98	27	5	22
28 do		2			113	37	150	137	100	37	8	29
29 do		8	3	4	117	33	150	132	102	30	1	29
30 do				3	146	54	200	167	115	52	12	40
31 do		2	1	1	118	32	150	126	102	24	9	15
32 do		1	1		106	44	150	119	80	39	11	28
33 do				2	144	81	225	208	133	75	27	48
34 do		1			93	57	150	156	101	55	15	40
35 do			2	3	120	30	150	132	102	30	5	25
36 do		1		6	97	53	150	143	93	50	12	38
37 do				3	107	43	150	121	78	43	5	38
38 do		4			146	54	200	162	111	51	16	35
39 do		1			186	37	223	128	99	29	5	24
40 do		2		1	128	22	150	44	122	22	4	18
41 do				2	146	54	200	172	121	51	16	35
42 do				3	112	38	150	143	106	37	9	28
43 do					106	44	150	124	84	40	6	34
44 do					98	27	125	103	77	26	3	23
45 do					94	31	175	108	79	29	9	20
46 do		2		3	121	54	150	163	110	53	6	47
1 Ward 5		3		4	113	37	150	153	118	35	6	29
11 do					121	29	125	136	110	26	7	19
14 do					112	38	150	147	109	38	6	32
15 do					91	34	150	118	84	34	7	27
30 do					117	33	150	155	124	31	7	24
31 do					119	31	150	121	96	25	12	13
					153	42	175	143	105	38	7	31
Totals	11	59	50	86	9,576	3,572	13,148	11,465	8,015	3,356	709	2,647
Majority for Gooderham												1,938

Toronto, West, Seat "A"

Ward 5	No.				Noble	Hunter	Cra	fowl
Ward 5	2			149	51	200	170	119	51		7	43
do	3			74	26	100	65	39	26	1	3	23
do	5			106	19	125	101	82	19	2	5	13
do	6	3		134	16	150	107	91	16	2	4	10
do	7	1		178	22	200	162	140	22		2	18
do	8	1	1	126	49	175	138	96	42	1	8	34
do	9			126	49	175	158	11	47	2	7	39
do	10	1		127	73	200	172	101	71	4	5	64
do	11			121	48	175	139	93	46	1	4	38
do	12	1	1	121	29	150	116	90	26		4	21
do	13	2		146	29	175	129	102	27		4	23
do	16											

RETURN from the Records of the GENERAL ELECTION to the Legislative Assembly, 1911 —*Continued.*

Electoral District: Toronto, West—Seat "A"—Con.

THOMAS HURST, Returning Officer.

Numbers of Polling Places	Crawford	Hinter	Noble	Total No. of Votes Polled	No. of Votes Remaining Unpolled	No. of Names on the Polling Lists	No. of Ballot Papers sent out to each Polling Place	Used Ballot Papers	Unused Ballot Papers	Rejected Ballot Papers	Cancelled Ballot Papers	Declined Ballot Papers	Ballot Papers taken from Polling Places
Ward 5, No. 17	27	7	..	36	84	120	150	39	111	3	..	..	..
do 18	19	6	1	25	118	143	175	26	149	1	..	..	..
do 19	21	6	1	28	89	117	150	30	120	2	4	..	..
do 20	43	8	..	52	105	157	200	56	144	..	1	..	..
do 21	45	22	..	67	83	150	175	68	107	1	..	..	..
do 22	45	8	3	56	84	140	175	57	118	..	..	..	..
do 23	49	5	3	57	70	127	175	57	118	1	1	..	..
do 24	39	6	..	45	92	137	150	47	128	5	..	1	..
do 25	26	7	1	33	86	119	125	38	112	1	..	..	..
do 26	22	6	1	29	71	100	175	30	95	1	3	..	..
do 27	29	2	2	32	60	92	125	33	117	..	..	..	..
do 28	46	11	..	58	77	135	175	58	119	5	..	..	..
do 29	41	10	2	53	93	146	175	56	156	..	..	2	..
do 32	39	5	..	44	11	155	200	44	141	2	..	1	2
do 33	23	4	..	29	117	146	175	34	150	..	..	..	..
do 34	21	4	4	25	121	154	175	25	167	1	..	..	1
do 35	26	5	2	31	104	159	200	33	145	8	3	..	..
do 36	40	11	..	55	76	149	175	55	102	..	..	..	..
do 37	58	15	..	73	61	100	200	73	140	1	..	..	..
do 38	29	8	4	39	109	161	175	42	121	..	..	2	..
do 39	38	14	2	52	95	123	200	60	102	..	..	..	..
do 40	21	7	..	28	60	108	150	29	101	..	..	1	2
do 41	35	12	1	48	61	109	150	48	111	..	..	..	..
do 42	35	12	1	48	69	107	150	39	126	1	..	..	..
do 43	30	7	..	38	83	130	175	49	..	..	..	..	..
do 44	34	13	..	47	..	..	..	49	..	..	..	..	..

do	.... " 45	29	6	1	36	54	90	125	38	87	....	2	....	....
do	.... " 50	47	9	2	58	64	122	150	59	91	1	....	....	....
do	.... " 51	43	13	....	56	121	177	200	57	143	1	....	....	....
do	.... " 52	39	14	....	53	94	147	175	54	121	....	....	1	....
do	.... " 53	27	15	2	44	95	139	175	46	129	2	....	....	....
do	.... " 54	40	8	2	50	107	157	200	52	148	....	....	2	....
do	.... " 55	33	5	2	40	142	182	225	40	185	....	....	....	....
do	.... " 56	29	17	1	47	101	148	175	47	128	....	....	....	....
do	.... " 57	29	15	2	46	108	154	200	49	151	....	....	3	....
do	.... " 58	24	12	1	37	70	107	150	41	109	4	....	....	....
do	.... " 59	24	3	....	27	83	110	150	29	121	....	....	2	....
do	.... " 60	23	12	1	36	91	127	175	36	139	....	....	....	....
do	.... " 61	32	6	2	40	60	100	125	40	85	....	....	....	....
do	.... " 62	47	13	1	61	117	178	225	64	161	1	2	....	....
do	.... " 63	28	10	....	38	90	128	175	38	137	....	....	....	....
do	.... " 64	24	6	....	30	71	101	150	32	118	2	....	....	....
do	.... " 65	32	8	....	40	57	97	125	41	84	1	....	....	....
do	.... " 66	53	12	1	66	110	176	225	66	159	....	....	....	....
do	.... " 67	34	10	....	44	94	138	175	46	129	2	....	....	....
do	.... " 68	25	7	....	32	66	98	125	34	91	....	....	2	....
do	.... " 69	44	12	1	57	97	154	200	58	142	1	....	....	....
do	.......Nos. part 70 and 73	41	13	3	57	41	198	225	59	166	....	....	2	....
do	..........................No. 74	27	7	1	35	92	127	175	36	139	1	....	....	....
do	.... " 75	36	7	2	45	139	184	225	47	178	....	2	....	....
do	.... " 76	34	11	2	47	132	179	225	57	168	10	....	....	....
do	.... " 77	46	8	....	54	123	177	225	56	169	2	....	....	....
do	.... " 78	38	8	....	46	97	143	175	53	122	7	....	....	....
do	.... " 79	22	1	1	24	110	134	175	31	144	....	....	7	....
bo	.... " 80	27	5	3	35	107	142	175	35	140	....	....	....	....
do	.... " 81	31	8	1	40	96	136	175	40	135	....	....	....	....
do	.... " 82	37	4	3	44	131	175	200	44	156	....	....	....	....
do	.... " 83	34	16	3	53	117	170	200	54	146	1	....	....	....
do	.... " 84	25	2	2	29	85	14	150	34	116	5	....	....	....
do	.... " 85	22	7	....	29	79	108	150	34	116	....	....	5	....
do	.... " 86	49	10	2	61	123	184	225	63	162	2	....	....	....
do	.... " 87	30	8	3	41	101	142	175	41	134	....	....	....	....
do	.... " 88	16	8	2	26	105	131	175	33	142	7	....	....	....
do	.... " 89	36	8	2	46	132	178	225	47	178	1	....	....	....
Ward 6	..........................No. 1	21	9	1	31	74	105	150	34	116	1	2	....	....
do	.... " 2	34	16	....	50	115	165	200	63	137	13	....	....	....
do	.... " 3	34	21	3	58	147	205	250	63	187	4	1	....	....
do	.... " 4	20	13	1	34	115	149	175	34	41	....	....	....	....
do	.... " 5	24	5	....	29	82	115	150	32	118	....	1	2	....
do	.... " 6	47	6	4	57	96	153	200	61	139	4	....	....	....
do	.... " 7	32	9	2	43	82	125	150	45	105	1	....	1	....

RETURN from the Records of the GENERAL ELECTION to the Legislative Assembly, 1911.—*Continued.*

Electoral District	Numbers of Polling Places	Crawford	...fter.	Noble	Total No. of Votes Polled	No. of Votes Remaining Unpolled	No. of Names on the Polling Lists	No. of Ballot Papers sent out to each Polling Place	Used Ballot Papers	Unused Ballot Papers	Rejected Ballot Papers	Cancelled Ballot Papers	Declined Ballot Papers	Ballot Papers taken from Polling Places
Toronto, West—(Seat "A"—Con.)	Table 6	34	19	2	55	103	158	200	57	143	2			
	do 9	26	11	2	39	53	92	125	39	86	1			
	do 10	32	14	1	47	113	160	200	48	152			5	
	do 11	46	14		61	133	194	225	66	159	2			
	do 12	35	8	2	43	77	120	150	45	105	5		3	
	do 13	32	8	1	42	98	140	175	47	128			2	
	do 14	37	14	1	51	97	148	175	51	124	8			
	do 15	35	12		48	102	150	175	51	124			2	
	do 16	44	9	3	54	126	180	200	54	171	8	1	2	
	do 17	38	8	1	47	108	155	200	57	143	4			
	do 18	42	13	3	55	101	156	175	55	145	1		1	
	do 19	33	12		45	76	121	175	45	130	4			
	do 20	28	7	1	45	95	133	200	46	129				
	do 21	26	7	3	38	124	158	200	37	163	1		3	
	do 22	37	9	1	34	123	162	200	43	157	4		2	
	do 23	40	16		39	116	172	225	58	142	1			
	do 24	34	13	1	56	143	197	175	55	170	1			
	do 25	41	9	3	54	83	128	175	47	128	1			
	do 26	29	15	2	45	82	139	200	61	114	4		1	
	do 27	42	10	1	57	128	168	150	40	160	1	1		
	do 28	30	12	1	40	106	161	150	55	142	1		3	
	do 29	42	15	3	55	68	116	150	51	99	3		2	
	to 30	30	12	2	48	75	115	200	41	109				
	do 31	26	12		40	80	124	200	48	102	1			
	do 32	32	8		44	65	123	200	58	142				
	od 33	50	9	7	58	107	155	200	49	151	1			

148	138	131	152	169	139	151	154	185	41	159	124	139	132	129	143	108	165	119	143	152	109	131	121	97	80	155	209	139	140	122	102	81	128	147	99	136	132	138	121	117	105	123	41	140
52	62	69	48	56	61	49	71	40	59	41	76	61	43	46	57	42	60	31	57	48	41	44	54	28	20	45	66	61	60	53	48	44	47	28	26	39	43	37	29	33	20	27	34	35
200	200	200	200	225	200	200	225	200	200	200	200	175	200	150	150	200	200	150	175	175	125	100	200	275	200	200	175	150	125	175	175	125	175	175	150	150	125	150	175	175				
174	174	160	159	192	153	154	200	185	164	169	166	155	150	145	168	113	210	116	149	164	112	139	154	88	68	173	238	166	168	147	117	103	136	138	92	147	129	143	124	120	100	11	148	131
123	116	102	116	136	96	106	129	145	106	130	90	94	110	99	115	75	150	85	98	116	71	99	108	63	51	133	176	11	110	95	74	59	90	111	67	109	86	109	89	81	87	14	97	
51	58	58	43	56	57	48	71	40	58	39	76	61	40	46	53	38	60	31	51	48	41	40	46	25	17	40	62	55	58	52	43	44	46	27	25	38	43	34	28	31	19	24	34	34
8	17	6	1	8	7	6	15	6	10	10	16	15	11	10	17	6	12	8	13	10	8	12	6	10	4	14	16	14	13	13	18	8	4	4	9	9	6	6	4	2	8	5		
40	39	49	42	47	48	40	53	33	48	28	59	45	28	36	36	32	48	23	37	36	32	26	38	15	13	25	43	39	42	37	30	25	37	23	19	33	32	25	20	24	15	21	23	27
34	35	36	37	38	39	40	41	42	43	44	45	46	47	48	49	50	51	52	53	54	55	56	57	58	59	60	61	62	63	64	65	66	67	68	69	70	71	72	73	74	75	76	77	78

Return from the Records of the General Election to the Legislative Assembly, 1911.—*Continued.*

Electoral District	Numbers of Polling Places	Crawford	Hunter	Noble	Total No. of Votes Polled	No. of Votes Remaining Unpolled	No. of Names on the Polling Lists	No. of Ballot Papers sent out to each Polling Place	Used Ballot Papers	Unused Ballot Papers	Rejected Ballot Papers	Cancelled Ballot Papers	Declined Ballot Papers	Ballot Papers taken from Polling Places
Toronto, West—Seat "A"—Con. Ward 6	No. 79	23	4	3	27	85	112	150	29	121	2			
do	" 80	39	12	4	54	102	156	175	58	117	4			
do	" 81	33	10	2	47	110	157	200	49	151	1		1	
do	" 82	24	4		30	97	127	150	30	120			1	
do	" 83	12	8		31	110		175	32	143	2		1	
do	" 84	51	4	3	19	96	115	150	20	130	3			
do	" 85	42	10	4	65	139	204	200	67	183	3			
do	" 86	22	11	3	56	134	190	225	59	166	2			
do	" 87	30	9	2	33	95	128	150	37	113	4			
do	" 88	40	7	2	39	141	180	225	41	184	5		4	4
do	" 89		9		49	72	121	150	57	93				
do	" 90	33	14	1	48	100	148	200	53	147				
Totals		5,469	1,519	215	7,203	16,369	23,572	29,500	7,579	21,921	243	33	100	
Majority for Crawford		3,950												

Electoral District	Numbers of Polling Places	McPherson	Watt		Total No. of Votes Polled	No. of Votes Remaining Unpolled	No. of Names on the Polling Lists	No. of Ballot Papers sent out to each Polling Place	Used Ballot Papers	Unused Ballot Papers	Rejected Ballot Papers	Cancelled Ballot Papers	Declined Ballot Papers	Ballot Papers taken from Polling Places
Toronto, West—Seat "B" Ward 5	No. 2	34	15		49	121	170	200	49	151				
do	" 3	21	6		27	38	65	100	27	73				
do	" 5	13	5		18	83	101	125	18	107			1	
do	" 6	9	7		16	91	107	150	16	134				
do	" 7	16	8		24	138	162	200	24	176				
do	" 8	30	12		42	96	138	175	42	126	5			
do	" 9	39	9		48	110	158	175	48	127			1	

			4				4			1											2					6	4	2		2				3											
2	1									6																1																		
4			4	3		1		2		2	1				2			1	8		6								3				3			3			2					
127	128	121	146	111	124	170	120	118	118	120	104	97	95	142	123	144	130	141	175	167	120	57	159	90	123	102	100	138	76	114	141	118	121	130	147	188	128	157	109	121	139	85	163	138
73	47	29	29	39	26	30	55	57	57	55	46	28	30	33	52	56	45	34	25	25	33	55	68	41	60	27	48	50	37	49	36	59	57	54	45	53	37	47	43	41	29	36	40	62	37
200	175	150	175	150	150	200	175	175	175	150	125	125	175	175	200	175	175	200	175	125	200	150	150	150	150	175	125	150	200	175	175	175	175	200	225	175	200	150	150	175	125	225	175	
172	139	116	129	120	143	117	157	150	140	127	137	119	100	92	135	146	155	146	146	154	159	149	100	161	123	108	109	107	130	90	122	177	139	157	182	148	154	107	110	127	100	178	128	
103	98	88	100	85	117	90	106	93	84	72	94	91	72	60	83	96	110	112	121	123	104	81	62	109	96	66	59	70	87	54	67	122	95	97	106	145	101	111	69	81	94	62	116	91
69	41	28	29	35	26	27	51	57	56	55	43	28	28	32	52	50	45	34	25	31	55	68	38	52	27	42	50	37	43	36	55	55	52	42	51	37	47	43	38	29	33	38	62	37
9	8	6	6	13	8	7	11	16	14	9	6	10	6	2	12	12	7	9	6	5	18	14	8	15	9	11	14	7	13	5	9	11	12	15	15	6	18	13	14	5	13	8	12	9
60	33	22	23	22	18	20	40	41	42	46	37	18	22	30	40	38	38	25	19	26	37	54	30	37	18	31	36	30	30	31	46	44	40	27	36	31	29	30	24	24	20	30	50	28
10	11	12	13	16	17	18	19	20	21	22	23	24	25	26	27	28	29	32	33	34	35	36	37	38	39	40	41	42	43	44	45	50	51	52	53	54	55	56	57	58	59	60	61	62	63
do	do	do	do	do	do	do	do	do	do	do	do	do	do	do	do	do	do	do	do	do	do	do	do	do	do	do	do	do	do	do	do	do	do	do	do	do	do	do	do	do	do	do	do	do	do

Return from the Records of the General Election to the Legislative Assembly, 1911.—*Continued.*

Electoral District	Numbers of Polling Places	Names of Candidates and No. of Votes Polled for each		Total No. of Votes Polled	No. of Votes Remaining Unpolled.	No. of Names on the Polling Lists.	No. of Ballot Papers sent out to each Polling Place.	Used Ballot Papers.	Unused Ballot Papers.	Rejected Ballot Papers.	Cancelled Ballot Papers.	Declined Ballot Papers.	Ballot Papers taken from Polling Places.
		Watt.	**Sin.**										
Toronto. West—Seat "B".—Con. Ward 5	64	8	22	30	71	101	150	30	120				
do	65	7	34	41	56	97	125	41	84				
do	66	12	52	64	112	176	225	64	161			2	
do	67	9	35	44	94	138	175	46	129	2		6	
do	68	4	26	30	68	98	125	30	92	1			
do	69	12	45	57	97	154	200	58	142	1			
do Nos. pt. 70 and ....No. 73		17	36	53	145	198	225	59	166				
do	74	10	24	34	93	127	175	34	41		1	4	4
do	75	11	37	48	136	184	225	49	176	1			
do	76	13	30	43	136	179	225	56	182				
do	77	11	44	55	122	177	175	41	169				
do	78	12	29	41	102	143	175	26	134				
do	79	2	22	24	110	134	175	43	149		2		
PP do	80	14	29	43	99	142	200	34	132				
do	81	9	25	34	102	136	150	43	157	2			
Po do	82	7	36	43	132	175	150	54	146				
to do	83	20	22	50	120	170	225	30	120		1		
do	84	8	23	30	84	74	175	30	120				
do	85	7	45	30	78	108	225	63	162	3			
do	86	16	28	61	123	184	175	33	142				1
do	87	5	34	33	109	142	225	23	152				
do	88	7	16	23	108	131	200	47	178				
do	89	13	34	47	131	178	250	34	116	3			
Ward 6	No. 1	10	20	30	75	105		43	157				
do	2	7	36	43	122	165		43	186	3			
do	3	20	41	61	144	205		64					

No.											do
4	5	1	143	32	175	149	122	27	9	18	do
5	4	8	118	32	150	115	89	26	2	24	do
6			136	64	200	153	100	53	8	45	do
7	1	7	105	45	150	125	81	44	11	33	do
8	2	3	143	57	200	158	108	50	20	30	do
9	4		86	39	125	92	55	37	9	28	do
10	5		152	48	200	160	116	44	13	31	do
11	3	1	164	61	225	194	133	61	13	48	do
12	3	4	105	45	150	120	80	40	8	32	do
13	4	4	136	39	175	140	101	39	7	32	do
14			124	51	175	148	100	48	14	34	do
15	2	8	124	51	225	150	103	47	12	35	do
16		1	163	62	200	180	126	54	12	42	do
17	4	4	153	47	200	155	108	47	10	37	do
18			145	55	175	156	105	51	13	38	do
19	5		130	45	175	121	78	43	12	31	do
20		1	139	36	200	133	97	36	10	26	do
21		9	163	37	200	158	125	33	7	26	do
22		3	157	43	225	162	127	35	6	29	do
23	5	8	146	54	175	172	118	54	13	41	do
24		5	170	55	200	197	147	50	14	36	do
25		6	128	47	200	128	84	44	9	35	do
26			114	61	150	139	82	57	17	40	do
27		5	160	40	150	168	128	40	9	31	do
28	5		144	56	200	161	105	56	15	41	do
29		1	99	51	200	116	70	46	13	33	do
30		5	109	41	200	115	75	40	14	26	do
31		1	102	48	200	124	86	38	12	26	do
32	1		142	58	200	123	68	55	10	45	do
33		6	151	49	200	155	114	41	13	28	do
34			148	52	225	174	127	47	9	38	do
35			136	64	200	174	117	57	22	35	do
36			147	53	225	160	107	53	14	39	do
37	4		152	48	225	159	116	43	5	38	do
38	3		175	50	200	192	142	50		50	do
39			140	60	200	153	98	55	13	42	do
40	2	1	151	49	200	154	110	44	5	39	do
41	6		148	77	200	200	127	73	24	49	do
42			183	42	175	185	143	42	11	31	do
43	4	6	141	59	175	164	111	53	9	44	do
44			159	41		169	130	39	12	27	do
45		6	124	76		166	97	69	11	58	do
46	2		139	61		155	100	55	13	42	do
47	6		132	43		150	111	39	12	27	do
48	4	2	127	48		145	99	46	7	39	do

RETURN from the Records of the GENERAL ELECTION to the Legislative Assembly, 1911.—*Continued.*

Electoral District	No. of Polling Place	Watt	McPherson	Total No. of Votes Polled	No. of Votes Remaining Unpolled	No. of Names on the Polling Lists	No. of Ballot Papers sent out to each Polling Place	Used Ballot Papers	Unused Ballot Papers	Rejected Ballot Papers	Cancelled Ballot Papers	Declined Ballot Papers	Ballot Papers taken from Polling Places
Toronto, West—Seat "B"—Con. Ward 6	49	10	39	49	119	168	200	57	143				7
do	50	8	30	38	75	113	150	42	108	1		1	
do	51	14	48	62	148	210	225	64	161				
do	52	8	22	30	86	116	150	33	117	3			
do	53	12	35	47	102	149	200	47	153				
do	54	12	33	45	119	164	200	48	152				5
do	55	6	32	38	74	112	150	42	108				1
do	56	15	24	39	100	139	175	44	131	4			
do	57	12	37	42	112	154	125	28	97	3			
do	58	4	12	24	64	88	100	14	86	6			
do	59	12	10	14	54	68	200	44	156				
do	60	20	29	41	132	173	275	66	209				
do	61	22	40	60	178	238	200	55	145	1			
do	62	13	33	55	111	166	200	60	140				
do	63	10	42	55	113	168	175	54	121	4		1	
do	64	12	38	48	99	147	150	47	93				
do	65	14	30	42	75	117	125	38	87				
do	66	10	24	38	65	103	175	47	128	1			
do	67	5	36	46	90	136	175	29	146				
do	68	6	20	25	113	138	175	26	99	4			
do	69	9	18	24	114	92	175	36	139	1			
do	70	13	24	33	86	147	175	45	130	3			
do	71	7	30	43	109	129	175	37	138				
do	72	7	27	34	97	143	175	29	130				
do	73	5	20	27	88	124	150	33	138			2	
do	74		27	32		120			127			1	

Victoria East—Robert Mercer Mason—By Acclamation. ISAAC NAYLOR, Returning Officer.

No.									
75 do	16	4	20	80	100	125	20	105	
76 do	20	3	23	88	111	150	28	122	
77 do	22	13	35	113	148	175	35	140	
78 do	26	9	35	96	131	175	35	140	
79 do	21	5	26	86	112	150	29	121	
80 do	36	17	53	103	156	175	57	118	
81 do	33	17	50	107	157	200	52	148	
82 do	19	11	30	97	127	150	30	120	
83 do	21	10	31	110	141	150	32	143	
84 do	14	7	21	94	115	175	25	125	
85 do	44	20	64	140	204	250	67	183	
86 do	39	14	53	137	190	225	60	165	
87 do	21	15	36	92	128	150	37	113	
88 do	31	12	43	137	180	225	43	182	
89 do	38	14	52	69	121	150	57	93	
90 do	29	16	45	103	148	200	50	150	
Totals	5,225	1,749	6,974	16,598	23,572	29,500	7,378	22,122	
Majority for McPherson	3,476								

Victoria West..... JOHN JACKSON, Returning Officer.

	Johnston	Vrooman	Weeks					
Carden	No. 1	27	45	72	50	125	122	53
Dalton	No. 2	22	28	51	24	75	74	24
Eldon	No. 1	37	12	49	32	85	81	36
do	No. 2	11	15	27	25	75	52	48
Lindsay, E. Ward	No. 2	50	103	154	44	200	198	43
do	No. 3	60	94	155	57	225	212	68
do North	No. 1	81	65	148	71	225	219	77
do	No. 2	68	48	118	34	175	152	57
do	No. 3	54	55	114	67	200	181	85
S utho	No. 4	83	50	149	100	200	249	96
do	No. 1	97	63	167	55	225	222	57
do	No. 2	95	52	149	14	275	263	123
do	No. 3	11	45	168	68	235	236	66
do	No. 4	66	49	122	84	225	206	102
Mariposa	No. 1	119	47	169	172	350	341	179
do	No. 2	79	89	130	93	225	223	92
do	No. 3	72	50	177	101	300	278	123
do	No. 4	56	46	123	46	175	169	46
do				102	42	150	44	47

RETURN from the Records of the GENERAL ELECTION to the Legislative Assembly, 1911.—Continued.

Victoria, West— Con.

Numbers of Polling Places	Weeks	Vroonan	Johnston	Total No. of Votes Polled	No. of Votes remaining Unpolled	No. of Names on the Polling Lists	No. of Ballot Papers sent out to each Polling Place	Used Ballot Papers	Unused Ballot Papers	Rejected Ballot Papers	Cancelled Ballot Papers	Declined Ballot Papers	Ballot Papers taken from Polling Places
Mariposa .... No. 3	63	111	3	177	40	217	225	177	48				
do 4	89	60	1	150	54	204	225	152	73				
do 5	88	35	1	124	42	166	175	126	49				
do 6	52	27		79	27	106	125	78	47	2			
do 7	92	32	1	124	25	169	175	124	51	2			
do 8	24	30	4	55	30	85	100	55	45				
Ops .... No. 1	67	34	1	102	35	137	150	102	45			1	
do 2	32	43	3	79	27	106	125	79	46		1		
do 3	35	27		63	31	94	100	63	37				
do 4	57	22	1	82	34	116	125	82	43				
do 5	21	76	2	98	49	147	150	99	51	1			
do 6	30	45		77	32	109	150	78	47	1			
Woodville	82	27		109	18	127	150	109	41				
Totals	**1,732**	**1,836**	**94**	**3,662**	**1,743**	**5,405**	**5,745**	**3,697**	**2,048**	**19**	**12**	**6**	
Majority for Vroonan		104											

Waterloo, North.

Numbers of Polling Places	Euler	Lackner	Martin	Total No. of Votes Polled	No. of Votes remaining Unpolled	No. of Names on the Polling Lists	No. of Ballot Papers sent out to each Polling Place	Used Ballot Papers	Unused Ballot Papers	Rejected Ballot Papers	Cancelled Ballot Papers	Declined Ballot Papers	Ballot Papers taken from Polling Places
Berlin .... No. 1	39	103	38	180	66	246	25	30	5				
do 2	36	99	23	158	49	207	25	38	67				
do 3	47	135	20	202	74	276	80	82	98	1			
do 4	11	41	5	57	17	74	80	57	43			2	
do 5	47	86	11	145	52	197	25	45	80				
do 6	55	81	10	149	59	208	25	49	76	1		1	

Location	No.												
do	7				71	127	198	166	39	127	20	58	49
do	8				106	169	275	239	70	169	17	70	79
do	9				124	151	275	243	92	151	14	73	63
do	10				85	140	225	198	58	140	9	75	54
do	11				69	106	175	154	48	106	8	31	67
do	12				81	142	223	186	44	142	15	56	69
do	13				93	107	200	177	70	107	8	56	42
do	14				75	124	199	168	44	124	18	57	49
do	15				96	154	250	210	56	154	29	87	34
do	16				92	158	250	221	63	158	35	77	45
do	17				80	120	200	175	55	120	17	53	49
do	18				130	118	248	213	95	118	11	69	37
do	19				104	221	325	301	80	221	39	126	55
do	20				86	139	225	188	49	139	17	70	52
Waterloo	1				57	68	125	107	39	68	2	45	21
do	2				81	119	200	175	56	119	3	84	32
do	3				95	105	250	160	55	105	6	65	34
do	4		3		125	155	250	223	68	155	10	83	62
do	5				40	173	124	265	92	173	9	93	70
do	6				81	84	150	114	30	84	7	49	28
do	7				92	69	200	128	59	69	5	39	25
do	8				75	108	226	176	68	108	4	41	63
Elmira	1				69	151	298	207	56	151	5	77	69
Waterloo Tp	1				85	229	175	285	56	229	8	125	96
do	2				43	90	125	153	63	90		57	32
do	3				160	82	323	107	137	82	3	23	59
do	4				80	163	200	300	56	163	1	59	98
do	5				89	120	224	176	77	120	9	57	62
Wellesley Tp	1				76	135	150	212	54	135		28	98
do	2				86	74	250	218	54	74	1	52	22
do	3				107	164	225	207	89	164	3	105	58
do	4				66	118	225	190	31	118	2	38	73
do	5				70	159	275	238	33	159	3	59	97
do	6				77	205	250	231	58	205	4	102	99
do	7				53	173	148	98	58	173		59	109
Woolwich Tp	1				74	72	176	119	26	72	1	8	63
do	2				47	74	250	155	45	74		13	60
do	3				82	129	200	229	26	129	1	38	91
do	4				103	168	223	174	61	168	1	21	145
do	5				109	97	125	187	77	97	2	38	58
do	6				56	114	150	95	73	114		35	77
do	7				70	69	150	116	36	69		28	41
Totals		5	5	25	4,094	6,414	10,508	9,220	2,806	6,414	454	3,059	2,866

Majority for Lackner 193

GEORGE DAVIDSON,
Returning Officer.

RETURN from the Records of the GENERAL ELECTION to the Legislative Assembly, 1911.—*Continued.*

Electoral District: Waterloo, South

WILLIAM R. PLUM, Returning Officer.

Numbers of Polling Places	Maguire	Pattinson	Taylor, Jr.	Total No. of Votes Polled	No. of Votes Remaining Unpolled	No. of Names on the Polling Lists	No. of Ballot Papers sent out to each Polling Place	Used Ballot Papers	Unused Ballot Papers	Rejected Ballot Papers	Cancelled Ballot Papers	Declined Ballot Papers	Ballot Papers taken from Polling Places
Ayr Village .... No. 1	6	74	11	191	13	204	225	192	33	1			
Galt .... No. 2	9	41	15	65	92	157	175	65	110				
do .... A to L ...... No. 3	28	56	38	122	103	225	225	122	103				
do .... M to Z ...... No. 4	14	43	22	79	70	149	150	80	70				
do .... No. 5	27	62	48	137	147	284	300	137	163		1		
do .... A to L ...... No. 6	10	57	40	107	176	283	300	107	193			1	
do .... M to Z ...... No. 7	17	66	36	119	89	208	225	119	106				
do .... No. 8	14	52	34	100	78	178	175	101	74		1		
do .... A to L ...... No. 9	9	45	75	90	82	172	175	91	84			1	
do .... M to Z ...... No. 10	34	76	37	185	125	310	325	186	139	2	1	1	
do .... No. 11	39	63	51	139	96	235	249	139	110	3			
do .... No. 12	16	77	28	44	127	271	151	130	59				
do .... A to K ...... No. 1	22	46	24	90	60	150	250	59	106				
do .... L to Z ...... No. 2	39	74	29	41	99	240	225	137	138	1			
do .... No.	24	39	18	87	139	226	150	107	50				
do .... No.	29	42	19	100	54	154	200	100	58				
do .... No.	30	93	50	41	67	208	150	142	37				
New Hamburg ...... No.	16	78	33	113	44	157	150	113	45				
North Dumfries ... No.	36	11	82	197	117	314	275	197	59			1	
do	3	69	29	105	47	152	75	105	21				
do	1	132	33	54	71	121	125	54	76				
do	2	23	87	49	19	286	125	49	87				
do	1	15	62	11	72	73	200	21	43				
....	2	22	66	82	92	203	125	82	63			1	
....	3	18		87	46	128	150	87					

Waterloo (left table)

Preston	No. 1				85	165	250	240	75	165	19	127	19
do (M to Z)	No. 1				72	153	225	203	50	153	9	120	24
do	No. 2			1	122	278	400	384	106	278	21	215	42
do (M to Z)	No. 2				179	221	400	396	176	220	26	166	28
Waterloo Township	No. 1		1		64	86	150	170	85	85	58	24	3
do	No. 2	1			46	104	150	170	65	103	17	81	5
do	No. 3				47	103	150	155	67	103	46	44	13
do	No. 4				99	101	200	208	52	101	38	52	11
do	No. 5			1	50	75	125	122	107	75	40	34	1
do	No. 6				63	62	125	117	47	61	36	24	1
Wilmot Township	No. 1				53	147	200	202	56	147	96	50	
do	No. 2				84	116	200	190	55	116	65	51	
do	No. 3				11	89	300	187	74	89	28	60	
do	No. 4	1			104	196	200	303	98	196	110	85	1
do	No. 5				93	82	175	171	87	82	10	72	
do	No. 6		1		74	101	175	157	56	101	29	71	1
Totals		5	5	8	3,631	5,143	8,774	8,638	3,513	5,125	1,773	2,770	582
Majority for Pattinson												997	

Welland (right table) — Monroe, Fraser

											Monroe	Fraser
Bertie	No. 1				50	50	100	82	33	49	25	24
do	No. 2				72	78	150	137	59	78	35	43
do	No. 3				67	133	200	148	15	133	64	69
do	No. 4				77	148	225	220	72	148	77	71
do	No. 5				42	58	100	90	33	57	18	39
do	No. 6			1	96	204	300	287	84	203	105	98
Bridgeburg	No. 1				149	126	275	256	132	124	40	84
do (A to M)	No. 1			2	80	45	125	125	80	45	13	32
do (N to Z)	No. 2				87	38	150	110	72	38	9	29
Chippawa	No. 1				71	129	200	200	72	128	51	77
Crowland	No. 2				84	94	125	125	32	45	64	29
do	No. 3				55	66	150	134	70	64	24	40
Fort Erie	No. 1				90	70	125	102	32	70	32	38
the	No. 2			1	149	154	250	242	90	152	62	90
do	No. 3				80	93	150	44	48	93	38	58
do	No. 4				54	119	175	118	25	119	40	53
do	No. 5		1	2	32	160	250	172	53	159	62	57
do	No. 6				56	63	100	244	85	63	72	87
do	No. 7			1	90	56	100	94	31	56	21	42
Niagara Falls	No. 1 A	5	1		37	37	75	83	27	37	4	52
					44	64	100	59	22	64	7	30
					38	64	100	87	23	64	27	37

RETURN from the Records of the GENERAL ELECTION to the Legislative Assembly, 1911.—*Continued.*

Electoral District	Numbers of Polling Places	Fraser	Monroe	Total No. of Votes Polled	No. of Votes remaining Unpolled	No. of Names on the Polling Lists	No. of Ballot Papers sent out to each Polling Place	Used Ballot Papers	Unused Ballot Papers	Rejected Ballot Papers	Cancelled Ballot Papers	Declined Ballot Papers	Ballot Papers taken from Polling Places
Welland—Con.	a Falls ... B	102	72	174	65	39	350	178	172	2	1		1
	do ... 2 ... A to M	88	63	51	102	253	275	152	123	3			1
	do ... 3 ... N to Z	70	78	48	84	232	250	153	97	1			
	do ... 4 ... A to M	55	40	95	39	34	120	95	55	1	1		
	do ... 4 ... N to Z	65	48	13	89	93	200	114	86	1			
	do ... 5 ... A to M	41	27	68	48	16	125	69	56	2	1		
	do ... 5 ... N to Z	81	90	71	115	286	15	173	127				
	do ... 6 ... A to M	54	29	83	81	64	225	85	90	3			3
	do ... 6 ... N to Z	61	54	15	95	210	99	117	108	2			
	do ... 7 A ... A to M	38	18	56	43	99	325	58	41	4			
	do ... 7 B ... N to Z	83	39	122	70	192	225	126	199		1		
	do ... 8 ... A to M	48	15	63	111	01	225	65	60				
	do ... 8 ... N to Z	33	64	197	62	88	175	203	22	1	3		
	Bt Colborne ... No. 1	69	32	01	54	63	225	105	70	3			
	do ... No. 2	99	56	45	40	209	175	155	70	2	1		
	ad ... No. 1	93	33	126	42	66	125	126	49	3			
	do ... 2	63	82	65	57	209	125	146	79				
	do ... 3	37	28	65	78	107	75	66	59		1		
	do ... 4	25	17	49	51	96	125	43	32				
	bl Town ... No. 1	66	24	34	64	212	250	49	76	1			
	do ... 2	31	68	80	44	31	30	136	72	1	3		
	do ... 3	132	69	61	35	232	125	103	82		2		
	do ... 4	82	36	92	24	127		168	48		3		
	do	63	19	90		14		102	58	1			
		70	29					92	35				
			20					90					

Wellington, West

Municipality	No.								
Bd Tp	1			1	31	69	90	91	22	69	23	46
do	2			2	67	83	30	124	42	82	41	41
do	3			2	68	57	125	89	34	55	28	27
do	4				57	68	125	115	49	66	27	39
do	5				46	54	90	75	21	54	26	28
do	6		1	1	39	61	90	90	29	61	31	30
W... Md	1				139	111	250	279	168	111	54	57
do	2A				253	147	90	374	228	46	86	60
do	2B				39	86	225	201	116	85	38	47
do	3			1	96	54	30	139	85	54	31	23
do	4				139	136	275	170	34	36	84	52
do	5				158	117	275	268	151	17	75	42
Wil Hy	1				40	85	125	117	33	84	53	31
do	2	7	11	45	44	106	30	139	33	06	69	37
Totals					**4,815**	**6,284**	**11,09**	**10,173**	**3,956**	**6,217**	**2,706**	**3,511**
Majority for Fraser												**805**

Wellington, East

Municipality	No.	Richardson	Craig						
Luther, West	1	24	48			52	73	125	98	26	72
do	2	24	32			44	56	100	94	38	56
do	3	42	41			42	83	125	13	30	83
do	4	39	31	1		55	70	125	07	37	70
do	5	49	46			30	91	125	19	24	95
do	6	66	58			51	124	175	46	32	124
Lutr Tp	1	75	41			51	16	200	30	42	16
do	2	48	34	2		84	83	125	16	64	82
do	3	53	26			42	79	150	142	34	79
do	4	34	66			71	90	150	129	63	90
do	5	57	23			50	82	125	101	29	90
do	6	27	27			64	64	100	81	21	54
do	7	24	26	3		46	50	75	59	27	50
Garafraxa West	1	10	23			25	33	75	55	9	33
do	2	32	29			42	61	100	76	25	61
do	3	27	17			39	63	75	68	24	61
do	4	16	17			27	55	100	84	21	48
do	5	37	49	2		37	16	200	72	18	63
do	6	51	46	1		45	102	125	171	56	54
Belwood Village		55	32			64	68	171	05	70	10
Mt Forest, N. Ward		34	46			98	88	150	46	39	101
do S. "		41	56			57	88	100	141	59	66
do E. "		60	23			87	16		87	25	87
do W. "	1	43				34	66			21	66
Nichol	2					34	66	100			

RETURN from the Records of the GENERAL ELECTION to the Legislative Assembly, 1911.—Continued.

Electoral District	Numbers of Polling Places	Names of Candidates and No. of Votes Polled for each		Total No. of Votes Polled	No. of Votes remaining Unpolled	No. of Names on the Polling Lists	No. of Ballot Papers sent out to each Polling Place	Used Ballot Papers	Unused Ballot Papers	Rejected Ballot Papers	Cancelled Ballot Papers	Declined Ballot Papers	Ballot Papers taken from Polling Places
		Craig.	Richardson.										
Wellington, East—Con. Nichol	3	32	63	95	17	112	125	96	29	1			
do	4	27	40	67	35	102	125	67	58				
Elora	1	57	84	141	34	175	200	142	58	1			
do	No. 2	45	120	165	36	201	225	165	59				
Erin Tp	1	21	94	115	58	173	175	115	60				
do	2	33	63	96	34	130	150	96	54		1		
do	3	63	70	133	33	166	175	133	42		4		
do	4	47	66	113	35	148	175	113	62	1			
do	5	30	42	72	59	131	150	72	78				
do	6	62	94	156	69	225	225	157	68	1			
Erin Village	No. 1	68	54	122	28	150	175	122	53	1			1
Fergus	2	113	81	194	51	245	210	195	55				
do		113	83	196	68	264	275	197	78	15			
Totals		1,595	1,932	3,527	1,361	4,888	5,500	3,547	1,953	15			
Majority for Richardson			37										

Electoral District	Numbers of Polling Places	McIntosh.	Schofield.	Total No. of Votes Polled	No. of Votes remaining Unpolled	No. of Names on the Polling Lists	No. of Ballot Papers sent out	Used Ballot Papers	Unused Ballot Papers	Rejected Ballot Papers	Cancelled Ballot Papers	Declined Ballot Papers	Ballot Papers taken
Wellington, South. Guelph City	No. 1A	62	96	158	85	243	250	160	90	2			
do	1B	31	53	84	22	106	125	86	39	2			1
do	2A	54	82	136	70	206	200	136	64				
do	2B	28	55	83	39	122	125	86	39				
do	3	55	126	181	30	211	250	181	69	3			
do	4	70	112	182	84	266	250	184	66	1	1		

												Subdivision
			39	111	150	154	45	109	77		32	do ... 5
			58	142	200	197	55	142	88		54	do ... 6
			93	157	250	249	93	156	95		61	do ... 7
		1	54	146	200	202	58	144	77		67	do ... 8
		2	38	87	125	120	33	87	45		42	do ... 9
	1		46	204	250	271	69	202	132		70	do ... 10
	2	1	59	166	225	237	71	166	90		76	do ... 11
		2	72	178	250	240	63	177	102		75	do ... 12
		3	24	126	150	156	34	122	69		53	do ... 13
			49	176	125	232	59	173	88		85	do ... 14A
		1	37	88	125	122	34	88	52		36	do ... 14B
		2	60	190	250	245	55	190	105		86	do ... 15
			74	202	276	275	74	201	115		73	do ... 16
		3	94	157	251	233	78	155	82		26	do ... 17A
		3	12	88	100	118	31	87	61		48	do ... 17B
			43	132	175	187	55	132	84		16	do ... 18A
	1	1	12	88	100	110	25	85	69		29	do ... 18B
			16	84	225	114	33	81	52		62	do ... 19
	2		42	183	150	227	45	182	87		67	Eramosa Tp. No. 1
			42	108	150	144	36	108	46		53	do ... 2
			36	114	150	148	34	114	47		56	do ... 3
1			50	100	225	136	37	99	46		55	do ... 4
			125	100	125	135	37	98	42		101	do ... 5
		1	27	98	200	120	23	97	47		102	do ... No. 1
			52	148	200	207	59	148	66		51	do ... 2
1	2	1	31	169	126	213	45	168	26		62	do ... 3
			49	77	200	119	42	77	62		81	do ... 4
			75	125	175	189	65	124	44		68	do ... 5
		1	74	126	300	171	46	125	68		44	do ... No. 1
			39	136	175	181	45	136	46		30	do ... 2
			210	90	125	130	40	90	45		45	do ... 3
		3	150	75	125	113	38	75	82		60	do ... 4
			45	130	149	170	43	127	22		63	do ... 5
			43	82		117	35	82	20		53	Pi ... No. 1
		1	42	83		111	28	83	67			do ... 2
			28	121		156	36	120				do ... 3
3	**6**	**35**	**2,407**	**5,420**	**7,827**	**7,453**	**2,079**	**5,374**	**2,912**	**2,462**	**Totals**
									450		Majority for Scholfield

WILLIAM WALLACE WHITE,
Returning Officer.

RETURN from the Records of the GENERAL ELECTION to the Legislative Assembly, 1911.—*Continued.*

Electoral District	Numbers of Polling Places		Names of Candidates and No. of Votes Polled for each		Voters at each Polling Place			Ballot Papers sent out and how disposed of in each Polling Place						
			Chambers.	McEwing.	Total No. of Votes Polled.	No. of Votes Remaining Unpolled.	No. of Names on the Polling Lists.	No. of Ballot Papers sent out to each Polling Place.	Used Ballot Papers.	Unused Ballot Papers.	Rejected Ballot Papers.	Cancelled Ballot Papers.	Declined Ballot Papers.	Ballot Papers taken from Polling Places.
Wellington, West..	Village of Art hr	No. 1	64	53	117	41	158	175	118	57	1			
	do	No. 2	69	42	111	33	44	169	112	57	1	2		
	Village of Clifford....	No. 1	67	65	132	24	156	150	134	16				
	Village of Drayton....	No. 2	99	88	187	33	220	225	188	37	1			
	Town of Harriston....	No. 1	57	18	75	21	96	125	76	49	1			
	do	No. 2	43	16	59	12	71	100	59	41				
	do	No. 3	55	18	73	26	99	150	74	26	1			
	do	No. 4	63	19	82	18	100	150	82	68				
	do	No. 5	58	31	89	21	110	150	89	61				
	Town of Palmerston to— North Ward	No. 1	73	34	107	61	168	225	107	118				
	West Ward	No. 2	104	27	131	96	227	200	131	69				
	East	No. 3	119	40	159	130	289	250	164	86		3		
	Township of	No. 1	40	100	140	18	158	175	140	10				
	do	No. 2	54	70	124	24	148	150	124	51				
	do	No. 3	36	91	127	15	142	125	127	23				
	do	No. 4	49	34	83	17	100	150	83	42				
	do	No. 5	40	67	107	24	131	100	107	43	2			
	do	No. 6	38	55	93	27	120	150	95	5				
	Township of Maryboro	No. 1	56	46	102	37	139	175	103	47				
	do	No. 2	46	68	114	37	151	250	115	60	2			
	do	No. 3	86	96	182	46	228	125	183	67	1			
	do	No. 4	32	42	74	18	92	150	74	51	1			
	do	No. 5	79	14	123	18	141	125	123	27	1			
	do	No. 6	51	34	85	14	99	150	85	40				
	Township of Peel	No. 1	58	99	157	20	177	200	158	42	1			

GEORGE M. FOX, Returning Officer.

Wentworth, North.

		2		13							2		Majority
do	2		1	26	80	106	98	20	78	59	19		
do	3			31	94	125	103	9	94	42	52		
do	4		1	55	121	176	184	64	120	79	41		
do	5			61	114	175	142	29	113	69	44		
do	6	1	1	74	101	175	145	44	101	57	44		
do	7			58	92	150	124	32	92	50	42		
Totals		2	9	13	1,498	3,453	4,951	4,460	1,029	3,431	1,653	1,778	
Majority for Chambers												125	Lawson.

McWard	1			82	243	326	292	49	243	92	151
do	2	1	6	56	219	275	256	38	218	72	146
Foundry	1		3	68	230	298	286	57	229	66	157
Valley do	2			72	178	250	218	40	178	72	106
do	1	1	1	51	199	250	231	32	199	79	117
do	2			44	81	125	97	16	81	33	49
do	1	2		40	85	125	110	25	85	33	52
do	2		1	53	172	150	208	36	172	127	42
do	3		1	31	119	225	136	17	119	68	51
do	4		1	75	150	125	191	41	150	110	50
do	5			28	97	150	116	19	97	55	41
do	6		4	47	103	125	127	24	103	68	35
do	7			45	55	100	70	16	54	38	15
do	8		1	48	77	125	103	26	77	52	24
do	9			45	80	125	110	30	80	57	23
do	1			55	70	125	91	21	70	54	16
do	2		2	43	82	125	103	21	82	35	47
do	3			2	123	125	142	19	123	61	62
do	4			29	96	125	118	22	96	62	34
Wt.				30	70	100	78	8	70	36	30
do				25	100	125	110	10	100	60	40
do				26	74	100	86	12	74	47	26
do				35	99	100	109	10	99	51	48
do				97	65	275	81	16	65	25	40
East		1		45	178	200	274	96	178	83	92
do			2	64	155	225	167	12	155	63	91
do				42	161	125	189	28	161	74	87
do		1			83		111	28	83	61	22
Totals		4	20	1,304	3,444	4,748	4,210	769	3,441	1,723	1,694
Majority for McQueen		2								29	

RETURN from the Records of the GENERAL ELECTION to the Legislative Assembly, 1911.—*Continued.*

Electoral District	Numbers of Polling Places		Names of Candidates and No. of Votes Polled for each			Voters at each Polling Place			Ballot Papers sent out and how disposed of in each Polling Place						
		No.	Barrett.	Reed.	Regan.	Total No. of Votes Polled.	No. of Votes Remaining Unpolled.	No. of Names on the Polling Lists.	No. of Ballot Papers sent out to each Polling Place.	Used Ballot Papers.	Unused Ballot Papers.	Rejected Ballot Papers.	Cancelled Ballot Papers.	Declined Ballot Papers.	Ballot Papers taken from Polling Places.
Wentworth South..	An[cas]ter	1		43	7	52	36	88	125	52	73	2			
	do	2	4	55	22	83	29	112	125	83	42	2		2	
	do	3	12	40	60	114	96	210	250	114	136	1	1	1	
	do	4	1	76	97	176	59	235	250	176	74				
	do	5		93	21	98	56	170	200	98	86	1		1	
	do	6	1	67	29	85	61	159	175	85	77				
	do	7		66	17	54	29	114	100	54	40				
	do	8		38	16	24	24	78	75	24	46			1	1
	Barton	1		3	18	73	26	50	150	73	51				
	do	2	2	23	48	58	61	134	125	58	77	3	2		
	do	3	2	13	42	45	58	116	225	45	67	1	1		
	do	4	3	19	26	92	73	118	75	92	105	3			
	do	5		23	59	44	115	207	225	44	133			2	
	do	6	9	23	21	135	19	63	300	135	31			1	
	do	7		51	80	128	82	217	225	128	90				
	do	8	4	15	72	134	145	273	300	134	172	3	3		
	do	9	36	34	53	171	122	213	200	171	91				
	do	10	45	37	87	63	52	293	150	63	129		1		
	do	11	44	38	22	87	87	115	125	87	62	2		2	
	Annex	12	3	25	37	93	34	174	150	93	113	1	1	1	
	Binbrook	1	22	44	48	111	29	127	150	111	57				
	do	2	1	61	49	77	26	140	150	77	39	1		2	
	do	3	1	42	34	105	19	103	125	105	48			1	
	Glanford	1		68	34	121	29	124	200	121	45				
	do	2	1	69	52	135	29	150	200	135	79				
	do	3		76	56		39	174			65	1			1

ROBERT H. LEWIS,
Returning Officer.

Saltfleet (and totals)

	No.											
Saltfleet	1	109	191	300	283	92	191	96	84	8	2	
do	2	64	136	200	192	56	136	88	46	2	2	1
do	3	50	75	125	120	45	75	45	26	2	1	
do	4	77	98	175	155	57	98	62	36			
do	5	57	68	125	95	37	58	27	27	3		
do		96	104	200	176	72	104	71	30	3		
Totals		2,481	3,144	5,625	4,978	1,844	3,134	1,496	1,391	209	25	7	6
Majority for Regan								105					

York East

	No.	Annis	McCowan
To, Ward 1	69	2	14
do	70	4	31
do	71	3	17
do	72	16	35
do	73	7	14
do	74	15	41
do	75	18	24
do	76	6	35
do	77	3	47
do	78	9	57
do	79	13	38
do	80	9	18
Ward 2	Nos. 61 and 62	26	24
To	1	89	43
do	2	89	33
do	3	22	37
do	4	10	17
do	5	7	36
Stouffville	6	28	12
do	7	15	11
North	1	6	32
	2	23	11
York Tp		4	39
do A to L	10	35	24
do M to Z	11	18	25
do A to L	12	27	63
do M to Z	13	5	38
do	14		16
		6	127
		6	59
		9	18
		9	

York East

RETURN from the Records of the GENERAL ELECTION to the Legislative Assembly, 1911.—*Continued.*

Electoral District	Numbers of Polling Places	Names of Candidates and No. of Votes Polled for each — N.	Names of Candidates and No. of Votes Polled for each — Annis.	To. 1 No. of Votes Polled	No. of Votes Remaining Unpolled	No. of Names on the Polling Lists	No. of Ballot Papers sent out to each Polling Place	Used Ballot Papers	Unused Ballot Papers	Rejected Ballot Papers	Cancelled Ballot Papers	Declined Ballot Papers	Ballot Papers taken from Polling Places
York, East—Con.	No. 1 Markham Tp	41	48	89	69	158	165	89	76				
	do 2	33	16	49	50	99	65	49	56				
	do 3	36	30	66	53	119	77	66	61				
	do 4	47	47	94	77	171	13	94	79				
	do 5	71	62	33	98	231	31	33	98				
	do 6	27	50	77	65	142	32	77	75	1			
	do 7	20	25	45	49	158	02	45	57				
	do 8	22	61	83	75	137	167	84	83	1			
	do 9	38	49	71	66	150	140	71	69	1			
	do 10	24	51	89	61	125	25	90	65	1			
	do 11	80	41	65	60	172	28	65	64	3	1		
	...m Village 1	57	44	24	48	112	26	25	53	1			
	do 2	59	29	86	67	191	80	87	39				
	do ...d Hill	57	65	24	97	173	17	25	81				
	Scarboro Tp 1	59	19	76	91	193	80	76	98				
	do 2	60	43	92	91	152	61	82	53			1	
	do 3	71	41	01	51	184	93	14	79	3			
	do 4	29	42	13	71	107	10	14	64	1			
	do 5	45	28	57	50	139	50	57	96				
	do 6	49	41	86	53	195	07	86	67				
	do 7	53	61	10	85	154	62	11	89		1		
	do 8	22	41	94	60	131	36	95	92				
	No. 15	27	5	27	44	136	40	27					
	Ward L. Toronto 60	30	10	37	99	123	30	37				1	
	do 61	30	7	37	86	133	11	38					
	do 62		8	38	95								

Municipality / Poll	Lennox	Sn.									
do No. 63	18	10	28	110	138	146	28	118			
do No. 64	48	9	57	95	152	162	67	105			
do No. 65	36	8	44	136	180	175	44	131			3
do No. 66	23	8	31	79	110	110	31	79			
do No. 67	12	9	20	117	137	140	20	120			
do No. 68	20	9	29	120	149	157	29	128			
Totals	**2,337**	**1,555**	**3,892**	**5,504**	**9,396**	**9,825**	**3,915**	**5,910**	**15**	**5**	**3**
Majority for McCowan	**782**										
King No. 1	93	59	152	16	168	210	45	55	2		1
do No. 2	57	62	19	8	127	90	19	41			2
do No. 3	120	83	203	35	238	260	205	55		5	
do No. 4	80	92	172	21	193	235	74	61	1		1
do No. 5	84	54	128	13	41	175	133	42			3
do No. 6	86	96	200	34	234	275	203	72	2		
do No. 7	60	56	142	38	180	210	45	65			
do No. 8	49	49	99	14	123	90	10	50			
do No. 9	24	22	71	16	87	120	71	49	1		
do No. 10	128	40	64	13	77	10	64	46			
Whitchurch No. 1	47	61	189	64	253	275	189	86			1
do No. 2	40	96	143	46	189	225	143	82		5	
do No. 3	91	89	129	30	159	185	129	56			
do No. 4	48	69	90	42	202	95	61	64			
do No. 5	44	79	127	43	70	35	133	62			
do No. 6	70	36	80	39	119	200	80	55			
East Gwillimbury No. 1	52	77	147	40	187	30	147	53	1		
do No. 2	84	64	16	11	127	225	16	34			
do No. 3	71	99	183	14	197	175	183	42			
do No. 4	79	57	128	25	153	225	128	47			
do No. 5	63	98	177	23	200	30	178	47			
do No. 6	77	45	108	26	34	200	108	42			
North Gwillimbury No. 1	86	68	45	23	168	185	45	55			
do No. 2	61	53	39	16	45	180	139	46			
do No. 3	50	61	122	25	147	125	122	58			
Georgina No. 1	79	24	74	22	96	185	75	50	2	1	
do No. 2	77	59	138	18	46	35	39	46			
do No. 3	57	12	89	16	65	175	91	44			
do No. 4	84	67	124	15	139	40	124	51	2	1	1
Holland &c.	57	24	108	13	121	175	57	39			
do &c.	119	62	181	29	210	250	183	67	2	2	2

York, North

RETURN from the Records of the GENERAL ELECTION to the Legislative Assembly, 1911.—*Continued.*

Electoral District	Numbers of Polling Places	Names of Candidates and No. of Votes Polled for each.		Total No. of Votes Polled.	No. of Votes Remaining Unpolled.	No. of Names on the Polling Lists.	No. of Ballot Papers sent out to each Polling Place.	Used Ballot Papers.	Unused Ballot Papers.	Rejected Ballot Papers.	Cancelled Ballot Papers.	Declined Ballot Papers.	Ballot Papers taken from Polling Places.
		Walton.	Lennox.										
York, North—Con.	North Ward	65	113	178	25	203	235	178	57	—	—	—	
	Centre do	68	80	148	16	164	200	149	51	1	—	—	
	S'uth do	57	134	191	34	225	250	192	58	2	2	1	
	Newmarket— St. George Ward ... A to N	[10	71	181	51	232	275	183	92	—	—	—	8
	do ... O to Z	35	53	88	25	113	150	99	57	3	—	—	
	St. Andrews do ... A to Z	78	110	188	33	221	260	193	67	5	2	—	
	do ... N to M	56	54	110	12	122	150	111	39	1	—	1	
	St. Patricks do ... A to M	106	98	204	53	257	285	204	81	—	—	—	
	do ... N to Z	42	56	98	36	134	160	98	62	—	—	—	
	Totals	2,530	3,023	5,553	1,073	6,626	7,830	5,604	2,226	25	17	8	
	Majority for Lennox		493										
		Verral.	Godfrey.										
York, West	Ward 3 ... No. 84	17	17	34	41	75	100	36	64	—	1	1	
	do ... " 85	19	22	41	61	102	100	41	59	—	—	—	
	do ... No. 86	15	23	38	82	120	124	39	85	1	—	—	
	Ward 4 ... " 74	2	7	9	15	24	25	9	16	—	—	—	
	do ... " 88	13	49	62	118	180	199	63	136	—	—	—	
	Ward 5 ... No. 90	13	40	53	118	171	174	53	121	1	—	—	
	do ... " 91	10	47	57	69	126	150	57	93	1	—	—	
	do ... " 92	8	19	27	58	85	100	27	73	—	—	—	

York, West—Con. — SAMUEL RYDING, Returning Officer.

No.	Location	Godfrey	Verral						
No. 93	do	17	6	23	61	84	100	24	76
No. 91	Ward 6	18	5	23	93	116	126	24	102
92	do	30	1	31	87	118	125	31	94
93	do	18	7	25	84	109	125	25	100
94	Ward 7	66	19	85	165	250	260	85	175
1	do	26	15	41	88	129	150	41	109
2	do	26	9	35	84	119	150	35	94
3	do	34	15	49	92	141	150	49	101
4	do	40	11	51	98	9	150	51	99
5	do	27	8	35	96	81	148	36	112
6	do	27	5	32	98	130	300	33	267
7	do	39	10	49	88	137	145	50	95
8	do	21	7	28	69	97	101	28	73
9	do	32	8	40	95	135	150	40	111
10	do	47	11	58	92	150	150	60	89
11	do	45	15	60	65	125	149	61	90
12	do	44	17	61	85	146	150	51	76
13	do	29	22	51	84	135	150	49	89
14	do	31	18	49	69	118	150	61	77
15	do	36	25	61	79	140	150	73	113
16	do	47	26	73	76	9	175	62	80
17	do	41	20	61	90	151	125	45	107
18	do	28	17	45	77	122	181	74	61
19	do	44	27	71	104	175	100	39	81
20	do	28	11	39	52	91	125	44	104
21	do	29	13	42	60	102	150	46	97
22	do	30	16	46	79	125	174	77	122
No. 1	Vaughan	38	37	75	70	145	200	78	107
2	do	23	54	77	95	172	200	93	120
3	do	34	59	93	76	169	250	130	123
4	do	64	65	129	97	168	200	77	111
5	do	56	21	77	91	44	175	64	103
6	do	42	22	64	80	140	175	72	94
7	do	43	44	72	68	165	200	106	114
8	do	28	62	105	60	184	201	87	41
No. 1	Etobicoke	74	11	85	99	226	251	110	103
2	do	83	23	106	120	258	275	172	98
3	do	44	25	169	89	171	174	76	126
4	do	58	18	76	95	222	224	98	106
5	do	72	26	98	124	193	200	94	75
6	do	47	47	74	99	137	150	75	75
7	do	38	36	94	63	138	151	95	56
8	do	38	56		44				

RETURN from the Records of the GENERAL ELECTION to the Legislative Assembly, 1911.—*Continued.*

Electoral District	Numbers of Polling Places	Godfrey		Total No. of Votes Polled	No. of Votes remaining Unpolled	No. of Names on the Polling Lists	No. of Ballot Papers sent out to each Polling Place	Used Ballot Papers	Unused Ballot Papers	Rejected Ballot Papers	Cancelled Ballot Papers	Declined Ballot Papers	Ballot Papers taken from Polling Places
York, West—Con.	No. 3	6	17	17	68	103	250	36	214				
	do 4	31	17	17	50	73	75	23	52				
	do 5	14	9	9	76	128	177	52	125				
	do 6	54	22	22	65	88	99	23	76				
	do A to M 7	45	9	9	159	235	250	78	172		1		
	do N to Z 7	14	13	13	144	18	75	54	121				
	do 8	7	6	6	231	258	275	27	248				
	do 9	23	6	6	157	170	150	13	137				
	do 15	17	1	1	263	292	175	30	145	1			
	do 16	37	6	6	167	168	147	19	128				
	do 17	77	21	21	223	210	176	43	179	1			
	do A ΦM 18	41	4	4	117	321	325	99	77	2	1	1	
	do N to Z 18	105	21	21	31	162	47	46	279	3			
	do A to Z 19	79	36	36	46	257	175	127	320				
	Woodbridge 1	36	52	52	62	61	160	16	59				1
	Weston ... 2	28	47	47	44	30	125	90	47	2			
	do 3	39	53	53	52	121	176	78	84	3			
	do 4	18	47	47	80	44	30	92	84				
	?lico 1	94	33	33	41	45	299	66	160	2			
	do 2	48	14	14	97	159	175	66	109				
	Totals	2,847	1,522	4,369	6,727	11,106	12,415	4,424	7,991	31	15	9	3
	Majority for Godfrey	1,325											

EIGHTH REPORT

OF THE

BUREAU OF ARCHIVES

FOR THE

PROVINCE OF ONTARIO

BY

ALEXANDER FRASER, LL.D., F.S.A. Scot. (Edin.), etc.

Provincial Archivist

1911

PRINTED BY ORDER OF

THE LEGISLATIVE ASSEMBLY OF ONTARIO

TORONTO:

'rinted and Published by L. K. CAMERON, Printer to the King's Most Excellent Majesty

1912

Printed by
WILLIAM BRIGGS,
29-37 Richmond Street West,
TORONTO

His Honour COL. SIR JOHN MORISON GIBSON, K.C.M.G., LL.D. etc., etc.

Lieutenant-Governor of the Province of Ontario.

IT PLEASE YOUR HONOUR:

I have the pleasure to present herewith for the consideration of Your Honour Report of the Bureau of Archives of Ontario for 1911.

Respectfully submitted,

ARTHUR J. MATHESON,

Provincial Treasurer.

RONTO, 1912.

[3]

LIEUT. COL. THE HONOURABLE ARTHUR JAMES MATHESON, K. C., M.
etc., *Treasurer of Ontario.*

SIR,—I have the honour to submit to you the following Report in conn
with the Bureau of Archives for the Province of Ontario.

I have the honour to be, Sir,

Your obedient servant,

ALEXANDER FRASER,

Provincial Arch

Toronto, 31st December, 1911.

CONTENTS.

Report

of the

Ontario Bureau of Archives

PREFATORY

No volumes of Ontario Archives have been more in demand than those containing the Journals of the Legislature and Legislative Council of Upper Canada, since the appearance of the first volume in 1909. It cannot be otherwise than gratifying that an interest sincere and widespread is thus manifested in the sources of our Provincial history.

The Ontario Bureau of Archives invites the co-operation of the growing class of students of local history throughout the Province, and will gratefully receive and carefully preserve papers and documents—especially of an official character—placed in its collection.

The contents of the volume now given to the public, calls for no special comment from the Provincial Archivist, than that no trace has been yet found of the missing numbers for the years 1794, 1795, 1796, 1797, 1809, 1813, and 1815, and that the search shall not be abandoned.

As in preceding volumes the aim has been to furnish a literal reproduction of the original MSS.; no liberty has been taken with the form in which the Clerk of the House recorded the proceedings.

Continuing with the Journals for 1812, the MSS. for the next Report is already in the printers' hands.

ALEXANDER FRASER,

Provincial Archivist.

[7]

The Journals

OF THE

EGISLATIVE ASSEMBLY

OF

Upper Canada

FOR THE YEARS

1805, 1806, 1807, 1808, 1810, 1811

VOLUME TWO

Ontario Archives, 1911

JOURNAL

OF THE

HOUSE OF ASSEMBLY

OF

UPPER CANADA

From the first day of February to the
second day of March,

1805.

Both days inclusive.

In the forty-fifth year of the Reign of

KING GEORGE THE THIRD.

It being the first session of the Fourth Provincial
Parliament of this Province.

JOURNAL

OF THE

HOUSE OF ASSEMBLY

OF

UPPER CANADA

1805.

PETER HUNTER, Lieutenant Governor.

PROCLAMATION.

George the Third, by the Grace of God of the United Kingdom of Great Britain and Ireland King, Defender of the Faith.

To all our loving Subjects, GREETING.

Whereas by our Proclamation, bearing date the ninth day of March last, we thought fit by and with the advice of our Executive Council to Prorogue our Provincial Parliament until the sixteenth day of this present month of April, at which time in our Town of York you were held and constrained to appear. But we taking into our Royal consideration the ease and convenience of our loving subjects, have thought fit, by and with the advice of our Executive Council, to relieve you and each of you of your attendance at the time aforesaid, hereby convoking, and by these presents enjoining you and each of you, that on the twenty-fourth day of May next ensuing you meet us in our Provincial Parliament in our Town of York, there to take into consideration the state and welfare of our Province of Upper Canada, and therein to do as may seem necessary. Herein fail not.

In Testimony Whereof we have caused these our letters to be made patent, and the Great Seal of our said province to be hereunto affixed. Witness our trusty and well beloved Peter Hunter, Esquire, our Lieutenant Governor of our said Province, and Lieutenant General Commanding our Forces in our Provinces of Upper and Lower Canada, at York this Tenth day of April, in the year of Our Lord, One thousand, eight Hundred and four, and in the Forty-fourth year of our Reign.

Wm. JARVIS, Secretary.   P.H.

PETER HUNTER, Lieutenant Governor.

PROCLAMATION.

George the Third, by the Grace of God of the United Kingdom of Great Britain and Ireland, King, Defender of the Faith.

To our well beloved and faithful, the Legislative Councillors of our Province of Upper Canada, and to our beloved and faithful, the Knights, Citizens and Burgesses of the House of Assembly of our said Province, called and chosen to our present Provincial Parliament of our said Province, and to all our loving subjects to whom these presents may come, GREETING.

Whereas we have thought fit, by and with the advice of our Executive Council of our said Province of Upper Canada, to dissolve this present Provincial Parliament of our said Province, which now stands prorogued to the Twenty-fourth day of May, instant. We do for that end publish this our Royal Proclamation, and do hereby dissolve the said Provincial Parliament accordingly. And the Legislative Councillors, and the Knights, Citizens and Burgesses of the House of Assembly are discharged from their meeting and attendance on Thursday, the said Twenty-fourth day of May, instant. And we being desirous and resolved that as soon as may be to meet our people of our said Province, and to hear their advice in Provincial Parliament, do hereby make known our Royal will and pleasure to call a New Provincial Parliament, and do hereby further declare that with the advice of our said Executive Council we have this day given orders for the issuing out writs in due form for calling a new Provincial parliament in our said province, which writs are to bear teste on Tuesday, the Fifteenth day of this present month of May, and to be returned on Monday, the second day of July next.

In Testimony Whereof we have caused these our letters to be made patent, and the Great Seal of our Province to be hereunto affixed. Witness our well beloved and trusty Peter Hunter, Esquire, our Lieutenant Governor of our said Province, and Lieutenant General Commanding our Forces in our Provinces of Upper and Lower Canada, at York, in the Province of Upper Canada, this Fourteenth day of May, in the year of Our Lord, One thousand, eight hundred and four, and in the forty-fourth year of our reign.

                                                                                              P.H.
WM. JARVIS, Secretary.

By a further Proclamation of His Excellency, Peter Hunter, Esquire, Lieutenant Governor of the Province of Upper Canada, and Lieutenant General commanding His Majesty's Forces in the Provinces of Upper and Lower Canada, etc., etc., etc., dated at York the Twenty-seventh day of June, one thousand eight hundred and four, the meeting of the Legislative Council and House of Assembly stands prorogued to the Tenth day of August next.

By a further Proclamation of His Excellency, Peter Hunter, Esquire, Lieutenant Governor of the Province of Upper Canada, and Lieutenant General commanding His Majesty's Forces in the Province of Upper and Lower Canada, etc., etc., etc., dated at York the Third day of August, one thousand eight hundred and four, the meeting of the Legislative Council and House of Assembly stands prorogued to the Seventeenth day of September next.

By a further proclamation of His Excellency, Peter Hunter, Esquire, Lieutenant Governor of the Province of Upper Canada, and Lieutenant General Commanding His Majesty's Forces in the provinces of Upper and Lower Canada, etc., etc., etc., dated at York, the Thirteenth day of September, one thousand eight hundred and four, the meeting of the Legislative Council and House of Assembly stands prorogued to the Twenty-fifth day of October next.

By a further proclamation of His Excellency, Peter Hunter, Esquire, Lieutenant Governor of the Province of Upper Canada, and Lieutenant General Commanding His Majesty's Forces in the provinces of Upper and Lower Canada, etc., etc., etc., dated at York the Eighteenth day of October, one thousand eight hundred and four, the meeting of the Legislative Council and House of Assembly stands prorogued to the Third day of December next.

By a further Proclamation of His Excellency, Peter Hunter, Esquire, Lieutenant Governor of the Province of Upper Canada, and Lieutenant General commanding His Majesty's Forces in the provinces of Upper and Lower Canada, etc., etc., etc., dated at York the First day of December, one thousand eight hundred and four, the meeting of the Legislative Council and House of Assembly stands prorogued to the Tenth day of January, one thousand eight hundred and five.

PETER HUNTER, Lieutenant Governor.

PROCLAMATION.

George the Third, by the Grace of God of the United Kingdom of Great Britain and Ireland King, Defender of the Faith.

To our beloved and faithful Legislative Councillors of our Province of Upper Canada, and to our Knights, Citizens and Burgesses of our said Province, to the Provincial Parliament of our Town of York, on the Tenth day of January to be commenced, held, called and elected, and to every of you, GREETING.

Whereas by our Proclamation, bearing date the First day of December last, we thought fit, by and with the advice of our Executive Council, to prorogue our said Provincial Parliament until the Tenth day of January, one thousand eight hundred and Five, at which time in Our Town of York you were held and constrained to appear. But we, taking into our Royal consideration the ease and convenience of our loving subjects, have thought fit, by and with the advice and consent of Our Executive Council to relieve you, and each of you, of your attendance at the time aforesaid, hereby convoking, and by these presents enjoining you, and each of you, that on the First Day of February, next, which will be in the Year of Our Lord One Thousand Eight Hundred and Five, you meet us in Our Provincial Parliament in Our Town of York for the actual dispatch of Public Business, there to take into consideration the state and welfare of Our said Province of Upper Canada, and therein to do as may seem necessary. Herein Fail not.

In testimony whereof we have caused these Our Letters to be made patent, and the Great Seal of Our said Province to be hereunto affixed. Witness Our Trusty and Well beloved Peter Hunter, Esquire, Our Lieutenant Governor of Our said Province, and Lieutenant General Commanding Our Forces in Our Provinces of Upper and Lower Canada, this twenty-eighth day of December in the Year of Our Lord One Thousand Eight Hundred and Four, and in the Forty-fifth Year of Our Reign.

P.H.

WM. JARVIS, Secretary.

UPPER CANADA.

George the Third, by the Grace of God of the United Kingdom of Great Britain and Ireland King, Defender of the Faith.

To Our Trusty and Well beloved William Jarvis and Donald McLean, Esquires, GREETING.

Whereas by a certain Act of Parliament, passed in the thirty first year of Our Reign, entitled "An Act to repeal certain parts of an Act passed in the fourteenth year of His Majesty's Reign, entitled 'An Act for making more effectual provision for the Government of the Province of Quebec in North America, and to make further provision for the Government of the said Province;'" it is among other things provided that no Member either of the Legislative Council or Assembly in either of the Provinces of Upper or Lower Canada shall be permitted to sit or vote therein until he shall have taken and subscribed the Oath therein set forth, either before the Governor or Lieutenant Governor of such Province, or person administering the Government therein, or before some person or persons authorized by the said Governor, Lieutenant Governor or other person as aforesaid. Now therefore, know Ye that we have constituted and authorized, and by these presents do constitute and authorize you the said William Jarvis and Donald McLean, Esquires to administer the Oath in the above mentioned Act of Parliament set forth unto the Members of the House of Assembly of Our said province of Upper Canada, conformably to the form therein mentioned and provided.

Witness His Excellency Peter Hunter, Esquire, Lieutenant Governor of the Province of Upper Canada and Lieutenant General Commanding His Majesty's Forces in the Provinces of Upper and Lower Canada, this thirteenth day of January in the Year of Our Lord One Thousand Eight Hundred and Five, and the Forty Fifth Year of His Majesty's Reign.

                                              P.H.

(Signed) WM. JARVIS, Secretary.

OFFICE OF ENROLMENTS, UPPER CANADA.

1st February, 1805.

Return of the names of the Members chosen to serve in the House of Assembly in the Provincial Parliament for this Province, called to meet this day by virtue of Writs of Election issued by Order of His Excellency Peter Hunter, Esquire, Lieutenant Governor, bearing teste the Fifteenth Day of May last, as appears by the said Writs duly returned into this Office by the Returning Officers of the several Counties and Ridings respectively, as commanded.

Counties and Ridings.	Representatives Chosen.	Returning Officers.
Glengarry and Prescott..............	Alex. McDonell & W. B. Wilkinson, Esquires	G. Munro, Esq.
Stormont and Russell..............	Robert J. D. Gray, Esq.	J. Anderson. Esq.
Dundas	John Crysler, Esq................	G. Munro, Esq.
Grenville	Samuel Sherwood, Esq............	Wm. Fraser, Esq.
Leeds	Peter Howard, Esq...............	Wm. Fraser. Esq.
Frontenac	Allan McLean, Esq.	Wm. Coffin, Esq.
Lennox and Addington............	Thomas Dorland, Esq............	Alex. Fisher, Esq.
Prince Edward...................	Ebenezer Washburn, Esq.........	Arch. McDonell, Esq.
Hastings and Northumberland.....	David McG. Rogers. Esq..........	John Peters, Esq.
Durham, Simcoe and E. Riding York	Angus McDonell, Esq.	Wm. Allan. Esq.
W. York, 1st Lincoln and Haldimand	Solomon Hill & Robert Nellis, Esqs	Abraham Nellis, Esq.
2nd, 3rd and 4th Lincoln	Isaac Swazey & Ralph Clench, Esqs	Thomas Merritt, Esq.
Norfolk, Oxford and Middlesex	Benajah Mallory, Esq............	Wm. Spurgin. Esq.
Kent	John McGregor, Esq.	Abraham Tredell.Esq
Essex	Matthew Elliot & David Cowan,Esqs	Samuel Hands, Esq.

Donald McLean, Esq.,   (Signed) W. Jarvis, Secretary
    Clerk Commons Ho. Assy.   and Keeper of Rolls.

HOUSE OF ASSEMBLY, UPPER CANADA.

York, Friday, 1st February, 1805.

At the First Session of the Fourth Parliament of Upper Canada, begun and held in the Town of York, on Friday, the First day of February, in the Forty fifth Year of the Reign of Our Sovereign Lord George the Third, by the Grace of God of the United Kingdom of Great Britain and Ireland, King, Defender of the Faith, and in the Year of Our Lord One Thousand Eight Hundred and Five. His Excellency, the Lieutenant Governor, having by his proclamation here-unto annexed, dated at York the Fourteenth day of May, 1804, dissolved the last Provincial Parliament, and by his Writs of Summons issued under the Great Seal of the Province, bearing Teste at York on Tuesday, the Fifteenth day of May, 1804, calling a new Provincial Parliament, and appointed the same to meet and to sit on the second day of July next ensuing, and having prorogued the same from time to time until this day,—William Jarvis and Donald MacLean Esquires, Commissioners appointed by Dedimus Potestatem for administering the Oath to the Members of the House of Assembly of the said Province of Upper Canada, came about eleven o'clock in the forenoon into the House of Assembly of the said Province, where William Jarvis, Esq., Keeper of the Rolls, delivered to Donald MacLean, Esq., Clerk of the Assembly, the Roll containing the list of the names of such Members as has been returned to serve in the Provincial Parliament, a copy whereof is hereunto annexed. The Commissioners did administer the Oath appointed to the Members who appeared, which being done, and the Members having subscribed the Roll containing the Oath, they repaired to their seats in the Assembly accordingly.

After which a message was delivered by Mr. George Lawe, Gentleman Usher of the Black Rod.

Gentlemen,—

His Excellency the Lieutenant Governor commands the Members of this Honorable House to attend His Excellency immediately, in the Legislative Council Chamber.

Accordingly the Members went up to attend His Excellency, where being,

The Honorable Speaker of the Legislative Council said.

Gentlemen of the House of Assembly,

I have it in command from His Excellency the Lieutenant Governor to signify to you that it is his will and pleasure that you do return to the House to which you belong, and there to elect one of your number to be your Speaker, whom you shall present for the approbation of His Excellency at the Bar of this House to-morrow at one o'clock.

And the Members being returned.

Prayers were read.

Ralf Clench Esquire, Knight, one of the Representatives for the second, third, and fourth Ridings of the County of Lincoln, stood up and addressed him-self to the Clerk, who standing up pointed to him and then sat down, proposed to the House for their Speaker, Alexander McDonell, Esquire, in which motion he was seconded by Robert Nellis, Esquire, Knight, one of the Representatives for the West Riding of the Counties of Lincoln and Haldimand.

The Clerk having declared Alexander McDonell, Esquire, unanimously elected, he was led to the Chair by Ralf Clench and Robert Nellis, Esquires.

After the Speaker was led to the Chair he addressed the House as follows.
Gentlemen of the House of Assembly,—
I fell much gratitude for the Honor you have conferred on me by placing
me in this Chair, and I shall strenuously endeavour to merit the continuance of
your good opinion.
And thereupon he sat down in the Chair.
Then the Mace, which before lay under the Table, was laid upon the Table.
David McGregor Rogers, Esquire, addressing himself to Mr. Speaker Elect,
moved that this House do adjourn until to-morrow at one o'clock.
The House adjourned accordingly until one o'clock to-morrow.

Saturday, 2nd February, 1805.

Prayers were read.
The House being met, and Mr. Speaker Elect having taken the Chair,
A message was delivered by Mr. George Lawe, Gentleman Usher of the Black
Rod.
Mr. Speaker,
It is His Excellency the Lieutenant Governor's pleasure that this Honorable
House do immediately attend His Excellency in the Legislative Council Chamber.
Accordingly Mr. Speaker elect, with the Members, went up to the Legislative
Council and Chamber,
Where being, The Honorable Speaker of the Legislative Council asked if
they had chosen their Speaker.
Alexander McDonell, Esquire, was presented as their Speaker Elect.
Then the Honorable Speaker of the Legislative Council said,
The Lieutenant Governor commands me to say that he is perfectly satisfied
with the choice of the Assembly, and doth allow and confirm you, Mr. McDonell
to be its Speaker.
Then Mr. Speaker addressed himself,
May it Please Your Excellency,—
The Honor which the House of Assembly have conferred upon me in choosing
me their Speaker is as great as the important duties of the Office are above my
abilities.
My zeal, however ardent, not sufficiently compensating for my incapacity,
I most respectfully implore the excuse and commands of Your Excellency.
I most humbly claim in the name of the Assembly the freedom of speech and
generally all the like privileges and liberties as are enjoyed by the Commons of
Great Britain, our Mother Country.
Then the Honorable Speaker of the Legislative Council said,
The Lieutenant Governor commands me to assure the Assembly that it may
depend on the unlimited enjoyment of all its past privileges.
And then Mr. Speaker further claimed that the proceedings of the Repre-
sentatives may receive the most favorable construction, and that whatever the
Speaker shall say which might be taken in evil part may be imputed to his ignorance
and not unto the Assembly, that he may resort again to their House for declaration
of their true intent, and that his error may be pardoned.
Then the Honorable Speaker of the Legislative Council said,—
Mr. Speaker,
The Lieutenant Governor directs me to assure the Assembly that he will
always be perfectly disposed to put the most favorable construction on every proceeding and word, both of the House and its Speaker.

Then Mr. Speaker said that as often as necessity for His Majesty's Service and the good of the Commonwealth shall require, the House of Assembly may have access to the person of His Majesty's Representative in this Province.

Then the Honorable Speaker of the Legislative Council said,—

Mr. Speaker,

The Lieutenant Governor commands me to say that the Assembly may always depend on having access to his Person at seasonable hours.

The House being returned,

Mr. Speaker reported that the House had been in the Legislative Council Chamber, where His Excellency had been pleased to approve the choice the House had made of him to be their Speaker, and that he had in their name, and on their behalf, by humble petition to His Excellency, laid claim to all their rights and privileges, that they may enjoy freedom of speech in their debates and have access to His Excellency's person as occasion may require, and that all their proceedings may receive from His Excellency the most favorable construction; which he said His Excellency had confirmed to them by granting their privileges in as simple a manner as ever they were granted and allowed.

Then Mr. Speaker did again return his humble thanks to the House for the very great Honor they had now done him, and did assure them of a continuance of his fidelity in their service, humbly requesting their protection and assistance to him in the discharge of his great trust, and of their indulgence to him in the pardon of his failings and imperfections in it.

Mr. Speaker further reported that when the House attended His Excellency this day in the Legislative Council Chamber, His Excellency was pleased to make a speech to both Houses of the provincial Parliament, of which, Mr. Speaker said, he had, to prevent mistakes, obtained a copy, which he read to the House, and is as follows. Videlicet.

Honorable Gentlemen of the Legislative Council

and

Gentlemen of the House of Assembly:—

Since the last session of the Legislature of this Province, in pursuance of the authority vested in me by an Act passed therein, respecting the repairing and laying out of Public Highways and building of bridges, I have by proclamation appointed Commissioners, and have taken such other measures as have appeared to me to be the best suited for carrying into effect the provisions of that Act.

I have also, by the authority of the Legislature, appointed Commissioners for the purpose of entering into a Provisional Agreement with those of Lower Canada, respecting the duties and drawbacks on goods and merchandise passing from the one Province to the other. These Commissioners, I have no doubt, have executed the trust committed to their charge by that appointment with fidelity and care. I have ordered the provisional Agreement entered into to be laid before you for the obtaining of the sanction and confirmation of this Legislature.

I embrace this opportunity of congratulating you on the success which hath attended the first efforts of the cultivation of hemp in this Province. The reward with which the Trustees of the Society instituted at London for the encouragement of Arts, Manufactures and Commerce have been pleased to honor the labours of the industrious farmer will, I trust, still further stimulate his exertions and in every laudable pursuit incite this infant Colony to the practice of that industry and diligence which will promote the interests of the individual.

Gentlemen of the House of Assembly,—

I have directed the Public Accounts to be laid before you, and am persuaded that you will examine them with that attention which the nature of the subject requires.

Honorable Gentlemen of the Legislative Council
and
Gentlemen of the House of Assembly,

I forbear on this occasion to point out in particular the subjects which may now call for your investigation and care. The knowledge which you respectively possess of the situation and interest of the Inhabitants of this widely extended Province will enable you to discover where the aid of the Legislature may still be necessary. And it shall be my endeavour at all times to co-operate with you in the enacting of such laws as may best promote the true object of all Legislation— the Public Good. ·

Mr. Clench moved, seconded by Mr. Nellis, that Mr. Sherwood, Mr. McLean and Mr. Wilkinson be a Committee to draft an Address to His Excellency the Lieutenant Governor in answer to His Excellency's Speech.

It was ordered accordingly.

Mr. Rogers then moved, seconded by Mr. Swazey, for leave to bring up two Petitions from the Inhabitants of the District of Newcastle.

Leave was accordingly granted.

Mr. Rogers then moved, seconded by Mr. Swazey, for leave to bring in a Bill to alter certain parts of an Act, passed in the forty second year of His Majesty's Reign, entitled "An Act to provide for the administration of Justice in the District of Newcastle" on Monday next.

Accordingly leave was given.

Mr. Sherwood moved, seconded by Capt. Cowan, that the Speaker do give notice at the Lieutenant Governor's Office as soon as possible that the seats of the Members of the House of Assembly for the Counties of Stormont and Russell, and of Durham, Simcoe, and the East Riding of York are vacated.

It was ordered accordingly.

Mr. Wilkinson then moved, seconded by Mr. Sherwood, for leave to bring up the Petition of the Inhabitants of Lancaster, on Monday next.

Leave was accordingly granted.

Then Mr. Sherwood moved, seconded by Mr. Clench, for leave to bring in a Bill on Monday next, to regulate the trial of controverted elections or returns of Members to serve in Parliament.

Accordingly leave was granted.

On motion of Mr. Clench, seconded by Mr. Sherwood, the House adjourned until Monday next.

Monday, 4th February, 1805.

Prayers were read.

Mr. Speaker informed that in obedience to the commands of this House he had sent notice to His Excellency the Lieutenant Governor that the seats of the Members of the House of Assembly for the Counties of Stormont and Russell, of Durham, Simcoe and the East Riding of York are vacated.

Mr. Wilkinson moved, seconded by Mr. Clench, for leave to bring up the Petition of the Inhabitants of the Town of Cornwall on Wednesday next.

Leave was accordingly granted.

Mr. Clench, seconded by Mr. Swazey, moved for leave to bring up the Petition of the Grand Jury and other Inhabitants of the District of Niagara on Wednesday next; and also for leave to bring up another Petition from a number of the Inhabitants of the said District of Niagara on the same day.

Accordingly leave was given.

Mr. McLean, one of the Committee named to draft an Address of thanks to His Excellency the Lieutenant Governor for his Speech to both Houses of Parliament on opening the present Session, reported that the Committee had prepared an Address accordingly, which he was directed to submit to the House whenever it shall be pleased to receive the same.

The Report was ordered to be received.

Which Report he read in his place, and then delivered in the same at the Table, where it was again read by the Clerk.

On motion of Mr. Sherwood, seconded by Mr. Swazey, the House resolved itself into Committee to go into the consideration of the draft of the Address in answer to His Excellency's Speech to both Houses of Parliament at the opening of the present Session.

Mr. Speaker left the Chair.

Mr. Crysler was called to the Chair of the Committee.

Mr. Speaker resumed the Chair.

Mr. Crysler reported that the Committee had gone through the draft of the Address to His Excellency the Lieutenant Governor, without any amendment, which he was directed to submit to the House whenever it shall be pleased to receive the same.

Ordered, That the Report be now received.

Which Report was accepted, and the Address is as follows:

To His Excellency Peter Hunter, Esquire, Lieutenant Governor of the Province of Upper Canada, and Lieutenant General Commanding His Majesty's Forces in the Provinces of Upper and Lower Canada, &c. &c. &c.

May it please Your Excellency,—

We, His Majesty's most dutiful and loyal subjects, the Commons of Upper Canada, in Parliament assembled, return you our thanks for Your Excellency's Speech, and for your condescension in informing us of the measures that you have been pleased to take to carry into effect the law passed in the last Session of Parliament relative to the Public Highways.

It is with pleasure we learn that the Commissioners on the part of our Sister Colony, Lower Canada, have agreed with those whom Your Excellency has been pleased to appoint for this Province, and we hope that their proceedings have been such as will merit the approbation of every branch of the Legislature.

We feel highly gratified for the benevolent attention which Your Excellency manifests to that important part of the Community, the industrious farmer, and we trust with confidence that under your auspices, and from the patronage of our Parent Country, the cultivation of Hemp, and every other useful branch of Agriculture, will rapidly increase, and will highly conduce to the prosperity of this Province.

When the Public Accounts are laid before us, they shall be attentively investigated, and we sincerely pledge ourselves to promote every measure which by the Legislature may be deemed necessary for the Public Welfare.

Commons House of Assembly,
4th February, 1805.

Mr. Rogers then moved, seconded by Mr. Swazey, that the draft of the

Address to His Excellency as reported by the Committee be engrossed, and that messengers be appointed to wait upon His Excellency to know when he will be pleased to receive this House with its Address.

Ordered accordingly.

Then Mr. Sherwood, seconded by Mr. Mallory, moved, That Messrs. Swazey and Rogers do wait upon his Excellency the Lieutenant Governor to know when he will please to receive the House with its Address.

Which was ordered accordingly.

The Clerk of this House informed Mr. Speaker that the Clerk of the Peace for the different Districts in this Province (except the District of London) did send him returns of all the rateable property in their respective Districts, in compliance with the eighth section of the Act for the more uniform collection of Assessments throughout this Province.

Mr. Speaker then ordered the different returns made by the Clerks of the Peace to be laid on the Table, and afterwards to be entered in a book to be of Record in this House.

Mr. Rogers moved, seconded by Mr. Clench, that the Order of the Day for the first reading of the Bill for the District of Newcastle be discharged, and that leave be given him to bring in the said Bill on Tuesday next.

Leave was accordingly given.

On motion of Mr. Sherwood, seconded by Captain Cowan, the House adjourned.

Tuesday, 5th February, 1805.

Prayers were read.

Mr. Swazey reported that in obedience to the Order of this House the Messengers had waited upon His Excellency the Lieutenant Governor to know when he would be pleased to receive this House with its Address; and that His Excellency was pleased to appoint this day at two o'clock in the afternoon.

Read, two Petitions from the District of Newcastle, which are as follows:

To the Honorable the Legislative Council and House of Assembly of the Province of Upper Canada in Parliament assembled.

The Petition of the Inhabitants of the District of Newcastle,

Humbly Showeth,

That the place appointed by Law for building a Gaol and Court House in the District of Newcastle appears to Your Petitioners to be inconvenient.

Your Petitioners therefore pray that so much of an Act entitled "An Act to provide for the Administration of Justice within the District of Newcastle" as directs that a Gaol and Court House should be built in the Town of Newcastle may be repealed, and that it may be lawful for Your Petitioners to cause a Gaol and Court House to be built in some part near the centre of the said District.

And as in duty bound they will ever pray.

Signed by Robert Baldwin, Lieut. of the County of Durham, John Spenser, Leonard Soper, Joseph Keeler, Elias Jones, Elias Smith, Senior, Benjamin Marsh, Asa Burnham, Joel Merriman, John Peters, Sheriff, Timothy Porter, Coroner, D. McG. Rogers, Clerk of the Peace, and one hundred and twenty-three others.

To the Representatives of the Province of Upper Canada in Provincial Parliament Assembled,

The Petition of sundry Inhabitants of the District of Newcastle,

Humbly showeth,

That Your Petitioners feel themselves much alarmed at the destruction that is made with the deer in this district by driving and hunting them with dogs at all seasons of the year, which in a short time will inevitably destroy and drive them all out of the country, whereas were they only to be taken at a certain season, it would not prevent their decrease, and they would be of great service to the inhabitants who want the meat in this new settlement, and could take them without dogs.

That in order to preserve the deer Your Petitioners conceive that were they only to be taken between the twentieth of August and the first of January they would not be wantonly destroyed, and every inhabitant might share an equal benefit from them.

Your Petitioners therefore humbly submit the business to your consideration, and pray that such provision may be made in that behalf as to you in your wisdom shall seem meet.

And your Petitioners as in duty bound shall ever pray.
31st December, 1804.

Signed by { Henry Frint, John Frint, Samuel Turney, Joel Merriman, & ninety-eight others.

Read for the first time, an Act to alter certain parts of an Act passed in the forty-second year of His Majesty's Reign, entitled "An Act to provide for the Administering of Justice in the District of Newcastle."

On motion of Mr. Clench, seconded by Mr. McLean, the said Bill was ordered to be read a second time on Monday next.

On motion of Mr. Swayze, seconded by Mr. Washburn, the house adjourned till twelve o'clock at noon.

The House being met agreeable to adjournment,

By command of His Excellency, the Lieutenant Governor, William Jarvis, Esquire, Keeper of the Rolls, delivered in at the Bar a copy of the Provisional Agreement made and entered into on the part of the Commissioners of this Province and those duly authorized on the part of Lower Canada, which is as follows, viz.

Provisional Agreement made and entered into by the undersigned Commissioners, viz.

The Honorable Richard Cartwright, the Honorable Robert Hamilton, and Samuel Sherwood, Esquire, upon the part of the Province of Upper Canada, appointed by His Excellency, Peter Hunter, Esquire, of the Province by Commission bearing date the Twenty second day of March in the Year of Our Lord One Thousand Eight Hundred and Four, in the Forty Fourth Year of His Majesty's Reign, under authority of an Act of the Legislature thereof passed in the thirty seventh year of His Majesty's Reign, entitled "An Act to authorize the Lieutenant Governor to nominate and appoint certain Commissioners for the purposes therein mentioned; and the Honorable James McGill, John Richardson, Samuel Gerrard, Joseph Perinault, Morrice Blondeau, Esquire, Commissioners on the part of Lower Canada, appointed by an Act of the Legislature thereof, passed in the Forty Fourth Year of His Majesty's Reign, entitled 'An Act for appointing Commissioners to treat with Commissioners appointed, or to be appointed, on the part of Upper Canada for the purposes therein mentioned.'"

The said Commissioners having met and communicated to each other their respective powers and authority, and having taken into consideration and maturely deliberated upon the objects of their appointment, and finding that no material alteration hath taken place in the relative situation of the two Provinces so as to require any change in the existing provisions for ascertaining the respective proportions of duties and drawbacks on articles imported at the Port of Quebec, or otherwise, it is unanimously agreed that the Articles of Agreement at present subsisting between the two Provinces be further continued, and be in force as if they were here particularly inserted until the First Day of March in the Year of Our Lord One Thousand Eight Hundred and nine.

Done at Montreal, the Fifth day of July, in the Year of Our Lord One Thousand Eight Hundred and Four, and the Forty Fourth Year of His Majesty's Reign, having signed four copies of the same tenor and date.

(Signed)

Richard Cartwright.
R. Hamilton.
Samuel Sherwood.
James McGill.
John Richardson.
Samuel Gerrard.
Jos. Perinault.
Mce. Blondeau.

Office of Enrolments, Upper Canada,
5th February, 1805.

[I do hereby certify the foregoing to be a true copy of the original deposited with the Archives of this Province.

(Signed) Wm. Jarvis, Keeper of the Rolls.]

On motion of Mr. Rogers, seconded by Mr. Howard, the House adjourned to half past one o'clock in the afternoon.

The House having met agreeable to adjournment,

Mr. Speaker, attended by the House, went up at the hour appointed with the Address of this House to His Excellency the Lieutenant Governor, and being returned, Mr. Speaker reported that the House had attended His Excellency with its Address, to which he had been pleased to make the following answer.

Gentlemen of the House of Assembly:—

I return you my best thanks for your respectful Address, and have no doubt but that your deliberations and exertions will effectually promote the happiness and prosperity of His Majesty's Subjects in this Province.

Mr. Wilkinson moved, seconded by Mr. McLean, for leave to bring in a Bill on Monday next for the more regular appointment of Parish and Town Officers throughout this Province.

Leave was accordingly granted.

On motion of Mr. Nellis, seconded by Mr. Washburn, the House adjourned.

Wednesday, 6th February, 1805.

Prayers were read.

Read for the first time, An Act to regulate the trial of Controverted Elections or returns of Members to serve in Parliament.

Mr. Sherwood, seconded by Mr.Clench, moved that the Bill for the trial of Controverted Elections be read a second time to-morrow.

Ordered accordingly.

Read, The Petition of the Inhabitants of the Township of Lancaster, which is as follows, viz:

To the Honorable the Commons of Upper Canada in Parliament assembled.

The Petition of the several persons whose names are hereunto subscribed, for themselves and on behalf of the Inhabitants of the Township of Lancaster.

Humbly Sheweth,—

That Your Petitioners are subject to many great and material disadvantages from the extent of the Township of Lancaster, it consisting of eighteen concessions deep.

That the Commissioners of the Highways, Assessors, Collectors, &c., are obliged to perform a double proportion of duty to the Officers of other Townships, and from the situation of the country and bad state of the roads the duty is rendered extremely difficult.

That Your Petitioners conceive the forming of a new Township from the ninth concession of Lancaster to the first concession of Hawkesbury would obviate the present inconvenience of Your Petitioners.

Wherefore Your Petitioners pray Your Honorable House will take the business into consideration, and to give them such relief as to Your Honorable House shall seem meet, and Your Petitioners will ever pray.

Alexander McMillian, J.P., Alexander McDonnell, J.P., Alex'r Rose, John McDonald, John Kennedy, Alexander McLeod, Norman McLeod, Finley McDonell, and twenty others.

Then Mr. Wilkinson moved, seconded by Captain Cowan, for leave to bring in a Bill to-morrow for the division of the Township of Lancaster.

Leave was accordingly granted.

On motion of Mr. Swazey, seconded by Mr. Mallory, the House adjourned.

Thursday, 7th February, 1805.

Prayers were read.

Mr. McLean moved, seconded by Mr. Sherwood, for leave to bring in a Bill to-morrow entitled "An Act to revive and continue an Act to ratify and confirm certain Provisional Articles of Agreement entered into by the respective Commissioners of this Province and Lower Canada, met at Montreal on the fifth day of July, One thousand eight hundred and four, for carrying the same into effect, and also to continue an Act passed in the thirty ninth year of His Majesty's Reign."

Then Mr. Howard moved, seconded by Mr. Sherwood, for leave to bring in a Bill on Monday next for an Act to alter certain parts of an Act entitled "An Act to provide for the appointment of Parish and Town Officers throughout this Province."

Accordingly leave was given.

Mr. Wilkinson, seconded by Mr. Sherwood, moved for the Order of the Day.

Then was read for the second time, "An Act to regulate the trial of Controverted Elections, or returns of Members to serve in Parliament."

On motion of Mr. Sherwood, seconded by Mr. McLean, the House resolved itself into Committee to take the said Bill into their consideration.

Mr. Speaker left the Chair.

Mr. Wilkinson was called to the Chair of the Committee.

Mr. Speaker resumed the Chair.

And Mr. Wilkinson reported that the Committee had gone through the Bill and had made some amendments thereto, which he was directed to report to the

3 A.

House.   He then read the Report in his place and afterwards delivered the same with the Bill in at the Table, where it was again read by the Clerk.

Which Report was accepted.

Mr. McLean moved, seconded by Mr. Sherwood, that the Bill as now read be engrossed, and read a third time to-morrow.

Ordered accordingly.

Read for the first time, An Act for the division of the Township of Lancaster, which was ordered to be read a second time to-morrow.

Mr. Rogers then moved, seconded by Mr. Swayze, for leave to bring up the petition of the Inhabitants of the County of Leeds.

Leave was accordingly granted.

House adjourned.

Friday, 8th February, 1805.

Prayers were read.

Mr. McLean moved, seconded by Mr. Sherwood, that so much of the Order of the Day be dispensed with as requires this day the bringing in of the Bill entitled "An Act to continue an Act to ratify and confirm certain Provisional Articles of Agreement, entered into by the respective Commissioners of this Province and Lower Canada, at Montreal on the fifth day of July One Thousand Eight Hundred and Four, and for carrying the same into effect, and also to continue an Act passed in the thirty-ninth year of His Majesty's Reign," and that leave be given to bring in the same on Monday next.

Ordered accordingly.

Mr. Rogers, seconded by Mr. Swayze moved, that the Order of the Day for the third reading of the engrossed Bill to regulate the trial of Controverted Elections be discharged, and that the said Bill be recommitted this day.

The House accordingly resolved itself into Committee on the said Bill.

Mr. Speaker left the Chair.

Mr. Washburn was called to the chair of the Committee.

Mr. Speaker resumed the Chair.

And Mr. Washburn reported that the Committee had gone through the Bill, and had made some amendments thereto, which he was directed to report to the House whenever it shall be pleased to receive the same.   And he read the Report in his place, and afterwards delivered the same in at the Table, where it was again read by the Clerk.

Which Report was accepted.

Mr. McLean, seconded by Mr. Sherwood, moved that the Bill as now amended be engrossed and read a third time this day.

Ordered accordingly.

Read for the second time, A Bill entitled, "An Act for the division of the Township of Lancaster."

On motion of Mr. Washburn, seconded by Mr. Clench, the House resolved itself into Committee to go into the consideration of the said Bill.

Mr. Speaker left the Chair.

Mr. Sherwood was called to the chair of the Committee.

Mr. Speaker resumed the Chair.

And Mr. Sherwood reported that the Committee had gone through the Bill, and had made an amendment thereto, which amendment he read in his place, and afterwards delivered the Bill and amendment in at the Table, where it was again read by the Clerk.

And the said amendment being again read, and the question being thereupon put, it was agreed to by the House.

Mr. Wilkinson moved, seconded by Mr. Rogers, that the Bill as amended be engrossed and read a third time to-morrow.

It was ordered accordingly.

An engrossed Bill entitled "An Act to regulate the trial of Controverted Elections, or returns of Members to serve in Parliament" was read for the third time.

Mr. Rogers then moved, seconded by Mr. Washburn, that the following clause be inserted after the second clause of the said Bill.

"Provided that nothing herein contained in respect to the statement of the grounds or reasons required to be made in the petition shall affect the petitions prepared to be laid before the House during this session of Parliament."

A division thereupon ensued; the names being called for they were taken down, and are as follows.

Yeas	Nays
MESSRS. ROGERS	MESSRS. NELLIS
SWAYZE	CLENCH
WASHBURN	HOWARD
DORLAND	HILL
	McGREGOR
	McLEAN
	SHERWOOD
	MALLORY
	COWAN
	WILKINSON

The same passed in the negative by a majority of six.

On motion of Mr. Sherwood, seconded by Mr. McLean,

Resolved, That the Bill do pass, and that the title be "An Act to regulate the trial of Controverted Elections, or Returns of Members to serve in Parliament."

Mr. Clench then moved, seconded by Mr. Dorland, that Messrs. Sherwood, Cowan and McLean do carry up the Bill to the Legislative Council, and do request their concurrence thereto.

Which was ordered accordingly.

Mr. Sherwood moved, seconded by Mr. McLean, that no petition shall be read in the House by the Clerk, complaining of an undue election, until it be known whether the Bill now before the House to regulate contested elections or returns of Members to serve in Parliament will be passed into a Law.

A division took place, the names being called for they were taken down, and are as follows, viz:

Yeas	Nays
MESSRS. COWAN	MESSRS. ROGERS
MALLORY	WASHBURN
SHERWOOD	DORLAND
McLEAN	SWAYZE
McGREGOR	WILKINSON
HOWARD	
HILL	
CLENCH	
NELLIS	

Carried in the affirmative by a majority of four.

The House accordingly resolved the same.

On motion of Mr. Rogers, seconded by Mr. Washburn, the House adjourned.

Saturday, 9th February, 1805.

Prayers were read.

Mr. Wilkinson moved, seconded by Mr. McLean, for leave to bring in a Bill on Monday next for the regulation of Special Juries throughout the Province.

Leave was accordingly given.

An engrossed Bill entitled "An Act for the division of the Township of Lancaster" was read for the third time.

The Bill then passed and was signed by Mr. Speaker.

Mr. Clench moved, seconded by Mr. Swayze, that Messrs. Rogers, Wilkinson, and Dorland be a Committee to carry up to the Honorable the Legislative Council the Bill for the division of the Township of Lancaster, and to request their concurrence.

Ordered accordingly..

House adjourned till Monday next.

Monday, 11th February, 1805.

Prayers were read.

Mr. Rogers reported that the Messengers did carry up to the Honorable Legislative Council the Bill entitled "An Act for the division of the Township of Lancaster," to which Bill they requested their concurrence.

Mr. Sherwood, one of the Messengers named to carry up to the Legislative Council a Bill entitled "An Act to Regulate the trial of Controverted Elections, or Returns of Members to serve in Parliament," reported that they did bring up the same, to which they requested their concurrence.

Mr. Wilkinson moved, seconded by Mr. Rogers, that so much of the Order of the Day as gives him leave to bring in a Bill for the appointment of Town Officers, may be discharged.

The Leave was discharged accordingly.

Agreeable to the Order of the Day, was read for the second time an Act to alter certain parts of an Act passed in the forty second year of His Majesty's Reign, entitled "an Act to provide for the administration of Justice in the District of Newcastle."

Mr. Rogers then moved, seconded by Mr. Swayze, that the House do now resolve itself into Committee to take into consideration the Bill for the District of Newcastle.

The House accordingly resolved itself into Committee.

Mr. Speaker left the Chair.

Mr. Howard was called to the chair of the Committee.

Mr. Speaker resumed the Chair.

Mr. Howard reported that the Committee had gone through the consideration of the said Bill, to which they had made some amendment, which he was directed to submit to the House whenever it shall be pleased to receive the same.

The House then resolved that the said Report be now received.
Which Report was then received and accepted.

Mr. Rogers, seconded by Mr. Swayze, moved that the Bill for the District of Newcastle be engrossed and read a third time to-morrow.

Ordered accordingly.

Then was read for the first time, An Act to provide for the appointment of Parish and Town Officers throughout the Province.

Mr. Rogers then moved, seconded by Mr. Howard, That the Bill for the appointment of Parish and Town Officers be read a second time to-morrow.

Which was ordered accordingly.

The Bill entitled, "An Act to revive and confirm an Act to ratify and confirm certain Provisional Articles of Agreement entered into by the respective Commissioners of this Province and Lower Canada, met at Montreal on the fifth Day of July, One thousand eight hundred and four, for carrying the same into effect, and also to continue an Act passed in the thirty ninth Year of His Majesty's Reign" was read for the first time.

Then Mr McLean moved, seconded by Mr. Washburn for leave to bring in a Bill on Wednesday next to Regulate the Curing, Packing, and Inspecting of Beef and Pork to be exported from this Province."

Leave was accordingly granted.

Mr. Washburn then moved, seconded by Mr. McLean for leave to bring in a Bill on Tuesday next to repeal an Act passed in the fortieth year of His Majesty's Reign, entitled "An Act to alter the method of performing Statute Duty on the Highways and Roads within this Province, and to make further provisions for the same."

Accordingly leave was given.

Mr. Sherwood, seconded by Mr. Nellis, moved that leave be given to Messrs. Wilkinson and Crysler to absent themselves from their attendance in this House for four days of this week.

Leave of absence was accordingly given.

On motion of Mr. Nellis, seconded by Mr. Dorland, the House adjourned till half past one o'clock in the afternoon.

The House being met,

A message from the Hon. Legislative Council by Mr. Burns, Master in Chancery.

Mr. Speaker,—

I am commanded by the Honorable Legislative Council to inform this House that they have passed the Bill entitled "An Act to regulate the trial of Controverted Elections, or returns of Members to serve in Parliament," sent up from this House, to which they have made some amendments, to which amendments they request the concurrence of this House.

And then he withdrew.

Which Bill as amended was then read.

On motion of Mr. Sherwood, seconded by Mr. Clench, the House resolved itself into Committee to enter into the consideration of the said Bill as amended by the Legislative Council.

Mr. Speaker left the Chair.

Mr. Wilkinson was called to the chair of the Committee.

Mr. Speaker resumed the Chair, and Mr. Wilkinson reported that the Committee had gone through the Bill as amended, which he was directed to report as amended by the Legislative Council whenever the House would be pleased to receive the same.

It was then ordered to receive the Report.

Which Report was received and accepted.

On motion of Mr. Sherwood, seconded by Mr. McLean, the House adjourned till twelve o'clock at noon to-morrow.

Tuesday, 12th February, 1805.

Prayers were read.

The engrossed Bill entitled "An Act to provide for the administration of justice in the District of Newcastle" was read a third time.

On motion of Mr. Rogers, seconded by Mr. Hill,

Resolved, That the Bill do pass, and that the title be "An Act to alter certain parts of an Act passed in the forty second year of His Majesty's Reign, entitled 'An Act to provide for the administration in the District of Newcastle,'"

The House divided upon the question the names being called for they were taken down and are as follows, viz:

Yeas	Nays
MESSRS. SHERWOOD	MESSRS. CLENCH
MALLORY	WASHBURN
ROGERS	
COWAN	
HILL	
HOWARD	
NELLIS	
DORLAND	
WILKINSON	
CRYSLER	
McGREGOR	
McLEAN	

It was accordingly resolved in the affirmative by a majority of ten.

On motion of Mr. Sherwood, seconded by Mr. Rogers,

Ordered, That Mr. Rogers and Mr. Howard do carry the Bill to the Legislative Council, and request their concurrence, and that they do also carry up to the Legislative Council the Petition from the Inhabitants of the District of Newcastle.

Ordered accordingly.

Read for the second time, The Bill to regulate Town and Parish Officers.

On motion of Mr. Howard, seconded by Mr. Rogers, the House resolved itself into Committee to go into the consideration of the said Bill.

Mr. Speaker left the Chair.

Mr. McLean was called to the chair of the Committee.

Mr. Speaker resumed the Chair.

And Mr. McLean reported that the Committee had gone through the consideration of the said Bill without any amendment, which he was directed to report whenever the House shall be pleased to receive the same.

Ordered, That the Report be now received.

The Report was then received and accepted.

Mr. Howard moved, seconded by Mr. Nellis, that the Bill for the further appointment of Parish and Town Officers be engrossed and read a third time to-morrow.

Ordered accordingly.

Read a second time, The Bill entitled "An Act to revive and continue an Act to ratify and confirm certain Provisional Articles of Agreement entered into by the respective Commissioners of this Province and Lower Canada, met at Montreal on the fifth day of July, One thousand Eight Hundred and Four, for carrying the same into effect; and also to continue an Act passed in the thirty ninth year of His Majesty's Reign."

On motion of Mr. McLean, seconded by Mr. Sherwood, the House resolved itself into Committee to go into the consideration of the said Bill.

Mr. Speaker left the Chair.

Mr. Washburn was called to the chair of the Committee.

Mr. Speaker resumed the Chair.

Mr. Washburn reported that the Committee had gone through the consideration of the said bill without any amendment, which he was directed to report to the House whenever it shall be pleased to receive the same.

The House then resolved that the said Report be now received.

Which Report was received and accepted.

Mr. McLean then moved, seconded by Mr. Wilkinson, that the Bill now read be engrossed and read a third time to-morrow.

Ordered accordingly.

Mr. Sherwood moved, seconded by Capt. Cowan, that Mr. McLean and Mr. Wilkinson do inform the Legislative Council that the Assembly have concurred in the amendments made by them to the Bill for regulating Controverted Elections.

Thereupon a question having arisen, whether or not a Bill could be debated which had passed the Assembly, had been sent to the Legislative Council, there amended, then sent back to the Assembly and the amendments concurred in by it, on the day after concurring in such amendments.

The question having been referred to the Speaker, he decided that the Bill should again be debated because a clause in that Bill made mandatory in the Assembly what of right is optional; namely, opening or shutting the doors at pleasure.

On appeal to the House against the decision of the Speaker, the House decided against the Speaker.

Mr. Rogers then moved, seconded by Mr. Clench, in amendment, that after the word "that" in Mr. Sherwood's motion, the rest of the motion be expunged, and that the following words be inserted, "the amendments made by the Honorable the Legislative Council to the Bill entitled 'An Act to regulate the trial of Controverted Elections or Returns of Members of the House of Assembly,' be recommitted."

The same being carried in the affirmative, the House accordingly resolved itself into Committee to go into the consideration of the amendments made to the said Bill.

Mr. Speaker left the Chair.

Mr. Wilkinson was called to the Chair of the Committee.

Mr. Speaker resumed the Chair.

Mr. Wilkinson reported that the Committee had gone through the consideration

of the said amendments, to which they had made no amendment, which he was
directed to report to the House whenever the House would be pleased to receive
the same.

Mr. Rogers then moved, seconded by Mr. Clench, that the report of the
Committee of the Whole House on the Bill to regulate the Trial of Controverted
Elections be not accepted.

A division thereupon took place; the names were ordered to be taken down,
and are as follows,

Yeas.	Nays
MESSRS WILKINSON	MESSRS. SHERWOOD
McGREGOR	COWAN
CLENCH	MALLORY
WASHBURN	HILL
DORLAND	CRYSLER
SWAYZE	HOWARD
	NELLIS
	McLEAN

The same passed in the negative by a majority of one:

Then the amendments made by the Legislative Council were read as engrossed,
and passed.

Mr. Sherwood moved, seconded by Mr. Nellis, that Mr. McLean and Captain
Cowan do inform the Legislative Council that the House of Assembly have
concurred in their amendments to the Bill to regulate Controverted Elections.

Which was ordered accordingly.

Mr. Wilkinson then moved, seconded by Mr. Sherwood, that leave of absence
be given to Ralf Clench, Esquire, for four days in this week.

Leave of absence was accordingly given.

Mr. Rogers moved, seconded by Mr. Swayze, for leave to bring up the Petition
of James Covill, of Elizabethtown.

Leave was accordingly given, and the said Petition was ordered to lie on
the Table.

Mr. Washburn moved, seconded by Mr. Dorland, that so much of the Order
of this Day be discharged as gives him leave for the first reading of the Road
Bill, and that he have leave to bring in the same on Saturday next.

Accordingly leave was given.

Read, Two Petitions from the District of Niagara.

To the Honorable Provincial Parliament of Upper Canada:

We, the subscribers, Inhabitants of the said Province, and faithful subjects
to His Majesty, and at all times ready and willing to support the operating laws
in his Dominions; and being possessed of that inalienable right of free men to
make known to our law makers and rulers such grievances as we may think we
labour under, do beg leave under mature consideration and confidence of the
truth and propriety thereof, to most humbly suggest to Your Honors that the law
of said Province prohibiting distillers selling any of their distilled liquors under
three gallons is not so happily calculated as in our opinion may be for the general
good of His Majesty's subjects, for many are under a necessity at times for some
of this liquor, but either for the want of abilities, or from principles of prudence
are prevented of receiving those comforts of the country to which their hand
labour entitles them.

We beg leave further to suggest that no detriment can accrue to the revenue by giving the distillers license to sell one gallon, as in our opinion few retailers or inn keepers would have any objection to an alteration of said law.

The limits of this Petition will not give an opportunity to state all the reasons in support thereof, which will actually be in your possession.

We therefore most humbly pray that Your Honors would take this subject into your wise consideration, and repeal said law in such a manner that the distillers may sell one gallon; or otherwise order and direct so that the law touching the same may be, as all laws should be, for the general benefit of the public weal; and as in duty bound we shall ever pray.

Lanty Shannors,* Inn-keeper.
Ezekiel Woodruff.
Sam'l VanWick, Inn-keeper.
John Fralick.
John + Camp (his mark).
and fifty-six others.

To the Honorable the Legislative Council and House of Assembly for the Province of Upper Canada.

The Petition of the subscribers, Inhabitants of the District of Niagara.

Humbly prays,

That the Legislature may at their next meeting take into their serious consideration the laws respecting highways and Roads throughout this Province, and make such alterations or amendments to the same as to them in their wisdom may appear meet. Your Petitioners beg leave to intimate that under the existing law it is difficult to determine which are really and legally Highways, the Commissioners being frequently divided in opinion with respect to the construction to be put on said laws, and from the circumstance of the Justices of the Peace being all Commissioners of the Highways and Roads, and nothing mandatory or compulsory on them to act when required, and as it would be unfair that those gentlemen, who do sacrifice much of their time to their duty as Justices, should be forced to leave their homes for days in acting as Commissioners, without an adequate allowance being made them for their trouble and expense; and as many of these gentlemen would probably not wish to act in the line of Commissioners.

Your Petitioners are therefore of opinion that it would tend to the ease of the Inhabitants and the welfare of the District to have a certain number of disinterested persons to be overseers or Commissioners of the Highways in each and every District, and that an allowance should be made to them from the different District Treasurers to be raised by a tax for that immediate purpose, making it compulsory on them on all occasions when thereto required to lay out, alter, or amend any road or roads throughout their respective District or Division. However, all this is submitted to the Honorable the Legislature for their consideration, which Your Petitioners pray may meet with due and mature deliberation.

And your Petitioners as in duty bound will ever pray.

(Signed) { John Pettit.
          Levi Lewis.
          Richard Griffin.
          Wm. Kennedy.
          and fifteen others.

On motion of Mr. Sherwood, seconded by Mr. Wilkinson,

The House adjourned till twelve o'clock to-morrow noon.

*Shannon?

Wednesday, 13th February, 1805.

Prayers were read.

Read for the first time, "An Act to regulate the curing, packing, and inspection of Beef and Pork."

On motion of Mr. McLean, seconded by Mr. Dorland,

Ordered, That the said Bill be read a second time on Monday next.

Ordered accordingly.

The engrossed Bill entitled "An Act to make provisions for further appointment of Parish and Town Officers throughout this Province," was read for the third time.

On motion of Mr. Howard, seconded by Mr. Nellis,

Resolved, That the Bill do pass, and that the title be "An Act to make provisions for further appointments of Parish and Town Officers throughout this Province."

Mr. Sherwood moved, seconded by Mr. Nellis, that Messrs. Howard and Dorland do carry the said Bill to the Legislative Council and request their concurrence.

Ordered accordingly.

The engrossed Bill, entitled "An Act to ratify and confirm certain Articles of Agreement entered into on the part of the Commissioners of Upper and Lower Canada," was read the third time.

On motion of Mr. McLean, seconded by Mr. Rogers,

Resolved, That the Bill do pass, and that the title be "An Act to ratify and confirm certain Provisional Articles of Agreement entered into by the respective Commissioners of this Province and Lower Canada at Montreal on the fifth day of July, One thousand eight hundred and four, relative to duties, and for carrying the same into effect; and also to continue an Act passed in the thirty-ninth year of His Majesty's Reign, and continued by an Act passed in the forty-first year of His Majesty's Reign."

Mr. Sherwood moved, seconded by Mr. Mallory, that Messrs. McLean and Hill do carry the said Bill to the Legislative Council and request their concurrence.

It was ordered accordingly.

On motion of Mr. Sherwood, seconded by Mr. Clench,—That any Member of the House may bring up a Petition and deliver the same to the Clerk to be laid on the Table, without leave.

The House resolved the same.

Mr. Clench moved, seconded by Mr. McGregor, for leave to bring in a Bill on Monday next to amend an Act passed in the forty-third year of His Majesty's Reign, entitled "An Act to enable married women having Real Estate more conveniently to alien and convey the same."

Leave was accordingly granted.

Mr. McGregor moved, seconded by Mr. Clench, for leave to bring in a Bill for the relief of Insolvent Debtors, on Friday next.

Leave was accordingly granted.

Mr. Rogers, seconded by Mr. Clench, moved that a Committee be appointed to request a conference with the Honorable the Legislative Council on the most proper means of speedily obtaining the Royal assent to an Act to regulate the Trial of Controverted Elections.

A division thereupon ensued; the names were called for and were taken down, and are as follows,

Yeas.	Nays.
MESSRS. CLENCH	MESSRS. McLEAN
ROGERS	SHERWOOD
HILL	COWAN
SWAYZE	DORLAND
WASHBURN	HOWARD
	MALLORY

The same passed in the negative by a majority of one.

On motion of Mr. Sherwood, seconded by Mr. McGregor, the House adjourned till twelve o'clock at noon to-morrow.

Thursday, 14th February, 1805.

Prayers were read.

Messrs. Howard and Dorland reported that they had brought up to the Honorable Legislative Council the Bill entitled "An Act for the further appointment of Parish and Town Officers," and did request their concurrence.

Mr. McLean, one of the Messengers named to carry up to the Honorable Legislative Council the Bill entitled "An Act to ratify and confirm certain Provisional Articles of Agreement entered into by the respective Commissioners of this Province and Lower Canada at Montreal, on the fifth day of July, One thousand eight hundred and four; relative to Duties, and for carrying the same into effect; and also to continue an Act passed in the thirty-ninth year of His Majesty's Reign, and continued by an Act passed in the forty-first year of His Majesty's Reign," reported that they did carry up the said Bill to the Honorable the Legislative Council and did request their concurrence.

By command of His Excellency, the Lieutenant Governor, William Jarvis, Esquire, Secretary of the Province, appeared at the Bar of the House, whereat he delivered the Provincial Public Accounts.

And then he withdrew.

Which Accounts were read, and are as follows,

SCHEDULE OF ACCOUNTS laid before the House of Assembly.

No. 1. The Inspector's list of names of persons licensed as Shop and Innkeepers in the several Districts of the Province of Upper Canada, for the year ending 5th of April, 1804. These returns were not received in time to be laid before the Legislature in 1804.

No. 2. The Inspector's list of names of such persons as have been licensed to work Stills in the several Districts of the Province of Upper Canada for the year ending the 5th April, 1804. These returns were not received in time to be laid before the Legislature in 1804.

No. 3. The Inspector's list of names of persons licensed as Shop and Innkeepers in the several Districts of the Province of Upper Canada for the year ending 5th April, 1805.

No. 4. The Inspector's list of names of such persons as have been licensed to work Stills in the several Districts of the Province of Upper Canada for the year ending the 5th of April, 1805.

No. 5. Provincial Revenue of the Crown arising from duties collected on Goods imported under authority of Acts of the Provincial Parliament, between the 1st January and the 31st December, 1804, including such duties as have not been heretofore stated.

No. 6. Provincial Revenue of the Crown arising from Duties collected on goods imported under authority of Acts of the Parliament of Great Britain between the 1st January and the 31st December, 1804.

No. 7. Abstract of Warrant issued by His Excellency, Lieutenant General Peter Hunter, Lieutenant Governor of the Province of Upper Canada, for moneys charged against the funds arising from Duties imposed by the Provincial Legislature.

No. 8. Supplementary abstract statement of moneys collected within the several Districts of the Province of Upper Canada, on Shop-keepers, Inn-keepers and Still Licenses for the year ending the 5th April, 1804, after deducting ten per cent. allowed to the Inspectors by the Act of the forty-third of the King.

No. 9. Supplimentary Abstract Statement of moneys collected within the several Districts of the Province of Upper Canada on Shop and Innkeepers licenses for the year ending 5th April, 1804, under authority of Acts of the Parliament of Great Britain, after deducting ten per cent. allowed to the Inspectors by the Act of the forty-third of the King.

No. 10. Abstract statement of moneys collected within the several Districts of the Province of Upper Canada on Shop, Innkeepers and Still Licenses, for the year ending the 5th of April, 1805, as far as the returns have been received, after deducting ten per cent. allowed to the Inspector by the Act of the forty-third of the King.

No. 11. Abstract Statement of moneys collected within the several Districts of the Province of Upper Canada on Shop and Innkeepers Licenses for the year ending the 5th of April, 1805, under authority of Acts of the Parliament of Great Britain so far as the returns have been received, after deducting ten per cent. allowed to the Inspectors by the Act of the 43rd of the King.

No. 12. General account of articles on which duties on importation are imposed by the Legislature of Lower Canada, which have passed Coteau du Lac upwards from the 1st of January to the 30th of June, 1804, agreeable to the written accounts thereof received, or as ascertained on examination of carriages according to the Act.

No. 13. General account of articles on which duties on importation are imposed by the Legislature of Lower Canada, which have passed Coteau du Lac upwards from the 1st July to the 31st December, 1804, agreeable to the written account thereof received, or as ascertained on examination of carriages according to the Act.

No. 14. Account of lighthouse tonnage duties collected for the year ending 31st December, 1804.

No. 15. Account of Cash received by the Honorable Peter Russell, Receiver General, for Fines and Forfeitures, under authority of Acts of the Provincial Parliament between the 5th February, 1804, and the 5th February, 1805.

No. 16. Account of Cash received by the Honorable Peter Russell, Receiver General, for fines and forfeitures under the authority of Acts of the Parliament of Great Britain, between the 5th of February, 1804, and the 5th February, 1805.

No. 17. General state of cash received by the Honorable Peter Russell, Receiver General, for duties and fines, under authority of Acts of the Parliament of Great Britain, between the 5th February, 1804, and the 5th February, 1805.

No. 18. General state of receipts and payments by the Honorable Peter Russell, Receiver General, for the duties and fines under authority of the Acts of the Provincial Parliament between the 5th of February, 1804, and the 5th of February, 1805.

Inspector General's Office, (Signed) John McGill,
York, 4th February, 1805. Inspr. Genl.
P. P. Accounts.

(For Accounts and Statements see Appendix.)

On motion of Mr. Sherwood, seconded by Mr. Clench, the House adjourned till twelve o'clock at noon.

Friday, 15 February, 1805.

Prayers were read.

Read for the first time, The Bill for giving relief to insolvent debtors.

Mr. McGregor then moved, seconded by Mr. Sherwood, that the Bill for the Relief of Insolvent Debtors be read a second time to-morrow.

Ordered accordingly.

Mr. Sherwood, seconded by Mr. Clench, moved that the Order for the second reading of the Bill for inspecting Beef and Pork, on Monday next be discharged, and that the same be read a second time this day.

Ordered accordingly.

Read a second time, The Bill to regulate the curing, packing and inspection of Beef and Pork.

Mr. McLean then moved, seconded by Mr. Clench, that the House do now resolve itself into Committee to take into consideration the said Bill.

The House resolved itself into Committee accordingly.

Mr. Speaker left the Chair.

Mr. Dorland was called to the chair of the Committee.

Mr. Speaker resumed the Chair.

And Mr. Dorland reported that the Committee had directed him to report a progress, and asked for leave to sit again this day.

Leave was accordingly granted.

A message from the Legislative Council by Mr. Burns, Master in Chancery.

Mr. Speaker,

I am commanded by the Honorable the Legislative Council to inform this House that they have passed an Act "to ratify and confirm certain Provisional articles of Agreement entered into by the respective Commissioners of this Province and Lower Canada, at Montreal on the 5th day of July, One Thousand Eight Hundred and Four, relative to duties, and for carrying the same into effect; and also to continue an Act passed in the thirty-ninth year of His Majesty's Reign, continued by an Act passed in the forty-first year of His Majesty's Reign" with some amendments, to which they request the concurrence of this House.

The amendments were then read.

Mr. Sherwood gave notice that to-morrow he would move the House to go into Committee to take into consideration the amendments made by the Legislative Council to the Bill to confirm the Provisional Agreement entered into by the Commissioners named by this Province and Lower Canada.

The House again resolved itself into Committee on the Bill to regulate the curing, packing, and inspection of Beef and Pork.

Mr. Speaker left the Chair.

Mr. Dorland again took the chair of the Committee.

Mr. Speaker resumed the Chair.

Mr. Dorland reported that the Committee had gone through the consideration of the said Bill, to which they had made some amendments, which he was directed to report whenever the House shall be pleased to receive the same.

Ordered, That the Report be now received.

Which Report was received and accepted.

Mr. McLean moved, seconded by Mr. Mallory, that the Bill now reported be engrossed, and read a third time to-morrow.

Ordered accordingly.

On motion of Mr. Swayze, seconded by Mr. Washburn, the House adjourned till twelve o'clock to-morrow at noon.

Saturday, 16th February, 1805.

Prayers were read.

Mr. Rogers moved, seconded by Mr. Dorland, for leave to bring in a Bill for the better preservation of Deer, on Monday next.

Leave was accordingly given.

Read, The Petition of the Magistrates of the Home District, which is as follows.

To the Honorable the House of Assembly of the Province of Upper Canada.

The Petition of the Magistrates of the Home District,

Humbly Sheweth,

That the assessments and rates, as by law established in and for the said District, have been found inadequate to discharge the burthens and expenses incident thereto.

That the Gaol of the said District has fallen into great decay, and requires, for the safety and comfort of the Prisoners, many needful and necessary reparations.

That for the purpose of discharging the said necessary burthens and expenses, and for the repairing of the said Gaol, the aid of the Legislature is necessary.

Your Petitioners therefore humbly request that Your Honorable House will take the premises into consideration and grant them such relief therein as you in your wisdom shall think fit.

And Your Petitioners as in duty bound shall ever pray.

(Signed)   Wm. Jarvis, Chairman,
                          in Special Sessions.
                  Wm. Allen
                  Jno. McGill
                  D. Cameron
                  Jas. Macaulay
                  Alexr. Wood.

York, 13th Feb'y, 1805.

Then was read for the first time a Bill to regulate the Statute Labour to be done on Public Roads and Highways throughout this Province.

Mr. Washburn, seconded by Mr. Dorland, moved that the said Bill be read a second time on Monday next.

Which was ordered accordingly.

Then was read for the second time the Insolvent Debtors Bill.

On motion of Mr. McGregor, seconded by Mr. Rogers, the House resolved itself into Committee to take the said Bill into consideration.

Mr. Speaker left the Chair.

Mr. Rogers was called to the chair of the Committee.

Mr. Speaker resumed the Chair.

And Mr. Rogers reported that the Committee had gone through the consideration of the said Bill, to which they made an amendment, which he was directed to report whenever the House shall be pleased to receive the same.

It was then resolved that the Report be now received.

The Report was then received and accepted.

Mr. McGregor then moved, seconded by Mr. Rogers, that the said Bill be engrossed and read a third time on Monday next.

Ordered accordingly.

Then was read the engrossed Bill for the inspection of Pork and Beef.

On motion of Mr. McLean, seconded by Mr. Sherwood,

Resolved, That this Bill do pass, and that the title be "An Act to regulate the curing, packing and inspection of Beef and Pork."

The Bill then passed and was signed by Mr. Speaker.

Mr. Rogers moved, seconded by Mr. Swayze, that Messrs Sherwood, McLean, and Mallory do carry up the said Bill to the Legislative Council, and request their concurrence in passing the same.

It was ordered accordingly.

Mr. Clench, seconded by Mr. Sherwood, moved for leave to bring in on Tuesday next a Bill to authorize the Justices of the Peace for the Home District in Quarter Sessions assembled to increase the assessment in said District.

Leave was accordingly given.

Mr. McLean moved, seconded by Mr. Sherwood, for leave to bring in a Bill on Monday next to purchase a Philosophical Apparatus.

Accordingly leave was granted.

Mr. Sherwood, seconded by Mr. Swayze, moved for leave to bring in a Bill on Monday next to alter the time of issuing Tavern and Still licenses.

Leave was given.

On motion of Mr. Sherwood, seconded by Mr. McLean, the House resolved itself into Committee to go into the consideration of the amendments made by the Legislative Council to a Bill entitled "An Act to ratify and confirm certain Provisional Articles of Agreement entered into by the respective Commissioners of this Province and Lower Canada."

Mr. Speaker left the Chair.

Mr. Hill was called to the chair of the Committee.

Mr. Speaker resumed the Chair.

Mr. Hill reported that the Committee had gone through the amendments made by the Legislative Council, without any amendment, which he was directed to report whenever the House will be pleased to receive the same, which Report he read in his place, and afterwards handed it in at the Table, when it was again read by the Clerk.

The House then resolved that the said Report be now received. It was accordingly received and accepted.

On motion of Mr. Sherwood, seconded by Mr. McLean,

Ordered, that Messrs Clench and Cowan do go up and inform the Honorable the Legislative Council that this House have concurred in the amendments made by them to the Bill for ratifying the Provisional Agreement with Lower Canada.

Mr. Clench, one of the Messengers named to inform the Legislative Council that this House did concur in the amendments made by them to an Act to ratify and confirm certain Articles of Agreement entered into by the respective Commissioners of this Province and Lower Canada, reported that they had carried up the said Message to the Legislative Council.

On motion of Mr. Swayze, seconded by Mr. Clench, the House adjourned till Monday next at twelve o'clock at noon.

Monday, 18th February, 1805.

Prayers were read.

Mr. Sherwood moved, seconded by Mr. Nellis, for leave to bring in a Bill to-morrow for the speedy recovery of rents from lands reserved for the Crown and Clergy. Leave was accordingly given.

Mr. Rogers gives notice that he will on to-morrow move that an humble address be presented to His Excellency the Lieutenant Governor praying that he will be pleased to issue his Warrant to the Clerk of this House for the sum of Sixteen Pounds Five Shillings currency, to enable him to purchase twenty copies of the Provincial Statutes of this Province, to be delivered to the Members of the House of Assembly representing the Counties of Hastings and Northumberland, and also six copies to be delivered to the Magistrates in the County of Durham, in the District of Newcastle, the copies of the Statutes intended for the said Counties being lost in His Majesty's Schooner "Speedy."

Mr. Clench moved, seconded by Mr. Sherwood, that the Order of the Day, so far as relates to the leave given to introduce a Bill to amend an Act passed in the forty-third year of His Majesty's Reign, entitled, "An Act to enable married women having Real Estate more conveniently to alien and convey the same," be discharged.

The same passed in the negative.

Mr. Clench, seconded by Mr. Sherwood, moved that so much of the Order of the Day as relates to the leave given to bring in on this day a Bill to amend an Act passed in the forty-third year of His Majesty's Reign entitled "An Act to enable Married Women having Real Estate more conveniently to alien and convey the same," be discharged, and that leave be given to bring in the same on Wednesday next. Accordingly leave was given.

Read for the first time, A Bill for the preservation of Deer throughout this Province.

Mr. Rogers then moved, seconded by Mr. Nellis, that the Bill for the preservation of Deer be read a second time to-morrow. Which was carried in the negative.

Read for the second time, An Act to alter the Statute Labour to be done on the Highways and Public Roads throughout this Province.

Mr. Washburn, seconded by Mr. Clench, moved that the House do now resolve itself into Committee to take the Road Bill into consideration.

The House accordingly resolved itself into Committee. Mr. Speaker left the Chair. Mr. Nellis was called to the chair of the Committee. Mr. Speaker resumed the Chair.

And Mr. Nellis reported that the Committee had made a progress, and directed him to ask for leave to sit again this day.

Leave was accordingly given.

A Message from the Legislative Council by Mr. Burns, Master in Chancery.

Mr. Speaker,

I am commanded by the Legislative Council to inform this House that they have passed an Act to afford relief to those persons who may be entitled to claim lands in this Province as heirs or devisees of the nominees of the Crown in cases where no patent hath issued to such lands.

And then he withdrew.

Agreeable to leave granted, the House again resolved itself into Committee to go into the further consideration of the Public Roads throughout this Province.

Mr. Speaker left the Chair. Mr. Nellis was again called to the Chair of the Committee. Mr. Speaker resumed the Chair.

Mr. Nellis reported that the Committee had made a progress, and directed him to ask leave to sit again this day. Leave was accordingly given.

A Message from the Legislative Council by Mr. Burns, Master in Chancery.

Mr. Speaker,

I am commanded by the Honorable Legislative Council to inform this House that they have passed the Bill entitled "An Act to make provision for further appointments of Parish and Town Officers throughout this Province," with some amendments, to which they desire the concurrence of the House of Assembly.

And then he withdrew.

The amendments to the said Bill were then read for the first time.

The House according to leave given again resolved itself into Committee to go into the further consideration of the Road Bill.

Mr. Speaker left the Chair. Mr. Nellis again took the Chair of the Committee. Mr. Speaker resumed the Chair.

Mr. Nellis reported that the Committee had gone through the consideration of the said Bill, to which they had made some amendments, which amendments he was directed to report to the House whenever it shall be pleased to receive the same.

Resolved, That the Report be now received.

The Report was accordingly received and accepted.

Mr. Sherwood then moved, seconded by Mr. Nellis, that the Bill as amended be engrossed and read a third time on Wednesday next. Ordered accordingly.

A Message from the Legislative Council by Mr. Burns, Master in Chancery.

Mr. Speaker,

I am commanded by the Legislative Council to inform this House that they passed the Bill entitled "An Act to alter certain parts of an Act passed in the forty-second year of His Majesty's Reign, entitled 'An Act to provide for the Administration of Justice in the District of Newcastle,'" with some amendments, to which they request the concurrence of the House of Assembly.

And then he withdrew.

4 A.

Then were read for the first time the amendments made to the said Bill.

Read, the engrossed Bill for the relief of Insolvent Debtors, for the third time.

On motion of Mr. McGregor, seconded by Captain Cowan,

Resolved, That the Bill do pass, and that the title be "An Act for the relief of Insolvent Debtors."

The Bill then passed, and was signed by Mr. Speaker.

Mr. Sherwood then moved, seconded by Mr. Rogers, that Mr. Clench and Mr. McGregor do carry up the said Bill to the Honorable the Legislative Council and request their concurrence.

Ordered accordingly.

Then was read for the first time a Bill for appropriating a certain sum of money for the purchase of a Philosophical Apparatus for the use of this Province.

Mr. McLean then moved, seconded by Mr. Sherwood, that this Bill be read a second time on Wednesday next. Which was ordered accordingly.

Then was read for the first time the Tavern and Still License Bill.

Mr. Mallory gave notice that he shall move to-morrow that the House do then resolve itself into Committee to take into its consideration the Public Accounts.

Read for the first time, An Act to afford relief to those persons who may be entitled to claim lands in this Province as heirs or devisees of the nominees of the Crown, in cases where no patent hath issued for such lands, sent down from the Legislative Council for concurrence.

Mr. Rogers then moved, seconded by Mr. Sherwood, that the Bill entitled "An Act to afford relief to those persons who may be entitled to claim lands in this Province as heirs or devisees of the nominees of the Crown, in cases where no. Patent hath issued for such lands," be read a second time on Thursday next.

Ordered accordingly.

Then Mr. Rogers moved, seconded by Mr. Swayze, that the House do now resolve itself into Committee to take into consideration the amendments made by the Honorable the Legislative Council to the Bill for the District of Newcastle.

The House accordingly resolved itself into Committee.

Mr. Speaker left the Chair.

Mr. Clench was called to the Chair of the Committee.

Mr. Speaker resumed the Chair.

And Mr. Clench reported that the Committee had gone into the consideration of the said amendments, and that the Committee did direct him to report the Bill as amended by the Legislative Council whenever the House shall be pleased to receive the same.

Resolved, That the said Report be now received.

Which Report was then received and accepted.

Mr. Sherwood then moved, seconded by Mr. Swayze, that Messrs. Rogers and McGregor do inform the Honorable the Legislative Council that this House have concurred in the amendments made by them to the Newcastle Bill.

Ordered accordingly.

Mr. Howard then moved, seconded by Mr. Sherwood, that the House do now resolve itself into Committee to take into consideration the amendments made by the Honorable the Legislative Council to a Bill entitled "An Act to make further provision for the appointment of Parish and Town Officers."

The House accordingly resolved itself into Committee.

Mr. Speaker left the Chair.

Mr. McLean was called to the Chair of the Committee.

Mr. Speaker resumed the Chair.

· Mr. McLean reported that the Committee had gone through the consideration of the amendments made to the said Bill, without any amendments, which he was directed to report whenever the House is pleased to receive the same.

It was then Ordered, that the said Report be now received.

The said Report was then received and accepted.

On motion of Mr. Sherwood, seconded by Mr. Swayze,—that Messrs. Rogers and McGregor do inform the Honorable Legislative Council that this House hath concurred in the amendments made by them to an Act to provide for the Administration of Justice in the District of Newcastle.

It was ordered accordingly.

On motion of Mr. Swayze, seconded by Mr. Nellis, the House adjourned.

Tuesday, 19th February, 1805.

Prayers were read.

Mr. Rogers moved, seconded by Mr. Dorland, that an Address be presented to His Excellency the Lieutenant Governor praying that he will be pleased to issue his Warrant in favor of the Clerk of the House of Assembly for the sum of Sixteen Pounds, Five Shillings, to enable him to purchase twenty copies of the Provincial Statutes of this Province to be delivered to the Members of the House of Assembly representing the Counties of Hastings and Northumberland and also six copies of the said Statutes to be delivered to His Majesty's Justices of the Peace in the County of Durham in the District of Newcastle; the copies of the Statutes of this Province intended for the said Counties being lost in His Majesty's Schooner "Speedy." Ordered accordingly.

Read for the first time, An Act increasing the Assessments and Rates in the Home District.

Mr. Clench, seconded by Mr. McGregor, moved that this Bill be read a second time on Thursday next. Which passed in the negative.

Then was read for the first time An Act for the speedy recovery of rents arising from the lands reserved for the Crown.

Mr. Sherwood moved, seconded by Mr. Clench, that this Bill be read a second time to-morrow. Ordered accordingly.

Mr. Sherwood moved, seconded by Mr. Swayze, that this House do present an Address to His Excellency the Lieutenant Governor, praying him to advance the sum of twenty-five Pounds to the Clerk of the House towards paying the Copying Clerks.

Mr. Sherwood then moved, seconded by Captain Cowan, that Messrs. Clench and Howard be a Committee to draft an Address to His Excellency the Lieutenant Governor, praying that he may be pleased to advance Twenty-five Pounds to the Clerk of this House towards paying Copying Clerks. Which was ordered accordingly.

Then Mr. Clench informed the House that the Committee had drafted an Address to His Excellency the Lieutenant Governor, which he was ready to submit to the House whenever it shall be pleased to receive the same.

The House then resolved that the said Address be now received.

Mr. Clench then read the same in his place, which he delivered in at the Table, and was once more read by the Clerk, and is as follows.

To His Excellency Peter Hunter, Esquire, Lieutenant Governor of the Province of Upper Canada and Lieutenant General commanding His Majesty's Forces in the Provinces of Upper and Lower Canada.

May it please your Excellency,

We, His Majesty's most dutiful and loyal subjects, the Commons of Upper Canada in Parliament assembled, do most humbly pray that Your Excellency will be pleased to order an advance of Twenty-five Pounds Currency to be made to the Clerk of this House, on account towards defraying the expenses of Copying Clerks during the present Session, and that the same be charged to the fund by law appropriated for that purpose.

Commons House of Assembly,
    19th February, 1805.

On motion of Captain Cowan, seconded by Mr. McGregor,

The said Address was ordered to be engrossed.

Mr. Mallory moved, seconded by Mr. Sherwood, that this House do now resolve itself into Committee to take into consideration the Public Accounts.

The House accordingly resolved itself into Committee.

Mr. Speaker left the Chair. Mr. Dorland was called to the Chair of the Committee. Mr. Speaker resumed the Chair.

Mr. Dorland reported that the Committee had gone through the consideration of the Provincial Public Accounts, which he was directed to report to the House whenever it shall be pleased to receive the same.

Then Mr. Rogers moved, seconded by Mr. Washburn, that the Report of the Committee be not received.

On Mr. Speaker having put the question a division thereupon took place, the names being called for they were taken down, and are as follows.

Yeas.	Nays.
MESSRS. COWAN	MESSRS. ROGERS
McGREGOR	WASHBURN
McLEAN	DORLAND
HOWARD	
CLENCH	
CRYSLER	
MALLORY	
NELLIS	
HILL	
SWAYZE	

The same passed in the negative by a majority of seven.

Then Mr. Dorland read the Report in his place, and delivered the same in at the Table, where it was again read by the Clerk, and is as follows.

THE COMMITTEE REPORT:—

	£.	s.	d.
That there remains in the Receiver General's hands from last year, as per No. 13	1,566	2	11⅛
That the Revenues arising from duties in Lower Canada for the last Year, though not as yet paid, but supposed to amount to	1,400	0	0
That it appears to the Committee that there is due upon Still, Shop, and Tavern Licenses for the year ending on the 5th of April next as per Nos. 3 & 4	701	0	0
	£3,667	2	11⅛

Of which there is appropriated annually for the current expenses of the two Houses £790.

And also appropriated annually for printing the laws £80 ....

	870	0	0
	2,797	2	11⅛

The Committee further report that it is their opinion that One Hundred ought to be paid out of the unappropriated moneys above mentioned to each of the Commissioners who were authorized by His Excellency the Lieutenant Governor to treat with Commissioners from Lower Canada.

Which Report was then received and accepted.

On motion of Mr. Sherwood, seconded by Capt. Cowan,

Ordered, That Mr. Rogers and Mr. Washburn be a Committee to draft an Address to His Excellency the Lieutenant Governor, praying that he may be pleased to issue his Warrant for Sixteen Pounds Five Shillings for the purpose of purchasing twenty-six copies of the Provincial Statutes, to be delivered to the Members representing Counties of Hastings and Northumberland, and to the Magistrates of the County of Durham in the District of Newcastle.

Which was ordered accordingly.

Then Messrs. Rogers and Washburn reported that in obedience to the Commands of this House they had drafted an address to His Excellency the Lieutenant Governor, which they are ready to submit to the House whenever it should be pleased to receive the same.

The House then resolved that the said Address be now received and read.

. Then Mr. Rogers read the said Address in his place, which he afterwards delivered in at the Table where it was again read by the Clerk, and is as follows.

     To His Excellency Peter Hunter Esquire, Lieutenant Governor of The Province of Upper Canada, and Lieutenant General Commanding His Majesty's Forces in the Provinces of Upper and Lower Canada, &c, &c, &c.

May it please Your Excellency:—

We, His Majesty's most dutiful and loyal subjects, the Commons of Upper Canada in Parliament assembled, do most respectfully pray that it may please Your Excellency to issue Your Warrant in favour of the Clerk of the House of

Assembly for the sum of Sixteen Pounds Five Shillings, to be employed in purchasing twenty copies of the Provincial Statutes of this Province, to be delivered to the Members of the House of Assembly representing the Counties of Hastings and Northumberland, and also six copies of the said Provincial Statutes to be delivered to His Majesty's Justices of the Peace in the County of Durham in the District of Newcastle; the copies of the Statutes of this Province intended for the said Counties being lost in His Majesty's Schooner "Speedy," which sum of money the Commons will make good during the next Session of Parliament.
Commons House of Assembly,
    19th February, 1805.

Then, on motion of Mr. Hill, seconded by Mr. Mallory,
Ordered, That the said Address be engrossed.
The said Address was then read as engrossed, and signed by Mr. Speaker.
Mr. Sherwood moved, seconded by Mr. Nellis, that Messrs. Swayze and Rogers do wait upon His Excellency the Lieutenant Governor to know when he will be pleased to receive the Addresses of this House voted this day, and that they do also present the same at the time His Excellency may appoint.
Which was ordered accordingly.
Mr. Washburn, seconded by Mr. Howard, moved for leave to bring in a Bill on Friday next to establish a Fund for the support of one or more Public Schools in each and every District within this Province. Leave was accordingly given.
Then Mr. Sherwood moved, seconded by Mr. Clench, for leave to bring in a Bill to-morrow to make good the money paid by His Excellency the Lieutenant Governor in consequence of several Addresses of this House in the last Session of Parliament. Accordingly leave was granted.
Messrs Clench and McGregor reported that they had carried up to the Legislative Council the Bill entitled "An Act for the relief of insolvent debtors," and did request their concurrence.
On motion of Mr. Crysler, seconded by Mr. Howard, the House adjourned.

Wednesday, 20th February, 1805.

Prayers were read.
Messrs. Swayze and Rogers reported that in obedience to the Commands of this House they had presented the two Addresses of this House, voted yesterday, to His Excellency the Lieutenant Governor, who was pleased to return the following answer to them.

Gentlemen:—
I readily accede to the prayer contained in your Address, and shall issue my Warrant upon the Receiver General for the sum of Sixteen Pounds Five Shillings, to be applied for the purpose therein mentioned.

Gentlemen:—
I readily accede to the request in your Address, and shall issue my Warrant for the sum of Twenty-Five Pounds, the sum of money therein prayed for.

Then was read for the first time, "A Bill to enable Married Women having Real Estate to convey the same."

Mr. Rogers moved, seconded by Mr. Nellis, that the Bill just now read be read a second time to-morrow. Ordered accordingly.

Mr. Howard, seconded by Mr. Nellis, moved that the Order of the Day for the third reading of the Road Bill be discharged, and that the said Bill be recommitted.

The House accordingly resolved itself into Committee.

Mr. Speaker left the Chair.

Mr. Nellis was called to the chair of the Committee.

Mr. Speaker resumed the Chair.

Mr. Nellis reported that the Committee had gone through the consideration of the said Bill, to which they had made some amendments, which he was directed to report to the House whenever it shall be pleased to receive the same.

The House then resolved that the Report be now received.

The Report was then received and accepted.

Mr. McLean moved, seconded by Mr. Washburn, that so much of the Order of the Day be discharged as relates to the second reading of the Bill entitled "An Act to purchase a Philosophical Apparatus," and that the same be read on Monday next. Ordered accordingly.

Read for the second time, "A Bill for the more speedy and effectual recovery of the Crown and Clergy reserve rents."

On motion of Mr. Sherwood, seconded by Mr. Clench, the House resolved itself into Committee on the said Bill.

Mr. Speaker left the Chair.

Mr. Mallory was called to the chair of the Committee.

Mr. Speaker resumed the Chair.

And Mr. Mallory reported that the Committee had gone through the consideration of the said Bill to which they had made some amendments, which he was directed to report whenever the House should be pleased to receive the same.

The House then resolved that the said Report be now received.

Which Report was then received and accepted.

Read for the first time, "A Bill for granting to His Majesty a certain sum of money out of the Provincial Fund for the purpose therein mentioned."

Mr. Sherwood moved, seconded by Mr. Clench, that this Bill be read a second time to-morrow. Ordered accordingly.

Mr. Howard, seconded by Mr. McLean, moved that this House do vote an Address to His Excellency the Lieutenant Governor, praying him to advance the sum of Three Hundred Pounds to the Commissioners appointed by this Province to treat with the Commissioners of Lower Canada. Ordered accordingly.

Mr. Howard moved, seconded by Mr. Clench, that Messrs McLean and McGregor be a Committee to draft an Address to His Excellency the Lieutenant Governor, praying that he may be pleased to pay Three Hundred Pounds to the Commissioners appointed by this Province to treat with Commissioners of Lower Canada. Which was ordered accordingly.

Mr. McLean, one of the Committee appointed to draft an Address to His Excellency the Lieutenant Governor, reported that they had drafted the Address, which they were ready to submit to the House whenever it shall be pleased to receive the same.

The House then resolved that the Address be now received.

The Address was then received and read, and is as follows.

To His Excellency Peter Hunter, Esquire, Lieutenant Governor of the Province of Upper Canada, and Lieutenant General Commanding His Majesty's Forces in the Provinces of Upper and Lower Canada, &c, &c, &c.

May it please Your Excellency,—

We, His Majesty's most dutiful and loyal subjects, the Commons of Upper Canada in Parliament assembled, do most humbly pray that Your Excellency will be pleased to issue your Warrant to the Receiver General to pay to the Hon. Robert Hamilton, Esquire, The Honorable Richard Cartwright, Esquire, and Samuel Sherwood, Esquire, the Commissioners appointed by Your Excellency on the part of this Province to treat with Commissioners appointed on the part of the Province of Lower Canada, each the sum of One Hundred Pounds, which we, the Commons of Upper Canada will make good to Your Excellency in the next Session of Parliament.

Commons House of Assembly,
    20th Feb'y, 1805.

The said Address was then signed by Mr. Spear.

Mr. McLean moved, seconded by Capt. Cowan, that Messrs. Clench and McGregor do wait on His Excellency the Lieutenant Governor, to know when he will receive the Address relative to the Commissioners, and also to present the same. Which was ordered accordingly.

Which was ordered accordingly.

Capt. Cowan moved, seconded by Mr. McLean, for leave to bring in a Bill to-morrow to make provision for the Sheriffs of the Districts who are not already provided for by law. Leave was accordingly granted.

Matthew Elliott, Esquire, who had previously taken the Oath, and had subscribed the Rolls containing the same took his seat in the House.

Read, the Petition of William Fraser, Esquire.

To His Excellency Peter Hunter, Esquire, Lieutenant Governor of His Majesty's Province of Upper Canada, the Honorable the Legislative Council, and the Honorable the Commons House of Assembly in Parliament assembled.

The Petition of William Fraser, Junior, Esquire, respectfully represents,

That Your Petitioner has for several years held the place of Sheriff of the District of Johnstown, and has diligently performed his duty to the best of his abilities without receiving any salary or any other remuneration for the various services attached to his Office, except the fees arising from Civil Suits which are not by any means adequate to afford him a decent support.

Your Petitioner therefore most humbly submits his case to the wisdom of the Legislature, and presumes to hope from the justice of Parliament for the same provision which has been made for others in his situation.

And as in duty bound he will ever pray, &c. &c.

Johnstown,   (Signed) William Fraser.
    8th Jan'y, 1805.

On motion of Mr. Sherwood, seconded by Mr. Nellis,

Ordered, That the Bill entitled "An Act for the speedy recovery of the rents arising from the lands reserved for the Crown and for the maintenance and support of a Protestant Clergy within this Province" be engrossed and read a third time to-morrow.

Mr. Washburn, seconded by Mr. Dorland, moved for leave to bring in a Bill on to-morrow to alter the present mode of swearing witnesses before the Grand Jury.

On the question being put the House divided, upon which the Speaker gave his vote that leave be given to bring in the Bill to-morrow.

Leave was accordingly given.

Mr. Sherwood gave notice that he will move to-morrow to fill up the blank in the first clause in the Bill for the speedy recovery of the rents of Crown and Clergy Reserves with the word "eight."

On motion of Mr. Howard, seconded by Mr. Mallory, it is ordered that the Bill for the better regulation of Statute Labour to be performed on the Highways and Roads be engrossed as amended, and read a third time to-morrow.

On motion of Mr. Clench, seconded by Capt. Cowan, the House adjourned till twelve o'clock to-morrow at noon.

Thursday, 21st February, 1805.

Prayers were read.

Read for the second time, the Bill to afford relief to persons claiming lands as Heirs to Nominees of the Crown.

Mr. McLean, seconded by Mr. Rogers, moved that the House do now resolve itself into Committee to take into consideration the said Bill.

Accordingly the House resolved itself into Committee on the said Bill.

Mr. Speaker left the Chair.

Mr. McGregor was called to the chair of the Committee.

Mr. Speaker resumed the Chair.

Mr. McGregor reported that the Committee had gone through the consideration of the said Bill without any amendment, which he was directed to report whenever the House shall be pleased to receive the same.

The House then resolved that the said Report be now received.

Which Report was received and accepted.

Read for the second time, The Bill to enable Married Women having Real Estate to the more easily alien and convey the same.

On motion of Mr. Mallory, seconded by Mr. Rogers, the House resolved itself into Committee on the said Bill.

Mr. Speaker left the Chair.

Capt. Cowan was called to the chair of the Committee.

Mr. Speaker resumed the Chair.

Capt. Cowan reported, that the Committee had gone through the consideration of the said Bill, without any amendments, which he was directed to report whenever the House shall be pleased to receive the same.

The House then resolved that the Report be now received.

Which Report was then received and accepted.

Mr. Rogers moved, seconded by Mr. Swayze, that the Bill for enabling Married Women having Real Estate more conveniently to alien the same be engrossed, and read a third time to-morrow.

Ordered accordingly.

Read for the second time, The Bill for applying a certain sum of money advanced by His Majesty through his Lieutenant Governor in pursuance of Addresses from this House.

On motion of Mr. Sherwood, seconded by Mr. Clench, the House resolved itself into Committee on the said Bill.

Mr. Speaker left the Chair.

Mr. Crysler was called to the chair of the Committee.

Mr. Speaker resumed the Chair.

Mr. Crysler reported that the Committee had gone through the consideration of the said Bill without any amendment. Which report was received and accepted.

On motion of Mr. Sherwood, seconded by Mr. McLean, Ordered, That the said Bill be engrossed and "Plaintiff" be inserted.

Which passed in the negative.

On the main question being put the House divided, the names being called for were taken down, and are as follows.

Yeas.
MESSRS. MALLORY
ROGERS
HILL
DORLAND
CLENCH
McLEAN

.Nays.
MESSRS. SHERWOOD
COWAN
McGREGOR
HOWARD
NELLIS
CRYSLER
SWAYZE

The same passed in the negative by a majority of one.

Mr. Sherwood, seconded by Capt. Cowan, moved that the Bill do pass.

The Bill accordingly passed.

Mr. Rogers, seconded by Mr. Hall, moved for leave to bring in a Bill on to-morrow to repeal so much of an Act passed in the fortieth year of His Majesty's Reign, entitled "An Act for the more equal representation of the Commons of this Province in Parliament, and for the better defining the qualifications of Electors," as regards the qualification of Electors.

Leave was accordingly granted.

Mr. Howard moved, seconded by Capt. Cowan, that Mr. Nellis and Mr. Swayze do carry up to the Honorable the Legislative Council the Bill entitled "An Act to alter the mode of performing the Statute Labour on the Highways and Roads throughout this Province," and request their concurrence.

Ordered accordingly.

Mr. Sherwood gave notice that he shall move to-morrow the Bill to alter the time of issuing Licenses be then read a second time.

On motion of Mr. Mallory, seconded by Mr. Swayze,

The House adjourned.

Friday, 22nd February, 1805.

Prayers were read.

Mr. Washburn moved, seconded by Mr. Howard, that so much of the Order of the Day be discharged as orders that the School Bill be read this Day, and that leave be given to bring in the same on Monday next.

Leave was granted accordingly.

The engrossed Bill entitled "an Act for applying a certain sum of money therein mentioned to make good certain moneys issued and advanced by His Majesty to the Lieutenant Governor in pursuance of two Addresses," was read a third time.

On motion of Mr. Clench, seconded by Mr. Sherwood,

Resolved, That the Bill do pass, and that the title be "An Act for applying a certain sum of money therein mentioned to make good certain moneys issued and advanced by His Majesty through his Excellency the Lieutenant Governor in pursuance of two Addresses."

Mr. Rogers, seconded by Mr. Nellis, moved that Messrs. Sherwood and Clench do carry up to the Honorable the Legislative Council the Bill for making good certain moneys advanced by His Majesty through the Lieutenant Governor, and to request their concurrence. Which was ordered accordingly.

Read for the first time, The Bill to repeal so much of an Act passed in the fortieth year of His Majesty's Reign, entitled "an Act for the more equal representation of the Commons of this Province in Parliament, and for the better defining the qualifications of Electors,". as regards the qualifications of Electors.

Mr. Rogers moved, seconded by Mr. Hill, that the Bill defining the qualifications of Electors be read a second time on Monday. Ordered accordingly.

The engrossed Bill entitled, An Act to amend an Act passed in the thirty-third year of His Majesty's Reign, entitled "An Act to enable Married Women having Real Estate more easily to alien the same," was read a third time.

On motion of Mr. Sherwood, seconded by Mr. Swayze,

Resolved, That this Bill do pass, and that the title be "An Act to amend an Act passed in the thirty-third year of His Majesty's Reign, entitled "An Act to enable Married Women having Real Estate more easily to alien the same."

Mr. McLean moved, seconded by Mr. Rogers, that Captain Cowan and Mr. Hill do carry up to the Honorable the Legislative Council the Bill sent down by them for concurrence, entitled "An Act to afford relief to those persons who may be entitled to claim lands in this Province as heirs or devisees of the Nominees of the Crown, in cases where no Patent hath issued for such lands," and inform them that this House have concurred in passing the same. Ordered accordingly.

On motion of Mr. Sherwood, seconded by Mr. Swayze,

Was read for the second time the Bill for altering the time of issuing licenses in this Province.

Mr. Sherwood moved, seconded by Mr. Clench, that the House do now resolve itself into Committee to take this Bill into consideration.

The House accordingly resolved itself into Committee.

Mr. Speaker left the Chair.

Mr. Howard was called to the Chair of the Committee.

Mr. Speaker resumed the Chair.

Mr. Howard reported that the Committee had gone through the consideration of the said Bill, to which they had made some amendments, which he was directed to report whenever the House shall be pleased to receive the same.

The House then resolved that the said Report be now received, which Report was received and accepted.

Mr. Rogers moved, seconded by Mr. Swayze, that the Bill for altering the time of issuing Licenses be engrossed and read a third time to-morrow.

Ordered accordingly.

Mr. Clench, seconded by Captain Eliott, moved for leave to bring in on to-morrow a "Bill to amend an Act for granting money for the further encouragement of the Growth and Cultivation of Hemp." Leave was granted accordingly.

On motion of Mr. Washburn, seconded by Mr. Dorland, the House adjourned.

Saturday, 23rd February, 1805.

Prayers were read.

Captain Cowan, one of the Messengers named by this House to return to the Honorable Legislative Council a Bill sent down by them for the concurrence of this House, entitled "An Act to afford relief to those persons who may be entitled to claim lands in this Province as Heirs or Devisees of the Nominees of the Crown, in cases where no Patent hath issued," reported that they had carried up the said Bill.

Then Mr. Nellis, first named to carry up to the Honorable Legislative Council the Bill entitled "An Act to alter the mode of performing Statute Labour on the Highways and Roads throughout this Province," reported that they had carried up the said Bill to which they requested their concurrence.

Then was read the third time the engrossed Bill for altering the time of issuing Licences for keeping Houses of Entertainment, or Stills for the purpose of distilling spirituous liquors.

Mr. Howard then moved, seconded by Mr. Crysler, that in the tenth line, the second section after the word "the" be inserted "Inspector."

Which was ordered accordingly.

On motion of Mr. Howard, seconded by Mr. Crysler,

Resolved, That the Bill do pass, and that the title be "An Act for altering the time of issuing Licences for the keeping of a House or any other place of public Entertainment, or for the retailing of Wine, Brandy, Rum, or any other spirituous liquors, or for the having or using of Stills for the purpose of distilling spirituous liquors, and for repealing so much of an Act passed in the forty-third year of His Majesty's Reign as relates to the periods of paying into the hands of the Receiver General the monies collected by the Inspector of each and every District throughout this Province for such licences."

Mr. Nellis, seconded by Mr. Washburn, moved that Messrs. Howard and Crysler do carry up to the Honorable the Legislative Council the Bill entitled "An Act for altering the time of issuing Licences for the keeping of a house or any other place of public entertainment, or for the retailing of Wine, Brandy, Rum or any other spirituous liquors, or for the having or using of Stills for the purpose of distilling spirituous liquors and for repealing so much of an Act passed in the forty-third year of His Majesty's Reign as relates to the periods of paying into the hands of the Receiver General the monies collected by the Inspector of each and every District throughout this Province for such Licences," and request their concurrence.

Also the Bill entitled "An Act for the speedy recovery of the rents arising from the Lands reserved for the Crown, and for the maintenance and support of a Protestant Clergy within the Province," and request their concurrence in passing the same.

And also a Bill entitled "An Act to amend an Act passed in the thirty-third year of Hs Majesty's Reign, entitled 'An Act to enable married women having

Real Estate more easily to alien the same,' " and also to request their concurrence thereto. Which was ordered accordingly.

Then was read for the first time the Bill for giving further encouragement for the Cultivators of Hemp throughout this Province.

Mr. Clench, seconded by Mr. Howard, moved that the said Bill be read a second time on Monday next. Ordered accordingly.

Messrs. Clench and McGregor reported that in obedience to the commands of this House they had presented to His Excellency, the Lieutenant Governor, the Address of this House voted on the twentieth instant, to which he was pleased to return the following answer.

Gentlemen,

I accede to the request contained in the Address of the House of Assembly of the twentieth instant, and shall accordingly issue my Warrants on the Receiver General to pay to the Honorable Richard Cartwright, Esquire, the Honorable Robert Hamilton, Esquire, and Samuel Sherwood, Esquire, the Commissioners appointed by me on the part of this Province to treat with Commissioners appointed on the part of Lower Canada, each of them respectively the sum of One Hundred Pounds.

York, Feb'y 22nd, 1805.

Mr. Clench, one of the Messengers named to carry up to the Legislative Council an Act for applying a certain sum of money therein mentioned to make good certain moneys advanced by His Majesty through the Lieutenant Governor in pursuance of two Addresses, reported that they had carried up the said Bill and did request their concurrence.

The Speaker informed the House that application had been made to him in writing by the Clerk of the House, which he then read, and is as follows, viz.

Mr. Speaker,

The Clerk respectfully informs this House that the wages now due the Copying Clerks exceeds the sum appropriated by law for that purpose; he therefore prays that he may receive the permission and sanction of this House to employ Copying Clerks to assist him in doing the duty of this House.

Commons House of Assembly,   (Signed) Donald Maclean,
23rd February, 1805.   Clerk Assembly.

A Message from the Honorable Legislative Council by Mr. Burns, Master in Chancery:

Mr. Speaker,—

The Honorable Legislative Council have commanded me to inform this House that they have passed the Bill entitled "An Act to regulate the Curing, Packing and Inspection of Beef and Pork," with some amendments, to which they request the concurrence of the House of Assembly.

And then he withdrew.

The amendments were then read for the first time.

Mr. Howard then moved, seconded by Mr. Washburn, that the House do now resolve itself into Committee to take into consideration the said amendments.

The House accordingly resolved itself into Committee to go into the consideration of the said amendments.

Mr. Speaker left the Chair.

Mr. Dorland was called to the Chair of the Committee.

Mr. Speaker resumed the Chair.

Mr. Dorland reported that the Committee had made a progress, and that he was directed to ask for leave to sit again this day.

Leave was accordingly granted.

A Message from the Honorable Legislative Council by Mr. Burns, Master in Chancery.

Mr. Speaker,

I am commanded by the Legislative Council to .inform this Honorable House. that they have concurred in passing the Bill sent up from this House entitled "An Act for granting relief to Insolvent Debtors," without any amendment.

The House again resolved itself into Committee to go into the further consideration of the Beef and Pork Inspection Bill.

Mr. Speaker left the Chair.

Mr. Dorland was again called to the Chair of the Committee.

Mr. Speaker resumed the Chair.

And Mr. Dorland reported that the Committee had gone through the consideration of the said amendments, and that he was directed to report the Bill as amended by the Legislative Council, whenever the House shall be pleased to receive the same.

The House then resolved that the said Report be now received.

The Report was then received and accepted.

Which amendments were ordered to be engrossed.

Mr. McLean then moved, seconded by Mr. Nellis, that Mr. Washburn and Mr. Mallory do inform the Honorable Legislative Council that this House have concurred in the amendments made in and to an Act for the regulating, curing and packing of Pork and Beef.

Which was ordered accordingly.

Mr. Howard, one of the Messengers named to carry up to the Legislative Council the three Bills following, viz.

The Bill entitled "An Act for altering the time of issuing Licenses for the keeping of a house or any other place of public entertainment, or for the retailing of Wine, Brandy, Rum, or any other Spirituous Liquor, or for the having and using Stills for the purpose of distilling Spirituous Liquors, and for repealing so much of an Act passed in the Forty-third year of His Majesty's Reign as relates to the periods of paying into the hands of the Receiver General the moneys collected by the Inspector of each and every District throughout this Province for such Licences."

Also the Bill entitled "An Act for the speedy recovery of the rents arising from the lands reserved for the Crown and for the maintenance and support of a Protestant Clergy within this Province."

And also the Bill entitled "An Act to amend an Act passed in the Thirty-third year of His Majesty's Reign, entitled 'An Act to enable married women having Real Estate more easily to alien the same,'" reported that they had carried up the said Bills to the Legislative Council and did request their concurrence therein.

On motion of Mr. Clench, seconded by Captain Cowan, the House adjourned till eleven o'clock at noon on Monday next.

Monday, 25th February, 1805.

Prayers were read.

Read for the first time, A Bill for establishing Schools in the different Districts in this Province.

Mr. Washburn then moved, seconded by Mr. Clench, that the said Bill be read a second time to-morrow. Ordered accordingly.

Read for the second time the Bill for defining the qualification of Electors. On motion of Mr. Rogers, seconded by Mr. Nellis, the House resolved itself into Committee to go into the consideration of the Bill for the better defining the qualifications of Electors.

Mr. Speaker left the Chair.

Mr. Washburn was called to the Chair of the Committee.

Mr. Speaker resumed the Chair.

Mr. Washburn reported that the Committee had made a progress, and had directed him to ask for leave to sit again this day.

Leave was accordingly granted.

A Message from the Honorable Legislative Council, by Mr. Burns, Master in Chancery.

Mr. Speaker,

I am commanded by the Legislative Council to inform this House that they have concurred in passing the Bill entitled "An Act for applying a certain sum of money therein mentioned to make good certain moneys issued and advanced by His Majesty's Lieutenant Governor in pursuance of two Addresses," without any amendments.

And then he withdrew.

The House again resolved itself into Committee to go into the further consideration of the Bill for the Better Defining the Qualification of Electors.

Mr. Speaker left the Chair.

Mr. Washburn was called to the Chair of the Committee.

Mr. Speaker resumed the Chair.

Mr. Washburn reported that the Committee had made a progress, and did direct him to ask for leave to sit again this day. Leave was accordingly given.

A Message from the Legislative Council by Mr. Burns, Master in Chancery.

Mr. Speaker,

I am commanded by the Legislative Council to inform this House that they have concurred in passing an Act for altering the Time for issuing Licences for the keeping a house or any other place of public entertainment, or for the retailing of Wine, Brandy, Rum, or any other Spirituous Liquors, or for the having and using of Stills, for the purpose of distilling spirituous liquors, and for repealing so much of An Act passed in the Forty-third year of His Majesty's Reign as relates to the periods of paying into the hands of the Receiver General the moneys collected by the Inspector of each and every District throughout this Province for such Licences, sent up by this House, without any amendment.

And then he withdrew.

The House again resolved itself into Committee to go into the further consideration of the Qualification of Electors.

Mr. Speaker left the Chair.

Mr. Washburn again took the Chair of the Committee.

Mr. Speaker resumed the Chair.

Mr. Washburn reported that the Committee had gone through the consideration of the said Bill without any amendment, which he was directed to submit to the House whenever it shall be pleased to receive the same.

The House then resolved that the said Report be now received.

Which Report was received and accepted.

Mr. Rogers then moved, seconded by Mr. Clench, that the Bill for the better defining the Qualification of Electors be engrossed and read a third time to-morrow.

Ordered accordingly.

Read for the second time a Bill for the further encouragement of the growth and cultivation of Hemp within this Province.

Mr. Clench moved, seconded by Mr. Washburn, that this House do now resolve itself into Committee to take the Bill into consideration.

The House accordingly resolved itself into Committee.

Mr. Speaker left the Chair.

Mr. Swayze was called to the Chair of the Committee.

Mr. Speaker resumed the Chair.

And Mr. Swayze reported that the Committee had gone through the consideration of the said Bill without any amendment, which he was directed to report whenever the House shall be pleased to receive the same.

The House then resolved that the Report be now received.

Which Report was received and accepted.

Mr. Clench moved, seconded by Mr. Nellis, that the Bill be engrossed and read a third time to-morrow. Ordered accordingly.

Mr. Sherwood moved, seconded by Mr. Clench, that the Fifth Rule of this House, requiring a day's previous notice being given to make a motion, be dispensed with. Which was ordered accordingly.

On motion of Mr. Sherwood, seconded by Mr. Clench,

Ordered, That it be made a Rule of this House that no Petition complaining of an undue election shall be read until the Petitioner or Petitioners shall give security to pay such costs as the House may order in case the Petition shall be considered groundless, and the sitting Member or Members duly elected.

The House accordingly resolved the same.

Mr. Nellis moved, seconded by Mr. Clench, that leave of absence from this House be granted to Isaac Swayze, Esquire, for six days.

Leave of absence was accordingly granted.

On motion of Mr. Clench, seconded by Mr. Howard, the House adjourned.

Tuesday, 26th February, 1805.

Prayers were read.

Read, the engrossed Bill entitled "An Act to repeal certain parts of an Act passed in the fortieth year of His Majesty's Reign."

On motion of Mr. Rogers, seconded by Mr. Clench,

Resolved, That the Bill do pass, and that the title be "An Act to repeal certain parts of an Act passed in the Fortieth year of His Majesty's Reign, entitled 'An Act for the more equal representation of the Commons of this Province in Parliament, and for the better defining the Qualification of Electors.'"

The Bill then passed, and was signed by Mr. Speaker.

Mr. Rogers moved, seconded by Mr. Clench, that Mr. Washburn and Mr. Dorland do carry up the said Bill to the Honorable the Legislative Council and request their concurrence.

Which was ordered accordingly.

On motion of Mr. Washburn, seconded by Mr. Clench, the House resolved itself into Committee to go into the consideration of the Bill for establishing Schools in the different Districts throughout this Province.

Mr. Speaker left the Chair.

Mr. Washburn was called to the Chair of the Committee.

Mr. Speaker resumed the Chair.

Mr. Washburn reported that the Committee had made a progress and directed him to ask leave to sit again to-morrow.

Leave was accordingly granted.

The House then adjourned to half past one o'clock in the afternoon. The House being met,

Mr. Washburn reported that they had carried up to the Honorable Legislative Council a Bill entitled "An Act for the more equal representation of the Commons of this Province in Parliament, and for the better defining the Qualification of Electors," and did request their concurrence.

The engrossed Bill furthering the cultivation and growth of Hemp within this Province was read for the third time.

On motion of Mr. Clench, seconded by Mr. Nellis,

Resolved, That this Bill do pass, and that the title be "An Act to amend an Act passed in the Forty-fourth year of His Majesty's Reign, entitled 'An Act for granting to His Majesty a certain sum of Money for the further encouragement of the growth and cultivation of Hemp within this Province, and the exportation thereof.' "

The Bill then passed, and was signed by Mr. Speaker.

Mr. Nellis moved, seconded by Mr. Hill, that Messrs. Wilkinson and Crysler do carry the said Bill up to the Legislative Council, and request their concurrence.

Mr. Wilkinson reported that they had carried up to the Legislative Council the said Bill, and did request their concurrence.

A Message from the Legislative Council by Mr. Burns, Master in Chancery. Mr. Speaker,

I am commanded by the Honorable Legislative Council to inform this House that they have returned a Bill sent up from this House entitled "An Act for the more speedy recovery of rents arising from the lands reserved for the Crown, and for the maintenance and support of a Protestant Clergy within this Province," which they have passed with some amendments, to which they request the concurrence of the House of Assembly.

And then he withdrew.

Which amendments were then read.

On motion of Mr. Rogers, seconded by Mr. Dorland, the House adjourned till twelve o'clock at noon to-morrow.

5 A.

Wednesday, 27th February, 1805.

Prayers were read.

Mr. Washburn moved, seconded by Mr. Mallory, that the House do now resolve itself into Committee to go into the consideration of the Bill for establishing Schools in the different Districts.

The House accordingly resolved itself into Committee to go into the further consideration of the said Bill.

Mr. Speaker left the Chair.

Mr. Wilkinson was called to the Chair of the Committee.

Mr. Speaker resumed the Chair.

Mr. Wilkinson reported that the Committee had made a progress, and desired him to ask for leave to sit again.

On the question being put for leave to sit again, it passed in the negative.

Mr. Sherwood, seconded by Mr. Mallory, moved that the House do resolve itself into Committee to go into the consideration of the amendments made by the Honorable Legislative Council in and to a Bill entitled "An Act for the more speedy recovery of the rents due on Crown and Clergy reserves."

On the question being put, the House was divided; Mr. Speaker then gave his vote that the House shall go into the consideration of the said amendments.

The House accordingly resolved itself into Committee.

Mr. Speaker left the Chair.

Mr. Mallory was called to the Chair of the Committee.

Mr. Speaker resumed the Chair.

Mr. Mallory reported that the Committee had directed him to inform the House that a Conference be requested with the Honorable the Legislative Council on the subject of the amendments made by them to the said Bill, which he was desired to report, whenever the House shall be pleased to receive the same.

The House then resolved that the Report be now received, which Report was then received and accepted, and ordered accordingly.

William Jarivs, Esquire, came to the Bar of the House and did inform Mr. Speaker that William Weekes, Esquire, had taken the Oath as prescribed by the Statute, and did sign the Roll.

Then David McGregor Rogers and Ralph Clench, Esquires, introduced William Weekes, Esquire, Knight, representing the Counties of Durham, Simcoe and East Riding of York, who took his seat accordingly.

Mr. Sherwood moved, seconded by Capt. Elliott, that Messrs. Rogers, McLean, Dorland and Weekes be a Committee to confer with the Honorable the Legislative Council on the amendments made by them in and to a Bill for the recovery of the Rents of Crown and Clergy Reserves, which was ordered accordingly.

Then Mr. Sherwood moved, seconded by Mr. Nellis, that Messrs Rogers and Elliott do wait upon the Honorable the Legislative Council, and inform them that this House requests a conference on the amendments made by them to the Bill for the recovery of Crown and Clergy Rents. Ordered accordingly.

A Message from the Honorable Legislative Council by Mr. Burns, Master in Chancery.

Mr. Speaker,—

I am commanded by the Honorable Legislative Council to inform this House that they have passed an Act to amend an Act passed in the forty-fourth year of His Majesty's Reign, entitled "An Act for granting to His Majesty a certain sum of money for the further encouragement of the growth and cultivation of Hemp within this Province, and the exportation thereof" without any amendment. And then he withdrew.

Mr. Rogers reported that they had carried up the Message requesting a conference with the Honorable Legislative Council on the subject matter of the amendments made by them in and to the Bill for the more speedy recovery of the Crown and Clergy Rents.

A written Message from the Honorable Legislative Council by Mr. Burns, Master in Chancery.

Mr. Speaker,—

I am directed by the Honorable Legislative Council to inform you that they have acceded to the Message sent unto them by the House of Assembly of this date, and that they have appointed a Committee to meet a Committee of the House of Assembly forthwith in the Council Chamber, in conference upon the amendments made in and to the Bill for the recovery of Crown and Clergy Rents.

Legislative Co. Chamber,   (Sd) Rich'd Cartwright,
   27th Feb'y 1805.   Speaker.

Members present: Mr. Speaker, Messrs. Clench, Nellis, Sherwood, McGregor, Crysler, Hill, Mallory.

Mr. Speaker then adjourned the House for want of a quorum.

Thursday, 28th February, 1805.

, Prayers were read.

The Committee of the House of Assembly appointed to confer with a Committee of the Honorable the Legislative Council on the amendments made in a Bill entitled "An Act for the speedy recovery of the Rents arising from the lands reserved for the Crown and for the maintenance and support of a Protestant Clergy within this Province" beg leave to report that the Committee of the Honorable the Legislative Council will agree to modify the first amendment so that Executors or Administrators shall not be liable to pay the rents due from the Testator or Intestate, unless they should have assets in their hands sufficient to answer the same at the time of its being demanded.

The Committee of the Legislative Council persist in the amendment made by them which goes to expunge the fourth clause of the Bill, laying it down as a principle from which they will not depart that Lessees shall pay rent from the date of their application; which amendment your Committee could not agree to.

All which is humbly submitted by order of the Committee.

York, 28th Feb'y 1805.   (Sd) D. McG. Rogers.

Which Report was accepted.

Mr. Weekes gave notice that he will move this House to-morrow, that it be expedient to enter into the consideration of the disquietude which prevails in this Province by reason of the administration of Public Affairs.

Mr. Rogers moved, seconded by Mr. Weekes, that this House do now resolve itself into Committee to take into their consideration the contingent account of the two Houses of Parliament, and that the Committee have power to send for such persons and papers as they shall judge necessary.

The House resolved itself into Committee accordingly.

Mr. Speaker left the Chair.

Mr. Weekes was called to the Chair of the Committee.

Mr. Speaker resumed the Chair.

Mr. Weekes reported that the Committee of the Whole House on taking into consideration the Contingent Accounts of the Legislative Council and the House of Assembly resolved that the Chairman do report progress, and ask leave to sit again to-morrow. Leave was accordingly granted.

Mr. Clench, seconded by Mr. McGregor, moved that Hugh Carpac, the person at present employed by this House as Messenger and Fire lighter, be recommended to be established as such with an annual allowance to be made him.

Which was ordered accordingly.

Mr. Clench moved, seconded by Mr. Crysler, that leave of absence be granted to Mr. Mallory for the present session of Parliament.

Leave of absence was granted accordingly.

On motion of Mr. Mallory, seconded by Mr. McGregor, the House adjourned till to-morrow at twelve o'clock.

Friday, 1st March, 1805.

Prayers were read.

Mr. Weekes moved, seconded by Mr. Rogers, that it is expedient for this House to enter into the consideration of the disquietude which prevails in the Province by reason of the administration of Public Offices.

On the question being put, thereupon a division took place; the names being called for they were taken down, and are as follows.

Yeas.	Nays.
MESSRS. MALLORY	MESSRS. McGREGOR
ROGERS	ELLIOTT
WASHBURN	COWAN
WEEKES	McLEAN
	SHERWOOD
	HILL
	DORLAND
	CRYSLER
	WILKINSON
	HOWARD

The same passed in the negative by a majority of six.

Agreeable to the Order of the Day the House resolved itself into Committee on the Contingent Accounts of both Houses of Parliament for the present Session.

Mr. Speaker left the Chair.

Mr. Weekes was called to the Chair of the Committee.

Mr. Speaker resumed the Chair.

Mr. Weekes reported that the Committee had gone through the consideration of the Contingent Accounts of the Legislative Council and this House, and that they had come to several resolutions thereon, which he was directed to submit to the House, and he read the Report in his place, and afterwards delivered the same in at the Table, where it was read throughout by the Clerk.

And the said Resolutions are as follows.

* Resolved, That it is the opinion of the Committee that there is due to sundry persons, agreeable to the annexed account sent down from the. Hon. the Legislative Council, and signed by their Speaker, for services performed during the present session, £27. 14. 4¾.

Resolved, That it is the opinion of the Committee that it will be expedient to advance the Clerk of the Legislative Council the sum of £20. to enable him to purchase a supply of stationery for the use of the ensuing session of Parliament.

Resolved, That it is the opinion of the Committee, that there is due to sundry persons, agreeable to the annexed account for articles furnished for the use of this House, and for services performed during the present Session, £104. 9. 1.

Resolved, That it is the opinion of the Committee that it is expedient to advance the sum of £30. to the Clerk of the House of Assembly to enable him to purchase a supply of stationery for the use of the next Session of Parliament.

On motion of Mr. Sherwood, seconded by Mr. Wilkinson,

Resolved, That this House doth concur in the foregoing resolutions reported from the Committee.

York, 27th February, 1805.

GOVERNMENT OF UPPER CANADA,
       To George Lawe,
              Gentleman Usher of the Black Rod.

No. 1.	To amount of William Allan's account for sundries furnished the House of Parliament	4.	2.	2½
No. 2.	To amount of Thos. Moseley's account for sundries furnished the Legislative Council	1.	1.	7
No. 3.	To amount of John Bassell's account for his attendance on the Legislative Council	11.	16.	3
No. 4.	To amount of John Bennett's account for copy of the Provincial Statutes for the Legislative Council...		12.	6
No. 5.	To amount of Eleanor Bassell's account for scrubbing the Legislative Council Chamber and Office	1.	17.	6
No. 6.	To amount of Phipp Aingers' account for cleaning the Stoves of the Legislative Council Chamber	2.	0.	7½
No. 7.	To Caleb Humphrey's account for repairing the Gallery between the Parliament Buildings	1.	3.	9

£22.   14.   4¾

Amounting to Twenty-two Pounds, Fourteen Shillings and Fourpence Three Farthings.

To the Clerk of the Legislative Council for extra allowance to Copying Clerks 5.   0.   0

(Signed) Richard Cartwright,
                         Speaker.

Commons House of Assembly,
       28th February, 1805.

Contingent Account of the Honorable House of Assembly for the first Session of the Fourth Parliament.

To Duncan Cameron's account	£6.	3.	9
To Duncan Cameron as Executor to Judge Cochrane	39.	2.	2½
To John Bennett's account	5.	15.	0
To Henry Hale's account		15.	0
To John McBeath's account	7.	4.	0
To Postage of a letter from the Clerk of the Peace, Western District, enclosing the Assessment rate		2.	3
To The Doorkeeper's account	5.	8.	1
To Isaac Columbes's account	1.	5.	10½
To Philip Clinger's account	2.	0.	0
To Hugh Garfrae, Messenger's account	10.	0.	0
To John Dettor's* for extra copying	3.	10	6
To William Connors for Copying	2.	10.	0
To Charles Willcocks for Copying	3.	16.	0
To William Baldwin for copying	7.	0.	0
To allowance made the Clerk to complete the business of the present Session	10.	0.	0
	£104.	9.	1

The Honorable the Assembly in account current with Donald MacLean, Clerk, for stationery furnished for the use of the first session of the fourth Parliament.

Dr.

To cash paid Duncan Cameron for stationery bought for the use of the first session of the fourth Parliament, as per receipt	£23.	17.	6
To Mr. Neilson's account for parchment, as per receipt ..	6.	2.	6
To Paid Charles Willcocks for copying done for the use of the present session, as per receipt	18.	0.	0
To Paid William Baldwin for copying done for the use of the present session, as per receipt	7.	0.	0
	£55.	0	0

Cr.

By cash received by virtue of an Address from the House of Assembly, dated 6th March, 1804, for the purpose of purchasing stationery for the use of the present session	£30.	0.	0
By cash received by virtue of an Address presented to His Excellency, the Lieutenant Governor, from the House of Assembly, dated the 19th Feb'y, 1805, on account of Copying Clerks, being the sum allowed by law annually for that purpose	25.	0.	0
	£55.	0.	0

* Detlor?

On motion of Captain Cowan, seconded by Mr. McGregor,

Resolved, that an humble Address be presented to His Excellency, the Lieutenant Governor, to request that he will be pleased to issue his Warrant in favor of George Lawe, Gentleman Usher of the Black Rod, for the sum of £22. 14. 4¾, to enable him to pay the Contingent Account of the Legislative Council during this Session; and also that His Excellency may be pleased to issue his Warrant in favor of James Clarke, Esquire, Clerk of the Legislative Council, for the sum of £25, for the purpose of paying extra Copying Clerks employed by him during this session, and for the purpose of purchasing stationery for the use of the next session of Parliament. And that His Excellency will be further pleased to issue his Warrant in favor of Donald McLean, Esquire, Clerk of the House of Assembly, for the sum of £104. 9. 1, for the purpose of paying the extra Copying Clerks employed by him this Session, and the other contingent accounts of the House of Assembly during this Session of the Legislature. And that His Excellency be also pleased to advance the Clerk of the House of Assembly the sum of £30, to enable him to purchase stationery for the use of the next Session of Parliament.

Then Mr. Wilkinson moved, seconded by Captain Cowan, that Messrs. Weekes and McLean be a Committee to draft an Address to His Excellency, the Lieutenant Governor, praying that he may be pleased to issue his Warrants for the payment of the several contingencies of both Houses of Parliament for the present Session, and for the purchase of stationery for both Houses for the ensuing Session of the Legislature, which was ordered accordingly.

Mr. Weekes reported that the Committee appointed to draft an Address to His Excellency, the Lieutenant Governor, had done so, which they were ready to submit to the House whenever it should be pleased to receive the same.

The House then resolved that the said Address be now received.

Mr. Weekes then read the Address in his place, which he then delivered in at the Table, and it was again read by the Clerk, and is as follows:

To His Excellency Peter Hunter, Esquire, Lieutenant Governor of the Province of Upper Canada and Lieutenant commanding His Majesty's Forces in the Provinces of Upper and Lower Canada, &c, &c, &c.

May it please Your Excellency,

We, His Majesty's most dutiful and loyal subjects, the Commons of Upper Canada in Parliament assembled, do most humbly pray that it may please Your Excellency to issue your Warrant directed to the Receiver General, requiring him to pay unto Mr. George Lawe, Gentleman Usher of the Black Rod, the sum of twenty-two Pounds, fourteen shillings and fourpence three farthings, in order to enable him to answer and satisfy certain contingent expenses of the Legislative Council during the present Session; and also that it may please Your Excellency to issue your Warrant, directed to the Receiver General requiring him to pay unto James Clarke, Esquire, Clerk of the Legislative Council, the sum of five pounds, to enable him to answer and satisfy the wages of extra Copying Clerks employed during the present session of Parliament; and the further sum of Twenty pounds to enable him to provide a supply of stationery for the use of the ensuing Session of Parliament, and that Your Excellency be further pleased to issue your Warrant, directed to the Receiver General, requiring him to pay unto Donald MacLean,

Esquire, Clerk of the Commons House of Assembly, the sum of One hundred and four pounds, nine shillings and one penny, in order to enable him to answer and satisfy the Contingent expenses of the Commons House of Assembly, including the wages of extra Copying Clerks during the present Session; and also Your Excellency's Warrant to the Receiver General, requiring him to pay the sum of Thirty pounds to enable him to purchase a supply of stationery for the use of the ensuing Session of Parliament, which several sums of money the Commons will make good to Your Excellency the next Session of Parliament.
Commons House of Assembly,
1st March, 1805.

Then, on motion of Captain Cowan, seconded by Captain Elliott,
Ordered, That the said Address be now engrossed.
The said Address as engrossed was then read, which passed, and was signed by Mr. Speaker.
On motion of Mr. Rogers, seconded by Mr. Weekes,
Ordered, That Captain Cowan and Mr. McGregor do present the said Address to His Excellency the Lieutenant Governor.
On motion of Mr. Howard, seconded by Mr. Crysler, the House adjourned.

Saturday, 2nd March, 1805.

Prayers were read.
Captain Cowan and Mr. McGregor reported that in obedience to the Order of the House they had waited upon His Excellency, the Lieutenant Governor, and presented to him the Address of this House voted yesterday.
To which His Excellency was pleased to return the following. answer:
Gentlemen,
I accede to the Address of the House of Assembly of the 1st of March, 1805, and shall issue my Warrants accordingly.
York, 2nd March, 1805.
A Message from His Excellency, the Lieutenant Governor, by Mr. George Lawe, Gentleman Usher of the Black Rod.
Mr. Speaker,
I am commanded by His Excellency, the Lieutenant Governor, to acquaint this Honorable House that it is His Excellency's pleasure that the Members thereof do forthwith attend upon His Excellency in the Legislative Council Chamber.
Accordingly Mr. Speaker with the House went up to attend His Excellency, when His Excellency was pleased to give in His Majesty's name the Royal assent to the following Public and Private Bills:
An Act to regulate the Trial of Controverted Elections or Returns of Members to serve in Parliament.
An Act to alter certain parts of An Act passed in the Forty-second year of His Majesty's Reign, entitled "An Act to provide for the Administration of Justice in the District of Newcastle."
An Act to make Provision for Further Appointments of Parish and Town Officers throughout this Province.
An Act for the Relief of Insolvent Debtors.
An Act to regulate the Curing, Packing and Inspection of Beef and Pork.

An Act for altering the Time of Issuing Licences for the keeping of a house or any other place of public entertainment, or for the Retailing of Wine, Brandy, Rum or any other Spirituous Liquors, or for the having or using of Stills for the purpose of distilling Spirituous Liquors; and for repealing so much of an Act passed in the Forty-third year of His Majesty's Reign, as relates to the periods of paying into the hands of the Receiver General the moneys collected by the Inspector of each and every District throughout this Province for such Licences.

An Act to afford Relief to those who may be entitled to claim Lands in this Province, as Heirs or Devisees of the Nominees of the Crown, in cases where no Patent hath issued for such Lands.

Mr. Speaker then said,

May it please Your Excellency to approve of the three Bills which the House of Assembly, with the concurrence of the Legislative Council, have passed for aid to His Majesty.

An Act to ratify and confirm certain Provisional Articles of Agreement entered into by the respective Commissioners of this Province and Lower Canada at Montreal on the fifth day of July, one thousand eight hundred and four, relative to duties, and for carrying the same into effect; and also to continue an Act passed in the Thirty-ninth year of His Majesty's Reign, and continued by an Act passed in the Forty-first year of His Majesty's Reign.

An Act for applying a certain sum of money therein mentioned to make good certain moneys issued and advanced by His Majesty through the Lieutenant Governor in pursuance of two Addresses.

An Act to amend an Act passed in the Forty-fourth year of His Majesty's Reign, entitled "An Act for granting to His Majesty a certain sum of money for the further encouragement of the Growth and cultivation of Hemp within this Province, and the exportation thereof.

And then His Excellency was pleased to make the following Speech to both Houses.

Honorable Gentlemen of the Legislative Council
and
Gentlemen of the House of Assembly.

The ability and diligence with which you have conducted the business of the Public enables me, at this early period, to close this Session of the Legislature.

I have with pleasure assented in His Majesty's name to the Bill by which the Lands bestowed by the bounty of the Crown will be transmitted and secured to the Heirs, and according to the will of the original objects of that bounty.

The regulations which have been enacted respecting the improvement and management of some of the most essential articles of our produce meet with our approbation, and, I trust, will contribute to render that produce a permanent source of supply and of wealth to this Province.

The other laws which have passed, will, I hope, effectuate the salutary purposes for which they were intended, and prove, that in the discharge of your duty, you have not been unmindful of the important trust committed to your care.

I now close this Session of the Legislature, fully confiding that in your respective Counties and Districts as Magistrates or as private individuals you will at all times give additional force and effect to the laws of this Province by your exertions and example.

After which the Honorable Speaker of the Legislative Council said:—
Gentlemen of the Legislative Council,
                                and
Gentlemen of the House of Assembly:—
It is His Excellency the Lieutenant Governor's will and pleasure that the Provincial Parliament be prorogued until Monday the eighth day of April next, to be then here held, and this Provincial Parliament is accordingly prorogued until Monday the eighth day of April next.

[I do hereby certify that the above and what is written on the foregoing pages is a true copy of the Journal of the House of Assembly of Upper Canada, being the first session of the Fourth Provincial Parliament, assembled at York on the first day of February last, agreeable to the Proclamation of His Excellency, Peter Hunter, Esquire, Lieutenant Governor of the Province of Upper Canada, and Lieutenant General Commanding His Majesty's Forces in the Province of Upper and Lower Canada, and prorogued by His Excellency the 2nd day of March last.
York, Upper Canada,   Donald MacLean,
    27th April, 1805.   Clerk Assembly.]

        [Certified to be a true copy.

                        George Mayer,
            Librarian and Keeper of the Records,
                        Colonial Office, 25th August, 1855.]

JOURNAL

OF THE

HOUSE OF ASSEMBLY

OF

UPPER CANADA

From the fourth day of February to the
third day of March,

1806.

Both days inclusive.

In the forty-sixth year of the Reign of

KING GEORGE THE THIRD.

Being the second session of the fourth provincial parliament
of this province.

JOURNAL

OF THE

HOUSE OF ASSEMBLY

OF

UPPER CANADA

1806.

PETER HUNTER, Lieutenant Governor.

PROCLAMATION.

George the Third, by the Grace of God of the United Kingdom of Great Britain and Ireland King, Defender of the Faith.

To Our beloved and faithful Legislative Councillors of Our Province of Upper Canada, and to Our Knights, Citizens and Burgesses of Our said Province to the Provincial Parliament at the Town of York on the Eighth Day of April to be commenced, held, called and elected, and to every of you, Greeting.

Whereas by Our Proclamation bearing date the Second Day of March last we though fit, by and with the advice of Our Executive Council, to prorogue Our said Provincial Parliament until the Eighth day of this present Month of April, at which time in Our Town of York you were held and constrained to appear,— But We taking into Our Royal consideration the ease and convenience of Our Loving Subjects have thought fit, by and with the advice and consent of Our Executive Council to relieve you and each of you of your attendance at the time aforesaid, hereby convoking, and by these presents enjoining you and each of you that on the Fifteenth Day of May next ensuing you meet us in Our Provincial Parliament in Our Town of York there to take into consideration the state and welfare of Our said Province of Upper Canada, and there to do as may seem necessary,—Herein fail not.

In testimony whereof we have caused these Our Letters to be made patent, and the Great Seal of Our said Province to be hereunto affixed:—Witness Our Trusty and Well Beloved Peter Hunter, Esquire, Lieutenant Governor of our said Province, and Lieutenant General Commanding Our Forces in Our Province of Upper and Lower Canada, at York, this Second Day of April in the Year of Our Lord One Thousand Eight Hundred and Five, and in the Forty-Fifth Year of Our Reign.

P.H.

Wm. Jarvis, Sec'y.

By a further Proclamation of His Excellency Peter Hunter, Esquire, Lieutenant Governor of the Province of Upper Canada, and Lieutenant General Commanding His Majesty's Forces in the Province of Upper and Lower Canada &c. &s. &c. dated at York the Tenth Day of May, One Thousand Eight Hundred and Five the meeting of the Legislative Council and House of Assembly stands prorogued to the Twenty-First Day of June, One Thousand Eight Hundred and Five.

By a further Proclamation of His Excellency Peter Hunter, Esquire, Lieutenant Governor of the Province of Upper Canada, and Lieutenant General Commanding His Majesty's Forces in the Provinces of Upper and Lower Canada &c. &c. &c. dated at the Town of York the Fourteenth Day of June, One Thousand Eight Hundred and Five, the meeting of the Legislative Council and House of Assembly stands prorogued to the Twenty-ninth Day of July, One Thousand Eight Hundred and Five.

By a further Proclamation of His Excellency Peter Hunter, Esquire, Lieutenant Governor of the Province of Upper Canada, and Lieutenant General Commanding His Majesty's Forces in the Provinces of Upper and Lower Canada &c. &c. &c. dated at York, the Twenty-sixth day of July, One Thousand Eight Hundred and Five, the meeting of the Legislative Council and House of Assembly stands prorogued to the Sixth Day of September, One Thousand Eight Hundred and Five.

By a further Proclamation of His Excellency Peter Hunter, Esquire, Lieutenant Governor of the Province of Upper Canada, and Lieutenant General Commanding His Majesty's Forces in the Province of Upper and Lower Canada &c. &c &c. dated at York, the Thirty-First Day of August One Thousand Eight Hundred and Five the meeting of the Legislative Council and House of Assembly stands prorogued to the Fifteenth Day of October, One Thousand Eight Hundred and Five.

ALEX'R GRANT, President.

PROCLAMATION.

George the Third, by the Grace of God of the United Kingdom of Great Britain and Ireland King, Defender of the Faith.

To Our Beloved and Faithful Legislative Councillors of Our Province of Upper Canada, and to Our Knights, Citizens and Burgesses of Our said Province to the Parliament of Our Town of York on the Fifteenth Day of October, to be commenced, held called and elected, and to every of you, Greeting.

Know ye that we have thought fit, by and with the advice of Our Executive Council of Our said Province, to convoke, and by these presents do convoke and enjoin you and each of you that on the Fifteenth Day of October next ensuing you meet us in Our Provincial Parliament in Our Town of York, there to take into consideration the state and welfare of Our said Province of Upper Canada, and there in to do as may seem necessary. Herein Fail not.

In testimony whereof we have caused these- Our Letters to be made patent and the Great Seal of Our said Province to be hereunto affixed. Witness Our Trusty and Well beloved Alexander Grant, Esquire, Our President administering the Government of Our said Province of Upper Canada at York, this Seventeenth day of September, in the Year of Our Lord One Thousand Eight Hundred and Five, and Forty-Fifth of Our Reign.

A.G.

Wm. Jarvis, Sec'y.

By a further Proclamation of His Honor Alexander Grant, Esquire, President administering the Government of the Province of Upper Canada &c. &c. &c. dated at York the Eleventh Day of October, One Thousand Eight Hundred and Five, the meeting of the Legislative Council and House of Assembly stands prorogued to the thirteenth day of December, One Thousand Eight Hundred and Five.

By a-further Proclamation of His Honor Alex'r Grant, Esquire, President administering the Government of the Province of Upper Canada, dated at York the Fourteenth day of November One Thousand Eight Hundred and Five, the meeting of the Legislative Council and House of Assembly stands prorogued to the Thirteenth day of December, One Thousand Eight Hundred and Five.

By a further Proclamation of His Honor Alex'r Grant, Esquire, President administering the Government of the Province of Upper Canada &c. &c. dated at York the Twenty-Sixth day of December One Thousand Eight Hundred and Five, the meeting of the Legislative Council and House of Assembly stands prorogued to the First day of February, One Thousand Eight Hundred and Six.

ALEX'R GRANT, President,

PROCLAMATION.

George the Third, by the Grace of God of the United Kingdom of Great Britain and Ireland King, Defender of the Faith.

To Our Beloved and Faithful Legislative Councillors of Our Province of Upper Canada, and to Our Knights, Citizens and Burgesses of Our said Province to the Provincial Parliament at Our Town of York on the First Day of February, to be commenced, held, called and elected, and to every of you, Greeting.

Whereas by Our Proclamation bearing date the Twenty-Sixth Day of December last we thought fit, by and with the advice of Our Executive Council to convoke Our said Provincial Parliament to meet us on the First day of February for the actual dispatch of Public Business, at which time in Our Town of York you were held and constrained to appear, but we taking into Our Royal consideration the ease and convenience of Our Loving Subjects have thought fit by and with the consent of Our Executive Council to relieve you and each of you of your attendance at the time aforesaid, hereby convoking, and by these presents enjoining you and each of you that on Tuesday the Fourth day of February you will meet us in Our Provincial Parliament in Our Town of York for the actual dispatch of Public Business, there to take into consideration the state and welfare of Our said Province of Upper Canada, and there to do as may seem necessary. Herein Fail not.

In testimony whereof we have caused these Our Letters to be made patent, and the Great Seal of Our said Province to be hereunto affixed.

Witness Our trusty and well beloved Alexander Grant Esquire, Our President administering the Government of Our said Province of Upper Canada, at York, this Thirty-First Day of January in the Year of Our Lord One Thousand Eight Hundred and Six, and Forty-Sixth Year of Our Reign.

Wm. Jarvis, Sec'y.   A.G.

HOUSE OF ASSEMBLY, UPPER CANADA.

Tuesday, 4th February, 1806.

At the Second Session of the Fourth Parliament of Upper Canada, begun and held in the Town of York on Tuesday the Fourth day of February, in the Forty-Sixth Year of the Reign of Our Sovereign Lord George the Third, by the

Grace of God of the United Kingdom of Great Britain and Ireland, King, Defender of the Faith, and in the Year of Our Lord One Thousand Eight Hundred and Six.

His Excellency the late Peter Hunter, Esquire, Lieutenant Governor, and. His Honor Alexander Grant Esquire, President, did by their several proclamations as annexed prorogue the meeting of the Provincial Parliament until this day.

The House being met, prayers were read.

A Message by Mr. George Lawe, Gentleman Usher of the Black Rod.

Mr. Speaker,

It is His Honor the President's pleasure that this Honorable House do immediately attend him in the Honorable Legislative Council Chamber.

The House went up accordingly, and being returned,

Mr. Speaker reported that the House had attended His Honor the President in the Legislative Council Chamber, where his Honor had been pleased to open the present Session by a most gracious Speech to both Houses, and that to prevent mistakes he had obtained for the information of the House a copy of His Honor's Speech, which was read as follows.

Honorable Gentlemen of the Legislative Council
and
Gentlemen of the House of Assembly.

By the much lamented death of Lieutenant Governor Hunter the administrationtion of the Government of this Province hath devolved on me. I most sincerely condole with you on that melancholy event. His faithful and meritorious services to the Public in this part of His Majesty's Dominions will be long felt and remembered. It shall be my endeavour to imitate and follow his example.

Since the last Session of this Legislature, Commissioners have been appointed for carrying into effect the provisions of an Act for affording relief to those persons who may be entitled to claim lands in this Province as Heirs or Devisees of the Nominees of the Crown. To such lands I make no doubt by the exertions and abilities of those Gentlemen to whom that important trust is delegated the Public will soon see the most important benefits from the operations of that Statutory Law.

I forbear on the present occasion to point out particular objects for your deliberations, being convinced that your knowledge of the respective situations of His Majesty's Subjects whom you here represent will be the surest guide to direct you in the enacting of such laws as may still be necessary for their security and comfort (as well as in the continuing of laws heretofore made but now about to expire) whose beneficial effects we have already felt and experienced.

Gentlemen of the House of Assembly,

I have ordered the Public Accounts to be laid before you, not doubting but that you will pay that attention in the examination of them which the nature, of the subject requires.

Honorable Gentlemen of the Legislative Council
and
Gentlemen of the House of Assembly,

It is with the highest satisfaction that I congratulate you on the great Naval Victory which lately hath crowned the success of His Majesty's Arms, though our joy is not unmixed, as we have deeply to regret the loss of one of the bravest and most able defenders of his King and of His Country.

May Great Britain, Our Parent State, ever have such men to fight her battles, and may she by the blessing of Providence be enabled to defend herself and her widely extended Dominions from the assaults of her enemies, and transmit her Territories with her invaluable Constitution unimpaired to the latest posterity.

Mr. Speaker then adjourned the House for want of a quorum.

Present: Mr. Speaker, Messrs. Dorland, Nellis, Howard, Hill, Weekes, Mallory, McLean, Cowan, Elliott.

Wednesday, 5th February, 1806.

Prayers were read.

Mr. Jarvis came to the Bar of this House and there did inform Mr. Speaker that D'Arcy Bolton, Esquire, did take the Oath as prescribed by the Statute, and did sign the Roll.

Then Allan McLean and Matthew Elliott, Esquires, introduced D'Arcy Boulton, Esquire, Knight, representing the County of Stormont and Russell and took his seat accordingly.

Mr. Nellis then moved, seconded by Mr. Hill, that Messrs. Weekes, McLean, Dorland and Capt. Elliott be a Committee to draft an Address to His Honor the President in answer to his Speech.

Mr. Weekes moved in amendment, seconded by Capt. Elliott, that Mr. Nellis, Mr. Howard, and Mr. Mallory be added after the word Elliott to Mr. Nellis' motion. Which was carried in the affirmative, and ordered accordingly.

On motion of Mr. Weekes, seconded by Mr. Mallory, the House adjourned.

Thursday, 6th February, 1806.

Prayers were read.

Capt. Elliott, from the Committee appointed to draw up an Address of thanks to His Honor the President for His Speech to both Houses in opening the present Session, reported that the Committee had prepared an Address accordingly, which he was directed to submit to the House whenever it should be pleased to receive the same.

Ordered, That the Report be now received.

And he read the report in his place, and then delivered in the same at the Table, where it was again read by the Clerk once throughout, as follows:

To the Honorable Alexander Grant, Esquire, President, administering the Government of the Province of Upper Canada, &c.

May it please Your Honor,

We, His Majesty's most dutiful and loyal subjects, the Commons of Upper Canada in Parliament assembled, beg leave to present to you our gratulations on your accession to the administration of the Government of this Province.

We affect not to describe to you the career in which disinterested virtue may display itself in exercising the high prerogative of the Representative of a gracious and benevolent Sovereign, but we cherish the fond hope that you, in your relation to Majesty and from your experience in the Public concerns of this Country, will in the administration of the Government of it preserve unsullied this important trust.

We derive much pleasure from being informed that the Act of the last Session of this Parliament for affording relief to those persons who may be entitled to claim Lands in this Province as Heirs or Devisees of the Crown in cases where no patent

6 A.

hath issued for such Lands, will in its operation prove a salutary law, as we feel impressed with the principle that the protection of the subject and the security of his property ought to be legibly evinced in every act of legislation in which a regard to our happy constitution can find either ascendency or support.

We shall with cheerful assiduity devote our attention to the Public Accounts, and shall feel ourselves happy in submitting to you such observations as may be deemed essential, either in the retrenchment of the expenditure of the Public moneys or in devising the means of a more necessary application of them.

We feel more than ordinary pleasure in your communication of His Majesty's late Naval Victory, and though we may much regret the fall of the illustrious Nelson in that action, yet we cannot refrain from expressing our sensations of joy. May our Navy be permanent, and its successes perpetual.

Commons House of Assembly,
                6th February, 1806.   (Signed) Alex. McDonell,
                                                                                    Speaker.

On motion of Mr. Weekes, seconded by Mr. Solicitor General,

Ordered, That the Address be engrossed.

The Address as engrossed was then read, passed, and signed by Mr. Speaker.

On motion of Mr. Nellis, seconded by Mr. Dorland,

Ordered, That Captain Cowan, Mr. Howard and Mr. Mallory do wait upon His Honor, the President, to know when he will be pleased to receive this House with its address.

Captain Cowan, accompanied by the other messengers, reported that in obedience to the order of this House they had waited upon His Honor, the President, to know His Honor's pleasure when he would receive the House with its address; and that His Honor was pleased to appoint this day at three o'clock in the afternoon to receive the House.

Mr. Speaker then read a paper by permission of the House, which was ordered to be inserted in the Journal, and is as follows, viz.

The Speaker begs the indulgence of the House to have inserted on its Journals that he does not concur in opinion with the House in the new mode which it has adopted in Addressing the President: it has been the uniform and established practice in addressing Presidents administering a Government to say "To His Honor," and not "To the Honorable." The former appellation, the Speaker humbly conceives to be more respectful, and more comprehensive than the latter. Mr. President Russell was invariably addressed by the former appellation during his administration of the Government of this Province; as Mr. President Dunn actually is in that of Lower Canada.

At the Hour appointed Mr. Speaker attended by the House went up to his Honorable President with the Address of this House.

And being returned, Mr. Speaker reported that the House had attended upon His Honor with its Address, to which His Honor had been pleased to make the following answer:

Gentlemen of the House of Assembly,

I return you my best thanks for your respectful Address, and have no doubt but that your deliberations and exertions will effectually promote the happiness and prosperity of His Majesty's subjects in this Province.

On motion of Mr. Nellis, seconded by Mr. Hill, the House adjourned.

Friday, 7th February, 1806.

Prayers were read.

Mr. Weekes moved, seconded by Mr. Dorland, for leave to bring in on Wednesday next a Bill to amend an Act passed in the Forty-third year of the King, entitled "An Act for the more equal representation of the Commons of this Province in Parliament, and for the better defining the qualification of Electors." Leave was accordingly given.

On motion of Captain Cowan, seconded by Mr. McLean, the House adjourned.

Saturday, 8th February, 1806.

Prayers were read.

Mr. Weekes moved, seconded by Mr. Nellis, that the Petition brought up from Mr. Mallory for the relief of the People called Methodists be now read.

Accordingly the said Petition was read by the Clerk at the Table, and is as follows:

To the Honorable House of Commons for the Province of Upper Canada in Session assembled.

The Petition of the Religious Community called Methodists, Humbly Showeth,

That the Members of the Methodist Society in this Province of Upper Canada are numerous, and a large majority of the principal ones are of those people called U. E. Loyalists, or their descendants, having fled from their former homes or habitations and joined the Royal British Standard, to which they have since firmly adhered, and in whose defence, should the necessity of the case again require it, Your Petitioners trust their loyalty in maintaining the rights of the best of Sovereigns would be as conspicuous as it heretofore has been.

Your Petitioners being liable to all the Statutes, Duties, Services, pains and penalties with those of other religious societies in this Province, and not having an equal participation with them in their religious rites, which we, Your Petitioners, think a great grievance, having confidence in the friendship of many of your respectable body with whom we are acquainted, and hoping the rest with whom me are not acquainted to be equally friendly, have presumed once more to solicit your Honorable House among whom we know there are men well acquainted with our religious tenets and also our sufferings—we, Your Petitioners, have not the least doubt from the liberality of your House but that every step will be taken, and everything done for us, that can consistently with our glorious Constitution. At the same time we would not forget to offer you our sincere thanks for your kind disposition, manifested towards us on the presentment of our former Petition.

We, Your Petitioners, therefore humbly pray that an Act may be passed in our favor, giving authority to our preachers, most of whom are Missionaries from the States, and a number more who are residents in this Province regularly ordained, to solemnize the religious rites of Marriage, as well as to confirm all past marriages performed by them.

This requisition we, Your Petitioners, pray may be taken into your serious consideration, and we trust that our request will appear so reasonable that its purport will meet your unanimous approbation, while ease will be given to the minds and consciences of a numerous body of the Inhabitants of this Province.

And we, Your Petitioners, will then as now and shall as in duty bound ever pray.

(Signed)   Samuel Coates,
                  John Embury,
                  Jeremiah Lovess*,
                  and about 235 others.

Mr. Dorland then moved, seconded by Mr. Nellis, for leave to bring in on Tuesday next a Bill for removing doubts respecting the affirmation of the people called Quakers. Leave was accordingly granted.

The Clerk of this House has the honor of informing Mr. Speaker and the House that the Clerks of the Peace for the different Districts in this Province did send him returns of all the rateable property in their respective Districts, in compliance with the Eighth section of the Act for the more uniform collection of Assessments throughout this Province, except the Clerk of the Peace for the Western District.

Mr. Speaker then ordered the different returns received from the Clerks of the Peace to be laid on the Table and to be entered in a book to be of record in this House.

Captain Eliott, seconded by Mr. Mallory, moved for leave to bring in on Friday next a Bill for making provisions for the laying out and repairing the Roads and Bridges throughout this Province. Leave was accordingly given.

Mr. Weekes gave notice that he will on Monday next move this House to resolve itself into a Committee to take into consideration the state of the Province.

Mr. Howard moved, seconded by Mr. Dorland for leave to bring in a Bill on Friday next to revise an Act passed in the Forty-third year of the King, relative to Assessments and Rates, and to make further provisions for the same. Accordingly leave was granted.

Mr. Mallory, seconded by Mr. Howard, then moved for leave to bring in a Bill on Friday next to give relief to a Religious Society called Methodists throughout this Province. Leave was accordingly given.

On motion of Mr. Dorland, seconded by Mr. Nellis, the House adjourned until Monday next.

Monday, 10th February, 1806.

Prayers were read.

Ordered, That when the copy of an Address from this House is sent to the Secretary of the Governor, Lieutenant Governor, or person administering the Government for his perusal to be prepared with his answer to such address, the Clerk do add the name of the Speaker thereto, viz. "(Signed) B. C."

Agreeably to the notice given,

Mr. Weekes moved, seconded by Mr. Mallory, that the House do now resolve itself into a Committee to take into consideration the state of the Province.

The House accordingly resolved itself into Committee.

The Speaker left the Chair.

Mr. Howard was called to the Chair of the Committee.

Mr. Speaker resumed the Chair.

Mr. Howard reported that the Committee had made some progress, and had directed him to ask for leave to sit again this day.

*Loveless.

Ordered, that the said Committee have leave to sit again this day.

Mr. Weekes then moved, seconded by Mr. Howard, that the Committee appointed to take into consideration the state of the Province have leave to call before them such witnesses and to examine such papers as may be necessary on their deliberation of this question.

The House then resolved, That the Committee have power to send for persons and papers.

Mr. Weekes moved, seconded by Mr. Dorland, that the House do now resolve itself into Committee to go into the further consideration of the state of the Province.

The House accordingly resolved itself into Committee.

Mr. Speaker left the Chair.

Mr. Howard again took the Chair of the Committee.

Mr. Speaker resumed the Chair.

Mr. Howard reported that the Committee had made some progress, and directed him to move for leave to sit again to-morrow.

Ordered, That the said Committee have leave to sit again to-morrow.

On motion of Mr. Dorland, seconded by Mr. Washburn, the House adjourned.

Tuesday, 11th February, 1806.

Prayers were read.

Mr. Howard moved, seconded by Mr. Nellis, that the Petition from the Inhabitants of the District of Johnstown be now read.

The said Petition was then read, and is as follows, viz.

To the Honorable the House of Assembly for the Province of Upper Canada.

The Petition of the subscribers, Inhabitants of the District of Johnstown in said Province, humbly represents,

That the District of Johnstown extends about fifty-six miles on the River St. Lawrence, that the Counties of Grenville and Leeds are the only inhabited Counties in said District.

That the County of Leeds originally contained ten Townships, two of which Escott, and Yonge, are now comprised in one; that the County of Grenville contains only seven Townships, whose population in the whole is not more than half so great as that of the County of Leeds. That the Court House and Gaol in the District of Johnstown are situated in the Town of Johnstown in the County of Grenville, within seven miles of the division line between the said District and the Eastern District. That the said Court House and Gaol were erected in pursuance of an Act passed in the Thirty-second year of the King for the express purpose of accommodating the inhabitants of that part of the Province, then known by the name of the Eastern District. That since the last mentioned period the present District of Johnstown has been formed by dividing the said Eastern District conformably to an Act passed in the Thirty-eighth year of the King, entitled "An Act for the better division of the Province." That the remote situation of the said Court House and Gaol from the centre of the said District of Johnstown precluded in a great degree the inhabitants of said District from enjoying the conveniences which the Legislature had undoubtedly in view when the last mentioned Act was framed. That previous to the division of the Eastern District before mentioned the General Quarter Sessions of the Peace were alternately holden at Cornway and Johnstown, and the inhabitants of the said District of Johnstown attended the said Session as Jurymen only twice a year at the said Court House in Johnstown, that since the said division the said inhabitants are obliged to attend the General Quarter Sessions of the Peace to serve on Juries four times in each year, and to travel the same distance for that purpose as formerly. That if the Court House and Gaol were placed in a more central situation the expense and the trouble of attending the Court to serve on Juries would be more equally divided and the benefits intended to be granted by the said Act of the Thirty-eighth of the King would be more generally experienced. That the said Court House and Gaol in the Town of Johnstown is in a ruinous and almost irreparable state.

Your Petitioners therefore humbly pray that Honorable House of Assembly to form a Bill calculated to enable the inhabitants of the said District of Johnstown to build a new Gaol and Courthouse near or about Mr. Daniel Jones's Mill in the front of the first Concession of Elizabethtown in the County of Leeds aforesaid. Your Petitioners humbly conceive that the said situation is the most eligible of any in the said District of Johnstown for the purpose aforesaid, being at the distance of twenty-three miles from the lower extremity of said District, and as far towards the centre of the same as convenience will allow; and your Petitioners as in duty bound will ever pray.

                    (Signed)   Wm. Buell,
                                        David Manhart,
                                        Lewis P. Sherwood,
                                              and about 107 others.
District of Johnstown,
    December 20th, 1806.

Mr. Howard then moved, seconded by Mr. Nellis, for leave to bring in a Bill on Thursday next to enable the inhabitants in the District of Johnstown to erect and build a Court House and Gaol in the Township of Elizabethtown.

Leave was accordingly granted.

Then was read for the first time a Bill for removing doubts respecting the affirmation of the people called Quakers.

Mr. Nellis moved, seconded by Mr. Dorland, that the said Bill be read a second time to-morrow. Ordered accordingly.

Mr. Weekes then moved, seconded by Mr. Mallory, that this House do now resolve itself into Committee to take into their further consideration the state of the Province.

The House accordingly resolved itself into Committee.

Mr. Speaker left the Chair.

Mr. Howard took the Chair of the Committee.

Mr. Speaker resumed the Chair.

And Mr. Howard reported that the Committee had made some progress, and had directed him to ask for leave to sit again to-morrow.

The House accordingly resolved that the Committee have leave to sit again to-morrow.

Read, A Letter from the Speaker of the Honorable the Legislative Council to the Speaker of this House as follows, viz.

Legislative Council Chamber,
11th February.

Mr. Speaker,—

I think it proper to inform you that Wm. Warren Baldwin Esquire, hath been duly appointed a Master in Chancery, and as such will be employed in making the necessary communications from the Legislative Council to the House of Assembly during the present Session.

I have the honor to be, with much regard,

Sir,

Your Very Obedient Servant,

Richard Cartwright,
Speaker, Legislative Co.

The Honorable the Speaker
of the House of Assembly.

On motion of Mr. Dorland, seconded by Capt. Cowan, the House adjourned.

Wednesday, 12th February, 1806.

Prayers were read.

Mr. Weekes moved, seconded by Mr. Mallory that so much of the Order of the Day as gives leave to bring in a Bill this day to alter and amend an Act made for the more equal representation of the people and for the qualification of Electors be discharged, and leave given to bring in the same on Saturday next.

Ordered accordingly.

Then was read for the second time the Bill for removing debts respecting the affirmation of the people called Quakers.

Mr. Nellis moved, seconded by Capt. Elliott, that this House do now resolve itself into Committee to take into consideration the Bill for removing doubts respecting the affirmation of Quakers.

The House accordingly resolved itself into Committee.

Mr. Speaker left the Chair.

Mr. McLean was called to the Chair of the Committee.

Mr. Speaker resumed the Chair.

Mr. McLean reported that the Committee had made some progress and had directed him to ask for leave to sit again to-morrow.

Ordered, That the Committee have leave to sit again to-morrow.

Agreeable to the Order of the Day the House resolved itself into Committee to go into the further consideration of the state of the Province.

Mr. Speaker left the Chair.

Mr. Howard took the Chair of the Committee.

Mr. Speaker resumed the Chair.

Mr. Howard reported that the Committee had come to several resolutions, which he was directed to report to the House whenever the House should be pleased to receive the same.

Ordered, That the Report be now received.

And he read the Report in his place and afterwards delivered the same in at the Table, where it was again read by the Clerk, and is as follows:

Resolved, That it is the opinion of this Committee that it is expedient that they do recommend to the House that an Address be presented to His Honor the President, praying that U. E. Loyalists applying for grants of lands may be permitted to locate lands by agent as heretofore, and that the demand of extra fees under the table of fees of January 1804 be discontinued.

Resolved, That it is the opinion of this Committee that it is expedient to recommend to the House that an Address be presented to His Honor the President, praying that persons known by the description of Military Claimants who have from inability of means, infirmity of health or other untoward circumstances been hitherto unable to make their claims or to procure titles for lands under the proclamation made for that purpose, do now receive such quota or portion of lands as they might have been entitled to receive had they made an early application under such privileges as Military Claimants originally obtained grants of the waste lands of the Crown.

Resolved, That it is the opinion of this Committee, that the Roads throughout the greater part of this Province are in such a state that it is expedient to devise some means for the repair of them.

Resolved, That it is the opinion of this Committee that seminaries for the education of youth are highly necessary in this Province.

The said resolutions were then received and accepted.

Mr. Sherwood moved, seconded by Capt. Cowan, that Mr. Weekes, Mr. McLean, and Mr. Solicitor General be a Committee to prepare addresses upon the resolutions of the House relative to the sons of U. E. Loyalists and Military Claimants.

Which was ordered accordingly.

The Solicitor General then moved, seconded by Capt. Elliott for leave to bring in a Bill to enable His Majesty to grant to aliens part of the waste lands of the Crown within this Province.

A division thereupon took place, and the names were ordered to be taken down, and are as follows:

Yeas.	Nays.
MESSRS. SOL'R GEN.	MESSRS. NELLIS
WASHBURN	COWAN
ELLIOTT	SHERWOOD
	MALLORY
	McLEAN
	WEEKES
	HOWARD
	DORLAND
	HILL
	CRYSLER
	CLENCH

The same was carried in the negative by a majority of eight.

Mr. Sherwood moved, seconded by Mr. Nellis, for leave to bring in a Bill on Monday next to alter and amend an Act passed in the thirty-third year of the King, entitled "An Act to provide for the nomination and appointment of Parish and Town Officers within this Province." Leave was accordingly granted

On motion of Mr. Nellis, seconded by Capt. Elliott, the House adjourned.

Thursday, 13th February, 1806.

Prayers were read.

Read for the first time, An Act for erecting a Court House and Gaol in the Township of Elizabethtown in the district of Johnstown.

Mr. Howard then moved, seconded by Mr. Nellis, that the Bill to enable the Inhabitants in the District of Johnstown to erect and build a Court House and Gaol in the Township of Elizabethtown be read a second time to-morrow. Ordered accordingly.

Agreeable to the Order of the Day, the House resolved itself into Committee to go into the further consideration of the Bill for removing doubts respecting the affirmation of the people called Quakers.

Mr. Speaker left the Chair.

Mr. McLean took the Chair of the Committee.

Mr. Speaker resumed the Chair.

Mr. McLean reported that the Committee had gone through the consideration of the said Bill, to which they had made some amendments, which he was directed to report to the House whenever it should be pleased to receive the same.

The Report was then received and accepted.

Mr. Sherwood moved, seconded by Mr. Dorland, that the Bill relative to Quakers be engrossed and read a third time to-morrow. Ordered accordingly.

Mr. Howard then moved, seconded by Mr. Mallory for leave to bring in a Bill on Monday next to alter an Act passed in the thirty-eighth of the King; entitled "An Act to alter the method of performing Statute Duty on the Highways and Roads within this Province." Leave was accordingly granted.

Mr. Weekes, from the Committee appointed to draft two addresses to His Honor the President, reported that they had prepared two addresses grounded on two resolutions of this House, which they were ready to submit to this House whenever it should be pleased to receive the same.

Ordered, That the draft of the said Addresses be now received.

He then read the two Addresses in his place, and then delivered in the same at the Table, where they were again read through by the Clerk, and are as follows:

To His Honor Alexander Grant, President administering the Government of the Province of Upper Canada, &c. &c.

May it please Your Honor,

We, His Majesty's dutiful and loyal subjects, the Commons of Upper Canada in Parliament assembled, taking into consideration the state of this Province, and having due regard to such means as may tend to promote harmony and tranquility amongst all descriptions of His Majesty's people, humbly beg leave to represent to you that several persons of the description of those who have adhered to the unity of the Empire and to whom it has been held out that the Bounty of our Most Gracious Sovereign would be extended by grant of a certain portion of lands on applying for the same, are precluded from receiving His Gracious Favor by reason of the difficulty of access to the seat of Government at York, and of the expense of attending therein. We therefore entreat you that you in your kind consideration for their situation and in your laudable design of carrying the Royal promise into effect, will dispense with their personal attendance and permit them by their agents to lay their claims before Your Honor in Council, and also to do such further acts towards obtaining grants for lands through their agents as the exigency of their case may require.

We also with due respect beg leave to represent to you that the infant state of wealth and commerce in this country renders persons applying for grants of lands incapable of paying large fees for the same to the Land Granting Department, and that the additional fee required under the table of Fees of the 1st of January, 1804, is incommensurate with their means, and has caused much discontent.

We therefore entreat that you in your solicitude for promoting the welfare and prosperity of all descriptions of His Majesty's dutiful subjects will in your Council direct that they may be relieved from the payment of this fee, or that you will take such other measures for absolving them therefrom as to you in your wisdom may seem meet.

Commons House of Assembly,
13th February, 1806.

To His Honor Alexander Grant, Esquire, President administering the Government of the Province of Upper Canada, &c. &c.

May it please Your Honor,

We, His Majesty's dutiful and loyal subjects, the Commons of Upper Canada in Parliament assembled, deeply impressed with sentiments of loyalty and attachment to His Majesty's person and Government, and studious to devise such means as may induce discord or dissatisfaction to give place in every breast to an unity of affection to the common Father of his people, beg leave to represent to you that a number of persons under the description of Military Claimants have, from inability of means, infirmity of health, or other untoward circumstances, been hitherto unable to make claims or to procure titles for lands under the Proclamations made for compensating them in lands for their Military services.

We rest satisfied that when we advert to the character of the soldier who exhausted his vigor and his years in the service of his King, and who sought for naught but victory in the battle of his Country, your feelings will be sufficiently roused to his condition, and that you will extend to him as the reward of his zeal and loyalty that bounty which was early intended by our Gracious Sovereign, and which neither time nor residence (much less poverty or distress) ought to amend or diminish.

We therefore hope that you will in your Council and wisdom grant to persons of this description (even at this late period) such quota or portion of land as they might have been entitled to receive had they made an early application, and under such privileges as Military Claimants formerly received grants of the waste lands of the Crown.

Commons House of Assembly,
13th February, 1806.

On motion of Mr. Sherwood, seconded by Captain Cowan, the two Addresses were ordered to be engrossed and read to-morrow.

On motion of Mr. Nellis, seconded by Captain Cowan, the House adjourned.

Friday, 14th February, 1806.

Prayers were read.

Captain Eliott moved, seconded by Mr. Mallory, that so much of the Order of the Day as directs that a Bill for the repair of Roads and Bridges be brought in this Day be discharged, and that leave be given to bring in the same on Wednesday next.

The said Order was discharged, and leave given to bring in the Bill next Wednesday.

Mr. Howard then moved, seconded by Mr. Dorland, that so much of the Order of the Day as relates to the Assessment Bill be discharged.

Ordered accordingly.

Then was read for the first time the Bill for affording relief to the society of people called Methodists in this Province.

Mr. Mallory moved, seconded by Mr. Sherwood, that any Rule of this House that prevents the second reading of a Bill in the same day be dispensed with in this instance, and that the Bill relative to Methodists be now read a second time.

Accordingly the said Bill was read for the second time.

Agreeable to the Order of the Day was read for the second time the Bill for erecting a Gaol and Court House in the District of Johnstown.

William Jarvis, Esquire, Secretary of the Province, delivered in at the Bar of this House the Public Provincial Accounts as Per Schedule, which was read by the Clerk at the Table, and are as follows.

SCHEDULE OF ACCOUNTS LAID BEFORE THE HOUSE OF ASSEMBLY.

No. 1. The Inspector's list of Names of persons licensed as Shop and Innkeepers in the several Districts of the Province of Upper Canada for the year ending the 5th of April, 1805. These returns were not received in time to be laid before the Legislature in 1805.

No. 2. The Inspector's list of names of such persons as have been licensed to work Stills in the several Districts of the Province of Upper Canada for the year ending the 5th April, 1805. These returns were not received in time to be laid before the Legislature in 1805.

No. 3. The Inspector's list of names of persons licensed as Shop and Innkeepers in the several Districts of the Province of Upper Canada, from the 5th April, 1805, to the   January, 1806.

No. 4. The Inspector's list of names of such persons as have been licensed to work Stills in the several Districts of the Province of Upper Canada from the 1st April, 1805, to the 5th April, 1806.

No. 5. Provincial Revenue of the Crown arising from Duties collected on goods imported under authority of Acts of the Provincial Parliament, between the 1st January and 31st December, 1805, including such duties as have not heretofore been stated.

No. 6. Provincial Revenue of the Crown arising from duties collected on goods imported under authority of Acts of the Parliament of Great Britain, between the 1st January and the 31st December, 1805, including such duties as have not heretofore been stated.

No. 7. Abstract of Warrants issued by His Excellency Peter Hunter, Esquire, Lieutenant Governor, and His Honor Alexander Grant, Esquire, President of the Province of Upper Canada, for moneys charged against the funds arising from duties imposed by the Provincial Legislature.

No. 8. Supplementary abstract statement of moneys collected within the several Districts of the Province of Upper Canada on Shop, Innkeepers and

Still Licences, for the year ending the 5th April, 1805; after deducting ten per cent. allowed to the Inspectors by the Act of the Forty-third of the King.

No. 9. Abstract statement of moneys collected within the several Districts of the Province of Upper Canada on Shop, Innkeepers and Still Licences, issued between the 5th April, 1805, and 5th January, 1806, so far as the returns have been received after deducting ten per cent. allowed to the Inspector by the Act of the Forty-third of the King.

No. 10. Abstract statement of moneys collected within the several Districts of the Province of Upper Canada on Shop and Innkeepers Licences, issued between the 5th April, 1805, and 5th January, 1806, under authority of Acts of the Parliament of Great Britain, so far as the returns have been received after deducting ten per cent. allowed to the Inspectors by the Act of the Forty-third of the King.

No. 11. General account of articles on which duties on importation are imposed by the Legislature of Lower Canada, which have passed Coteau-du-Lac upwards from the 1st January to the 30th June, 1805, agreeable to the written accounts thereof received, or as ascertained on examination of carriages according to the Act.

No. 12. General account of articles on which duties on importation are imposed by the Legislature of Lower Canada, which have passed Coteau-du-Lac upwards from the 1st July to the 31st December, 1805, agreeable to the written accounts thereof received, or as ascertained on examination of carriages according to the Act.

No. 13. Account of Lighthouse tonnage duty collected for the year ending the 31st December, 1805.

No. 14. Account of cash received by the Honorable Peter Russell, Receiver General, for fines and forfeitures, under authority of Acts of the Provincial Parliament, between the 5th February, 1805, and 5th February, 1806.

No. 15. Account of cash received by the Honorable Peter Russell, Receiver General, for fines and forfeitures under authority of Acts of the Parliament of Great Britain, between the 5th February, 1805, and 5th February, 1806.

No. 16. General state of cash received by the Honorable Peter Russell, Receiver General, for duties and fines under authority of Acts of the Parliament of Great Britain, between the 5th February, 1805, and the 5th February, 1806.

No. 17. General state of receipts and payments by the Honorable Peter Russell, Receiver General, for duties and fines and likewise appropriations made under authority of Acts of the Provincial Parliament, between the 4th February, 1805, and 9th February, 1806.

Inspector General's Office,   (Signed) John McGill,
York, 5th February, 1806.   Inspr. Genl. P.P. Ac'ts.

(For accounts as per Schedule, see appendix.)

Then was read for the third time the Bill for giving relief to the Societies of Quakers, Mennonists and Tunkers.

Mr. Weekes moved, seconded by Mr. Sherwood, that after the word "Quakers" the words "Mennonists and Tunkers" be inserted throughout the Bill.

Ordered accordingly.

Mr. Weekes moved, seconded by Mr. Sherwood, that the Bill be engrossed as amended. Ordered accordingly.

The Speaker then read the two Addresses as engrossed, voted to be presented to His Honor, the President, which passed, and were signed by the Speaker.

Mr. Sherwood then moved, seconded by Captain Cowan, that Mr. Weekes and Mr. Howard do wait upon His Honor, the President, to know at what time he will be pleased to receive the two Addresses of this House; and also that they present the said Addresses to him at such time as he may be pleased to appoint. Ordered accordingly.

On motion of Mr. Howard, seconded by Mr. Nellis, the House resolved itself into Committee to go into the consideration of the Bill for erecting a Gaol and Courthouse in the Township of Elizabethtown, District of Johnstown.

Mr. Speaker left the Chair.

Mr. Dorland was called to the Chair of the Committee.

Mr. Speaker resumed the Chair.

Mr. Dorland reported that the Committee had made a progress, and that he was directed to ask for leave to sit again next Monday.

Resolved, That the Committee have leave to sit again on Monday next.

On motion of Mr. Solicitor General, seconded by Mr. Sherwood, the House resolved itself into Committee to go into the consideration of a Bill for giving relief to the Society of people called Methodists.

Mr. Speaker left the Chair.

Mr. Weekes was called to the Chair of the Committee.

Mr. Speaker resumed the Chair.

Mr. Weekes reported that the Committee had gone through the consideration of the said Bill, to which the Committee had made some amendments, which he was directed to report whenever the House should be pleased to receive the same.

Resolved, That the said Report be now received.

Mr. Washburn then moved, seconded by Mr. Mallory, that the Methodist Bill be engrossed and read a third time to-morrow. Ordered accordingly.

On motion of Captain Cowan, seconded by Mr. Nellis, the House adjourned.

Saturday, 15th February, 1806.

Prayers were read.

Read for the first time, A Bill for the better defining the qualifications of Electors.

Mr. Weekes moved, seconded by Mr. Howard, that the said Bill be read a second time on Monday next. Ordered accordingly.

Read for the third time, the engrossed Bill for affording relief to the Society called Methodists.

On motion of Mr. Mallory, seconded by Mr. McLean,

Resolved, That the Bill do now pass, and that the title be "An Act to afford relief to the Religious Society called Methodists."

The Bill then passed and was signed by the Speaker.

Mr. Dorland then moved, seconded by Mr. Nellis, that the Bill for relieving Dissenters of the Religious Societies of Quakers, Mennonists and Tunkers from certain legal disabilities, be now read as engrossed.

The said Bill was read as engrossed for the third time.

Mr. Weekes moved, seconded by Mr. Dorland, that this Bill do pass, and that the title be "An Act for relieving Dissenters of the Religious Societies of Quakers, Mennonists and Tunkers from certain legal disabilities."

The House resolved the same; the Bill accordingly passed, and was signed by the Speaker.

Mr. Washburn moved, seconded by the Solicitor General, that Mr. Mallory and Mr. Hill be a Committee to carry. up the Methodist Bill to the Honorable Legislative Council, and request their concurrence thereto. Ordered accordingly.

Mr. Nellis then moved, seconded by Mr. Dorland, that Mr. McLean, Mr. Crysler and Mr. Mallory be a Committee to carry up to the Honorable Legislative Council the Bill for affording relief to the Societies called Quakers, Mennonists and Tunkers, and request their concurrence thereto.

Mr. McLean moved in amendment, seconded by Mr. Howard, that the name of McLean be left out and the name of Dorland substituted.

Which was carried in the affirmative and ordered accordingly.

The main question being then put, the same passed in the negative.

Mr. Solicitor General then moved, seconded by Captain Elliott, for leave to bring in a Bill on Tuesday next to continue an Act passed in the Forty-third year of His Majesty's Reign, entitled "An Act·for the better securing to His Majesty, his Heirs and Successors, the due collection and receipt of certain duties therein mentioned." Leave was accordingly granted.

Mr. Washburn, seconded by Mr. Nellis moved for leave to bring in a Bill on Tuesday next to grant support to the Poor within this Province.

Accordingly leave was given.

On motion of Captain Cowan, seconded by Captain Elliott, the House adjourned until Monday next at twelve o'clock at noon.

Monday, 17 February, 1806.

Prayers were read.

Mr. Howard moved, seconded by Mr. Nellis, that so much of the Order of the Day as relates to the Statute Labour Bill be discharged, and that leave be given to bring it in on Friday next. Ordered accordingly.

Agreeable to the Order of the Day, the House resolved itself into Committee to go into the further consideration of the Bill for erecting a gaol and Court-house in the District of Johnstown.

Mr. Speaker left the Chair.

Mr. Dorland took the Chair of the Committee.

Mr. Speaker resumed the Chair.

Mr. Dorland reported that the Committee had gone through the consideration of the said Bill, to which they had made some amendments, which he was directed to report whenever the House should be pleased to receive the same.

The House then resolved that the said Report be now received and accepted.

The said Report was then accordingly received and accepted.

Mr. Howard, seconded by Mr. Weekes, moved that the Johnstown Bill be engrossed and read a third time to-morrow. Ordered accordingly.

Read for the second time, The Bill for the better defining the Qualification of Electors.

Mr. Dorland, one of the Messengers named to carry up to the Legislative Council the Bill for relieving Dissenters of the Religious Societies of Quakers, Mennonists, and Tunkers, from certain disabilities; reported that they had carried up the same and did request their concurrence thereto.

Mr. Weekes moved, seconded by Mr. Rogers, that the House do to-morrow resolve itself into a Committee to take the Bill for the better defining the Qualification of Electors into consideration. The House resolved the same.

Then was read for the first time, The Bill for regulating the duty of Parish and Town Officers throughout the Province.

Mr. Sherwood then moved, seconded by Mr. McLean, that so much of the Rules of this House as prevents a Bill from being read a second time in the same day be dispensed with, and that leave be given to read this Bill a second time this day. The same passed in the negative.

Mr. Rogers, seconded by Mr. Weekes, moved that the Bill relative to Parish and Town Officers be read a second time to-morrow. Ordered accordingly.

Mr. Sherwood moved, seconded by Mr. Rogers, for leave to bring in a Bill to-morrow to provide for the payment of costs after Judgment.

Leave was accordingly granted.

Then was read the Petition of John Bennett, Government printer, which is as follows, viz.

To the Honorable the Legislative Council and House of Assembly.

The Petition of John Bennett, Government Printer,

Humbly Showeth,

That Your Petitioner as Printer to His Majesty was appointed to print the Laws and Journals of the House of Assembly of the Province of Upper Canada, for which service a sum not exceeding three hundred pounds currency was voted by Parliament. After the first impression Your Petitioner by letter informed His Excellency, the late Lieutenant Governor, that the work performed would not, according to the schedule with which he was furnished, calculated in Quebec in the year 1789, when paper, printing materials, wages, and even the necessaries of life, were to be had at much more reasonable rates than at present, amount to near the sum voted for that purpose; and was given to understand by the Lieutenant Governor's Secretary that he was to receive the whole sum voted by the Legislature for printing the Laws and Journals, and His Excellency's Warrants for the full amount were always ready, either before or as soon as the work could be completed.

Sometime afterwards His Honor, Chief Justice Allcock, demanded of Your Petitioner what sums received by him for printing the Laws and Journals; on being informed, said he would put a stop to the printing of the Journals; that the receipt of such a sum was mere robbery, &c. &c. &c., that he would represent him to the Governor, and that the money should be refunded. On stating his situation to His Excellency, Your Petitioner was again told by His Honor that as sure as God was his Maker he should receive a letter requesting him to give up his office were any more complaints made to the Governor.

Your Petitioner was next commanded to attend His Excellency, who demanded whether he had been paid for printing the Laws and Journals, and by what authority payment was made; on being informed the money was paid by virtue of His Excellency's own Warrants, he observed the money was voted for himself, and not for the printer, who was ordered immediately to retire to make out his accounts without delay and to present them to the Inspector General of Public Provincial Accounts for examination.

Shortly afterwards Your Petitioner was given to understand that the sum of three hundred and seventy-five pounds, Halifax currency, was to be refunded by him, nearly two thirds of which sum have actually been stopped by retaining his contingencies.

Upon what principle this deduction is founded your Petitioner could never learn, nor has he ever witnessed a precedent; all the satisfaction or information he could possibly derive relative to the subject was "You are getting too rich, sir."

The duty required of Your Petitioner was duly performed, and no complaint ever alleged; consequently he received the money appropriated therefore and applied the same to the purchase of new printing materials and stationery to a considerable amount, and to other purposes, and had that work exceeded the sum a loss would then have accrued, as it was to have been done for that particular sum. The difficulties and embarassments into which such a measure would infallibly involve him represented to the Governor, but they were represented in vain—no redress could be obtained.

The situation of Your Petitioner is therefore distressing in the extreme, and has left him deeply in arrears in Lower Canada. In short, all he now receives from Government is a salary of One hundred Pounds, ninety-one Pounds, five shillings of which is to be yearly paid to an assistant, and sometimes a trifling contingent account which Government do not think proper to retain. Thus circumstance he is entirely deprived of the means of making the necessary remittances for the articles used in the process of his business.

Two people exclusive of your Petitioner were employed in printing the Revised Statutes, done at the wish of the Government, at the rate of fourteen dollars a week, for upwards of eighteen months, together with other heavy expenses attending the same; at the completion of which your Petitioner confidently and anxiously expected to have been able to have satisfied these demands, but the money for the copies taken by the Government was detained, and those flattering prospects have now vanished, and he has to anticipate the dreary and disheartening prospect of beginning the world anew, involved in debt, without even the slender means he possessed on his arrival in the country. The refunding of three hundred and seventy five pounds, Halifax currency, will ultimately ruin him; he therefore humbly hopes Your Honorable House will take his case into consideration, and grant him such relief as to you in your wisdom may seem meet. And Your Petitioner, as in duty bound, will ever pray.

(Signed) John Bennett,
York, Upper Canada,   Government Printer.
12th February, 1806.

On motion of Mr. Sherwood, seconded by Mr. Weekes,

Ordered, That the House do now resolve itself into a Committee to take into its consideration the Public Accounts.

The House accordingly resolved itself into Committee.

Mr. Speaker left the Chair.

Mr. Hill was called to the Chair of the Committee.

Mr. Speaker resumed the Chair.

Mr. Hill reported a progress, and was directed to ask for leave to sit again to-morrow.

Resolved, That the Committee have leave to sit again to-morrow.

On motion of Mr. Sherwood, seconded by Captain Elliott, the House adjourned.

Tuesday, 18th February, 1806.

Prayers were read.

Read for the first time, An Act to continue an Act for the better securing to His Majesty certain duties therein mentioned.

The Solicitor General moved, seconded by Capt. Cowan, that the second reading of the Act for continuing the collection of certain duties within this Province be appointed for to-morrow. Ordered accordingly.

Agreeable to the Order of the Day the House resolved itself into Committee to go into the consideration of the Bill for the better defining the qualifications of Electors.

Mr. Speaker left the Chair.

Mr. Nellis was called to the Chair of the Committee.

Mr. Speaker resumed the Chair.

Mr. Nellis reported that the Committee had gone through the consideration of the said Bill, to which they had made some amendments, which he was directed to report whenever the House should be pleased to receive the same.

The House then resolved that the Report be now received.

Which Report was then received and accepted.

Mr. Washburn then moved, seconded by Mr. Nellis, that so much of the Order of the Day be discharged as relates to the bringing in a Bill for the support of the poor within this Province. Which was ordered accordingly.

Mr. Rogers moved, seconded by Mr. Nellis, that the Committee appointed to carry up the Bill for the relief of the Methodists to the Legislative Council do also carry up four petitions. Ordered accordingly.

Mr. Weekes then moved, seconded by Mr. Sherwood, that the Bill for amending an Act for the more equal representation of the Commons be engrossed, and read a third time to-morrow. Which was ordered accordingly.

Read for the third time, The engrossed Bill for erecting a Gaol and Court House in the District of Johnstown.

Mr. Howard, seconded by Mr. Sherwood, moved that the title of the Johnstown Bill be "An Act to enable the Inhabitants of the District of Johnstown to erect and build a Court House and Gaol in the Township of Elizabethtown."

The House accordingly resolved the same.

The Bill then passed and was signed by the Speaker.

Mr. Nellis then moved, seconded by Mr. Dorland, that Mr. Howard and Mr. Washburn be a Committee to carry up the said Bill to the Honorable the Legislative Council and request their concurrence thereto. Ordered accordingly.

Read for the second time, The Bill for regulating the duty of Parish and Town Officers.

On motion of Mr. Sherwood, seconded by Mr. Rogers, the House resolved itself into Committee to go into the consideration of the said Bill.

Mr. Speaker left the Chair.

Mr. Mallory was called to the Chair of the Committee.

Mr. Speaker resumed the Chair.

7 A.

Mr. Mallory reported that the Committee had made a progress, and that he was directed to ask for leave to sit again on Thursday next.

Leave was accordingly granted.

Read for the first time, An Act to amend the Law.

Mr. Sherwood moved, seconded by Mr. Rogers, that the said Act be read a second time to-morrow. Ordered accordingly.

Capt. Cowan, seconded by the Solicitor General, moved for leave to bring in to-morrow a Bill to provide for several Sheriffs in this Province.

Leave was accordingly granted.

Mr. Washburn, seconded by Mr. Nellis, moved that so much of the Order of the Day be discharged as relates to the Public Accounts, and that leave be given to take them into consideration to-morrow. Ordered accordingly.

Mr. Sherwood moved, seconded by Capt. Cowan, for leave to bring in a Bill to-morrow to appropriate a sum of money for the purpose of certain apparatus for the promoting of science. Leave was accordingly granted.

On motion of Mr. Sherwood, seconded by Capt. Cowan, the House adjourned until to-morrow at twelve o'clock at noon.

Wednesday, 19th February, 1806.

Prayers were read.

Read for the second time, an Act to continue an Act for the better securing to His Majesty the due collection of certain duties therein mentioned.

. Mr. Mallory, one of the Messengers named to carry up to the Honorable the Legislative Council the Bill to afford relief to the Society of people called Methodists, reported that they had carried up the same, and did request their concurrence thereto, as also the four petitions ordered to accompany it.

Mr. Sherwood reported that the Messengers named to carry up to the Honorable Legislative Council the Act for erecting a Gaol and Court House in the Township of Elizabethtown, District of Johnstown, had carried up the same, and did request their concurrence thereto.

Mr. Weekes moved, seconded by Mr. Rogers, that after the word "Britain" the words in the seventh line of the fourth clause of the Bill entitled "An Act to repeal certain parts of an Act passed in the Fourteenth year &c." be .engrossed, and the following words inserted, "passed in the Thirty-First year of His Majesty's Reign, entitled 'An Act to repeal certain parts of an Act passed in the Fourteenth Year of His Majesty's Reign, entitled 'An Act for making more effectual provision for the Government of the Province of Quebec in North America, and to make further provision for the Government of the said Province.'" Ordered. accordingly.

Read a second time, the Bill to amend the Law.

Mr. Sherwood moved, seconded by Mr. Rogers, that the House do now resolve itself into Committee on the Bill to amend the Law.

The House accordingly resolved itself into Committee on the said Bill.

Mr. Speaker left the Chair.

Capt. Cowan was called to the chair of the Committee.

Mr. Speaker resumed the Chair.

Capt. Cowan reported that the Committee had gone through the consideration of the said Bill without any amendments.

Mr. Sherwood moved, seconded by Mr. Mallory, that the Bill to amend the Law be engrossed, and read a third time to-morrow.

A division thereupon took place, the names being called for they were taken down and are as follows:

Yeas.	Nays.
MESSRS. COWAN	MESSRS. NELLIS
SHERWOOD	MALLORY
SOLICITOR GEN.	McLEAN
WEEKES	DORLAND
HOWARD	HILL
CRYSLER	CLENCH
WASHBURN	

Carried in the affirmative by a majority of one.

The Bill was accordingly ordered to be engrossed.

Mr. Rogers then moved, seconded by Mr. Weekes, that the Bill to provide for the Sheriffs be read a second time on Friday next. Ordered accordingly.

Mr. Sherwood moved, seconded by Capt. Elliott, that the Order of the Day to bring in the Road Bill be discharged for to-day, and that leave be given him to bring it in to-morrow. Which was ordered accordingly.

Agreeable to the Order of the Day the House resolved itself into Committee on the Provincial Public Accounts.

Mr. Speaker left the Chair.

Mr. Hill took the chair of the Committee.

Mr. Speaker resumed the Chair.

Mr. Crysler then moved, seconded by Mr. Clench, that Messrs. Weekes, Dorland, Rogers, Nellis and Washburn be a Select Committee to examine the Public Accounts, and that they do report to this House as soon as possible, and that the said Committee have power to send for such persons or papers as they shall think necessary. Ordered accordingly.

Read for the first time, a Bill to appropriate a certain sum of money for the purpose of an apparatus to promote science.

Mr. Sherwood then moved, seconded by Capt. Elliott, for the second reading of the Bill for promoting science on Friday next. Ordered accordingly.

Read for the third time as engrossed, the Bill for the better defining the qualification of Electors.

Mr. Weekes then moved, seconded by Mr. Rogers, that the said Bill do pass, and that the title be, an Act to alter and amend an Act for the more equal representation of the Commons of the Province, and for the better defining the qualifications of Electors."

The House resolved the same.

The Bill then passed, and was signed by the Speaker.

Mr. Sherwood then moved, seconded by Mr. McLean, that Mr. Weekes and Mr. Crysler be a Committee to carry up this Bill to the Legislative Council. Which was ordered accordingly.

On motion of Mr. Sherwood, seconded by Capt. Cowan, the House adjourned until twelve o'clock to-morrow at noon.

Thursday, 20th February, 1806.

Prayers were read.

Read for the third time, the Bill to amend the Law.

The Bill then passed and was signed by Mr. Speaker.

Mr. Weekes, one of the Messengers named to carry up to the Honorable Legislative Council the Act for the better defining the qualifications of Electors, reported that they had carried up the said Bill, and did request their concurrence thereto.

Mr. Rogers then moved, seconded by Mr. Weekes, that Mr. Sherwood and the Solicitor General be a Committee to carry up to the Honorable Legislative Council the Bill to amend the Law, and to request their concurrence in passing the same. Ordered accordingly.

Agreeable to the Order of the Day, the House resolved itself into a Committee to go into the consideration of the Bill for regulating the appointment of Town and Parish Officers.

Mr. Speaker left the Chair.

Mr. Mallory was called to the chair of the Committee.

Mr. Speaker resumed the Chair.

Mr. Mallory reported that the Committee had gone through the consideration of the said Bill, to which they had made some amendments, which he was directed to report whenever the House shall be pleased to receive the same.

The House then resolved that the Report be now received.

On motion of Mr. Sherwood, seconded by Mr. Nellis, the said Bill was ordered to be engrossed and read a third time on Saturday next.

Read for the first time, the Road Bill.

On motion of Mr. Mallory, seconded by Mr. Nellis, the said Bill was ordered to ·be read a second time on Saturday next.

Mr. Washburn moved, seconded by Mr. Howard, for leave to bring in a Bill on to-morrow to repeal so much of an Act passed in the thirty-fifth of the King, entitled "An Act to regulate the practice of Physic and Surgery" as relates to the Governor, Lieut. Governor, or person administering the Government, to order and appoint a Board of Surgeons to examine persons applying, and grant license to these approved of to practise physic, surgery and mid-wifery, and make further provision for the same. Leave was accordingly granted.

Mr. Weekes gave notice that he would on Saturday next move that this House do appoint a Committee to prepare an Address to Our Most Gracious Sovereign, laying before His Majesty the substance of two addresses presented by this House to His Honor the President on the 14th Inst, and praying that Our Most Gracious Sovereign, in his parental solicitude for his subjects in this Province, will take the matter of such Addresses into consideration.

Mr. Rogers moved, seconded by Mr. Weekes, that the Rule of this House that directs that no petition complaining of an undue Election shall be read until the Petitioner or Petitioners shall give security to pay such costs as the House may order, in case the petition shall be considered groundless, and the sitting Members duly elected, be rescinded. The same passed in the negative.

On motion of Capt. Elliott, seconded by Mr. Nellis, the House adjourned until twelve o'clock to-morrow at noon.

Friday, 21st February, 1806.

Prayers were read.

William Jarvis, Esquire, Secretary of the Province, came to the Bar of the House, and there did deliver answers to two addresses of this House presented to His Honor the President on the fourteenth instant, which answers were signed by His Honor; which the Speaker then read, the Members standing up, and are as follows, viz.

Gentlemen of the Commons House of Assembly:—

It is the sons of the persons mentioned in one of the Addresses presented by you the thirteenth of this month who are required by the regulations of the Executive Government of this Province personally to appear, in order to obtain grants of the lands bestowed on them by the bounty of the Crown.

The Frauds for some time committed by the agent of persons assuming that character, rendered the personal appearance of such claimants a measure of the highest expediency.

But as it is my wish to contribute to the ease and accommodation of His Majesty's Subjects in this Province of every description, as well as at all times to pay proper attention to your representations, I shall, aided by the advice of the Executive Council take into consideration whether the evils above stated may not be obviated consistent with indulgence as to personal appearance to the sons of those persons who adhere to the unity of the Empire, whose local situation may render it difficult for them to comply with the above regulations.

The Table of Fees of the Ninth January, 1804, is under the authority of instructions of that date communicated by one of His Majesty's principal Secretaries of State to the late Lieutenant Governor.

(Signed) Alex'r Grant,
President.

Gentlemen of the Commons House of Assembly:—

I will take into serious consideration what is stated in your Address to me respecting Military Claimants, as no one can wish more than I do to contribute to the comfort and happiness of that highly meritorious class of individuals.

(Signed) Alex'r Grant,
President.

Mr. Howard then moved, seconded by Mr. Crysler, that so much of the Order of the Day as relates to the Statute Labour Bill be discharged.

Ordered accordingly.

Read for the second time the Bill for allowing Salaries to different Sheriffs in this Province.

Capt. Cowan moved, seconded by Mr. Sherwood, that the House do now resolve itself into a Committee to take this Bill into consideration.

The House accordingly resolved itself into Committee.

Mr. Speaker left the Chair.

Mr. Solicitor General was called to the chair of the Committee.

Mr. Speaker resumed the Chair.

Mr. Solicitor General reported a progress, and asked for leave to sit again this day. Leave was accordingly granted.

Mr. Solicitor General, one of the Messengers named to carry up to the Honorable Legislative Council the Bill entitled "An Act to amend the Law," reported that they had carried up the same, and did request their concurrence thereto.

The House again resolved itself into Committee to go into the further consideration of a Bill for allowing salaries to Sheriffs.

Mr. Speaker left the Chair.

Mr. Solicitor General again took the chair of the Committee.

Mr. Speaker resumed the Chair.

The Solicitor General reported that the Committee had gone through the consideration of the Bill, to which they had made some amendments, which he was directed to report to the House whenever it should be pleased to receive the same.

Mr. Clench then moved, seconded by Mr. Dorland, that the Report be not received.

A division thereupon took place; the names being called for they were taken down and are as follows, viz.

Yeas.	Nays.
MESSRS. DORLAND	MESSRS. ELLIOTT
CLENCH	COWAN
HILL	SHERWOOD
NELLIS	WASHBURN
WEEKES	SOL'R GEN.
McLEAN.	ROGERS.
	HOWARD.
	CRYSLER.

The same was carried in the negative by a majority of two.

The Report was then received and accepted.

Mr. Rogers then moved, seconded by Mr. Howard, that the Bill for allowing salaries to the Sheriffs be engrossed, and read a third time to-morrow.

Which was ordered accordingly.

Agreeable to the Order of the day was read for the second time a Bill to appropriate a certain sum of money for the purchase of apparatus to promote science.

Mr. Sherwood moved, seconded by Capt. Cowan, that the House do now resolve itself into Committee to take the said Bill into consideration.

The House accordingly resolved itself into Committee to go into the consideration of the said Bill.

Mr. Speaker left the Chair.

Mr. Clench was called to the Chair of the Committee.

Mr. Speaker resumed the chair.

Mr. Clench reported that the Committee had gone through the consideration of the said Bill, to which they had made some amendments, which he was directed to report to the House whenever it shall be pleased to receive the same.

The House then resolved that the said Report be now received and accepted.

On motion of Mr. Clench, seconded by Capt. Cowan,

Ordered, That the said Bill be engrossed and read a third time to-morrow.

Read for the first time, the Bill for regulating the practice of Physic and Surgery.

Mr. Washburn moved, seconded by Mr. Sherwood, that the Bill to regulate the practice of Physic and Surgery be read a second time to-morrow.

Ordered accordingly.

Then the Clerk, by order of the House, read the bond of Samuel Ryerse, Esquire, respecting the contested election of Benajah Mallory, Esquire, the sitting Member for the Counties of Norfolk, Oxford and Middlesex, which is as follows, viz.:

Know all men by these presents that we, Samuel Ryerse, of the District of London in the Province of Upper Canada, and Samuel Smith of the County of York and Home District, of the Province aforesaid, are held and firmly bound unto Benajah Mallory, of the District of London and Province aforesaid, Esquire, in the sum of One Hundred Pounds of lawful money, to be paid to the said Benajah Mallory, his Heirs, Assigns or certain Attornies, in which payment well and truly to be made we bind ourselves, our Heirs and Assigns, firmly by these presents.

Signed with our hands, sealed with our seals, and dated at York this twenty-first day of February in the Year of Our Lord One Thousand Eight Hundred and Six.

Whereas the said Benajah Mallory has been returned as a Member to represent the District of London in the provincial Parliament of Upper Canada, and whereas the said Samuel Ryerse contests the legality of his holding a seat therein.

Now, therefore, the condition of this obligation is such, that if the above bounden, or either of them, shall produce such proofs of the legal incapacity of the said Benajah Mallory as will induce the Honorable the Commons House of Assembly to dispossess the said Benajah Mallory of his seat therein or in default thereof will pay such sum or sums of money to the said Benajah Mallory for his costs as the Honorable the Commons House of Assembly then this obligation will be null and void, or otherwise remain in full force and effect.

(Signed)   Samuel Ryerse.
            Samuel Smith.

Signed and sealed
in presence of
(Signed)   John McDonell.
            J. Boucherville.

Then the House ordered that the Clerk file the Bond upon the Records of the House, there to be kept until the decision of the said contested election by this Honorable House take place.

Then the Clerk, by order of the House, read at the Table the petition of Samuel Ryerse, Esquire, respecting the said contested election, which is as follows, viz.:

To the Honorable the Commons House of Assembly of the Province of Upper Canada, in Provincial Parliament assembled.

The Petition of Samuel Ryerse of Woodhouse, in the District of London, Esquire,

Respectfully Sheweth,

That at the late election holden in and for the said District of London for a Member to represent the said District in Your Honorable House of Assembly, Benajah Mallory, the now sitting member, and your petitioner were candidates, the Returning Officer, William Spurgin, declared the said Benajah Mallory duly elected.

Your Petitioner therefore comes forward to state to Your Honorable body that the said Benajah Mallory has been illegally and unduly returned, being by the thirty-first of His present Majesty rendered ineligible to a seat in the Parliament, having both before and since the election been a preacher and teacher of the Religious Society or Sect called Methodists, all of which Your Petitioner is ready to verify, and is ready to give any security Your Honorable House may deem necessary.

Your petitioner therefore most humbly prays that a day may be assigned him to be heard, by Counsel or otherwise, at the Bar of Your Honorable House in support of the charge as afore stated, and that such steps may be taken as you in your wisdom may think proper to compel the attendance of such witnesses as Your Petitioner may deem necessary to support his charge against the aforesaid Benajah Mallory as a Preacher and Teacher of the Religious Society or Sect called Methodists.

And Your Petitioner as in duty bound will ever pray.

(Signed)   Sam'l Ryerse.

Then the House resolved that the Petition of Samuel Ryerse contains grounds and reasons sufficient, if substantiated, to make the election of Benajah Mallory, Esquire, void.

Mr. Sherwood then moved, seconded by Mr. Clench, that Friday, the seventh day of March next ensuing, at twelve o'clock at noon, be appointed for to take into consideration the merits of the Petition of Samuel Ryerse, Esquire, complaining of the undue Election and return of Benajah Mallory, Esquire, now sitting Member in this House, returned for the Counties of Norfolk, Oxford and Middlesex.

The House accordingly resolved that the said day and hour be appointed to hear the merits of the said contested election.

On motion of Mr. Clench, seconded by Capt. Elliott, the House adjourned until ten o'clock in the forenoon to-morrow.

Saturday, 22nd February, 1806.

Prayers were read.

Read for the third time, the engrossed Bill for giving salaries to Sheriffs.

Mr. Weekes then moved, seconded by Mr. Sherwood, that the following make an additional clause to the said Bill: "And be it further enacted by the authority aforesaid, that this Act shall remain in force for ten years, and to the end of the then next present Session of Parliament."

Mr. Nellis moved in amendment to the additional clause proposed, that in line the third the word "ten" be expunged, and that the word "seven" be inserted in lieu thereof. Which passed in the negative.

The main question was then put, and carried in the negative.

Mr. Sherwood then moved, seconded by Capt. Cowan, that the Bill do pass, and that the title be "An Act to make provision for several Sheriffs in this Province." Which passed in the negative.

Then was read for the third time the engrossed Act for promoting Science.

Mr. Sherwood then moved, seconded by Mr. Clinch, that the Bill do pass, and that the title be "An Act to purchase certain apparatus for promoting Science."

A division thereupon took place; the names being called, for they were taken down, and are as follows, viz.:

Yeas.	Nays.
MESSRS. McLEAN.	MESSRS. HOWARD.
COWAN.	ROGERS.
SOL'R GENERAL.	HILL.
WEEKES.	DORLAND.
ELLIOTT.	NELLIS.
WASHBURN.	
CRYSLER.	
CLENCH.	

Carried in the affirmative by a majority of three, the Bill then passed and was signed by Mr. Speaker.

Mr. Washburn moved, seconded by Mr. Crysler, that Mr. Clench and Captain Cowan be a Committee to carry up to the Legislative Council the said Bill, and to request their concurrence thereto. Ordered accordingly.

Read for the second time, the Bill to regulate the practice of Physic and Surgery.

Mr. Clench, one of the Messengers named to carry up to the Honorable Legislative Council the Bill to purchase apparatus for promoting science, reported that they had carried up the said Bill and did request their concurrence thereto.

Mr. Washburn moved, seconded by Mr. Clench, that the House do on Monday next resolve itself into Committee to take into consideration the Bill to regulate the practice of Physic and Surgery.

The House accordingly resolved the same.

Read for the third time, the engrossed Bill for regulating the appointment of Parish and Town Officers.

Mr. Sherwood then moved, seconded by Mr. Rogers, that the Bill do pass, and that the title be "An Act to alter and amend an Act passed in the thirty-third year of His Present Majesty's Reign, entitled 'An Act to provide for the nomination and appointment of Parish and Town Officers.'"

Ordered accordingly.

The Bill then passed, and was signed by the Speaker.

Mr. Sherwood moved, seconded by Captain Eliott, that Mr. Rogers and Mr. Nellis do carry up the said Bill to the Honorable Legislative Council, and request their concurrence thereto. Accordingly it was ordered.

Mr. Weekes gives notice that he will on Monday next move that this House do resolve itself into a Committee to take into consideration the necessity of Addressing our Most Gracious Sovereign on the subject of two Addresses from this House, presented on the thirteenth instant to His Honor the President.

Mr. Weekes moved, seconded by Mr. Rogers, for leave to bring in on Monday next a Bill for establishing Public Schools in this Province.

Leave was accordingly given.

Mr. Sherwood, seconded by Mr. Solicitor-General, moved that the following clause be added to the Sheriffs' Salary Bill: "And be it further enacted by the authority aforesaid that this Act shall be and continue in force eight years from and after passing of the same, and from thence to the end of the then next ensuing session of the Provincial Parliament, and no longer."

Carried in the affirmative, and ordered accordingly.

Mr. Sherwood then moved, seconded by Mr. Rogers, that the Bill do pass, and that the title be "An Act to make provision for Sheriffs in this Province."

The House accordingly resolved the same.

Mr. Rogers, one of the Messengers named to carry up to the Honorable Legislative 'Council the Bill to altar and amend an Act passed in the thirty-third year of His present Majesty's Reign, entitled, "An Act to provide for the nomination and appointment of Parish and Town Officers," reported that they had carried up the said Bill and did request their concurrence thereto.

Then was read the Petition of Captain Joseph Brant, which is as follows:

To the Honorable the Commons House of Assembly in Parliament Assembled, &c., &c., &c.

The Petition of Captain Joseph Brant, Respectfully Sheweth,

That in the year 1775, when the war between Great Britain and her Colonies had commenced, the Mohawk Nation, always faithful to the cause of the King, took a decided and active part, and leaving their families to the mercy of the enemy brought off the Indian Department through a hostile country into Canada; where their conduct was highly approved by Sir Guy Carleton, who, in a public council with the Indians, desired them to take up the hatchet and defend their rights; he then solemnly engaged that we should be remunerated for any losses we might sustain during the war.

Some years after, when it was foreseen that the contest was likely to take an unfavorable turn, we stated our situation to the late Sir Frederick Haldimand, then Governor and 'Commander-in-Chief, and requested a confirmation of General Carleton's promise, by which it was understood that the Indians who had lost their lands should receive an equivalent in this country, and at all events have them as fully confirmed as those they were possessed of before the war; and the grant which we afterwards obtained is now before your Honorable House.

The lands thus granted, although from the quantity and situation by no means an equivalent for our losses, we cheerfully accepted, in full confidence that they should be our own property, at least as much so as those we had sacrificed by joining the British Standard at the commencement of the war.

After thus obtaining these lands, which are delineated on the map, which is also before Your Honorable House, we, with the approbation of General Haldimand, settled some white families on the tract (many of whom had served with us) for the purpose of making roads and teaching our people the benefit of agriculture, etc. I am sorry to say that our grievances commenced upon the establishment of the present Government of Upper Canada, by whom it was contemplated to curtail us of a great part of this tract.

Considering ourselves under the protection of His Majesty, it becomes a duty we owe to ourselves and our posterity candidly to state the difficulties we labour under. Divisions have been fomented amongst the Indians by Mr. Claus, the Deputy Superintendent, which may lead to serious consequences. He has taken the most unjustifiable means to destroy our former transactions, for which purpose he brought a party of Senecas from Buffalo Creek, to whom he dictated a paper purporting to make void all we had done respecting the lands in question; although he must have known that these Indians who live within the limits of the United States have, in their present situation, no right to interfere in the disposal of our lands. This will appear by referring to General Haldimand's grant.

We cannot see what interest it can be to the Government to tie our hands in regard to the disposal of our own property, or that Mr. Claus, through the means he has in his power, should disunite us.

That a small spot of ground of so little consequence to the British Nation should become a matter of contention we cannot suppose to be their intention, but if, unfortunately for us, this should be the case, and if ever this small tract is considered as too large for the former services and losses of the Indians, in God's name let them confirm the one half.

We are aware that all representations of this nature should come through the Indian Department, but as they have long since ceased from paying attention to our complaints, we are under the necessity of appealing to your Honorable House in hopes of obtaining relief through such means as you in your wisdom shall see fit.

In behalf of the Indians,

(Signed) JOSEPH BRANT,

York, 14th February, 1806.   Agent.

Read for the third time as engrossed, the Bill to make provision for several Sheriffs in this Province, which passed, and was signed by the Speaker.

Mr. Washburn moved, seconded by Mr. Nellis, that Mr. Sherwood and Mr. Crysler do carry up to the Legislative Council the Bill, and request their concurrence thereto. Ordered accordingly.

Mr. Mallory gave notice that he will on Wednesday next move that this House resolve itself into a Committee to take into consideration the prayer of Captain Brant's petition.

Mr. Sherwood, seconded by Mr. Clench, moved that the Speaker be authorized to issue summons to require the attendance of witnesses either for the sitting member, Mr. Mallory, or the Petitioner, Mr. Ryerse.

The House accordingly resolved the same.

On motion of Captain Eliott, seconded by Mr. Nellis, the House adjourned until Monday next at twelve o'clock at noon.

Monday, 24th February, 1806.

Prayers were read.

Agreeable to the Order of the Day, the House resolved itself into Committee to go into the consideration of the Bill for regulating the practice of Physic and Surgery.

Mr. Speaker left the Chair.

Mr. Sherwood was called to the Chair of the Committee.

Mr. Speaker resumed the Chair.

Mr. Sherwood reported that the Committee had gone through the consideration of the said Bill, to which they had made some amendments, which he was directed to report to the House whenever it should be pleased to receive the same.

The Report was then received and accepted.

Mr. Washburn then moved, seconded by Mr. Clench, that the Bill to regulate the practice of Physic and Surgery be engrossed and read a third time to-morrow. Ordered accordingly.

A message from the Honorable Legislative Council by Mr. Baldwin, Master-in-Chancery.

Mr. Speaker,—

The Honorable the Legislative Council have concurred in passing the Bill entitled "An Act to amend the Law," sent up from this House, to which they have made some amendments, to which amendments they request the concurrence of this House.

And then he withdrew.

Mr. Weekes then moved, seconded by Mr. Rogers, that this House do resolve itself into a Committee to take into consideration the necessity of addressing Our Most Gracious Sovereign on the subject of two addresses from this House presented on the 13th instant to His Honor the President.

A division thereupon took place; the names being called for they were taken down, and are as follows, viz.:

Yeas.	* Nays.
MESSRS. MALLORY.	MESSRS. SHERWOOD.
WEEKES.	NELLIS.
ROGERS.	ELLIOTT.
CLENCH.	COWAN.
	DORLAND.
	SOLICITOR-GENERAL.
	WASHBURN.
	HILL.
	CRYSLER.
	McLEAN.

Carried in the negative by a majority of six.

Read, the amendments made by the Honorable Legislative Council to an Act entitled "An Act to amend the Law."

On motion of Mr. Sherwood, seconded by Capt. Cowan, the House resolved itself into Committee to go into the consideration of the said amendments.

Mr. Speaker left the Chair.

Mr. Crysler was called to the Chair of the Committee.

Mr. Speaker resumed the Chair.

Mr. Crysler reported that the Committee had gone through the amendments made by the Legislative Council to the said Bill without any amendments, which he was directed to report whenever the House should be pleased to receive the same.

The said Report was then received and accepted.

On motion of Mr. Sherwood, seconded by Mr. Nellis,

Ordered, that the Bill as amended be engrossed.

Capt. Cowan, seconded by Mr. Nellis, moved, that Mr. Sherwood and Mr. Solicitor-General do inform the Legislative Council that this House have agreed to the amendments made by them to the Act to amend the Law.

Ordered accordingly.

Mr. Mallory moved, seconded by Capt. Elliott, that the Road Bill be read a second time this day.

The said Bill was accordingly read for the second time.

Mr. Nellis then moved, seconded by Capt. Cowan, that this House do resolve itself into Committee on to-morrow to take the Road Bill into consideration.

Ordered accordingly.

The Solicitor General moved, seconded by Mr. Sherwood, that the House do resolve itself in a committee this day on the Duty Bill.

The House accordingly resolved itself into Committee to go into the consideration of the said Bill.

Mr. Speaker left the Chair.

Mr. Washburn was called to the chair of the Committee.

Mr. Speaker resumed the Chair.

Mr. Washburn reported that the Committee had gone through the consideration of the said Bill, to which the Committee had made some amendments, which he was directed to report whenever the House should be pleased to receive the same.

The said Report was then received and accepted.

The Solicitor General moved, seconded by Capt. Elliott, that the said Bill be engrossed and read a third time to-morrow. Ordered accordingly.

Mr. Clench then moved, seconded by Mr. McLean, that there be a call of the House on Wednesday next. Ordered accordingly.

Mr. Rogers moved, seconded by Mr. Nellis, that the Order of the House which gives Mr. Weekes leave to bring in a Bill on to-morrow to provide for Schools in this Province be discharged, and that leave be given to him to bring in the said Bill this day. Ordered accordingly.

And the said Bill was read by the Clerk at the Table for the first time.

Mr. Rogers then moved, seconded by Mr. Nellis, that the Bill to provide for Schools in this Province be read a second time to-morrow.

It was ordered accordingly.

On motion of Mr. Nellis, seconded by Mr. Crysler, the House adjourned until twelve o'clock to-morrow at noon.

Tuesday, 25th February, 1806.

Prayers were read.

Agreeable to the Order of the Day the House resolved itself into Committee on the Road Bill.

Mr. Speaker left the Chair.

Mr. Rogers was called to the chair of the Committee.

Mr. Speaker resumed the Chair.

Mr. Rogers reported progress, and asked for leave to sit again to-morrow.

Leave was granted accordingly.

Read a third time, the engrossed Bill for the better securing to His Majesty, His Heirs and Successors, the due collection and receipt of certain Duties therein mentioned.

Mr. Solicitor General moved, seconded by Mr. Rogers, that the Bill do pass, and that the title be "An Act to continue an Act passed in the forty-third year of His Majesty's Reign, entitled "An Act for the better securing to His Majesty, His Heirs and Successors, the due collection and receipt of certain Duties therein mentioned.

The Bill then passed, and was signed by the Speaker.

On motion of Mr. Sherwood, seconded by Mr. McLean,

Ordered, That the Solicitor General and Mr. Nellis do carry up the said Bill to the Legislative Council, and request their concurrence therein.

Read for the third time as engrossed, The Bill to regulate the practice of Physic and Surgery.

Mr. Solicitor General, one of the Messengers named to carry up to the Legislative Council the Bill for the better securing to His Majesty, His Heirs and Successors, the due collection and receipt of certain Duties therein mentioned, reported that they had carried up the said Bill and did request their concurrence thereto.

Mr. Washburn moved, seconded by Mr. Rogers, that the title of the Bill be "An Act to amend certain parts of an Act passed in the thirty-fifth year of His Majesty's Reign, entitled 'An Act to regulate the Practice of Physics and Surgery.'"

Ordered accordingly.

The Bill then passed, and was signed by Mr. Speaker.

Mr. Rogers moved, seconded by Mr. Weekes, that Mr. Washburn and Mr. Hill do carry up to the Honorable Legislative Council the Bill to provide for the licensing of Physicians and Surgeons, and to request their concurrence in passing the same. Ordered accordingly.

Read for the second time, the Bill for erecting Public Schools in the different Districts in this Province.

On motion of Mr. Weekes, seconded by Mr. Sherwood, the House resolved itself into Committee to go into consideration of the said Bill.

Mr. Speaker left the Chair.

Mr. McLean was called to the chair of the Committee.

Mr. Speaker resumed the Chair.

Mr. McLean reported that the Committee had made a progress, and that he was directed to ask leave to sit again to-morrow.

Leave was accordingly granted.

Mr. Weekes, from the Select Committee to whom was referred the Provincial Public Accounts, reported the proceedings of the Committee therein and he read the Report in his place, and afterwards delivered the same in at the Table, where it was read by the Clerk, and is as follows, viz.:

The Committee appointed to examine the Public Accounts and to report thereon, having examined the same, and agreed upon the following Report, viz.:

Your Committee have in the first place examined the amount of Duties on Stills, and also on Shop and Tavern Licenses contained in the Supplementary Accounts for the year 1805, and not accredited in the Public Accounts of that year, as marked Nos. 1 and 2, and find on comparing the same with the document marked 8, which has a reference thereto, that a sum of £7. 4s. 1½d. is short credited in the Public Accounts, the same after deducting ten per cent. for the Inspector, making £78. 5s. 6½d.

Your Committee have examined the Duties on Stills, and also on Shop and Tavern Licenses, and find on a calculation of the duties chargeable on the specific number of gallons set forth in the Account marked No. 9, and also of the number of Shop and Tavern Licenses, that the same far exceeds the amount of the sum credited in the General Account of Receipts and disbursements marked No. 17, the same, after deducting ten per cent. for Inspectors, making £1,092. 5s. 11d.

Your Committee have examined the Account of goods imported under authority of Acts of the Provincial Parliament marked No. 5, and find the duties on the same to amount to the sum of £488. 12s. ⅛d.

Your Committee have examined the Account marked No. 6, relating to the like Duties, and find the same to make £113. 10s. 7⅝. Sterling, equal to Provincial Currency £126. 2s. 10¼d.

Your Committee have examined the Account marked No. 13, for Tonnage or Light House Duty, and find the same to amount, exclusive of outstanding sums though credited in the General Account but £79. 3s. ¼d. to £96. 5s. 6¼d.

Your Committee have examined the Account marked No. 14, for Fines and Forfeitures, and find the same to amount to £12. 10s.

Your Committee have examined the Account marked No. 15, and find a sum for Fines and Forfeitures of £29. 17s. 7¼. sterling £33. 4s.

Your Committee have examined the Account marked No. 17, and find a balance of last year's funds remaining in the Receiver General's hands of £166. 2s. 11⅛d.

Your Committee have examined the same Account, and find a sum received from Lower Canada under the Provincial Agreement, £1,414. 6s. 8d.

Your Committee find in the same Account a sum received from John Bennett, Printer of £61. 6s. 5½d.

Your Committee find in the same Account a payment received from George Lukes, for Duties and arrears of Duties on Stills, £62. 17s. 9¾d.

Your Committee find the whole amount of the sums received for the year ending the 5th February, 1806, to amount to £3,632. 9s. 9¾d.

Your Committee find the amount of the sums payable out of the said fund under authority of this Parliament, including £400 for Public Buildings to be as follows, viz. £1,789. 0.½d.

Donald McLean, Esq.	25.	0	0
Hon. Richd. Cartwright	100.	0.	0
Hon. Robt. Hamilton ....·	100	0.	0
Sam'l. Sherwood, Esq.	100	0.	0
James Clarke, Esq.	25.	0.	0
George Lawe, Gent.	22.	14.	3
James Clarke	5.	0.	0
James Clarke	3.	16.	10½
Donald McLean	16.	5.	0
Donald McLean	.3.	5.	0
Donald McLean	104.	9.	1
Donald McLean	30.	0.	0
James Clarke	125.	0.	0
George Lawe	50.	0.	0
David Burns, Esq	50.	0.	0
Rev. Jno. Stewart	50.	0.	0
Hugh McLean	20.	0.	0
The Speaker of the Commons House of Assembly....	200.	0.	0
Donald McLean	125.	0.	0
Thos. Ridout, Esq	50.	0.	0
Rev. Robt. Addison	50.	0.	0
Thos. Ridout, ...			
Johnson	20.	0.	0
John Symington	33.	10.	10
For Public Buildings, annually	400.	0.	0
For printing the Laws	80.	0.	0

£1,789.   1.   ½

Your Committee find that a balance is now remaining in the Receiver General's hands after deducting the aforesaid disbursements of £1,743. 9s. 9¼d.

Your Committee find that the following sums remain in the Receiver General's hands of moneys appropriated by Act of Parliament, as hereafter set forth,

For Roads	£725.	0.	0
For the Purchase of Hemp	900.	0.	0
For the Purchase of Hemp Seed	423.	11.	0
A sum voted to support the War	500.	0.	0
For the purchase of Hemp in Wm. Allan's hands	100.	0.	0
For the purchase of the Statute Laws of England, in the hands of Henry Alcott, Esq	175.	0.	0
	£2,823.	11.	0

Your Committee find that several items are introduced in the General Account of disbursements, not authorized by the Provincial Parliament making in manner following £617. 13s. 7d.

Your Committee find that out of the sum of £1,000 appropriated by Act of Parliament for Roads, an advance of £250 of the same has been made to Thos. Talbot, Esq, which Your Committee understand has not been laid out according to the provisions of the Act.

Your Committee find that several sums have been annually returned as outstanding which are not brought into the General Account of the receipts and expenditures of the Province.

Your Committee find that the balance stated to be in the Receiver General's hands by the General Account of Receipts and Expenditures laid before the House is only £933. 9s. 10½d.

All which is humbly submitted.

(Signed) W. Weekes,
Chairman of Committee.

Commons House of Assembly,
25th February, 1806.

Mr. Washburn, one of the Messengers named to carry up to the Honorable Legislative Council the Bill to regulate the practice of Physic and Surgery, reported that they had carried up the same, and requested their concurrence thereto.

Mr. Weekes moved, seconded by Mr. Rogers, that the House do now resolve itself into Committee to take into consideration the Report of the Select Committee on the Provincial Public Accounts.

The House accordingly resolved itself into Committee.

Mr. Speaker left the Chair.

Mr. Dorland was called to the chair of the Committee.

Mr. Speaker resumed the Chair.

Mr. Dorland reported a progress, and asked for leave to sit again.

Leave was granted accordingly.

Mr. Sherwood gave notice that he shall move to-morrow that the accounts of the Contingent Expenses of the two Houses of Parliament for the present Session be laid before this House.

Mr. Weekes gave notice that he will to-morrow move the House to address His Honor the President praying that the Officers of this House be paid their salaries in future half yearly.

Read, the Petition of Duncan Cameron Esquire, which is as follows, viz: To the Honorable the Commons of Upper Canada, in Parliament assembled.

The humble Petition of Duncan Cameron, Administrator of the Goods and Chattels of the late Hon. Mr. Justice Cochrane,

Humbly Sheweth,

That Your Petitioner in submitting to Your Honorable House his demand for 62 volumes of Debrett's Parliamentary Register, which Your Honorable House purchased of Your Petitioner as part of the effects of the said Mr. Justice Cochrane, was then ignorant of the price paid for said Books in England, and only charged the average price of ten shillings per volume.

That Your Petitioner has since found amongst Mr. Cochrane's papers the charge made by the Bookseller for six of the volumes, which average fourteen shillings and nine pence sterling per volume.

Your Petitioner therefore prays that you will take the same into consideration, and make such order thereon as to you shall seem meet.

And Your Petitioner will ever pray.

(Signed) D. Cameron.

On motion of Capt. Elliott, seconded by Capt. Mallory, the House adjourned until to-morrow at twelve o'clock at noon.

Wednesday, 26th February, 1806.

Prayers were read.

The Order of the Day for the call of the House being read,

Ordered, That the House be now called over.

The House was accordingly called over, and several of the Members appeared, and the names of such Members as made default to appear were taken down, and are as follows, viz:

Wm. B. Wilkinson.
Peter Howard.
Allan McLean.
Isaac Swayzey (sick, excused.)
Benajah Mallory.
John McGregor.

Agreeable to the Order of the Day the House resolved itself into Committee to go·into the consideration of the Bill for amending and laying out Public Roads throughout the Province.

Mr. Speaker left the Chair.

Mr. Rogers was called to the chair of the Committee.

Mr. Speaker resumed the Chair.

Mr. Rogers reported that the Committee had made a progress, which he was directed to report, and to ask leave to sit again this day.

Leave was accordingly granted.

A Message from the Legislative Council by Mr. Baldwin, Master in Chancery.

8 A.

Mr. Speaker:—

I am commanded by the Honorable Legislative Council to inform this House that they have passed the Bill to alter and amend an Act, passed in the thirty-third year of His present Majesty's Reign, entitled "An Act to provide for the nomination and appointment of Parish and Town Officers," to which they have made some amendments, to which amendments they request the concurrence of this House. And then he withdrew.

Agreeable to leave given, the House again resolved itself into Committee to go into the further consideration of the Bill for amending the Roads through this Province.

Mr. Speaker left the Chair.

Mr. Rogers again took the chair of the Committee.

Mr. Speaker resumed the Chair.

Mr. Rogers reported that the Committee had made a progress, and that he was directed to ask for leave to sit again this day.

Leave was accordingly granted.

A Message from the Legislative Council by Mr. Baldwin, Master in Chancery. Mr. Speaker:—

The Legislative Council have passed the Bill entitled "An Act to make provision for several Sheriffs in this Province," to which they have made several amendments, to which amendments they desire the concurrence of the House of Assembly.

And also the Legislative Council have passed the Bill entitled "An Act to continue an Act passed in the forty-third year of His Majesty's Reign, entitled 'An Act for the better securing to his Majesty, His Heirs and Successors, the due collection and receipt of certain duties therein mentioned.'"

And also the Legislative Council have passed the Bill entitled "An Act to purchase certain apparatus for promoting science," with amendments, to which amendments they desire the concurrence of the House of Assembly.

And then he withdrew.

Agreeable to leave given the House again resolved itself into Committee to go into the further consideration of the Road Bill.

Mr. Speaker left the Chair.

Mr. Rogers again took the chair of the Committee.

Mr. Speaker resumed the Chair.

Mr. Rogers reported progress, and asked for leave to sit again to-morrow.

Leave was accordingly given.

Agreeable to the Order of the Day the House resolved itself into Committee to go into the consideration of the Bill for establishing schools in the different Districts in this Province.

Mr. Speaker left the Chair.

Mr. McLean was called to the chair of the Committee.

Mr. Speaker resumed the Chair.

And Mr. McLean reported that the Committee had made a progress, and directed him to ask for leave to sit again to-morrow.

Leave was accordingly granted.

Mr. Mallory moved, seconded by Mr. Nellis, that this House do now resolve itself into a Committee to take into its consideration the Petition of Capt. Brant.

The House accordingly resolved itself into Committee.

Mr. Speaker left the Chair.

Mr. Weekes was called to the chair of the Committee.

· Mr. Speaker resumed the Chair, and Mr. Weekes reported that the Committee had made a progress, and that he was directed to ask for leave to sit again to-morrow. Leave was accordingly granted.

Mr. Sherwood moved, seconded by Capt. Cowan, that the House do now resolved itself into a Committee to take into consideration the amendments made by the Legislative Council to the Bill for procuring apparatus for promoting science.

Which passed in the negative.

On motion of Mr. Howard, seconded by Mr. Rogers, the House adjourned.

Thursday, 27th February, 1806.

Prayers were read.

Agreeable to the Order of the Day the House resolved itself into a Committee to go into the consideration of the Bill for laying out Public Roads throughout this Province.

Mr. Speaker left the Chair.

Mr. Rogers was called to the Chair of the Committee.

Mr. Speaker resumed the Chair.

Mr. Rogers reported a progress and asked for leave to sit again.

Leave was accordingly granted.

Agreeable to the Order of the Day, the House resolved itself into a Committee to go into the consideration of the Bill for establishing Public Schools in the different Districts in this Province.

Mr. Speaker left the Chair.

Mr. McLean was called to the Chair of the Committee.

Mr. Speaker resumed the Chair.

Mr. McLean reported progress, and asked for leave to sit again this day.

Leave was accordingly granted.

A Message by Mr. Baldwin, Master-in-Chancery.

Mr. Speaker,—

I am commanded by the Honorable Legislative Council to inform this House that they have passed a Bill entitled "An Act to amend certain parts of an Act passed in the thirty-fifth year of His Majesty's reign, entitled 'An Act to regulate the practice of Physic and Surgery,' " to which they have made some amendments, to which they request the concurrence of the House of Assembly.

And then he withdrew.

The House again resolved itself into a Committee to go into the further consideration of the Bill for establishing Public Schools in the different Districts in this Province.

Mr. Speaker left the Chair.

Mr. McLean again took the chair of the Committee.

Mr. Speaker resumed the Chair.

Mr. McLean reported that the Committee had gone through the consideration of the said Bill, to which they had made several amendments, which he was directed to report to the House whenever it shall be pleased to receive the same.

Mr. Clench then moved, seconded by Captain Elliott, that the Report be not received.

A division thereupon took place, the names being called for, they were taken down, and are as follows, viz.:

Yeas.	Nays.
MESSRS. CLENCH.	MESSRS. NELLIS.
ELLIOTT.	COWAN.
	SHERWOOD.
	SOL'R GENERAL.
	MALLORY.
	WEEKES.
	ROGERS.
	DORLAND.
	WASHBURN.
	HILL.
	HOWARD.
	McLEAN.

The same was carried in the negative by a majority of ten.

The Report was then received and accepted.

Mr. Weekes then moved, seconded by Mr. Howard, that the said Bill be engrossed and read a third time to-morrow. Which was ordered accordingly.

Mr. Sherwood moved, seconded by Mr. McLean, that the House do now resolve itself into a Committee to go into the further consideration of the Road Bill.

The House accordingly resolved itself into Committee.

Mr. Speaker left the Chair.

Mr. Rogers was called to the Chair of the Committee.

Mr. Speaker resumed the Chair.

Mr. Rogers reported that the Committee had gone through the Bill with some amendments, which he was directed to report whenever the House should be pleased to receive the same.

The House then resolved that the said Report be now received and accepted.

Mr. Rogers then moved, seconded by Mr. Clench, that the Bill to provide for the opening and amending of the Public Highways throughout this Province be engrossed and read a third time to-morrow. Ordered accordingly.

Agreeable to the Order of the Day, the House resolved itself into a Committee to go into the consideration of Captain Joseph Brant's Petition.

Mr. Speaker left the Chair.

Mr. Weekes was called to the chair of the Committee.

Mr. Speaker resumed the Chair.

Mr. Weekes reported that the Committee was of opinion that the prayer of the said Petition was entitled to a further consideration, and that it be recommended to the House to take it into consideration early in the next Session of Parliament.

The House accordingly Resolved: That the prayer of the said Petition be taken into consideration early in the next ensuing Session of the Provincial Parliament.

Mr. Sherwood then moved, seconded by Captain Elliott, for leave to bring in a Bill to make provision for several Sheriffs in this Province.

Leave was then granted.

He then read the said Bill in his place, and delivered the same in at the Table, where it was again read throughout by the Clerk for the first time.

Mr. Weekes then moved that the said Bill be now read for the second time.

The said Bill was accordingly read for the second time.

On motion of Mr. Sherwood, seconded by Mr. Rogers, the House resolved itself into Committee to go into the consideration of the said Bill.

Mr. Speaker left the Chair.

Mr. Nellis was called to the Chair of the Committee.

Mr. Speaker resumed the Chair.

Mr. Nellis reported that the Committee had gone through the said Bill without any amendment.

On motion of Mr. Sherwood, seconded by Captain Cowan, the said Bill was ordered to be engrossed and read a third time this day.

Then was read as engrossed for the third time the Bill for allowing Salaries to certain Sheriffs in this Province.

Mr. Sherwood then moved that the Bill do pass, and that the title be "An Act to make provision for certain Sheriffs in this Province."

The Bill then passed and was signed by the Speaker.

Mr. Sherwood moved, seconded by Mr. Solicitor-General, for leave to bring in a Bill this day to procure certain Apparatus for promoting Science.

Leave was accordingly granted.

The said Bill was then read for the first time.

On motion of Mr. Clench, seconded by Mr. Rogers, the said Bill was read for the second time.

On motion of Mr. Sherwood, seconded by the Solicitor-General, the House resolved itself into Committee to go into the consideration of the said Bill.

Mr. Speaker left the Chair.

Mr. Mallory was called to the chair of the Committee.

Mr. Speaker resumed the Chair.

Mr. Mallory reported that the Committee had gone through the consideration of the said Bill without any amendment.

On motion of Mr. Clench, seconded by Captain Cowan, the said Bill was ordered to be engrossed and read a third time this day.

The said Bill as engrossed was read for the third time.

Mr. Sherwood then moved, seconded by the Solicitor-General, that the said Bill do pass, and that the title be "An Act to procure certain Apparatus for the promotion of Science."

The Bill then passed, and was signed by the Speaker.

Mr. Rogers then moved, seconded by Mr. Mallory, that Mr. Sherwood and Captain Cowan do carry up to the Honorable Legislative Council the Bill to provide for several Sheriffs and the Bill for purchasing certain Apparatus for promoting Science, and to request their concurrence in passing the same.

Mr. Solicitor-General then moved, seconded by Captain Cowan, for leave to bring in a Bill for applying a certain sum of money therein mentioned to make good certain moneys issued and advanced by His Majesty through the Lieutenant-Governor in pursuance of Addresses of this House.

Leave was accordingly granted.

On motion of Mr. Washburn, seconded by Mr. Dorland,

Ordered, That the amendments made by the Legislative Council to the engrossed Bill entitled "An Act to amend certain parts of an Act passed in the thirty-fifth year of His Majesty's reign, entitled 'An Act to regulate the practice of Physic and Surgery,'" be now taken into consideration.

Accordingly the House resolved itself into Committee to take the case into consideration.

Mr. Speaker left the Chair.

Captain Cowan was called to the Chair of the Committee.

Mr. Speaker resumed the Chair.

Captain Cowan reported that the Committee had gone through the consideration of the said Bill as amended by the Honorable Legislative Council, which he was directed to report whenever the House shall be pleased to receive the same.

The House then received the Report and concurred in the amendments made by the Legislative Council.

Mr. Sherwood moved, seconded by Mr. Clench, that Messrs. Rogers and Hill do inform the Legislative Council that this House has concurred in the amendments made by them to the Bill entitled, "An Act to amend certain parts of an Act passed in the thirty-fifth year of His Majesty's reign, entitled 'An Act to regulate the practice of Physic and Surgery." Ordered accordingly.

Mr. Sherwood, one of the Messengers named to carry up to the Legislative Council the Act to procure certain Apparatus for the promotion of Science, and also the Act to make provision for Sheriffs in this Province, reported that they had carried up the said Bills, and did request their concurrence thereto.

Mr. Weekes moved, seconded by Mr. Clench, that this House do resolve itself into a Committee to-morrow to take into consideration the Report on the Public Accounts. Ordered accordingly.

On motion of Mr. Sherwood, seconded by Mr. Clench, the House resolved itself into a Committee to go into the consideration of the amendments made by the Honorable Legislative Council to the Bill for the nomination of Parish and Town Officers.

Mr. Speaker left the Chair.

Mr. Clench was called to the chair of the Committee.

Mr. Speaker resumed the Chair.

Mr. Clench reported a progress, and asked for leave to sit again this day.

Leave was accordingly granted.

A Message from the Honorable Legislative Council by Mr. Baldwin, Master-in-Chancery.

Mr. Speaker,—

I am commanded by the Legislative Council to inform this House that they have passed the Bill sent up from this House entitled "An Act to make provision for certain Sheriffs in this Province" without any amendment.

And then he withdrew.

The House, agreeable to leave given, resolved itself into Committee to go into the further consideration of the Bill to nominate Parish and Town Officers.

Mr. Speaker left the Chair.

Mr. Clench again took the chair of the Committee.

Mr. Speaker resumed the Chair.

Mr. Weekes then moved, seconded by Mr. Rogers, that this House do resolve itself into a Committee to consider the propriety of an Address to His Honor, the President, praying that the Officers of the Legislative Council and Assembly may be paid their salaries half-yearly.

The House accordingly resolved itself into a Committee.

Mr. Speaker left the Chair.

Mr. Sherwood was called to the chair of the Committee.

Mr. Speaker resumed the Chair.

Mr. Sherwood reported that it is the opinion of the Committee that the Officers of the Legislative Council and House of Assembly suffer much inconvenience from the delay of payment of their salaries until the end of the year, and that the Committee recommend that the House do request a conference with the Legislative Council to prepare a joint Address to His Honor, the President, upon the subject of the same. Which report was received and accepted.

Mr. Rogers then moved, seconded by Mr. Weekes, that Mr. McLean and Mr. Clench be a Committee to request a conference with the Legislative Council on the subject of a joint Address to His Honor, the President, for the payment of the salaries of the Officers of the two Houses of Parliament half-yearly, and that they also be a Committee on the part of this House to manage the said conference, if agreed to by the Legislative Council. Which was ordered accordingly.

Friday, 28th February, 1806.

Prayers were read.

Read for the third time as engrossed, the Bill for establishing Schools in the different Districts throughout this Province.

Mr. Washburn then moved, seconded by Mr. Clench, that the said Bill be now recommitted, which passed in the negative.

Mr. Weekes moved, seconded by Mr. Sherwood, that the Bill do pass, and that the title be "An Act for the more general dissemination of learning throughout the Province."

The Bill then passed, and was signed by the Speaker.

Mr. Sherwood then moved, seconded by Mr. Clench, that this House do request a Conference with the Legislative Council upon the amendments made by them to a Bill relative to Parish and Township Officers. Ordered accordingly.

Mr. Weekes moved, seconded by Mr. Clench, that Mr. Sherwood and Captain Cowan do carry up to the Legislative Council the Bill for the more general dissemination of learning throughout the Province, and to request their concurrence thereto. Which was ordered accordingly.

Mr. Rogers moved, seconded by Mr. Washburn, that Mr. Sherwood and Capt. Cowan do go up and request a Conference with the Honorable Legislative Council in the amendments made by them to the Bill to amend an Act for the nomination and appointment of Parish and Town Officers.

The same was ordered accordingly.

Then was read for the third time as engrossed, the Bill for laying out and repairing Roads throughout this Province.

Mr. Rogers then moved, seconded by Mr. Weekes, that the Bill do pass, and that the title be "An Act to repeal an Act passed in the forty-fourth year of His Majesty's reign, entitled, 'An Act for granting to His Majesty a certain sum of money out of the funds applicable to the uses of this Province to defray the expenses of amending and repairing the Public Highways and Roads, laying out and building new Roads, and building Bridges in the several Districts thereof, and to make further provision for the opening and amending of the said Roads.' "

The House resolved the same; the Bill passed, and was signed by the Speaker.

Mr. Rogers moved, seconded by Mr. Weekes, that Mr. Sherwood and Capt. Cowan do carry up to the Honorable Legislative Council the said Bill, and do request their concurrence in passing the same. Ordered accordingly.

Read for the first time, an Act for applying a certain sum of money for the purpose therein mentioned.

The Solicitor-General moved, seconded by Mr. McLean, that the Act for applying a certain sum of money therein mentioned to make good certain moneys issued and advanced by His Majesty through His late Lieutenant-Governor in pursuance of the several Addresses of this House be now read a second time.

The said Bill was accordingly read for the second time.

Mr. Solicitor-General then moved, seconded by Mr. McLean, that the House do now resolve itself into Committee to go into the consideration of the said Bill.

The House accordingly resolved itself into Committee to go into the consideration of the said Bill.

Mr. Speaker left the Chair.

Mr. Washburn was called to the chair of the Committee.

Mr. Speaker resumed the Chair.

Mr. Washburn reported that the Committee had gone through the Bill, and had made several amendments thereto, which he was directed to report to the House whenever it should be pleased to receive the same.

The House then resolved that the said Report be now received.

The said Report was then received and accepted.

On motion of the Solicitor-General, seconded by Mr. McLean, the said Bill was ordered to be engrossed and read a third time to-morrow.

A Message from the Legislative Council by Mr. Baldwin, Master-in-Chancery.

Mr. Speaker:—

The Honorable the Legislative Council have passed the Bill entitled "An Act to procure certain apparatus for the promotion of science, sent up from the Honorable House, without any amendments.

And then he withdrew.

In obedience to the order of the House Mr. Clench and Mr. McLean reported that they had brought up to the Honorable Legislative Council the Message of this House, and is as follows, viz:

Mr. Speaker:—

The Commons do request a Conference with the Honorable Legislative Council on the subject of a joint Address to His Honor the President for the payment of the salaries of the Officers of the two Houses half yearly.

Commons House of Assembly,　　　　　　　　　　　　(Signed) A. McDonell,
28th February, 1806.　　　　　　　　　　　　　　　　　　　　Speaker.

Messrs. Sherwood and Capt. Cowan, in obedience to the order of this House, did carry up to the Honorable Legislative Council the following Message, viz: Mr. Speaker:—

The Commons request a Conference with the Honorable Legislative Council upon the amendments made by them to the Bill entitled "An Act to alter and amend an Act, passed in the thirty-third year of His present Majesty's Reign, entitled 'An Act to provide for the nomination of Parish and Town Officers.

Commons House of Assembly,　　　　　　　　　　　　(Signed) Alex'r McDonell,
28th February, 1806.　　　　　　　　　　　　　　　　　　　　Speaker.

Mr. McLean, one of the Messengers named to carry up a Message to the Honorable Legislative Council, reported that they had carried up the said Message.

Then Mr. Sherwood, one of the Messengers named to carry up to the Honorable Legislative Council the Bill entitled "An Act for the more general dissemination of learning throughout the Province," reported that they had carried up the said Bill and did request their concurrence thereto.

Mr. Sherwood, one of the Messengers named to request a Conference with the Honorable Legislative Council, further reported that they had carried up the said message.

Agreeable to the Order of the Day, the House resolved itself into a Committee to go into the further consideration of the Provincial Public Accounts.

Mr. Speaker left the Chair.

Mr. Dorland was called to the chair of the Committee.

Mr. Speaker resumed the Chair.

Mr. Dorland reported a progress, and asked for leave to sit again.

Leave was accordingly granted.

A written Message from the Honorable Legislative Council by Mr. Baldwin, Master in Chancery.

Mr. Speaker:—

A Committee of the Legislative Council are now ready to meet a Committee of the House of Assembly in the Legislative Council Chamber, as well on the subject of a joint Address to His Honor the President for the payment of the salaries of the two Houses of Parliament half yearly, as on the subject of amendments made by them to the Bill entitled "An Act to authorize and amend an Act passed in the thirty-third year of His present Majesty's Reign, entitled 'An Act to provide for the nomination of Parish and Town Officers.

Legislative Council Chamber, (Signed) Rich'd Cartwright,
28th February, 1806. Speaker Leg. Co.

And then he withdrew.

The House again resolved itself into a Committee to go into the further consideration of the Provincial Public Accounts.

Mr. Speaker left the Chair.

Mr. Dorland again took the Chair of the Committee.

Mr. Speaker resumed the Chair.

Mr. Dorland reported that the Committee had gone through the consideration of the Provincial Public Accounts, and had come to several resolutions, which he was directed to submit to the House, and he read the Report in his place; and afterwards delivered the same in at the Table, where it was again read by the Clerk. And the said Resolutions are as follows:

Resolved, That it is the opinion of the Committee that several sums of money have been paid out of the Provincial Treasury without the authority of Parliament or a vote of this House, amounting to £617. 13s. 7d.

Resolved, That it is the opinion of the Committee that the rights and privileges of the Commons House of Assembly in this Province have been violated by the application of several sums of the moneys in the Provincial Treasury to various purposes without the assent of Parliament or a vote of the Commons House of Assembly, and this Committee do therefore recommend to the Commons House of Assembly to address His Honor the President, praying that no moneys be issued in future without the assent of Parliament, or a vote of the House of Assembly, and that the sum of £617. 13s. 7d. be replaced in the Provincial Treasury, to be at the disposal of Parliament.

The following is the Schedule of moneys paid out of the Provincial Treasury in the year ending on February, 1806, without the consent of Parliament or a vote of the Commons House of Assembly.

Mr. John Bennett, Government Printer, being the amount of his salary as Government Printer, and the rent of an Office from the 1st January, to the 30th June, 1805, inclusive £50. 0. 0

Mr. Hugh McLean, being his half yearly allowance as Usher of the Court of King's Bench, from 1st January to 30th June, 1805, inclusive .... 5 .0. 0

Mr. Isaac Pilkington, being his half yearly allowance as keeper of the Court of King's Bench from 1st January to 30th June, 1805, inclusive .... 5 .0. 0

Mr. John Bennett, Government Printer, being the amount of his account for printing proclamations & laws of the first session of the fourth Provincial Parliament of this Province, and publications in the Gazette &c. between the 1st January and 30th June, 1805, inclusive 63. 5. 10

William Jarvis, Esq. Secretary of the Province, being the amount of his Fees on divers Public instruments &c. between the 1st January and 30th June, 1805, inclusive.... 38. 4. 0

William Jarvis, Esq. Register of the Province, being the amount of his Fees on divers public instruments &c. between the 1st January, and 30th June, 1805, inclusive ... 4. 15. 9

David Burns, Esq. Clerk of the Crown and Pleas, equal to £8. sterling, being the amount of his Contingent Account between 1st January and 30th June, inclusive 8. 17. 9¼

Thomas Scott, Esq. Attorney General, equal to £32. 4s. sterling, being the amount of his Contingent Account between 1st January and 30th June inclusive 35. 15. 6½

William Samuel Currey, Esq. Administrator to the Estate of the late Lieutenant Governor, Peter Hunter, Esq. being the amount of his Fees on divers Public instruments due to the said Lieut. Governor Peter Hunter, Esquire, from the 1st January to the 30th of June, 1805, inclusive... 42. 0. 0

Mr. John Bennett, Government Printer, being the amount of his Salary as Government Printer, and the rent on an Office from 1st July to the 31st December, 1805, inclusive 50. 0. 0

Mr. Hugh McLean, being his half yearly allowance as
Usher of the Court of King's Bench, from the 1st July to
the 31st December, 1805, inclusive 5.   0.   0

Mr. Isaac Pilkington, being his half yearly allowance as
Keeper of the Court of King's Bench from the 1st July to
the 31st December, 1805, inclusive 5.   0.   0

Mr. John Bennet, Government Printer, being the
amount of his account for printing notices, licenses, money
warrants, proclamations and bonds between the 1st July
and 31st December, 1805, inclusive 11.   15.   0

D'Arcy Boulton, Esq. Solicitor General, equal to
£30. 18s. sterling, being the amount of his contingent
account from the 1st July to the 31st December, 1805, inc...   34.   6.   8

William Jarvis, Esq. Secretary of the Province, being
the amount of his fees of divers Public instruments between
the 1st July and the 31st December, 1805, inclusive 43.   11.   0

William Samuel Currey, Esq. administrator to the estate
of the late Lieutenant Governor Peter Hunter, Esq. being
the amount of fees on divers Public instruments due to the
said late Lieutenant Governor Peter Hunter, Esq. from the
1st July to the 31st August, 1805, inclusive 70.   0.   0

William Jarvis, Esq., Register of the Province, being
the amount of his fees on divers Public instruments between
1st July to the 31st August, 1805, inclusive 7.   4.   3

William Allan, Esq. being the amount of fees on divers
public instruments due to Mr. President Grant between the
11th September and the 31st December, 1805, inclusive....   24.   0.   0

Thomas Scott, Esq. Attorney General, equal to £36. 6s.
sterling, being the amount of his Contingent account between the 1st July and the 31st December, 1805, inclusive   95.   17.   9¼

Mr. William Smith, being for materials furnished and
repairs made to the passage of communication between the
two Houses of the Legislature 18.   0.   0

————————————
£617.   .13.   7
————————————

Mr. Rogers moved, seconded by Mr. Weekes, that Mr. Sherwood and Captain
Cowan be added to the Committee appointed to confer with a Committee of the
Legislative Council on the subject of an Address to His Honor the President,
requesting him to alter the mode of paying the salaries of the Officers of the
two Houses of Parliament. Ordered accordingly.

Mr. Rogers then moved, seconded by Mr. Weeks, that Messrs. Sherwood, McLean, Clench and Cowan be a Committee to confer with a Committee of the Honorable Legislative Council on the amendments made by them to an Act for amending the Act relative to Parish and Town Officers.

The same was ordered accordingly.

On motion of Mr. Rogers, seconded by Mr. Nellis, the House adjourned for half an hour.

The House being met,

Mr. Sherwood, one of the Messengers named to confer with a Committee of the Honorable Legislative Council on the subject matter of amendments made by them to a Bill sent up from this House, entitled "An Act for the nomination of Parish and Town Officers throughout this Province," reported that they had met a Committee of the Honorable Legislative Council and that they had mutually agreed to the several amendments made to the said Bill, except that made to the ninth clause, prep. eighth line, third after the word "meeting" the rest of the clause be withdrawn.

Mr. Sherwood also reported that the Honorable Legislative Council had concurred in jointly addressing His Honor the President that the salaries of the Officers of both Houses of Parliament should be paid half yearly as the same becomes due.

Mr. Sherwood then moved, seconded by Capt. Elliott, that the amendments made to the Parish and Town Officers Bill as agreed upon by the Committee of Conference be adopted by this House, and that a Committee be appointed to inform the Legislative Council of the same. Ordered accordingly.

On motion of Mr. Sherwood, seconded by Capt. Elliott,

Ordered, that Messrs. Rogers and Nellis do carry the following message up to the Legislative Council.

Mr. Speaker:—

The House of Assembly have agreed to the Report of their Committee of Conference on the Bill entitled "An Act to alter and amend an Act passed in the thirty-third year of His present Majesty's Reign entitled 'An Act to provide for the nomination and appointment of Parish and Town Officers, and also to repeal certain parts of an Act passed in the thirty-third year of His Majesty's Reign, entitled, 'An Act to authorize and direct the laying and collecting of assessments and rates in every district in this Province, and to provide for the payment of the wages of the Members of the House of Assembly,' " and have adopted all the amendments made by this Honorable House except the one agreed to be withdrawn by the Committee of both Houses.

(Signed) Alex'r McDonell,
Commons House of Assembly,   Speaker.
28th February, 1806.

Mr. Washburn moved, seconded by the Solicitor General, that the House do now resolve itself into a Committee to go into the consideration of John Bennett's Petition. The same passed in the negative.

Mr. Weekes moved, seconded by Mr. Rogers, that an Address be presented to His Honor, the President, praying that he may be pleased to order that the salaries of the Officers of both Houses of Parliament be paid half yearly.

Mr. Clench then moved, seconded by Captain Cowan, that Messrs. Rogers and Weekes be a Committee to draft an Address to His Honor, the President, praying that he may be pleased to order the salaries to be paid to the respective Officers of both Houses of Parliament half yearly, as the same becomes due.

Which was ordered accordingly.

Mr. Rogers, one of the Committee appointed to draft an Address to His Honor, the President, praying that the salaries of the Officers of both Houses should be paid half yearly as the same becomes due, reported that they had drafted an Address to His Honor, the President, which they were ready to submit to the House whenever it should be pleased to receive the same.

It was then resolved that the said Address be now received.

He then read the Address in his place, and afterwards delivered the same in at the Table, where it was again read by the Clerk, and is as follows, viz.:

To His Honor Alexander Grant, Esquire, President administering the Government of the Province of Upper Canada, etc., etc., etc.

May it please Your Honor.

We, His Majesty's dutiful and loyal subjects, the Legislative Council and Commons of Upper Canada assembled, beg leave to state to Your Honor that the Officers and others attending the Legislative Council and House of Assembly suffer much inconvenience from the delay of payment of their respective salaries until the end of the year in which the same become payable.

We therefore entreat Your Honor to direct that they may be paid half yearly as the other officers of the Civil Government are paid.

The said Address was then ordered to be engrossed.

The said Address as engrossed was then read, passed, and signed by the Speaker.

Mr. McLean moved, seconded by Mr. Sherwood, that Messrs. Weekes and Boulton be a Committee to prepare an Address to the President in pursuance of the resolutions of the House upon the report of the Committee on the Provincial Public Accounts. Ordered accordingly.

Read, The Petition of sundry Inhabitants of the Western District, which is as follows, viz.:

To the Honorable the House of Representatives of His Majesty's Province of Upper Canada, in Provincial Parliament assembled.

The Petition of the Magistrates in General Quarter Sessions assembled, and others, Freeholders of the Western District.

Most Humbly Showeth,

That the Act of the forty-third of George the Third for the further altering and amending an Act, passed in the thirty-third year of His present Majesty's Reign, entitled "An Act to encourage the destroying of wolves and bears in different parts of this Province," has fallen with a great weight on this District; that a quarter part of the whole assessments have been consumed in discharging the claims made on the Treasurer under the authority of the same.

Your Petitioners further represent that the District, from causes which have already been laid before this Honorable House, is greatly in debt, and which they can see no prospect of paying off while the assessments are appropriated in the manner directed by the said Act.

They therefore humbly pray a repeal of the same so far as it relates to this District.

And your petitioners as in duty bound will ever pray.

(Signed) William Smith,
Hector S. McKay,
John Sparlman,
Sandwich, the 26th day of January, 1806.   and about 32 others.

Mr. Rogers then moved, seconded by Mr. Weekes, that Captains Cowan and Elliott do wait upon His Honor, the president, to know when he will be pleased to receive the Address of the two Houses of Parliament, praying him to order that the salaries of their Officers may be paid half yearly; and that those gentlemen be a joint Committee with a Committee of the Honorable Legislative Council, to present the said Address at what time His Honor will be pleased to appoint to receive the same. The same was ordered accordingly.

Mr. Rogers reported that the Messengers had carried up the Message of this House concurring in the conference held by a Committee of both Houses this day on the subject matter of amendments made in and to an Act for the nomination of Parish and Town officers.

On motion of Captain Cowan, seconded by the Solicitor General, the House adjourned until to-morrow at twelve o'clock at noon.

Saturday, First March, 1806.

Prayers were read.

Captain Cowan, one of the Messengers named to wait upon His Honor, the President, to know at what time he would be pleased to receive the Joint Address of the Legislative Council and this House, reported that His Honor was pleased to say that he would receive it this day at twelve o'clock.

A Message from the Honorable Legislative Council by Mr. Baldwin, Master in Chancery.

Mr. Speaker,—

I am commanded by the Honorable Legislative Council to inform this House that they have concurred and passed the Bill entitled "An Act to repeal an Act passed in the forty-fourth year of His Majesty's Reign, entitled 'An Act for the granting to His Majesty a certain sum of money out of the funds applicable to the uses of this province to defray the expense of amending and repairing the Public Highways and Roads, laying out and opening new Roads and building Bridges in the several Districts thereof; and to make further provision for the opening and amending the said Roads,'" without any amendment.

And then he withdrew.

Captain Cowan, one of the Messengers named to carry up to His Honor, the President, the Joint Address of the two Houses of Legislature, reported that they had carried up the same; to which His Honor was pleased to return the following answer:

Gentlemen of the Commons House of Assembly,

In reply to your Address requesting that the salaries of the officers and others attending Your House may be paid half yearly as the other Civil Officers of Government are paid, I shall readily meet your wishes and give the necessary directions for that purpose.

Read for the third time as engrossed, the Bill for applying a certain sum of money therein mentioned to make good moneys advanced by His Majesty through the Lieutenant Governor.

Mr. Solicitor General then moved, seconded by Mr. McLean, that the Bill do pass, and that the title be "An Act for applying a certain sum of money therein mentioned to make good certain moneys issued and advanced by His Majesty through the late Lieutenant Governor, in pursuance of several Addresses."

The Bill then passed, and was signed by the Speaker.

Mr. McLean then moved, seconded by Mr. Dorland, that Mr. Boulton and Captain Cowan do carry up to the Legislative Council the said Bill.

Ordered accordingly.

Mr. Solicitor General, one of the Messengers named to carry up to the Honorable Legislative Council the Bill to make good several sums of money issued by His Majesty through the late Lieutenant Governor in pursuance of several Addresses, reported that they had carried up the said Bill and did request their concurrence thereto.

Mr. Weekes, one of the Committee appointed to draft an Address to His Honor, the President, reported that they had drafted an Address, which they were ready to submit to the House whenever it should be pleased to receive the same.

The House then resolved that the said Report be now received.

He then read the draft of the Address in his place, and then gave it in at the Table, where it was once more read by the Clerk, and is as follows, viz.

To His Honor, Alexander Grant, Esquire, President administering the Government of the province of Upper Canada, etc., etc., etc.

May it please Your Honor,

We, His Majesty's most dutiful and loyal subjects, the Commons of Upper Canada in Parliament Assembled, have, conformably to an early assurance to Your Honor, taken into consideration the Public Accounts of the Province, and have, on a due investigation of the same, to report to you that the first and most constitutional privilege of the Commons has been violated in the application of moneys out of the Provincial Treasury to various purposes without the assent of Parliament or a vote of the Commons House of Assembly.

The comment on this departure from constituted authority and fiscal establishment must be more than painful to all who appreciate the advantages of our happy Constitution, and who wish their continuance to the latest posterity; but however studious we may be to abstain from stricture we cannot suppress the mixed emotions of relative condition, we feel it as the representatives of a free people, we lament it as the subjects of a beneficent Sovereign, and we hope that you, in your relation to both, will more than sympathize in so extraordinary an occurrence.

We beg leave to annex hereto a schedule of the moneys so misapplied, amounting to Six Hundred and Thirteen Pounds, Thirteen Shillings, and Sevenpence, and trust that you will not only order that sum to be replaced in the Provincial Treasury, but will also direct that no moneys be issued thereout in future without the assent of Parliament or a vote of the Commons House of Assembly.

Commons House of Assembly,   (Signed) Alexander McDonell,
1st March, 1806.   Speaker.

Then, on motion of Mr. Dorland, seconded by Mr. Nellis,
Ordered, That the said Address be engrossed.

Accordingly the said Address was engrossed, was read, passed, and signed by the Speaker.

The Solicitor General then moved, seconded by Mr. McLean, that Mr. Rogers and Mr. Dorland do wait upon His Honor the President to know when he will be pleased to receive the House with its Address.   Ordered accordingly.

A Message from the Honorable Legislative Council by Mr. Baldwin, Master in Chancery.

Mr. Speaker:—

The Honorable Legislative Council have passed the Bill sent up from this Honorable House, entitled "An Act for applying a certain sum of money therein mentioned to make good certain moneys issued and advanced by His Majesty through the Lieutenant Governor in pursuance of several Addresses" without any amendment.

And then he withdrew.

On motion of Mr. Nellis, seconded by Mr. Dorland, the House adjourned for one quarter of an hour.

The House being met,

Mr. Rogers, one of the Messengers named to wait upon His Honor the President, reported that in obedience to the Orders of the House the Messengers had waited upon His Honor the President to know his pleasure when he would receive this House with its Address and that His Honor was pleased to appoint Monday the third instant at ten o'clock in the forenoon to receive this House with its Address.

On motion of Mr. Nellis, seconded by Mr. Hill,

The House resolved itself into Committee on the Contingent Accounts of both Houses of Parliament for the present Session.

Mr. Speaker left the Chair.

Mr. Crysler was called to the chair of the Committee.

Mr. Speaker resumed the Chair.

Mr. Crysler reported that the Committee had gone through the consideration . of the Contingent Accounts of the Legislative Council and this House, and that they had come to several Resolutions thereon, which he was directed to submit to the House; and he read the Report in his place, and afterwards delivered the same in at the Table, where it was again read by the Clerk.

And the said Resolutions are as follows:

Resolved, that it is the opinion of the Committee that there is due to sundry persons, agreeable to the annexed account sent down from the Legislative Council, and signed by their Speaker, for services performed during the present Session £33 13s. 7d.

Resolved, that it is the opinion of this Committee that there is due to the sundry persons, agreeable to the annexed account for articles furnished for the use of this House, and for services performed during the present Session, £39 8s. 11½d.

Resolved, that it is the opinion of this Committee that the sum of £15 be allowed to the Clerk to enable him to complete the business of the present Session.

Resolved, that it is the opinion of the Committee that it is expedient to advance the sum of £30 to the Clerk of the House of Assembly to enable him to purchase a supply of stationery for the use of the next Session of Parliament.

Resolved, that it is the opinion of the Committee that Hugh Carfrae be allowed annually for his attendance on this House as Messenger and Firelighter the sum of £15.

Resolved, that there is due to Duncan Cameron, Esq., Administrator of the estate of the late Mr. Justice Cochrane, the sum of £18 for books purchased for the use of the House of Assembly the last and present Session, as per account.

On motion of Mr. Rogers, seconded by Mr. Washburn,

Resolved, that this House doth concur in the foregoing Resolutions reported from the Committee.

The Honorable Legislative Council
           to George Lawe Dr.

To W. Allan's Acct. for sundries furnished for the Legislative Council	£5	1	5
To John Bassett's Account for his attendance on the Legislative Council	12	16	3
To William Smith's Account for sundry repairs to the Legislative Council Chamber and Office	1	10	0
For Sarah Hay's Account for scouring the Office and Chamber of the Legislative Council	2	6	9
For Philip Clinger's Acct. for cleaning the stoves and making two holdfasts to secure the pipes of the stoves of the Legislative Council Chamber and Office	1	10	0
For Elinor Bassett's Acct. for hemming and washing the towels of the Legislative Council Chamber and Office		9	2
For making a Press for the security of the Records, etc., of the Legislative Council, and furnishing all materials for the same	5	0	0
For extra Copying Clerks	5	0	0
Prov. Curr'y	£33	13	7

York, 1st March, 1806.

Approved.   (Signed)   Richd. Cartwright,
                                           Speaker.

York, Upper Canada, Mar. 1, 1806.

The Contingent Account of the Commons House of Assembly, for the Second Session of the Fourth Provincial Parliament.

Due to John McBeath	£8	10	6
" Philip Clinger	1	5	0
" William Allan		6	10½
" Duncan Cameron	1	10	7½
" Alex'r. Wood	1	17	6
" Thomas Ridout Johnson	8	0	9½
" The Postmaster at York		2	8
" Allowance made to complete the business of the present Session, and for other contingencies during the recess of Parliament	15	0	0
" Cash voted to procure stationery for the use of the ensuing Session of the Provincial Parliament	30	0	0
" Charles Willcocks for extra copying	6	0	0

9 A.

"   Samuel B. Cozens   Do.   6   5   0
"   John Cameron and others for Do. 5 10   0
"   Allowance to Hugh Carfrae, Messenger and Firelighter to
         House of Assembly for services during this Session....   15   0   0

Passed the Commons House of Assembly,   £99   8 11½
    1st March, 1806.

The House of Assembly in Account Current with Donald McLean, Clerk of the
    Assembly, for Stationery furnished for the use of the Second Session of the
    Fourth Provincial Parliament.

Dr.
1805.
    To Cash paid John Nelson for stationery bought for the use of
        the Second Session of the Fourth Parliament, as per receipt £27   5   5
    To freight of two barrels bulk from Montreal, supposed 18s. 6d.
        per bar., to Kingston 1 17   0
    To freight from Kingston to York, 'at 5s.   10   0
    To balance due by Donald McLean, the Clerk   7   7

                                                          £30   0   0

The House of Assembly in Account Current with Donald McLean, Clerk of the
    Assembly, for stationery furnished for the use of the Second Session of the
    Fourth Provincial Parliament.

                                                                 Cr.
1805.
    By Lieut.-Gov. Hunter's Warrant to enable me to provide a supply
        of stationery for the use of the House of Assembly at the
        ensuing session, pursuant to an Address from the House of
        Assembly dated 1st March, 1805 .... £30   0   0

                                                          £30   0   0

    Errors excepted.
York, 26th Feb'y, 1806.   (Signed) Donald McLean.
                                                         Clerk Assembly.

The House of Assembly in Account Current with Donald McLean, Clerk of the
                                Assembly.
Dr.
1806.
    To Cash paid Chas. Willcocks for copying, as per receipt £10   0   0
    Do. Saml. D. Cozens for Do., as per receipt   11   0   0
    Do. John Cameron for Do. as per receipt   4   0   0

            Prov. Cur'y............................. £25   0   0

1806.   Cr.
By amount of His Honor the President's Warrant in my favor as by
   law appropriated £25   0   0

                          Prov. Cur'y............................. £25   0   0

Errors excepted.   (Signed) Donald McLean,
York, 26th Feb'y, 1806.   Clerk Assembly.

The Honorable House of Assembly
              to the Estate of the Honorable Mr. Justice Cochrane,   Dr.

So much short charged on 62 volumes of Debrett's Parliamentary
   Register, sold and delivered in February, 1805 .... £16   7   2
Two volumes Debrett's Parliamentary Register at 16s. 5d.......   1 12 10

                          Halifax Cur'y............................. £18   0   0

   Mr. Rogers then moved, seconded by Mr. Nellis, that the Solicitor-General
and Mr. Washburn be a Committee to draft an Address to His Honor the President
requesting him to issue his Warrant for the payment of certain sums of money
agreeable to the several Resolutions of the Committee on the Contingent Accounts
of this House. Which was ordered accordingly.
   Mr. Solicitor-General reported that the Committee appointed to draft an
Address to His Honor the President had done so, which they were ready to submit
to the House whenever it should be pleased to receive the same.
   The House then resolved that the said Address be now received.
   The Solicitor-General then read the Address in his place, and delivered it in
at the Table, when it was again read by the Clerk, and is as follows, viz.:
                        To His Honor Alexander Grant, Esquire,
                        President Administering the Government of
                        the Province of Upper Canada, etc., etc.
   May it Please Your Honor,—
   We, His Majesty's Most dutiful and Loyal Subjects, the Commons of Upper
Canada in Parliament assembled, do most humbly pray that it may please Your
Honor to issue your warrant directed to the Receiver-General, requiring him to
pay unto Mr. George Lawe, Gentleman Usher of the Black Rod, the sum of Thirty-
three Pounds Thirteen Shillings and Sevenpence, in order to enable him to
answer and satisfy certain contingent expenses of the Legislative Council during
the present Session.
   And also that it may please Your Honor to issue Your Warrant directed to
the Receiver-General, requiring him to pay unto Donald McLean, Esquire, Clerk
of the House of Assembly, the sum of Sixty-nine Pounds, Eight Shillings and
Elevenpence Halfpenny to enable him to answer and satisfy certain Contingent
Expenses of the House of Assembly during the present Session.
   And that Your Honor be further pleased to issue your Warrant, directed
to the Receiver-General, requiring him to pay the sum of Thirty Pounds to enable
him to purchase a supply of stationery for the use of the ensuing Session of Parliament, which several sums of money the Commons will make good to Your Honor
the next Session of Parliament.
Commons House of Assembly,   (Signed) Alexander McDonell,
      1st March, 1806.   Speaker.

Then, on motion of Captain Cowan, seconded by Mr. Howard,

Ordered, That the said Address be now engrossed,

The said Address as engrossed was then read, passed, and signed by the Speaker.

On motion of Mr. Rogers, seconded by Mr. Nellis,

Ordered, That Captain Cowan and Captain Elliott do present the said Address to His Honor the President at such time as he may be pleased to appoint to receive the same.

On motion of Mr. Washburn, seconded by Mr. Crysler, the House adjourned till Monday at nine o'clock in the forenoon.

Monday, 3rd March, 1806.

Prayers were read.

Captain Cowan reported that the Messengers had waited upon His Honor, the President, with the Address of this House voted on the first instance, to which His Honor was pleased to return the following answer, viz.:

Gentlemen of the Commons House of Assembly,—

Agreeable to your Address of the 1st March, I shall issue Warrants for the purposes therein mentioned.

York, Upper Canada,

3rd March, 1806.

On motion of Mr. Clench, seconded by Mr. Sherwood,

Ordered, That an Address to His Honor, the President, for the payment of Eighteen Pounds to Duncan Cameron, Esquire, as Executor to the Estate of the late Judge Cochrane, being the amount due for certain books purchased of him for the use of the House of Assembly, the last session and the present.

Ordered accordingly.

Captain Cowan moved, seconded by Mr. Crysler, that Messrs. McLean and Rogers be a Committee to draft an Address to His Honor, the President, praying that he may be pleased to issue his Warrant to the Clerk of this House, to enable him to pay Duncan Cameron Esquire, Thirteen Pounds, due to the Estate of the late Judge Cochrane, as per account laid before this House accompanied by a petition.

Mr. McLean and Mr. Rogers informed the House that agreeably to an order of this House they had drafted an Address to His Honor, the President, which they are ready to submit to the House whenever it shall be pleased to receive the same.

The House then resolved that the said Address be now received and read.

The said Address was then delivered in at the Table to the Clerk and by him read, and is as follows:

> To His Honor Alexander Grant, Esquire, President administering the Government of the Province of Upper Canada, etc., etc.

May it Please Your Honor,—

We, His Majesty's most dutiful and loyal subjects, the Commons of Upper Canada in Parliament assembled, do most respectfully pray that it may please Your Honour to issue your Warrant to the Clerk of the House of Assembly for the sum of Eighteen Pounds, to enable him to pay Duncan Cameron, Esquire, Ad-

ministrator to the Estate of the late Mr. Justice Cochran, for books purchased for the use of the House of Assembly; which sum of money the Commons will make good in the next session of Parliament.
Commons House of Assembly,
3rd March, 1806.

On motion of Mr. Dorland, seconded by Mr. Washburn, the said Address was ordered to be engrossed.
The Address as engrossed then passed, and was signed by the Speaker.
On motion of Mr. Weekes, seconded by Mr. Howard,
Ordered, That the said Address be presented to His Honor, the President, by Captains Cowan and Elliott at such time as he may be pleased to receive the same.
Captain Cowan reported that the Messengers had waited upon His Honor, the President, with the Address voted this day, to which he was pleased to return the following answer, viz.:
Gentlemen of the Commons House of Assembly,—
Agreeable to your Address of the third March, I shall issue a Warrant for the purpose therein mentioned.
York, Upper Canada,
3rd March, 1806.

Mr. Sherwood then moved, seconded by Mr. Clench, that the trial of the election of Benajah Mallory, Esquire, be deferred to the third day of the next Session of Parliament, and that the Speaker have authority during the Recess to issue orders for the attendance of witnesses. Ordered accordingly.
Mr. Sherwood, seconded by Mr. Clench, moved that the Contingent Accounts of this House shall be hereafter signed by the Speaker, and that he shall cause to be sent to the Governor, Lieutenant-Governor, or person administering the Government for the time being, four copies of the same signed by him, immediately after the close of each session, as the only voucher for the expenditure of the Session; and that the heading of the said Contingent Account shall be "The Contingent Account of the Commons House of Assembly for the (as the case may be) Provincial Parliament."
The House accordingly resolved the same.
At the hour appointed Mr. Speaker and the House attended upon His Honor, the President, with the Address of this House, and being returned, Mr. Speaker reported that the House had attended upon His Honor, the President, with the Address, and that His Honor was pleased to make the following answer:
Gentlemen of the Commons House of Assembly,—
I learn with regret from your Address of the first March that a degree of dissatisfaction prevails in the Commons House of Assembly with respect to the application of a sum of money stated to amount to Six Hundred and Seventeen Pounds Thirteen Shillings and Seven Pence.
At the time of my accession to the administration of the Government I found that various items similar to those in the Schedule accompanying your Address had been charged against the Provincial Government and acquiesced in for two years preceding, and I directed the usual mode to be followed in making up the accounts which I ordered to be laid before you during the present session.
The money in question has been undoubtedly applied to purposes useful and necessary for the general concerns of the Province.
I am, however, desirous to give every reasonable satisfaction to the House of

Assembly; I shall direct the matter to be immediately investigated, and, if there has been error in stating the account, take measures to have it corrected and obviated for the time to come.

York, Upper Canada,   (Signed) Alexander Grant,
3rd March, 1806.   President.

Mr. Weekes then moved, seconded by Mr. Rogers, that the House do resolve itself into a Committee to take into consideration the answer of His Honor, the President, to our Address of this day.

The House accordingly resolved itself into a Committee.

Mr. Speaker left the Chair.

Mr. Howard was called to the Chair of the Committee.

Mr. Speaker resumed the Chair.

Mr. Howard reported that the Committee had passed a Resolution which he was directed to report whenever the House shall be pleased to receive the same.

On the question being put for the Report being received, the House being divided,

Mr. Speaker then gave his vote for the Report not being received.

A Message from His Honor, the president, by Mr. George Lawe, Gentleman Usher of the Black Rod.

Mr. Speaker,

I am commanded by His Honor, the President, to acquaint this Honorable House that it is His Honor's pleasure that the Members thereof do forthwith attend upon His Honor in the Legislative Council Chamber.

Accordingly Mr. Speaker with the House went up to attend His Honor, when His Honor was pleased to give in His Majesty's name the Royal assent to the following Public and Private Bills.

An Act to alter and amend an Act passed in the Thirty-third year of His present Majesty's Reign, entitled "An Act to provide for the nomination and appointment of Parish and Town Officers, and also to repeal certain parts of an Act passed in the Thirty-third year of His present Majesty's Reign, entitled 'An Act to authorize and direct the laying and Collection of Assessments and Rates in every District in this province, and to provide for the payment of wages to the Members of the House of Assembly.'"

An Act to repeal an Act passed in the Thirty-fifth year of His Majesty's Reign, entitled "An Act to regulate the practice of Physic and Surgery."

His Honor was pleased to reserve the following Bill for the signification of His Majesty's pleasure thereon.

An Act to authorize the Sheriff to levy all necessary costs incurred in any suit brought in any of His Majesty's Courts of Law in this Province.

Mr. Speaker then said,

May it please Your Honor to approve of the five Bills which the Assembly, with the concurrence of the Legislative Council, have passed for aid to His Majesty.

An Act to make provision for certain Sheriffs in this province.

An Act to procure certain Apparatus for the promotion of Science.

An Act to repeal an Act passed in the Forty-fourth year of His Majesty's Reign, entitled "An Act for granting to His Majesty a certain sum of money out of the fund applicable to the uses of this Province, to defray the expenses of amending and repairing the Public Highways and Roads, laying out and opening new Roads, and building Bridges in the Several Districts thereof, and to make further provisions for the opening and amending new Roads."

An Act to continue an Act passed in the Forty-third year of His Majesty's Reign, entitled "An Act for the better securing to His Majesty, His Heirs and Successors, the due collection and receipt of certain Duties therein mentioned."

An Act for applying a certain sum of money therein mentioned to make good certain moneys issued and advanced by His Majesty through the Lieutenant-Governor in pursuance of several Addresses.

To which His Honor was also pleased to give the Royal assent in His Majesty's name.

His Honor, the president, was then pleased to make the following Speech to both Houses of Parliament.

Honorable Gentlemen of the Legislative Council,
and
Gentlemen of the House of Assembly.

Having dedicated a considerable portion of your time to the service of the Public, I think it proper to close this session of the Legislature.

The Bills to which I have now given the Royal assent contain, some of them, objects of the highest importance to the public.

By the opening of Roads and construction of Bridges, while the safety and comfort of the individual will be promoted, the commerce and riches of this Province will necessarily be extended and increased.

The encouragement which you have given for the procuring of the means necessary for communicating of useful and ornamental knowledge to the rising generation meets with my approbation, and I have no doubt will produce the most salutary effects.

The other Bills which have now passed will, I trust, effectuate the beneficial purpose for which they were intended.

I dismiss you with the pleasing hope that the Laws enacted for the good of this province will derive additional strength and energy from your exertions, influence and example.

(Signed)　　Alexander Grant,
York, Upper Canada, 3rd March, 1806.　　　　　　　　　President.

After which the Honorable Speaker of the Legislative Council said,
Gentlemen of the Legislative Council,
and
Gentlemen of the House of Assembly.

It is His Honor, the president's will and pleasure that this provincial Parliament be prorogued until Saturday, the 'Twelfth day of April next, to be then here held, and this provincial Parliament is accordingly prorogued until Saturday, the Twelfth day of April next.

[I do hereby certify that the above and what is written on the foregoing pages is a true copy of the Journal of the House of Assembly in Upper Canada, being of the Second Session of the Fourth Provincial parliament assembled in the Town of York on the Fourth day of February last agreeably to the Proclamation of His

Honor, Alexander Grant, Esquire, President administering the Government of Upper Canada, and prorogued by His Honor the Third day of March last.

York, Upper Canada,   Donald McLean,
   16th April, 1806.]   Clerk Assembly.

[Certified to be true copies from the original records in the Colonial Office.

                                                  Geo. Mayer,
Colonial Office, Downing Street,   Librarian and Keeper of the Records.
   8th September, 1850.]

JOURNAL

OF THE

HOUSE OF ASSEMBLY

OF

UPPER CANADA

From the second day of February to the

ninth day of March,

1807.

Both days inclusive.

In the forty-seventh year of the Reign of

KING GEORGE THE THIRD.

Being the third session of the fourth provincial parliament of
this province.

JOURNAL

OF THE

HOUSE OF ASSEMBLY

OF

UPPER CANADA

1807.

ALEXANDER GRANT, President.

PROCLAMATION.

George the Third, by the Grace of God of the United Kingdom of Great Britain and Ireland, King, Defender of the Faith.

To our beloved and faithful Legislative Councillors of our Province of Upper Canada, and to Our Knights, Citizens and Burgesses of Our said Province, to the Provincial Parliament at our Town of York on the Twelfth Day of April, to be commenced, held, called and elected, and to every of you GREETING.

Whereas by Our Ploclamation bearing date the Third day of March last, we thought fit, by and with the advice of Our Executive Council, to prorogue Our said Provincial Parliament until the Twelfth day of April next ensuing, at which time, in Our Town of York, you are held and constrained to appear; but we, taking into our Royal consideration the ease and convenience of our loving subjects, have thought fit, by and with the advice and consent of Our Executive Council, to relieve you and each of you of your attendance at the time aforesaid, hereby convoking, and by these presents enjoining you and each of you that on the Twentieth day of May next ensuing you meet us in Our Provincial Parliament in Our Town of York, there to take into consideration the state and welfare of Our said Province of Upper Canada, and there to do as may seem necessary. Herein fail not.

In Testimony Whereof we have caused these Our Letters to be made Patent, and the Great Seal of Our said Province to be hereunto affixed;

Witness Our well beloved Alexander Grant, Esquire, Our President administering the Government of Our said Province of Upper Canada, at York, this Eighth day of April, in the Year of Our Lord, One thousand eight hundred and six, and in the Forty-sixth year of Our Reign.

WM. JARVIS, Secretary.   A. G.

By a further proclamation of His Honor, Alexander Grant, Esquire, President administering the Government of the Province of Upper Canada, &c., &c., dated at York the Fifteenth day of May, One thousand eight hundred and six, the meeting of the Legislative Council and House of Assembly stands prorogued to the Twenty-seventh day of June next.

By a further Proclamation of His Honor, Alexander Grant, Esquire, President administering the Government of the Province of Upper Canada, &c., &c., dated at York, the twentieth day of June One Thousand Eight Hundred and Six, the Meeting of the Legislative Council and House of Assembly stands prorogued to the fourth day of August next.

By a further proclamation of His Honor Alexander Grant, President administering the Government of the Province of Upper Canada &c., dated at York the first day of August One Thousand Eight Hundred and Six, the Meeting of the Legislative Council and House of Assembly stands prorogued to the eleventh day of September next.

PROCLAMATION.

FRANCIS GORE, Lieutenant-Governor.

George the Third, by the Grace of God of the United Kingdom of Great Britain and Ireland King, Defender of the Faith.

To Our beloved and faithful Legislative Councillors of Our Province of Upper Canada, and to Our Knights, Citizens and Burgesses of Our said Province, to the Provincial Parliament at Our Town of York, on the fourth day of August, to be commenced, held, called and elected, and to every of you, GREETING.

Whereas by Our Proclamation bearing date the first day of August, we thought fit, by and with the advice of Our Executive Council, to prorogue Our said Provincial Parliament until the eleventh day of September next, at which time in Our Town of York you were held and constrained to appear; but we, taking into Our Royal consideration the ease and convenience of Our loving subjects, have thought fit, by and with the advice and consent of Our Executive Council, to relieve you and each of you of your attendance at the time aforesaid, hereby convoking, and by these presents enjoining you and each of you that on the thirteenth day of October next ensuing you meet us in Our Provincial Parliament in Our Town of York, there to take into consideration the state and welfare of Our said Province of Upper Canada, and there to do as may seem necessary. Herein fail not.

In testimony whereof we have caused these Our Letters to be made patent, and the Great Seal of Our said Province to be hereunto affixed.

Witness Our trusty and well beloved Francis Gore, Esquire, Our Lieutenant-Governor of Our said Province of Upper Canada, at York, this twenty-ninth day of August, in the Year of Our Lord One Thousand Eight Hundred and Six, and Forty Sixth Year of Our Reign.

WM. JARVIS, Secy.   F. G.

By a further Proclamation of His Excellency Francis Gore, Esquire, Lieutenant-Governor of the Province of Upper Canada, &c., &c., dated at York, the sixth day of October One Thousand Eight Hundred and Six, the Meeting of the Legislative Council and House of Assembly stands prorogued to the twentieth day of November next.

By a further Proclamation of His Excellency Francis Gore, Esquire, Lieutenant-Governor of the Province of Upper Canada, &c., &c., dated at York the fourteenth day of November, One Thousand Eight Hundred and Six, the Meeting of the Legislative Council and House of Assembly stands prorogued to the twenty-sixth day of December next.

PROCLAMATION.

FRANCIS GORE, Lieutenant-Governor.

George the Third, by the Grace of God of the United Kingdom of Great Britain and Ireland King, Defender of the Faith.

To Our beloved and faithful Legislative Councillors of Our Province of Upper Canada, and to Our Knights, Citizens and Burgesses of Our said Province, to the Provincial Parliament at Our Town of York on the twenty-sixth day of December, to be commenced, held, called and elected, and to every of \you, GREETING.

Whereas by Our Proclamation bearing date this fourteenth day of November, we have thought fit, by and with the advice of Our Executive Council, to prorogue Our said Provincial Parliament until the twenty-sixth day of December instant, at which time in Our Town of York you were held and constrained to appear; but we, taking into Our Royal consideration the ease and convenience of Our Loving subjects, have thought fit, by and with the advice and consent of Our Executive Council, to relieve you and each of you of your attendance at the time aforesaid, hereby convoking, and by these presents enjoining you and each of you that on the second day of February next, which will be in the Year of Our Lord One Thousand Eight Hundred and Seven, you meet us in Our Provincial Parliament in Our Town of York, for the actual dispatch of public business, there to take into consideration the state and welfare of Our said Province of Upper Canada, and there to do as may seem necessary. Herein fail not.

In testimony whereof we have commanded these Our Letters to be made Patent, and the Great Seal of Our said Province to be hereunto affixed.

Witness Our trusty and well beloved Francis Gore, Esquire, Our Lieutenant-Governor of Our said Province of Upper Canada, at York this nineteenth day of December, in the Year of Our Lord One Thousand Eight Hundred and Six, and Forty-seventh year of Our Reign.

WM. JARVIS, Sec. F. G.

HOUSE OF ASSEMBLY, UPPER CANADA.

York, 2nd February, 1807.

At the third Session of the Fourth Parliament of Upper Canada, begun and held in the Town of York, on Monday, the second day of February, in the forty-seventh year of the Reign of Our Sovereign Lord George the Third, by the Grace of God of the United Kingdom of Great Britain and Ireland King, Defender of the Faith, and in the Year of Our Lord One Thousand Eight Hundred and Seven.

His Honor Alexander Grant, Esquire, late President administering the Government of Upper Canada, and His Excellency Francis Gore Esquire, Lieutenant-Governor, having by their several proclamations as annexed prorogued the meeting of the Provincial Parliament until this day,

The House being met, Prayers were read.

A Message from His Excellency the Lieutenant-Governor by Mr. George Lawe, Gentleman Usher of the Black Rod.

Mr. Speaker:—

It is His Excellency the Lieutenant-Governor's pleasure that this Honorable House do immediately attend him in the Legislative Council Chamber.

The House went up accordingly, and being returned, Mr. Speaker reported that the House had attended His Excellency the Lieutenant-Governor in the Legislative Council Chamber, where His Excellency had been pleased to open the present session by a Speech to both Houses; and that to prevent any mistakes he had obtained for the information of the House a copy of His Excellency's Speech, which was read as follows:

Honorable Gentlemen of the Legislative Council,
and
Gentlemen of the Assembly:—
It is with great satisfaction I now meet you for the first time in Parliament.
From the very short period of my residence in this Province I shall not take
upon myself to call your attention to any particular object of legislation, convinced that your experience and knowledge of this Colony will fully enable you to
enact such salutary laws as will tend to its prosperity, and I have no doubt of your
attention being directed to such Acts of the Provincial Parliament as will necessarily expire unless continued by the Legislature.

Gentlemen of the House of Assembly:—
I have ordered the proper Officer to lay the Provincial Accounts before you,
and have given instructions that the unappropriated sums of money raised under
the authority of this Parliament, taken out of the Provincial Treasury, and applied
to the payment of certain public contingent expenses in the year 1805, as stated
in the accounts laid before you during the last session of this Legislature, shall be
replaced. I am, however, fully confident that you will unite with me in sentiments of loyalty and gratitude, while reflecting on the very liberal supplies annually
afforded to this Province by the bounty of Our Parent State for its necessary expenditures. And it will be for the House of Assembly to consider whether some
appropriation of the Revenue ought not to be made on its part to relieve (as far
as its resources will permit) the Mother Country from the Burthen of the Contingent Expenses incidental to the support of the Civil Government, and the administration of Justice in this Province.

Honorable Gentlemen and Gentlemen:—

I trust that your zeal for the public good will induce you to occupy your time
in the faithful discharge of your duty, and be assured of my cordial co-operation
when you direct your attention to the welfare and happiness of His Majesty's
subjects.

William Jarvis, Esquire, one of the Commissioners appointed by Dedimus
Potestatem, to administer the Oaths to the members of the House of Assembly,
came to the Bar, and did inform Mr. Speaker that Robert Thorpe, Esquire, had
taken the Oath as prescribed by the Statute, and did sign the Roll.

Then Ralph Clench and Robert Nellis, Esquires, introduced Robert Thorpe,
Esquire, Knight representing the Counties of Durham and Simcoe, and the East
Riding of the County of York, who took his seat accordingly.

At three o'clock p.m. Mr. Speaker adjourned the House for want of a Quorum.

Members present, Mr. Speaker, Messrs. McGregor, Cowan, Clench, Nellis,
Swayze, Mallory, Justice Thorpe and Solicitor General.

Tuesday, 3rd February, 1807.

Prayers were read.
Mr. Clench moved, seconded by Mr. Dorland, that Messrs. Solicitor General,
McLean and Swayze be a Committee to prepare an Address to His Excellency the
Lieutenant-Governor in answer to His Speech.
Ordered accordingly.
On motion of Mr. Clench, seconded by Mr. Hill, the House adjourned.

Wednesday, 4th February, 1807.

Prayers were read.

Agreeably to the Order of the Day at one o'clock the House took up the consideration of Samuel Ryerse's Petition, which laid over since the last Session, complaining of the undue return of Benajah Mallory, a sitting Member in this House.

In conformity to an Act passed in the first session of the fourth Provincial Parliament entitled "An Act to regulate the trial of controverted elections," the Speaker and Members then present were then sworn at the Table by the Clerk.

Members present,—Mr. Speaker, Mr. Justice Thorpe, Messrs. Dorland, Swayze, Hill, McLean, Clench, Nellis, Solicitor General, Cowan and McGregor.

Mr. Stewart, Counsel for Mr. Ryerse, was heard at the Bar of the House in support of the allegations set forth in Mr. Ryerse's Petition, complaining of the undue return of Benajah Mallory, Esquire, and concluded by addressing the House as follows, viz:

To the Honorable the Speaker and the Members of the House of Assembly.

Gentlemen:—

In the case of the controverted election of Benajah Mallory, Esquire, on the Petition of Samuel Ryerse,

I humbly beg leave to state that due exertions have been used to serve the subpœnas commanding the attendance of several material and necessary witnesses. in support of the petition, but the said witnesses have not as yet attended Your Honorable House, they having the whole of this day. I, therefore, humbly beg leave to state on the part of the Petitioner that I am unable to proceed at present in the trial with safety to the Petitioner.

Mr. Solicitor General moved, seconded by Mr. Clench, that the further consideration of the Petition of Samuel Ryerse, complaining of an undue election, be deferred until to-morrow morning at ten o'clock, in consequence of the representations of the Petitioner's Counsel respecting the summons.

Which was ordered accordingly.

Mr. McLean moved, seconded by Mr. McGregor, for leave to bring in a Bill on Saturday next for granting to His Majesty duties on Licenses to Hawkers, Pedlars. and Petty Chapmen.

Leave was accordingly granted.

On motion of Capt. Cowan, seconded by Mr. Nellis, the House adjourned.

Thursday, 5th February, 1807.

Prayers were read.

Agreeably to the Order of the Day the House went into the further consideration of the contested election of Ryerse and Mallory.

Mr. Stewart, Counsel for Mr. Ryerse, delivered in at the Bar the following affidavit, which was read at the Table by the Clerk, and is as follows:

Niagara }
District }

Before me, Samuel Hatt, Esquire, one of His Majesty's Justices of the Peace in and for the District aforesaid personally appeared John Baptiste Rousseau of Ancaster in the aforesaid District, Gent, who, being duly sworn, deposeth and saith that on the sixteenth day of January last he saw Adrian Marlett of Barton, Surveyor, receive a subpœna requiring him to appear before the Provincial Parliament to be holden at York in this present month of February.

Sworn before me at Ancaster,
2nd February, 1807.

S. Hatt, J. P.   (Sd.)   B. Rousseau.

Mr. Stewart then prayed the House for further delay as follows:

To the Honorable the Speaker and the Members of the House of Assembly.

· Gentlemen:—

Two material and necessary witnesses having refused to obey your commands to attend your Honorable House as evidence on the part of Samuel Ryerse, Esquire, the petitioner against the sitting Member, Benajah Mallory, Esquire, I have been under the necessity of summoning other evidences, which I trust will arrive in the course of the day, and therefore, humbly pray your indulgence in adjourning the trial until to-morrow.

Which the House rejected.

Four witness were then sworn at the Bar in support of Mr. Ryerse's petition, viz.: Andrew VanEvery, John Galbreath, Joseph Baker and John Detter.*

Mr. Solicitor-General moved, seconded by Captain Cowan, that no further proceedings take place in the trial of the Contested Election now before this House until to-morrow morning at ten o'clock.

The House accordingly resolved the same.

On motion of Captain Cowan, seconded by Mr. Nellis, the House adjourned.

Friday, 6th February, 1807.

Prayers were read.

Agreeable to the Order of the Day the House went into the further consideration of Mr. Mallory's contested Election.

Mr. Solicitor General moved, seconded by Mr. Nellis, that the Petition be dismissed, the allegations therein being unsupported by evidence.

A division ensued; the names were called for and taken down as follows:

Yeas	Nays
MESSRS. NELLIS.	MESSRS. COWAN
SOL'R-GENERAL	McLEAN
HILL	DORLAND
THORPE	McGREGOR
CLENCH	
SWAYZE	

Majority of two in the affirmative.

The Petition was accordingly dismissed.

Mr. Solicitor General, from the Committee appointed to draft an Address of thanks to His Excellency, the Lieutenant Governor, for his Speech to both Houses at the opening of the present Session, reported that the Committee had prepared an Address accordingly, which he was directed to submit to the House whenever it should be pleased to receive the same.

It was then Ordered that the Report be now received.

Which Report he read in his place, and then delivered the same in at the Table, where it was again read by the Clerk.

Mr. Rogers, seconded by Mr. Swayze, moved that this House do now resolve itself into a Committee to take into their consideration the draft of the Address to His Excellency, the Lieutenant Governor.

The House accordingly resolved itself into Committee.

Mr. Speaker left the Chair.

Detlor.

Mr. Dorland was called to the Chair of the Committee.

Mr. Speaker resumed the Chair.

Mr. Dorland reported that the Committee had gone through the consideration of the draft of an Address to His Excellency the Lieutenant Governor, to which they had made no amendments, which he was directed to report to the House whenever it should be pleased to receive the same.

Ordered, That the Report be now received.

Which Report was accepted, and the Address is as follows:

> To His Excellency, Francis Gore, Esquire, Lieutenant Governor of the Province of Upper Canada, &c., &c., &c.

May it please Your Excellency,

We, His Majesty's most dutiful and loyal subjects, the Commons of Upper Canada, in Parliament assembled, beg leave to express to Your Excellency our most sincere satisfaction on meeting you at this time in Parliament.

And although Your Excellency hath only generally directed our attention to the welfare of the Province, we trust every exertion on our part will be used in framing such laws as will tend to advance the agricultural and commercial interests of this Province, as well as the prosperity of His Majesty's subjects of every description.

We shall review carefully the expiring laws, and adopt such as appear expedient to continue.

As soon as the Public Accounts, which we have no doubt will be exhibited in the most full and ample manner, are laid before us, our time shall be devoted to the investigation of them.

We cheerfully embrace the present occasion to express our full satisfaction of Your Excellency's directions relative to certain moneys that have been taken from the Provincial Treasury without either the authority or concurrence of Parliament.

It has at all times been our earnest desire to offer to our most gracious Sovereign any money that could be spared from the Provincial Treasury, but our fears are, from the unimproved state of this Province, that our resources must be appropriated to the internal improvement of itself. Should it still appear to us, on examination of the Public Accounts, that any sum of consequence remains in the Treasury worthy of being appropriated to His Majesty to relieve the Parent Country from the burden and support of this Province, we shall consider it our first duty to crave our Most Gracious Sovereign's acceptance of it.

If zeal to discharge the important trusts delegated to us were the only circumstance that impressed itself forcibly on our minds, our task would be easy, but when we consider that the welfare and happiness of His Majesty's subjects in this Province depend on the salutary laws that may be passed, no sacrifice can be too great on our parts to effect this purpose.

Confiding in Your Excellency's support and co-operation wherever the welfare and happiness of His Majesty's subjects in this Province are concerned, no effort of ours shall be wanting in the faithful discharge of our duty.

House of Assembly,   (Signed) Alexander McDonell,
6th Feb'y, 1807.   Speaker.

Mr. Rogers moved, seconded by Mr. Swayze, that the Address to the Lieutenant Governor be engrossed, and that Messengers be named to wait upon His Excellency to know when he will be pleased to receive the same.

10 A.

The Address as engrossed was then read, passed, and signed by the Speaker.

Mr. Clench, seconded by Mr. Mallory, moved that Messrs. Rogers and McGregor do wait upon His Excellency, the Lieutenant Governor, to know when he will be pleased to receive this House with its Address in answer to His Excellency's Speech.

Which was ordered accordingly.

Mr. Justice Thorpe gave notice that he will on to-morrow move that this House do resolve itself into a Committee to take into their consideration the state of the Roads in this Province.

Mr. Nellis, seconded by Mr. Cowan, moved that Messrs. Solicitor General and McLean be a Committee to report to the House the laws about to expire.

Which was ordered accordingly.

Mr. Nellis again moved, seconded by Captain Cowan, that leave of absence be granted to Ralph Clench, Esquire, for eight days.

Leave was accordingly granted.

The Solicitor General moved, seconded by Mr. Nellis, for leave to bring in a Bill to amend an Act for the regulation of Special Juries.

Leave was accordingly granted.

On motion of Mr. Rogers, seconded by Mr. Hill, the House adjourned.

Saturday, 7th February, 1807.

Prayers were read.

Mr. Rogers, accompanied by the other Messengers, reported that in obedience to the Order of this House they had waited upon His Excellency's Lieutenant Governor, to know His Excellency's pleasure when he would receive the House with its Address, and that His Excellency was pleased to appoint this day at half past twelve o'clock to receive the House with its Address.

Agreeably to the Order of the Day Mr. McLean brought in a Bill for licensing Hawkers, Pedlars and Petty Chapmen, which was read for the first time by the Clerk at the Table.

Mr. McLean moved, seconded by Mr. McGregor, that the Bill entitled "An Act for licensing Hawkers, Pedlars and Petty Chapmen" be read for the second time on Monday next. Ordered accordingly.

At the hour appointed Mr. Speaker and the House went up with the Address of this House in answer to His Excellency the Lieutenant Governor's Speech to both Houses of Parliament at the opening of the present Session, and being returned,

Mr. Speaker reported that the House had attended upon His Excellency the Lieutenant Governor with its Address, to which His Excellency had been pleased to return the following answer.

Gentlemen of the House of Assembly:—

Accept my thanks for this Address, and for the satisfaction you express at meeting me at this time in Parliament.

I rely upon your assurances that you will direct your attention to the welfare and interest of this Province.

It will be a source of the highest satisfaction to me to co-operate with you in every measure conducive to the happiness and prosperity of His Majesty's subjects.

The Speaker having reminded the House that two men who had been summoned by him to attend this House to give evidence in the controverted election of Ryerse and Mallory had refused obedience to his summons.

Debates than ensued on points of privilege.

Noel DeL'Isle was then examined at the Bar of the House, and being asked whether within his knowledge Adrian Marlett had received a summons signed by the Speaker, requiring his attendance as a witness on the trial of the contested election between Ryerse and Mallory,

Answered that Marlett told him that he had been summoned, but that he would not attend, and doubted whether he was obliged to attend, not having been summoned in a regular manner.

Mr. Solicitor General moved, seconded by Mr. Rogers, that the Speaker may issue his Warrant to apprehend Adrian Martell and bring him before this House for a contempt in not obeying the summons of the Speaker to attend this House. Which was ordered accordingly.

Mr. Solicitor General again moved, seconded by Mr. Clench, that the Speaker do issue his Warrant to apprehend Levi Lawrence, and bring him before the House for a contempt in not obeying a summons of the Speaker to attend this House. Ordered accordingly.

Mr. Justice Thorpe, seconded by Mr. Nellis, moved that this House do now resolve itself into a Committee of the Whole House, to take into consideration the state of the Roads in this Province.

The House accordingly resolved itself into Committee.

Mr. Speaker left the Chair.

Mr. Clench was called to the chair of the Committee.

Mr. Speaker resumed the Chair.

Mr. Clench reported that the Committee had made a progress, and had desired him to ask for leave to sit again on Monday next.

Leave was accordingly given.

On motion of Mr. Swazey, seconded by Mr. Hill, the House adjourned.

Monday, 9th February, 1806.

Prayers were read.

Mr. Speaker reported that in obedience to the commands of this House he had issued his Warrants to apprehend and bring to the bar of this House Adrian Marlett and Levi Lawrence, to answer to the contempt shewn by them to the Speaker's summons.

Read for the first time, a Bill relative to Special Juries.

Mr. Solicitor General moved, seconded by Mr. Clench, that the Special Jury Bill be read a second time to-morrow. Ordered accordingly.

Read, the Petition of Duncan Cameron, John Birkier, Alexander Wood, George Playter and sundry other Freeholders of the Counties of Durham and Simcoe and the East Riding of the County of York, setting forth the ineligibility of Mr. Justice Thorpe as a Member in this Honorable House, for the aforesaid Counties and Riding, which is as follows.

To The Honorable the Representatives of the Commons of Upper Canada in Parliament assembled.

The Petition of the undersigned Freeholders of the East Riding of the County of York and Counties of Durham and Simcoe.

Most Respectfully Sheweth:—

That His Majesty's Writ, bearing date the Twenty-first of November now last past, did issue for the election of a Knight to represent the East Riding of the

County of York and the Counties of Durham and Simcoe in the Assembly of this Province in the place of William Weekes, Esquire, deceased.

That William Allan, of York, Esquire, was duly appointed Returning Officer for the said Riding and Counties, and did, on the Twenty-ninth day of December, proceed to such election.

That Robert Thorpe, Esquire, one of His Majesty's Judges in the Court of his Bench in this Province, and Thomas Barnes Gough, of York, Esquire, were the only candidates nominated by the respective Freeholders then and there present.

That Your petitioners previous to the closing of the poll, the election not being determined on view, did protest against the return of the said Robert Thorpe for the reason and causes hereafter set forth.

That the said Robert Thorpe has been returned as a Member for the said Riding and Counties, he having a majority of votes, to wit, two hundred and sixty-eight, and the said Thomas Barnes Gough only one hundred and fifty-nine votes, whereas Your Petitioners humbly conceive that the said Thomas Barnes Gough should have been returned Member of the said Riding and Counties for the reasons and causes following to wit.

That the said Robert Thorpe, at the time of such election, was, and still is one of His Majesty's Judges of the Court of his Bench in this Province.

That in England none of the Judges of the Court of King's Bench, Common Pleas, Barrons of the Exchequer who have judicial places, can be chosen Knight, Citizen or Burgess in Parliament.

That having adopted in this Province the law of England as a rule of decision, the said Robert Thorpe was not then and now is not eligible in this Province to sit as a Member in Your Honorable House of Assembly, that in the attainment of such an object as Judge, who decides on the life, liberty and property of His Majesty's subjects, must necessarily be liable to the frailties and passions incident to human nature, and may therefrom imbibe partialities, prejudices or prepossessions repugnant to and at war with the purity of the unsullied ermine, inimical to the independence and dignified administration of the law, and subversive of the free and constitutional liberties of His Majesty's subjects.

That Your Petitioners have further to state with great deference to Your Honorable House that this procedure is unconstitutional, inasmuch as being an attempt to clothe, arm and blend in one person, the conflicting powers, authorities and jurisdiction of the Legislature and Judicial functions contrary to the spirit of good government and the immemorial usage and custom of the Commons of England, whose rules of conduct Your Honorable House has adopted as the criterion of your decisions, where not otherwise specially provided for,

Wherefore your Petitioners, conceiving that the said Robert Thorpe was not lawfully returned, and that Thomas Barnes Gough was duly elected, pray that the said return may be reformed and amended, and the name of Thomas Barnes Gough be inserted on the roll, and the name of Robert Thorpe erased therefrom.

And as in duty bound your Petitioners will ever pray.

York, 4th February, 1807.

Then read the Petition of Thomas Barnes Gough, Esquire, complaining-of the undue return of Mr. Justice Thorpe to represent the County of Durham, the East Riding of the County of York and the County of Simcoe; and praying that the return may be reformed and amended, which is as follows.

To the Honorable House of Assembly of the Province of Upper Canada.

The Petition of Thomas Barnes Gough, of York, in said Province.

Most Respectfully Showeth,

That His Majesty's Writ bearing date the Twenty-first day of Nevember now last past did issue for the election of a Knight to represent the County of Durham, the East Riding of the County of York, and the County of Simcoe, in the Assembly of this Province, in the place of William Weekes, Esquire, deceased.

That William Allan, of York, Esquire, was duly appointed Returning Officer for the said Counties and Riding, and did on the twenty-ninth day of December proceed to such election.

That Robert Thorpe, Esquire, one of His Majesty's Judges in the Court of his Bench in this Province, and Your Petitioner were the only candidates nominated by the respective Freeholders then and there present.

That Your Petitioner, previous to the commencement of a poll, the election not being determined on view, did protest against the nomination of the said Robert Thorpe for the reasons and causes hereafter set forth.

That the said William Allan, notwithstanding, did proceed to take a poll, and did adjourn the same from day to day until the third day of January following, when the said election was determined.

That the said Robert Thorpe has been returned as a Member for the said Counties and Riding, he having a majority of votes, to wit, two hundred and sixty-nine, and Your Petitioner only one hundred and fifty-nine.

Whereas Your petitioner humbly conceives that he should have been returned Member for the said Counties and Riding, for the reasons and causes following, to wit,

That the said Robert Thorpe, at the time of such election, was, and still is, one of His Majesty's Judges of the Court of his Bench in this Province.

That in England none of the Judges of the Court of King's Bench, Common Pleas, or Barrons of the Exchequer, who have judicial places can be chosen Knight, Citizen, or Burgess in Parliament.

That having adopted in this Province the law of England as a rule of decision, the said Robert Thorpe was then, and now is, not eligible in this Province to sit as a Member in Your Honorable House of Assembly.

That Your Petitioner has further to state with great deference to Your Honorable House that the precedent is unconstitutional, inasmuch as being an attempt to clothe, arm and blend in one person the conflicting powers, authorities and jurisdiction of the Legislative and Judicial functions, contrary to the spirit of good government and the immemorial usage and custom of the Commons of England, whose rule or conduct Your Honorable House has adopted as the criterion of your decision when not otherwise specially provided for.

Wherefore, your Petitioner, conceiving that the said Robert Thorpe was not lawfully returned, and that Your Petitioner was duly elected, and ought to have been returned, prays that the said return may be reformed and amended, and the name of your Petitioner be inserted on the roll and the name of Robert Thorpe erased therefrom.

York, 2nd day February, 1807.   (Signed) Thomas Barnes Gough.

Mr. Rogers moved, seconded by Mr. Clench, that the House do now resolve itself into Committee to take into their consideration whether the grounds contained in the Petition of the Inhabitants of the Home District, if true and sufficient to make the election of the sitting Member void.

The House accordingly resolved itself into Committee.

Mr. Speaker left the Chair.

Captain Cowan was called to the Chair of the Committee.

Mr. Speaker resumed the Chair.

Captain Cowan reported progress and asked for leave to sit again this day.
Leave was granted accordingly.

William Jarvis, Esquire, Secretary of the Province, came to the Bar of the
House, and delivered in, by order of His Excellency, the Lieutenant Governor,
the Public Provincial Accounts as per Schedule, which was read by the Clerk at
the Table, and are as follows:

SCHEDULE OF ACCOUNTS LAID BEFORE THE HOUSE OF ASSEMBLY.

No. 1. The Inspector's list of names and persons licensed as Shop and Inn-
keepers in the several Districts of the Province of Upper Canada, between the 5th
of April, 1805, and 5th January, 1806. These returns were not received in time
to be laid before the Legislature in 1806.

No. 2. The Inspector's list of names of persons licensed as Shop and Inn-
keepers in the several Districts of the Province of Upper Canada, from the 5th
January, 1806, to the 5th January, 1807.

No. 3. The Inspector's list of names of such persons as have been licensed
to work Stills in the several Districts of the Province of Upper Canada, from the
5th January, 1806, to the 5th January, 1807.

No. 4. Provincial Revenue of the Crown arising from duties collected on
Goods imported under authority of Acts of the Provincial Parliament, between
the 1st January and 31st December, 1806, including such duties as have not been
heretofore stated.

No. 5. Provincial Revenue of the Crown arising from duties collected on
Goods imported under authority of Acts of the Parliament of Great Britain, between
the 1st January and the 31st December, 1806, including such duties as have not
heretofore been stated.

No. 6. Abstract of Warrants issued by His Honor, Mr. President Grant and
His Excellency, Francis Gore, Esquire, Lieutenant Governor of the Province of
Upper Canada, for moneys charged against the funds arising from duties imposed
by the Provincial Legislature.

No. 7. Supplementary abstract statement of moneys collected within the
several Districts of the Province of Upper Canada on Shop and Inn-Keepers
Licenses, issued between the 5th April, 1805, and 5th January, 1806, under authority of Acts of the Provincial Parliament after deducting ten per cent. allowed to
the Inspector by the Act of the Forty-third of the King.

No. 8. Supplementary Abstract Statement of moneys collected within the
several Districts of the Province of Upper Canada on Shop and Inn-Keepers
Licenses issued between the 5th April, 1805, and 5th January, 1806, under authority of Acts of the Parliament of Great Britain, after deducting ten per cent.
allowed to the Inspectors.

No. 9. Abstract Statement of moneys collected within the several Districts
of the Province of Upper Canada on Shop, Inn-keepers and Still licenses, issued
between the 5th January, 1806, and 5th January, 1807, so far as the returns have
been received, after deducting ten per cent. allowed to the Inspectors by the Act of
the Forty-third of the King.

No. 10. Abstract Statement of moneys collected within the several Districts of the Province of Upper Canada on Shop and Inn-keepers licenses issued between the 5th January, 1806, and 5th January, 1807, under authority of Acts of the Parliament of Great Britain, so far as the returns have been received, after deducting ten per cent. allowed to the Inspectors.

No. 11. General Account of articles on which duties on importation are imposed by the Legislature of Lower Canada which have passed Coteau Du Lac upwards from 1st of January to 30th June, 1806, agreeable to the written account thereof received, or as ascertained on examination of carriages according to the Acts.

No. 12. Account of tonnage Lighthouse duty collected for the year ending 31st December, 1806.

No. 13. Account of cash received by the Honorable Peter Russell, Receiver General, for Fines and Forfeitures, under authority of Acts of the Provincial Parliament, between the 5th February and 31st December, 1806.

No. 14. Account of cash received by the Honorable Peter Russell, Receiver General, for Fines and Forfeitures, under authority of Acts of the Parliament of Great Britain, between the 5th February and 31st December, 1806.

No. 15. General State of Cash received by the Hon. Peter Russell, Receiver General, for Duties and Fines, under authority of Acts of the Parliament of Great Britain, between the 5th February and 31st December, 1806.

No. 16. General State of Receipts and Payments by the Hon. Peter Russell, Receiver General, for Duties and Fines, and likewise Appropriations made under authority of Acts of the Provincial Parliament between the 5th February and 31st December, 1806.

No. 17. General Account of articles on which Duties on Importation are imposed by the Legislature of Lower Canada, which have passed Coteau du Lac upwards, from 1st July to the 31st December, 1806, agreeable to the written accounts thereof received, or as ascertained on examination of carriages according to the Act.

Inspector General's Office,   (Signed) John McGill,
York, 2nd Feb'y, 1807.   Insp. Gen'l Pub. Pro. Accts.
(For Accounts as per Schedule see Appendix.)

The House again resolved itself into a Committee on the Petition of certain Freeholders of the Home District against the eligibility of Mr. Justice Thorpe's sitting as a member of this House.

Mr. Speaker left the Chair.

Capt. Cowan again took the chair of the Committee.

Mr. Speaker resumed the Chair.

Capt. Cowan reported progress, and asked for leave to sit again to-morrow.

Leave was accordingly granted.

Mr. McLean moved, seconded by Mr. McGregor, that so much of the Order of this Day as relates to the Hawkers' and Pedlars' Bill be discharged, and that it be read for the second time to-morrow. Ordered accordingly.

The House accordingly resolved itself into Committee on the Public Roads throughout this Province.

Mr. Speaker left the Chair.

Mr. Clench was called to the chair of the Committee.

Mr. Speaker resumed the Chair.

Mr. Clench reported progress, and asked for leave to sit again on Thursday next. Ordered accordingly.

Read, the Petition from the London and Western Districts respecting Highways and Public Roads, which is as follows:

To the Honorable House of Assembly of His Majesty's Province of Upper Canada, in Parliament Assembled.

The petition of sundry Inhabitants of the London and Western Districts of the said Province,

Most Humbly Sheweth,

That by an Act of the Legislature of this Province, passed in the forty-sixth year of His Majesty's Reign relative to Public Highways and Roads in the Province it was among other things enacted, That the Road which should be deemed the Public Highway throughout the Province as far as the same extends through the District of London should be as follows, namely: commencing at the Indian Mill on the Grand River, thence along the road leading through the Township of Burford to the Delaware Town on the River Thames and across the said River, thence down the River to the tract of land commonly known as the Moravian grant.

That your petitioners have from experience found that if the said Road should be opened and followed in its present direction, namely, on are north side of the River Thames, it would be productive of many and great inconveniences to His Majesty's subjects, for the following among other reasons

First, because that the River Thames at particular seasons is very difficult to cross, and attended with much danger, and sometimes it is for several days together altogether impassable.

Second, because that on the north side of the said River Thames the lands through which the said Road would pass have not yet been purchased by His Majesty, and of course there are no inhabitants settled thereon.

Third, because that it would be attended with great expense and labour, owing to the great depth and number of rivers, to cut out the said road and erect the necessary bridges thereon, and which, without settlers, would be continually out of repair.

That your Petitioners humbly conceive it would be of great benefit and attended with many advantages to His Majesty's subjects, if the said road was laid out from the Township of Oxford on the South side of the River Thames to the Moravian Grant in the London District.

That your Petitioners have every reason to believe that the lands are equally advantageous on the south for the laying out of a road as on the north side, and that it would be thereby considerably shortened, and, as the lands are all located on the south side, it would tend to the more speedy selling and improvement of the lands, and be the means of keeping the road open and in good repair.

Your Petitioners therefore humbly pray that Your Honorable House will take this their prayer into consideration, and upon proper evidence to be adduced to substantiate the facts stated in the present petition, will make such alterations in the said Act as Your Honorable House in your wisdom shall deem meet.

And your Petitioners as in duty bound will ever pray.

(Signed) Wm. Smith,
Wm. Mills,
Geo. B. Hale,
T. McKee,

Sandwich, 13th Jan., 1807.   and several others.

Mr. Rogers moved, seconded by Mr. Clench, that the petitions from the Districts of London and Western District be referred to the Committee of the whole House on the state of the roads in this Province.
Ordered accordingly.
Read, the petition from the District of Niagara, which is as follows:
To the Honorable the Commons of Upper Canada in Parliament assembled.

The petition of a number of His Majesty's subjects residing at or near the River of Niagara,
Humbly Sheweth,
That your Petitioners must of necessity make use of the water of the River Niagara, which contains the carcases of creatures thrown into it by certain persons, and that these carcases are not unfrequently lodged within a few rods of our houses, by which the water is unfit to use.
It is therefore our humble request that you would be pleased to take such measures as may terminate this grievance, and we as in duty bound shall ever pray.

                                                    (Signed) Saml. Sheet,
                                                              John Palmer,
                                                              Daniel Abel,
Willoughby, 20th Jany., 1807.   and several others.

Mr. Solicitor-General moved, seconded by Capt. Cowan, for leave to bring in a Bill on Wednesday next, to amend an Act passed in the thirty-third year of His present Majesty's reign, entitled, "An Act to confirm and make valid certain marriages heretofore contracted in the country now comprised within the Province of Upper Canada, and to provide for the future solemnization of marriage within the same." Leave was accordingly granted.

Mr. Washburn moved, seconded by Mr. Mallory, for leave to bring in a Bill on Wednesday next to provide a fund for the support of one Public School in each and every District within this Province. Leave was accordingly granted.

Mr. Solicitor-General moved, seconded by Capt. Cowan, for leave to bring in a Bill on Wednesday next to continue and amend an Act entitled "An Act particularizing the property, real and personal, which during the continuance thereof shall be subject to assessment and rates, and fixing the several valuations at which each and every particular of such property shall be rated and assessed."
Leave was granted accordingly.

Mr. Rogers moved, seconded by Mr. Nellis, that the names of the Members of this House be called over on Thursday next. Ordered accordingly.

On motion of Mr. Mallory, seconded by Mr. Hill, the House adjourned until to-morrow at twelve o'clock at noon.

Tuesday, 10th February, 1807.

Prayers were read.
Agreeably to the Order of the Day was read for the second time a Bill to amend an Act passed in the fortieth year of the Reign of His Majesty, entitled, "An Act for the Regulation of Special Juries."
Mr. Solicitor-General moved, seconded by Capt. Cowan, that the House do resolve itself into a Committee on the Special Jury Bill.

The House accordingly resolved itself into a Committee.
Mr. Speaker left the Chair.
Mr. Hill was called to the chair of the Committee.
Mr. Speaker resumed the Chair.
Mr. Hill reported that the Committee had made a progress and that he was directed to ask for leave to sit again. Leave was accordingly granted.
Mr. Solicitor General then moved, seconded by Capt. Cowan, that so much of the Order of the Day as applies to the petition from the Home District be discharged, and that the Committee have leave to sit again to-morrow.
Which passed in the negative.
The House then, agreeably to the Order of the Day resolved itself into a Committee to go into the further consideration of the Petition complaining of the undue return of Mr. Justice Thorpe to sit as Member to represent the Counties of Durham, Simcoe, and the East Riding of the County of York.
Mr. Speaker left the Chair.
Mr. Cowan was called to the chair of the Committee.
Mr. Speaker resumed the Chair.
Mr. Cowan reported that the Committee had made a progress, and had directed him to ask for leave to sit again this day. Leave was accordingly granted.
A Message from His Excellency the Lieutenant-Governor, signed by His Excellency, was delivered to the Speaker by William Halton, Esq. Secretary to His Excellency, which Message was read, all the members standing up, and the same is as follows, viz:—
Francis Gore, Lieutenant-Governor.
The Lieutenant-Governor thinks it proper to acquaint the House of Assembly that he has received from Mr. President Dunne, administering the Government of Lower Canada, the copy of an Act of the Legislature of that Province, passed in the month of March, One Thousand Eight Hundred and Five, entitled, "An Act to provide for the erection of a Common Gaol in the Districts of Quebec and Montreal, by which additional duties have been imposed on certain goods, etc., imported into the Province from the United States of America," and the Lieutenant-Governor submits it to the consideration of the House of Assembly whether the Legislature of this Province is not called upon, by the existing Agreement with the Province of Lower Canada, to impose similar duties upon the like articles imported into this Province from the United States of America.
Government House, York,   F. G.
10th Feb'y, 1807.

Agreeable to leave given the House then resolved itself into a Committee to go into the further consideration of the petition complaining of the undue return of Mr. Justice Thorpe as Member to represent the Counties of Durham, Simcoe, and the East Riding of the County of York.
Mr. Speaker left the Chair.
Mr. Cowan again took the chair of the Committee.
Mr. Speaker resumed the Chair.
Mr. Cowan reported that the Committee had gone through the consideration of the said Petition, which he was directed to report whenever the House should be pleased to receive the same.
The House then resolved that the Report be now received.
The Report was then unanimously received, and read by the Clerk at the Table, which Report is as follows:

Resolved, That it is the opinion of the Committee that the Petition of the nhabitants of the Home District, complaining of the undue election of Mr. Justice Thorpe, does not contain sufficient grounds, if true, to make the election f the sitting Member for the Counties of Durham and Simcoe and the East Riding of the County of York void.

The House accordingly resolved the same.

Mr. Rogers then moved, seconded by Mr. Clench, that the further consideration of the Petition of Thomas Barnes Gough be deferred for three months, the grounds contained in the Petition being not sufficient to make the return complained of void. Which was ordered accordingly.

Read for the second time, a Bill for granting to His Majesty duties on licenses o Hawkers, Pedlars and Petty Chapmen.

On motion of Mr. McLean, seconded by Mr. McGregor, the House resolved tself into a Committee to go into the consideration of the said Bill.

Mr. Speaker left the Chair.

Mr. Howard was called to the chair of the Committee.

Mr. Speaker resumed the Chair.

Mr. Howard reported that the Committee had made a progress, and had lirected him to ask for leave to sit again to-morrow.

Leave was granted accordingly.

On motion of Mr. Rogers, seconded by Mr. Mallory, the House adjourned ntil twelve o'clock to-morrow at noon.

Wednesday, 11th February, 1807.

Prayers were read.

Mr. Solicitor General moved, seconded by Mr. McLean, that the House do now resolve itself into a Committee to take into consideration His Excellency the Lieutenant Governor's Message, delivered by his Secretary yesterday.

The House accordingly resolved itself into a Committee.

Mr. Speaker left the Chair.

Mr. McLean was called to the chair of the Committee.

Mr. Speaker resumed the Chair.

Mr. McLean reported that it was the opinion of the Committee that an humble address should be presented to His Excellency the Lieutenant Governor, thanking him for his communication by message yesterday.

Which Report was accepted.

Mr. Nellis then moved, seconded by Mr. Clench, that Mr. Justice Thorpe and Mr. Rogers be a Committee to draft an Address to His Excellency the Lieutenant Governor in answer to his message yesterday.

Which was ordered accordingly.

Read for the first time, an Act to confirm and make valid certain marriages in this Province.

On motion of Mr. Solicitor General, seconded by Mr. McLean,

Ordered, That the said Marriage Act be read a second time to-morrow.

Mr. Washburn then moved that so much of the Order of the Day as relates to his bringing in a Bill this day to provide a fund for the support of Public Schools in this Province be discharged, and that he have leave to bring in the same to-morrow. Ordered accordingly.

Mr. Solicitor General moved, seconded by Mr. McLean, that so much of the order of the Day as respects the Assessment Bill be discharged, and that the said Bill be read to-morrow. Which was ordered accordingly.

Agreeably to the Order of the Day the House resolved itself into a Committee to go into the consideration of the Hawkers and Pedlars Bill.

Mr. Speaker left the Chair.

Mr. Howard took the Chair of the Committee.

Mr. Speaker resumed the Chair.

Mr. Howard reported that the Committee had made a progress, and that he was directed to ask for leave to sit again.

Leave was accordingly granted.

Mr. Justice Thorpe, one of the Committee appointed to draft an Address to His Excellency the Lieutenant Governor, in answer to his Message of yesterday, reported that they had done so, which they were ready to submit to the House whenever it should be pleased to receive the same.

The House then resolved that the said Address be now received.

Mr. Justice Thorpe accordingly read the Address in his place and delivered it in at the Table, where it was again read by the Clerk, and is as follows.

To His Excellency, Francis Gore, Esquire, Lieutenant Governor of the Province of Upper Canada, etc.

May it Please Your Excellency:—

We, His Majesty's faithful and loyal subjects, the Commons of Upper Canada, in Parliament assembled, respectfully return thanks to Your Excellency for your Message of yesterday, communicating your having received from Mr. President Dunn, administering the Government of Lower Canada, the copy of an Act of the Legislature of that Province, passed in One Thousand Eight Hundred and Five, entitled "An Act to provide for the erection of a Common Gaol in the Districts of Montreal and Quebec," by which additional duties have been imposed on certain goods, etc., imported into that Province, and submitting to our consideration whether we are not called upon by the existing Agreement with the Province of Lower Canada to impose similar duties on the like articles imported from the United States into this Province; and we respectfully assure Your Excellency that we will take the same into our most serious consideration.

Commons House of Assembly,   (Signed) Alex. McDonell,
11th Feby., 1807.   Speaker.

Then, on motion of Mr. Rogers, seconded by Mr. Hill,

Ordered, That the said Address be now engrossed.

The said Address as engrossed was then read, passed, aand signed by the Speaker.

Mr. Solicitor General then moved, seconded by Mr. Clench, that Messrs. McLean, Washburn and McGregor do wait upon His Excellency the Lieutenant Governor to know when it will be his pleasure to receive the Address of this House in answer to his Message of yesterday, and that those gentlemen do present the same.

Ordered accordingly.

Mr. Solicitor General moved, seconded by Mr. Swayze, for leave to bring in a Bill on Friday next, to revive, continue and amend an Act, passed in the forty-second year of His Present Majesty, entitled "An Act to enable the Governor,

Lieutenant Governor or person administering the Government of this Province, to appoint one or more additional Port or Ports of Entry within this Province, and to appoint one or more Collectors at the same respectively.

Leave was granted accordingly.

On motion of Mr. McGregor, seconded by Mr. Nellis, the House adjourned.

Thursday, 12th February, 1807.

Prayers were read.

Agreeably to the Order of the Day the House resolved itself into a Committee to go into the further consideration of the Road Bill.

Mr. Speaker left the Chair.

Mr. Clench took the Chair of the Committee.

Mr. Speaker resumed the Chair.

Mr. Clench reported progress, and asked for leave to sit again.

Leave was accordingly granted.

Mr. Clench moved, seconded by Mr. Dorland, that the Solicitor General, Mr. Justice Thorpe, Messrs. McLean, Hill and Cowan be a Special Committee to settle a plan to be laid before the House for the improvement of the Roads of this Province.

Ordered accordingly.

The Order of the Day for the call of the House being read,

Ordered, that the House be now called.

The House was accordingly called over, and several of the Members appeared, and the names of such Members as made default to appear were taken down, and are as follows: W. B. Wilkinson, J. Crysler, Samuel Sherwood, Matthew Elliott,— out of the Province.

Read for the second time the Bill entitled "An Act to amend certain parts of an Act passed in the thirty-third year of His Majesty's Reign, entitled 'An Act to confirm and make valid certain marriages heretofore contracted in the country now composed within the Province of Upper Canada, and to provide for the future solemnization of marriages within the same.' "

Mr. Rogers then moved, seconded by Mr. Cowan, that this House do now resolve itself into a Committee to go into the consideration of the said Bill.

The House accordingly resolved itself into Committee.

Mr. Speaker left the Chair.

Mr. Rogers was called to the chair of the Committee.

Mr. Speaker resumed the Chair.

Mr. Rogers reported progress, and asked for leave to sit again.

Leave was granted accordingly.

Read for the first time, the School Bill.

Mr. Washburn moved, seconded by Mr. Rogers, that the School Bill be read a second time to-morrow. Ordered accordingly.

Read for the first time, the Bill entitled "An Act to continue and amend an Act and to render more effectual an Act passed in the forty-third year of His present Majesty, entitled 'An Act particularizing the property, real and personal, which, during the continuance thereof, shall be subject to assessments and rates.' "

Mr. Rogers moved, seconded by the Solicitor General, that the Bill to revive and continue the Assessment Bill be read a second time to-morrow.

Ordered accordingly.

Mr. McLean, one of the Messengers named to wait upon His Excellency the Lieutenant Governor with the Address of this House in answer to his Message, reported that they had waited upon the Lieutenant Governor with the said Address, to which he was pleased to make the following answer.

Gentlemen of the House of Assembly:—

I thank you for this Address, and have much satisfaction in observing your readiness to attend to my message of the 10th instant.

Government House, York,

13th Feby, 1807.

Mr. McLean moved, seconded by Mr. Clench, that the House do now resolve itself into Committee to take into consideration the Public Provincial Accounts.

The House accordingly resolved itself into Committee.

Mr. Speaker left the Chair.

Mr. McGregor was called to the chair of the Committee.

Mr. Speaker resumed the Chair.

Mr. McGregor reported that the Committee do recommend to the House that a Select Committee be appointed to examine the Provincial Public Accounts and report the state of the Provincial Revenue to the House.

Which report was accepted, and ordered accordingly.

Mr. Justice Thorpe then moved, seconded by Mr. Nellis, that Messrs. Rogers, McLean, Clench, McGregor and Howard be a Committee to examine the Public Provincial Accounts and report the state of the Provincial Revenue to the House and that the said Committee have power to send for such persons or papers as they may think necessary for their information. Ordered accordingly.

On motion of Mr. Mallory, seconded by Mr. Hill, the House adjourned.

Friday, 13th February, 1807.

Prayers were read.

Read for the first time, an Act for appointing Collectors and Ports of Entry.

Mr. Solicitor General moved, seconded by Mr. Rogers, that the Collectors Bill be read a second time to-morrow.

Which was ordered accordingly.

Read for the second time, the Bill for establishing Public Schools throughout this Province.

Mr. Washburn moved, seconded by Mr. Dorland, that the House do now resolve itself into a Committee to take into consideration the School Bill.

The House accordingly resolved itself into Committee.

Mr. Speaker left the Chair.

Mr. Mallory was called to the chair of the Committee.

Mr. Speaker resumed the Chair.

Mr. Mallory reported that the Committee had made a progress, and that he was directed to ask for leave to sit again on Monday next.

Resolved, That the Committee have leave to sit again on Monday.

Read for the second time, the Bill laying assessments throughout this Province.

Mr. Solicitor General then moved, seconded by Mr. Cowan, that this House do now resolve itself into a Committee on the Assessment Bill.

The House accordingly resolved itself into a Committee.

Mr. Speaker left the Chair.

Mr. Swayze was called to the chair of the Committee.

Mr. Speaker resumed the Chair.

And Mr. Swayze reported progress, and asked for leave to sit again. Leave was accordingly granted.

Read, the Petition of William Willcocks, Esquire, which is as follows.

To the Honorable the Speaker and, the Honorable the Members of the Commons House of Assembly in Parliament assembled.

The petition of William Willcocks

Humbly Sheweth,

That Your Petitioner has been Judge of the Home District Court for more than seven years, and (he presumes to flatter himself) has discharged his duty therein to the satisfaction of the public.

That his fees having never exceeded Ten Pounds a year, which he is informed is not the case in the other Districts, are entirely unequal to his labours, being obliged to attend four times in a year and at every Quarter Sessions to try causes.

Your Petitioner therefore humbly prays that you will be pleased to take his case into your consideration and grant him such a salary as in your wisdom you may think adequate to his situation as a Judge,

And your petitioner as in duty bound will ever pray.

York, 10th Feb'y, 1807.   (Sd.) William Willcocks.

Then was read the Petition of Charles Willcocks, Gentleman, which is as follows:

To the Honorable the Speaker and the Honorable the Members of the Commons House of Assembly in Parliament assembled.

The Petition of Charles Willcocks, Gentleman, Humbly Sheweth,

That Your Petitioner has attended this Honorable House as its copying Clerk four sessions of Parliament, and he presumes to flatter himself that he has acted in his station to the satisfaction of the Clerk of the House, and of the Honorable Members thereof.

That he was honored with a Commission (under the Seal of the then Speaker, Mr. Beasley) as Special Messenger, and did his duty as such. Your Petitioner depending entirely for support upon his small abilities as Scrivener takes the liberty of requesting that Your Honorable House may be pleased to take his case into consideration and allow him such salary during pleasure for his attendance each session of Parliament, and for bringing up the Journal for the House after its close, as in your wisdom you shall think meet.

And Your Petitioner as in duty bound will ever pray.

York, 10th Feb'y, 1807.   (Sd.) Chas. Willcocks.

Read, the Petition of the Inhabitants of the Townships of Mersia, Gosfield and Colchester, which is as follows.

To the Honorable the Members of the House of Assembly of Upper Canada in Parliament assembled.

The Inhabitants of the Townships of Mersia, Gosfield and Colchester, seeing with regret the insufficiency of their District Gaol in the Town of Sandwich, which in its present state is so confined and incommodious that an unfortunate debtor (although probably an honest, industrious man) must be confined in the same dungeon or cell with the greatest criminal, which is repugnant to human feeling, and unprecedented in civilized society.

They at the same time see the inability of the funds arising from the present taxes in their District to build a new Gaol, or even to make the absolutely neces- sary additions and repairs to the present one, sensible that such means must be raised within the District, they humbly beg leave to point out to the Honorable House of Assembly a mode of raising the necessary sum in a manner the least injurious to the poorer and most industrious part of the District.

With this view and to obtain so desirable a purpose they humbly recommend to the Honorable House to pass an Act imposing a duty of tax upon all curricles, caleches or other pleasure carriages within the District, which, if it only amounted to two shillings and sixpence currency upon each annually, would, in all probability, raise a sum adequate to the object in view in the course of three or four years.

The Inhabitants of the said Townships trust that the Honorable House of Assembly (studious for the prosperity and welfare of the Province in general) will take their proposition into their serious consideration.

(Signed) Wm. Buchanan,

Joseph Quick,

Alex'r Duff,

Colchester, 29th Dec., 1807.   and several others.

Mr. Clench moved, seconded by Mr. Mallory, for leave to bring in a Bill on Monday to regulate the practice of Physic and Surgery within this Province.

Leave was accordingly granted.

On motion of Mr. Clench, seconded by Capt. Cowan, the House adjourned until Monday at twelve o'clock at noon.

Monday, 16th February, 1807.

Prayers were read.

Mr. Speaker informed the House that he had received a letter from Mr. Mallory, a Member of this House, apologizing for the necessity of his being absent from this House for a few days without leave.

Read for the second time an Act to enable the Lieutenant Governor to appoint one or more Ports of Entry, and one or more Collectors within this Province.

Mr. Solicitor General moved, seconded by Mr. Clench, that the House do now resolve itself into Committee to take into consideration the Collectors' Bill.

The House accordingly resolved itself into a Committee.

Mr. Speaker left the Chair.

Mr. Nellis was called to the chair of the Committee.

Mr. Speaker resumed the Chair.

Mr. Nellis reported that the Committee had gone through the consideration of the said Bill, to which they had made several amendments, which he was directed to report whenever the House should be pleased to receive the same.

Resolved, That the Report be now received.

The Report was then received and accepted.

Mr. Solicitor General then moved, seconded by Mr. Rogers, that the Collectors' Bill be engrossed and read a third time to-morrow.

Which was ordered accordingly.

Agreeable to the Order of the Day, the House resolved itself into Committee to go into the further consideration of the Bill for establishing Public Schools throughout this Province.

Mr. Speaker left the Chair.

Mr. Crysler was called to the chair of the Committee.

Mr. Speaker resumed the Chair.

Mr. Crysler reported that the Committee had made a progress, and had directed him to ask for leave to sit again. Leave was accordingly given.

Mr. Clench moved, seconded by Mr. Howard, that so much of the Order of the Day as relates to the bringing in a Bill for regulating the Practice of Physic and Surgery be discharged, and that leave be given him to bring in the same on Thursday next. Leave was accordingly granted.

Mr. Washburn then moved, seconded by Mr. Swayze, for leave to bring in a Bill on Wednesday next to alter the present mode of collecting the Duty on Shop and Tavern Keepers Licenses within this Province. Leave was accordingly given.

Mr. Rogers moved, seconded by Mr. Dorland, that this House do now resolve itself into Committee to take into their further consideration the Bill for Licensing Hawkers, Pedlars, and Petty Chapmen.

The House accordingly resolved itself into Committee.

Mr. Speaker left the Chair.

Mr. Howard was called to the chair of the Committee.

Mr. Speaker resumed the Chair.

Mr. Howard reported progress, and asked for leave to sit again this day. Leave was accordingly given.

A Message from the Honorable Legislative Council by Mr. Baldwin, Master-in-Chancery:—

Mr. Speaker,—

I am commanded by the Legislative Council to inform this House that they have passed an Act to extend the benefits of an Act, passed in the thirty-seventh year of His Majesty's reign, entitled "An Act for the more easy barring of Dower and to repeal certain parts of the same," and then he withdrew.

According to leave given the House again resolved itself into Committee to go into the further consideration of the Act for licensing Hawkers and Pedlars.

Mr. Speaker left the Chair.

Mr. Howard again took the chair of the Committee.

Mr. Speaker resumed the Chair.

Mr. Howard reported a progress and asked for leave to sit again to-morrow. Leave was accordingly granted.

Mr. Rogers then moved, seconded by Mr. Justice Thorpe, that Messrs. Sherwood, Dorland and Capt. Elliott be added to the Committee appointed by the House to report the most eligible means of repairing the roads in this Province. Ordered accordingly.

Read for the first time, an Act sent down from the Honorable Legislative Council for the more easy receiving of Dower.

Mr. Solicitor General then moved, seconded by Mr. Sherwood, that the Bill for the more easy barring of Dower be read a second time to-morrow.

Which was ordered accordingly.

On motion of Mr. Solicitor General, seconded by Capt. Elliott, the House resolved itself into a committee to go into the consideration of His Excellency the

11 A.

Lieutenant-Governor's message, respecting Duties laid by the Province of Lower Canada on goods imported from the United States of America.

Mr. Speaker left the chair.

Mr. Elliott was called to the chair of the Committee.

Mr. Speaker resumed the Chair.

Mr. Elliott reported that the Committee had made a progress, and that he was directed to ask for leave to sit again. Leave was accordingly granted.

On motion of Mr. Swayze, seconded by Mr. Hill, the House adjourned until twelve o'clock to-morrow at noon.

Tuesday, 17th February, 1807.

Prayers were read.

Agreeably to the Order of the Day was read for the third time, an engrossed Act for appointing Collectors and Ports of Entry.

The Solicitor General moved, seconded by Capt. Elliott, that the Bill do pass, and that the title be "An Act to revive and continue an Act passed in the forty-second year of His present Majesty, entitled 'An Act to enable the Governor, Lieutenant Governor, or person administering the Government of the Province to appoint one or more additional Port or Ports of Entry, Place or Places of Entry within this Province, and to appoint one or more Collector or Collectors at the same respectively.' "

The House resolved the same.

The Bill then passed, and was signed by the Speaker.

Mr. Solicitor General then moved, seconded by Capt. Elliott, that Messrs. McLean and Dorland do carry up to the Honorable Legislative Council the said Act, and do request their concurrence thereto, which was ordered accordingly.

Agreeably to the Order of the Day the House resolved itself into Committee on the Hawkers and Pedlars Bill.

Mr. Speaker left the Chair.

Mr. Howard was called to the chair of the Committee.

Mr. Speaker resumed the Chair.

Mr. Howard reported that the Committee had gone through the consideration of the said Bill, to which they had made several amendments, which he was directed to report whenever the House should be pleased to receive the same.

The Report was then received and accepted.

Mr. McLean moved, seconded by Mr. Washburn, that the Hawkers and Pedlars Bill be engrossed and read a third time to-morrow, which was ordered accordingly.

On motion of Mr. Hill, seconded by Mr. Washburn, the House adjourned until ten o'clock to-morrow.

Wednesday, 18th February, 1807.

Prayers were read.

Read for the first time, the Bill to alter the mode of collecting Duties upon Licenses.

Mr. Washburn moved, seconded by Mr. Howard, that the License Bill be read a second time to-morrow. Ordered accordingly.

Read the second time, the Bill for Barring Dower.

The House resolved itself into Committee to go into the consideration of the said Bill.

Mr. Speaker left the Chair.
Mr. Washburn was called to the chair of the Committee.
Mr. Speaker resumed the Chair.
Mr. Washburn reported progress, and asked for leave to sit again to-morrow.
Leave was granted accordingly.
The House resolved itself into Committee on the Assessment Bill.
Mr. Speaker left the Chair.
Mr. Swazey was called to the chair of the Committee.
The Speaker resumed the Chair.
Mr. Swazey reported progress and asked for leave to sit again on Monday next. Leave was granted accordingly.

Mr. Rogers, from the Select Committee to whom was referred the Provincial Public Accounts, reported the proceedings of the Committee thereon, and he read the Report in his place, and afterwards delivered the same in at the Table, where it was again read by the Clerk, and is as follows, viz.:—

Report of the Select Committee appointed to examine the Public Accounts, Third Session, Fourth Provincial Parliament:—

The Committee took into their consideration the Accounts marked Nos. 1 and 7, and find that there has been collected upon Shop and Innkeepers·Licenses between the 5th April, 1805, and the 5th January, 1806, not brought into the accounts of that year £4 14 6

Upon examining the Accounts Nos. 2, 3, and 9 the Committee find that the Duties arising from Licenses on Shop, Innkeepers and Stills, issued between the 5th January, 1806, and the 5th January, 1807, as far as the accounts have come to hand, after deducting ten per cent. for Inspectors, amount to......   1074 9 2½

Your Committee understand that not any of the Duties collected under the authority of British Acts of Parliament are credited to the Provincial Treasury. They beg leave to submit to the House whether all moneys raised in this Province under any authority whatsoever is or is not at the disposal of the Provincial Legislature.

The Committee observe that in the Accounts laid before the House of Assembly, Two Pounds Provincial Currency on each Shop and Tavern License is supposed to be collected under authority of a British Act of Parliament, they submit to the House whether the said sum of Two Pounds is not levied under the authority of an Act of the Provincial Legislature passed in the thirty-third year of His Present Majesty's Reign, and whether the said sum is not appropriated by the last-mentioned Act for the payment of the salaries of the Officers of the Legislative Council and House of Assembly.

The Committee next took into their consideration the account of Duties collected on Goods imported from the United States between the 1st January and the 31st December, 1806, No. 4, and find the amount of the same, after deducting the expense of collection 528 5 2⅝

Upon examining the Account of Fines and Forfeitures, No. 13, we find that the sum received on account of the same

between the 5th February, 1806, and the 1st February, 1807,
amounts to 14 15   6
     The Committee took into consideration the Account marked
No. 12, and find that there has been collected on account of
Tonnage and Lighthouse Duty for the year ending 31st December, 1806 ....   90 14   6
     Your Committee find that the sum of £31 0s. 11¾d. has
been received from the Collectors on account of Lighthouse
Duties collected for the year 1805, stated as outstanding 5th
February, 1806, including the sum of £24 5s. 3d. due to the
Collector of the Port of Kingston for duties to the said period
which was omitted to be stated as outstanding the 5th February,
1806   31   0 11¾
     Your Committee upon examining the account of articles
upon which Duties upon importation are imposed by the Legislature of Lower Canada, and which have passed Coteau du Lac
upwards, from the 1st January to the 30th June, 1806, No. 11,
and also the account of the same nature from the 1st of July
to the 31st December, 1806, marked No. 17, find the money to
be received by this Province according to the Duties heretofore
accounted for to this Province, will probably amount to about..   1694   0   0
     Your Committee beg leave to observe that the Province of
Lower Canada do not account to this Province for any duties
which they collect under the authority of British Acts of
Parliament.
     The Committee next proceeded to take into their considera-
tion the supplementary account marked No. 8, and find that
there has been collected on Shop and Innkeepers Licenses
between the 5th April, 1805, and the 5th January, 1806, and
not before accounted for 8 10   1 2/10
     Upon examining the Account No. 10 we find that the
amount of Duties upon Licenses to Shop and Innkeepers between
5th January, 1806, and 5th January, 1807, supposed to be levied
under a British Act of Parliament, amounts to   424   8   9 6/10
     Your Committee, upon examining the Account of Duties
collected upon goods imported from the United States between
the 1st January and the 31st December, 1806, under British Acts
of parliament, according to No. 5 amounts to 240 18   4½
     The sums received for Fines and Forfeitures under British
Acts of Parliament between the 5th February and 31st December,
1806, marked No. 14, amounts to 116 19   8½
     The Committee do not observe in any of the Public Accounts
that the sum taken from the Provincial Treasury last year without any authority has been replaced.
     Your Committee observe that the Province of Lower Canada
have not paid to this Province any sum on account of the
additional Duties laid by them in 1805, and that the probable
amount of such Duties will be for the period commencing 25th
March, and ending 31st December, 1805, £1,000, and that the
probable amount of the said Duties from the 1st January to
the 31st December, 1806 will be £1,280.

The Committee have it not in their power to state correctly what the amount of Duties levied in Lower Canada upon articles passing into Upper Canada under British Acts of Parliament are, the amount of articles liable to Duty passing Coteau du Lac not mentioning from what part the same are imported. The Committee beg leave to submit the following Account to the House.

General Account of Duties collected in Upper Canada under Acts of the Provincial Parliament including this Province's proportion of Duties collected in Lower Canada to the 31st December, 1805, between the 5th January, 1806, and the 5th January, 1807, including all the sums outstanding the 5th February, 1806, and the 2nd February, 1807.

Cash received by the Receiver General for duties on Shop, Innkeepers and Still Licenses outstanding the 5th of February, 1806 . ... 164 14 9¼

Cash received by the Receiver General for duties on goods imported, outstanding the 5th February, 1806 .... 61 12 8⅞

Amount of Duty on Shop and Tavern Licenses not accounted for the 5th February, 1806. .... 4 14 6

Amount of duties on Shop, Innkeepers' and Still licenses issued between 5th January, 1806, and 5th January, 1807, net Revenue. 1074 9 2½

Amount of duties on goods imported from the United States up to the 31st Decr., 1806, after deducting expense of collection. 528 5 2⅝

The sum received for Fines and Forfeitures between 1st Jan. and 31st Dec., 1806. .... 14 15 6

This Province's proportion of Duties received from Lower Canada for the year ending the 31st December, 1805......... 1364 13 10½

Cash received from Wm. Springer and J. Ward, Inspectors, for Duties on Still worked in 1802 and 1803 without License. 17 14 1½

Amount of duties collected for the purpose of erecting Lighthouses, &c. 90 14 6

Cash received on account of Lighthouse Duties collected for the year ending 31st December, 1805, stated as outstanding on 5th February, 1806, also the sum of £24. 5. 3. due by the Collector of the Port of Kingston for Duties collected to said period omitted to be stated as outstanding 5th February, 1806. 31 0 11¾

Due from Joseph Anderson, Esq., Collector of Customs, to the 31st December, 1806 .... 11 7½

Due from Colin McNabb, late Collector of Customs at Niagara, since 1802. .... 87 0 10¾

Amount of Cash remaining in the Receiver General's hands the 4th February, 1806. .... 933 9 10¼

£4373 17 9½

Paid by the Receiver General last year,
Mr. Pres. Grant's and Lieut. Gov. Gore's
Warrants £3137 1 2½
For Public Buildings 400 0 0
Receiver General's allowance on all the
money collected 90 3 10

3627 5 0½

Remaining of last year's Revenue.................... 746 12 9
Cash expected from Lower Canada.................... 1694 0 0

2440 12 9
Deduct the Balance of Lighthouse Duty appropriated.... 59 18 11

Provincial Currency £2380 13 10

General Account of all the Duties collected under British Acts of Parliament between the 5th January, 1806, and the 5th January, 1807, including all sums outstanding to the 5th January 1807.

Cash received by the Receiver General on Shop and Tavern
Licenses, not accounted for 5th February, 1806 .... 8 10 12/10
Amount of duties upon Shop and Innkeepers Licenses
between 5th January, 1806, and 5th Jan'y, 1807 .... 424 8 9 6/10
Amount of duties on goods imported from the United
States between 1st January and 31st December, 1806........ 240 18 4½
The sum arising from Fines and Forfeitures between the
5th February and 31st December, 1806. .... 116 19 8½

Sterling £790 16 11 8/10

Account of sums appropriated by law to
be paid.
To Six Sheriffs annually £50 each £300 0 0
For Public Buildings. 400 0 0
Officers of the two Houses of Parliament. 790 0 0
Copying Clerks. 50 0 0
Printing the Laws. 80 0 0

Provincial Curr'y. £1620 0 0

Account of Money in the Receiver
General's Office.
To support the War. 500 0 0
Of the sums of money appropriated for
Hemp, but not applied. 1423 11 0
Buildings appropriated, but not applied 1200 0 0
For purchasing the British Statutes, but
not applied. 175 0 0

£3298 11 0

All which is humbly submitted,
By Order of the Committee.
(Signed) D. McG. ROGERS, Chairman.

The 18th February, 1807.

Mr. Rogers then moved, seconded by Mr. Swazey, that this House do now resolve itself into Committee to take into their further consideration the Public Accounts of this Province.   The House resolved itself into Committee accordingly.
Mr. Speaker left the Chair.
Mr. McGregor was called to the chair of the Committee.
Mr. Speaker resumed the Chair.
Mr. McGregor reported progress, and asked for leave to sit again on Monday next.   Leave was granted accordingly.
Mr. McLean, one of the Messengers named to carry up to the Honorable Legislative Council the Bill for allowing the Governor, Lieutenant Governor, or person administering the Government of this Province, to appoint Ports of Entry and Collectors therein, reported that they had carried up the said Bill and did request their concurrence thereto.
On motion of Capt. Cowan, seconded by Capt. Elliott, the House adjourned until to-morrow at twelve o'clock at noon.

Thursday, 19th February, 1807.

Prayers were read.
Mr. Clench moved, seconded by Mr. Rogers, that so much of the Order of the Day as relates to the bringing in a Bill for regulating the practice of Physic and Surgery be discharged.   The same was discharged accordingly.
Read for the second time, the Bill for regulating the issuing of tavern and shop licenses.
Mr. Washburn then moved, seconded by Mr. Rogers, that this House do now resolve itself into a Committee to take into consideration the License Bill.
The House accordingly resolved itself into Committee to take the said Bill into consideration.
Mr. Speaker left the Chair.
Mr. Solicitor General was called to the Chair of the Committee.
Mr. Speaker resumed the Chair.
Mr. Solicitor General reported that he was directed to report to the House, whenever it should be pleased to receive the same, that it was the opinion of the Committee that the further consideration of the said Bill be deferred for three months, which report was accepted, and ordered accordingly.
Agreeably to the Order of the Day, the House resolved itself into Committee to go into the consideration of the Bill sent down by the Honorable Legislative Council for barring dower.
Mr. Speaker left the Chair.
Mr. Washburn was called to the Chair of the Committee.
Mr. Speaker resumed the Chair.
Mr. Washburn reported that the Committee had gone through the consideration of the said Bill, to which the Committee had made several amendments, which he was directed to report to the House whenever it should be pleased to receive the same.
The House then resolved that the said Report be now received.
The Report was accordingly received.
Mr. Rogers then moved, seconded by the Solicitor General, that the amendments made by this House to the Act entitled "An Act to extend the provisions

of an Act for the more easy barring of dower" be engrossed, and that the said amendments be read a third time to-morrow. Ordered accordingly.

Mr. Justice Thorpe, Chairman of the Special Committee appointed to inquire into the state of the Public Roads and Highways throughout this Province, reported as follows:

Commissioners to be appointed in each District to establish from one end of this Province to the other a Road, upon which such moneys as the House shall think fit are to be expended, which Commissioners shall be invested with power to employ a surveyor whenever they shall think it necessary.

The Roads to begin at Point Au Boudet, and proceed to Cornwall. The Road from the Western line of Cornwall to Kingstown to be established where it was laid out by the surveyor Pennoyer, under the authority of Lord Dorchester, the Road through the Midland District to lead through Kingston, Ernesttown, Richmond, the Mohawk tract, Thurlow, and Sidney, where it is now laid out, and usually wrought by the Statute Labour Commissioner, to be appointed in the Newcastle, Home, District of Niagara, District of London, and in the Western District. The road from Sidney through Murray, Cramatha, Haldimand, Hamilton, Hope, Clark and Darlington, from thence through Whitby, Pickering, and Scarborough to the Town of York, thence through the Mississugua tract to the head of the Lake, from thence pursue Dundas Street until you arrive at the Indian Mohawk lands on the Grand River, then in a direct course to an old Indian village on the River Thames, passing through the Indian Lands, Burford, Norwich, Durham, Dorchester, Westminster, Southwold, Dunwich, Aldborough, Orford, Howard and Chatham, from thence to Sandwich and Amherstburgh as at present laid out.

The Commissioners to be empowered to alter the prescribed road in the event of their finding it necessary on survey.

Six Commissioners for each District who shall have power to call in the aid of a surveyor.

The Commissioners to act for the upper part of the district to be appointed from the lower part, and vice versa.

The road established by the Commissioners not to be altered but by the authority of Parliament. A sum of money to be appropriated and divided in each district.

The Act passed last year entitled, etc., to be repeated.

The proceedings of the Commissioners to be reduced to writing with courses, and one copy to be filed with the Clerk of the Peace and another to be transmitted to the Clerk of the House of Assembly.

The lands on the affected roads belonging to individuals not resident in the district to be liable to a tax, and in default of payment to be sold. The money to be applied on the highway.

An Address to be presented to the Lieutenant Governor representing the propriety and necessity of raising a fund from the waste lands of the Crown, to be at the disposal of Parliament for the purpose of accomplishing this most desirable end, and on completing a great highway throughout this Province.

The House then resolved itself into Committee on the said Report.

Mr. Speaker left the Chair.

Mr. Clench took the Chair of the Committee.

Mr. Speaker resumed the Chair.

Mr. Clench reported that the Committee had made a progress, and had directed him to ask for leave to sit again. Leave was accordingly granted.

Mr. Washburn moved, seconded by Mr. Dorland, that the House do now resolve itself into Committee to take into consideration the School Bill.

The House accordingly resolved itself into Committee.

Mr. Speaker left the Chair.

Mr. Crysler was called to the Chair of the Committee.

Mr. Speaker resumed the Chair.

Mr. Crysler reported that the Committee had made a progress, and that he was directed to ask for leave to sit again to-morrow. Leave was given accordingly.

On motion of Mr. Sherwood, seconded by Captain Elliott, the House adjourned till twelve o'clock to-morrow at noon.

Friday, 20th February, 1807.

Prayers were read.

Read, the Affidavit of Thomas Horner, which is as follows:

(Niagara District.)

Personally came before me, Samuel Hatt, Esquire, one of His Majesty's Justices of the Peace for the said District, Thomas Horner, of the Township of Blenheim and District of London, Esquire, who, being duly sworn, deposeth and saith, That he did, on or about the twenty-second day of January last past, serve a subpœna on Levi Lawrence, of Burford, in the District of London, Yeoman, the contents of which was as follows, viz.:

To Levi Lawrence, of Burford, Yeoman,

By virtue of the authority to me given by the Honorable the Commons House of Assembly, I hereby summon and require you to attend in your proper person at York on the third day of the next Session of Parliament to give testimony in the controverted Election of Benajah Mallory, Esquire, the sitting Member for Norfolk, Oxford and Middlesex, on the Petition of Samuel Ryerse, Esquire.

(Signed) Alex'r. McDonell,
Speaker.

And further this deponent saith not.

(Signed) THOMAS HORNER.

Sworn before me at Ancaster,
11th of February, 1807.
(Signed) S. HATT, J.P.

Mr. Sherwood moved, seconded by Captain Elliott, that the prisoners be called to the Bar and stand there without the Serjeant-at-Arms, and that questions put by any member shall be proposed to the Speaker, and by him put to the Prisoner. Ordered accordingly.

Adrian Morlot was then brought to the Bar, and there did answer such questions as were put to him.

A Message from the Honorable the Legislative Council by Mr. Baldwin, Master-in-Chancery:

Mr. Speaker,—I am commanded by the Honorable Legislative Council to inform this House that they have concurred in passing an Act to revise an Act passed in the forty-second year of His present Majesty, entitled, "An Act to enable the Governor, Lieutenant-Governor, or person administering the Government of this Province to appoint one or more additional Port or Ports, Place or Places of

Entry within this Province, and to appoint one or more Collector or Collectors at the same respectively.

And then he withdrew.

Mr. Sherwood moved, seconded by Mr. Swazey, that the prisoner be discharged and that the Speaker do inform him that he is discharged from the insufficiency of the summons, the irregularity of the service, and the want of providing means for his support; but that had no other reason appeared to the House than an injury to his private concerns he would have been severely punished.

The Speaker accordingly informed him of the same, and then the prisoner was discharged from the Bar.

Levi Lawrence was then brought to the Bar, and after answering divers questions put to him, he was, by Order of the House, discharged from the Bar.

Mr. Justice Thorpe moved, seconded by Mr. Washburn, that so much of the Order of the day as regards the Barring Dower Bill be dispensed with, and that the third reading be deferred until Monday next. Ordered accordingly.

Agreeably to the Order of the Day the House resolved itself into a Committee to go into the further consideration of the Bill for establishing Public Schools in the several districts throughout this province.

Mr. Speaker left the Chair.

Mr. Crysler was called to the Chair of the Committee.

Mr. Speaker resumed the Chair.

Mr. Crysler reported that the Committee had made a progress, and had directed him to ask for leave to sit again on Monday next. Leave was accordingly granted.

Then was read for the third time as engrossed the Bill for granting to His Majesty duties on licenses to Hawkers, Pedlars and Petty Chapmen, and for regulating their trade.

Mr. McLean then moved, seconded by Mr. Clench, that the Bill do pass, and that the title be "An Act for granting to His Majesty duties on Licenses to Hawkers, Pedlars, and Petty Chapmen, and other trading persons therein mentioned."

The Bill then passed, and was signed by Mr. Speaker.

Mr. Sherwood then moved, seconded by Mr. Swazey, that Messrs. Clench and McLean do carry up the Bill for Licensing Hawkers, Pedlars, and Petty Chapmen to the Honorable Legislative Council and request their concurrence thereto. Ordered accordingly.

The House then ordered that the reasonable expense of Levi Lawrence be paid him, and that the Special Messenger do charge the same in his account of disbursements.

Thereafter the House resolved that Adrian Marlet should not be allowed his expenses, he being reprimanded for showing contempt to the order of this House.

On motion of Mr. Clench, seconded by Mr. Howard, the House adjourned until Monday next at twelve o'clock noon.

Monday, 23rd February, 1807.

Prayers were read.

Mr. Speaker informed the House that the Serjeant-at-Arms had requested the indulgence of this House in granting him permission to be absent for a short time from his attendance on this House, and that he be permitted to appoint Joseph Cenequy, Gentleman, as his deputy.

Agreeably to the Order of the Day, the House resolved itself into a Committee to go into the further consideration of the Bill particularizing the property which shall be subject to assessment and rates throughout this Province.

Mr. Speaker left the Chair.

Mr. Swazey was called to the Chair of the Committee.

Mr. Speaker resumed the Chair.

Mr. Swazey reported that the Committee had made a progress, and had directed him to ask for leave to sit again to-morrow. Leave was accordingly granted.

Mr. Sherwood moved, seconded by the Solicitor General, for leave to bring in a Bill to-morrow to alter and amend the existing laws relative to the Court of King's Bench in this Province. Leave was granted accordingly.

Mr. Sherwood again moved, seconded by the Solicitor General, for leave to bring in a Bill to-morrow to provide a salary for another Judge of the Court of King's Bench in this Province, and to repeal an Act appropriating money for Public Buildings at York. Leave was accordingly given.

Mr. McGregor moved, seconded by Mr. Sherwood, for leave to bring in a Bill to-morrow to repeal the several Acts now in force giving bounties for killing wolves. Leave was granted accordingly.

On motion of Mr. Rogers, seconded by Mr. Clench, ordered, that what had not been gone through of the Order of the Day be taken into consideration to-morrow.

On motion of the Solicitor General, seconded by Captain Elliott, the House adjourned.

Tuesday, 24th February, 1807.

Prayers were read.

Read for the first time, the Judicature Bill.

Mr. Clench, one of the Messengers named to carry up to the Honorable Legislative Council the Bill for Licensing Hawkers, Pedlars, and Petty Chapmen, reported that they did carry up the said Bill, and did request their concurrence thereto.

Mr. Sherwood then moved, seconded by Mr. Nellis, that the Judicature Bill be read a second time on Saturday next. Ordered accordingly.

Read for the first time, an Act to repeal the Appropriation for Public Buildings.

Mr. Sherwood moved, seconded by Mr. Nellis, that the Bill for repealing the Appropriation of money for erecting Public Buildings be read a second time on Saturday next. The same was ordered accordingly.

Read for the first time, an Act to repeal the Bounty for Destroying Wolves.

Mr. McGregor moved, seconded by Mr. Sherwood, that the Bill for repealing the Bounty for Destroying Wolves be read a second time to-morrow. Ordered accordingly.

Agreeably to the Order of the Day the House resolved itself into a Committee to go into the further consideration of the Assessment Act.

Mr. Speaker left the Chair.

Mr. Swazey was called to the Chair of the Committee.

Mr. Speaker resumed the Chair.

Mr. Swazey reported that the Committee had made a progress, and had directed him to ask for leave to sit again to-morrow. Leave was accordingly granted.

Read, the petition of Isaac Swazey, Esquire, which is as follows:
To the Honorable the Commons House of Assembly of the Province of Upper
Canada in Parliament assembled.

The Petition of Isaac Swazey, Inspector for the District of Niagara,
Humbly Sheweth,

That Your Petitioner has been commissioned Inspector of Licenses for the
District of Niagara. That in consequence of the power vested in him by law he
collected a considerable sum of money for Duties on Licenses issued 5th January,
1806.

That on the night of the twenty eighth day of January, 1806, his House was
broken open and he was robbed of large sums of money of his own private property
and the public. That amongst the said money was the sum of One Hundred and
Seventy Eight Pounds, Five Shillings and Eightpence Farthing, Provincial
currency, collected on account of Duties on Shop, Tavern and Still Licenses issued
the said 5th January, 1806.

Your Petitioner presumes he has always been punctual in his payments, and
diligent in the discharge of his duty as Inspector, and he believes that he will be
able to prove to the Honorable House that the said sum was not lost by any negligence or inattention on his part.

Wherefore, Your Petitioner prays that the House will take his case into consideration, and grant him such relief as they in their wisdom shall think meet; and
Your Petitioner, as in duty bound, will ever pray.

(Signed)   ISAAC SWAZEY.
York, 19th February, 1807.

Mr. Rogers moved, seconded by Mr. Solicitor General, that the petition of
Isaac Swazey be referred to the Committee of the Whole House on the Public
Accounts. Ordered accordingly.

The Clerk of the House has the honor of informing Mr. Speaker and the
House that the Clerks of the Peace for the different Districts in this Province did
send him returns of all the rateable property in their respective Districts, in compliance with the eighth section of the Act for the more uniform laying of Assessments throughout this Province.

The Speaker then ordered the different returns received from the Clerks of the
Peace to be laid upon the Table, and to be entered in a Book, to be of record in this
House.

The House then resolved itself into a Committee to go into the further consideration of the Provincial Public Accounts.

Mr. Speaker left the Chair.

Mr. McGregor was called to the chair of the Committee.

Mr. Speaker resumed the Chair.

And Mr. McGregor reported that the Committee had made a progress, and did
request him to ask for leave to sit again. Leave was accordingly granted.

Mr. Rogers then moved, seconded by Mr. Washburn, that he may have leave
to bring in a Bill for the relief of Isaac Swazey, Inspector for the District of
Niagara, to-morrow. Leave was accordingly granted.

On motion of Mr. Rogers, seconded by Mr. Washburn,

Ordered, That what had not been gone through of the Order of this Day be
taken into consideration to-morrow.

On motion of the Solicitor General, seconded by Capt. Cowan, the House
adjourned.

Wednesday, 25th February, 1807.

Prayers were read.

Read for the second time, The Bill to repeal the Bounty for destroying Wolves. On motion of Mr. Rogers, seconded by Mr. Dorland, the House resolved itself nto a Committee to go into the consideration of the said Bill.

Mr. Speaker left the Chair.

Mr. Justice Thorpe was called to the chair of the Committee.

Mr. Speaker resumed the Chair.

Mr. Justice Thorpe reported that the Committee had gone through the consideration of the said Bill, to which they had made an amendment, which he was directed to report to the House when it should be pleased to receive the same.

The House then resolved that the said Report be now received.

The Report was accordingly received, and is as follows:

Be repealed so far as respects the Western District, the District of London, the Home District, the District of Newcastle, the District of Johnstown and the Eastern District.

On motion of Mr. Rogers, seconded by Mr. Sherwood, the House again resolved itself into a Committee to reconsider the amendment made to the said Bill.

Mr. Speaker left the Chair.

Mr. Justice Thorpe again took the chair of the Committee.

Mr. Speaker resumed the Chair.

Mr. Justice Thorpe reported that it is the opinion of the Committee that the former amendment made to the said Bill be withdrawn. Which Report was accepted, and ordered accordingly.

Mr. McGregor then moved, seconded by Capt. Cowan, that the said Bill be engrossed and read a third time to-morrow. Ordered accordingly.

Then read for the third time, as amended, and engrossed, The Act for Barring Dower, which then passed and was signed by the Speaker.

Mr. Justice Thorpe moved, seconded by Mr. Rogers, that Messrs. Sherwood and McLean do go up and inform the Legislative Council that this House has passed the Bill for Barring Dower, as amended, to which amendments they request their concurrence. Ordered accordingly.

Read for the first time, An Act for the relief of Isaac Swazey, Esquire.

Mr. Rogers moved, seconded by Mr. Nellis, that the Bill for the relief of Isaac Swazey be read a second time on Friday next. Which was ordered accordingly.

Agreeably to the Order of the Day the House resolved itself into a Committee to go into the further consideration of the Assessment Act.

Mr. Speaker left the Chair.

Mr. Swazey was called to the chair of the Committee.

Mr. Speaker resumed the Chair.

Mr. Swazey reported that the Committee had gone through the consideration of the said Bill, to which the Committee had made several amendments, which he was directed to report whenever the House should be pleased to receive the same.

The Report was then received and accepted.

Mr. Howard moved, seconded by Mr. Swazey, that the Assessment Bill be engrossed and read a third time to-morrow. Ordered accordingly.

The House then resolved itself into a Committee on the School Bill.

Mr. Speaker left the Chair.

Mr. Crysler was called to the chair of the Committee.

Mr. Speaker resumed the Chair.

Mr. Crysler reported that the Committee had gone through the consideration of the said Bill, to which they had made several amendments, which he was directed to report whenever the House should be pleased to receive the same. The Report was then received and accepted.

The Solicitor General then moved, seconded by Mr. Sherwood, for leave to bring in a Bill on Friday next, granting to His Majesty, His Heirs and Successors, to and for the uses of this Province the like Duties on goods and merchandize brought into this Province from the United States of America as are now imposed and levied on similar articles brought from the United States and Lower Canada. Leave was accordingly granted.

On motion of Mr. Justice Thorpe, seconded by Mr. Clench, was read the petition of Thomas Barnes Gough, and is as follows:

To the Honorable House of Assembly of the Province of Upper Canada in Parliament assembled.

The Petition of Thomas Barnes Gough, of York, in said Province,

Most Respectfully Sheweth,

That Your Petitioner did respectfully petition Your Honorable House on the first day of the present session against the election and return of Robert Thorpe, Esquire, as a Knight to represent the County of Durham, the East Riding of the County of York, and the County of Simcoe in Your Honorable House in the place of the late William Weekes, Esq.

That Your Petitioner has at a great expense procured a Counsel from a distant part of this Province to support the grounds and prayer of his Petition.

That Your Petitioner has learned, with regret, that Your Honorable House has postponed the consideration thereof for three months.

Your petitioner, throwing himself on the justice and liberality of Your Honorable House, prays that you will be pleased to take the same into your consideration, and permit him to be heard by his Counsel in support of the allegations thereof at as early a period of this Session as Your Honorable House shall deem meet.

(Signed) THOS. BARNES GOUGH.

York, 18th February, 1807.

Mr. Rogers then moved, seconded by Mr. Dorland, that the petition of Thomas Barnes Gough be taken into consideration this day three months.

Which was carried in the negative.

On motion of Mr. Clench, seconded by Mr. McGregor, the House resolved itself into a Committee to go into the consideration of the Petition of Thos. Barnes Gough.

Mr. Speaker left the Chair.

Mr. Sherwood was called to the chair of the Committee.

Mr. Speaker resumed the Chair.

Mr. Sherwood reported that it was the opinion of the Committee that the further consideration of the said Petition be deferred for three months.

Mr. Solicitor General then moved, seconded by Capt. Cowan, that the Report be not received.

A division took place, the names being called for were taken down, and are as follows:

Yeas	Nays
MESSRS. SOL'R. GEN.	MESSRS. McGREGOR
SHERWOOD	CLENCH
COWAN	MALLORY
McLEAN	ROGERS
NELLIS	HILL
CRYSLER	DORLAND
	HOWARD
	WASHBURN

The same passed in the negative by a majority of two.

The Report was then received and accepted, and ordered accordingly.

Mr. Washburn then moved, seconded by Mr. Crysler, that the School Bill be engrossed and read a third time on Friday next. Ordered accordingly.

Mr. Rogers moved, seconded by Mr. Hill, that leave be given him to bring in a Bill to establish the fees of the Clerks of the Peace, and to provide for certain costs, to-morrow. Leave was accordingly granted.

On motion of Mr. Clench, seconded by Mr. Nellis, the House adjourned.

Thursday, 26th February, 1807.

Prayers were read.

Read for the third time, as engrossed, The Act to repeal several Acts granting Bounties for destroying Wolves.

Mr. McGregor then moved, seconded by Mr. Sherwood, that the Bill do pass, and that the title be "An Act to repeal the several Acts now in force, giving bounties for destroying Wolves."

Mr. Speaker having put the question for the Bill passing, a division took place, the names being called for they were taken down, and are as follows:

Yeas	Nays
MESSRS. SOL'R. GEN.	MESSRS. CLENCH
SHERWOOD	McLEAN
McGREGOR	WASHBURN
COWAN	SWAZEY
NELLIS	HILL
ROGERS	MALLORY
HOWARD	
THORPE	
CRYSLER	

The same was carried in the affirmative by a majority of three.

The Bill then passed, and was signed by the Speaker.

Then was read for the third time, as engrossed, the Assessment Act.

Mr. Rogers moved, seconded by Mr. Swazey, that the further consideration of the Assessment Bill be postponed for three months, and that the Speaker do direct that copies be printed for the use of the Members, which passed in the negative.

Mr. Clench then moved, seconded by Mr. Justice Thorpe, that the Assessment Bill be recommitted.

On the question being put a division took place; the names being called for, they were taken down, and are as follows:

Yeas	Nays
MESSRS. CLENCH	MESSRS. SOL'R. GEN.
McLEAN	SHERWOOD
SWAZEY	COWAN
ROGERS	McGREGOR
WASHBURN	NELLIS
THORPE	HOWARD
DORLAND	HILL
	MALLORY
	CRYSLER

The same passed in the negative by a majority of two.

The Solicitor General then moved, seconded by Mr. Sherwood, that the Bill do pass, and that the title be "An Act to repeal the several Acts now in force in this Province, relative to Rates and Assessments, and also to particularize the property, real and personal, which, during the continuance thereof, shall be subject to Assessments and Rates, and fixing the several valuations at which each and every particular of such property shall be rated and assessed."

The Bill then passed, and was signed by the Speaker.

The Solicitor General then moved, seconded by Capt. Cowan, that Messrs. Howard and Sherwood do carry up the Assessment Act to the Legislative Council, and do inform them that the House of Assembly have passed the same, and request their concurrence thereto. Ordered accordingly.

Read for the first time, The Fee Bill.

Mr. Rogers then moved, seconded by Mr. Swazey, that the Bill for establishing the Fees of the Clerk of the Peace be read a second time to-morrow. Ordered accordingly.

By order of the House was read the Petition of sundry Inhabitants of the District of Johnstown, which is as follows:

To the Honorable House of Assembly for the Province of Upper Canada.

The petition of the Subscribers, Inhabitants of the District of Johnstown, Humbly Represents,

That the District of Johnstown extends about fifty six miles on the River St. Lawrence. That the Counties of Grenville and Leeds are the only inhabited Counties in said District, That the County of Leeds originally contained ten Townships, two of which, Escott and Yonge, are now comprised in one, that the County of Grenville contains only seven Townships, whose population is not more than half as great as that of the County of Leeds. That the Court House and Gaol in the District of Johnstown is situated in the Town of Johnstown in the County of Grenville, within seven miles of the division line between the said District and the Eastern District; that the said Court House and Gaol were erected in pursuance of an Act passed in the thirty second year of the King, for the express purpose of accommodating the Inhabitants of that part of the Province, then known by the name of the Eastern District, conformably to an Act passed in the thirty eighth year of the King, entitled, "An Act for the better division of this Province." That the remote situation of the Court House and Gaol from the centre of the said District of Johnstown precludes in a great degree the inhabitants of the said

District from enjoying the conveniences which the Legislature undoubtedly had in view when the last mentioned Act was passed. That previous to the division of the Eastern District aforementioned the General Quarter Sessions of the Peace were alternately holden at Cornwall and Johnstown, and the Inhabitants of the said District of Johnstown attended the said sessions as Jury men only twice a year at the said Court House in Johnstown. That since the said division the said inhabitants were obliged to attend the General Quarter Sessions of the Peace to serve on juries four times in each year, and to travel the same distance for that purpose as formerly. That if the Court House and Gaol were placed in a more central situation, the expense and trouble of attending the Courts to serve on juries would be more equally divided, and the benefits intended to be granted by the said Act of the thirty eighth year of the King, would be more effectually experienced. That the said court House and Gaol in the Town of Johnstown is in a ruinous and almost irreparable state.

Your Petitioners, therefore, humbly pray the Honorable House of Assembly to frame a Bill calculated to enable the inhabitants of the said District of Johnstown to build a new Gaol and Court House on the front end of lots Nos. 10, 11, or 12, in the first Concession of the Township of Elizabethtown, in the County of Leeds aforesaid.

Your Petitioners humbly conceive that the said situation is the most eligible of any in said District of Johnstown for the purposes aforesaid, being at the distance of twenty three miles from the lower extremity of said District, as far towards the centre of the same as convenience will allow,

And Your Petitioners, as in duty bound, will ever pray.

We, the subscribers, hereby authorize Mr. Charles Jones to insert our names to any general petition which may be addressed to the Honorable House of Assembly for the purposes mentioned in the body of the foregoing Petition.

(Signed) :   Matthew Howard, Stephen Howard, Alex'r McLean, Jr., Samuel Wright, and several others.

District of Johnstown,
    Decr. 1806.

On motion of Mr. Clench, seconded by Mr. Swazey, was read the Petition of sundry inhabitants of the District of Niagara, and is as follows.

To the Honorable the Speaker and Members of the House of Assembly at York :—

The Petition of the Magistrates and principal Inhabitants living on the road along the road between the Lakes Ontario and Erie and its vicinity :—

Sheweth,—

That the Bridge crossing the mouth of the Chippewa Creek, upwards of three hundred feet in length, is so much decayed as to render the passing unsafe, and has twice endangered the lives of passengers and teams by breaking down.

Your Petitioners deem it necessary to enlarge on the utility (and, indeed, necessity) of a bridge. Then, since it is so well known to many of the Gentlemen in Your House, particularly those representing this part of the Province, but presume to say that no road in this district is more travelled than the road above mentioned.

The law authorizing the Magistrates in Quarter Sessions to draw on the County Treasurer for the repair of highways and bridges does not allow them to exceed the sum of Fifty Pounds for any one bridge, which, in the present exigence is far too small a sum.

12 A.

Your Petitioners, therefore, pray that the Legislative Body will be pleased to authorize the Magistrates of Niagara District in Quarter Sessions assembled, to apply an additional sum of Two Hundred Pounds of the County money to defray the expense of building a bridge across the mouth of Chippewa Creek, or make such other provisions as the necessity of the case requires, and which in your wisdom shall seem meet.

And Your petitioners will pray.

John Warren, Sr., Thomas Cummings, Sam'l Street, Sr., Douglas, and several others.

Mr. Solicitor General then moved, seconded by Captain Cowan, for leave to bring in a Bill on Saturday next for building a Gaol and Court House in Eliza-bethtown, in the District of Johnstown. Leave was accordingly granted.

Mr. Rogers then moved, seconded by Mr. Swazey, that this House do now resolve itself into a Committee to take into their further consideration the Public Accounts.

Accordingly the House resolved itself into Committee.

Mr. Speaker left the Chair.

Mr. McGregor took the chair of the Committee.

Mr. Speaker resumed the Chair.

And Mr. McGregor reported that the Committee had made a progress, and had directed him to ask for leave to sit again this day. Leave was accordingly granted.

A Message from the Legislative Council by Mr. Baldwin, Master in Chancery: Mr. Speaker,—

I am commanded by the Legislative Council to inform this Honorable House that they have passed a Bill for the relief of Clerks to Attorneys who may have served their Clerkships without being bound by contracts in writing, to which they request the concurrence of this House.

And then he withdrew.

The said Bill was then read for the first time.

On motion of the Solicitor General, seconded by Capt. Cowan, the said Bill was ordered to be read for the second time to-morrow.

The House again resolved itself into a Committee to go into the further con-sideration of the Public Provincial Accounts.

Mr. Speaker left the Chair.

Mr. McGregor was called to the chair of the Committee.

Mr. Speaker resumed the Chair.

Mr. McGregor reported that the Committee had made a progress, and that he was directed to ask for leave to sit again to-morrow. Leave was accordingly granted.

On motion of Mr. McGregor, seconded by Mr. Nellis, ordered, that the House be called over to-morrow.

The House resolved itself into a Committee to go into the further consideration of the Special Jury Bill.

Mr. Speaker left the Chair.

Mr. Hill was called to the chair of the Committee.

Mr. Speaker resumed the Chair.

Mr. Hill reported that the Committee had made some progress, and that he was directed to ask for leave to sit again on Monday next. Leave was accordingly granted.

The House then resolved itself into a Committee to go into the further consideration of the Marriage Bill.

Mr. Speaker left the Chair.

Mr. Rogers was called to the chair of the Committee.

Mr. Speaker resumed the Chair.

Mr. Rogers reported that the Committee had made a progress, and had directed him to ask for leave to sit again on Monday next. Leave was accordingly granted to sit again on Monday next.

The House then resolved itself into a Committee to take into their further consideration the state of the roads throughout this Province.

Mr. Speaker left the Chair.

Mr. Clench took the chair of the Committee.

Mr. Speaker resumed the Chair.

Mr. Clench reported that the Committee had made a progress, and had asked for leave to sit again this day. Leave was accordingly granted.

Mr. Justice Thorpe moved, seconded by Mr. Rogers, that the Committee of the Whole House on the state of the roads be empowered to examine such persons as they shall think necessary in order to obtain information with respect to the state of the roads in the different districts. Ordered accordingly.

The House again resolved itself into a Committee.

Mr. Speaker left the Chair.

Mr. Clench again took the chair of the Committee.

Mr. Speaker resumed the Chair.

And Mr. Clench reported that the Committee do recommend to the House that the Select Committee on the Public Highways and Roads throughout this Province, be a Committee to draft a Bill grounded on their Report to this House. The House resolved the same, and ordered accordingly.

On motion of Capt. Cowan, seconded by Capt. Elliott, the House adjourned.

Friday, 27th February, 1807.

Prayers were read.

Read for the second time, the Bill for granting relief to Isaac Swazey, Esquire.

Mr. Rogers moved, seconded by Mr. Nellis, that the House do now resolve itself into a Committee to take into their consideration the Bill for the relief of Isaac Swazey, and that the Committee have power to examine such persons as they may think proper. Ordered accordingly.

The House then resolved itself into a Committee to go into the consideration of the said Bill.

Mr. Speaker left the Chair.

Mr. Clench was called to the chair of the Committee.

Mr. Speaker resumed the Chair.

Mr. Clench reported that the Committee recommended that the further consideration of the Bill for granting relief to Isaac Swazey, Esquire, be postponed until the first week in the next ensuing Session of the Provincial Parliament.

Mr. Rogers moved, seconded by Mr. Howard, that the Report be not received.

A division thereupon took place; the names being called for, they were taken down, and are as follows:

Yeas.	Nays.
MESSRS. MALLORY,	MESSRS. ELLIOTT.
HOWARD.	COWAN.
ROGERS.	McGREGOR.
SHERWOOD.	McLEAN.
CRYSLER.	NELLIS.
	WASHBURN.
	HILL.
	THORPE.
	CLENCH.
	DORLAND.

Which passed in the negative by a majority of five.

The Report was then received and accepted, and ordered accordingly.

Mr. Rogers moved, seconded by Mr. Clench, that Isaac Swazey have leave to withdraw his Petition and the affidavits annexed to it. Leave was accordingly granted.

Read for the second time, the Bill to regulate the Fees to be taken by the Clerks of the Peace throughout this Province.

On motion of Mr. Rogers, seconded by Mr. Mallory, the House resolved itself into a Committee to take into their consideration the said Fee Bill.

Mr. Speaker left the Chair.

Mr. Crysler was called to the Chair of the Committee.

Mr. Speaker resumed the Chair.

Mr. Crysler reported a progress, and asked for leave to sit again this day. Leave was accordingly granted.

A Message from the Honorable Legislative Council by Mr. Baldwin, Master-in-Chancery:

'Mr. Speaker,—

I am commanded by the Honorable Legislative Council to inform this House that the Legislative Council have concurred with the House of Assembly in that part of their amendment to the Bill entitled, "An Act to extend the benefits of an Act passed in the thirty-seventh year of His Majesty's reign, entitled, 'An Act for the more easy Barring of Dower and to repeal certain parts of the same,'" which instead of "Great Britain or Ireland" substitutes the words "The United Kingdom of Great Britain and Ireland," also to that part which declares that no omission which has heretofore occurred in the registry of a Certificate of Dower barred shall vitiate the same, but do not concur with the other amendments, and request a conference thereon.

(Signed) THOMAS SCOTT,
Speaker.

Legislative Council Chamber,
27th February, 1807.

And also the Legislative Council have passed an Act sent up by this Honorable House entitled "An Act for granting to His Majesty Duties and Licenses to Hawkers, Pedlars and Petty Chapmen, and for regulating their trade," to which they made some amendments, to which amendments they request the concurrence of this House.

And also that they have passed an Act to repeal part of an Act passed in the thirty-seventh year of His present Majesty, entitled, "An Act for regulating the practice of the Court of King's Bench," to which they request the concurrence of this House, and then he withdrew.

Read for the first time, the amendments made by the Legislative Council to the Act for licensing Hawkers, Pedlars and Petty Chapmen.

Mr. Rogers then moved, seconded by Mr. Howard, that a Committee be appointed to confer with a Committee of the Legislative Council on the amendments made by them to a Bill for extending the provisions of an Act for Barring Dower, which was ordered accordingly.

Mr. Rogers again moved, seconded by Mr. Howard, that Messrs. Sherwood, McLean, Dorland and McGregor be a Committee to confer with a Committee of the Legislative Council on the amendments made to a Bill for extending the provisions of an Act for Barring of Dower. Ordered accordingly.

On Motion of Mr. Sherwood, seconded by Mr. Crysler, ordered, that Messrs. Clench and McGregor do carry up to the Legislative Council the following message:

Mr. Speaker,

We are directed by the Commons to inform Your Honorable House that they have appointed a Committee to manage on their part a conference upon the subject of their amendments in and to the Bill entitled "An Act for Barring Dower," and that their Managers will attend Your Committee at any time Your Honorable House may think fit to appoint.

(Signed) ALEXANDER MCDONELL,
Speaker,

Commons House of Assembly,
27th February, 1807.

Mr. Clench, one of the Messengers named to carry up to the Legislative Council the Message from this House, reported that they had carried up the said Message.

Mr. McLean then moved, seconded by Mr. Sherwood, that the amendments made by the Legislative Council to a Bill entitled "An Act for granting to His Majesty Duties on Licenses to Hawkers, Pedlars and Petty Chapmen, and for regulating their trade," be rejected, and that he have leave to bring in a Bill to-morrow granting to His Majesty certain Duties on Licenses to Hawkers, Pedlars, Petty Chapmen and other trading persons. Leave was accordingly granted.

Read for the first time, An Act sent down from the Legislative Council to repeal an Act passed in the thirty-seventh year of His present Majesty entitled " An Act to regulate the practice of the Court of King's Bench."

The House again, agreeably to leave given, resolved itself into a Committee, to go into the further consideration of the Fees to be taken by the Clerks of the Peace.

Mr. Speaker left the Chair.

Mr. Crysler again took the Chair of the Committee.

Mr. Speaker resumed the Chair.

Mr. Crysler reported a progress, and asked for leave to sit again this day. Leave was accordingly granted.

A Message from the Legislative Council by Mr. Baldwin, Master in Chancery.

Mr. Speaker,

The Committee of conference of the Legislative Council on the amendments to the Bill entitled " An Act to extend the benefits of An Act passed in the thirty-seventh year of His Majesty's Reign, entitled ' An Act for the more easy Barring of Dower, and to repeal certain parts of the same, are now ready to meet the Committee of the House of Assembly in the Legislative Council Chamber.

(Signed) THOMAS SCOTT,
Speaker.

Legislative Council Chamber,
27th February, 1807.

And then he withdrew.

Mr. Sherwood, first named in the conference requested by the Legislative Council in the amendments made by this House to the Act for extending the benefits of an Act passed in the thirty-seventh year of His Majesty's Reign, entitled "An Act for the more easy Barring of Dower and to repeal certain parts of the same," reported that the Committee of the Commons House of Assembly declined withdrawing the amendments made by this House to that Bill.

Agreeably to leave given, the House again resolved itself into Committee to go into the further consideration of the Clerks of the Peace Bill.

Mr. Speaker left the Chair.

Mr. Crysler again took the Chair of the Committee.

Mr. Speaker resumed the Chair.

Mr. Crysler reported a progress, and asked for leave to sit again on Monday next. Leave was accordingly granted.

On motion of Mr. Howard, seconded by Mr. Nellis,

Ordered, That what had not been gone through of the Order of this Day be taken into consideration to-morrow.

On motion of Mr. Justice Thorpe, seconded by Mr. Washburn, the House adjourned until to-morrow at twelve o'clock at noon.

Saturday, 28th February, 1807.

Prayers were read.

Read for the second time, the Judicature Bill.

On motion of Mr. Sherwood, seconded by Mr. McGregor, the House resolved itself into a Committee to go into the consideration of the said Bill.

Mr. Speaker left the Chair.

Captain Cowan was called to the Chair of the Committee.

Mr. Speaker resumed the Chair.

Captain Cowan reported that the Committee had made a progress, and directed him to ask for leave to sit again on Monday next. Leave was accordingly granted.

Read for the second time, the Bill to repeal the Act for Public Buildings.

Read for the third time as engrossed, the Bill for establishing a Public School in each District in this Province.

Mr. Justice Thorpe moved, seconded by Mr. Howard, that the School Bill be recommitted on Monday next. Ordered accordingly.

Then was read for the first time the Bill for Licensing Hawkers, Pedlars and Petty Chapmen.

Mr. McLean then moved, seconded by Mr. Sherwood, that the Hawkers and Pedlars Bill be read for a second time on Monday next. Which was ordered accordingly.

On motion of Mr. Crysler, seconded by Mr. Hill,

Ordered, That so much of the Order of this Day be dispensed with as relates to the second reading of the Act for granting relief to Attorneys' Clerks, and that the said Bill be read on Monday next.

Mr. Justice Thorpe moved, seconded by Mr. Howard, that the Public Accounts shall be the first business on the Order of the Day until they are finished. Which passed in the negative.

Mr. Rogers moved, seconded by Mr. Sherwood, that the order made yesterday on the Bill for the relief of Isaac Swazey be discharged, and that he have leave to produce further evidence in support of the facts stated in his Petition.

The House divided thereon; the names being called for were taken down as follows:

Yeas	Nays
MESSRS. CRYSLER	MESSRS. DORLAND
MALLORY	CLENCH
McGREGOR	NELLIS
SHERWOOD	ELLIOTT
ROGERS	THORPE
WASHBURN	McLEAN
COWAN	
HILL	
HOWARD	

Majority of three in the affirmative.

The order was accordingly discharged, and leave was given to produce further evidence in support of the facts stated in his Petition.

On motion of Mr. Howard, seconded by Mr. Hill, ordered, that what had not been gone through of the Order of this Day be taken into consideration on Monday next.

On motion of Captain Cowan, seconded by Captain Elliott, the House adjourned until Monday next.

Monday, 2nd March, 1807.

Prayers were read.

Agreeably to the Order of the Day the House resolved itself into a Committee to go into the further consideration of the Judicature Bill.

Mr. Speaker left the Chair.

Captain Cowan was called to the Chair of the Committee.

Mr. Speaker resumed the Chair.

Captain Cowan reported that the Committee recommended to the House that the Judicature Bill be printed, and that ten copies be sent to each Member of the House of Assembly, the Legislative Council, to Mr. Justice Powell, the Attorney General (when he arrives) and fifty copies to His Excellency, the Lieutenant Governor; and that a Bill of this nature be brought in at the next session of Parliament. Which Report was received and accepted. And Ordered accordingly.

The House then resolved itself into a Committee to go into the further consideration of the Bill for establishing the Fees to be taken by the Clerks of the Peace throughout this Province.

Mr. Speaker left the Chair.

Mr. Crysler was called to the Chair of the Committee.

Mr. Speaker resumed the Chair.

Mr. Crysler reported a progress, and asked for leave to sit again this day. Leave was accordingly granted.

A Message from the Legislative Council by Mr. Baldwin, Master in Chancery.

Mr. Speaker,

I am commanded by the Legislative Council to inform this Honorable House that they have passed an Act sent up from this House, entitled " An Act to repeal the several Acts now in force giving bounties for destroying Wolves," to which they have made some amendments, to which amendments they request the concurrence of this House.

And then he withdrew.

The amendments were then read for the first time.

On motion of Mr. Sherwood, seconded by Mr. McGregor, they were ordered to be read a second time to-morrow.

The House again resolved itself into a Committee to go into the further consideration of the Fees to be taken by the Clerks of the peace.

The Speaker left the Chair.

Mr. Crysler again took the Chair of the Committee.

Mr. Speaker resumed the Chair.

Mr. Crysler reported that the Committee had gone through the consideration of the said Bill, to which the Committee had made several amendments, which he was directed to submit to the House whenever it shall be pleased to receive the same.

The House then resolved that the Report be now received.

The Report was accordingly received.

The Solicitor General moved, seconded by Mr. Dorland, that the Clerk of the Peace Fee Bill be engrossed and read a third time to-morrow. Ordered accordingly.

Then was read for the third time, as engrossed, the Bill for establishing Schools in this Province.

Mr. McLean moved, seconded by Mr. Sherwood, that the Bill do pass, and that the title be " An Act to establish Public Schools in each and every District of this Province.

The Speaker then put the question, Shall the Bill pass. A division took place, the names being called for they were taken down, and are as follows:

Yeas	Nays
MESSRS. SOL'R. GEN.	MESSRS. CRYSLER
SHERWOOD	JUS. THORPE
ELLIOTT	HILL
COWAN	ROGERS
McGREGOR	
McLEAN	
CLENCH	
SWAZEY	
NELLIS	
WASHBURN	
MALLORY	

Carried in the affirmative by a majority of seven.

The Bill then passed, and was signed by the Speaker.

Mr. McLean then moved, seconded by Capt. Elliott, that Messrs. Washburn and Swazey be a Committee to carry the School Bill up to the Legislative Council and request their concurrence thereto. Which was ordered accordingly.

Then was read for the second time, the Hawkers and Pedlars Bill.

On motion of Mr. Clench, seconded by Capt. Cowan, the House resolved itself into a Committee to go into the consideration of the said Bill.

Mr. Speaker left the Chair.

Mr. Dorland was called to the chair of the Committee.

Mr. Speaker resumed the Chair.

Mr. Dorland reported that the Committee had gone through the consideration of the said Bill, to which the Committee had made an amendment, which he was directed to report to the House whenever it should be pleased to receive the same.

The House then resolved that the Report be now received.

The Report was accordingly received.

Mr. Clench then moved, seconded by Mr. Nellis, that the Bill relating to Hawkers, Pedlars and Petty Chapmen be engrossed, and read a third time this day. Ordered accordingly.

The said Bill was then read for the third time as engrossed.

Mr. McLean then moved, seconded by Mr. Sherwood, that the Bill do pass, and that the title be " An Act for granting to His Majesty duties on Licenses to Hawkers, Pedlars and Petty Chapmen, and other Trading persons therein mentioned.

The Bill then passed, and was signed by the Speaker.

Mr. Clench then moved, seconded by Mr. McGregor that the Messengers named to carry up to the Honorable Legislative Council the Bill for establishing Public Schools do also carry up the Bill entitled " An Act for granting to His Majesty duties on Licenses to Hawkers, Pedlars and Petty Chapmen, and other trading persons." Which was ordered accordingly.

The Solicitor General, seconded by Mr. Rogers, then moved that the Attorneys Bill be read a second time this day. The said Bill was accordingly read a second time.

Mr. Solicitor General, seconded by Mr. Swazey, moved that this House do now resolve itself into a Committee on the Attorneys Bill. The House accordingly resolved itself into a Committee.

Mr. Speaker left the Chair.

Mr. Hill was called to the chair of the Committee.

Mr. Speaker resumed the Chair.

Mr. Hill reported that the Committee had gone through the consideration of the said Bill without any amendment, which he was directed to report to the House whenever it should be pleased to receive the same.

The Report was then received and accepted.

The said Bill was then read for the third time, passed, and signed by the Speaker.

Mr. Sherwood then moved, seconded by Mr. Justice Thorpe, for leave to bring in a Bill to-morrow to enable the Practitioners at the Bar in this Province to take a greater number of Clerks than by law they are now limited to take. Leave was accordingly granted.

Mr. Solicitor General moved, seconded by Mr. McLean, that Mr. Washburn and Mr. Swazey do carry up the Bill entitled " An Act for the relief of Clerks to Attorneys who may have served their clerkship without being bound by contract in writing " to the Legislative Council, and inform them that this House have concurred in passing the same without any amendments. Ordered accordingly.

Read for the first time, The Johnstown Court House Bill.

On motion of the Solicitor General, seconded by Mr. McLean, the said Bill was read for the second time.

The Solicitor General moved, seconded by Mr. Crysler, for leave to bring in ' a Bill to-morrow to regulate the payment of several orders of Sessions made by the Quarter Sessions in the Eastern District previous to the establishment of the District of Johnstown. Leave was accordingly granted.

Mr. Justice Thorpe again gave notice that he will to-morrow move an Address to the Lieutenant Governor, on the subject of the claims of U. E. Loyalists, their children, and also the claims of the military claimants.

On motion of Mr. Dorland, seconded by Mr. Washburn, the House adjourned.

Tuesday, 3rd March, 1807.

Prayers were read.

Mr. Rogers moved, seconded by Mr. Solicitor General, that the House do now resolve itself into a Committee to take into their consideration the Bill for the relief of Isaac Swazey, Esquire.

The House accordingly resolved itself into a Committee.

Mr. Speaker left the Chair.

Mr. Speaker was called to the chair of the Committee.

Mr. Speaker resumed the Chair.

Mr. Clench reported that the Committee had made a progress, and had directed him to ask for leave to sit again to-morrow. Leave was accordingly granted.

Read for the second time, a Bill entitled "An Act to repeal the several Acts now in force giving bounties for destroying Wolves," as amended.

On motion of Mr. Sherwood, seconded by Mr. Solicitor General, the house resolved itself into a Committee to go into the consideration of the amendments made by the Legislative Council to the Bill entitled "An Act to repeal the several Acts now in force, giving bounties for destroying Wolves."

Mr. Speaker left the Chair.

Mr. Howard was called to the chair of the Committee.

Mr. Speaker resumed the Chair.

Mr. Howard reported that the Committee had concurred in the amendments made by the Legislative Council to the Bill entitled " An Act to repeal the several Acts now in force, giving bounties for destroying Wolves," which he was to report to the House whenever it should be pleased to receive the same.

Ordered, that the said Report be now received.

Ordered, that the Solicitor General and Captain Cowan do carry the following message to the Legislative Council:

Mr. Speaker,—

We are commanded by the House of Assembly to inform this Honorable House that it has concurred in the amendments made by this Honorable House to an Act entitled "An Act to repeal the several Acts now in force, giving bounties for destroying Wolves."

(Signed) Alexr. McDonell,

Commons House of Assembly,   Speaker.
3rd March, 1807.

Read for the third time, as engrossed, the Bill entitled "An Act to establish the Fees of the Clerks of the Peace, and to regulate the Fees in the several Courts of Quarter Sessions throughout this Province."

Mr. Sherwood then moved, seconded by the Solicitor General, that this Bill do pass, and that the title be "An Act to establish the Fees of the Clerks of the Peace, and to regulate the Fees in the several Courts of Quarter Sessions throughout this Province."

The Bill then passed and was signed by the Speaker.

Read for the first time the Bill entitled, "An Act to authorize the Practitioners at the Bar in this Province to take such number of Clerks as is therein mentioned," and that the said Bill be read a second time to-morrow.

Mr. Rogers moved, seconded by Mr. Mallory, that the Solicitor General and Capt. Cowan do carry up to the Legislative Council the Bill for establishing the Fees of the Clerks of the Peace, and to request their concurrence thereto. Ordered accordingly.

Mr. Washburn, one of the Messengers named to carry up to the Legislative Council the Bill for licensing Hawkers, Pedlars and Petty Chapmen, reported that they had carried up the same, to which they requested their concurrence.

And also an Act for establishing Public Schools in each and every District in this Province to which they also requested their concurrence, and also the message of this House.

Read for the first time, the Bill for paying of money to individuals in the District of Johnstown.

The Solicitor General moved, seconded by Mr. Sherwood, that the Johnstown and Eastern District Bill be read a second time to-morrow. Ordered accordingly.

The Solicitor General then moved, seconded by Mr. Sherwood, that the House do on to-morrow resolve itself into a Committee on the Johnstown Court House Bill, which was accordingly ordered.

Mr. Thorpe gave notice that he would to-morrow move an Address to the Lieutenant Governor on the claims of the U. E. and Military Claimants.

Read for the first time, the Duty Bill.

Mr. Solicitor General, seconded by Mr. Sherwood, moved that the Duty Bill be read a second time to-morrow. Ordered accordingly.

Mr. Justice Thorpe moved, seconded by Mr. Rogers, for leave to bring in a Bill to-morrow for the preservation of Salmon. Leave was accordingly granted.

Mr. Rogers moved, seconded by the Solicitor General, that the names of the members of this House be called over to-morrow. Ordered accordingly.

Mr. Swazey then moved, seconded by Mr. Crysler, for leave to bring in a Bill to-morrow to remove doubts respecting the eligibility of the Judges of His Majesty's Court of King's Bench to sit in the House of Assembly in this Province. Leave was accordingly granted.

On motion of Capt. Cowan, seconded by Mr. Mallory, the House adjourned.

Wednesday, 4th March, 1807.

Prayers were read.

Read for the first time, an Act for the better Preservation of Salmon.

On motion of Mr. Justice Thorpe, seconded by Mr. Mallory,

Ordered, that the said Bill be read a second time to-morrow.

Read for the second time, an Act for allowing Practitioners at the Bar in this Province to take such number of Clerks as therein mentioned.

On motion of Mr. Sherwood, seconded by Mr. Clench, the House resolved itself into a Committee to go into the consideration of the said Bill.

Mr. Speaker left the Chair.

Mr. McGregor was called to the chair of the Committee.

Mr. Speaker resumed the Chair.

Mr. McGregor reported that the Committee had gone through the consideration of the said Bill without any amendment, which report was accepted.

On motion of Mr. Sherwood, seconded by Mr. McGregor,

Ordered, that the said Bill be engrossed and read a third time to-morrow.

Read for the second time, the Bill for giving relief to those who held orders on the District Treasury of Johnstown.

On motion of the Solicitor General, seconded by Mr. Sherwood, the House resolved itself into a Committee to go into the consideration of the said Bill.

Mr. Speaker left the Chair.

Mr. Hill was called to the chair of the Committee.

Mr. Speaker resumed the Chair.

Mr. Hill reported that the Committee had gone through the consideration of the said Bill without any amendment, which Report was received and accepted.

On motion of Mr. Solicitor General, seconded by Mr. Sherwood, the said Bill was ordered to be engrossed and read a third time to-morrow.

Agreeably to the Order of the Day, the House resolved itself into a Committee to go into the consideration of the District of Johnstown Court House and Gaol Bill.

Mr. Speaker left the Chair.

Mr. McLean was called to the chair of the Committee.

Mr. Speaker resumed the Chair.

Mr. McLean reported that the Committee had made a progress, and directed him to ask for leave to sit again to-morrow. Leave was accordingly granted.

Mr. Justice Thorpe then moved, seconded by Mr. Washburn, that the House should now resolve itself into a Committee on the claims of the U. E. and Military Claimants.

The House divided thereon, the names being called for they were taken down, and are as follows:

Yeas.	Nays.
MESSRS. CLENCH.	MESSRS. SOL'R GEN.
McGREGOR.	CRYSLER.
DORLAND.	MALLORY.
ROGERS.	ELLIOTT.
HILL.	COWAN.
JUSTICE THORPE.	McLEAN.
WASHBURN.	SHERWOOD.
	NELLIS.
	SWAZEY.

Which was carried in the negative by a majority of one.

Then was read for the second time the Bill for granting duties to His Majesty on Goods and Merchandise imported from the United States of America, as are paid in the Province of Lower Canada.

On motion of Mr. Solicitor General seconded by Mr. Swazey, the House resolved itself into a Committee to go into the consideration of the said Bill.

Mr. Speaker left the Chair.

Mr. Rogers was called to the chair of the Committee.

Mr. Speaker resumed the Chair.

Mr. Rogers reported that the Committee had gone through the consideration of the said Bill, to which they had made some amendments, which he was directed to report to the House whenever it shall be pleased to receive the same.

The House then resolved that the Report be now received: He then read the report in his place, and then delivered the same in at the Table, where it was again read by the Clerk, and is as follows:

That the said Act shall continue to be in force to the first day of March in the year of Our Lord, One Thousand Eight Hundred and Nine, and no longer.

The Report was then received and accepted.

On motion of the Solicitor General, seconded by Capt. Elliott, ordered, that the said Bill be engrossed and read a third time to-morrow.

The Order of the Day for the call of the House being read,

Ordered, that the House be now called over.

The House was accordingly called over, and the only member absent is W. E. Wilkinson.

Read for the first time, the Bill to remove doubts respecting the eligibility of the Judges of His Majesty's Court of King's Bench to sit in the House of Assembly in this Province.

Mr. Washburn then moved, seconded by Mr. Justice Thorpe, that the Bill relative to Judges of the Court of King's Bench be read a second time this day three months.

The House divided thereon, the names being called for they were taken down, and are as follows:

Yeas	Nays
MESSRS. MALLORY	MESSRS. SOL'R. GEN.
CLENCH	CRYSLER
McGREGOR	ELLIOTT
NELLIS	COWAN
ROGERS	McLEAN
HOWARD	SHERWOOD
HILL	SWAZEY
WASHBURN	
THORPE	
DORLAND	

The same was carried in the affirmative by a majority of three. And Ordered accordingly.

Mr. Rogers then moved, seconded by Mr. Sherwood, that this House do now resolve itself into a Committee to take into their further consideration the Bill for the relief of Isaac Swazey. The same passed in the negative.

Mr. Rogers then moved, seconded by Mr. Clench, that the House do now resolve itself into a Committee to take into their further consideration the Provincial Public Accounts.

The House accordingly resolved itself into a Committee.

Mr. Speaker left the Chair.

Mr. McGregor was called to the Chair of the Committee.

Mr. Speaker resumed the Chair.

Mr. McGregor reported that the Committee had made a progress, and directed him to ask for leave to sit again to-morrow. Leave was accordingly granted. On motion of Capt Elliott, seconded by Mr. McGregor, the House adjourned.

Thursday, 5th March, 1807.

Prayers were read.

Read for the second time, The Bill entitled " An Act for the better Preservation of Salmon."

Mr. Justice Thorpe then moved, seconded by Mr. Swazey, that the House do now resolve itself into a Committee to go into the consideration of the said Bill.

A division thereupon took place, the names being called for they were taken down, and are as follows:

Yeas	Nays
MESSRS. SOL'R. GEN.	MESSRS. CLENCH
COWAN	DORLAND
SHERWOOD	HILL
McGREGOR	
McLEAN	
HOWARD	
ROGERS	
SWAZEY	
THORPE	

The same was carried in the affirmative by a majority of six.

The House accordingly resolved itself into a Committee.

Mr. Speaker left the Chair.

Mr. Sherwood was called to the chair of the Committee.

Mr. Speaker resumed the Chair.

Mr. Sherwood reported that the Committee had gone through the consideration of the said Bill, to which they had made several amendments, which he was directed to report whenever the House should be pleased to receive the same.

The House then resolved that the said Report be now received and accepted.

Read for the third time, as engrossed, A Bill to authorize Practitioners in the Law to take a certain number of Clerks.

Mr. Sherwood then moved, seconded by the Solicitor General, That the Bill do pass, and that the title be " An Act to authorize Practitioners in the Law in this Province to take such a number of Clerks as is therein mentioned."

The Bill then passed and was signed by the Speaker.

Mr. Rogers moved, seconded by Mr. Swazey, that Messrs. Sherwood and McLean do carry up to the Legislative Council the Bill for allowing Attornies more Clerks, and to request their concurrence in passing the same. Ordered accordingly.

Read for the third time, as engrossed, a Bill for the payment of certain debts due by the Eastern District.

Mr. Sherwood then moved, seconded by the Solicitor General, that the Bill do pass, and that the title be " An Act to regulate the payment of certain debts due by the Eastern District before the establishment of the District of Johnstown."

The said Bill then passed, and was signed by the Speaker.

A Message from the Legislative Council by Mr. Baldwin, Master in Chancery.

Mr. Speaker,

I am Commanded by the Legislative Council to inform this Honorable House that they have passed a Bill entitled "An Act to establish Public Schools in each and every District of this Province " without any amendment.

And then he withdrew.

Mr. Solicitor General then moved, seconded by Mr. Swazey, that Messrs. Sherwood and McLean do carry up the Eastern District Bill to the Legislative Council, and inform them that the House of Assembly have passed the same, and request the concurrence of the Legislative Council to the same.

And also that Messrs Sherwood and McLean do carry up the Duty Bill to the Legislative Council, and inform them that the House of Assembly have passed the same, and request their concurrence thereto. Ordered accordingly.

Mr. Howard then moved, seconded by Mr. Dorland, that so much of the Order of this Day as relates to the House going into a Committee to go into the consideration of the Johnstown Court House Bill be discharged, and that leave be given for the House to go into Committee to-morrow on the said Bill. Ordered accordingly.

Mr. Sherwood, first named to carry up several Bills to the Legislative Council, reported that they had carried up an Act to Authorize Practitioners in the Law in this Province to take such number of Clerks as is therein mentioned.

And also an Act to regulate the payment of certain debts due by the Eastern District before the establishment of Johnstown.

And also a Bill entitled, "An Act for granting to His Majesty, His Heirs and Successors, to and for the uses of this Province the like duties on goods and merchandize brought into this Province from the United States of America as are now paid on goods and merchandize imported from the United States of America into the Province of Lower Canada.

On motion of Mr. Solicitor General, seconded by Mr. McLean, the House resolved itself into a Committee on the Marriage Bill.

Mr. Speaker left the Chair.

Mr. Rogers was called to the chair of the Committee.

Mr. Speaker resumed the Chair.

Mr. Rogers reported that the Committee had made a progress, and directed him to ask leave to sit again this day. Leave was accordingly granted.

A Message from the Legislative Council, by Mr. Baldwin, Master in Chancery.

Mr. Speaker,

I am commanded by the Legislative Council to inform this Honorable House that they have passed an Act entitled "An Act to repeal the several Acts now in force in this Province relative to Rates and Assessments, and also to particularize the property, real and personal, which, during the continuance thereof, shall be subject to Assessments and Rates, and fixing the several valuations at which each and every particular of such property shall be rated and assessed," to which they made several amendments, to which amendments they request the concurrence of this House.

And then he withdrew.

The House again resolved itself into a Committee to go into the further consideration of the Marriage Act.

Mr. Speaker left the Chair.

Mr. Rogers again took the chair of the Committee.

Mr. Speaker resumed the Chair.

Mr. Rogers reported that the Committee had made a progress, and had directed him to ask for leave to sit again this day. Leave was accordingly granted.

A Message from the Legislative Council by Mr. Baldwin, Master in Chancery.
Mr. Speaker,—
I am commanded by the Legislative Council to inform this Honorable House
that they have passed an Act entitled " An Act for granting to His Majesty duties
on Licenses to Hawkers, Pedlars and petty Chapmen, and other Trading persons,"
without any amendment.
And then he withdrew.
The House again resolved itself into a Committee to go into the further con-
sideration of the Marriage Act.
Mr. Speaker left the Chair.
Mr. Rogers again took the chair of the Committee.
Mr. Speaker resumed the Chair.
And Mr. Rogers reported that the Committee had gone through the con-
sideration of the said Bill, to which the Committee had made several amendments,
which he was directed to report to the House whenever it should be pleased to
receive the same.
The Report was then accordingly received and accepted.
Mr. Solicitor General then moved, seconded by Mr. McLean, that the Marriage
Act be engrossed, and read for the third time to-morrow. Ordered accordingly.
Mr. Rogers then moved, seconded by Mr. Sherwood, that the House do now
resolve itself into a Committee to take into their further consideration the Bill for
the relief of Isaac Swazey.
Which passed in the negative.
On motion of Mr. Solicitor General, seconded by Mr. Clench, the House
resolved, That it is the opinion of this House that on the night of the 28th day of
January One Thousand Eight Hundred and Six, Isaac Swazey, Esquire, Inspector
of Revenue for the District of Niagara, was robbed in his house by some persons
unknown of the sum of One hundred and seventy-eight Pounds, five Shillings and
eight pence currency, being money by him collected as Inspector; and that he was
at the same time severely beat and wounded.
The House then resolved itself into a Committee to go into the further con-
sideration of the Provincial Public Accounts.
Mr. Speaker left the Chair.
Mr. McGregor took the Chair of the Committee.
Mr. Speaker resumed the Chair.
And Mr. McGregor reported that the Committee had made a progress, and did
direct him to ask for leave to sit again. Leave was accordingly granted.
On motion of Mr. Washburn, seconded by Captain Cowan, the House adjourned.

Friday, 6th March, 1807.

Prayers were read.
Read for the third time, the Bill for the Preservation of Salmon.
Mr. McLean moved, seconded by Mr. Sherwood, that the words " Midland
District " in the first clause of the Bill be expunged. Which was ordered accord-
ingly.
Mr. Justice Thorpe then moved, seconded by Mr. Mallory, that the words
" this Province " be expunged, and " the aforesaid District " substituted, and that
the words " for and during the aforesaid month of September, October, and
November " be expunged. Which was ordered accordingly.

On motion of Mr. Sherwood, seconded by Mr. McLean, the House resolved itself into a Committee to go into the consideration of the amendments made by the Honorable Legislative Council to the Act entitled " An Act for laying Assess- ments throughout this Province."

Mr. Speaker left the Chair.

Mr. Mallory was called to the chair of the Committee.

Mr. Speaker resumed the Chair.

Mr. Mallory reported that the Committee had gone through the consideration of the amendments made by the Honorable Legislative Council to said Act, to which the Committee concurred; which he was directed to report to the House whenever it should be pleased to receive the same.

The Report was then received, and the House concurred in the said amendments.

On motion of Mr. McLean, seconded by Mr. Howard,

Ordered, That a Message be sent up to the Honorable Legislative Council to acquaint them that this House did concur in the amendments made by them to the Act for laying Assessments and Rates throughout this Province.

Mr. McLean then moved, seconded by the Solicitor General, that the Marriage Act, as engrossed, be recommitted.

The House accordingly resolved itself into a Committee to go into the further consideration of the Marriage Act.

Mr. Speaker left the Chair.

Mr. Rogers was called to the Chair of the Committee.

Mr. Speaker resumed the Chair.

Mr. Rogers reported that the Committee had gone through the consideration of the said Bill, to which the Committee had made several amendments, which he was directed to report to the House whenever it should be pleased to receive the same.

The House then resolved, That the said Report be now received.

Mr. McLean moved, seconded by the Solicitor General, that the Marriage Bill be engrossed, and read a third time to-morrow. Ordered accordingly.

On motion of the Solicitor General, seconded by Mr. Howard, the House resolved itself into a Committee on the District of Johnstown Court House Bill.

Mr. Speaker left the Chair.

Mr. McLean was called to the Chair of the Committee.

Mr. Speaker resumed the Chair.

Mr. McLean reported that the Committee had gone through the consideration of the said Bill, to which they had made several amendments, which he was directed to submit to the House whenever it should be pleased to receive the same.

The House then resolved that the said Report be now received.

The Report was accordingly received.

On motion of the Solicitor General, seconded by Mr. Howard, the said Bill as amended was ordered to be engrossed and read a third time to-morrow.

Mr. Solicitor General moved, seconded by Mr. Crysler, for leave to bring in a Bill to-day for applying certain sums of money therein mentioned to make good certain moneys issued and advanced by His Majesty through His Honor, Mr. President Grant, in pursuance of two addresses of this House. Leave was accordingly granted.

The said Bill was read for the first time.

On motion of Mr. McLean, seconded by Mr. Sherwood, the said Bill was read for the second time.

13 A.

On motion of Mr. Rogers, seconded by Mr. Clench, the House resolved itself into a Committee to go into the consideration of the said Bill.

Mr. Speaker left the Chair.

Mr. Swayzey was called to the Chair of the Committee.

Mr. Speaker resumed the Chair.

Mr. Swayzey reported that the Committee had gone through the consideration of the said Bill without any amendments.

On motion of the Solicitor General, seconded by Mr. McLean, the said Bill was ordered to be engrossed and read a third time to-morrow.

Mr. Thorpe moved, seconded by Mr. Rogers, that the Bill for the Preservation of Salmon do pass, and that the title be "An Act for the Preservation of Salmon."

The Bill then passed and was signed by the Speaker.

Mr. Solicitor General moved, seconded by Captain Cowan, that Messrs. Rogers and Howard do carry the said Act up to the Legislative Council, and that they do request their concurrence thereto; and also the Message of this House.

Mr. Speaker,

We are commanded by the House of Assembly to inform this Honorable House that they have concurred in the amendments made by the Honorable the Legislative Council to an Act entitled "An Act to repeal the several Acts now in force in this Province relative to Rates and Assessments, and also to particularize the property, real and personal, which, during the continuance thereof, shall be subject to Assessments and Rates; and fixing the several valuation at which each and every particular of such property shall be rated and assessed.

(Signed) Alex'r McDonell,

Speaker.

Commons House of Assembly,
6th March, 1807.

On motion of Mr. Sherwood, seconded by Mr. Rogers,

Ordered, That the Clerk of the House do lay before the House the account of expenditures incurred for the use thereof since the close of the last session, on Monday next.

On motion of Mr. McGregor, seconded by Captain Elliott, the House adjourned.

Saturday, 7th March, 1807.

Prayers were read.

Mr. Rogers, one of the Messengers named, reported that in obedience to the commands of this House they had carried up to the Honorable Legislative Council the Act for the better Preservation of Salmon in several Districts of this Province, to which they requested their concurrence.

And also the Message of this House to the Honorable Legislative Council, acquainting them that this House had concurred in the amendments made by them to the Act for the more uniformly laying Assessments and Rates throughout this Province.

Mr. Sherwood then moved, seconded by Mr. Clench, that this House do resolve that they will relinquish the sum of Six hundred and seventeen Pounds, thirteen Shillings and seven pence, applied by the late Governor Hunter to the use of this Province without the concurrence of the other branches of the Legislature, and that an Address be presented to His Excellency, the Lieutenant Governor, to that effect.

The House divided upon the question: the names being called for, they were taken down, and are as follows.

Yeas.	Nays.
MESSRS. CRYSLER	MESSRS. WASHBURN
SOL'R GENERAL	THORPE
SHERWOOD	
McGREGOR	
ELLIOTT	
McLEAN	
COWAN	
CLENCH	
NELLIS	
HOWARD	
ROGERS	
SWAZEY	
HILL	

The same was carried in the affirmative by a majority of ten. The Address was ordered accordingly.

On motion of Mr. Sherwood, seconded by Mr. McLean,

Ordered, That the Solicitor General and Mr. Clench be a Committee to draft an Address to His Excellency, the Lieutenant Governor, for the purpose aforesaid.

Messrs. Solicitor General and Clench informed the House that agreeable to the commands of this House they had drafted an Address to His Excellency, the Lieutenant Governor, which they were ready to submit to the House whenever it should be pleased to receive the same.

The House then resolved, that the said Address be now received, which he read in his place, and afterwards delivered in the same at the Table, where it was again read by the Clerk, and is as follows:

To His Excellency, Francis Gore, Esquire, Lieutenant Governor of the Province of Upper Canada, &c. &c. &c.

May it please Your Excellency,

We, His Majesty's most dutiful and loyal subjects, the Commons of Upper Canada, in Parliament Assembled, beg leave to inform Your Excellency that we have relinquished the sum of Six hundred and seventeen Pounds, thirteen Shillings and seven pence, paid by the late Lieutenant Governor Hunter without the concurrence of the other branches of the Legislature; as we are convinced that the same was expended for the public use, and for the benefit of this Province. Commons House of Assembly, 7th March, 1807.

On motion of Mr. Sherwood, seconded by Captain Cowan, the said Address was ordered to be engrossed.

The Address as engrossed was then read, passed and signed by the Speaker.

On motion of Mr. Sherwood, seconded by Mr. McLean,

Ordered, That the Solicitor General and Mr. Clench do present to His Excellency, the Lieutenant Governor, the said Address at such time as he may be pleased to receive the same.

Read for the third time, as engrossed, an Act for applying certain sums of money therein mentioned to make good certain moneys issued and advanced by His Majesty through his Honor, Mr. President Grant, in pursuance of two Addresses of this House.

Mr. Rogers then moved, seconded by Mr. Swazey, that the said·Bill do pass. The Bill accordingly passed, and was signed by the Speaker.

Mr. Clench then moved, seconded by Mr. McGregor, that Mr. Nellis and Captain Elliott do carry the said Bill to the Honorable the Legislative Council and request their concurrence thereto. Which was ordered accordingly.

Then was read for the third time, as engrossed an Act to make Marriages heretofore contracted in this Province -valid.

The Solicitor General then moved, seconded by Mr. Crysler, that the Bill do pass, and that the title be "An Act to conform and make valid certain Marriages heretofore contracted, and to provide for the future solemnization thereof." The other "An Act to extend the provisions of a former Act and to Provide for the future solemnization of Marriage."

The Bill then passed and was signed by the Speaker.

Mr. McLean then moved, seconded by Mr. Solicitor General, that Mr. Nellis and Captain Elliott do carry up to the Legislative Council the Marriage Act, and request their concurrence thereto.

Read for the third time, as engrossed, the Johnstown Court House Bill.

Mr. Howard then moved, seconded by Mr. McLean, that the Bill do pass, and that the title be "An Act to enable the Inhabitants in the District of Johnstown to erect and build a Court House and Gaol in the Township of Elizabethtown.

The Bill accordingly passed and was signed by the Speaker.

Mr. Rogers then moved, seconded by Captain Elliott, that Messrs. Howard and Crysler do carry up to the Honorable the Legislative Council the Bill for erecting a Court House and Gaol in the District of Johnstown, and request their concurrence in passing the same. Ordered accordingly.

Mr. Washburn gave notice that he intends in the course of the next Session of Parliament to move this House to take into its consideration whether it would not be for the public good of the Newcastle District to repeal the Act that formed the same, and make other provision for that part of the Province.

A Message from the Honorable Legislative Council by Mr. Baldwin, Master in Chancery.

Mr. Speaker,

I am commanded by the Honorable Legislative Council to inform this House that they have concurred in passing an Act to authorize Practitioners in the Law in this Province to take such a number of Clerks as therein mentioned, without any amendments.

And also an Act for granting to His Majesty, His Heirs and Successors, to and for the uses of this Province, the like Duties on Goods and Merchandize brought into this Province from the United ·States of America as are now paid on Goods and ·Merchandize imported from the United States of America into the Province of Lower Canada, without any amendment.

And then he withdrew.

Mr. Nellis, first named, reported that they had carried up to the Honorable Legislative Council the Act for applying certain sums of money therein mentioned to make good certain moneys issued and advanced by His Majesty through His

Honor, Mr. President Grant, in pursuance of two several Addresses, and did request their concurrence thereto.

And also an Act to confirm and make valid certain marriages heretofore contracted in this Province, and did request their concurrence thereto.

A Message from the Legislative Council by Mr. Baldwin, Master in Chancery.

Mr. Speaker,

I am Commanded by the Legislative Council to inform this Honorable House that they have concurred in passing an Act to regulate the payment of certain debts due by the Eastern District before the establishment of the District of Johnstown, without any amendment.

And also an Act for applying certain sums of money therein mentioned to make good certain moneys issued and advanced by His Majesty, through His Honor Mr. President Grant, in pursuance of two Addresses, without any amendment.

And then he withdrew.

On motion of Capt. Elliott, seconded by Capt. Cowan the House adjourned until nine o'clock on Monday morning.

Monday, 9th March, 1807.

Prayers were read.

Mr. Clench, one of the Messengers named to wait upon His Excellency the Lieutenant Governor with the Address of this House, voted on the 7th inst, reported that they had waited upon His Excellency with the said Address, to which he had been pleased to return the following answer.

Gentlemen:—

Your Address informing me that you have relinquished the sum of Six Hundred and Seven Pounds, thirteen Shillings and seven Pence, paid by the late Lieutenant Governor Hunter without the concurrence of the other branches of the Legislature, gives me the greatest satisfaction. It shows that in the proceedings on this subject the House of Assembly have been actuated by proper motives, and I feel much gratified at the honor which will be reflected on this Colony by the handsome manner in which you have thus put an end to them.

Government House, York, 8th March, 1807.

A Message from the Honorable Legislative Council by Mr. Baldwin, Master in Chancery.

Mr. Speaker,

I am commanded by the Legislative Council to inform this Honorable House that they have concurred in passing an Act for the better Preservation of Salmon.

And also that they have concurred in passing an Act establishing the Fees of the Clerks of the Peace, and to regulate the Fees in the several Courts of Quarter Sessions throughout this Province to which they have made several amendments, to which amendments they request the concurrence of this House.

And then he withdrew.

The amendments made to the said Bill were then read.

Mr. Sherwood then moved, seconded by the Solicitor General, that the House do now resolve itself into a Committee to go into the consideration of the amendments made by the Honorable Legislative Council to an Act entitled "An Act for regulating the Fees to be taken in the several Courts of Quarter Sessions throughout this Province.

The House divided thereon, the names being called for they were taken down, and are as follows.

Yeas.	Nays.
MESSRS. ELLIOTT	MESSRS. HILL
SOL'R GEN.	CLENCH
SHERWOOD	DORLAND
COWAN	
McGREGOR	
SWAZEY	
NELLIS	
HOWARD	
ROGERS	
CRYSLER	

The same was carried in the affirmative by a majority of seven.
The House accordingly resolved itself into a Committee.
Mr. Speaker left the Chair.
Mr. Crysler was called to the chair of the Committee.
Mr. Speaker resumed the Chair.
And Mr. Crysler reported that the Committee had gone through the consideration of the said amendments, and that he was directed to report to the House that it was the opinion of the Committee that the amendments made by the Legislative Council should be adopted.
Which Report the House resolved should be received and accepted.
The Report was accordingly accepted.
On motion of Mr. Sherwood, seconded by Capt. Cowan,
Ordered, That Messrs. Rogers and Dorland do carry up to the Legislative Council the following message.
Mr. Speaker,
We are commanded by the House of Assembly to inform this Honorable House that they have concurred in the amendments made by this House to an Act entitled "An Act to establish the Fees of the Clerks of the Peace, and to regulate the Fees in the several Courts of Quarter Sessions throughout this Province.
(Signed) Alex'r McDonell,
Commons House of Assembly,   Speaker.
9th March, 1807.

On motion of Mr. Sherwood, seconded by the Solicitor General, the House resolved itself into a Committee to take into their consideration the Contingent Accounts of both Houses of Parliament for both Houses of Parliament for the present Session.
Mr. Speaker left the Chair.
Mr. Nellis was called to the chair of the Committee.
Mr. Speaker resumed the Chair.
Mr. Nellis reported that the Committee had gone through the consideration of the Contingent Accounts of the Legislative Council and this House, and that they had come to several Resolutions thereon, which he was directed to submit to the House. And he then read the several Resolutions in his place, and afterwards delivered the same in at the Table, where they were again read by the Clerk.
And the said Resolutions are as follows:

Resolved, That it is the opinion of the Committee that it is expedient to advance the sum of Twenty Pounds to the Clerk of the Legislative Council, to enable him to purchase a supply of stationery for the use of the next Session of Parliament; and the sum of Six Pounds be allowed to him to enable him to complete the business of the present Session, over and above the sum appropriated by law, for the paying of copying clerks, making in all Twenty Six Pounds.

Resolved, That it is the opinion of this Committee that there is due to sundry persons, agreeable to the annexed account sent down from the Hon. Legislative Council and signed by their Speaker, for services performed during the present Session the sum of Fifty-five Pounds, Six Shillings and Eightpence Halfpenny, and that there is due George Lawe, Gentleman Usher of the Black Rod, Twenty-five Pounds for articles furnished and services rendered the two Houses of Parliament previous to the present Session, making in all Eighty Pounds Six Shillings and Eight Pence Halfpenny.

Resolved, That it is the opinion of this Committee that there is due to sundry persons for articles furnished for the use of this House, and services performed during the present Session, One Hundred and Sixteen Pounds Fourteen Shillings.

Resolved, That it is the opinion of this Committee that it is expedient to advance the Clerk of this House thirty Pounds to enable him to purchase a supply of stationary for the use of the ensuing Session of Parliament.

Resolved, That it is the opinion of this Committee, that Hugh Carfrae be allowed for his attendance this Session as Messenger and Firelighter to this House, and for every Session thereafter that he shall be employed in that capacity, the sum of Twenty Pounds.

Resolved, That it is the opinion of this Committee that the sum of Fifty Pounds be paid to the Church or Town Wardens of each of the following Townships, viz: Sandwich, Niagara, York, Newcastle, Augusta and Cornwall, to be expended upon the Church of each of the said Towns or Townships respectively, and also to the Church or Town Wardens of the Township of Adolphustown the sum of Fifty Pounds, to be expended upon the Court House in the said Township, which is used as a Church.

Estimate of a sum of money necessary to procure stationery
for the Honorable the Legislative Council for the ensuing Session.   £20   0   0
Of sum necessary to pay a Copying Clerk for bringing up the
business of the present Session.   5   0   0
                                                            ─────────────
                                                              £25   0   0

(Signed)   JNO. POWELL, C. L. O.
Approved, (Signed) THOS SCOTT, Speaker.

The Honorable the Legislative Council,
                            To John Powell, Their Clerk, Dr.
To this sum for the payment of Copying Clerks, exclusive of
the £25 appropriated for that purpose £1 10   0
Amount of William Allen's Account for Stationery furnished
for the Legislative Council. 10 10   3

York, 9th March, 1807.   £12   0   3
(Signed) JNO. POWELL, C. L. C.
Examined and approved,
(Signed)   THOS. SCOTT, Speaker.

Government of Upper Canada,
         to George Lawe, Dr.

To amount of Wm. Allan's Account	£17	5	2½
" " John McBeath, Account ....:..	15	2	0
" " John Bassell's Account	14	7	6
" " Ellinor Bazzel's Account		9	6
" " Sarah Hay's Account	4	15	0
" " Philip Clinger's Account	2	5	0
" " John Edgill's Account	1	2	6
	£55	6	8½

· George Lawe, Gentleman Usher of the Black Rod, maketh Oath and saith that the above Account of Fifty-five Pounds, Six Shillings and Eightpence Halfpenny is just and true to the best of his knowledge and belief.

(Signed)   GEORGE LAWE.

Sworn before me this 7th day of March, 1807.

(Signed)   THOS. SCOTT, C. J.

9th March, 1807, York, Upper Canada.

The Contingent Account of the Commons House of Assembly, for the third Session of the Fourth Provincial Parliament.

Due to John McBeath	£33	18	6
" Duncan Cameron	2	9	2½
" Titus G. Simons ....•...	4	14	9
" John Bennett	11	5	0
" Noel Delisle	15	5	0
" Philip Clinger	2	12	6
" Thos. Ridout	1	0	0
" Quetton St. George		15	7½
" Alex'r. Wood		9	4½
" Thos. R. Johnson .·...........................	9	6.	½
" William Allan		11	10½
" The Postmaster at York	·	8	0
To Cash voted to procure stationery for the use of the ensuing Session of the Prov. Parliament	30	0	0
Due the Copying Clerks beyond what is allowed by Law for that purpose	32	12	7
To Stationery beyond the sum advanced for that purpose of procuring Stationery for the present Session	1	5	2
Allowance to Hugh Carfrae, Messenger and Firelighter to the House of Assembly for services during the present Session	20	0	0
	£166	14	0

Commons House of Assembly,
   9th March, 1807.

(Signed)·ALEX'R. McDONELL, Speaker.

The Honorable the House of Assembly in Account Current with their Clerk.
Dr.
1806. Ap'l 22nd.
. To Cash paid Samuel Cozens for copying during the Recess of
Parliament as per receipt £5 3 10
    To Do. Do. Charles Willcocks, as per receipt. 2 10 0
    To Do paid Hugh Carfrae as per receipt 2 6 3

                                                            10 0 1
    To balance due by Donald McLean 4 19 11

                                                       £15 19 11
                                                              Cr.
1806, Ap'l 22nd.
By Cash allowed to complete the business of the Session £15 0 0

                                                        £15 0 0

                    (Signed) DONALD McLEAN, Clerk Assembly.

The Honorable the House of Assembly in Account for Stationery with their Clerk,
For the Third Session of the Fourth Provincial Parliament.
Dr.
1807, Jany. 8th.
    To Alexander Wood £5 19 0
    " D. Cameron 2 4 6
    " William Allan 3 15 11½
    " J. Walkers, for Parchment 8 2 10
    " H. Drean, for bringing Do 2 6
    " 1½ Reams demy paper at 80s. 6 0 0
    Paper Borrowed and to be returned of the same quality
ream, 7 quires at 80s. 5 8 0

                                                       £31 12 9½

    To Balance due the Clerk 1 5 2
                                                              Cr.
By Balance remaining in my hands since last year 7 7
By the President's Warrant advanced for Stationery 30 0 0
By Balance due the Clerk. 1 5 2½

                                                       £31 12 9½

    Errors excepted.   9th March, 1807.
                    (Signed) DONALD McLEAN.

The Honorable House of Assembly in Account Current with their Clerk, for
    Copying Clerks during the Third Session of the Fourth Parliament.
Dr.
    To Charles Willcocks £12 0 0
    " Joseph Shaw 17 15 0

To Stephen Heward 6 2 0
" Hugh Heward 10 0 0
" John McDonell 2 0 0
" John Higgins 14 15 0

                                                        £62 12 6

                                                                    Cr.
By Balance of Cash remaining unexpended by an Allowance
made last session for completing the business of that Session
during the Recess of Parliament £14 19 11
By the amount of His Excellency the Lieutenant Governor's
Warrant in my favour, as by Law appropriated for paying of
Copying Clerks 25 0 0
To Balance due to the Clerk 32 12 6

Errors Excepted. 9th March, 1807.
                              Donald McLean, Clerk Assembly.

Mr. Rogers then moved, seconded by Mr. Hill, that the Resolution of the Committee of the Whole House with regard to churches in York, Niagara, Sandwich, Augusta, Cornwall, and the Court House in Adolphustown be not adopted by this House.

The House divided upon the question.

The names being called for they were taken down as follows, viz.:

Yeas.	Nays.
MESSRS. SWAZEY.	MESSRS. SOL'R GEN.
ROGERS.	SHERWOOD.
COWAN.	ELLIOTT.
HILL.	CLENCH.
THORPE.	McGREGOR.
NELLIS.	DORLAND.
	CRYSLER.

And the same was carried in the negative by a majority of one.

On motion of Mr. Sherwood, seconded by the Solicitor General,

Resolved, that this House do now concur in the foregoing Resolutions reported from the Committee of the Whole House on the Contingent accounts of the two Houses of Parliament.

Resolved, that an Humble Address be presented to His Excellency the Lieutenant Governor, to request His Excellency that he will be pleased to issue his Warrant in favour of George Lawe, Usher of the Black Rod, for the sum of Eighty Pounds Six Shillings and Eightpence Halfpenny, and his warrant in favour of John Powel, Esquire, Clerk of the Legislative Council, for the sum of Twenty-six Pounds, and also his Warrant in favour of Donald McLean, Esq., Clerk of the House of Assembly, for the sum of One Hundred and Sixty-six Pounds Fourteen Shillings; and also the sum of Fifty Pounds to be paid to the Church or Town Wardens of each of the following Townships, viz., Sandwich, Niagara, York and Cornwall, and also to the Church or Town Wardens of the Township of Adolphustown, the sum of Fifty Pounds.

On motion of Mr. Sherwood, seconded by Capt. Elliott,

Ordered, that the Solicitor General and Mr. Clench be a Committee to draft an Address to His Excellency the Lieutenant Governor in conformity to the several Resolutions of the House this day.

Mr. Solicitor General reported that the Committee had drafted an Address to His Excellency the Lieutenant Governor grounded on the several Resolutions of the House this day, which he was ready to submit to the House whenever it should be pleased to receive the same.

Mr. Sherwood then moved, seconded by Capt. Cowan, that the Address be now received.

The House divided upon the question, and the names were taken down, and are as follows:—

Yeas.	Nays.
MESSRS. SOL'R GEN.	MESSRS. SWAZEY.
COWAN.	ROGERS.
SHERWOOD.	HILL.
McGREGOR.	NELLIS.
CLENCH.	
DORLAND.	
CRYSLER.	

Majority of three in the affirmative.

· Mr. Solicitor General then read the Address in his place, and afterwards delivered the same in at the table, where it was again read by the Clerk, and is as follows:

To His Excellency Francis Gore, Esquire, Lieutenant Governor of the Province of Upper Canada, etc.

May it Please Your Excellency,

We, His Majesty's most dutiful and loyal subjects, the Commons of Upper Canada in Parliament assembled, do most humbly pray that it may please Your Excellency to issue your Warrant directed to the Receiver General requiring him to pay to Mr. George Lawe, Usher of the Black Rod, the sum of Eighty Pounds Six Shillings and Eightpence Halfpenny; to John Powell, Esquire, Clerk of the Legislative Council, the sum of One Hundred and Sixty-six Pounds Fourteen Shillings. And whereas we have resolved that the sum of Fifty Pounds be paid to the Church or Town Wardens of each of the following Townships, viz.: Sandwich, Niagara, York, Augusta, and Cornwall, to be expended upon the Church of each of the said Towns or Townships respectively; and also to the Church or Town Wardens of the Township of Adolphustown the sum of Fifty Pounds, to be expended upon the Court House in said Township, which is used as a Church.

We therefore do most humbly pray that Your Excellency will be pleased to issue your Warrants to carry the said Resolution into effect, and the Commons will make good the several sums of money to Your Excellency at the next Session of Parliament.

Commons House of Assembly, 9th March, 1807.

The Address then passed and was signed by the Speaker.

On motion of Mr. Sherwood, seconded by Mr. Dorland,

Ordered, that the Solicitor General and Mr. Clench do present the said Address to His Excellency the Lieutenant Governor at such time as he may be pleased to receive the same.

On motion of Mr. Hill, seconded by Mr. Nellis, the House adjourned.

Tuesday, 10th March, 1807.

Prayers were read.

Mr. Solicitor General reported that the Messengers had waited upon His Excellency, the Lieutenant Governor, with the Address of this House of yesterday, and that His Excellency had been pleased to return the following answer: Gentlemen,—

I shall, in compliance with this Address, issue my Warrants to the Receiver General to pay the several sums mentioned therein to the Usher of the Black Rod. Clerk of the Legislative Council, and Clerk of the House of Assembly.

I shall also issue my Warrant to the Receiver General to enable the House to carry their Resolution into effect that the sum of Fifty Pounds be paid to the Church or Town Wardens of each of the following Townships, viz.: Sandwich, Niagara, York, Augusta and Cornwall, to be expended upon the Church of each of the said Towns or Township respectively, and also the Church or Town Warden of the Township of Adolphustown, the sum of Fifty Pounds, to be expended upon the Court House in that Township, which is used as a Church.

Government House, York,
9th March, 1807.

The House was then pleased to order that the Speaker should apply to His Excellency, the Lieutenant Governor, for the sum of Fifteen Pounds, to be given to the Clerk of this House to enable him to complete the business of the present Session during the Recess of Parliament; to be by him accounted for to this House the next Session, which sum this House will make good to His Excellency during the next Session of the Provincial Parliament.

The Names of the Members present were taken down and are as follows, *vide licit*:

Mr. Speaker, Messrs. Sol'r General, Sherwood, Crysler, Elliott, McGregor, Clench, Nellis, Rogers, Justice Thorpe, Washburn, Hill, McLean, Cowan, Swazey, Dorland.

A Message from His Excellency, the Lieutenant Governor, by Mr. George Lawe, Gentleman Usher of the Black Rod.

Mr. Speaker,—

I am commanded by His Excellency, the Lieutenant Governor, to inform this Honorable House that it is His Excellency's pleasure that the Members thereof do forthwith attend upon His Excellency in the Legislative Council Chamber.

Accordingly Mr. Speaker with the House went up to attend His Excellency, when His Excellency was pleased to give in His Majesty's name the Royal assent to the following Public and Private Bills:

An Act to revive and continue an Act passed in the Forty-second year of His present Majesty, entitled "An Act to enable the Governor, Lieutenant Governor, or Person Administering the Government of this Province, to appoint one or more additional Port or Ports, Place or Places of Entry within this Province, and to appoint one or more Collector or Collectors at the same respectively."

An Act to repeal the several Acts now in force giving Bounties for Destroying Wolves.

An Act to establish the Fees of the Clerks of the Peace, and to regulate the Fees in the several Courts of Quarter Sessions throughout this Province.

An Act to authorize Practitioners in the Law in this Province to take such a number of Clerks as is therein mentioned.

An Act to regulate the payment of certain Debts due by the Eastern District before the establishment of the District of Johnstown.

An Act for the better Preservation of Salmon.

An Act for the relief of Clerks to Attornies who may have served their Clerkships without being bound by contract in writing.

Mr. Speaker then said,—

May it please Your Excellency to approve of the five Bills which the Assembly, with the concurrence of the Legislative Council, have passed for aid to His Majesty.

An Act to repeal the several Acts now in force in this Province relative to Rates and Assessments, and also to particularize the property, real and personal, which during the continuance thereof, shall be subject to assessments and rates, and fixing the several valuations at which each and every particular of such property shall be rated and assessed.

An Act to establish Public Schools in each and every District of this Province.

An Act for applying certain sums of money therein mentioned to make good certain moneys issued and advanced by His Majesty through His Honor, Mr. President Grant, in pursuance of two Addresses.

An Act for granting to His Majesty Duties on Licences to Hawkers, Pedlars and Petty Chapmen, and other trading persons therein mentioned.

An Act for granting to His Majesty, His Heirs and Successors, to and for the uses of this Province, the like Duties on Goods and Merchandize brought into this Province from the United States of America as are now paid on Goods and Merchandize imported from the United States of America into the Province of Lower Canada. ·

To which five Acts His Excellency, the Lieutenant Governor, was pleased to give the Royal assent in His Majesty's name.

His Excellency, the Lieutenant Governor, was then pleased to make the following Speech to both Houses of Parliament:

Honorable Gentlemen of the Legislative Council
and
Gentlemen of the House of Assembly,—

In closing the Session of the Legislature I must express the sense I entertain of the attention with which you have executed the important trusts committed to your care.   •

I have with particular approbation, assented, in His Majesty's name, to the Acts whereby Public Schools will now be established in the different Districts of this Province, fully sensible of the importance of such institutions to the education and morals of the rising generation in this Infant Colony. In the prosecution of this laudable object you may rely on my attention and care. ·

The regulations which have been enacted for increasing the Public Revenue will, I trust, produce that salutary end; and I here must express my satisfaction, when considering the liberal manner in which the House of Assembly has conducted itself respecting the Revenues of this Province; entertaining the pleasing hope that its Revenue may soon be more adequate to its necessities, and that it will, at no very distant period, be enabled to relieve our Parent State from part of that burthen which it has on our account so generously sustained.

The other Bills which I have assented to will, I trust, promote the end of all legislation, the public good.

I now put an end to this Session of the Legislature, confiding that in the different parts of this widely extended Province to which you respectively belong, good order in society, obedience to the laws, and loyalty to the King will effectually be promoted by your influence and example.

After which the Honorable Speaker of the Legislative Council said:—

Gentlemen of the Legislative Council
and
Gentlemen of the House of Assembly,—

It is His Excellency the Lieutenant Governor's will and pleasure that this Provincial Parliament be prorogued until Saturday, the eighteenth day of April next, to be then here held; and this Provincial Parliament is accordingly prorogued until Saturday, the eighteenth day of April next.

I do hereby certify that the above and what is written on the foregoing pages in a transcript of the Journal of the House of Assembly in Upper Canada, being the Third Session of the Fourth Provincial Parliament, assembled in the Town of York on the Second day of February last, agreeably to the Proclamation of His Excellency, Francis Gore, Esq., Lieutenant Governor of the Province of Upper Canada; and prorogued by His Excellency on the Tenth day of March last.

Donald McLean,

Clerk of the House of Assembly.

Clerk of the Assembly's Office,
York, 11th May, 1807.

[Certified to be true copies from the original records in the Colonial Office.

George Mayer,

Librarian and Keeper of the Records.

Colonial Office, Downing Street,
24th September, 1856.]

JOURNAL

OF THE

HOUSE OF ASSEMBLY

OF

UPPER CANADA

From the twentieth day of January to the
sixteenth day of March,

1808,

Both days inclusive.

In the forty-eighth year of the Reign of

KING GEORGE THE THIRD.

Being the fourth session of the Fourth Provincial
Parliament of this Province.

JOURNAL

OF THE

HOUSE OF ASSEMBLY

OF

UPPER CANADA

1808.

FRANCIS GORE, Lieutenant Governor.

PROCLAMATION.

George the Third, by the Grace of God, of the United Kingdom of Great Britain and Ireland, King, Defender of the Faith.

To Our beloved and faithful Legislative Councillors, of Our Province of Upper Canada, and to Our Knights, Citizens and Burgesses of Our said Province, to the Provincial Parliament of Our Town of York, on the Eighteenth day of April to be commenced, held, called and elected, and to every of you, GREETING.

Whereas by Our Proclamation, bearing date the Tenth day of March last, we thought fit, by and with the advice of Our Executive Council, to prorogue Our Provincial Parliament until the Eighteenth day of this present month of April, at which time, in Our Town of York, you were held and constrained to appear,— But we, taking into Our Royal consideration the ease and convenience of Our loving subjects, have thought fit, by and with the advice of Our Executive Council, to relieve you, and each of you, of your attendance at the time aforesaid; hereby convoking, and by these presents enjoining you, and each of you, that on the Twenty-sixth day of May next ensuing you meet us in Our Provincial Parliament, in Our Town of York, there to take into consideration the state and welfare of Our Province of Upper Canada, and there to do as may seem necessary. Herein fail not.

In Testimony Whereof we have caused these Our Letters to be made Patent, and the Great Seal of Our said Province to be hereunto affixed.

Witness Our trusty and well beloved Francis Gore, Esquire, Our Lieutenant-Governor of Our said Province, at York, this Thirteenth day of April, in the year of Our Lord, One Thousand Eight Hundred and Seven, and in the Forty-seventh year of Our Reign.

F. G.

WM. JARVIS, Secretary.

By a further Proclamation of His Excellency, Francis Gore, Esquire, Lieutenant-Governor of the Province of Upper Canada, etc., etc., etc., dated at York, the Twentieth day of May, One Thousand Eight Hundred and Seven, the meeting of the Legislative Council and House of Assembly stands prorogued to the Third day of July, One Thousand Eight Hundred and Seven.

14 A.   189

By a further Proclamation of His Excellency, Francis Gore, Esquire, Lieutenant-Governor of the Province of Upper Canada, etc., etc., etc., dated at York,
the Twenty-sixth day of June, One Thousand Eight Hundred and Seven, the
meeting of the Legislative Council and House of Assembly stands prorogued
to the Tenth day of August, One Thousand Eight Hundred and Seven.

By a further Proclamation of His Excellency, Francis Gore, Esquire, Lieutenant-Governor of the Province of Upper Canada, etc., etc., etc., dated at York,
the Sixth day of August, One Thousand Eight Hundred and Seven, the meeting
of the Legislative Council and House of Assembly stands prorogued to the Seventeenth day of September, One Thousand Eight Hundred and Seven.

By a further Proclamation of His Excellency, Francis Gore, Esquire, Lieutenant-Governor of the Province of Upper Canada, etc., etc., etc., dated at York,
the Eleventh day of September, One Thousand Eight Hundred and Seven, the
meeting of the Legislative Council and House of Assembly stands prorogued
to the Twenty-third day of October, One Thousand Eight Hundred and Seven.

By a further Proclamation of His Excellency, Francis Gore, Esquire, Lieutenant-Governor of the Province of Upper Canada, etc., etc., etc., dated at York,
the Sixteenth day of October, One Thousand eight Hundred and Seven, the
meeting of the Legislative Council and House of Assembly stands prorogued to
the Thirteenth day of November, One Thousand Eight Hundred and Seven.

By a further Proclamation of His Excellency Francis Gore, Esquire, Lieutenant Governor of the Province of Upper Canada, etc., etc., etc., dated at York,
the Twenty-fourth day of November, One Thousand Eight Hundred and Seven.
the meeting of the Legislative Council and House of Assembly stands prorogued
to the Sixth day of January, One Thousand Eight Hundred and Eight.

FRANCIS GORE, Lieutenant-Governor.

PROCLAMATION.

George the Third, by the Grace of God, of the United Kingdom of Great
Britain and Ireland, King, Defender of the Faith.
To Our loving subjects, GREETING.
Whereas by our Proclamation, bearing date the Twenty-third day of November
last, we thought fit, by and with the advice of Our Executive Council, to prorogue
the Provincial Parliament until the Sixth day of January next ensuing; at which
time, in Our Town of York, you were held and constrained to appear,—But we,
taking into our royal consideration the ease and convenience of Our loving subjects, have thought fit, by and with the advice of Our Executive Council, to relieve
you, and each of you, of your attendance at the time aforesaid; hereby convoking,
and by these presents enjoining you, and each of you, that on the Twentieth day
of January next ensuing, you meet us in Our Provincial Parliament, in Our
Town of York, for the actual despatch of business; there to take into consideration
the state and welfare of Our said Province of Upper Canada, and there to do as
may seem necessary. Herein fail not.

In Testimony Whereof we have caused these Our Letters to be made Patent, and the Great Seal of Our said Province to be hereunto affixed. Witness Our Trusty and well beloved Francis Gore, Esquire, Our Lieutenant-Governor of Our said Province, at York, this Twenty-third day of December, in the Year of Our Lord, One Thousand Eight Hundred and Seven, and in the Forty-eighth year of Our Reign.

WILLIAM JARVIS, Secretary.   F. G.

HOUSE OF ASSEMBLY, UPPER CANADA.

York, Wednesday, 20th January, 1808.

At the Fourth Session of the Fourth Parliament of Upper Canada, begun and held in the Town of York, on Wednesday, the Twentieth day of January, in the Forty-eighth year of the Reign of Our Sovereign Lord, George the Third, by the Grace of God, of the United Kingdom of Great Britain and Ireland, King, Defender of the Faith, etc.; and in the Year of Our Lord, One Thousand Eight Hundred and Eight.

His Excellency, the Lieutenant-Governor, having prorogued the meeting of Parliament until the Eighteenth day of April, One Thousand Eight Hundred and Seven; and by His Proclamations annexed, having further prorogued the same from time to time until this day,—
The House being met,
A Message by Mr. George Lawe, Gentleman Usher of the Black Rod.
Mr. Speaker,—
It is His Excellency the Lieutenant-Governor's pleasure that this Honorable House do immediately attend him in the Legislative Council Chamber.
The House went up accordingly; and being returned,—
Mr. Speaker reported that the House had attended His Excellency, the Lieutenant-Governor, in the Legislative Council Chamber, where His Excellency had been pleased to open the present Session by a most gracious Speech to both Houses, and that to prevent mistakes he had obtained for the information of the House a copy of His Excellency's Speech, which was read as follows:—
Honorable Gentlemen of the Legislative Council
and
Gentlemen of the Assembly.—
It is with the highest satisfaction that I express on this occasion the sentiments which I entertain of that spirit of loyalty which was lately so conspicuously and universally displayed on calling out the Militia of this Province.
The zeal and unanimity which at that time prevailed, and the voluntary offers of service which were then tendered, evince that His Majesty's subjects in this Colony have a King whom they love, and a Constitution which they are ready to defend.
Since the last Session of this Legislature the necessary measures have been taken on my part, and on that of the Trustees appointed by me, for the establishing of Public Schools; institutions which I trust will be the means, not only of communicating useful knowledge to the youth of this Province, but also of instilling into their minds principles of religion and loyalty.
I think it proper to remind you that the Act for affording relief to those

persons who may be entitled, as Heirs or Devisees of the Nominees of the Crown, to land in this Province, will shortly expire; it will be for you to consider the expediency of the further continuation of that Act.

Your past experience, as well as your local knowledge, renders you particularly qualified to discover what still may be wanting to secure the peace, welfare and good government of the Province. To promote this important purpose I am well assured will be the object of your deliberations, as it shall be the ruling principle of my conduct.

Gentlemen of the House of Assembly,—

I shall give orders to the proper officer to lay before you the Public Accounts, not doubting but they will be considered with that attention which the nature of the subject requires.

Honorable Gentlemen of the Legislative Council
                    and
Gentlemen of the House of Assembly,—

The events of the times, and the particular situation of this Province, require from you more than an ordinary degree of attention and care.

From the short experience that I have had during the last Session of the Legislature, I entertain a well founded confidence that firmness with moderation will govern your conduct on the present occasion, and that you will convince His Majesty's subjects in this Colony that the authority with which you are invested by the Constitution has not been delegated to you in vain.

Members present: The Speaker, Messrs. Solicitor General, Sherwood, Washburn, Swazey, Crysler and Dorland.

Mr. Speaker adjourned the House for want of a quorum.

Thursday, 21st January, 1808.

Prayers were read.
Present: Mr. Speaker, Messrs. Solicitor General and Swazey.
At twelve o'clock Mr. Speaker adjourned the House for want of a quorum.

Friday, 22nd January, 1808.

Prayers were read.
Present: The Speaker and Mr. Washburn.
At eleven o'clock the Speaker adjourned the House for want of a quorum.

Saturday, 23rd January, 1808.

Prayers were read.
Present: The Speaker, and Messrs. Dorland and Washburn.
At half past ten o'clock the Speaker adjourned the House for want of a quorum, until ten o'clock on Monday morning.

Monday, 25th January, 1808.

Prayers were read.
Present: Mr. Speaker, Messrs. Solicitor General, Elliott, Cowan, Dorland, Swazey, and Washburn.
At eleven o'clock the Speaker adjourned the House for want of a quorum.

Tuesday, 26th January, 1808.

Prayers were read.

Read, His Excellency, the Lieutenant-Governor's Speech to both Houses of Parliament at the opening of the present Session.

Mr. Washburn moved, seconded by Mr. Swazey, that Messrs. Solicitor General, Sherwood and McGregor be a Committee to draft an Address to His Excellency, the Lieutenant-Governor, in answer to His Speech; two of which to make a quorum, and to report the same to the House to-morrow. Ordered accordingly.

William Jarvis, Esquire, one of the Commissioners appointed by dedimus potestatem to administer the oath to the Members of the House of Assembly, came to the Bar, and did inform Mr. Speaker that Joseph Willcocks, Esquire, had taken the Oath as prescribed by the Statute, and did sign the Roll.

Then Joseph Willcocks, Esquire, Knight, representing the West Riding of the County of York, the First Riding of the County of Lincoln, and the County of Haldimand, came within the Bar and took his seat accordingly.

Mr. Solicitor General moved, seconded by Captain Elliott, for leave to bring in a Bill to-morrow the better to ascertain and secure Titles to Lands in this Province. Leave was accordingly given.

Mr. Solicitor General again moved, seconded by Captain Elliott, that it is the opinion of this House that the Seventeenth Rule adopted by this House embraces the Rule of the British House of Commons of the Twenty-third February, One Thousand Six Hundred and Eighty-eight, which passed in the negative.

On motion of Captain Elliott, seconded by the Solicitor General, the House adjourned.

Wednesday, 27th January, 1808.

Prayers were read.

Mr. Solicitor General moved, seconded by Captain Elliott, that so much of the Order of this Day as respects the bringing in a Bill to ascertain and secure Titles of Lands in this Province be discharged, and that he have leave to bring in the said Bill to-morrow. Ordered accordingly.

Mr. Solicitor General, from the Committee appointed to draft an Address of thanks to His Excellency, the Lieutenant-Governor, for his Speech to both Houses at the opening of the present Session, reported that the Committee had prepared an address accordingly, which he was directed to submit to the House whenever it should be pleased to receive the same. Ordered, that the report be now received, which report he read in his place, and then delivered the same in at the Table, where it was again read by the Clerk. Mr. Sherwood then moved, seconded by the Solicitor General, that the House do now resolve itself into a Committee to take the Address into consideration. The House accordingly resolved itself into a Committee. Mr. Speaker left the Chair. Mr. Solicitor General was called to the Chair of the Committee.

Mr. Speaker resumed the Chair. Mr. Solicitor General reported that the Committee had gone through the draft of an address to His Excellency, the Lieutenant-Governor, to which they had made no amendments, which he was directed to report to the House whenever it should be pleased to receive the same. Ordered, that the Report be now received, which Report was accepted, and the Address is as follows:—

To His Excellency, Francis Gore, Esquire, Lieutenant-Governor of the Province of Upper Canada, etc., etc., etc.

May it please Your Excellency,—

We, His Majesty's loyal subjects, the Commons of Upper Canada, in Parliament Assembled, beg leave to return to Your Excellency our dutiful acknowledgements for your gracious Speech.

We sincerely congratulate Your Excellency on the ardent zeal and attachment to Our Sovereign and Constitution manifested by the Militia, and we trust that the same patriotic and loyal spirit pervades all ranks of His Majesty's subjects in this Colony.

We highly applaud the prompt and efficacious measures adopted by Your Excellency to carry into effect the provision of an Act, passed in the last Session of Parliament, for the establishment of Public Schools; and we pleasingly anticipate from these institutions the most substantial benefit to the rising generation in this Province.

We beg leave to assure Your Excellency that we feel it to be our duty, and that it shall be the object of our continual consideration, to adopt such measures as will best tend to secure the peace, welfare and good government of this Province; and we are sensible from our experience that in providing for these important and interesting objects we may rely upon Your Excellency's co-operation and assistance.

The momentous events of the times strongly impress upon our minds the necessity of directing all our counsels to the preservation and support of that excellent Constitution from which we derive all the blessings following from true and rational liberty.

We hope our future firmness and moderation to merit a continuance of that highly gratifying approbation which Your Excellency is pleased to express of our former conduct; and also to convince our fellow subjects in this Colony that we only desire to promote their real interest and prosperity

Commons, House of Assembly,

York, 27th January, 1808.

On motion of Mr. Sherwood, seconded by Captain Cowan, the Address was ordered to be engrossed. The Address as engrossed was then read, passed, and signed by the Speaker. Mr. Sherwood then moved, seconded by Captain Cowan, that Messrs. Howard and Dorland do wait upon His Excellency, the Lieutenant-Governor, to know when it will be his pleasure to receive this House with its Address in answer to His Speech. Ordered accordingly.

Mr. Willcocks moved, seconded by Mr. Howard, for leave to bring in a Bill on Saturday next, to renew the Act for granting a bounty for destroying of Wolves in this Province. Leave was accordingly granted.

Mr. Howard then moved, seconded by Mr. Willcocks, for leave to bring in a Bill on Monday next, to alter the method of performing Statute Labour on the Highways and Roads throughout this Province. Accordingly leave was granted.

On motion of Mr. Willcocks, seconded by Mr. Mallory, the House adjourned.

Thursday, 28th January, 1808.

Prayers were read.

Mr. Howard, accompanied by the other Messenger, reported that in obedience to the order of this House they had waited upon His Excellency the Lieutenant-

Governor to know His Excellency's pleasure, when he would receive this House with its Address; and that His Excellency was pleased to appoint this day, at twelve o'clock at noon to receive the House with its Address.

Then was read for the first time a Bill, the better to ascertain and secure Titles to Lands in this Province.

Mr. Solicitor General moved, seconded by Captain Cowan, that the Bill for ascertaining and securing titles to lands in this Province be read a second time on Tuesday next. Ordered accordingly.

Mr. Solicitor General then moved, seconded by Captain Cowan, for leave to bring in a Bill on Tuesday next to amend certain parts of an Act, passed in the Thirty-third year of His Majesty's Reign, entitled "An Act to confirm and make valid certain marriages heretofore contracted in the country, now comprised within the Province of Upper Canada, and to provide for the future solemnization of marriages within the same." Leave was accordingly given.

At the hour appointed, Mr. Speaker and the House went up with the Address of this House to His Excellency the Lieutenant-Governor; and being returned,—

Mr. Speaker reported that the House had attended on His Excellency the Lieutenant-Governor with its Address, to which His Excellency had been pleased to make the following answer:—

Gentlemen of the House of Assembly:—

I return you my thanks for your loyal and dutiful Address.

The zeal which you discover for the preservation of that excellent Constitution from which you derive so many blessings is honorable to yourselves, and worthy of that situation in which you are placed.

I have no doubt but that by your conduct you will convince your fellow subjects that your only desire is to promote their prosperity and interest.

Government House,

     28th January, 1808.

Mr. Washburn then moved, seconded by the Solicitor General, for leave to bring in a Bill on Wednesday next to alter in some measure the present demand for shop and tavern licenses in this Province, and make other provisions for the same. Leave was accordingly given.

Mr. Willcocks gave notice that he intends to move to-morrow for a Resolution of the House, whether any Member shall have free access to the Journals of the House, and take extracts therefrom.

Mr. Dorland moved, seconded by Captain Elliott, for leave to bring in a Bill on Monday next to amend an Act, passed in the Forty-sixth year of His Majesty's Reign, entitled "An Act for the nominating and appointing Parish and Town Officers in this Province." Leave was granted.

Read, the Petition of the Inhabitants of the Townships of Toronto, Trafalgar, and Nelson, which is as follows:—

To the Honorable Speaker and other Members of the House of Assembly at York, in the Province of Upper Canada:

The Petition of the Inhabitants of Toronto, Trafalgar, and Nelson,

Humbly Sheweth,—

That whereas we, Your Petitioners, are settled in a wild, uncultivated part of the country, and consequently are obliged to bring our provisions and other necessaries from a distant part, and as our passage along Dundas Street is entirely obstructed by the River Credit, the Sixteen and Twelve Mile Creeks, the banks of which, especially the two latter, are inaccessible to any carriage or beast of burthen, so that we are obliged to carry our necessaries over our backs, or to bring them round by the old road, which is attended with the greatest inconvenience, both with respect to the additional distance and badness of the road. Our Statute labour on the roads is quite inadequate to the arduous task of bridging these creeks, nor are we able to raise contributions equivalent to the labour. If they be permitted to remain in their present situation it will prove very injurious to the growth of our settlement by rendering miserable those who are settled, and discouraging others from coming in. Numbers have been obliged to leave their habitations during the winter, and retire to a place where the necessaries of life are to be had more conveniently, to the great injury of their private affairs. It is, therefore, the prayer of Your Petitioners that you take our situation into your consideration, and endeavour to find means to extricate us from this evil.

Your Petitioners further beg leave to represent that they will use their most strenuous exertions in assisting to level the banks of said Creeks, and also to make other parts of the street passable. Encouraged by this pleasing consideration, that your ears are ever open to the plaintive voice of distress, and that your chief concern is the public good, we have ventured to lay our petition before you, willing to indulge the flattering hopes that you will be able to afford us the necessary relief.

And Your Petitioners, as in duty bound, shall ever pray.

Nelson, 2nd January, 1808.

John Chisholm, Thomas Atkinson, Alexander Brown, Daniel Reiley, George King, James Davidson, John Day, and sixty-nine others.

Then Mr. Howard moved, seconded by Mr. Swazey, that so much of the Order of the Day for Monday next as gave him leave to bring in on that day a Bill to alter the method of performing Statute Labour on the Highways and Roads throughout this Province be discharged, and that leave be given to him to bring in on that day a Bill to alter the method of regulating the laying out of Highways and Roads throughout this Province, and to alter the method of performing the Statute Labour thereon. Ordered accordingly.

Then Mr. Mallory moved, seconded by Mr. Dorland, for leave to bring in a Bill on Monday next to authorize the inhabitants of the County of Haldimand to hold Annual Town Meetings, for the purpose of electing Town and Parish Officers. Accordingly leave was given.

On motion of the Solicitor General, seconded by Captain Cowan, the House adjourned until twelve o'clock at noon to-morrow.

Friday, 29th January, 1808.

Prayers.

William Jarvis, Esquire, Secretary of the Province, came to the Bar of the House and delivered in, by order of His Excellency the Lieutenant-Governor, the Public Provincial Accounts as per Schedule, which was read, and are as follows, viz.:—

Schedule of Accounts laid before the House of Assembly.

No.-1. The Inspector's List of names of persons licensed as Shop and Inn-keepers in the several Districts of Upper Canada, between the 5th January, 1806, and the 5th of January, 1807; these returns not received in time to be laid before the Legislature in 1807.

No. 2. The Inspector's List of names of persons licensed as Shop and Inn-keepers in the several Districts of the Province of Upper Canada, from the 5th January, 1807 to the 5th January, 1808.

No. 3. The Inspector's List of names of such persons as have been licensed to work Stills in the several Districts of the Province of Upper Canada, from the 5th January, 1807 to the 5th January, 1808.

No. 4. Provincial Revenue of the Crown arising from duties collected on goods imported under authority of Acts of the Provincial Parliament, between the 1st January and the 31st December, 1807, including such duties as have not been heretofore stated.

No. 5. Provincial Revenue of the Crown arising from duties collected on goods imported under authority of Acts of the Parliament of Great Britain, be-tween the 1st January and the 31st December, 1807, including such duties as have not been heretofore stated.

No. 6. Abstract of Warrants issued by His Excellency, Francis Gore, Esquire, Lieutenant-Governor of the Province of Upper Canada, for moneys charged against the funds arising from duties imposed by the Provincial Legislature.

No. 7. Supplementary Abstract Statement of moneys collécted within the several Districts of the Province of Upper Canada, on Shop, Innkeepers, and Still licenses, issued between the 5th January, 1806, and 5th January, 1807, under authority of Acts of the Provincial Parliament, after deducting 10 per cent. allowed to the Inspectors by the Act of the 43rd of the King.

No. 8. Supplementary Abstract Statement of moneys collected within the several Districts of the Province of Upper Canada, on Shop and Innkeepers licenses, issued between the 5th January, 1806, and the 5th January, 1807, under authority of Acts of the Parliament of Great Britain, after deducting 10 per cent. allowed to the Inspectors of the Act of the 43rd of the King.

No. 9. Abstract Statement of moneys collected within the several Districts of the Province of Upper Canada, on Shopkeepers and Still licenses, issued be-tween the 5th January, 1807, and the 5th January, 1808, so far as the returns have been received, after deducting 10 per cent. allowed to the Inspectors by the Act of the 43rd of the King.

No. 10. Abstract Statement of moneys collected within the several Districts of the Province of Upper Canada, on Shop and Innkeepers licenses, issued be-tween the 5th January, 1807, and the 5th January, 1808, under authority of Acts of the Parliament of Great Britain, so far as the returns have been received, after deducting 10 per cent. allowed to the Inspectors by the Act of the 43d of the King.

No. 11. General Account of articles on which duties on importation are im-posed by the Legislature of Lower Canada, which have passed Coteau du Lac upwards from the 1st January to the 30th June, 1807, agreeable to the written accounts thereof received, or as ascertained on examination of carriages according to the Act.

No. 12. Account of Lighthouse Tonnage Duty collected for the year ending the 31st December, 1807.

No. 13. Account of moneys collected within the several Districts of the Province of Upper Canada, on licenses issued to Hawkers, Pedlars and Petty Chapmen, for the year ending the 5th April, 1808, after deducting 10 per cent. allowed to the Inspectors by the Act of the 43d of the King.

No. 14. Account of cash received by the Hon. Peter Russell, Receiver General, for Fines and Forfeitures, under authority of Acts of the Parliament, from the 1st January to the 31st December, 1807.

No. 15. Account of cash received by Hon. Peter ·Russell, Receiver General, for Fines and Forfeitures under authority of Acts of the Parliament of Great Britain, between the 1st January and the 31st December, 1807.

No. 16. General State of cash received by Hon. Peter Russell, Receiver General, for Duties and Fines under authority of Acts of the Parliament of Great Britain, between the 1st January and the 31st December, 1807.

No. 17. General State of receipts and payments by Hon. Peter Russell, Receiver General, for Duties and Fines, and likewise appropriations made under authority of Acts of the Provincial Parliament, between the 1st January and the 31st December, 1807.

No. 18. General Account of articles on which duties on importation are imposed by the Legislature of Lower Canada, which have passed Coteau du Lac upwards from the 1st July to the 31st December, 1807, agreeable to the written accounts thereof received, or as ascertained on examination of carriages according to the Act.

INSPECTOR GENERAL'S OFFICE,   JOHN McGILL,
York, 27th January, 1808.   Inspector Gen., Pub. Pro. Accts.

(For Accounts as per above Schedule see Appendix.)

Mr. Willcocks moved, seconded by Mr. Mallory, that each and every Member of this House shall, at all times during the sitting of Parliament, have free access to the Journals of the House, and take abstracts therefrom.

A division thereupon took place. The names being called for, they were taken down and are as follows:—

Yeas: Nays:
MESSRS. DORLAND   MESSRS. SOLICITOR GENERAL
        MALLORY   COWAN
        WILLCOCKS.   ELLIOTT
                                                  SHERWOOD
                                                  McGREGOR
                                                  CRYSLER
                                                  SWAZEY
                                                  WASHBURN
                                                  NELLIS
                                                  HOWARD.

The same was carried in the negative by a majority of seven.

Mr. Howard moved, seconded by Mr. Dorland, for leave to bring in a Bill on Tuesday next to have the Journals of the House of Assembly printed annually. Leave was accordingly given.

By Order of the House was read a Paragraph from a newspaper entitled "The Upper Canada Guardian, or Freeman's Journal," printed at Niagara, by Joseph Willcocks, dated Thursday, the first day of October, One Thousand Eight Hundred and Seven, which was ordered to lie on the Table.

On motion of Captain Cowan, seconded by Mr. Nellis, the House adjourned.

Saturday, 30th January, 1808.

Prayers were read.

Read for the first time, a Bill for allowing a bounty for destroying Wolves. Mr. Willcocks moved, seconded by Mr. Rogers, that a Bill for reviving the Act allowing a bounty for destroying of Wolves in this Province be read a second time on Tuesday next. Ordered accordingly.

Captain Cowan gave notice that he would move on Wednesday next for the House to go into a Committee to take into consideration that part of a paragraph in the "Upper Canada Guardian" that relates to this House. Mr. Sherwood moved, seconded by Mr. Swazey, that a copy of the paragraph published in the "Upper Canada Guardian" of the 1st of October last, relative to bribery, be sent to each Member of this House, which was ordered accordingly.

Mr. Solicitor General moved, seconded by Mr. Sherwood, that Messrs. Rogers, McGregor, Cowan, Crysler and Nellis be a Committee to take into consideration the Provincial Public Accounts, and report the same to the House. Ordered accordingly.

Mr. Solicitor General moved, seconded by Captain Cowan, that Captain Elliott have leave of absence from attending his duty in Parliament during the present Session. Leave of absence was accordingly given.

On motion of Mr. Sherwood, seconded by Captain Cowan, the House adjourned until twelve o'clock at noon on Monday next.

Monday, 1st February, 1808.

Prayers were read.

Read for the first time, the Bill for the better defining the duty of Parish and Town Officers.

Mr. Dorland moved, seconded by Mr. Rogers, that a Bill for the better regulation of Parish and Town Officers be read a second time to-morrow. Ordered accordingly.

Mr. Howard moved, seconded by Mr. Rogers, that so much of the Order of the Day as gives leave to bring in a Bill this day to alter the method of regulating, laying out and amending the Highways and Public Roads throughout this Province, and for altering the method of performing Statute Labour thereon be discharged. It was ordered accordingly.

Read for the first time, the Bill for Regulating the election of Parish and Town Officers in the County of Haldimand. Mr. Mallory moved, seconded by Mr. Nellis, that the Bill for enabling the Inhabitants of the County of Haldimand to elect Town and Parish Officers be read a second time to-morrow. Ordered accordingly.

The House then resolved that six copies of the Provincial Statutes be purchased for this House.

Read, the petition from the London District, which is as follows:—
The Honorable the Members of the House of Parliament of Upper Canada, now convened.

The humble Petition of us, His Majesty's most loyal subjects,

Most Humbly Sheweth:—

That in your wisdom in your last Session of Parliament you were pleased to vote a certain sum of money for the use of a Public School in this District, said School to be under the direction of certain Trustees, appointed by His Majesty's Representative for that purpose.

That Your Humble petitioners see with regret from what has taken place that your laudable intentions are frustrated, and the money (in our present situation) is totally lost to the Public.

That the Trustees, having nominated a teacher that insists on being paid double the sum for his labours as those we have had before (of equal service to us), which measures have put it out of the power of the public to reap that advantage which was designed them.

That Your Humble Petitioners referring this to wise and better judgments hope Your Honorable House will take this infant District into Your consideration, and if you in your wisdom should think it expedient, the money appropriated to one school be divided into four equal parts to four different schools.

And Your Petitioners, as in duty bound, will ever pray.

John Backhose, Titus Finch, James McCall, Silas Secord, Abram Smith, and sixty others.

On motion of Mr. Sherwood, seconded by Mr. Swazey, the House adjourned.

Tuesday, 2nd February, 1808.

Prayers were read.

Read for the second time, the Bill for receiving the bounty on killing Wolves. Mr. Willcocks moved, seconded by Mr. Nellis, that this House do now resolve itself into a Committee to take into consideration the Bill for reviving the bounty for destroying of Wolves in this Province. The House accordingly resolved itself into a Committee. Mr. Speaker left the Chair. Captain Cowan was called to the Chair of the Committee. Mr. Speaker resumed the Chair. Captain Cowan reported that the Committee had made a progress, and had directed him to ask for leave to sit again on Thursday next. Resolved, that the Committee do sit again on Thursday next.

Read for the second time, the Bill for repealing part of an Act, passed in the Forty-sixth year of His Majesty's Reign, entitled "An Act to provide for the nomination and appointment of Parish and Town Officers." Mr. Dorland moved, seconded by Mr. Swazey, that the House do now resolve itself into a Committee to take the said Bill into consideration. The House accordingly resolved itself into a Committee. Mr. Speaker left the Chair. Mr. Clench was called to the Chair of the Committee. Mr. Speaker resumed the Chair. Mr. Clench reported that the Committee had made a progress, and that he was directed to ask for. leave to sit again to-morrow. Leave was accordingly granted.

Read for the second time, the Bill for to enable the Inhabitants of the County of Haldimand, in the District of Niagara, to elect Parish and Town Officers. Mr. Mallory moved, seconded by Mr. Solicitor General, that the House do now resolve itself into a Committee to take into consideration the Bill for authorizing the inhabitants of the County of Haldimand to hold annual Town meetings. The House accordingly resolved itself into a Committee on the said Bill. Mr. Speaker left the Chair. Mr. Crysler was called to the Chair of the Committee. Mr. Speaker resumed the Chair. Mr. Crysler reported that the Committee had gone through the consideration of the said Bill without any amendment.

Mr. Mallory moved, seconded by Mr. Solicitor General, that the Bill for appointing Parish and Town Officers in the County of Haldimand be engrossed, and read a third time on Friday next. Ordered accordingly.

Read for the second time, the Bill the better to ascertain and secure titles to lands in this Province.

Read for the first time, A Bill to amend certain parts of the Marriage Act. Mr. Solicitor-General moved, seconded by Mr. Mallory, that the Marriage Act be read a second time on Thursday next. which was ordered accordingly.

Read for the first time, A Bill for printing annually the Journals of this House. Mr. Howard then moved, seconded by Mr. Dorland, that the Bill for printing annually the Journals of this House be read a second time on Monday next.

Mr. Sherwood moved, seconded by Mr. Howard, for leave to bring in a Bill to-morrow for establishing a Court of Common Pleas in each and every District of this Province. Leave was accordingly granted.

Mr. Sherwood then moved, seconded by Mr. Swazey, for leave to bring in a Bill to-morrow for the regulation of Special Juries. Accordingly leave was given.

Mr. Sherwood moved, seconded by Mr. Swazey, for leave to bring in a Bill to-morrow to repeal an Act appropriating money for Public Buildings at York. Leave was granted.

On motion of Mr. Solicitor-General, seconded by Mr. Mallory, the House adjourned.

Wednesday, 3rd February, 1808.

Prayers were read.

Mr. Washburn moved, seconded by Mr. Dorland, that so much of the Order of this Day as gives leave to bring in a Bill to alter the present regulation of Shop and Tavern Licenses be discharged. The Order was discharged accordingly.

Agreeably to the Order of the Day the House resolved itself into a Committee to go into the consideration of the Bill for regulating Parish and Town Officers. Mr. Speaker left the chair. Mr. Clench was called to the chair of the Committee. Mr. Speaker resumed the Chair. Mr. Clench reported that the Committee had gone through the consideration of the said Bill, to which they had made some amendments, which he was directed to report to the House whenever it should be pleased to receive the same. Resolved, That the Report be now received. Mr. Dorland moved, seconded by Mr. Nellis, that the Bill for the better regulation of Parish and Town Officers be engrossed, and read a third time on Thursday next. Ordered accordingly.

Read for the first time, A Bill for establishing a Court of Common Pleas in this Province. Mr. Sherwood then moved, seconded by Mr. Nellis that the Court of Common Pleas Bill be read a second time on Saturday next, which was ordered accordingly.

Read for the first time, A Bill for defining the qualification of Special Juries. Mr. Sherwood then moved, seconded by Mr. Nellis, that the Bill relative to Special Juries be read a second time on Friday next.
Ordered accordingly.

Read for the first time, A Bill for repealing an Act passed in the forty fourth year of His Majesty's Reign, for erecting Public Buildings in the Town of York. Mr. Sherwood then moved, seconded by Mr. Swazey that the Bill to repeal the law granting money for Buildings in York be read a second time to-morrow. The same was ordered accordingly.

Mr. Clench moved, seconded by Mr. Sherwood, for leave to bring in a Bill on Monday next to regulate the Practice of Physic and Surgery. Leave was accordingly given.

Mr. Clench moved, seconded by Mr. Rogers, for leave to bring in a Bill on Monday next, to increase the Representatives of the people of this Province. Leave was granted.

On motion of Mr. Sherwood, seconded by Mr. Clench, the House adjourned.

Thursday, 4th February, 1808.

Prayers were read.

Agreeably to the Order of the Day, the House resolved itself into a Committee to go into the further consideration of the Bill for allowing a bounty for killing Wolves. Mr. Speaker left the chair. Captain Cowan was called to the chair of the Committee.

Mr. Speaker resumed the Chair, and Capt. Cowan reported that the Committee had made a progress, and had directed him to ask for leave to sit again to-morrow. Leave was accordingly given.

Read for the second time, A Bill for confirming and making valid certain marriages contracted in this Province. On motion of Mr. Solicitor-General, seconded by Mr. Dorland, the House resolved itself into a Committee to go into the consideration of the Bill for making valid certain marriages contracted in this Province. Mr. Speaker left the chair. Mr. Dorland was called to the chair of the Committee.

Mr. Speaker resumed the Chair, and Mr. Dorland reported that the Committee had gone through the consideration of the said Bill without any amendment, which he was directed to report whenever the House should be pleased to receive the same. The House then resolved that the Report be now received. The Report was accordingly received and accepted. Mr. Solicitor-General moved, seconded by Mr. McLean, that the Marriage Bill be engrossed and read a third time to-morrow. Ordered accordingly.

Read for the third time, The engrossed Bill for the nomination of Parish and Town Officers. On motion of Mr. Solicitor-General, seconded by Mr. McLean, the House resolved itself into a Committee to go into the further consideration of the Bill for the nomination and Appointment of Parish and Town Officers. Mr. Speaker left the chair. Mr. Clench was called to the chair of the Committee.

Mr. Speaker resumed the chair, and Mr. Clench reported that the Committee had gone through the consideration of the said Bill, to which they had made several amendments, which he was directed to report to the House whenever it should be pleased to receive the same. The report was then ordered to be received.

Mr. Rogers moved, seconded by Mr. Swazey, that the Bill for the further regulation and appointment of Parish and Town Officers be engrossed, and read a third time to-morrow, which was ordered accordingly.

Read for the second time, the Bill to repeal a certain Act passed in the forty-fourth year of His Majesty's Reign, entitled "An Act appropriating a certain sum of money annually to defray the expense of erecting certain Public Buildings to and for the uses of this Province." Mr. Sherwood moved, seconded by Mr. McLean, that the House do now resolve itself into a Committee to take into consideration the Bill to Repeal the Law granting móney for erecting Public Buildings in York. The House accordingly resolved itself into a Committee. Mr. Speaker left the Chair. Mr. Howard was called to the chair of the Committee.

Mr. Speaker resumed the Chair, and Mr. Howard reported that the Committee had gone through the consideration of the said Bill to which they had made an amendment, which he was directed to report to the House whenever it should be pleased to receive the same.

Resolved that the Report be now received. The Report was accordingly received and accepted.

On motion of Mr. Sherwood, seconded by Mr. Clench, the said Bill was ordered to be engrossed, and read a third time to-morrow.

Read, the Petition of John Cameron, Printer to the King's Most Excellent Majesty, which is as follows:

To the Honorable the House of Assembly of Upper Canada in Parliament assembled.

The Petition of John Cameron,

Most Humbly Sheweth,—

That Your Petitioner is desirous of obtaining permission from Your Honorable House to publish the Debates and Proceedings thereof during the present Session in the *York Gazette* in such manner as Your Petitioner can obtain them without having access to the Journals. This request is most respectfully submitted by the Petitioner, who, as in duty bound, will ever pray.

(Signed) JOHN CAMERON,
York, 4th February, 1808.

On motion of Mr. Clench, seconded by Mr. Sherwood, ordered, that John Cameron, His Majesty's Printer in this Province, have leave to publish the debates of this House without having access to the Journals. It was so ordered accordingly.

On motion of Captain Cowan, seconded by Mr. McGregor.

The House adjourned.

Friday, 5th February, 1808.

Prayers were read.

Read for the third time, as engrossed, the Bill for authorizing the Nomination of Parish and Town Officers in the County of Haldimand.

On motion of Mr. Clench, seconded by Mr. Swazey, the House resolved itself into a Committee of the Whole to go into the further consideration of the whole Bill. Mr. Speaker left the Chair. Mr. Crysler was called to the chair of the Committee.

Mr. Speaker resumed the Chair, and Mr. Crysler reported that the Committee had made a progress and had directed him to ask for leave to sit again to-morrow. Ordered, that the committee have leave to sit again to-morrow to go into the further consideration of the said Bill.

Agreeably to the Order of the Day the House resolved itself into a Committee to go into the further consideration of the Bill for granting a Bounty for destroying Wolves in this Province. Mr. Speaker left the Chair. Capt. Cowan took the chair of the Committee.

Mr. Speaker resumed the Chair, and Capt. Cowan reported that the Committee had made a progress and had directed him to ask for leave to sit again this day. Leave was accordingly granted.

A message from the Honorable the Legislative Council by Mr Baldwin, Master in Chancery,

Mr. Speaker,—

I am commanded by the Honorable the Legislative Council to inform this House that they have passed a Bill entitled "An Act to extend the benefits of an Act passed in the thirty-seventh year of His Majesty's Reign, entitled 'An Act for the more easy barring of Dower,' and to repeal certain parts of the same," to which they request the concurrence. of this House.

And then he withdrew. Which Act, on motion of Mr. Rogers, seconded by Mr. Howard, was read for the first time. Mr. Rogers then moved, seconded by Mr. Howard, that the Bill to extend the benefit of an Act for Barring of Dower be read a second time on Wednesday next, which was ordered accordingly.

Agreeably to leave given, the House again resolved itself into a Committee to go into the further consideration of the Bill for granting a bounty for destroying of Wolves.

Mr. Speaker left the Chair. Capt. Cowan took the chair of the Committee.

Mr. Speaker resumed the Chair. Capt. Cowan reported that the Committee had made a progress, and had directed him to ask for leave to sit again on Wednesday next. Ordered, that the Committee have leave to sit again on Wednesday next.

Read for the second time, the Bill respecting Special Juries. Mr. Sherwood moved, seconded by Mr. Swazey, that the House do now resolve itself into a Committee to take the said Bill into consideration. The House accordingly resolved itself into Committee. Mr. Speaker left the Chair. Mr. Rogers was called to the chair of the Committee.

Mr. Speaker resumed the Chair, and Mr. Rogers reported that the Committee had made a progress and had directed him to ask for leave to sit again to-morrow. Ordered, that the Committee have leave to sit again to-morrow.

Ordered, that so much of the Order of the Day as gave leave to read the Marriage Bill for the third time, be discharged, and that the said Bill be read for the third time to-morrow.

Then was read for the third time, the Bill for the Regulation of Parish and Town Officers. On motion of Mr. Dorland, seconded by Mr. Washburn, Resolved, That the Bill do pass, and the title be "An Act for the better Regulation of Parish and Town Officers throughout this Province." The Bill then passed, and· was signed by the Speaker. Mr. Rogers moved, seconded by Mr. Nellis, that Messrs. Dorland and Washburn be a Committee to carry up to the Honorable the Legislative Council the Bill entitled "An Act for the Better

Regulation of Parish and Town Officers throughout this Province," and request their concurrence thereto. Ordered accordingly.

Read for the third time, the Bill to repeal an Act passed in the forty-fourth year of His Majesty's Reign, appropriating certain sums of money for Public Buildings in this Province. On motion of Mr. Sherwood, seconded by Mr. Nellis, Resolved, That the Bill do pass, and that the title be "An Act to repeal an Act passed in the forty-fourth year of His Majesty's Reign, entitled 'An Act appropriating a certain sum of money annually, to defray the expenses of erecting certain Public Buildings to and for the uses of this Provinces.'"   The Bill accordingly passed, and was signed by the Speaker.

Mr. Rogers then moved, seconded by Mr. Swazey, that Mr. Sherwood and Capt. Cowan be a Committee to carry up to the Honorable the Legislative Council the Bill to repeal an Act for appropriating money for Public Buildings in this Province, and to request their concurrence thereto. Ordered accordingly.

The Solicitor-General moved, seconded by Mr. McLean, for leave to bring in a Bill to-morrow to enable the inhabitants of the District of Johnstown to erect and build a Court House and Gaol in the Township of Elizabethtown. Leave was granted accordingly.

Mr. Howard then moved, seconded by Mr. Rogers for leave to bring in a Bill on Monday next to alter the method of laying out, amending and keeping in repair the Public Highways and Roads throughout this Province, and to alter the mode of performing Statute Labour thereon. Accordingly leave was given.

On motion of Capt. Cowan, seconded by Mr. Swazey, the House adjourned.

Saturday, 6th February, 1808.

Prayers were read.

Read for the second time, the Bill for establishing a Court of Common Pleas in this Province. Mr. Sherwood moved, seconded by Mr. Clench, that the House do now resolve itself into a Committee to take the said Bill into consideration. The House accordingly resolved itself into a Committee. Mr. Speaker left the Chair. Mr. Mallory was called to the chair of the Committee.

Mr. Speaker resumed the Chair, and Mr. Mallory reported that the Committee had made a progress, and had directed him to ask for leave to sit again on Monday next. Resolved, That the Committee have leave to sit again on Monday next.

Agreeably to the Order of the Day, the House resolved itself into a Committee to go into the consideration of the Bill for the Nomination of Parish and Town Officers in the County of Haldimand. Mr. Speaker left the chair. Mr. Crysler was called to the Chair of the Committee.

Mr. Speaker resumed the Chair, and Mr. Crysler reported that the Committee had gone through the consideration of the said Bill, to which they had made no amendments, which he was directed to report to the House whenever it should be pleased to receive the same. Resolved, That the Report be now received.

The Report was accordingly received and accepted.

Mr. Mallory then moved, seconded by Mr. Nellis, that the Bill for the nomination of Parish and Town Officers in the County of Haldimand be read a third time on Monday next. Ordered accordingly.

15 A.

On motion of Mr. Sherwood, seconded by Mr. Solicitor-General, ordered, that so much of the Order of this Day as respects the Special Jury Bill and the Bill for making valid certain marriages heretofore contracted in this Province be postponed; and that the said Bills do make a part of the Order of the Day for Monday next. Read for the first time, the Bill for erecting a Gaol and Court House in the District of Johnstown. On motion of the Solicitor-General, seconded by Mr. Howard, the said Bill was ordered to be read a second time on Monday next.

Mr. Rogers gave notice that he will on Monday next move that the Petition of William Firth, Esquire, be referred to a Committee of the Whole House on thé Bill for establishing a Court of Common Pleas, and that the said Committee do have power to hear the Petitioner in support of the facts alleged in his Petition.

On motion of Mr. Swazey, seconded by Mr. Crysler, the House adjourned.

Monday, 8th February, 1808.

Prayers were read.

Mr. Howard moved, seconded by Mr. Mallory, that so much of the Order of the Day as relates to the second reading of the Bill for Printing the Journals be discharged. Ordered accordingly.

On motion of Mr. Clench, seconded by Mr. McGregor, ordered, that so much of the Order of this Day as gave him leave to read for the first time a Bill for regulating the Practice of Physic and Surgery be discharged, and that he have leave to bring in the same to-morrow.

. Read for the first time, a Bill for increasing the representation of the Commons in this Province. Mr. Clench then moved, seconded by Mr. Swazey, that the said Bill be read a second time on Thursday next, which was ordered accordingly.

Read for the first time, a Bill for improving and laying out the Public Highways and Roads throughout this Province. The House then ordered that twenty copies of the said Bill be printed for the use of the members.

Mr. Rogers moved, seconded by Mr. Dorland, that the Petition of William Firth, Esquire, be now read. A division thereupon took place; the names being called for, they were taken down, and are as follows:

Yeas.	Nays.
MESSRS. ROGERS.	MESSRS. SOLICITOR-GENERAL
DORLAND	McLEAN .
	COWAN
	SHERWOOD
	MALLORY
	CLENCH
	McGREGOR
	SWAZEY
	HOWARD
	WASHBURN

Carried in the negative by a majority of eight.

Agreeably to the Order of the Day the House resolved itself into a Committee to go into the further consideration of the Common Pleas Bill.

Mr. Speaker left the Chair. Mr. Mallory took the Chair of the Committee. Mr. Speaker resumed the Chair. Mr Mallory reported that the Committee had made a progress, and directed him to ask for leave to sit again to-morrow. Leave was accordingly given.

Mr. Sherwood, accompanied by the other Messengers, reported that they had carried up to the Honorable Legislative Council the Bill entitled "An Act to repeal an Act passed in the forty-fourth year of His Majesty's Reign, entitled 'An Act appropriating a certain sum of money annually to defray the expense of erecting certain Public Buildings to and for the uses of this Province.'" and did request their concurrence thereto.

Mr. Dorland, one of the Messengers named to carry up to the Honorable Legislative Council the Bill entitled "An Act for the better regulation of Parish and Town Officers throughout this Province," reported that they did carry up the same, and did request their concurrence thereto. Then was read for the third time, as engrossed, the Bill for the nomination of Parish and Town Officers in the County of Haldimand. On motion of Mr. Mallory, seconded by Mr. Sherwood, ordered, that the title of the Bill for the nomination of Parish and Town Officers in the County of Haldimand be "An Act to authorize the Inhabitants of the County of Haldimand to hold Annual Meetings for the purpose of electing Parish and Town Officers." The Bill then passed, and was signed by the Speaker. Mr. Rogers then moved, seconded by Mr. Sherwood, that Messrs. Mallory and Nellis do carry up to the Honorable the Legislative Council the Bill respecting the County of Haldimand, and request their concurrence thereto. Ordered accordingly.

On motion of Captain Cowan, seconded by Mr. Sherwood, ordered, that what remains on the Order of this Day be postponed, and that the same make a part of the Order of the Day to-morrow.

Captain Cowan moved, seconded by Mr. McLean, for leave to bring in a Bill to revive and continue an Act entitled "An Act to provide for the appointment of Returning Officers for the several Counties within this Province." Leave was accordingly given.

The Solicitor General moved, seconded by Captain Cowan, for leave to bring in a Bill to-morrow to explain, amend, and reduce into one Act of Parliament the several Laws now in force relating to the raising and training the Militia of this Province. Accordingly leave was given.

On motion of Mr. McGregor, seconded by Mr. Clench, the House adjourned.

Tuesday, 9th February, 1808.

Prayers were read.

Read for the first time, the Bill to regulate the Practice of Physic and Surgery. Mr. Clench then moved, seconded by Mr. Swazey, that the said Bill be read a second time on Saturday next, which was ordered accordingly.

Read for the second time, the Johnstown Court House and Gaol Bill. On motion of the Solicitor General, seconded by Mr. Crysler, the House resolved itself into Committee to go into the consideration of the said Bill. Mr. Speaker left the Chair. Mr. Nellis was called to the chair of the Committee.

Mr. Speaker resumed the Chair. Mr. Nellis reported that the Committee had made a progress, and had directed him to ask for leave to sit again to-morrow. Leave was accordingly given.

Read for the first time, the Bill for continuing the Act for appointing Returning Officers throughout this Province, which was ordered to be read a second time to-morrow.

Read for the first time, the Militia Bill. On motion of the Solicitor General seconded by Mr. Clench, ordered, that the Militia Bill be read for the second time on Monday next.

Agreeably to the Order of the Day, the House resolved itself into a Committee of the Whole to go into the further consideration of the Bill to establish a Court of Common Pleas in this Province. Mr. Speaker left the Chair. Mr. Mallory took the Chair of the Committee.

Mr. Speaker resumed the Chair, and Mr. Mallory reported that the Committee had made a progress, and had directed him to ask for leave to sit again to-morrow. Ordered, that the Committee have leave to sit again to-morrow.

Agreeably to the Order of the Day, the House resolved itself into a Committee to go into the further consideration of the Special Jury Bill. Mr. Speaker left the Chair. Mr. Rogers took the Chair of the Committee.

Mr. Speaker resumed the Chair. Mr. Rogers reported that the Committee had gone through the consideration of the said Bill, to which they had made some amendments, which he was directed to report to the House whenever it should be pleased to receive the same. Ordered, that the Report be now received. The Report was accordingly received and accepted. Mr. Rogers then moved, seconded by Mr. Sherwood, that the Bill as amended be engrossed, and read a third time to-morrow. Ordered accordingly.

Argeeably to the Order of the Day, the House resolved itself into a Committee to go into the Consideration of the Marriage Bill. Mr. Speaker left the Chair. Mr. Dorland was called to the chair of the Committee.

Mr. Speaker resumed the Chair, and Mr. Dorland reported that the Committee had gone through the consideration of the said Bill, to which they had made some amendments, which he was directed to report to the House whenever it should be pleased to receive the same.

The House then resolved that the Report be now received. The Report was then received and accepted. On motion of Mr. McLean, seconded by the Solicitor General, ordered, that the said Bill be engrossed and read a third time on Friday next.

On motion of Mr. Solicitor General, seconded by Mr. Clench, ordered, that twenty-five Copies of the Militia Bill be printed for the use of the members of this House.

On motion of the Solicitor General, seconded by Mr. Rogers, ordered, that the House will on Friday next resolve itself into a Committee to go into the consideration of the Bill the better to ascertain and secure Titles to Lands in this Province.

Mr. Washburn moved, seconded by Mr. McLean, for leave to bring in a Bill to-morrow to alter the present duty paid on Shop and Tavern Licences in this Province. Leave was accordingly given.

On motion of Mr. Clench, seconded by Mr. Howard, the House adjourned.

Wednesday, 10th February, 1808.

Prayers were read.

Read for the third time, the Act for Barring of Dower. Mr. Mallory moved, seconded by Mr. Willcocks, that the House do now resolve itself into a Committee to take into consideration the Bill for Barring of Dower. Mr. Mallory moved, seconded by Mr. Willcocks, that the House do now resolve itself into a Committee to take into consideration the Bill for Barring of Dower. The House accordingly resolved itself into a Committee to go into the consideration of the said Bill. Mr. Speaker left the Chair. Mr. Sherwood was called to the chair of the Committee.

Mr. Speaker resumed the Chair, and Mr. Sherwood reported that the Committee had gone through the consideration of the said Bill without any amendment, which he was directed to report to the House whenever it should be pleased to receive the same. Ordered, that the Report be now received. The Report was accordingly received and accepted. On motion of the Solicitor General, seconded by Capt. Cowan, the said Act was ordered to be read for the third time to-morrow.

Agreeably to the Order of the Day, the House resolved itself into a Committee to go into the further consideration of the Bill for granting a bounty for destroying of Wolves. Mr. Speaker left the Chair. Capt. Cowan took the chair of the Committee.

Mr. Speaker resumed the Chair, and Capt. Cowan reported that the Committee had gone through the consideration of the said Bill, to which they had made several amendments, which he was directed to report to the House whenever it should be pleased to receive the same. The House then resolved that the Report be now received. The Report was then received and accepted.

Mr. Rogers then moved, seconded by Mr. Willcocks, that the Bill granting a bounty for destroying Wolves be engrossed, and read a third time to-morrow. Ordered accordingly.

The Solicitor General then moved, seconded by Capt. Cowan, that the Johnstown District Court House Petition, and the Subscription Papers from the said District be now read. Ordered accordingly. The Clerk then read the Petition and subscription papers from the District of Johnstown, which was as follows:—

To His Excellency Francis Gore, Esquire, Lieutenant Governor of the Province of Upper Canada, etc., etc., etc., the Honorable the Legislative Council, and the Honorable House of Assembly in Parliament convened.

The Petition of the Subscribers, Inhabitants of the District of Johnstown, Humbly Prays,—

That an Act may be passed to enable the inhabitants of said District to build a Court House and Gaol on the front of Lot No. 11 or 12 in the First Concession of Elizabethtown, in said District, in lieu of the Court House and Gaol now standing in the Town of Johnstown.

And in Duty bound, Your Petitioners will ever Pray, November 9th, 1807.

Robert McLean, David D. Jones, Nehemiah Seaman, Simon Powers, Reuben Sherwood, Adriel Sherwood, Stephen Baldwin, Jacob Church, and Five Hundred and Twenty others in sundry lists.

We, the subscribers, Inhabitants of the District of Johnstown, do severally bind ourselves to pay the sums affixed to our respective names to such person or persons as shall be appointed by the Magistrates in Quarter Sessions assembled to receive the same, for the express purpose of erecting and building a Court

House and Gaol on the front end of lot No. 10, 11, or 12 in the first Concession of Elizabethtown, in the District of Johnstown aforesaid.

District of Johnstown,
    Dec'r, 1806.

Several persons, inhabitants of the District of Johnstown, have subscribed the sum of Three Hundred and Sixty Pounds, as per original lists, for the purposes above stated.

Mr. Solicitor General moved, seconded by Mr. McLean, that so much of the Order of the Day as regards the going into a Committee on the Johnstown Court House Bill be discharged, and that the House do go into Committee to-morrow to take into consideration the said Bill. Ordered accordingly.

Mr. Mallory, one of the messengers named to carry up to the Honorable Legislative Council the Act to authorize the inhabitants of the County of Haldimand to hold Annual Meetings for the purpose of electing Town and Parish Officers, reported that they had carried up the said Act, and did request their concurrence thereto.

Read for the second time, the Bill for continuing an Act entitled "An Act to provide for the appointment of Returning Officers for the several Counties within the Province." Capt. Cowan then moved, seconded by Mr. Nellis, that the House do now resolve itself into a Committee to take into consideration the Bill for continuing the Act for the appointment of Returning Officers for the several Counties within this Province. The House accordingly resolved itself into a Committee. Mr. Speaker left the Chair. Mr. McLean was called to the chair of the Committee.

Mr. Speaker resumed the Chair. and Mr. McLean reported that the Committee had gone through the consideration of the said Bill without any amendment, which he was directed to report to the House whenever it should be pleased to receive the same. Ordered, that the Report be now received. The Report was accordingly received and accepted. Capt. Cowan then moved, seconded by Mr. Rogers, that the Bill for appointing Returning Officers be engrossed, and read a third time to-morrow, which was ordered accordingly.

Agreeably to the Order of the Day the House resolved itself into a Committee to go into the further considertion of the Bill to establish a Court of Common Pleas in this Province. Mr. Speaker left the Chair. Mr. Mallory took the chair of the Committee.

Mr. Speaker resumed the Chair, and Mr. Mallory reported that the Committee had made a progress, and had directed him to ask for leave to sit again to-morrow. Ordered, that the Committee have leave to sit again to-morrow.

Read for the third time, as engrossed, the Bill to Regulate Special Juries. On motion of Mr. Sherwood, seconded by Mr. Nellis, resolved, that the Bill do pass, and that the title be "An Act for the better regulation of Special Juries." The Bill accordingly passed, and was signed by the Speaker. Mr. Washburn moved, seconded by Mr. Mallory, that Messrs. Sherwood and Nellis do carry up to the Honorable the Legislative Council the Bill for the better regulation of Special Juries, and request their concurrence thereto. Ordered accordingly.

Then was read for the first time, the Bill for the better regulation of granting Tavern Licenses. Mr. Washburn moved, seconded by Mr. Dorland, that the Bill to alter Tavern Licenses within this Province be read a second time to-morrow, which was ordered accordingly.

Mr. Sherwood gave notice that he will move to-morrow that the ·Common Pleas Bill be engrossed, and read for the third time.

On motion of Mr. McGregor, seconded by 'Mr. Clench, the House adjourned.

Thursday, 11th February, 1808.

Prayers were read.

Agreeably to the Order of the Day, the House resolved itself into a Committee to go into the further consideration of the Court of Common Pleas Bill. Mr. Speaker left the Chair. Mr. Mallory took the chair of the Committee.

Mr. Speaker resumed the Chair, and Mr. Mallory reported that the Committee had gone through the consideration of the said Bill, to which the Committee had made several amendments, which he was directed to report to the House whenever it should be pleased to receive the same. Resolved, that the Report be now received. The Report was accordingly received and accepted.

Read for the second time, the Bill for increasing the representation of the Commons of this Province.

Ordered, that petitions, memorials and other papers addressed to this House shall be presented by the Member in his place, by permission of the House, who shall be answerable to this House that they do not contain improper matter.

Read, the Petition of the inhabitants of the Town of York, which is as follows:—

To the Honorable the Legislative Council, and the Honorable Commons House of Assembly of Upper Canada in Parliament assembled.

The Humble Petition of the undersigned, Inhabitants of the Town of York, in the Home District.

Sheweth,—

That the population of the Town of York, as well as the County of Durham, the East Riding of the County of York, and the County of Simcoe is much increased during the last seven years.

That from the extent of population Your Petitioners presume to think that they are not sufficiently represented, and humbly beg leave to suggest that it would be highly beneficial to increase the number of Representatives.

That as the Inhabitants of the Town of York are now very numerous, Your Petitioners take the liberty of suggesting that if they were permitted to send one Representative to the House of Assembly, the evil complained of would be in some measure removed.

Your Petitioners therefore most respectfully pray that an Act may be passed during the present Session of Parliament permitting the Inhabitants of the Town of York, to send a Representative to the House of Assembly, unconnected with the County Representation.

And Your Petitioners, as in duty bound, will ever pray.

George Playter, ·William Allan, D. Cameron, W. C. Hewitt, ·Saml. Ridout, Alexr. Wood, Thos. Hamilton, Benjn.· Cozens, Joshua Leech, Eli Playter, and twenty-five others.

Mr. Clench moved, seconded by Mr. Sherwood, that so much of the Order of the Day as relates to the bringing in a Bill for increasing the representation of the Commons in Parliament be discharged, and that he have leave to bring in the same on Monday next. Ordered accordingly.

Read for the third time, the Bill sent down from the Legislative Council for the more easy barring of Dower. Which, on motion of the Solicitor General, seconded by Capt. Cowan, passed, and was signed by the Speaker. Mr. Rogers then moved, seconded by Mr. Sherwood, that the Solicitor General and Capt. Cowan do inform the Honorable and Legislative Council that the House of Assembly have concurred in passing the Bill for extending the provisions of an Act-for the more easy Barring of Dower. Ordered accordingly.

Read for the third time, as engrossed, the Bill granting a bounty for destroy-ing of Wolves in several Districts of this Province. Mr. Willcocks moved, seconded by Mr. Rogers, that the proviso in the Bill reviving the bounty for killing Wolves be expunged. Ordered accordingly.

Mr. Willcocks, seconded by Mr. Rogers, moved that the Bill do pass, and that the title be "An Act to encourage the destroying of Wolves in several Districts of this Province." Ordered accordingly.

The said Bill then passed, and was signed by the Speaker.

The Solicitor General, one of the Messengers named to return to the Honor-able Legislative Council an Act passed by them entitled "An Act to extend the benefits of an Act passed in the thirty-seventh year of His Majesty's reign, en-titled 'An Act for the more easy Barring of Dower,' and to repeal certain parts of the same," reported that they had carried up the said Act, and did inform them that this House had concurred in passing the same.

Agreeably to the Order of the Day, the House resolved itself into a Com-mittee on the Johnstown Court House and Gaol Bill. Mr. Speaker left the Chair. Mr. Nellis was called to the chair of the Committee.

Mr. Speaker resumed the Chair, and Mr. Nellis reported that the Committee had gone through the consideration of the said Bill, to which they had made several amendments, which he was directed to report to the House whenever it should be pleased to receive the same. Resolved, that the report be now received. The Report was accordingly received and accepted. Mr. Solicitor General moved, seconded by Mr. Nellis, that the Johnstown Court House and Gaol Bill be en-grossed, and read for the first- time to-morrow. Ordered accordingly.

Mr. Mallory, one of the Messengers appointed to carry up to the Honorable Legislative Council the Act authorizing the inhabitants of the County of Haldi-mand to hold Annual Meetings for the purpose of electing Town and Parish Officers, reported that they had carried up to the Honorable Legislative Council the said Act, and did request their concurrence thereto.

Read for the third time, the Bill for appointing Returning Officers for each and every County within this Province.

Mr. Sherwood, one of the messengers named to carry up to the Honorable Legislative Council the Act for the better regulation of Special Juries, reported that they had carried up the said Act, and did request their concurrence thereto.

Read for the second time, the Bill for the regulation of Tavern Licenses. Mr. Washburn moved, seconded by Mr. Crysler, that the House do to-morrow resolve itself into a Committee to go into the consideration of the Tavern License Bill. Ordered accordingly.

Mr. Sherwood then moved, seconded by Mr. Clench, that the Common Pleas Bill be engrossed, and read a third time to-day. Ordered accordingly. Read for the third time, as engrossed, the Bill for establishing a Court of Common Pleas in this Province. Mr. Sherwood moved, seconded by Mr. Clench, that the said Bill do pass, and that the title be "An Act for the establishment of a Court of

Common Pleas in each and every District of this Province." A division thereupon took place, the names being called for, they were taken down, and are as follows:

Yeas.	Nays.
MESSRS. SOL'R Gen.	MESSRS. WILLCOCKS
McLEAN	ROGERS
COWAN	
SHERWOOD	
McGREGOR	
CLENCH	
SWAZEY	
NELLIS	
HOWARD	
MALLORY	
WASHBURN	
CRYSLER	

The same was carried in the affirmative by a majority of ten. The Bill then passed and was signed by the Speaker. The Solicitor General moved, seconded by Mr. McLean, that Messrs. Sherwood and Clench do carry up to the Honorable the Legislative Council the said Bill, and request their concurrence thereto, which was ordered accordingly.

Mr. McLean moved, seconded by Mr. Clench, for leave to bring in a Bill to make provision for the Judges of the Court of Common Pleas in this Province. Leave was accordingly given.

Read for the first time, the Bill to make provision for the Judges of the Court of Common Pleas in this Province. Mr. McLean then moved, seconded by Mr. Sherwood, that the Bill to make provision for the Judges of the Court of Common Pleas be read a second time on Monday next. Ordered accordingly.

On motion of Mr. Clench, seconded by Mr. Dorland, the House adjourned.

Friday, 12th February, 1908.

Prayers were read.

On motion of Mr. Rogers, seconded by Mr. Nellis, ordered, that Messrs. Washburn and Willcocks do carry up to the Honorable the Legislative Council the Act to encourage the destroying of Wolves in several Districts in this Province, and to request their concurrence thereto. Ordered accordingly.

Read for the third time, the Bill for erecting a Court House and Gaol in the District of Johnstown. Mr. Solicitor General then moved, seconded by Mr. Mc-Lean, that the Bill do pass, and that the title be "An Act for building a Court House and Gaol in the Township of Elizabethtown in the District of Johnstown." The Bill then passed and was signed by the Speaker. Mr. Rogers moved, seconded by Mr. Nellis, that the Solicitor General and Mr. Howard do carry up to the Honorable Legislative Council the Act enabling the inhabitants of the District of Johnstown to erect and build a Gaol and Court House in the Township of Elizabethtown, in said District, and to request their concurrence thereto, which was ordered accordingly.

Read for the third time, as engrossed, a Bill to make valid certain marriages heretofore contracted in this Province. The Solicitor General then moved, seconded by Mr. McLean, that the Bill do pass, and that the title be "An Act to amend certain parts of an Act passed in the thirty-third year of His Majesty's reign, entitled, 'An Act to confirm and make valid certain Marriages heretofore contracted in the country now comprised within the province of Upper Canada.'" Mr. Rogers then moved, seconded by Mr. McLean, that the Solicitor General and Mr. Howard do carry up to the Honorable the Legislative Council the Marriage Act, and to request their concurrence thereto. Ordered accordingly.

Agreeably to the Order of the Day the House resolved itself into a Committee to go into the further consideration of the Bill for securing titles to lands in this Province. Mr. Speaker left the Chair. Mr. Washburn was called to the chair of the Committee.

Mr. Speaker resumed the Chair, and Mr. Washburn reported progress, and asked for leave to sit again this day. Leave was accordingly granted.

A Message from the Honorable Legislative Council by Mr. Baldwin, Master-in-Chancery:

Mr. Speaker,—

I am commanded by the Honorable Legislative Council to inform this Honorable House that they have passed an Act, sent up from this House, entitled "An Act for the better regulation of Parish and Town Officers throughout this Province," with amendments, to which amendments they request the concurrence of this House.

And then he withdrew.

Agreeably to leave given, the House again resolved itself into a Committee to go into the further consideration of the Bill for the better securing titles to lands in this Province. Mr. Speaker left the Chair. Mr. Washburn again took the chair of the Committee.

Mr. Speaker resumed the Chair. Mr. Washburn reported that the Committee had made a progress, and had directed him to ask for leave to sit again to-morrow. Leave was accordingly granted.

Mr. Solicitor General, one of the messengers named to carry up to the Honorable Legislative Council an Act to amend certain parts of an Act, passed in the thirty-third year of His Majesty's reign, entitled "An Act to confirm and make valid certain marriages heretofore contracted in the country now comprised within the Province of Upper Canada," reported that they had carried up the said Bill to the Honorable the Legislative Council, and did request their concurrence thereto; and also an Act for building a Court House and Gaol in the Township of Elizabethtown in the District of Johnstown, to which they did request their concurrence in passing the same.

Mr. Washburn, one of the messengers named to carry up to the Honorable Legislative Council the Act to encourage the destroying of Wolves in several Districts of this Province, reported that they had carried up the said Act to the Honorable Legislative Council, and did request their concurrence thereto.

Agreeably to the Order of the Day, the House resolved itself into a Committee to go into the consideration of the Bill for the regulation of Tavern Licenses in this Province. The Speaker left the Chair. Mr. Willcocks was called to the chair of the Committee.

Mr. Speaker resumed the Chair, and Mr. Willcocks reported that the Committee had made a progress, and had directed him to ask for leave to sit again to-morrow. Leave was accordingly granted.

Mr. Rogers then moved, seconded by Mr. Nellis, that the amendments made by the Honorable the Legislative Council to the Bill for the regulation of Parish and Town officers be read. The said amendments were then read accordingly. Mr. Rogers then moved, seconded by Mr. Nellis, that the House do now resolve itself into a Committee to go into the consideration of the amendments made by the Honorable Legislative Council to the Bill for the regulation of Parish and Town Officers. The House accordingly resolved itself into a Committee. Mr. Speaker left the Chair. Capt. Cowan was called to the chair of the Committee.

Mr. Speaker resumed the Chair. Capt. Cowan reported that the Committee had gone through the consideration of the amendments made to the said Bill, and that the Committee had directed him to report to the House, whenever it should be pleased to receive the same, that the Committee had concurred in the amendments made in and to the said Act by the Legislative Council. Mr. Rogers then moved, seconded by Mr. Mallory, that Messrs. Howard and Nellis do inform the Honorable Legislative Council that they have concurred in and adopted the amendments made by them in and to the Act for the regulation of Parish and Town Officers.

Mr. Speaker,—

We are commanded by the Commons House of Assembly to acquaint this Honorable House that it has concurred in adopting the amendments made by the Legislative Council in and to the Act entitled "An Act for the better regulation of Parish and Town Officers throughout this Province."

Commons House of Assembly,   Alexr. McDonell,
12th February, 1808.   Speaker.

Which was ordered accordingly.

Mr. Howard then moved, seconded by Mr. Rogers, for leave to bring in a Bill to-morrow to extend the jurisdiction of the several Courts of Requests within this Province. Leave was accordingly granted.

Mr. Washburn gave notice that he will move to-morrow for leave to bring in a Bill to amend an Act passed in the thirty-seventh year of His Majesty's reign, entitled "An Act for the more easy Barring of Dower in this Province."

The Solicitor General moved, seconded by Capt. Cowan, for leave to bring in a Bill on Monday next for the more just admeasurement of Fuel within the Town and Township of York. Leave was accordingly granted.

On motion of Mr. McGregor, seconded by Mr. Clench, the House adjourned.

Saturday, 13th February, 1808.

Prayers were read.

Read for the first time, the Bill for regulating the Court of Requests. Mr. Rogers moved, seconded by Mr. Nellis, that the Bill to extend the jurisdiction of the Court of Requests be read a second time on Monday. Ordered accordingly.

Agreeably to the Order of the Day, the House resolved itself into a Committee to go into the consideration of the Bill for regulating the Practice of Physic and Surgery in this Province. Mr. Speaker left the Chair. Mr. Crysler was called to the chair of the Committee.

Mr. Speaker resumed the Chair, and Mr. Crysler reported that the Committee had made a progress and had directed him to ask for leave to sit again. Leave was accordingly granted.

Agreeably to the Order of the Day, the House resolved itself into a Committee to go into the further consideration of the Bill for the Better establishing of Titles to Lands in this Province. Mr. Speaker left the Chair. Mr. Washburn was called to the chair of the Committee.

Mr. Speaker resumed the Chair, and Mr. Washburn reported that the Committee had made a progress, and had directed him to ask for leave to sit again on Monday next. Ordered, that the Committee have leave to sit again on Monday next.

Agreeably to the Order of the Day, the House resolved itself into a Committee to go into the further consideration of the Bill for regulating the granting of Tavern Licenses. Mr. Speaker left the Chair. Mr. Willcocks took the chair of the Committee.

Mr. Speaker resumed the Chair, and Mr. Willcocks reported that the Committee had made a progress, and had directed him to ask for leave to sit again. Leave was accordingly granted.

Mr. Rogers in his place delivered in at the table the Account and Vouchers delivered to him by William Allan, Esquire, one of the Commissioners appointed by His Excellency the late Lieutenant Governor Hunter, for the purchase of Hemp, which Account is as follows:

An Account of Hemp purchased by William Allan, Esq., as one of the Commissioners appointed by His Excellency the late Lieutenant Governor Hunter, for the Home District.

1804.	No.			
May 5	1	To Cash paid Matthew Cline for 1 cwt. 0 qr. 0 lbs.	£2 0 0
1805.				
Feb. 12	2	Paid Timothy Rogers for 4 cwt. 2 qr. 0 lbs.	9 0 0
Dec. 28	3	Paid to James Rogers for 5 cwt. 0 qr. 0 lbs.	12 10 0
1806.				
Feb. 15	4	Paid Elisha Dexter for 3 cwt. 0 qr. 0 lbs.	6 0 0
Feb. 25	5	Paid Ulrick Burkholder for 3 cwt.	7 10 0
Dec. 5	6	Paid Ulrick Burkholder for 4 cwt. 3 qrs.	9 10 0
1807.				
Mar. 7	7	Paid John Kock for 6 cwt. 0 qr. 10 lbs.	15 4 - 4½
Apl. 4	8	Paid N. Coves for 1 qr. 3 cwt. 1 lb.	4 7 11½
Jne. 25	9	Paid Peter Brillinger for 1 qr. 2 cwt. 8 lbs.	3 18 6
1808.				
Jan. 10	10	Paid Ulrick Burkholder for 7 cwt.	17 10 0
Jan. 5	11	Paid Ulrick Burkholder for 4 cwt. 14 lbs.	10 6 3
Jan. 18	12	Paid Wm. Macklin for 3 cwt. 23 lbs.	2 7 9
		Paid for packing and shipping do.	1 5 0
			101 9 10

Brot. forward	£101	9 10
By Cash received from the Receiver General on account	100	0 0
Balance due William Allan	1	9 10

Errors excepted.
York, 18th January, 1808.

W. Allan, Commissioner.

Mr. Washburn moved, seconded by Mr. Nellis, for leave to bring in a Bill on Monday next to amend an Act passed in the thirty-seventh year of His Majesty's reign, entitled "An Act for the more easy Barring of Dower in this Province." Leave was accordingly given.

Mr. Howard then moved, seconded by Mr. Rogers, that the House do resolve itself into a Committee on Monday next to go into the consideration of the Bill for regulating, laying out and amending the Highways and Roads throughout this Province. The House accordingly resolved the same.

On motion of Mr. Sherwood, seconded by Mr. McLean, the House adjourned until eleven o'clock in the forenoon, on Monday next.

Monday, 15th February, 1808.

Prayers were read.

On motion of the Solicitor General, seconded by Mr. Clench, ordered, that the second reading of the Militia Bill be postponed until Wednesday next.

Mr. Clench then moved, seconded by Mr. Nellis, that so much of the Order of the Day as relates to the second reading of the Bill for increasing the representation of the Commons of this Province be discharged, and that leave be given that the said Bill be read a second time to-morrow, which was ordered accordingly.

Read for the second time, the Bill for granting salaries to Judges. On motion of Mr. Sherwood, seconded by Mr. Clench, the House resolved itself into a Committee to go into the consideration of the said Bill. Mr. Speaker left the Chair. Mr. Dorland was called to the Chair of the Committee.

Mr. Speaker resumed the Chair. Mr. Dorland reported that the Committee had made a progress, and had directed him to ask for leave to sit again to-morrow. Leave was accordingly given.

Read for the second time, the Bill for extending the Jurisdiction of the Court of Requests. Mr. Howard then moved, seconded by Mr. Nellis, that the House do resolve itself into a Committee on Wednesday next to take into consideration the Court of Requests Bill. Ordered accordingly.

Agreeably to the Order of the Day the House resolved itself into a Committee to go into the further consideration of the Bill for the securing Titles to Lands in this Province. Mr. Speaker left the Chair. Mr. Washburn was called to the Chair of the Committee.

Mr. Speaker resumed the Chair, and Mr. Washburn reported that the Committee had made a progress, and had directed him to ask for leave to sit again to-morrow. Leave was accordingly granted.

Mr. Washburn then moved, seconded by Mr. Howard, that so much of the Order of the Day as relates to the bringing in of a Bill to amend certain parts of an Act passed in the thirty-seventh year of His Majesty's reign, entitled "An Act for the more easy Barring of Dower," be discharged, and that he have leave to bring in a Bill to-morrow to repeal the whole of the said Act, and to make other provisions for the same. Leave was accordingly given.

Read for the second time, the Bill for laying out and keeping in repair the Public Highways and Roads throughout the Province. Agreeably to the Order of the Day the House resolved itself into a Committee to go into the consideration of the said Bill. Mr. Speaker left the Chair. Mr. McGregor was called to the chair of the Committee.

Mr. Speaker resumed the Chair, and Mr. McGregor reported that the Committee had made a progress, and that he was directed to ask for leave to sit again to-morrow. Ordered, that the Committee have leave to sit again to-morrow.

Mr. Clench gave notice that he will move to-morrow that the House do resolve itself into a Committee to go into the further consideration of the Bill for regulating the practice of Physic, Surgery and Midwifery in this Province.

Mr. Clench moved, seconded by Mr. Sherwood, for leave to bring in a Bill to-morrow to establish a Court of Quarter Sessions, and a Court of Requests, at Saint Joseph's, on the Island of Saint Joseph's, in the Western District. Leave was accordingly given.

On motion of Mr. Clench, seconded by Mr. McGregor, the House adjourned.

Tuesday, 16th February, 1808.

Prayers read.

The Clerk of this House has the honor of respectfully informing Mr. Speaker and the House that the Clerks of the Peace for the different Districts in this Province did send him returns of all the rateable property in their respective Districts, in compliance with the Tenth Section of the Act passed during the last Session of the Legislature, for the more uniform laying of Assessments and Rates throughout this Province.

Read for the first time, the Bill for the more easy Barring of Dower. Mr. Washburn moved, seconded by Mr. Rogers, that the Bill for the more easy Barring of Dower be read a second time to-marrow, which was ordered accordingly.

Mr. Clench then moved, seconded by Mr. Sherwood, that the House do now resolve itself into a Committee to go into the consideration of the Bill for increasing the Representation of the Commons in this Province. The House, accordingly resolved itself into a Committee. Mr. Speaker left the Chair. Mr. Howard was called to the Chair of the Committee.

Mr. Speaker resumed the Chair, and Mr. Howard reported that the Committee had made a progress, and had directed him to ask for leave to sit again to-morrow. Ordered, that the Committee have leave to sit again to-morrow.

Agreeably to the Order of the Day the House resolved itself into a Committee on the Bill for allowing Salaries to the Judges of the Court of Common Pleas, to be appointed in this Province. Mr. Speaker left the Chair. Mr. Dorland took the Chair of the Committee.

Mr. Speaker resumed the Chair, and Mr. Dorland reported that the Committee had gone through the consideration of the said Bill, to which they had made several amendments, which he was directed to report to the House whenever it should be pleased to receive the same. Resolved, that the Report be now received and accepted. On motion of Mr. Sherwood, seconded by Mr. Clench, ordered, that the said Bill be engrossed and read a third time to-morrow.

Agreeably to the Order of the Day the House resolved itself into a Committee to go into the further consideration of the Bill for laying out and repairing the Public Highways and Roads throughout this Province. Mr. Speaker left the Chair. Mr. McGregor took the chair of the Committee.

Mr. Speaker resumed the Chair, and Mr. McGregor reported that the Committee had made a progress, and had directed him to ask for leave to sit again this day. Leave was accordingly granted.

A Message from the Honorable Legislative Council by Mr. Baldwin, Master in Chancery.

Mr. Speaker,

I am commanded by the Honorable the Legislative Council to inform this House that they have passed an Act, sent up from this House, entitled "An Act for the better regulation of Special Juries," to which they have made several amendments, to which amendments they request the concurrence of this House in passing the same.

And then he withdrew.

Agreeably to leave given the House again resolved itself into a Committee to go into the further consideration of the Bill for establishing Public Roads and Highways throughout this Province. Mr. Speaker left the Chair. Mr. McGregor again took the Chair of the Committee.

Mr. Speaker resumed the Chair, and Mr. McGregor reported that the Committee had made a progress, and had directed him to ask for leave to sit again to-morrow. Ordered, that the Committee have leave to sit again to-morrow.

Read for the first time, the Bill for establishing a Court of Quarter Sessions and a Court of Requests in the Island of Saint Joseph's, in this Province. On motion of Mr. Clench, seconded by Captain Cowan, ordered, that the said Bill be read for the second time to-morrow.

On motion of Mr. Swazey, seconded by Mr. Crysler, the House adjourned until eleven o'clock to-morrow in the forenoon.

Wednesday, 17th February, 1808.

Prayers were read.

Read for the second time, a Bill for the more easy Barring of Dower. Mr. Washburn moved, seconded by Mr. Mallory, that the House do now resolve itself into a Committee to go into the consideration of the Bill to alter the present mode of Barring Dower. The House accordingly resolved itself into a Committee. Mr. Speaker left the Chair. Mr. Clench was called to the Chair of the Committee.

Mr. Speaker resumed the Chair, and Mr. Clench reported that the Committee had made a progress, and had directed him to ask for leave to sit again. Ordered, that the Committee have leave to sit again.

Agreeably to the Order of the Day the House resolved itself into a Committee to go into the consideration of the Bill for the more equal Representation of the Commons in Parliament. Mr. Speaker left the Chair. Mr. Howard was called to the Chair of the Committee.

Mr. Speaker resumed the Chair, and Mr. Howard reported that the Committee had made a progress, and had directed him to ask for leave to sit again this day. Leave was accordingly granted.

By Command of His Excellency, the Lieutenant-Governor, William Jarvis, Esquire, Secretary of the Province, delivered in at the Bar the General Account of articles on which duties on importation are imposed by the Legislature of Lower Canada, which have passed Coteau du Lac upwards from the First July to the Thirty-first December, One Thousand Eight Hundred and Seven, which was read by the Clerk at the Table, and ordered to be joined to the other Public Accounts, and forms Number Eighteen.

Mr. Clench moved, seconded by Mr. Sherwood, that the House do now resolve itself into a Committee to go into the further consideration of the Bill for regulating the Practice of Physic, Surgery and Midwifery within this Province. The House accordingly resolved itself into a Committee to go into the consideration of the said Bill. Mr. Speaker left the Chair. Mr. Crysler was called to the Chair of the Committee.

Mr. Speaker resumed the Chair, and Mr. Crysler reported that the Committee had made a progress, and had directed him to ask for leave to sit again. Resolved, that the Committee have leave to sit again.

Agreeably to the Order of the Day the House resolved itself into a Committee to go into the further consideration of the Bill to secure Titles to Lands in this Province. Mr. Speaker left the Chair. Mr. Washburn took the Chair of the Committee.

Mr. Speaker resumed the Chair, and Mr. Washburn reported that the Committee had made a progress, and had directed him to ask for leave to sit again. Leave was accordingly granted.

Read for the third time, as engrossed, the Bill for allowing Salaries to Judges of the Court of Common Pleas, to be appointed in this Province. Mr. Sherwood then moved, seconded by Mr. Clench, that the Bill do pass, and that the title be " An Act to provide for the support of Judges of the Court of Common Pleas." A division thereupon took place; the names being called for, they were taken down, and are as follows:—

Yeas:	Nays:
MESSRS. CRYSLER	MESSRS. WILLCOCKS
SOLICITOR GENERAL	HOWARD
COWAN	ROGERS
SHERWOOD	SWAZEY
CLENCH	DORLAND.
NELLIS	
WASHBURN	
MALLORY	
McLEAN.	

The same was carried in the affirmative by a majority of four. The Bill then passed, and was signed by the Speaker.

Mr. Rogers then moved, seconded by Mr. Swazey, that Messrs. Sherwood and McLean do carry up to the Honorable the Legislative Council the Bill to provide Salaries for Judges of the Court of Common Pleas, and to request their concurrence thereto. Ordered accordingly.

Agreeably to the Order of the Day the House resolved itself into a Committee to go into the further consideration of the Bill for laying out and amending the Public Highways and Roads throughout this Province. Mr. Speaker left the Chair. Mr. Rogers was called to the Chair of the Committee.

Mr. Speaker resumed the Chair, and Mr. Rogers reported that the Committee had made a progress, and had directed him to ask for leave to sit again. Leave was accordingly given.

Mr. Clench then moved, seconded by Mr. Swazey, that so much of the Order of the Day as relates to the second reading of the Bill for establishing Courts of

Quarter Sessions and Requests in the Island of Saint Joseph's be discharged, and that the same be read on Friday next, which was ordered accordingly.

Read for the third time, as engrossed, the Bill for continuing an Act passed in the Thirty-third year of His Majesty's Reign, to provide for the appointment of Returning Officers in this Province. The Solicitor General then moved, seconded by Captain Cowan, that the Bill do pass, and that the title be " An Act to continue an Act passed in the Thirty-third year of His Majesty's Reign, entitled 'An Act to provide for the appointment of Returning Officers of the several Counties within this Province.'" The Bill then passed, and was signed by the Speaker. Mr. Solicitor General then moved, seconded by Mr. Crysler, that Captain Cowan and Mr. Clench do carry up to the Honorable Legislative Council the Act to continue an Act passed in the Thirty-third year of His Majesty's Reign, entitled " An Act to provide for the appointment of Returning Officers for the several Counties within this Province," and to request their concurrence thereto, which was ordered accordingly.

Mr. Sherwood, one of the Messengers named to carry up to the Legislative Council an Act to provide for the support of the Judges of the Court of Common Pleas, reported that they had carried up the same, and did request their concurrence thereto.

Mr. Clench then moved, seconded by Mr. Swazey, that so much of the Order of the Day as relates to the second reading of the Bill for increasing the Representation of the Commons of this Province in Parliament be discharged. Ordered accordingly.

Read, the Petition from the Trustees appointed by His Excellency, the Lieutenant-Governor, in the District of London, by virtue of an Act passed in the last Session of the Legislature, entitled " An Act to establish Public Schools in each and every District of this Province," which is as follows:—

To the Honorable the Commons of Upper Canada in Parliament assembled.

The Memorial of the Trustees appointed and acting under the District School Bill for the District of London,

Most respectfully represents, That soon after they received their appointment they proceeded to discharge the trust reposed in them, by recommending to His Excellency the Lieutenant-Governor a person whom they considered properly qualified to fill the situation of District School Master, who, in consequence of such recommendation, was duly appointed.

That the person so nominated on receiving notice of his appointment attended for the purpose of performing the duties attached to the situation, but neither School House nor Scholars could be procured in Townsend, the place pointed out by the Statute.

Your Memorialists therefore trust that Your Honorable House, taking into consideration the important object contemplated by the Statute, and the impossibility of carrying it into effect under existing circumstances, will deem it expedient to amend the Act, so that the School may be opened and kept in the Village of Dover, in the Township of Woodhouse, where a School House would be built, as appears by the accompanying subscription lately set on foot, and sufficient accommodation procured for those coming from distant parts of the District.

And Your Memorialists, as in duty bound, will ever pray.

Samuel Ryerse, John Cottman, Joseph Ryerse, Thomas Welch, Trustees.

16 A.

Mr. Mallory then moved, seconded by Mr. Howard, for leave to bring in a Bill on Saturday next to change the place of holding the Public School in the District of London. Leave was accordingly granted.

On motion of Mr. Swazey, seconded by Mr. Rogers, the House adjourned.

Thursday, 18th February, 1808.

Prayers were read.

Read, the Petition of the Inhabitants of the District of London, which is as follows:—

To the Honorable the Speaker and Members of the House of Commons of Upper Canada:

The Petition of the undersigned, Inhabitants of the District of London, Humbly Showeth,—

That the operation of that part of an Act entitled "An Act to repeal the several Acts now in force in this Province, relative to Rates and Assessments, etc., etc., passed in the Forty-seventh year of His present Majesty's Reign, which directs that all real property shall be rated and assessed in the District where the owner of the property so rated and assessed resides, and the moneys arising by tax thereon shall be paid for the use and benefit of such District into the hands of the Treasurer thereof is peculiarly hard upon this District.

Your Petitioners are inhabitants of a very extensive and newly settled District, not very populous or wealthy; their annual public expenditures are nearly equal, if not quite, to that of any other District; and the money raised under the Act above mentioned, which is now paid into the Treasury of this District, is entirely inadequate to defray the necessary expenses; insomuch that the Magistrates have been under the necessity of involving the District already so largely in debt that there seems scarcely any possibility of ever being extricated by any means but the interference of the Legislature.

Your Petitioners beg leave to state that the quantity of land rated and assessed in this District does not exceed One Hundred and Twenty Thousand acres, and that they are led to believe that there is not less than Eight Hundred Thousand acres of land located, and subject to taxation in this District; so that the taxes raised upon Six Hundred and Eighty Thousand acres of land are now paid into the Treasuries of other. Districts, which, if paid for the use of this, would ᑢlace it in a respectable and independent situation.

They also beg leave to suggest that to subject all lands located in this Province to taxation, whether the owner thereof reside therein or not, would, they humbly conceive, be extremely beneficial to the Province in general.

Your Petitioners therefore humbly pray that Your Honorable House would be pleased to take this District into consideration, so far as relates to the present mode of paying taxes, and procure the repeal of so much of the aforesaid Act as directs the payment of the money raised by tax upon land into the Treasury of the District, where the owner of such land resides; and enact in lieu thereof that in future all land located, or that may be hereafter located, in this Province, shall be subject to taxation; whether the owner thereof is a resident of the Province or not, and that such land shall be rated and assessed in the District where it may be situated, and that the money raised thereon shall be paid to and for the use of such District.

And Your Petitioners, as in duty bound, will ever pray.

John Bostwick, Samuel Ryerse, J.P., Henry Bostwick, R. W. Dease, C.P., Thomas Welch, J.P., Peter Peeple, J.P., Nathan P. Barnham, J.P., Edward Watson, J.P., Elrick Crosby, Henry VanAllen, H. Alexander, John Williams, and One Hundred and Sixty-four others.

Then was read the Petition of the Inhabitants of the Township of Grimsby, which is as follows:—

To the Honorable the Knights, Burgesses and Citizens of the Province of Upper Canada in Parliament convened.

The Petition of some of the Freeholders, and all Inhabitants, Householders of the Town of Grimsby, and adjacent thereto, in the said Province, Sheweth,—

That by an Act passed in the Thirty-eighth year of His present Majesty George the Third, entitled "An Act to alter the method of performing Statute Duty on the Highways and Roads within this Province," your Petitioners humbly conceive themselves to be aggrieved.

That by the said Act, Statute Labour is to be performed in the following manner, viz.: That every Inhabitant, Householder, included or inserted in or upon the Assessment Roll of any Parish, Township, reported Township or place, shall, in proportion to the estimate of his real and personal property thereon, be taken, rated, and held liable to work on the Highways and Roads in each and every year as follows, that is to say. If his property be rated at not more than One Hundred Pounds, then his proportion of labor shall not exceed six days. If at more than One Hundred Pounds, and not more than Two Hundred Pounds, eight days. If at more than Two Hundred Pounds, and not more than Three Hundred Pounds, twelve days.

That Your Petitioners, under and by virtue of said Act, humbly think their labour on the Highways is very much out of proportion, there being no more days than twelve exacted from the Freeholder of considerable property, and he who is worth but Three Hundred Pounds.

That Your Petitioners, the Householders, humbly consider themselves in a very great degree burdened by the labor rated by the said Act, which amounts to six days, being half as much for the poor man, who does not own an acre of land, or a team to injure the roads, and whose whole property does not exceed Twenty Pounds, as the gentleman possessed of from Five to Ten Thousand Pounds.

Your Petitioners therefore hope Your Honors will take their cases into serious consideration, and use your endeavours to have such alterations and amendments in the said Act, in such manner as your Petitioners may be relieved, and do such other matters and things in the alteration and amendments as to Your Honors in Your wisdom shall seem meet.

And Your Petitioners will pray.

John Wolverton, Daniel Palmer, Smith Griffin, William Feligh, John Kennedy, George Hughes, and twenty-six others.

The Petition of the Inhabitants of the Township of Beasley was then read, which is as follows:—

To the Honorable the Legislature of the Province of Upper Canada.

The Petition of the undersigned Inhabitants of the Township of Brand, commonly called Beasley's Township, or Block No. 2.

Humbly Sheweth,—

That several of our Township inhabitors takes kegs and barrels full of spirits from the Distillers and trades with the Indians, which causes them to get drunk and lie about and not follow their hunting, and their young ones starving for hunger, going about begging and halloing for victuals before our doors like beasts, and at the same time often the old ones coming along and being drunk, scaring ourselves and our families by their bad behaviour.

And whereas it is known by us that a certain Abraham Stouffer, of our Township, was shot by a drunken Indian through his arm and other places, and was then in danger of his life; such sufferings causes us to petition to Your Honorable Assembly to take into consideration what is said, and prevent such trading by an Act.

And Your Petitioners, as in duty bound, will ever pray.

Beasley's Township, 2nd Jan., 1808.

John Shoop,

Joseph Barringer,

and Twenty-five others.

Mr. Rogers moved, seconded by Mr. Willcocks, that the amendments made by the Honorable Legislative Council, in and to an Act for the better regulation of Special Juries be now read. The said Bill was accordingly read for the first time as amended by the Honorable Legislative Council. Agreeable to the Order the said Bill was read for the second time.

On motion of Mr. Rogers, seconded by Mr. Nellis, the House resolved itself into a Committee to go into the consideration of the amendments made by the Honorable Legislative Council in and to the Act for the better regulation of Special Juries. Mr. Speaker left the Chair. Mr. Nellis was called to the Chair of the Committee.

Mr. Speaker resumed the Chair, and Mr. Nellis reported that the Committee had made a progress, and had directed him to ask for leave to sit again to-morrow. Ordered, that the Committee have leave to sit again to-morrow.

Mr. Rogers gave notice that he will move to-morrow, that the Militia Bill be read a second time.

Mr. Rogers moved, seconded by Mr. Howard, that the Rule of this House that requires one day's previous notice be discharged, so far as it prevents the Road Bill from being again committed, and that the House do now resolve itself into a Committee to go into the consideration of the said Bill.

Ordered, that the said Rule be now dispensed with, and that the House do now resolve itself into a Committee to go into the consideration of the said Bill. The House accordingly resolved itself into a Committee. Mr. Speaker left the Chair. Mr. Rogers took the Chair of the Committee.

Mr. Speaker resumed the Chair, and Mr. Rogers reported that the Committee had made a progress, and had directed him to ask for leave to sit again this day. Ordered, that the Committee have leave to sit again this day.

A Message from the Honorable Legislative Council by Mr. Baldwin, Master in Chancery,

Mr. Speaker,—

I am commanded by the Honorable the Legislative Council to inform this House that they have passed an Act sent up from this House, entitled " An Act to authorize the inhabitants of the County of Haldimand to hold Annual Meetings for the purpose of electing Parish and Town Officers," to which they have made several amendments, to which amendments they request the concurrence of this House in passing the same, and then he withdrew.

The House again resolved itself into a Committee to go into the further consideration of the Road Bill. Mr. Speaker left the Chair. Mr. Rogers again took the Chair of the Committee.

Mr. Speaker resumed the Chair, and Mr. Rogers reported that the Committee had made a progress, and had directed him to ask for leave to sit again to-morrow. Ordered, that the Committee have leave to sit again to-morrow.

Captain Cowan rose up in his place, and did inform the House that an Honorable Member (W. Willcocks) had made use of language out of doors derogatory to the honor and integrity of this Honorable House, and nearly in these words: "That the Members of the House of Assembly dared not to proceed in the prosecution they had commenced against him. He was sorry they did not continue it; it would have given him an opportunity of proving they had been bribed by General Hunter; and that he had a Member of the House ready to come forward and give testimony to that effect." The Gentlemen that were present were Titus Simons, Samuel S. Willmott, Surveyor of Lands, and Dr. James Glennon, Practitioner of Physic in this Town.

Upon motion of Mr. Sherwood, seconded by Mr. Clench, ordered, that the House do now resolve itself into a Committee of Privileges of the Whole House, to take into its consideration the said information.

The House accordingly resolved itself into said Committee. Mr. Speaker left the Chair. Mr. Swazey was called to the Chair of the Committee.

Mr. Speaker resumed the Chair, and Mr. Swazey reported to the House that the Committee had come to several Resolutions on the subject referred, which they had directed him to report to the House whenever it would be pleased to receive the same. Ordered that the report be now received, and he read the report in his place, and, having delivered the same at the Table, it was again read throughout by the Clerk, and is as follows:—

Resolved, that it is the opinion of this Committee that the expressions said to be made use of by Mr. Joseph Willcocks are false, slanderous and highly derogatory to the dignity of this House.

Resolved, that it is the opinion of the Committee that the Speaker be authorized to send for any witness that he may think necessary, to be examined at the Bar of this House, touching the information given to this House by Captain Cowan, a Member of this House, against Joseph Willcocks.

Resolved, that it is the opinion of the Committee that a day be fixed by the House for the trial of Mr. Joseph Willcocks, a Member of this House.

The Solicitor General, seconded by Captain Cowan, moved that the House do concur with the Committee in their Resolutions just reported. The House accordingly concurred in the said Resolutions. Ordered. that the Clerk will give Mr. Willcocks a copy of the paper read by Captain Cowan. Captain Cowan moved, seconded by Mr. Solicitor General, that Saturday next be appointed for the day of trial of Mr. Joseph Willcocks. Ordered accordingly. Mr. Willcocks moved, seconded by Mr. Rogers, that he be permitted to remain in his place during his trial, and that he be also permitted to put such interrogatories to the evidences as may seem to him necessary, which was ordered accordingly.

Mr Mallory moved, seconded by Mr. Washburn, for leave to bring in a Bill on Monday next to alter and better regulate the present mode of assessing Wild Lands in the District of London. Accordingly leave was given.

Mr. Washburn moved, seconded by Mr. Swazey, for leave to bring in a Bill to-morrow to disenable any Judge of the Court of King's Bench or Common Pleas, or any Judge of the District Courts, from being a Member of the House of Assembly in this Province. Leave was granted accordingly.

On motion of Mr. Washburn, seconded by Mr. Dorland, the House adjourned.

Friday, 19th February, 1808.

Prayers were read.

Read for the first time, the amendments made by the Honorable the Legislative Council in and to a Bill entitled "An Act to authorize the inhabitants of the County of Haldimand to hold Annual Meetings for the purpose of electing Town and Parish Officers."

Read for the second time, the Bill for holding Special Sessions of the Peace, and a Court of Requests in the Town of Saint Joseph's, in the Western District. Mr. Clench then moved, seconded by Mr. McGregor, that the House do now resolve itself into a Committee to go into the consideration of the Bill for establishing a Court of Special Sessions and a Court of Requests at Saint Joseph's, on the Island of Saint Joseph's. The House accordingly resolved itself into a Committee. Mr. Speaker left the Chair. Mr. Mallory was called to the Chair of the Committee.

Mr. Speaker resumed the Chair, and Mr. Mallory reported that the Committee had made a progress, and had directed him to ask for leave to sit again to-morrow. Ordered, that the Committee have leave to sit again to-morrow.

Agreeable to the Order of the Day, the House resolved itself into a Committee to go into the consideration of the amendments made by the Honorable the Legislative Council to an Act for the better regulation of Special Juries. Mr. Speaker left the Chair. Mr. Nellis was called to the Chair of the Committee.

Mr. Speaker resumed the Chair, and Mr. Nellis reported that the Committee had gone through the consideration of the said amendments, to which they concurred, which he was directed to report to the House whenever it should be pleased to receive the same. The House resolved that the report be now received, and that the amendments be adopted. Mr. Sherwood, seconded by Mr. Nellis, moved that Messrs. Rogers and Swazey do inform the Honorable the Legislative Council that this House have concurred with the amendments made by them in and to an Act for the better regulation of Special Juries, which was ordered accordingly. Mr. Speaker,—

We are commanded by the Commons House of Assembly to acquaint this Honorable House, that it has concurred in adopting the amendments made by the Legislative Council, in and to the Act entitled "An Act for the better regulation of Special Juries."

                                                    (Signed) ALEXANDER MCDONELL,
Commons House of Assembly,   Speaker.
19th February, 1808.

Mr. Rogers then moved, seconded by the Solicitor General, that the Bill to. explain, amend and reduce into one Act of Parliament the several laws now in force, relative to the raising and training of the Militia of this Province be now read for the second time. The said Bill was accordingly read for the second time. Mr. Rogers moved, seconded by Mr. Nellis, that the House do now resolve itself into a Committee to go into the consideration of the Militia Bill. The House accordingly resolved itself into a Committee to go into the consideration of the said Bill. Mr. Speaker left the Chair. Captain Cowan was called to the Chair of the Committee.

Mr. Speaker resumed the Chair and Captain Cowan reported that the Committee had made a progress, and had directed him to ask for leave to sit again on Monday next. Ordered, that the Committee have leave to sit again on Monday next.

Agreeably to the Order of the Day, the House resolved itself into a Committee to go into the further consideration of the Road Bill. Mr. Speaker left the Chair. Mr. Rogers took the Chair of the Committee.

Mr. Speaker resumed the Chair, and Mr. Rogers reported that the Committee had gone through the consideration of the said Bill, to which they had made several amendments, which he was directed to report to the House whenever it should be pleased to receive the same. Ordered, that the Report be now received.

Mr. Mallory then moved, seconded by Mr. Dorland, that the Road Bill be engrossed, and read for the third time on Monday next. Ordered accordingly.

Mr. Washburn moved, seconded by Mr. Dorland, that so much of the Order of the Day as relates to the bringing in a Bill this day to exclude the Judges of the Court of King's Bench, Common Pleas, and the District Courts from having a seat in the House of Assembly be discharged, and that he have leave to bring in the same on Monday next. The Order was accordingly discharged, and leave given to bring in the said Bill on Monday next.

Mr. Solicitor General gave notice that he will move to-morrow for leave to read for the first time a Bill for the more just admeasurement of Firewood within the Town and Township of York.

Mr. Willcocks moved, seconded by Mr. Mallory, for leave to bring in a Bill on Thursday next to amend an Act passed in the Forty-seventh year of His Majesty's Reign, entitled "An Act to establish Public Schools in each and every District of this Province." Leave was accordingly granted.

On motion of the Solicitor General, seconded by Mr. Swazey, the House adjourned.

Saturday, 20th February, 1808.

Prayers were read.

Captain Cowan, one of the Messengers named to carry up to the Honorable the Legislative Council the Act to continue an Act passed in the Thirty-third year of His Majesty's Reign, entitled "An Act to provide for the appointment of Returning Officers of the several Counties within this Province," reported that they had carried up the said Act and did request their concurrence in passing the same.

Mr. Rogers, first named to carry up to the Honorable the Legislative Council the Message from this House of yesterday, reported that they had carried up the same.

Mr. Mallory moved, seconded by Mr. Dorland, that so much of the Order of the Day, as relates to the bringing in a Bill respecting the Public School in the

District of London, be discharged, and that leave be given him to bring in the same on Tuesday next. Accordingly so much of the Order of the Day was discharged, and leave was given him to bring in the same on Tuesday next.

Mr. Speaker informed the House that agreeable to the Order of this House he had issued his summons, commanding the attendance of Titus Simons, Samuel S. Willmott, Surveyor of Lands, and Dr. Glennon, Practitioner of Physic, in the Town of York, at the Bar of this House this day, at ten o'clock in the forenoon, to give evidence touching the information now before this House respecting Joseph Willcocks, one of its Members. On motion of Mr. Solicitor General, seconded by Captain Cowan, ordered, that the proceedings of this House on the Eighteenth instant, relating to Joseph Willcocks, one of its Members, be now read. The proceedings were accordingly read. Dr. Glennon was then called to the Bar, to give evidence touching the charges exhibited against Joseph Willcocks, a Member of this House. Samuel S. Willmott was next called to the Bar, to give testimony touching the charges exhibited against Joseph Willcocks, a Member of this House. The evidence on the part of the House was closed. Mr. Willcocks, by permission, cross-examined the witnesses. Mr. Willcocks moved, seconded by Mr. Sherwood, that he may be permitted to call such witnesses in his behalf as may seem to him necessary. Permission was accordingly given him to examine such evidence as he thought necessary. After the evidence on the part of Mr. Willcocks had been gone through, Captain Cowan moved, seconded by Mr. Sherwood, that it is the opinion of this House that Joseph Willcocks is guilty of the charge alleged against him. The House unanimously resolved the same. Captain Cowan then moved, seconded by Mr. Sherwood, that Joseph Willcocks be taken into the custody of the Sergeant at Arms and be committed to the Common Gaol of this District. Resolved unanimously, that Joseph Willcocks be committed to the Common Gaol of the District, and that the Speaker do issue his warrant for that purpose. Mr. Speaker then read the Warrant which he signed by order of the House, and is as follows:—

Alexander McDonell, Esquire, Speaker of the Honorable the Commons House of Assembly.

To the Sheriff of the Home District, GREETING.

By virtue of the power and authority in me vested by the Honorable the Commons House of Assembly, you are hereby ordered and required to receive into the Common Gaol of your District the body of Joseph Willcocks, and him safely to keep until discharged by due course of law, the said Joseph Willcocks having been convicted of a contempt of the Commons House of Assembly.

Given under my hand and seal at York,   (Signed) ALEXANDER McDONELL,
    this 20th day of February, 1808.   Speaker.

Mr. Clench moved, seconded by Mr. Nellis, that so much of the Order of this Day as relates to the second reading of the Bill to establish Courts of Quarter Sessions and Requests at Saint Joseph's, on the Island of Saint Joseph's, be discharged, and that leave be given to bring the same in on Monday next. The order was discharged, and leave was given to bring the said Bill in on Monday next.

Mr. Clench gave notice that he will on Monday next move, that this House do then go into Committee of the Whole, to go into the further consideration of the Bill for increasing the representation of the Commons of this Province in Parliament.

Mr. Clench gave notice that he will on Monday next move, that this House do then resolve itself into a Committee, to go into the further consideration of the Bill for regulating the practice of Physic, Surgery and Midwifery within this Province.

The Solicitor General gave notice that he will move on Monday next, that the House do then resolve itself into a Committee to go into further consideration of the Land Commission Bill.

Read for the first time the Bill for the more just admeasurement of Firewood within the Town and Township of York. On motion of Mr. Solicitor General, seconded by Captain Cowan, ordered, that the said Bill be read for the second time on Monday next.

Read, a Petition form the Inhabitants of York, Home District, which is as follows :—

To the Honorable the Commons of Upper Canada in Parliament assembled.

The Petition of the Undersigned Inhabitants of York, Humbly Showeth,—

That Your Petitioners, desirous of improving the Streets in the aforesaid Town of York, and whereas if it may be thought expedient to alter the present mode of applying the Statute Duty on the Highways and Roads, and for the better amending and keeping in repair the streets in the aforesaid Town of York; Your Petitioners therefore pray that for each and every Householder bounding on any street in the aforesaid Town shall be compelled to make good and keep in repair one equal half of the street adjoining his lot or premises, and for the better performance of the same the Overseer of Highways at all times shall see that this duty be faithfully done.

And your Petitioners, as in duty bound, will ever pray.

William Knott, Patrick Hartney, Paul Marian, Daniel Laughlin, Thomas Hamilton, Benjamin Cozens, John VanTanter, Daniel Tiers, and twenty-one others.

On motion of Captain Cowan, seconded by Mr. McLean, the House adjourned until Monday next.

Monday, 22nd February, 1808.

Prayers were read.

The Sergeant-at-Arms reported that in obedience to the command of this Honorable House he delivered Joseph Willcocks, Esquire, Member representing West York, first Lincoln, and Haldimand, into the custody of the Sheriff of this District, and also the Speaker's Warrant to him directed.

Mr. Mallory moved, seconded by Mr. Nellis, that so much of the Order of this Day as relates to the Bill for the better regulation of rating and assessing Wild Lands in the District of London be discharged. Ordered accordingly.

Read for the third time, as engrossed, the Bill for laying out Public Highways and Roads in this Province. On motion of Mr. Howard, seconded by Mr. Dorland the House resolved itself into a Committee to go into the further consideration of the said Bill. Mr. Speaker left the Chair. Mr. Rogers took the Chair of the Committee. Mr. Speaker resumed the Chair, and Mr. Rogers reported that the Committee had made a progress, and had directed him to ask for leave to sit again this day. Leave was accordingly granted.

A Message from the Honorable the Legislative Council by Mr. Baldwin, Master in Chancery.

Mr. Speaker,—

I am commanded by the Honorable the Legislative Council to inform this House that they have passed an Act, sent up from this House, to amend certain parts of an Act passed in the thirty-third year of His Majesty's Reign, entitled "An Act to confirm and make valid certain marriages heretofore contracted in the Country now comprised within the Province of Upper Canada," to which they have made some amendments, to which amendments they request the concurrence of this House in passing the same.

Also an Act for building a Court House and Gaol in the Township of Eliza-bethtown in the District of Johnstown, to which they have made several amend-ments and to which amendments they desire the concurrence of this House in pass-ing the same.

And also that they have passed an Act, sent up from this House, entitled "An Act to continue an Act passed in the thirty-third year of His Majesty's Reign, entitled, 'An Act to provide for the appointment of Returning Officers for the several Counties within this Province," without any amendments.

And then he withdrew.

The House again resolved itself into a Committee to go into the further consideration of the Bill for establishing Public Highways and Roads throughout this Province. Mr. Speaker left the chair. Mr. Rogers again took the Chair of the Committee.

. Mr. Speaker resumed the Chair. and Mr. Rogers reported that the Committee had made a progress and had directed him to ask for leave to sit again to-morrow. Leave was accordingly granted.

Read for the first time, the amendments made by the Honorable the Legis-lative Council to the Act for erecting a Court House and Gaol at Elizabethtown, in the District of Johnstown. Mr. Solicitor General, seconded by Mr. McLean, moved that the said Bill be now read for the second time. The said Bill was accordingly read for the second time. On motion of Mr. Solicitor General, seconded by Mr. Sherwood, the House resolved itself into a Committee to go into the consideration of the amendments made by the Honorable the Legislative Coun-cil in and to the Johnstown Court House and Gaol Bill. Mr. Speaker left the Chair. Mr. Swazey was called to the chair of the Committee.

Mr. Speaker resumed the Chair, and Mr. Swazey reported that the Committee had gone through the consideration of the said amendments, and that he was directed to report to the House whenever it should be pleased to receive the same, that the amendments as made by the Honorable Legislative Council be adopted. The House accordingly resolved that the amendments as made by the Honorable Legislative Council be adopted.

On motion of Mr. Solicitor General, seconded by Mr. McLean, the amend-ments made by the Honorable Legislative Council to an Act to confirm and make valid certain Marriages heretofore contracted in the county now comprised within the Province of Upper Canada was read for the first time. Mr. Rogers then moved, seconded by the Solicitor General, that the amendments made by the Honorable Legislative Council to the Marriage Act be read a second time to-morrow, which was ordered accordingly.

Mr. Washburn moved, seconded by Mr. Sherwood, that so much of the Order of the Day as relates to the bringing in a Bill to prevent the Judges of the Court of King's Bench, the Judges of the Court of Common Pleas, and District Judges, from being eligible to hold a seat in the House of Assembly of this Province, be discharged, and that he have leave to bring in the same on any other day during the present Session of Parliament, which was ordered accordingly.

Read for the second time, the Bill for establishing Courts of Quarter Sessions and Requests in the Island of Saint Joseph's. Mr. Clench moved, seconded by Mr. McGregor, that the House do now resolve itself into a Committee to go into the consideration of the Bill for establishing Courts of Quarter Sessions and Requests at Saint Joseph's, in the island of Saint Joseph's. The House accordingly resolved itself into a Committee. Mr. Speaker left the Chair. Mr. Crysler was called to the Chair of the Committee.

Mr. Speaker resumed the Chair, and Mr. Crysler reported that the Committee had gone through the consideration of the said Bill, to which they had made several amendments, which he was directed to report to the House whenever it should be pleased to receive same.

Ordered, that the Report be now received, and that the amendments be adopted. The House accordingly resolved that the amendments made by the Honorable Legislative Council to the said Act be adopted.

Mr. Clench then moved, seconded by Mr. Sherwood, that the House do now resolve itself into a Committee to go into the further consideration of the Bill for regulating the practice of Physic, Surgery, and Midwifery in this Province. The House accordingly resolved itself into a Committee to go into the consideration of the said Bill. Mr. Speaker left the Chair. Mr. Crysler took the Chair of the Committee.

Mr. Speaker resumed the Chair, and Mr. Crysler reported that the Committee had made a progress, and had directed him to ask for leave to sit again to-morrow. Leave was granted accordingly.

Mr. McGregor, seconded by Mr. Sherwood, moved for leave to bring in a Bill to-morrow to amend and keep in repair the Public Highways and Roads through a part of the Counties of Essex and Kent, in the Western District. Leave was accordingly granted.

Mr. Sherwood moved, seconded by Mr. Rogers, for leave to bring in a Bill to-morrow to regulate the Fees to be taken in the Court of King's Bench. Accordingly it was given.

Mr. Rogers, seconded by Mr. Sherwood, moved that so much of the Order of the Day as has not been proceeded upon remain as part of the Order of the Day for to-morrow, and that this House do now adjourn until twelve o'clock at noon to-morrow.

The House accordingly discharged the Order of the Day, and ordered that the House meet to-morrow at twelve o'clock noon.

Tuesday, 23rd February, 1808.

Prayers were read.

Read for the first time, the Bill to regulate the Fees to be taken in the Court of King's Bench. Mr. Sherwood then moved, seconded by Mr. Dorland, that the Bill to regulate the Fees to be taken in the Court of King's Bench be read a second time to-morrow, which was ordered accordingly.

Agreeably to the Order of the Day, the House resolved itself into a Committee to go into the further consideration of the Bill for laying out and establishing Public Highways and Roads throughout this Province. Mr. Speaker left the Chair. Mr. Rogers took the chair of the Committee.

Mr. Speaker resumed the Chair, and Mr. Rogers reported that the Committee had gone through the consideration of the said Bill, to which they had made several amendments, which he was directed to report to the House whenever it shall be pleased to receive the same. Ordered, that the Report be now received. The Report was accordingly received and accepted.

Mr. Howard then moved, seconded by Mr. Nellis, that the Bill for establishing Public Highways and Roads throughout this Province be read for the third time to-morrow, which was ordered accordingly.

Mr. Rogers then moved, seconded by Mr. Nellis, that the Solicitor General and Mr. Howard do inform the Honorable the Legislative Council that this House have concurred in adopting the amendments made by them in and to the Johnstown Court House and Gaol Act. Ordered accordingly.

Agreeably to the Order of the Day the House resolved itself into a Committee to go into the further consideration of the Militia Bill. Mr. Speaker left the Chair. Capt. Cowan took the Chair of the Committee.

Mr. Speaker resumed the Chair, and Capt. Cowan reported that the Committee had made a progress, and had directed him to ask for leave to sit again to-morrow. Ordered, that the Committee have leave to sit again to-morrow.

Agreeably to the Order of the Day, the House resolved itself into a Committee to go into the consideration of the Bill to regulate the practice of Physic, Surgery, and Midwifery. Mr. Speaker left the Chair. Mr. Crysler was called to the chair of the Committee.

Mr. Speaker resumed the Chair, and Mr. Crysler reported that the Committee had gone through the consideration of the said Bill, to which they had made several amendments, to which he was directed to request the concurrence of this House. The House accordingly concurred in the said amendments.

Mr. Clench then moved, seconded by Mr. Sherwood, that the Bill for regulating the practice of Physic, Surgery and Midwifery in this Province be engrossed, and read a third time to-morrow. The said Bill was ordered to be engrossed and read a third time to-morrow.

Read for the first time, the Bill for keeping in repair the Public Highways and Roads leading through the Counties of Essex and Kent, in the Western District. Mr. McGregor then moved, seconded by Mr. Sherwood, that the said Bill be read for the second time to-morrow. The said Bill was accordingly ordered to be read the second time to-morrow.

On motion of Mr. McGregor, seconded by Capt. Cowan, ordered, that so much of the Order of this Day as has not been proceeded upon remain as part of the Order of the Day for to-morrow.

On motion of Mr. Clench, seconded by Mr. Sherwood, the House adjourned until eleven o'clock in the forenoon to-morrow.

Wednesday, 24th February, 1808.

Prayers were read.

Read for the third time, as engrossed, the Bill for regulating the practice of Physic, Surgery and Midwifery throughout this Province. On motion of Mr. Clench, seconded by Mr. Sherwood, the said Bill was ordered to be recommitted.

The House accordingly resolved itself into a Committee to go into the further consideration of the said Bill. Mr. Speaker left the Chair. Mr. Crysler was called to the Chair of the Committee.

Mr. Speaker resumed the Chair, and Mr. Crysler reported that the Committee had made a progress, and that he was directed to ask for leave to sit again tomorrow. Accordingly leave was granted to sit again to-morrow. The Solicitor General, one of the messengers named to carry up to the Honorable Legislative Council a Message of this House, reported that they had carried up the same.

Mr. Howard, seconded by Mr. Nellis, moved that the Order of the Day, so far as relates to the Court of Requests Bill, be discharged, which was ordered accordingly.

Agreeably to the Order of the Day the House resolved itself into a Committee to go into the consideration of the Bill for increasing the representation of the Commons of this Province in Parliament. Mr. Speaker left the Chair. Mr. Crysler was called to the Chair of the Committee.

Mr. Speaker resumed the Chair, and Mr. Crysler reported that the Committee had made a progress, and had directed him to ask for leave to sit again to-morrow.

Agreeably to the Order of the Day the House resolved itself into a Committee of the Whole, to go into the further consideration of the Bill for securing Titles to Lands in this Province. Mr. Speaker left the Chair. Mr. Washburn was called to the Chair of the Committee.

Mr. Speaker resumed the Chair, and Mr. Washburn reported that the Committee had made a progress, and had directed him to ask for leave to sit again to-morrow. Leave was accordingly granted.

Read for the second time, the amendments made by the Honorable Legislative Council in and to an Act, sent up from this House, entitled "An Act to amend certain parts of an Act passed in the Thirty-third year of His Majesty's Reign, entitled 'An Act to confirm and make valid certain Marriages heretofore contracted in the country now comprised within the Province of Upper Canada. On motion of Mr. Solicitor General, seconded by Mr. Rogers, the House resolved itself into a Committee, to go into the consideration of the amendments made by the Honorable Legislative Council in and to the said Act. Mr. Speaker left the Chair. Mr. Nellis was called to the Chair of the Committee.

Mr. Speaker resumed the Chair, and Mr. Nellis reported that the Committee had made a progress, and that he was directed to acquaint the House that the Committee had recommended that a Conference be held with the Legislative Council, on the subject matter of the amendments made by them to an Act entitled "An Act to confirm and make valid certain Marriages heretofore contracted in this Province," which Report was accepted. Then Mr. Sherwood moved, seconded by Capt. Cowan, that the Solicitor General, Messrs. Rogers, Washburn and McLean, be a Committee to request a Conference with the Honorable Legislative Council on the amendments made by them in and to the Act entitled "An Act to confirm and make valid certain Marriages heretofore contracted in the country now comprised within the Province of Upper Canada," and also that they be a Committee from this House to hold the Conference therewith. The same was ordered accordingly.

Mr. Speaker,

The House of Assembly request a Conference with the Honorable Legislative Council, on the subject matter of amendments made by them in and to an Act, sent up from this House, entitled "An Act to amend certain parts of an Act

passed in the Thirty-third year of His Majesty's Reign, entitled ' An Act to confirm and make valid certain Marriages heretofore contracted in the country now
comprised within the Province of Upper Canada.' "
                                (Signed)   ALEXR. MCDONELL, Speaker.
Commons House of Assembly,
    24th February, 1808.
    Read for the second time, the Bill for establishing the Fees to be taken in the
Court of King's Bench.
    On motion of Mr. Sherwood, seconded by Capt. Cowan, the House resolved
itself into a Committee to go into the consideration of the said Bill. Mr. Speaker
left the Chair. Mr. McGregor was called to the Chair of the Committee.
    Mr. Speaker resumed the Chair, and Mr. McGregor reported that the Com-
mittee had made a progress, and had directed him to ask for leave to sit again
to-morrow. Leave was granted accordingly.
    On motion of Mr. Howard, seconded by Mr. Nellis, ordered, that so much of
the Order of this Day as has not been proceeded upon remain as a part of the
Order of the Day for to-morrow.
    On motion of Mr. Dorland, seconded by Mr. Nellis, the House adjourned until
twelve o'clock at noon to-morrow.

                        Thursday, 25th February, 1808.

    Prayers were read.
    Read for the third time, as engrossed, the Bill for establishing Public High-
ways and Roads throughout this Province. On motion of Mr. McLean, seconded
by Capt. Cowan, the House resolved itself into a Committee to go into the further
consideration of the said Bill. Mr. Speaker left the Chair. Mr. Rogers was called
to the Chair of the Committee.
    Mr. Speaker resumed the Chair, and Mr. Rogers reported that the Committee
had made a progress, and had directed him to ask for leave to sit again to-morrow.
Ordered, that the Committee have leave to sit again to-morrow.
    Agreeably to the Order of the Day, the House resolved itself into a Committee
to go into the further consideration of the Militia Bill. Mr. Speaker left the Chair.
Captain Cowan took the Chair of the Committee.
    Mr. Speaker resumed the Chair, and Captain Cowan reported that the Com-
mittee had made a progress, and had directed him to ask for leave to sit again
to-morrow. Ordered, that the Committee have leave to sit again to-morrow.
    Mr. Solicitor General, seconded by Mr. Rogers, moved that so much of the
Order of this Day as has not been proceeded upon do make a part of the Order of
the Day to-morrow, which was ordered accordingly.
    Mr. Solicitor General moved, seconded by Captain Cowan, for leave to bring
in a Bill on Saturday next to alter and amend an Act for granting to His Majesty
a certain sum of money for the further encouragement of the growth and cultivation of Hemp within this Province, and the exportation thereof. Leave was given
accordingly.
    Mr. Clench gave notice that he will move to-morrow that the Bill for establish-
ing Courts of Quarter Sessions at Saint Joseph's, in the Island of St. Joseph's, be
engrossed and read a third time.
    On motion of Mr. Clench, seconded by Mr. Nellis, the House adjourned.

Friday, 26th February, 1808.

Prayers were read.

Read for the second time, the Bill for establishing Public Highways and Roads through the Counties of Essex and Kent in the Western District. Mr. McGregor moved, seconded by Mr. Dorland, that the House do now resolve itself into a Committee, to go into the consideration of the said Bill. · The House accordingly resolved itself into a Committee to go into the consideration of the said Bill. Mr. Speaker left the Chair. Mr. Solicitor General was called to the Chair of the Committee.

Mr. Speaker resumed the Chair, and Mr. Solicitor General reported that the Committee had gone through the consideration of the said Bill without any amendment, which he was directed to report to the House whenever it should be pleased to receive the same. Ordered, that the Report be now received. The Report was accordingly received and accepted.

Mr. McGregor then moved, seconded by Mr. Rogers, that the Bill for establishing Public Roads and Highways through the Counties of Essex and Kent be engrossed, and read a third time to-morrow, which was ordered accordingly.

Mr. Nellis moved, seconded by Mr. Mallory, that the Order of the Day so far as respects the School Bill be discharged. Accordingly the Order was discharged.

Agreeably to the Order of the Day the House resolved itself into a Committee to go into the further consideration of the Bill for regulating the practice of Physic, Surgery and Midwifery in this Province. Mr. Speaker left the Chair. Mr. Crysler took the Chair of the Committee.

Mr. Speaker resumed the Chair, and Mr. Crysler reported that the Committee had gone through the Consideration of the said Bill, to which they had made several amendments, which amendments he was directed to report to the House whenever it shall be pleased to receive the same. A division thereupon took place, the names being called for, they were taken down, and are as follows:—

Yeas:	Nays:
MESSRS. DORLAND	MESSRS. ROGERS
SOLICITOR GENERAL	SWAZEY
McLEAN	NELLIS
COWAN	MALLORY
SHERWOOD	
McGREGOR	
CLENCH	
CRYSLER	
HOWARD	
WASHBURN	

The same was carried in the affirmative by a majority of six. The Report was then received and accepted. Mr. Clench moved, seconded by Mr. Sherwood, that the said Bill be engrossed, and read a third time to-morrow, which was ordered accordingly.

Agreeably to the Order of the Day the House resolved itself into a Committee to go into the consideration of the Bill for increasing the representation of the Commons of this Province in Parliament. Mr. Speaker left the Chair. Mr. Howard was called to the Chair of the Committee.

Mr. Speaker resumed the Chair, and Mr. Howard reported that the Committee had made a progress, and had directed him to ask for leave to sit again to-morrow. Ordered, that the Committee have leave to sit again to-morrow.

Agreeably to the Order of the Day the House resolved itself into a Committee to go into the consideration of the Bill for securing Titles to Lands in this Province. Mr. Speaker left the Chair. Mr. Washburn was called to the Chair of the Committee.

Mr. Speaker resumed the Chair, and Mr. Washburn reported that the Committee had made a progress, and had directed him to ask for leave to sit again this day. Leave was accordingly granted.

A Message from the Honorable the Legislative Council by Mr. Baldwin, Master in Chancery.

Mr. Speaker,

The Honorable the Legislative Council inform the House of Assembly that they accede to their request of a Conference upon the subject matter of the amendments made by them in and to an Act, sent up from this House, entitled " An Act to amend certain parts of an Act passed in the Thirty-third year of His Majesty's Reign entitled ' An Act to confirm and make valid certain Marriages heretofore contracted in the country now comprised within the Province of Upper Canada,' " and that a Committee of this House will be ready to confer with them thereupon in the Legislative Council Chamber immediately after the rising of this House to-day.

Legislative Council Chamber,   (Signed)   THO'S SCOTT,
Friday, 26th February, 1808.   Speaker.

And then he withdrew.

The House again resolved itself into a Committee to go into the further consideration of the Bill to secure Titles to Lands in this Province. Mr. Speaker left the Chair. Mr. Washburn again took the Chair of the Committee.

Mr. Speaker resumed the Chair, and Mr. Washburn reported that the Committee had gone through the consideration of the said Bill, to which they had made several amendments, which he was directed to report to the House whenever it shall be pleased to receive the same. Resolved, that the Report be now received and accepted.

Mr. Sherwood moved, seconded by Captain Cowan, that the Land Commission Bill be engrossed, and read a third time to-morrow. Ordered accordingly.

Agreeably to the Order of the Day the House resolved itself into a Committee to go into the consideration of the Bill for regulating the Fees to be taken in the Court of King's Bench. Mr. Speaker left the Chair. Mr. McGregor was called to the Chair of the Committee.

Mr. Speaker resumed the Chair, and Mr. McGregor reported that the Committee had gone through the consideration of the said Bill, to which they had made several amendments, which he was directed to report to the House whenever it shall be pleased to receive the same. Ordered, that the Report be now received. The Report was accordingly received and accepted. Mr. Sherwood then moved, seconded by Captain Cowan, that the said Bill be engrossed, and read for the third time to-morrow, which was ordered accordingly.

Mr. Rogers moved, seconded by Mr. Clench, that Mr. Sherwood be added to the Committee appointed by this House to confer with the Honorable the Legislative Council, on the subject matter of the amendments made by them in and to the Marriage Act. Ordered accordingly.

The Solicitor General, seconded by Captain Cowan, moved that so much of the Order of this Day as directs the Militia Bill to be recommitted this day be now discharged, and that it remain first on the Order of the Day to-morrow for that purpose, which passed in the negative.

Then Mr. Rogers moved, seconded by Mr. Sherwood, that so much of the Order of the Day as relates to the going into Committee on the Road, Militia, and School Bills, be discharged, and that the same be committed to-morrow. Accordingly the said Bills were discharged and ordered to stand as a part of the Order of the Day to-morrow.

Mr. Clench moved, seconded by Mr. McGregor, for leave to bring in a Bill on Monday next to empower the Commissioners of the Peace to regulate a Police in several Towns within this Province. Leave was accordingly granted.

On motion of Captain Cowan, seconded by Mr. Dorland, the House adjourned.

Saturday, 27th February, 1808.

Prayers were read.

Messrs. Rogers, Sherwood, Washburn and McLean reported:—

Mr. Speaker,

The Committee of the House of Assembly, appointed to confer with the Honorable Legislative Council on the amendments made by them to the Bill to confirm certain Marriages contracted in this Province, have met the Committee of the Honorable Legislative Council, and the only reason given by them for making the amendments, Press the 4th, line the 5th, was that it was improper to provide for irregular Marriages heretofore contracted, as it would encourage irregularities in the future. You Committee thought that the state of the country required that all marriages heretofore contracted should be confirmed.

By Order of the Committee.

(Signed D. McG. ROGERS.

Agreeably to the Order of the Day the House resolved itself into a Committee to go into the further consideration of the Bill for establishing Public Highways and Roads throughout this Province. Mr. Speaker left the Chair. Mr. Rogers took the Chair of the Committee.

Mr. Speaker resumed the Chair, and Mr. Rogers reported that the Committee had gone through the consideration of the said Bill, to which they had made several amendments, which he was directed to report to the House whenever it should be pleased to receive the same. The House then resolved that the said Report be now received and accepted. Mr. Howard moved, seconded by Mr. Dorland, that the Bill for establishing Public Highways and Roads throughout this Province be engrossed, and read a third time on Monday next. Ordered accordingly.

Agreeably to the Order of the Day the House resolved itself into a Committee to go into the further consideration of the Militia Bill. Mr. Speaker left the Chair. Captain Cowan took the Chair of the Committee.

Mr. Speaker resumed the Chair, and Captain Cowan reported that the Committee had made a progress, and had directed him to ask for leave to sit again this day. Leave was accordingly granted.

A written Message from the Honorable the Legislative Council by Mr. Baldwin, Master in Chancery.

17 A.

Mr. Speaker,

The Honorable the Legislative Council adhere to their amendments to an Act entitled " An Act to amend certain parts of an Act passed in the Thirty-third year of His Majesty's Reign, entitled 'An Act to confirm and make valid certain Marriages heretofore contracted in the Country now comprised within the Province of Upper Canada.' "

Legislative Council Chamber,   (Signed)   THO'S SCOTT,
February 27th, 1808.   Speaker. -

And then he withdrew.

The House again resolved itself into a Committee to go into further consideration of the Militia Bill. Mr. Speaker left the Chair. Captain Cowan again took the Chair of the Committee.

Mr. Speaker resumed the Chair, and Captain Cowan reported that the Committee had made a progress, and had directed him to ask for leave to sit again on Monday next. Ordered, that the Committee have leave to sit again on Monday next.

Mr. Mallory moved, seconded by the Solicitor General, that so much of the Order of the Day as relates to the London District School Bill be discharged, and that he have leave to bring in the same on Monday next. The said Order was discharged, and leave given to bring in the said Bill on Monday next.

Read for the first time, the Bill to encourage the growth and cultivation of Hemp in this Province. Mr. Solicitor General, seconded by Captain Cowan, moved that the Bill for the growth and cultivation of Hemp be read a second time on Monday next. Ordered accordingly.

Read for the third time, as engrossed, the Bill for regulating Statute Labour in the Counties of Essex and Kent, in the Western District. Mr. McGregor moved, seconded by Mr. Sherwood, that the Bill do pass, and that the title be " An Act for the better regulation of Statute Labour in the Counties of Essex and Kent, in the Western District." The Bill accordingly passed, and was signed by the Speaker. Mr. Rogers then moved, seconded by Mr. Howard, that Captain Cowan and Mr. Crysler do carry up to the Honorable the Legislative Council the Act for the better regulating the Statute Labour in the Counties of Essex and Kent, in the Western District, and request their concurrence thereto, which was ordered accordingly.

Read for the third time, as engrossed, the Bill for regulating the practice of Physic, Surgery and Midwifery in this Province. Mr. Clench moved, seconded by Mr. Dorland, that the Bill do pass, and that the title be "An Act to regulate the practice of Physic, Surgery and Midwifery in this Province." The Bill then passed, and was signed by the Speaker. Mr. Washburn then moved, seconded by Mr. Nelson, that Messrs. Clench and Dorland do carry up to the Honorable the Legislative Council the Act to regulate the practice of Physic, Surgery and Midwifery within this Province, and do request their concurrence thereto. Ordered accordingly.

Mr. Clench, seconded by Mr. Dorland, moved that so much of the Order of the day as relates to the Bill for increasing the representation of the Commons of this Province in Parliament be discharged, and that it remain as a part of the Order of the Day for Monday next. The said Order was discharged accordingly, and, ordered, that the same shall remain as a part of the Order of the Day for Monday next.

Read for the third time, as engrossed, the Bill the better to ascertain and secure the Titles to Lands in this Province. The Bill then passed, and was signed by the Speaker.

Mr. Sherwood, seconded by Mr. Rogers, moved that the Committee appointed to carry up to the Honorable the Legislative Council the Act for regulating the practice of Physic, Surgery and Midwifery in this Province, do also carry up the Act for the better securing Titles to Lands in this Province; and request their concurrence thereto. Which was ordered accordingly.

Read for the third time, as engrossed, the Bill for establishing the Fees to be taken in the Court of King's Bench. Mr. Sherwood then moved, seconded by Mr. Rogers, that the Bill do pass, and that the title be "An Act for the better regulating the Fees to be taken in the Court of King's Bench." The Bill then passed, and was signed by the Speaker.

Mr. Washburn then moved, seconded by Mr. Nellis, that Messrs. Sherwood and Nellis do carry up to the Honorable the Legislative Council the Act for the better regulating the Fees to be taken in the Court of King's Bench, and request their concurrence thereto.

Mr. Sherwood, seconded by Mr. Rogers, moved, in amendment to Mr. Washburn's motion, that the Committee named to carry up to the Honorable the Legislative Council the Act for the better regulating the Statute Labour in the Counties of Essex and Kent, in the Western District, do also carry up the Act for the better regulating the Fees to be taken in the Court of King's Bench; and request their concurrence thereto, which passed in the negative.

The main question was then put, which was carried in the affirmative, and ordered accordingly.

On motion of Captain Cowan, seconded by the Solicitor General, the House adjourned until Monday next.

Monday, 29th February, 1808.

Prayers were read.

Read for the third time, as engrossed, the Bill for establishing Public Highways and Roads throughout the Province. Mr. Howard then moved, seconded by Mr. Dorland, that the Bill do pass, and that the title be "An Act to provide for the laying out, amending, and keeping in repair the Public Highways and Roads in this Province; and to repeal the laws now in force for that purpose." The Bill accordingly passed, and was signed by the Speaker. Mr. Rogers then moved, seconded by Mr. Swazey, that Messrs. Howard and Dorland do carry up to the Honourable the Legislative Council the Act entitled "An Act to provide for the laying out, amending, and keeping in repair the Public Highways and Roads in this Province and to repeal the laws now in force for that purpose," which was ordered accordingly.

Agreeably to the Order of the Day the House resolved itself into a Committee to go into the further consideration of the Bill for the better regulation of the Militia. Mr. Speaker left the Chair. Captain Cowan took the Chair of the Committee.

Mr. Speaker resumed the Chair, and Captain Cowan reported that the Committee had made a progress, and had directed him to ask for leave to sit again this day. Leave was accordingly granted to sit again this day.

A message from the Honorable the Legislative Council by Mr. Baldwin, Master in Chancery.

Mr. Speaker,

I am commanded by the Honorable the Legislative Council to inform this House that they have passed an Act, sent up from this House, entitled, " An Act for the establishment of a Court of Common Pleas in each and every District of this Province," to which they have made several amendments, to which amendments they request the concurrence of this House.

And also an Act sent up from this House, entitled, " An Act to provide for the support of Judges of the Court of Common Pleas," to which they have made several amendments, to which amendments they request the concurrence of this House. And then he withdrew.

The House again resolved itself into a Committee to go into the further consideration of the Bill for the better regulation of the Militia. Mr. Speaker left the Chair. Captain Cowan again took the chair of the Committee.

Mr. Speaker resumed the Chair, and Captain Cowan reported that the Committee had made a progress, and had directed him to ask for leave to sit again to-morrow. Leave was accordingly granted.

Read for the first time, the Bill for the establishing of a Police in several Towns in this Province. Mr. Howard then moved, seconded by Mr. Swazey, that the Bill for establishing a Police in several Towns in this Province be read a second time to-morrow. Ordered accordingly.

The Solicitor General moved, seconded by Mr. McLean, that so much of the Order of this Day as has not been proceeded upon remain as part of the Order of the Day for to-morrow. The said Order was discharged for this day, and ordered, that it do make a part of the Order of the day for to-morrow.

On motion of the Solicitor General, seconded by Captain Cowan, the House adjourned.

Tuesday, 1st March, 1808.

Prayers were read.

Mr. Howard, one of the Messengers named to carry up to the Honorable the Legislative Council the Act entitled " An Act to provide for the laying out, amending, and keeping in repair the Public Highways and roads in this Province; and to repeal the laws now in force for that purpose," reported that they had carried up the said Act, and did request their concurrence in passing the same.

Read for the first time, the amendments made by the Honorable the Legislative Council in and to an Act, sent up from this House, entitled " An Act for the establishment of a Court of Common Pleas in each and every District of this Province." Mr. Sherwood then moved, seconded by Mr. McGregor, that the amendments made by the Honorable the Legislative Council in and to an Act sent up from this House, entitled " An Act for the establishment of a Court of Common Pleas in each and every District of this Province" be read a second time on this day three months. The House accordingly resolved the same.

Solicitor General, seconded by Captain Cowan, moved that the House do now resolve itself into a Committee to go into the consideration of the Bill to encourage the growth and cultivation of Hemp in this Province, and the exportation thereof. The House accordingly resolved itself into a Committee to go into the consideration of the said Bill. Mr. Speaker left the Chair. Mr. Dorland was called to the chair of the Committee.

Mr. Speaker resumed the Chair, and Mr. Dorland reported that the Committee had made a progress, and had directed him to ask for leave to sit again. The Report was not received, and the Committee had no leave to sit again.

Agreeably to the Order of the Day the House resolved itself into a Committee to go into the consideration of the Bill for increasing the representation of the Commons of this Province. Mr. Speaker left the Chair. Mr. Howard was called to the chair of the Committee.

Mr. Speaker resumed the Chair, and Mr. Howard reported that the Committee had made a progress, and had directed him to ask for leave to sit again to-morrow. Leave was accordingly granted.

Read for the first time, the Bill for establishing a Public School in the District of London. Mr. Mallory then moved, seconded by Mr. Howard, that the London District School Bill be read a second time to-morrow. Mr. Speaker having put the question, a division thereupon took place. The names being called for, they were taken down and are as follows:—

Yeas.	Nays.
MESSRS. MALLORY	MESSRS. SOLICITOR GENERAL
ROGERS	COWAN
HOWARD.	McLEAN
	SHERWOOD
	McGREGOR
	CLENCH
	SWAZEY
	NELLIS
	WASHBURN
	CRYSLER.

The same was carried in the negative by a majority of seven.

Read for the second time, the Bill to establish a Police in several Towns within this Province. On motion of Mr. Clench, seconded by Mr. Swazey, the House resolved itself into a Committee to go into the consideration of the said Bill. Mr. Speaker left the Chair. Mr. Washburn was called to the chair of the Committee.

Mr. Speaker resumed the Chair, and Mr. Washburn reported that the Committee had made a progress, and had directed him to report that further progress be postponed.

Agreeably to the Order of the Day, the House resolved itself into a Committee to go into the further consideration of the Militia Bill. Mr. Speaker left the Chair. Captain Cowan took the chair of the Committee.

Mr. Speaker resumed the Chair, and Captain Cowan reported that the Committee had made a progress, and had directed him to ask for leave to sit again to-morrow, and, that it should be the first on the Order of the Day for to-morrow. It was accordingly granted that the Committee should sit again to morrow, and ordered, that the said Bill be the first thing on the Order of the Day for to-morrow.

Mr. Clench gave notice that he will move to-morrow that the Bill for establishing Courts of Quarter Sessions and Requests at St. Joseph's be engrossed and read a third time to-morrow.

Mr. Washburn then moved, seconded by the Solicitor General, for leave to bring in a Bill to-morrow for granting to His Majesty a certain sum of money for the further encouragement of the growth and cultivation of Hemp in this Province. Leave was accordingly granted.

The Solicitor General moved, seconded by Mr. McLean, for leave to bring in a Bill to-morrow to alter and amend an Act passed in the last Session of the Legislature, for the establishment of Public Schools in each and every District of this Province. Leave was accordingly granted.

On motion of Captain Cowan, seconded by Mr. Nellis, the House adjourned.

Wednesday, 2nd March, 1808.

Prayers were read.

Agreeably to the Order of the Day the House resolved itself into a Committee to go into the further consideration of the Bill for the better regulation of the Militia. Mr. Speaker left the Chair. Captain Cowan took the chair of the Committee.

The Speaker resumed the Chair, and Captain Cowan reported that the Committee had made a progress, and had directed him to ask for leave to sit again to-morrow. Leave was accordingly granted.

Agreeably to the Order of the Day the House resolved itself into a Committee to go into the further consideration of the Bill for the more equal representation of the Commons of this Province. Mr. Speaker left the Chair. Mr. Howard took the chair of the Committee.

Mr. Speaker resumed the Chair, and Mr. Howard reported that the Committee had gone through the consideration of the said Bill, to which they had made several amendments, which he was directed to report to the House whenever it should be pleased to receive the same. Ordered, that the Report be now received. The Report was accordingly received and accepted.

Mr. Clench then moved, seconded by Mr. Rogers, that the Bill for increasing the representation of the Commons of this Province in Parliament be engrossed, and read a third time to-morrow, which was ordered accordingly.

Read for the first time, A Bill for the encouragement, and to promote the cultivation of Hemp within this Province. Mr. Washburn moved, seconded by Mr. Mallory, that so far as the fifth Rule of this House, which directs that one day's previous notice shall be given before any question shall be put, be now dispensed with, and that the Bill to grant a certain sum of money to His Majesty for the further encouragement of the growth and cultivation of Hemp be read a second time this day. The same passed in the negative. Mr. Washburn then moved, seconded by Mr. Mallory, that the said Bill be read for the second time to-morrow, which was ordered accordingly.

Read for the first time, A Bill to repeal a certain part of an Act passed in the forty-seventh year of His Majesty's Reign, entitled " An Act to establish Schools in each and every District of this Province. The Solicitor General then moved, seconded by Mr. McLean, that the said Bill be read for the second time to-morrow, which was ordered accordingly.

Mr. Sherwood then moved, seconded by Mr. Clench, that the Contingent expenses of both Houses of Parliament be laid before this House to-morrow. The same was ordered accordingly.

Mr. Speaker then read, by permission of the House, a representation made by the Clerk of this House, which is as follows:—

The Clerk of the House of Assembly has the honor of representing most respectfully to the Representatives of the Commons of Upper Canada in Parliament Assembled,

That he was appointed Clerk to the Honorable House in the year 1801, with a salary of £125 per annum at the time he was appointed. The funds appropriated by Law for the payment of the salaries of the Officers of the Legislative Council and House of Assembly, and the Contingent Expenses thereof, were not very productive; since then they became more than abundant for that purpose.

Having the Honor of being Clerk to so high and dignified a branch of the Legislature of this Province, it makes the situation respectable, to which is attached great responsibility, notwithstanding his salary is not better than that of the inferior Clerks in any of the Public Offices, whose salaries are paid by the Crown, and to whose situation there is no responsibility attached.

Owing to the very extravagant prices of every article in this place, although painful to him to relate, he has the mortification to state that since his first appointment his salary has fallen greatly short of what is absolutely necessary to provide even the indispensable common necessaries of life with the most rigid economy, which upwards of seven years' experience has fatally proved to him.

Your Clerk therefore respectfully submits to the superior judgment of the Representatives of the Commons of Upper Canada in Parliament Assembled, the making of such an augmentation to his present salary as may be thought suitable to so respectable and responsible a situation as Clerk of the third and important branch of the Legislature of Upper Canada.

Clerk Assembly's Office,   (Signed) Donald McLean,
York, 2nd Mar., 1808.   Cl'k. Assembly.

Which was ordered to lie on the Table, and to be taken into consideration to-morrow.

On motion of Mr. Clench, seconded by Mr. Howard, the House adjourned.

Thursday, 3rd March, 1808.

Prayers were read.

Agreeably to the Order of the Day the House resolved itself into a Committee to go into the consideration of the Bill for the better regulation of the Militia of this Province.

Mr. Speaker left the Chair. Captain Cowan took the chair of the Committee.

Mr. Speaker resumed the Chair, and Captain Cowan reported that the Committee had gone through the consideration of the Bill for the better regulation of the Militia, to which they had made several amendments, to which amendments he was directed to report to the House whenever it should be pleased to receive the same. Ordered, that the Report be now received. The Report was accordingly received and accepted.

The Solicitor General then moved, seconded by Captain Cowan, that the Militia Bill be engrossed, and read a third time to-morrow, which was ordered accordingly.

Read for the third time, as engrossed, the Bill for the more equal representation of the Commons of this Province in Parliament.

A Message from the Honorable the Legislative Council by Mr. Baldwin, Master in Chancery.

Mr. Speaker,

I am commanded by the Honorable the Legislative Council to inform this House that they have passed an Act, sent up from this House, entitled "An Act the better to ascertain and secure the titles to Lands in this Province," to which they have made several amendments, to which amendments they request the concurrence of this House in passing the same.

And then he withdrew.

Then Mr. Rogers moved, seconded by Mr. Dorland, that the word "one" be expunged, and the words "represented by two" in lieu thereof in the sixth line of the third press. in the Bill for increasing the Representation of the Commons of this Province in Parliament. A division thereupon took place. The names being called for they were taken down and are as follows:—

Yeas.	Nays.
MESSRS. SHERWOOD	MESSRS. SOL'R General
HOWARD	COWAN
ROGERS	McGREGOR
DORLAND.	CRYSLER
	CLENCH
	McLEAN
	WASHBURN
	MALLORY.

The same passed in the negative by a majority of four. Mr. Sherwood then moved, seconded by Mr. Rogers, that the Bill do pass, and that the title be " An Act for the better Representation of the Commons of this Province in Parliament." Ordered accordingly. The Bill then passed and was signed by the Speaker.

Mr. Rogers, seconded by Mr. Sherwood, moved that Messrs. Clench and Crysler do carry up to the Honorable the Legislative Council the Act for the better Representation of the Commons of this Province in Parliament, and do request their concurrence thereto. Which was ordered accordingly.

On motion of Capt. Cowan, seconded by Mr. McGregor, the House adjourned.

Friday, 4th March, 1808.

Prayers were read.

Mr. Rogers moved, seconded by Mr. Mallory, that the amendments made by the Honorable the Legislative Council in and to an Act for the better securing the Titles to Lands in this Province be now read for the first time. Accordingly the said amendments were read for the first time. Mr. Rogers again moved, seconded by Mr. Howard, that the said amendments be read for the second time to-morrow. Ordered accordingly.

Mr. Washburn moved, seconded by the Solicitor General, that the House do now resolve itself into a Committee, to go into the consideration of the Bill to encourage the growth and cultivation of Hemp in this Province. The House accordingly resolved itself into a Committee to go into the Consideration of the said Bill. Mr. Speaker left the Chair. Mr. McLean was called to the chair of the Committee. Mr. Speaker resumed the Chair, and Mr. McLean reported that the Committee had made a progress, and had directed him to ask for leave to sit again this day. Leave was accordingly granted.

A message from the Honorable the Legislative Council by Mr. Baldwin, Master in Chancery.

Mr. Speaker,

I am commanded by the Honorable the Legislative Council to inform this House that they have passed an Act, sent up from this House, entitled " An Act to provide for the laying out, amending and keeping in repair the Public Highways and Roads in this Province, and to repeal the laws now in force for that purpose." to which they have made several amendments, to which amendments they request the concurrence of this House in passing the same.

And also an Act, sent up from this House, entitled " An Act for the better regulating the Statute Labour in the Counties of Essex and Kent, in the Western District," to which they have also made several amendments, to which amendments they also request the concurrence of this House in passing the same.

And then he withdrew.

Agreeably to leave given the House again resolved itself into a Committee to go into the further consideration of the Bill to Encourage the Growth and Culti- vation of Hemp in this Province. Mr. Speaker left the Chair. Mr. McLean again took the chair of the Committee.

Mr. Speaker resumed the Chair, and Mr. McLean reported that the Com- mittee had made a progress, and had directed him to ask for leave to sit again.

Read for the second time, The Bill for authorizing the Trustees of the Public School in the District of London, or the majority of them, to establish the said School in such part of the said District as they may deem proper for the same.

Mr. Crysler, one of the Messengers named to carry up to the Honorable the Legislative Council the Act for the better representation of the Commons of this Province in Parliament, reported that they had carried up the same, and did re- quest their concurrence thereto.

Mr. Solicitor General moved, seconded by Capt. Cowan, that the House do now resolve itself into a Committee to go into the consideration of the London District School Bill. The House accordingly resolved itself into a Commtitee to go into the consideration. of the said Bill. Mr. Speaker left the Chair. Mr. Dorland was called to the chair of the Committee. Mr. Speaker resumed the Chair, and Mr. Dorland reported that the Committee had gone through the con- sideration of the said Bill, to which they had made several amendments, which he was directed to report to the House whenever it shall be pleased to receive the same. On Mr. Speaker having put the question, shall the Report be now received, a division thereupon took place. The names being called for they were taken down, and are as follows:

Yeas.	Nays
MESSRS. SOLR. GENERAL	MESSRS. MALLORY
COWAN	HOWARD
SHERWOOD	ROGERS
McLEAN	DORLAND
McGREGOR	
CLENCH	
WASHBURN –	
CRYSLER	

The same was carried in the affirmative by a majority of four. The Report was accordingly received and accepted. Mr. Solicitor General then moved, seconded by Mr. Sherwood, that the School Bill be engrossed, and read a third time to-morrow, which was ordered accordingly.

Read for the third time, as engrossed, the Bill for raising and training the Militia of this Province. Mr. Solicitor General moved, seconded by Capt. Cowan, that the Bill do pass, and that the title be " An Act to explain, amend, and reduce to one Act of Parliament the several laws now in being for the raising and training the Militia of this Province," which was ordered accordingly. The Bill then passed and was signed by the Speaker. Then Mr. McLean moved, seconded by Mr. Sherwood, That Mr. Solicitor General and Capt. Cowan do carry up to the Honorable the Legislative Council the Militia Act, and request their concurrence thereto. Ordered accordingly.

Read for the third time, as engrossed, the Bill to establish a Court of Quarter Sessions at Saint Joseph's, in the Western District.

Mr. Clench then moved, seconded by Mr. Sherwood, that the Bill do pass, and that the title be " An Act to establish a Court of Quarter Sessions in the Town of Saint Joseph's, in the Island of Saint Joseph's, in the Western District of this Province." The Bill then passed, and was signed by the Speaker. Mr. Rogers then moved, seconded by Mr. Mallory, that Mr. McGregor and Capt. Cowan do carry up to the Honorable the Legislative Council the Act to establish a Court of Quarter Sessions in the Town of Saint Joseph's, on the Island of Saint Joseph's, in the Western District of this Province, and request their concurrence thereto. Ordered accordingly.

The Solicitor General moved, seconded by Capt. Cowan, for leave to bring in a Bill to-morrow for applying a certain sum of money therein mentioned to make good certain moneys issued and advanced by His Majesty, through the Lieutenant Governor, in pursuance of an Address of this House.

On motion of Mr. Sherwood, seconded by Mr. Clench, ordered, that the Contingent Accounts of both Houses of Parliament for the present Session be the first on the Order of the Day for to-morrow.

Mr. Clench gave notice that he will on to-morrow move that this House do, draft an Address to His Excellency the Lieutenant Governor, indicative of the high sense entertained by this House of His Excellency's Administration, and the great attention that has been paid by him to that meritorious class of persons the U. E. Loyalists and Military Claimants; and that the House do then resolve itself into a Committee to go into the consideration of the same.

Mr. McLean, seconded by Mr. McGregor, moved that the amendments made by the Honourable the Legislative Council to the Act for the better regulating the Statute Labour in the Counties of Essex and Kent, in the Western District of this Province, be now read for the first time. The said Act, as amended by the Honorable the Legislative Council, was accordingly read for the first time. Mr. McGregor then moved, seconded by Mr. McLean, that the said amendments be read for the second time to-morrow, which was ordered accordingly.

Mr. Washburn gave notice that he will move to-morrow that the petition of the Inhabitants of the County of Prince Edward, respecting the Commerce of this Province, be read, and that it do make a part of the Order of the Day for to-morrow for that purpose.

On motion of Mr. McGregor, seconded by the Solicitor General, the House adjourned.

Saturday, 5th March, 1808.

Prayers were read.

Mr. Rogers, from the Select Committee to whom was referred the Public Provincial Accounts, reported the proceedings of the Committee thereon. He read the Report in his place, and afterwards delivered in the same at the Table, where it was again read by the Clerk, and is as follows:—

REPORT OF THE SELECT COMMITTEE OF THE HOUSE OF ASSEMBLY ON THE PUBLIC ACCOUNTS.

The Committee, having taken into their consideration the Accounts that have been laid before them, from No. 1 to No. 18 beg leave to state

That the Balance remaining in the Receiver General's hands the 31st Decr. 1807, appears to be £2497 18 5⅛

That there is outstanding for Duties on Shop, Innkeepers, and Still Licenses, issued between the 5th January, 1807, and 5th January, 1808 (No. 9) as far as the Accounts have come to hand 558 18 7¾

Also that there is outstanding on Duties collected on goods imported from the United States, between the 1st Jany. and the 31st Decr., 1807, as far as the Returns have been made........ 172 10 2⅞

And also for Duties collected in 1802, from Colin McNabb, Collector, Niagara 87 0 10¾

That there is outstanding for Tonnage on vessels appropriated for Lighthouses 36 0 8¼

And that there is outstanding on Licenses to Hawkers, Pedlars and Petty Chapmen 70 0 0

That there is due from Lower Canada one years additional duties to 31st Decr., 1806 .... 1322 0 1¾

That the amount to be received from Lower Canada for duties on Imports, including additional duties to 31st Decr., 1807, will be 2800 0 0

£7544 9 0½

The Balance of Lighthouse Duty appropriated £116 8 3¼

Also the Receiver General's allowance of 3 per cent. on £924. 10s. 5⅝d. outstanding the 27th January, 1808, for duties collected in this Province 27 14 8½

Will be due six Sheriffs the 3rd March, 1808 .... 300 0 0

Also will be due Schoolmasters the 10th March, 1808. ...... 600 0 0

The Receiver General will be entitled to 3½ per cent. on the sum of £4,122. 0s. 1¾d., to be received from Lower Canada duties collected to 31st Decr. 1807 .... 144 5 4¾

Will be wanted for printing the laws, say 80 0 0

For the Contingencies of the two Houses of Parliament,- including a supply of stationery for next Session in 1807 ...... 288 0 8

For copying Clerks, appropriated by law £25. each. 50 0 0

Balance £5938 0 0

£7544 9 0½

Sums of money in the Receiver General's hands, appropriated but not applied.

For to support the War (by vote)	£500	0	0
Public Buildings, (York).	1600	0	0
Purchasing British Statutes.	175	0	0
To encourage and promote the culture and exportation of Hemp	423	11	0
	£2698	11	0

In the hands of Mr. McGill for the purchase of Hempseed.. £3 11 3

N. B. The sum collected under British Acts of Parliament is Provincial Currency, which is not brought into the Provincial Treasury, or any account before the House how the same is disposed of. 619 3 0

The Committee observe that the Officers of the two Houses of Parliament are paid up to the 7th January, 1808, and that nothing will be due before the 7th July, next; and as the Inspector will pay the money collected the first of June next, there will be a sufficient sum collected to answer the demand at that time.

Mr. Sherwood moved, seconded by the Solicitor General, that the School Bill be the first thing on the Order of the Day, to be read for the third time. On Mr. Speaker having put the question, Messrs. Rogers, Dorland and Howard retired from their seats. The names of the Members present were taken down, and are as follows:—The Speaker, Messrs. Washburn, McLean, Solicitor General, Cowan, Sherwood, McGregor, Crysler, Clench and Mallory.

The Speaker then adjourned the House, for want of a quorum, until Monday next.

Monday, 7th March, 1808.

At eleven o'clock the Speaker took the Chair and adjourned the House for want of a quorum.

Present, The Speaker and Mr. Mallory.

Tuesday, 8th March, 1808.

Prayers were read.

Mr. Speaker, on his having taken the Chair, informed the House that on the division of a question relative to the third reading of a Bill last Saturday three Members thought proper to quit their seats, and thus left the House without a quorum.

Thus situated he conceived it his duty to dispatch an express, requiring the attendance of two of the Members from the District of Niagara.

To the activity of the Gentleman who was dispatched with the summons, and the persevering zeal of one of the Honorable Members so summoned the Colony is indebted for being once more able to proceed on the business now before it.

Mr. Washburn, seconded by Mr. Sherwood, then moved that the following Order be inserted on the Journals of the House:—

Ordered, that it be inserted upon the Journals of this House, that, on Saturday last, when a question was about to be put by the Speaker, David McGregor Rogers, Thomas Dorland, and Peter Howard, Esquires, Members of the House, then present in their places, departed the House without leave, whereby the House was left without a quorum.

Ordered, that it be further inserted upon the Journals, that the House do approve of the conduct of the Speaker in sending an Express for Messrs. Nellis and Swazey, absent by consent; and that the expense incident to such express shall form a part of the Contingent Expenses of this House. The House unanimously resolved the same.

Mr. Sherwood, seconded by Mr. Clench, moved that the School Bill be now read for the third time. The School Bill as engrossed, was accordingly read for the third time.

Mr. Sherwood then moved, seconded by Mr. Washburn, that the Bill do pass, and that the title be "An Act to amend an Act, passed in the forty seventh year of His Majesty's Reign, entitled 'An Act to establish Public Schools in each and every District of this Province.'" A Division thereupon took place. The names being called for they were taken down, and are as follows:—

Yeas	Nays
MESSRS. SOL'R. GENERAL	MR. MALLORY
McLEAN	
COWAN	
SHERWOOD	
McGREGOR	
CLENCH	
WASHBURN	
NELLIS	
CRYSLER	

The same was carried in the affirmative by a majority of eight. The Bill then passed, and was signed by the Speaker. Mr. Sherwood then moved, seconded by Mr. Nellis, that the Solicitor General and Mr. Washburn do carry up to the Honorable the Legislative Council the Act entitled " An Act to amend an Act, passed in the forty seventh year of His Majesty's Reign, entitled 'An Act to establish Public Schools in each and every District of this Province,' " and request their concurrence thereto, which was ordered accordingly.

Ordered, that the Contingent Accounts for the Present Session of the Legislative Council and this House do lie on the Table, and are as follows:—

Contingent Expenses of the Clerk of the Legislative Council's Office, for the Year 1808.

	£	s	d
Amount of William Allan's Account for Stationery furnished the last Session.	4	10	9
Duncan Cameron's Account for Do. furnished the last Session	6	0	0
William and James Crooks' Account for parchment for the present Session.	4	7	6
Estimate for Stationery for the ensuing Session	20	0	0
Estimate for Clerks to bring up the business of the present Session	10	0	0
	£44	18	3

Approved,

(Signed) THOS. SCOTT, Speaker.

GOVERNMENT OF UPPER CANADA,
To George Lawe, Dr.

To Amount of William Allan's Acct.	£40	0	10½
" " " John Mcbeath's Acct.	3	16	9
" " " P. Clinger's Acct.	2	6	0
" " " Lewis Bright's Acct.		3	9
" " " Mary Jobbett's Acct.	2	7	6
" " " Thos. Doneldson's Acct.	1	10	0
" " " Francis Friday's Acct.		5	0
" " " Elinor Bassell's Acct.		14	9
" " " John Bassell's Acct.	20	0	0
	£71	4	7½

Amounts to Seventy One Pounds, Four Shillings and Sevenpence Halfpenny Currency.

Personally came and appeared before me the above named George Lawe, who maketh Oath, and saith the above account is Just and True in all particulars, to the best of his knowledge and belief.

Sworn before me this eighth day of March, 1800.

(Signed)   THOS. SCOTT, C.J.

York, Upper Canada, 3rd March, 1808.   The Contingent Account of the Commons House of Assembly for the 4th Session of the 4th Provincial Parliament.

Due Messrs. Cameron and Bennett	£15	15	0
" John McBeath	12	11	6
" Alexander Wood	5	0	0
" Isaac Columbus		10	0
" Duncan Cameron	9	12	1
" William Allan	1	9	0¾
" William Wells	4	10	0
" Hugh Carfrae	8	3	1¼
" Philip Clinger	3	15	6
" Donald McLean for postage of a letter from the Clerk of the Peace of the Western District, on the Public Service		1	4
" Titus Simons	3	0	0
" Samuel J. Wilmott	5	11	9
" Henry Hale	7	7	6
" Allowance to complete the business of the present Session	30	0	0
" Allowance to provide Stationery for the ensuing Session of Parliament	40	0	0
" Copying Clerks, due this day	76	15	0
" Balance due for Stationery over and above the Thirty Pounds advanced to procure Stationery	3	16	2½
" Hugh Carfrae, as Messenger	20	0	0

" Expense of an express sent for Messrs. Nellis and Swazey   25   0   0
" To defray expense of Mr. Willcock's imprisonment ..   8   0   0

£280 18 0¾

Commons House of Assembly 8th March, 1808.
(Signed)   ALEXR. McDONELL, Speaker.

Dr. The Honorable the House of Assembly, in Account with their Clerk.
To Cash paid Joseph Shaw for washing in the Office of the
House of Assembly during the recess of Parliament, as per receipt   £9 10   0
To Cash paid Hugh Carfrae for attending the Office during
the recess of Parliament. 3 17   6
To Balance remaining in the Clerk's hands, and carried to the
credit of the copying Clerk's account ....   1 ·12   6

£15   0   0

Clerk of the House of Assembly's Office, York, 3rd March, 1808.
Errors Excepted.   DONALD McLEAN, Clk. Assy.

Cr. The Honorable the House of Assembly in Account Current with their Clerk.
By Cash received in advance to complete the business of the
Session during the recess of Parliament £15   0   0

£15   0   0

By Balance carried to the credit of the Copying Clerks this
Session £1 12   6
The Honorable the House of Assembly in Account Current with their
Clerk for Stationery for the Fourth Session Fourth Provincial Parliament.
Dr.

William Allan £7   8   9
Alexander Wood 2 16   3
Duncan Cameron   11   1 10½
William and James Crooks   10   6   3
Quetton St. George 1 17   3
Henry Drean 5 10

£33 16   2½

To Balance Due £3 16   2½
Cr.
By Cash received in advance for the Purchase of Stationery   £30   0   0
By Balance due 3 16. 2½

£33 16   2½

Errors excepted.
Clerk of the Ho. Assembly's Office, York, 3rd March, 1808.
DONALD McLEAN, Clk. Assy.

The Honorable House of Assembly in Account Current with their Clerk for Copying Clerks during the Fourth Session of the Fourth Provincial Parliament. Dr.

To Joseph Shaw	£30	2	6
To Edward McMahon	30	7	6
To Allan McLean	24	10	0
To John Higgins	18	7	6
	£103	7	6

To Balance due	£76	15	0

Cr.

By Balance remaining unexpended by an allowance made Last Session for completing the business of that Session during the recess of Parliament £1 12 6

By Amount of His Excellency the Lieut. Governor's Warrant in my favour, as by law appropriated for paying of copying Clerks 25 0 0

Balance due the Clerk 76 15 0

£103 ·7 6

Clk. Ass'ys Office, York, 8th Mar. 1808.

Errors excepted.   DONALD McLEAN, Clk. Assembly.

On motion of the Solicitor General, seconded by Captain Cowan, the House resolved itself into a Committee to take into their consideration the contingent accounts of both Houses of Parliament for the present Session. Mr. Speaker left the Chair. Mr. Sherwood was called to the Chair of the Committee.

Mr. Speaker resumed the Chair, and Mr. Sherwood reported that the Committee had gone through the consideration of the Contingent Accounts of both Houses of Parliament, and that they had come to several resolutions thereon, which he was directed to submit to the House. He then read in his place the said resolutions, and then delivered the same in at the Table, where they were again read by the Clerk, and the said Resolutions are as follows :—

Resolved, that it is the opinion of this Committee that it is expedient to advance to the Clerk of the Legislative Council the sum of Twenty Pounds, to enable him to purchase stationery for the use of the next Session of Parliament, and the sum of Ten Pounds be allowed to him to enable him to complete the business of the present Session, over and above the sum appropriated by Law for the paying of Copying Clerks; and the further sum of Fourteen Pounds, Eighteen Shillings and Three Pence, to pay a balance due from the last Session's Contingent Accounts, making in all Forty-four Pounds, Eighteen Shillings and Three Pence, as certified by the Speaker of the Legislative Council.

Resolved, that it is the opinion of this Committee that there is due to sundry persons, agreeable to Mr. George Lawe, Gentleman Usher of the Black Rod's account, certified by the Speaker of the Legislative Council, for services performed during the present Session, the sum of Fifty Pounds, Four Shillings and Seven Pence halfpenny.

Resolved, that it is the opinion of this Committee that there be allowed to the Messenger of the Legislative Council the sum of Twenty Pounds for each and every session of Parliament.

Resolved, that it is the opinion of this Committee, that there is due to sundry persons for articles furnished for the use of this House, and services performed during the present Session, the sum of Two Hundred and Ten Pounds, Eighteen Shillings.

Resolved, that it is the opinion of this Committee that it is expedient to allow the Clerk of this House Forty Pounds, to enable him to purchase a supply of stationery for the use of the ensuing Session of Parliament.

Resolved, that it is the opinion of this Committee that the sum of Thirty Pounds be allowed the Clerk of this House to complete the business of the present Session of Parliament.

Resolved, that an humble Address be presented to His Excellency, the Lieutenant Governor, to request that His Excellency will be pleased to issue his Warrant in favor of John Powell, Esquire, Clerk of the Honorable the Legislative Council, for the sum of Forty-four Pounds, Eighteen. Shillings and Three pence. To Mr. George Lawe, Gentleman Usher of the Black Rod, for the sum of Seventy Pounds, Four Shillings and Seven Pence Halfpenny, including Twenty Pounds to John Bassell, as Messenger and Firelighter to the Legislative Council. To Donald McLean, Esquire, Clerk of the House of Assembly, for the sum of Two Hundred and Eighty Pounds, Eighteen Shillings.

Resolved, that the House doth concur in the several resolutions reported from the Committee.

On motion of Captain Cowan, seconded by Mr. McLean, ordered, that Messrs. Sherwood and Clench be a Committee to draft an Address to His Excellency, the Lieutenant Governor, in conformity to several resolutions of the House this day.

Mr. Sherwood, from the Committee named to draft an Address to His Excellency, the Lieutenant Governor, grounded on the several resolutions of the House this day, reported that the Committee had drafted an Address, which they were ready to submit to the House whenever it shall be pleased to receive the same.

The House then resolved that the Address be now received.

Mr. Sherwood then read the Address in his place, and afterwards delivered the same in at the Table, where it was again read by the Clerk and is as follows:

To His Excellency, Francis Gore, Esquire, Lieutenant Governor of Province of Upper Canada, &c., &c.

May it please Your Excellency,

We, His Majesty's most dutiful and loyal subjects, the Commons of Upper Canada, in Parliament assembled, do most humbly pray that it may please Your Excellency to issue Your Warrants, directed to the Receiver General, requesting him to pay to John Powell, Esquire, the sum of Forty-four Pounds, Eighteen Shillings and Three pence; to Mr. George Lawe, Usher of the Black Rod, the sum of Seventy Pounds, Four Shillings and Seven pence; to Donald McLean, Esquire, Clerk of the House of Assembly, the sum of Two Hundred and Eighty Pounds, Eighteen Shillings; to enable them to pay the contingent expenses of the present Session, and to provide a supply of stationery for the ensuing session of Parliament.

We therefore do most humbly pray that Your Excellency will be pleased to issue your Warrants for that purpose, and the Commons will make good the several sums of money to Your Excellency at the next Session of Parliament.

Commons House of Assembly, 8th March, 1808.

On motion of Mr. Nellis, seconded by Mr. Mallory, ordered, that the said Address be engrossed. The said Address, as engrossed, was then read, passed, and

18 A.

signed by the Speaker. Mr. Sherwood moved, seconded by Capt. Cowen, that Messrs. McLean and Washburn be a Committee to present the said Address to His Excellency, the Lieutenant Governor, at such time as he may be pleased to receive the same, which was ordered accordingly.

Read for the first time, a Bill for applying a certain sum of money therein mentioned to make good moneys advanced by His Majesty, through the Lieutenant Governor. On motion of Mr. Clench, seconded by Mr. McGregor, the said Bill was read for the second time. On motion of Mr. Washburn, seconded by Mr. Mallory, the House resolved itself into a Committee to go into the consideration of the said Bill. Mr. Speaker left the Chair. Mr. Clench was called to the Chair of the Committee. Mr. Speaker resumed the Chair, and Mr. Clench reported that the Committee had gone through the consideration of the said Bill, to which they had made an amendment, which he was directed to report to the House whenever it shall be pleased to receive the same. Ordered, that the Report be now received.

The Report was accordingly received.

Captain Cowan moved, seconded by Mr. Crysler, that the said Bill be engrossed, and read a third time this day. Ordered accordingly. The said Bill was read for the third time as engrossed. The Solicitor General then moved, seconded by Captain Cowan, that the Bill do pass, and that the title be "An Act for applying certain sums of money therein mentioned to make good certain moneys issued and advanced by His Majesty, through the Lieutenant Governor, in pursuance of an Address." The Bill then passed, and was signed by the Speaker.

The Solicitor General then moved, seconded by Mr. McLean, that Captain Cowan and Mr. McGregor do carry up to the Honorable the Legislative Council the Act for applying certain sums of money therein mentioned, and request their concurrence thereto.

Messrs. Solicitor General and Washburn reported that they had carried up to the Honorable the Legislative Council the Act entitled "An Act to amend an Act passed in the Forty-seventh year of His Majesty's Reign entitled ' An Act to establish Public Schools in each and every district of this Province,' " and did request their concurrence thereto.

The Solicitor General and Captain Cowan reported that they had carried up to the Honorable the Legislative Council an Act entitled " An Act to explain, amend and reduce to one Act of Parliament the several Laws now in being for raising and framing the Militia of this Province," and did request their concurrence in passing the same; and, also, an Act entitled " An Act to establish a Court of Quarter Sessions in the Town of Saint Joseph's, on the Island of Saint Joseph's, in the Western District of this Province," and did also request their concurrence thereto.

Agreeably to notice given, Mr. Clench read in his place, by permission of the House, an Address to His Excellency, the Lieutenant Governor; and then delivered the same in at the Table, where it was again read by the Clerk, and is as follows:

To His Excellency, Francis Gore, Esquire, Lieutenant Governor of the Province of Upper Canada, &c., &c., &c.

May it please Your Excellency,

We, His Majesty's dutiful and loyal subjects, the Commons of the Province of Upper Canada, in Parliament assembled, beg leave to renew our professions of attachment and loyality to His Majesty's person and Government; and as many of His Majesty's subjects in this Province have heretofore evinced the zeal and sincerity of those professions at the expense and privation of everything but life, we trust they will always be actuated by the same spirit, should occasion require it.

Permit us, before we surrender the important trust that has been delegated to us, to express to Your Excellency our acknowledgements for the many benefits this Province has derived under your administration; and, though we shall not presume to enumerate them, we cannot avoid noticing the relief Your Excellency has so graciously extended to these meritorious people, the Loyalists, who adhered to the unity of the Empire; and the Military Claimants.

As we can with confidence assure our constituents of Your Excellency's unceasing attention, and ardent desire to promote the welfare and happiness of His Majesty's subjects in this Province, and, as it is our duty, it shall also be our 'pride to inculcate a love of order, harmony and union among them, and to cherish and mature their attashment to the happiest of constitutions and the best of Sovereigns.

With reverential thankfulness to the great disposer of events for the uninterrupted blessings of peace, which we have in so peculiar a manner enjoyed since the first establishmnet of the Province, we shall offer up our supplications to Him for the continuation of His mercies, and that He may be graciously pleased to order and direct your counsels that they may tend to His glory, your honor, and the happiness of the people; and impress them with an awful sense of their dependence on the obligations to Him.

Commons House of Assembly, March, 1808.

Mr. Clench then moved, seconded by Mr. Nellis, that the House do resolve itself into a Committee to go into the consideration of the said Address. The House accordingly resolved itself into a Committee. Mr. Speaker left the Chair. Mr. McGregor was called to the Chair of the Committee. Mr. Speaker resumed the Chair, and Mr. McGregor reported that the Committee had gone through the consideration of the said Address without any amendments, which he was directed to report to the House whenever it shall be pleased to receive the same. Resolved, that the Report be now received. On motion of Mr. Clench, seconded by Mr. Nellis, Ordered, that the said Address be engrossed and read to-morrow. Mr. Sherwood then moved, seconded by Mr. McLean, that Messrs. Clench, Crysler and Nellis do present the said Address to His Excellency, the Lieutenant Governor, which was ordered accordingly.

Read for the second time, the amendments made by the Honorable the Legislative Council in and to the Essex and Kent Road Act. Mr. McGregor then moved, seconded by Mr. Sherwood, that the House do now resolve itself into a Committee to go into the consideration of the amendments made by the Honorable the Legislative Council in and to the Essex and Kent Road Act. The House accordingly resolved itself into a Committee. Mr. Speaker left the Chair. The Solicitor General was called to the Chair of the Committee. Mr. Speaker resumed the Chair, and Mr. Solicitor General reported that the Committee had gone through the consideration of the said amendments, which he was directed by the Committee to report to the House, whenever it should be pleased to receive the same, that the amendments made by the Honorable Legislative Council in and to the said Act be adopted by this House. The said Report was accordingly received, and the amendments adopted. Mr. McLean then moved, seconded by Mr. Sherwood, that Captain Cowan and Mr. McGregor do inform the Honorable the Legislative Council that this House have adopted the amendments made by them in and to the Essex and Kent Road Act, which was ordered accordingly.

Then Mr. McLean, seconded by Mr. Crysler, moved that the amendments made by the Honorable the Legislative Council in and to the Act entitled "An Act to provide for the laying out, amending, and keeping in repair the Public Highways and Roads in this Province, and to repeal the Laws now in force for that purpose" be now read for the first time. The said amendments were accordingly read for the first time. Mr. McLean then moved, seconded by Mr. Crysler, that the said amendments be read for a second time to-morrow, which was ordered accordingly.

Read for the second time, the amendments made by the Honorable the Legislative Council in and to the Act entitled " An Act for the better securing the Titles to Lands in this Province." On motoin of the Solicitor General, seconded by Mr. McLean, the House resolved itself into a Committee to go into the consideration of the said amendments. Mr. Speaker left the Chair. Captain Cowan was called to the Chair of the Committee.

Mr. Speaker resumed the Chair, and Mr. Cowan reported that the Committee had gone through the consideration of the said amendments, which amendments the Committee had recommended to be adopted by this House; and that the House do acquaint the Honorable the Legislative Council of the same, which Report was received, and ordered accordingly. Mr. Solicitor General, then moved, seconded by Mr. Sherwood, that Captain Cowan and Mr. McGregor do acquaint the Honorable the Legislative Council that this House doth concur in adopting the amendments made by them in and to the Act for the better securing the Titles to Lands in this Province, which was ordered accordingly.

A Message to the Honorable the Legislative Council.
Mr. Speaker,

We are commanded by the Commons House of Assembly to acquaint this Honorable House that it has concurred in adopting the amendments made by the Legislative Council in and to the Act entitled " An Act the better to ascertain and secure the Title to Lands in this Province."
Commons House of Assembly, 8th March, 1808.

(Signed)   ALEX'R McDONELL, Speaker.

Then Captain Cowan moved, seconded by Mr. McLean, for leave to bring in a Bill this day to amend an Act to encourage the growth and cultivation of Hemp in this Province. Leave was accordingly granted, and the said Bill was accordingly read for the first time. Captain Cowan again moved, seconded by Mr. McGregor, that the Bill to encourage the cultivation and growth of Hemp in this Province be read a second time to-morrow. Ordered accordingly.

Mr. Clench then moved, seconded by Mr. Sherwood, for leave to bring in a Bill to-morrow to augment the salary of the Clerk of the Legislative Council and the Clerk of the House of Assembly. Leave was accordingly granted.

Mr. Solicitor General then moved, seconded by Mr. McLean, for leave to bring in a Bill this day to repeal so much of an Act passed in the Forty-sixth year of His Majesty's Reign, entitled " An Act for the better securing to His Majesty, His Heirs and Successors, the due collection and receipt of certain duties therein mentioned," as limits the continuance of the aforesaid Act to the term of two years. Leave was granted accordingly. And the said Bill was then read for the first time. Mr. Solicitor General, seconded by Captain Cowan, moved that the Bill for the due collection and receipt of certain duties therein mentioned be read a second time to-morrow. The same was ordered accordingly.

Mr. McLean, seconded by Mr. Crysler, moved for leave to bring in a Bill this day for granting to His Majesty a certain sum of money out of the funds applicable to the uses of this Province, to defray the expense of amending and repairing the Public Highways and Roads, laying out and opening new roads, and building Bridges in the several Districts thereof.

Leave was accordingly granted, and the said Bill was then read for the first time. Mr. McLean moved, seconded by Mr. Crysler, that the Bill for granting to His Majesty a certain sum of money for laying out and repairing the Public Highways and Bridges be read for the second time to-morrow, which was ordered accordingly.

Messrs. Cowan and McGregor reported that they had carried up to the Honorable the Legislative Council the Act for applying certain sums of money therein mentioned to make good certain moneys issued and advanced by His Majesty, through the Lieutenant Governor, in pursuance of an Address; and did request their concurrence thereto.

Also the message of this House that it had concurred in adopting the amendments made by the Honorable the Legislative Council in and to an Act, sent up from this House, entitled "An Act to continue an Act passed in the Forty-fifth year of His Majesty's Reign, entitled 'An Act to afford relief to those persons who may be entitled to claim lands in this Province as Heirs or Devisees of the Nominees of the Crown, in cases where no Patent hath issued for such lands; and further to extend the benefits of the said Act.'"

And also the message of this House that it has concurred in adopting the amendments made by the Honorable the Legislative Council in and to an Act for the better regulating the Statute Labor in the Counties of Essex and Kent, in the Western District.

The Solicitor General gave notice that he will move to-morrow that the House do then resolve itself into a Committee to consider of the propriety of addressing Our gracious Sovereign on the subject matter of the cultivation of Hemp within this Province.

Mr. McLean, seconded by Mr. Crysler, moved for leave to bring in a Bill this day for granting to His Majesty an annual sum of money for the purpose therein mentioned. Leave was accordingly granted, and the said Bill was accordingly read for the first time. Mr. McLean, seconded by Mr. Crysler, again moved that the Bill for granting to His Majesty an annual sum of money for the purpose therein mentioned be read a second time to-morrow. Ordered accordingly.

Mr. Washburn then moved, seconded by Mr. Mallory, that this House do resolve that there be granted to Donald McLean the sum of   for his former services as Clerk of this House. The same passed in the negative.

On motion of Capt. Cowan, seconded by Mr. McGregor, the House adjourned until nine o'clock in the forenoon to-morrow.

Wednesday, 9th March, 1808.

Prayers were read.

Agreeable to the Order of the Day was read as engrossed an Address voted yesterday to be presented to His Excellency the Lieutenant Governor, indicative of the high sense entertained by this House of His Excellency's administration, and his great attention to that meritorious class of people, the Loyalists, who adhered to the unity of the Empire during the Revolution in America; and Military Claimants.

The Address then passed, and was signed by the Speaker.

Mr. Clench then moved, seconded by Mr. Nellis, that the Address to His Excellency the Lieutenant Governor, instead of being presented by a Committee, as resolved yesterday, be presented by the Speaker with the whole House, at such time as His Excellency may be pleased to appoint, which was unanimously ordered.

Mr. Clench, seconded by Mr. Crysler, again moved that Messrs. McLean and Washburn do wait upon His Excellency the Lieutenant Governor to know when it will be His Excellency's pleasure to receive the House with its Address. Ordered accordingly.

Agreeably to the Order of the Day was read for the second time the amendments made by the Honorable the Legislative Council in and to an Act for establishing Public Highways and Roads throughout this Province. Mr. Clench then moved, seconded by Mr. Nellis, that the House do now resolve itself into a Committee to go into the consideration of the amendments made by the Honorable the Legislative Council in and to the Act entitled "An Act to provide for the laying out, amending and keeping in repair the Public Highways and Roads in this Province; and to repeal the laws now in force for that purpose." The House accordingly resolved itself into a Committee. Mr. Speaker left the Chair. Capt. Cowan was called to the chair of the Committee.

Mr. Speaker resumed the Chair, and Capt. Cowan reported that the Committee had made a progress, and had directed him to ask for leave to sit again this Day. Leave was accordingly granted.

Mr. Washburn, one of the messengers named to wait upon His Excellency the Lieutenant Governor, reported that in obedience to the command of this House they had waited upon His Excellency the Lieutenant Governor, and that His Excellency was pleased to appoint this day at the hour of one o'clock to receive the House with its Address.

At the hour appointed Mr. Speaker, attended by the House, went up to His Excellency the Lieutenant Governor with its Address.

And being returned:—Mr. Speaker reported that the House had attended upon His Excellency the Lieutenant Governor with its Address, to which His Excellency had been pleased to return the following answer.

Gentlemen of the House of Assembly,

Your loyalty to the King, and the favorable sentiments which you are pleased to express respecting my conduct, afford me the highest satisfaction.

While no stranger to the zeal with which many of His Majesty's subjects in this Province have served the best of Kings, and their sufferings in that service, it is particularly gratifying to me to become an instrument of dispensing the bounty of the Crown to men who so well deserve it.

I unite with you in imploring the Great Ruler of the Universe that he may be pleased to continue to this Province the blessings of peace, but if it should be ordained otherwise by Infinite Wisdom I trust and hope that the loyalty so conspicuously displayed in times past by many of its inhabitants will engage them again to stand forth in the cause of their country; and that their children, the objects of His Majesty's peculiar favour and bounty, following such an example will, with a generous and virtuous emulation, tread in the steps of their fathers, and that all His Majesty's subjects in this Province, having experienced the blessings of the happy Constitution under which we live, will show themselves on every occasion ready to defend it.

I have no doubt that the same zeal for the prosperity of the Province which has governed your public conduct will continue to animate you in private life, and that your endeavours will never be wanting in every situation to promote the Public Good.

Government House,
York, 9 Mar. 18^8.

Read for the second time, the Bill to encourage the growth and cultivation of Hemp in this Province. Capt. Cowan then moved, seconded by Mr. Nellis, that the House do now resolve itself into a Committee to go into the consideration of the Bill to encourage the growth and cultivation of Hemp in this Province. The House accordingly resolved itself into a Committee. Mr. Speaker left the Chair. The Solicitor General was called to the chair of the Committee.

Mr. Speaker resumed the Chair, and the Solicitor General reported that the Committee had gone through the consideration of the said Bill, to which they had made several amendments, which he was directed to report to the House whenever it should be pleased to receive the same. The Report was then ordered to be received and accepted. Capt. Cowan again moved, seconded by Mr. Sherwood, that the Hemp Bill be engrossed, and read a third time to-morrow. Which was ordered accordingly.

Read for the first time, the Bill for increasing the Salaries of the Clerks of the Legislative Council and House of Assembly. Mr. Clench then moved, seconded by Mr. Nellis, that the Bill for increasing the salary of the Clerk of the Legislative Council and the Clerk of the House of Assembly be read a second time to-morrow, which was ordered accordingly.

Read for the second time, The Bill for the due collection of certain Duties therein mentioned. On motion of the Solicitor General, seconded by Mr. McGregor, the House resolved itself into a Committee to go into the consideration of the said Bill. Mr. Speaker left the Chair. Mr. McLean was called to the chair of the Committee.

Mr. Speaker resumed the Chair, and Mr. McLean reported that the Committee had gone through the consideration of the said Bill without any amendment, which he was directed to report to the House whenever it should be pleased to receive the same. It was then ordered that the Report be now received and accepted.

Mr. Solicitor General then moved, seconded by Mr. McGregor, that the Bill for securing to His Majesty, His Heirs and successors, the due collection and receipt of certain duties therein mentioned be engrossed, and read a third time to-morrow. Ordered accordingly.

Then Mr. McLean moved, seconded by Mr. Sherwood, that the House do now resolve itself into a Committee to go into the consideration of the Bill for granting to His Majesty a certain sum of money therein mentioned for the purpose of amending and repairing the Roads, opening and laying out new roads, and building and repairing bridges within this Province. The House accordingly resolved itself into a Committee. Mr. Speaker left the Chair. Mr. Nellis was called to the chair of the Committee.

Mr. Speaker resumed the Chair, and Mr. Nellis reported that the Committee had gone through the consideration of the said Bill, to which they had made several amendments, which he was directed to report to the House whenever it should be pleased to receive the same. Mr. Clench then moved, seconded by Mr. Mallory, that the Report be now received. A division thereupon took place; the names being called for they were taken down, and are as follows:—

Yeas.	Nays.
MESSRS. SOL'R GENERAL	MESSRS. CLENCH
McGREGOR	MALLORY
COWAN	
McLEAN	
SHERWOOD	
NELLIS	
CRYSLER	

The same was carried in the affirmative by a majority of six. The Report was then received and accepted.

Mr. McLean, seconded by Mr. Sherwood, moved that the Bill for granting to His Majesty a sum of money for Public Roads and Bridges throughout this Province be engrossed and read a third time to-morrow. Ordered accordingly.

The Solicitor General then moved, seconded by Mr. McLean, that the House do now resolve itself into a Committee to go into the consideration of the propriety of Addressing His Excellency the Lieutenant Governor on the subject of the encouragement of the growth and cultivation of hemp in this Province. The House accordingly resolved itself into a Committee. Mr. Speaker left the Chair. Mr. Clench was called to the chair of the Committee.

Mr. Speaker resumed the Chair, and Mr. Clench reported that the Committee had made a progress, and had directed him to ask for leave to sit again to-morrow. Leave was accordingly granted.

Read for the second time, The Bill for granting to His Majesty a certain sum of money annually, for the purposes therein mentioned. Mr. McLean moved, seconded by Mr. Sherwood, that the House do now resolve itself into a Committee, to go into the consideration of the Bill for granting to His Majesty a sum of money annually for the purposes therein mentioned. The House accordingly resolved itself into a Committee. Mr. Speaker left the Chair. Mr. Washburn was called to the Chair of the Committee. Mr. Speaker resumed the Chair. Mr. Washburn reported that the Committee had gone through the consideration of the said Bill, to which they had made an amendment, which he was directed to report to the House whenever it should be pleased to receive the same. Ordered, that the Report be now received. The Report was accordingly received and accepted. Then Mr. McLean moved, seconded by Mr. Sherwood, that the Bill for granting to His Majesty an annual sum of money for the purposes therein mentioned be engrossed, and read a third time to-morrow. Ordered accordingly.

Agreeably to leave given, the House again resolved itself into a Committee to go into the further consideration of the amendments made by the Honorable the Legislative Council in and to the Act entitled "An Act to ascertain what shall be taken and deemed to be Public Highways and Roads in this Province. Mr. Speaker left the Chair. Capt. Cowan again took the chair of the Committee.

Mr. Speaker resumed the Chair, and Capt. Cowan reported that the Committee had made a progress, and that he was directed to report that the further considera-tion of the said amendments be postponed for nine months, which report was received, and ordered accordingly.

By permission of the House, Capt. Cowan read in his place an Address to His Excellency the Lieutenant Governor, and then delivered the same in at the Table, where it was again read by the Clerk, and is as follows:—

To His Excellency Francis Gore, Esquire, Lieutenant Governor of the Province of Upper Canada, &c., &c., &c.:

May it please Your Excellency,

We, His Majesty's most dutiful and loyal subjects, the Commons of Upper Canada, in Parliament assembled, have taken into our serious consideration the great danger to the lives and property of His Majesty's subjects navigating on Lake Ontario; and having examined the Fund appropriated by an Act passed in the Forty-Third Year of His Majesty's Reign, for the purposes of erecting and keeping in repair Lighthouses on the Isle Forest, Missasauga Point, Gibraltar Point. We find that the moneys arising from Tonnage Duties levied in virtue of the said Act are not at present sufficient to complete the same. But being anxious, as far as in us lies, to render the navigation less dangerous by the immediate construction of Lighthouses authorized by the said Act to be erected on those points and places.

We humbly pray Your Excellency to direct a Lighthouse to be built with all convenient speed on the place known by the name of Gibralter Point; and this House will make good the expenses thereof out of any of the unappropriated moneys in the hands of the Receiver General until the funds established by the said Act of the forty-third year of His Majesty's Reign shall be sufficient to repay the same.

Commons House of Assembly,
9th March, 1808.

On motion of Capt. Cowan, seconded by Mr. McGregor, the House resolved itself into a Committee to go into the consideration of the said Address. Mr. Speaker left the Chair. Mr. Crysler was called to the chair of the Committee.

Mr. Speaker resumed the Chair, and Mr. Crysler reported that the Committee had gone through the consideration of the said Address, without any amendment, which he was directed to report to the House whenever it should be pleased to receive the same. The House then resolved that the Report be now received. The Report was accordingly received and accepted. On motion of Mr. McLean, seconded by the Solicitor General, Ordered that the said Address be engrossed. The said Address as engrossed was read, passed, and signed by the Speaker. Mr. Sherwood then moved, seconded by Mr. Clench, that Capt. Cowan and Mr. McGregor do present the said Address to His Excellency the Lieutenant Governor, which was ordered accordingly.

Messrs. McLean and Washburn reported that in obedience to the command of this House they had waited upon His Excellency the Lieutenant Governor, with the Address of this House respecting the Contingent Expenses of the Honorable the Legislative Council and this House for the present Session, and that His Excellency was pleased to say that he would issue his Warrants for that purpose.

On motion of Mr. Nellis, seconded by Mr. Crysler, the House adjourned.

Thursday, 10th March, 1808.

Prayers were read.

A Message from the Honorable the Legislative Council by Mr. Baldwin, Master in Chancery.

Mr. Speaker,

I am commanded by the Honorable the Legislative Council to inform this House that they have passed an Act, sent up from this House, entitled "An Act for applying certain sums of money therein mentioned to make good certain moneys issued and advanced by His Majesty, through the Lieutenant Governor, in pursuance of an Address from this House," without any amendment.

And then he withdrew.

Capt. Cowan and Mr. McGregor reported that, agreeably to the command of this House, they had waited upon His Excellency the Lieutenant Governor with the Address of this House, voted yesterday, to which His Excellency had been pleased to return the following answer.

Gentlemen of the House of Assembly,

It will afford me great satisfaction in complying with the wishes of the House of Assembly expressed in this Address; especially as the motives which have induced the House to propose so necessary an establishment have for their object the safety of the lives and properties of His Majesty's subjects.

Government House,
York, 10 Mar. 1808.

Read for the third time, as engrossed, the Bill for granting to His Majesty an annual sum of money as therein mentioned. Mr. McLean then moved, seconded by the Solicitor General, that the Bill do pass, and that the title be "An Act for granting to His Majesty an annual sum of money for the purposes therein mentioned." The Bill accordingly passed, and was signed by the Speaker. The Solicitor General then moved, seconded by Mr. McLean, that Messrs. Clench and Washburn do carry up to the Honorable the Legislative Council the Act for granting to His Majesty an annual sum of money for the purposes therein mentioned, and request their concurrence thereto, which was ordered accordingly.

Read for the third time, as engrossed, the Bill for the better securing to His Majesty, His Heirs and Successors, the due collection and receipt of certain duties therein mentioned. Then the Solicitor General moved, seconded by Mr. McLean, that the Bill do pass, and that the title be "An Act to repeal certain parts of an Act passed in the forty-sixth year of His Majesty's Reign, entitled 'An Act to continue an Act passed in the forty-third year of His Majesty's Reign, entitled an Act for the better securing to His Majesty, His Heirs and Successors, the due collection and receipt of certain duties therein mentioned.'" The Bill then passed, and was signed by the Speaker. The Solicitor General again moved, seconded by Mr. McLean that Messrs. Clench and Washburn do carry up to the Honorable the Legislative Council the said Bill, and request their concurrence thereto. The same was ordered accordingly.

Read for the third time, as engrossed, The Bill for the further encouragement of Hemp. Capt. Cowan then moved, seconded by Mr. Sherwood, that the Bill do pass, and that the title be "An Act for the further encouragement of the growth and cultivation of hemp within this Province, and for the exportation thereof." The Bill accordingly passed, and was signed by the Speaker.

Mr. Mallory moved, seconded by Mr. Sherwood, that Messrs. Clench and Washburn do carry up to the Honorable the Legislative Council the said Bill, and request their concurrence thereto. Ordered accordingly.

Then was read for the third time, as engrossed, the Bill for amending and repairing the Public Highways and Bridges. Mr. McLean then moved, seconded by the Solicitor General, that the Bill do pass, and that the title be "An Act for granting to His Majesty a certain sum of money out of the funds applicable to the uses of this Province, to defray the expenses of amending and repairing the Public Highways and Roads, laying out and opening new roads, and building bridges in the several Districts thereof. The Bill then passed, and was signed by the Speaker. Mr. McLean moved, seconded by Mr. McGregor, that Messrs. Clench and Washburn do carry up to the Honorable the Legislative Council the said Act, and do request their concurrence thereto, which was ordered accordingly.

Messrs. Clench and Washburn, the messengers named to carry up to the Honorable the Legislative Council several Acts from this House, reported that in obedience to the command of this House they had carried up to the Honorable the Legislative Council an Act entitled "An Act for granting to His Majesty an annual sum of money for the purposes therein mentioned," to which they did request their concurrence.

Also an Act entitled "An Act to repeal certain parts of An Act passed in the forty-sixth year of His Majesty's Reign, entitled "An Act to continue an Act passed in the forty-third year of His Majesty's Reign, entitled 'An Act for the better securing to His Majesty, His Heirs and Successors, the due collection and receipt of certain duties therein mentioned,'" to which they did also request their concurrence.

Another Act entitled "An Act for granting to His Majesty a certain sum of money out of the funds applicable to the uses of this Province, to defray the expenses of repairing and amending the Public Highways and Roads, laying out and opening new roads and building bridges in the several Districts thereof," and did request their concurrence in passing the same.

And also an Act entitled "An Act for the further encouragement of the growth and cultivation of hemp within this Province, and for the exportation thereof," and did request their concurrence thereto.

Read for the second time, The Bill for increasing the Salary of the Clerk of the Honorable the Legislative Council and the Clerk of the House of Assembly. Mr. Mallory then moved, seconded by Mr. Nellis, that the House do now resolve itself into a Committee, to go into the consideration of the Bill for increasing the salary of the Clerk of the Honorable the Legislative Council, and the Clerk of the House of Assembly. The House accordingly resolved itself into a Committee. Mr. Speaker left the Chair. Mr. Crysler was called to the chair of the Committee.

Mr. Speaker resumed the Chair, and Mr. Crysler reported that the Committee had gone through the consideration of the said Bill, to which they had made several amendments, which he was directed to report to the House whenever it should be pleased to receive the same. . Ordered, that the Report be now received. The Report was accordingly received and accepted. Mr. Clench then moved, seconded by Mr. Mallory, that the said Bill be engrossed, and read a third time to-morrow. Ordered accordingly.

Agreeably to the Order of the Day, the House resolved itself into a Committee to go into the further consideration of an Address to His Excellency the Lieutenant Governor, for promoting the cultivation and exportation of hemp. Mr. Speaker left the Chair. Mr. Clench was called to the chair of the Committee.

Mr. Speaker resumed the Chair, and Mr. Clench reported that the Committee had gone through the consideration of the said Address, to which they had made several amendments, which he was directed to report to the House, whenever it should be pleased to receive the same. The House then resolved that the Report be now received. The Report was accordingly received and accepted. On motion of Mr. McGregor, seconded by Capt. Cowan, ordered, that the said Address as amended be engrossed.

On motion of the Solicitor General, seconded by Capt. Cowan, the said Address was read as engrossed, and is as follows:

To His Excellency Francis Gore, Esquire, Lieutenant Governor of the Province of Upper Canada, etc., etc., etc.

May it please Your Excellency,—

We, His Majesty's most dutiful and loyal subjects, the Commons of Upper Canada, in Parliament assembled, being fully convinced of the advantages which would undoubtedly result from the encouragement of the growth and cultivation of hemp in this Province, have raised and applied from the Provincial Funds for that purpose the sum of One Thousand Seven Hundred Pounds.

It is with pleasure we represent to Your Excellency that the small advances we have been enabled to make in this important branch of agriculture plainly, evince that the Province of Upper Canada, both from climate and soil is well adapted to the growth of that valuable article.

But though we have ventured to state that the soil of this Province is peculiarly favorable to the culture of hemp, yet we respectfully beg leave to submit to Your Excellency that before we can more strenuously press that subject on the Canadian farmers we must be assured that the commodity when raised will be purchased in the country, and that the paternal hand of His Majesty will be graciously extended in dispelling difficulties which prevent them at present from accomplishing in its fullest strength so desirable an object. The inhabitants are incapable of waiting for the return of sales; but that obstruction may be remedied by appointing agents in the country, by which means the energy of the Province would be exerted, and the most valuable benefits result. And, if it should appear expedient to Your Excellency that this obstacle should be overcome in the manner which we have presumed to state, His Majesty's subjects in this Colony would glow with the pleasing reflection of being serviceable to the parent State by exertions which, in the end, would prove highly profitable to themselves.

We, therefore, His Majesty's most dutiful and loyal subjects, most respectfully suggest that the subject matter of this Address were made known to His Majesty, which we presume to hope Your Excellency will effect, he would deign to take the same into his Royal consideration, and if, on the one hand, His Majesty shall judge it expedient to encourage the culture of hemp in this Province, on the other we shall gratefully concur in adopting every measure within our reach, corresponding with His Majesty's views.

Commons House of Assembly,
10th March, 1808.

The Address then passed, and was signed by the Speaker.

Then Mr. Sherwood moved, seconded by Mr. Mallory, that this House do request a conference with the Honorable the Legislative Council, on the subject matter of the amendments made by them in and to an Act sent up from this House, entitled "An Act to provide for the support of Judges of the Court of Common Pleas," and that Messrs. Clench and Washburn be a Committee to request the same. Ordered accordingly.

A Written message to the Honorable the Legislative Council:

Mr. Speaker,—

We are commanded by the Commons House of Assembly to request that a conference be had with this Honorable House on the subject matter of the amendments made by this House in and to an Act entitled "An Act to provide for the support of Judges of the Court of Common Pleas.

Commons House of Assembly,   (Signed) ALEX'R MCDONELL,
10th March, 1808.   Speaker.

Capt. Cowan then moved, seconded by Mr. Mallory, that Messrs. Clench, McLean, Solicitor General, Washburn, McGregor and Sherwood be a Committee to confer with the Honorable the Legislative Council upon the subject matter of the amendments made by them in and to an Act sent up from this House, entitled "An Act to provide for the support of Judges of the Court of Common Pleas," which was ordered accordingly.

Messrs. Clench and Washburn reported that they had carried up to the Honorable the Legislative Council the message of this House, requesting a conference with them upon the subject matter of the amendments made by them in and to an Act sent up from this House, entitled "An Act to provide for the support of Judges of the Court of Common Pleas."

Mr. McGregor moved, seconded by Mr. Sherwood, that the House do now resolve itself into a Committee to go into the consideration of the propriety of presenting an Address to His Excellency the Lieutenant Governor upon the subject of establishing a more regular communication by post in this Province. The House accordingly resolved itself into a Committee. Mr. Speaker left the Chair. Mr. McLean was called to the chair of the Committee.

Mr. Speaker resumed the Chair, and Mr. McLean reported that the Committee had gone through the consideration of the said Address, to which they had made several amendments, which amendments he was directed to report to the House whenever it should be pleased to receive the same. Ordered, that the Report be now received. The Report was accordingly received and accepted.

On motion of the Solicitor General, seconded by Mr. McGregor, the said Address, as amended, was ordered to be engrossed.

On motion of Capt. Cowan, seconded by Mr. Nellis, the said Address was read as engrossed.

The Address then passed, and was signed by the Speaker, and is as follows:
To His Excellency Francis Gore. Esquire, Lieutenant Governor of the Province of Upper Canada, etc., etc., etc.

May it please Your Excellency,—

We, His Majesty's most dutiful and loyal subjects, the Commons of Upper Canada, in Parliament assembled, beg leave to state that the Post Office now established by His Majesty's Government continues but five months in the year in this Province, and that it would greatly conduce to the convenience and benefit of the Inhabitants if a regular communication by post were established during the whole year.

Fully convinced that Your Excellency is anxiously desirous to promote the welfare and best interests of His Majesty's subjects under your Government, we respectfully approach Your Excellency to request that you will be pleased to make such a representation to His Majesty's Ministers, relative to the better establishment of a Post Office in this Colony, as Your Excellency may think proper to procure the desired effect.

Commons House of Assembly,
10th March, 1808.

Mr. Clench then moved, seconded by Mr. Mallory, that Messrs. McGregor, Nellis and Sherwood do wait upon His Excellency the Lieutenant Governor with the said Address.

A Written Message from the Honorable the Legislative Council, by Mr. Baldwin, Master-in-Chancery.

Mr. Speaker,—

The Honorable the Legislative Council has agreed that a Committee of their . House shall meet a Committee of this House of Assembly, in conference, upon the matter of the amendments made by the Legislative Council in and to an Act to provide for the support of Judges of the Court of Common Pleas, in the Legislative Council Chamber, to-morrow, at ten o'clock a.m.

Legislative Council Chamber,   (Signed) THOS. SCOTT,
York, 10th March, 1808.   Speaker.

And then he withdrew.

Mr. Sherwood moved, seconded by Mr. Clench, that the Solicitor General, Messrs. Crysler, Washburn and Mallory be a Committee to present to His Excellency the Lieutenant Governor the Address of this House, relative to the culture of hemp in this Province, which was ordered accordingly.

On motion of Mr. Mallory, seconded by Mr. Crysler, the House adjourned.

Friday, 11th March, 1808.

Prayers were read.

Mr. Solicitor General moved, seconded by Mr. Washburn, that the Committee appointed to confer with a Committee of the Honorable the Legislative Council, upon the subject matter of amendments made by the Legislative Council in and to the Act to provide for the support of Judges of the Court of Common Pleas, do now report to the House.

Accordingly Mr. Solicitor General, with the other Members of the Committee appointed to confer with a Committee of the Honorable the Legislative Council, upon the subject matter of the amendments made by them in and to the Act sent up from this House, entitled "An Act to provide for the support of Judges of the Court of Common Pleas," reported that the Committee from this House did meet the Committee appointed by the Legislative Council, and that it had been agreed upon by them to recommend to the Honorable the Legislative Council another amendment, to be substituted in lieu of the former, which Report was read by the Clerk at the Table.

Read for the third time, as engrossed, the Bill for increasing the salaries of the Clerk of the Legislative Council and the Clerk of the House of Assembly. The Solicitor General moved, seconded by Mr. Clench, that the Bill do pass, and that the title be "An Act for granting to His Majesty a certain sum of money out of the Provincial Fund, to increase the salary of the Clerk of the Legislative Council and the Clerk of the House of Assembly. The Bill then passed, and was signed by the Speaker. The Solicitor General then moved, seconded by Mr. McLean, that Messrs. Clench and Crysler do carry up to the Honorable the Legislative Council the said Act, and request their concurrence thereto, which was ordered accordingly.

Mr. McLean gave notice that he will move to-morrow for a call of the House.

Messrs. McGregor, Nellis and Sherwood reported that, agreeably to the command of this House, they had waited upon His Excellency the Lieutenant Governor with the Address of this House voted yesterday, for the more regular communication with Lower Canada by Post throughout the year, to which His Excellency had been pleased to return the following answer:

Gentlemen of the House of Assembly,—

I am so perfectly sensible that the Inhabitants of this Province would derive considerable benefit were a regular Post established, that I shall cheerfully transmit your Address to His Majesty's Ministers, to be laid before the King, with my best support.

Government House, York,
11th March, 1808.

The Solicitor General, Messrs. Crysler, Washburn and Mallory reported that, in obedience to the commands of this House they had waited upon His Excellency the Lieutenant Governor with the Address of this House, voted yesterday, relative to the cultivation and exportation of hemp in and from this Province, to which His Excellency was pleased to return the following answer:

Gentlemen of the House of Assembly,—

It is most gratifying to me to observe that the House of Assembly have directed their attention to the laudable purpose of encouraging the growth and culture of hemp in this Province.

No delay shall take place on my part in making the representations suggested in this Address to His Majesty's Ministers, and be assured that every exertion shall be made by me to dispel the difficulties which now impede this important branch of agriculture.

Government House, York,
11th March, 1808.

A Written Message from the Honorable the Legislative Council, by Mr. Baldwin, Master-in-Chancery:

Mr. Speaker,—

The Honorable the Legislative Council cannot accede to the further amendment proposed to be made by the Commons House of Assembly in and to an Act intituled "An Act to provide for the support of Judges of the Court of Common Pleas."

Legislative Council Chamber,   (Signed) THOMAS SCOTT,
York, 11th March, 1808.   Speaker.

Another Message from the Honorable the Legislative Council, by Mr. Baldwin, Master-in-Chancery:

Mr. Speaker,—

I am Commanded by the Honorable the Legislative Council to inform this House that they have concurred in passing an Act sent up from this Honorable House, entitled "An Act to amend an Act passed in the forty-seventh year of His Majesty's reign, entitled 'An Act to establish Public Schools in each and every District of this Province.'"

And then he withdrew.

The Solicitor General moved, seconded by Mr. McLean, that this House do now resolve that Hugh McLean, the person who has attended the Commissioners under an Act of the Parliament of this Province for the relief of the Heirs and Devisees of the Nominees of the Crown, be allowed for the last three years' attendance the sum of Ten Pounds, and that the Speaker be authorised to write a letter to His Excellency the Lieutenant Governor, requesting him to issue his Warrant for that amount; and that this House will make good the same the next Session of Parliament, which was ordered accordingly.

On motion of Mr. McLean, seconded by Capt. Cowan, the House adjourned until twelve o'clock at noon to-morrow.

Saturday, 12th March, 1808.

Prayers were read.

A message from the Honorable the Legislative Council by Mr. Baldwin, Master-in-Chancery:

Mr. Speaker,—

I am commanded by the Honorable the Legislative Council to inform this House that they have concurred in passing an Act sent up from this House, entitled "An Act for the further encouragement of the growth and culture of hemp within this Province, and for the exportation thereof," without any amendment.

Also, an Act sent up from this Honorable House. entitled "An Act for granting to His Majesty a certain sum of money out of the Provincial Fund, to increase the Salary of the Clerk of the Legislative Council and the Clerk of the House of Assembly," without any amendment.

Also, an Act sent up from this House, entitled "An Act for granting to His Majesty a certain sum of money out of the Funds applicable to the uses of this Province, to defray the expenses of amending and repairing the Public Highways and Roads, laying out and opening new roads. and building bridges in the several Districts thereof," without any amendment.

Also an Act sent up from this Honorable House, entitled "An Act to repeal certain parts of an Act passed in the forty-sixth year of His Majesty's reign, entitled "An Act to continue an Act passed in the forty-third year of His Majesty's reign, entitled 'An Act for the better securing to His Majesty, His Heirs and Successors, the due collection and receipt of certain duties therein mentioned,'" without any amendment.

And also an Act sent up from this Honorable House, entitled "An Act for granting to His Majesty an annual sum of money for the purpose therein mentioned," without any amendment.

And then he withdrew.

Capt. Cowan moved, seconded by Mr. Clench, for leave to bring in a Bill this day to provide for the support of Judges hereafter to be appointed for this Province. Leave was accordingly given, and the said Bill was read for the first time. Capt. Cowan then moved, seconded by Mr. Clench, that the Bill to provide a salary for Judges hereafter to be appointed for this Province be read a second time this day, which passed in the negative. Mr. Clench, seconded by Mr. Washburn, moved that the said Bill be read a second time on Monday next. Ordered accordingly.

The Solicitor General moved, seconded by Capt. Cowan, that it be resolved by this House that the subscription papers accompanying the petition to this House respecting the Johnstown Courthouse be transmitted by the Clerk of this House to the Chairman of the Quarter Sessions of the District of Johnstown. The House accordingly resolved the same.

At three o'clock the Speaker adjourned the House for want of a quorum.

Present :—Mr. Speaker, Messrs. Cowan, Solicitor General, Washburn, and McLean.

Monday, 14th March, 1808.

Prayers were read.

On motion of Captain Cowan, seconded by Mr. McGregor, the House adjourned for two hours.

The House being met:

A Message from the Honorable the Legislative Council by Mr. Baldwin, Master-in-Chancery.

Mr. Speaker,—

I am commanded by the Honorable the Legislative Council to inform this House that they have passed an Act sent up from this Honorable House entitled "An Act to explain, amend, and reduce to one Act of Parliament, the several laws now in being for the raising and training the Militia of this Province." Mr. Mallory moved, seconded by Mr. Nellis, that the amendments made by the Honorable the Legislative Council in and to the Act for the better regulation of the Militia of this Province " be now read for the first time. The said amendments were accordingly read for the first time. Mr. Solicitor General moved, seconded by Mr. McLean, that the said amendments be read a second time to-morrow. Ordered accordingly.

On motion of the Solicitor General, seconded by Mr. McLean, the House adjourned.

Tuesday, 15th March, 1808.

Prayers were read.

Agreeably to the Order of the Day, was read for the second time the amendments made by the Honorable the Legislative Council in and to the Act for the raising and training the Militia of this Province. On motion of Mr. Clench, seconded by Mr. Nellis, the House resolved itself into a Committee to go into consideration of the amendments made by the Honorable the Legislative Council in and to the said Act. Mr. Speaker left the Chair. Captain Cowan was called to the Chair of the Committee.

Mr. Speaker resumed the Chair, and Captain Cowan reported that the Committe had gone through the consideration of the said amendments, and that he was directed to report that the Committee approved of the Bill as amended by the Honorable the Legislative Council, and did recommend that the Bill as amended be adopted by the House. The House accordingly resolved that the amendments made by the Honorable the Legislative Council to the said Bill be adopted. The amendments were accordingly adopted. Mr. Sherwood moved, seconded by Mr. Crysler, that Messrs. Clench and Cowan do inform the Honorable the Legislative Council that this House hath concurred in adopting the amendments made by them in and to the Act for the raising and training the Militia of this Province. Ordered accordingly.

Mr. Speaker,—

We are commanded by the Commons House of Assembly to acquaint the Honorable House that they have concurred in adopting the amendments made by the Legislative Council in and to the Act entitled "An Act to explain, amend, and reduce to one Act of Parliament, the several laws now in being for raising and training the Militia of this Province.

Commons House of Assembly,   (Signed) ALEX'R McDONELL,
15th March, 1808.   Speaker.

19 A.

A Message from the Honorable the Legislative Council, by Mr. Baldwin, Master-in-Chancery.

Mr. Speaker,—

I am commanded by the Honorable the Legislative Council to acquaint this House that they have passed an Act, sent up from the House, entitled "An Act for the better representation of the Commons of this Province in Parliament," to which they have made several amendments, to which amendments they request the concurrence of this House.

And then he withdrew.

On motion of Mr. Clench, seconded by Mr. Nellis, the amendments to the said Act were read for the first time. Captain Cowan then moved, seconded by Mr. McGregor, that the said amendments be now read for the second time. The said amendments were accordingly read for the second time. Mr. Clench then moved, seconded by Mr. Mallory, that the House do now resolve itself into a Committee to go into the consideration of the amendments made by the Honorable the Legislative Council in and to the Act sent up from this House, entitled "An Act for the better representation of the Commons of this Province in Parliament." The House accordingly resolved itself into a Committee. Mr. Speaker left the Chair. Mr. Crysler was called to the chair of the Committee.

Mr. Speaker resumed the Chair, and Mr. Crysler reported that the Committee had gone through the consideration of the said amendments, and that he was directed to report to the House, whenever it should be pleased to receive the same, that the Committee recommended that the amendments made by the Honorable the Legislative Council to the said Act be adopted. The House then resolved that the said amendments be adopted. Mr. Sherwood then moved, seconded by Mr. Crysler, that Messrs. Clench and Nellis do inform the Honorable the Legislative Council that this House have concurred in adopting the amendments made by them in and to the Act for the better representation of the Commons of this Province in Parliament, which was ordered accordingly.

Mr. Speaker,—

We are commanded by the Commons House of Assembly to acquaint this Honorable House that they have concurred in adopting the amendments made by the Legislative Council, in and to the Act entitled "An Act for the better representation of the Commons of this Province in Parliament, and to repeal part of an Act, passed in the fortieth year of His Majesty's reign, entitled 'An Act for the more equal representation of the Commons of this Province in Parliament; and for the better defining the qualifications of Electors.'"

Commons House of Assembly,   (Signed) ALEX'R McDONELL,
15th March, 1808.   Speaker.

Mr. Washburn moved, seconded by Mr. Clench, that the Petition of the inhabitants of the County of Prince Edward, relative to the Commerce of this Province, be now read, and that the same be inserted on the Journals of this House, and recommended to be taken into consideration by any future Parliament, which was ordered accordingly, and the Petition is as follows:—

To the Gentlemen Commons, Members of the House of Assembly of the Province of Upper Canada in Parliament assembled.

We, His Majesty's most loyal and dutiful subjects, Inhabitants of the County of Prince Edward, in the Midland District, and Province aforesaid,

Deeply impressed with a sense of the present confined situation of the Commerce of this Country, think it our indispensable duty, for the present and future prosperity thereof. to lay before you what we conceive a true and just statement cf it, and the much-to-be lamented method of purchasing and exporting, etc., of every commodity we can furnish for exportation, at the Ports of Quebec and Montreal, to which places we are obliged to take and dispose of each and every article we can furnish for the purpose aforesaid.

We find that by a prohibition of all vessels (the English excepted) from entering the aforesaid Ports to be the greatest misfortune attending our situation. First, it throws the whole trade of these ports into the hands of a few individuals residing therein, which governs all our commerce.   Secondly, it causes a combination between them to fix prices on all imports and exports, which we are sorry to say they have generally done to our direct damage.   Thirdly, it causes all imports and exports to be carried on in chartered vessels.   Fourthly, it prohibits us from any advantage or profit arising from a trade with any foreign Kingdom, State, or Country, even where our fellow subjects are permitted to trade.   And, finally, it excludes us from any privilege in trade, except trusting our all in that line in the hands of the aforesaid individuals which have had, and still hold, the power of allowing us whatever price they please for all exports, and in return compel whatever price they please to charge for all imports of merchandize which come solely through their hands, imported as aforesaid in a few chartered vessels.   And we are aware that for several years past the exports have employed more than double the number of chartered vessels than the imports have; which, of course, leaves more than half the aforesaid vessels to come in under ballast, and cannot be expected to take freights on the same reasonable terms as if they were freighted in and out, which serves as one of the many politics or excuses which these individuals make use of for taking our produce, lumber, and every article we can furnish for exportation at a very reduced price to what might otherwise be allowed by them.

We can, with confidence, and from a long experience, namely, since we have been able to furnish a single article for exportation. assure you that nothing but a scarcity of whatever commodity was most wanting would cause it to command a fair price in the aforesaid market, which is principally owing to the combined situation of the commerce as aforesaid, and are severally of opinion that the only and sure method of causing a medium of contrast or spirit of opposition (which we think to a certain degree necessary in trade in these more enlightened days of the world) would be to admit a free trade to and from the aforesaid Ports, with all Nations and People with whom his Majesty is at peace, and allowing commerce.

We are also well aware that without it it is almost impossible for the farmers, who, under their all wise Creator, are the main pillar and support of all nations and countries, to receive a just reward for all their labours.

We have the satisfaction to observe that this country is blessed with seemingly all that Nature could do for it—a good market for the produce of our labours excepted—and Providence has placed an industrious people therein to till the fertile soil, who, no doubt would follow their ploughs and reap their harvest with smiles on their countenances, could they only be satisfied that they were to receive a reasonable price for what they might have left after supporting their families.

We also lament that the situation of the commerce of so great and good a country as this Province might be under the aid of Providence, which we hope may guide all our councils, and inspire every branch of our Legislature with a sense of the obligation they are under to give all assistance in their power to have the commercial situation there, placed on the best, most favorable and permanent footing that its remote situation from a market can possibly admit of.

We hope you will join us in opinion, and we look up to you for redress, for not only this, but all other grievances that we have a right to complain of, at least as you in your situation can assist or take notice of, which we conceive to extend to every matter or thing which doth or may tend to harm the welfare or prosperity of your constituents, or benefit the same.

We also request you will communicate this to the other two branches of the Legislature in what manner you think most proper, and at the same time request their aid in adopting measures the most fit and speedy to remedy the aforesaid grievances.

We are also aware that nothing can be done to insure a free trade as aforesaid, short of obtaining His Majesty's consent, occasioned by stipulation in the present treaty of amity, commerce and navigation, between His Majesty and the United States of America; at least as far as that nation is concerned; and trust that you will see with us the immediate necessity of an endeavor to obtain the privilege aforesaid, and, through a petition, or by some other means that may be thought proper, make the same known to our most gracious Sovereign.

We also assure you that we are willing to accept it under every restriction as to duties, etc., which might otherwise tend to harm His Majesty or his subjects in general; and we are confident that the obtaining the above mentioned privilege would be a means of thousands of good subjects emigrating immediately to this country.

It is with regret we have to observe that our above stated situation renders us incapable of being that benefit to our most gracious Sovereign, in conjunction with our fellow subjects in other parts of his Dominions, that our inclination leads us to be.

We conclude this our prayer and statement, having given only the outlines of our opinion on the above important subject, as we conceive it, and with a sanguine hope that you will think with us that there is an actual necessity of endeavoring by the best and surest method of obtaining it to enhance the price of every article we can furnish for exportation.

We also flatter ourselves that our fellow subjects throughout the Province will join us in opinion, and hope to see some abler pen employed in adopting the most salutary measures to be taken in the pursuit thereof; at the same time trusting that you will seriously reflect on this subject, and pay it the respect which in your wisdom you may deem it worthy of.

And your Petitioners, as in duty bound, will ever pray.

Solomon Spafford, Simeon Washburn, Stephen Palen, Sampson Striker, Silas Dyne, Gilbert Palen, and one hundred and twenty-three others.

The Speaker reported that, in obedience to the command of this House, he had written to His Excellency, the Lieutenant-Governor, requesting him to issue his warrant, in favor of Hugh McLean, for the sum of Ten Pounds; in consideration of his past services as Messenger, attending the Commissioners who are appointed under an Act of the Parliament of this Province to afford relief to persons claiming lands in this Province as Heirs or Devisees of the Nominees of the Crown in cases where no Patent hath issued for such lands—to which he received no answer.

On motion of Mr. Crysler, seconded by Mr. McGregor, the House adjourned.

Wednesday, 16th March, 1808.

Prayers were read.

Messrs. Clench and Nellis reported that, in obedience to the command of this House, they had carried up to the Honorable the Legislative Council the Message of this House, acquainting them that this House had concurred in adopting the amendments made by the Honorable the Legislative Council in and to an Act sent up from the House, entitled "An Act for the better representation of the Commons of this Province in Parliament, and to repeal part of an Act passed in the Fortieth year of His present Majesty's Reign, entitled 'An Act for the more equal representation of the Commons of this Province in Parliament, and for the better defining the qualifications of electors.'"

And also that they had carried up another message of this House to the Honorable the Legislative Council, acquainting them that this House have concurred in adopting the amendments made by them in and to an Act sent up from this House, entitled "An Act to explain, amend, and reduce to one Act of Parliament the several laws now in being for the raising and training the Militia of this Province."

The Clerk reported to the House the expenditure of his office since the Eighth instant, being the day the Contingent Accounts were approved and passed by this House, and is as follows:—

THE HONORABLE THE HOUSE OF ASSEMBLY, in account with their Clerk for Copying Clerks and other contingencies between the 9th and 16th March, 1808, both days:

Dr.	Inclusive.			
To Joseph Shaw		£7.	5s.	0d.
" Edward McMahon		7	10	0
" Allan McLean		5	10	0
" John Higgins		7	5	0
" Messenger's Account		1	17	1
Balance . .			12	11
		£30.	0s.	0d.

			Cr.	
By Cash to be received	£30.	0s.	0d.
	£30.	0s.	0d.

By balance that will be in the Clerk's hands. .   12s.   11d.

The Order of the Day for the call of the House being read, ordered, that the House be now called over. The House was accordingly called over, and the names of all the members were taken down, and are as follows, viz.:—The Speaker, W. B. Wilkinson (dead), D'Arcy Boulton, John Crysler, Samuel 'Sherwood, Peter Howard (absent), Allan McLean, Thomas Dorland (absent), Ebenezer Washburn, David McGregor Rogers (absent), Robert Thorpe (beyond sea, excused), Joseph Willcocks (Committed to Gaol by and for contempt of this House), Robert Nellis, Isaac Swayze (absent), Matthew Elliott (absent by leave), David Cowan, Esquires.

On motion of Captain Cowan, seconded by the Solicitor General,

Resolved, that it be inserted upon the Journals of this House, that on the last day the Commons House of Assembly sat, in the Fourth Session of the Fourth Provincial Parliament of this Province, being the Sixteenth day of March. On the names of the Members being called it appeared that David McGregor Rogers, Thomas Dorland and Peter Howard, Esquires, were absent without leave, since the Fifth day of March last past, when they left the House without a quorum, with a determined resolution not to return unless the majority of the House would acquiesce in their measures. That in consequence thereof the business of the House was suspended until the attendance of Robert Nellis, Esquire, who was sent for to his place of residence, he being absent on leave; by which means a quorum was formed, and the House of Assembly enabled to resume the business of the Session.

The House unanimously resolved the same.

Captain Cowan, seconded by Mr. McLean, moved that Joseph Willcocks be this day discharged from imprisonment, and that the Speaker do issue his warrant for that purpose. The Speaker accordingly issued his Warrant, which is as follows:—

Alexander McDonell, Esquire, Speaker of the Honorable the Commons House of Assembly,

To the Sheriff of the Home District, GREETING.

By virtue of the power and authority in me vested by the Commons House of Assembly, you are hereby ordered and required to discharge from your custody this day, Joseph Willcocks, Esquire, who was, on the Twentieth day of February last past, committed to the Gaol of the Home District, he having on that day been convicted of a contempt of the said House of Assembly; and for so doing this shall be your sufficient warrant.

Given under my hand and seal at York this Sixteenth day of March, 1808.
                                  (Signed) ALEXANDER McDONELL,
                                                              Speaker.

On motion of Mr. McGregor, seconded by Mr. Clench, the House adjourned for one hour.

The House being met:—

A Message from His Excellency the Lieutenant-Governor by Mr. George Lawe, Gentleman Usher of the Black Rod:—

Mr. Speaker,—

I am commanded by His Excellency, the Lieutenant-Governor to inform this Honorable House, that it is His Excellency's pleasure that the Members thereof do forthwith attend upon His Excellency in the Legislative Council Chamber.

Accordingly, Mr. Speaker, with the House, went up to attend His Excellency, when His Excellency was pleased to give, in His Majesty's name, the Royal assent to the following Public and Private Bills, viz:—

An Act for the better regulation of Parish and Town Officers throughout this Province.

An Act for the better regulation of Special Juries.

An Act to continue an Act passed in the Thirty-third year of His Majesty's Reign, entitled "An Act to provide for the appointment of Returning Officers of the several Counties within this Province."

An Act for building a Court House and Gaol in the Township of Elizabeth-town, in the District of Johnstown.

An Act for the better regulating the Statute Labour in the Counties of Essex and Kent in the Western District.

An Act to continue an Act passed in the Forty-fifth year of His Majesty's Reign, entitled "An Act to afford relief to those persons who may be entitled to claim lands in this Province as Heirs or Devisees of the Nominees of the Crown, in cases where no Patent hath issued for such lands, and further to extend the benefits of the said Act."

An Act to explain, amend, and reduce to one Act of Parliament, the several Laws now being for the raising and training the Militia of this Province.

An Act for the better representation of the Commons of this Province in Parliament, and to repeal part of an Act passed in the Fortieth year of His Majesty's Reign, entitled "An Act for the more equal representation of the Commons of this Province, and for the better defining the qualification of Electors."

An Act to extend the benefits of An Act passed in the Thirty-seventh year of His Majesty's Reign, entitled "An Act for the more easy Barring of Dower, and to repeal certain parts of the same."

Mr. Speaker then said:

May it please Your Excellency to approve of the Seven Bills, which the Assembly, with the concurrence of the Legislative Council, have passed for aid to His Majesty:—

An Act for applying certain sums of money therein mentioned to make good certain moneys issued and advanced by His Majesty through the Lieutenant-Governor in pursuance of an Address.

An Act to amend an Act passed in the Forty-seventh year of His Majesty's Reign, entitled "An Act to establish Public Schools in each and every District of this Province."

An Act for granting to His Majesty an annual sum of money for the purposes therein mentioned.

An Act for granting to His Majesty a certain sum of money out of the funds applicable to the uses of this Province, to defray the expenses of amending and repairing the Public Highways and Roads, laying out and opening new Roads, and building Bridges in the several Districts thereof.

An Act for the further encouragement of the growth and cultivation of Hemp within this Province, and for the exportation thereof.

An Act for granting to His Majesty a certain sum of money out of the Provincial Fund, to increase the salary of the Clerk of the Legislative Council, and the Clerk of the House of Assembly.

An Act to repeal certain parts of an Act passed in the Forty-sixth year of His Majesty's Reign, entitled "An Act to continue an Act passed in the Forty-third year of His Majesty's Reign, entitled 'An Act for the better securing to His Majesty, his Heirs and Successors, the due collection and receipt of certain duties therein mentioned.' "

To which seven Bills His Excellency, the Lieutenant Governor, was pleased to give the Royal assent in His Majesty's name.

And then His Excellency, the Lieutenant Governor, was pleased to make the following Speech to both Houses of Parliament.

Honorable Gentlemen of the Legislative Council,
    and
Gentlemen of the House of Assembly,
    The unusual length to which this Session of the Legislature has been prolonged
by an event that could not have been foreseen, will not, I trust, operate as a
material inconvenience to your private affairs. It will, however, be your pride to
reflect that instead of repining at any expense of labour or of time, your zealous
exertions for the Public service have terminated honorably to yourselves and
advantageously to the Public.
    In times like the present, of uncertainty and of danger, the first care of every
good man is the safety of his country. The salutary provisions enacted by you in
the Bill for regulating the Militia of this Province are the most substantial proofs
that this has been the governing principle of your conduct.
    The Act for extending the representation of the Commons in the House of
Assembly I consider as a measure beneficially conducive to the dearest interests
of the subjects of this Province at large; I therefore cheerfully concur in the
adoption of it.
    I am much gratified also to have in my power to observe that the growth and
cultivation of Hemp in this Colony, the soil of which is so well calculated for that
desirable branch of agriculture, has not escaped the serious attention of the House
of Assembly; and no endeavors shall be wanting on my part to give activity to
the measures which they have suggested to produce an abundant supply of an
article of the first necessity to the Mother Country.
    Your wisdom in providing against the difficulties of an Inland Communica-
tion, with a prudent management of the sums you have appropriated for the
laying out and repairing the public Roads and Bridges, will, I trust, considerably
improve them. They are, however, generally in so imperfect a state, that I have
it in contemplation to call the next Session of the Legislature at a season of the
year better calculated for an easy access to the Seat of Government.
    The relations of amity which happily existed between Great Britain and the
United States of America have been in some degree interrupted, and I regret that
during this Session I have not been enabled to lay before you any communication
on this interesting subject. But I cherish the hope that the voice of wisdom and
of moderation will ultimately prevail, and that the people of the United States
will justly appreciate the good will of His Majesty, and that two nations may not
be involved in the calamities of War, whose mutual interests plainly point to
peace and commercial intercourse; from whence naturally arises opulence, prosperity, and happiness to nations. It is, however, our essential duty to be prepared
for every event, and, should occasion call for it, to be ready with firmness to defend
the just rights of our King and the interests of his people.
    I now close this Session of the Legislature, which, from its constitution, must
soon be dissolved, fully confident that your utmost efforts will be exerted in
promoting peace, harmony and good morals amongst the great body of the people;
and that the same zeal for the prosperity of this Province which has distinguished
your public character will govern and animate your private conduct.
    After which the Honorable the Speaker of the Legislative Council said:
    It is His Excellency the Lieutenant-Governor's will and pleasure that this
Provincial Parliament be prorogued until Friday, the Twenty-second day of
April next, to be then here held; and the Provincial Parliament is accordingly
prorogued until Friday, the Twenty-second day of April next.

[I do hereby certify that the above and what is written on the foregoing pages is a transcript of the Journal of the House of Assembly in Upper Canada, being the Fourth Session of the Fourth Provincial Parliament assembled in the Town of York, on the Twentieth day of January last, agreeably to the Proclamation of His Excellency, Francis Gore, Esquire, Lieutenant-Governor of the Province of Upper Canada; and prorogued by His Excellency on the Sixteenth day of March last.

Clerk of the Assembly's Office, York,   DONALD MCLEAN,
        13th May, 1808.   Clerk Assembly.]

[Certified to be true copies from the original records in the Colonial Office.

                                    GEORGE MAYER,
                        Librarian and Keeper of the Records.

Colonial Office, Downing Street,
        October, 1856.]

JOURNAL

OF THE

HOUSE OF ASSEMBLY

OF

UPPER CANADA

From the first day of February to the
twelfth day of March,
1810.
Both days inclusive.
In the Fiftieth Year of the Reign of

KING GEORGE THE THIRD

Being the Second Session of the Fifth Provincial
Parliament of this Province.

JOURNAL

OF THE

HOUSE OF ASSEMBLY

OF

UPPER CANADA

1810.

FRANCIS GORE, Lieutenant-Governor.

PROCLAMATION.

GEORGE THE THIRD, by the Grace of God, of the United Kingdom of Great Britain and Ireland, King, Defender of the Faith:

To all Our Loving Subjects, GREETING.

WHEREAS, by Our proclamation, bearing date the ninth day of March last, we thought fit, by and with the advice of our Executive Council, to prorogue Our Provincial Parliament until the fourteenth day of this present month of April, at which time, in Our Town of York, you were held and constrained to appear; but we, taking into Our Royal consideration the ease and convenience of Our loving subjects, have thought fit, by and with the advice of Our Executive Council, to relieve you, and each of you, of your attendance at the time aforesaid, hereby convoking, and by these presents enjoining you, and each of you, that on the twenty-second day of May next ensuing you meet us in Our Provincial Parliament, in our Town of York, there to take into consideration the state and welfare of Our Province of Upper Canada, and therein to do as may seem necessary. Herein fail not.

In testimony whereof we have caused these Our Letters to be made patent, and the Great Seal of Our said Province to be hereunto affixed. Witness Our Trusty and Well beloved Francis Gore, Esquire, Our Lieutenant Governor of Our said Province, at York, this seventh day of April, in the Year of Our Lord One Thousand Eight Hundred and Nine, and in the Forty-ninth year of Our Reign.

(Signed)   F. G.

WM. JARVIS, Secretary.

By a further proclamation of His Excellency Francis Gore, Esquire, Lieutenant Governor of the Province of Upper Canada, &c., &c., dated at York, the tenth day of May, One Thousand Eight Hundred and Nine, the Meeting of the Legislative Council and House of Assembly stands prorogued to the twenty-ninth day of June, One Thousand Eight Hundred and Nine.

⸴ By a further Proclamation of His Excellency Francis Gore, Esquire, Lieutenant Governor of the Province of Upper Canada, &c., &c., &c., dated at York, the twenty-third day of June, One Thousand Eight Hundred and Nine, the Meeting of the Legislative Council and House of Assembly stands prorogued to the fifth day of August, One Thousand Eight Hundred and Nine.

By a further Proclamation of His Excellency Francis Gore, Esquire, Lieutenant Governor of the Province of Upper Canada, &c., &c., &c., dated at York.

[281]

the twenty-eighth day of July, One Thousand Eight Hundred and Nine, the Meeting of the Legislative Council and House of Assembly stands prorogued to the twelfth day of September, One Thousand Eight Hundred and Nine.

By a further Proclamation of His Excellency Francis Gore, Esquire, Lieutenant Governor of the Province of Upper Canada, &c., &c., &c., dated at York, the ninth day of October, One Thousand Eight Hundred and Nine, the Meeting of the Legislative Council and House of Assembly stands prorogued to the twenty-eighth day of November, One Thousand Eight Hundred and Nine.

By a further Proclamation of His Excellency Francis Gore, Esquire, Lieutenant Governor of the Province of Upper Canada, &c., &c., &c., dated at York, on the eighteenth day of November, One Thousand Eight Hundred and Nine, the Meeting of the Legislative Council and House of Assembly stands prorogued to the fourth day of January, One Thousand Eight Hundred and Ten.

FRANCIS GORE, Lieutenant Governor.

PROCLAMATION.

GEORGE THE THIRD, by the Grace of God, of the United Kingdom of Great Britain and Ireland, King, Defender of the Faith:

To Our beloved and faithful Legislative Councillors of Our Province of Upper Canada, and to Our Knights, Citizens and Burgesses of Our said Province to the Provincial Parliament at Our Town of York, on the fourth day of the Month of January next ensuing, to be commenced, held, called and elected, and to every of you, GREETING.

WHEREAS, by Our Proclamation, bearing date the eighteenth day of November last, we thought fit, by and with the advice of Our Executive Council, to prorogue Our Provincial Parliament until the fourth day of the Month of January next ensuing; at which time, in Our Town of York, you were held and constrained to appear; but we, taking into Our Royal consideration the ease and convenience of Our loving subjects, have thought fit, by and with the advice of Our Executive Council, to relieve you, and each of you, of your attendance at the time aforesaid, hereby convoking, and by these presents enjoining you, and each of you, that on the first day of February next ensuing you meet us in Our Provincial Parliament in Our Town of York, for the actual dispatch of public business, there to take into consideration the state and welfare of Our Province of Upper Canada, and therein to do as may seem necessary.

Herein fail not.

In Testimony whereof we have caused these Our Letters to be made patent, and the Great Seal of Our said Province to be hereunto affixed.

Witness Our Trusty and Well beloved Francis Gore, Esquire, Our Lieutenant Governor of Our said Province, at York, this eleventh day of December, in the Year of Our Lord One Thousand Eight Hundred and Nine, and in the Fiftieth Year of Our Reign.

(Signed)   F. G.

(Signed)   WM. JARVIS, Secretary.

HOUSE.OF ASSEMBLY.

YORK, Thursday, 1st February, 1810.

At the Second Session of the Fifth Parliament of Upper Canada, begun and held in the Town of York, on Thursday, the fifth day of February, in the Fiftieth year of the Reign of Our Sovereign Lord, George the Third, by the Grace of God, of the United Kingdom of Great Britain and Ireland, King, Defender of the Faith, and in the Year of Our Lord One Thousand Eight Hundred and Ten.

His Excellency the Lieutenant Governor, having prorogued the Meeting of Parliament until the fourteenth day of April, One Thousand Eight Hundred and Nine, and by his proclamations annexed having further prorogued the same from time to time until this day.

The House being met, prayers were read.

A Message by Mr. George Lawe, Gentleman Usher of the Black Rod.

Mr. Speaker,

It is His Excellency the Lieutenant-Governor's pleasure that this Honorable House do immediately attend him in the Legislative Council Chamber.

The House went up accordingly, and being returned:—

Mr. Speaker reported that the House attended His Excellency in the Legislative Council Chamber, where His Excellency had been pleased to open the following Session by a most gracious Speech to both Houses, and that to prevent mistakes he had obtained for the information of the House a copy of His Excellency's Speech, which was read as follows:—

Honorable Gentlemen of the Legislative Council,

and

Gentlemen of the House of Assembly:—

On reviewing the situation of this Province I am happy in stating to you that I do not perceive any occurrence as taking place to interrupt its commerce or internal prosperity since the last Session of the Legislature.

It would have been an additional source of satisfaction to me to have been able to announce to you the restoration and renewal of friendship and amity between Great Britain and the United States of America, which, until of late, have so happily existed; and should the repeated efforts of His Majesty to accomplish so desirable an end not succeed, I trust that his brave and loyal subjects in this Province will evince, as many of them have already done, an unconquerable attachment to their King and Constitution.

Your respective situations in the Province will enable you to discover what may be still wanting to increase the happiness and prosperity of your fellow subjects, and to direct your deliberations to those points which may require Legislative assistance. It is the honorable task you are now called upon to perform.

It is incumbent upon me to call your attention to the evils resulting from the unskilful surveys of lands in this Province, instances of which have been reported to me by the Judges on their return from the circuits. A subject of such importance, will, I have no doubt, engage your most serious consideration.

Gentlemen of the House of Assembly,

I have directed the Public Accounts to be laid before you, in order that they may undergo such an examination as the nature of the subject requires.

Honorable Gentlemen of the Legislative Council,

and

Gentlemen of the House of Assembly,

It is unnecessary for me to recommend to you an unremitting zeal for the Public Service, and a steady prosecution of those objects which may promote the general interests of the Province, as a prompt and faithful discharge of these duties will be most conducive to the interests of your constituents.

Henry Maule, Esquire, the Member returned at the last General Election to represent the County of Dundas, being heretofore unable to attend his duty in Parliament, appeared this day, and took the Oath as appointed by the Statute, and did subscribe the Roll. He accordingly repaired to his seat in the House.

Benajah Mallory, Esquire, the Member returned to represent the Counties of Oxford and Middlesex, being heretofore unable to attend his duty in Parliament, appeared this day, and took the Oath as appointed by the Statute, and did subscribe the Roll. He accordingly repaired to his seat in the House.

Donald McLean, Esquire, one of the Commissioners appointed by *dedimus potestatem* to administer the Oath to the Members of the House of Assembly, came to the Bar, and did inform Mr. Speaker, that John Wilson, Esquire, had taken the Oath, as prescribed by the Statute, and did sign the Roll. Then Thomas B. Gough and David McGregor Rogers, Esquires, introduced John Wilson, Esquire, Knight representing the West Riding of the County of York, who took his seat accordingly.

Mr. Rogers gave notice that he will to-morrow move that this House do then resolve itself into a Committee to take into consideration His Excellency's Speech at the opening of the present Session.

Mr. Gough gave notice that he will to-morrow move for a call of the House on Monday next.

On motion of Mr. Rogers, seconded by Mr. Gough, the House adjourned.

Friday, 2nd February, 1810.

Prayers were read.

The Sergeant-at-Arms being absent by leave in Europe, Thomas Hamilton, Gentleman, was permitted by the House to act as Deputy Sergeant-at-Arms.

Mr. Gough, seconded by Mr. Rogers, moved that the petition of the inhabitants of the Counties of Lennox and Addington be now brought up, and that it do lie upon the Table. Ordered accordingly.

Mr. Rogers, seconded by Mr. Mallory, moved that the House do now resolve itself into a Committee to take into consideration His Excellency the Lieutenant-Governor's Speech at the opening of the present Session. The House accordingly resolved itself into a Committee. Mr. Speaker left the Chair. Mr. Mallory was called to the Chair of the Committee.

Mr. Speaker resumed the Chair, and Mr. Mallory reported that the Committee had made a progress, and directed him to ask for leave to sit again to-morrow. Leave was accordingly granted to sit again to-morrow.

Mr. Gough, seconded by Mr. Rogers, moved that this House be called over on Monday next. Ordered accordingly.

Mr. Wilcox moved, seconded by Mr. Mallory, for leave to bring in on Monday next, a Bill to alter and amend certain parts of an Act, passed in the fortieth year of His Majesty's Reign, entitled "An Act for the more equal representation of the Commons of this Province in Parliament, and for the better defining the qualifications of Electors." Leave was accordingly granted.

Mr. Willcocks, seconded by Mr. Rogers, moved for leave to bring in a Bill on Thursday next, to repeal certain parts of an Act passed in the forty-eighth year of

His Majesty's Reign, entitled "An Act to amend an Act passed in the forty-seventh year of His Majesty's Reign, entitled 'An Act to establish Public Schools in each and every District of this Province.'" Leave was accordingly granted.

Thomas Fraser and Henry Marcle, Esquires, rose in their places and acquainted the House that John Brownell, Member representing the Counties of Stormont and Russell, died in the month of December last. Therefore Capt. Fraser moved, seconded by Mr. Marcle, that the Speaker do acquaint His Excellency the Lieutenant-Governor that John Brownell, a Member of the House of Assembly, representing the Counties of Stormont and Russell, is dead, and that His Excellency be requested to issue a Writ for the election of a Knight to represent the same in the room of deceased. Ordered accordingly.

Mr. Gough, seconded by Mr. Rogers, moved for leave to bring in a Bill to-morrow for applying a certain sum of money therein mentioned to make good certain moneys issued and advanced by His Majesty, through the Lieutenant-Governor. Leave was accordingly granted.

Mr. Willcocks, seconded by Mr. Sovereign, moved that the third Rule of this House be now dispensed with, and that he have leave to bring in a Bill on Tuesday next to alter and amend an Act passed in the forty-ninth year of His Majesty's reign, entitled "An Act for granting a sum of money in aid of the building of a bridge across the Grand River." Ordered, that the said Rule be dispensed with on this occasion, and leave given to bring in the said Bill.

Mr. Mallory moved, seconded by Mr. Willcocks, that the third Rule of this House be dispensed with, and that he have leave to bring in on Tuesday next, a Bill to authorize the inhabitants of the County of Haldimand to hold Annual Meetings for the purpose of electing Parish and Town Officers. The said rule was accordingly dispensed with on this occasion, and leave was granted to bring in the said Bill on Tuesday next.

Mr. Mallory again moved, seconded by Mr. Willcocks, to bring in a Bill on Thursday next, to repeal so much of an Act passed in the forty-third year of His Majesty's Reign, as extends to the payment of the Members of the House of Assembly, and to make further provision for the same." Leave was granted accordingly.

Mr. Willcocks, seconded by Mr. Sovereign, moved for leave to bring in a Bill on Monday next, to alter and amend an Act, passed in the forty-eighth year of His Majesty's Reign, entitled "An Act for granting to His Majesty an annual sum of money, for the purposes therein mentioned." On Mr. Speaker having put the question, a division thereupon took place. The names being called for, they were taken down, and are as follows:—

Yeas.	Nays.
MESSRS. JAS. WILSON	MESSRS. FRASER.
WILLCOCKS	SECORD
MARCLE	C. WILSON.
GOUGH	
SOVEREIGN	
BURRITT	
ROGERS	
MALLORY	
JNO. WILSON	
ROBLIN	
LEWIS.	

20 A.

Carried in the affiirmative by a majority of eight. Leave was accordingly granted to bring in the said Bill on Monday next.

On motion of Mr. C. Wilson, seconded by Capt. Fraser, the House adjourned.

Saturday, 3rd February, 1810.

Prayers were read.

The Speaker reported that, in obedience to the commands of this House, he had sent notice to His Excellency the Lieutenant-Governor that the seat of the Member of the House of Assembly for the Counties of Stormont and Russell is vacant.

Mr. Burritt moved, seconded by Capt. Fraser, for leave to bring up a petition from the inhabitants of the County of Grenville, for the purpose of holding the Courts alternately in the Town of Johnstown and the Township of Elizabethtown, in the District of Johnstown. Leave was accordingly granted, and the said Petition ordered to lie on the Table.

Mr. Mallory moved, seconded by Mr. Sovereign, for leave to bring up the petition of the inhabitants of Block Number Two on the Grand River, in the West Riding of the County of York. Leave was granted accordingly, and the Petition was ordered to lie on the Table.

Read for the first time, the Bill to make good moneys advanced by the Lieutenant-Governor. Mr. Rogers moved, seconded by Mr. Gough, that the Bill for appropriating a sum of money to make good moneys advanced by the Lieutenant-Governor be read a second time on Monday, the 12th instant. Ordered accordingly.

Agreeably to the Order of the Day, the House resolved itself into a Committee to take into consideration the draft of an Address to His Excellency the Lieutenant-Governor, in answer to his Speech at the opening of the Legislature. Mr. Speaker left the Chair. Mr. Mallory was called to the Chair of the Committee.

Mr. Speaker resumed the Chair, and Mr. Mallory reported that the Committee had gone through the consideration of the said draft, which he was directed to report to the House whenever it should be pleased to receive the same. On Mr. Speaker having put the question on the Report's being received, a division thereupon took place. The names being called for they were taken down, and are as follows :—

Yeas.	Nays.
MESSRS. BURRITT	MESSRS. JNO. WILSON
MARCLE	FRASER
GOUGH	ROGERS
ROBLIN	WILLCOCKS
MALLORY	
JAS. WILSON	
LEWIS	
SECORD	
C. WILSON	
SOVEREIGN	

Carried in the affirmative by a majority of eight. The Report was accordingly received.

Capt. Fraser then moved, seconded by Mr. Secord, that the said draft of the Address be engrossed, and read this day, which was ordered accordingly.

On motion of Mr. Mallory, seconded by Mr. Secord, Ordered, That Messrs. Burritt, Crowell, Wilson, Fraser and Marcle do wait upon His Excellency the Lieutenant-Governor, to know at what time he will be pleased to receive the House with its Address in answer to His Excellency's Speech.

Mr. C. Wilson moved, seconded by Mr. Secord, for leave to bring in a Bill on Saturday next for appropriating a certain sum of money for the purpose of establishing Common Schools in each and every District, and to alter and amend an Act passed in the forty-seventh year of His Majesty's Reign, entitled " An Act to establish Public Schools in each and every District in this Province,"

On Mr. Speaker having put the question, a division thereupon took place. The names being called for they were taken down, and are as follows:—

Yeas.	Nays.
MESSRS. FRASER	MESSRS. ROBLIN
MARCLE	WILLCOCKS
BURRITT	ROGERS
GOUGH	JNO. WILSON
SECORD	SOVEREIGN
JAS. WILSON	MALLORY
LEWIS	
C. WILSON.	

Carried in the affirmative by a majority of two. Leave was accordingly granted to bring in the said Bill.

Mr. Roblin, seconded by Mr. Rogers, moved for leave to bring in a Bill on Wednesday next, to extend the benefits of an Act passed in the thirty-seventh year of His Majesty's Reign, entitled " An Act for the more easy barring of dower." Leave was accordingly granted.

Read as engrossed, The Address to His Excellency the Lieutenant-Governor, which then passed, and was signed by the Speaker, and is as follows:—

To His Excellency Francis Gore, Lieutenant-Governor of the Province of Upper Canada, &c., &c., &c. :—

May it please Your Excellency,

We, His Majesty's dutiful and loyal subjects, the Commons of the Province of Upper Canada in Parliament assembled, beg leave to return you our unfeigned and sincere thanks for Your Excellency's Speech to both Houses of Parliament upon opening of the present Session.

We contemplate with satisfaction the increasing commerce and internal prosperity of this Province since our last Session.

We lament that His Majesty's repeated efforts for the restoration and renewal of friendship and amity between the United Kingdom of Great Britain and Ireland, and the United States of America, have heretofore failed of accomplishing so desirable an end; yet we cherish a hope that the wisdom and policy of that Nation will direct them to embrace His Majesty's overtures, should His Majesty's efforts prove unavailing to attain the happy event. We trust the confidence Your Excellency has so flatteringly expressed in the bravery and loyalty of His Majesty's subjects in this Province will be fully justified, animated with a continual desire to maintain that character, which many of them have purchased with all but life, and ever exert themselves to manifest their unconquerable attachment to their King and Constitution, and to repel any attempt to alienate their attachment from either.

The recommendation of Your Excellency to discover from our respective situations what may still be wanting to increase the happiness and prosperity of our fellow subjects shall meet our earnest and grateful attention, and we shall endeavor to direct our deliberations to those points which may require legislative assistance.

Your Excellency's calling our attention to provide a remedy for the unskilful surveys of lands in this Province is a further proof of the unremitting watchfulness of Your Excellency to the interests of His Majesty's subjects in this Province, and shall meet our most deliberate investigation.

The Public Accounts shall likewise undergo such an examination as the nature of the subject requires.

We shall endeavour, agreeable to Your Excellency's recommendation, to use an unremitting zeal for the public service, and a steady prosecution of those objects which may promote the general interests of the Province, and a prompt and faithful discharge of the honorable task we now have to perform, and will be most conducive to the interests of our constituents.

Commons House of Assembly,   (Signed) SAML. STREET,
York, 3rd February, 1810.   Speaker.

Mr. Sovereign moved, seconded by Mr. Willcocks, for leave to bring in a Bill on Thursday next, to repeal certain parts of an Act passed in the forty-seventh year of His Majesty's reign, the better to ascertain the mode of assessing wild lands in this Province. Leave was granted.

On motion of Mr. C. Wilson, seconded by Mr. Lewis, the House adjourned until Monday next.

Monday, 5th February, 1810.

Prayers were read.

Mr. Burritt, accompanied by the other Messengers, reported that, in obedience to the Order of this House, they had waited upon His Excellency the Lieutenant-Governor, to know His Excellency's pleasure when he would receive the House with its Address, and that His Excellency was pleased to appoint this day at one o'clock in the afternoon to receive the House with its Address.

On motion of Mr. Gough, seconded by Mr. Secord, the House adjourned for half an hour.

The House being met, agreeable to adjournment, at the hour appointed Mr. Speaker and the House went up with the Address of this House to His Excellency the Lieutenant-Governor, and being returned, Mr. Speaker reported that the House had attended upon His Excellency, the Lieutenant-Governor, with its Address, to which His Excellency had been pleased to make the following answer:—

Gentlemen of the House of Assembly,

Your expressions of zeal and loyalty afford me the highest gratification. They are the honorable pledges of that fidelity which the original settlement of this Province was intended to assure, and which, I trust, will be rendered perpetual in yourselves and in your posterity.

Mr. Speaker also informed the House that he had received from Major Hatton, His Excellency the Lieutenant-Governor's Secretary, an answer to the letter written him by order of this House on the third instant, which is as follows:—

LIEUTENANT-GOVERNOR'S OFFICE,
YORK, 4th February, 1810.

SIR,—

I have had the honor of receiving and laying before the Lieutenant-Governor your letter of yesterday's date in the name of the House of Assembly, to inform

His Excellency that John Brownell, Esquire, Member representing the Counties of Stormont and Russell is dead, and that those Counties are at present unrepresented. His Excellency desires me to inform you that he will cause a new writ to be issued for those Counties without delay.

I have the honor to be, Sir,

Your most obedient humble servant,
(Signed) W. M. HALTON,
Secretary.

To His Honor the Speaker
of the House of Assembly.

Agreeably to the Order of the Day, the House was called over, when several of the Members appeared, and the names of such members as made default to appear were taken down and are as follows:—

Alex'r McDonnell, Allan McLean, John McGregor, Matthew Elliott, Tho's Mears, Tho's Wilson (sick in town, excused), and J. B. Baby.

Mr. Gough gave notice that he will to-morrow move that the House do take into consideration measures to enforce the punctual attendance of its Members.

Agreeably to the Order of the Day was read for the first time a Bill for the reduction of the salary of the Adjutant-General of the Militia of this Province. Mr. Willcocks moved, seconded by Mr. Rogers, that the Bill for reducing the salary of the Adjutant-General of the Militia be read a second time on Thursday next. Ordered accordingly.

On motion of Mr. Mallory, seconded by Mr. Secord, the Petition of the Inhabitants of Block number Two on the Grand River was read. Mr. Mallory, seconded by Mr. Willcocks, moved for leave to bring in a Bill on Thursday next for granting a certain sum of money to the Inhabitants of Block number Two on the Grand River in the West Riding of the County of York, for the purpose of opening and improving roads. Leave was accordingly granted.

Mr. Gough, seconded by Mr. Sovereign, moved for leave to bring in a Bill on Wednesday next for the more easy recovery of debts in this Province, and other purposes. Accordingly leave was granted.

Mr. Willcocks moved, seconded by Mr. Rogers, for leave to bring in a Bill to-morrow to repeal an Act passed in the forty-eighth year of His Majesty's Reign, entitled " An Act for granting to His Majesty a certain sum of money out of the Provincial Fund, to increase the salary of the Clerk of the Legislative Council and the Clerk of the House of Assembly. On Mr. Speaker having put the question for leave to bring in the Bill, a division thereupon took place. The names being called for, they were taken down, and are as follows:—

Yeas.	Nays.
MESSRS. GOUGH	MESSRS. FRASER
WILLCOCKS	BURRITT
ROGERS	MARCLE
DORLAND	HOWARD
ROBLIN	SECORD
SOVEREIGN	LEWIS
JOHN WILSON	McNABB
	C. WILSON
	MALLORY

So it passed in the negative by a majority of two.

Mr. Gough, seconded by Mr. Rogers, moved for leave to bring in a Bill on Wednesday next to prevent the fraudulent sale and transfer of lands in this Province. Leave was accordingly granted.

Mr. Gough, seconded by Mr. Sovereign, moved for leave to bring in a Bill on Wednesday next for the regulation of Lands, and also for the more exactly ascertaining the boundaries of lands in this Province. Accordingly leave was granted.

Mr. Rogers, seconded by Mr. Howard, moved for leave to bring in a Bill to-morrow to alter the mode of laying out, opening and keeping in repair the Public Highways in this Province. Leave was accordingly granted.

Mr. Howard moved, seconded by Mr. John Wilson, for leave to bring in a Bill on Wednesday next to regulate the practice of Physic and Surgery in this Province. Leave was granted.

On motion of Mr. Gough, seconded by Mr. Marcle, the House adjourned.

Tuesday, 6th February, 1810.

Prayers were read.

Agreeable to the Order of the Day was read for the first time a Bill to enable the Inhabitants of the County of Haldimand to hold Town Meetings for the purpose of electing Parish and Town Officers. Mr. Mallory moved, seconded by Mr. Willcocks, that the said Bill be read a second time to-morrow, which was ordered.

Agreeably to the Order of the Day was read for the first time a Bill for the laying out, amending and keeping in repair the Public Highways and Roads, and for the better regulation of performing the Statute Labour thereon. Mr. Rogers then moved, seconded by Mr. Mallory, that the said Bill be read for the second time to-morrow. It was ordered accordingly.

William Jarvis, Esquire, Secretary of the Province, came to the Bar of the House, and delivered in by order of His Excellency the Lieutenant-Governor the Provincial Public Accounts, the Schedule of which was read by the Clerk at the Table, and is as follows:—

Schedule of Accounts laid before the House of Assembly.

No. 1. General accounts of articles on which duties on importation are imposed by the Legislature of Lower Canada which have passed Coteau du Lac upwards from the 1st of January to the 30th of June, 1809, agreeable to the written accounts thereof received, or as ascertained on examination of carriages according to the Act.

No. 2. The Inspector's list of names of persons licensed as Shop and Innkeepers in the several Districts of the Province of Upper Canada, between the 5th of January, 1808, and the 5th of January, 1809. These returns were not received in time to be laid before the Legislature in 1809.

No. 3. The Inspector's returns of Still licenses issued in the Midland and Niagara District, which expired on the 5th of January, 1809. These returns were not received in time to be laid before the Legislature in 1809.

No. 4. The Inspector's list of names of persons licensed as Shop and Innkeepers in the several Districts of the Province of Upper Canada, from the 5th of January, 1809, to the 5th January, 1810.

No. 5. The Inspector's list of names of such persons as have been licensed to work Stills in the several Districts of the Province of Upper Canada, from the 5th of January, 1809, to the 5th of January, 1810.

No. 6. Account of moneys collected within the several Districts of the Province of Upper Canada on Licenses issued to Hawkers, Pedlars and Petty Chapmen, for the year ending the 5th of April, 1809. The returns were not received in time to be laid before the Legislature during the last Session, after deducting ten per cent. allowed to the Collectors by the Act of the Forty-seventh of the King.

No. 7. Account of Moneys collected within the several Districts of the Province of Upper Canada on Licenses issued to Hawkers, Pedlars and Petty Chapmen, for the year ending the 5th of April, 1810 (so far as the returns have been received), after deducting the Collectors' allowance of ten per cent.,· and the sums repaid to such persons as have obtained certificates of residence agreeable to the Act of the Forty-seventh of the King.

No. 8. Provincial Revenue of the Crown arising from duties collected on goods imported under Acts of the Provincial Parliament, between the 1st of January and the 31st of December, 1809, including such duties as have not hitherto been stated.

No. 9. Provincial Revenue of the Crown arising from duties collected on Goods imported under authority of Acts of the Parliament of Great Britain, between the 1st of January and the 31st December, 1809, including such duties as have not been heretofore stated.

No. 10. Abstract of Warrants issued by His Excellency, Francis Gore, Esquire, Lieutenant-Governor of the Province of Upper Canada, for moneys charged against the funds arising from duties imposed by the Provincial Legislature.

No. 11. Account of Lighthouse tonnage duty collected for the year ending the 31st December, 1809, so far as the returns have been received, including such duties as have not been heretofore stated.

No. 12. Supplementary abstract statement of moneys collected within the several Districts of the Province of Upper Canada, on Shop and Inn-keepers and Still licenses issued between the 5th of January, 1808, and 5th of January. 1809, under authority of Acts of the Provincial Parliament, after deducting ten per cent. allowed to the Inspectors by the Act of the Forty-third of the King.

No. 13. Supplementary abstract statement of moneys collected within the several Districts of the Province of Upper Canada, on Shop and Inn-keepers Licenses issued between the 5th of January, 1808, and the 5th of January, 1809, under authority of Acts of the Parliament of Great Britain, after deducting ten per cent. allowed to the Inspectors by the Act of the Forty-third of the King.

No. 14. Abstract statement of moneys collected within the several Districts of the Province of Upper Canada on Shop, Inn-keepers and Still licenses issued between the 5th of January, 1809, and the 5th of January, 1810 (so far as the returns have been received), after deducting ten per cent. allowed to the Inspectors by the Act of the Forty-third of the King.

No. 15. Abstract statement of moneys collected within the several Districts of the Province of Upper Canada on Shop and Inn-keepers licenses issued between the 5th of January, 1809, and the 5th of January, 1810, under authority of Acts of the Parliament of Great Britain (so far as the returns have been received), after deducting ten per cent. allowed to the Inspectors by the Act of the Forty-third of the King.

No. 16. General state of Cash received by the Receiver-General for duties and fines, under authority of Acts of the Parliament of Great Britain between the 1st of January and the 31st of December, 1809.

No. 17. General state of receipts and payments by the Receiver-General for duties and fines, likewise appropriations made under authority of the Acts of the Provincial Parliament between the 1st January and the 31st December, 1809.

York, 5th February, 1810.

(For Public Accounts as per Schedule see appendix.)

Read for the first time a Bill for granting a sum of money for erecting a Bridge across the Grand River. Mr. Willcocks then moved, seconded by Mr. Mallory, that the Bill for erecting a Bridge across the Grand River be read a second time to-morrow, which was ordered accordingly.

Mr. Mallory moved, seconded by Mr. Burritt, that the Petition of the Inhabitants of the County of Grenville be now read. The Petition was accordingly read:—

To the Commons House of Assembly of the Province of Upper Canada.

The Petition of the Magistrates and principal Inhabitants of the County of Grenville

Most humbly showeth,.

That by an Act passed in the Forty-eighth year of His Majesty's Reign it was enacted that it should and might be lawful for the Justices of the Peace for the District of Johnstown, in General Quarter Sessions assembled, to fix upon a site or situation on the front of· Lot Number Ten, Eleven or Twelve on the first concession of the Township of Elizabethtown, adjoining the King's Highway, where a Court House and Gaol might be erected, and also that as soon as the Justices of the Peace in General Quarter Sessions assembled, or the majority of them, should be satisfied that the said Court House and Gaol would be sufficiently finished, the said Court House and Gaol should be declared the Court House and Gaol of the said District of Johnstown.

That the Inhabitants of the County of Grenville have been at great expense in building and finishing a Gaol and Court House in the Town of Johnstown, and building houses in the said Town for the accommodation of the Court of the said District, which, for no reason but the ambition and interest of a few individuals, have been moved to Elizabethtown.

That the County of Grenville and the Counties in the rear thereof contain more inhabitants than the Counties above, and therefore, although the Court House and Gaol in Elizabethtown are nearly in the centre of the District, they are not in the centre of the settlement.

That the situation of the Court House and Gaol in Elizabethtown renders it inconvenient for the inhabitants of the County of Grenville to attend the several Courts of the said District to discharge their public and private duties. .

Your Petitioners therefore pray that the Court of the said District of Johnstown may be held alternately in the Town of Johnstown and Elizabethtown, each County supporting their respective Gaols, by which means Your Petitioners will be enabled to attend their Public and private concerns.

And Your Petitioners, as in duty bound, will ever pray.

Andrew Adams, Joel Hatton, Peleg Spencer, John Culbreath, and one hundred and thirteen others.

Also another Petition of the same tenor with sixty-two signatures.

Mr. Burritt moved, seconded by Mr. Secord, for leave to bring in a Bill on Saturday next for the purpose of holding the Courts alternately in the town of Johnstown and the Township of Elizabethtown, and to repeal so much of an Act passed in the Forty-eighth year of His Majesty's Reign as relates to the Gaol and Court House in the District of Johnstown. Accordingly leave was granted.

Mr. Willcocks, seconded by Mr. Rogers, moved for leave to bring in a Bill on Saturday next to extend the Jurisdiction of the Court of Requests in this Province. Leave was granted.

Mr. McNabb moved, seconded by Mr. Dorland, that Captain Frazer, Mr. Gough, Mr. Rogers and Mr. Howard be a Committee to examine the Provincial Public Accounts. The House accordingly ordered the same.

Mr. Gough moved, seconded by Mr. Secord, that the Petition of the Inhabitants of the Counties of Lennox and Addington and Prince Edward be now read. The Petition was read accordingly, and is as follows:—

To the Honorable the Representatives of the Province of Upper Canada, in the House of Commons assembled.

The Petition of the undersigned inhabitants, Freeholders of the United Counties of Lennox and Addington, and the County of Prince Edward (except Ameliasburgh), in the Midland District.

Humbly Showeth,

That John Roblin and James Wilson, two of the Members returned as Representatives for the said Counties, have not been duly and lawfully elected and chosen, inasmuch as the said John Roblin and James Wilson, at the time of their being returned as Members of the House of Assembly for this Province, then were, and for many years before, and still are public Preachers and Teachers in that Society or Community of people called Methodists. Your Petitioners therefore humbly represent that the said John Roblin and James Wilson are not eligible to seats, or to be returned as Members of the House of Assembly of this Province; and pray that the said John Roblin and James Wilson may not be permitted to hold seats in Your Honorable House, and that the same may be vacated.

And Your Petitioners, as in duty bound, will ever pray.

Adolphustown, 25th January, 1810.

(Signed) John Ferguson, Reuben Bedell, Ebenezer Washburn, Simeon Washburn, and Thirteen others.

Mr. Gough moved, seconded by Mr. C. Wilson, that the said Petition be taken into consideration on Saturday next, which was ordered accordingly.

Mr. Willcocks moved, seconded by Mr. Mallory, for leave to bring in a Bill to-morrow to repeal an Act passed in the forty-sixth year of His Majesty's Reign, entitled " An Act to make provision for certain Sheriffs in this Province." On Mr. Speaker having put the question, a division thereupon took place. The names being called for, they were taken down, and are as follows:—

Yeas.	Nays.
MESSRS. GOUGH	MESSRS. BURRITT
JOHN WILSON	MARCLE
SECORD	FRAZER
MALLORY	DORLAND
ROGERS	C. WILSON.
WILLCOCKS	
HOWARD	
ROBLIN	
JAMES WILSON	
LEWIS	
McNABB	
SOVEREIGN	

Carried in the affirmative by a majority of seven. Leave was accordingly granted to bring in the said Bill to-morrow.

Mr. Gough then moved, seconded by Mr. Rogers, that the House do now resolved itself into a Committee, to take into consideration a mode of compelling the Members of this House to attend their duty in Parliament. The House accordingly resolved itself into a Committee. Mr. Speaker left the Chair. Capt. Frazer was called to the chair of the Committee. Mr. Speaker resumed the Chair, and Capt. Frazer reported that the Committee had come to a Resolution, which he was directed to report to the House whenever it should be pleased to receive the same. Ordered, that the Report be now received. The Report was accordingly received and accepted, and is as follows:—

Resolved, that the Members who were absent when the House was called over yesterday be ordered into, and considered at this time as in the custody of the Serjeant at Arms, and shall not be discharged therefrom until they shall have paid the customary fees established in the Parliament of the United Kingdom in like cases, unless they shall shew to the satisfaction of this House sufficient cause for such absence.

Mr. Willcocks gave notice that he will to-morrow move that this House do address His Excellency the Lieutenant-Governor, requesting His Excellency to cause the proper Officer to lay before this Honorable House a Statement of all such moneys as have been appropriated by the Legislature for the repairing of the Public Highways and Roads within this Province, from the year One Thousand Eight Hundred and Three to the year One Thousand Eight Hundred and Nine, inclusive.

On motion of Mr. Burritt, seconded by Mr. Marcle, the House adjourned.

Wednesday, 7th February, 1807.

Prayers were read.

Read for the first time, The Bill for the more equal representation of the Commons of this Province in Parliament, and for the better defining the qualifications of Electors. Mr. Willcocks moved, seconded by Mr. Rogers, that the Bill for altering the representation of the Commons be read a second time to-morrow, which was ordered accordingly.

Read for the first time, a Bill for the more easy Barring of Dower. Mr. Roblin then moved, seconded by Mr. Rogers, that the Bill for the more easy barring of Dower be read a second time to-morrow. Ordered accordingly.

Read for the first time, a Bill for the more easy recovery of Debts. Mr. Gough moved, seconded by Mr. Rogers, that the Bill for the more easy recovery of Debts be read a second time to-morrow. Which was ordered accordingly.

Read for the first time, a Bill to prevent the fraudulent sale of Lands. Mr. Gough then moved, seconded by Mr. Roblin, that the Bill to prevent the fraudulent sale of Lands be read a second time to-morrow. Ordered accordingly.

Read for the first time, a Bill for the Regulation of the Practice of Physic and Surgery.

Mr. Howard then moved, seconded by Mr. C. Wilson, that the Physic and Surgery Bill be read a second time to-morrow.

Mrs. Speaker having put the question, a division thereupon took place. The names being called for they were taken down, and are as follows:—

Yeas.	Nays.
MESSRS. McNABB	MESSRS. GOUGH
BURRITT	JNO. WILSON
FRAZER	SECORD
MARCLE	MALLORY
HOWARD	SOVEREIGN
McLEAN	WILLCOCKS
ROGERS	JAS. WILSON
LEWIS	ROBLIN.
DORLAND	
C. WILSON.	

Carried in the affirmative by a majority of two.   The said Bill was then ordered to be read a second time to-morrow.

Read for the second time, the Bill for enabling the inhabitants of the County of Haldimand to hold Town Meetings, for the purpose of electing Parish and Town Officers.   Mr. Mallory moved, seconded by Mr. Howard, that the House do now resolve itself into a Committee to take into consideration the Bill to authorize the Inhabitants of the County of Haldimand to hold Town Meetings, for the purpose of electing Parish and Town Officers.   The House accordingly resolved itself into a Committee.   Mr. Speaker left the Chair.   Mr. Burritt was called to the chair of the Committee.

Mr. Speaker resumed the Chair, and Mr. Burritt reported that the Committee had gone through the consideration of the said Bill, to which they had made several amendments, which amendments he was directed to report to the House whenever it should be pleased to receive the same.   Ordered, that the Report be now received. The Report was accordingly received and accepted.   Mr. Mallory then moved, seconded by Mr. Willcocks, that the County of Haldimand Parish and Town Officers Bill be engrossed, and read a third time to-morrow, which was ordered accordingly.

Read for the second time, the Bill for laying out, amending, and keeping in repair the Public Highways and Roads, and for the better regulation of the Statute Labour thereon.   Mr. Rogers moved, seconded by Mr. Mallory, that the House do now resolve itself into Committee to go into the consideration of the said Bill.   The House accordingly resolved itself into Committee to go into the consideration of the said Bill.   Mr. Speaker left the Chair.   Mr. Howard was called to the chair of the Committee.

Mr. Speaker resumed the Chair, and Mr. Howard reported that the Committee had made a progress, and had directed him to ask for leave to sit again to-morrow. Leave was granted to sit again to-morrow.

Mr. Gough moved, seconded by Mr. Willcocks, that as Mr. McLean had this day attended in his place, and paid his fees, he be now discharged from the custody of the Serjeant at Arms.   Ordered accordingly.

Agreeably to the Order of the Day was read for the second time, the Bill for granting money to build a bridge across the Grand River.   Mr. Willcocks moved, seconded by Mr. Mallory, that the House do now resolve itself into a Committee to go into the consideration of the Bill for erecting a Bridge across the Grand River.   The House accordingly resolved itself into a Committee to go into the consideration of the said Bill.   Mr. Speaker left the Chair.   Mr. McLean was called to the chair of the Committee.

Mr. Speaker resumed the Chair, and Mr. McLean reported that the Committee had made a progress, and had directed him to ask for leave to sit again to-morrow. Leave was accordingly granted.

Read for the first time, The Bill for the reduction of the salaries of certain Sheriffs in this Province. Mr. Willcocks moved, seconded by Mr. Mallory, that the Bill for reducing the Sheriffs' salaries be read a second time to-morrow. On Mr. Speaker having put the question, a division thereupon took place. The names being called for, they were taken down, and are as follows:—

Yeas.	Nays.
MESSRS. JNO. WILSON	MESSRS. FRAZER
SECORD	McNABB
WILLCOCKS	BURRITT
MALLORY	GOUGH
JAS. WILSON	HOWARD
ROBLIN.	ROGERS
	SOVEREIGN
	LEWIS
	McLEAN.

The same passed in the negative by a majority of three.

Mr. McNabb, seconded by Mr. Burritt, moved for leave to bring in a Bill on Tuesday next, to raise the duties on licenses to Hawkers, Pedlars, and Petty Chapmen throughout this Province. Leave was accordingly granted.

Mr. Willcocks moved, seconded by Mr. Rogers, that this House do address His Excellency the Lieutenant-Governor, requesting His Excellency to direct to be laid before it all such Reports as may have been furnished him by the Commissioners of the Public Highways respecting the disbursement of the several sums of money which have been appropriated by the Legislature of this Province, subsequent to the year One Thousand Eight Hundred and Three, for the amending and keeping in repair of the Public Highways and Roads; and if such Reports have not been furnished to His Excellency he will be pleased to direct that the said Commissioners do lay before this Honorable House full statements of the sums they have respectively received, and the manner in which they have been applied. Ordered accordingly.

On motion of Mr. McNabb, seconded by Mr. Burritt, the House adjourned.

Thursday, 8th February, 1810.

Prayers were read.

Mr. Gough moved, seconded by Mr. Rogers, for leave to bring up two petitions from sundry Menonists and Tunkers. Leave was accordingly granted.

Agreeably to the Order of the Day was read for the first time, a Bill to repeal the Act establishing Public Schools in this Province. Mr. Willcocks moved, seconded by Mr. Rogers, that the Bill for repealing the School Act be read a second time on Saturday next, which was ordered accordingly.

Read for the first time, a Bill to make further provision for the payment of wages to the Members of the House of Assembly. Mr. Mallory then moved, seconded by Mr. Lewis, that the Bill to repeal certain parts of an Act passed in the thirty-third year of His Majesty's Reign, relative to the payment of wages to the Members of the House of Assembly, be read a second time to-morrow. Ordered accordingly.

Agreeably to the Order of the Day was read for the second time, The Bill for the more equal representation of the Commons in Parliament, and for altering the qualifications of Electors.

Mr. Mallory moved, seconded by Mr. Secord, that so much of the Order of the Day as relates to the bringing in a Bill this Day to grant money to the inhabitants of Block No. 2 be dispensed with this day, and that he have leave to bring in the same to-morrow. Ordered accordingly, and leave was given to bring in the said Bill to-morrow.

Mr. Willcocks moved, seconded by Mr. Rogers, that the House do now resolve itself into a Committee to take into consideration the Bill for altering the qualification of Electors. The House accordingly resolved itself into a Committee. Mr. Speaker left the Chair. Mr. James Wilson was called to the chair of the Committee.

Mr. Speaker resumed the Chair, and Mr. Wilson reported that the Committee had gone through the consideration of the said Bill, to which they had made several amendments, which he was directed by the Committee to report to the House whenever it should be pleased to receive the same. Ordered, that the Report be now received.

Mr. Willcocks, seconded by Mr. Sovereign, moved that the Bill for altering the qualification of Electors be engrossed, and read for the third time to-morrow. Which was ordered accordingly.

Mr. Roblin moved, seconded by Mr. Secord, that the House do now resolve itself into a Committee, to go into the consideration of the Dower Bill. The House accordingly resolved itself into a Committee. Mr. Speaker left the Chair. Mr. Dorland was called to the chair of the Committee.

Mr. Speaker resumed the Chair, and Mr. Dorland reported that the Committee had gone through the consideration of the said Bill, to which they have made several amendments, which he was directed to report to the House whenever it should be pleased to receive the same. Ordered, that the Report be now received and accepted.

Mr. Roblin again moved, seconded by Mr. James Wilson, that the Bill for the more easy barring of Dower be engrossed, and read a third time to-morrow, which was ordered accordingly.

Read for the second time, the Bill for the more easy Recovery of Debts. Mr. Gough moved, seconded by Mr. Sovereign, that the House do now resolve itself into a Committee, to go into the consideration of the said Bill. The House resolved itself into a Committee accordingly, to go into the consideration of the said Bill. Mr. Speaker left the Chair. Mr. Roblin was called to the chair of the Committee.

Mr. Speaker resumed the Chair, and Mr. Roblin reported that the Committee had made a progress, and had directed him to ask for leave to sit again to-morrow. Leave was accordingly granted to sit again to-morrow.

Read for the second time, the Bill to prevent the fraudulent sale and transfer of Lands.

Mr. Gough then moved, seconded by Mr. Rogers, that the House do now resolve itself into a Committee, to go into the consideration of the Bill to prevent the fraudulent sale of Lands. The House accordingly resolved itself into a Committee to go into the consideration of the said Bill. Mr. Speaker left the Chair. Mr. McNabb was called to the chair of the Committee.

Mr. Speaker resumed the Chair, and Mr. McNabb reported that the Committee had made a progress, and had directed him to ask for leave to sit again to-morrow. Leave was accordingly granted to sit again to-morrow.

Read for the second time, The Bill to regulate the Practice of Physic and Surgery. Mr. Howard moved, seconded by Mr. Mallory, that the House do now resolve itself into a Committee to go into the consideration of the Bill to regulate the Practice of Physic and Surgery. The House accordingly resolved itself into a Committee to go into the consideration of the said Bill. Mr. Speaker left the Chair. Mr. Rogers was called to the chair of the Committee.

Mr. Speaker resumed the Chair, and Mr. Rogers reported that the Committee had come to a Resolution that the said Bill be taken into consideration on this day three months, which report was accepted, and ordered accordingly.

Read for the third time, as engrossed, the Bill to enable the inhabitants of the County of Haldimand to hold Annual Town Meetings. On motion of Mr. Mallory, seconded by Mr. Willcocks, resolved, that the Bill do pass, and that the title be "An Act to authorize the inhabitants of the County of Haldimand to hold Annual Meetings, for the purpose of electing Parish and Town Officers." The Bill then passed, and was signed by the Speaker.

Mr. Rogers then moved, seconded by Mr. Dorland, that Messrs. Mallory and Willcocks do carry up to the Honorable the Legislative Council the Bill entitled "An Act to authorize the inhabitants of the County of Haldimand to hold Annual Meetings, for the purpose of electing Parish and Town Officers," and to request their concurrence in passing the same, which was ordered accordingly.

Mr. Willcocks moved, seconded by Mr. Roblin, that Messrs. Gough, Howard and John Wilson be a Committee to draft an Address to His Excellency the Lieutenant Governor, relative to the disbursement of money for the repairing and amending the Public Highways and Roads in this Province, which was ordered accordingly.

Mr. Mallory moved, seconded by Mr. C. Wilson, that the Road Bill be discharged from the Order of the Day, and that it be the first on the Order of the Day for to-morrow. The House accordingly ordered the same.

Agreeably to the Order of the Day, the House resolved itself into a Committee to go into the further consideration of the Grand River Bridge Bill. Mr. Speaker left the Chair. Mr. McLean again took the chair of the Committee.

Mr. Speaker resumed the Chair, and Mr. McLean reported that the Committee had gone through the consideration of the said Bill, to which it had made several amendments, which he was directed to report to the House whenever it should be pleased to receive the same. The House accordingly resolved that the Report be now received. Mr. Willcocks then moved, seconded by Mr. Sovereign, that the Bill for erecting a bridge across the Grand River be engrossed, and read a third time to-morrow. Ordered accordingly.

Mr. Willcocks moved, seconded by Mr. John Wilson, that so much of the Order of the Day as relates to the Adjutant-General's Salary Bill be dispensed with, and that it do make a part of the Order of the Day for to-morrow, which was ordered accordingly.

Mr. Willcocks, seconded by Mr. James Wilson, again moved for leave to bring in a Bill on Monday next, to reduce the Salary of the Speaker of the House of Assembly. On Mr. Speaker having put the question a division thereupon took place. The names being called for they were taken down and are as follows:—

Yeas.	Nays.
MESSRS. JNO. WILSON.	MESSRS. McNABB
HOWARD	MARCLE
ROGERS	FRAZER
JAS. WILSON	BURRITT
. ROBLIN	SOVEREIGN
WILLCOCKS.	GOUGH
	McLEAN
	SECORD
	LEWIS
	DORLAND
	C. WILSON
	MALLORY.

Which passed in the negative by a majority of six.

Mr. Willcocks, seconded by Mr. Mallory, moved for leave to bring in a Bill on Monday next, to lay a duty on License to Public Billiard Tables. Leave was accordingly granted.

Mr. Howard moved, seconded by Mr. McLean, for leave to bring in a Bill on Monday next to grant relief to indigent persons in this Province. Leave was granted.

On motion of Mr. McNabb, seconded by Mr. Burritt, the House adjourned.

Friday, 9th February, 1810.

Prayers were read.

Mr. Howard moved, seconded by Mr. Willcocks, that so much of the Order of the Day as respects the Road Bill, being first on the Order of this Day, be dispensed with, and that it be the second thing that shall be taken up by the House this Day, which was ordered accordingly.

Read for the second time, the Bill for reducing the Salary of the Adjutant-General of the Militia. Mr. Willcocks then moved, seconded by Mr. Roblin, that the House do now resolve itself into a Committee to take into consideration the Bill for reducing the salary of the Adjutant-General of the Militia. The House accordingly resolved itself into a Committee. Mr. Speaker left the Chair. Mr. Gough was called to the chair of the Committee.

Mr. Speaker resumed the Chair, and Mr. Gough reported that the Committee had gone through the consideration of the said Bill, to which they had made no amendments, which he was directed to report to the House whenever it should be pleased to receive the same. On Mr. Speaker having put the question for the Report being received, a division thereupon took place. The names being called for they were taken down and are as follows:—

Yeas.	Nays.
MESSRS. GOUGH	MESSRS. McNABB
JNO. WILSON	BURRITT
DORLAND	MARCLE
HOWARD	FRASER
MALLORY	McLEAN
WILLCOCKS	SECORD
LEWIS	C. WILSON
SOVEREIGN	
JAS. WILSON	
ROBLIN	

Carried in the affirmative by a majority of three.   The Report was then accordingly received and accepted. Mr. Willcocks moved, seconded by Mr. Jas. Wilson, that the Bill for reducing the salary of the Adjutant of the Militia be engrossed, and read a third time to-morrow, which was ordered accordingly.

Agreeably to the Order of the Day the House resolved itself into a Committee, to go into the further consideration of the Road Bill.   Mr. Speaker left the Chair. Mr. Howard again took the chair of the Committee.

Mr. Speaker resumed the Chair, and Mr. Howard reported that the Committee had directed him to inform the House that they had gone through the consideration of the said Bill, to which they had made several amendments, which he was directed to report whenever the House should be pleased to receive the same.   The House accordingly resolved that the Report be now received.

Read for the second time, The Bill for altering the mode of payment of wages to the Members of the House of Assembly.

Mr. Gough moved, seconded by Mr. C. Wilson, that the excuse of Messrs. Baby and McGregor, of being detained by the inclemency of the weather, be deemed sufficient, and that they be discharged from the custody of the Serjeant-at-Arms without paying Fees.   Accordingly Messrs. Baby and McGregor were excused, and discharged from the custody of the Serjeant-at-Arms without paying Fees.

The Serjeant-at-Arms came to the Bar of the House, and informed the Speaker that Capt. Elliott, now in his custody by an Order of the House, was prevented from attending in his place in consequence of the bad state of his health.   Mr. Gough therefore moved, seconded by Mr. C. Wilson, that Capt. Elliott be discharged from the custody of the Serjeant-at-Arms, without paying Fees.

Mr. Mallory, seconded by Mr. Sovereign, moved that the House do now resolve itself into a Committee, to go into the consideration of the Bill for making further provision for the payment of wages to the Members of the House of Assembly.   The House accordingly resolved itself into a Committee to go into the further consideration of the said Bill.   Mr. Speaker left the Chair.   Mr. John Wilson was called to the chair of the Committee.

Mr. Speaker resumed the Chair, and Mr. Wilson reported that the Committee had made a progress, and had directed him to ask for leave to sit again this day three months.   Leave was accordingly granted for the Committee to sit again this day three months.

Read for the first time, a Bill for granting a sum of money to the inhabitants of Block No. Two on the Grand River.   Mr. Mallory then moved, seconded by Mr. Willcocks, that the Bill for granting money to the inhabitants of Block No. Two on the Grand River, for the purpose of opening and repairing roads, be read a second time   to-morrow, which passed in the negative.   The said Bill was then ordered to be read for the second time on this day three months.

Read for the third time, as engrossed, the Bill for the better defining the qualifications of Electors.   On motion of Mr. Willcocks, seconded by Mr. Jas. Wilson, resolved, that the said Bill do pass, and that the title be "An Act for the better defining the qualifications of Electors for the Commons of Upper Canada."   The Bill accordingly passed, and was signed by the Speaker.

Read for the third time, as engrossed, the Bill for the more easy Barring of Dower.   On motion of Mr. Roblin, seconded by Mr. Willcocks, resolved that the said Bill do pass, and that the title be "An Act further to extend the benefits of an Act passed in the thirty-seventh year of His Majesty's reign, entitled 'An Act for the more easy Barring of Dower.'"   The Bill then passed, and was signed by the Speaker.

Mr. Willcocks, seconded by Mr. Roblin, moved that Messrs. Dorland and James Wilson do carry up to the Legislative Council the Bill entitled "An Act for the better defining the qualifications of Electors to the Commons of Upper Canada," and request their concurrence in passing the same, which was ordered accordingly.

Mr. Willcocks again moved, seconded by Mr. C. Wilson, that Messrs. Howard and Roblin do carry up to the Honorable the Legislative Council the Bill entitled "An Act further to extend the benefits of an Act passed in the thirty-seventh year of His Majesty's reign, entitled 'An Act for the more easy Barring of Dower,'" and request their concurrence in passing the same. Ordered accordingly.

Mr. Willcocks, accompanied by the other Messengers, informed the House that they had carried up to the Honorable the Legislative Council the Act entitled "An Act to authorize the inhabitants of the County of Haldimand to hold Annual Town Meetings for the purpose of electing Town and Parish Officers," and did request their concurrence in passing the same.

Mr. Gough moved, seconded by Mr. Secord, that so much of the Order of the Day as relates to the Bills for the more easy recovery of Debts, and for preventing the fraudulent sale of Lands, be dispensed with; and that they do make a part of the Order of the Day for Monday next, which was ordered accordingly.

Read for the third time, as engrossed, the Bill for granting money for erecting a bridge across the Grand River, in the District of Niagara. On motion of Mr. Willcocks, seconded by Mr. Howard, resolved, that the said Bill do now pass, and that the title be "An Act for granting an additional sum of money for the purpose of erecting a bridge across the Grand River." The Bill accordingly passed and was signed by the Speaker. Mr. Willcocks, seconded by Mr. Howard, again moved, that Messrs. McGregor and John Wilson do carry up to the Honorable the Legislative Council the Bill for granting money for building a bridge across the Grand River, and to request their concurrence in passing the same, which was ordered accordingly.

Mr. McLean moved, seconded by Mr. Lewis, for leave to bring up sundry petitions from the inhabitants of the District of Niagara and the West Riding of York, with a subscription list. Leave was accordingly granted to bring up the said petitions and subscription papers, which were ordered to lie upon the Table.

On motion of Mr. C. Wilson, seconded by Mr. Secord, the House adjourned.

Saturday, 10th February, 1810.

Prayers were read.

Mr. Gough moved, seconded by Mr. Burritt, that the petitions of the Mennonists and Tunkers be now read. The said Petitions were accordingly read, and are as follows: .

To the Honorable the Speaker and Members of the House of Commons of Upper Canada, in Parliament assembled.

The Petition of the Society of people called Mononists and Tunkers, Humbly Sheweth,

That by an Act of the Province, passed in the thirty-third year of His Majesty's reign, Your Petitioners, after producing a certificate from three or four respectable people, one of whom must be a preacher in the Society to which they belong, shall pay in time of peace Four Dollars a year, and in time of invasion or insurrection Twenty Dollars a year, for which favorable law and liberty of conscience we are thankful to God and the Government under which we live. And

' 21 A.

whereas many of Our Sons now under age and incapable of judging in matters of conscience, are not as yet actually considered as Church members, and cannot of course secure the necessary certificates, we therefore humbly pray the same indulgence may be extended to them that is granted to ourselves, their parents, that is that they may be exempted from serving in the Militia by paying the commutation money until they arrive at the age of twenty-one, or until they be admitted as Church Members.

And Your Petitioners further pray that your Honorable Body will take into your consideration the many difficulties which poor people, with large families, have to labour under in new settlements, and if you in your wisdom should deem meet to lessen the burden of our commutation money Your Petitioners, as in duty bound, shall ever pray.

Signed by two Preachers, two Elders, and thirty-five members of the Society of Mennonists and Tunkers.

The other Petition is of the same tenor as the above, with thirty-four signatures to it.

Mr. Gough, seconded by Mr. Willcocks, moved for leave to bring in a Bill on Monday next for the relief of minors of the Religious Societies of Mennonists and Tunkers. Leave was granted to bring in the said Bill on Monday next.

Read for the first time, a Bill for establishing township schools in this Province.

Mr. C. Wilson moved, seconded by Mr. Lewis, that the said Bill be read a second time on Monday next. The said Bill was accordingly ordered to be read a second time on Monday next.

Mr. Burritt moved, seconded by Mr. Gough, for leave to withdraw his motion and Petition for leave to bring in a Bill this Day for holding the Courts alternately in the Town of Johnstown and the Township of Elizabethtown, in the District of Johnstown. Leave was accordingly granted to withdraw the Petition and motion.

Mr. Willcocks, seconded by Mr. Secord, moved that so much of the Order of the Day as relates to the Bill for extending the jurisdiction of the Court of Requests be dispensed with this day, and that it be placed on the Order of the Day for Thursday next, which was ordered accordingly.

Mr. McNabb moved, seconded by Mr. Gough, that upon the information of Mr. McGregor of the state of health of the family of Mr. McDonell, that Mr. McDonnell be excused from attending his duty in Parliament during the Session, and that he be discharged from the custody of the Serjeant at Arms without paying fees. Mr. McDonell was accordingly excused from attending this Session, and discharged from the custody of the Serjeant at Arms without paying fees.

Mr. Gough moved, seconded by Mr. C. Wilson, that the House do now resolve itself into a Committee to go into the consideration of the Petition of the Freeholders of the United Counties of Lennox and Addington, and the County of Prince Edward. The House accordingly resolved itself into a Committee to go into the consideration of the said Petition. Mr. Speaker left the Chair. Mr. Lewis was called to the Chair of the Committee.

Mr. Speaker resumed the Chair, and Mr. Lewis reported that the Committee had made a progress, and had directed him to ask for leave to sit again on Monday next.

Mr. McNabb, seconded by Mr. Burritt, moved that so much of the Order of the Day as has not been proceeded upon be dispensed with for this day, and that it be on the Order of the Day for Monday next, which was ordered accordingly.

On motion of Mr. Willcocks, seconded by Mr. McNabb, the House adjourned until Monday next.

Monday, 12th February, 1810.

Prayers were read.

Agreeably to the Order of the Day the House resolved itself into a Committee to go into the merits of the Petition of the Freeholders of the Counties of Lennox and Addington, and the County of Prince Edward, against the eligibility of Messrs. Roblin and Wilson holding their seats in the House. Mr. Speaker left the Chair. Mr. Lewis was called to the Chair of the Committee.

Mr. Speaker resumed the Chair, and Mr. Lewis reported that the Committee had come to a resolution, which he was directed by the Committee to report, whenever the House should be pleased to receive the same. Ordered, that the Report be now received. The Report was accordingly received and accepted, and is as follows, viz. :—

Resolved, that it appears to this Committee that there is sufficient grounds in the Petition of the Freeholders of the Counties of Lennox and Addington, and the County of Prince Edward, against John Roblin and James Wilson, to proceed to trial; and that the House do proceed to the trial of each separately.

A Message from the Honorable the Legislative Council by Mr. Baldwin, Master in Chancery:

Mr. Speaker,

I am commanded by the Honorable the Legislative Council to acquaint this Honorable House that it has passed an Act entitled "An Act to render the Justices of the Peace more safe in the execution of their duty," to which they request the concurrence of this House in passing the same.

And then he withdrew.

On motion of Mr. Howard, seconded by Mr. McLean, ordered, that the said Bill be now read. The same Bill was accordingly read for the first time. Mr. Howard, seconded by Mr. McLean, moved that the Bill brought down from the Honorable the Legislative Council, entitled "An Act to render the Justices of the Peace more safe in the execution of their duty," be read a second time to-morrow, which was ordered accordingly.

Mr. Gough moved, seconded by Mr. Willcocks, that the House do proceed to the trial of the Controverted Election of James Wilson, Esquire, sitting member of this House, representing the County of Prince Edward (except Ameliasburgh) on Monday, the Twenty-sixth instant. Ordered accordingly.

Mr. Gough again moved, seconded by Mr. Willcocks, that the House do proceed to the trial of the Controverted election of John Roblin, Esquire, one of the sitting Members, representing the United Counties of Lennox and Addington, on Tuesday, the Twenty-seventh instant. The House accordingly resolved the same.

Then the House ordered that the Petitioners against the eligibility of James Wilson, sitting Member of this House, by themselves or Attorney, do give bond with two sufficient sureties, jointly and severally, in the sum of two hundred pounds, Provincial currency, to indemnify the said James Wilson his expenses, should he keep his seat as returned to represent the County of Prince Edward (except Ameliasburgh).

The House having been pleased to approve of Duncan Cameron, Esquire, and Mr. John Cameron, both of the Town of York, as joint security on the above amount:—

The House also have been pleased to order that the Petitioners against the eligibility of John Roblin, Esquire, sitting Member of this House, by themselves or attorney do give bond, with two sufficient sureties, jointly and severally, in the sum of Two Hundred Pounds, Provincial Currency, to indemnify the said John Roblin his expenses, should he keep his seat as returned as one of the Members representing the United Counties of Lennox and Addington. The House having been pleased to approve of Duncan Cameron, Esquire, and Mr. John Cameron, both of the Town of York, as joint security on the above amount.

Read for the second time, a Bill to repeal part of an Act passed in the forty-eighth year of His Majesty's Reign, entitled "An Act to amend an Act passed in the forty-seventh year of His Majesty's Reign, entitled "An Act to establish Schools in each and every District in this Province." Mr. Willcocks, seconded by Mr. Sovereign, moved that the House do now resolve itself into a Committee, to take into consideration the School Bill. The House accordingly resolved itself into a Committee. Mr. Speaker left the Chair. Mr. Lewis was called to the Chair of the Committee. Mr. Speaker resumed the Chair, and Mr. Lewis reported that the Committee had come to a resolution that the said Bill be not adopted. On Mr. Speaker having put the question, a division thereupon took place. The names being called for, they were taken down, and are as follows:—

Yeas.	Nays.
MESSRS. McNABB	MESSRS. GOUGH
BURRITT	JOHN WILSON
FRAZER	HOWARD
MARGLE	MALLORY
ELLIOTT	WILLCOCKS
BABY	BORLAND
McLEAN	JAMES WILSON
McGREGOR	ROBLIN
C. WILSON	SOVEREIGN
LEWIS	SECORD

The House being divided; Mr. Speaker gave his vote for the Report being received. The Report was then accordingly received and adopted.

Mr. Willcocks moved, seconded by Mr. Secord, that so much of the Order of the Day as relates to the Bill for reducing the salary of the Adjutant General of the Militia, be postponed until Thursday next, and that it be on the Order of that Day.

Mr. Howard, seconded by Mr. Secord, moved that the House do now resolve itself into a Committee to go into the consideration of the Road Bill. The House accordingly resolved itself into a Committee to go into the consideration of the said Bill. Mr. Speaker left the Chair. Mr. Howard was called to the Chair of the Committee.

Mr. Speaker resumed the Chair, and Mr. Howard reported that the Committee had gone through the consideration of the said Bill, to which they had made several amendments, which he was directed to report to the House whenever it should be pleased to receive the same. Ordered, that the Report be now accepted. Mr. Howard then moved, seconded by Mr. James Wilson, that the Road Bill be engrossed, and read a third time to-morrow. Ordered accordingly.

Read for the second time, the Bill to make good moneys issued and advanced by His Majesty, through His Excellency, the Lieutenant Governor, in pursuance of two addresses. Mr. McLean then moved, seconded by Mr. Howard, that the House do now resolve itself into a Committee, to go into the consideration of the said Bill. The House accordingly resolved itself into a Committee. Mr. Speaker left the Chair. Mr. Willcocks was called to the Chair of the Committee. Mr. Speaker resumed the Chair, and Mr. Willcocks reported that the Committee had made a progress, and had directed him to ask for leave to sit again on Wednesday next. Ordered, that the Committee have leave to sit again on Wednesday next.

Read for the first time, a Bill for laying a .duty on Billiard Tables in this Province. Mr. Willcocks then moved, seconded by Mr. Sovereign, that the Bill for Licensing Billiard Tables be read a second time to-morrow, which was ordered accordingly.

Mr. Howard then moved, seconded by Mr. Mallory, that so much of the Order of the Day as gives him leave to bring in a Bill this day for the relief of indigent persons, be postponed; and that he have leave to bring in the same on Thursday next. Ordered accordingly.

Agreeably to the Order of the Day the House resolved itself into a Committee, to go into the consideration of the Bill to prevent the fraudulent sale of lands. Mr. Speaker left the Chair. Mr. McNabb was called to the Chair of the Committee.

Mr. Speaker resumed the Chair, and Mr. McNabb reported that the Committee had gone through the consideration of the said Bill without any amendment, which he was directed to report whenever the House should be pleased to receive the same. Ordered, that the Report be now received. Mr. Gough then moved, seconded by Mr. McNabb, that the Bill to prevent the fraudulent sale of lands be engrossed, and read a third time to-morrow, which was ordered accordingly.

Mr. Willcocks then moved, seconded by Mr. Lewis, for leave to bring in a Petition from the Freeholders of the Townships of Ancaster and Barton. Leave was accordingly granted, and the said Petition was ordered to lie upon the Table.

Read for the first time, a Bill for the relief of Mennonists and Tunkers. Mr. Gough then moved, seconded by Mr. Sovereign, that the Bill for the relief of Minors of the Societies of Mennonists and Tunkers be read a second time to-morrow. Ordered accordingly.

Mr. C. Wilson moved, seconded by Mr. Lewis, that so much of the Order of the Day as has not been proceeded upon be postponed for this day, and that it be on the Order of the Day for to-morrow. Ordered accordingly.

On motion of Mr. Willcocks, seconded by Mr. C. Wilson, ordered, that the Speaker do direct the Serjeant at Arms to procure a Carpet for this House, and green baize for the several tables therein, and also that he be directed to get lined with suitable cloth the pew appropriated for the members of this House in the Church in the Town of York.

Mr. Mallory then moved, seconded by Mr. Sovereign, for leave to bring in a Bill on Friday next for the better regulation of Tavern Licenses within this Province. Leave was accordingly granted.

Mr. Mallory again moved, seconded by Mr. Sovereign, for leave to bring in a Bill to-morrow to repeal certain parts of an Act passed in the forty-third year of His Majesty's Reign, entitled "An Act to provide for the payment of

wages to the Members of the House of Assembly, and to make further provision
for the payment of the same." Leave was accordingly granted.

Mr. Howard, seconded by Mr. Mallory, moved that it be a Rule of this
House that the Members thereof do meet at the usual hour of ten o'clock in
the forenoon, adjourn at three in the afternoon, and meet again at six in the
afternoon of the same day, for the purpose of despatching Public Business.   On
Mr. Speaker having put the question a division thereupon took place.   The names
being called for, they were taken down, and are as follows:—

Yeas.	Nays.
MESSRS. JOHN WILSON	MESSRS. MARCLE
HOWARD	FRAZER
SOVEREIGN	BABY
ROBLIN	McLEAN
MALLORY	GOUGH
	WILLCOCKS
	McNABB
	SECORD
	BURRITT
	DORLAND
	JAMES WILSON
	LEWIS
	C. WILSON

The same passed in the negative by a majority of eight.

Mr. McLean moved, seconded by Mr. Gough, for leave to bring in a Bill
on Wednesday next, for the division of certain Districts in this Province.   Leave
was accordingly granted.

On motion of Mr. Gough, seconded by Mr. Willcocks, resolved, that this
House, having received information of the death of Mrs. Rogers, wife of David
McGregor Rogers, Esquire, a Member of this House, do, as a mark of our esteem
for, and sympathy with him on the distressing event, at its rising to-morrow
adjourn until Thursday next; in order that the Members of this House may
attend at the funeral; and that the Order of the Day for Wednesday be postponed,
and that it do make a part of the Order of the Day for Thursday next.   The
House accordingly resolved the same.

Mr. McLean moved, seconded by Mr. Marcle, for leave to bring in a Bill on
Wednesday next, for granting to His Majesty a certain sum of money applicable
to the uses of this Province, to defray the expenses of amending and repairing
the Public Highways and Roads, laying out and opening New Roads, and building
Bridges, from the Township of Cornwall to the line dividing this Province from
the Province of Lower Canada.   Leave was accordingly granted.

On motion of Mr. Lewis, seconded by Mr. Secord, the House adjourned.

Tuesday, 13th February, 1810

Prayers were read.

The Clerk of this House has the honor of informing Mr. Speaker and the
House that the Clerks of the Peace of the different Districts in this Province
did send him returns of all the rateable property in their respective Districts, in
compliance with the tenth section of the Act for the more uniform laying of

Assessments and Rates throughout this Province. Mr. Speaker then ordered that the different returns received from the Clerks of the Peace be laid on the Table, to be entered in a Book to be of Record in this House.

Mr. Gough, seconded by Mr. Willcocks, moved for leave to bring up the petition of certain inhabitants of the Home District. Leave was accordingly granted to bring up the said Petition.

Then the Clerk, by order of the House, read two Bonds respecting the Controverted Election of James Wilson, Esquire, the sitting Member representing the County of Prince Edward (excepting the Township of Ameliasburgh) and John Roblin, Esquire, one of the sitting Members, representing the united Counties of Lennox and Addington, which are as follows.

Know all men by these presents, that we, Duncan Cameron, of the Town of York aforesaid, His Majesty's Printer, both of the Home District and Province of Upper Canada, are held and finally bound unto James Wilson of the County of Prince Edward, in the Midland District, of the Province aforesaid, Esquire, in the sum of Two Hundred Pounds of lawful money, to be paid to the said James Wilson, his heirs, executors, administrators or assigns, for which payment well and truly to be made, we bind ourselves, our heirs, executors and administrators firmly by these presents.

Signed with our hands, sealed with our seals, and dated at York, this Fourteenth day of February, in the Year of Our Lord One Thousand Eight Hundred and Ten.

Whereas the said James Wilson has been returned as Member to represent the County of Prince Edward (except Ameliasburgh) in the Provincial Parliament of Upper Canada; and whereas several of the inhabitants, freeholders thereof, contest the legality of his holding a seat therein, now know ye that if the above bounden Duncan Cameron and John Cameron, or either of them, their heirs, executors, administrators or assigns shall after the House of Assembly have decided the said Return, pay or cause to be paid unto the said James Wilson all such costs and charges as he or they shall be directed to pay by the House, then the said obligation to be null and void; otherwise to be and remain in full force and virtue.

Signed, Sealed and Delivered　　　　　　　　(Signed) D. CAMERON (Seal)
　　　in the presence of　　　　　　　　　　　　　　J. CAMERON (Seal)
　　　　　　　　　　　　　　　　　　　　　　　(Signed) J. McDONELL
　　　　　　　　　　　　　　　　　　　　　　　　　　　H. CARFRAE.

Know all men by these presents that we, Duncan Cameron, of the Town of York, Esquire, and John Cameron, of the Town of York aforesaid, His Majesty's Printer, both of the Home District of the Province of Upper Canada, are held and firmly bound unto John Roblin, of the United Counties of Lennox and Addington in the Midland District of the Province aforesaid, Esquire, in the sum of Two Hundred Pounds of lawful money, to be paid to the said John Roblin, his heirs, executors, administrators or assigns, for which payment to be well and truly made we bind ourselves, our heirs, executors, administrators and assigns firmly by these presents.

Signed with our hands, sealed with our seals, and dated at York, this Fourteenth day of February, in the Year of Our Lord One Thousand Eight Hundred and Ten.

Whereas the said John Roblin has been returned as one of the Members to represent the United Counties of Lennox and Addington in the Provincial Parliament of Upper Canada, and whereas several of the inhabitants, Freeholders thereof, contest the legality of his holding a seat therein.

Now know ye, that if the above Duncan Cameron and John Cameron, or either of them, their heirs, executors, administrators or assigns, shall, after the House of Assembly have decided the said Return, pay or cause to be paid unto the said John Roblin all such costs and charges as he or they shall be directed to pay by the House, then the said obligation to be null and void, otherwise to be and remain in full force and virtue.

Signed, Sealed and Delivered   (Signed) J. MacDONELL
   in the presence of   H. CARFRAE.
                                              (Signed) D. CAMERON (Seal)
                                                      J. CAMERON (Seal)

Agreeably to the Order of the Day, the House resolved itself into a Committee to go into the further consideration of the Bill for the more easy Recovery of Debts. Mr. Speaker left the Chair. Mr. Roblin took the chair of the Committee.

Mr. Speaker resumed the Chair, and Mr. Roblin reported that the Committee had gone through the consideration of the said Bill, to which they had made several amendments, which he was directed to report to the House whenever it should be pleased to receive the same. Ordered, that the Report be now received.

Mr. Gough then moved, seconded by Mr. C. Wilson, that the Bill for the more easy recovery of debts be engrossed, and read for the third time on Thursday next, which was ordered accordingly.

Read for the Second time, the Bill for establishing Common Schools in the several Districts of this Province. Mr. C. Wilson, seconded by Mr. Lewis, moved that the House do now resolve itself into a Committee to go into the consideration of the School Bill. The House accordingly resolved itself into a Committee to go into the consideration of the said Bill. Mr. Speaker left the Chair. Mr. Sovereign was called to the chair of the Committee.

Mr. Speaker resumed the Chair, and Mr. Sovereign reported that the Committee had made a progress, and had directed him to ask for leave to sit again this day. Leave was accordingly granted to sit again this day.

A Message from the Honorable the Legislative Council by Mr. Baldwin, Master in Chancery.

Mr. Speaker,

I am commanded by the Honorable the Legislative Council to acquaint this House that they have passed an Act sent up from this House, entitled " An Act to authorize the inhabitants of the County of Haldimand, to hold annual Town Meetings for the purpose of electing Town and Parish Officers," to which they have made several amendments, to which amendments they request the concurrence of this House.

And then he withdrew.

Mr. Willcocks then moved, seconded by Mr. Sovereign, that the amendments made by the Honorable the Legislative Council to the Act to authorize the inhabitants of Haldimand to hold annual Town Meetings, for the purpose of electing Town and Parish Officers, be now read. The said amendments were accordingly read for the first time. Mr. Willcocks again moved, seconded by Mr. Sovereign, that the said amendments be read for the second time on Thursday next, which was ordered accordingly.

Agreeably to leave given the House again resolved itself into a Committee to go into the further consideration of the Bill for establishing Common Schools in this Province. Mr. Speaker left the Chair. Mr. Sovereign was called to the chair of the Committee.

Mr. Speaker resumed the Chair, and Mr. Sovereign reported that the Committee had made a progress, and had directed him to ask for leave to sit again on Friday next. Leave was accordingly granted to sit again on Friday next.

Mr. McNabb then moved, seconded by Mr. Burritt that so much of the Order of the Day as relates to the Bill for imposing an additional duty on Licenses to Hawkers and Pedlars, be now dispensed with, and that it be on the Order of the Day for Saturday next. Ordered accordingly.

Mr. Willcocks, seconded by Mr. Sovereign, moved that so much of the Order of the Day as respects the Bill for extending the jurisdiction of the Court of Requests, be now dispensed with, and that the same be on the Order of the Day for Monday next, which was ordered accordingly.

Read for the Second time, a Bill sent down from the Honorable the Legislative Council entitled "An Act to render Justices of the Peace more safe in the execution of their duty." Mr. G. Wilson moved, seconded by Mr. Howard, that the House do now resolve itself into a Committee to go into the consideration of the said Bill. The House accordingly resolved itself into a Committee. Mr. Speaker left the Chair. Mr. G. Wilson was called to the chair of the Committee.

Mr. Speaker resumed the Chair, and Mr. Wilson reported that the Committee had come to a Resolution that the further consideration of the said Bill be postponed for three months. On Mr. Speaker having put the question, a division thereupon took place. The names being called for they were taken down, and are as follows:—

Yeas.	Nays.
MESSRS. GOUGH	MESSRS. McNABB
JNO. WILSON	FRAZER
HOWARD	BURRITT
WILLCOCKS	MARCLE
MALLORY	BABY
ROBLIN	McLEAN
SOVEREIGN	LEWIS
SECORD	C. WILSON
JAS. WILSON	McGREGOR
DORLAND	

The same was carried in the affirmative by a majority of one. And the further consideration of the said Bill was accordingly postponed for three months.

Read for the third time, as engrossed, the Bill for laying out, amending and keeping in repair, the public Highways and Roads throughout this Province. On motion of Mr. Howard, seconded by Mr. Sovereign, resolved, that the Bill do now pass, and that the title be "An Act to provide for the laying out, amending, and keeping in repair the public Highways and Roads in this Province, and to repeal the laws now in force for that purpose." The Bill accordingly passed, and was signed by the Speaker. Mr. Mallory then moved, seconded by Mr. Sovereign, that Mr. Gough and Capt. Frazer do carry up to the Honorable the Legislative Council the Act entitled "An Act to provide for the laying out, amending, and keeping in repair the public Highways and Roads in this Province, and to repeal the laws now in force for that purpose," and to request their concurrence in passing the same, which was ordered accordingly.

Then was read for the second time, the Bill for laying a duty on Billiard Tables.

Read for the first time, a Bill to make further provision for the payment of wages to the Members of the House of Assembly. Mr. Mallory then moved, seconded by Mr. Sovereign, that the Bill to make further provision for the payment of wages to the Members of the House of Assembly, be read for the second time on Thursday next, which was ordered accordingly.

Read for the third time, as engrossed, the Bill to prevent the fraudulent sale of lands. On motion of Mr. Gough, seconded by Mr. Sovereign, resolved, that the Bill do pass, and that the title be " An Act to prevent the fraudulant sale and transfer of lands in this Province." The Bill accordingly passed, and was signed by the Speaker. Mr. Howard then moved, seconded by Mr. Sovereign, that Messrs. Gough and Frazer do carry up to the Honorable the Legislative Council the Act entitled " An Act to prevent the fraudulent sale and transfer of lands in this Province," and request their concurrence thereto, which was ordered accordingly.

Mr. Burritt moved, seconded by Mr. McLean, that so much of the Order of the Day as has not been proceeded with be postponed until Thursday next. Ordered accordingly.

Mr. Willcocks, seconded by Mr. McNabb, moved that the Members of this House with its Officers do meet here at the hour of eleven o'clock in the forenoon to-morrow, for the purpose of going in a body to attend the funeral of the late Mrs. Rogers, wife of David McGregor Rogers, Esquire, a Member of this House. The House accordingly resolved the same.

On Motion of Mr. Marcle, seconded by Mr. Burritt, the House adjourned until Thursday next.

Thursday, 15th February, 1810.

Prayers were read.

Read for the second time, the Bill for the relief of Mennonists and Tunkers. Mr. Gough moved, seconded by Mr. Willcocks, that the House do now resolve itself into a Committee, to go into the consideration of the Bill for the relief of Mennonists and Tunkers. The House accordingly resolved itself into a Committee, to go into the consideration of the said Bill. Mr. Speaker left the Chair. Mr. McGregor was called to the Chair of the Committee.

Mr. Speaker resumed the Chair, and Mr. McGregor reported that the Committee had gone through the consideration of the said Bill without amendment, which was directed to report to the House whenever it should be pleased to receive the same. Ordered, that the Report be now received. The Report was accordingly received and accepted. Mr. Gough then moved, seconded by Mr. McNabb, that the Bill for the relief of Mennonists and Tunkers be engrossed, and read a third time to-morrow, which was ordered accordingly.

Mr. Willcocks, seconded by Mr. Mallory, moved that so much of the Order of the Day as relates to the Bill for granting money to replace moneys advanced by the Lieutenant Governor, be dispensed with for this day, and that the same be on the Order of the Day for Thursday next, which was passed in the negative.

Mr. Gough then moved, seconded by Mr. Burritt, that the House do now resolve itself into a Committee, to go into the consideration of the Bill for granting to his Majesty a certain sum of money in lieu of moneys issued and advanced by the Lieutenant Governor, in pursuance of two addresses. The House accordingly resolved itself into a Committee to go into the consideration of the said Bill. Mr. Speaker left the Chair. Mr. Willcocks was called to the chair of the Committee.

Mr. Speaker resumed the Chair, and Mr. Willcocks reported that the Committee had gone through the consideration of the said Bill, to which they had made no amendments, which he was directed to report to the House whenever it should be pleased to receive the same. Ordered, that the Report be now received. Mr. Gough, seconded by Mr. McNabb, moved that the said Bill be engrossed, and read a third time on Thursday the twenty-second instant. Ordered, that the said Bill be engrossed, and read a third time on Thursday, the twenty-second instant.

Mr. McLean moved, seconded by Mr. James Wilson, that so much of the Order of the Day as relates to the Bill for the creation of a new District, be dispensed with, and that the same be on the Order of the Day to-morrow. The same was dispensed with, and so ordered accordingly.

Mr. McLean, seconded by Mr. Howard, again moved, that so much of the Order of the Day as relates to the Bill for granting money for the repairing of roads and bridges from Cornwall to the line dividing this Province from that of Lower Canada, be dispensed with for this day, and that he have leave to bring in the same to-morrow. It was accordingly dispensed with, and leave given to bring in the same to-morrow.

Mr. Willcocks, seconded by Mr. Roblin, moved that so much of the Order of the Day, as regards the Bill for reducing the salary of the Adjutant General of the Militia, be now dispensed with, and that the same be on the Order of the Day for Monday next. Ordered accordingly.

Read for the first time, a Bill for the relief of casual indigent persons in this Province. Mr. Howard then moved, seconded by Mr. Willcocks, that the Bill to make provision for needy persons be read a second time to-morrow. Ordered that the said Bill be read for the second time to-morrow.

Read for the third time, as engrossed, the Bill for the more easy recovery of debts. On motion of Mr. Gough, seconded by Mr. Willcocks, resolved, that the Bill do now pass, and that the title be "An Act for the more easy recovery of Debts in this Province, and other purposes." The Bill then accordingly passed, and was signed by the Speaker. Mr. Mallory moved, seconded by Mr. Roblin, that Messrs. Willcocks and McNabb do carry up to the Honorable the Legislative Council the Act entitled "An Act for the More Easy Recovery of Debts in this Province, and other purposes," and requests their concurrence thereto. Ordered accordingly.

Messrs. Gough and Frazer, the messengers named to carry up to the Honorable the Legislative Council two Acts from this House, reported that, in obedience to the commands of this House, they had carried up to the Honorable the Legislative Council an Act entitled "An Act to prevent the fraudulent sale and transfer of lands in this Province," to which they did request their concurrence.

Also an Act entitled "An Act to provide for the laying out, amending and keeping in repair the Public Highways and Roads in this Province, and to repeal the laws now in force for that purpose," to which they did request their concurrence in passing the same.

Messrs. McGregor and John Wilson, the messengers named to carry up to the Honorable the Legislative Council the Act from this House entitled "An Act for granting an additional sum of money for the purpose of erecting a bridge across the Grand River," reported that they had carried up the same, and did request their concurrence thereto.

Messrs. Howard and Roblin, the messengers ordered to carry up to the Honorable the Legislative Council an Act from this House, entitled "An Act further to extend the benefits of an Act passed in the thirty seventh year of His Majesty's Reign, entitled ' An Act for the more easy Barring of Dower,' " reported that they had carried up the said Act, and did request their concurrence in passing the same.

Mr. Mallory, seconded by Mr. Willcocks, moved that the House do now resolve itself into a Committee to go into the consideration of the amendments made by the Honorable the Legislative Council, in and to an Act entitled "An Act to authorize the inhabitants of the County of Haldimand to hold Annual Meetings, for the purpose of electing Town and Parish Officers."

The House accordingly resolved itself into a Committee, to go into the consideration of the said amendments. Mr. Speaker left the Chair. Mr. Baby was called to the Chair of the Committee.

Mr. Speaker resumed the Chair, and Mr. Baby reported that the Committee had gone through the consideration of the said amendments, and that he was directed by the Committee to recommend that the said amendments be adopted by this House. Mr. Mallory then moved, seconded by Mr. Roblin, that the said amendments be engrossed and read a third time to-morrow. Which was ordered accordingly.

Messrs. Willcocks and McNabb, the Messengers ordered to carry up to the Honorable the Legislative Council an Act from this House entitled "An Act for the more easy recovery of Debts in this Province, and other purposes," reported that in obedience to the commands of this House they had carried up the said Act, and did request their concurrence in passing the same.

Mr. Mallory, seconded by Mr. Sovereign, moved that the House do now resolve itself into a Committee to go into the consideration of the Bill for making further provision for the Payment of Wages to the Members of this House. The House accordingly resolved itself into a Committee. Mr. Speaker left the Chair. Captain Frazer was called to the Chair of the Committee.

Mr. Speaker resumed the Chair, and Captain Frazer reported that the Committee had gone through the consideration of the said Bill, to which they had made several amendments, which he was directed to report to the House whenever it should be pleased to receive the same. On Mr. Speaker having put the question for the Report being received, a division thereupon took place. The names being called for, they were taken down, and are as follows:—

Yeas.	Nays.
MESSRS. BURRLTT	MESSRS. FRAZER
JOHN WILSON	MARCLE
HOWARD	GOUGH
MALLORY	ELLIOTT
ROBLIN	McGREGOR
WILLCOCKS	BABY
SECORD	LEWIS
SOVEREIGN	McLEAN
DORLAND	
McNABB	
JAMES WILSON	
C. WILSON	

Carried in the affirmative by a majority of four. The Report was accordingly received. Mr. Mallory then moved, seconded by Mr. Secord, that the Bill for making further provision for the Payment of Wages to the Members of the House of Assembly be engrossed, and read a third time to-morrow, which was ordered accordingly.

Mr. Gough, from the Committee appointed to draft an Address to His Excellency the Lieutenant-Governor, requesting that His Excellency would be pleased to furnish the House with such Reports as have been made by the Commissioners appointed under the authority of the several Acts of this Province, appropriating moneys for improving the Highways and Roads, subsequent to the year One Thousand Eight Hundred and Three; reported that the Committee had drafted an Address, which he was directed by the Committee to submit to the House whenever it should be pleased to receive the same. The House then Ordered that the Address be now received. He then read the Address in his place, and afterwards delivered in the same at the Table, where it was again read by the Clerk, and is as follows:—

To His Excellency, Francis Gore, Esquire, Lieutenant-Governor of the Province of Upper Canada, etc., etc., etc.

May it please Your Excellency,

We, His Majesty's dutiful and loyal subjects, the Commons of the Province of Upper Canada in Parliament Assembled, being anxious faithfully to discharge the duties of the important task we have to perform, beg leave humbly to request Your Excellency will be pleased to direct to be laid before this House, all such reports as may have been received by the late Lieutenant-Governor Hunter, Mr. President Grant, and by Your Excellency, from the Commissioners of Public Highways, respecting the disbursements of the several sums of money which have been appropriated by the Legislature of this Province in conformity to several Acts thereof subsequent to the year One Thousand Eight Hundred and Three, for amending and repairing the Public Highways and Roads, laying out and opening new Roads and building Bridges in the several Districts thereof; and if such report has not been furnished to Your Excellency, that you will be pleased to direct the said Commissioners to lay before this House full statements of the sums they have respectively received and the manner in which they have been applied.

Commons House of Assembly,
19th February. 1810.

Mr. Gough then moved, seconded by Mr. Burritt, that the House do on to-morrow resolve itself into a Committee to go into the consideration of the said Address. The same was ordered accordingly.

Mr. McLean moved, seconded by Mr. Marcle, for leave to bring in a Bill to-morrow for granting to His Majesty a certain sum of money out of the funds applicable to the uses of this Province, to defray the expenses of amending and repairing the Roads and Bridges in the several Districts thereof. Leave was accordingly granted.

Mr. Howard, seconded by Mr. Sovereign, moved for leave to bring in a Bill on Monday next to prevent irregularity at Elections in future. Leave was granted accordingly.

Mr. Howard again moved, seconded by Mr. Sovereign, for leave to bring in a Bill on Monday next, to authorize the Justices of the Peace throughout this Province to convict in a summary way any person or persons coming into or travelling through this Province, and exhibiting in Public any play or Show therein. Accordingly leave was granted.

Mr. Gough then moved, seconded by Mr. C. Wilson, that the Bill for ascertaining the Boundaries of Lands in this Province be read to-morrow. Ordered that the said Bill be read to-morrow.

Mr. Mallory gave notice that he will to-morrow move that this House do address His Excellency, the Lieutenant-Governor, to request that His Excellency will be pleased to direct the Adjutant-General to lay before this House the state of the Militia of this Province.

Mr. Gough, seconded by Mr. Lewis, moved that the petition of the Inhabitants of the Home District be now read. The said Petition was accordingly read, and is as follows:—

To the Honorable the House of Assembly of Upper Canada, in Parliament Assembled.

The Petition of the Inhabitants of the Home District in said Province,

Most humbly Showeth,

That Your Petitioners, by the blessing of God, have experienced great benefits from the Salmon Fishery; and whereas divers persons do catch them at a time when they are not eatable, and selling them to the Inhabitants and Public for good, and fearing that by catching them so, at a time when they ought to spawn, it will be the means of destroying them altogether, Your Petitioners therefore most humbly pray that the Honorable House will pass an Act to prohibit the catching salmon after the Fifteenth of October, and also that no mill-gates be hoisted, or no sluices be stopped for the purpose of stopping or catching said salmon.

And Your petitioners, as in duty bound, will ever pray.

(Signed) Nicholas Delong, Wm. Cooper, Oliver Prentice, John Holly, James Weiant, Michael Miller, and forty other signatures.

On Motion of Mr. Howard, seconded by Mr. McLean, the House adjourned.

Friday, 16th February, 1810.

Prayers were read.

Mr. Gough moved, seconded by Mr. Willcocks, for leave to bring in the Petition of the Inhabitants of the Township of Toronto in the Home District. Leave was granted to bring up the said Petition.

Mr. Speaker informed the House that application in writing had been made to him by the Clerk of the House, which he read, and is as follows:—

Mr. Speaker,

The Clerk respectfully informs the House that the wages now due the Copying Clerks exceed the sum appropriated by law for that purpose; he therefore prays the permission and sanction of this House to employ Copying Clerks in his Office.

Commons House of Assembly,

16th February, 1810.   (Signed) DONALD McLEAN,
                                                     Clerk, Assembly.

Mr. Willcocks, seconded by Mr. Secord, moved that the Clerk be authorized to employ such number of Copying Clerks as may be found necessary during the present Session. Mr. Speaker did then, by permission of the House, authorize the Clerk to employ Copying Clerks to assist him in his Office.

Mr. Mallory moved, seconded by Mr. Sovereign, that so much of the Order of the Day as relates to leave for him to bring in a Bill this day for the better regulating Tavern Licenses in this Province be dispensed with, and that he have leave to bring in the same on Tuesday next. The same was dispensed with, and leave given to bring in the same on Tuesday next.

Agreeably to the Order of the Day, the House resolved itself into a Committee to go into the consideration of the Bill for establishing Common Schools in this Province. Mr. Speaker left the Chair. Mr. Sovereign was called to the Chair of the Committee.

Mr. Speaker resumed the Chair, and Mr. Sovereign reported that the Committee had made a progress, and had directed him to ask for leave to sit again on Monday next. Leave was granted to sit again on Monday next.

Read for the third time, as engrossed, the Bill for the relief of Mennonists and Tunkers. On motion of Mr. Gough, seconded by Mr. Sovereign, resolved, that the Bill do pass, and that the title be "An Act for the relief of Minors of the Societies of Mennonists and Tunkers."

The Bill then passed, and was signed by the Speaker.

Mr. Willcocks, seconded by Mr. Mallory, moved that Messrs. Gough and Burritt do carry up to the Honorable the Legislative Council the Act entitled "An Act for the relief of Minors of the Societies of Mennonists and Tunkers," and request their concurrence thereto, which was ordered accordingly.

On motion of Mr. McLean, seconded by Mr. Howard, was read the Petitions and subscription paper of the Inhabitants of the District of Niagara, and the West Riding of the County of York, praying that the site of the intended Town may be at Coot's Paradise; which are as follows:—

To the Commons House of Assembly of the Province of Upper Canada, in Parliament assembled.

The Petition of the Inhabitants of part of the District of Niagara, the County of Haldimand, and the West Riding of the County of York,

Humbly Showeth,

That Petitions were forwarded to Your Honorable House last Session, praying the creation of a new District from a part of the Niagara District, the West Riding of the County of York, and the County of Haldimand.

That Your Petitioners have heard the Beach was named in Your Honorable House as the most central place for the County Town.

Your Petitioners humbly beg leave to remind Your Honorable House that the proposed place at the Beach is entirely on private property, which originally belonged to the family of the late Captain Brant, which by him was in part parcelled out into small and irregular tracts, and sold to individuals without any allowance or reserves for roads, either to lands sold, or in any way through it; and in which from this circumstance, there is at present great confusion, as well as strife and contention, about roads; and from this trouble made to prevent roads being carried through that tract it is not to be supposed as it becomes more valuable it will be less contended for.

That in the neighborhood of the Beach no supplies or materials for building, or accommodation, are to be procured at present from the country immediately round it, and as a further bar to convenience or comfort to be expected there in the new purchase, three or four concessions only are purchased, and the few settlers in them have everything to buy for themselves, and it will be no more convenience for the persons who in all probability will compose the Bench of Justices to attend there than at York or Niagara, it being too far generally for them to go and return the same day; and as your Petitioners contemplate the present division as merely temporary, for when a further purchase is made in the late purchased tract, and it becomes tolerably populous, there will be territory enough for two districts.

That the Inhabitants in every stage of settlement in this Province, who settled on Dundas Street, were required to perform a settlement duty in consequence of being indulged with lots on the Great Western Road; that Governor Simcoe, seeing so advantageous and proper a situation, with the advice and concurrence of the Executive Council, reserved at the head of the water communication, from which Dundas Street proceeds to the westward, a Town plot, in which are reserves for the purpose of erecting all the various public buildings, place of worship, etc., necessary in a County Town; which we conceive to be in the heart of a good settlement, from which every supply may easily be drawn to make persons settled in a Town comfortable, and that the river, down which all the produce from this part of the country, as well as further westward, must necessarily pass, has been cleared out last Summer at the expense of private individuals; that boats of a very considerable magnitude may now commodiously be brought up to the town reserve, and that access by land to and from it is easy and good by the various roads which pass through and to it.

That Your Petitioners have further to remark to Your Honorable House that the natural requisites for building a town with are very near to the reserve: there is plenty of good limestone and timber, that the reserve is well watered, healthy, and immediately in the neighborhood of all the mills in this part of the Country.

Wherefore Your Petitioners pray Your Honorable House may take their case into consideration, and if a division in the district should be found expedient, the original town plot reserve at the head of the water communication may be appropriated for the county town, and, as in duty bound, your Petitioners will ever pray.

(Signed) Richard Hatt, Wm. Nellis, Eph. L. Philips, Wm. Hepbourne, Andrew Nellis, Jun., Henry Ellis, and eighty-two other signatures.

Four other petitions to the same purpose, with four hundred and sixty-six signatures, were brought up and laid on the Table.

And also was read a paper of which the following is a copy:—

To the Commons House of Assembly of the Province of Upper Canada, in Parliament met.

Whereas several petitions have gone forward to Your Honorable House, stating that a division of the districts has been solicited, and praying that the place originally appropriated under the administration of Governor Simcoe might be applied as the County Town for the new district, that is, the village reserved at the head of the water communication at Coot's Paradise; and should it appear to the wisdom of Your Honorable House that the village above recited is the most proper place, and Your Honorable House should deem it proper to name the reserve above mentioned as the place for the County Town, and it passes into a law, then, and in that case, we, the subscribers, do bind ourselves, our heirs and administrators, jointly and severally, to subscribe and pay the sum affixed to our respective names, for the purpose of furnishing materials and defraying the expenses in erecting a Gaol and Court House in the aforesaid town plot, at the head of the water communication, at Coot's Paradise in Ancaster and Flamboro' West.

January 29th, 1810.

Richard Hatt, five hundred dollars.

W. G. Hepburne, one hundred dollars.

Titus G. Simons, one hundred dollars.
Manuel Overfield, two hundred dollars.
Hector S. McKay, two hundred dollars.
Caleb Forsythe, one hundred dollars.
And seventy-two other signatures, subscribing the sum of two thousand seven
hundred and sixty dollars.

On motion of Mr. Willcocks, seconded by Mr. Mallory, was read another
Petition of the Inhabitants of the Township of Nelson, East and West Flamboro',
Beverley, Blocks Nos. 1, 2 and 3 on the River Ouse (more commonly known as
the Grand River) Salt Fleet, Barton, Ancaster, Glanford, and Binbrook, including
that part of the County of Haldimand which lies between the Onondaga Village
and the Dundas Street, which is as follows:—

To the Honorable the Commons House of Assembly in Parliament assembled.
We, the inhabitants, freeholders of the Townships of Nelson, East and West
Flamboro', Beverley, Blocks 1, 2 and 3 on the River Ouse (more commonly known
as the Grand River), Saltfleet, Barton, Ancaster, Glanford and Binbrook, including that part of the County of Haldimand which lies between the Onondaga Village and the Dundas Street, labouring under many inconveniences, and attended
with heavy expenses, which necessarily occur in travelling from our remote situation to the places of public business; and having ample means to erect and support public buildings nigh home, are desirous of being separated from the Counties
of York and Lincoln, and becoming established in our own; and that a Bill nominating the head of the Beech in the Township of Nelson to be the proper place for
the County Town did pass Your Honorable House last Session:—

And we, humbly conceiving that you did not receive the most accurate information respecting the most eligible site for a new County Town, and the incalculable inconvenience that must necessarily await the inhabitants if established
in that part of the proposed district; beg leave humbly to present those objections
which appear to us most prominent.   `

In the first place the materials necessary for the erection of public buildings
cannot be procured without enormous difficulty and expense; neither is the situation
a central one,—of course it will not remedy the great evil of which we complain
in travelling such an immense distance in attending to the several Courts of Justice, etc., as above stated. That the settlements adjacent to the proposed place
are new and unproductive, consequently destitute of all articles immediately necessary for the establishment of a County Town.

We beg leave also to inform Your Honorable House that we are apprised of
a petition intended to be brought before you, recommending the head of Coot's
Paradise as a proper place for the County Town, which was at an early period,
and in the infancy of this country, ordered by General Simcoe to be laid out into
Town lots; but from the unhealthy situation of the place, owing to the ground
being principally low, and the waters overflowing both in Spring and Fall, it being
at the head of a long frog marsh which is navigable only at particular seasons of
the year, all attempts to establish a town in that quarter of the district have proved
unsuccessful, and is now only sought for by those who wish to promote their personal interest on the inconvenience and expense of four-fifths of the inhabitants
of the proposed district.

Therefore Your Petitioners take the liberty of recommending to Your Honorable House the south side of Burlington Bay, and nigh the head, on the main
Road leading to the Grand River, Dundas Street, etc., on Number 14 in the
22 A.

second concession of the Township of Barton, owned by James Durand and Nathaniel Hughson, as the most convenient part of the proposed district for the inhabitants and the public in general; having immediately adjacent a sufficiency of building timber, a redundancy of excellent stone and water that may be commanded at the pleasure and to the convenience of every individual at a trifling expense; together with conveniences of every other kind suitable to the establishment of a County Town.

We beg leave also to mention that the Road already opened on the division line leading from the said lot, and distant only one mile and a quarter to the best harbour on Burlington Bay, with every access to the water, there being no impediment to a free communication to the water's edge or to interrupt the navigation of small crafts to the immediate boundary of the water.

We also pledge ourselves that James Durand or Nathaniel Hughson will each or either of them appropriate such a quantity of lands as shall be deemed necessary for the public buildings, etc.

We therefore humbly request that Your Honorable House will be pleased in your wisdom to establish the County Town at the last mentioned place.

And Your Petitioners, as in duty bound, will ever pray.

(Signed) John Drake, Ezra Barnum, M. Marcle, Elijah Secord, Benj. Springer, Rich'd Beasley, Thomas Dowlin, Thos. Shaw, and two hundred and fifty-four other subscribers.

Read for the first time, a Bill for the creation of a new district. Mr. McLean moved, seconded by Mr. Howard, that the Bill for the creation of a new district be read a second time on Monday next, which was ordered accordingly.

Read for the second time, the Bill for the relief of indigent persons in this Province. Mr. Howard then moved, seconded by Mr. Mallory, that the House do now resolve itself into a Committee to take into consideration the Bill to make provision for the poor. The House accordingly resolved itself into a Committee, to go into the consideration of the said Bill. Mr. Speaker left the Chair. Mr. Burritt was called to the Chair of the Committee.

Mr. Speaker resumed the Chair, and Mr. Burritt reported that the Committee had made a progress, and had directed him to ask for leave to sit again on Monday next. Leave was accordingly granted to sit again on Monday next.

Mr. Gough, one of the messengers named to carry up to the Honorable the Legislative Council the Act entitled "An Act for the relief of minors of the Society of Mennonists and Tunkers," reported that, in obedience to the commands of this House, they had carried up the same, and did request their concurrence thereto.

Read for the third time, as engrossed, the amendments made by the Honorable the Legislative Council in and to the Act entitled "An Act to authorize the inhabitants of the County of Haldimand to hold Annual Meetings, for the purpose of electing Town and Parish Officers." The said amendments as read were then adopted by the House. Mr. Howard then moved, seconded by Mr. Secord, that Messrs. C. Wilson and Mallory do acquaint the Honorable the Legislative Council that this House concurred in and to the amendments made by them to the Act entitled "An Act to authorize the inhabitants of the County of Haldimand to hold Annual Town Meetings, for the purpose of electing Town and Parish Officers. Ordered accordingly.

A Written Message to the Honorable the Legislative Council by Messrs. C. Wilson and Mallory.

MR. SPEAKER,—
We are commanded by the Commons House of Assembly to acquaint this Honorable House that they have concurred in adopting the amendments made by the Honorable the Legislative Council, in and to the Act entitled "An Act to authorize the inhabitants of the County of Haldimand to hold Annual Meetings, for the purpose of electing Town and Parish Officers."

Commons House of Assembly,
16th February, 1810.   (Signed) SAM'L STREET,
                                                            Speaker.

Read for the third time, as engrossed, the Bill for altering the mode of payment of wages to the Members of the House of Assembly. Mr. Willcocks moved, seconded by Mr. Sovereign, that the said Bill be re-committed to-morrow, which was ordered accordingly.

Agreeably to the Order of the Day, the House resolved itself into a Committee to go into the consideration of the draft of an Address to His Excellency the Lieutenant Governor, respecting the expenditure of the various sums of money granted by the Parliament of this Province for the purpose of amending and repairing the Highways and Bridges, subsequent to the year one thousand eight hundred and three. Mr. Speaker left the Chair. Mr. Howard was called to the Chair of the Committee.

Mr. Speaker resumed the Chair, and Mr. Howard reported that the Committee had gone through the consideration of the said Address, without any amendments, which he was directed to report to the House whenever it should be pleased to receive the same. Ordered, that the Report be now received. On motion of Mr. Willcocks, seconded by Mr. Gough, ordered, that the said Address be engrossed, and read a third time to-morrow.

Read for the first time, A Bill for granting a sum of money for the purpose of amending and repairing the Highways and Bridges in this Province. Mr. McLean, seconded by Mr. Wilson, moved that the Bill for appropriating money for roads and bridges, be read a second time on Tuesday next, which was ordered accordingly.

Mr. McNabb moved, seconded by Mr. Burritt, that so much of the Order of the Day as has not been proceeded upon, be now dispensed with, and that the same be on the Order of the Day to-morrow. The same was dispensed with, and ordered accordingly.

On motion of Mr. Burritt, seconded by Mr. McGregor, the House adjourned.

Saturday, 17th February, 1810

Prayers were read.

Read for the first time, A Bill for the more accurately ascertaining the boundaries of lands in this Province. Mr. Gough then moved, seconded by Mr. C. Wilson, that the Bill for ascertaining the boundaries of lands be read a second time on Thursday next, which was ordered accordingly.

Read for the first time, A Bill for laying an additional duty on licenses to Hawkers, Pedlars, and Petty Chapmen. Mr. McNabb moved, seconded by Capt. Frazer, that the Bill for raising the duty on licenses to Hawkers and Pedlars be read a second time on Wednesday next. Mr. Gough, seconded by Mr. Sovereign, moved as an amendment to Mr. McNabb's motion, that the words "this day three months" be inserted, which was carried in the affirmative.

The main question accordingly passed in the negative, and the said Bill was ordered to be read on this day three months.

Mr. Willcocks, seconded by Mr. Roblin, moved that so much of the Order of the Day as relates to the Bill for altering the mode of payment of the wages to the Members of the House of Assembly, be dispensed with, and that the same be on the Order of the Day for Monday next. Which was ordered accordingly.

Mr. Willcocks again moved, seconded by Mr. Roblin, that the Address to His Excellency the Lieutenant Governor, respecting the disbursement of public money upon the highways and roads, be re-committed on Monday next. The House accordingly resolved the same.

Mr. Gough, seconded by Mr. Willcocks, moved for leave to bring in a Bill on Monday next, to amend an Act passed in the forty-seventh year of His Majesty's Reign, entitled "An Act for the preservation of Salmon." Leave was accordingly granted.

Mr. Speaker then read a letter from William Hatton, Esquire, Secretary to His Excellency the Lieutenant Governor, which is as follows:—

Lieutenant Governor's Office,
16th February, 1810.

SIR:—

In compliance with your letter of yesterday's date, I have the honor of transmitting to you fifty copies of the Acts passed in 1809, and I regret that it is not in my power to send you more than twelve of those passed in 1808, as they are nearly the whole number which remain in the Lieutenant Governor's Office.

I have the honor to be,
Sir,
Your most obedient humble Serv't
(Signed) WM. HATTON.

His Honor the Speaker of the
House of Assembly.

Mr. McNabb moved, seconded by Mr. Burritt, for leave to bring in a Bill on Tuesday next, to lay a tax on Dogs in this Province. Leave was accordingly granted.

On motion of Mr. McNabb, seconded by Mr. Marcle, the House adjourned until Monday next.

Monday, 19th February, 1810.

Prayers were read.

Agreeably to the Order of the Day, the House resolved itself into a Committee, to go into the consideration of the Bill for altering the mode of paying the wages to the Members of the House of Assembly. Mr. Speaker left the Chair. Capt. Frazer was called to the Chair of the Committee.

Mr. Speaker resumed the Chair, and Capt. Frazer reported that the Committee had gone through the consideration of the said Bill, to which they had made several amendments, which he was directed to report to the House whenever it should be pleased to receive the same. Ordered, that the Report be now received.

Mr. Mallory moved, seconded by Mr. Rogers, that the Bill to alter the mode of payment of wages to the Member of the House of Assembly be engrossed, and read a third time to-morrow. Ordered accordingly.

A Message from the Honorable the Legislative Council, by Mr. Burns, Master in Chancery.

MR. SPEAKER,—

I am commanded by the Honorable the Legislative Council to acquaint this House that they have passed an Act entitled "An Act for preventing the forgery and counterfeiting of foreign Bills of Exchange, and of Foreign Notes, and Orders for the Payment of Money," to which they request the concurrence of this House in passing the same.

Also that they have passed an Act, sent up from this House, entitled "An Act for granting an additional sum of money for the purpose of erecting a bridge across the Grand River," to which they have made several amendments, to which amendments they request the concurrence of this House.

And then he withdrew.

Read for the first time, An Act sent down from the Honorable the Legislative Council entitled "An Act to prevent forging and counterfeiting foreign Bills of Exchange." Mr. Howard then moved, seconded by Mr. Sovereign, that the Bill brought down from the Legislative Council for preventing the forging and counterfeiting foreign Bills of Exchange, be read a second time on Wednesday next, which was ordered accordingly.

Read for the first time, the amendments made by the Honorable the Legislative Council, in and to the Act sent up from this House, entitled "An Act for granting an additional sum of money, for the purpose of erecting a bridge across the Grand River." Mr. Willcocks then moved, seconded by Mr. Mallory, that the amendments made by the Honorable the Legislative Council to a Bill entitled "An Act for granting an additional sum of money, for the purpose of erecting a bridge across the Grand River," be read a second time to-morrow. Ordered accordingly.

Mr. C. Wilson, one of the messengers named to carry up to the Honorable the Legislative Council the Message of this House, respecting the Act entitled "An Act to authorize the inhabitants of the County of Haldimand to hold Annual Meetings, for the purpose of electing Town and Parish Officers," reported that they did carry up the same message to the Legislative Council.

Agreeably to the Order of the Day, the House resolved itself into a Committee, to go into the further consideration of the Address to His Excellency the Lieutenant Governor, respecting the expenditure of money on the highways and roads. Mr. Speaker left the Chair. Mr. Howard was called to the Chair of the Committee.

Mr. Speaker resumed the Chair, and Mr. Howard reported that the Committee had gone through the consideration of the said Address, to which they had made no amendment, which he was directed to report to the House whenever it should be pleased to receive the same. Ordered, that the report be now received and accepted. Mr. Rogers, seconded by Mr. Jas. Wilson, moved that the Address to His Excellency the Lieutenant Governor be engrossed, and that messengers be appointed to wait upon His Excellency with the same, which was ordered accordingly.

Read for the first time, A Bill to extend the Jurisdiction of the Court of Requests. Mr. Willcocks then moved, seconded by Mr. Sovereign, that the Bill for extending the jurisdiction of the Court of Requests be read a second time to-morrow, which was ordered accordingly.

Read for the third time, as engrossed, the Bill for the reduction of the salary of the Adjutant General.

Mr. Willcocks then moved, seconded by Mr. Roblin, that the Bill do now pass, and that the title be, "An Act to amend an Act passed in the forty-eighth year of His Majesty's Reign, entitled ' An Act for granting to His Majesty an, Annual Sum of Money, for the purposes therein mentioned.' " On Mr. Speaker having put the question, a division thereupon took place. The names being called for, they were taken down, and are as follows:—

Yeas.	Nays.
MESSRS. GOUGH	MESSRS. BURRITT
JNO. WILSON	MARCLE
WILLCOCKS	ELLIOTT
ROGERS	BABY
SECORD	McGREGOR
HOWARD	McLEAN
SOVEREIGN	McNABB
MALLORY	C. WILSON
ROBLIN	
DORLAND	
LEWIS	
JAS. WILSON	

Carried in the affirmative by a majority of four. The Bill then passed, and was signed by the Speaker. Mr. McGregor, seconded by Mr. Howard, then moved that Messrs. Willcocks and Mallory do carry up to the Legislative Council the Act entitled " An Act to amend an Act passed in the forty-eighth year of His Majesty's Reign, entitled ' An Act for granting to His Majesty an Annual Sum of Money for the purposes therein mentioned,' " and request their concurrence thereto. Ordered accordingly.

Mr. Howard, seconded by Mr. Sovereign, moved that so much of the Order of the Day as gives leave to bring in a Bill for the better regulation of elections in this Province, be dispensed with for this day, and that he have leave to bring in the same to-morrow. The same was dispensed with, and ordered accordingly.

Read for the first time, A Bill for the discouragement of Public Plays and Exhibitions in this Province. Mr. Howard then moved, seconded by Mr. Jas. Wilson, that the Bill for the discouragement of Plays and Shows, be read a second time to-morrow. Ordered accordingly.

Agreeably to the Order of the Day, the House resolved itself into a Committee, to go into the consideration of the School Bill. Mr. Speaker left the Chair. Mr. Sovereign took the chair of the Committee.

Mr. Speaker resumed the Chair, and Mr. Sovereign reported that the Committee had made a progress, and had directed him to ask for leave to sit again to-morrow. Leave was granted to sit again to-morrow.

Read as engrossed, the Address to His Excellency the Lieutenant Governor, which passed, and was signed by the Speaker.

Mr. Willcocks moved, seconded by Mr. Frazer, that Messrs. McGregor and Frazer do wait upon His Excellency the Lieutenant Governor, to know when he will be pleased to receive the Address of this House; and that the same gentlemen do present the same at such time as His Excellency shall be pleased to appoint, which was ordered accordingly.

Read for the first time, A Bill for the preservation of Salmon. Mr. Gough then moved, seconded by Mr. Mallory, that the Bill for the further preservation of Salmon be read a second time to-morrow. Ordered accordingly.

Mr. McNabb moved, seconded by Mr. Dorland, that so much of the Order of the Day as has not been proceeded upon be dispensed with for this Day, and that it be on the Order of the Day for to-morrow, which was ordered accordingly.

Mr. McNabb again moved, seconded by Mr. Dorland, for leave to bring in a Bill on Wednesday next, to alter the construction of Mill dams on the River Moira, so that rafts of timber and crafts may pass over them in safety. Leave was accordingly granted.

Mr. Willcocks moved, seconded by Mr. Sovereign, for leave to bring in a Bill on Wednesday next, to repeal an Act passed in the fourty-fourth year of His Majesty's Reign, entitled "An Act to repeal certain parts of an Act, passed in the thirty-fourth year of His Majesty's Reign, entitled 'An Act to establish a Supreme Court of Civil and Criminal Jurisdiction, and to regulate the Court of Appeal, and to authorize His Majesty's Court of King's Bench in this Province, to regulate certain fees, costs and charges therein mentioned.'" Leave was accordingly granted.

Mr. Rogers gave notice, that he will to-morrow move that the House do request the Judges of the Court of King's Bench to direct that there be laid before this House, as soon as it can be done, a list of all such fees as have been by them allowed in consequence of the power in them vested by an Act passed in the forty-fourth year of His Majesty's Reign.

Mr. McLean, seconded by Mr. Dorland, moved for leave to bring in a Bill on Wednesday next, for the relief of the different Districts of this Province from such charges as may arise from Bastard Children being born within this Province. Leave was accordingly granted.

Mr. McGregor gave notice that he will to-morrow move, that no new Bill be brought into the House after Saturday next.

On motion of Mr. Willcocks, seconded by Mr. Mallory, the House adjourned.

Tuesday, 20th February, 1810.

Prayers were read.

Mr. Gough, seconded by Mr. Mallory, moved that the petition of the inhabitants of the Township of Toronto be now read.

The said Petition was accordingly read, and is as follows:—

To the Honorable the Commons House of Assembly in Parliament assembled.

The humble Petition of the undersigned inhabitants of the Township of Toronto, in the Home District,

Respectfully Sheweth,

That Your Petitioners reside in the said Township, on or near Dundas Street, leading from Cooper's Mills on the River Humber to the head of Lake Ontario.

That Your Petitioners have not the means of getting to Cooper's Mills to get their grain ground, there being no established road for four miles or thereabouts.

That Your Petitioners are willing to make a road there at their own expense in the event of the same being established. They are also willing to erect a bridge across the Humber at their own expense.

Your Petitioners presume to state that the road as now marked out by the inhabitants avoids all swamps and mountains, and is as direct as it is capable of being and that there is no part of the labour necessary but they are willing to perform, except a bridge across the River Credit, on the Dundas Road.

Your Petitioners therefore respectfully pray that the Honorable House will be pleased to pass a Bill establishing the said road, and give such pecuniary assistance to effect the building of a bridge across the River Credit, as to the wisdom of this Honorable House shall seem meet.

And Your Petitioners, as in duty bound, will ever pray.

York, February 9th, 1810.

(Signed) Allen Robinett, Jr., William Cooper, Allen Robinett, Caleb Humphrey, and thirty-three others.

Mr. Gough moved, seconded by Mr. Willcocks, for leave to bring in a Bill on Thursday next, for granting a sum of money in aid of building a bridge over the River Credit, adjoining Dundas Street, between the Townships of Etobicoke and Toronto, in the Home District. Leave was accordingly granted.

Mr. Willcocks gave notice that he will to-morrow move, that the House do resolve itself into a Committee, to take into consideration the Bill for imposing a tax upon Billiard Tables in this Province.

Mr. Gough, seconded by Mr. Mallory, moved for leave to bring up the Petition of Augustus Jones, Deputy Surveyor. Leave was accordingly granted to bring up the said Petition.

Mr. Rogers moved, seconded by Mr. Willcocks, that the Judges of His Majesty's Court of King's Bench in this Province be requested by the Speaker to lay before this House, as soon as it can be conveniently done, a list of all such fees as have been by them allowed in consequence of the power in them vested by an Act passed in the forty-fourth year of His Majesty's Reign. Ordered accordingly.

Read for the second time, the Bill for the creation of a new District. Mr. McLean then moved, seconded by Mr. Howard, that the House do now resolve itself into a Committee to go into the consideration of the new District Bill. The House accordingly resolved itself into a Committee to go into the consideration of the said Bill. Mr. Speaker left the Chair. Mr. Burritt was called to the chair of the Committee.

Mr. Speaker resumed the Chair. And Mr. Burritt reported that the Committee had made a progress, and had directed him to ask for leave to sit again to-morrow. Leave was accordingly granted to sit again to-morrow.

Agreeably to the Order of the Day, the House resolved itself into a Committee, to go into the consideration of the Bill to make provision for the Poor. Mr. Speaker left the Chair. Mr. Burritt took the chair of the Committee.

Mr. Speaker resumed the Chair, and Mr. Burritt reported that the Committee had gone through the consideration of the said Bill, to which they had made several amendments, which he was directed to report to the House whenever it should be pleased to receive the same. The House then resolved that the Report be now received and accepted. Mr. Howard, seconded by Mr. James Wilson, moved that the Poor Bill be engrossed, and read for the third time to-morrow, which was ordered accordingly.

Mr. Mallory moved, seconded by Mr. Gough, that so much of the Order of the Day as gives him leave to bring in a Bill this Day, to regulate Tavern Licenses, be dispensed with for this day, and that he have leave to bring the same in on Thursday next. The same was dispensed with, and ordered accordingly.

Read for the second time, the Bill for granting a sum of money for repairing the Roads and Bridges. Mr. McLean then moved, seconded by Mr. James Wilson, that the House do now resolve itself into a Committee, to go into the consideration of the Bill for appropriating a sum of money for the purpose of repairing the

Roads and Bridges in this Province. The House accordingly resolved itself into a Committee, to go into the consideration of the said Bill. Mr. Speaker left the Chair. Mr. Howard was called to the chair of the Committee.

Mr. Speaker resumed the Chair, and Mr. Howard reported that the Committee had made a progress, and had directed him to ask for leave to sit again to-morrow. Leave was accordingly granted to sit again to-morrow.

Read for the first time, the Bill for discouraging the practice of keeping useless cur dogs. Mr. McNabb then moved, seconded by Mr. C. Wilson, that the Bill for discouraging the practice of keeping useless cur dogs, be read a second time to-morrow. Ordered accordingly.

Read for the third time, as engrossed, the Bill to alter the mode of paying wages to the Members of the House of Assembly. On motion of Mr. Mallory, seconded by Mr. Roblin, resolved, that the Bill do pass, and that the title be " An Act to alter the mode of paying wages to the Members of the House of Assembly." The Bill then passed, and was signed by the Speaker. Mr. Rogers moved, seconded by Mr. Dorland, that Messrs. Secord and McNabb do carry up to the Honorable, the Legislative Council, the Bill entitled "An Act to alter the mode of paying the wages of the Members of the House of Assembly," and request their concurrence in passing the same. Mr. Howard, seconded by Mr. Burritt, moved as an amendment to Mr. Rogers' motion, that the names " Secord and McNabb " in Mr. Rogers motion be expunged and the names " Mallory and John Wilson " be inserted, which was carried in the affirmative, and ordered accordingly. The main question accordingly passed in the negative.

Read for the second time, the amendments made by the Legislative Council, in and to the Grand River Bridge Bill. Mr. Willcocks then moved, seconded by Mr. Mallory, that the House do now resolve itself into a Committee, to go into the consideration of the amendments made by the Honorable the Legislative Council in and to the Act sent up from this House, entitled " An Act for granting an additional sum of money for erecting a bridge across the Grand River." On Mr. Speaker having put the question, a division thereupon took place. The names being called for were taken down, and are as follows:—

Yeas.	Nays.
MESSRS. McNABB	MESSRS. BURRITT
J. WILSON	MARCLE
MALLORY	GOUGH
WILLCOCKS	FRAZER
SOVEREIGN	BABY
JAS. WILSON.	HOWARD
	McLEAN
	C. WILSON
	McGREGOR
	SECORD
	DORLAND
	LEWIS
	ROGERS.

The same passed in the negative by a majority of eight. Mr. Willcocks, seconded by Mr. Mallory, moved for leave to bring in a Bill to-morrow, for the purpose of granting a sum of money, to erect a bridge across the Grand River. Leave was accordingly granted.

A Message from the Honorable the Legislative Council, by Mr. Baldwin, Master in Chancery.

Mr. Speaker,

I am commanded by the Honorable the Legislative Council to inform this House that they have passed an Act, entitled "An Act to declare the Common Goals in the several Districts of this Province to be Houses of Correction for certain purposes," to which they request the concurrence of this House in passing the same.

And also that they have passed an Act sent up from this House, entitled "An Act for the relief of Minors of the Society of Mennonists and Tunkers," to which they have made several amendments, to which amendments they request the concurrence of this House in passing the same.

And then he withdrew.

Read for the first time, the Act sent down from the Honorable the Legislative Council, entitled "An Act to declare the Common Gaols of this Province to be Houses of Correction for certain purposes. Mr. McLean then moved, seconded by Mr. Rogers, that the said Bill be read for the second time on Thursday next, which was ordered accordingly.

Then was read for the first time, the amendments made by the Honorable the Legislative Council, in and to an Act sent up from this House, entitled "An Act for the relief of Minors of the Societies of Mennonists and Tunkers." Mr. Gough then moved, seconded by Mr. McNabb, that the said amendments be read a second time on Wednesday next, which was ordered accordingly.

Messrs. Mallory and J. Wilson reported that, in obedience to the commands of this House, they had carried up to the Honorable the Legislative Council the Act entitled "An Act to alter the mode of paying the wages of the Members of the House of Assembly," to which they did request their concurrence in passing the same.

Read for the second time, a Bill for extending the jurisdiction of the Court of Requests. Mr. Willcocks then moved, seconded by Mr. Secord, that the House do now resolve itself into a Committee, to go into the consideration of the said Bill. The House accordingly resolved itself into a Committee. Mr. Speaker left the Chair. Mr. McLean was called to the chair of the Committee.

Mr. Speaker resumed the Chair, and Mr. McLean reported that the Committee had made a progress, and had directed him to ask for leave to sit again to-morrow. Leave was accordingly granted to sit again to-morrow.

Read for the first time, the Bill for preventing bribery and corruption at future elections in this Province. Mr. Howard then moved, seconded by Mr. James Wilson, that the said Bill be read a second time to-morrow. Ordered accordingly.

Mr. McGregor then moved, seconded by Mr. Marcle, that no new Bills be introduced into this House after Saturday next. Passed in the negative.

Mr. Burritt moved, seconded by Mr. Dorland, that so much of the Order of the Day, as has not been proceeded on, be dispensed with for this day, and that the same be the first on the Order of the Day for to-morrow, which was ordered accordingly.

Mr. Rogers gave notice, that he will to-morrow move, that it be a standing Rule of this House, that all business remaining on the Order of the Day and not proceeded on when the House adjourns, shall stand as a part of the Order of the next day.

Mr. Gough gave notice, that he will to-morrow move, that ten o'clock be the hour appointed on the respective days fixed on for taking into consideration the Petition complaining of the undue election of Messrs. James Wilson and John Roblin, and that the Speaker do give the Petitioners and the Sitting Members, or their respective agents, notice thereof in writing, accompanied with an order to attend this House at the time appointed, either in person, or by their counsel or agents.

On motion of Mr. McGregor, seconded by Mr. Burritt, the House adjourned.

Wednesday, 21st February, 1810.

Prayers were read.

Mr. Howard, seconded by Mr. Roblin, moved that the House do now resolve itself into a Committee, to go into the consideration of the Show Bill. The House accordingly resolved itself into a Committee, to go into the consideration of the said Bill. Mr. Speaker left the Chair. Mr. Jas Wilson was called to the chair of the Committee.

Mr. Speaker resumed the Chair, and Mr. Wilson reported that the Committee had made a progress, and had directed him to ask for leave to sit again to-morrow. Leave was accordingly granted to sit again to-morrow. Agreeably to the Order of the Day, the House resolved itself into a Committee to go into the consideration of the School Bill. Mr. Speaker left the Chair. Mr. Sovereign took the chair of the Committee.

Mr. Speaker resumed the Chair, and Mr. Sovereign reported that the Committee had gone through the consideration of the said Bill, to which they had made several amendments, which he was directed to report to the House whenever it should be pleased to receive the same. On Mr. Speaker having put the question for the Report being received a division thereupon took place. The names being called for they were taken down and are as follows:—

Yeas.	Nays.
MESSRS. McNABB	MESSRS. MARCLE
BURRITT	FRAZER
J. WILSON	BABY
HOWARD	C. WILSON
SOVEREIGN	LEWIS
ROGERS	McLEAN.
MALLORY	
WILLCOCKS	
J. WILSON	
DORLAND	
GOUGH	
ROBLIN	
SECORD	

Carried in the affirmative by a majority of seven. The Report was accordingly received and accepted. Mr. Gough then moved, seconded by Mr. Rogers, that the School Bill be engrossed, and read a third time to-morrow, which was ordered accordingly.

Read for the second time, the Bill for the preservation of Salmon. Mr. Gough then moved, seconded by Mr. Sovereign, that the House do now resolve itself into a Committee, to go into the consideration of the Salmon Bill. The House accordingly resolved itself into a Committee, to go into the consideration of the said Bill.

Mr. Speaker left the Chair. Mr. Dorland was called to the chair of the Committee. Mr. Speaker resumed the Chair, and Mr. Dorland reported that the Committee had gone through the consideration of the Bill, to which they had made several amendments, which amendments he was directed to report to the House whenever it shall be pleased to receive the same. Ordered, that the Report be now received and accepted. Mr. Gough, seconded by Mr. Mallory, then moved that the Salmon Bill be engrossed, and read a third time to-morrow. Ordered accordingly.

Read for the second time, the Bill for preventing the Forging and Counterfeiting of Foreign Bills of Exchange. Mr. Howard then moved, seconded by Mr. Secord, that the House do now resolve itself into a Committee, to go into the consideration of the said Bill. The House accordingly resolved itself into a Committee, to go into the consideration of the said Bill. Mr. Speaker left the Chair. Mr. Roblin was called to the chair of the Committee.

Mr. Speaker resumed the Chair, and Mr. Roblin reported that the Committee had made a progress, and had directed him to ask for leave to sit again to-morrow. Leave was accordingly granted to sit again to-morrow.

Read for the first time, the Bill to alter the construction of mill-dams. Mr. Gough then moved, seconded by Mr. Willcocks that the Mill-dam Bill be read a second time this day three months. The said Bill was accordingly ordered to be read again on this day three months.

Read for the first time, the Bill for the better regulation of the Fees taken in the Court of King's Bench in this Province. Mr. Willcocks, seconded by Mr. Sovereign, moved that the Bill for regulating the Fees to be taken in the Court of King's Bench be read a second time to-morrow. On Mr. Speaker having put the question, a division thereupon took place. The names being called for they were taken down, and are as follows:—

	Yeas.		Nays.
MESSRS.	GOUGH	MESSRS.	McNABB
	MARCLE		FRAZER
	BABY		McLEAN.
	ELLIOTT		
	J. WILSON		
	HOWARD		
	WILLCOCKS		
	ROGERS		
	C. WILSON		
	MALLORY		
	SECORD		
	ROBLIN		
	DORLAND		
	LEWIS		
	SOVEREIGN.		

Carried in the affirmative by a majority of twelve, and the said Bill was ordered to be read for the second time to-morrow.

Mr. Gough moved, seconded by Mr. Lewis, that ten o'clock in the morning be the hour appointed on the respective days fixed on for taking into consideration the petition of the Freeholders of the Counties of Lennox, Addington and Prince Edward, complaining of the undue election of Messrs. James Wilson and John Roblin, and that the Speaker do give the Petitioners and the Sitting Members, or their respective agents, notice thereof in writing; accompanied with an order to attend this House at the time appointed, either in person or by their Counsel or Agent. The House accordingly resolved the same.

Mr. Rogers, seconded by Mr. Gough, moved that it be a standing Rule of this House that all matters remaining on the Order of the Day unproceeded upon when the House adjourns shall stand as the first part of the Order of the next day. The House unanimously resolved the same.

On Motion of Captain Elliott, seconded by Mr. Gough, the House adjourned.

Thursday, 22nd February, 1810.

Prayers were read.

A message from the Honorable the Legislative Council, by Mr. Baldwin, Master in Chancery.

Mr. Speaker,

I am commanded by the Honorable the Legislative Council to inform this House that they have passed an Act sent up from this House entitled "An Act to extend the benefits of an Act passed in the thirty-seventh year of His Majesty's Reign, entitled 'An Act for the more easy Barring of Dower,'" to which they have made several amendments, to which amendments they request the concurrence of the House in passing the same. And then he withdrew.

Read the first time, the amendments made by the Honorable the Legislative Council in and to the Act sent up from this House, entitled "An Act to extend the benefits of an Act passed in the thirty-seventh year of His Majesty's Reign, entitled 'An Act for the more easy Barring of Dower.'" Mr. Rogers then moved, seconded by Mr. McNabb, that the amendments to the Dower Bill be read a second time to-morrow, which was ordered accordingly.

Captain Frazer and Mr. McGregor, the Messengers ordered to wait upon His Excellency, the Lieutenant-Governor, to know when His Excellency would be pleased to receive the Address of this House, reported that they had waited upon His Excellency, and that he was pleased to appoint this day at the hour of twelve o'clock at noon.

The Messengers being returned, reported that they had waited upon His Excellency, the Lieutenant-Governor, and did present to His Excellency the Address which passed this House on the nineteenth instant, respecting the expenditure of moneys on the Public Highways and Roads in this Province; to which His Excellency was pleased to make the following answer.

Gentlemen of the House of Assembly,

I shall direct the Commissioners of the Public Highways to furnish accounts of the disbursements of the several sums of money which have been appropriated by the Legislature for Public Roads, and intrusted to them for expenditure, in order that they may be laid before you.

22nd February, 1810.

Mr. Rogers, seconded by Mr. Willcocks, moved that so much of the Rules of this House as require one day's previous notice to be given be dispensed with so far as to allow him to make a motion for an Address to His Excellency, the Lieutenant-Governor, to request His Excellency to direct the Judges of His Majesty's Court of King's Bench in this Province, to lay before this House an account of all such fees as have been allowed to them in consequence of the power vested in them by an Act of the Parliament of this Province, passed in the Forty-fourth year of His Majesty's Reign. The said Rule was accordingly dispensed with on this occasion.

Mr. Rogers then moved, seconded by Mr. Willcocks, that an Address be presented to His Excellency, the Lieutenant-Governor, to request that His Excellency will be pleased to direct the Judges of His Majesty's Court of King's Bench in this Province to lay before this House a list of all such fees as have been by them allowed, in consequence of the power in them vested by an Act passed in the forty-fourth year of His Majesty's Reign. Which was ordered accordingly.

Mr. Rogers again moved, seconded by Mr. Willcocks, that Messrs. Gough and Burritt be a committee to draft an Address to His Excellency, the Lieutenant-Governor, agreeably to the resolution of the House this day; and that they do report the same with all convenient speed. The same was ordered accordingly.

Mr. Gough, from the Committee appointed to draft an Address to His Excellency, the Lieutenant-Governor, reported that they had drafted an Address to His Excellency, which he was directed by the Committee to report to the House whenever it shall be pleased to receive the same. Ordered that the report be now received. The report was accordingly received.

He then read the draft of the Address in his place, and afterwards delivered the same in at the Table, where it was read again by the Clerk, and is as follows:—

To His Excellency Francis Gore, Esquire, Lieutenant-Governor of the Province of Upper Canada, &c., &c., &c.

May it please Your Excellency,

We, His Majesty's most dutiful and loyal subjects, the Commons of Upper Canada, in Parliament assembled, conceiving it necessary in order to enable us to discharge our duty in Parliament that we should be made acquainted with the fees taken in His Majesty's Court of King's Bench, do most respectfully request that Your Excellency will be pleased to direct the Judges of His Majesty's Court of King's Bench in this Province to lay before this House an account of all such fees as by them have been allowed in consequence of the power vested in them by an Act passed in the forty-fourth year of His Majesty's Reign.

Mr. Rogers then moved, seconded by Mr. Willcocks, that the Draft of an Address to His Excellency, the Lieutenant-Governor, be engrossed, and that Messengers be appointed to wait upon His Excellency to know when he will be pleased to receive the Address of this House; and to present the same at such time as His Excellency shall be pleased to appoint, which was ordered accordingly. The said Address as engrossed was read, passed, and signed by the Speaker.

Mr. Rogers moved, seconded by Mr. Willcocks, that Messrs. Baby and McNabb do wait upon His Excellency the Lieutenant-Governor, to know when he will be pleased to receive the Address of this House, and that those gentlemen do present the same at such time as His Excellency shall be pleased to appoint. Ordered accordingly.

Mr. Rogers then moved, seconded by Mr. Roblin, that the Order of the Day on the Grand River Bill be now proceeded upon. The said Bill was accordingly read for the first time. Mr. Willcocks moved, seconded by Mr. Mallory, that so much of the rules of this House as requires one day's previous notice be now dispensed with, so far as relates to a Bill for granting an additional sum of money for the purpose of erecting a bridge across the Grand River. The said Rule was accordingly dispensed with. Mr. Willcocks again moved, seconded by Mr. Sovereign, that the Bill for granting an additional sum of money for the purpose of erecting a bridge across the Grand River be now read a second time. The said Bill was accordingly read for the second time. On motion of Mr. Willcocks, seconded by Mr. Sovereign, the House resolved itself into a Committee, to go into the consideration of the said Bill. Mr. Speaker left the Chair. Mr. McNabb was called to the chair of the Committee.

Mr. Speaker resumed the Chair, and Mr. McNabb reported that the Committee had gone through the consideration of the said Bill, without any amendment, which he was directed to report to the House whenever it should be pleased to receive the same. Ordered, that the report be now received. The Report was accordingly received and accepted. Mr. Willcocks moved, seconded by Mr. Sovereign, that the Bill for granting an additional sum of money, for building a bridge across the Grand River, be engrossed, and read a third time to-morrow. Ordered accordingly.

Mr. McLean moved, seconded by Mr. Howard, that so much of the Order of the Day be discharged as gives leave to bring in a Bill for the relief of the different Districts of this Province, from such charges as may arise from bastard children born within this Province. The said Order was accordingly discharged.

Mr. Willcocks moved, seconded by Mr. Roblin, that the House do now resolve itself into a Committee, to go into consideration of the Bill for imposing a tax upon Billiard Tables. The House accordingly resolved itself into a Committee. Mr. Speaker left the Chair. Mr. Rogers was called to the chair of the Committee.

Mr. Speaker resumed the Chair, and Mr. Rogers reported that the Committee had made a progress, and had directed him to ask for leave to sit again to-morrow. Leave was accordingly granted to sit again to-morrow.

Agreeably to the Order of the Day, the House resolved itself into a Committee, to go into the consideration of the Bill for the creation of a new District. Mr. Speaker left the Chair. Mr. Burritt was called to the chair of the Committee.

Mr. Speaker resumed the Chair, and Mr. Burritt reported that the Committee had made a progress, and had directed him to ask for leave to sit again to-morrow. Leave was accordingly granted to sit again to-morrow.

Read for the third time, as engrossed, the Bill to make provision for the poor in this Province. On motion of Mr. Howard, seconded by Mr. McGregor, resolved that the Bill do pass, and that the title be " An Act to make provision for the poor throughout this Province." The Bill then passed and was signed by the Speaker. Mr. Mallory moved, seconded by Mr. Dorland, that Messrs. Howard and Lewis do carry up to the Honorable the Legislative Council the Act entitled " An Act to make provision for the poor throughout this Province," and request their concurrence thereto. The House accordingly resolved the same.

Mr. Mallory moved, seconded by Mr. Willcocks, that the petition of Augustus Jones, Deputy Surveyor, be now read. The Petition of Augustus Jones, Deputy Surveyor, was accordingly read, and is as follows:—

To the Honorable the Commons House of Assembly of the Province of Upper Canada, in Parliament assembled.

The Petition of Augustus Jones, Deputy Surveyor, Humbly Sheweth,

That Your Petitioner was employed as Assistant Surveyor at Niagara in the year 1789, by the then Deputy Surveyor of the District, Philip Frey, Esq., by the desire of the Commanding Officer and the concurrence of the then established Law Board, and has been continued in the Surveyor General's Department ever since; that during the periods of June, 1787, and February, 1789, Your Petitioner, with his party, surveyed the greatest part of fifteen Townships, containing 2,537 lots of 100 acres each, amounting in all to Five Hundred and Twenty-Six Pounds, Fifteen Shillings, and Two-Pence, Provincial Currency, no part of which has been paid Petitioner, owing to the irregularity of Mr. Frey's Accounts, he having about that time obtained leave of absence to visit his father in the State of New York, from whence he never returned.

That your Petitioner nevertheless continued the survey in the absence of Mr. Frey, until after the division of the Province of Quebec, and a Surveyor General for this Province was appointed, and your Petitioner's accounts were regularly paid. After such division of the Province of Quebec Your Petitioner made out an attested copy of his accounts of surveying the fifteen Townships, and laid them before the Law Board, who gave him the necessary certificates and recommendations, which were sent to the Surveyor General at Quebec, through the Surveyor General of this Province, and which, together with the documents, are now in that Office.

Your Petitioner begs leave to state that the irregularity of Mr. Frey's accounts, his absence from the Province, and the unexpected division thereof, has so operated against Your Petitioner that he has, without any fault on his part, been deprived both of his own wages, as well as the expenses incurred in performing the aforesaid surveys.

Your Petitioner therefore humbly prays that Your Honorable Body will be pleased to consider his case, and grant him such relief as the nature thereof may require. Should any documents be required by Your Honorable House Your Petitioner is ready to produce such as are in existence, and which he presumes will be satisfactory.

And your Petitioner, as in duty bound, will ever pray.

(Signed)   AUGUSTUS JONES, Deputy Surveyor.
York, 19th February, 1810.

Mr. McNabb moved, seconded by Capt. Frazer, for leave to bring in a Bill on Saturday next to alter the construction of mill-dams throughout this Province on navigable streams, where rafts of timber and crafts might otherwise pass down in safety. Accordingly leave was granted.

On motion of Mr. Mallory, seconded by Mr. Willcocks, the House adjourned.

Friday, 23d, February, 1810.

Prayers were read.

Messrs. McNabb and Baby, the messengers ordered to wait upon His Excellency the Lieutenant Governor with the Address of this House, reported that they had waited upon His Excellency the Lieutenant-Governor, and did present His Excellency the said Address, to which His Excellency was pleased to make the following answer:—

Gentlemen of the House of Assembly,—

I shall direct an Account of the Fees allowed by the Court of King's Bench, under the authority of an Act passed in the forty-fourth year of His Majesty's Reign, to be laid before you.

23d February, 1810.

Capt. Frazer moved, seconded by Mr. Willcocks, for leave to bring in the Petition of John Brikie, Esquire. Leave was accordingly granted to bring up the said Petition.

Mr. Rogers, seconded by Mr. Gough, moved that the Order of the Day for the third reading of the Bill for applying a certain sum of money to make good moneys issued and advanced by His Majesty, through the Lieutenant-Governor, in pursuance of Addresses of this House, be discharged, and that the said Bill be recommitted to-morrow, which was ordered accordingly.

Mr. Willcocks moved, seconded by Mr. Gough, that so much of the Order of the Day, as directs the third reading of the Bill for limiting the duration of the

Act establishing schools, be discharged, and that the said Bill be now re-committed. The said Order was discharged accordingly, and the House resolved itself into a Committee, to go into the further consideration of the said Bill. Mr. Speaker left the Chair. Mr. Gough was called to the chair of the Committee.

Mr. Speaker resumed the Chair, and Mr. Gough reported that the Committee' had gone through the consideration of the said Bill, to which they had made several amendments, which amendments he was directed to report to the House whenever the House shall be pleased to receive the same. Ordered, that the Report be now received and accepted. Mr. Willcocks moved, seconded by Mr. Jas. Wilson, that the School Bill be engrossed, and read a third time to-morrow. Ordered accordingly.

Read for the third time, as engrossed, the Bill for granting money for erecting a bridge across the Grand River. On motion of Mr. Willcocks, seconded by Mr. Sovereign, resolved, that the Bill do pass, and that the title be " An Act granting an additional sum of money for erecting a bridge across the Grand River. The Bill then passed, and was signed by the Speaker. Mr. Mallory moved, seconded by Mr. Sovereign, that Messrs. Dorland and Roblin do carry up to the Honorable the Legislative Council the Act for granting an additional sum of money for the purpose of erecting a bridge across the Grand River, and request their concurrence thereto, which was ordered accordingly.

Mr. Howard gave notice that he will to-morrow move, that the House do resolve itself into a Committee, to take into consideration the Bill for the discouragement of Public Plays and Puppet Shows in this Province.

Mr. Gough moved, seconded by Mr. Lewis, that the Order of the Day for the third reading of the Bill for the preservation of Salmon, be discharged, and that the House do now resolve itself into a Committee to take the said Bill into consideration. The said Order was accordingly discharged, and the House resolved itself into a Committee, to go into the consideration of the said Bill. Mr. Speaker left the Chair. Mr. Jas. Wilson was called to the chair of the Committee.

Mr. Speaker resumed the Chair, and Mr. Wilson reported that the Committee had gone through the consideration of the said Bill, to which they had made several amendments, which he was directed to report to the House whenever it shall be pleased to receive the same. Ordered, that the Report be now received. The Report was accordingly received and accepted. Mr. Gough then read, seconded by Mr. Dorland, that the Salmon Bill be engrossed, and read a third time to-morrow. Ordered accordingly.

Mr. Howard, one of the messengers named to carry up to the Honorable the Legislative Council, the Act entitled " An Act to make provision for the poor throughout this Province," reported that they had carried up the said Act, and did request their concurrence thereto.

Agreeably to the Order of the Day, the House resolved itself into a Committee, to go into the consideration of the Bill for appropriating money for the purpose of repairing the highways and roads throughout this Province. Mr. Speaker left the Chair. Mr. Howard was called to the chair of the Committee.

Mr. Speaker resumed the Chair, and Mr. Howard reported that the Committee had made a progress, and had directed him to ask for leave to sit again to-morrow. Leave was accordingly granted to sit again to-morrow.

Mr. Rogers, seconded by Mr. Dorland, moved that the Order of the Day, respecting the Dower Bill, be now proceeded on. Accordingly was read for the second time the amendments made by the Honorable the Legislative Council, in and to
23 A.

the Dower Bill. Mr. Rogers then moved, seconded by Mr. Roblin, that the House do now resolve itself into a Committee, to go into the consideration of the said amendments. The House accordingly resolved itself into a Committee. Mr. Speaker left the Chair. Mr. Lewis was called to the chair of the Committee.

Mr. Speaker resumed the Chair, and Mr. Lewis reported that the Committee had gone through the consideration of the said amendments, which he was directed to report to the House whenever it shall be pleased to receive the same. Ordered that the Report be now received. The Report was accordingly received and accepted. Mr. Howard moved, seconded by Mr. Dorland, that the amendments made by the Honorable the Legislative Council, in and to the Dower Bill, be read a third time to-morrow. Which was ordered accordingly.

Read for the second time, the Bill sent down from the Legislative Council for making Gaols Houses of Correction for certain purposes. Mr. Rogers then moved, seconded by Mr. Howard, that the House do now resolve itself into a Committee, to go into the consideration of the Bill for making Gaols Houses of Correction for certain purposes. The House accordingly resolved itself into a Committee, to go into the consideration of the said Bill. Mr. Speaker left the Chair. Mr. Willcocks was called to the chair of the Committee.

Mr. Speaker resumed the Chair, and Mr. Willcocks reported that the Committee had gone through the consideration of the said Bill without any amendments, which he was directed to report whenever the House shall be pleased to receive the same. Ordered that the Report be now received. Mr. Howard then moved, seconded by Mr. Roblin, that the Bill sent down from the Legislative Council for making the Common Gaols Houses of Correction, be read a third time to-morrow, which was ordered accordingly.

Mr. Mallory gave notice, that he will to-morrow move that this House do then resolve itself into a Committee to go into the consideration of the Petition of Augustus Jones.

Mr. Gough gave notice, that it appears to this House that there is not a sufficient number of the statutes of this Province for the use and necessary accommodation of the House and the Members thereof, and that —— copies thereof ought to be printed. And that an Address be presented to His Excellency, the Lieutenant-Governor, requesting him to order the same to be done, and to issue his warrant to the Receiver General to pay the expense thereof, not exceeding the sum of —— Pounds, and that this House will make good the same.

On motion of Mr. C. Wilson, seconded by Mr. Lewis, the House adjourned.

Saturday, 24th February, 1810.

Prayers were read.

Read for the third time, as engrossed, the Bill for limiting the duration of the Act establishing Public Schools in this Province. On motion of Mr. Willcocks, seconded by Mr. Sovereign, resolved, that the Bill do pass, and that the title be " An Act to repeal certain parts of an Act passed in the forty-eighth year of His Majesty's Reign, entitled ' An Act to amend an Act passed in the forty-seventh year of His Majesty's Reign' entitled ' An Act to establish Public Schools in each and every District of this Province.'" The Bill accordingly passed, and was signed by the Speaker. Mr. Mallory, seconded by Mr. Secord, moved that Messrs. Dorland and Howard do carry up to the Honorable the Legislative Council the Act entitled " An Act to repeal certain parts of an Act passed in the forty-eighth year of His Majesty's Reign, entitled ' An Act to amend an Act passed in the forty-seventh year of His Majesty's Reign, entitled 'An Act to establish Public Schools in each and every District of this Province,'" and request their concurrence thereto. Ordered accordingly.

Read for the third time, as engrossed, the Bill for the preservation of Salmon. On motion of Mr. Gough, seconded by Mr. Secord. Resolved, That the Bill do pass, and that the title be "An Act to extend the provisions of an Act passed in the forty-seventh year of His Majesty's Reign, entitled 'An Act for the preservation of Salmon.'" The Bill then passed, and was signed by the Speaker. Mr. Rogers moved, seconded by Capt. Elliott, that Messrs. Gough and John Wilson do carry up to the Honorable the Legislative Council the Act entitled "An Act to extend the provisions of an Act passed in the forty-seventh year of His Majesty's Reign, entitled 'An Act for the preservation of Salmon,'" and request their concurrence thereto, which was ordered accordingly.

Read for the third time, the Dower Bill, as amended by the Legislative Council, which amendments were adopted by the House. Mr. Rogers then moved, seconded by Capt. Elliott, that Messrs. Howard and Dorland do inform the Legislative Council that this House has concurred in adopting the amendments made by them, in and to the Act entitled "An Act further to extend the benefits of an Act passed in the thirty-seventh year of His Majesty's Reign, entitled 'An Act for the more easy Barring of Dower.'" The same was ordered accordingly; and the message is as follows:—

Mr. Speaker,—

We are commanded by the Commons House of Assembly to acquaint this Honorable House that they have concurred in adopting the amendments made by the Legislative Council, in and to the Acts entitled "An Act further to extend the benefits of an Act passed in the thirty-seventh year of His Majesty's Reign, entitled 'An Act for the more easy Barring of Dower.'"

Commons House of Assembly,
24th February, 1810.

(Signed) SAML. STREET, *Speaker.*

Read for the third time, the Bill sent down from the Honorable Legislative Council, entitled "An Act to render the Gaols in the several Districts of this Province Houses of Correction for certain purposes," to which Act the House concurred. Mr. Rogers, seconded by Mr. Howard, moved that Messrs. McLean and Fraser do inform the Honorable the Legislative Council that this House has concurred in adopting the Act sent down from the Legislative Council entitled "An Act to render the Gaols in the several Districts of this Province Houses of Correction for certain purposes." Ordered accordingly; and the message is as follows:—

Mr. Speaker,—

We are commanded by the Commons House of Assembly to acquaint this Honorable House that they have concurred in and to the Act entitled "An Act to render the Gaols in the several Districts of this Province Houses of Correction for certain purposes."

(Signed) SAML. STREET, *Speaker.*

Commons House of Assembly,
24th February, 1810.

Mr. McNabb moved, seconded by Mr. Burritt, that so much of the Order of the Day as relates to the Bill for discouraging the practice of keeping useless dogs and curs, be discharged. The said Order was accordingly discharged.

Read for the second time, the amendments made by the Legislative Council, in and to the Act for the relief of minors of the Society of Mennonists and Tunkers. Mr. Gough then moved, seconded by Mr. Secord, that the House do now resolve itself into a Committee to go into the consideration of the amendments made by the Honorable the Legislative Council, in and to the Act for the relief of minors of the Societies of Mennonists and Tunkers. The House accordingly resolved itself into a Committee, to go into the consideration of the said amendments. Mr. Speaker left the Chair. Mr. Secord was called to the chair of the Committee.

Mr. Speaker resumed the Chair, and Mr. Secord reported that the Committee had gone through the consideration of the said amendments, which amendments he was directed by the Committee to recommend that the House doth concur thereto. The House accordingly concurred in adopting the said amendments. Mr. Gough again moved, seconded by Mr. Secord, that the amendments made by the Legislative Council, in and to the Bill for the relief of minors of the Societies of Mennonists and Tunkers be read a third time on Wednesday next, which was ordered accordingly.

Mr. Gough, one of the messengers ordered to carry up to the Honorable the Legislative Council the Act entitled " An Act to extend the provisions of an Act passed in the forty-seventh year of His Majesty's Reign, entitled ' An Act for the preservation of Salmon,' " reported that they had carried up the said Bill to the Legislative Council, and did request their concurrence in passing the same.

Messrs. Howard and Dorland, the Members ordered to carry up to the Honorable the Legislative Council the Message of this House, that this House has concurred in adopting the amendments made by the Legislative Council, in and to the Act for the more easy Barring of Dower, reported that they had carried up the same,

And also that they had, in obedience to the command of this House, carried up to the Legislative Council, the Act entitled " An Act to repeal certain parts of an Act passed in the forty-eighth year of His Majesty's Reign, entitled ' An Act to amend an Act passed in the forty-seventh year of His Majesty's Reign, entitled ' An Act to establish Public Schools in each and every District of this Province,' " to which they did request their concurrence in passing the same.

Agreeably to the Order of the Day, the House resolved itself into a Committee, to go into consideration of the Court of Requests Bill. Mr. Speaker left the Chair. Mr. McLean was called to the chair of the Committee.

Mr. Speaker resumed the Chair, and Mr. McLean reported that the Committee had made a progress, and had directed him to ask for leave to sit again this day. Leave was accordingly granted to sit again this day.

A message from the Honorable the Legislative Council, by Mr. Baldwin, Master in Chancery.

Mr. Speaker,—

I am commended by the Legislative Council to acquaint this House that they have passed an Act entitled " An Act to provide for obtaining the benefits of the process of outlawry in Civil Actions within this Province," to which they request the concurrence of this House in passing the same.

And then he withdrew.

The said Bill was then read for the first time.

Mr. Rogers moved, seconded by Mr. Gough, that the Bill to provide for the process of outlawry be read a second time on Monday next, which was ordered accordingly.

Agreeably to leave given, the House again resolved itself into a Committee, to go into the further consideration of the Court of Requests Bill. Mr. Speaker left the Chair. Mr. McLean again took the chair of the Committee.

Mr. Speaker resumed the Chair, and Mr. McLean reported that the Committee had made a progress, and had directed him to ask for leave to sit again on Monday next. Leave was accordingly granted to sit again on Monday next.

Read for the second time, the Bill to prevent Bribery and Corruption at Elections for the Commons of this Province. Mr. Howard then moved, seconded by Mr. Gough, that the House do now resolve itself into a Committee to go into the consideration of the said Bill. The House accordingly resolved itself into a Committee. Mr. Speaker left the Chair. Mr. C. Wilson was called to the chair of the Committee.

Mr. Speaker resumed the Chair, and Mr. C. Wilson reported that the Committee had made a progress and had directed him to ask for leave to sit again on Tuesday next. Leave was accordingly granted to sit again on Tuesday next.

Mr. Mallory moved, seconded by Mr. Willcocks, that the House do now resolve itself into a Committee, to go into the consideration of the petition of Augustus Jones. The House accordingly resolved itself into a Committee to go into the consideration of the said Petition. Mr. Speaker left the Chair. Mr. Mallory was called to the Chair of the Committee.

Mr. Speaker resumed the Chair, and Mr. Mallory reported that the Committee had made a progress, and had directed him to ask for leave to sit again. Ordered, that the Committee have leave to sit again.

Read for the first time, the Bill for altering the construction of Mill-dams on navigable streams throughout this Province.

Mr. McNabb then moved, seconded by Captain Frazer, that the Bill for altering the construction of Mill-dams be read a second time on Tuesday next. Ordered, that the said Bill be read a second time on Tuesday next.

Mr. Gough, seconded by Mr. Dorland, moved for leave to bring in a Bill on Monday next for printing the Statutes of this Province, which passed in the negative.

Mr. Mallory moved, seconded by Mr. Howard, for leave to bring in a Bill on Monday next to repeal part of the Act passed in the thirty-fourth year of His Majesty's Reign, and also part of an Act passed in the thirty-seventh year of His Majesty's Reign, respecting Sheriffs in this Province; and to make further provision for the same. Leave was accordingly granted.

Mr. McLean, seconded by Mr. James Wilson, moved for leave to bring up the Petition of William Jarvis, Esquire. Leave was accordingly granted.

On motion of Mr. McNabb, seconded by Mr. Willcocks, the House adjourned until Monday next.

Monday, 26th February, 1810.

Prayers were read.

Read for the third time, the Amendments made by the Honorable the Legislative Council, in and to the Act for the relief of Minors of the Societies of Mennonists and Tunkers. Mr. Gough then moved, seconded by Mr. Secord, that the amendments made by the Honorable the Legislative Council in and to the Act entitled " An Act for the relief of Minors of the Societies of Mennonists and Tunkers," be now adopted by the House. The said amendments were accordingly adopted by the House. Mr. Rogers, seconded by Mr. McNabb, moved that Messrs. Gough and Secord do acquaint the Legislative Council that this House has concurred in adopting the amendments made by them in and to the Act entitled " An Act for the relief of Minors of the Societies of Mennonists and Tunkers." The same was ordered accordingly; and the Mesage is as follows :—

Mr. Speaker,

We are commanded by the Commons House of Assembly to acquaint this Honorable House that they have concurred in adopting the amendments made by the Legislative Council in and to the Act entitled "An Act for the relief of Minors of the Societies of Mennonists and Tunkers."
Commons House of Assembly,
26th February, 1810.   (Signed)   SAM'L STREET, Speaker.

On motion of Mr. Gough, seconded by Captain Elliott, the House resolved itself into a Committee, to go into the consideration of the Bill for appropriating money to make good moneys issued and advanced by His Majesty through the Lieutenant-Governor, in pursuance of two Addresses of this House. Mr. Speaker left the Chair. Mr. Rogers was called to the chair of the Committee.
Mr. Speaker resumed the Chair, and Mr. Rogers reported that the Committee had made several amendments, which amendments he was directed to report to the House whenever it shall be pleased to receive the same. Ordered, that the Report be now received. The Report was accordingly received and accepted. Mr. Gough then moved, seconded by Mr. Marcle, that the Appropriation Bill as amended be engrossed, and read a third time to-morrow, which was ordered accordingly.
Agreeably to the Order of the Day, the House went into the consideration of the Petition of the Inhabitants, Freeholders of the Incorporated Counties of Lennox and Addington, and the County of Prince Edward (except the Town of Ameliasburgh), complaining that James Wilson, Esquire, the sitting Member representing the County of Prince Edward (except Ameliasburgh) was not duly and lawfully elected and chosen.
In conformity to an Act passed in the First Session of the Fourth Provincial Parliament, entitled "An Act to regulate the Trial of Controverted Elections," the Speaker and the Members present were sworn by the Clerk at the Table.
Members present:—The Speaker, Thomas B. Gough, James McNabb, Thomas Frazer, Henry Marcle, Stephen Burritt, Matthew Elliott, J. B. Baby, Peter Howard, Allan McLean, John Wilson, John McGregor, Crowell Wilson, Joseph Willcocks, Benajah Mallory, John Roblin, Philip Sovereign, Thomas Dorland, Levi Lewis, David Secord, D. McG. Rogers.   e
The Clerk then read at the Table the Petition of the Inhabitants, Freeholders of the United Counties of Lennox and Addington, and the County of Prince Edward (except Ameliasburgh).
The Solicitor-General came to the Bar as Counsel for James Wilson, Esquire, the sitting Member. A place was allotted for him by the House within the Bar, but not to be a precedent hereafter.
John McDonell, Esquire, Barrister-at-Law, of Counsel for the Petitioners of the Counties of Lennox, Addington and Prince Edward, complaining that James Wilson, Esquire, the sitting Member, was not duly and lawfully elected and chosen, came to the Bar. A place was allotted for him by the House within the Bar, but not to be a precedent in the future.
John Lowe, one of the witnesses in support of the Petition of the Inhabitant Freeholders of the County of Prince Edward (except Ameliasburgh) was sworn at the Bar.
John McDonell, Esquire, Counsel for the Petitioners, by permission of the House began to examine witnesses on the part of the said Petitioners.
The Solicitor-General did also obtain the permission of the House to cross-

examine such witnesses as were brought forward in support of the Petition of the Freeholders of the County of Prince Edward (except Ameliasburgh).

A Message from the Honorable the Legislative Council by Mr. Baldwin, Master in Chancery.

Mr. Speaker,

I am commanded by the Honorable the Legislative Council to inform this House that they have passed an Act, sent up from this House, entitled "An Act to provide for the laying out, amending and keeping in repair the public highways and roads in this Province, and to repeal the law now in force for that purpose," to which they have made several amendments, to which amendments they request the concurrence of this House.

And then he withdrew.

The House again went into the consideration of the Controverted Election. Tobias Ryckman, a witness in support of the Petition, was sworn at the Bar. The evidence of Tobias Ryckman, the witness for the petitioners, having been gone through, the Clerk of the Crown appeared at the Bar, and delivered in a written paper, signed by himself, which was read by the Clerk at the Table, and is as follows :—

The Clerk of the Crown and of the Common Pleas, in pursuance of directions to him given, begs leave respectfully to state to the House of Assembly that no Rule or Order has been pronounced by the Court of King's Bench to ascertain, determine, declare and adjudge what fees shall or may be taken, or be allowed to be taken, by any Clerk of the Crown, Counsel, Attorney, Sheriff, Officer or other person, in consequence of the power vested in the said Court by an Act passed in the forty-fourth year of His present Majesty's Reign; excepting the Rule of Easter Term, 46 Geo. III., whereby it is ordered that in future the quantum of costs on all proceedings in this Court be governed by the Rule of Allowance in Westminster Hall; and that the practice of this Court do conform in all possible respects to that laid down in Tidd and Sellon.

(Signed)   JOHN SMALL,

Clerk of the Crown, etc.

Peter Valleau, on evidence also for the Petitioners, was sworn at the Bar, as was also in his place, John Roblin, Esquire, a Member of this House, in support of the Petition.

Mr. McLean then moved, seconded by Mr. John Wilson, that the further consideration of the contested Election be postponed until ten o'clock to-morrow morning, which was ordered accordingly.

Agreeably to the Order of the Day was read for the second time the Bill for the more accurate adjustment of the Survey and admeasurement of Lands in this Province.

Mr. Gough then moved, seconded by Mr. Burritt, that the House do on Wednesday next resolve itself into a Committee to take into consideration the Bill for the more accurate admeasurement of Lands in this Province, and for the better ascertaining the boundaries thereof. The same was ordered accordingly.

Then was read for the first time the amendments made by the Legislative Council in and to the Act for keeping in repair the Highways and Roads.   Mr. Howard then moved, seconded by Mr. Dorland, that his amendments made by the Legislative Council in and to the Road Bill be read a second time to-morrow, which was ordered accordingly.

On motion of Mr. Lewis, seconded by Mr. C. Wilson, the House adjourned.

Tuesday, 27th February, 1810.

Prayers were read.

Agreeably to the Order of the Day was read for the third time, as engrossed, the Bill for appropriating a sum of money to make good moneys advanced by the Lieutenant-Governor in pursuance of several Addresses of this House. On motion of Mr. Gough, seconded by Captain Elliott, resolved, that the Bill do pass, and that the title be "An Act for applying a certain sum of money therein mentioned to make good certain moneys issued and advanced by His Majesty through the Lieutenant-Governor, in pursuance of several Addresses of this House." The Bill then passed, and was signed by the Speaker. Mr. Howard moved, seconded by Mr. Baby, that Messrs. Gough and Dorland do carry up to the Legislative Council the act entitled "An Act for applying a certain sum of money therein mentioned to make good certain moneys issued and advanced by His Majesty through the Lieutenant-Governor, in pursuance of several Addresses of this House," and request their concurrence in passing the same, which was ordered accordingly.

On motion of Mr. Howard, seconded by Mr. James Wilson, the House resolved itself into a Committee, to go into the consideration of the Bill for the discouragement of Public Plays and Shows in this Province. Mr. Speaker left the Chair. Mr. James Wilson was called to the Chair of the Committee.

Mr. Speaker resumed the Chair, and Mr. Wilson reported that the Committee had made a progress, and had directed him to ask for leave to sit again to-morrow.

Leave was accordingly granted to sit again to-morrow.

Agreeably to the Order of the Day, the House went into the further consideration of the Controverted Election of James Wilson, Esquire.

John Lowe, was called to the Bar, and re-examined by the Council for the Petitioners; as was also Peter Valleau.

Mr. Gough then moved, seconded by Mr. Secord, that the further consideration of the Petition of the Freeholders of the County of Prince Edward be adjourned until to-morrow, and that the Petitioners do pay to the sitting Member, James Wilson, Esquire, such additional expense as he may incur by such indulgence to them, which was ordered accordingly.

Agreeably to the Order of the Day, the House resolved itself into a Committee to go into the consideration of the Bill to prevent Forgery in this Province. Mr. Speaker left the Chair. Mr. Roblin was called to the Chair of the Committee.

Mr. Speaker resumed the Chair, and Mr. Roblin reported that the Committee had made a progress, and had directed him to ask for leave to sit again to-morrow. Leave was granted accordingly.

Read for the second time, the Bill to regulate the Fees to be taken in the Court of King's Bench. Mr. Willcocks then moved, seconded by Mr. Rogers, that the Bill for regulating the Fees to be taken in the Court of King's Bench be referred to a Committee of the whole House, which was ordered accordingly.

Agreeably to the Order of the Day, the House resolved itself into a Committee to go into the consideration of the Bill for laying a Duty upon Billiard Tables. Mr. Speaker left the Chair. Mr. Rogers was called to the Chair of the Committee.

Mr. Speaker resumed the Chair, and Mr. Rogers reported that the Committee had gone through the consideration of the said Bill, to which they had made several amendments, which amendments he was directed to report to the House whenever it shall be pleased to receive the same. Ordered, that the Report be now received. Mr. Willcocks then moved, seconded by Mr. Roblin, that the Bill for imposing a Tax upon Billiard Tables be engrossed, and read a third time to-morrow, which was ordered accordingly.

Agreeably to the Order of the Day the House resolved itself into a Committee, to go into the consideration of the Bill for creating a new District. Mr. Speaker left the Chair. Mr. Burritt was called to the Chair of the Committee.

Mr. Speaker resumed the Chair, and Mr .Burritt reported that the Committee had made a progress, and had directed him to ask for leave to sit again this day. Leave was accordingly granted to sit again this day.

A Message from the Honorable the Legislative Council by Mr. Baldwin, Master in Chancery.

Mr. Speaker,

I am commanded by the Honorable the Legislative Council to inform this House that they have passed an Act, sent up from this House, entitled " An Act granting an additional sum of money for erecting a Bridge across the Grand River," without any amendment.

And then he withdrew. -

Mr. Gough, one of the Messengers named to carry up to the Honorable the Legislative Council the Act entitled " An Act applying a certain sum of money therein mentioned to make good moneys issued and advanced by His Majesty through the Lieutenant--Governor in pursuance of several Addresses of this House," reported that they had carried up the said Bill, and request their concurrence in passing the same.

Mr. Gough, one of the Messengers named to carry up the Message of this House to the Honorable the Legislative Council, that this House had concurred in the amendments made by the Legislative Council in and to the Act entitled " An Act for the relief of minors of the Societies of Mennonists and Tunkers," reported that they had carried up the same.

Agreeably to leave given, the House again resolved itself into a Committee to go into the consideration of the Bill for the creation of a New District. Mr. Speaker left the Chair. Mr. Burritt again took the Chair of the Committee.

Mr. Speaker resumed the Chair, and Mr. Burritt reported that the Committee had gone through the consideration of the said Bill, to which they had made several amendments, which he was directed to report to the House whenever it shall be pleased to receive the same. Ordered, that the Report be now received.

On motion of Mr. Willcocks, seconded by Mr. Rogers, the House adjourned.

Wednesday, 28th February, 1810.

Prayers were read.

Read for the third time, as engrossed, the Bill for laying a Duty upon Billiard Tables. On motion of Mr. Willcocks, seconded by Mr. James Wilson, resolved, that the Bill do pass, and that the title be " An Act for Licensing Billiard Tables." The Bill accordingly passed, and was signed by the Speaker. Mr. McNabb, seconded by Mr. Baby, moved that Messrs. Willcocks and Sovereign do carry up to the Honorable the Legislative Council the Act entitled " An Act for Licensing Billiard Tables," and request their concurrence thereto, which was ordered accordingly.

Agreeably to the Order of the Day, the House resolved itself into a Committee, to go into the further consideration of the Bill for appropriating a sum of money for improving the roads and building Bridges throughout the Province. Mr. Speaker left the Chair. Mr. Howard was called to the Chair of the Committee.

Mr. Speaker resumed the Chair, and Mr. Howard reported that the Committee had made a progress, and had directed him to ask for leave to sit again this day. Ordered, that the Committee have leave to sit again this day.

Agreeably to the Order of the Day, the House went into the further considera-
tion of the Petition of the Inhabitants of the County of Prince Edward (except
Ameliasburgh) stating that James Wilson, Esquire, the sitting Member, was not
duly and lawfully elected and chosen. Mr. McNabb, Esquire, a Member of this
House, was sworn in his place as an evidence in support of the Petition of the
Freeholders of the County of Prince Edward (except Ameliasburgh).

A Message from the Honorable the Legislative Council by Mr. Baldwin,
Master in Chancery.

Mr. Speaker,

I am commanded by the Honorable the Legislative Council to acquaint this
House that they have passed an Act, sent up from this House, entitled " An Act
to extend the provisions of an Act passed in the forty-seventh year of His Majesty's
Reign, entitled " An Act for the Preservation of Salmon," to which they have made
several amendments, to which amendments they request the concurrence of this
House.

And then he withdrew.

The amendments made by the Honorable the Legislative Council were then
read for the first time. Mr. Gough then moved, seconded by Mr. Lewis, that the
amendments made by the Legislative Council in and to the Salmon Bill be read
a second time to-morrow, which was ordered accordingly.

Agreeably to leave given, the House again resolved itself into a Committee to
go into the further consideration of the Bill for appropriating money for Roads and
Bridges. Mr. Speaker left the Chair. Mr. Howard again took the Chair of the
Committee.

Mr. Speaker resumed the Chair, and Mr. Howard reported that the Committee
had made a progress, and had directed him to ask for leave to sit again this day.
Leave was accordingly given to sit again this day.

A Message from His Excellency, the Lieutenant-Governor, signed by His Excellency, was presented by William Hatton, Esquire, His Excellency's Secretary, which
Message was read, all the Members of the House being uncovered, and is as
follows :—

(Signed) FRANCIS GORE, Lieutenant-Governor.

The Lieutenant-Governor thinks it proper to acquaint the House of Assembly
that, with a view to encourage the infant manufactures in this Province, a contract
has been made to supply His Majesty's ships and vessels on these lakes with cordage
of our own manufacture.

It is therefore expedient that the Commissioners for the purchase of hemp,
under the provisions of the Statute passed in the forty-first year of His Majesty's
Reign, should be at liberty to dispose of the same without its being transported out
of the Province, and the Lieutenant-Governor submits to the wisdom of the House
to make a provision to that effect.

28th February, 1810.   F. G.

Mr. McLean moved, seconded by Mr. Rogers, that the House do on to-morrow
resolve itself into a Committee, to go into the consideration of His Excellency the
Lieutenant-Governor's Message to this House. The House accordingly resolved the
same.

Agreeably to leave given, the House resolved itself into a Committee to go into
the further consideration of the Bill for granting money for the purpose of amending and repairing the roads and bridges. Mr. Speaker left the Chair. Mr. Howard
again took the Chair of the Committee.

Mr. Speaker resumed the Chair, and Mr. Howard reported that the Committee had gone through the consideration of the said Bill, to which they had made several amendments, which he was directed to report whenever the House should be pleased to receive the same. Ordered, that the Report be now received. Mr. McLean then moved, seconded by Mr. Jas. Wilson, that the Bill for appropriating money for roads and bridges be engrossed, and read a third time on Thursday next, which was ordered accordingly.

Mr. Willcocks then moved, seconded by Mr. Secord, that the further consideration of the Contested Election of James Wilson, Esquire, be postponed until to-morrow. Ordered accordingly.

Read for the second time, the Bill to provide for obtaining the benefits of the process of outlawry in Civil Actions.

Mr. Gough then moved, seconded by Mr. C. Wilson, that the House do to-morrow resolve itself into a Committee, to go into the consideration of the outlawry Bill, which was ordered accordingly.

Mr. Mallory moved, seconded by Capt. Frazer, that so much of the Order of the Day as gives leave to bring in a Bill to regulate Tavern Licenses in this Province, be discharged. The said was accordingly discharged.

Agreeably to the Order of the Day, the House resolved itself into a Committee to go into the consideration of the Bill to prevent Bribery and Corruption at Elections. Mr. Speaker left the Chair. Mr. C. Wilson took the Chair of the Committee.

Mr. Speaker resumed the Chair, and Mr. Wilson reported that the Committee had gone through the consideration of the said Bill, to which they had made several amendments, which he was directed to report to the House whenever it shall be pleased to receive the same. Ordered, that the Report be now received.

Mr. McLean moved, seconded by Mr. John Wilson, that the Bill for creating a New District be engrossed, and read a third time to-morrow, which was ordered accordingly.

Mr. Howard then moved, seconded by Mr. Rogers, that the Bill to prevent Bribery and Corruption at Elections be engrosssed and read a third time to-morrow. Ordered accordingly.

On motion of Mr. Burritt, seconded by Mr. McNabb, the House adjourned.

Thursday, 1st March, 1810.

Prayers were read.

Read for the first time, a Bill respecting Sheriffs in this Province. Mr. Mallory moved, seconded by Mr. Secord, that the Bill respecting Sheriffs be read a second time to-morrow. Ordered accordingly.

Read for the second time, the amendments made by the Honorable the Legislative Council in and to the Bill for the further preservation of Salmon. Mr. Gough then moved, seconded by Captain Elliott, that the House do now resolve itself into a Committee, to go into the consideration of the amendments made by the Honorable the Legislative Council in and to the Bill for the further preservation of Salmon. The House accordingly resolved itself into a Committee. Mr. Speaker left the Chair. Mr. Baby was called to the Chair of the Committee.

Mr. Speaker resumed the Chair, and Mr. Baby reported that the Committee had gone through the consideration of the said amendments, and that he was directed by the Committee to report to the House that the amendments be adopted. The Report was then received, and ordered accordingly. Mr. Gough then moved,

seconded by Capt. Frazer, that the amendments made by the Honorable the Legislative Council, in and to the Salmon Bill, be read a third time-to-morrow, which
was ordered accordingly.

Agreeably to the Order of the Day Mr. Speaker put the question for the third
reading of the Bill to prevent Bribery and Corruption at Elections in this Province.
A division thereupon took place; the names being called for were taken down, and
are as follows:—

Yeas.	Nays.
MESSRS. BURRITT	MESSRS. McNABB
GOUGH	FRAZER
ROGERS	BABY
J. WILSON	SECORD.
HOWARD	
C. WILSON	
WILLCOCKS	
ROBLIN	
LEWIS	
MALLORY-	

Carried in the affirmative by a majority of six, and the said Bill was accordingly read for the third time. On motion of Mr. Howard, seconded by Mr. Willcocks, resolved, that the Bill do now pass, and that the title be " An Act to prevent
Bribery and Corruption at any future election of a Member to serve in the House
of Assembly in this Province." On Mr. Speaker having put the question a division
thereupon took place. The names being called for they were taken down, and are
as follows:—

Yeas.	Nays.
MESSRS. BURRITT	MESSRS. McNABB
GOUGH	FRAZER
ELLIOTT	MARCLE
WILSON	BABY
HOWARD	McGREGOR
C. WILSON	SECORD
ROGERS	McLEAN.
WILLCOCKS	
JAMES WILSON	
ROBLIN	
LEWIS	
MALLORY	

Carried in the affirmative by a majority of five. The Bill then passed, and
was signed by the Speaker.

Mr. Rogers moved, seconded by Mr. Willcocks, that Messrs. Howard and
Burritt do carry up to the Honorable the Legislative Council the Bill to prevent
Bribery and Corruption at elections, and request their concurrence in passing the
same. Ordered accordingly.

Agreeably to the Order of the Day, the House resolved itself into a Committee
to go into the consideration of the Court of Requests Bill. Mr. Speaker left the
Chair. Mr. McLean was called to the Chair of the Committee.

Mr. Speaker resumed the Chair, and Mr. McLean reported that the Committee had gone through the consideration of the said Bill, to which they had made several amendments, which he was directed to report to the House whenever it should be pleased to receive the same. Ordered, that the Report be now received. The Report was accordingly received and accepted.

Mr. Willcocks then moved, seconded by Mr. Mallory, that the Bill for extending the jurisdiction of the Court of Requests be engrossed, and read a third time to-morrow, which was ordered accordingly.

Mr. Willcocks, seconded by Mr. Rogers moved, that the further consideration of the contested election of James Wilson, Esquire, be postponed until to-morrow. The same was accordingly postponed until to-morrow.

Read for the second time, the Bill for altering the construction of Mill-dams in this Province.

Agreeably to the Order of the Day, the House resolved itself into a Committee to go into the consideration of the Message from His Excellency the Lieutenant-Governor. Mr. Speaker left the Chair. Mr. McGregor was called to the Chair of the Committee.

Mr. Speaker resumed the Chair, and Mr. McGregor reported that the Committee had come to a resolution, which he was directed to report whenever the House should be pleased to receive the same. Ordered, that the Report be now received. Accordingly the Report was unanimously received and is as follows:—

The Committee do recommend that a respectful address be presented to His Excellency the Lieutenant-Governor, thanking him for his message of the 28th ult. respecting the contract made for the sale of hemp, the growth of this Province; and that the Committee do take into its consideration the adoption of measures to carry the Lieutenant-Governor's Message into effect.

Mr. Rogers moved, seconded by Mr. Willcocks, that Messrs. McLean and Gough be a Committee to draft an address to His Excellency the Lieutenant-Governor, agreeably to the resolution of the House this day, respecting the culture of hemp in the Province, which was ordered accordingly. Mr. Gough moved, seconded by Captain Elliott, for leave to bring in a Bill to-morrow to repeal and amend part of an Act passed in the forty-fourth year of His Majesty's Reign, for encouraging the growth and cultivation of hemp in this Province. Leave was accordingly granted.

Mr. McNabb moved, seconded by Mr. Burritt, that the House do now resolve itself into a Committee to go into the consideration of the Bill to alter the construction of Mill-dams. Ordered accordingly.

Read for the second time, the amendments made by the Legislative Council in and to the Act for laying out, amending and keeping in repair the Public highways and roads in this Province. Mr. Howard then moved, seconded by Mr. Rogers, that the House do now resolve itself into a Committee to go into the consideration of the amendments made by the Legislative Council in and to the Act for laying out, amending and keeping in repair the Highways and Roads. The House accordingly resolved itself into a Committee to go into the consideration of the amendments made to the said Bill. Mr. Speaker left the Chair. Captain Frazer was called to the Chair of the Committee.

Mr. Speaker resumed the Chair, and Captain Frazer reported that the Committee had made a progress, and had directed him to ask for leave to sit again this day. Ordered, that the Committee have leave to sit again this day.

A Message from the Honorable the Legislative Council by Mr. Baldwin, Master in Chancery.

Mr. Speaker,

I am commanded by the Honorable the Legislative Council to inform this House that they have passed an Act, sent up from this House, entitled "An Act for applying a certain sum of money therein mentioned, to make good moneys issued and advanced by His Majesty through the Lieutenant-Governor, in pursuance of several Addresses of this House," without any amendment.

And then he withdrew.

Mr. Gough, from the Committee appointed to draft an Address to His Excellency, the Lieutenant-Governor, in answer to His Excellency's Message to this House, respecting the sale of Hemp in this Province, reported that they had drafted an Address, which he was directed by the Committee to submit to the House whenever it shall be pleased to receive the same. Ordered, that the draft of an Address be now received. He then read the draft of the Address in his place, and afterwards delivered in the same at the Table, where it was again read by the Clerk throughout. Mr. Gough, seconded by Mr. Roblin, moved that the House do now resolve itself into a Committee to go into the consideration of the draft of the Address to the Lieutenant-Governor. The House accordingly resolved itself into a Committee, to go into the consideration of the draft of an Address to the Lieutenant-Governor. Mr. Speaker left the Chair. Mr. Burritt was called to the Chair of the Committee.

Mr. Speaker resumed the Chair, and Mr. Burritt reported that the Committee had gone through the consideration of the Address without any amendment, which he was directed to report to the House whenever it should be pleased to receive the same. Ordered, that the Report be now received.

Mr. Gough then moved, seconded by Mr. Burritt, that the Address to His Excellency, the Lieutenant-Governor, be engrossed, and read a third time this day. Ordered accordingly.

The said Address was then read as engrossed, which passed, and was signed by the Speaker, and the same is as follows :—

To His Excellency, Francis Gore, Esquire, Lieutenant-Governor of the Province of Upper Canada, etc., etc., etc.

May it please Your Excellency,

We, His Majesty's dutiful and loyal subjects, the Commons of Upper Canada in Parliament assembled, beg leave to return you our most respectful thanks for Your Excellency's Message to this House of the Twenty-eighth ultimo, respecting the contract made for the sale of Hemp, the growth of this Province ; and to assure Your Excellency that this Housse will immediately take into their consideration the adopting of measures to carry into effect an object so highly advantageous to the general interests of this Province.

Commons House of Assembly,   (Signed) SAMUEL STREET,
    1st March, 1810.   Speaker.

Mr. Rogers then moved, seconded by Mr. Willcocks, that Messrs. Gough and Howard do wait upon His Excellency, the Lieutenant-Governor, to know when His Excellency will be pleased to receive the Address of this House respecting Hemp ; and that those gentlemen do present the said Address at such time as His Excellency shall be pleased to appoint. Which was ordered accordingly.

Agreeably to leave given, the House again resolved itself into a Committee, to go into the further consideration of the amendments made by the Legislative Council in and to the Bill for laying out, amending and keeping in repair the Public

Highways and Roads. Mr. Speaker left the Chair. Captain Frazer was called to the Chair of the Committee.

Mr. Speaker resumed the Chair, and Captain Frazer reported that the Committee had made a progress, and had directed him to ask for leave to sit again tomorow. Leave was accordingly granted to sit again to-morrow.

On the motion of Mr. Burritt, seconded by Mr. Marcle, the House adjourned.

Friday, 2nd March, 1810.

Prayers were read.

Messrs. Gough and Howard, the Messengers ordered to wait upon His Excellency, the Lieutenant-Governor, to know at what time His Excellency would be pleased to receive the Address of this House, respecting the encouragement of the culture of hemp in this Province, reported that they had waited on His Excellency, and that His Excellency was pleased to appoint this Day at the hour of eleven o'clock in the forenoon to receive the said Address.

At the hour appointed, the Messengers ordered to present the Address of this House to His Excellency, the Lieutenant-Governor, went up with the said Address accordingly, and being returned, reported that they had presented the said Address to His Excellency, the Lieutenant-Governor, to which His Excellency was pleased to make the following answer:—

Gentlemen of the House of Assembly,

I thank you for this Address, and it affords me much satisfaction to find you are so well disposed to adopt measures for the encouragement of the infant manufactures of this Province.

Government House, York,
    2nd March, 1810.

Agreeably to the Order of the Day, was read for the third time the amendments made by the Legislative Council in and to the Bill for the further Preservation of Salmon. Mr. Gough then moved, seconded by Mr. Lewis, that Messrs. McGregor and Baby be a Committee to inform the Honorable the Legislative Council that this House has concurred in the amendments made by them in and to the Salmon Bill. Ordered accordingly.

Mr. Speaker,—

We are commanded by the Commons House of Assembly to acquaint this Honorable House that they have concurred in adopting the amendments made by the Legislative Council in and to the Act entitled "An Act to extend the provisions of an Act passed in the forty-seventh year of His Majesty's Reign, entitled 'An Act for the Preservation of Salmon.'"

Commons House of Assembly,   (Signed) SAM'L STREET,
    2nd March, 1810.   Speaker.

Mr. McLean moved, seconded by Mr. Howard, that the the third reading of the Bill for the division of Districts be discharged, and that the said Bill be recommitted. The same was accordingly discharged, and the said Bill was ordered to be recommitted. The House then resolved itself into a Committee to go into the consideration of the said Bill. Mr. Speaker left the Chair. Mr. Burritt was called to the Chair of the Committee.

Mr. Speaker resumed the Chair, and Mr. Burritt reported that the Committee had gone through the consideration of the said Bill, to which they had

made several amendments, which he was directed to report to the House whenever
it should be pleased to receive the same.

On Mr. Speaker having put the question for the Report being received, a
division thereupon took place. The names being called for, they were taken down,
and are as follows:—

Yeas.	Nays.
MESSRS. McNABB	MESSRS. C. WILSON
BURRITT	SECORD
FRAZER	ELLIOTT
MARCLE	
GOUGH	
BABY	
McLEAN	
HOWARD	
ROGERS	
McGREGOR	
LEWIS	

Carried in the affirmative by a majority of eight. The Report was accordingly
received.

Read for the third time, as engrossed, the Bill to extend the Jurisdiction of
the Court of Requests. On motion of Mr. Howard, seconded by Mr. Gough,
Resolved, That the Bill do pass, and that the title be "An Act to extend the
Jurisdiction of the Court of Requests throughout this Province." The Bill then
passed, and was signed by the Speaker. Mr. Rogers moved, seconded by Captain
Elliott, that Messrs. C. Wilson and McNabb do carry up to the Honorable the
Legislative Council the Act entitled "An Act to extend the Jurisdiction of the
Court of Requests throughout this Province," and request their concurrence thereto,
which was ordered accordingly.

Mr. McLean moved, seconded by Mr. Howard, that so much of the Rules
of this House as requires one day's previous notice before certain questions can
be put, be now dispensed with inasmuch as it respects the third reading of the
Bill for the division of sundry Districts. The said Rule was accordingly dispensed
with as far as respects the said Bill. Mr. McLean again moved, seconded by Mr.
Howard, that the Bill for the division of sundry Districts be engrossed, and read
a third time this day, which was ordered accordingly.

Agreeably to the Order of the Day, the House resolved itself into a Committee, to go into the further consideration of the amendments made by the
Legislative Council in and to the Bill for laying out, amending and keeping in
repair the Highways and Roads. Mr. Speaker left the Chair. Captain Frazer
was called to the Chair of the Committee. Mr. Speaker resumed the Chair, and
Captain Frazer reported that the Committee had come to a resolution that a
conference be requested with the Honorable the Legislative Council in and upon
the amendments made by them in and to the Act entitled "An Act for laying
out, amending and keeping in repair the Public Highways and Roads in this
Province; and to repeal the laws now in force for that purpose," which he was
directed to report to the House whenever it shall be pleased to receive the same.
Ordered, that the Report be now received. The Report was accordingly received.
Mr. Gough then moved, seconded by Mr. Burritt, that Messrs. Rogers and Howard
do carry up to the Honorable the Legislative Council a message from this House,

requesting a conference with them on the subject of the amendments made by the Legislative Council in and to the Road Bill, which was ordered accordingly, and the message is as follows:—

MR. SPEAKER,—

I am commanded by the Commons House of Assembly to request a conference with the Honorable the Legislative Council on the subject matter of the amendments made by them in and to an Act entitled "An Act to provide for the laying out, amending, and keeping in repair the Public Highways and Roads in this Province; and to repeal the laws now in force for that purpose.

Commons House of Assembly,   (Signed) SAM'L STREET,
2nd March, 1810.   Speaker.

On motion of Mr. McLean, seconded by Mr. Gough, resolved, that the Speaker be directed to order medical assistance immediately to attend on Benajah Mallory, Philip Sovereign, Joseph Willcocks, John Roblin, John Wilson and James Wilson; and report the state of their health at the Bar of this House.

On Mr. Speaker having put the question a division thereupon took place. The names being called for they were taken down, and are as follows:—

Yeas.	Nays.
MESSRS. McNABB	MESSRS. HOWARD
FRAZER	ROGERS
BURRITT	LEWIS
MARCLE	
McGREGOR	
BABY	
McLEAN	
GOUGH'	
ELLIOTT	
C. WILSON	
SECORD	

Carried in the affirmative by a majority of eight. The Speaker did then order Doctors Richardson and Lee to visit those gentlemen, and enquire into the state of their health, and report the same to the House as soon as possible.

Messrs. Wilson and McNab, the messengers appointed to carry up to the Honorable the Legislative Council the Act entitled "An Act to extend the jurisdiction of the Court of Requests throughout this Province," reported that they had carried up the same, and did request their concurrence thereto.

Messrs. Rogers and Howard, the Members named to carry up to the Honorable the Legislative Council the message of the House, requesting a conference with them, reported that they had carried up to the Legislative Council the said message.

Read for the third time, as engrossed, the Bill for the creation of a new District.

Doctors Richardson and Lee came to the Bar of the House, and did acquaint the Speaker that, in obedience to his orders, they had called at the lodgings of several of the Members, absent from this House on account of indisposition, and have the honor of making a written report of the state of health of Joseph Willcocks, James Wilson, John Wilson, and John Roblin, Esquires, which report is as follows:—

24 A.

Mr. Speaker,—

We have seen and examined Mr. Willcocks, Mr. James Wilson, Mr. John Wilson, and Mr. Roblin, and are of opinion, from Mr. Willcocks' statement, and from his present state, that it would not be proper for him to attend the House this day. Mr. James Wilson states that he has taken medicine this morning, but we think (if it is absolutely necessary) he might attend in his place. The other two gentlemen complain very much, but have taken no medicine; we think they might come to the House, whether they would remain it is impossible for us to say. These gentlemen all state that they think they will be able to attend to-morrow. We are of the same opinion.

(Signed) R. RICHARDSON.

W. LEE.

A written message from the Honorable the Legislative Council, by Mr. Baldwin, Master in Chancery.

Mr, Speaker,—

A Committee of the Honorable the Legislative Council will meet a Committee of the House of Assembly forthwith in the Legislative Council Chamber, to confer on the subject matter of the amendments made by them in and to a Bill entitled "An Act to provide for the laying out, amending, and keeping in repair the Public Roads and Highways in this Province, and to repeal the laws now in force for that purpose."

Legislative Council Chamber,   (Signed) THOS. SCOTT,
    2nd March, 1810.   Speaker.

Mr. Gough, seconded by Mr. McNabb, moved that Messrs. Rogers, Howard, McLean and C. Wilson be a Committee of conference, to meet a Committee of the Honorable the Legislative Council, on the subject matter of the amendments made by them in and to the Road Bill, which was ordered accordingly.

Mr. Rogers, from the Committee appointed by this House to confer with a Committee of the Honorable the Legislative Council on the subject matter of the amendments made by the Legislative Council in and to the Bill, reported that they had met the managers on the part of the Legislative Council, and have reason to believe that the Legislative Council will so modify their amendments as to do away with the objections made by the House of Assembly.

Read for the first time, A Bill respecting the Sale of Hemp in this Province. Mr. Gough moved, seconded by Mr. Secord, that the Hemp Bill be read a second time to-morrow, which was ordered accordingly.

A written message from the Honorable the Legislative Council by Mr. Baldwin, Master in Chancery:—

Mr. Speaker,—

The Honorable the Legislative Council have acceded to the alteration agreed upon this day by the Committees of Conference upon the subject matter of the amendments made by them in and to a Bill entitled " An Act to provide for the laying out, amending and keeping in repair of the Public Highways and Roads in this Province, and to repeal the laws now in force for that purpose

Legislative Council Chamber,   (Signed) THOS. SCOTT,
    2nd March, 1810.   Speaker.

And then he withdrew.

Read for the third time, as engrossed, the Bill for appropriating a sum of money for repairing roads and bridges throughout this Province.

On motion of Mr. McLean, seconded by Mr. Gough, the House adjourned.

Saturday, 3rd March, 1810.

Prayers were read.

Mr. Burritt moved, seconded by Mr. Gough, that the memorial of John Beikie, Esquire, be now read.

The said memorial was accordingly read, and is as follows:—

To the Honorable the Speaker and the Honorable the Members of the House of Assembly.

The Memorial of John Beikie Most Respectfully Sheweth,

That Your Memorialist has done the work of Clerk to the Commission under the Heir and Devisee Acts, since the 1st June, 1805, to the present time.

That he has constantly furnished the Commission with stationery, for which he has had no allowance, there being none made, either under the former or the present Act. That he feels confident the duty has been faithfully discharged towards the Public, and therefore humbly prays that his past services may be considered, and that he may be allowed for stationery.

And Your Memorialist will ever pray.

York, 1st March, 1810.   (Signed) JOHN BEIKIE.

Mr. Rogers moved, seconded by Mr. Gough, for leave to bring up the Petition of Hugh McLean, Door-keeper to the Commissioners for securing titles to lands in this Province. The said petition was accordingly brought up, and ordered to lie upon the Table.

Mr. Rogers moved, seconded by Mr. Gough, that the House be cleared of strangers. The House was accordingly cleared of strangers. The door being opened, Mr. Burritt then moved, seconded by Capt. Elliott, that the House do now enter into the consideration of the Contested Election of James Wilson, Esquire.

The House accordingly proceeded on the merits of the Petition of the Freeholders of the County of Prince Edward (except Ameliasburgh), complaining of the undue return of James Wilson, Esquire, to represent that County in the House of Assembly. The Solicitor-General, of Counsel for James Wilson, Esquire, the sitting Member, by permission of the House, proceeded upon the defence in behalf of James Wilson, Esquire, to whom John McDonell, Esquire, Barrister-at-Law, by permission of the House, replied.

After Counsel having been heard in support of the allegations set forth in the petition of the Freeholders of the County of Prince Edward, and that on the part of the sitting Member, they were ordered to retire within the Bar. The House then examined Mr. McNabb, a Member of this House, touching the merits of the said petition. Mr. Rogers then moved, seconded by Mr. Gough, that John Dettor be examined by the House, which was ordered accordingly. John Dettor was then called to the Bar and sworn.

Mr. Gough, seconded by Mr. McGregor, moved that the House do now resolve that it appears to this House that the Petitioners complaining of the undue election and return of James Wilson, Esquire, the sitting Member representing the County of Prince Edward (except Ameliasburgh), have proved the allegations of their petition; it being the opinion of this House that he comes within the contemplation of the twenty-first clause of an Act of the Parliament of Great Britain, passed in the thirty-first year of His Majesty's Reign, entitled, " An Act to repeal certain parts of an Act, passed in the fourteenth year of His Majesty's Reign, entitled ' An Act to make further provision for the Government of the Province of Quebec, in North America, and to make further provision for the Government of the said

Province,'" and has therefore vacated his seat. On Mr. Speaker having put the question, a division thereupon took place. The names being called for, they were taken down and are as follows:—

Yeas.	Nays.
MESSRS. McNABB	MESSRS. J. WILSON
BURRITT	HOWARD
FRAZER	WILLCOCKS
MARCLE	ROGERS
ELLIOTT	ROBLIN
BABY	LEWIS
GOUGH	
McLEAN	
G. WILSON	
SECORD	
McGREGOR	

Carried in the affirmative by a majority of five. The House accordingly resolved the same.

On motion of Mr. Burritt, seconded by Mr. Marcle, the House adjourned.

Monday, 5th March, 1810.

Prayers were read.

Agreeably to the Order of the Day, was read for the third time, as engrossed, the Bill for appropriating money for amending and repairing the highways and roads.

On motion of Mr. McLean, seconded by Capt. Frazer, resolved, that the Bill do pass and that the title be " An Act for granting to His Majesty a certain sum of money out of the funds applicable to the uses of this Province, to defray the expenses of amending and repairing the Public Highways and Roads, laying out and opening New Roads, and building Bridges in the several Districts thereof." The Bill then passed, and was signed by the Speaker.

Agreeably to the Order of the Day, was read for the third time, as engrossed, the Bill for appropriating money for amending and repairing the highways and roads.

On motion of Mr. McLean, seconded by Captain Frazer, resolved, that the Bill do pass, and that the title be " An Act for granting to His Majesty a certain sum of money out of the funds applicable to the uses of this Province, to defray the expenses of amending and repairing the Public highways and roads, laying out and opening new roads, and building bridges in the several Districts thereof." The Bill then passed, and was signed by the Speaker.

Agreeably to the Order of the Day, was read for the third time, as engrossed, a Bill for the division of sundry Districts. On motion of Mr. McLean, seconded by Mr. Jas. Wilson, resolved, that the Bill do now pass, and that the title be " An Act for the better division of sundry Districts of this Province, and to constitute a District therefrom, called the District of Nelson, and to provide for the administration of justice in the said District." The Bill then passed and was signed by the Speaker. Mr. McLean, seconded by Mr. Gough, moved that Messrs. Rogers and Lewis do carry up to the Honorable the Legislative Council the Bill entitled " An Act for the better division of sundry Districts of this Province, &c.," and that they may have permission to take up the petitions and subscription paper relative to the said Bill, and that they do also carry up to the Legislative Council the Act entitled " An Act for the appropriation of a sum of money for roads and bridges throughout this Province." The same was ordered accordingly.

Agreeably to the Order of the Day, the House resolved itself into a Committee, to go into the consideration of the Bill for regulating the Fees in the Court of King's Bench. Mr. Speaker left the Chair. Mr. Roblin was called to the Chair of the Committee.

Mr. Speaker resumed the Chair, and Mr. Roblin reported that the Committee had gone through the consideration of the said Bill, to which they have made several amendments, which he was directed to report to the House whenever it shall be pleased to receive the same. Ordered, that the Report be now received. The Report was accordingly received and accepted. Mr. Willcocks, seconded by Mr. Secord, moved that the Bill for regulating the Fees to be taken in the Court of King's Bench be re-committed this day. Ordered accordingly.

Mr. Gough moved, seconded by Capt. Elliott, that the House do now resolve itself into a Committee, to go into the consideration of the Hemp Bill.

The House accordingly resolved itself into a Committee, to go into the further consideration of the said Bill. Mr. Speaker left the Chair. Mr. McNabb was called to the Chair of the Committee.

Mr. Speaker resumed the Chair, and Mr. McNabb reported that the Committee had gone through the consideration of the said Bill, to which they have made several amendments, which he was directed to report to the House whenever it shall be pleased to receive the same. Ordered, that the Report be now received.

The report was accordingly received and accepted.

Mr. Gough, seconded by Capt. Elliott, again moved that the fifth Standing Rule of this House be now dispensed with, as far as it relates to the Hemp Bill. The said Rule was accordingly dispensed with as far as respects the said Bill. Mr. Gough then moved, seconded by Capt. Elliott, that the Hemp Bill be engrossed, and read a third time this Day, which was ordered accordingly.

Agreeably to the Order of the Day, the House resolved itself into a Committee, to go into the consideration of the Bill to prevent the forging and counterfeiting of Foreign Bills of Exchange. Mr. Speaker left the Chair. Mr. Roblin was called to the Chair of the Committee.

Mr. Speaker resumed the Chair, and Mr. Roblin reported that the said Bill be read again on this day three months, which he was directed by the Committee to report to the House whenever it shall be pleased to receive the same. Mr. Rogers moved, seconded by Mr. McLean, that the Report of the Committee be not received, but that the Committee be directed to sit again to-morrow. The same was ordered accordingly.

Read for the third time, as engrossed, the Bill to prevent the exportation of Hemp from this Province. On motion of Mr. Gough, seconded by Mr. Baby, resolved, that the Bill do pass, and that the title be " An Act to amend an Act, passed in the forty-fourth year of His Majesty's reign, entitled ' An Act for granting to His Majesty a certain sum of money, for the further encouragement of the growth and cultivation of Hemp within this Province and the exportation thereof.' " The Bill then passed, and was signed by the Speaker. Mr. Gough, seconded by Mr. Mallory, moved that Messrs. Rogers and Lewis do carry up to the Legislative Council the Bill entitled " An Act to amend an Act passed in the forty-fourth year of His Majesty's Reign, entitled ' An Act for granting to His Majesty a certain sum of money for the further encouragement of the growth and cultivation of hemp within this Province, and the exportation thereof.' " Ordered accordingly.

Agreeably to the Order of the Day, the House resolved itself into a Committee, to go into the consideration of the Bill for discouraging Public Plays and Shows in this Province. Mr. Speaker left the Chair. Mr. Rogers was called to the Chair of the Committee.

Mr. Speaker resumed the Chair, and Mr. Rogers reported that the Committee had gone through the consideration of the said Bill, to which they had made an amendment, which he was directed to report whenever the House should be pleased to receive the same. Ordered, that the report be now received. The Report was accordingly received and accepted. Mr. Howard then moved, seconded by Mr. Willcocks, that the Bill to prevent Public Plays and Exhibitions be engrossed, and read a third time to-morrow, which was ordered accordingly.

Agreeably to the Order of the Day, the House resolved itself into a Committee, to go into the consideration of the Bill respecting Land Surveyors, and the admeasurement of land in this Province. Mr. Speaker left the Chair. Mr. John Willson was called to the Chair of the Committee.

Mr. Speaker resumed the Chair, and Mr. John Wilson reported that the Committee had come to a resolution, which he was directed to report to the House whenever it should be pleased to receive the same. Ordered, that the Report be now received.

The Report was accordingly received, and is as follows —

The Committee do recommend to the House that the Bill respecting Land Surveyors and the better ascertaining the boundaries of lands, be printed, and that four copies thereof be delivered to each Member of this House.

The House accordingly concurred with the Committee, and the said Bill was ordered to be printed for the use of the Members.

Messrs. Rogers and Lewis, the messengers named to carry up to the Honorable the Legislative Council the Act entitled " An Act for granting to His Majesty a certain sum of money out of the funds applicable to the uses of the Province, to defray the expenses of amending and repairing the Public Highways and Roads, laying out and opening new roads, and building bridges in the several districts thereof," reported that they had carried up the same, and did request their concurrence thereto.

Also that they had carried up to the Legislative Council the Act entitled " An Act for the better division of sundry Districts of the Province, and to constitute a District therefrom, called the District of Nelson; and to provide for the administration of justice in the said District," with the petition and subscription paper of the Petitioners for the new District, to which they did request their concurrence.

Also an Act entitled " An Act to amend an Act passed in the forty-fourth year of His Majesty's Reign, entitled ' An Act for the granting to His Majesty a certain sum of money for the further encouragement of the growth and cultivation of hemp within this Province, and for the exportation thereof,' " to which they did request their concurrence in passing the same.

Messrs. McGregor and Baby, the Messengers named to carry up to the Honorable the Legislative Council the Message of concurrence from this House respecting the amendments made by the Legislative Council, in and to the Bill for the preservation of Salmon, reported that they had carried up the said Message.

Mr. Willcocks, seconded by Mr. Rogers, moved that the Order of the Day for recommitting the Bill for regulating the Fees of the Officers of the Court of King's

Bench be discharged, and that the said Bill be engrossed, and read a third time to-morrow, which was ordered accordingly.

Agreeably to the Order of the Day, the House went into the consideration of the Petition of the Inhabitants, Freeholders of the United Counties of Lennox and Addington, and the County of Prince Edward (except Ameliasburgh), complaining that John Roblin, Esquire, one of the sitting Members, representing the United Counties of Lennox and Addington, was not duly and lawfully elected and chosen.

In conformity to an Act passed in the First Session of the Fourth Provincial Parliament, entitled " An Act to regulate the Trial of Controverted Elections," the Speaker and the Members present were sworn by the Clerk at the Table. Members present:

The Speaker, Thomas B. Gough, James McNabb, Thomas Frazer, Henry Marcle, Stephen Burritt, Matthew Elliott, J. Willson, Peter Howard, Alexander McLean, John McGregor, C. Willson, Joseph Willcocks, Benajah Mallory, Levi Lewis, D. McG. Rogers, Philip Sovereign.

The Clerk at the Table read the Petition of the Inhabitant Freeholders of the United Counties of Lennox and Addington, and the County of Prince Edward (except Ameliasburgh).

John McDonell, Esquire, Barrister-at-Law, of Counsel for the Petitioners of the United Counties of Lennox and Addington, and the County of Prince Edward (except Ameliasburgh), complaining that John Roblin, Esquire, was not duly and lawfully elected and chosen, came to the Bar. A place was allotted for him by the House within the Bar, but not to be a precedent hereafter.

A Message from the Honorable the Legislative Council by Mr. Baldwin, Master in Chancery.

Mr. Speaker:

I am commanded by the Honorable the Legislative Council to inform this House that they have passed an Act, sent up from this House, entitled " An Act for granting to His Majesty a Duty upon Billiard Tables," to which they have made several amendments, to which they request the concurrence of this House.

And then he withdrew, and Mr. Willcocks moved, seconded by Mr. Gough, for leave to bring in a Bill to-morrow for Licensing Billiard Tables.

On Mr. Speaker having put the question, a division thereupon took place. The names being called for, they were taken down, and are as follows:—

Yeas:	Nays:
MESSRS. GOUGH	MESSRS. McNABB
McLEAN	FRAZER
J. WILLSON	BURRITT
HOWARD	MARCLE
WILLCOCKS	BABY
ROGERS	SECORD
ROBLIN.	G. WILLSON
	MALLORY
	SOVEREIGN
	McGREGOR
	LEWIS
	ELLIOTT.

The same was carried in the negative by a majority of five.

Then John Lowe, an evidence in support of the Petition of the Inhabitants of the United Counties of Lennox and Addington, and the County of Prince Edward, was sworn at the Bar. John McDonell, Esquire, Counsel for the Petitioners, by permission of the House began to examine witnesses on the part of the said Petitioners. John Roblin, Esquire, sitting Member petitioned against, cross-examined the witness. Peter Valleau, Tobias Ryckman and Joseph Trompeau were sworn and severally examined by the Counsel for the Petitioners, and cross-exaimed by the sitting Member.

On motion of Mr. Mallory, seconded by Mr. Sovereign, the House adjourned.

Tuesday, 6th March, 1810.

Prayers were read.

Mr. Willcocks moved, seconded by Mr. Sovereign, that the Rule of the House which requires one day's notice, be dispensed with, as far as relates to the Billiard Table Bill, and that he have leave to bring in the said Bill this day. The said Rule was accordingly dispensed with on this occasion, and leave was granted to bring in the said Bill this day.

Then was read for the first time a Bill for Licensing Billiard Tables. Mr. Willcocks moved, seconded by Mr. Sovereign, that the Bill for Licensing Billiard Tables be read a second time this day. The said Bill was accordingly read for the second time. Mr. Willcocks again moved, seconded by Mr. Sovereign, that the House do now resolve itself into a Committee, to go into the consideration of the said Bill. Mr. Speaker left the Chair. Mr. Gough was called to the Chair of the Committee.

Mr. Speaker resumed the Chair, and Mr. Gough reported that the Committee had gone through the consideration of the said Bill, without any amendment, which he was directed by the Committee to report to the House whenever it shall be pleased to receive the same. Ordered, that the Report be now received.

Mr. Willcocks, seconded by Mr. Sovereign, moved that the Bill for imposing a Duty upon Billiard Tables be engrossed, and read a third time this day. Ordered accordingly.

Mr. McNabb, seconded by Mr. Burritt, moved that the Petition of William Jarvis, Esquire, be now read. The said Petition was accordingly read, and is as follows:—

To the Honorable the Commons House of Assembly of Upper Canada, in Provincial Parliament assembled.

The Petition of William Jarvis, Esquire, Keeper of the Rolls.

Most respectfully showeth,

That since the establishment of a Parliament in this Province your Petitioner has been Keeper of the Rolls, for which service your Petitioner has never received any remuneration.

Your Petitioner therefore prays the Honorable House will be pleased to take this Petition into their consideration, and make him such annual allowance as the nature of the trust reposed in him shall to them seem meet. .

And in duty bound will ever pray.

(Signed) WM. JARVIS.

23rd February, 1810.   Keeper of the Rolls.

Mr. Gough moved, seconded by Mr. Burritt. that the Speaker do order the Bill for the ascertaining the Boundaries of Lands in this Province to be printed, in conformity to the resolution of this House yesterday. Mr. Speaker did then order the said Bill to be printed.

Read for the third time, as engrossed, the Bill to prohibit Public Plays and Shows in this Province. On motion of Mr. Howard, seconded by Mr. Roblin, resolved, that the Bill do pass, and that the title be " An Act to prevent all Plays of interludes, Puppet Shows, Rope Dancers, or Stage Plays from performing in this Province for hire or gain." The Bill accordingly passed and was signed by the Speaker.

Read for the third time, as engrossed, the Bill for regulating the Fees in the Court of King's Bench.

On motion of Mr. Willcocks, seconded by Mr. Secord, resolved, that the Bill do pass, and that the title be "An Act to repeal an Act passed in the forty-fourth year of His Majesty's Reign, entitled 'An Act to repeal certain parts of an Act passed in the thirty-fourth year of His Majesty's Reign, entitled 'An Act to repeal certain parts of an Act passed in the thirty-fourth year of His Majesty's Reign, entitled 'An Act to establish a Superior Court of Civil and Criminal Jurisdiction, and to regulate the Court of Appeal; and to authorize His Majesty's Court of King's Bench in this Province to regulate certain Fees, Costs and Charges therein mentioned.'" The Bill then passed, and was signed by the Speaker.

Mr. Rogers, seconded by Mr. Secord, moved that Messrs. Howard and Will-cocks do carry up to the Honorable the Legislative Council the Bill entitled "An Act to prevent all Plays of interludes, Puppet Shows, Rope Dancers, or Stage Plays from performing in this Province for hire or gain."

And also the Bill entitled "An Act to repeal an Act passed in the forty-fourth year of His Majesty's Reign, entitled 'An Act to repeal certain parts of an Act passed in the thirty-fourth year of His Majesty's Reign, entitled 'An Act to estab-lish a Superior Court of Civil and Criminal Jurisdiction, and to regulate the Court of Appeal; and to authorize His Majesty's Court of King's Bench in this Province to regulate certain Fees, Costs and Charges therein mentioned,'" and request their concurrence in passing the said Acts. Ordered accordingly.

Agreeably to the Order of the Day, the House resolved itself into a Committee to go into the consideration of the Bill to prevent Forgery and the Counterfeiting of Foreign Bills of Exchange. Mr. Speaker left the Chair. Mr. Roblin was called to the chair of the Committee.

Mr. Speaker resumed the Chair, and Mr. Roblin reported that the Committee had gone through the consideration of the said Bill, to which they had made several amendments, which amendments he was directed to report to the House whenever it shall be pleased to receive the same. The House resolved that the Report be now received.

Mr. Gough gave notice, that he will to-morrow move that the House do then resolve itself into a Committee, to consider of an Address to Our Most Gracious Sovereign, congratulating him on his having entered into the fiftieth year of his Reign.

Mr. McLean moved, seconded by Mr. McGregor, that the fifth Rule of this House be now dispensed with, as far as relates to the third reading of the Bill to prevent forgery this day. The said Rule was accordingly dispensed with on this occasion.

Mr. McLean again moved, seconded by Mr. McGregor, that the amendments made in and to the Bill for preventing forgery, be engrossed, and that the Bill as amended be read a third time this day. The same was ordered accordingly.

Read for the third time as engrossed, the Bill for licensing Billiard Tables. On motion of Mr. Willcocks, seconded by Mr. Mallory, resolved, that the Bill do pass, and that the title be "An Act for granting to His Majesty a duty upon Billiard Tables." The Bill then passed and was signed by the Speaker.   Mr. Gough, seconded by Mr. C. Wilson, moved that Messrs. Willcocks and John Wilson do carry up to the Honorable the Legislative Council the Bill entitled "An Act for granting to His Majesty a duty upon Billiard Tables," and request their concurrence thereto.

Mr. Willcocks gave notice, that he will to-morrow move that the House do then resolve itself into a Committee, for the purpose of adopting some eligible method to remunerate Samuel Street, Esq., our Honorable Speaker, for the great and unparalleled expenses he has been at in supporting the high dignity of his station during the present Session.

Mr. Rogers, seconded by Mr. Sovereign, moved that the House do now resolve itself into a Committee, to go into the consideration of the amendments made by the Legislative Council, in and to the Bill for the better regulating the Statute Labour on the highways and roads, as modified by the Committee of conference of the two Houses, which met thereupon.   The House accordingly resolved itself into a Committee to go into the consideration of the said amendments.   Mr. Speaker left the Chair.   Mr. Lewis was called to the chair of the Committee.

Mr. Speaker resumed the Chair, and Mr. Lewis reported that the Committee had gone through the consideration of the amendments, made by the Legislative Council, in and to the Bill for laying out, amending and keeping in repair the Public Highways and Roads in this Province, as modified by the Committee of Conference of the two Houses, which he was directed to report to the House whenever it shall be pleased to receive the same.   Ordered, that the Report be now received.   Mr. Rogers then moved, seconded by Mr. Gough, that the fifth Rule of this House be dispensed with as far as respects the amendments made to the Road Bill, and that the said amendments be now read a third time.   The said Rule was dispensed with on this occasion and the said amendments were ordered to be read a third time this day.

Messrs. Howard and Willcocks, the messengers ordered to carry up to the Honorable the Legislative Council two Acts from this House, reported that in obedience to the commands of this House, they had carried up to the Legislative Council the Act entitled "An Act to prevent all Plays of Interludes, Puppet Shows, Rope Dancers and Stage Plays from performing in this Province for hire or gain."

And also the Act entitled "An Act to repeal an Act passed in the forty-fourth year of His Majesty's Reign, entitled 'An Act to repeal certain parts of an Act passed in the thirty-fourth year of His Majesty's Reign, entitled 'An Act to establish a Superior Court of Civil and Criminal Jurisdiction, and to regulate the Court of Appeal; and to authorize His Majesty's Court of King's Bench in the Province to regulate certain Fees, Costs and Charges therein mentioned,' " to which two Bills they did request the concurrence of the Legislative Council.

Messrs. Willcocks and John Willson, the messengers named to carry up to the Honorable the Legislative Council an Act from this House, entitled "An Act for granting to His Majesty a duty upon Billiard Tables," reported that they had carried up the said Act, and did request their concurrence thereto.

Read for the third time, as engrossed, the amendments made by the Legislative Council, in and to the Road Bill, as modified by the Committee of conference which met thereupon, which amendments were then adopted by the House, passed, and signed by the Speaker.

Mr. Gough then moved, seconded by Mr. Mallory, that Messrs. Rogers and Secord do inform the Legislative Council that this House has concurred in adopting the amendments made by the Legislative Council in and to the Road Bill, as modified by the Committee of conference. Ordered accordingly, and the message of conference is as follows:—

Mr. Speaker,

We are directed by the Commons House of Assembly to inform this Honorable House that the House of Assembly have agreed to pass the Bill entitled "An Act to provide for the laying out, amending and keeping in repair the Public Highways and Roads in this Province, and to repeal the laws now in force for that purpose," with the amendments, as modified by the Committee of conference of the Honorable the Legislative Council and the House of Assembly.

Commons House of Assembly,   (Signed)   SAM'L STREET,
6th March, 1810.   Speaker.

Mr. Willcocks gave notice, that he will move to-morrow, that the House do then resolve itself into a Committee for the purpose of adjusting the allowances to be made to the Counsel and Witnesses in the case of the petitioners of the County of Prince Edward against James Wilson, Esquire, late a Member of this House.

Messrs. Rogers and Secord, the messengers ordered to carry up to the Legislative Council the message of this House respecting the amendments made by the Legislative Council, in and to the Road Bill, as modified by the Committee of conference, reported that they had carried up the said message.

Read for the first time, a Bill for erecting a Bridge across the River Credit, on the Dundas Road. Mr. Gough then moved, seconded by Mr. Willcocks, that the Bill for erecting a Bridge across the River Credit be read a second time to-morrow, which was ordered accordingly.

Read for the third time, as amended by this House, the Bill sent down from the Honorable the Legislative Council for preventing forgery and the counterfeiting of Foreign Bills of Exchange; which passed, and was signed by the Speaker. Mr. Rogers then moved, seconded by Capt. Elliott, that Messrs. McLean and Frazer do inform the Legislative Council that this House have passed the Bill sent down by them for the prevention of forgery, with amendments. The same was ordered accordingly. Messrs. McLean and Frazer, the messengers ordered to carry up an Act sent down from the Legislative Council, entitled "An Act for preventing forgery, and the counterfeiting of Foreign Bills of Exchange, and Foreign notes, and Orders for the payment of money," reported that they had carried up the said Act as amended, to which amendments they did request the concurrence of the Legislative Council.

Agreeably to the Order of the Day, the House went into the further consideration of the Contested Election of John Roblin, Esquire, one of the sitting Members, representing the united Counties of Lennox and Addington.

Daniel Bidel was sworn at the Bar, and examined by the Counsel for the Petitioners, and cross-examined by John Roblin, Esquire, the sitting Member.

James McNabb, Esquire, a Member of this House, was sworn in his place, and examined by the Counsel for the Petitioners, and cross-examined by John Roblin, Esquire, the sitting Member.

Thomas Dorland, Esquire, a Member of this House, was sworn in his place, and examined by the Counsel for the Petitioners, and cross-examined by the sitting Member.

John Willson was sworn at the Bar, and examined by the Counsel for the Petitioners, and cross-examined by the sitting Member.

The evidence on the part of the Petitioners having been gone through, John Roblin, Esquire, the sitting Member, was permitted by the House to call evidence to confute the allegations set forth in the petition of the Inhabitants, Freeholders of the United Counties of Lennox and Addington.

Tobias Ryckman was again called to the Bar, and re-examined by John Roblin, Esquire, the sitting Member, and cross-examined by the Counsel for the Petitioners.

Then John Willson, Esquire, a Member of this House, was sworn in his place as a witness on the part of John Roblin, Esquire, the sitting Member, and cross-examined by the Counsel for the Petitioners.

On motion of Mr. Willcocks, seconded by Mr. Mallory, the House adjourned.

Wednesday, 7th March, 1810.

Prayers were read.

Mr. Burritt moved, seconded by Mr. McNabb, that Thomas Dorland, Esquire, a Member of this House, have leave of absence during the remainder of this Session, in consequence of the bad state of his health. Ordered, that Mr. Dorland have leave of absence.

Mr. Rogers, seconded by Mr. Lewis, moved that the Petition of Hugh McLean be now read. The said Petition was accordingly read, and is as follows:—

To the Honorable the Commons House of Assembly of Upper Canada.

The petition of Hugh McLean, of York,

Humbly Sheweth,

That the Commissioners appointed under and by virtue of an Act of the Provincial Parliament, passed in the forty-eighth year of His Majesty's Reign, entitled "An Act to continue an Act passed in the forty-fifth year of His Majesty's Reign, entitled 'An Act to afford relief to those persons who may be entitled to claim lands as heirs or Devisees of the Nominees of the Crown, in cases where no patent hath issued for such lands, and further to extend the benefits of the said Act,'" employed Your Petitioner as Doorkeeper and Messenger to the Commission during their sittings in the year 1809.

That Your Petitioner during twenty days performed the duties of such situation to the best of his ability (as will appear by the annexed certificates) and hath not received any compensation for the same.

Your Petitioner therefore humbly prays Your Honorable House to grant him such remuneration for his service as to your wisdom may seem meet.

And Your Petitioner, as in duty bound, will every pray.

York, 28th February, 1810.   (Signed)   HUGH McLEAN.

Mr. Rogers moved, seconded by Mr. Willcocks, that the Petitions of William Jarvis, John Beikie, and Hugh McLean, be referred to the Committee which shall be appointed to investigate the Contingent Accounts of this Session of Parliament. The same was ordered accordingly.

Agreeably to the Order of the Day, the House went into the further consideration of the Contested Election of John Roblin, Esquire, one of the sitting Members, representing the united Counties of Lennox and Addington.

George Duggan was sworn at the Bar as a witness on the part of John Roblin,

Esquire, the sitting Member, who was then examined by him, and cross-examined by the Counsel for the Petitioners.

· Tobias Ryckman was again called to the Bar, and re-examined by the sitting Member, and cross-examined by the Counsel for the Petitioners.

John Willson, Esquire, a Member of this House was re-examined in his place by the sitting Member, and cross-examined by the Counsel for the Petitioners.

Peter Valleau was again called to the Bar and re-examined by the sitting Member, and cross-examined by the Counsel for the Petitioners.

John Lowe was also called to the Bar, and re-examined by the sitting Member and cross-examined by the Counsel for the Petitioners.

John Willson, Esquire, a Member of this House, was again re-examined in his place.

George Duggan was again called to the Bar, and re-examined.

Daniel Bidel was also called to the Bar, and re-examined by the House.

The evidence on the part of John Roblin, Esq., having been gone through, the Counsel for the Petitioners was then ordered to withdraw without the Bar.

A written message from the Honorable the Legislative Council, by Mr. Baldwin, Master in Chancery:—

Mr. Speaker,

The Honorable the Legislative Council have concurred in the amendments made by the Commons House of Assembly in and to a Bill entitled " An Act for preventing the Forgery and Counterfeiting of Foreign Bills of Exchange, and of Foreign Notes, and Orders for the Payment of Money."

(Signed) THO's SCOTT, Speaker.

Legislative Council Chamber,
7th March, 1810.

The Legislative Council have also passed an Act sent up from this House, entitled "An Act to amend an Act passed in the forty-fourth year of His Majesty's Reign, entitled ' An Act for granting to His Majesty a certain sum of money for the further growth and cultivation of hemp within this Province, and the exportation thereof,' " without any amendment.

And also an Act sent up from this House entitled " An Act for granting to His Majesty a certain sum of money out of the funds applicable to the uses of this Province, to defray the expenses of amending and repairing the Public Highways and Roads, laying out and opening new roads, and building bridges in the several Districts thereof," without any amendment.

And then he withdrew.

Mr. Gough, seconded by Mr. McGregor, moved, that it appears to this House that the Petition of the United Counties of Lennox and Addington, complaining of the undue election and return of John Roblin, Esquire, one of the sitting Members, representing the said Counties, have fully proved the allegations of their petition, and that he is ineligible to a seat in this House.

On Mr. Speaker having put the question a division thereupon took place. The names being called for, they were taken down, and are as follows:—

Yeas.   Nays.
MESSRS. BURRITT   MESSRS. J. WILLSON
    MARCLE   HOWARD
    McGREGOR   LEWIS
    GOUGH   ROGERS
    BABY   WILLCOCKS
    McLEAN   MALLORY
    McNABB
    SECORD
    C. WILLSON
    SOVEREIGN
    ELLIOTT
    FRAZER

Carried in the affirmative by a majority of six; and the seat of John Roblin, Esquire, is accordingly become vacant.

Mr. Gough then moved, seconded by Capt. Elliott, that the Speaker do inform His Excellency the Lieutenant Governor, that there is a vacancy in this House for a Member to represent the County of Prince Edward, (except Ameliasburgh) in the room of James Wilson, Esquire, he having vacated his seat; also that there is a vacancy in this House for one of the Members to represent the United Counties of Lennox and Addington, in the room of John Roblin, Esquire, he having vacated his seat under the twenty-first clause of an Act passed in the thirty-first year of His Majesty's Reign, entitled :— (Omitted in MS.)

Mr. Rogers, seconded by Mr. Willcocks, moved as an amendment to Mr. Gough's motion that the words " he having vacated his seat," be expunged, and that the words " his seat having been declared vacant " be inserted; and that the remainder of the motion after the word " also " be expunged.

Which was carried in the affirmative.

The main question was then put, which passed in the negative.

Mr. Rogers gave notice, that he will to-morrow move that the Clerk of this House be directed to furnish John Willson with such extracts from the Journals of this House as he may require, in order to enable him to prove the Resolutions of this House on the Petition complaining of the undue return of Richard Beasley, Esquire, which Petition was heard and returned last Session of Parliament.

Mr. Howard, seconded by Mr. Willcocks, moved that this House do to-morrow take into consideration the accounts of the evidence attending this House on the contested election of John Roblin and James Willson, Esquires.   Ordered accordingly.

On motion of Mr. Willcocks, seconded by Mr. Rogers, the House adjourned.

Thursday, 8th March, 1810.
Prayers were read.

Mr. Gough moved, seconded by Capt. Frazer, that the House do now resolve itself into a Committee, to consider of a congratulatory Address to Our Most Gracious Sovereign, on his having entered into the fiftieth year of his Reign. The House accordingly resolved itself into a Committee, to go into the consideration of the same. Mr. Speaker left the Chair. Mr. Willcocks was called to the chair of the Committee.

Mr. Speaker resumed the Chair, and Mr. Willcocks reported :—

Resolved, that the Committee do unanimously recommend to the House that a dutiful and loyal Address be presented to His Majesty, to congratulate him upon the fiftieth anniversary of His Majesty's accession to the Throne, and to implore the Divine Being to continue his protection and preservation of a life so dear to all His Majesty's subjects.

Mr. McLean moved, seconded by Mr. Marcle, that Messrs. Gough, Willcocks and McNabb be a Select Committee to draft an Address, conformably to the foregoing Resolution. Ordered accordingly.

Mr. Gough, from the Committee appointed to draft an Address to His Majesty, conformable to the resolution of the House this day, reported that they had drafted an Address accordingly, which the Committee were ready to submit to the House whenever it should be pleased to receive the same. The House unanimously resolved that the draft of an Address be now received. He then read the draft of the Address in his place, and then delivered the same in at the Table, where it was again read by the Clerk.

A message from the Honorable the Legislative Council by Mr. Baldwin, Master in Chancery.

Mr. Speaker,

I am commanded by the Honorable the Legislative Council to inform this House that they have passed an Act sent up from this House, entitled " An Act for granting to His Majesty a duty upon Billiard Tables," without any amendment.

Also that they have passed an Act sent up from this House, entitled " An Act to repeal an Act passed in the forty-fourth year of His Majesty's Reign, entitled ' An Act to repeal certain parts of an Act passed in the thirty-fourth year of His Majesty's Reign, entitled ' An Act to establish a Superior Court of Civil and criminal Jurisdiction, and to regulate the Court of Appeal, and to authorize His Majesty's Court of King's Bench in this Province to regulate certain Fees, Costs and Charges therein mentioned,' " without any amendment.

And then he withdrew.

Mr. Gough, seconded by Mr. Burritt, moved that the Contingent Accounts of the present Session of Parliament be laid before the House this day, which was ordered accordingly.

Mr. Gough again moved, seconded by Mr. J. Willson, that the draft of the Address to His Majesty be read a second time this day. The draft of the Address to His Majesty was accordingly read. On motion of Mr. Gough, seconded by Mr. Rogers, the House resolved itself into a Committee to go into the consideration of the said Address. Mr. Speaker left the Chair. Mr. Willcocks was called to the chair of the Committee.

Mr. Speaker resumed the Chair, and Mr. Willcocks reported that the Committee had gone through the consideration of the said Address, without any amendment, which he was directed to report to the House whenever it shall be pleased to receive the same. Ordered that the Report be now received. On motion of Mr. Howard, seconded by Mr. Lewis, the said Address was ordered to be engrossed and read this day.

The Address to His Majesty was read as engrossed, which passed, and was signed by the Speaker, and is as follows, viz. :—

To the King's Most Excellent Majesty.

Most Gracious Sovereign:—

We, Your Majesty's most dutiful and loyal subjects, the Commons of Upper Canada, in Parliament assembled, humbly pray Your Majesty to accept our warmest congratulations on the happy event of Your Majesty having attained the fiftieth year of your Reign; an event so pleasing to all Your Majesty's subjects in this remote Colony, that it hath pleased Almighty God to preserve the life of Your Majesty until this period; while one and all are imploring the Great Disposer of Events still to cherish and preserve a life so dear as that of Our Most Beloved King.

Let it not be considered ostentatious from the humble Commons of Upper Canada to offer their prayers for the life endeared to the subjects of this Province by the most Parental affection: Your Majesty having afforded your loyal subjects of this Province an asylum in the hour of distress, when nothing was left them but their loyalty to their King, their lives, and their honor.

Permit us, Sire, to assure Your Majesty that none of Your subjects are animated with a more fervent zeal of loyalty and attachment to Your Sacred Person and Government than Your Majesty's subjects of Upper Canada.

Commons House of Assembly,

Friday, 9th March, 1810.   (Signed) SAM'L STREET, Speaker.

Mr. McLean moved, seconded by Mr. Howard, that an Address be presented to His Excellency the Lieutenant Governor, requesting that His Excellency will be pleased to transmit through the accustomed channel to His Majesty, an Address from the Representatives of the Commons of Upper Canada in Parliament assembled. The House accordingly resolved the same. Mr. McLean moved, seconded by Mr. McGregor, that Messrs. Gough, Howard and Rogers be a Committee to draft the said Address to His Excellency the Lieutenant Governor, which was ordered accordingly.

Mr. Gough, from the Committee appointed to draft an Address to His Excellency the Lieutenant Governor, reported that the Committee had drafted an Address accordingly, which was ready to submit to the House whenever it should be pleased to receive the same. Ordered, that the Report be now received. He then read the Report in his place, and delivered the same in at the Table, where it was again read by the Clerk. On motion of Mr. Baby, seconded by Capt. Frazer, the House resolved itself into a Committee, to go into the consideration of the said Address. Mr. Speaker left the Chair. Mr. J. Willson was called to the chair of the Committee.

Mr. Speaker resumed the Chair, and Mr. Willson reported that the Committee had gone through the consideration of the said Address, to which they have made no amendments, which he was directed to report to the House whenever it shall be pleased to receive the same. Resolved, that the Report be now received. On motion of Capt. Frazer, seconded by Mr. Burritt, ordered, that the said Address be engrossed, and read this day. The said Address, as engrossed, was read, passed, and signed by the Speaker, and is as follows:—

To His Excellency, Frances Gore, Esquire, Lieutenant Governor of the Province of Upper Canada, &c., &c., &c.

May it please Your Excellency,

We, His Majesty's most dutiful and loyal subjects, the Commons of the Province of Upper Canada, in Parliament assembled, having unanimously agreed upon a congratulatory Address to His Majesty upon the fiftieth anniversary of His Majesty's accession to the Throne, have to request Your Excellency will be pleased to transmit the same through the accustomed channel, to be presented to His Majesty in the name of the Commons of the Province of Upper Canada.

Commons House of Assembly,

8th March, 1810.   (Signed) SAM'L STREET, Speaker.

Mr. Gough moved, seconded by Mr. Sovereign, that Captain Frazer and Mr. McNabb do wait upon His Excellency, the Lieutenant Governor to know when His Excellency will be pleased to receive this House with its congratulatory Address to His Majesty, and also an Address to His Excellency, requesting him to transmit the same. Ordered accordingly.

Mr. Mallory moved, seconded by Mr. John Willson, for leave to bring up the Petition of Thomas Hamilton, one of the Commissioners for superintending the amending and repairing of Roads and Bridges in the Home District of this Province; and that the rule of this House, which directs that there shall be two days notice before a Petition can be read, be dispensed with on the present occasion; and that the said Petition be now read.

The said Rule was accordingly dispensed with on the present occasion, and the Petition of Thomas Hamilton was brought up and read by the Clerk at the Table, and is as follows:

To the Honorable the Speaker and Members of the House of Assembly of Upper Canada in Parliament convened.

The Petition of Thomas Hamilton,

Humbly Showeth,

That Your Petitioner, having been appointed one of the Commissioners for the home district of this Province, in the year 1809 to superintend the repairing and amending the roads and bridges in the said District,

That Your Petitioner in calculating the probable expense of the causeway near the River Don, previous to the completion of the work, expected, and had reason to expect at that time, that the inhabitants of that neighborhood would assist in the raising of the same; but Your Petitioner has, to his great prejudice, been deceived, and has been obliged to pay out of his own money the sum of eighteen pounds, fifteen shillings, Provincial Currency, to complete the work.

Your Petitioner therefore prays that Your Honorable House will take his case into your consideration, and grant him such relief as you in your goodness may deem proper.

And Your Petitioner, as in duty bound, will ever pray.

York, 8th March, 1810.　　　　　　(Signed) THO'S HAMILTON.

Mr. Howard moved, seconded by Captain Elliott, that Mr. Mallory have leave of absence during the remainder of this Session of Parliament on account of the bad state of his health. Leave of absence was accordingly granted.

Mr. McLean moved, seconded by Mr. Rogers, that this House do now adjourn until nine o'clock to-morrow morning.

The House accordingly adjourned until nine o'clock to-morrow morning.

Friday, 9th March, 1810.

Prayers were read.

Messrs. Frazer and McNabb, the Messengers ordered to wait upon His Excellency, the Lieutenant Governor, to know at what time His Excellency would be pleased to receive this House with its Addresses to His Majesty and the Lieutenant Governor, reported that they had waited upon His Excellency, the Lieutenant Governor, and that His Excellency was pleased to appoint this day at the hour of two o'clock in the forenoon to receive the House with its addresses.

Agreeably to the Order of the Day the House resolved itself into a Committee, to go into the consideration of the expense incurred in consequence of the Contested

25 A.

Election of James Wilson and John Roblin, Esquires. Mr. Speaker left the Chair.
Mr. Secord was called to the Chair of the Committee.

Mr. Speaker resumed the Chair, and Mr. Secord reported that the Committee
had come to several resolutions, which he was directed to report whenever the
House should be pleased to receive the same. Ordered, that the Report be now
received. The Report was accordingly received, and is as follows:—

Resolved, that all the evidences that have attended on the late contested Elections of James Wilson and John Roblin, be allowed the sum of seven shillings and
six pence per day each, for the time they have attended.

Resolved, that it appears to the Committee that the House ought to pay to:

John Lowe for four days at 7s. 6d	£1	10	0
Peter Valleau for four days at 7s. 6d	1	10	0
Tobias Ryckman for four days at 7s. 6d	1	10	0
James Willson, two days at 7s. 6d.		15	0
Joseph Thompson, two days at 7s. 6d.		15	0
Daniel Bidel, two days at 7s. 6d.		15	0
	£6	15	0

They being necessarily detained for that time by this House.

Resolved, that it appears that the whole time John Lowe, Peter Valleau, and
Tobias Ryckman have been detained is twenty-one days each. That the time
James Willson has been detained is five days.

Resolved, that it appears to the Committee that the Petitioners against James
Wilson do pay to him the fee due his Counsel for two day's attendance.

Agreeably to the Order of the Day the Clerk laid before the House the Contingent Accounts of the two Houses of the Legislature for the present Session,
which were ordered to lie on the Table, and are as follows.

Estimate of sum necessary to furnish Stationery for the Legislative Council,
for the year 1811 £20 0 0

Approved by me,

York, 9th March, 1810. (Signed) THO's SCOTT, Speaker.

Government of Upper Canada, to George Lawe, Dr.

To amount of Wm. Allan's Account	£ 9	6	10½
" John Thompson's (the masons) Account	7	7	0
" John Bassell's (the masons) Account	20	13	9
" Margaret Bright's (the masons) Account	2	9	0
" John McBeth's (the masons) Account		18	0
" Philip Clinger's (the masons) Account	2	7	6
Halifax Currency	£43	2	1½

Amounting to Forty-three Pounds, Two Shillings and Three halfpence,
currency.

(Signed) GEORGE LAWE.

George Lawe maketh Oath and saith that the above account is just and true
in all its particulars to the best of his knowledge and belief.

Sworn before me this Tenth
day of March, 1810. THO's SCOTT, Speaker.

York, Upper Canada, 9th March, 1810.

The Contingent Account of the Commons House of Assembly, for the second Session of the Fifth Provincial Parliament.

To Matthew Dunham's Account	£19	5	7½
" James Lockwood's Account		17	2½
" Thomas Hamilton's Account	70	0	0
" Henry Hale's Account	1	5	0
" John McBeath's Account	4	16	7
" George Duggan's Account		10	0
" Philip Klinger's Account	2	7	6
" Sarah Herron's Account	3	11	3
" Quetton St. George's Account	30	17	10
" John Bassell's Account		7	6
" Hugh Carfrae's Account	23	10	4
" John Edgel's Account	6	0	0
" Carpet for the Church Pew	2	15	0
" Hugh Carfrae, being his yearly salary	20	0	0
" Thomas Hamilton, for extra services, taking care of furniture	10	0	0
" Allowance for witnesses detained by the House in the contested election of James Willson and John Roblin	6	15	0
" Hugh Carfrae for his extra services	10	0	0
" Allowance to Counsel in contested election	2	6	8
Provincial Currency	£152	5	6

York, 9th March, 1810.
House of Assembly
12th March, 1810.

(Signed) SAM'L STREET, Speaker.

York, Upper Canada, 10th March, 1810.

The Contingent Account of the Clerk of the Commons, House of Assembly's Office, for the second Session of the Fifth Provincial Parliament.

Due the Copying Clerks	£109	7	6
Balance due for Stationery	3	6	4½
Cash paid St. George for test		5	7½
Almanac			7½
Montreal newspapers	2	10	0
York Gazette	1	0	0
Mr. Allan's Account for postage	2	16	4
Mr. Wood's Account	8	9	9
Allowance for Stationery for the ensuing Session of Parliament	40	0	0
John Cameron	6	0	0
Provincial Currency	£173	16	2½

Commons House of Assembly,
10th March, 1810.

(Signed) SAM'L STREET, Speaker.

The Honorable the House of Assembly in Account Current with their Clerk for Copying Clerks, during the second Session of the Fifth Provincial Parliament.
Dr.

To Edward McMahon £27 15 0
" Charles Baynes 27 10 0
" Thomas Ridout 22 10 0
" George Kuck 17 5 0
" George Ridout 9 15 0
" Isaac Wood 1 10 0

    Provincial Currency £106 5 0

To Balance £31 5 0
" Edward MacMahon 1 0 0
" Charles Baynes 1 5 0
" Joseph Shaw 1 5 0
" Hugh Heward 1 5 0
Due Edward MacMahon for copying and comparing sundry
 writings in the Clerk of the Assembley's Office during the
 recess of Parliament 18 2 6

    Provincial Currency .... £104 - 7 6

                     Cr.
By Cash appropriated by law for Copying Clerks not yet
 received £25 0 0
By Balance 81 5 0

               £106 5 0
    Errors excepted.
York, 8th March, 1810.   (Signed) DONALD MACLEAN, Clerk Assembly.

The Honorable the House of Assembly in Account Current with the Clerk for Stationery for the second Session of the Fifth Provincial Parliament.
Dr.

To William James Crooks £32 14 0
" Alexander Wood 8 19 4½
" William Allan 5 5 6

              £46 18 10½
" Balance due £3 6 4½
                  Cr.
By Cash advanced for the purchase of stationery £40 0 0
" Four copies of the Provincial Statutes returned to Bennett
 being incomplete 3 0 0
" Balance due on Firewood 12 6
" Balance due 3 6 4½

              £46 18 10½
Errors excepted.
 York, 8th March, 1810.   (Signed) DONALD MACLEAN.

At the hour appointed the House went up with its Addresses to His Majesty and His Excellency the Lieutenant Governor.

The House being returned; Mr. Speaker reported that the House had waited upon His Excellency the Lieutenant Governor with its Addresses, to which His Excellency was pleased to return the following answer:—

Gentlemen of the House of Assembly:—

I participate with you in that pleasure which every loyal subject must feel on His Majesty's having entered into the Fiftieth year of His Reign.

I account it as particularly fortunate in being enabled to lay at His Majesty's feet the congratulations of men, many of whose fathers, and not a few who themselves, have with their lives and fortunes stood forth in the cause of their country and their King.

9th March, 1810.

Mr. Mallory moved, seconded by Mr. Gough, that the Petition of Thomas Hamilton be referred to the Committee on Contingent Accounts. Ordered accordingly.

Mr. C. Willson moved, seconded by Mr. McNabb, that this House do resolve that the pamphlet entitled " A view of the Province of Upper Canada," signed John Mills Jackson, contains a false, scandalous and seditious libel, comprising expressions of the most unexampled insolence and contumely towards His Majesty's Government in this Province, the grossest aspersions upon the House of Assembly, the Courts therein, and the Officers of the Civil Establishment of the said Government, and most manifestly tending to alienate the affections of the people from His Majesty's Government of this Province, to withdraw them from their obedience to the laws of the Country, and to excite them to insurrection.

Mr. Gough moved, seconded by Mr. Baby, that the further consideration of Mr. C. Willson's motion, seconded by Mr. McNabb, relative to the Pamphlet entitled " A view of the Province of Upper Canada," signed John Mills Jackson, be postponed until to-morrow. The House unanimously resolved the same.

On motion of Mr. McLean, seconded by Mr. Marcle, was read the pamphlet entitled " A view of the Province of Upper Canada," signed John Mills Jackson, or " A view of the Political situation of the Province of Upper Canada, in North America," in which her physical capacity is stated, the means of diminishing her burden, increasing her value, and securing her connection to Great Britain are fully considered. With notes and appendix. London, printed for W. Earle, No. 43, Albemarle Street, 1809."

On motion of Mr. Rogers, seconded by Mr. McLean the House adjourned.

Saturday, 10th March, 1810.

Prayers were read.

The House went into the Order of the Day for taking into consideration a motion made yesterday by Mr. C. Willson, seconded by Mr. McNabb, that the House do resolve that the Pamphlet entitled " A View of the Province of Upper Canada," signed John Mills Jackson, contains a false, scandalous and seditious libel, comprising expressions of the most unexampled insolence and contumely towards His Majesty's Government of this Province; the grossest aspersions upon the House of Assembly, the Courts of Justice therein, and the Officers of the Civil Establishment of the said Government, and most manifestly tending to alienate the affections of the people from His Majesty's Government of this Province, to withdraw them from their obedience to the laws of the Country and to excite them to insurrection. The House unanimously resolved the same.

Mr. Gough, seconded by Mr. McNabb, moved that the House do present an
Address to His Excellency the Lieutenant Governor, expressive of its abhorrence
and detestation of an infamous and seditious libel, signed John Mills, Jackson;
and that Messrs. C. Willson, McLean and McGregor be a Select Committee to
draft the same, which was ordered accordingly.

Mr. C. Willson, seconded by Mr. Gough, moved that the Phamplet entitled
" A view of the Province of Upper Canada," signed John Mills Jackson, be preserved among the Records of this House. The House unanimously ordered the
same.

Mr. Gough then moved, seconded by Mr. C. Willson, that the names of the
Members present be taken down. The names of the Members present were accord-
ingly taken down, and are as follows, viz.:—The Speaker, James McNabb, Stephen
Burritt, Henry Markle, J. B. Baby, Allan McLean, Philip Sovereign, J. B. Gough,
Peter Howard, Joseph Willcocks, D. McG. Rogers, Thomas Frazer, Matthew
Elliott, David Secord, John McGregor, Levi Lewis, Crowell Willson, and John
Willson, Esquires.

Mr. Gough, seconded by Mr. McLean, moved, that Mr. Sovereign have leave of
absence for the remainder of the Session, which passed in the negative.

Mr. McLean, from the Committee appointed to draft an Address to His Excellency, the Lieutenant-Governor, approbatory of His Excellency's administration
of the Government of this Province, and testifying their abhorrence and detestation of a Pamphlet signed John Mills Jackson, reported that the Committee had
drafted an Address accordingly, which they were ready to submit to the House whenever it should be pleased to receive the same. Ordered, that the Report be now
received. He then read the draft of the Address in his place, and afterwards
delivered the same in at the Table, where it was again read by the Clerk.   On
motion of Mr. Gough, seconded by Mr. C. Willson, the House resolved itself into
a Committee to go into the consideration of the said Address. Mr. Speaker left the
Chair. Mr. C. Willson was called to the Chair of the Committee.

Mr. Speaker resumed the Chair, and Mr. C. Willson reported that the Committee had gone through the consideration of the said Address without any amendment which he was directed by the Committee to report to the House, whenever
it shall be pleased to receive the same.

On Mr. Speaker having put the question for the Report being received a
division thereupon took place.

The names being called for, they were taken down, and are as follows:—

Yeas.	Nays.
MESSRS. FRAZER	MESSRS. J. WILLSON
BABY	HOWARD
McLEAN	WILLCOCKS
BURRITT	ROGERS
GOUGH	
McNABB	
SECORD	
ELLIOTT	
McGREGOR	
MARCLE	
C. WILLSON	
LEWIS	
SOVEREIGN	

Carried in the affirmative by a majority of nine. The Report was accordingly received.

Mr. McLean, seconded by Mr. Baby, moved that the said Address be engrossed, and read this day. Ordered accordingly.

Mr. Rogers, from the Select Committee to whom was referred the Public Provincial accounts, reported the proceedings of the Committee thereon. He read the Report in his place, and then delivered the same in at the Table, where it was again read by the Clerk, and is as follows, viz:—

Report of the Select Committee appointed to take into consideration the Public Accounts of this Province, the second Session of the Fifth Provincial Parliament.

The Committee upon examining the accounts numbered 10 and 17 find that all moneys that have been paid out of the Provincial Treasury last year are paid by proper authority, and that there remained in the Receiver General's hands the 31st Dec. 1809, a balance of £922 1 8

Upon examining the Account No. 14 we find that there was outstanding the 31st Dec. 1809 of duties collected on Shop, Innkeepers, and Still Licenses, issued between the 5th Jan. 1809 and the 5th Jan., 1810, as far as the acc'ts have been reecived 617 8 0¾

A.—Upon examining the Account No. 8 we find that there was outstanding 31st Dec., 1809, of duties collected on goods imported from the United States, as far as the accounts have been furnished by the Collectors, the sum of 97 12 9¼

B—It appears by the Account No. 7, that there was outstanding 31st Dec., 1809, of duties collected on Licenses issued to Hawkers, Pedlars and Petty Chapmen for the year ending the 5th of April, 1810, as far as the accounts have come to hand, the sum of 178 17 3¼

By a note added to the account No. 17 it appears that there has been paid to the Receiver General's Agent at Montreal, the sum of £4,645. 10. 2 provincial currency, which the Committee is only this Province's proportion of duties up to the 31st December, 1808 .... 4645 10 2

C—There is due from the Province of Lower Canada one year's duties on goods brought into this Province between the 1st Jan., and the 31st Dec., 1809, which may amount to...... 4908 0 5¼

£11439 10 4¾

A—The Committee observe that the Accounts are not furnished by some of the Collectors of Customs in the manner that by law they ought to be, and that if those accounts were regularly furnished it would probably appear that there are considerable sums of money in the hands of those Collectors, above the sum above stated.

B—By the Act imposing duties on Licenses issued to Hawkers, Pedlars and Petty Chapmen, the Collector is allowed ten per cent. on the money collected; but being obliged in certain cases to pay back the whole sum that has been paid, the Province suffers a loss of Sixteen Shillings on each sum so paid.

C—The Committee cannot by any means in their power ascertain what reductions the last sum to be received from Lower Canada is liable to. A large sum is kept back each year. They submit whether the House ought not to be informed on what account those sums are kept back.

A large sum of money is annually collected at the Port of Quebec, for duties under British Acts of Parliament, which sum they are informed is never accounted for to this Province in any manner.

There was in the hands of the Receiver-General 31st December, 1809, the District of Johnstown proportion of money appropriated for roads, forty-ninth of Geo. III. £200   0   0
There is due six Sheriffs 2nd March, 1810   300   0   0
The Balance of Lighthouse Duty appropriated, but not applied supposing the sum taken from the Lighthouse at York to . be taken out of the General Fund 314 13 8½

                                                        £814 13 8½

Account of money in the hands of the Receiver-General, appropriated, but not applied.
To Support the War, by vote £500   0   0
To Purchase the British Statutes   175   0   0
For erecting Public Buildings in York 2,400   0   0

                                                        £3,075   0   0

Account of money collected under British Acts of Parliament, not accounted for.
On Shop and Innkeepers Licenses issued between 5th Jan., 1809, and 5th Jan., 1810, No. 15 ....   £468   3   7 2-10
For duties collected on goods imported from the United States between the 1st Jan., and 31st Dec., 1809, as far as the accounts have come to hand, No. 9   129   0   0 1-4
For fines and forfeitures between 1st Jan., and the 31st Dec., 1809, No. 16   27   5   9 1-4

                                                        £624   9   4 3-5

The Committee observe that the fines, etc., imposed in the several Courts are in the Accounts supposed to be levied under British Acts of Parliament. They submit to the House whether they can be properly be said to be so imposed.

There is due from Colin McNabb, late Collector of Customs at the Port of Niagara, since 1802 ....   £87   0 10¼

The Committe think that it is improper for the Public money to remain in any individual's hands, especially for such a length of time. When money is collected from the Public it ought as soon as possible to be paid into the Provincial Treasury, that the Public might have the use of it.

All which is humbly submitted.

                              By Order of the Committee,
                              (Signed) D. McG. ROGERS,.
York, 8th March, 1810.   Chairman.

Agreeably to the Order of the Day, the House resolved itself into a Committee, to go into the consideration of the Contingent Accounts of the two Houses of Parliament. Mr. Speaker left the Chair.

Mr. Sovereign was called to the Chair of the Committee.

Mr. Speaker resumed the Chair, and Mr. Sovereign reported that the Committee had come to several resolutions, which he was directed to report to the House, whenever it shall be pleased to receive the same. On Mr. Speaker having put the question for the Report being received a division thereupon took place. The names being called for they were taken down and are as follows:—

Yeas.	Nays.
MESSRS. C. WILSON	MESSRS. J. WILLSON
GOUGH	WILLCOCKS
BABY	ROGERS
BURRITT	HOWARD.
McGREGOR	
SECORD	
McLEAN	
ELLIOTT	
MARCLE	
SOVEREIGN	
LEWIS	
FRAZER.	

Carried in the affirmative by a majority of eight. Mr. Sovereign then reported that the Committee had gone through the consideration of the Contingent Accounts of both Houses of Parliament, and that they had come to several resolutions thereon. He then read in his place the said resolutions and afterwards delivered the same in at the Table, where they were again read by the Clerk, and are as follows, viz.:—

Resolved, that it is the opinion of this Committee that it is expedient to advance to the Clerk of the Legislative Council, the sum of Twenty Pounds to enable him to purchase stationery for the use of the next Session of Parliament. (£20.)

Resolved, that it is the opinion of this Committee that there is due to George Lawe, Gentleman Usher of the Black Rod, agreeably to his account, as certified by the Speaker of the Legislative Council, for sundry contingent expenses thereof during the present Session, the sum of Forty-Three Pounds Two Shillings and One Penny Halfpenny. (£43 2s. 1½d.)

Resolved, that it is the opinion of this Committee that there is due to the Clerk of the House of Assembly, for disbursements in his Office, and for paying of Copying Clerks during the recess and the present Session One Hundred and Thirty-Three Pounds Sixteen Shillings and Twopence Halfpenny. (£163 16s. 2½d)

Resolved, that it is the opinion of this Committee that it is expedient to advance to the Clerk of the House of Assembly, the sum of Forty Pounds, to enable him to procure a supply of stationery for the use of the next Session of Parliament. (£40.)

Resolved, that it is the opinion of this Committee that there is due to sundry persons for articles purchased by the Serjeant-at-Arms for the use of the House of

Assembly during the recess and the present Session, One Hundred and Forty-Three Pounds Three Shillings and Tenpence. (£143 3s. 10d.)

Resolved, that it is the opinion of this Committee that the evidences that have attended on the late Contested Election of James Wilson and John Roblin, be allowed the sum of Six Pounds Fifteen Shillings, as a compensation to them for the time they were necessarily detained by the House. (£6 15s. 0d.)

Resolved, that it is the opinion of this Committee, that there be paid Two Pounds Six Shillings and Eightpence, Counsel Fees for two days attendance having been necessarily detained by the House. (£2 6s. 8d.)

Resolved, that it is the opinion of this Committee that the sum of Fifty Pounds be allowed to William Jarvis, Esq., Keeper of the Rolls, for his services as such to this date. (£50.)

Resolved, that it is the opinion of this Committee that it is expedient to allow the Commissioners appointed in the Home District for amending highways and bridges to make good money by them, more than was granted last Session of Parliament, Eighteen Pounds Fifteen Shillings. (£18 15s. 0d.)

Resolved, that it is the opinion of this Committee, that there is due to John Beikie for Stationery furnished and services attending the Commissioners under the Act to afford relief to those persons who may be entitled to claim lands in this Province as Heirs or Devisees of the Nominees of the Crown, for. five years past, including Five Pounds to Hugh McLean, as Messenger to the Commissioners during the last year. (£35.)

On motion of Mr. McNabb, seconded by Mr. Burritt, resolved, that the House do now concur in the foregoing resolutions reported from the Committee.

Resolved, that an humble Address be presented to His Excellency the Lieutenant-Governor, to request that His Excellency will be pleased to issue his Warrant in favour of John Powell, Esquire, Clerk of the Legislative Council, for the sum of Twenty Pounds, to enable him to purchase stationery for the use of the ensuing Session of Parliament.

To George Lawe, Gentleman Usher of the Black Rod, for the sum of Forty Three Pounds Two Shillings and One Penny Halfpenny, for the payment of the contingent expenses of the Legislative Council during the present Session of Parliament.

To Donald McLean, Esquire, Clerk of the House of Assembly, for the sum of One Hundred and Seventy-Three Pounds Sixteen Shillings and Twopence Halfpenny, to enable him to pay the contingent expenses of his Office, and for printing done for this House, and to procure a supply of Stationery for the ensuing Session of Parliament.

To the Serjeant-at-Arms One Hundred and Fifty-Two Pounds Five Shillings and Sixpence, to enable him to pay for sundry articles furnished during the recess and the present Session of Parliament, including allowance made to witnesses and Counsel fee in the Contested Election of James Wilson and John Roblin.

To William Jarvis, Esquire, Keeper of the Rolls, for his services as such to this date, Fifty Pounds.

To the Commissioners appointed in the Home District for amending highways and bridges, to make good money expended by them more than was granted last year, Eighteen Pounds Fifteen Shillings.

To Mr. John Beikie, for stationery and services attending the Commissioners under the Devisee Act, Thirty-Five Pounds, including Five Pounds allowed to Hugh McLean, the Messenger, as wages during the last year.

Mr. Rogers moved, seconded by Mr. Willcocks, that the Clerk of this House be directed to furnish John Willson, Esquire, with certified copies from the Journals of this House, to enable him to prove the resolutions entered into when this House took into their consideration the petition of the said John Willson and the Freeholders of the West Riding of the County of York, which was heard and determined last year. Which was ordered accordingly.

Mr. Rogers again moved, seconded by Mr. Willcocks, that the Clerk be directed to furnish D'Arcy Boulton, Esquire, with a certified copy of the resolutions of this House which directs the Petitioners against James Willson, Esquire, to pay him the Fees of his counsel for two days. Ordered accordingly.

Mr. McLean moved, seconded by Mr. Gough, that the engrossed Address to His Excellency, the Lieutenant-Governor be now read. On Mr. Speaker having put the question for the Address being read as engrossed, a division thereupon took place. The names being called for they were taken down and are as follows:—

Yeas.	Nays.
MESSRS. BABY	MESSRS. J. WILLSON
McLEAN	HOWARD
BURRITT	WILLCOCKS
GOUGH	ROGERS.
McNABB	
SECORD	
ELLIOTT	
McGREGOR	
MARCLE	
C. WILLSON	
LEWIS	
SOVEREIGN	

Carried in the affirmative by a majority of eight.

The said Address, as engrossed, was then passed, and signed by the Speaker, and is as follows:—

To His Excellency, Francis Gore, Esquire, Lieutenant-Governor of the Province of Upper Canada, etc., etc., etc.

May it please Your Excellency.

We, His Majesty's dutiful and loyal subjects, the Commons of Upper Canada, in Parliament assembled, beg leave to assure Your Excellency of our approbation of Your Excellency's administration of the Government of this Province, which, since your arrival among us, has increased in wealth, prosperity and commerce, far execeding our most sanguine expectations, aided by your wise and liberal exertions to promote the same.

We should not intrude upon Your Excellency at this time to express the general sentiment of the people of this Province did not we feel ourselves called upon and impelled by a sense of that duty which we owe to our constituents, His Majesty's loyal subjects of this Province to you, Sir, as administering the Government thereof; and to that August Sovereign whom we regard as the Father of his people, only to express our abhorrence and indignation at a pamphlet now before us, addressed to the King, Lords and Commons of the United Kingdom of Great Britain and Ireland, containing in almost every page the most gross and false aspersions on Your Excellency and His Majesty's Executive Government, the House of Assembly, and the loyal inhabitants of this Province, under the signature of John Mills Jackson, tending to misrepresent a brave and loyal portion of His Majesty's Subjects. The Commons of Upper Canada, as the organ of the People, consider the author and publisher of such false and libellous pamphlets as a character endeavouring to alienate the minds of the unwary from His Majesty's Government, and to diminish the parental affection of His Majesty to his liege subjects in this Province, which with gratitude we proudly acknowledge to have experienced an ample and abundant share of.

In addressing Your Excellency we feel a satisfaction in repeating our approbation of Your Excellency's administration of this Government, without entering into the details, which would exceed the bounds of an Address.

We humbly request Your Excellency will be pleased to represent us to His Majesty in our true character, as loyal subjects, to remove any impression which such libel may have made, or might make under such imputation.

Commons House of Assembly,   (Signed)   SAMUEL STREET,
10th March, 1810.   Speaker.

Mr. John Willson gave notice that he will, early in the next Session of Parliament, bring forth petitions of the inhabitants of the West Riding of York (except the Township of Toronto), the Townships of Saltfleet, Ancaster, Barton and Binbrook in the first Riding of the County of Lincoln, and that part of the County of Haldimand between Dundas Street and the Onondaga Village, praying the same may be formed into a new District.

Mr. Gough, seconded by Mr. McGregor, moved that Messrs. Howard and Sovereign do wait upon His Excellency, the Lieutenant-Governor, to know at what time His Excellency will be pleased to receive the Address of this House, respecting the libel signed John Mills Jackson, and that those gentlemen do present the same at such time as His Excellency shall be pleased to appoint. Mr. Speaker having put the question a division thereupon took place. The names being called for they were taken down and are as follows, viz:—

Yeas.	Nays.
MESSRS. BABY	MESSRS. J. WILLSON
McLEAN	HOWARD
BURRITT	WILLCOCKS
GOUGH	ROGERS.
McNABB	
SECORD	
ELLIOTT	
McGREGOR	
MARCLE	
LEWIS	
SOVEREIGN	

Carried in the affirmative by a majority of eight. Messrs. Howard and Sovereign were accordingly ordered to present the said Address at such time as His Excellency would be pleased to receive the same. On motion of Mr. McNabb, seconded by Mr. Marcle, the House adjourned until Monday next.

Monday, 12th March, 1810.

Prayers were read.

Read, a letter from William Hatton, Esquire, Secretary to His Excellency the Lieutenant-Governor, which is as follows: —

Lieutenant-Governor's Office,
York, 10th March, 1810.

Sir,

I have the honor to inform you by command of the Lieutenant-Governor, that His Excellency has been pleased to appoint Monday, the 12th inst., at twelve o'clock at noon, for the prorogation of the two Houses of the Legislature of this Province.

I have the honor to be, Sir,
Your most obedient humble servant,
(Signed) Wᴹ. HATTON, Secretary.

The Honorable the Speaker of the
Commons House of Assembly.

Messrs. Howard and Sovereign reported that, in obedience to the order of the House they had waited upon His Excellency the Lieutenant-Governor, to know His Excellency's pleasure, when he would be pleased to receive the Address of this House, voted the 10th instant, and that His Excellency was pleased to appoint this day, at the hour of eleven o'clock in the forenoon, to receive the said Address.

At the time appointed, Messrs. Howard and Sovereign, the messengers ordered to present to His Excellency the Lieutenant-Governor, the Address of this House voted the 10th instant, went up with the Address, and did present the same to His Excellency the Lieutenant-Governor, to which Address His Excellency was pleased to return the following answer, viz.:—

Gentlemen of the House of Assembly,

The publication which you mention contains the most gross misrepresentations of the principles, temper, and situations of every class of His Majesty's subjects in this Province, and is calculated to produce the most pernicious effects.

The approbation which you have been pleased to express respecting my conduct, merits my acknowledgement and thanks.

It shall be my duty to convey the sentiments of His Majesty's faithful and loyal Commons of Upper Canada to the foot of the Throne.

12th March, 1810.

Mr. Gough, seconded by Mr. Lewis, moved that Messrs. McLean and Howard be a Committee to draft an Address to His Excellency the Lieutenant-Governor, praying him to issue his Warrants for paying the contingent accounts of the two Houses of Parliament for the present Session. Ordered accordingly.

Mr. McLean, from the Committee appointed to draft an Address to His Excellency the Lieutenant-Governor, requesting His Excellency to issue his Warrants for the payment of the contingent accounts of the present Session of Parliament, reported that he had drafted an Address accordingly, which they were ready to submit to the House, whenever it should be pleased to receive the same. Ordered, that the Report be now received. He then read in his place the draft of the said Address, and afterwards delivered it in at the Table where it was again read by the Clerk. Mr. Gough, seconded by Mr. McNabb, moved that the House do now resolve itself into a Commitee, to go into the consideration of the said Address. The House accordingly resolved itself into a Committee to go into the consideration of the said Address. Mr. Speaker left the Chair. Mr. Mallory was called to the Chair of the Committee.

Mr. Speaker resumed the Chair, and Mr. Mallory reported that the Committee had gone through the consideration of the said Address, without any amendment, which he was directed by the Committee to report to the House, whenever it should be pleased to receive the same. Ordered, that the Report be now received. The Report was accordingly received and accepted. Mr. Gough then moved, seconded by Mr. McNabb, that the said Address be engrossed, and read a third time this day. Ordered accordingly.

Read as engrossed, the Address to His Excellency the Lieutenant-Governor, respecting the contingent accounts of the present Session, which then passed, and was signed by the Speaker, and is as follows:—

To His Excellency, Francis Gore, Esquire, Lieutenant-Governor of the Province of Upper Canada, etc., etc., etc.

May it please Your Excellency,

We, His Majesty's most dutiful and loyal subjects, the Commons of Upper Canada, in Parliament assembled, do most humbly pray that it may please Your Excellency to issue Your Warrants, directed to the Receiver-General, requiring him to pay to John Powell, Esquire, Clerk of the Legislative Council, the sum of Twenty Pounds; to Mr. George Lawe, Usher of the Black Rod, the sum of Forty-Two Pounds Two Shillings and One Penny Halfpenny; to Donald McLean, Esquire, Clerk of the House of Assembly, One Hundred and Seventy-Three Pounds Sixteen Shillings and Twopence Halfpenny; to Mr. Thomas Hamilton, Deputy Sergeant-at-Arms, One Hundred and Fifty-Two Pounds Five Shillings and Sixpence; to enable them to pay the contingent expenses of the present Session, and to provide a supply of stationery for the ensuing Session of Parliament; to William Jarvis, Esquire, Keeper of the Rolls, for his Commissioners appointed in the Home District for amending highways and bridges, to make good money expended by them more than was granted last year, Eighteen Pounds Fifteen Shillings; to Mr. John Beikie, for stationery and service attending the Commissioners under the Act to afford relief to those persons who may be entitled to claim lands in this Province as Heirs or Devisees of the Nominees of the Crown, including the Messengers wages, Thirty-Five Pounds.

We therefore do most humbly pray that Your Excellency will be pleased to issue your Warrants to carry the said resolutions into effect; and the Commons will make good the several sums of money to Your Excellency at the next Session of Parliament.

Commons House of Assembly,   (Signed)   SAMUEL STREET,
12th March, 1810.   Speaker.

Mr. Gough, seconded by Mr. Baby, moved that Messrs. McNabb and Frazer do wait upon His Excellency the Lieutenant-Governor, to know at what time His Excellency will be pleased to receive the Address of this House respecting the contingent accounts; and that they do present the same at such time as His Excellency shall be pleased to appoint. Ordered accordingly.

Messrs. McNabb and Frazer, the messengers named to wait upon His Excellency the Lieutenant-Governor to know at what time His Excellency would be pleased to receive the Address of this House, voted this day reported that His Excellency was pleased to say that he would receive it this day at eleven o'clock.

Mr. McNabb reported that the Messengers had waited upon His Excellency, the Lieutenant-Governor, with the Address of this House of this day, and that His

Excellency was pleased to answer that he would give the necessary orders to comply therewith.

The names of the Members present were taken down, and are as follows:— The Speaker, Thomas Frazer, J. E. Baby, Allen McLean, Stephen Burritt, J. B. Gough, James McNabb, David Secord, Matthew Elliott, John McGregor, Benajah Mallory, Henry Marcle, Crowel Willson, Levi Lewis, Philip Sovereign, John Willson, Peter Howard, Joseph Willcocks, David McGregor Rogers, Esquires.

A Message from His Excellency, the Lieutenant-Governor, by Mr. George Lawe, Gentleman Usher of the Black Rod:—

Mr. Speaker,

I am commanded by His Excellency, the Lieutenant-Governor, to acquaint this Honorable House that it is His Excellency's pleasure that the Members thereof do forthwith attend upon His Excellency in the Legislative Council Chamber.

Accordingly Mr. Speaker, with the House, went up to attend His Excellency, when His Excellency was pleased to give, in His Majesty's name, the Royal assent to the following Public and Private Bills, viz.

An Act to authorize the Inhabitants of the County of Haldimand to hold Annual Meetings for the purpose of electing Town and Parish Officers.

An Act further to extend the benefits of an Act passed in the thirty-seventh year of His Majesty's Reign, entitled "An Act for the more easy Barring of Dower."

An Act to provide for the laying out, amending and keeping in repair the public Highways and Roads in this Province; and to repeal the laws now in force for that purpose."

An Act to extend the provisions of an Act passed in the forty-seventh year of His Majesty's Reign, entitled "An Act for the preservation of Salmon."

An Act for the relief of Minors of the Societies of Mennonists and Tunkers.

An Act to render the Gaols in the several Districts of this Province Houses of Correction for certain purposes.

An Act for preventing the Forgery and Counterfeiting of Foreign Bills of Exchange, and Foreign Notes, and Orders for the Payment of Money.

An Act to repeal an Act passed in the forty-fourth year of His Majesty's Reign, entitled "An Act to repeal certain parts of an Act passed in the thirty-fourth year of His Majesty's Reign, entitled 'An Act to establish a Supreme Court of Civil and Criminal Jurisdiction, and to regulate the Court of Appeal and to authorize His Majesty's Court of King's Bench in this Province to regulate certain Fees, Costs and Charges therein mentioned.'"

Mr. Speaker then said,

May it please Your Excellency to approve of the five Bills which the Assembly, with the concurrence of the Legislative Council, have passed in aid of His Majesty, which are as follows:—

An Act for granting an additional sum of money for the purpose of erecting a Bridge across the Grand River.

An Act for applying a certain sum of money therein mentioned to make good moneys issued and advanced by His Majesty through the Lieutenant-Governor in pursuance of several Addresses of this House.

An Act for granting to His Majesty a duty upon Billiard Tables.

An Act to amend an Act passed in the forty-ninth year of His Majesty's Reign, entitled "An Act for granting to His Majesty a certain sum of money for the further encouragement of the growth and cultivation of Hemp within this Province, and the exportation thereof."

An Act for granting to His Majesty a certain sum of money out of the funds applicable to the uses of this Province, to defray the expenses of amending and repairing the Public Highways and Roads, laying out and opening New Roads, and building Bridges in the several Distrits thereof, to which five Bills His Excellency the Lieutenant-Governor was pleased to give the Royal assent in His Majesty's Name.

And then His Excellency was pleased to make the following Speech to both Houses:—

Honorable Gentlemen of the Legislative Council
and
Gentlemen of the House of Assembly.

In closing this Session of the Legislature I with pleasure embrace the opportunity of expressing my approbation of that zeal with which you have discharged the duties committeed to your care.

The regulations which you have enacted respecting the Statute Labour on the Highways, as well as the liberal appropriation of money for the purpose of laying out and amending certain Roads, and of building of Bridges, I consider as an honorable testimony of the attention which you have paid to objects of Public utility and benefit.

By the extension of the powers delegated to the Commissioners for purchasing Hemp, the growth of this Province, a facility will be obtained of establishing Manufacturers of that valuable article among ourselves.

The laws which are now passed for the prevention and punishment of Forgery and Counterfeiting Foreign Bills of Exchange, and other security for the payment of money, which we have adopted from our Parent State, will, I trust, put a stop to a crime so detrimental to the interests of civil society in every country.

I entertain the hope that the other Bills passed by you, and to which I have assented in His Majesty's name, will produce the salutary end for which they were intended.

But, Gentlemen, before I prorogue this Session of the Legislature, I cannot deny myself the satisfaction of uniting my congratulations with yours on the happy event of His Majesty having entered into the fiftieth year of His Reign. To few Sovereigns has it been granted for so long a period to reign in the hearts and affections of his people. May his subjects ever bear in mind the security and protection which they have enjoyed under his Government; may his valuable life, if it should please Almighty God, be still prolonged for their benefit; and may we in this Province, who have been specially favored by His bounty, manifest our gratitude by attachment to his person and government, and by obedience to his laws.

12th March, 1810.

After which the Honorable Speaker of the Legislative Council said:—

It is His Excellency, the Lieutenant-Governor's will and pleasure that this Provincial Parliament be prorogued until Monday, the Sixteenth day of April next, to be then here held; and the Provincial Parliament is hereby prorogued accordingly until Monday the Sixteenth day of April next.

[I do hereby certify that the above and what is written on the foregoing pages is a true transcript of the Journal of the House of Assembly in Upper Canada, being the Second Session of the Fifth Provincial Parliament assembled in the Town of

York on Thursday, the First day of February last; agreeably to the Proclamation of His Excellency, Francis Gore, Esquire, Lieutenant-Governor of the Province of Upper Canada, etc., etc., etc., and prorogued by His Excellency on the Twelfth day of March last.

DONALD MACLEAN,
Clerk, Commons House of Assembly.

Clerk of the Assembly's Office,
York, 12th June, 1810.]

[Certified to be true copies from the original Records in the Colonial Office.
GEORGE MAYER, Librarian and Keeper of the Records.

Colonial Office, Downing Street,
. 26th May, 1856.]

26 A.

JOURNAL

OF THE

HOUSE OF ASSEMBLY

OF

UPPER CANADA

From the first day of February to the

thirteenth day of March,

1811.

Both days inclusive.

In the fifty-first year of the Reign of

KING GEORGE THE THIRD

Being the Third Session of the Fifth Provincial
Parliament of this Province.

JOURNAL

[OF THE

HOUSE OF ASSEMBLY

OF

UPPER CANADA

1811.

FRANCIS GORE, Lieutenant-Governor.

PROCLAMATION.

George the Third, by the Grace of God, of the United Kingdom of Great Britain and Ireland, King, Defender of the Faith.

To Our Beloved and Faithful Legislative Councillors of Our Province of Upper Canada, and to Our Knights, Citizens, and Burgesses of Our said Province to the Provincial Parliament, at Our Town of York, on the Sixteenth day of April, to be commenced, held, called and elected, and to every of you, GREETING.

Whereas by Our Proclamation, bearing date the Twelfth day of March last, we thought fit, by and with the advice of Our Executive Council, to prorogue Our Provincial Parliament until the Sixteenth day of this present month of April, at which time, in Our Town of York, you were held and constrained to appear; but we, taking into Our Royal consideration the ease and convenience of Our loving subjects, have thought fit, by and with the advice of Our Executive Council, to relieve you, and each of you, of your attendance at the time aforesaid; hereby convoking, and by these presents enjoining you, and each of you, that on the Twenty-fifth day of May next ensuing you meet us in Our Provincial Parliament in Our Town of York, there to take into consideration the state and welfare of Our Province of Upper Canada, and therein to do as may seem necessary. Herein Fail Not.

In Testimony Whereof we have caused these Our Letters to be made Patent, and the Great Seal of Our said Province to be hereunto affixed. Witness Our trusty and well-beloved Francis Gore, Esquire, Lieutenant-Governor of Our said Province, at York, this second day of April, in the year of Our Lord One Thousand Eight Hundred and Ten, and in the Fiftieth year of Our Reign.

F. G.

William Jarvis, Secretary.

By a further Proclamation of His Excellency, Francis Gore, Esquire, Lieutenant-Governor of the Province of Upper Canada, &c., &c., &c., dated at York, the Eighteenth day of May, One Thousand Eight Hundred and Ten, the Meeting of the Legislative Council and House of Assembly stands prorogued to the Second day of July, One Thousand Eight Hundred and Ten.

[385]

By a further Proclamation of His Excellency, Francis Gore, Esquire, Lieutenant-Governor of the Province of Upper Canada, &c., &c., &c., dated at York, the Twenty-second day of June, One Thousand Eight Hundred and Ten, the meeting of the Legislative Council and House of Assembly stands prorogued to the Tenth day of August, One Thousand Eight Hundred and Ten.

By a further Proclamation of His Excellency, Francis Gore, Esquire, Lieutenant-Governor of the Province of Upper Canada, &c., &c., &c., dated at York the First day of August, One Thousand Eight Hundred and Ten, the meeting of the Legislative Council and House of Assembly stands prorogued to the Fifteenth day of September, One Thousand Eight Hundred and Ten.

By a further Proclamation of His Excellency, Francis Gore, Esquire, Lieutenant-Governor of the Province of Upper Canada, &c., &c., &c., dated at York, the First day of September, One Thousand Eight Hundred and Ten, the Meeting of the Legislative Council and House of Assembly stands prorogued to the Twenty-third day of October, One Thousand Eight Hundred and Ten.

By a further Proclamation of His Excellency, Francis Gore, Esquire, Lieutenant-Governor of the Province of Upper Canada, &c., &c., &c., dated at York, the Sixteenth day of October, One Thousand Eight Hundred and Ten, the Meeting of the Legislative Council and House of Assembly stands prorogued to the Thirtieth day of November, One Thousand Eight Hundred and Ten.

By a further Proclamation of His Excellency, Francis Gore, Esquire, Lieutenant-Governor of the Province of Upper Canada, &c., &c., &c., dated at York, the Twentieth day of November, One Thousand Eight Hundred and Ten, the meeting of the Legislative Council and House of Assembly stands prorogued to the Seventh day of January, One Thousand Eight Hundred and Eleven.

FRANCIS GORE, Lieutenant-Governor.

PROCLAMATION.

George the Third, by the Grace of God, of the United Kingdom of Great Britain and Ireland, King, Defender of the Faith.

To Our Beloved and Faithful Legislative Councillors of Our Province of Upper Canada, and to Our Knights, Citizens and Burgesses of Our said Province to the Provincial Parliament at Our Town of York, on the Seventh day of January next ensuing, to be commenced, held, called and elected, and to every of you, GREETING.

Whereas by our Proclamation, bearing date the Twentieth day of November last, we thought fit, by and with the advice of Our Executive Council, to prorogue Our Provincial Parliament until the Seventh day of January; at which time, in Our Town of York, you were held and constrained to appear; but we, taking into our Royal consideration the ease and convenience of Our loving subjects, have thought fit, by and with the advice and consent of Our Executive Council, to relieve you, and each of you, of your attendance at the time aforesaid; hereby convoking, and by these presents enjoining you, and each of you, that on the First day of February next ensuing you meet us in our Provincial Parliament, in Our Town of York, for the actual despatch of Public Business; there to take into consideration the state and welfare of Our Province of Upper Canada, and therein to do as may seem necessary. Herein Fail not.

In testimony whereof we have caused these Our Letters to be made patent and the Great Seal of Our said Province to be hereunto affixed. Witness Our Trusty and Well beloved Francis Gore, Esquire, Our Lieutenant-Governor of Our said Province, at York, the Twenty-fourth day of December, in the Year of Our Lord One Thousand Eight Hundred and Ten, and in the Fiftieth Year of Our Reign.

(Signed) F. G.

(Signed) WILLIAM JARVIS, Secretary.

HOUSE OF ASSEMBLY.

YORK, Friday, 1st February, 1811.

At the Third Session of the Fifth Parliament of Upper Canada, begun and held at the Town of York on Friday, the first day of February, in the Fifty-first year of the reign of Our Sovereign Lord George the Third, by the Grace of God, of the United Kingdom of Great Britain and Ireland, King, Defender of the Faith, and in the Year of Our Lord One Thousand Eight Hundred and Eleven.

His Excellency the Lieutenant-Governor having prorogued the meeting of Parliament until the Sixteenth day of April, One Thousand Eight Hundred and Ten; and by his proclamations annexed having further prorogued the same from time to time until this day.

The House being met :—

The Clerk informed the Speaker that during the recess of Parliament His Excellency the Lieutenant-Governor has been pleased to appoint William Stanton, Esquire, to be Serjeant at Arms of this Honorable House, vice Thomas Ridout, Esquire, resigned.

Mr. Speaker then desired the Serjeant at Arms to attend his duty in this House.

The Serjeant at Arms took his place accordingly.

A message from His Excellency the Lieutenant-Governor by Mr. George Lawe, Gentleman Usher of the Black Rod.

Mr. Speaker,

It is His Excellency the Lieutenant-Governor's pleasure that this Honorable House do immediately attend him in the Legislative Council Chamber.

The House went up accordingly; and being returned :—

Mr. Speaker reported that the House attended His Excellency the Lieutenant-Governor in the Legislative Council Chamber, where His Excellency had been pleased to open the present Session by a most gracious Speech to both Houses; and that, to prevent mistakes, he had obtained for the information of this House a copy of His Excellency's Speech, which was read by the Clerk at the Table, and is as follows :—

Honorable Gentlemen of the Legislative Council
and
Gentlemen of the House of Assembly :—

When Europe is desolated by the calamities of war, and nations with their Kings degraded and oppressed; whilst in other countries life and property are held at the will of the conqueror, and liberty is but an empty name; you, gentlemen, are called together by a kind and gracious Sovereign, not for the purpose of ambition or of power, but peacefully to consult and to promote your own happiness.

Undeserving of such blessings must such subjects be, who, under these circumstances, are not deeply impressed with thankfulness to God and loyalty to the King.

Your past conduct, Gentlemen, bears ample testimony to your loyalty.

Thus animated, you will with zeal perform that important task committed to your care; and your knowledge of this widely extended Province will enable you to direct that zeal to its proper objects, and effectually to promote the comfort and the prosperity of your fellow subjects.

I think it proper on this occasion to call your attention to the expediency of continuing for a limited time an Act passed in the forty-ninth year of His Majesty's reign, to ratify and confirm the Provisional Articles of Agreement entered into between this Province and that of Lower Canada.

Gentlemen of the House of Assembly,

Having communicated your wishes with respect to the establishment of a regular Post in this Province to be communicated to His Majesty, I am now enabled to inform you that this subject is under particular consideration.

I have directed the Public Accounts to be laid before you, not douting but that you will consider them with your accustomed care and attention.

Honorable Gentlemen of the Legislative Council
and
Gentlemen of the House of Assembly,

Thus gratefully acknowledging the advantages and the privileges which we enjoy, let us remember that their continuance greatly depends upon our own conduct. It is by removing from our minds partiality, prepossession and prejudice, that we can hope, either as Legislators or as individuals to be of real benefit to the community.

Banishing, then, everything from our thoughts that may weaken or divert our attention from the love of our country, let us now cordially unite in the enacting of such laws as may best tend to the peace, welfare, and good Government of this Province.

Donald McLean, Esquire, one of the Commissioners appointed by *dedimus potestatem* to administer the Oath to the Members of the House of Assembly, came to the Bar, and did inform Mr. Speaker that Willet Casey, John Stinson and Abraham Marsh, Esquires, had taken the oath as prescribed by the Statute, and did sign the roll. ·

Then Stephen Burritt and Thomas Dorland, Esquires, introduced Willet Casey, Esquire, Knight representing the Counties of Lennox and Addington; and also John Stinson, Esquire, Knight representing the County of Prince Edward; (except the Township of Ameliasburgh). They took their seats accordingly.

Thomas Frazer and Henry Marcle, Esquires, introduced Abraham Marsh, Esquire, Knight representing the Counties of Stormont and Russell, who took his seat accordingly.

Mr. Dorland seconded by Mr. Elliott moved that Messrs. Gough, Burritt, and C. Wilson be a Committee to draft an Address to His Excellency the Lieutenant-Governor, in answer to his Speech, which was ordered accordingly.

Capt. Fraser gave notice, that he will to-morrow move that the quorum of this House be reduced from fifteen to eleven, including the Speaker.

Mr. Gough gave notice, that he will to-morrow move for a call of the House this day week.

On motion of Mr. Dorland, seconded by Mr. Lewis, the House adjourned.

Saturday, 2nd February, 1811.

Prayers were read.

Mr. Fraser, seconded by Mr. Burritt, moved that the quorum of this House be reduced from fifteen to eleven, including the Speaker, which was unanimously ordered.

Mr. Burritt, by leave, brought up the Petition from the inhabitants of the County of Grenville in the District of Johnstown; and likewise a Petition from the inhabitants of the County of Dundas, in the Eastern District, which were ordered to lie on the Table.

Mr. Gough, by leave, brought up the Petition of the inhabitants of Block No. 2 on the Grand River, in the West Riding of the County of York, which was ordered to lie on the Table.

Mr. Gough moved, seconded by Mr. C. Wilson, that there be a call of the House on Wednesday next. Ordered accordingly.

Mr. Gough, from the Committee appointed to draft an Address to His Excellency the Lieutenant-Governor, in answer to his Speech to both Houses at the opening of the present Session, reported that the Committee had prepared an Address accordingly, which he was ready to submit to the House, whenever it should be pleased to receive the same. Ordered, that the Report be now received. And he read the Report in his place, and then delivered the same at the Table, where it was again read by the Clerk once throughout. Mr. Dorland, seconded by Mr. Gough, moved that the House do now resolve itself into a Committee, to go into the consideration of the said Address. Mr. Speaker left the Chair. Capt. Fraser was called to the Chair of the Committee.

Mr. Speaker resumed the Chair, and Capt. Fraser reported that the Committee had gone through the consideration of the said Address without any amendment, which he was directed to report, whenever the House should be pleased to receive the same. The House resolved that the Report be now received. The Report was accordingly received. Mr. Burritt then moved, seconded by Mr. Markle, that the draft of the said Address be engrossed, and that messengers be appointed to wait on His Excellency the Lieutenant-Governor to know when he will be pleased to receive the same. Ordered accordingly.

Mr. Gough, seconded by Mr. C. Wilson, moved that Messrs. Elliott, Fraser and Dorland, do wait upon His Excellency the Lieutenant-Governor, to know when he will be pleased to receive this House with its Address in answer to His Excellency's Speech, which was ordered accordingly.

Mr. Gough again moved, seconded by Mr. C. Wilson, for leave to bring in a Bill on Monday next, for applying a certain sum of money therein mentioned, to make good certain moneys issued and advanced by His Majesty, through the Lieutenant-Governor in pursuance of an Address of this House. Leave was accordingly granted.

Read as engrossed, the Address to His Excellency the Lieutenant-Governor, which then passed, and was signed by the Speaker, and is as follows:—

To His Excellency Francis Gore, Esquire, Lieutenant-Governor of the Province of Upper Canada, &c., &c., &c.

May it please Your Excellency:—

We, His Majesty's most dutiful and loyal subjects, the Commons of the Province of Upper Canada, in Parliament assembled, beg leave to return you our warmest thanks for Your Excellency's Speech at the opening of the present Session.

Being conscious of the purposes for which our kind and gracious Sovereign has called us together and taught by the awful example of the calamities of war which desolate Europe, and of nations with their Kings degraded and oppressed, we fully feel the urgent necessity which behoves us peacefully to consult to promote our own happiness, and preserve that real liberty we enjoy. Undeserving, indeed, must we be, under such circumstances, were we not deeply impressed with thankfulness to God, and loyalty to our King.

If our past conduct, as Your Excellency has been pleased to express, bears ample testimony to our loyalty, we trust it will remain unimpaired by our future.

We shall zealously endeavor to promote the comfort and prosperity of our fellow subjects, by directing our attention to those objects, which, from our knowledge of this widely extended Province, may appear to us to lead thereto.

Agreeably to your Excellency's recommendation of the expediency of continuing for a limited time an Act passed in the forty-ninth year of His Majesty's reign, to ratify and confirm the Provisional Articles of Agreement entered into between this Province and that of Lower Canada, shall come under our immediate consideration.

Your Excellency's information respecting the establishment of a regular Post in this Province demands our grateful acknowledgements, and is a further proof of your unremitting attention to the interests of this Province.

When we receive the Public Accounts, they shall as usual, undergo an investigation with care and attention.

Gratefully acknowledging the privileges and advantages we enjoy, and conscious that their continuance greatly depends upon our own conduct, we shall cordially unite with Your Excellency and the other branch of the Legislature in the enacting of such laws as may best tend to the peace, welfare, and good Government of this Province, and shall divest our minds of every partiality, prepossession, and prejudice, except such as loyalty to the King, attachment to the Constitution, and love of our Country may inspire.

Commons House of Assembly, Saturday, 2nd Feby. 1811.

(Signed) Sam'l Street, Speaker.

On motion of Mr. Dorland, seconded by Mr. Fraser, the House adjourned until Monday.

Monday, 4th February, 1811.

Prayers were read.

Capt. Elliott, accompanied by the other messengers, reported that, in obedience to the order of this House, they had waited upon His Excellency the Lieutenant-Governor, to know His Excellency's pleasure, when he would receive the House with its Address; and that His Excellency was pleased to appoint to-morrow, at twelve o'clock at noon, to receive the House with its Address.

Read for the first time, A Bill for making good several sums of money, advanced by the Lieutenant-Governor, in pursuance of an Address of this House. Mr. Gough moved, seconded by Capt. Elliott, that the said Bill be read a second time to-morrow week, which was ordered accordingly.

Mr. Gough, seconded by Mr. Lewis, moved for leave to bring in a Bill, on Wednesday next, to continue for a limited time an Act passed in the forty-ninth year of His Majesty's reign, entitled "An Act for the continuing for a limited time the Provisional Agreement entered into between this Province and Lower Canada, at Montreal, on the fifth day of July, 1804, relative to duties; also for continuing for a limited time the several Acts of the Parliament of this Province now in force relating thereto." Leave was accordingly given. .

On motion of Mr. Burritt, seconded by Mr. Baby, the House adjourned.

Tuesday, 5th February, 1811.

Prayers were read.

At the hour appointed, Mr. Speaker and the House went up with the Address of this House to His Excellency the Lieutenant-Governor, and being returned;

Mr. Speaker reported that the House had attended upon His Excellency the Lieutenant-Governor with its Address; to which His Excellency had been pleased to make the following answer.

Gentlemen of the House of Assembly:—

I thank you for this expression of your loyalty, and persuade myself that in declaring your prejudice in favour of our King, our Constitution and our Country you faithfully deliver the sentiment of those you represent.

5th February, 1811.

Mr. Rogers moved, seconded by Mr. Mallory, for leave to bring up the Petition of Benjamin Marsh, Esquire, of the Township of Hope. Leave was accordingly granted, and the said petition ordered to lie upon the Table.

Mr. J. Willson, seconded by Mr. Gough, moved that the petition of Block No. 2 be now read.

The said petition of the inhabitants of Block Number two on the Grand River was read, and is as follows:—

To the Honorable House of Assembly, in their Legislative capacities assembled.

The Petition of the inhabitants of Block Number Two, Grand River in the West Riding of the County of York;

Humbly Sheweth,

That your Petitioners are settled at the western extremity of the said County, unconnected with any settlement within a distance of seventeen miles.

That your Petitioners have expended considerable sums of money in improving their lands, and have suffered many hardships and inconveniences inseparable from the situation that attends the improvement of new countries.

And that Your Petitioners have expended the sum of One Thousand Dollars, exclusive of their voluntary labour in opening a road from the Block aforesaid to the inhabited part of the County, in the neighborhood of the head of Lake Ontario.

Notwithstanding these exertions, the road is barely passable to travel, and Your Petitioners find that their funds are exhausted, and pray your honorable body will grant them the sum of one hundred pounds to enable them to complete the said road.

And your Petitioners as in duty bound, will ever pray.

Benjamin Bomberger, Jacob Stromer, Jacob Sipes, David Skome, J. F. Lesser, Samuel Stouffer, and eighty-seven other subscribers.

Mr. Burritt moved, seconded by Capt. Fraser, that the petition of the inhabitants of the Counties of Grenville and Dundas be now read.

The said Petitions were then read, and are as follows:—

To the Honorable the Legislative Council and House of Assembly of the Province of Upper Canada in Parliament assembled, &c., &c.

The humble representation and Petition of the subscribers, inhabitants of the County of Dundas, Respectfully Showeth,

That your Petitioners feel themselves in duty bound, as loyal subjects to His Majesty, by all means in their power to promote the peace, welfare and prosperity of their country.

That situated as they are at present, they humbly conceive it a duty they owe to themselves and posterity to petition the Honorable, Legislative and House of

Assembly to take such measures as in your wisdom shall seem best to form the said County of Dundas and the County of Grenville into a new District, and to establish by law the place for erecting a Court House and Gaol, as near the centre of the said Counties as may be most convenient, the establishment of which your Petitioners are sensible will be a great improvement to this part of the country, and spur to industry, which is their greatest object.

Your Petitioners beg leave to communicate to your Honorable Houses the essential reasons that induced them to urge this request from the following propositions:

First, A great part of the inhabitants of this County are at the distance of forty or fifty miles from the Surrogate Office, Registrar's Office, &c., &c.

Secondly, Your Petitioners never could obtain any of the public money from the District Treasury (though they have often applied for it to the session) to assist in opening new roads, and building bridges which are much wanted.

Thirdly, They have but two Magistrates in the County that act, seldom more than one attends the Quarter Sessions at Cornwall, where there is no less than ten Magistrates in the circle of three miles, and many more near at hand; which makes a vast majority, and always over-rules one or more from this County, and have actually appropriated the moneys of the District fund to suit their own convenience.

Also Your Petitioners are well informed that several hundred pounds of the District money is wholly lost in the hands of the Treasurers and Collectors, the accounting for the same it is agreed by the said majority of Magistrates to omit and pass over, and bury all past losses in oblivion, and try to do better in time to come; thus leaving a precedent on their records that Your Petitioners fear will prove injurious to their country, and do not wish to countenance. Your Petitioners confide in both the Honorable Houses, and hope that they may be pleased to pass an Act constituting the said County of Dundas and the County of Grenville, with the Counties in the rear, (whose Magistrates and principal inhabitants Your Petitioners have conferred with, and find them desirous of the same event), into a new District.

And Your Petitioners, as in duty bound, will ever pray.

Capt. M. Jesse Wright, George Stobentson, Andrew Berkley, Luke de Pencian, John Slever, Sen'r, Philip Tedderley, and one hundred and seventy-four others.

To the Honorable the Legislative Council and House of Assembly of the Province of Upper Canada.

The Petition of the Magistrates and principal inhabitants of the Counties of Dundas and Grenville,

Most Humbly Showeth,

That by virtue of an Act passed in the forty-eighth year of His Majesty's reign, enacting that it should be lawful for the Justices of the Peace for the District of Johnstown, in General Quarter Sessions assembled, or the major part of them to fix upon a site or situation for a Court House and Gaol in the front end or ends of Lots Numbers Ten, Eleven or Twelve in the First Concession of Elizabethtown, adjoining the King's highway. A majority of the Justices of the Peace so assembled did fix upon a site or situation in front of Lot Number   for the above purpose, and that in pursuance of a vote of Sessions a Court House and Gaol are now building on the said lot.

That the said measure carried in Sessions by a majority of the Justices will subject the inhabitants of the County of Grenville to some loss and many inconveniences. In the Town of Johnstown, which is laid out in acre lots with a park lot with better than six acres to each lot, several individuals have been at consider-able expense in building and improvements, with the two-fold view of serving them-selves and of accommodating the public; a view which they are not ashamed to avow, as they humbly conceive it to be reasonable, and as they presume that considerations of individuals and private interest have not been wholly excluded, but notoriously well known from the motives of those who projected a. Court House at Elizabeth-town.

The inhabitants of Grenville at large must be also greatly incommoded by attending on all the Courts of Quarter Sessions and District Courts at the new Court House, which they deem the greater hardship that they have a Court House of their own, where the public business of the County might be heard and deter-mined.

That Your Petitioners being thus incommoded by the building of the new Court House, and forming no inconsiderable part of the population of the District, though they have been thrown into a minority in the above measure, humbly think themselves entitled to some consideration from the Legislature; and therefore beg leave to suggest the adoption of one of the following alternatives, which, with little or no prejudice to the public interest, will do away in some measure with the in-conveniences and embarrassments they have just reason to apprehend.

Namely, as the Counties of Dundas and Grenville with the Counties imme-diately in the rear, would make a compact District of forty miles in front, with a Court House and Gaol already built nearly in the centre.

The Legislature would be pleased to pass an Act for forming the said Counties into a separate District, or, if this should be deemed inconvenient in the present state of things, that the Legislature would empower the inhabitants of the County of Grenville to hold the May and November Sessions and District Courts at Johns-town as usual, leaving the remaining terms in the year to be held in the new Court House, for the accommodation of the upper part of the District, that each Division shall support its own Court House, Gaol and Prison, out of its own rates and assessments, without burthening the public with any new office, except that of one expert Treasurer, which is no burthen at all, as he only receives the percentage, which without any other expense incident to this plan it is hoped will be thought of little importance, compared to the advantages that will accrue to Your Petition-ers from so equitable a scheme.

Therefore your Petitioners are actuated to lay before His Excellency, the Lieutenant-Governor, and the Honorable Legislative Council and House of As-sembly our grievances, in hope of a favourable redress, as it has not been of a monetary consideration with us; we have been consulting with our aforesaid join-ing Counties for some years past, and finding them then and now firmly of the same opinion with us, as appears by the Petition to that purport laid before the Legislature.

Therefore we earnestly pray that in your great wisdom you will be pleased to grant that inestimable favor above mentioned.

And Your Petitioners, as in duty bound, will ever pray.

Solomon Snyder, Thomas Williams, Tobias Stabey, Robert Parker, William Snyder, Jun'r, Hacole Stabey, and three hundred and sixty-three others.

Mr. Burritt again moved, seconded by Mr. Marcle, for leave to bring in a Bill on Monday next for the purpose of annexing the County of Grenville in the District of Johnstown, and the County of Dundas, in the Eastern District, and those Coun-ties in the rear of them; and that the said Counties become a separate District. Leave was accordingly given.

Mr. Gough, seconded by Mr. Dorland, moved for leave to bring in a Bill to-morrow to amend an Act passed in the forty-ninth year of His Majesty's reign, entitled "An Act to explain, amend, and reduce into one Act the several laws now in force for the raising and training the Militia of this Province." Accordingly leave was granted.

On motion of Mr. Dorland, seconded by Captain Fraser, the House adjourned.

Wednesday, 6th February, 1811.

Prayers were read.

Agreeably to the Order of the Day the House was called over, when several of the members appeared; and the names of such as made default to appear were taken down, and are as follows:—

Alexander McDonell, Thomas Mears, Peter Howard (excused on account of sickness in his family), Allan McLean, James McNabb, Philip Sovereign, John McGregor, Matthew Elliot.

Mr. Gough gave notice that he will to-morrow move that the members who were absent when the House was called over this day be ordered into and considered as at this time in the custody of the Serjeant at Arms, and shall not be discharged therefrom until they shall have paid the customary fees established in the Parliament of Great Britain in like cases, unless they shall show to the satisfaction of this House sufficient cause for such absence.

Mr. Burritt moved, seconded by Mr. Rogers, that the present attendance of Peter Howard, Esquire, be dispensed with in this House, in consequence of sickness in his family. Which was ordered accordingly.

Read for the first time, a Bill for continuing the Provisional Articles of Agreement with Lower Canada. Mr. Gough then moved, seconded by Mr. Secord, that the Provisional Agreement Bill be read a second time to-morrow. Ordered accordingly.

Read for the first time, a Bill to amend the Militia Act. Mr. Gough again moved, seconded by Mr. Secord, that the Bill to amend the Militia Act be read a second time to-morrow. Which was ordered accordingly.

Mr. Mallory, seconded by Mr. Rogers, moved for leave to bring up the Petition of Henry Bostwick, Esquire, and others.

Leave was accordingly granted, and the said Petition was ordered to lie on the Table.

Mr. Willcocks gave notice that he will move on Thursday next that the House do resolve itself into a Committee of the Whole, to take into consideration the necessity of an Address to His Excellency, the Lieutenant-Governor, requesting that His Excellency will be pleased to lay before this House, as soon as convenience will permit, a statement of all moneys which have been collected and paid by all persons who have absented themselves from Militia training, or who have paid any moneys under and by virtue of the several Militia Laws now or heretofore in force in this Province; and to what uses the said moneys have been applied.

Mr. Mallory moved, seconded by Mr. C. Wilson, for leave to bring in a Bill to-morrow to repeal an Act passed in the forty-sixth year of the King, to make a provision for certain Sheriffs in this Province. Accordingly leave was granted.

On motion of Mr. Dorland, seconded by Mr. Mallory, the House adjourned.

Thursday, 7th February, 1811.

Prayers were read.

Mr. Gough moved, seconded by Mr. C. Willson, that the Members who were absent when the House was called over yesterday be ordered into and be considered at this time as in custody of the Serjeant at Arms, and shall not be discharged therefrom until they have paid the customary fees established in the Parliament of the United Kingdom in like cases, unless they show to the satisfaction of this House sufficient cause for such absence. Which was ordered accordingly.

Mr. Gough again móved, seconded by Mr. C. Willson, that Messrs. Elliot and Sovereign, who have attended this day, and made excuses to the satisfaction of this House for their absence at the call of the House yesterday, be discharged from the custody of the Serjeant at Arms without paying fees. The House accordingly ordered the same.

Read for the second time the Provisional Agreement Bill. Mr. Gough, seconded by Mr. Dorland, moved that the Bill for continuing the Provisional Agreement with Lower Canada be referred to a Committee of the Whole House on Saturday next. Ordered accordingly.

Read for the second time, the Bill to amend the Militia Law.

Mr. Gough then moved, seconded by Mr. C. Willson, that the House do now resolve itself into a Committee, to take the Bill to amend the Militia Law into consideration. The House accordingly resolved itself into a Committee. Mr. Speaker left the Chair. Mr. Dorland was called to the Chair of the Committee.

Mr. Speaker resumed the Chair. Mr. Dorland reported that the Committee had made a progress, and had directed him to ask for leave to sit again this day. Leave was accordingly granted to sit again this day.

William Jarvis, Esquire, Secretary of the Province, came to the Bar of the House, and delivered in, by order of His Excellency the Lieutenant-Governor, the Provincial Public Accounts; and also the Hemp and Road Accounts.

Agreeably to leave given, the House resolved itself again into a Committee to go into the further consideration of the Bill to amend the Militia Law. Mr. Speaker left the Chair. Mr. Dorland again took the Chair of the Committee.

Mr. Speaker resumed the Chair, and Mr. Dorland reported that the Committee had made a progress, and had directed him to ask for leave to sit again to-morrow. Leave was accordingly granted to sit again to-morrow.

Read, the Schedule of the Road and Hemp Accounts, and also read, the Schedule of the Provincial Public Accounts, which are as follows:—

SCHEDULE OF ACCOUNTS laid before the House of Assembly.

No. 1. General account of articles on which duties on importatin are imposed by the Legislature of Lower Canada, which have passed Coteau du Lac upwards from the 1st of January to the 30th of June, 1810, agreeable to the written accounts thereof received, or as ascertained on examination of carriages according to the Act.

No. 2. The Inspector's list of names of persons licensed as Shop and Inn-keepers in the several Districts of the Province of Upper Canada, between the 5th of January, 1809, and the 5th of January, 1810. These returns were not received in time to be laid before the Legislature in 1810.

No. 3. The Inspector's return of Still Licenses issued in the Midland, Niagara, and London Districts, which expired on the 5th of January, 1810. These returns were not received in time to be laid before the Legislature in 1810.

No. 4. The Inspector's list of names of persons licensed as Shop and Inn-keepers in the several Districts of the Province of Upper Canada, from the 5th January, 1810, to the 5th January, 1811.

No. 5. The Inspector's list of names of such persons as have been licensed to work Stills in the several Districts of the Province of Upper Canada, from the 5th of January, 1810, to the 5th of January, 1811.

No. 6. Account of moneys collected within the several Districts of the Province of Upper Canada on Licenses issued to Hawkers, Pedlars and Petty Chapmen, for the year ending the 5th of April, 1810, (the returns were not received in time to be laid before the Legislature during the last Session), after deducting ten per cent. allowed to the Collectors by the Act of the 47th of the King.

No. 7. Account of moneys collected within the several Districts of the Province of Upper Canada on licenses issued to Hawkers, Pedlars and Petty Chapmen, for the year ending the 5th of April, so far as the returns have been received, after de-ducting ten per cent. and the sums repaid to such persons as have obtained cer-tificates of residence, agreeable to the Act of the 47th of the King.

No. 8. Provincial Revenue of the Crown arising from duties collected on goods imported under authority of Acts of the Provincial Parliament, between the 1st of January and the 31st of December, 1810, including such duties as have not been heretofore stated.

No. 9. Provincial Revenue of the Crown arising from duties collected on goods imported under authority of Acts of the Parliament of Great Britain between the 1st of January and the 31st of December, 1810, including such duties as have not been heretofore stated.

No. 10. Abstracts of Warrants issued by His Excellency Francis Gore, Esquire, Lieutenant-Governor of the Province of Upper Canada, for moneys charged against the funds arising from duties imposed by the Provincial Legislature.

No. 11. Account of lighthouse tonnage duties collected for the year ending the 31st December, 1810 (so far as the returns have been received), including such duties as have not been heretofore stated.

No. 12. Supplementary Abstract Statement of moneys collected within the several Districts of the Province of Upper Canada on Shop, Inn-keepers and Still Licenses, issued between the 5th of January, 1809, and 5th of January, 1810, under authority of Acts of the Provincial Parliament, after deducting ten per cent. allowed the Inspectors by the Act of the 43rd of the King.

No. 13. Supplementary Abstract Statement of moneys collected within the sev-eral Districts of the Province of Upper Canada, on Shop and Inn-keepers Licenses issued between the 5th of January, 1809, and the 5th of January, 1810, under authority of Acts of the Parliament of Great Britain, after deducting ten per cent. allowed to the Inspectors by the Act of the 43rd of the King.

No. 14. Abstract Statement of moneys collected within the several Districts of the Province of Upper Canada, on Shop, Inn-keepers and Still Licenses, issued between the 5th of January, 1810, and the 5th of January, 1811, so far as the returns have been received, after deducting ten per cent., allowed to the Inspectors by the Act of the 43rd of the King.

No. 15. Abstract Statement of moneys collected within the several Districts of the Province of Upper Canada on Shop and Inn-keepers' Licenses, issued between the 5th of January, 1810, and the 5th of January, 1811, under authority of Acts of the Parliament of Great Britain, so far as the returns have been received, after deducting ten per cent. allowed the Inspectors by the Act of the 43rd of the King.

No. 16. General state of cash received by the Receiver-General for duties and fines under authority of Acts of the Parliament of Great Britain, between the 1st of January and the 31st of December, 1810.

No. 17. General state of receipts and payments by the Receiver-General for duties and fines (likewise appropriations made) under authority of Acts of the Provincial Parliament, betwen the 1st of January and 31st of December, 1810.

No. 18. General account of articles on which duties on importation are imposed by the Legislature of Lower Canada, which have passed Coteau du Lac upwards from the 1st of July to the 31st of December, 1810, agreeable to the written accounts thereof, or as ascertained on examination of carriages according to the Act.

York, 4th February, 1811.   JOHN McGILL,
                                             Insp'r Gen. P. P. Accts.

(For Public Accounts as per Schedule see Appendix.)

Mr. Willcocks moved, seconded by Mr. Secord, that so much of the Order of the Day as relates to an Address to His Excellency, the Lieutenant-Governor, on the subject of Militia Fines be dispensed with, and that the same be on the Order of the Day for Saturday next. Ordered accordingly.

Read for the first time, the Bill to repeal the Act allowing a Salary to Sheriffs. Mr. Mallory then moved, seconded by Mr. Willcocks, that the Sheriff Bill be read a second time to-morrow. On Mr. Speaker having put the question, a division thereupon took place. The names being called for, they were taken down, and are as follows.

Yeas.	Nays.
MESSRS. MARKLE,	MESSRS. GOUGH,
MARSH,	· BURRITT,.
CASEY,	BABY,
JOHN WILSON,	FRASER,
MALLORY,	STINSON,
SECORD,	ROGERS,
WILLCOCKS,	ELLIOT,
HOWARD,	LEWIS,
SOVEREIGN,	DORLAND,
	FRAZER.

The same passed in the negative by a majority of one.

Mr. Willcocks, seconded by Mr. Gough, moved for leave to bring in a Bill on Monday next to repeal an Act passed in the forty-seventh year of His Majesty's reign, intituled " An Act to establish Public Schools in each and every District of this Province. Leave was accordingly granted.

27 A.

Mr. Willcocks moved, seconded by Mr. Sovereign, for leave to bring in a Bill on Monday next, to repeal an Act passed in the forty-seventh year of His Majesty's reign, intituled " An Act for granting to His Majesty an annual sum of money for the purposes therein mentioned." Accordingly leave was granted.

Mr. Willcocks again moved, seconded by Mr. Rogers, for leave to bring in ·a Bill, on Wednesday next for the purpose of making ineligible to a seat in this House any person or persons who shall hold, sustain or enjoy ·an office, place or appointment of profit or emolument in and by virtue of any Commission derived immediately from His Majesty, or of any Commission derived from His Excellency the Lieutenant-Governor or person administering the Government of this Province, Registers of Counties only excepted.

On Mr. Speaker ·having put the question a division thereupon took place.

The names being called for, they were taken down, and are as follows: —

Yeas.	Nays.
MESSRS. MARSH,	MESSRS. GOUGH,
CASEY,	BURRITT,
JOHN WILSON,	BABY,
MALLORY,	FRASER,
SECORD,	MARKLE,
STINSON,	ELLIOT,
WILLCOCKS,	LEWIS,
HOWARD,	C. WILLSON.
ROGERS,	
DORLAND,	
SOVEREIGN,	

Carried in the affirmative by a majority of three.

Mr. Howard moved, seconded by Mr. Secord, for leave to bring in a Bill, on Tuesday next, to prevent bribery at any future election in this Province. Leave was accordingly given.

Mr. Howard again moved, seconded by Mr. John Wilson, for leave to bring in a Bill, on Wednesday next, to regulate the Practice of Physic and Surgery in this Province. Accordingly leave was granted.

Mr. Gough, seconded by Mr. C. Willson, moved, that Mr. McLean having appeared in his place be discharged from the custody of the Serjeant at Arms upon paying his fees. Which was ordered accordingly.

Mr. Mallory moved, seconded by Mr. Baby, for leave to bring in a Bill, to-morrow, to amend an Act passed in the thirty-fourth year of His Majesty's reign, respecting the service of Writs, Summonses and declarations issuing out of the Court of King's Bench, and other Courts in this Province. Leave was accordingly granted.

Mr. Rogers, seconded by Mr. Burritt, moved, that the petition of Benjamin Marsh, Esquire, be referred to the Committee of this House on Public Accounts. Ordered accordingly.

On the motion of Capt. Fraser, seconded by Capt. Elliott, the House adjourned.

Friday, 8th February, 1811.

Prayers were read.

Agreeably to the Order of the Day, the House resolved itself into a Committee, to go into the consideration of the Bill to amend the Militia Law. Mr. Speaker left the Chair. Mr. Dorland was called to the Chair of the Committee.

Mr. Speaker resumed the Chair, and Mr. Dorland reported the Committee had made progress, and had directed him to ask for leave to sit again on Monday next. Ordered, that the Committee have leave to sit again on Monday next.

Mr. Gough moved, seconded by Mr. Dorland, that Mr. McNabb, having this day appeared in his place, and made an excuse to the satisfaction of the House, be discharged from the custody of the Serjeant at Arms without paying fees. Ordered accordingly.

Mr. Mallory, seconded by Mr. Dorland, moved that so much of the Order of the Day as gives him leave to bring in a Bill this day to amend an Act passed in the thirty-fourth year of His Majesty's Reign, respecting the service of Writs, Summonses and Declarations, issuing out of the Court of King's Bench and other Courts in this Province, be dispensed with, and that he have leave to bring in the same on Monday next, which was ordered accordingly.

Mr. Burritt, seconded by Capt. Elliott, that Messrs. Rogers, Howard, Dorland and McNabb, be a Committee to examine the Public Accounts. The same was ordered accordingly.

Mr. Burritt again moved, seconded by Mr. C. Willson, that Messrs. Elliot, Baby, Fraser, Gough and Secord, be a Committee to examine into those parts of the Public Accounts which respect Roads and Hemp. The House accordingly ordered the same.

Mr. McNabb, seconded by Mr. G. Williamson, moved for leave to bring in a Bill, on Tuesday next, to alter the construction of Mill-dams upon navigable streams of water, so that rafts and crafts may pass over them in safety. Leave was accordingly granted.

Mr. McNabb again moved, seconded by Capt. Fraser, for leave to bring in a Bill, on Tuesday next, to raise the duty upon Licenses to Hawkers, Pedlars and Petty Chapmen in this Province. Accordingly leave was granted.

Mr. Mallory, seconded by Mr. McLean, moved for leave to bring in a Bill, on Friday next, to repeal the laws and ordinances of the Province of Quebec now in force in this Province, and to make further provision for the same. Leave was granted to bring in the said Bill.

Mr. Howard moved, seconded by Mr. Rogers, for leave to bring in a Bill, on Thursday next, to continue and amend an Act passed in the forty-seventh year of His Majesty's Reign, relative to Assessments and Rates in this Province. Leave was accordingly granted.

Mr. John Wilson moved, seconded by Mr. Mallory, for leave to bring in a Bill, on Wednesday next, for granting a sum of money to the Petitioners of Block No. 2 on the Grand River, for the purpose of repairing the road from thence to Dundas Mills, which was passed in the negative.

On motion of Mr. McLean, seconded by Mr. J. Wilson, the House adjourned until eleven o'clock to-morrow.

Saturday, 9th February, 1811.

Prayers were read.

Agreeably to the Order of the Day, the House resolved itself into a Committee, to go into the consideration of the Provisional Agreement Bill. Mr. Speaker left the Chair. Mr. Burritt was called to the Chair of the Committee.

Mr. Speaker resumed the Chair, and Mr. Burritt reported that the Committee had made some progress, and had directed him to ask for leave to sit again on Saturday next. Ordered, that the Committee have leave to sit again on Saturday next.

Mr. Willcocks moved, seconded by Mr. Rogers, that this House do now resolve itself into a Committee to take into consideration an Address to His Excellency the Lieutenant-Governor, respecting the Militia Fines.

The House accordingly resolved itself into a Committee to go into the consideration of the said Address. Mr. Speaker left the Chair. Mr. McLean was called to the Chair of the Committee.

Mr. Speaker resumed the Chair, and Mr. McLean reported that it is the opinion of the Committee, that an Address be presented to His Excellency the Lieutenant-Governor, requesting His Excellency to lay before this House, as soon as convenience will permit, certified accounts of all fines which have been collected and paid under and by virtue of the several Militia Laws now and heretofore in force in this Province; which he was directed to report, whenever the House should be pleased to receive the same. Ordered that the report be now received.

Mr. Willcocks then moved, seconded by Mr. Rogers, that Messrs. Gough and McLean be a Committee to draft an Address to His Excellency the Lieutenant-Governor, agreeably to the Report of the Committee of the whole House upon Militia Fines, which was ordered accordingly.

Mr. McLean, seconded by Capt. Fraser, moved for leave to bring in a Bill, on Monday next, to repeal part of an Act, passed in the thirty-seventh year of His Majesty's Reign, intituled "An Act for regulating the Court of King's Bench." Leave was accordingly granted.

Mr. Howard moved, seconded by Mr. Gough, for leave to bring up a petition from the inhabitants of the District of Johnstown. Leave was accordingly granted, and the said petition was ordered to lie upon the Table.

Mr. Mallory moved, seconded by Mr. Rogers, that the petition of Henry Bostwick and others be now read. Accordingly the said Petition was then read by the Clerk at the Table, and is as follows:

To the Honorable Members of the House of Commons, in Provincial Parliament assembled.

The Memorial of the undersigned

Most Respectfully Showeth,

That during the Fourth Session of the Fourth Provincial Parliament, a petition was presented to that Honorable Body, signed by a number of the Trustees of the Public Schools for the District of London, praying the removal of the said School from Townsend to the Village of Dover, in the Township of Woodhouse.

That in consequence of that petition the Trustees were authorized by an Act passed in that Session to establish it where they might think proper intending, it is persumed, to meet the object of the petition.

That immediately after the promulgation of that Act Your Memorialists called upon the Trustees with a large subscription, (exceeding one hundred pounds, Provincial Currency) subscribed by the inhabitants in and near the Village of Dover, for the purpose of erecting a House for the use of the Public School, and at the same time requested an order for the establishment of it in the said Village.

The order which accompanies this was given. Your Memorialists were then authorized by the Subscribers to collect the subscriptions, and superintend the building of the house, in consequence of which Your Memorialists immediately contracted for the necessary materials, and with carpenters, &c., to build the house.

That after Your Memorialists had gone to a very great expense, and had contracted for every material to finish the house they were suddenly told by the Trustees, without any previous communication or intimation of their design, that they had changed their minds, and had determined to establish the School in Charlotteville, not offering any rational motive for their conduct, excepting that as we had not completed the house at the time limited in their order they did not conceive themselves any longer bound to us; at which time it was utterly impossible for Your Memorialists to have finished the house, owing to the late opening of the water communication. The nails which were purchased the Fall before were at Fort Erie, and could not be procured until late in the month of May. This circumstance was well known to the Trustees.

·That at the time Your Memorialists procured the order for the˜ School, they offered to the Trustees a house for the teacher, in the neighborhood of Dover, where he would immediately have had a very respectable School until the Public School House would be finished; but this offer was rejected.

That Your Memorialists have been at a very great expense (relying upon the faith of the Trustees) to erect the house, which could now be finished in a short time, and that they have no means of indemnifying themselves, should the School be permanently established in Charlotteville; the subscription being for the express purpose of building a house for the use of the Public School, and the deed for the land whereon the house is erected is given to the Trustees in trust for the same purpose.

Wherefore Your Memorialists most respectfully pray that Your Honorable House, taking into consideration the allegations herein contained, will direct by law that the Public School for the District of London shall be permanently established in the Township of Woodhouse, at the place where the house erected for that purpose is situated. ·

And Your Memorialists, as in duty bound, will ever pray.

Henry Van Allen, Abraham Rulpelge, Henry Bostwick.
Woodhouse, District of London.

On motion of Mr. McLean, seconded by Mr. Marsh, the House adjourned till Monday next, at eleven o'clock in the forenoon.

Monday, 11th February, 1811.

Prayers were read.

Read for the first time, the Bill to form Grenville and Dundas into a separate District.

Mr. Burritt, seconded by Capt. Fraser, moved, that the Bill for forming the Counties of Grenville and Dundas into a separate District be read a second time · on Wednesday next, which was ordered accordingly.

Read for the first time, the Bill to repeal the Act allowing the Adjutant General a salary.

Mr. Willcocks moved, seconded by Mr. Mallory, that the Bill for repealing the Act which authorizes the Adjutant General of the Province to receive a salary out of the Provincial Fund, be read a second time to-morrow. On Mr. Speaker having put the question, a division thereupon took place. The names being called for, they were taken down, and are as follows:—

Yeas.	Nays.
MESSRS. MARSH	MESSRS. BURRITT
CASEY	FRASER
JOHN WILSON	MARKLE
HOWARD	GOUGH
SOVEREIGN	McLEAN
STINSON	C. WILLSON
WILLCOCKS	ELLIOTT
ROGERS	BABY
MALLORY	McNABB
DORLAND	
LEWIS	

Carried in the affirmative by a majority of two. Accordingly the said Bill was ordered to be read for the second time to-morrow.

Agreeably to the Order of the Day the House resolved itself into a Committee, to go into the further consideration of the Bill to amend the Militia Law. Mr. Speaker left the Chair. Mr. Dorland took the Chair of the Committee.

Mr. Speaker resumed the Chair, and Mr. Dorland reported the Committee had made progress, and had directed him to ask for leave to sit again to-morrow. Ordered, that the Committee have leave to sit again to-morrow.

Read for the first time, the Bill to repeal part of an Act passed in the thirty-fourth year of the King, and to regulate the practice of the Courts of Justice.

Mr. Mallory then moved, seconded by Mr. Dorland, that the Bill to repeal part of an Act passed in the thirty-fourth year of the King, and to make further provision for the same, be read a second time to-morrow. Ordered accordingly.

Mr. Willcocks moved, seconded by Mr. Sovereign, that so much of the Order of the Day as relates to the School Bill be dispensed with, and that the same be on the Order of the Day for to-morrow, which was ordered accordingly.

Read for the first time, the Bill to regulate the practice of the Court of King's Bench. Mr. McLean then moved, seconded by Mr. Gough, that the Bill intituled "An Act to repeal part of an Act passed in the thirty-seventh year of His Majesty's Reign, intituled 'An Act for regulating the practice of the Court of King's Bench,'" be read a second time to-morrow, which was ordered accordingly.

Mr. Gough, one of the Committee appointed to draft an Address to His Excellency, the Lieutenant-Governor, respecting the receipts and expenditures of Militia Fines, reported that the Committee had prepared an Address accordingly; which he was directed to submit to the House whenever it should be pleased to receive the same. Ordered, that the report be now received. He then read the report in his place, and delivered in the same at the Table, where it was again read by the Clerk.

Mr. Gough moved, seconded by Mr. Rogers, that the draft of the Address to His Excellency, the Lieutenant-Governor, be engrossed and read this day, which was ordered accordingly.

Mr. Willcocks gave notice that he will move to-morrow that this House do resolve itself into a Committee to take into consideration the necessity of an Address to His Excellency, the Lieutenant-Governor, upon the propriety of holding two Circuits in the year in each and every District of this Province.

Mr. Willcocks moved, seconded by Mr. Mallory, for leave to bring in a Bill on Thursday next to reduce the salary of the Speaker of the House of Assembly. On Mr. Speaker having put the question, a division thereupon took place. The names being called for, they were taken down, and are as follows:—

Yeas.	Nays.
MESSRS. J. WILSON	MESSRS. McNABB
HOWARD	BURRITT
SOVEREIGN	FRASER
WILLCOCKS	MARCLE
ROGERS	MARSH
MALLORY	GOUGH
SECORD	McLEAN
	CASEY
	STINSON
	ELLIOTT
	BABY
	DORLAND
	LEWIS

Carried in the negative by a majority of six.

Mr. McLean moved, seconded by Mr. Gough, for leave to bring in a Bill on Wednesday next, intituled "An Act to repeal part of an Act passed in the thirty-eighth year of His present Majesty, intituled 'An Act to amend part of an Act passed in the thirty-fourth year of the Reign of His Majesty, intituled 'An Act to establish a Superior Court of Civil and Criminal Jurisdiction, and to regulate the Court of Appeals; and also to amend and repeal part of an Act passed in the thirty-seventh year of the Reign of His Majesty, intituled 'An Act for regulating the practice of the Court of King's Bench, and to make further provision respecting the same.'" Leave was accordingly granted.

Mr. Gough, seconded by Mr. Dorland, moved that the Address to His Excellency, the Lieutenant-Governor, respecting Militia Fines, as engrossed, be now read. Accordingly the said Address, as engrossed, was read, passed, and signed by the Speaker; and is as follows:—

To His Excellency, Francis Gore, Esquire, Lieutenant-Governor of the Province of Upper Canada, &c., &c., &c.

May it please Your Excellency,—

We, His Majesty's most dutiful and loyal subjects, the Commons of the Province of Upper Canada, in Parliament assembled, being anxious faithfully to discharge the important task we have to perform, beg leave humbly to request Your Excellency will be pleased to direct to be laid before this House, as soon as convenience will permit, copies of the certified accounts of all fines which have been collected and paid under and by virtue of the several Militia Laws now and heretofore in force in this Province, and to what purposes the same have been applied.

Commons House of Assembly,

Monday, 11th February, 1811.

(Signed) Sam'l Street, Speaker.

Mr. Gough again moved, seconded by Captain Fraser, that Messrs. Rogers and Willcocks do wait upon His Excellency, the Lieutenant-Governor, to know when His Excellency will be pleased to receive the Address of this House, and that these gentlemen do present the same at such time as His Excellency shall be pleased to appoint, which was ordered accordingly.

On motion of Mr. McLean, seconded by Captain Fraser, the House adjourned to eleven o'clock to-morrow forenoon.

Tuesday, 12th February, 1811.

Prayers were read.

Mr. McLean moved, seconded by Mr. Rogers, for leave to bring up a Petition from sundry inhabitants of the Eastern District. Leave was accordingly granted, and the said Petition ordered to lie upon the Table.

Mr. McLean again moved, seconded by Mr. Gough, for leave to bring up a Petition from sundry inhabitants of the Province, relative to boundaries of land. Accordingly leave was granted, and the said Petition was ordered to lie upon the Table.

Read, the Petition of Sundry Inhabitants of the District of Johnstown, which is as follows:—

To the Honorable the Commons House of Assembly of Upper Canada, in Parliament assembled.

The Petition of the subscribers, Inhabitants of the District of Johnstown, Respectfully Showeth,—

That Your Petitioners are informed that an attempt will be made to procure a law to be passed for holding the Courts of Justice alternately at Johnstown and Elizabethtown in this District.

That the several Courts are now directed by law to be held at Elizabethtown, which place is central, and a large Court House and Gaol has been lately erected at a great expense. This law wisely provides for the general good, and were it altered we conceive that much injury would result to the community without producing any other good effect than gratifying the interests of a very few individuals. In the event of such alterations of the law a new Court House and Gaol must necessarily be built at Johnstown, as the old one is decayed. The District would thereby be subject to an expense which it is not able to bear; the Quarter Sessions, instead of being composed of one body, would probably consist of two parties, formed of the respective Justices who might reside in the vicinity of each Court House. From hence would result contrary measures, which would not only tend to induce indecent animosity, but also embarrass and even pervent justice.

This District is not very large, having some years since been divided from the Eastern District; one Court House and Gaol are therefore amply sufficient for all the purposes of Justice.

Your Petitioners therefore pray that no Bill may be suffered to pass through Your Honorable House for holding the Courts of Justice in this District at any other place than Elizabethtown

(Signed)—Sam'l McNish, Alexander McLean, Peter Purvis, Archibald Mc-Lean, Samuel Griffin, John Shipman, and one hundred and seventy other persons.

Mr. McLean moved, seconded by Mr. Gough, for leave to bring up a Petition from sundry inhabitants of this Province, relative to the division of the Home and Niagara District.

Leave was accordingly granted, and the said Petition ordered to lie upon the Table.

Read, a Letter from Alexander McDonnell, Esquire, a Member of this House, which is as follows:—

Sir:—   Baldoon, 21st January, 1811.

Although I am perfectly aware that an application for leave of absence during the ensuing Session will appear unreasonable, I cannot reconcile to myself the not soliciting it, preferring to be called importunate to failing in respect to the House; I must therefore, through you, Sir, request the indulgence of the House in forgiving an absence which from many circumstances is rendered unavoidable.

I have the Honor to be, Sir,

Your Humble Servant,

(Signed) Alex'r McDonnell.

The Honorable the Speaker of the House of Assembly.

Mr. Howard, seconded by Mr. Rogers, moved for leave to bring up a Petition from a number of the principal inhabitants of the District of Johnstown. Leave was accordingly granted, and the said Petition was ordered to lie upon the Table.

On Motion of Mr. Willcocks, seconded by Mr. Rogers, the House adjourned.

Wednesday, 13th February, 1811.

Prayers were read.

Read for the first time, the Bill to prevent charge and expense at Elections.

Mr. Howard then moved, seconded by Mr. Rogers, that the Bill for preventing Charge and Expense at Elections be read a second time to-morrow. Ordered accordingly.

Mr. Willcocks, seconded by Mr. Rogers, moved that the House do now resolve itself into a Committee to go into consideration of the Adjutant General's Salary Bill. The House accordingly resolved itself into a Committee, to go into the consideration of the said Bill. Mr. Speaker left the Chair. Mr. Howard was called to the Chair of the Committee.

Mr. Speaker resumed the Chair, and Mr. Howard reported that the Committee had gone through the consideration of the said Bill, to which they had made no amendments, which he was directed to report to the House whenever it should be pleased to receive the same. The House divided upon the question, and the names were taken down as follows:—

Yeas.	Nays.
MESSRS. McNABB	MESSRS. BURRITT
MARSH	FRASER
CASEY	MARKLE
JOHN WILSON	GOUGH
STINSON	BABY
HOWARD	McLEAN
MALLORY	ELLIOTT
WILLCOCKS	C. WILLSON
ROGERS	
SECORD	
DORLAND	
LEWIS	
SOVEREIGN	

Carried in the affirmative by a majority of five, and the said Report was accordingly received.

Mr. Willcocks then moved, seconded by Mr. Rogers, that the Bill for taking away the Salary from the Adjutant General of this Province be engrossed, and read a third time to-morrow, which was ordered accordingly.

Agreeably to the Order of the Day the House resolved itself into a Committee, to go into the further consideration of the Bill to amend the Militia Law. Mr. Speaker left the Chair. Mr. Dorland was called to the Chair of the Committee.

Mr. Speaker resumed the Chair, and Mr. Dorland reported that the Committee had gone through the consideration of the said Bill, to which they had made several amendments, which he was directed to report to the House whenever it should be pleased to receive the same. Ordered, that the Report be now received. Mr. Gough then moved, seconded by Mr. C. Wilson, that the Militia Bill be engrossed, and read a third time to-morrow, which was ordered accordingly.

Read for the second time, the Bill to repeal part of an Act passed in the thirty-fourth of the King, to regulate the practice of the Courts of Justice. Mr. Mallory then moved, seconded by Mr. Rogers, that this House do now resolve itself into a Committee, to take into consideration the Bill to repeal a part of the thirty-fourth of the King, and to make further provision for the same. The House accordingly resolved itself into a Committee. Mr. Speaker left the Chair. Mr. McNabb was called to the Chair of the Committee.

Mr. Speaker resumed the Chair, and Mr. McNabb reported that the Committee had made a progress, and had directed him to ask for leave to sit again to-morrow. Ordered, that the Committee have leave to sit again to-morrow.

Read for the second time, the Bill to repeal the School Act. Mr. Willcocks then moved, seconded by Mr. Dorland, that the Bill for repealing the School Law be read a second time to-morrow, which was ordered accordingly.

Read for the second time the Bill to repeal part of an Act which regulates the practice of the Court of King's Bench. Mr. McLean then moved, seconded by Mr. Gough, that the House do now resolve itself into a Committee, to take into consideration the Bill intituled "An Act to repeal part of an Act passed in the thirty-seventh year of His Majesty's Reign, intituled 'An Act for regulating the practice of the Court of King's Bench.'" The House accordingly resolved itself into a Committee. Mr. Speaker left the Chair. Mr. Rogers was called to the Chair of the Committee.

Mr. Speaker resumed the Chair, and Mr. Rogers reported that the Committee had gone through the consideration of the Bill without any amendments, which he was directed to report whenever the House should be pleased to receive the same. On Mr. Speaker having put the question, shall the report be now received? a division thereupon took place. The names being called for, they were taken down, and are as follows:—

Yeas.	Nays.
MESSRS. McNABB	MESSRS. MARKLE
BURRITT	MARSH
FRASER	CASEY
GOUGH	JOHN WILSON
McLEAN	HOWARD
STINSON	MALLORY
C. WILLSON	WILLCOCKS
LEWIS	ROGERS
BABY	ELLIOTT
DORLAND	SECORD
	SOVEREIGN

So it passed in the negative by a majority of one, and the Report was accordingly rejected.

Mr. Willcocks moved, seconded by Mr. Rogers, that the House do now resolve itself into a Committee, to take into consideration the expediency of an Address to His Excellency, the Lieutenant-Governor, upon the necessity of holding two Circuits in the year, in each and every District of this Province. The House accordingly resolved itself into a Committee, to take into consideration the same. Mr. Speaker left the Chair. Mr. Gough was called to the Chair of the Committee.

Mr. Speaker resumed the Chair, and Mr. Gough reported that it is the opinion, of this Committee that it be necessary and expedient to present an Address to His Excellency, the Lieutenant-Governor, praying that His Excellency will be pleased to direct that two circuits may be holden in the year, in each and every District of this Province; which he was directed to report whenever the House should be pleased to receive the same.   Ordered, that the report be now received.

Mr. Willcocks then moved, seconded by Mr. Rogers, that Messrs. Mallory and Casey be a Committee to draft an Address to His Excellency, the Lieutenant-Governor upon the expediency of His Excellency's directing two Circuits to be holden in the year in each and every District of this Province, which was ordered accordingly.

Mr. Gough moved, seconded by Captain Fraser, that the House do now resolve itself into a Committee, to take the Appropriation Bill into consideration. The House accordingly resolved itself into a Committee, to take the said Bill into consideration. Mr. Speaker left the Chair. Mr. John Wilson was called to the Chair of the Committee.

Mr. Speaker resumed the Chair, and Mr. Wilson reported that the Committee had gone through the consideration of the said Bill, to which they had made an amendment, which he was directed to report to the House whenever it should be pleased to receive the same.   Ordered, that the Report be now received.

Mr. Gough then moved, seconded by Captain Elliott, that the Appropriation Bill be engrossed, and read a third time to-morrow, which was ordered accordingly.

Read for the first time, a Bill for the purpose of making ineligible to a seat in this House any person or persons who shall hold, sustain, or enjoy any office, place, or appointment of profit or emolument, in and by virtue of any commission derived immediately from His Majesty, or of any commission derived from His Excellency, the Lieutenant-Governor, or person administering the Government of this Province, Registrars of Counties only excepted.   Mr. Willcocks then moved, seconded by Mr. Mallory, that the Bill for preventing Officers of Government from being eligible to a seat in the House of Assembly be read a second time on Monday next. On Mr. Speaker having put the question, a division thereupon took place. The names being called for, they were taken down, and are as follows:—

Yeas.	Nays.
MESSRS. McLEAN	MESSRS. McNABB
GOUGH	BURRITT
MALLORY	FRASER
WILLCOCKS	MARSH
ROGERS	MARKLE
HOWARD	J. WILSON
	CASEY
	SOVEREIGN
	STINSON
	C. WILLSON
	SECORD
	ELLIOTT
	BABY
	LEWIS
	DORLAND

Carried in the negative by a majority of nine.

Mr. Howard moved, seconded by Captain Elliott, that so much of the Order of the Day as respects the Physic and Surgery Bill be dispensed with, and that it be on the Order of the Day for Saturday next. Ordered accordingly.

Read for the second time, the Bill to form Grenville and Dundas Counties into a separate District. Mr. Burritt then moved, seconded by Captain Fraser, that the House now resolve itself into a Committee, to go into consideration of the Bill for the division of the District of Johnstown and the Eastern District. The House accordingly resolved itself into a Committee, to take the said Bill into consideration. Mr. Speaker left the Chair. Mr. Lewis was called to the Chair of the Committee.

Mr. Speaker resumed the Chair, and Mr. Lewis reported that the Committee had made a progress, and had directed him to ask for leave to sit again this day three months. Ordered, that the Committee have leave to sit again on this day three months.

Read for the first time, a Bill to repeal an Act for regulating the Practice of the Court of King's Bench, and to make further provision for the same.

Mr. McLean then moved, seconded by Captain Fraser, that the Bill intituled "An Act to repeal part of an Act passed in the thirty-eighth year of His present Majesty, intituled 'An Act to amend part of an Act passed in the thirty-fourth year of His Majesty's Reign, intituled 'An Act to establish a Superior Court of Civil and Criminal Jurisdiction, and to regulate the Court of Appeals, and also to amend and repeal part of an Act passed in the thirty-seventh year of His Majesty's Reign, intituled 'An Act for regulating the Practice of the Court of King's Bench,' and to make further provision respecting the same," be read a second time on Friday next, which was ordered accordingly.

Read for the first time, the Bill for altering the construction of Mill-dams.

Mr. McNabb then moved, seconded by Mr. C. Willson, that the Bill for altering the construction of Mill-dams be read a second time on Friday next, which was ordered accordingly.

Mr. Burritt moved, seconded by Mr. McNabb, for leave to bring in a Bill on Monday next for the purpose of holding Quarter Sessions, the District Courts, alternately at the Town of Johnstown, in the County of Grenville, and in the Township of Elizabethtown in the County of Leeds, in the District of Johnstown. Leave was accordingly granted.

Mr. Rogers, one of the messengers appointed to wait upon His Excellency, the Lieutenant-Governor, with the Address of this House, respecting the Militia Fines, reported that they had accordingly waited upon His Excellency with the said Address, to which His Excellency had been pleased to make the following answer.

Gentlemen of the House of Assembly:—

I shall at all times be ready to pay every attention to the representation of the House of Assembly, of abuses that may exist, which properly come within their cognizance.

12th, February, 1811.

Mr. Willcocks moved, seconded by Mr. Rogers, for leave to bring in a Bill, on Tuesday next, to extend the jurisdiction of the Court of Requests. Leave was accordingly granted.

On motion of Mr. Willcocks, seconded by Mr. Mallory, the House adjourned.

Thursday, 14th February, 1811.

Prayers were read.

Read for the first time, the Assessment Bill.

Mr. Howard then moved, seconded by Mr. Willcocks, that the Assessment Bill be read a second time to-morrow, which was ordered accordingly.

Read for the second time, the Bill to prevent Charge and Expense at Elections.

Mr. Howard again moved, seconded by Mr. Willcocks, that the House do now resolve itself into a Committee, to take into consideration the Election Bill. The House accordingly resolved itself into a Committee. Mr. Speaker left the Chair. Mr. Willcocks was called to the Chair of the Committee.

Mr. Speaker resumed the Chair, and Mr. Willcocks reported that the Committee had made a progress, and directed him to ask for leave to sit again this day. Leave was accordingly granted for the Committee to sit again this day.

A Message from the Honorable the Legislative Council, by Mr. Baldwin, Master in Chancery:—

Mr. Speaker,—

I am commanded by the Honorable the Legislative Council to acquaint this House that it has passed an Act, intituled "An Act to provide for obtaining the benefit of the process of outlawry in Civil Actions within this Province," to which they request the concurrence of this House in passing the same.

And then he withdrew.

. Read for the first time, the Bill to provide for obtaining the benefit of the process of outlawry in Civil Actions within this Province. Mr. McBean then moved, seconded by Mr. Baby, that the Outlawry Bill be read a second time to-morrow, which was ordered accordingly.

Agreeably to leave given, the House again resolved itself into a Committee, to go into the further consideration of the Bill to prevent Charge and Expense at Elections. Mr. Speaker left the Chair. Mr. Willcocks again took the Chair of the Committee.

Mr. Speaker resumed the Chair, and Mr. Willcocks reported that the Committee had gone through the consideration of the said Bill to which they had made several amendments, which amendments he was directed to report to the House whenever it should be pleased to receive the same.

On Mr. Speaker having put the question, shall the Report be now received? a division thereupon took place. The names being called for, they were taken down, and are as follows:—

Yeas.	Nays.
MESSRS. BURRITT	˙MESSRS. FRASER
MARSH	BABY
GOUGH	McLEAN
CASEY	SOVEREIGN
HOWARD	ELLIOTT
JOHN WILSON	LEWIS
STINSON	
MALLORY	
WILLCOCKS	
ROGERS	
C. WILLSON	
DORLAND	
SECORD	

Carried in the affirmative by a majority of seven, and the said Report was accordingly received.

Mr. Howard then moved, seconded by Mr. Rogers, that the Bill to prevent bribery at Elections be engrossed, and read a third time to-morrow, which was ordered accordingly.

Read for the third time, as engrossed, the Bill to repeal an Act allowing the Adjutant General of this Province a Salary.

Mr. Willcocks then moved, seconded by Mr. Rogers, that the Adjutant General's Bill do now pass, and that the title be "An Act to repeal an Act, passed in the forty-eighth year of His Majesty's Reign, intituled 'An Act for granting to His Majesty an annual sum of money for the purposes therein mentioned.' "

On Mr. Speaker having put the question, shall the Bill now pass? a division thereupon took place. The names being called for they were taken down, and are as follows:—

Yeas.	Nays.
MESSRS. MARSH	MESSRS. FRASER
CASEY	BURRITT
JOHN WILSON	BABY
HOWARD	GOUGH
STINSON	ELLIOTT
MALLORY	C. WILLSON
SOVEREIGN	McLEAN
WILLCOCKS	
ROGERS	
LEWIS	
DORLAND	
SECORD	
McNABB	

Carried in the affirmative by a majority of six. The Bill accordingly passed, and was signed by the Speaker.

Mr. Mallory, seconded by Mr. Rogers, then moved that Messrs. Sovereign and Willcocks be appointed to carry up the Bill to reduce the Salary of the Adjutant General to the Honorable the Legislative Council and request their concurrence in passing the same, which was ordered accordingly.

Agreeably to the order of the Day, the House resolved itself into a Committee, to go into the further consideration of the Bill to repeal part of an Act passed in the thirty-fourth of the King, and to make further provision for the same. Mr. Speaker left the Chair. Mr. McNabb took the Chair of the Committee.

Mr. Speaker resumed the Chair, and Mr. McNabb reported that the Committee had made a progress, and had directed him to ask for leave to sit again on Monday next. Leave was accordingly granted to sit again on Monday next.

Read for the third time, as engrossed, the Bill to amend the Militia Law. On motion of Mr. Gough, seconded by Mr. Sovereign, resolved, that the Bill do pass, and that the title be "An Act to amend an Act passed in the forty-eighth year of His Majesty's Reign, intituled 'An Act to explain, amend, and reduce to one Act the several laws now in force for the raising and training the Militia of this Province.'" The Bill then passed and was signed by the Speaker.

Mr. Gough again moved, seconded by Mr. Mallory, that Messrs. Dorland and Casey be appointed to carry up the Bill to amend the Militia Laws to the Legislative Council, and request their concurrence thereto, which was ordered accordingly.

Read for the second time, the Bill to repeal the School Act. Mr. Willcocks then moved, seconded by Mr. Rogers, that this House do on to-morrow resolve itself into a Committee, to take into consideration the School Bill, which was ordered accordingly.

Read for the first time, the Bill to lay an additional duty upon Hawkers and Pedlars. Mr. McNabb then moved, seconded by Mr. Fraser, that the Hawker and Pedlar Bill be read a second time on Saturday next, which was ordered accordingly.

Read for the third time, as engrossed, the Appropriation Bill. On motion of Mr. Gough, seconded by Capt. Elliott, resolved, that the Bill do now pass, and that the title be "An Act for applying a certain sum of money therein mentioned to make good moneys issued and advanced by His Majesty, through the Lieutenant-Governor, in pursuance of an Address of this House." The Bill then passed, and was signed by the Speaker.

Mr. Gough again moved, seconded by Capt. Elliott, that Messrs. Dorland and Casey do carry up the Appropriation Bill to the Legislative Council, and request their concurrence thereto, which was ordered accordingly.

Mr. John Wilson moved, seconded by Mr. Burritt, that the petition of sundry inhabitants of the Home and Niagara Districts be now read.

The said petition was then read, and is as follows:—

To the Commons House of Assembly of the Province of Upper Canada, in Provincial Parliament.

The Petition of the Inhabitants of the Townships of Trafalgar, Nelson, Flamboro', Beverley, Blocks Nos. 1, 2, and 3 on the Grand River, County of Haldimand; Ancaster, Glanford, Barton and Saltfleet,

Humbly Showeth,— •

That Your Petitioners, having sent forth Petitions to Your Honorable House the last Session, praying a division of the District of Niagara and the Home District, that a new District might be created, and the Town Plot reserved at the head of the water communication of Coot's Paradise under the administration of Governor Simcoe, might be appropriate for the County Town.

That the same passed Your Honorable House; but from the circumstance of certain regulations of the Honorable the Legislative Council not having been at that time complied with, through ignorance in Your Petitioners, the Bill was not passed in the Council; but, as Your Petitioners now conceive the regulations have been complied with, they again come forward as last year.

Wherefore Your Petitioners pray Your Honorable House to take their case again into consideration, and that Your Honorable House will revive the Bill passed last Session, and that the Town Plot reserved at the head of the water communication may again be named for the County Town, and the subscriptions annexed to the petitions last year are still continued.

And Your Petitioners, in duty bound, will ever pray.

Daniel Morden, Solomon Mills, Henry Haiffman, Moses Morden, John Flees, John Will, and seven hundred and ten other Petitioners.

Mr. John Wilson then moved, seconded by Mr. Willcocks, for leave to bring in a Bill on Monday next, to form part of the Niagara and Home Districts into a separate District. Leave was accordingly granted.

Mr. Mallory moved, seconded by Mr. Willcocks, for leave to bring in a Bill, on Wednesday next, to better regulate Tavern Licenses throughout this Province. Accordingly leave was granted.

Mr. McLean moved, seconded by Mr. Gough, that the petition of sundry inhabitants of this Province, relative to boundaries of land, be now read. The said petition was then read, and is as follows:—

To the Honorable the Legislative Council and the Commons of the House of Assembly, in Provincial Parliament assembled.

The Petition of Sundry Inhabitants of this Province, most humbly sheweth,

That We, His Majesty's most dutiful and loyal subjects, believing it would be conducive to great advantage, and to the furtherance of peace and prosperity of His Majesty's subjects in this Province, the settlement and establishment of the boundary lines (enclosing the Townships) without any alteration of their original courses. For this end, therefore, Your Petitioners express satisfaction for what was brought forward last winter, intituled "An Act concerning Land Surveyors, and the admeasurement of land, and for the better and more exactly ascertaining the boundaries of lands in this Province." Your Petitioners, therefore, humbly request that this Bill may be established into a law, believing it is founded on justice, equity and would be conducive of a most general settlement, not only of the Township of Kingston, but of the Province at large, that all Licensed Surveyors, in running out the limits or division lines, shall cause this survey to coincide and agree with the boundary lines of the Townships and Concessions so ascertained and established; and the lines so ascertained and established, according to the Bill alluded to, may be firm and permanent. Your petitioners, therefore, believing this would establish peace and order, leave it to impartial consideration, and, as in duty bound, will ever pray, and for the prosperity of Government.

Done at Kingston, the 10th January, 1811.

Jervis Worden, John Brewer, Daniel Ferris, Samuel Ryder, and fifty-nine others.

Mr. Gough moved, seconded by Mr. Howard, for leave to bring in a Bill, on Saturday next, for more clearly ascertaining the boundaries of lands in this Province. Leave was accordingly granted.

Mr. Rogers, seconded by Mr. Willcocks, moved for leave to bring in a Bill, to-morrow, to obviate certain doubts which have arisen in the practice of the Court of King's Bench in this Province. Leave was granted accordingly.

Mr. Mallory, one of the Committee named to draft an Address to His Excellency the Lieutenant-Governor, upon the expediency of His Excellency's directing two circuits to be holden in the year in each and every District of this Province, reported that the Committee had drafted an Address accordingly, which he was directed to submit to the House whenever it should be pleased to receive the same. Ordered, that the Report be now received.

And he read the Report in his place, and then delivered in the same at the Table, where it was again read by the Clerk, and is as follows:—

To His Excellency Francis Gore, Esquire, Lieutenant-Governor of the Province of Upper Canada, &c., &c., &c.

May it please Your Excellency:

We, His Majesty's most dutiful and loyal subjects, the Commons of Upper Canada, in Parliament assembled, viewing with peculiar satisfaction the increased and increasing population and prosperity of this Province in general, and not insensible to the vast importance attached to the speedy administration of justice to all classes of His Majesty's Subjects, in every District thereof, beg leave humbly to represent to Your Excellency our full conviction that it would tend in a large degree to promote the Public welfare were two Circuits to be holden yearly in each and every District within this Province.

We therefore request Your Excellency will be pleased, pursuant to the powers and authority with which Your Excellency is invested, in and by an Act of this Province, passed in the thirty-fourth year of His Majesty's Reign, intituled "An Act to establish a Superior Court of Civil and Criminal Jurisdiction, and to regulate the Court of Appeal," to order and direct Commissioners of Assize and Nisi Prius and Oyer and Terminer, to issue unto each and every District in this Province, twice in every year.

Mr. Willcocks then moved, seconded by Capt. Elliott, that this House do now resolve itself into a Committee, to take into consideration the Address to His Excellency the Lieutenant-Governor, upon the subject of two Circuits to be holden in the year in each and every District of this Province. The House accordingly resolved itself into a Committee. Mr. Speaker left the Chair. Mr. Secord was called to the chair of the Committee.

Mr. Speaker resumed the Chair, and Mr. Secord reported that the Committee had made a progress, and had directed him to ask for leave to sit again this day three months. Leave was accordingly granted to sit again this day three months.

On motion of Capt. Elliott, seconded by Mr. Baby, the House adjourned.

Friday, 15th February, 1811.

Prayers were read.

Read for the second time, the Bill to alter the construction of Mill-dams.

The Clerk of this House has the honor respectfully to acquaint Mr. Speaker and the House that the Clerks of the Peace of the different Districts of this Province did send him returns of all the rateable property in their respective Districts, in compliance with the tenth section of the Act for the more uniform laying of

28 A.

Assessments and Rates throughout this Province. Mr. Speaker then ordered the different returns received from the Clerks of the Peace to be laid on the Table, and to be entered in a book to be of record in this House.

Mr. McNabb moved, seconded by Mr. Dorland, that this House do now resolve itself into a Committee, to take into consideration the Mill-dam Bill. The House accordingly resolved itself into a Committee. Mr. Speaker left the Chair. Mr. C. Willson was called to the chair of the Committee.

Mr. Speaker resumed the Chair, and Mr. C. Willson reported that the Committee had made a progress, and had directed him to ask for leave to sit again on Monday next. Leave was accordingly granted to sit again on Monday next.

Messrs. Sovereign and Willcocks, the messengers ordered to carry up to the Honorable the Legislative Council an Act intituled " An Act to repeal an Act passed in the forty-eighth year of His Majesty's Reign, intituled ' An Act for granting to His Majesty an annual sum of money for the purposes therein mentioned,' " reported that they had carried up the said Act, and did request their concurrence in passing the same.

Mr. Dorland, one of the messengers ordered to carry up to the Honorable the Legislative Council the Act intituled " An Act to amend an Act passed in the forty-eighth year of His Majesty's Reign, intituled ' An Act to explain, amend, and reduce into one Act the several laws now in force for the raising and training the Militia of this Province.' "

And also an Act intituled " An Act for applying a certain sum of money therein mentioned, to make good certain moneys issued and advanced by His Majesty, through the Lieutenant-Governor, in pursuance of an Address of this House,' " reported that they had carried up the said Acts, to which Acts they had requested the concurrence of the Legislative Council in passing the same.

Mr. Rogers, seconded by Mr. Willcocks, moved that this House do now resolve itself into a Committee, to take into their consideration the Lieutenant-Governor's answer to the Address of this House, requesting the Accounts of the Militia Fines received and paid under the authority of the laws now in force in this Province. On Mr. Speaker having put the question for the House to resolve itself into a Committee, a division thereupon took place. The names being called for they were taken down and are as follows :—

Yeas.	Nays.
MESSRS. CASEY	MESSRS. McNABB
JOHN WILSON	BURRITT
HOWARD	FRASER
SOVEREIGN	BABY
WILLCOCKS	MARSH
MALLORY	GOUGH
ROGERS	McLEAN
SECORD	ELLIOTT
DORLAND	C. WILLSON
STINSON	LEWIS

The House being divided:—

Mr. Speaker gave the casting vote for the House not to resolve itself into a Committee to take into consideration His Excellency the Lieutenant-Governor's answer.

Mr. Gough moved, seconded by Mr. Secord, that so much of the Order of the Day, as respects the second reading of the Bill to repeal part of an Act passed in the thirty-seventh year of His present Majesty's Reign, for regulating the practice of the Court of King's Bench, be dispensed with; and that it be on the Order of the Day for to-morrow, which was ordered accordingly.

Read for the second time, the Assessment Bill. ·Mr. Howard then moved, seconded by Mr Mallory, that the House do now resolve itself into a Committee, to take into consideration the Assessment Bill. The House accordingly resolved itself into a Committee. Mr. Speaker left the Chair. Mr. Mallory was called to the Chair of the Committee.

Mr. Speaker resumed the Chair, and Mr. Mallory reported that the Committee had made a progress, and had directed him to ask for leave to sit again to-morrow. Leave was accordingly granted for the Committee to sit again to-morrow.

Read for the second time, the Bill to provide for obtaining the benefits of the process of outlawry in Civil Actions within this Province. Mr. McLean then moved, seconded by Mr. Gough, that the House do now resolve itself into a committee, to take into their consideration a Bill intituled "An Act to provide for obtaining the benefits of .the process of outlawry in Civil Suits within this Province." The House accordingly resolved itself into a Committee. Mr. Speaker left the Chair. Capt. Fraser was called to the chair of the Committee.

Mr. Speaker resumed the Chair, and Capt. Fraser reported that the Committee had made a progress, and had directed him to ask for leave to sit again to-morrow. Leave was accordingly granted for the Committee to sit again to-morrow.

Read for the third time, as engrossed, the Bill to prevent Charge and Expense at Elections. On motion of Mr. Howard, seconded by Mr. Rogers, resolved, that the Bill do now pass, and that the title be "An Act to prevent Charge and Expense at Elections of Members to serve in the House of Assembly in this Province." The Bill accordingly passed, and was signed by the Speaker. Mr. Mallory moved, seconded by Capt. Fraser, that Messrs. Howard and Marsh do carry up to the Honorable the Legislative Council the Bill to prevent Charge and Expense at Elections, and request their concurrence thereto, which was ordered accordingly.

Agreeably to the Order of the Day the House resolved itself into a Committee, to go into the consideration of the Bill to repeal the School Act. Mr. Speaker left the Chair. Mr. Sovereign was called to the chair of the Committee.

Mr. Speaker resumed the Chair, and Mr. Sovereign reported that the Committee had gone through the consideration of the said Bill without any amendment, which he was directed to report whenever the House should be pleased to receive the same. On Mr. Speaker having put the question, shall the Report be now received? A division thereupon took place. The names being called for they were taken down and are as follows:—

Yeas.	Nays.
MESSRS. MARSH	MESSRS. BURRITT
DORLAND	FRASER
GOUGH	McLEAN
CASEY	BABY
JOHN WILSON	ELLIOTT
HOWARD	
MALLORY	
WILLCOCKS	
ROGERS	
STINSON	
SECORD	
LEWIS	
SOVEREIGN	
C. WILLSON ·	

Carried in the affirmative by a majority of nine, and the Report was accordingly received. Mr. Willcocks then moved, seconded by Mr. Rogers, that the School Bill be engrossed, and read a third time to-morrow. Ordered accordingly.

Read for the first time, the Bill to obviate doubts which have arisen in the Court of King's Bench. Mr. Rogers then moved, seconded by Mr. Dorland, that the Bill for obviating certain doubts that have arisen in the practice of the Court of King's Bench, be read a second time to-morrow, which was ordered accordingly.

Read for the first time, the Bill to repeal the laws and ordinances of the Province of Quebec. Mr. Mallory then moved, seconded by Mr. Willcocks, that the Bill to repeal the laws and ordinances of the Province of Quebec, now in force in this Province, be read a second time on Monday next. Ordered accordingly.

Mr. Dorland moved, seconded by Mr. Rogers, for leave to bring up a petition from the inhabitants of the Midland District. Leave was accordingly granted, and the said petition ordered to lie upon the Table.

Mr. Mallory moved, seconded by Mr. McLean, for leave to bring up the petition of the inhabitants of Trafalgar, Nelson, Flamboro, East and West, Beverley, Barton, Ancaster, Blocks Nos. 1, 2, and 3, County of Haldimand, Dundas, and other Townships. Leave was accordingly granted, and the said petition was ordered to lie upon the Table.

On motion of Capt. Elliott, seconded by Mr. Secord, the House adjourned.

Saturday, 16th February, 1811.

Prayers were read.

Agreeably to the Order of the Day the House resolved itself into a Committee, to go into the further consideration of the Bill to continue the Provisional agreement with Lower Canada. Mr. Speaker left the Chair. Mr. Burritt took the chair of the Committee.

Mr. Speaker resumed the Chair, and Mr. Burritt reported that the Committee had made a progress, and had directed him to ask for leave to sit again on Thursday next. Leave was accordingly granted to sit again on Thursday next.

Read for the first time, the Bill for the more regular Practice of Physic and Surgery in this Province. Mr. Howard then moved, seconded by Mr. Dorland, that the Physic and Surgery Bill be read a second time on Saturday next, which was ordered accordingly.

Read for the first time, A Bill respecting Land Surveyors, and the Admeasurement of Land in this Province. Mr. Gough then moved, seconded by Mr. Secord, that the Bill for ascertaining the boundary lines of land be read a second time on Wednesday next, which was ordered accordingly.

Mr. McLean moved, seconded by Mr. Stinson, that so much of the Order of the Day as relates to the going into Committee on the Bill relative to the Practice of the Court of King's Bench, be discharged, and that the same be on the Order of the Day for Monday. Ordered accordingly.

On the Order of the Day being read for the House to resolve itself into a Committee to go into the consideration of the Assessment Bill. Mr. Howard moved, seconded by Mr. Willcocks, that the Order of the Day, so far as it respects the Assessment Bill, be discharged. Mr. Mallory, seconded by Mr. C. Willson, moved in amendment, that all the words of Mr. Howard's motion after "Willcocks" be struck out, and the following substituted. "That the House will resolve itself into a Committee to go into the consideration of the Assessment Bill on Thursday next." The House divided upon the question, and the names were taken down as follows:—

Yeas.	Nays.
MESSRS. McNABB	MESSRS. JOHN WILSON
BURRITT	HOWARD
MARSH	WILLCOCKS
McLEAN	ROGERS
GOUGH	CASEY
C. WILLSON	
FRASER	
ELLIOTT	
SECORD	
LEWIS	
DORLAND	
BABY	
STINSON	
MALLORY	
SOVEREIGN	

Carried in the affirmative by a majority of ten.

The main question was then put, which passed in the negative.

Agreeably to the Order of the day, the House resolved itself into a Committee, to go into the consideration of the Bill for obtaining the Process of Outlawry.

Mr. Speaker left the Chair.

Capt. Fraser took the chair of the Committee.

Mr. Speaker resumed the Chair.

And Capt. Fraser reported that the Committee had made a progress, and had directed him to ask for leave to sit again on Monday next.

Leave was accordingly granted for the Committee to sit again on Monday next.

Read for the second time, the Bill for obviating certain doubts which have arisen in the Practice of the Court of King's Bench.

Mr. Rogers then moved, seconded by Mr. Dorland, that the House do now resolve itself into a Committee, to take into consideration the Bill to obviate certain doubts which have arisen in the Practice of the Court of King's Bench, in this Province.

The House accordingly resolved itself into a Committee.

Mr. Speaker left the Chair.

Mr. Burritt was called to the chair of the Committee.

Mr. Speaker resumed the Chair.

And Mr. Burritt reported that the Committee had gone through the consideration of the said Bill, without any amendment, which he was directed to report whenever the House should be pleased to receive the same.

Ordered, That the Report be now received.

Mr. Rogers moved, seconded by Mr. Burritt, that the Bill for obviating certain doubts which have arisen in the Practice of the Court of King's Bench, be engrossed, and read a third time on Monday next.

Which was ordered accordingly.

Read for the second time, the Bill to continue the Act laying an additional duty on Hawkers and Pedlars.

Mr. McNabb then moved, seconded by Mr. Burritt, that the House do now resolve itself into a Committee, to take into consideration the Hawkers' and Pedlars' Bill.

The House accordingly resolved itself into a Committee.

Mr. Speaker left the Chair. Mr. Howard was called to the Chair of the Committee.

Mr. Speaker resumed the Chair. and Mr. Howard reported that the Committee had made a progress, and had directed him to ask for leave to sit again on Monday next. Leave was accordingly granted to sit again on Monday next.

Mr. Mallory moved, seconded by Mr. C. Willson, for leave to bring in a Bill, on Tuesday next, to amend and explain an Act passed in the thirty-eighth year of His Majesty's Reign, to establish a Court of Civil and Criminal jurisdiction, and to regulate the Court of Appeal. Accordingly leave was granted.

On motion of Mr. McLean, seconded by Mr. Dorland, the House adjourned to Monday next, at eleven o'clock in the forenoon.

Monday, 18th February, 1811.

Prayers were read.

Agreeably to the Order of the Day, the House resolved itself into a Committee, to go into the further consideration of the Bill to repeal part of the Act passed in the thirty-fourth year of His Majesty's Reign, and to make further provision for the same. Mr. Speaker left the Chair. Mr. McNabb took the chair of the Committee.

Mr. Speaker resumed the Chair, and Mr. McNabb reported that the Committee had made a progress, and had directed him to ask for leave to sit again this day. Leave was accordingly granted for the Committee to sit again this day.

Mr. Gough moved, seconded by Mr. Rogers, that Mr. McGregor, one of the defaulters at the call of this House, having appeared in his place and made an excuse to the satisfaction of the House, be discharged from the custody of the Serjeant at Arms without paying fees. The House accordingly ordered the same.

Agreeably to leave given, the House again resolved itself into a Committee, to go into the further consideration of the Bill to repeal part of an Act passed in the thirty-fourth of the King. Mr. Speaker left the Chair. Mr. McNabb took the chair of the Committee.

Mr. Speaker resumed the Chair, and Mr. McNabb reported that the Committee had made a progress, and had directed him to ask for leave to sit again on Wednesday next. Leave was accordingly granted for the Committee to sit again on Wednesday next.

Read for the first time, the Bill for holding the Courts alternately in the Towns of Johnstown and Elizabethtown. Mr. Burritt then moved, seconded by Mr. McNabb that the Bill for holding the Courts alternately in the District of Johnstown be read a second time to-morrow, which was ordered accordingly.

Read for the first time, the Bill to form a new District out of the Home and Niagara Districts. Mr. John Willson then moved, seconded by Mr. Lewis, that the Bill for forming a new District be read a second time on Wednesday next, which was ordered accordingly.

Read for the third time, as engrossed, the Bill to repeal the School Act. Mr. Willcocks then moved, seconded by Mr. Sovereign, that the School Bill do now pass, and that the title be, "An Act to repeal part of an Act passed in the forty-eighth year of His Majesty's Reign intituled 'An Act to amend an Act passed in the forty-seventh year of His Majesty's Reign, intituled 'An Act to establish Public Schools in each and every District of this Province.' " The House divided upon the question, and the names were taken down as follows:—

Yeas	Nays
MESSRS. DORLAND	MESSRS. McNABB
GOUGH	BURRITT
MARSH	FRASER
STINSON	McLEAN
CASEY	McGREGOR
JOHN WILLSON	BABY
HOWARD	ELLIOTT
MALLORY	
C. WILLSON	
WILLCOCKS	
ROGERS	
SECORD	
LEWIS	
SOVEREIGN	

Carried in the affirmative by a majority of seven. The Bill then passed, and was signed by the Speaker.

A message from the Honorable the Legislative Council by Mr. Baldwin, Master in Chancery.

Mr. Speaker,

I am commanded by the Honorable the Legislative Council to inform this House that they have passed an Act sent up from this House, intituled "An Act for applying a certain sum of money therein mentioned to make good certain moneys issued and advanced by His Majesty through the Lieutenant Governor in pursuance of an Address of this House," without any amendment.

And then he withdrew.

Mr. Howard, one of the messengers named to carry up to the Honorable the Legislative Council an Act intituled "An Act for preventing Charge and

Expense at Elections of Members to serve in the House of Assembly in this Province," reported that they had carried up the said Act, and did request their concurrence in passing the same.

Mr. Rogers moved, seconded by Mr. Mallory, that Messrs. Dorland and Stinson do carry up to the Hon. the Legislative Council the Act intituled "An Act to repeal part of an Act passed in the forty-eighth year of His Majesty's Reign, intituled 'An Act to amend an Act passed in the forty-seventh year of His Majesty's Reign, intituled 'An Act to establish Public Schools in each and every District of this Province,' " and request their concurrence thereto. Ordered accordingly.

Read for the second time, the Bill to repeal the laws and ordinances of the Province of Quebec. Mr. Mallory then moved, seconded by Mr. Stinson, that the House do now resolve itself into a Committee, to take into consideration the Bill to repeal the laws and ordinances of the Province of Quebec now in force in this Province. The House accordingly resolved itself into a Committee. Mr. Speaker left the Chair. Mr. Dorland was called to the chair of the Committee.

Mr. Speaker resumed the Chair, and Mr. Dorland reported that the Committee had made a progress, and had directed him to ask for leave to sit again to-morrow. Leave was accordingly granted.

Agreeably to the Order of the Day, the House resolved itself into a Committee, to take into consideration the Bill for obtaining the benefits of the Process of Outlawry in Civil Actions within this Province. Mr. Speaker left the Chair. Capt. Fraser took the chair of the Committee.

Mr. Speaker resumed the Chair, and Capt. Fraser reported that the Committee had made a progress, and had directed him to ask for leave to sit again on Wednesday next. Leave was granted for the Committee to sit again on Wednesday next.

Read for the third time, as engrossed, the Bill for obviating certain doubts in the Court of King's Bench.

On motion of Mr. Rogers, seconded by Mr. Gough, resolved, that the Bill do now pass, and that the title be "An Act to obviate certain doubts which have arisen in the Court of King's Bench in this Province." The Bill then passed, and was signed by the Speaker.

Agreeably to the Order of the Day, the House resolved itself into a Committee, to go into the consideration of the Bill to continue the Act laying a duty upon Hawkers and Pedlars, and to make further provision for the same. Mr. Speaker left the Chair. Mr. Howard was called to the chair of the Committee.

Mr. Speaker resumed the Chair, and Mr. Howard reported that the Committee had made a progress, and had directed him to ask for leave to sit again to-morrow. Leave was accordingly granted for the Committee to sit again to-morrow.

Mr. Mallory moved, seconded by Mr. Secord, that Messrs. Rogers and Casey do carry up to the Honorable the Legislative Council the Act intituled "An Act to obviate certain doubts which have arisen in the practice of the Court of King's Bench in this Province," and to request their concurrence thereto. Which was ordered accordingly.

Mr. McLean moved, seconded by Mr. Gough, for leave to bring in a Bill to-morrow, to amend an Act passed in the thirty-fifth year of His Majesty's Reign, intituled "An Act for the Public Registering of Deeds, Conveyances, Wills and other incumbrances which shall or may affect any Lands, Tenements, or Hereditaments within this Province. Leave was accordingly granted.

On motion of Mr. Gough, seconded by Mr. Elliott, the House adjourned.

Tuesday, 19th February, 1811.

Prayers were read.

Read for the second time, the Bill for holding Courts alternately in the Towns of Johnstown and Elizabethtown. Mr. Burritt then moved, seconded by Mr. McNabb, that the House do now resolve itself into a Committee, to take into consideration the Bill for holding Courts alternately in the District of Johnstown. The House accordingly resolved itself into a Committee. Mr. Speaker left the Chair. Mr. McNabb was called to the chair of the Committee.

Mr. Speaker resumed the Chair, and Mr. McNabb reported that the Committee had made some progress, and had directed him to ask for leave to sit again this day three months. Leave was accordingly granted to sit again this day three months.

Read for the first time, The Bill for extending the jurisdiction of the Court of Requests. On motion of Mr. Willcocks, seconded by Mr. Rogers. Ordered, that the said Bill be read a second time on Thursday next.

Mr. Speaker informed the House that application in writing had been made to him by the Clerk of the House, which he read, and is as follows.

Mr. Speaker,

The Clerk respectfully informs the House that the wages now due the Copying Clerks exceeds the sum appropriated by law for that purpose. He therefore prays the permission and sanction of this House to employ Copying Clerks in his Office.

Commons House of Assembly,   (Signed) DONALD McLEAN,
        18th February, 1811.   Clk. Assy.

Agreeably to the Order of the Day the House resolved itself into a Committee, to go into the consideration of the Bill to amend the Assessment Act. Mr. Speaker left the Chair. Mr. Mallory took the chair of the Committee.

Mr. Speaker resumed the Chair, and Mr. Mallory reported that the Committee had made some progress, and had directed him to ask for leave to sit again to-morrow. Leave was accordingly granted for the Committee to sit again to-morrow.

Mr. Gough moved, seconded by Mr. Dorland, for leave to bring in a Bill, on Thursday next, for ascertaining damages on Protested Bills of Exchange, and fixing the rate of interest in this Province. Leave was accordingly granted.

On motion of Mr. McLean, seconded by Mr. Marsh, the House adjourned.

Wednesday, 20th February, 1811.

Prayers were read.

Mr. Rogers, one of the messengers named to carry up to the Honorable the Legislative Council the Act intituled "An Act to obviate certain doubts which have arisen in the practice of the Court of King's Bench in this Province," reported that they had carried up the said Act, and did request their concurrence in passing the same.

Agreeably to the Order of the Day, the House resolved itself into a Committee, to go into the further consideration of the Bill to alter the construction of Mill-dams. Mr. Speaker left the Chair. Mr. C. Willson was called to the chair of the Committee.

Mr. Speaker resumed the Chair, and Mr. C. Willson reported that the Committee had made a progress, and had directed him to ask for leave to sit again on Saturday next. Leave was accordingly granted for the Committee to sit again on Saturday next.

Read for the first time, the Bill to amend an Act passed in the thirty-eighth year of His Majesty's reign, for establishing a Criminal Court of Jurisdiction in this Province. Mr. Mallory then moved, seconded by Mr. Rogers, that the Bill to explain and amend an Act passed in the thirty-eighth year of His Majesty's reign be read a second time to-morrow, which was ordered accordingly.

Agreeably to the Order of the Day, the House resolved itself into a Committee to go into the further consideration of the Bill to continue and amend the Act lay-ing a duty upon Hawkers and Pedlars in this Province. Mr. Speaker left the Chair. Mr. Howard took the chair of the Committee. Mr. Speaker resumed the Chair, and Mr. Howard reported that the Committee had made a progress, and had directed him to ask for leave to sit again this day. Leave was accordingly granted for the Committee to sit again this day.

Mr. Mallory moved, seconded by Mr. Willcocks, that the petition of the inhabitants of Trafalgar, Nelson, Flamboro' (east and west), Saltfleet, Barton, Ancaster, Blocks 1, 2, and 3, County of Haldimand, and other Townships be now read. The said petition was then read, and is as follows:

To the Honorable the House of Assembly of the Province of Upper Canada in Parliament assembled.

The Petition of the Inhabitants of Trafalgar, Nelson, Flamboro' (east and west), Beverley, Blocks 1, 2, and 3, in Haldimand, North West of Dundas Street in the West Riding of the County of York, also in Haldimand, South East of Dundas Street, to a line extended from the East angle of the Gore of Townsend to the South corner of the Townships of Binbrook, Saltfleet, Glanford, Barton and Ancaster in the District of Niagara.

Humbly Sheweth,

That Your Petitioners at present labour under many inconveniences owing to their situations being so remote from those parts of the Districts of York and Niagara where the Courts of Law are held, and other public business of the country transacted; occasioning to Your Petitioners serious loss of time, heavy expenses, and in the instances of barring of dowers much difficulty to their families. Your Petitioners might well enlarge upon this score were they not satisfied that Your Honorable House will at once be aware of them, more particularly when it is considered how populous the several named Townships are, and the necessity that the various local interests of an extensive, growing part of the country, should have more steady and minute attention paid to them than is practicable under existing circumstances. From these considerations Your Petitioners earnestly beg leave to call the attention of Your Honorable House, and to pray that in your wisdom an Act may be passed separating the Townships inhabited by Your Petitioners from the Districts of York and Niagara, and forming them into a new District and County. Your Petitioners have great satisfaction in being able to assure Your Honorable House that from the flourishing state of their parts of the Districts of York and Niagara, and the respectability and known good order of the inhabitants, every means that are requisite for giving immediate force and stability to the proposed new District, and to meet the attendant pecuniary exigencies may be found therein.

While thus addressing Your Honorable House, Your Petitioners cannot forbear recommending to your notice an object of the greatest solicitude, being that Your Honorable House, in the event of a division taking place, will be pleased to select a situation for the County Town, where, both from a present view of the country, and the probability of its progress, it may not hereafter prove ineligible; and where healthfulness and general conveniency abound.

Your Petitioners are informed that situations have been recommended to Your Honorable House as well adapted for the purpose, and Your Petitioners flatter themselves with the hope that if urged with the private motives of individuals any should be proposed that do not embrace the true interests of the country, they may meet with a merited reception. Your Petitioners conceive it will not be deemed unacceptable their accompanying their Petition with a map of the proposed New District, and have marked thereon, for the consideration of Your Honorable House, a spot which they are of opinion is well calculated, not only at present, but with a contemplative view of what may be looked for from the future prosperity of this flourishing settlement; it will be found upon the south side, and near the head of Burlington Bay, viz., Lot Number Fourteen in the Second Concession of the Township of Barton, upon the main Western Road of the Province, and where various country roads concentrate. This spot is peculiar for its natural advantages, the site being handsome and extensive; abounding with fine springs of water, excellent building stone and other materials, firewood, etc.; and within one mile and a quarter of the best harbour in the Bay. Your Petitioners are prepared to assure Your Honorable House that the proprietors of the Lot herein alluded to and the lots adjoining it are ready to appropriate gratuitously sufficient lands upon which to erect Public Buildings, and also to dispose of Thirty acres of land to be laid out in Town lots at the price of Twenty-five Dollars per acre.

Your Petitioners have only further to assure Your Honorable House with the greatest reverence and respect, that, as in duty bound, they will ever pray.

(Signed) Augustus Jones, E. Jones, Isaac Samson, Wm. Davis, Jun'r, John Springstead, Walter Bates, and three hundred and seventy-eight others.

Read for the second time, the Bill concerning Land Surveyors, and the admeasurement and boundaries of Lands in this Province. Mr. Gough then moved, seconded by Mr. Howard, that the House do now resolve itself into a Committee to take into consideration the Bill for better ascertaining the boundaries of lands in this Province. The House accordingly resolved itself into a Committee. Mr. Speaker left the Chair. Mr. John Willson was called to the Chair of the Committee.

Mr. Speaker resumed the Chair, and Mr. John Willson reported that the Committee had made some progress, and directed him to ask for leave to sit again to-morrow. Leave was accordingly granted for the Committee to sit again to-morrow.

Mr. Dorland, one of the Messengers named to carry up to the Honorable Legislative Council the Act intituled "An Act to repeal part of an Act passed in the forty-eighth year of His Majesty's reign, intituled 'An Act to amend an Act passed in the forty-seventh year of His Majesty's Reign, intituled "An Act to establish Public Schools in each and every District of this Province,"'" reported that they had carried up the said Act, and did request their concurrence in passing the same.

Mr. Gough moved, seconded by Mr. Dorland, that the Petition of the Inhabitants of the Midland District be now read.

The said Petition was then read, and is as follows:

To the Honorable the Legislative Council and Commons House of Assembly, in Provincial Parliament assembled.

The Petition of the Inhabitants of the Midland District,

Humbly Sheweth,

That we, His Majesty's most dutiful and loyal subjects, believe it would be to great advantage, and to the peace and prosperity of His Majesty's subjects in this Province, if the settlement and establishment of the boundary lines enclosing the Townships could be without any alteration of their original courses. For that end and intent Your Petitioners express their satisfaction with what was brought forward last winter, intituled "An Act concerning Land Surveyors, and the ascertaining the boundaries, and the admeasurements of lands in this Province."

Your Petitioners, therefore, humbly request that the Act alluded to may be passed into a law, believing that it is founded on justice and equity.

And Your Petitioners, as in duty bound, will ever pray.

(Signed) Simon McNabb, Leonard W. Meyers, Gilbert Harris, George W. Meyers, Stephen Gilbert, Owen Phonlin, and ten other Petitioners.

Read for the first time, the Bill to amend the Act for the Public Registering of Deeds, Conveyances, Wills and other incumbrances which shall be made, or may affect any lands, tenements, or hereditaments within this Province."

Mr. McLean then moved, seconded by Mr. Gough, that the Bill intituled "An Act to amend an Act intituled 'An Act for the Public Registering of Deeds, Conveyances, Wills, and other incumbrances which shall be made or may affect any lands, tenements or hereditaments within this Province,' " be read for the second time on Friday next, which was ordered accordingly.

Agreeably to the Order of the Day the House resolved itself into a Committee to go into the further consideration of the Bill to repeal part of an Act passed in the thirty-fourth year of His Majesty's reign and to make further provision for the same. Mr. Speaker left the Chair. Mr. McNabb took the chair of the Committee.

Mr. Speaker resumed the Chair, and Mr. McNabb reported that the Committee had directed him to ask for leave to sit again on Friday next. Ordered, that the Committee have leave to sit again on Friday next.

Read for the second time, the Bill to form a separate District from part of the Home and Niagara District.

Mr. John Willson then moved, seconded by Mr. Mallory, that this House do, on to-morrow, resolve itself into a Committee to take into consideration the Bill for forming a new District, which was ordered accordingly.

Agreeably to the Order of the Day, the House resolved itself into a Committee to go into the further consideration of the Bill for obtaining the benefits of the process of Outlawry. Mr. Speaker left the Chair. Captain Fraser took the Chair of the Committee.

Mr. Speaker resumed the Chair, and Captain Fraser reported that the Committee had made progress, and had directed him to ask for leave to sit again on Friday next. Leave was accordingly granted.

Agreeably to the Order of the Day the House resolved itself into a Committee to go into the consideration of the Bill to amend the Assessment Act. Mr. Speaker left the Chair. Mr. Mallory took the chair of the Committee.

Mr. Speaker resumed the Chair, and Mr. Mallory reported that the Committee had made a progress, and had directed him to ask for leave to sit again this day. Leave was accordingly granted to sit again this day.

A Message from the Honorable the Legislative Council, by Mr. Baldwin, Master in Chancery:

Mr. Speaker,

I am commanded by the Honorable the Legislative Council to acquaint this House that they have passed an Act, sent up from this House, intituled "An Act to amend an Act passed in the forty-eighth year of His Majesty's reign, intituled 'An Act to explain, amend, and reduce into one Act, the several laws now in force for the raising and training of the Militia of this Province,'" to which they have made several amendments, and to which amendments they request the concurrence of this House.

And then he withdrew.

The amendments made by the Honorable the Legislative Council to the Bill for amending the Militia Law were then read for the first time. Mr. Rogers then moved, seconded by Mr. Gough, that the amendments made by the Legislative Council to the Militia Bill be read for a second time to-morrow, which was ordered accordingly.

Mr. Speaker reminded the House of the application made by the Clerk through him to this House yesterday, for its permission for him to employ Copying Clerks in his office during the present Session of Parliament. The House then directed Mr. Speaker to permit the Clerk to employ the necessary Copying Clerks in his office for this Session. Mr. Speaker then ordered the Clerk to employ the necessary Copying Clerks in his office during the present Session.

Agreeably to leave given, the House again resolved itself into a Committee to go into the further consideration of the Assessment Bill. Mr. Speaker left the Chair. Mr. Mallory again took the Chair of the Committee.

Mr. Speaker resumed the Chair, and Mr. Mallory reported that the Committee had made a progress, and had directed him to ask for leave to sit again to-morrow. Leave was accordingly granted for the Committee to sit again to-morrow.

Mr. Willcocks moved, seconded by Mr. Secord, for leave to bring in a Bill on Monday next to alter and amend so much of an Act passed in the forty-eighth year of His Majesty's reign, intituled "An Act to explain, amend, and reduce to one Act of Parliament, the several laws now in being for the raising and training the Militia of this Province," as relates to the application of Militia Fines. Leave was accordingly granted.

On motion of Mr. Willcocks, seconded by Mr. Mallory, the House adjourned.

Thursday 21st February, 1811.

Prayers were read.

Agreeably to the Order of the Day, the House resolved itself into a Committee to go into the further consideration of the Bill to repeal the Laws and Ordinances of the Province of Quebec. Mr. Speaker left the Chair. Mr. Dorland was called to the chair of the Committee.

Mr. Speaker resumed the Chair, and Mr, Dorland reported that the Committee had gone through the consideration of the said Bill, without any amendment, which he was directed to report whenever the House should be pleased to receive the same.

Ordered, that the Report be now received.

Mr. Mallory then moved, seconded by Mr. John Willson, that the Bill to repeal the laws and ordinances of the Province of Quebec now in force in this Province be engrossed, and read a third time to-morrow, which was ordered accordingly.

Agreeably to the Order of the Day the House resolved itself into a Committee to go into the further consideration of the Bill to continue the Provisional Agreement with Lower Canada. Mr. Speaker left the Chair. Mr. Burritt took the chair of the Committee.

Mr. Speaker resumed the Chair, and Mr. Burritt reported that the Committee had made some progress, and had directed him to ask for leave to sit again on Monday next. Leave was accordingly granted for the Committee to sit again on Monday next.

Read for the second time, the Bill for extending the jurisdiction of the Court of Requests. Mr. Willcocks then moved, seconded by Mr. Rogers, that the House do now resolve itself into a Committee to take into consideration the Bill for extending the Jurisdiction of the Court of Requests. The House accordingly resolved itself into a Committee. Mr. Speaker left the Chair. Mr Lewis was called to the chair of the Committee.

Mr. Speaker resumed the Chair, and Mr. Lewis reported that the Committee had made some progress, and had directed him to ask for leave to sit again this day. Leave was accordingly granted for the Committee to sit again this day.

A message from His Excellency the Lieutenant Governor, signed by His Excellency, was presented by William Halton, Esquire, His Excellency's Secretary, which message was read, all the Members of the House being uncovered, and the same is as follows:—

(Signed) Francis Gore, Lt.-Governor.

The Lieutenant Governor thinks proper to acquaint the House of Assembly that he has directed the several officers commanding the Regiments of Militia to furnish a detailed account of the application of the moneys arising from the fines, penalties, and forfeitures, levied under the authority of the Act, to explain, amend, and reduce to one Act of Parliament the several laws now in force for the raising and training of the Militia of this Province.

The neglect of the Statute to make provision for any control over the discretion of the respective Officers entrusted with this duty may have given occasion to abuses which may require legislative provision to correct.

The Lieutenant Governor will, therefore, on receipt of the several returns, which he fears cannot be expected during this Session of Parliament, direct them to be laid before the House of Assembly, 21st February, 1811.

F. G.

Agreeably to the Order of the Day, the House resolved itself into a Committee to go into the further consideration of the Bill to extend the Jurisdiction of the Court of Requests. Mr. Speaker left the Chair. Mr. Lewis again took the Chair of the Committee.

Mr. Speaker resumed the Chair, and Mr. Lewis reported that the Committee had made a progress, and had directed him to ask for leave to sit again to-morrow. Leave was accordingly granted to sit again to-morrow.

Agreeably to the Order of the Day, the House resolved itself into a Committee to go into the further consideration of the Bill to revive and amend the Bill laying duties upon Hawkers and Pedlars in this Province. Mr. Speaker left the Chair. Mr. Howard took the Chair of the Committee.

Mr. Speaker resumed the Chair, and Mr. Howard reported that the Committee had made a progress, and had directed him to ask for leave to sit again to-morrow. Leave was accordingly granted for the Committee to sit again to-morrow.

Mr. McLean moved, seconded by Mr. Dorland, for leave to bring in a Bill on Saturday next to amend and repeal part of an Act passed in the fortieth year of His Majesty's reign, intituled "An Act to provide for the laying out, amending, and keeping in repair the Public Highways and Roads in this Province, and to re-peal the laws now in force for that purpose." Leave was granted accordingly.

Read for the first time, the Bill for ascertaining the damages on protested Bills of Exchange, and fixing the rate of interest in this Province.

Mr. McLean moved, seconded by Mr. C. Willson, for leave to bring up the Petition of Isaac Swayze. Leave was accordingly granted, and the said Petition ordered to lie upon the Table.

Mr. Gough, seconded by Mr. Dorland, moved that the Bill for ascertaining the damages on protested Bills of Exchange, etc., be read a second time to-morrow, which was ordered accordingly.

On motion of Mr. Willcocks, seconded by Mr. John Wilson, the House adjourned.

Friday, 22nd February, 1811.

Prayers were read.

Mr. Gough moved, seconded by Captain Fraser, that the House do on to-morrow resolve itself into a Committee to take into consideration His Excellency the Lieutenant Governor's Message to this House received yesterday, which was ordered accordingly.

Read for the second time, the Bill to amend an Act passed in the thirty-eighth year of His Majesty's reign, respecting the authority of Magistrates to arrest persons leaving the Province.

Mr. Mallory then moved, seconded by Mr. Willcocks, that this House do now resolve itself into a Committee to take into their consideration the Bill to amend and explain an Act passed in the thirty-eighth year of His Majesty's reign, respecting the authority of Magistrates.

The House accordingly resolved itself into a Committee. Mr. Speaker left the Chair. Mr. Willcocks was called to the chair of the Committee.

Mr. Speaker resumed the Chair, and Mr. Willcocks reported that the Committee had gone through the consideration of the said Bill, to which they had made several amendments, which he was directed to report whenever the House should be pleased to received the same. Ordered, that the Report be now received.

Mr. Mallory then moved, seconded by Mr. Dorland, that the Bill to amend an Act passed in the thirty-eighth year of His Majesty's reign, relative to Magistrates, be engrossed and read a third time to-morrow, which was ordered accordingly.

Agreeably to the Order of the Day, the House resolved into a Committee to go into the further consideration of the Bill concerning Land Surveyors, and the ad-measurement and boundaries of land in this Province. Mr. Speaker left the Chair. Mr. John Willson took the Chair of the Committee.

Mr. Speaker resumed the Chair, and Mr. John Willson reported that the Committee had made some progress, and had directed him to ask for leave to sit again to-morrow. Leave was accordingly given for the Committee to sit again to-morrow.

Mr. Mallory moved, seconded by Mr. Willcocks, for leave to bring in a Bill on Tuesday next to alter and amend certain parts of an Act passed in the forty-eighth year of His Majesty's reign, intituled "An Act for the better regulation of Special Juries." Leave was granted accordingly.

On motion of Mr. Dorland, seconded by Mr. C. Willson, the House adjourned.

Saturday, 23rd February, 1811.

Prayers were read.

Read for the third time, as engrossed, the Bill to repeal the Laws and Ordinances of the Province of Quebec. On motion of Mr. Mallory, seconded by Mr. Sovereign, resolved, that the Bill do now pass, and that the title be "An Act to repeal all the Laws and Ordinances of the Province of Quebec now in force in this Province." The Bill then passed, and was signed by the Speaker. Mr. Rogers then moved, seconded by Mr. Howard, that Messrs. Mallory and Sovereign be named to carry up to the Honorable the Legislative Council the Bill for repealing the Quebec Ordinances, and to request their concurrence thereto, which was ordered accordingly.

Agreeably to the Order of the Day, the House resolved itself into a Committee to go into the further consideration of the Bill to form a separate District out of the Home and Niagara Districts. Mr. Speaker left the Chair. Mr. Secord was called to the chair of the Committee.

Mr. Speaker resumed the Chair, and Mr. Secord reported that the Committee had made a progress, and directed him to ask for leave to sit again on Tuesday next. Leave was accordingly granted for the Committee to sit again on Tuesday next.

Agreeably to the Order of the Day, the House resolved itself into a Committee to go into the further consideration of the Bill to lay a duty upon Hawkers, Pedlars, and Petty Chapmen in this Province. Mr. Speaker left the Chair. Mr. Howard took the Chair of the Committee.

Mr. Speaker resumed the Chair, and Mr. Howard reported that the Committee had gone through the consideration of the said Bill, to which they had made several amendments, which he was directed to report to the House whenever it should be pleased to receive the same. Ordered, that the Report be now received. Mr. McLean then moved, seconded by Mr. McNabb, that the Bill intituled "An Act to lay a duty upon Hawkers, Pedlars, and Petty Chapmen, be engrossed, and read a third time on Monday next, which was ordered accordingly.

Mr. Mallory, one of the Messengers named to carry up to the Honorable the Legislative Council the Act intituled "An Act to repeal all the Laws and Ordinances of the Province of Quebec now in force in this Province, reported that they had carried up the said Act, to which they requested their concurrence in passing the same.

Agreeably to the Order of the Day, the House resolved itself into a Committee to take into consideration His Excellency the Lieutenant Governor's Message to this House, received the twenty-first instant. Mr. Speaker left the Chair. Mr. C. Willson was called to the chair of the Committee.

Mr. Speaker resumed the Chair, and Mr. C. Willson reported that it is the opinion of this Committee that a respectful Address be presented to His Excellency, the Lieutenant Governor, to return our grateful acknowledgments for His Excellency's Message to the House of the twenty-first instant, and to thank His Excellency for having given directions to the several Officers commanding the Regiments of Militia to furnish a detailed account of the moneys arising from the fines, penalties and forfeitures, levied under the authority of the Act to explain, amend, and reduce to one Act of Parliament, the several laws now in being for the raising and training the Militia of this Province; in compliance with the prayer of the Address of this House to His Excellency, and to assure His Excellency if after receiving those accounts it shall appear that abuses have existed which may require legislative aid to control, that this House, in conjunction with the other branch of the Legislature, will adopt measures to bring the delinquents to justice; and to prevent such offences being committed in future, which he was directed to report whenever the House should be pleased to receive the same.

The House accordingly ordered that the Report be now received and accepted.

Mr. McLean then moved, seconded by Captain Fraser, that Messrs. Gough and McNabb be a Committee to draft an Address to His Excellency, the Lieutenant Governor, in answer to His Excellency's Message and report the same as soon as convenient, which was ordered accordingly.

Mr. Gough, one of the Committee named to draft an Address to His Excellency the Lieutenant Governor, in answer to His Excellency's Message to this House, received the twenty-first instant, reported that they had drafted an Address accordingly, which he was directed to submit to the House whenever it should be pleased to receive the same. Ordered, that the Report be now received, and he read the Report in his place, and then delivered it in to the Clerk at the Table.

Mr. McLean then moved, seconded by Captain Fraser, that the House do now resolve itself into a Committee of the Whole, to take into their consideration the Address to His Excellency, the Lieutenant Governor, in answer to his Message. The House accordingly resolved itself into a Committee. Mr. Speaker left the Chair. Mr. McGregor was called to the Chair of the Committee.

Mr. Speaker resumed the Chair, and Mr. McGregor reported that the Committee had gone through the consideration of the said Address, without any amendment, which he was directed to report whenever the House should be pleased to receive the same. Ordered, that the Report be now received.

Mr. Gough then moved, seconded by Mr. Rogers, that the Address to His Excellency, the Lieutenant Governor, be engrossed, and read a third time this day; and that Messrs. Fraser and Elliott be appointed a Committee to wait upon His Exccllency, to know when he will be pleased to receive the same, and to present the same at such time as His Excellency shall be pleased to appoint, which was ordered accordingly.

Mr. Gough again moved, seconded by Mr. Willcocks, that the two Select Committees appointed to examine the Public Accounts be, and they are hereby respectfully authorized to call for such persons and papers as they may find necessary for their information on the said Accounts. Ordered accordingly.

Agreeably to the Order of the Day, the House resolved itself into a Committee to go into the further consideration of the Bill to amend the Assessment Act. Mr. Speaker left the Chair. Mr. Mallory took the Chair of the Committee.

Mr. Speaker resumed the Chair, and Mr. Mallory reported that the Committee had made some progress, and had directed him to ask for leave to sit again on Monday next._ Leave was accordingly granted for the Committee to sit again on Monday next.

Read, as engrossed, the Address to His Excellency, the Lieutenant Governor, in answer to His Excellency's Message, which is as follows:

To His Excellency Francis Gore, Esquire, Lieutenant Governor of the Province of Upper Canada, etc., etc., etc.

29 A.

May it please Your Excellency,

We, His Majesty's dutiful and loyal subjects, the Commons of Upper Canada, in Parliament assembled, beg leave to return to Your Excellency our grateful acknowledgment for Your Excellency's Message to this House of the twenty-first instant; also to request Your Excellency to accept our thanks for the directions Your Excellency has been pleased to issue to the several Officers commanding the Regiments of Militia, to furnish a detailed account of the moneys arising from the fines, penalties, and forfeitures, levied under the authority of the Act to explain, amend and reduce to one Act of Parliament the several laws now in being for the raising and training the Militia of this Province; in compliance with the prayer of an Address of this House to Your Excellency.

We also beg leave to assure Your Excellency if, after receiving those accounts, it shall appear that abuses have existed which may require legislative aid to control, that this House will endeavor to adopt measures to bring the delinquents to justice, and to prevent such offences being committed in future.

Passed the Commons House of Assembly, 23rd February, 1811.

(Signed) SAMUEL STREET, Speaker.

Which then passed and was signed by the Speaker. Mr. Willcocks moved, seconded by Mr. Rogers, for leave to bring in a Bill on Monday next to alter and amend the practice now in force respecting criminal prosecution in the Courts of King's Bench, and Oyer and Terminer in this Province. Leave was accordingly granted.

Read for the first time, the Bill to amend the Road Act. Mr. McLean then moved, seconded by Captain Fraser, that the Bill intituled "An Act to repeal and amend part of an Act passed in the fiftieth year of His Majesty's reign, to provide for laying out and amending the Highways and Roads in this Province; be read a second time on Thursday next, which was ordered accordingly.

On motion of Mr. C. Willson, seconded by Captain Fraser, the House adjourned to Monday next.

Monday, 25th February, 1811.

Prayers were read.

Captain Fraser, one of the Messengers named to wait upon His Excellency, the Lieutenant Governor, with the Address of this House, in answer to His Excellency's Message of the twenty-first instant, reported that they had waited upon His Excellency with the said Address.

Read for the second time, the amendments made by the Honorable the Legislative Council in and to the Bill for amending the Militia Law.

Mr. Gough then moved, seconded by Mr. Rogers, that the House do now resolve itself into a Committee to take into consideration the amendments made by the Honorable the Legislative Council to the Bill for amending the Militia Law. The House accordingly resolved itself into a Committee. Mr. Speaker left the Chair. Captain Fraser was called to the Chair of the Committee.

Mr. Speaker resumed the Chair, and Captain Fraser reported that it is the opinion of this Committee that a conference be requested with the Honorable the Legislative Council on the amendments made to the Bill for amending the Militia Law, which he was directed to report whenever the House should be pleased to receive the same. Ordered, that the Report be now received.

Mr. Rogers then moved, seconded by Mr. Dorland, that Messrs. McGregor and Stinson be a Committee to request a conference with the Honorable the Legislative Council on the amendments made by them to the Bill for amending the Militia Law, which was ordered accordingly.

Mr. Speaker,—

The House of Assembly request a conference with the Honorable Legislative Council on the subject matter of amendments made by them in and to an Act, sent up from this House; intituled "An Act to amend an Act passed in the forty-eighth year of His Majesty's reign, intituled 'An Act to explain, amend, and reduce into one Act the several laws now in force for the raising and training the Militia of this Province.   (Signed) SAMUEL STREET, Speaker.

Commons House of Assembly, Monday, 25th Feb'y, 1811.

Mr. McNabb moved, seconded by Mr. Baby, that so much of the Order of the Day be dispensed with as relates to the third reading of the Hawkers and Pedlars Bill, and that the same be recommitted to-morrow.   Ordered accordingly.

Agreeably to the Order of the Day, the House resolved itself into a Committee to go into the further consideration of the Assessment Bill.   Mr. Speaker left the Chair.   Mr. Mallory took the Chair of the Committee.

Mr. Speaker resumed the Chair, and Mr. Mallory reported that the Committee had gone through the consideration of the said Bill, to which they had made several amendments, which he was directed to report whenever the House should be pleased to receive the same.   Ordered, that the Report be now received.   Mr. Howard then moved, seconded by Mr. Gough, that the Assessment Bill be engrossed and read a third time to-morrow, which was ordered accordingly.

Mr. McLean moved, seconded by Mr. Rogers, that the House do now resolve itself into a Committee, to take into their consideration the amendments to the Register Act.   The House accordingly resolved itself into a Committee.   Mr. Speaker left the Chair.   Mr. McLean was called to the Chair of the Committee.

Mr. Speaker resumed the Chair, and Mr. McLean reported that the Committee had made a progress, and had directed him to ask for leave to sit again to-morrow.   Leave was accordingly granted for the Committee to sit again to-morrow.

Agreeably to the Order of the Day, the House resolved itself into a Committee to go into the further consideration of the Bill to repeal an Act passed in the thirty-fourth year of His Majesty's reign, respecting the duty of Sheriffs. Mr. Speaker left the Chair.   Mr. McNabb took the Chair of the Committee.

Mr. Speaker resumed the Chair, and Mr. McNabb reported that the Committee had gone through the consideration of the said Bill, to which they had made several amendments, which he was directed to report whenever the House should be pleased to receive the same.   Ordered, that the Report be now received. Mr. Mallory then moved, seconded by Mr. Howard, that the Sheriffs Bill be engrossed and read a third time to-morrow, which was ordered accordingly.

Mr. Willcocks moved, seconded by Mr. Secord, for leave to bring in a Bill to-morrow to repeal an Act or Ordinance of Quebec to prevent persons practising Physic and Surgery within the Province of Quebec, or Midwifery in the Towns of Quebec and Montreal without License.   Leave was accordingly granted.

On motion of Mr. McLean, seconded by Mr. Rogers, the House adjourned to eleven o'clock to-morrow forenoon.

Tuesday, 26th February, 1811.

Prayers.

Mr. Mallory moved. seconded by Mr. Dorland; for leave to bring up the Petition of the inhabitants in the vicinity of Lake Ontario.   Leave was accordingly granted, and the said petition ordered to lie upon the Table.

Read for the third time, as engrossed, the Bill to amend an Act passed in the thirty-eighth year of His Majesty's Reign, respecting Civil and Criminal Courts of Justice. On motion of Mr. Mallory, seconded by Mr. Dorland, resolved, that the Bill do now pass, and that the title be "An Act to amend and explain an Act passed in the thirty-eighth year of His Majesty's Reign, intituled 'An Act to establish a Superior Court of Civil and Criminal jurisdiction, and to regulate the Court of Appeal.'" The Bill then passed, and was signed by the Speaker.

Mr. Mallory then moved, seconded by Mr. Dorland, that Messrs. McNabb and Lewis do carry up to the Honorable the Legislative Council the Bill intituled "An Act to amend and explain an Act passed in the thirty-eighth of the King, respecting Civil and Criminal Courts," and request their concurrence in passing the same, which was ordered accordingly.

Read for the third time, as engrossed, the Bill to repeal part of an Act passed in the thirty-fourth year of His Majesty's Reign, respecting the duties of Sheriffs. On motion of Mr. Mallory, seconded by Mr. C. Willson, resolved, that the Bill do pass, and that the title be "An Act to regulate the duty of Sheriffs, and for other purposes therein mentioned." The Bill then passed, and was signed by the Speaker. Mr. Mallory again moved, seconded by Mr. C. Willson, that Messrs. McNabb and Lewis be named to carry up to the Honorable the Legislative Council the Bill to regulate the duty of Sheriffs, and for other purposes therein mentioned, and to request their concurrence in passing the same, which was ordered accordingly.

Read for the third time, as engrossed, the Assessment Bill.

Read for the first time, the Bill to repeal the Quebec ordinance respecting the Practice of Physic and Surgery. Mr. Willcocks moved, seconded by Mr. Secord, that the Bill for repealing the Ordinance of the twenty-eighth of the King, which restricts persons from practising Physic, Surgery and Midwifery, without a license, be read a second time to-morrow, which was ordered accordingly.

Agreeably to the Order of the Day the House resolved itself into a Committee, to go into the further consideration of the Bill concerning Land Surveyors, and the admeasurement of land in this Province. Mr. Speaker left the Chair. Mr. Willcocks took the chair of the Committee. Mr. Speaker resumed the Chair, and Mr. Willcocks reported that the Committee had made some progress, and directed him to ask for leave to sit again this day. Leave was accordingly granted for the Committee to sit again this day.

A message from the Honorable the Legislative Council, by Mr. Baldwin, Master in Chancery.

Mr. Speaker,

I am commanded by the Honorable the Legislative Council to acquaint this House that they have passed an Act intituled "An Act further to amend an Act passed in the forty-seventh year of His Majesty's Reign intituled 'An Act to establish Public Schools in each and every District of this Province,'" to which they request the concurrence of this House in passing the same.

And also that they have passed an Act sent up from this House, intituled, "An Act to obviate certain doubts which have arisen in the practice of the Court of King's Bench of this Province," to which they have made several amendments, to which amendments they request the concurrence of this House in passing the same.

And then he withdrew.

Read for the first time, the Act sent down from the Honorable the Legislative Council, intituled "An Act further to amend the Act establishing Public Schools in this Province." Mr. Gough then moved, seconded by Mr. Dorland, that the School Bill be read a second time this day three months, which was ordered accordingly.

Also read for the first time, the amendments made by the Honorable the Legislative Council in and to an Act sent up from this House, intituled "An Act to obviate certain doubts which have arisen in the practice of the Court of King's Bench in this Province.

Mr. Rogers then moved, seconded by Mr. C. Willson, that the amendments made by the Honorable the Legislative Council to the Bill for obviating certain doubts which have arisen in the practice of the Court of King's Bench in this Province, be read a second time to-morrow, which was ordered accordingly.

Agreeably to leave given the House again resolved itself into Committee, to go into the further consideration of the Bill concerning Land Surveyors, and the admeasurement of land in this Province. Mr. Speaker left the Chair. Mr. Willcocks again took the chair of the Committee.

Mr. Speaker resumed the Chair, and Mr. Willcocks reported that the Committee had made some progress, and directed him to ask for leave to sit again to-morrow. Leave was accordingly granted for the Committee to sit again to-morrow.

On motion of Mr. Howard, seconded by Mr. Dorland, resolved, that the Assessment Bill do now pass, and that the title be "An Act to repeal an Act passed in the forty-seventh year of His Majesty's Reign intituled 'An Act to repeal the several Acts now in force in this Province, relative to Rates and Assessments, and also to particularize the property, real and personal, which, during the continuance thereof shall be subject to Rates and Assessments, and fixing the several valuations at which each and every particular of such property shall be rated and assessed, and to make further provision for the same.'" The Bill then passed, and was signed by the Speaker.

Mr. McLean moved, seconded by Mr. Baby, that Messrs. Howard and Casey do carry up to the Honorable the Legislative Council the Assessment Bill, and request their concurrence in passing the same, which was ordered accordingly.

Agreeably to the Order of the Day the House resolved itself into a Committee, to go into the further consideration of the Bill for to continue the Act laying duties upon Hawkers and Pedlars in this Province. Mr. Speaker left the Chair. Mr. Howard took the chair of the Committee.

Mr. Speaker resumed the Chair, and Mr. Howard reported that the Committee had gone through the consideration of the said Bill, to which they had made several amendments, which he was directed to report whenever the House should be pleased to receive the same. The House divided on the question, and the names were taken down as follows:—

Yeas.	Nays.
MESSRS. FRASER	MESSRS. SECORD
McNABB	HOWARD
GOUGH	MARSH
STINSON	MALLORY
CASEY	J. WILSON
ROGERS	C. WILLSON
McGREGOR	WILLCOCKS
BURRITT	ELLIOTT
MARKLE	LEWIS
BABY	
McLEAN	
DORLAND	

Carried in the affirmative by a majority of three, and the Report was accordingly received.

Mr. McNabb then moved, seconded by Capt. Fraser, that the Hawker and Pedlar Bill be engrossed, and read a third time to-morrow, which was ordered accordingly.

Mr. McNabb, one of the messengers named to carry up to the Honorable the Legislative Council the Act intituled "An Act to amend and explain an Act passed in the thirty-eighth year of His Majesty's Reign, intituled 'An Act to establish a Superior Court of Civil and Criminal jurisdiction, and to regulate the Court of Appeal,'" and also an Act intituled "An Act to regulate the duty of Sheriffs, and for other purposes therein mentioned," reported that they had carried up the said Acts, to which they requested their concurrence in passing the same.

Mr. McLean moved, seconded by Mr. Baby, for leave to bring in a Bill to-morrow, intituled "An Act for the relief of Creditors against absconding debtors." Leave was accordingly granted.

Read, the Petition of Isaac Swayze, which is as follows:—

To the Honorable the Commons House of Assembly of the Province of Upper Canada.

The Petition of Isaac Swayze, of Niagara, most humbly sheweth,

That Your Petitioner did heretofore humbly shew to Your Honorable House that a burglary had been committed upon his house on the night of the 28th January, 1806, at which time he was robbed of the sum of One Hundred and Seventy-eight Pounds, Provincial currency, then in his possession, and received by him as Inspector of Licenses for the District of Niagara, for duties on Shop, Tavern, and Still Licenses, issued 5th January, 1806, exclusive of private property and money received on account of the District of Niagara, and that Your Petitioner was at the same time very dangerously wounded.

Your Petitioner now begs leave to press upon your consideration the honorable testimony of such facts as were then adduced by him, on which your resolution of the fifth day of March, 1807, was founded; and humbly prays that Your Honorable House would be pleased to afford him that relief which in your wisdom you shall think the circumstances of his unfortunate case may require.

And Your Petitioner, as in duty bound, will ever pray.

(Signed) ISAAC SWAYZE.

Mr. C. Willson then moved, seconded by Mr. McLean, for leave to bring in a Bill, on Thursday next, for the relief of Isaac Swayze, Esquire, which passed in the negative.

On motion of Mr. Willcocks, seconded by Mr. Mallory, the House adjourned.

Wednesday, 27th February, 1811.

Prayers were read.

Read for the third time, as engrossed, the Bill to continue the Act laying Duties upon Hawkers and Pedlars in this Province.

Mr. McNabb then moved, seconded by Mr. Burritt, that the Hawker and Pedlar Bill do pass, and that the title be "An Act to repeal an Act passed in the forty-seventh year of His Majesty's Reign, intituled 'An Act for granting to His Majesty duties on Licenses to Hawkers, Pedlars, and Petty Chapmen, and other trading persons therein mentioned; and further for granting to His Majesty certain duties on Licenses to Hawkers, Pedlars and Petty Chapmen, and other trading persons therein mentioned.'" The House divided upon the question, and the names were taken down as follows:—

Yeas.	Nays.
MESSRS. McNABB	MESSRS. SECORD
FRASER	MARSH
BURRITT	MALLORY
CASEY	HOWARD
GOUGH	JOHN WILSON
McGREGOR	WILLCOCKS
McLEAN	ELLIOTT
ROGERS	LEWIS
STINSON	C. WILLSON
MARKLE	
DORLAND	
BABY	

Carried in the affirmative by a majority of three. The Bill then passed, and was signed by the Speaker. Mr. McNabb again moved, seconded by Mr. C. Willson, that Messrs. Dorland and Baby do carry up to the Honorable the Legislative Council the Hawker and Pedlar Bill, and request their concurrence in passing the same, which was ordered accordingly.

Mr. Rogers moved, seconded by Mr. Howard, for leave to bring up the Petition of the inhabitants of the Townships of Darlington, Clarke and Hope, in the District of Newcastle. Leave was accordingly granted, and the said Petition ordered to lie upon the Table.

Agreeably to the Order of the Day, the House resolved itself into a Committee, to go into the further consideration of the Bill concerning Land Surveyors, and the admeasurement of land in this Province. Mr. Speaker left the Chair. Mr. Willcocks took the chair of the Committee.

Mr. Speaker resumed the Chair, and Mr. Willcocks reported that the Committee had made a progress, and had directed him to ask for leave to sit again to-morrow. Leave was accordingly granted by the Committee to sit again to-morrow.

Mr. Howard, one of the messengers named to carry up to the Honorable the Legislative Council the Bill intituled "An Act to repeal an Act passed in the forty-seventh year of His Majesty's Reign, intituled 'An Act to repeal the several Acts now in force in this Province, relative to Rates and Assessments, and also to particularize the property, real and personal, which, during the continuance thereof shall be subject to rates and assessments; and fixing the several valuations at which each and every particular of such property shall be rated and assessed; and to make further provision for the same,'" reported that they had carried up the said Act, to which they requested their concurrence in passing the same.

Mr. Dorland, one of the messengers named to carry up to the Honorable the Legislative Council the Act intituled "An Act to repeal an Act passed in the forty-second year of His Majesty's Reign, intituled 'An Act for granting to His Majesty duties on Licenses to Hawkers, Pedlars and Petty Chapmen, and other trading persons therein mentioned; and further for granting to His Majesty certain duties on Licenses to Hawkers, Pedlars and Petty Chapmen, and other trading persons therein mentioned,'" reported that they had carried up the said Act, and did request their concurrence in passing the same.

Mr. McGregor, one of the messengers named to carry up the message of this House, requesting a conference with the Honorable the Legislative Council, in and to the amendments made by them to the Militia Law, reported that they had carried up the same.

Agreeably to the Order of the Day, the House resolved itself into a Committee. to go into the further consideration of the Bill for the Provisional Agreement with Lower Canada. Mr. Speaker left the Chair. Mr. Burritt took the chair of the Committee.

Mr. Speaker resumed the Chair, and Mr. Burritt reported that the Committee had made some progress, and had directed him to ask for leave to sit again to-morrow. Leave was accordingly granted for the Committee to sit again to-morrow.

Read for the second time, the Bill to amend the Road Act.

Mr. McLean then moved, seconded by Mr. McGregor, that the House do now resolve itself into a Committee of the whole, to take into their consideration the Bill intituled "An Act to amend and repeal part of an Act passed in the fiftieth year of His Majesty's Reign, intituled 'An Act for laying out and amending the Public Highways and Roads.'"

The House accordingly resolved itself into a Committee. Mr. Speaker left the Chair. Mr. Stinson was called to the chair of the Committee.

Mr. Speaker resumed the Chair, and Mr. Stinson reported that the Committee had made some progress, and had directed him to ask for leave to sit again this day. Leave was accordingly granted for the Committee to sit again this day.

A message from the Honorable the Legislative Council by Mr. Baldwin, Master in Chancery.

Mr. Speaker,

I am commanded by the Honorable the Legislative Council to inform this House that they have passed an Act intituled "An Act for the benefit of the Creditors of such persons who have died indebted beyond what their personal estate can discharge," and to which they request the concurrence of this House in passing the same.

And also a written message from the Honorable the Legislative Council, concerning a conference with this House, respecting the amendments to the Militia
Law.

And then he withdrew.

Read for the first time, the Bill sent down from the Honorable the Legislative
Council intituled "An Act for the benefit of the creditors of such persons who have
died indebted beyond what their personal estate can discharge." Mr. Rogers then
moved, seconded by Mr. C. Willson, that the Bill for the benefit of creditors of
persons deceased, be read a second time on Saturday next, which was ordered
accordingly.

Then was read the written message sent down from the Honorable the Legislative Council, respecting the conference on amendments made to the Militia Bill,
which is as follows :—

Mr. Speaker,—

The Legislative Council have appointed a Committee to confer with the
Committee of the Commons House of Assembly on the subject matter of amendments made by them in and to a Bill intituled "An Act to amend an Act passed
in the forty-eighth year of His Majesty's Reign, intituled 'An Act to explain,
amend, and reduce into one Act, the several laws now in force for the raising and
training the Militia of this Province,' " in the Legislative Council Chamber, at
the rising of this House.

Legislative Council Chamber,   (Signed) Thos. Scott,
Wednesday, 27th Feb'y., 1811.   Speaker.

Mr. C. Willson moved, seconded by Mr. McNabb, that Messrs. Howard, Dorland, Rogers, Gough and John Willson be a Committee of conference from this
House, to meet a Committee of the Honorable Legislative Council on the subject
matter of the amendments made by them in and to the Bill for amending the Militia
Law, which was ordered accordingly.

Agreeably to leave given, the House again resolved itself into a Committee, to
go into the further consideration of the Bill to amend the Road Act. Mr, Speaker
left the Chair. Mr. Stinson again took the chair of the Committee.

Mr. Speaker resumed the Chair, and Mr. Stinson reported that the Committee
had gone through the consideration of the said Bill, to which they had made several
amendments, which he was directed to report whenever the House should be pleased
to receive the same. Ordered that the Report be now received.

Mr. McLean then moved, seconded by Mr. Rogers, that the Bill intituled "An
Act to amend and repeal parts of an Act passed in the fiftieth year of His Majesty's
Reign, intituled 'An Act to provide for the laying out and amending the roads &c,' "
be engrossed and read a third time to-morrow, which was ordered accordingly.

Mr. Howard, one of the Committee appointed to confer with the Honorable
the Legislative Council, on the subject matter of amendments made by them to
the Militia Law, reported that the Committee had conferred accordingly, and that
the Legislative Council adhered to their amendments in and to the said Bill.

Read for the first time, the Bill for the relief of creditors against absconding
debtors.

Mr. McLean then moved, seconded by Mr. McGregor, that the Bill intituled
"An Act for the Relief of Creditors against Absconding Debtors," be read a second
time on Friday next, which was ordered accordingly.

On motion of Mr. C. Willson, seconded by Mr. Mallory, the House adjourned to eleven o'clock to-morrow.

Thursday, 28th February, 1811.

Prayers were read.

Mr. Gough, by permission of the House, laid on the Table a Petition from the inhabitants of York, Trafalgar, and other Townships.

Agreeably to the Order of the Day, the House resolved itself into a Committee, to go into the further consideration of the Bill to continue the Provisional Agreement with Lower Canada. Mr. Speaker left the Chair. Mr. Burritt took the Chair of the Committee.

Mr. Speaker resumed the Chair, and Mr. Burritt reported that the Committee had gone through the consideration of the said Bill without any amendment, which he was directed to report whenever the House should be pleased to receive the same. Ordered, that the Report be now received. Mr. Gough then moved, seconded by Capt. Elliott, that the Provisional Agreement Bill be engrossed, and read a third time to-morrow, which was ordered accordingly.

Read for the second time, the amendments made by the Honorable the Legislative Council to the Bill for obviating certain doubts in the Court of King's Bench. Mr. Rogers then moved, seconded by Mr. McLean, that the House do now resolve itself into a Committee, to take into consideration the amendments made by the Legislative Council in and to the Bill for obviating certain doubts that have arisen in the practice of the Court of King's Bench. The House accordingly resolved itself into a Committee. Mr. Speaker left the Chair. Mr. Casey was called to the Chair of the Committee.

Mr. Speaker resumed the Chair, and Mr. Casey reported that the Committee had come to a resolution that a conference be requested with the Honorable, the Legislative Council in and to the subject matter of amendments made by them in and to the Act intituled "An Act for obviating doubts which have arisen in the practice of the Court of King's Bench in this Province," which he was directed to report to the House whenever it shall be pleased to receive the same. Ordered that the Report be now received, and the Report was received accordingly.

Mr. Rogers then moved, seconded by Mr. Lewis, that Messrs. McLean and Baby be a Committee to request a conference with the Honorable the Legislative Council on the amendments made to a Bill for obviating certain doubts that have arisen in the practice of the Court of King's Bench, which was ordered accordingly, and the message is as follows:—

Mr. Speaker,—

The House of Assembly request a conference with the Honorable the Legislative Council on the subject matter of the amendments made by them in and to the Act intituled "An Act to obviate certain doubts which have arisen in the practice of the Court of King's Bench in this Province.

Commons House of Assembly,   (Signed) Samuel Street,
Thursday, 28 Feby., 1811.   Speaker.

Agreeably to the Order of the Day the House resolved itself into a Committee, to go into the further consideration of the Bill to amend the Register Act. Mr. Speaker left the Chair. Mr. McLean took the Chair of the Committee.

Mr. Speaker resumed the Chair, and Mr. McLean reported that the Committee had made some progress, and had directed him to ask for leave to sit again this day. Leave was accordingly granted for the Committee to sit again this day.

Read for the third time as engrossed, the Bill to amend and repeal part of the Road Act. On motion of Mr. McLean, seconded by Capt. Elliott, resolved, that the Bill do now pass, and that the title be "An Act to amend and repeal part of an Act passed in the fiftieth year of His Majesty's Reign, intituled 'An Act to provide for the laying out, amending and keeping in repair the Public Highways and Roads in this Province; and to repeal the laws now in force for that purpose.'" The Bill then passed, and was signed by the Speaker. Mr. Rogers then moved, seconded by Mr. Lewis, that Messrs. McLean and Baby do carry up to the Honorable the Legislative Council the Bill for altering the Road Act, and to request their concurrence thereto, which was ordered accordingly.

Mr. McLean, one of the Messengers named to carry up to the Honorable the Legislative Council the Act intituled "An Act to amend and repeal part of an Act passed in the fiftieth year of His Majesty's Reign, intituled 'An Act to provide for the laying out, amending and keeping in repair the Public Highways and Roads in this Province; and to repeal the laws now in force for that purpose,'" reported that they had carried up the said Act, and did request their concurrence in passing the same. Also that they carried up to the Honorable the Legislative Council the message of this House, requesting a conference with them.

Agreeably to leave given, the House again resolved itself into a Committee, to go into the further consideration of the Bill to amend the Register Act. Mr. Speaker left the Chair. Mr. McLean again took the Chair of the Committee.

Mr. Speaker resumed the Chair, and Mr. McLean reported that the Committee had made a progress, and had directed him to ask for leave to sit again this day. Leave was accordingly granted for the Committee to sit again this day.

A Message from the Honorable the Legislative Council by Mr. Baldwin, Master in Chancery:—

Mr. Speaker,—

The Legislative Council have appointed a Committee, to confer with the Committee of the Commons House of Assembly on the subject matter of amendments made by them, in and to a Bill intituled "An Act for obviating certain doubts which have arisen in the practice of the Court of King's Bench in this Province," at the rising of this House, in the Legislative Council Chamber.

Legislative Council Chamber,   (Signed) Thos. Scott,
Thursday, 28th Feby., 1811.   Speaker.

Mr. Dorland then moved, seconded by Mr. C. Willson, that Messrs. McLean, Baby, Stinson and Rogers be a Committee to confer with a Committee of the Honorable the Legislative Council, on the amendments made by them in and to the Bill for obviating certain doubts which have arisen in the practice of the Court of King's Bench, which was ordered accordingly.

Agreeably to leave given, the House again resolved itself into a Committee, to go into the further consideration of the Bill to amend the Register Act. Mr. Speaker left the Chair. Mr. McLean again took the Chair of the Committee.

Mr. Speaker resumed the Chair, and Mr. McLean reported that the Committee had gone through the consideration of the said Bill, to which they had made several amendments, which he was directed to report whenever the House should be pleased to receive the same. Ordered, that the Report be now received and accepted.

Mr. McLean then moved, seconded by Mr. Burritt, that the Bill intituled "An Act to amend and Act passed in the thirty-fifth year of His Majesty's Reign, intituled 'An Act for the Public Registering of Deeds,'" be engrossed, and read a third time to-morrow, which was ordered accordingly.

'Agreeably to the Order of the Day, the House resolved itself into Committee, to go into the further consideration of the Bill concerning Land Surveyors, and the boundaries of land in this Province. Mr. Speaker left the Chair. Mr. Willcocks took the Chair of the Committee.

Mr. Speaker resumed the Chair, and Mr. Willcocks reported that the Committee had made some progress, and had directed him to ask for leave to sit again to-morrow. Leave was accordingly granted for the Committee to sit again to-morrow.

Read for the first time, the Bill respecting the prosecution of libels in the Court of King's Bench in this Province.

Mr. Willcocks then moved, seconded by Mr. Secord, that the Libel Bill be read a second time to-morrow, which was ordered accordingly.

Read for the first time, the Bill for altering the application of Militia Fines.

Mr. Gough, by leave of the House, brought forward and laid on the Table the Petition of William Allan, Esquire.

Mr. Willcocks moved, seconded by Mr. Secord, that the Bill for altering the application of the Militia Fines be read a second time to-morrow, which was ordered accordingly.

Read for the second time, the Bill for repealing the Ordinance of Quebec, relative to the practice of Physic, Surgery and Midwifery. Mr. Willcocks, seconded by Mr. Lewis, then moved that the House do now resolve itself into a Committee to take into consideration the Bill for repealing the Ordinance of Quebec, relative to the practice of Physic, Surgery and Midwifery. The House accordingly resolved itself into a Committee. Mr. Speaker left the Chair. Mr. McLean was called to the Chair of the Committee.

Mr. Speaker resumed the Chair, and Mr. McLean reported that the Committee had gone through the consideration of the said Bill, without any amendments, and that he was directed to report whenever the House should be pleased to receive the same. Ordered that the Report be now received.

Mr. Willcocks again moved, seconded by Capt. Elliott, that the Bill for repealing the Ordinance of Quebec relative to the practice of Physic and Surgery, be engrossed, and read a third time to-morrow, which was ordered accordingly.

Mr. Howard moved, seconded by Capt. Elliott for leave to bring in, to-morrow, a Bill to appropriate money for roads throughout this Province. Leave was granted accordingly.

On motion of Mr. Dorland, seconded by Mr. Lewis, the House adjourned to eleven o'clock to-morrow.

Friday, 1st March, 1811.

Prayers were read.

Mr. Mallory, seconded by Mr. McNabb, moved for leave to bring up the Petition of Almarin James, late from the State of New York. Leave was accordingly granted, and the said petition ordered to lie on the Table.

Mr. Mallory again moved, seconded by Capt. Elliott, that the sixth Rule of this House be dispensed with, so far as relates to the Petition of Almarin James, and that the said Petition be now read. The House accordingly resolved that the said Rule be dispensed with, and that the said Petition be now read.

The said Petition was accordingly read, and is as follows :—

To the Honorable the Commons of Upper Canada, in Parliament Assembled, and the Honorable the Legislative Council of the said Province.

The Petition of Almarin James, late of Whitestone, in the State of New York.

Humbly Showeth,—

That your Petitioner begs leave to state to Your Honorable Bodies that he possesses a new invented method of carrying on the distilling business to a greater degree of perfection than heretofore experienced, by the power of steam.

Your Petitioner can also, by steam, make grist mills and saw mills do business to as much advantage as if effected by water.

He also can, by the power of steam, improve chemistry, and supply various branches for domestic utility, equal to what the power of water can effect. He therefore begs leave to submit with great deference, this, his useful discovery to your consideration, and to solicit an exclusive right to this his discovery for the period of seven years, secured to him in such manner as to Your Honorable Bodies in your wisdom shall seem meet.   .

And Your Petitioner, as in duty bound, will ever pray.

York, 1st March, 1811.

(Signed) Almarin James.

He hereafter submits his prices to your consideration, viz.:
·For the benefit of a Grist Mill, $35.   ·
For the benefit of a Saw-Mill $35
For the benefit of Distilleries, $25.

And every kind of machinery going by water in equal proportion.

These are to certify that I have seen in operation upon a small scale the contrivance for distillery in wooden vessels by steam, introduced into this Province by Almarin James, and that it appeared completely to answer the purpose.

York, 1st February, 1811.

(Signed) Richard Cartwright.

Home District, York, 26th Feby., 1811.

I hereby certify that the bearer, Almarin James of the Town of Kingston, Midland District, has this day come before me and taken the Oath of allegiance according to law.

(Signed) W. Allen, J. P.

Whereas Almarin James, a citizen of the United States hath alleged that he has invented a new and useful improvement, being a steam still, which improvement has not been known before his application, and we, the undersigners, are well acquainted with the said James, and do verily believe him, the said James, to be the true inventor thereof.

Whitestone, January 27th, 1811.

(Signed) Levi Rice, David Tucker, William Simons, Daniel Ferguson, James Patterson, Reuben Ferguson, Joseph Ferguson, William Fields, Aaron Baby.

I do hereby certify that I was present at an experiment made by Almarin James on new invented stills, and, as far as I can judge, will answer a good purpose, and save the distiller a great deal of money in setting his business in operation.   ·

As witness my hand, at Kingston, this 12th day of February, 1811.

(Signed) John Canning.

Read for the third time, as engrossed, the Bill to continue the Provisional Agreement with Lower Canada.

On motion of Mr. Gough, seconded by Mr. Lewis, resolved, that the Bill do now pass, and that the title be "An Act to continue and amend an Act passed in the forty-ninth year of His Majesty's Reign, intituled 'An Act for the continuing for a limited time the Provisional Agreement entered into between this Province and Lower Canada, at Montreal, on the fifth day of July, One Thousand Eight Hundred and Four, relative to duties; also for continuing for a limited time the several Acts of the Parliament of this Province now in force relating thereto.'" The Bill then passed and was signed. Mr. Gough again moved, seconded by Mr. Rogers, that Messrs. McNabb and Marsh do carry up to the Honorable the Legislative Council the Provisional Agreement Bill, and request their concurrence in passing the same, which was ordered accordingly.

Mr. McLean, from the Committee appointed from this House to confer with a Committee of the Honorable the Legislative Council on the subject matter of the amendments made by the Legislative Council in and to the Bill for obviating certain doubts which have arisen in the practice of the Court of King's Bench in this Province, reported that they had met the Managers on the part of the Legislative Council and they have reason to believe that the Legislative Council will consent to modify their amendments as to do away the objections made by the House of Assembly.

Read for the third time, as engrossed, the Bill to repeal an Ordinance of Quebec, relative to the practice of Physic, Surgery and Midwifery. On motion of Mr. Willcocks, seconded by Mr. Rogers, resolved, that the Bill do pass, and that the title be "An Act to repeal an Ordinance of the Province of Quebec, passed in the twenty-eighth year of His Majesty's Reign, intituled 'An Act or Ordinance to prevent persons practising Physic and Surgery within the Province of Quebec, or Midwifery in the Towns of Quebec and Montreal, without License.'" The Bill then passed, and was signed by the Speaker.

Mr. Willcocks again moved, seconded by Mr. Rogers, that Messrs. C. Willson and Mallory do carry up to the Honorable Legislative Council the Bill for repealing the Ordinance of Quebec, respecting Physic and Surgery, and request their concurrence in passing the same, which was ordered accordingly.

Mr. McLean moved, seconded by Mr. Rogers, that the Order of the Day relative to the third reading of the Registry Bill be discharged, and that the same be now recommitted. The House accordingly resolved itself into a Committee, to go into the further consideration of the Bill to amend the Register Act. Mr. Speaker left the Chair. Mr. Gough was called to the Chair of the Committee.

Mr. Speaker resumed the Chair, and Mr. Gough reported that the Committee had gone through the consideration of the said Bill, to which they had made several amendments, which he was directed to report whenever the House should be pleased to receive the same. Ordered, that the Report be now received.

Mr. Rogers then moved, seconded by Mr. Gough, that the Bill for registering Deeds and Judgments be engrossed, and read a third time to-morrow, which was ordered accordingly.

Agreeably to the Order of the Day, the House resolved itself into a Committee, to go into the further consideration of the Bill concerning Surveyors, and the Admeasurement of Land in this Province. Mr. Speaker left the Chair. Mr. Willcocks took the Chair of the Committee.

Mr. Speaker resumed the Chair, and Mr. Willcocks reported that the Committee had gone through the consideration of the said Bill, to which they had made several amendments, which he was directed to report whenever the House should be pleased to receive the same. Ordered, that the Report be now received. Mr. Howard then moved, seconded by Mr. Mallory, that the Survey Bill be engrossed, and read a third time to-morrow, which was ordered accordingly

Read for the first time, the Bill for appropriating a sum of money for repairing the roads and Bridges   Mr. Howard then moved, seconded by Mr. Sovereign, that the Bill for appropriating money for the Public Roads be read a second time on Monday next, which was ordered accordingly.

Mr. McNabb, one of the Messengers named to carry up to the Honorable the Legislative Council the Act intituled "An Act to continue and amend an Act passed in the forty-ninth year of His Majesty's Reign, intituled 'An Act for the continuing for a limited time the Provisional Agreement entered into between this Province and Lower Canada, on the fifth day of July, one thousand eight hundred and four, relative to duties; also for continuing for a limited time the several Acts of the Parliament of this Province now in force relating thereto,'" reported that they had carried up the said Act, to which they requested their concurrence in passing the same.

Mr. C. Willson, one of the Messengers named to carry up to the Honorable the Legislative Council the Act intituled "An Act to repeal an Ordinance of the Province of Quebec, passed in the twenty-eighth year of His present Majesty's Reign, intituled 'An Act or Ordinance to prevent Persons practising Physic and Surgery within the Province of Quebec, or Midwifery within the Towns of Quebec and Montreal, without License,'" reported that they had carried up the said Act, to which they requested their concurrence in passing the same.

Mr. Gough moved, seconded by Mr. Dorland, that the House do now resolve itself into a Committee, to take into their further consideration the amendments made by the Honorable the Legislative Council in and to the Act sent up from this House for amending the Militia Law. The House accordingly resolved itself into a Committee. Mr. Speaker left the Chair. Mr. Mallory was called to the Chair of the Committee.

Mr. Speaker resumed the Chair, and Mr. Mallory reported that the Committee had gone through the consideration of the said Act, and had adopted the amendments made thereto by the Honorable the Legislative Council, which he was directed to report whenever the House should be pleased to receive the same. Ordered, that the Report be now received.

Mr. Gough then moved, seconded by Mr. Rogers, that the amendments made by the Honorable the Legislative Council to the Bill for amending the Militia Laws be read a third time to-morrow, which was ordered accordingly.

Mr. Mallory moved, seconded by Captain Elliott, for leave to bring in a Bill to-morrow to repeal the third clause of an Act, passed in the forty-eighth year of His Majesty's Reign, intituled "An Act to amend an Act, passed in the forty-seventh year of His Majesty's Reign, to establish Public Schools in each and every District in this Province.'" Mr. Rogers, in amendment, seconded by Mr. Gough, moved that the word "to-morrow" in Mr. Mallory's motion be struck out, and in lieu thereof, the words "this day three months" be inserted. The question as amended was carried in the affirmative, and ordered accordingly.

On motion of Mr. Dorland, seconded by Mr. Lewis, the House adjourned.

Monday, 2nd March, 1811.

Prayers were read.

Read for the third time, as engrossed, the amendments made by the Legislative Council in and to the Bill to amend the Militia Bill. Mr. Gough then moved, seconded by Mr. C. Willson, that the House do concur in the amendments made by the Honorable the Legislative Council in and to the Bill for amending the Militia Law, and that Messrs. Dorland and Rogers do carry up the Message of concurrence of this House thereto, which was ordered accordingly, and the message of concurrence is as follows:—

Mr. Speaker,—

The House of Assembly have concurred in the amendments made by the Honorable the Legislative Council in and to an Act intituled "An Act to amend an Act, passed in the forty-eighth year of His Majesty's Reign, intituled 'An Act to explain, amend, and reduce into one Act, the several laws now in force for the raising and training the Militia of this Province.' "

Commons House of Assembly   (Signed) Samuel Street, Speaker.
2nd March, 1811.

A Message from the Honorable the Legislative Council, by Mr. Baldwin, Master in Chancery.

Mr. Speaker,—

I am commanded by the Honorable, the Legislative Council to inform this House that they have passed an Act, sent up from this House, intituled "An Act to repeal an Act, passed in the forty-seventh year of His Majesty's Reign, intituled 'An Act to repeal the several Acts now in force in this Province, relative to Rates and Assessments, and also to particularize the property, real and personal, which, during the continuance thereof, shall be subject to Rates and Assessments; and fixing the several valuations at which each and every particular of such property shall be rated and assessed, and to make further provision for the same," to which they have made several amendments, to which amendments they request the concurrence of this House, in passing the same.

And also a written message from the Honorable the Legislative Council, which is as follows:—

Mr. Speaker,—

The Honorable the Legislative Council have concurred in the alteration proposed in the Committee of Conference, to the amendments made by them in and to an Act intituled "An Act to obviate certain doubts which have arisen in the practice of the Court of King's Bench in this Province."

Legislative Council Chamber,

Saturday, Mar. 2nd, 1811.   (Signed) Tho's. Scott, Speaker.

And then he withdrew.

Read for the first time, the amendments made by the Honorable the Legislative Council in and to the Bill to obviate certain doubts which have arisen in the Practice of the Court of King's Bench in this Province. Mr. Rogers then moved, seconded by Mr. Casey, that the amendments made by the Honorable the Legislative Council in and to the Bill for obviating certain doubts which have arisen in the Practice of the Court of King's Bench in this Province be read a second time on Monday next, which was ordered accordingly.

Mr. Willcocks moved, seconded by Mr. Secord, that so much of the Order of the Day as relates to the third reading of the Bill concerning the Boundaries of Land in this Province, be dispensed with, and that the House do now resolve itself into a Committee to reconsider the said Bill. The House accordingly resolved itself into a Committee. Mr. Speaker left the Chair. Mr. Burrit was called to the Chair of the Committee.

Mr. Speaker resumed the Chair, and Mr. Burritt reported that the Committee had made some progress, and had directed him to ask for leave to sit again on Monday next. Leave was accordingly granted for the Committee to sit again on Monday next.

Read for the second time, the Bill for the relief of Creditors against Absconding Debtors. Mr. McLean then moved, seconded by Capt. Elliott, that the House do now resolve itself into a Committee, to take into consideration the Bill intituled "An Act for the relief of Creditors against Absconding Debtors. The House accordingly resolved itself into Committee. Mr. Speaker left the Chair. Mr. Dorland was called to the Chair of the Committee.

Mr. Speaker resumed the Chair, and Mr. Dorland reported that the Committee had made a progress, and had directed him to ask for leave to sit again this day. Leave was accordingly granted for the Committee to sit again this day.

A Message from the Honorable the Legislative Council by Mr. Baldwin, Master in Chancery.

Mr. Speaker,—

I am commanded by the Honorable the Legislative Council to inform this House that they have passed an Act sent up from this House, intituled "An Act to repeal an Act passed in the forty-seventh year of His Majesty's Reign, intituled "An Act for granting to His Majesty duties on Licenses to Hawkers, Pedlars, Petty Chapmen, and other trading persons, therein mentioned, and further for granting to His Majesty certain duties on Licenses to Hawkers, Pedlars and Petty Chapmen, and other trading persons therein mentioned," to which they have made several amendments, to which amendments they request the concurrence of this House in passing the same.

And then he withdrew.

Agreeably to leave given the House again resolved itself into a Committee, to go into the further consideration of the Bill for the relief of Creditors against Absconding Debtors. Mr. Speaker left the Chair. Mr. Dorland again took the Chair of the Committee.

Mr. Speaker resumed the Chair, and Mr. Dorland reported that the Committee had made some progress, and had directed him to ask for leave to sit again on Monday next. Leave was accordingly granted for the Committee to sit again on Monday next.

Read for the second time, the Bill for the relief of the Creditors of such persons who have died indebted beyond what their personal estate can discharge. Mr. Gough then moved, seconded by Mr. Willcocks, that the Bill for the benefit of the Creditors of such persons as died indebted beyond what their personal estates can discharge, be read a second time this day three months, which was ordered accordingly.

30 A.

- Mr. J. Willson then moved, seconded by Mr. Willcocks, for leave to bring up the Petition of Augustus Jones. Leave was accordingly granted, and the said petition was ordered to lie on the Table.

Mr. Willcocks then moved, seconded by Mr. Mallory, that so much of the rules of this House be dispensed with as relates to the Petition of Augustus Jones, and that the said Petition be now read. The said Rule was accordingly dispensed with, on this occasion, and the Petition of Augustus Jones was accordingly read by the Clerk at the Table, and is as follows:—

To the Honorable the Commons House of Assembly of the Province of Upper Canada, in Provincial Parliament assembled, &c., &c.

The Memorial of Augustus Jones of Niagara District, D. P. S.

Most Humbly Showeth,—

That Your Memorialist was, in the month of June, 1787, employed by the order of the then Commanding Officer at Niagara and the Magistrates, to execute certain surveys under P. R. Frey, D. C. S., and continued in such service under the said P. R. Frey from the 11th June, 1787, to the month of February, 1789, during which time there were almost fifteen Townships surveyed (which included the first settlers at Niagara.)

That Mr. Frey having left this Province before the said Survey was entirely completed Your Memorialist has never received any remuneration whatever, either for his own loss of time and salary, or the disbursements for the wages allowed the hands employed, and other incidental expenses made; amounting in all to £526. 15. 1 3-4 Provincial Currency; as will fully appear by the Accounts accompanying this, together with the Land Board Certificate.

Wherefore Your Memorialist most humbly prays that Your Honorable House will be pleased to take his case into consideration; and grant him such relief as your House in your wisdom may think the circumstance of it requires.

And Your Memorialist, as in duty bound, shall ever pray.

York, 2nd March, 1811.   Augustus Jones, D. P. S.

Mr. Mallory then moved, seconded by Mr. J. Willson, that the fifth Rule of this House be dispensed with, so far as it relates to the Petition of Augustus Jones, and that the House do now resolve itself into a Committee, to take into consideration the said Petition, which passed in the negative.

Mr. Mallory again moved, seconded by Mr. John Willson, for leave to bring in a Bill on Monday next, to give relief to Augustus Jones, which also passed in the negative.

Agreeably to the Order of the Day, the House resolved itself into a Committee, to go into the further consideration of the Bill to form a separate District from a part of the Niagara and Home Districts. Mr. Speaker left the Chair. Mr. Secord was called to the Chair of the Committee.

Mr. Speaker resumed the Chair, and Mr. Secord reported that the Committee had gone through the consideration of the said Bill, and had come to a resolution that the said Bill be read this day three months, which he was directed to report whenever the House should be pleased to receive the same. The House divided upon the question, and the names were taken down as follows:—

Yeas.	Nays.
MESSRS. BURRITT	MESSRS. MARSH
FRASER	J. WILLSON
STINSON	MALLORY
GOUGH	ROGERS
MCLEAN	WILLCOCKS
DORLAND	SECORD
McGREGOR	CASEY
MARKLE	LEWIS
ELLIOTT	
BABY	
C. WILLSON	

which was carried in the affirmative by a majority of three, and the said Resolution was accordingly adopted, and the said Bill was ordered to be read this day three months.

Read for the second time, the Bill for ascertaining the damages on Bills of Exchange

Mr. Gough then moved, seconded by Mr. McGregor, that the House do now resolve itself into a Committee, to take into consideration the Bill for ascertaining damages on Bills of Exchange. The House accordingly resolved itself into a Committee. Mr. Speaker left the Chair. Mr. Casey was called to the Chair of the Committee.

Mr. Speaker resumed the Chair, and Mr. Casey reported that the Committee had gone through the consideration of the said Bill without any amendment, which he was directed to report whenever the House should be pleased to receive the same. Ordered, that the Report be now received.

Mr. Gough then moved, seconded by Mr. Rogers, that the Bill for ascertaining the damages on protested Bills of Exchange be engrossed, and read a third time on Monday next, which was ordered accordingly.

Mr. Mallory moved, seconded by Mr. John Willson, for leave to bring in a Bill, on Monday next, for the purpose of giving encouragement to new and useful inventions in this Province. Leave was accordingly granted.

Mr. McLean, seconded by Capt. Elliott, moved for leave to bring in a Bill, on Monday next, to repeal an Act passed in the forty-seventh year of His Majesty's Reign, intituled "An Act to repeal the several Acts now in force in this Province, relative to Rates and Assessments, and also to particularize the property, real and personal, which, during the continuance thereof, shall be subject to Rates and Assessments; and fixing the several valuations at which each and every particular of such property shall be rated and assessed. Leave was accordingly granted.

Mr. McLean again moved, seconded by Mr. Dorland, for leave to bring in a Bill, on Monday next, intituled "An Act to repeal an Act passed in the forty-seventh year of His Majesty's Reign, intituled "An Act for granting to His Majesty duties on Licenses to Hawkers, Pedlars and Petty Chapmen, and other trading persons therein mentioned; and further for granting to His Majesty certain duties on Licenses to Hawkers, Pedlars and Petty Chapmen, and other trading persons therein mentioned, and to make further provision for the same.'" Leave was accordingly granted.

On motion of Mr. Dorland, seconded by Mr. C. Willson, the House adjourned until Monday next, at eleven o'clock in the forenoon.

Monday, 4th March, 1811.

Prayers were read.

Mr. McLean moved, seconded by Mr. Gough, that Mr. Mears be discharged from the custody of the Serjeant at Arms, without paying Fees, which was ordered accordingly.

Read for the third time, as engrossed, the Bill to amend the Register Act.

On motion of Mr. McLean, seconded by Mr. Gough, resolved, that the Bill do now pass, and that the title be "An Act to amend an Act passed in the thirty-fifth year of the Reign of His Majesty, intituled 'An Act for the Public Registering of Deeds, Conveyances, Wills and other Incumbrances which shall be made or may affect any lands, tenements or hereditaments within this Province.'" The Bill then passed, and was signed by the Speaker. Mr. Gough, seconded by Capt. Elliott, again moved, that Messrs. McLean and Mears do carry up to the Honorable the Legislative Council the Bill for amending the Register Act, and request their concurrence in passing the same, which was ordered accordingly.

Read for the third time, as engrossed, the Bill for ascertaining damages on Protested Bills of Exchange. On motion of Mr. Gough, seconded by Mr. G. Willson, resolved, that the Bill do pass, and that the title be "An Act to repeal an Ordinance of the Province of Quebec, passed in the seventeenth year of His Majesty's Reign, intituled 'An Ordinance for ascertaining damages on Protested Bills of Exchange, and fixing the Rate of Interest in the Province of Quebec; also to ascertain damages on Protested Bills of Exchange and fixing the Rate of Interest in this Province.'" The Bill then passed, and was signed by the Speaker.

Mr. Gough again moved, seconded by Mr. Dorland, that Messrs. McLean and Mears do carry up to the Honorable the Legislative Council the Bill for ascertaining damages on Protested Bills of Exchange, and request their concurrence in passing the same, which was ordered accordingly.

Mr. Mears moved, seconded by Mr. Howard, for leave to bring up the Petition of the inhabitants of the County of Prescott. Leave was accordingly granted, and the said Petition ordered to lie upon the Table.

Agreeably to the Order of the Day, the House resolved itself into a Committee, to go into the further consideration of the Bill for the better ascertaining the boundary lines of land in this Province. Mr. Speaker left the Chair. Mr. Burritt took the Chair of the Committee.

Mr. Speaker resumed the Chair, and Mr. Burritt reported that the Committee had gone through the consideration of the said Bill, to which they had made several amendments, which he was directed to report whenever the House should be pleased to receive the same. Ordered, that the Report be now received.

Mr. McLean, one of the messengers named to carry up to the Honorable the Legislative Council the Act intituled "An Act to amend an Act passed in the thirty-fifth year of His Majesty's Reign, intituled 'An Act for the public registering of Deeds, Conveyances, Wills and other incumbrances which shall be made or may affect any lands, tenements or hereditaments within the Province.

And also an Act intituled, "An Act to repeal an Ordinance of the Province of Quebec, passed in the seventeenth year of His Majesty's Reign, intituled 'An Ordinance, for ascertaining damages on protested Bills of Exchange, and fixing the rate of interest in the Province of Quebec; and to ascertain damages on Protested Bills of Exchange, and fixing the rate of interest in this Province,'" reported that they had carried up the said Acts, and requested their concurrence in passing the same.

Mr. Rogers, one of the Messengers ordered to carry up to the Honorable Legislative Council the Message of Concurrence of this House to the amendments made by them to the Militia Law, reported that they had carried up the said Message accordingly.

Mr. Howard moved, seconded by Mr. Rogers, that the Land Survey Bill be engrossed, and read a third time to-morrow, which was ordered accordingly

Read for the second time, the amendments made by the Legislative Council in and to the Bill for obviating certain doubts which have arisen in the practice of the Court of King's Bench. Mr. Rogers then moved, seconded by Mr. Secord, that the House do now resolve itself into a Committee, to take into their consideration the amendments made by the Legislative Council to a Bill to obviate certain doubts that have arisen in the practice of the Court of King's Bench. The House accordingly resolved itself into a Committee. Mr. Speaker left the Chair. Mr. Mears was called to the Chair of the Committee.

Mr. Speaker resumed the Chair, and Mr. Mears reported that the Committee had concurred in the amendments made by the Honorable the Legislative Council in and to the said Bill, which he was directed to report whenever the House should be pleased to receive the same. Ordered, that the Report be now received and accepted. Mr. Rogers then moved, seconded by Mr. Stinson, that the amendments made by the Honorable the Legislative Council to the Bill for obviating certain doubts that have arisen in the Practice of the Court of King's Bench be read a third time to-morrow, which was ordered accordingly.

  . Mr. Willcocks moved, seconded by Mr. Rogers, that the House do now resolve itself into a Committee, to take into consideration the Libel Bill.   .

The House divided upon the question, and the names were taken down as follows:—

. Yeas.	Nays.
MESSRS. GOUGH	MESSRS. BABY
DORLAND	McNABB
CASEY	MARSH
MALLORY	MEARS
HOWARD	FRASER
WILLCOCKS	BURRITT
ROGERS	ELLIOTT
STINSON	McGREGOR
SOVEREIGN	MARKLE
	LEWIS
	C. WILLSON
	McLEAN

Carried in the negative by a majority of two.

Agreeably to the Order of the Day, the House resolved itself into a Committee, to go into the further discussion of the Bill for the Relief of Creditors against Absconding Debtors. Mr. Speaker left the Chair. Mr. Dorland took the Chair of the Committee.

  . Mr. Speaker resumed the Chair, and Mr. Dorland reported that the Committee had made some progress, and directed him to ask for leave to sit again this day. Leave was accordingly granted for the Committee to sit again this day.

  . A Message from the Honorable the Legislative Council, by Mr. Burns, Master in Chancery:—

Mr. Speaker,—

I am commanded by the Honorable the Legislative Council to inform this House that they have passed an Act, sent up from this House, intituled "An Act to amend and repeal part of an Act, passed in the fiftieth year of His Majesty's Reign, intituled 'An Act to provide for the laying out, amending and keeping in repair the Public Highways and Roads in this Province, and to repeal the laws now in force for that purpose.'"

And also that they have passed an Act, sent up from this House, intituled "An Act to continue and amend an Act, passed in the forty-ninth year of His Majesty's Reign, intituled 'An Act for the continuing for a limited time the Provisional Agreement entered into between this Province and Lower Canada, at Montreal, on the fifth day of July, 1804, relative to duties; also for continuing for a limited time the several Acts of the Parliament of this Province now in force relating thereto,'" to which Acts they have made several amendments, and to which amendments they request the concurrence of this House in passing the same.

And then he withdrew.

Read for the first time, the amendments made by the Honorable the Legislative Council in and to the Bill for amending the Road Act.

Agreeably to leave given, the House again resolved itself into a Committee, to go into the further consideration of the Bill for the Relief of Creditors against Absconding Debtors. Mr. Speaker left the Chair. Mr. Dorland again took the Chair of the Committee.

Mr. Speaker resumed the Chair, and Mr. Dorland reported that the Committee had gone through the consideration of the said Bill, to which they had made several amendments; which he was directed to report whenever the House should be pleased to receive the same. Ordered, that the Report be now received. Mr. McLean then moved, seconded by Mr. Gough, that the Bill intituled "An Act for the Relief of Creditors against Absconding Debtors" be engrossed, and read a third time to-morrow, which' was ordered accordingly.

Mr. Gough moved, seconded by Mr. Dorland, for leave to bring in a Bill, to-morrow, to amend and continue for a limited time an Act, passed in the forty-ninth year of His Majesty's Reign, intituled "An Act for continuing for a limited time the Provisional Agreement entered into between this Province and Lower Canada, at Montreal, on the 5th day of July, 1804, relative to duties; also for continuing for a limited time the several Acts of the Parliament of this Province now in force relating thereto." Leave was accordingly granted.

Read for the first time, the Assessment Bill.

Mr. McLean then moved, seconded by Mr. Gough, that the Assessment Bill be read a second time to-morrow, which was ordered accordingly.

Read for the first time, the Bill to lay duties upon Hawkers, Pedlars and Petty Chapmen in this Province. Mr. McNabb then moved, seconded by Mr. McLean, that the Hawkers' and Pedlars' Bill be read a second time to-morrow, which was ordered accordingly.

Mr. Willcocks gave notice that he will move on the first day of the next Session that this House do resolve itself into a Committee, to take into consideration the necessity of enquiring into the cause why an account of Militia Fines, collected previous to the year 1808, should not be accounted for to this House

Mr Rogers, from the Select Committee, to whom was referred the Provincial Public Accounts, reported the proceedings of the Committee thereon.

He read the Report in his place, and then delivered the same in at the Table, where it was again read by the Clerk, and is as follows:

REPORT OF THE SELECT COMMITTEE appointed to take into their consideration the Public Accounts of this Province, the Third Session of the Fifth Provincial Parliament.

The Committee upon examining the Accounts Nos. 10 and 17 find that all the payments that have been made are by proper authority, and that there remained in the Receiver-General's hands the 31st December, 1810, a balance of £5096   1   9

Upon examining the account No. 14 we find that there was outstanding the 31st December, 1810, on duties collected on Shop, Innkeepers' and Still Licenses, issued between 5th January, 1810, and 5th January, 1811, as far as the accounts have been received ....   783 · 3   2¼

It appears by the account No. 8 that there was outstanding 31st December, 1810, of duties collected on goods imported from the United States, between 1st January and 31st December, 1810, as far as accounts have come to hand, the sum of   474   19   2½

It also appears by the account No. 7 that there was outstanding the 31st December, 1810, of duties collected on Licenses issued to Hawkers, Pedlars and Petty Chapman, for the year ending 5th April, 1811, as far as the accounts have come to hand....   232   0   6

There is due from Colin McNabb, late Collector at Niagara since 1802 ....   ·87   0   10¼

The amount of the duties to be received from Lower Canada for duties collected on goods imported into this Province between 1st January and 31st December, 1810, after deducting the expense of collection will probably amount to   4353   0   0

                                                                            £11026   5   6

Sums that will immediately be wanted:
The sum appropriated for roads, District of Johnstown ....   £200   0   0 ·
District of Johnstown, Western District   200   0   0
Six Sheriffs, due 3rd March next, £50 each   300   0   0

                                                                            £700   0   0

Some small sums will also be soon due to several School masters.

All the Officers of the two Houses of Assembly are paid up to the 7th January, 1811, inclusive.

The balance of Lighthouse duty in the hands of the Receiver-General last year, as stated by the Committee, was £314   13   8½

There has been collected to the 31st December, 1810, as far as the accounts have come to hand, £14 9s. 10½d., of which is yet outstanding   155   17   10½

                                                                            £470   11   7

The expenses of lighthouses last year:

York, to 31st December, 1809	£38	15	11			
York, to 30th June, 1810	29	7	0			
York, to 31st December, 1809	31	9	8			
Niagara, to 30th June, 1810	30	12	6			
				130	5	1

Balance in the Receiver-General's hands 340 6 6

Account of money in the Receiver-General's hands, appropriated but not applied

To support the War, by vote	500	0	0
To purchase the British Statutes	175	0	0
For Public Buildings at York	2800	0	0

£3475 0 0

Account of money raised under British Acts of Parliament not accounted for:

On Shop and Innkeepers' Licenses issued between 5th January, 1810, and 5th January, 1811, as far as the accounts are come to hand £620 9 2 4-10

For duties on goods imported from the United States, from 1st January to 31st December, 1810, as far as the returns have been received 328 19 9

To fines and forfeitures 115 16 8¾

£1065 5 8 3-20

The Committee cannot exactly state the sum to be received from Lower Canada for duties, as they do not know what the expense of collection will amount to; they presume, however, that the amount as stated will be the sum this Province will receive nearly.

The Committee observe that the fines, etc., imposed in the several Courts are in the accounts supposed to be levied under British Acts of Parliament; they submit to the House whether they can be properly said to be so levied.

The Committee observe that some of the Collectors of Customs do not furnish their accounts as by law they are required; neither do some of them pay in the money as they are required.

Two Pounds on each tavern and shop license is supposed to be levied under a British Act of Parliament, and the money not accounted for.

All which is humbly submitted.

By Order of the Committee.

(Signed) D. McG. ROGERS, Chairman.

Mr. Gough, one of the Select Committee appointed to examine the accounts of Commissioners of Roads in this Province, reported the proceedings of the Committee thereon, which he read in his place, and then delivered the same in at the Table, where it was again read by the Clerk, and is as follows:

Your Committee, to whom were referred the accounts of the Commissioners appointed under the several Acts of the Parliament of this Province for the amending and repairing the Public Highways and Roads, laying out and opening New Roads, and building Bridges in the several Districts thereof; also the accounts of the Commissioners for the purchase of Hemp,—beg leave to report as follows:

That they have examined the accounts of the different Districts for the money allotted for Roads in the following order. Of the money appropriated in the year 1804 warrants were only issued for the Home District, £150, and for the District of London, £250, which, being applied under the direction of the Lieutenant-Governor, by and with the advice and consent of the Executive Council, the accounts of the expenditure thereof have been audited and approved in Council.

EASTERN DISTRICT.

From this District there is no account of the expenditure of £200, appropriated in the year 1806, which was to be laid out under the directions of the Magistrates in General Quarter Sessions, and presume the same has been accounted for to them; the different sums granted for the years 1808, 1809, and 1810, appear to be duly accounted for, and there remains a balance unexpended in the hands of the Commissioners, Reverend John Strachan, Josh Anderson, and David Sheek, Esquires, £10 16s. 10¾d.

The Committee are informed that the work done in this District is insufficiently done in many parts, some of the causeways having been washed away for want of being properly covered.

DISTRICT OF JOHNSTOWN.

The Committee have the Treasurer's account of the sums paid by him in the year 1806, in compliance with the orders of the Magistrates in General Quarter Sessions, but the Treasurer has made no charge of Commission, although authorized by law to retain three per cent.

They have likewise received the Commissioner's accounts for the years 1808 and 1809, with a report of the Commissioners, of the money being properly applied; but they have no account of the expenditure of £200, appropriated for the year 1810, for which the Warrant has issued, as appears by the Inspector General's return, and remains to be accounted for by the Commissioners, £200.

MIDLAND DISTRICT.

The accounts from this District are minute in detail, accompanied with proper vouchers, verified on oath; there appears a balance due to the Honourable Richard Cartwright, one of the Commissioners £7 16 8
Also an error of 9 11

Due Sir Richard Cartwright £8   6   7

DISTRICT OF NEWCASTLE.

The Committee have received the Treasurer's account for 1806, which they conclude has been audited by the Magistrates in General Quarter Sessions, being expended under their direction.

Also the account of Alexander Fletcher, one of the Commissioners attested on oath, for the years 1808, 1809, and 1810, in whose hands a balance remains of £3. 8s. 6d.

Also the account of Elias Jones, Esquire, one of the Commissioners, accompanied with the vouchers for the expenditure of the appropriation of the years 1806, 1808 and 1809, by which there appears to be a balance in his hands of £1 11 11½

To which add short allowed by him received from the Treasurer in 1806, £19, instead of £19 17s. 6d. 17 6
                                                                                      £2   9   5½

Also paid him by Alexander Fletcher, Esquire, one of the Commissioners in the year 1810 123   3   4½

To be accounted for by Mr. Jones £125 12 10

The Committee have also Robert Baldwin, Esq., one of the Commissioners' account for the years 1808, 1809, and 1810, by which there appears a balance in his hands of...... £9 19   0

Also retained from Wilson until the work undertaken by him is completed 5 15   0

This sum not paid Leonard Soper, Esquire, but retained in Mr. Baldwin's hands, although charged in his account. Your Committee cannot but remark the impropriety of blending private transactions with Public accounts, as this charge refers to a yoke of oxen sold, which Mr. Soper states to be £13, and there is retained by Mr. Baldwin 18   2   6

His charge of commission at ten per cent., the law having made no provision for such charge, your Committee think they would not be justified in admitting it 21   5   0
                                                                                      £55   1   6

To be accounted for by the Commissioners £180 14   4

It has been suggested to the Committee by those residing where the money expended by Alexander Fletcher, Esquire, has been laid out, that sufficient work does not appear to be done adequate to the sums charged in his account with these remarks.

That cutting and clearing away underbrush is twice charged in the year 1809, first in the sum of £10 16s., and afterwards the additional sum of .... £2 ·10   0

Making 30 rods of causeway charged in 1809, but we apprehend was done in 1810, and included in the sum of £71 8s. 6d. that year paid sundry persons for work, and also that the causeway was made for 7s. 6d. per rod, amounting only to £11   15   0

                                            £14   5   0

The Committee having no vouchers from Mr. Fletcher, are incompetent to ascertain the above statement to a certainty, or the correctness of Mr. Fletcher's account, his charge of £4 for a bridge on the front road in Darlington, and no bridge was built, only some timber there, the greatest part of which was got out by Statute Labour.

There also appears a discontent in this district as to the mode and time in which the persons who performed the labour were paid, when they expected to be paid in cash when the work was done, were paid in goods out of stores in York, and in some cases not until twelve months after.

HOME DISTRICT.

The Committee have received the accounts of William Allan, Esquire, Treasurer for the year 1806, approved in General Quarter Sessions, and certified by the Chairman, on which there is a balance due the Treasurer of £0   8   2

Also the account of Samuel Smith, Esquire, one of the Commissioners for the expenditure of £200, appropriated in the year 1898, with vouchers, on which there is a balance due him of 0   3   9

                                     0   11   11

Due the Commissioner £0   11   11

Your Committee have no accounts from Mr. Thomas Hamilton, another of the Commissioners, of the appropriation received by him for the year 1809 .... £200   0   0

Additional sum paid him in pursuance of an Address to the Lieutenant-Governor 18   15   0

The appropriation for the year 1810 250   0   0

To be accounted for by Mr. Hamilton £463   15   0

DISTRICT OF NIAGARA.

The Committee have received the Treasurer's account of £150, the appropriation of the year 1806, which they conclude has been audited by the Magistrates in General Quarter Sessions.

They have also the account of Richard Hatt, Esquire, for part of the expenditures by him under the different appropriations of the years 1806, 1808, 1809, and 1810, on which there appears a balance due by him of £127 16 4

In addition thereto Mr. Hatt appears to have received from the Receiver General, by the Inspector General's Schedule, the full appropriation of the year 1810, being £250, and he only gives credit for £150, short 100 0 0

                                                     £227 16 4

He has also omitted to charge paid Samuel Street, Esquire, another of the Commissioners, and admitted in Mr. Street's account 50 0 0

To be accounted for by Mr. Hatt 177 16 4

Paid William Crooks on part of the road not expended, as appears per Joseph Edwards, Esquire's letter of the 17th January, 1811, to the Inspector General, to be accounted for . . 30 0 0

Also paid Thomas Dickson and Thomas Clark, not expended, as appears per do., and to be accounted for 20 0 0

Balance due on Samuel Street's account for the years 1809 and 1810 .... 60 4 10½

Balance in Joseph Edwards, Esquire's, hands for the year 1809 . . . . 153 2 9

To be accounted for by the Commissioners £441 3 11½

In Mr. Edwards' account is the charge of £3 0s. 5d. for expenses coming to York to receive the money in the year 1809. They suggest to the House the propriety of such a charge, more especially as so large a part thereof remains unexpended in his hands since June, 1809.

DISTRICT OF LONDON.

The Committee have received the account of the Treasurer, also of the Commissioners of the application of the appropriation of £300 for the year 1806, certified and approved in General Quarter Sessions, on which there is a balance due the Commissioners, Daniel Springer and Archibald McMillan, of £2 16s. 4½d.

Also the account of John Yeigh, one of the Commissioners for the year 1808, for the expenditure of £200, appropriated for that year, but unaccompanied by any vouchers.

Also Daniel Springer and Thomas Welsh, Commissioners, their account for the expenditure of £200, appropriated for the year 1809, but unaccompanied with any voucher. They have received no account from Robert Nichol of the application of £300, appropriated for the year 1810, and remains to be accounted for by him, £300.

In the foregoing accounts your Committee find the following sums charged by the respective Commissioners for personal attendance and rations, expenses of bringing the money from York, and risk, advertising and·taking in proposals, procuring a compass, etc., for which there is no provision made by law. The Committee submit to the House whether they ought to be admitted, viz.:—

Archibald McMillan, 1806	£6	7	6
James Burdick, 1806	5	8	9
Daniel Springer, 1806	15	15	0
Thomas Horner and Edward Watson, 1806	3	12	6
John Yeigh, 1808	14	0	0
Daniel Springer, 1809	13	6	3
Thomas Welsh, 1809	12	5	0
	£70	15	0

Exclusive thereof there is charged for surveying the roads during those years, £35. 5s. 1¼d.

WESTERN DISTRICT.

The Committee have the Treasurer's account for the year 1806, also the vouchers for the expenditure £250, appropriated for that year.

Also the account of John McGregor, Esquire, one of the Commissioners, with the vouchers for the expenditures of the moneys appropriated for the years 1808, 1809, and 1810, on which there appears to be due by him £194 19 3
To which add commission he charges, not provided by law.. 16 10 0

£211 9 3

Mr. McGregor also states that the axes, spades, &c., charged in his account are in his store, to remain till further occasion for them on the public roads.

Recapitulation of the different sums to be accounted for by the Commissioners of the respective districts, viz.:

Eastern	£74	16	10	3-4
Johnstown	200	0	0	
Newcastle	180	14	4	
Home	468	15	0	
Niagara	441	3	11½	
London (exclusive of personal services if disallowed)	300	0	0	
Western	211	9	3	
	£1876	19	5¼	

Due the Midland	£8	6	7
" Home		11	11
" London	2	16	4¼
	11	14	10¼

Total £1865 4 7

Although there is so large a sum unaccounted for by reason of some of the accounts not being returned, yet there remains a large sum still to be expended, and the Committee cannot but express their regret that more zeal and exertion, and a more rigid economy has not been exhibited to effect the beneficent intentions of the Legislature.

All which your Committee submit to this Honorable House.

(Signed) Tho's. B. Gough, M. Elliott, David Secord, J. B. Baby, Tho's. Fraser.

Mr. Mallory moved, seconded by Mr. John Wilson, that the House do resolve itself into a Committee, on Wednesday next, to take into their consideration the Report of the Select Committee on the Public Accounts, which was ordered accordingly.

On motion of Mr. Dorland, seconded by Mr. Gough, the House adjourned until eleven o'clock to-morrow forenoon.

Tuesday, 5th March, 1811.

Prayers were read.

Read for the third time, as engrossed, the amendments made by the Honourable the Legislative Council to the Bill intituled "An Act to extend Personal Arrest to the sum of Forty Shillings."

A message from the Honorable the Legislative Council by Mr. Baldwin, Master in Chancery:—

Mr. Speaker,—

I am commanded by the Honourable the Legislative Council to inform this House that they have passed an Act intituled "An Act to Regulate the Duty of Sheriffs, and for other purposes therein mentioned," to which they request the concurrence of this House in passing the same.

And then he withdrew.

Read for the first time, the Act sent down from the Legislative Council, intituled "An Act to regulate the Duty of Sheriffs, and for other purposes therein mentioned."

Mr. Rogers moved, seconded by Mr. Willcocks, that the Bill for obviating certain doubts that have arisen in the practice of the Court of King's Bench, amended by the Honorable the Legislative Council under the title of "An Act to extend Personal Arrest to the extent of Forty Shillings, and otherwise to regulate the practice in cases of personal arrest," do now pass as amended. The Bill accordingly passed as amended, and was signed by the Speaker.

Mr. Howard then moved, seconded by Mr. Willcocks, that Messrs. Rogers and Casey, do carry up to the Honorable the Legislative Council the Message of this House, that it has concurred in and to a Bill intituled "An Act to extend Personal Arrest to the sum of Forty Shillings, and otherwise to regulate the practice in cases of Personal Arrest," as amended by them, which was ordered accordingly.

And the message of concurrence was as follows:

Mr. Speaker,

The House of Assembly have concurred in the amendments made by the Honourable the Legislative Council, in and to an Act intituled "An Act to extend Personal Arrest to the sum of Forty Shillings and otherwise to regulate the practice in cases of Personal Arrest."

Commons House of Assembly,	(Signed) SAMUEL STREET,
5th March, 1811.	Speaker.

Mr. Mallory moved, seconded by Mr. Rogers, that the Bill sent down from the Legislative Council, to regulate the Duty of Sheriffs, be read a second time to-morrow, which was ordered accordingly.

Read for the third time, as engrossed, the Bill for the better ascertaining the boundaries of land in this Province. On motion of Mr. Howard, seconded by Mr. Rogers, resolved, that the Bill do now pass, and that the title be "An Act Concerning Land Surveyors, the Admeasurement of Land, and the More Accurately Ascertaining the Boundaries of Land in this Province." The Bill was then passed, and was signed by the Speaker.

Mr. Rogers then moved, seconded by Mr. Mallory, that Messrs. Howard and Stinson do carry up to the Honorable the Legislative Council the bill intituled "An Act Concerning Land Surveyors and the Admeasurement of Lands, and for More Accurately Ascertaining the Boundaries of Land in this Province," and request their concurrence in passing the same, which was ordered accordingly.

Mr. Rogers, one of the messengers named to carry up to the Honorable the Legislative Council the message of concurrence of this House to the amendments made by them in and to the Act intituled "An Act to extend Personal Arrest to Forty Shillings," reported that they had carried up the said message.

Read for the first time, the Bill to continue the Provisional Agreement with Lower Canada.

Mr. Gough then moved, seconded by Mr. Rogers, that the fifth Standing Rule of the House, which requires that any Member intending to move any question shall give one day's previous notice, be dispensed with, as far as it relates to the Provisional Agreement Bill. Ordered accordingly.

Mr. Gough again moved, seconded by Capt. Elliott, that the Provisional Agreement Bill be read a second time this day, which was ordered accordingly.

Mr. Howard, one of the messengers named to carry up to the Honorable the Legislative Council the Act intituled "An Act Concerning Land Surveyors, the Admeasurement of Land, and the More Accurately the Boundaries of Land in this Province," reported that they had carried up the said Act, to which they requested their concurrence in passing the same.

Read for the second time, the Bill to continue the Provisional Agreement with Lower Canada.

Mr. Gough then moved, seconded by Mr. McLean, that the House do now resolve itself into a Committee, to take into consideration the Provisional Agreement with Lower Canada. The House accordingly resolved itself into a Committee. Mr. Speaker left the chair. Mr. McNabb was called to the chair of the Committee.

Mr. Speaker resumed the chair, and Mr. McNabb reported that the Committee had gone through the consideration of the said Bill without any amendment, which he was directed to report whenever the House should be pleased to receive the same. Ordered that the report be now received.

Mr. Gough then moved, seconded by Mr. McLean, that the Provisional Agreement Bill be engrossed, and read a third time this day, which was ordered accordingly.

Read for the third time, as engrossed, the Bill to continue the Provisional Agreement with Lower Canada. On motion of Mr. Gough, seconded by Mr. McLean, resolved, that the Bill do now pass, and that the title be "An Act to amend and continue for a limited time, an Act passed in the forty-ninth year of His Majesty's reign, intituled 'An Act for continuing for a limited time the Pro-

visional Agreement entered into between this Province and Lower Canada, at
Montreal, on the 5th day of July, 1804, relative to duties; also for continuing for
a limited time the several Acts of the Parliament of this Province now in force
relating thereto.' " The Bill then passed, and was signed by the Speaker.

Mr. Gough again moved, seconded by Mr. McLean, that Messrs. McNabb
and Marsh do carry up to the Honorable the Legislative Council the Provisional
Agreement Bill, and request their concurrence in passing the same.   Ordered
accordingly.

Read for the second time, the Bill to lay a duty upon Hawkers, Pedlars and
Petty Chapmen.

Mr. McNabb then moved, seconded by Mr. Burritt, that the House do now
resolve itself into a Committee, to take into consideration the Hawker and Pedlar
Bill. The House accordingly resolved itself into a Committee.

Mr. Speaker left the Chair. Mr. Rogers was called to the chair of the Committee.

Mr. Speaker resumed the Chair, and Mr. Rogers reported that the Committee
had gone through the consideration of the said Bill, without any amendment,
which he was directed to report whenever the House should be pleased to receive
the same. Ordered, that the Report be now received.

Mr. McNabb again moved, seconded by Mr. Dorland, that the Hawker and
Pedlar Bill be engrossed, and read a third time to-morrow, which was ordered
accordingly.

Read for the second time, the Assessment Bill. Mr. Mallory then moved,
seconded by Mr. McLean, that the House do now resolve itself into a Committee,
to take into consideration the Assessment Bill. The House accordingly resolved
itself into a Committee. Mr. Speaker left the Chair. Mr. John Willson was
called to the chair of the Committee.

Mr. Speaker resumed the Chair, and Mr. Willson reported that the Committee had gone through the consideration of the said Bill, to which they had
made several amendments, which he was directed to report whenever the House
should be pleased to receive the same. Ordered, that the Report be now received.

Mr. McLean then moved, seconded by Mr. Gough, that the Assessment Bill
be engrossed, and read a third time to-morrow. Ordered accordingly.

Read for the second time, the Bill for the better Application of Militia Fines.
Mr. Willcocks then moved, seconded by Mr. Howard, that the House do now re-
solve itself into a Committee, to take into consideration the Bill for the Better
Application of Militia Fines. The House accordingly resolved itself into a Com-
mittee. Mr. Speaker left the Chair. Mr. Lewis was called to the chair of the
Committee.

Mr. Speaker resumed the Chair, and Mr. Lewis reported that the Committee
had gone through the consideration of the said Bill, to which they had made several
amendments, which he was directed to report whenever the House should be pleased
to receive the same. Ordered, that the Report be now received.

Mr. Willcocks then moved, seconded by Mr. Mallory, that the Bill for altering
the Application of Militia Fines be engrossed, and read a third time to-morrow,
which was ordered accordingly.

Read for the third time, as engrossed, the Bill for the relief of Creditors
against Absconding Debtors. Mr. McLean then moved, seconded by Capt. Elliott,
that the Bill for the Relief of Creditors against Absconding Debtors do now pass,

and that the title be "An Act for the Relief of Creditors against Absconding Debtors." The House divided upon the question, and the names were taken down as follows :—

Yeas.	Nays.
MESSRS. MEARS	MESSRS. MALLORY
BURRITT	WILLCOCKS
LEWIS	HOWARD
McGREGOR	
GOUGH	
CASEY	
SOVEREIGN	
STINSON	
McNABB	
JOHN WILLSON	
C. WILLSON	
MARKLE	
BABY	
DORLAND	
- McLEAN	
ELLIOTT	

Carried in the affirmative by a majority of fourteen. The Bill then passed, and was signed by the Speaker.

Mr. McLean again moved, seconded by Capt. Elliott, that Messrs. McNabb and Dorland do carry up to the Legislative Council the Bill intituled "An Act for the Relief of Creditors against Absconding Debtors," and request their concurrence in passing the same, which was ordered accordingly.

Read, the Petition of sundry inhabitants of the Home District, which is as follows.:—

To the Honorable House of Assembly of the Province of Upper Canada.

The Petition of the Subscribers, Inhabitants of the Townships of York, Etobicoke, Trafalgar, Toronto and Nelson.

Most humbly sheweth,

That Your Petitioners, as well as all other of His Majesty's subjects who travel the road leading from York to the western parts of this Province, are frequently put to very great inconveniences and danger, from the want of bridges across the Rivers Humber and Credit, particularly in the early part of the winter, and in the spring of the year, at which periods the ice is frequently in such a state as neither to admit of persons crossing on it or in boats.

That Your Petitioners would be very much benefited by the building of bridges across the said rivers near their mouths.

Therefore, Your Petitioners pray that Your Honorable House will be pleased to join in granting such a sum of money as will be necessary for that purpose.

And Your Petitioners, as in duty bound, will ever pray.

(Signed), Richard Beasley, John Emery, John Smith, John Mir, A. Cowell, Thos. Henton and eighty-five other petitioners.

Also read, the Petition of William Allan, Esq., one of the Commissioners for the purchasing of hemp, which is as follows :

31 A.

To the Honorable the House of Assembly of the Province of Upper Canada, &c., &c., &c.

The Petition of William Allan of York, one of the Commissioners appointed by His Excellency the Lieutenant-Governor for the purchase of hemp, and every part thereof.

Humbly Sheweth,

That Your Petitioner had the honor of being named as Commissioner for the purchase of hemp by the Late Lieutenant Governor, after the passing of the Act in 1804, and did continue to purchase and export the same, according to the best of his judgment, without making any charge for storage or commission till 1809; but on seeing at that period the account of one of the other Commissioners, wherein storage was charged at 50 per bundle, Your Petitioner thought, of course, that although the law did not provide for any allowance of commission, yet it was not contemplated by the Honorable House of Assembly that the Commissioners should take so much trouble, and run so great risk, without some allowance. Upon which Your Petitioner presumed to charge the said Commission. He, therefore, prays that the wisdom of the House will take into consideration and admit of the said Commission, charged previous to the passing of the late Act.

And Your Petitioner, as in duty bound, will ever pray, &c., &c., &c.

York, 28th February, 1811.   (signed) W. ALLAN.

Mr. Gough then moved, seconded by Mr. Sovereign, that the Petition of William Allan, Esquire, one of the Commissioners for the purchase and exportation of hemp, be referred to the Committee on the Contingent Accounts.   Ordered accordingly.

Mr. McLean moved, seconded by Capt. Elliott, that the amendments made by the Legislative Council, in and to the Bill intituled " An Act for amending the highways and roads," be read a second time on to-morrow, which was ordered accordingly.

Read for the first time, the Bill to encourage Useful Arts and Inventions in this Province.

Mr. Mallory then moved, seconded by Mr. Willcocks, that the Bill to encourage Useful Arts and Inventions in this Province be read a second time on to-morrow. The same was ordered accordingly.

On motion of Mr. Dorland, seconded by Mr. Stinson, the House adjourned until eleven o'clock to-morrow forenoon.

Wednesday, 6th March, 1811.

Prayers were read.

On motion of Mr. Willcocks, seconded by Mr. Mallory, ordered, that this House do, on to-morrow, resolve itself into a Committee upon Privileges of the House.

Read for the third time, as engrossed, the Bill for laying duties upon Hawkers and Pedlars in this Province.

Mr. McNabb then moved, seconded by Capt. Fraser, that the Bill do now pass, and that the title be " An Act to repeal an Act, passed in the forty-seventh year of His Majesty's Reign, intituled ' An Act for granting to His Majesty duties on Licenses to Hawkers, Pedlars and Petty Chapmen, and other trading persons therein mentioned; and further for granting to His Majesty duties on Licenses to Hawkers, Pedlars, and Petty Chapmen, and other trading persons therein mentioned.'" The House divided upon the question, and the names were taken down as follows:—

Yeas.	Nays.
MESSRS. MEARS	MESSRS. MALLORY
McNABB	HOWARD
FRASER	SECORD
GOUGH	WILLCOCKS
McLEAN	J. WILLSON
STINSON	LEWIS
CASEY	
ROGERS	
McGREGOR	
SOVEREIGN	
C. WILLSON	
MARKLE	
ELLIOTT	
BABY	
DORLAND	
MARSH	

Carried in the affirmative by a majority of ten. The Bill then passed, and was signed by the Speaker.

Mr. McLean moved, seconded by Mr. Baby, that Messrs. McNabb and Dorland do carry up to the Honorable the Legislative Council the Bill intituled " An Act to lay a duty upon Hawkers, Pedlars and Petty Chapmen," and request their concurrence in passing the same, which was ordered accordingly.

Read for the third time, as engrossed, the Assessment Bill.

Mr. McNabb, one of the messengers named to carry up to the Honorable the Legislative Council the Act intituled " An Act to amend and continue for a limited time an Act passed in the forty-ninth year of His Majesty's Reign, intituled ' An Act for continuing for a limited time the Provisional Agreement entered into between this Province and Lower Canada, at Montreal, on the fifth day of July, One Thousand Eight Hundred and Four, relative to duties; also for continuing for a limited time the several Acts of the Parliament of this Province now in force relating thereto.' "

Also an Act entituled " An Act for the Relief of Creditors against Absconding Debtors."

And also an Act intituled " An Act to repeal an Act, passed in the forty-seventh year of His Majesty's Reign, intituled ' An Act for granting to His Majesty duties on Licenses to Hawkers, Pedlars and Petty Chapmen, and other trading persons therein mentioned, and further for granting to His Majesty duties on Licenses to Hawkers, Pedlars and Petty Chapmen, and other trading persons therein mentioned,' " reported that they had carried up the said Act, to which they requested their concurrence in passing the same.

Mr. Willcocks moved, seconded by Mr. Rogers, that the Order of the Day for the third reading of the Bill for the Better application of Militia Fines be discharged, and that the said Bill be now recommitted. The House accordingly resolved itself into a Committee. Mr. Speaker left the Chair. Mr. Mears took the chair of the Committee.

Mr. Speaker resumed the Chair, and Mr. Mears reported that the Committee had gone through the consideration of the said Bill, to which they had made several amendments, which he was directed to report whenever the House should be pleased to receive the same. Ordered, that the Report be now received. Mr. Willcocks then moved, seconded by Mr. J. Willson, that the fifth Rule of this House be dispensed with, as far as it respects any question respecting a Bill for the more regularly accounting for Militia Fines, and that the said Bill be engrossed, and read a third time this day, which was ordered accordingly.

Read for the first time, the Bill for Regulating Special Juries. Mr. Mallory then Moved, seconded by Mr. Willcocks, that the Bill for regulating the mode of obtaining Special Juries be read a second time to-morrow. The same was ordered accordingly.

Mr. Howard moved, seconded by Mr. Mallory, that this House do now resolve itself into a Committee, to take into their consideration the Bill for appropriating money for the Roads.

Read the Petition of the inhabitants of the County of Prescott, which is as follows:—

To the Honorable the Commons House of Assembly, in Parliament assembled.

The Petition of the Subscribers, inhabitants of the County of Prescott, Eastern District, and Province of Upper Canada.

Humbly Sheweth,

That Your Memorialists beg leave to represent that they have long been settled in this County, and that from its situation on the Rapids of the Grand or Ottawa River they have suffered many and great inconveniences for want of a road in front of the Township of Hawksborough.

Your Memorialists further represent that many valuable settlers, after having passed several years above those rapids, seeing no prospect of having a sufficient road to transmit their produce by land, have actually removed below, and that the heavy expense and risk attendant on ascending the rapids have deterred many from moving to this country.

Your Memorialists further represent that having all these difficulties to encounter, that being cut off from the settlements in the other parts of the District and Province, except such communication as is kept open by individual exertion, the Statute Labour being insufficient to make roads from house to house, on account of the chief part of the lands being held by non-residents,—

Your Petitioners would therefore beg that Your Honorable House will be pleased to take their situation into consideration, and grant such a sum of money as they in their wisdom may think proper to be appropriated to the making a good cart road across the front of the Township of Hawksborough.

And Your Memorialists, as in duty bound, will ever pray.

County of Prescott, Feby. 1st, 1811.

(Signed) Jos. Fortune, Richd. Burnum, David Pattear and thirteen other petitioners.

The House then resolved itself into a Committee, to go into the consideration of the Bill for appropriating money for the roads. Mr. Speaker left the Chair. Mr. Willcocks was called to the chair of the Committee.

Mr. Speaker resumed the Chair, and Mr. Willcocks reported that the Committee had made a progress, and had directed him to ask for leave to sit again this day. Leave was accordingly granted for the Committee to sit again this day.

A message from the Honorable the Legislative Council by Mr. Baldwin, Master in Chancery:—

Mr. Speaker,

I am commanded by the Honorable the Legislative Council to acquaint this House that they have passed an Act sent up from this House, intituled "An Act to repeal an Ordinance of the Province of Quebec, passed in the twenty-eighth year of His present Majesty's Reign, intituled 'An Act or Ordinance to prevent persons practising Physic and Surgery within the Province of Quebec, or Midwifery in the Towns of Quebec or Montreal,'" to which they have made several amendments, and to which they request the concurrence of this House in passing the same.

And then he withdrew.

Read for the first time, the amendments made by the Legislative Council in and to the Bill to repeal the ordinance of Quebec respecting the practice of Physic, Surgery, and Midwifery.

On motion of Mr. McLean, seconded by Mr. McNabb, resolved, that the Assessment Bill do now pass, and that the title be "An Act to repeal an Act passed in the forty-seventh year of His Majesty's Reign, intituled 'An Act to repeal the several Acts now in force in this Province, relative to rates and Assessments; and also to particularize the property, real and personal, which, during the continuance thereof, shall be subject to Rates and Assessments, and fixing the several valuations at which each and every particular of such property shall be rated and assessed, and to make further provision for the same.'" The Bill then passed, and was signed by the Speaker. Mr. Willcocks moved, seconded by Mr. Howard, that Messrs. McLean and Mallory do carry up to the Honorable the Legislative Council the Assessment Act, and request their concurrence thereto, which was ordered accordingly.

Mr. McLean, one of the messengers named to carry up to the Honorable the Legislative Council the Act intituled "An Act to repeal an Act passed in the forty-seventh year of His Majesty's Reign, intituled 'An Act to repeal the several Acts now in force in this Province relative to Rates and Assessments; and also to particularize the Property, real and personal, which, during the continuance thereof, shall be subject to rates and Assessments; and fixing the several valuations at which each and every particular of such property shall be rated and assessed, and to make further provision for the same,'" reported that they had carried up the said Act, and did request their concurrence in passing the same.

Agreeably to leave given, the House again resolved itself into a Committee, to go into the further consideration of the Bill for appropriating money for the Public roads. Mr. Speaker left the Chair. Mr. Willcocks again took the chair of the Committee.

Mr. Speaker resumed the Chair, and Mr. Willcocks reported that the Committee had made some progress, and had directed him to ask leave to sit again to-morrow. Leave was accordingly granted for the Committee to sit again to-morrow.

On motion of Mr. Willcocks, seconded by Mr. Mallory, the House adjourned.

Thursday, 7th March, 1811.

Prayers were read.

Read for the third time, as engrossed, the Bill for the better Application of Militia Fines. On motion of Mr. Willcocks, seconded by Mr. Rogers, resolved, that the Bill do pass, and that the title be "An Act to amend an Act passed in the forty-eighth year of His Majesty's Reign, intituled 'An Act to explain, amend and reduce to one Act of Parliament, the several laws now in being for the raising and retaining the Militia of this Province.' " The Bill then passed, and was signed by the Speaker. Mr. Gough moved, seconded by Mr Lewis, that Messrs. Willcocks and John Willson do carry up to the Honorable ,the Legislative Council the Bill for amending the Militia Law, which was ordered accordingly.

Mr. Mallory moved, seconded by Mr. Dorland, that the House do now resolve itself into a Committee, to take into consideration the Bill to regulate the mode of obtaining Special Juries. The House accordingly resolved itself into a Committee. Mr. Speaker left the Chair. Mr. Mallory was called to the chair of the Committee.

Mr. Speaker resumed the Chair, and Mr. Mallory reported that the Committee had gone through the consideration of the said Bill, to which they had made several amendments, which he was directed to report whenever the House should be pleased to receive the same. Ordered, that the Report be now received.

A message from the Honorable the Legislative Council by Mr. Baldwin, Master in Chancery.

Mr. Speaker,

I am commanded by the Honorable the Legislative Council to acquaint this House that they have passed an Act sent up from this House, intituled "An Act to repeal an Ordinance of the Province of Quebec, passed in the seventeenth year of His Majesty's Reign, intituled 'An Ordinance for ascertaining damages on protested Bills of exchange, and fixing the rate of interest in the Province of Quebec ; also to ascertain damages on protested bills of exchange, and fixing the rate of interest in this Province,' " to which they have made several amendments, and to which they request their concurrence in passing the same. And then he withdrew.

Mr. Willcocks, seconded by Mr. Mallory, moved that the Special Jury Bill be engrossed, and read a third time to-morrow. The same was ordered accordingly.

Read for the first time, the amendments made by the Honorable the Legislative Council, in and to the Bill for ascertaining damages on Protested Bills of Exchange. Mr. Gough then moved, seconded by Mr. Dorland, that the amend' ments made by the Honorable the Legislative Council in and to the Bill for ascertaining the damages on Protested Bills of Exchange be read a second time to-morrow. Accordingly the said amendments were ordered to be read for the second time to-morrow.

Agreeably to the Order of the Day, the House resolved itself into a Committee, to take into consideration the Privileges of the House. Mr. Speaker left the Chair. Mr. Secord was called to the chair of the Committee.

Mr. Speaker resumed the Chair, 'and Mr. Secord reported that it is the opinion of this Committee that John Beikie, Esquire, Sheriff of the Home District, has been guilty of a breach of the Privileges of this House, by summoning a Member thereof, and the Officers of this House to attend as Jurors, while attending their duty in Parliament, which he was directed to report whenever the House should be pleased to receive the same. Ordered, that the Report be now received.

Mr. Rogers then moved, seconded by Mr. Dorland, that this House do direct the Speaker to inform John Beikie, Esquire, Sheriff of the Home District, that the House of Assembly have resolved that he has been guilty of a breach of privilege, in summoning a Member of this House, and some of its Officers, to attend as Jurors while they were engaged in their duty in the House ; but that the Assembly, being informed by several Members in their places that the said summonses were served by the Sheriff's Officers without his knowledge, do at this time admit that as an excuse, but they will expect that the Sheriff will take care that nothing of the like nature will happen in future, which was ordered and directed accordingly.

Mr. Willcocks, one of the messengers named to carry up to the Honorable the Legislative Council the Act intituled "An Act to amend part of an Act passed in the forty-eighth year of His Majesty's Reign, intituled 'An Act to explain, amend, and reduce to one Act of Parliament the several Laws now in being for the raising and training the Militia of this Province,'" reported that they had carried the said Act, to which they requested their concurrence in passing the same.

Mr. Gough, one of the Select Committee to whom was referred the Accounts of the Commissioners appointed for the Encouragement of the Cultivation and Exportation of Hemp, the growth of this Province, reported that Your Committee, to whom were referred the Accounts of the Commissioners appointed under the several Acts of the Parliament of this Province, for the encouragement of the Growth and Cultivation of Hemp within this Province, and the Exportation thereof, beg leave to report as follows.

That there appears in the hands of the Receiver General out of the sum of £750, granted for the purchase of Hemp seed and paying Bounties on Hemp, and paid to the Honorable John McGill and David William Smith, Esquires, 28th July, 1801, as appears per the accounts and letters of the Commissioners, Honorable John McGill and Thomas Scott, Esquires, dated 28th July, 1804, a balance of £480   0   0

Paid Hon. James Baby, Richard Cartwright, Robert Hamilton, and William Allan, Esquires, Commissioners appointed in pursuance of the Act of the 44th Geo. III   800   0   0
The Inspector General remarks that on the above warrant there was paid;
4 February, 1804, ... £100   0   0
6 February, 1809 700   0   0
                                        ——————— £1,280   0   0

Of which we find William Allan, Esquire, accounts in his account current.
15 January, 1808, for £100
15 January, 1809, for 300
                                          ——————— 400   0   0
To be accounted for by the above Commissioners........   880   0   0

The Committee have also the accounts of William Allan, Esquire, one of the Commissioners, wherein he acknowledges to have received as per the other side £400   0   0
From the Receiver General, and charged by him in the general account of the Provincial fund, therefore does not appear to be a part of the amount on the other side unaccounted for by the Commissioners   100   0   0

To which add commission charged by him
on his several accounts previous to the Act
of the 50th Geo. 3rd, which not being allowed
by law the Committee does not find themselves
justified in allowing 16.   17   4¼
                                                                         516   17   4¼

And he charges for the purchase of Hemp in the years
1804, 1805, 1806, 1807 and January, 1808, amounting to......   £516   17   4¼

And he charges for the purchase of Hemp in the years
1804, 1805, 1806, 1807, and January, 1808 amounting to ......

1809, Jan.	Cwt.	qrs.	lbs.					
For the pre- }	42	3	0	cost	£101	9	10	
ceding year. }	55	1	1	"	187	1	10½	
May 8, 1810.	21	1	5½	"	71	10	2¾	
May 15, in part } of 1809 & 1810. }	35	1	11	"	117	10	5½	477 12 4¾

Total cwt.   154   2   17½   Due by Mr. Allan,   ...   £39   4   11½

Of the foregoing hemp they have a copy of the account of
sales made in London of that shipped in the year 1808, net proceeds whereof amounts to £100. 7.9. Sterling, equal to Currency.   £122   13   0½

Of which they find only paid by the Honorable Richard
Cartwright into the Receiver General's hands   55   11   1¼

Appears due hereon £67   1   11¼

The other parcels of hemp, purchased by Mr. Allan, since ·
January, 1808, remain to be accounted for, viz.

Cwt.	qrs.	lbs.				
55	1	1	. cost	£187	1	10½
21	1	5½	"	71	10	2¾
35	1	11	"	117	10	5½
111	3	17½		£376	2	4¾

The two first parcels appear to be shipped for England, but the Committee
have no account of the sale thereof.

The last parcel has been sold to Mr. Mills, to`be manufactured in this
Province, agreeable to the act of the Fiftieth George third, which does not appear
to have been paid for.

The Committee also observe the sum of £100 in the Receiver General's account
paid Thomas Talbot, Esquire, one of the Commissioners for the purchase of hemp,
5th February, 1810, out of the Provincial Funds, but not out of the balance
stated to be unaccounted for by the Commissioners, the expenditure whereof is
unaccounted for by Mr. Talbot.

Recapitulation of amount to be accounted for by the Com-
missioners £880   0   0
William Allan   39   4   11½
Thomas Talbot 100   0   0
Hemp as above 111 cwt. 3 qrs. 17½ lbs.; cost 376   2   4¾
Honorable Richard Cartwright, on sales of Hemp in England   67   1   11¼

Tòtal £1,462   9   3½

The Committee further beg leave to observe that Mr. Allan, having made
no charge for weighing, storing, etc., of so dangerous a combustible, which must
be attended with much trouble   both receiving in and shipping, they submit to
the House the justice of allowing him in such manner as the House may think
proper the same commission as is allowed by the 50th Geo. 3rd, as a compensation
for his trouble.

Your Committee also beg leave to suggest that nothing remains of the sum
appropriated for the encouragement of the growth and cultivation of hemp, the
whole appropriation under the Act of the 44th George 3rd, appears to be drawn
from the Treasury, to wit.

By the Commissioners in 1805 .... £800
By Warrant to William Allan, 1810 100
By Warrant to Tho's. Talbot, 1810 100

Being the whole sum appropriated by law £1,000

And it appears that no further sum remains for the future encouragement
of the growth and cultivation of hemp than what may arise from the different
sums unaccounted for, and from the net proceeds of the hemp unaccounted for.

All which Your Committee respectfully submit to the House.

March, 7th, 1811.

(Signed) Thomas B. Gough, Thomas Fraser, M. Elliott, J. B. Baby, David
Secord.

Read, the Petition of sundry inhabitants of the District of Newcastle, which is
as follows.

To the Honorable the Members of the House of Assembly of the Province of
Upper Canada, in Parliament assembled.

The Petition of the several persons whose names are hereunto subscribed,
Inhabitants of the Townships Darlington, Clarke, and Hope, in the District of
Newcastle.

Humbly Sheweth,

That Dundas Street, through the Township of Clarke, is entirely obstructed
by fallen timber, and otherwise, so that travellers and the inhabitants of the
said Townships of Darlington, Clarke and Hope cannot pass and repass through
the said Township of Clarke on Dundas Street at any season of the year.

. That Your Petitioners further state that it is necessary to have the said
road opened for travellers. The sleighing continues much longer upon the said
road than upon the front, and that for upwards of eight miles there is no settlers
to open the same.

Your Petitioners therefore humbly pray that this Honorable House will
grant such sum of money for opening the same as they in their wisdom may
think proper.

Your Petitioners also further state that Mr. John Hartwell of the said Township of Clarke, will obligate himself to keep the said timber out of the road until there is sufficient inhabitants to repair the same.

And Your Petitioners, as in duty bound, will ever pray.

(Signed) Peletiah Soper, Zachariah Chesney, Wm. Orr, Ebenezer Hartwell, William Borland, Alex'r Fletcher, and nineteen other petitioners.

Agreeably to the Order of the Day, the House resolved itself into a Committee, to take into their consideration the Report of the Select Committee on the Public Accounts.

Mr. Speaker left the Chair. Mr. Sovereign was called to the chair of the Committee.

Mr. Speaker resumed the Chair, and Mr. Sovereign reported that the Committee had made a progress, and had directed him to ask for leave to sit again this day. Leave was accordingly granted for the Committee to sit again this day.

A message from the Honorable the Legislative Council by Mr. Baldwin, Master in Chancery:—

Mr. Speaker,

I am commanded by the Honorable the Legislative Council to inform this House that they have passed an Act sent up from this House, intituled "An Act to amend and continue for a limited time an Act passed in the forty-ninth year of His Majesty's Reign, intituled 'An Act for continuing for a limited time the Provisional Agreement entered into between this Province and Lower Canada, at Montreal, on the fifth day of July, One Thousand Eight Hundred and Four, relative to duties; also for continuing for a limited time the several Acts of the Parliament of this Province now in force relating thereto;'" also

An Act intituled "An Act to repeal an Act passed in the forty-seventh year of His Majesty's Reign, intituled 'An Act for granting to His Majesty duties on Licenses to Hawkers, Pedlars, and Petty Chapmen, and other trading persons therein mentioned, and further for granting to His Majesty duties on Licenses to Hawkers, Pedlars and Petty Chapmen, and other trading persons therein mentioned;" without any amendment. And then he withdrew.

Agreeably to leave given, the House again resolved itself into a Committee, to go into the further consideration of the Report of the Select Committee on the Public Accounts. Mr. Speaker left the Chair. Mr. Sovereign again took the chair of the Committee.

Mr. Speaker resumed the Chair, and Mr. Sovereign reported that the Committee had made some progress, and had directed him to ask for leave to sit again to-morrow. Leave was accordingly granted for the Committee to sit again to-morrow.

On motion of Mr. Gough, seconded by Mr. Dorland, the House adjourned.

Friday, 8th March, 1811.

Prayers were read.

Read for the third time, as engrossed, the Bill for the better regulation of Special Juries. On motion of Mr. Rogers, seconded by Capt. Elliott, resolved, that the Bill do pass, and that the title be "An Act to amend an Act, passed in the forty-eighth year of His Majesty's Reign, intituled 'An Act for the better regulation of Special Juries.'"

The Bill then passed and was signed by the Speaker.

Mr. Speaker acquainted the House that, in obedience to its commands he had drafted a letter to John Beikie, Esquire, Sheriff of the Home District, which he read, and was approved by the House, and is as follows.

Commons House of Assembly,

Sir:— March 7th, 1811.

I am directed by the Commons House of Assembly to acquaint you that you have been guilty of a breach of its Privilege, in summoning as Grand Jurors, (to attend a Court of Oyer and Terminer and General Gaol delivery) one of its Members, the Clerk and the Serjeant at Arms, and the Doorkeeper as a Petit Juror, during its sitting; but owing to several Members in their places having acquainted the House that you had informed them that it was done without your knowledge or privity, and having expressed your contrition to them, the House has been pleased at this time to accept of your excuse, in the expectation that a repetition will not be attempted.

I have the honor to be, Sir,

Your Most Obedient and Very Humble Ser't,

To John Beikie, Esquire, (Signed) SAMUEL STREET, Speaker.
Sheriff of the Home District.

Mr. Rogers again moved, seconded by Mr. Dorland, that Messrs. Willcocks and Mallory do carry up to the Honorable the Legislative Council the Special Jury Bill, and request their concurrence in passing the same, which was ordered accordingly.

Read for the second time, The amendments made by the Legislative Council, in and to the Bill for ascertaining damages on Protested Bills of Exchange.

Mr. Gough then moved, seconded by Mr. Rogers, that the House do now resolve itself into a Committee, to take into consideration the amendments made by the Honorable the Legislative Council to the Bill for ascertaining damages on Bills of Exchange. The House accordingly resolved itself into a Committee. Mr. Speaker left the Chair. Mr. Stinson was called to the chair of the Committee. Mr. Speaker resumed the Chair, and Mr. Stinson reported that the Committee had concurred in and to the amendments made by the Honorable the Legislative Council in and to the Bill for ascertaining damages on Protested Bills of Exchange, which he was directed to report whenever the House should be pleased to receive the same. Ordered, that the Report be now received.

Mr. Gough then moved, seconded by Mr. Dorland, that the fifth Standing Rule of this House, which requires that a Member intending to move any question shall give one day's previous notice, be dispensed with, as far as relates to the amendments made by the Honorable the Legislative Council to the Bill for ascertaining damages on Protested Bills of Exchange, which was ordered accordingly. Mr. Gough again moved, seconded by Capt. Elliott, that the amendments made to the Bill for ascertaining damages on Bills of Exchange be read a third time this day. Ordered accordingly. Read for the third time, the amendments made by the Honorable the Legislative Council, in and to the Bill for ascertaining the damages on Protested Bills of Exchange. Mr. Gough moved, seconded by Capt. Elliott, that the House do concur in the amendments made by the Honorable the Legislative Council to the Bill for ascertaining damages on Protested Bills of Exchange, and that Messrs. Willcocks and Mallory do carry up to the Honorable the Legislative Council the message of concurrence of this House thereto. The same was ordered accordingly.

The Bill then passed as amended, and the message of concurrence is as follows:—

Mr. Speaker,—

The House of Assembly have concurred in the amendments made by the Honorable the Legislative Council, in and to the Act intituled " An Act to repeal an Ordinance of the Province of Quebec, passed in the seventeenth year of His Majesty's Reign, intituled ' An Ordinance for acertaining the damages on Protested Bills of Exchange, and fixing the Rate of Interest in the Province of Quebec, also to ascertain damages on Protested Bills of Exchange, and fixing the rate of interest in this Province.' "

Commons House of Assembly,   (Signed) SAMUEL STREET,
8th March, 1811.   Speaker.

Read for the second time, the Bill sent down from the Honorable the Legislative Council, intituled "An Act to amend the process of the District Courts, and further to regulate the proceedings of Sheriffs." Mr. McLean then moved, seconded by Mr. Rogers, that the House do now resolve itself into a Committee, to take into consideration the Bill intituled " An Act to amend the process of the District Courts, and further to regulate the proceedings of Sheriffs." The House accordingly resolved itself into a Committee. Mr. Speaker left the Chair. Mr. C. Willson was called to the chair of the Committee.

Mr. Speaker resumed the Chair, and Mr. Willson reported that the Committee had gone through the consideration of the said Bill without any amendment, which he was directed to report whenever the House should be pleased to receive the same. Ordered that the report be now received.

Mr. Gough then moved, seconded by Mr. Rogers, that the Sheriffs' Bill be read a third time on to-morrow, which was ordered accordingly.

Read for the second time, the amendments made by the Legislative Council, in and to the Bill to amend the Road Act. Mr. McLean then moved, seconded by Mr. Mears, that the House do now resolve itself into a Committee, to take into consideration the amendments made by the Legislative Council, in and to the Road Act. The House accordingly resolved itself into a Committee. Mr. Speaker left the Chair. Mr. McGregor was called to the chair of the Committee.

Mr. Speaker resumed the Chair, and Mr. McGregor reported that the Committee had gone through the consideration of the said amendments, and had come to a resolution, that the said Bill be read again this day three months, which he was directed to report whenever the House should be pleased to receive the same. Ordered that the Report be now received, and that the said Bill be read again in three months hence.

Agreeably to the Order of the Day, the House resolved itself into a Committee, to go into the further consideration of the Bill to extend the jurisdiction of the Court of Requests. Mr. Speaker left the Chair. Mr. Lewis took the chair of the Committee. Mr. Speaker resumed the Chair, and Mr. Lewis reported that the Committee had gone through the consideration of the said Bill, without any amendment, which he was directed to report to the House whenever it should be pleased to receive the same. Ordered that the Report be now received.

Mr. Willcocks then moved, seconded by Mr. Rogers, that the Bill for extending the jurisdiction of the Court of Requests be engrossed, and read a third time to-morrow, which was ordered accordingly.

Agreeably to the Order of the Day, the House resolved itself into a Committee, to go into the further consideration of the Report of the Select Committee on the Public Accounts. Mr. Speaker left the Chair. Mr. Sovereign took the chair of the Committee.

Mr. Speaker resumed the Chair, and Mr. Sovereign reported that the Committee had made some progress, and had directed him to ask for leave to sit again this day. Leave was accordingly granted for the Committee to sit again this day.

A message from the Honorable the Legislative Council by Mr. Baldwin, Master in Chancery:—

Mr. Speaker,—

I am commanded by the Honorable the Legislative Council to acquaint this House that they have passed an Act sent up from this House, intituled " An Act to repeal an Act passed in the forty-seventh year of His Majesty's Reign, intituled ' An Act to repeal the several Acts now in force in the Province, relative to Rates and Assessments, and also to particularize the property, real and personal, which, during the continuance thereof, shall be subject to Rates and Assessments, and fixing the several valuations at which each and every particular of such property shall be rated and assessed,' and to make further provisions for the same," without any amendment.

And then he withdrew.

Mr. Willcocks, one of the messengers named to carry up to the Honorable the Legislative Council the Act intituled " An Act to amend an Act passed in the forty-eighth year of His Majesty's Reign, intituled ' An Act for the better Regulation of Special Juries,' " reported that they had carried up the said Act, and did request their concurrence in passing the same.

Also that they had carried up the message of concurrence of this House to the amendments made by the Honorable the Legislative Council, in and to the Bill for ascertaining damages on Protested Bills of Exchange.

Agreeably to leave given, the House again resolved itself into a Committee, to go into the further consideration of the Report of the Select Committee on the Public Accounts. Mr. Speaker left the Chair. Mr. Sovereign again took the chair of the Committee.

Mr. Speaker resumed the Chair, and Mr. Sovereign reported that the Committee had made a progress, and had directed him to ask for leave to sit again to-morrow. Leave was accordingly granted for the Committee to sit again to-morrow.

On motion of Mr. Dorland, seconded by Mr. Stinson, the House adjourned till 11 o'clock to-morrow.

Saturday, 9th March, 1811.

Prayers were read.

Read for the third time, the Bill sent down from the Honorable the Legislative Council, intituled " An Act to amend the Process of District Courts, and to regulate the proceedings of Sheriffs." Mr. Willcocks, seconded by Mr. Baby, then moved that the Bill from the Honorable the Legislative Council, intituled "An Act to amend the Process of the District Courts, and also further to regulate the Proceedings of Sheriffs in the sale of goods and chattels taken in execution," do now pass. The Bill then passed, and was signed by the Speaker.

Mr. Gough Moved, seconded by Mr. Willcocks, that Messrs. McLean and Casey do carry up to the Honorable the Legislative Council the message of concurrence of

this House in and to the Bill sent down by them, intituled " An Act to amend the
Process of the District Courts, and further to regulate the Proceedings of Sheriffs
in the sale of goods and chattels taken by them in execution," which was ordered
accordingly
And the message of concurrence is as follows:

Mr; Speaker:
The House of Assembly have passed an Act sent down from this Honorable
House, intituled " An Act to amend the Process of the District Courts, and also
further to regulate the Proceedings of Sheriffs in the sale of goods and chattels
taken by them on execution.

Commons House of Assembly,   (Signed) SAMUEL STREET,
Saturday, 9th March, 1811.   Speaker.

A message from the Honorable the Legislative Council, by Mr. Baldwin, Master
in ·Chancery.

Mr. Speaker,—
I am commanded by the Honorable the Legislative Council to acquaint this
House that they have passed an Act sent up from this House, intituled " An Act to
amend an Act passed in the thirty-fifth year of His Majesty's Reign, intituled ' An
Act for the Public Registering of Deeds, Conveyances, Wills and other incum-
brances, which shall.be made, or may affect any Lands, Tenements, or Heredita-
ments within this Province,' " to which they have made several amendments, to
which amendments they request the concurrence in passing the same.
And then he withdrew.
Read for the first time, the amendments made by the Honorable the Legislative
Council in and to the Bill to amend the Register Act.
Read for the third time, as engrossed, the Bill to extend the jurisdiction of the
Court of Requests. On motion of Mr. Willcocks, seconded by Mr. Casey, resolved,
that the Bill do now pass, and that the title be " An Act to extend the jurisdiction
of the Courts of Requests in this Province." The Bill then passed, and was signed
by the Speaker. Mr. Howard Moved, seconded by Mr. Rogers, that Messrs. Willcocks and Casey do carry up to the Honorable the Legislative Council the Bill
intituled " An Act to extend the jurisdiction of the Court of Requests in this
Province," which was ordered accordingly.
Agreeably to the Order of the Day, the House resolved itself into a Committee,
to go into the further consideration of the Bill for the appropriation of moneys for
the Public Roads. Mr. Speaker left the Chair. Mr. Willcocks was called to the
chair of the Committee.
Mr. Speaker resumed the Chair, and Mr. Willcocks reported that the Committee had gone through the consideration of the said Bill, to which they had made
several amendments, which he was directed to report whenever the House should
be pleased to receive the same. Ordered, that the Report be now received. Mr.
Howard then moved, seconded by Mr. Gough, that the Bill for the appropriation
of money for the roads be engrossed, and read a third time on Monday next, which
vas ordered accordingly.
. Mr. Howard again moved, seconded by Mr. C. Willson, that the Speaker of
`iis House do direct five hundred copies of the Bill concerning Land Surveyors
td the admeasurement of land, and for the better and more exactly ascertaining

the boundaries of lands in this Province, to be printed, for the purpose of their being distributed among the Members of the House of Assembly. Ordered accordingly.

Read, the Petition of William Jarvis, Esquire, Keeper of the Rolls, which is as follows:—

To the Honorable the Commons House of Assembly of Upper Canada, in Provincial Parliament assembled.

The Petition of William Jarvis, Esquire, Keeper of the Rolls.

Most Respectfully Sheweth,—

That since the establishment of a Parliament in this Province, Your Petitioner has been Keeper of the Rolls, for which service Your Petitioner has never received any remuneration, except Fifty Pounds Provincial Currency, which Your Honorable House was pleased to grant him during your Session in 1810.

Your Petitioner therefore prays that the Honorable House will be pleased to take this Petition into their consideration, and make him such an annual allowance as the nature of the trust reposed in him shall to them seem meet.

And in duty bound will ever pray.

(Signed) WILLIAM JARVIS,
2nd March, 1811. Keeper of the Rolls.

Mr. McLean moved, seconded by Mr. Burritt, that the House do resolve itself into a Committee on Monday next, to take into consideration the Contingent Account of Both Houses of Parliament, and that the Clerk do lay the same on the Table on that day, which was ordered accordingly.

Mr. Gough gave notice that he will on Monday next move for a new edition of the Laws of the Province to be printed.

Mr. McLean again moved, seconded by Mr. Howard, that the Petition of William Jarvis, Esquire, be referred to the Committee on Contingent Accounts. The same was ordered accordingly.

On motion of Mr. C. Willson, seconded by Mr. Secord, the House adjourned to Monday next.

Monday, 11th March, 1811.

Prayers were read.

Mr. McNabb moved, seconded by Mr. McLean, that the Appropriation Bill be recommended this day, which passed in the negative.

Read for the third time, as engrossed, the Bill for appropriating money for the Public Highways and Roads in this Province. Mr. Howard then moved, seconded by Mr. Rogers, that the following clause be added to the Bill for appropriating money on the roads, "Provided always, and be it further enacted by the authority aforesaid that it shall and may be lawful for the Commissioners to be appointed in and for the District of Johnstown to expend on the bridge on Daniel Jones' Mill Creek the sum of Forty Pounds out of the money granted by this Act for the said District of Johntown should it appear to them that the money is more wanted on that bridge than on the road in the said District before mentioned, anything in this Act to the contrary notwithstanding," which passed in the negative.

Mr. Willcocks, one of the messengers, named to carry up to the Honorable the Legislative Council the Bill intituled "An Act to extend the jurisdiction of the Courts of Requests in this Province," reported that they, had carried up the said Act, to which they requested their concurrence in passing the same.

Also that they had carried up the message of concurrence of this House to the Bill sent down from the Legislative Council, intituled "An Act to amend the Process of the District Courts, and also further to regulate the proceedings of Sheriffs in the sale of goods and chattels taken by them in Execution.

On motion of Mr. Mallory, seconded by Mr. Dorland, resolved, that the Appropriation Bill do now pass, and that the title be "An Act for granting to His Majesty a certain sum of money out of the funds applicable to the use of this Province, to defray the expenses of amending and opening the Public Highways and Roads, and building of Bridges in the several Districts thereof." The Bill then passed, and was signed by the Speaker. Mr. Mallory again moved, seconded by Mr. Baby that Messrs Willcocks and Howard do carry up to the Honorable the Legislative Council the Bill to appropriate money for opening and amending Roads, and building bridges in the several Districts of the Province, and request their concurrence in passing the same, which was ordered accordingly.

Agreeably to the Order of the Day, the House resolved itself into a Committee, to go into the further consideration of the Report of the Select Committee on the Public Accounts. Mr. Speaker left the Chair. Mr. Sovereign took the chair of the Committee.

Mr. Speaker resumed the Chair, and Mr. Sovereign reported that the Committee had come to several resolutions, which he was directed to report whenever the House should be pleased to receive the same. Ordered, that the Report be now received. The Report was accordingly received, and the Resolutions are as follows:—

Resolved, That it is the opinion of this Committee that the Commissioners for the Eastern District have not properly executed the trust reposed in them, by an injudicious application of the moneys committed to them for the purpose of amending and repairing the Highways in the said District.

Resolved, That it is the opinion of this Committee that the money appropriated by law for the District of Johnstown for 1808 and 1809 has been properly applied by the Commissioners of Highways for that District, and that the money appropriated in 1810 has not yet been expended.

Resolved, that it is the opinion of this Committee that the Commissioners of Highways in the Midland District have with propriety executed the trust reposed in them by the Legislature, and they highly approve of the regularity that appears in the accounts received from that District.

Resolved, that it is the opinion of this Committee that Charles Jones, Esquire, Commissioner of Highways in the District of Newcastle has with propriety accounted for the money that has been intrusted to him to lay out on the roads for the years 1808 and 1809, all the charges being accompanied by proper vouchers; and they presume the money now in his hands will be properly accounted for hereafter.

Resolved, that it is the opinion of this Committee, that the Commissioners of Roads appointed for the Western part of the District of Newcastle have misapplied the money committed to their charge for the amending and repairing the Public Highways and Roads in that part of the District, and that great dissatisfaction prevails on account of the improper conduct of the said Commissioners.

Resolved, that it is the opinion of this Committee, that the Commissioners for the Home District have properly executed their duty for the years 1806, 1807, 1808 and 1809, and that all the sums received by them up to that time appear to be duly accounted for. They presume that the sum granted for 1810 will here-after be properly applied and accounted for.

Resolved, that it is the opinion of this Committee that the Acting Commissioners of Highways appointed for the District of Niagara have neglected the trust reposed in them; that the sum of Four Hundred and Forty One pounds, Three Shillings and Elevenpence Halfpenny remains in their hands unaccounted for, and that no vouchers have been produced in confirmation of the sums said to be expended by the said Commissioners.

Resolved, that it is the opinion of this Committee that of the sum of Fifty Pounds, Provincial Currency, granted in the year 1810 for the road from Buchner's Bridge in Willoughby, to William Steele's in Humberstone, there has only been the sum of Thirty Pounds and One Shilling, New York Currency, expended on that Road, agreeable to the intention of the Legislature.

Resolved, that it is the opinion of this Committee that the Commissioners of Highways for the London District have abused their Office by the misapplication of the moneys committed to their care, and that Three Hundred Pounds rests in the hands of Mr. R. Nichols, a Commissioner, no part of which appears to have been applied to public uses.

Resolved, that it appears that the Commissioners of Highways in the Western District have faithfully executed the trust reposed in them by the Legislature, and have properly applied the sums intrusted to them.

Capt. Fraser moved, seconded by Mr. McNabb, that the sixth Rule of the House be dispensed with so far as it relates to the reading of the Petition of John Beikie, Esquire, and that the said Petition be now read.

The said Rule was accordingly dispensed with, and the Petition of John Beikie was then read, and is as follows:—

To the Honorable the Speaker and the Members of the Commons House of Assembly.

. The Memorial of John Beikie,

Respectfully Sheweth,

That Your Memorialist performed the duty of Clerk, during the year 1810, to the Commissioners appointed to carry into effect an Act of the Parliament of this Province, passed in the forty-eighth year of His Majesty's Reign, intituled " An Act to continue an Act passed in the forty-fifth year of His Majesty's Reign, intituled ' An Act to afford relief to those persons who may be entitled to claim lands in this Province as Heirs or Devisees of the Nominees of the Crown, in cases where no Patent hath issued for such lands, and further to extend the benefits of the said Act."

That Your Memorialist has been allowed a small compensation for services to the 31st December, 1809, and therefore prays that his case may be taken into consideration for the year 1810, and that such allowance may be made to him as the House shall think meet.

And Your Memorialist will ever pray.

9th March, 1811.   (Signed) JOHN BEIKIE.

Mr. Gough then moved, seconded by Capt. Fraser, that the petition of John Beikie, Esquire, be referred to the Committee on Contingent Accounts, which was ordered accordingly.

On motion of Mr. Gough, seconded by Mr. Dorland, resolved, that it is the opinion of this House that five hundred copies of the Provincial Statutes are re-

34 A.

quisite for the use of the House and the Province, and that this resolution be referred to the Committee on Contingent Accounts, to provide for the printing thereof.

Mr. Mallory moved, seconded by Mr. Willcocks, that a certain sum of money allowed to Levi Lawrence for attending the Bar of this House by virtue of a Warrant issued for him, be referred to the Committee on the Contingent Accounts, which was ordered accordingly.

Mr. Willcocks gave notice, that he will, on to-morrow, move an Address to His Excellency the Lieutenant Governor, upon the subject matter of several resolutions passed this House, relative to the conduct of certain Commissioners of Highways and Roads in this Province.

The Clerk, by order of the House, laid upon the Table the Contingent Accounts of both Houses of Parliament during the Recess and present Session, and are as follows:

Sum necessary for Stationery for the use of the Legislative Council for the year 1812 .... £20   0   0

Legislative Council Chamber   Approved,
March 11th, 1811.   (Signed) THOS. SCOTT, *Speaker.*

Province of Upper Canada
       to George Lawe, Dr.

No. 1 To Amt. of Wm Allan's Acct.	£15	1	10½
No. 2 To Amt of Joshua Leech's Acct.	10	5	0
No. 3 To Amt. of Margt. Bright Acct.	5	0	2
No. 4 To Amt. of Philip Klinger's Acct.	6	0	0
No. 5 To Amt. of John Basset's Acct.	20	0	0
	£56	8	10½

George Lawe maketh Oath, and saith that the above account is just and true to the best of his knowledge and belief.

Sworn before me, at York, the
12th day of March, 1811.   (Signed) THOS. SCOTT, Speaker.
                       York, Upper Canada, 11th March, 1811.

The Contingent Account of the Clerk of the Commons House of Assembly's Office, for the third Session of the fifth Provincial Parliament.

No. 1 Due the Copying Clerks	£105	10	0
1 Balance due for Station'y	12	0	4½
2 Almanac			7½
3 John Cameron	13	0	0
4 Mr. Allan's Acct. for Postage	2	13	6
5 Allowance for Stationery for the ensuing Session of Parliament	40	0	0
Provincial Currency	£173	4	6

Commons House of Assembly,
March 12th, 1811.   (Signed) SAML. STREET, Speaker.

The Honorable the House of Assembly in Account Current with the Clerk, for Stationery for the Third Session of the Fifth Provincial Parliament.

1810.

Aug. 11. No. 1 To William and James Crook's Acct.........	£35	3	6
1811. To William and James Crook's Acct........			
Feb. 18. No. 2 Imported parchment from the United States.	8	2	6
No. 3 To William Allan's Account	8	3	1½
No. 4 To Quetten St. George's Acc't		11	3
Provincial Currency	£52	0	4½
To Balance brought down	£12	0	4½
By Cash advanced for the purchase of Stationery..........	£40	0	0
By Balance due	12	0	4½
E. E. York, 12th March, 1811.	£52	0	4½

(Signed) DONALD MCLEAN, Clerk of the House of Assembly.

The Honorable the House of Assembly in account current with the Clerk for Copying Clerks, during the third Session of the fifth Provincial Parliament.

Dr. Acct.

No. 1 To Chas Baynes	£28	0	0
No. 2 To T. G. Ridout	28	10	0
No. 3 To William Shaw	23	0	0
No. 4 To George Kuch	23	0	0
No. 5 To Edward McMahon	9	0	0
No. 6 To Arch. McLean	8	0	0
No. 7 To Ed. McMahon for 34 days employment in the Office of the Clerk of the Assembly, copying and comparing sundry writings during the recess of Parliament, between 1st Apl. and 1st Aug., 1810, at 7s. 6d. per day	12	15	0
	£132	5	0

Copying Clerks, Credit side.

By Cash appropriated by Law for copying clerks, not yet received	£25	0	0
By Balance due the House of Assembly, not yet expended....	1	15	0
By Balance due	105	10	0
Provincial Currency	£132	5	0

E. E. York, 12th Mar., 1811.

(Signed) DONALD MCLEAN, *Clerk of the House of Assembly.*

York, Upper Canada, 12th March, 1811.

The Contingent Account of the Commons House of Assembly for the Third Session of the Fifth Provincial Parliament.

1	Thomas Hamilton's Account	£73	18	5
2	George Duggan's Account	7	0	0
3	Joshua Leach's Account	4	15	0
4	Alex'r Wood's Account	3	12	9
5	William Allan's Account	9	9	2
6	Hugh Carfrae's Contingent Account	23	18	11
7	Hugh Carfrae's usual allowance as Messenger	20	0	0
8	John Beikie	5	0	0
9	Hugh McLean	5	0	0
10	Benj. Marsh	13	7	6
11	Levi Lawrence	3	5	0
12	A. Janes	12	10	0
13	William Allan	16	17	4
14	Thos. Hamilton	5	0	0
15	William Jarvis, Esq.	50	0	0

Provincial Currency £253 14 1

Commons House of Assembly,

March 12th, 1811.   (Signed) SAML. STREET, Speaker.

Agreeably to the Order of the Day, the House resolved itself into a Committee to take into consideration the Contingent Accounts of both Houses of Parliament. Mr. Speaker left the Chair. Mr. Marsh was called to the chair of the Committee.

Mr. Speaker resumed the Chair, and Mr. Marsh reported that the Committee had made a progress, and had directed him to ask for leave to sit again to-morrow. Leave was accordingly granted for the Committee to sit again to-morrow.

On motion of Mr. Dorland, seconded by Mr. Stinson, the House adjourned.

Tuesday, 12th March, 1811.

Prayers were read.

Read, a letter from Wm. Halton, Esquire, Secretary to His Excellency the Lieutenant Governor, which is as follows:

Lieutenant Governor's Office, 11th March, 1811.

Sir,—I have the Honour to inform you, by command of the Lieutenant Governor, that His Excellency has been pleased to appoint Wednesday next, the thirteenth instant, at four o'clock in the afternoon, for the prorogation of the two Houses of the Legislature of this Province.

I have the honor to be, Sir, your most obedient humble servant,

(Signed) WM. HALTON, Secretary.

His Honor, the Speaker of the House of Assembly.

Agreeably to the Order of the Day, the House resolved itself into a Committee to go into the further consideration of the Contingent Accounts of the two Houses of Parliament. Mr. Speaker left the Chair. Mr. Marsh took the chair of the Committee.

Mr. Speaker resumed the Chair, and Mr. Marsh reported that the Committee had made some progress, and directed him to ask for leave to sit again this day, Leave was accordingly granted for the Committee to sit again this day.

A Message from the Honorable the Legislative Council by Mr. Baldwin, Master in Chancery:

Mr. Speaker,—
I am commanded by the Honorable the Legislative Council to acquaint this House that they have passed an Act sent up from this House, intituled "An Act for granting to His Majesty a certain sum of money out of the funds applicable to the uses of this Province to defray the expenses of amending and opening the Public Highways and Roads, and building of Bridges in the several Districts thereof," without any amendment, and then he withdrew.

Agreeably to leave given, the House again resolved itself into a Committee to go into further consideration of the Contingent Accounts of both Houses of Parliament. Mr. Speaker left the Chair. Mr. Marsh again took the Chair of the Committee.

Mr. Speaker resumed the Chair, and Mr. Marsh reported that the Committee had gone through the consideration of the Contingent accounts of the two Houses of Parliament, and that they had come to several resolutions therein, which he was directed to submit to the House whenever it should be pleased to receive the same. Ordered, that the Report be now received.

He then read in his place the said resolutions, and afterwards delivered the same in at the Clerk's table, where they were again read, and are as follows, viz.:

Resolved, that it is the opinion of this Committee that it is expedient to advance to the Clerk of the Legislative Council the sum of Twenty Pounds to enable him to purchase Stationery for the use of the ensuing Session of Parliament.
£20   0   0

Resolved, that it is the opinion of this Committee that there is due to George Lawe, Gentleman Usher of the Black Rod, agreeable to his account as certified by the Speaker of the Legislative Council, for sundry contingent expenses thereof during the present Session, the sum of Fifty Six Pounds, Eight Shillings and Tenpence Halfpenny £56   8 10½

Resolved, that it is the opinion of this Committee that there is due to the Clerk of the House of Assembly, for disbursements in his office. and for paying of Copying Clerks during the recess and the present Session, One Hundred and Thirty-three Pounds, Four Shillings and Sixpence £133   4   6

Resolved, that it is the opinion of this Committee, that it is expedient to advance to the Clerk of the House of Assembly the sum of Forty Pounds, to enable him to procure a supply of Stationery for the use of the next session of Parliament.
£40   0   0

Resolved, that it is the opinion of this Committee that there is due to sundry persons, for repairs done to the House of Assembly during the recess and present session, and also for articles purchased by the Serjeant at Arms for the use of the House of Assembly during the recess and present session, One Hundred and Forty-two Pounds, Fourteen Shillings and Threepence £142 14   3

And that he do also charge in his Contingent Account, and pay to the individuals therein named agreeable to the resolutions of this Committee, the several sums allowed to them, viz.:

To John Beikie, Esquire, Five Pounds .... £5   0 . 0
Hugh McLean, Five Pounds 5   0   0
Benj. Marsh, Thirteen Pounds Seven Shillings and Sixpence 13   7   6

Levi Lawrence, Three Pounds Five Shillings   3   5   0
A. Janes, Twelve Pounds Ten Shillings 12 10   0
William Allan, Esquire, Sixteen Pounds, Seventeen Shillings and
    Fourpence .. .. .ᶸ................................   16 17 .4
Thos. Hamilton, Five Pounds .... ˙ 5˙ 0   0
William Jarvis, Esquire, Fifty Pounds   50   0   0
Making in all One Hundred and Ten Pounds, Nineteen Shillings and Ten-
pence, which, including the amount of articles purchased by the Serjeant at Arms
during the recess and present session, and repairs done to the House, makes in
all Two Hundred and Fifty-three Pounds Fourteen Shillings and One Penny
                                                              £253 14 1
Resolved, that it is the opinion of this Committee that there be allowed to
John Beikie, Esq., for stationery purchased and services attending the Commis-
isoners under the Act to afford relief to those persons who may_ be entitled to
claim lands in this Province as Heirs or Devisees of the Nominees of the Crown,
for the year 1810, Five Pounds £5   0   0
To Hugh McLean; Messenger attending the said Commissioners, Five
Pounds, in all £10   0   0
Resolved, that it is the opinion of this Committee that the sum of Thirteen
Pounds, Seven Shillings and Sixpence be allowed to Benjamin Marsh, of the
Township of Hope, being the sum paid by him for a License to work a Still in the
year 1810, which Still was destroyed by fire £13 7   6
Resolved, that it is the opinion of this Committee that William Allan, Esquire,
one of the Commissioners for the purchase of hemp, during the years 1804, 1805,
1806, 1807, 1808, and 1809, for his trouble,·risk, and storing of hemp purchased by
him, be allowed, in lieu of commission, which not being allowed by law was de-
ducted from his account, Sixteen Pounds, Seventeen Shillings and Fourpence
                                                              £16 17 4
Resolved, that it is the opinion of this Committee that there be allowed Thomas
Hamilton, then Acting Deputy Serjeant at Arms, for extraordinary services
during the recess of Parliament, Five Pounds £5   0   0
Resolved, that it is the opinion of this Committee that the sum of Three
Pounds Five Shillings be allowed to Levi Lawrence for attending at the Bar
of the House of Assembly for the year 1807, as a witness in the contested Election,
the like sum having been then ordered by the House to be paid to him by the
Special Messenger, Noel De Lisle, but which he made appear he did not receive.
                                                              £3   5   0
Resolved, that it is the opinion of this Committee that there be allowed to A.
Janes, for making new discoveries, and introducing useful inventions into this
Province, Twelve Pounds Ten Shillings £12 10 0
Resolved, that it is the opinion of this Committee that there be allowed to
William Jarvis, Esquire, Fifty Pounds, as a compensation for services performed
as Keeper of the Rolls £50 0   0
On motion of Mr. Gough, seconded by Mr. McLean, resolved, that this House
doth concur in the foregoing resolutions reported from the Committee.
Resolved, that an humble Address be presented to His Excellency the Lieu-
tenant Governor, to request that His Excellency will be pleased to issue his War-
rant in favour of John Powell, Esquire, Clerk of the Honorable the Legislative
Council, for the sum of Twenty Pounds; to George Lawe, Gentleman Usher of the
Black Rod, for the sum of Fifty-six Pounds; to Donald McLean, Esquire, Clerk

of the House of Assembly, for the sum of One Hundred and Seventy-three Pounds Four Shillings and Sixpence; to William Stanton, Esquire, Sergeant at Arms, for the sum of Two Hundred and Fifty-three Pounds Fourteen Shillings and One Penny.

Also resolved, that it is the opinion of this Committee that an Humble Address be presented to His Excellency the Lieutenant Governor, requesting His Excellency will be pleased to issue his Warrant to the King's Printer, for the sum of Four Hundred Pounds, for compiling and printing five hundred copies of all the Acts of the Several Parliaments of this Province, including those of the present session, when the printing is completed; and the said Acts so compiled and printed shall be received from the Printer in compliance of a resolution entered into by the Committee.

On motion of Capt. Fraser, seconded by Mr. Marsh, ordered, that Messrs. Rogers and Howard be a Committee to draft an Address to His Excellency the Lieutenant Governor, in conformity to the several resolutions on the contingent account of both Houses of Parliament, which was ordered accordingly.

Mr. Rogers, from the Committee appointed to draft an Address to His Excellency the Lieutenant Governor, reported that the Committee had drafted an Address accordingly, which they were ready to submit whenever the House should be pleased to receive the same. The House then resolved that the draft of the said Address be now received. Mr. Rogers then read the draft of the Address in his place, and afterwards delivered the same in at the Clerk's table, where it was again read. On motion of Mr. McNabb, seconded by Mr. Markle, the House resolved itself into a Committee to go into the consideration of the said Address. Mr. Speaker left the Chair. Mr. McGregor was called to the chair of the Committee.

Mr. Speaker resumed the Chair, and Mr. McGregor reported that the Committee had gone through the consideration of the said Address without any amendment, which he was directed to report whenever the House should be pleased to receive the same Resolved, that the Report be now received. On motion of Mr. C. Willson, seconded by Mr. Secord, ordered, that the said Address on the Contingent Accounts of the two Houses of Parliament to His Excellency the Lieutenant Governor be engrossed and read to-morrow. The same was ordered accordingly.

On motion of Mr. McLean, seconded by Mr. Dorland, resolved, that an humble Address be presented to His Excellency the Lieutenant Governor, to request His Excellency will be pleased to issue his Warrant in favour of the King's Printer for the sum of Four Hundred Pounds, for compiling and printing five hundred copies of the Provincial Statutes, including those of the present Session. Resolved, that the House doth concur in the foregoing resolution reported by the Committee. On motion of Mr. C. Willson, seconded by Mr. Lewis, ordered, that Messrs. Gough and McLean be a Committee to draft an Address to His Excellency the Lieutenant Governor, in conformity to the resolution of the House this day relative to the printing of the laws. Mr. Gough from the Committee appointed to draft an Address to His Excellency the Lieutenant Governor, grounded on a resolution of the House this day, relative to the printing of the Provincial Statutes, reported that the Committee had drafted an Address accordingly, which they were ready to submit to the House, whenever it should be pleased to receive the same. The House then resolved that the draft of the said Address be now received. Mr. Gough then read the Address in his place, and afterwards delivered the same in at the Clerk's table, where it was again read. On motion of Mr. McNabb, seconded by Mr. Baby, the House resolved itself into a Committee to go into the consideration of the said Address. Mr.

Speaker left the Chair.   Mr. C. Willson was called to the chair of the Committee.   Mr. Speaker resumed the Chair, and Mr. C. Willson reported that the Committee had gone through the consideration of the said Address without any amendment, which he was directed to report whenever the House should be pleased to receive the same.   Resolved, that the Report be now received.   On motion of Mr. J. Willson, seconded by Mr. Mallory, ordered, that the said Address be engrossed and read to-morrow.

On motion of Capt. Elliott, seconded by Mr. Baby, the House adjourned.

Wednesday, 13th March, 1811.

Prayers were read.

Mr. Willcocks gave notice that he will, on the first day of the next Session, move that the House do resolve itself into a Committee to take into consideration the propriety of the Executive Government of this Province disposing of large quantities of lumber, and not accounting to the House of Assembly for the proceeds thereof.

Agreeably to the Order of the Day was read, as engrossed, the Address to His Excellency the Lieutenant Governor, respecting the Contingent Accounts of both Houses of Parliament during the present Session, which then passed and was signed by the Speaker, and is as follows, viz.:

To His Excellency Francis Gore, Esquire, Lieutenant Governor of the Province of Upper Canada, etc., etc., etc.

May it please Your Excellency,—

We, His Majesty's most dutiful and loyal subjects, the Commons of Upper Canada in Parliament assembled, do most humbly pray that it may please Your Excellency to issue your Warrants directed to the Receiver General, requiring him to pay to John Powell, Esquire, Clerk of the Legislative Council, the sum of Twenty Pounds; to George Lawe, Gentleman Usher of the Black Rod, the sum of Fifty-six Pounds; to Donald McLean, Esquire, Clerk of the House of Assembly, the sum of One Hundred and Seventy-three Pounds, Four Shillings and Sixpence; to William Stanton, Esquire, Serjeant at Arms, the sum of Two Hundred and Fifty-three Pounds, Fourteen Shillings and One Penny, to enable him to pay the Contingent Expenses of the present Session, and to provide a supply of Stationery for the ensuing Session of Parliament.

We therefore do most humbly pray that Your Excellency will be pleased to issue your Warrants to carry the said resolutions into effect, and the Commons will make good the several sums of money to Your Excellency at the next Session of Parliament.

Commons House of Assembly,   (Signed) SAMUEL STREET,
13th March, 1811.   Speaker.

Mr. McLean moved, seconded by Mr. Rogers, for leave to bring up Petitions from Sundry Inhabitants of the Province, relative to the incorporation of a bank. Leave was accordingly granted, and the said Petitions were ordered to lie on the Table.

Agreeably to the Order of the Day, was read as engrossed, an Address to His Excellency the Lieutenant Governor, requesting that he would be pleased to order five hundred copies of the Provincial Statutes to be printed, which Address passed, and was signed by the Speaker, and is as follows:

To His Excellency Frances Gore, Esquire, Lieutenant Governor of the Province of Upper Canada, etc., etc., etc.

May it please Your Excellency,—

We, His Majesty's most dutiful and loyal subjects, the Commons of Upper Canada in Parliament assembled, do most humbly pray that it may please Your Excellency to cause five hundred copies of all the Acts of the several Parliaments of this Province, including those of the present Session, to be printed, for the purpose of promulgating the laws generally throughout the Province; and that Your Excellency will be pleased to issue your warrant for the same, when the said number of copies are printed and delivered, which sum the Commons will make good to Your Excellency the next Session of Parliament.

Commons House of Assembly,   (Signed) SAMUEL STREET,
13th March, 1811.   Speaker.

Mr. Rogers moved, seconded by Mr. Baby, that Messrs. McGregor and McNabb do present to His Excellency the Lieutenant Governor the two Addresses of this House respecting the Contingent Accounts and the Printing of the Provincial Statutes, at such time as His Excellency will be pleased to receive them, which was ordered accordingly.

On motion of Capt. Elliott, seconded by Mr. Baby, the House adjourned for half an hour.

The House being met, Mr. McGregor, one of the Messengers named to present to His Excellency, the Lieutenant Governor, the two Addresses which passed the House this day, reported that, in obedience to the commands of this House, they had waited upon His Excellency the Lieutenant Governor, and did present the said two Addresses; and that His Excellency was pleased to answer that he would give the necessary orders to comply therewith. The names of the Members present were taken down, and are as follows:

The Speaker, Messrs. Tho's Fraser, Tho's Mears, Abraham March, Henry Markle, Stephen Burritt, James McNabb, David McG. Rogers, Thomas B. Gough, John Willson, Levi Lewis, Joseph Willcocks, Peter Howard, Allan McLean, John Stinson, Thomas Dorland, Willet Casey, Crowel Willson, Benajah Mallory, Philip Sovereign, John McGregor, Matthew Elliott, J. B. Baby, David Secord.

A Message from His Excellency the Lieutenant Governor, by Mr. George Lawe, Gentleman Usher of the Black Rod:

Mr. Speaker,—

I am commanded by His Excellency the Lieutenant Governor to acquaint this Honorable House that it is His Excellency's pleasure that the Members thereof do forthwith attend upon him in the Legislative Council Chamber.

Accordingly, Mr. Speaker, with the House, went up to attend His Excellency; when he was pleased to give, in His Majesty's name, the Royal assent to the following Public and Private Bills:

An Act to amend an Act passed in the forty-eighth year of His Majesty's reign, intituled "An Act to explain, amend and reduce to one Act of Parliament the several laws now in being for the raising and training the Militia of this Province."

An Act to amend the process of the District Courts, and also further to regulate the proceedings of Sheriffs, in the sale of goods and chattels taken by them in execution.

An Act to repeal an Ordinance of the Province of Quebec, passed in the seventeenth year of His Majesty's reign, intituled, "An Ordinance for ascertaining

Damages on Protested Bills of Exchange, and fixing the rate of interest in the Province of Quebec," also to ascertain the damages on Protested Bills of Exchange, and fixing the Rate of Interest in this Province.

An Act to extend Personal Arrest to the sum of Forty Shillings, and otherwise to regulate the practice in cases of personal arrest.

Mr. Speaker then said:—May it please Your Excellency to approve of the five Bills which the Assembly, with the concurrence of the Legislative Coucil, have passed in aid of His Majesty, which are as follows:

An Act for applying a certain sum of money therein mentioned to make good certain moneys issued and advanced by His Majesty through the Lieutenant-Governor in pursuance of an Address of this House.

An Act to repeal an Act passed in the forty-seventh year of His Majesty's Reign, intituled "An Act to repeal the several Acts now in force in this Province, relative to Rates and Assessments, and giving the several valuations at which each and every particular of such property shall be rated and assessed," and to make further provision for the same.

An Act to amend and continue for a limited time an Act passed in the forty-ninth year of His Majesty's Reign, intituled "An Act for continuing for a limited time the Provisional Agreement entered into between this Province and Lower Canada, at Montreal, on the fifth day of July, one thousand eight hundred and four, relative to Duties, also for continuing for a limited time the several Acts of the Parliament of this Province now in force, relating thereto."

An Act to repeal an Act passed in the forty-seventh year of His Majesty's Reign, intituled "An Act for granting to His Majesty's Duties on Licences to Hawkers, Pedlars, and Petty Chapmen, and other trading persons therein mentioned," and further for granting to His Majesty Duties on Licences to Hawkers, Pedlars, and Petty Chapmen, and other trading persons therein mentioned.

An Act for granting to His Majesty a certain sum of money out of the funds applicable to the use of this Province, to defray the expense of amending and opening the Public Highways and Roads, and building of Bridges in the several districts thereof.

To which five Bills His Excellency, the Lieutenant-Governor, was pleased to give the Royal assent in His Majesty's name.

And then His Excellency was pleased to make the following Speech to both Houses:

Honorable Gentlemen of the Legislative Council, and Gentlemen of the House of Assembly:—

In closing this Session of the Legislature I am happy in expressing the sense I entertain of the diligence and attention with which you have conducted the various objects of public concern that have come under your notice.

It is with pleasure I observe that your liberality is continued, and further extended, to the opening and amending of Roads and the Building of Bridges; as it is by a facility of communication, and of intercourse, that the interest of agriculture and commerce may be effectually promoted, and the industrial settler enabled to receive his merited reward.

The progressive state of improvement in this Province presents us with the most flattering prospects of success, and while it affords convincing proofs of what patient industry can accomplish, holds forth, also, a well-grounded hope, that by the fruits of our labour and the fertility of our soil we shall be enabled not only to insure plenty to ourselves, but, through the intervention of commerce, to become a valuable Colony to our Parent State.

The other laws which you have enacted, and to which I have now given the Royal assent merit also my approbation. It only remains for me to recommend that you will strengthen the laws of your country by your influence and example, and that added to your public exertions in this place, you will, as individuals, promote good order, industry and loyalty among your fellow subjects, as it is only by such means that we can expect or hope for the continuance of that comfort, security and liberty, which we, under the protection of our Parent State, and under the best of Kings, have hitherto enjoyed.

13th March, 1811.

After which, the Honorable Speaker of the Legislative Council said:—It is His Excellency the Lieutenant-Governor's will and pleasure that this Provincial Parliament be prorogued until Wednesday, the seventeenth day of April next, to be then here held; and the Provincial Parliament is accordingly prorogued until Wednesday, the seventeenth day of April next.

[I hereby certify that the above and what is written on the foregoing pages is a true transcript of the Journal of the House of Assembly in Upper Canada, being the Third Session of the Fifth Provincial Parliament, assembled in the Town of York, on Friday, the first day of February last, agreeably to the Proclamation of His Excellency, Francis Gore, Esquire, Lieutenant-Governor of the Province of Upper Canada, &c., &c., &c.; and prorogued by His Excellency on Wednesday, the thirteenth day of March last.

Clerk of Assembly's Office, York, 15th May, 1811.

DONALD MCLEAN, Clerk of the Commons House of Assembly.]

[Certified to be true copies from the original Records in the Colonial Office.

GEO. MAYER, Librarian and Keeper of the Records.

Colonial Office, Downing Street, 26th May, 1856.]

INDEX

33 A.

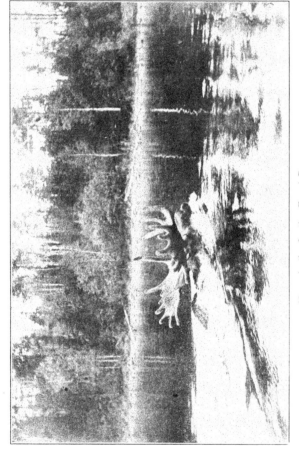

Moose in the Quetico Forest Reserve.

This unusually interesting photograph was taken by Mr. H. J. Bury, chief guide for the Commission, during its trip through the Quetico Forest Reserve. The animal came into the water less than 200 feet from where the party had halted for the midday meal, and commenced feeding on lily pad roots. He did not turn to leave the spot till almost touched with the paddle and two canoes followed him for some little distance. Mr. Bury obtaining several snap-shots.

FINAL REPORT

OF THE

Ontario Game and Fisheries Commission
1909-1911

Appointed to enquire into and report on all matters
appertaining to

The Game Fish, The Fisheries, and the Game of the Province of Ontario

PRINTED BY ORDER OF
THE LEGISLATIVE ASSEMBLY OF ONTARIO

TORONTO:
Printed and Published by L. K. CAMERON, Printer to the King's Most Excellent Majesty
1912.

Printed by
WILLIAM BRIGGS,
29-37 Richmond Street West,
TORONTO.

TABLE OF CONTENTS

——The illustrations in this report are principally from photographs taken by Captain R. M. Sims, D.S.O., the
Secretary of the Commission, and Mr. H. J. Bury, head guide to the Commission on its trip through the Quetico
Forest Reserve.

FINAL REPORT OF THE ONTARIO GAME AND FISHERIES COMMISSION

1909-1911

To the HONOURABLE JOHN MORISON GIBSON,

Lieutenant-Governor of the Province of Ontario.

MAY IT PLEASE YOUR HONOUR,—The undersigned, appointed by commission under the Great Seal of the Province, bearing date the seventeenth day of July, A.D. 1909, to make enquiries, take evidence, and report generally upon all matters appertaining to the game fish, the fisheries and the game of the Province of Ontario, which may injuriously affect the same, and any methods possible to increase their economic and other value to the masses of the people, begs leave herewith to submit his final report.

The instructions accompanying the Commission direct that the investigation shall include the following particulars:

(1) The condition of the fisheries and game within the Province of Ontario and the adjacent waters, including:

(2) The advisability of establishing provincial fish hatcheries, including the estimated cost of maintenance and construction, the best methods of operation, and other matters relating thereto;

(3) The alleged existence of contracts between fishermen within the Province of Ontario and foreign fish companies and individuals, together with the effect of such contracts (if any) upon the fisheries of Ontario;

(4) The matter of foreign fish companies and individuals encouraging breaches of the law on the part of fishermen, and others resident in Ontario;

(5) The qualifications, conditions of service, skill, efficiency (physical and otherwise), desirable for fisheries and game officials;

(6) The condition of the present equipment of the Department, together with the additional requirements (if any) in this regard in the matter of launches, boats, etc.;

(7) The advisability of the co-operation by the officers of other departments of the Government, and of other corporations, with the officers of the Department of Game and Fisheries, in assisting in the practical enforcement of the game laws and fishery regulations;

(8) Questions relating to the management of the public parks and forest reserves, especially in so far as the tourist sportsman traffic is concerned;

(9) All matters and things relating to fish and game which may assist in the efficient management of the Game and Fisheries Branch of the public service in Ontario, or be of economic advantage to the Province.

THE COMMERCIAL FISHERIES.

Depletion of the Fisheries.

It is hardly necessary for your Commissioner to call to your attention the fact that the commercial fisheries of the Great Lakes are rapidly dwindling, for scarcely a week elapses but that the lamentable diminution in one or other of the once flourishing fishing areas is strikingly recorded in the daily press. The grave significance of this state of affairs is not yet fully appreciated by the general public, mainly for the reason that, owing to conditions which will be hereinafter more fully discussed, the citizens of Ontario have not been educated to the economic value to themselves of the great fisheries lying at their very doors, or to the value of fish food as a factor in the daily dietary. The population of the Province, however, is rapidly increasing; the price of food rising higher and higher; and it is impossible to conceive that the day can be very far distant when the citizens of Ontario will awaken from their present lethargy, require from those in authority an accounting for the dissipation of their once splendid fisheries, and with no uncertain voice demand that the most drastic measures be forthwith adopted to save for themselves and for their children what is left of their fisheries, and, if possible, to restore them to something of their former prolificness.

There are still living in the Province men who can well recall the days when the waters of even Lake Ontario were literally teeming with whitefish, and to anyone hearing or reading their accounts it must readily occur that this magnificent fish, had it only been properly conserved, should have assumed in a populous Ontario the economic role of the deep-sea herring in the English markets. What a high-class, wholesome and, at the same time, cheap fish can mean to the welfare of the poorer classes of a populous community can hardly be over-estimated, a fact which can be attested to by anyone who has had experience of or even visited the more crowded areas of any of the greater English cities.

As a food the whitefish is, in all probability, the superior of the herring; the areas which it has inhabited are vast, and there can be little doubt but that under wise regulation, even without artificial assistance, the annual crop of this most excellent fish should have been sufficient to supply all the wants of the citizens of Ontario for a considerable time to come, while at the same time yielding a fair margin for export trade. That a neighboring nation should be consuming the great bulk of

Ontario's whitefish, leaving but a small margin at a high figure for her own citizens, will be discussed in a subsequent section; but the fact remains, however, that the diminution in the annual catch of whitefish has been so marked and persistent, in spite of increased and better appliances, that it must be open to the gravest doubt whether, under the present system of administration and regulation, the fisheries are not being actually destroyed, instead of merely depleted, for it must be remembered that to rehabilitate exhausted fisheries entails artificial production on a large scale; that artificial production on a large scale is only possible when there is an abundant supply of parent fish, and that the prolonged absence of schools of whitefish from certain of their former habitats may result, under the adaptable laws of nature, in a transformation of conditions such as to render those waters no longer as suitable for sustaining whitefish life.

In the Interim Report of this Commission reference was made to the sworn testimony, given to former Commissions, in regard to the immense quantities of whitefish that existed in the Great Lakes even forty and fifty years ago, and amongst other instances was cited that of 90,000 whitefish having been landed on Wellington Beach in one single haul of a net. What the average size of these fish may have been it is impossible to tell, but it seems safe to assume that it cannot have been less than approximately 2 lbs., thus making 180,000 lbs. of fish caught in a few hours, with a comparatively small amount of net, and with comparatively little effort or expense, in one tiny fraction of the whitefish area of Lake Ontario. When it is realized that the whitefish area of the Canadian portion of Lake Ontario is roughly one thousand four hundred square miles, some idea of the vast quantities of fish that must have existed in these waters can be gained, and the deplorable diminution that has occurred is very vividly brought home by a comprehension of the fact that, in spite of a steady increase in the quantity of nets used, for the fifteen years, 1892-1906, the average yearly catch for the whole 1,400 square miles of Lake Ontario's Provincial whitefish fisheries only just exceeded 250,000 lbs. Statistics are not available to show clearly the exact percentage of decrease since the days when the whitefish were so abundant, but, even if they were, it is doubtful whether they could more clearly emphasize the fact that it has been colossal than the brief comparison here made.

The decrease, however, far from having yet reached its limit, continues marked throughout almost all the whitefish areas of the Provincial waters, as the following short tables will show, and it is this alarming state of affairs which so strengthens the belief, as almost to make it a certainty, that unless stringent remedial measures are applied without delay, the fisheries will be, not merely depleted, but irredeemably destroyed.

CANADIAN WATERS OF LAKE SUPERIOR, 1892-1906.

Average yearly catch of whitefish:

1892–1896.. 1,123,000
1897–1901.. 591,000
1902–1906.. 462,000

CANADIAN WATERS OF NORTH CHANNEL AND LAKE HURON, EXCLUSIVE OF
GEORGIAN BAY, 1892-1906.

Average yearly catch of whitefish:

1892–1896.. 1,657,000
1896–1901.. 940,000
1902–1906.. 1,051,000

GEORGIAN BAY, 1892-1906.

Average yearly catch of whitefish:

1892–1896.. 1,535,000
1897–1901.. 450,000
1902–1906.. 423,000

CANADIAN WATERS OF LAKE ONTARIO, 1892-1906.

Average yearly catch of whitefish:

1892–1896.. 291,000
1897–1901.. 245,000
1902–1906.. 238,000

In dealing with fishing statistics it is always possible to gainsay the
conclusions arrived at from the comparison of any two particular years,
and in fact such comparison affords but a slender foundation on which
to base a sound argument owing to the fact that weather conditions and
other possible contingencies may greatly affect the success of the fishermen in individual years. Indeed, on more than one occasion interested
parties have availed themselves of the opportunities afforded by such
comparison, when localized and restricted to two years, to proclaim
through the public press that the commercial fisheries of the Province
were still in a flourishing condition. A period of fifteen years, however,
eliminates to a great extent this element of chance, and the averaging
of the catches in periods of five years enables a clear idea to be formed
of the extent of the loss or gain. It may, in fact, safely be said that outside of a few interested individuals whose desire for quick profit outweighs their appreciation of truthfulness, no one with any knowledge of
the condition of the Canadian Great Lake fisheries to-day will deny that
a steady decrease is occurring which must, unless something is soon done
to prevent it, result in the complete exhaustion of the fisheries. The
following short paragraph from a Sault Ste. Marie journal of November
25th, 1910, well illustrates this fact:

" LAKE SUPERIOR A FISHLESS SEA."

A despatch from Fort William says: " The catch of trout and whitefish in Lake Superior has never been so light as in the season now clos-

ing. The result of an all days's trip with one of the fish tugs is often not more than 300 pounds of fish, which is not enough to pay operating expenses. A half ton is considered an average catch on a single trip. That Lake Superior, known as the abode of the finest whitefish in the world, is fast becoming a fishless sea is a startling statement, but that is what the fishermen assert. Fishermen have been doing less business each year for some time. Tugs have been going farther and farther out each succeeding season, and now nets are set as much as five hours run from shore, but even in these unfrequented waters there are few fish."

Various reasons have been advanced from time to time to account for this decrease, some maintaining that the increased shipping on the waters was largely responsible; and others that it was due mainly to the pollution of spawning beds and feeding grounds owing to the sewage poured into the lakes at various points and other deleterious matter carried into them by streams and rivers boasting mills and manufactories on their banks. Doubtless each of these causes has played its part, but all the experts seem now to be agreed that without question the main and outstanding reason has been and is over-fishing. With this view your Commissioner is in entire accord.

In other departments of supply, such as domestic animals or plants, measures can be taken to increase the production of any particular species. Fresh land can be devoted to the purpose, new blood be introduced, or quicker breeding varieties imported or grafted. But, in dealing with fisheries, these channels of grappling adequately with the problem are closed for the reason that scientific knowledge of the life and domain of the fishes is exceedingly limited, chiefly owing to the obvious but greater difficulties that have been experienced in closely studying submarine conditions, so that for practical purposes only those areas already inhabited by any particular commercial fish are available for its exploitation, and the effects of the importation of new blood or new varieties are as yet so little understood as to be fraught with too much danger to make it advisable to undertake the experiment. Consequently to rehabilitate inland commercial fisheries exhausted through over-fishing there would appear to remain but two possible methods, namely, (a) by restrictive legislation, embracing alike the areas to be fished, the seasons of fishing, size limits, methods of capture, and, finally, the disposal of the fish when caught; (b) by artificial production, which in the sense here used implies the collection of spawn in vast quantities from parent fish on their natural spawning beds, its admixture, artificial incubation and hatching of the spawn, and, finally, the placing of the enormous quantities of fry or fingerlings thus obtained in the waters to be restocked.

The depletion of the fisheries of the Great Lakes has not been so sudden an occurrence as to have escaped the notice of experts and others interested in them on both sides of the boundary. Indeed the reverse has been the case, and as a result of the control of these fisheries being

vested in numerous and more or less independent authorities, namely, the
Federal Government of the United States, the Governments of Indiana,
Illinois, Michigan, Minnesota, New York, Ohio, Pennsylvania and Wisconsin, the Dominion Government of Canada and the Government of the
Province of Ontario, many and various expedients have been resorted to,
scientific investigations made, laws, regulations and restrictions introduced, and experiments in fish hatchery operations on a large scale instituted and tried out, so that before entering upon a discussion as to
the best means of rehabilitating the commercial fisheries of Ontario it
becomes necessary to review briefly the results that have been obtained
under various conditions prevailing in different localities throughout
the Great Lakes, and it is plain, also, that what scientific knowledge
there is of the lives, habits and distribution of the various fishes under
consideration should be clearly borne in mind, for more than once in the
history of the Great Lakes legislation has been introduced and enacted
to meet supposed conditions, quite at variance with the laws of nature,
owing entirely to the machinations of those whose misrepresentations
were the outcome of purely selfish interests. It would seem, however,
hardly to fall within the scope of a report of this nature to delve deeply
into the mysteries of scientific research in regard to each individual class
of fish, even were your Commissioner a scientific icthyologist, to which
distinction he lays no claim, and it is deemed, therefore, sufficient for the
purposes of this report to set out the salient features within the knowledge of present day science in regard to one most prominent variety, the
whitefish, while calling attention to the fact that, although all that is
said may not apply equally to every other variety of commercial fish,
much of it is directly pertinent and applicable in a slightly modified
form.

THE WHITEFISH.

There are three species of fishes commonly referred to as whitefish,
namely, the true whitefish (Coregonus Clupeiformis Mitchill), the Frost
Fish (Coregonus quadrilateralis), and the Sault Whitefish (Coregonus
labradoricus). Investigation has disclosed that the true whitefish is a
bottom feeder, as also that the depth at which it occurs most abundantly
is 10-35 fathoms.

This range is that occupied by the fish during eight or nine months
of the year, and is, therefore, undoubtedly its main feeding grounds. It
is likewise the area over which commercial fishing operations have been
carried on profitably at other times than during the migrations of the
fish. In discussing, then, the common or true whitefish it becomes at
once apparent that the area available to this fish is comparatively limited.
It is probably true that young whitefish of less than 1¼ lbs. are to be
caught in depths of water ranging from 20 feet up, but as these are immature fish and consequently unsuited for commercial purposes, this
fact does not materially affect the question of available whitefish area.

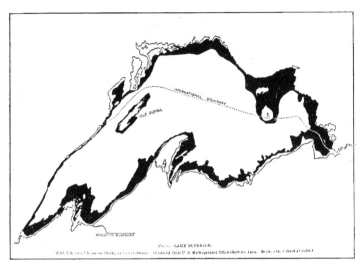

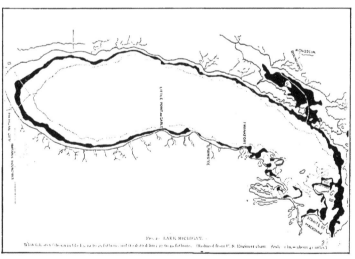

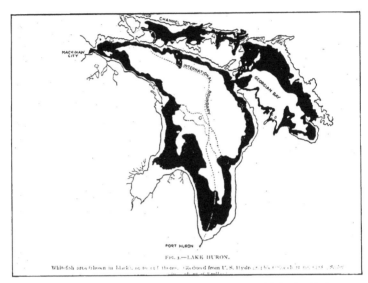

FIG. 3.—LAKE HURON.

Whitefish area (shown in black), 12 to 25 fathoms. (Reduced from U. S. Hydrographic Office chart no. 1975. Scale, about 8 miles.)

By kind permission of Mr. Paul Reighard, University of Michigan.

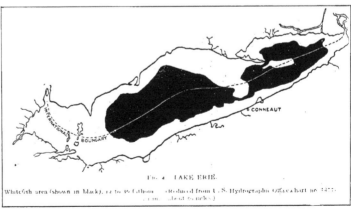

FIG. 4 LAKE ERIE.

Whitefish area (shown in black), 12 to 16 fathoms. (Reduced from U. S. Hydrographic Office chart no. 1475. Scale, about 6 miles.)

By kind permission of Mr. Paul Reighard, University of Michigan.

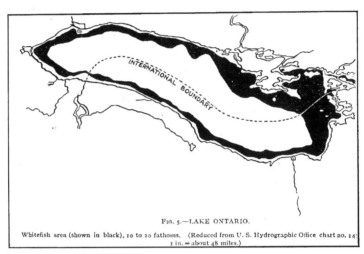

Fig. 5.—LAKE ONTARIO.

Whitefish area (shown in black), 10 to 20 fathoms.   (Reduced from U. S. Hydrographic Office chart no. 14?
1 in. = about 48 miles.)

By kind permission of Mr. Paul Reighard, University of Michigan.

Turning to the charts of the various lakes, it is evidently possible to mark clearly thereon the area afforded by each which is available for the sustenance of whitefish life. The result, including both Canadian and United States' waters, is found to be approximately as follows:

AREA, WHITEFISH AREA AND PERCENTAGE OF WHITEFISH AREA OF EACH OF THE GREAT LAKES.

——	Total area.	Whitefish area.	Percentage.
Lake Superior	32,000	7,400	23
Lake Michigan	22,000	2,600	12
Lake Huron	21,000	9,400	45
Lake Erie	9,500	4,100	43
Lake Ontario	6,500	2,200	34

Having plotted out these whitefish areas it will be noted that, with the exception of Lake Erie, the whitefish areas of the individual lakes, while varying considerably in breadth, more or less closely follow the sinuosities of the coast line, so that between the North and South or East and West boundaries, as the case may be, there intervenes a body of deep water unsuited to the true whitefish.

The evidence obtainable would appear to indicate that the whitefish does not wander at random throughout the areas available to it, but rather that it is local in its habits. In fact, those who frequently handle the fish can, as a general rule, easily distinguish between the fish of the various lakes. Twice a year, however, the whitefish leaves its habitual feeding grounds for shallower waters. In the southern lakes the first migration occurs about June or July (varying somewhat according to the latitude in the northern lakes), and the fish returns to the deeper water, as a rule, early in August. The cause of this migration has been much discussed, but perhaps the most plausible theory so far advanced is that this is the season of the year when the insect larvæ, on which the fish delight to feed, are most abundant in the shallower waters. The second migration occurs in October and November, according to latitude, and is for the purpose of spawning, continuing roughly for one month, during which period it is generally admitted that the fish do not eat. Both migrations would appear, from investigations that have been made, not to be a procession along the indentations of the shore, but rather a regular forward movement from the deeper waters of the normal feeding grounds into the shallower waters most convenient of access.

The natural spawning beds of the whitefish, so far as ascertained, consist of ledges of honeycombed and other similar rock, found in the shoaler portions of the lakes. The honeycombed rock, as the name implies, is dotted with innumerable small holes and cavities into which the eggs, as they are voided by the fish, may fall and remain comparatively secure from the depredations of spawn-eating fish, and also more or less free of the danger of being smothered by mud or other noxious deposits. The whitefish is not a nest-building fish, but is what is known as a

"School Spawner," approaching the spawning beds either singly or in schools, the female voiding her eggs irrespective of the proximity or otherwise of a male fish. The life of an unfertilized egg in the water is held to be exceedingly short, and it would appear to be a fair presumption that the same would equally apply to the germ contained in the milt of the male fish. The average number of eggs produced by the female whitefish is computed at approximately 35,000, assuming that the normal weight of the average commercial female whitefish is 2½ to 3 lbs., but the larger the fish grows, the more eggs she will usually produce, as many as 150,000 having been taken from a fish weighing eleven pounds. From the fact of the great quantities of eggs that must annually have been deposited, it has been deduced that under natural conditions the percentage of eggs hatched cannot have been very high, even in the days before commercial fishing on a large scale had been instituted, and before the spawning beds had possibly been polluted, for the normal yearly loss to swimming fish can hardly have attained such colossal proportions, and, as already indicated, the depositing of the eggs in the honeycombed rock affords considerable security against the ravages of enemies of the eggs. Consequently, it would appear that there are considerable grounds for the contention of many experts that only a very small proportion of the eggs, deposited under natural conditions, become fertilized. By some authorities this percentage is placed as low as one. On the other hand there has never been any question as to the vast quantities of whitefish that existed throughout the allotted areas in each of the Great Lakes prior to the advent of commercial fishing on a large scale, and from this fact alone it would not appear unreasonable to draw the conclusion that nature had perfected the spawning arrangements of the whitefish sufficiently to maintain an optimum population of them under normal conditions, in spite of the depredations of their enemies at the various stages of their lives, and in spite of the loss from other natural causes, even though such provision might obviously not be sufficient to meet the tremendous drain caused by excessive commercial fishing. The belief in the efficacy of nature's arrangements is strengthened, moreover, by sundry investigations which have been made as to the fertilization of the eggs of other school-spawning fish, in which it has proved exceedingly difficult to find any unfertilized eggs amongst many thousands examined on the spawning beds themselves, while the process of spawning was in progress.

What the actual percentage of eggs which are deposited and hatched under normal conditions may be, it would seem impossible at present to determine, but the percentage of eggs, collected from fish ripe for spawning, that can be hatched under artificial conditions, has been definitely ascertained; 75 per cent. is placing it at a very conservative estimate, and it must further be remembered that the eggs which are taken to the hatcheries are relieved of all danger from natural enemies, and the devastations of silt and other filth during the process of incubation, so that a considerable saving in fertilized eggs is thereby most certainly affected. Moreover, the fry obtained under artificial conditions appear just as hardy as those hatched in their natural state, although it would be impossible to compare the capabilities of such fry in looking after themselves when placed in the open waters with that of the percentage of fry naturally hatched and which have survived up to equal stages.

Consequently, viewing the comparative merits of natural and artificial hatching of whitefish spawn from an unbiassed standpoint, there would appear to be little doubt that the hatcheries can produce a very much greater percentage of fry from the eggs deposited than can nature unassisted, but that nature, which alone produced the millions of whitefish which crowded the waters before the advent of the modern commercial fisherman, is far too valuable an ally to be dispensed with altogether.

The whitefish, unlike many other varieties of fish, is in fair condition for eating at the time of spawning, for the reason that, owing to the low temperature of the water in October and November, the flesh is firm and flaky, and coming presumably fresh from bounteous summer feeding grounds, the fish itself is exceedingly fat.

From the above brief outline of the habits, life and domain of the whitefish, it would seem, then, that the following conclusions may be justly drawn:

(1) Under natural conditions only a comparatively small number of the eggs deposited are hatched.

(2) A greater number of eggs can be hatched by artificial means.

(3) In view of the fact that the average female whitefish produces 35,000 eggs, and that a percentage of these will be hatched by natural means, and a very high percentage can be hatched by artificial means, the destruction of immature fish—that is, fish which have not spawned at least once—is a great economic loss and detrimental to the welfare of the fisheries.

(4) The spawning seasons, spawning beds, and areas occupied mainly by immature fish can be accurately ascertained in each lake.

(5) The feeding grounds of the mature fish are known.

(6) The fish is largely local in its habits.

THE EFFECTS OF LEGISLATION ON THE WHITEFISH FISHERIES.

When first the diminution in the catch became apparent, the most obvious remedies were resorted to in the hopes of checking it, including the regulation of appliances, methods of capture and size of the mesh, the limitation of the numbers of nets in a given locality, the closing of certain areas and seasons, and, lastly, experiments in artificial propagation.

It was not to be expected that conditions should be precisely similar throughout the vast extent of the Great Lake fisheries, nor that all the authorities concerned in their control should see eye to eye in the matter of adopting the best possible means to suit their individual necessities, for it must be remembered that from the beginning political considerations have played no insignificant role in determining these matters on both sides of the boundary. Consequently, each authority having selected the remedies that seemed best in its judgment, there arose a situation of much complexity, in which the various regulations prevailing in adjacent waters not only served to increase the difficulties of efficient administration and enforcement of these various laws, but also rendered it almost impossible to test accurately the efficacy of this or that measure, for while regulations can obviously be localized to imaginary boundary lines, it is but rarely that in practice the fishery areas will be found to conform to the same, and to discover the real merits of a fishery enactment it is plainly necessary to have it in force throughout the whole of the particular fishing area affected. Moreover, each authority could, under this variegated system, attribute the continued decrease in its fisheries to the foolishness of its neighbors' regulations, a situation which, while it may be of temporary political convenience, plainly harbors a terrible economic folly from the viewpoint of a perpetuation of the fisheries and the welfare of the people concerned. For many years this fact has been recognized by experts on both sides of the boundary, with the result that a Joint Commission was appointed by the two Federal Governments concerned, and there has at length been drawn up a code of regulations which are to apply equally to all international waters of the Great Lake system. The date for the promulgation of this international code of regulations has not yet been fixed, but it would appear that it cannot now be much longer delayed, and in view of the fact that, once promulgated, it will remain in force for at least a term of five years, and that it deals decisively with the methods of capture and meshes of nets, it obviously becomes unnecessary for your Commissioner to discuss either of these questions. The code, however, deals with the limitation of nets only to the extent of defining the proximity of pound nets to each other, of series of pound nets to each other, and numbers in a series, and does not deal at all with the question of close seasons, and only generally with that of artificial propagation, and, since it is clearly stated in the opening paragraph of the code that domestic legislation is not affected otherwise than to the extent of the provisions of the code, it would seem reasonable to suppose that all these matters are left to the judgment of the authorities concerned. Consequently it would appear necessary to touch on each of these matters separately.

THE LIMITATION OF NETS.

That in virgin waters teeming with fish there exists an indissoluble relation between the amount of net used and the amount of fish caught is a fact too obvious to need explaining, and it is equally clear that in proportion as quantities of fish are removed from such waters, so will the rate of catch to each unit of net diminish. Consequently, when inland commercial fisheries have been exploited for some little while, even over vast but, nevertheless, strictly limited areas, such as that of the Great Lakes, there must come a time when the multiplication of nets ceases to be commercially profitable. It has, in fact, been held by many authorities that, since each area will only produce a certain amount of fish, dependent more or less on the natural and artificially assisted increase of previous years, it is extremely doubtful whether more fish are actually captured where the proportion of nets to the area is excessive than if the amount of nets was considerably reduced, and in any case that the situation is bound to adjust itself through economic causes, those weaker financially amongst the fishermen going to the wall in due course. In consequence, throughout a considerable portion of the Great Lake waters no effort at all has been made to restrict the numbers or lengths of nets in use.

In theory this argument is, in all probability, perfectly sound, but in practice, under the conditions which exist, its logic is questionable. In the first place it would seem to presuppose the prevalence of genuine rivalry among fishermen, each working for his own interests, and takes no stock of a condition where the vast majority of the fishermen are but the creatures of a great and powerful corporation. Secondly, it deduces that complete exhaustion will never actually occur, because such exhaustion would be commercially unprofitable. Here, again, is an assumption open to the gravest suspicion, for it takes no count of the operations of a great corporation which, in its avaricious cupidity for fat and immediate dividends, is but all too willing to extract the last ounce of fish food from any waters on which it can lay its grasp to-day, leaving to-morrow and the dim future to take care of itself. Thirdly, no account is taken of location by the champions of this argument, although it must be plain that where nets are thickly set in channels, or across narrows, along which the fish are wont to move as they wander over the area of their particular feeding grounds, the numbers of fish in that locality will of necessity very rapidly diminish. Undoubtedly, however, there is much strength in the premises of the argument itself, namely, that each area will only produce a certain amount of fish, and, even though extraneous conditions may be such as to prevent the automatic adjustment of the proper relation between nets and area, nevertheless the argument is useful as demonstrating the fact that a limitation of nets to the minimum quantity that will catch that amount must be an economic advantage, for the less the expense at which the fish is caught, the less ought to be the price to the consumer.

The price of fish has been rising steadily and there has been a corresponding tendency of recent years towards an increase in the quantities of nets, as the following table discloses:

AVERAGE FATHONS OF POUND AND GILL NETS IN USE IN CANADIAN WATERS 1892-1906.

	1892-1896	1897-1901	1901-1906
Lake Superior	151,500	243,800	206,000
Lake Huron	589,100	457,100	742,500
Georgian Bay	617,300	508,600	515,300
Lake Erie	65,500	124,800	207,200
Lake Ontario	171,800	212,700	214,000

On the American side, also, the general tendency towards an in-crease has been quite as pronounced, and several areas on the American side of the boundary are swept by a very much higher percentage of nets than is the case in any Canadian waters. On the whole it would appear, however, that the percentage of fish taken to the fathom of net is dis-tinctly in favour of the Canadian fishermen in those areas where the Americans have a great preponderance of nets over the Canadians and a fair comparison can be made, although more fish are taken on the American side. Taking the whitefish again as an example:—

STATE OF MICHIGAN, WATERS OF LAKE SUPERIOR, WHITEFISH AREA, 2,400 SQUARE MILES.

Years.	Average nets in fathoms.	Total pounds caught.	Percentage.
1892-1896	703,300	2,117,000	3.22
1897-1901	750,300	1,169,000	1.53
1902-1906	1,231,300	1,193,000	.91

CANADIAN WATERS OF LAKE SUPERIOR. WHITEFISH AREA, 3,600 SQUARE MILES.

Years.	Average nets in fathoms.	Total pounds caught.	Percentage.
1892-1896	151,500	1,123,000	9.27
1897-1901	243,800	591,000	2.48
1902-1906	206,000	462,000	2.32

STATE OF MICHIGAN WATERS OF LAKE HURON. WHITEFISH AREA. 3,200 SQUARE MILES.

Years.	Average nets in fathoms.	Total pounds caught.	Percentage.
1892-1896	525,400	501,000	.99
1897-1901	847,100	480,000	.79
1902-1906	991,700	515,000	.58

CANADIAN WATERS OF LAKE HURON AND NORTH CHANNEL, WHITEFISH AREA, 3,000 SQUARE MILES.

Years.	Average nets in fathoms.	Total pounds caught.	Percentages.
1892-1906	589,100	1,657,000	3.07
1897-1901	457,100	940,000	2.24
1902-1906	742,500	1,051,000	1.45

It must, of course, be noted that very extensive fish hatchery operations have been in force in the American waters above mentioned, while
on the Canadian side only comparatively trifling efforts have been made
in this direction in the case of the North Channel, and none in the case
of Lake Superior, but, having regard simply to the question of the limitation of nets, the tables above given are interesting as showing, firstly,
that the price of whitefish in Canada should have been considerably
less to the consumer than in the States in view of the less cost of
production as proved by the higher percentage of catch of the Canadian
nets, although, unfortunately, this has not been the case, and secondly,
that in the case of Lake Superior two apparently similar areas, in one
of which a considerably higher percentage of nets has been in use than
in the other, that is, an area with a limited as against an area with an
almost unlimited number of nets, both show a steady decrease, proving
apparently thereby that both were removing more fish than the available increase could withstand, which, again, should serve to emphasize
the very obvious fact that where the limitation of nets is carried to such
a point that the catch of the nets is less than the normal increase, the
result must be an augmentation of the numbers of fish in the waters.

It would seem then that in the limitation of nets there exists a
practical means of maintaining the balance between the yearly fish crop
and the annual increase to be anticipated in particular varieties of
fish, of affording the fish reasonable security against annihilation in
traversing narrows or channels, and, in a measure, of regulating the
cost of capture and in consequence, the price to the consumer.

CLOSE SEASONS.

The main object of a close season for fish is to enable the fish to
perform its breeding functions in security. It is the habit of practically all the more valuable commercial fresh-water fishes to journey to
the shoal places of the lakes, or up into the creeks and rivers, to spawn,
and consequently, during the period in which the fish is passing through
narrows or channels on its way to and from the spawning beds, or is
occupied on the beds in the business of reproduction, it is peculiarly
vulnerable to the attacks of the commercial net fisherman. Consequently, unless some protection is afforded to the fish at these periods
an enormous quantity of ripe spawn will remain undeposited, which
fact in its turn will evidently have a sinister effect on the natural
increase of a future year, that is, on the quantities of young fish available to take the place of those disappearing through natural processes
or owing to the operations of the commercial net fishermen.

Reference has been made in a preceding section to the fact that,
under the treatment of modern scientific hatchery equipment, a far
greater percentage of eggs can be hatched out than would take place in
the course of nature, but in the same section it was also attempted to
prove that under no circumstance could it be the part of wisdom to seek

to dispense altogether with the natural processes of reproduction. The success which has attended fish hatchery operations on a large scale has not tended, however, towards making this latter theory acceptable to the majority of fish-culturists. It has on the the contrary, had the effect of creating a belief among them that the results obtained by natural production were so insignificant that the process could safely be neglected provided there existed sufficient hatchery equipment to deal with the number of eggs obtainable. As a natural outcome of this theory, not only has the close season for fish during the breeding season been abandoned over a considerable number of the fishing areas in which great quantities of artificially hatched fry can be planted, but there has developed, also, a school of ardent fish-culturists which claims that inasmuch as the hatchery plants must be supplied with eggs to enable them successfully to carry out their proper functions, the breeding season of the fish is obviously the period in which, at all costs, fishery operations should be most vigorously conducted, the commercial net fishermen being instructed in the art of taking and mixing spawn, licensed only on condition that they do so, and paid by the hatcheries a small fixed sum for a given quantity of eggs, the fate of the parent fish being deemed immaterial in the light of the immense increase which it will have contributed to assure. Further, in the opinion of this school, even supposing close seasons to be deemed absolutely necessary, the logical time for such would be during those periods when the fish can be most readily caught, but when they are not laden with ripe spawn, such as the spring migration of the whitefish, referred to in a previous section. Whatever may be the merits of this contention it is quite plain that it must depend for its execution on the existence of an ample hatchery plant.

It can be shown that in those Canadian waters where practically no planting of fry has been effected, such as the fisheries of Lake Superior, data of which have already been given, in spite of a close season being in force during the alleged breeding season of the white-fish, the catch has steadily diminished, and the same can be shown in regard to Canadian waters, such as Lake Ontario, in which planting of fry has occurred on a moderate scale. This, however, can hardly be deemed proof that the close season is inefficacious, for a similar state of affairs can be disclosed⁻in certain of the American fishing areas, where no close season is in effect and artificial propagation is in full blast on a gigantic scale. It would seem, on the contrary, to suggest that, as evidently the annual catch is still in excess of the available in-crease, it cannot but be exceedingly unwise to neglect any possible means of assisting that increase, or, in other words, that the close season should be maintained until at least it has been demonstrated success-fully over a period of years that it can safely be dispensed with. Most particularly so must this be the case with Ontario, who herself possesses no hatchery equipment at all, but is entirely dependent on the Dominion

Government for even the modest efforts that are being made in this direction.

In dealing with this question, moreover, it must be remembered that, although almost throughout the Canadian waters of the great lakes there has existed a legal close season, this close season has been, unfortunately, far from rigorously enforced, owing in certain localities to the deliberate laxity or inefficiency of the officials whose duty it was to do so, and in others, such as the north shore of Lake Superior, to the lamentable lack of even the most obviously indispensable equipment to enable the officials to carry out the duties they were appointed and paid to perform.

Also, it is well known to those versed in fishery lore that the dates of the close season, as at present existing, do not in most cases tally with the actual period of breeding operations, for, firstly, the dates are fixed for the fisheries as a whole, whereas the difference in latitude will account for a normal variation of at least three weeks, and secondly, climatic conditions will every year exercise a considerable influence in hastening or retarding the general movement of the fish to the spawning beds.

In support of at least the first of these contentions may be quoted the conclusions arrived at by the Georgian Bay Fisheries Commission, who reported that after an examination of practically all the fishermen in the district, and those interested in, or having knowledge of, the fisheries they were forced to the conclusion that the whitefish spawned on an average fifteen days earlier in the northern and western waters of that area, than they did in the more southern and easterly, and consequently recommended that the close season for whitefish in the Georgian Bay region, north and west sections, should be from October 1 to January 1 following, and for the southern and eastern sections from October 15 to January 1 following. When such divergence as this in the dates of spawning of one particular variety of fish exists in waters so comparatively adjacent, it is easy to realize how much more must it be the case when the latitude and normal temperature of the waters are widely different.

It has been held by some authorities (amongst others the Georgian Bay Fisheries Commission, which, of course, included so great an expert as Professor Prince, the Dominion Commissioner of Fisheries), that on account of its voracious qualities, and general hardihood, the great lake trout does not require so much protection as does the more defence-less whitefish, and consequently that, even if the trout do congregate on the spawning beds considerably earlier than provided for by the close season afforded them for protection during this period, no great harm will be done by netting them at such times. This, however, would seem hardly to be a logical deduction, for whatever may be the relative defensive powers of fish in regard to each other, all are equally defence-less against the operations of the commercial net fisherman when they are congregated in throngs on the spawning beds, and the result of netting them at this period, must in each and every case be alike, namely depletion, unless, of course, some provision is made to care for the spawn.

It would appear then, that in so far as the fisheries of Ontario are concerned, the time has most certainly not yet arrived for the abandonment of the close season, but that on the contrary its continuance remains a most vital necessity; that in view of the steadily diminishing production of the Canadian great lake fisheries and of the absence of adequate fish hatchery plants it is imperative to obtain the utmost possible benefits from the close season; that these benefits can only be fully secured by the most rigid enforcement of the close season, which implies an adequate force of competent and honest officials supplied with an ample and efficient equipment; and, lastly, that some measures should be taken without delay to secure a revision of the dates of the various close seasons, so that they may tally with the actual dates of the spawning movements in the various areas of the Provincial fisheries.

CLOSE AREAS.

Nearly allied with the question of close seasons is that of close areas. It has been pointed out that for the greater portion of the year the mature fish inhabit certain areas which may be deemed their normal feeding grounds; that the immature fish will be frequently found at these periods in shallower water, and that the mature or commercial fish leave their regular feeding grounds at certain known periods of the year for the purpose of spawning, proceeding in general to certain well-known, or at least easily located, areas to perform their breeding functions.

The general principle of setting aside areas for the conservation of natural resources has been widely accepted, and is applied to-day in the matter of headwaters of river systems, forests, bird and animal life, perhaps nowhere more extensively so than in the Province of Ontario, but in the conservation of fish life in the great lakes it is conspicuous only by its almost total absence. Why this should be the case it is hard to explain, for plainly a principle, acknowledged to be so eminently beneficial to other great but exhaustible natural resources, could not well but prove itself equally advantageous in the conservation of fish life.

In the Report of the Dominion Fisheries Commission on the Fisheries of the Georgian Bay, a recommendation was made as to the setting aside of a considerable area, in which no commercial fishing whatever should be allowed, and rod and line angling only on the payment of a special fee. Although this most excellent recommendation was designed more particularly for the purpose of perpetuating in these waters the sporting fish, the black bass, the mascalonge, and the pickerel, doubtless, had it been acted upon, it would have had a beneficial effect, also, on the other classes of fish, for though the area selected did not apparently include any of the recognized feeding grounds of the commercial whitefish or great lake trout, on which these fish are to be caught in commercially profitable numbers, undoubtedly many of the immature fish of both varieties inhabit these waters, and would consequently have had complete protection. It would seem, indeed, that wherever considerable areas of water are known to sustain for the most part only the small or immature of the leading commercial fishes, whether or not sporting fish exist in them, such areas might all of them be set aside with advantage, for there is nothing more certain than that, if commercial fishing operations are conducted in such areas, the small or young fish, which predominate, will be destroyed in great numbers, for they will inevitably get into the nets, and this, even in the event of the enforcement of the size limit being sufficiently stringent as to prevent the fishermen getting them to the markets, must mean a most prodigious waste, whose effects cannot but be felt throughout the nearby fisheries in after years.

There are also certain other areas in which the fish are only to be caught at those periods of the year when they are spawning, or proceeding to the spawning beds. Unhappily, such areas, of which perhaps the Bay of Quinte is the most prominent example, sooner or later become the hunting grounds of a band of men who, appreciating the ease with which money is to be made by removing the fish as they crowd down the narrows, or arrive in schools on the spawning beds, undertake such operations regularly under the banner of legitimate commercial fishing, although for the most part they would be both incapable of and unwilling to pursue their normal calling on the open waters, and remaining satisfied with the profits they thus speedily make at the expense of the welfare of the whole fisheries are content to sit down for a large part of the year in totally unprofitable idleness. That if a close season is to be at all effective such areas should be definitely set aside from all commercial fishing, must be very plain to any unbiassed mind, for to allow fishing in them is at once to negative the results which are, avowedly, being sought.

It is, of course, absolutely certain that the so-called commercial fishermen in these areas would protest against the introduction of any such measures to the limits of their power, but it would seem that the interests of the public at large, which suffer so terribly through their operations, cannot but be held to outweigh the selfish interests of a comparatively small number of men, whose principal occupation is to profit by the slaughter of easily caught fish, to which every citizen of the Province has as much right as they, at the very season when those fish are about to be, or are actually engaged in, reproduction for the perpetuation of the fisheries. Moreover, the political significance of their outcry could not be but momentary, for even if the public did not at first appreciate that the claims of these men were unjust, the same public would no doubt quickly realize that there is plenty of work throughout Ontario for those anxious to find it, and would further most willingly open its ears to the legitimate and seductive argument of cheap fish food for the citizens of the Province.

The conclusions to be drawn from the above section would appear to be, then, that so long as it is necessary to maintain a close season, so long will it be highly beneficial to the general fisheries to set aside from commercial fishing such areas as are only made use of by the fish for the purposes of spawning, or which for the most part are only inhabited by the small or immature of the commercial fish.

A CLOSE PERIOD.

As a final recourse for the rehabilitation of an exhausted but not completely annihilated supply of animal life, there is no more apparent expedient than that of declaring a close period. This method has been tried out in regard to game and game birds in several localities with considerable success, but no government has as yet made the experiment in regard to commercial fisheries, although there are certain well known instances where such a measure would long since have proved an inestimable benefit. In the case of Ontario's Great Lake fisheries, although the decrease continues to be alarmingly marked, it must be remembered that at the present time the great bulk of the fish caught in Canadian waters finds its way into the markets of the greater American cities. Consequently, it would appear that the introduction of such a measure, which could not but entail considerable hardship on the citizens of the Province, need never be resorted to, until at least the experiment has been made of retaining Canadian fish for Canadian consumption only, an enactment which obviously would at once very considerably diminish the demand for, and consequently the drain on, the fish, for it would take no doubt some considerable time to develop a really extensive fish market throughout the Province, and this would afford the fisheries at least a period in which to recover from their exhaustion.

THE EFFECT ON THE WHITEFISH FISHERIES OF EXTENSIVE HATCHERY OPERATIONS.

In several sections of this report reference has already been made to the fish hatchery operations which have been and are being conducted in connection with the great lakes fisheries. It has been pointed out that so far as Canadian waters are concerned the Dominion Government alone has engaged in this enterprise, and at that not very extensively throughout the major portion of the fishery areas. On the other side of the border, however, a very different situation exists, for there the various States concerned in the control of the fisheries appear to vie with each other in the perfection and increase of their plants, despite the fact that the Federal Government is also largely interested in the same work.

Nothing that has been said in previous sections has been in the least intended to belittle the importance of these operations, for it is plain that if the fisheries are to continue to withstand the ever-increasing drain of a growing demand, too much attention cannot be paid to an undertaking in which seems to lie the greatest possible hope of preventing a further decrease without resort to very drastic legislative measures, and ultimately of effecting such an increase as will be capable of meeting the needs of a steadily increasing population.

In order to obtain some idea of the value of intensive planting it is necessary to select two areas which are administered under the same regulations, in one of which intensive planting has taken place, and in the other little or none. For this purpose the Canadian waters of Lake Erie and Lake Superior have been chosen, on the former of which the efforts of the Dominion Government fish hatcheries appear largely to have been centred, while in the latter no planting whatever has taken place, in the period selected, with the exception of a few hundred thousand fry on one occasion in the vicinity of Port Arthur, a present from the American authorities in return for the courtesy of being allowed to collect spawn from Canadian spawning beds during the close season. It must be noted, however, that in the case of Lake Superior an enormous body of deep water intervenes between the north and south shores, which the true whitefish will not cross, while in the case of Lake Erie, since practically the whole body of the lake is suitable for whitefish, there is no such intervening obstacle between the bulk of the Canadian and American fisheries, so that, although intensive planting on the American side has occurred in both lakes, it is only in Lake Erie that it will be likely to have been reflected in the Canadian fisheries, and, indeed, allowance must be made for this fact in considering the great divergence in the results disclosed.

AVERAGE PLANTS AND CATCH OF WHITEFISH IN THE CANADIAN WATERS OF LAKE ERIE. WHITEFISH AREA, 2,100 SQUARE MILES.

Year.	Plant.	Pounds caught.
1892–1896	45,900,000	199,000
1897–1901	60,500,000	354,000
1902–1906	62,000,000	355,000

AVERAGE PLANTS AND CATCH OF WHITEFISH IN THE CANADIAN WATERS OF LAKE SUPERIOR. WHITEFISH AREA, 3,600 SQUARE MILES.

Year.	Plant.	Pounds caught.
1892–1896	....	1,123,000
1897–1901	700,000	591,000
1902–1906	....	462,000

These figures would seem to demonstrate that intensive planting is capable of producing great results.

It is not sufficient, however, to have arrived at this conclusion. There remains to be examined the extent to which these hatchery and planting operations must be carried to produce effective results. An examination of the records of the Canadian waters of Lake Ontario, or of the American waters of Lake Superior, two examples of fishery areas in which moderate planting operations have been conducted, will show that in both instances the catch of fish has decreased, in spite of an increase in the amounts of net used.

AVERAGE YEARLY PLANT, CATCH AND FATHOMS OF NET IN USE IN THE CANADIAN WATERS OF LAKE ONTARIO. WHITEFISH AREA, 1,400 SQUARE MILES.

Year.	Plant.	Catch.	Fathoms.
1892–1896	4,200,000	291,000	171,800
1897–1901	4,820,000	245,000	212,700
1902–1906	3,600,000	238,000	214,000

AVERAGE YEARLY PLANT, CATCH AND FATHOMS OF NET IN USE IN THE AMERICAN WATERS OF LAKE SUPERIOR. WHITEFISH AREA, 2,400 SQUARE MILES.

Year.	Plant.	Catch.	Fathoms.
1892–1896	11,057,000	2,117,000	703,300
1897–1901	21,858,000	1,169,000	750,300
1902–1906	15,268,900	1,193,000	1,231,300

It would appear, then, to be demonstrated by the above two instances that in these particular waters the extent of the hatching and fry planting operations was insufficient in comparison with the amount of fishing being carried on.

From these two examples, taken in conjunction with the results obtained in Lake Erie, it would seem just to conclude that the effects of a plant should appear in a definite ratio on the fisheries, and that, consequently, it should be possible to determine what that ratio is. The practical difficulties in the way of such an investigation are, however, considerable, for, as it has already been pointed out, to arrive at definite results it is essential to consider fishery areas as a whole, and not according to the imaginary boundaries dividing the adjacent waters of states, provinces or nations. Thus, to determine definitely the ratio of plant to the square mile, or to the pound of fish caught, required to maintain decreasing fisheries to their existing capacity, it would be necessary to have the whitefish area of each lake or body of water systematically planted, for it is improbable that the local conditions of the individual areas would be sufficiently similar to produce like results in all of them. The greatest efforts in fry planting have, however, so far taken place in American waters, where the division of control is so great as to have rendered such systematic statistical research work almost impossible up to the present, but on the Canadian side of the boundary, over which there is, broadly speaking, but one control, the only obstacle in its way would appear to be the absence of a sufficiency of hatcheries to produce positive results, for, although, as has been pointed out above, owing to the peculiar disposition of the whitefish area in Lake Erie, the enormous American plant would have to be taken into consideration in that lake, in most other cases the great bodies of water intervening between the bulk of the Canadian and American fishery areas would render such investigations both possible and conclusive.

It is interesting to note, however, that attempts have already been made to determine the ratio from the statistics available, and although the accuracy of the results obtained may not be altogether above suspicion, none the less they would appear to be most useful as indicating the approximate figures that may be expected. Mr. Paul Reighard, of the University of Michigan, in a most interesting paper delivered before the Fourth International Fishery Congress, worked it out as follows:

A plant of 30,000 per square mile of whitefish area, or of 100 per pound of whitefish caught, is correlated, under existing conditions, with an increase of 72 per cent. in the catch;

A plant of 10,000, or 32 to the pound of whitefish caught, with a practically stationary whitefish product; a plant of 2,200, or 11 to the pound of whitefish caught, with a decrease of 26 per cent. in the whitefish product; pointing out, however, that as the whitefish increased under intensive planting it was quite possible that a less plant than 100 to the pound of fish caught would suffice to maintain the fisheries.

Assuming the cost of producing fry to be 2 cents per 1,000, which in all probability is placing it considerably too high, if Mr. Reighard's figures be taken as approximately correct, this would bring the cost of producing 1,000 pounds of whitefish to $2. In view of the fact that the price paid to the fishermen at present is never less than 5 cents per pound of whitefish, it would appear that extensive hatchery operations could not but prove economically a most profitable enterprise, for of recent years the supply has never equalled the demand and the Canadian markets are still capable of very considerable expansion.

From the above it would seem to be established that practical and economically profitable results can be obtained by conducting fish hatchery operations on a large scale; that in view of the continued decrease in the Provincial fisheries, steps should at once be taken to establish considerable Provincial fish hatchery plants; and that, hand-in-hand with the establishment of such plants, scientific investigations should be made to determine the extent to which the annual production of the hatcheries must be carried to produce positive results throughout the Provincial fisheries.

3 F.C.

SCIENTIFIC RESEARCH.

Attention has already been called to the fact that scientific knowledge of the lives and habits of the fishes is all too meagre, and in the preceding paragraph the necessity was established for proper statistical research in order to discover the extent of the fish hatchery operations which it is advisable for the Province to undertake. It is obvious that to solve problems affecting the supply of wild animal life, the fundamental necessity is an accurate knowledge of the life, habits and environment of the animal in question, be it fowl, beast or fish, and this necessity cannot but be enhanced when considerable expenditures of public moneys are contemplated, or actually being born, in the effort to find a satisfactory solution. Most particularly so must this be the case with the fisheries, for the difficulties, which from the outset beset the path of the scientific investigator, indicate only too well that his task can be none too easy, and that, therefore, immediate and continued efforts in this direction are indispensable if the desired results are ever to be obtained.

The direction such investigation should take is, at first glance, apparent in so far as the purely mechanical end of the fish hatchery operations is concerned, and to the extent, also, of methodical statistical research and the study of the life histories of the various fishes. But the field is by no means limited to these. Fishes, like all the other creatures possessed of life, not only require food to support that life, but are subject to a multitude of scourges and ailments which may not only affect their continued existence, or their reproductive powers, but may seriously impair their value as food for man, to the extent, even, of rendering them positively harmful to him.

Thus it will be seen that the field of scientific knowledge must not only embrace the care of the eggs or fry under its immediate charge, but must also grapple with the lives of the fish hatched, after they have been placed in the waters, in order to assist them against the ravages of disease, by attacking and if possible destroying its causes, and also to secure for them an abundance of proper food at all stages of their existence, which, in its turn, must imply an accurate appreciation of submarine conditions and an intimate acquaintance with the lives of an infinity of aquatic plants, minute animals and insects.

There remains also to be determined the relation of fishes to each other. Some fishes are known to be cannibalistic, and predaceous in regard to other forms of fish life; while other fishes, such as the carp, are accused of devouring the immature of more valuable species, although scientific support to such accusations has never been forthcoming. Some fishes again, such as the whitefish, which subsist chiefly on vegetable matter, such as is to be obtained on the bottoms of the areas which they inhabit, on insects and on the lesser varieties of mollusc and crustacean life, are known to be harmless; while others, such as the sturgeon and sucker, are accused of destructive spawn-eating propensities, although their guilt has never scientifically been established. The sucker, indeed, furnishes a good example of the comparative ignorance of the attributes of many fishes at present existing, for while many authorities and practically all commercial fishermen will unhesitatingly classify the fish as a deliberate spawn-seeker and eater, other authorities, including Dr. Forbes, and the well-known Provincial icthyologist, Mr. C. W. Nash, disclaim this propensity on the part of the sucker entirely. In fact careful examination of the stomachs of many suckers taken on or in the vicinity of spawning beds failed to disclose any other food than algæ, entomostraca and other low forms of animal life, while Mr. Nash, who also made the interesting experiment of keeping suckers, found that they refused at all times the spawn of other fishes, which was offered them, although they would greedily devour algæ, earthworms and various forms of insect life.

Before the institution of commercial fishing on a large scale apparently all the varieties of commercial fishes which now inhabit the waters (with the solitary exception of the imported carp), existed in them in great numbers, and it would appear, therefore, reasonable to assume that each species must have been assisting, to some extent, in preserving such a balance in the natural conditions prevailing below water as to render these suitable, not only for its own prolific existence, but for that of other varieties also; in fact, that a direct relationship did exist between the welfare of one variety and that of the other. On land the direct relationship between various forms of animal, insectivorous and vegetable life is receiving yearly ever-growing attention, some varieties being cultivated, preserved or introduced by reason of their beneficial influence or combative powers against some particular condition, while relentless war is being waged against other noxious species, often at enormous expense, but justified none the less by the great profit which it is known will accrue. Doubtless very similar conditions prevail below water as on land, but they are not at present understood. It is plain, however, that commercial fishery operations, when conducted vigorously against certain species and less vigorously or not at all against others, must sooner or later effect a considerable transformation in the normal conditions prevailing below water, by disturbing the natural balance. That this might easily result in a great increase in the numbers of more or less commercially useless varieties, such as the sucker, is but all too obvious, and if these fishes actually possess the harmful spawn-eating propensities attributed to them by some authorities, the direct baneful influence of their rapid multiplication on the numbers of the finer fishes can be readily appreciated. On the other hand, it is equally obvious that even such a fish as the sucker has its place in the scheme of nature, for it is well known that they were in great abundance when the white man first entered the country, so that, although in view of the effects of commercial fishing on the fisheries at large it might well be advisable to take steps to decrease the numbers of suckers and other coarse fish of little commercial value, it would not be safe to jump to the conclusion that all such fishes could be ruthlessly destroyed with advantage. In fact it is a matter for most careful, scientific study.

It has been shown in a preceding section that the establishment of a considerable Provincial fish hatchery plant is an urgent necessity if the fisheries are to be improved or even only maintained on their present footing, and that the success which has attended fish hatchery operations in certain of the waters of the great lakes is sufficient of itself to warrant such an undertaking.

From the present section it may be, then, concluded that in entering on this business there exists a real necessity to arrange at the same time for the energetic prosecution of scientific research. In this regard it may, perhaps, not be amiss to recall the fact that while Ontario has as great an interest in the fisheries of the great lakes as all the American States combined, she has, as yet, with the single exception of Mr. C. W. Nash's check list of the fishes of the Province, published by the Department of Education, contributed nothing to the proper scientific understanding of them, a condition which can hardly be held to become her dignity or the enterprise of her responsible authorities.

THE LICENSING OF NETS.

Attention is called in the Report of the Dominion Fisheries Commission on the Fisheries of the Georgian Bay to the apparent anomaly of charging a fixed license for a given quantity of nets, irrespective of the area in which this license is to be operative, and consequently irrespective of the catch, and it is recommended that, as a fair means of determining the value of a license, the catch should be taxed to the amount of $2 per ton of the finer species of fish and $1 per ton of the coarser varieties, the fishermen being required to make a sworn declaration as to their catch on an official form, which form, again, would have to be countersigned by the responsible government fishery official. In view of the fact that such a system would reverse the present system under which the value of the license is collected into the Treasury before it is issued, and that such a reversal is not altogether desirable, it is further suggested that the value of the license applied for be estimated for the catch of the previous season, and paid for before issuance on these terms, the balance in favor of or against the Government being adjusted when the final figures for the year have been compiled from the sworn returns of the fishermen and fishery overseers.

At the present time the value of the pound and gill net licenses in the Canadian waters of the great lakes is briefly as follows:

Pound Nets .... $50.00 per net

GILL NETS, LAKE SUPERIOR AND LAKE HURON, NORTH CHANNEL AND GEORGIAN BAY.

Sail or Rowboats with not more than   6,000 yards of net $10 00
Gasoline Launches with not more than 12,000 Yards of net 25 00
Tugs with not more than 30,000 yards of net 75 00
Tugs with not more than 60,000 yards of net 150 00

LAKE ERIE.

Sail or Rowboats with not more than 2,000 Yards of net $25 00
Gasoline Launches with not more than 4,000 Yards of net 75 00
Tugs with not more than 10,000 Yards of net 250 00

LAKE ONTARIO.

Sail or Rowboats with not more than 4,000 yards of net $10 00
Gasoline Launches with not more than 6,000 Yards of net 25 00
Tugs with not more than 10,000 yards of net 50 00

BAY OF QUINTE.

Between the Bridge at Belleville and the Village of Prinyer.

Sail or Rowboats with not more than 2,000 yards of net $25 00

The revenue derived from these licenses has been approximately as follows:

1908 .... $46,000
1909   56,000

What exact proportion of the expenditure of the Department of Game and Fisheries is solely debitable to the commercial fisheries it is impossible to determine, for a great many of its officials are largely concerned in the carrying out of other duties, such as the protection of the sporting fish, the collection of the non-resident anglers' tax and the protection of the game, while the same condition applies equally to the uses to which much of its equipment is put. It is plain, however, that if the expenditures on fish hatchery operations, which have been shown in previous sections of this report to be practically unavoidable if the fisheries are to be maintained, have to be undertaken, the Province cannot afford to do otherwise than collect as great a revenue from the commercial fisheries as they can reasonably bear, in order to meet, in part at least, this added charge.

Under the present system it is extremely doubtful whether the best results from the point of view of revenue are being obtained.

It is a matter of common knowledge that the Ontario fisheries of the great lakes are largely under the domination of a foreign corporation, and that, in consequence, the great bulk of the fish secured from these waters find their way to the American markets. It is perhaps not so well realized that the Government of the United States imposes a duty of ½ cent per pound on imported fish, and is, therefore, collecting yearly a very handsome revenue from the Canadian fisheries, whereas the Ontario Government, which has to bear the cost of protecting the fisheries, if not actually losing money on the transaction, is at least gaining no appreciable revenue therefrom, and at the same time in allowing

its commercial fisheries to be depleted to the advantage of a neighboring nation is failing to secure for the present population of the Province
the benefits that should properly be derived from this great asset, or to
assure a continuance of the same to future generations. In illustration
of this state of affairs may be cited the results of an investigation conducted by a gentleman, who is much interested in these matters, in
regard to one particular fishing station on Lake Superior. He computed
that from the licenses issued to the fishermen operating from this station
the Government secured a revenue of $310, and assumed that out of this
sum would have to be provided the salary of the overseer, the cost and
maintenance of his equipment and in addition some portion of the cost
of the annual or bi-annual inspection carried out by a senior official of
the Department of Game and Fisheries, pointing out that the sum available was none too ample for these various purposes. On the other hand
he ascertained that from the duty levied on the fish imported from this
station in the year of his investigation the Government of the United
States derived a revenue of approximately $2,600.

The price paid to the few would-be independent Canadian net fishermen for their fish by the alien corporation which practically controls
the output of the Canadian fisheries, is approximately 4 to 5 cents per
pound, and the fish retails in the greater American markets at from 12
to 40 cents per pound, so that the profit to the corporation is apparently
great. In addition to this, however, since the commercial control of the
fisheries lies principally in the hands of a foreign corporation, it is but
natural that citizens of a foreign nation should be largely concerned in
its exploitation, so that as the matter stands to-day it would appear that
while the cost of protection may be said to practically swallow up all
the revenue derived from the fisheries, not only is the United States
securing a considerable yearly revenue from them, the bulk of the profits and of the actual fish, but also no small proportion of the initial cost
of capture, a situation which is obviously most unsatisfactory.

It would seem, then, but just and reasonable that those who derive
the greatest benefit from the fisheries of the Province should be assessed
for the privilege on a somewhat higher scale than is in force to-day.

In this regard the notorious fact must be noted that in a great many
instances far greater lengths of gill nets are still made use of by tugs
than are called for in their licenses, it being usually claimed that if the
nets used were restricted to the legitimate amount, fishing operations
would cease to be profitable. It is plainly not advisable that such a
state of affairs should be permitted to continue. If it be deemed desirable to restrict the nets in a given area to the quantities called for on
the licenses issued, and it is true that the present limitations of lengths
prevent, in certain areas, commercially profitable operations, then there
should obviously be issued a lesser number of licenses, sanctioning
greater lengths for those areas, and all such cases should be promptly
and carefully investigated by the Department responsible, but under no

Unreeling the Nets.

Herring Fishing.

circumstances should a deliberate infringement of the privileges granted by a license be tolerated, as is all too frequently the case to-day.

Reference was made at the commencement of this section to the recommendation made by the Georgian Bay Fisheries Commission in regard to the matter of assessing the value of licenses. It would seem that such a system would undoubtedly be more equitable on the commercial fishermen than that at present in vogue, and, inasmuch as the tax would be levied on the catch, and not merely on the class or extent of net used, the Government would derive a proportionate benefit from any measures it enacted, or any expenditures it undertook, which resulted in an increased annual production of fish. Moreover, by adjusting the tax to the necessary proportions, without causing any undue hardship it could plainly be made to be profitable from the point of view of revenue, as the following figures indicate:

REVENUE FROM NET LICENSES.

1908—$46,000 approximately (the Department was unable to furnish the exact figures).

REVENUE BASED ON ESTIMATED CATCH.

1908—Fine Fish, 21,799,990 lbs. at $2 .... $43,600
1908—Coarse Fish, 5,800,651 lbs. at $1 5,800

Total Revenue $49,400

The tax being placed at $2 per 1,000 pounds of fine fish and $1 per 1,000 pounds of coarser fish.

By licensing the shippers and buyers, and requiring from them a sworn declaration as to the amount of fish handled and from whom purchased, in addition to the sworn declarations, before referred to, obtained from the net fishermen and countersigned by the responsible fishery overseer, it would appear probable that a considerable proportion of the illicit netting, which is at present being carried on, would automatically be put a stop to, owing to the practical obstacle presented to men so engaged of disposing of their catch, a fact which would not only be beneficial to the fisheries, but would also tend to increase the revenue of the Government, for it must always be remembered in considering the available fishery statistics of the great lakes that a very considerable quantity of fish is removed yearly from the lakes by illicit means which is never accounted for, and that in certain localities the licensed men have been known to meet with but very poor success, owing entirely to the extensive and successful operation of trap nets and other illicit contrivances in the waters in which they pursued their vocation.

It would appear, however, that the fisheries might justly be expected to produce an even greater revenue than that obtainable by the method above indicated.

In dealing with the timber resources of the Province it has become customary, when throwing open limits to the public, to invite tenders for them, or, in other words, to put them up to public auction. By this means a fair return for the privilege granted is assured to the public, for if the prices are obviously insufficient, it remains within the power of the Government to refuse the tenders, and under such conditions the general law of supply and demand will, in most cases, ensure a satisfactory figure being offered.

When the average cost of catching the fish, which may approximately be estimated at 3 cents per pound, all included, is compared with the average retail price of fish, 8 to 15 cents per pound at a conservative figure, it becomes plain that the concession granted by a fishing license has a considerable value, and, consequently, it would seem reasonable to conclude that there must exist therein a fair margin for public competition—that is, that a fee for the privilege should be obtainable over and above the regular tax on the catch, as suggested. It would seem, moreover, that as the value of the particular fishing concession would be liable to fluctuation, no better method than that of public tender could be devised to secure it. Such a system would obviously require a clear delimitation of the bounds of the concession, and a precise statement of the number of licenses, with privileges granted by them, that would be granted in any particular area.

The greatest desideratum in regard to the Provincial commercial fisheries is plainly that citizens of Ontario should, as far as possible, profit by catching the fish, and that the population of Ontario generally should profit to the greatest possible extent by the fish when it has been caught. Attention has, however, been called to the domination of a foreign corporation over the Provincial commercial fisheries, whereby a precisely opposite result is being at present attained. Evidently, if under prevailing conditions licenses were put up to auction, the bulk of them would, in all probability, still fall into the hands of the corporation referred to, to the detriment of the few independent Ontario fishermen, although even so a little additional revenue would be likely to accrue to the Government. If, however, it were possible to adjust matters so that the domination of the fish trust over the commercial fisheries of the Province could be curbed, and citizens of Ontario thereby encouraged to enter on the fishing business on a considerable scale as likely to prove a profitable venture to themselves, the system of putting fishing licenses up to auction, while enforcing a fixed tax on the catch, could not apparently but be profitable from the point of view of revenue, as an incentive to legitimate competition and thereby to trade, and, lastly, as an assurance that the exploitation of the fisheries would ultimately fall into the hands of an enterprising class of citizens of the Province. Various methods of producing such a situation will be discussed in a succeeding paragraph.

The main difficulties which would be encountered in introducing the system lie, apparently, in the facts (a) that the commercial fishing business has to be learned like any other vocation, more especially so in proportion as the water area increases in size, and that, consequently, it is probably more economical, in the case of large water areas at least, to encourage the development of a distinct class of commercial fishermen than to jeopardize the existence of such a class through the intrusion of others, ignorant of the business, but attracted by its speculative possibilities; (*b*) that after the elimination of the monopolies the uncertainty of obtaining licenses might deter enterprising provincial companies or individual fishermen from acquiring a sufficiency of nets or from erecting the freezing and storage plants necessary to conduct the business; (*c*) that considerable labor and expense would be involved in advertising for tenders; (*d*) that there are no doubt a number of men in the Province who, while possessed of little or no resources other than those obtained annually as the result of commercial fishing, have pursued their calling so long and have attained such an age that it would be impossible for them to turn to other means of livelihood in the event of their being unsuccessful in tendering for a license; (*e*) that if discrimination were instituted in one case—that is, if a higher tender was refused in favor of a lower it would open the road to all the evils of political patronage and influence. Undoubtedly some means of protection for the old fishermen would have to be devised, but this could easily be effected by refraining from putting up to tender the licenses of those who had engaged in commercial fishing in the Province any stated number of years. In regard, also, to the labor and expense involved in placing the licenses up to tender, these could be greatly lightened by fixing a term of years over which the license tendered for would be valid, subject, of course, to the licensee keeping within the law, and it is apparent that the cost of this small franchise could be expected to operate in the direction of securing a better observance of the laws, seeing that the licensee would have more at stake. How far, however, the other objections to the system would counterbalance its advantage can only be a matter of opinion and conjecture, but the privilege granted by a commercial fishing license is so great, and the advantages of such a system so attractive from many points of view, that, under proper administration of the fisheries, it might well be worth while at least to make an experiment in this direction.

It may be considered, then, from this section that the commercial fisheries should produce a greater revenue than they do at present; that a tax on the catch of fish would be more equitable on the fishermen than a license in proportion to the class or amount of net used; that the establishment of reasonable competition in the fishery business is greatly to be desired, and that such competition can best be assured by first breaking up the domination now exercised by an alien corporation over the commercial fisheries of the Province.

VARIOUS METHODS BY WHICH THE PROVINCIAL FISHERIES CAN BE
REHABILITATED, AND A STRONG FISH MARKET
DEVELOPED IN ONTARIO.

The situation disclosed in preceding sections renders it apparent
that at the present time the Province is not deriving even a reasonable
amount of benefit from the possession of immense fisheries, either in
revenue or fish food, and that, worse still, the once prolific fisheries are
dwindling with alarming rapidity. It has been shown, also, that by a
strict enforcement of the close season, by seeing to it that the dates of the
close season tally with the breeding seasons of the various fishes, by the
establishment of a series of fish hatchery plants and other measures, a
great deal can be accomplished in the direction of preventing a further
decrease, and ultimately of effecting an actual increase, in the product
of the fisheries, but it has also been pointed out that so long as an alien
corporation remains in practical control of the commercial output of the
fisheries, so long will the fish markets of the Province be of secondary
importance in comparison with those of greater American cities, and,
according to the measure of starvation that must prevail under such conditions, so will their growth continue to be stultified.

Fish companies and individual fishermen, who would be independent, have little chance of remaining so for any length of time. The
trust, through its agents, controls the bulk of the plant existent in the
Province which is indispensable for the conducting of the fishery business. It controls, also, in many instances the shipping facilities and the
ordinary channels of trade. For a time the independent fish company
or fishermen may succeed in disposing of their catch locally, but in
Ontario there is at present but small demand for the coarser varieties of
fish, and at certain seasons of the year these comprise the bulk of the
fishermen's catch. Then, if they should desire to dispose of their catch
outside of their immediate locality, they soon are swept into the toils of
the corporation, for unless they are willing to sell in the future all their
catch to it, the trust refuses to purchase any of the catch at all. It appears, indeed, that at no time will the corporation or its agents deal
with the independent men other than on the terms " all or nothing," so
that unless the company or fishermen are willing to lose their profits
and the fruits of their labors, or unless they can command sufficient
capital to make storage, shipping and market arrangements for themselves, which in some cases has been attempted but only with indifferent
and short-lived success, they must inevitably, sooner or later, bow to the
dictates of the corporation, and thus allow themselves to be swallowed
up by it. In certain cases definite contracts are drawn up, binding the
fishermen to sell only to the agents of the trust, and it seems more than
probable that in many cases also the corporation supplies the fishermen
with their nets, boats and other appliances, extracting part payment in
kind, but holding always a sufficient balance over their heads as to
ensure the continuance of their allegiance.

Contract or no contract, however, the result is the same, namely, that the truly independent fish company or fishermen cannot exist under the present conditions of the fishery trade for any length of time, and it must be clearly understood that the possession of a Canadian sounding title by a fish company is no guarantee either of Canadian proprietorship or independency. In fact, the reverse is, as a rule, the case.

It is plainly necessary, therefore, to examine carefully into what available means present themselves of effecting such a radical alteration in the situation as to place it on an economically sound basis, or, in other words, of breaking the domination of the American fish trust, placing the control of the fish crop in the hands of the citizens of the Province, and developing a proper fish market throughout Ontario, so that the people at large may profit by their fisheries and not be robbed of the profit for the benefit of the United States, while at the same time endeavoring to improve the general condition of the fisheries to the greatest possible extent.

Markets cannot be created in a day, even though the advantage of their establishment and rapid development were patent to everyone, neither can a great vested interest be attacked and shorn of its power without a considerable outcry being raised. The achievement of both objectives in the case of the fisheries would obviously involve the formulation of a strong, clear-cut policy, embracing the fundamental principles of conservation, economic exploitation and distribution, and the systematic and consistent execution of this policy over a period of years. Such a policy can only be evolved by a consideration of all the problems presented, without regard to the various authorities who may be concerned in its initial or subsequent introduction.

The control of the Canadian fisheries of the great lakes, however, is divided between the Dominion and Provincial Governments in such a way as to render impossible the adoption of a scheme, for the conservation and improvement of the fisheries and the development and regulation of an Ontario fish market, at all adequate to the necessities of the case, without considerable collaboration between them, and thus, even though, in all probability, the co-operation of the Dominion Government is to be anticipated in the event of a forceful fisheries policy being adopted by the Provincial Government, it becomes necessary, not only to inquire into the methods available for obtaining the desired results, but also as to how far these fall within the scope of Provincial legislation, and as to where it will be necessary to invoke the aid of the Dominion Government. Consequently the various available measures will first be discussed, and subsequently the relative powers of the two governments in regard to their enactment.

PROHIBITION OF EXPORT.

It has been pointed out that the great bulk of the product of the great lake fisheries at present finds its way into the markets of the

United States; 95 per cent., in fact, would in all probability prove to be a fairly accurate estimate. It is evident, therefore, that in such a measure as the prohibition of export there must, under existing conditions, lie great capabilities of very materially reducing the annual fish crop for a period of years, more especially in view of the fact already brought to notice that, although the potentialities of a great fish market in Ontario are apparent, actually the existing fish market is still in the most elementary stage of development.

It must also be equally clear that the indirect effect of such a measure could not but be the evolution of a far greater demand for fish throughout the Province, for prices would inevitably fall during the first periods of its enforcement, owing to the fact that many more men are engaged in the fishing business at present, and would probably be wishful of continuing it, than the demand under such conditions would warrant for at least several years to come, and consequently the surplus of supply over demand would bring about the usual result, a considerable reduction in values.

That the general public would only too joyfully take advantage of such a situation, is perfectly certain, and it is equally sure that the education of the general public to the value of fish food, or, in other words, the creation of a greater demand and thereby the upbuilding of a great Provincial fish market, is economically sound from the point of view of both business and health.

The introduction of such a measure, applicable to all classes of fish, would obviously disorganize the existing arrangements of the fish trust, and it would be compelled to seek other channels of supply, if the demands of its present markets were to continue to be filled. But with the troubles of this corporation the Province has no concern. It is true that the trust might commence to interest itself in the exploitation of the Ontario market, and thus continue to maintain its grip on the product of the fisheries to a limited extent, but even so, at least the citizens of the Province would profit by their fish to the extent of consuming them, a privilege which, broadly speaking, they are denied to-day.

There is no doubt but that the enactment of such a measure would meet with a storm of protest from the interests concerned, and from the tools employed by them in the prosecution of their business, the commercial net fishermen, for it is certain that the former would not relinquish one of its main sources of supply without making a great effort to retain it, and that it would be made to appear to the latter that their vocation and means of livelihood were being wantonly attacked. That for a time at least many of the net fishermen would have to seek other occupations cannot be denied, and it would be necessary to give ample notice of such a measure so as to enable the men to make suitable arrangements, or possibly even to purchase from them at an equitable valuation their boats, gear and other equipment, where such were beyond doubt the actual property of the men, but it must be remembered that the average annual profit to the man who does the actual fishing lies somewhere between $400 and $800 only, so that, although work is conducted during certain portions of the year only, and there are in consequence periods of idleness, which doubtless lend an additional attraction to the life in the view of many of those engaged in it, none the less it can hardly be deemed a profitable occupation in comparison with others under the conditions in which it exists to-day. There is, moreover, plenty of room for those who would have to abandon their calling in other walks of life in this Province, so that there would be no real hardship to them, and it would seem that the at least temporary disappearance of some proportion of them from this business could not but result in an amelioration of the condition of those who remained in it, seeing that what profits there were in the business would be divided amongst a less number of men, thus tending to raise the standard of life in the classes which engage in fishing, and creating a more remunerative and engaging prospect for those who would enter or re-enter this calling in due course as the necessities of a growing Ontario market required them.

It might be argued that if total prohibition of export were introduced for a term of years, there would be such a rapid increase in the numbers of coarse and predaceous fishes, owing to the lack of a market for these at least at first, that the more valuable and defenceless species, such as the whitefish, would derive very little actual benefit from the measure. It must be remembered, however, that total prohibition of export would, in all probability, only be introduced as one plank in a broad scheme for the conservation and development of the fisheries, and that accompanying it there would be, also, instituted an efficient system of fish hatcheries, whose first and chiefest attention would obviously be devoted to the more valuable fishes. It is indisputable, as has been shown in a preceding section, that the fish hatcheries can by modern scientific methods hatch a far greater percentage of the eggs of the parent fish than would be effected under natural conditions, and consequently, as the hatching system became perfected, the number of young fishes in the water as the result of one season's spawning would be vastly greater than the average now being attained by the same number of parent fish. This alone would seem to be sufficient to counteract the ill effects of giving the coarser and predaceous varieties even a somewhat protracted period of security from the American markets.

The principle of the prohibition of export, however, is not only capable of general application to the product of the fisheries, but in a more restricted sense to individual varieties of fish. Indeed, the alarming decrease in the annual catch of whitefish caused the Georgian Bay Fisheries Commission to recommend such a measure to the Dominion Government in regard to that particular species. Naturally, if the export of one or two varieties were prohibited by legislation, the fish trust could continue to purchase from the fishermen all their catch exclusive of the prohibited varieties, and probably would do so, so that, while the Ontario market was profiting to the extent of one or two of the finer varieties of fish, the great bulk of the other fishes would still be exported to the States.

By partial prohibition of export, therefore, unsupported by other measures, it would seem that not only would the power of the trust remain unshaken to a great extent, but that also the Ontario market would not receive the requisite impetus, for in dealing with such sources of food supply as the fisheries it is evidently necessary to take into account the requirements of all classes of the community, and to accomplish this, equal attention would have to be paid to the coarse as to the finer varieties of fish, for the former will in all probability always be the cheaper and, therefore, in greater demand by a considerable section of the population.

It must also be noted that the prohibition of export of particular varieties only would entail very strict supervision of shipments for export. The methods of packing fish in deep boxes and barrels are such that inspection is by no means easy at any time. It is well known, for instance, that no small numbers of black bass, the export of which sporting fish has already been prohibited, at present find their way to the fish markets of the States from certain localities, concealed in shipments of coarser fish. To make the protection of particular varieties of fish effective, in fact as in law, would appear to necessitate, therefore, a more thorough and searching inspection being carried out by a more conscientious and efficient body of officials than under present conditions is at all feasible.

If, however, such alterations were effected in the personnel and methods of the Department concerned as to make effective inspection possible of execution, and at the same time a method could be devised by which the Provincial fish market could be fostered in all classes of fish in spite of a continued export of large quantities of the coarser varieties to the already established markets for them in the States, it would seem that partial prohibition might have some weighty advantages over total prohibition, for in the first place it would not disorganize so abruptly the existing fishery business, and consequently would meet with less opposition, and secondly it would not leave in any doubt the possible undue increase in coarse fish referred to earlier in this section.

In any case there can be little doubt but that prohibition of export, even if applied only in modified form, would be a powerful factor in remedying the present deplorable condition both of Ontario's fisheries and of her fish market.

A PROVINCIAL FISH AGENCY.

The condition under which the fisheries are at present being conducted have already been indicated earlier in this report, and attention has been drawn to the fact that under these conditions healthy competition is practically eliminated, the yearly revenue of the majority of the fishermen is kept at a very low figure, and the fisherman himself becomes little more than the paid servant of the trust.

In other fish markets, such as those of the American Atlantic Fisheries, a situation more favourable to the net fisherman exists, inasmuch as there have become established certain firms who receive and market the fish of the individual fishermen on a fixed commission basis, and consequently the fisherman retains his independence and is in a position to profit directly by the fluctuations of the market, and a greater incentive is thereby afforded to initiative and enterprise. The existence of several firms in this commission business ensures competition and, consequently, a fair deal to the fishermen. Such a system, apparently, once prevailed over certain portions of the great lake fisheries, but it has completely disappeared in the evolution of the fish trust.

It is clear that the great bulk of the ordinary net fishermen could individually never succeed in storing, shipping and marketing their catch to advantage, for even were funds available, which is usually far from being the case, the very nature of their occupation precludes the possibility of their having sufficient leisure to attend satisfactorily to such details. Consequently, the presence of some form of middlemen who will receive, store and market the fish, either by direct purchase or on commission, would appear indispensable in connection with this business. That under normal conditions the competitive form of middleman, as represented by the commission houses of New York, is more equitable than the autocratic form, as represented by what might be termed the Chicago Fish Trust, both from the point of view of the fisherman and the consumer, would seem highly probable, but it is plain that if the profits of such commission houses could be reduced to a minimum, so as to but little more than cover the cost of operation, the profit to both fisherman and consumer would be correspondingly greater. This could be achieved only by the Government undertaking the work of the commission houses, or in other words, by the establishment of a Government Fish Agency. A strong plea in favour of such a measure is to be found in the report of the Georgian Bay Fisheries Commission, and, as no more clear or concise explanation of its advantages could very well be constructed, it is quoted at length:—

"A fish agency, or several such agencies, would be a much simpler matter   (i.e. than the successful Dominion Government sea-fish dryer at Souris, P.E.I.). The agent would merely act as receiver of the fish, as consignee from the fishermen, and pay them at current rates on the plan adopted at Souris, or at the government fish reduction works at various Atlantic points; he would place them in the Government refrigerator, unless the market required the fish at once, and would thus fill the orders as they reached him from the various markets in Canada and the United States. The fish agency would act as middleman between the fisherman and the market buyers, and would leave out of

4 F.C.

consideration the large monopolies, who seem to crush out all smaller enterprises and fair competition. These unscrupulous combines, who try, and with some success, owing to the lethargy of the public and its indifference to its best interests, to monopolize the whole fish business on both sides of the line; keep the fishermen in their clutches; dictate the price of fish in the wholesale and retail markets, and, from a Canadian point of view, work ruin to the fishing population and the fishing industries.

At least five advantages would follow from a fish agency scheme:—

(1) The control of the United States combines and monopolies would cease.

(2) The fisherman would have a central point to which he could with confidence send his catch of fish.

(3) The fisherman could rely on receiving full value for his fish, based on the current market prices.

(4) No waste of fish would occur, as the surplus of such fish as were not at the time in demand would be stored in the refrigerator until the demand came at a later date.

(5) The Canadian demand for fish would be met, and the large surplus would reach the United States markets. The present high price would allow of the payment of the duty imposed by the United States. Pickerel, it may be stated, have recently brought the surprising price in Chicago of forty cents per pound. Of course, the Canadian demand for our own fish would first be met before any foreign buyers were supplied."

It will be seen from the above extract what a powerful means would be afforded by such an agency, both for developing an adequate fish market in Ontario and for regaining commercial control of the fisheries by breaking the power of the fish trust, for not only would Ontario demands naturally be met before those of outside or foreign markets, but that demand could at the same time be carefully fostered and cultivated, and also, with sufficient storage appliances at its disposal, the Government would be entirely independent of the trust for securing its markets, and thus the domination and dictation of the trust would at one blow be annihilated. Moreover, from the existence in other markets of several prosperous commission houses in this line of business, it is obvious that, within reasonable bounds, the enterprise could not but be as profitable as it was deemed advisable to make it.

The effect of such a scheme in conjunction with that of partial prohibition of export is ably recited by the Georgian Bay Fisheries Commission, with especial reference to the whitefish, and a further quotation from that report is, therefore, made:—

"As we have pointed out, the whitefish in the Georgian Bay, and in fact all over Canada, so far as our knowledge and observation teaches us, is becoming almost depleted, and there is no one but who will say that the adoption of any measure, however radical it may be, which will preserve and increase the whitefish of Canada, is justifiable. The only class who can at all complain of such a measure would be United States citizens, and a handful of fishermen in Canada. As to the first class, we need not concern ourselves, and as to the fishermen, we firmly believe they will get in any event as high a price for the whitefish sold in Canada as they are now paid by the monopolistic companies who control their catch. That this measure would redound to the benefit of the Canadian citizen goes without question. We have met with innumerable complaints from all quarters of the Province that Canadians cannot get Canadian fish to eat, and the extraordinary fact has been brought out beyond dispute that a large percentage of the Canadian fish which is used by the Canadian consumer is caught in Canadian waters, goes to the United States markets, and is then brought back to Canada and sold. The great objection which the fishermen will have to the measure is that there is no fish market in Canada to consume all the whitefish which is caught, but we believe that such is not the case, and that, owing to the fast diminishing catch of whitefish which is occurring from year to year, and the vastly increasing population which is pouring into Canada, the Canadian consumer, if afforded opportunities of purchasing, will totally consume all the whitefish catch of the Dominion of Canada, and will pay as good a price as can be had for the fish to-day. More particularly, if the government fish agencies which we have recommended are established, will it assist the fisherman in disposing of his catch. There is no doubt that after the measure should become law, a great number of fishermen will build their own ice-houses and their own fishing stations, and not be dependent on the American companies for the necessities of their calling. But, for those who do not, if the government agencies are established, to which the fisherman knows that he can at once, and without extra trouble, dispose of his whitefish, it will, we believe, detract very materially, and in fact do away altogether with, any objection he might raise to the prohibition of the export of whitefish.

. . . .

If this recommendation be carried out, it must also be remembered that the American market is still open for the vast quantities of fish, forming two-thirds of the total catch of the Canadian fishermen, of trout and pickerel and other fish of coarser varieties, which find a ready sale in their markets; and we believe also that, as the Americans are dependent on our fish, the cutting off of one-third of their imports from Canada will necessarily raise the price to the Canadian catcher of those fish which can be taken into the United States."

It would seem, therefore, that through the operation of the two schemes together, the establishment of Provincial Fish Agencies and the prohibition of the export of certain varieties, a maximum of beneficial results could be obtained at a minimum of disorganization and friction, but that in any case the organization and establishment of Provincial Fish Agencies could not fail to be extremely advantageous, alike to the growth of the Provincial fish trade and to the citizens of the Province of Ontario.

THE IMPOSITION OF AN EXPORT DUTY ON FISH.

The chief advantage to be derived from the imposition of an export duty on fish would appear to be the revenue that would thus be obtained. It has been pointed out that at the present time the citizens of the United States are profiting to a far greater extent than the Canadians, both in revenue and in fish, from the Canadian fisheries of the great lakes, so that, although the markets of the United States are so firmly established and insistent in their demands for supply that in all probability they would still require all the Canadian fish that they could secure in spite of an export duty, the tax in itself would at least serve as a means of securing for the Canadians a reasonable compensation for the loss of the bulk of their fish.

It is improbable that the duty would in any serious way disturb the power of the fish trust, for that corporation could confidently be relied on to extract the amount of the tax from the consumer in the United States, who, to judge by the price of forty cents per pound, previously noted as having been paid in Chicago for pickerel, apparently is prepared to stand the cost, no matter almost what it may be, provided only that he gets the fish.

Similarly the production of the fisheries would not be seriously affected, as the demand would apparently continue to be as great as ever in the foreign markets, and this cause also would tend to prevent any general improvement in the condition of the Ontario fish market.

It is evident, however, that the above remarks are only applicable to a comparatively moderate tax, for there must exist a limit in cost which would break even the demands of the established American fish markets, and there is obviously no limit to the amount to which the export duty could be raised if desired. If such a measure, however, were contemplated, it would probably be on a broad general basis comprising all classes of fish, with an additional charge for the export of certain of the fine varieties of fish. In such a case the finer varieties would derive an advantage if the charge were raised sufficiently to effect a decrease in the demands of the American markets, and it would seem reasonable also to suppose that, in this event, the decrease in the quantities shipped to the American markets might well result in the creation of new and better markets in Ontario. The duty would have to be placed very high indeed, however, to achieve such desirable results.

In conjunction with the establishment of Provincial fish agencies, the imposition of an export duty on a sliding scale might prove advantageous in dealing with the demands from across the border, although it could never be quite so efficacious a measure as the total prohibition of export of the varieties it was desired to protect. It must, moreover, be remembered that, although it is most highly desirable to break the American commercial control of Ontario's fisheries, it would not be the part of wisdom to destroy the American markets for Ontario fish altogether, for during many years to come there should be, under a proper system, profit to be made by citizens of the Province in selling a considerable surplus catch of at least coarse fish to the Americans, which it is quite proper should be removed from the waters each year, but which otherwise would either be a drug on the Ontario market or else, perhaps, completely wasted.

It must also be noted that the remarks made in a previous section as to the inspection of fish would apply with great force should an export duty on fish ever be imposed, for fish piracy could be counted on to increase, and smuggling and juggling in varieties to be undertaken on a large scale, so that, without very strict and efficient inspection carried out by honest and capable officials, neither would the Government profit to the fullest extent in the matter of revenue, nor would the Provincial fish market or the fisheries themselves derive the fullest benefits to be anticipated from such a measure.

THE POWERS OF THE DOMINION AND PROVINCIAL GOVERNMENTS IN RELATION TO THE COMMERCIAL FISHERIES OF THE GREAT LAKES.

Under existing conditions, through the operation of the British North America Act, the Dominion of Canada is governed and administered as a whole by the Federal Government at Ottawa, and separately and individually in Provinces by the respective governments of the various Provinces. Naturally enough the British North America Act did not provide for all the contingencies which should eventually arise through the development of so vast a country in its allocation of power between the Dominion and Provincial Governments, but, broadly speaking, the lands, forests and waters within the boundaries of the respective Provinces were handed over to their governments to administer and govern, while to the Dominion Government was reserved the power of intervening in such administration in respect of measures affecting Canada as a whole.

In so far as the fisheries were concerned, whether maritime or inland, the attitude was taken by the Dominion Government that these were national, and consequently to be administered by federal authority. This view was ultimately accepted both by British Columbia and the

Maritime Provinces. The Canadian Fisheries of the great lakes, however, are conterminous with the southern boundaries of Ontario, and as these fisheries developed in value, and more citizens of the Province became engaged in their exploitation, it followed that Ontario's interest in these fisheries considerably augmented. Lying exclusively on the borders of her territory, it seemed to her government that Ontario was entitled to considerable voice in the administration of these fisheries. As time went on various matters of dispute in regard to them arose between the Government of Ontario and the Dominion Government, such an impasse being finally reached that the whole question was referred to the Privy Council for decision. On the basis of that decision was enacted the present system of what may be termed dual control.

Under this system the Dominion Government may, generally speaking, be said to regulate the conditions under which the fisheries are conducted, while the proprietory rights in relation to the fishes are vested in the Provincial Government, which issues licenses to those desirous of engaging in fishing operations.

It is not within the scope of this report to discuss the merits of this system, or to attempt to interpret in detail those points which, through decision of the Privy Council, still remain open to doubt and contention, but in view of the fact that glaring evils do exist in connection with the fisheries, which only very drastic measures can adequately remedy, it is necessary in this report to investigate carefully the extent to which Provincial legislation could alone institute such measures, without encroaching on the prerogative of the Dominion Government, and to what extent it would be necessary to invoke the aid of the Dominion Government in order to carry them into effect.

AN EFFICIENT PERSONNEL AND EQUIPMENT FOR A FISHERIES PROTECTIVE SERVICE.

In the Interim Report of this Commission attention was strongly called to the fact that both the personnel and equipment of the existing Provincial Fisheries Protective Service were in a lamentable state of inefficiency, and certain general recommendations were made on these heads with a view to remedying this state of affairs.

It is plain that in so far as the officials are concerned there can be no question either as to the right of the Provincial Government to appoint to these positions whomsoever it may select, nor as to the advisability of selecting for these posts only such men as are physically and morally suitable for them; but in regard to the equipment, the division of control of the fisheries somewhat complicates the question and appears to render a further examination into it necessary.

At the present time the Dominion Government maintains one large cruiser and employs a limited number of fishery inspectors to see that

Herring Fishing, Lake Huron.

the Dominion rulings in regard to the fisheries are observed, but the actual enforcement of the laws rests chiefly with the Provincial Government, which maintains a large staff of wardens, fishery overseers and inspectors, and incurs considerable expenditure in regard to the equipment for these officials, for this purpose. The large cruiser of the Dominion Government is eminently suitable for patrol work on the high seas of the great lakes, and for the supervision of the fish tugs engaged in operations over deep waters. With the exception of the "Edna Ivan," an ancient fish tug with indifferent cabin accommodation built upon it, which the Provincial Government again leased this year, the Province is possessed of no equipment in the very least degree suitable for this class of work, and, indeed, it would seem that such work, which is practically a policing of the fisheries against international fishing piracy, is distinctly the province of the Dominion Government. But in regard to all the vast extent of less exposed waters in which fishing operations are conducted, the Provincial Government, as has been pointed out, has assumed the burden of enforcing the general Dominion regulations in addition to those governing its own domestic arrangements, and by doing so has furnished conclusive proof not only of the very great importance it attaches to the protection of the fisheries, but also of a strong desire to retain as much control as possible over an interest which can affect to such a great degree the welfare of its citizens.

As previously recorded in this report, however, there has recently been drawn up a series of international regulations between Great Britain and the United States in regard to the fisheries of the great lakes, which, when promulgated, are to apply equally on both sides of the boundary, and there seems to be little doubt but that promulgation of these regulations will not long be delayed. The Commissioner who represented the United States in these negotiations has recommended to the United States Government that a suitable staff and equipment be provided and maintained by the Federal Government to enforce these regulations in so far as the American waters are concerned, and it would seem, therefore, reasonable to suppose that the Dominion Government should contemplate some such step also, unless very well assured that the Government of Ontario is prepared and willing adequately to undertake this work.

That the present equipment at the disposal of the Provincial Government is almost entirely unsuitable to the purposes on which it is employed has been set forth in no uncertain terms in the Interim Report of this Commission. In the face of a modern and efficient equipment, such as recommended to the Federal Government of the United States, it is evident that its lamentable deficiencies would become only the more apparent.

The whole question then would seem to resolve itself into a matter of policy on the part of the Provincial Government, to decide in fact whether it is expedient to spend the money necessary for the acquisition of an ample, suitable and efficient equipment, in order to retain control of the enforcement of the laws over what are practically its own fisheries, or whether to let this control pass altogether into the hands of the Dominion Government.

Duplication of the fisheries protective service would appear to be unnecessary and wasteful, and yet, seeing that the Dominion Government has entered upon an engagement with the Government of the United States to enforce certain regulations over the fisheries, it would seem unavoidable that it should take the matter into its own hands in the event of the Provincial Government being unwilling to adopt a progressive and suitable policy, both in regard to the selection of a staff and the provision of a proper equipment. Even should the Dominion Government decide to increase its staff and equipment, after promulgation of the international regulations, there can be little doubt but that the announcement by the Provincial Government, of its intention materially to improve its fishery protective service on modern lines, would be taken into consideration in determining the extent of such increase. In any case it is apparent that the more efficient and adequate the Provincial service, the more will the actual control of the fisheries continue to be exercised by the Province.

THE ESTABLISHMENT OF FISH HATCHERIES AND FISH AGENCIES.

In the United States practically all the individual States now maintain very extensive hatchery plants of their own, in addition to those supported by the Federal Government. It is plainly a purely domestic matter for each Province or State to decide for itself, and there can be no question as to the power of the Government of Ontario to do precisely as it chooses in this regard.

Similarly, the establishment of a Provincial Fish Agency would be a purely domestic arrangement, and as such within the absolute jurisdiction of the Provincial Government.

THE PROHIBITION OF EXPORT OF FISH.

The decision of the Privy Council in regard to the division of control in the matter of the great lake fisheries was a direct interpretation of the provisions of the British North America Act, and it was definitely established by this decision that the product of the great lake fisheries was the property of the Province, irrespective of whether or not the Dominion Government should see fit to levy a tax on the fisheries. The licenses issued to the commercial net fishermen by the Province are endorsed with the dates and areas for which the licenses are valid and other matters such as may from time to time be necessary, although, of course, such licenses are issued only with the understanding that fishing shall be carried on under the general rules and regulations enacted by the Dominion Government. The possession of a license, therefore, presumably entitles the licensee to the absolute possession of such fish as he may legally catch while fishing under the Dominion regulations and further restrictions of the Province, so that he is entitled to market his catch where and how he pleases. There is, however, no apparent reason why the license should not be endorsed with a provision to the effect that the fish, or certain specific classes of fish, must only be sold for home consumption, which, plainly, would be tantamount to a prohibition of export of the varieties of fish referred to. An analogous endorsement of a license occurs in the case of timber limits on Crown lands, the provision being to the effect that raw timber shall not be exported but must first be milled in the Province, and it is difficult to conceive that there should be any legal differentiation between the products of the forests and the fisheries, in so far as Provincial legislative powers are concerned, seeing that both, under the British North America Act, are the property of the Province, and consequently within Provincial jurisdiction.

In the case of the timber an Act was passed forbidding the export of raw timber cut on Crown lands, so that in the matter of restricting the sale of certain fishes to the home market a similar course might possibly be adopted by the Provincial Legislature, that is, indirect prohibition of export legislation might be introduced, the particular provisions of the Act in respect to the non-export of certain varieties of fish being, as in the case of timber, endorsed on each license issued.

A difficulty might arise through the actions of middlemen who, having purchased the fish from the fishermen on the understanding that it was for home consumption, might none the less decide to ship it abroad. In fact, under present conditions some such action on the part of the monopolies could reasonably be anticipated. Hence, to make the measure effective under Provincial Law, it would appear necessary to license the middlemen and retail fish dealers, and to endorse their licenses with a provision similar to that on the license of the commercial net fishermen. The Provincial Government can, of course, put under license any business or occupation it may select, and the endorsation of the license in the second and third channels of trade with a non-export or home consumption provision would clearly be valid if it were so in the case of the first, namely the commercial net fishermen.

Under the British North America Act are defined the jurisdictions of the Dominion and Provinces, but it occurs occasionally that, while one section apparently places a matter within the jurisdiction of the Province, another section can be interpreted as placing the same matter under Dominion authority. In such cases, if the question were contested, the Dominion ruling would apparently be held to prevail.

In regard to the question under review, although as has been shown the Province can possibly enact indirect legislation for the prohibition of the export of fishes, and certainly can virtually effect such prohibition of export by the endorsation of the licenses issued to the fishermen, there seems nevertheless to be little doubt that under the British North America Act the Dominion Government has authority to enact the prohibition of any or all classes of fish. Already Dominion legislation forbids the export of black bass, mascalonge and speckled trout. The Dominion authority to enact the measures prohibiting the export of these fishes has never been challenged in the courts, so that the action of the Dominion Government in these cases cannot be held to have established a conclusive precedent, but the acquiescence of the Provincial Government in the measures would at least tend to show tacit acknowledgement on its part of their validity, and it is obvious that there can be no legal distinction between sporting and commercial fishes in so far as jurisdiction is concerned.

A Dominion enactment would naturally affect all classes of the community, and this would put a stop to all legal exportation without recourse to the endorsation of the licenses issued to fishermen and fish dealers. It is evident also that whether enacted under Dominion or Provincial legislation, the greater the percentage of the total Ontario catch that was handled by a Provincial Fish Agency, the easier would become the enforcement of such a measure.

CLOSE SEASONS, A CLOSE PERIOD, AND CLOSE AREAS.

There is no question that the power of enacting close seasons falls exclusively within the jurisdiction of the Dominion Government. Attention has been called to the fact that, owing to the difference in latitude and climatic conditions, the present dates of the close seasons do not tally in many localities with the actual dates of spawning. The general distribution of the fisheries of the great lakes renders it, indeed, practically impossible to fix a short period for each variety of fish which will cover the widely divergent dates of spawning in all the different lakes, although no such difficulty would present itself if the duration of the close seasons were materially increased, as has been deemed advisable by many authorities, and as was recommended to the Dominion Government by the Georgian Bay Fisheries Commission in regard to the whitefish.

While, however, the power of the Dominion Government to fix such close seasons as its wisdom may direct is incontestable, and such seasons could not in any way be abbreviated by the Provincial Government, it is apparently within the powers of the Provincial Government to add to the Dominion close seasons, if it should so desire, by endorsing the commercial net licenses with dates which would make them valid for a shorter period than that allowed under Dominion regulation. Such at least is the opinion of the present Deputy Attorney-General of the

Province, Mr. J. R. Cartwright. If this be so, the Province evidently has it within its power to right the present unsatisfactory state of affairs, for it cannot be claimed that the Dominion dates are not suitable to some, at least, of the fishing areas of the great lakes, or that in a single instance they err either in commencing too soon or in being unduly prolonged.

A study of local conditions would appear then to be all that is necessary to enable the Province to institute close seasons which would tally with the actual dates of spawning in each individual locality.

It is further evident that by endorsing the licenses to cover the earliest possible dates at which spawning might commence, it would be possible for the Provincial Government to place the actual date on which fishing should cease within the discretion of its local fishery overseers, subject, of course, to the dates of the general Dominion close season. A system such as this would seem to afford the most logical solution to the problem of dealing adequately with the climatic influence on the commencement of the spawning run, but obviously, to be effective, it would be necessary for the Government fishery overseers to be considerably more conscientious and more thoroughly acquainted with fishing conditions than is usual to-day, for even a few days delay would mean considerable additional profit to the fishermen at the expense of the quantity of spawn which should have been deposited.

If the Provincial Government, as it would appear, has it within its authority to thus increase the close seasons enacted by the Dominion Government, it must evidently also have the power to stop fishing altogether by the refusal to issue licenses; in fact, of producing a longer or shorter close period and similarly of closing to commercial fishing any areas it may deem advisable.

A PROVINCIAL FISHERIES POLICY.

In the Interim Report of this Commission and in the preceding pages of this report an outline has been given of the general condition of the great lake fisheries and of the fish trade in the Province of Ontario, and sufficient has been said to show that stringent measures are essential to eradicate the glaring evils at the root of the present situation. The past history of the fisheries has furnished ample proof of the inefficacy of attempting to bolster up an avowedly unsound system with the flaccid pills of mildly remedial legislation, so that if it is desired to save, conserve and develop the fisheries to the maximum of their worth, and to obtain the greatest possible value from them for the benefit of the citizens of Ontario, a broad general policy in regard to them must be evolved and carried through systematically, despite the protests of the monopolies and their myrmidons, and despite the denunciations and vaporings of those more interested in retaining in their hands petty political patronage than in advancing the general welfare of the community. The rapidly increasing population of the Province renders the adoption of some such policy only the more urgent, for it is impossible to deny that year by year in the larger cities amongst a great many classes of the community the question of obtaining an abundance of wholesome and at the same time cheap food is growing ever harder of solution. Fish, which is admittedly the peer of any animal food, has never yet played its true economic role in the dietary of Ontario's population, and unless something is accomplished very soon in the direction of effecting a change in present conditions, it would appear that it would never have a chance to do so.

There can be no question that the Canadian fisheries of the great lakes are amply sufficient to-day to supply all the demands of the Canadian population adjacent to them, and, in spite of an increasing population, would be so for many years to come if the bulk of the supply was not diverted to other channels, but they cannot withstand the tremendous drain imposed on them to fill the insatiable demands of the great cities of the United States. The longer the present unsatisfactory condition is allowed to continue, the harder will it become to take the necessary measures to redress it.

In discussing the dual control in force over the Canadian fisheries but slight reference has as yet been made in regard to their international political aspect. It is plain, however, that this side of the question needs as careful consideration as any in the formulation of a broad fisheries policy. The situation which has arisen through the organization of an American monopoly to control the Canadian great lake fisheries renders it as impossible to argue that any of the more drastic corrective measures referred to in the previous sections of this report could be introduced without raising a howl of protest from the interests directly concerned, as without incurring considerable political opposition from the United States, for the deprivation of many of the larger fish markets in the United States of even a proportion of their accustomed supply of Canadian fish would be quite sufficient to ensure this latter, even though it is obvious that owing to the purely domestic nature of the measures international interference would be an unwarrantable intrusion into Provincial domestic affairs. Attention has been called to the fact that an international code of regulations has been framed for the general conduct of the great lake fisheries, and that the advantages to be derived by both nations from a fundamentally identical system of administration of the fisheries are very considerable. It has also been noted that the international code has not as yet been promulgated. How far the determination of the Provincial Government to break the power of the monopolies and to develop and exploit the Canadian fisheries of the great lakes for the benefit of the citizens of the Province would tend to further delay the promulgation of this code, or to produce modifications in it, it is impossible to determine, but at least it is evident that, as both parties to the code are greatly interested in its enactment, it would form to a certain extent a political lever in the hands of the United States

Government with which to approach the Dominion Government in any attempts to arrest the Provincial policy. The delay in promulgation has up to the present apparently been due to the efforts of representatives of certain of the fishing interests in the United States Senate, who claim that their particular localities will suffer through the restrictions imposed by the code, and in view of the fact that total or even partial prohibition of export of Ontario fish would adversely affect a very much greater number of American citizens than could the code, it is only reasonable to suppose that the hands of the present opponents of the code would be strengthened by many additional recruits, anxious to weild the sword of a prospective international code against the buckler of Ontario's domestic necessities. The Dominion Government, however, on which the brunt of international pressure must fall, has in the creation of its Commission of Conservation and in many other ways given evidence of the lively interest taken by it in all matters affecting the conservation of natural resources, and it is impossible to conceive that it could view otherwise than favourably the determination of the Provincial Government to conserve and exploit the fisheries of the great lakes on a fundamentally economic basis. Indeed, the whole question of the commercial fisheries of the great lakes is growing yearly in national and international importance to such an extent that it is doubtful whether any other course would be open to the Dominion Government than to endorse, assist, and forward a progressive Provincial fisheries policy by every means in its power, for obstruction on its part could not but be adjudged a retrogressive action by the great bulk of the Canadian people affected. The vital necessity for Ontario to secure for her present and future population the economic benefits from a magnificent commercial fishery must be apparent to every thinking citizen of Canada, and especially to its administrations, as likewise that tinkering with this great economic problem will never bring about its satisfactory elucidation. Hence it may at least safely be deemed improbable that the Dominion Government will either throw obstacles in the way, or challenge Ontario's authority to seek its solution by drastic measures, but will tender the Province its cordial co-operation to the extent of itself enacting such measures as the Provincial policy may require, and to the extent also of withstanding any international pressure that may be brought to bear to frustrate it.

In regard to the purely domestic political situation, it has already been pointed out that outside of the monopolies the only class that could be even temporarily adversely affected by the adoption of a forward and forceful fisheries policy would be the commercial net fishermen, who were either operating in certain restricted areas which it might be deemed expedient to close against commercial net fishing, or else under a prohibition of export measure were compelled to abandon their calling owing to a temporary lessening in the demand for fish. The numbers of these men are very small in comparison with the total population of the

Province, and although their distribution is such that in certain localities their influence is undoubtedly considerable, nevertheless it must
be conceded that the advantages to the Province, which would accrue
from the adoption of such a policy, could not fail to render it generally popular with the bulk of the population. Moreover, neither the
Provincial nor Dominion Government could be materially embarrassed
where both were conjointly involved in the adoption and carrying out
of a scheme to rehabilitate and perpetuate the fisheries.

It would seem, then, that the field is open and the occasion on the
whole propitious for the introduction by the Province of a fisheries
policy adequate to the necessities of the case, and it is impossible to deny
that such a step would be in the best interests of the Province. There
remains, then, but to recapitulate briefly what the salient features of
that policy should be.

The two outstanding evils at the root of the present situation are
the absolute inadequacy of the equipment and inefficiency of the Staff
of the Provincial Fisheries Service, and the commercial control of an
alien corporation. It is, therefore, to these that first and most careful
attention should be paid. To correct them the reorganization of the
Fisheries Service and the provision of a modern and adequate equipment should be undertaken without delay on the lines indicated in the
Interim Report of this Commission, and simultaneously there should be
established in Toronto a central fish agency on the lines indicated in this
report. Immediate action should also be taken to prevent the further
export of at least the two most valuable food fishes of the great lakes.
the whitefish and the great lake trout. In regard to checking the present
annual decrease in the catch and subsequently to effecting an increase
in it, the establishment of Provincial fish hatchery plants should be commenced forthwith, and side by side with this measure provision should
be made for adequate scientific superintendence of the hatcheries and
for scientific research work and statistical observations. The spawning
seasons of the various fishes in each and every locality should be closely
studied and provision made for the protection of the fish during those
periods in the manner indicated in this report. Such areas, also, as are
only inhabited by the commercial fishes when about to spawn, or by the
young and immature of the commercial fishes, should be carefully ascertained and set aside against commercial fishing for at least a considerable period of years.

It is evident that the policy outlined could not be carried out in a
moment, or without careful preparation and arrangement, and that not
only would the expenditures involved have to be spread over a period
of years, but that the whole question would require strong, consistent
and yet tactful treatment throughout the period of development, such
direction and impetus, in fact, as would be necessary in any walk of life
for the establishment of a great and prosperous industry. As was pointed
out in the Interim Report of this Commission, the method of adminis-

tration now in force is not adapted to the attainment of such an end. The abnormal expansion in all directions necessitates the undertaking of many other great public enterprises, and problems both difficult and intricate, but none the less requiring immediate solution, are constantly developing, so that it is impossible to conceive that a Minister, already so overloaded with vast responsibilities as must be a Minister in charge of so great and growing a Department as that of Public Works, should be able himself to devote either the requisite time or energy to the intricate and complex details surrounding the evolution of a fisheries policy calculated to produce a machinery equal to the task and likewise to foster and develop a demand for fish food among the citizens of the Province, who are as yet to a great extent unappreciative of its inherent economic value. Further, the delegation of such a duty to a subordinate official, even though that official were mentally and physically capable of discharging, it would inevitably result in the matter being treated as one of secondary importance, a fact which the present condition of the commercial fisheries situation would appear clearly to demonstrate, in so far at least as that where successive incumbents of a Ministerial office have had neither time nor opportunity to master even the basic principles of a problem, matters will be allowed to drift, or patchwork legislative remedies be deemed amply sufficient. Consequently it would seem apparent that the first step in the evolution of a new Provincial Fisheries Policy must be the establishment of an efficient authority to carry it out; the creation, in fact, of an executive controlling power, sufficiently stable to ensure the ultimate execution of plans laid over several years, and with sufficient time at its disposal to attend to all the intricate details on which the ultimate success of the policy must so largely depend.

The advantages to be derived through the elimination of party politics in the matter of petty appointments to the fisheries protective service were discussed in the Interim Report of this Commission, and it is evident that in the institution of such important measures as the establishment of a chain of fish hatchery plants, the provision of adequate and suitable equipment, the creation and development of a Provincial Fish Agency and the fixing of close periods and areas, the less political influence could be brought to bear on the executive chief, the greater would be the certainty of really permanent and satisfactory results being attained. The most obvious method of removing the fisheries from the sphere of party politics would be the creation of a small Commission to control them in conjunction with other matters of a somewhat kindred nature, as previously recommended by this Commission in its Interim Report, but, if such a course should be deemed inexpedient, at least some attempt should be made to place the control of Ontario's great commercial fisheries where they could receive the individual attention of the executive head which they both need and merit. The people of the Province cannot forever remain indifferent to the spoliation that is taking

5 F.C.

place, so that it would seem to be but the part of wisdom for the Government in some measure at least to anticipate their awakening.

GENERAL RECOMMENDATIONS IN REGARD TO THE GREAT LAKES COMMERCIAL FISHERIES.

In making the following recommendations your Commissioner desires explicitly to state that in his opinion the expenditure of money involved in various of the proposed measures would not be justified under the present system of administration of the fisheries, for without efficient direction and control adequate results could never be obtained.

With this proviso your Commissioner would most strongly recommend:

(1) That an executive power be created to deal with the great lake commercial fisheries and other kindred matters; if possible, by the creation of a small independent Commission after the model of the Temiskaming and Northern Ontario Railway Commission; or, failing this, by removing the control of the fisheries from the Department of Public Works and confiding it to some member of the Cabinet who is possessed of sufficient leisure to devote personal attention to the solution of its many great problems.

(2) That the reorganization of the outside service of the Department of Game and Fisheries be forthwith commenced; that only such of the fishery overseers as are capable of adequately discharging their duties shall be retained in the service; and that in future no man shall be engaged for such service whose qualifications for the position have not been definitely ascertained to be entirely satisfactory.

(3) That some form of Board be created to examine applicants for positions in the outside service of the Department of Game and Fisheries, and issue certificates of proficiency to such of them as are found to be suitable, both physically and morally, to undertake the duties they will be called upon to perform, and that without such certificate of proficiency no man shall be considered eligible for a position in the outside service of the Department of Game and Fisheries.

(4) That no official be employed in the outside service of the Department of Game and Fisheries who has any other business or occupation during such employment.

(5) That no official in the outside service of the Department of Game and Fisheries be paid less than $500 per annum, or a pro rata amount for limited periods.

(6) That steps be taken to acquire an adequate equipment for the Provincial Fisheries Protective Service on the lines indicated in the Interim Report of this Commission.

(7) That a central Provincial fish agency be established in Toronto with as little delay as possible, and branch agencies at such suitable ports as may be deemed desirable.

(8) That steps be taken to have the export of whitefish and lake trout prohibited for a term of at least five years by Dominion regulation, and that meanwhile the further export of these fishes be prevented by the endorsation of the licenses issued to fishermen and fish buyers with a provision to that effect.

(9) That the commercial net fisherman, as one condition of his license, shall be required to furnish monthly to the Department of Game and Fisheries, on a form provided by the Department for the purpose, a sworn return, showing the classes of fish and the weight of each variety caught, the number of shipments or sales made and the weight of same, and the names of the parties to whom the fish was shipped or sold, and that the signature of the local fishery overseer be required to be affixed to the return in sworn testimony of its accuracy.

(10) That fish buyers or wholesale fish merchants be put under license of $50 and retail fish merchants of $10 throughout the Province, and that, if necessary, these licenses be endorsed with the prohibition of export of whitefish and lake trout.

(11) That as a condition of license to the fish buyers and wholesale fish merchants they be required to render monthly to the Department of Game and Fisheries, on a form provided by that Department for the purpose, a sworn return of all purchases made and shipments of fish received, showing in each case the classes of fish, the weights of each variety, and the name of the consignor or vendor, together with a similar return of all bulk exports and Canadian shipments and a summary of local sales.

(12) That steps be taken to at once initiate a system of Provincial fish hatcheries, on a system which shall provide ultimately for a sufficiency of hatcheries to meet the needs of the Province in this direction.

(13) That the services of a duly qualified icthyologist be secured to report as to the suitability of sites for Provincial fish hatcheries, to superintend the construction of same and the installation of the necessary plants, and subsequently to exercise general supervision over the scientific work of the hatcheries and organize and develop a department of scientific research and statistical investigation.

(14) That a close study be made throughout the area of the commercial fisheries as to the usual dates of spawning of various fishes in the different areas.

(15) That the licenses of the commercial net fishermen in each locality be endorsed with dates which will render them invalid during the spawning of the more valuable fishes in that locality.

(16) That such areas as are only invaded by the more valuable commercial fishes during the spawning season or during other short periods in the summer months be closed altogether to commercial fishing for a term of at least five years.

(17) That such areas as are inhabited for the most part only by the

young or immature of the more valuable commercial fishes be carefully ascertained, and closed to all commercial gill or pound net fishing for a term of at least five years.

(18) That the whole fisheries be divided into a number of fishing areas for the purpose of carefully studying and determining the lengths of gill nets and the number of pound nets which can safely and advantageously be used in the same.

(19) That the value of each license be based on the value of the catch of the preceding year, the charge being fixed at the rate of $2.00 per 1,000 pounds of whitefish, herring, lake trout and pickerel, and $1.00 per 1,000 pounds of other fishes, and that the estimated value of each license be paid in advance, the balance in favor of or against the Government being adjusted at the end of the year from the sworn returns of the net fishermen attested to by the local fishery overseer.

(20) That, subsequent to the establishment of Provincial fish agencies and the introduction of a more effective system of administration of the fisheries, the experiment be made of placing the licenses in certain selected areas up to tender, power as usual being reserved to select such tenders as may be deemed the most advantageous.

COMMERCIAL FISHING IN THE LESSER LAKES OF THE PROVINCE.

The Province of Ontario is most liberally furnished with lakes of every size and description, most of them abounding, or at least once abounding, with fish of many varieties. In many of these lesser stretches of water there occur varieties of the commercial whitefish and trout, as well as the pickerel, ciscoes and other fish in more or less demand at the different fish markets of the States and Provinces, and as the decrease in the product of the great lake fisheries became marked, while the demand continued to increase, thus materially raising the market value of all classes of fish, it was but natural that the idea should be conceived of making use of the fish to be caught in the smaller bodies of water where such waters were reasonably accessible to adequate transportation facilities.

Experience in a short while proved that which was only to be expected, namely, that the smaller a body of water the less resisting power has it to the drain of vigorous commercial fishing, and, consequently, many of the inland lakes in which commercial fishing was carried on were soon absolutely depleted of all the finer forms of fish life, to the great detriment of the dwellers in the surrounding country.

There can be no doubt but that the logical economic function of the lesser lakes scattered throughout the Province is to supply wholesome fish food in the first instance to the poor settlers who open up the country and have at best a precarious existence, and subsequently as the country becomes more settled to the increasing population of the surrounding territory at cheap rates. In view of this fact it would seem most unwise to allow even one of the many lakes to be depleted of its finer fishes, especially when it is remembered that the depletion is taking place, not for the benefit of citizens of Ontario, but chiefly for that of a neighboring nation, for, as pointed out in previous sections of this report, the great bulk of the commercial fish catch is being, and has been, shipped abroad. Moreover, in such cases where sporting fish exist in these waters, they also have suffered to a like degree as the finer commercial fish, in spite of a ban having been, in certain cases, placed on their commercial use, for it is a well known fact that all is fish which comes into the commercial fisherman's net, and a price is paid by the foreign buyer for the interior contents of barrels and boxes laden with fish as well as for the fish which adorn the tops and bottoms of such shipments. The destruction of the sporting fish in these waters is greatly to be deplored, for it deprives the region of one of its chief attractions to the sportsman tourist, whose ready cash is such a valuable asset to the country at large.

It is usually argued by those engaged, or wishing to engage, in this business that the normal increase in these lakes is, as a rule, in excess of the sustaining or feeding power of the lakes and that, consequently, the majority of fish remain undersized and thin owing to a lack of sufficient food. It is also, of course, invariably and stoutly maintained that the sporting fish can by no possible means suffer any harm through commercial fishing operations. As to the latter of these contentions, experience as noted above, has proved the exact reverse. As to the former, it cannot be denied that there may in many instances be a substratum of truth in it, and yet it must also be acknowledged that if the fish now to be found inhabiting the waters after countless years of unimpeded natural reproduction are of such small size and poor quality as alleged, it is difficult to understand how it can be worth anybody's while to undertake commercial fishing for them as a means of profit making or livelihood. The probabilities would seem to be that a limited amount of commercial fishing might indeed result in the production of larger fish, owing to the greater amount of food available for a lesser number of fish, but that, on the other hand, the extent of reduction in quantities that can safely be accomplished in the first instance is strictly limited, and that thereafter to take more than the normal increase will result in the speedy depletion of the waters of the classes of fish removed from them. It would, of course, be impossible to lay down rigidly the exact amount of fish that might be removed from any of the lesser lakes for which it might be deemed advisable to issue commercial net licenses, but, on the other hand, it is evident that if the licensees were required to make sworn returns of the catch to the Government, the accuracy of the said returns being vouched for and attested by the responsible government inspector, it would very soon become apparent when the annual catch was markedly decreasing. Having once determined that the catch had seriously diminished, it would be a simple matter to give the particular lake a rest from commercial fishing for a period of years in order to permit of it restocking itself by natural means, as it would inevitably do if given the chance in sufficient time. That such a procedure would be the most economic method of handling these fisheries is evident, as it would eliminate all possibility of the lakes being depleted, and, at the same time, would avoid the expense of ultimately having to stock these waters by artificial means, a demand for which, in the case of those lakes which have already unfortunately been depleted, is certain eventually to arise.

Owing to the natural tendency of a licensee to derive the greatest possible benefit from the possession of his license, it is plain that the great majority of the licensees, if licenses on application, renewed to them yearly without question, could not be depended on to exercise impartial judgment in deciding when a rest from commercial fishing had become necessary and, consequently, the matter would have to be controlled and managed by the Government in order to attain the desired results, but it is interesting to note that in the western portion of the Province there is one inland lake fishery which has been conducted on these principles for many years by its regular licensees, with the result that in the years in which fishing is conducted the catch is good both in quantity and quality.

To ensure accuracy in returns from the licensees of inland lake fisheries, the inspection of their fisheries and shipments would have to be effective and efficient and it is, consequently, apparent that in those localities where adequate inspection cannot economically be provided at present, it would be advisable not to issue licenses for commercial fishing.

In all cases where commercial net licenses are issued for the inland lakes, the greatest care should also be taken to see that the licensees do not exceed the quantity or lengths of net called for on their license, and a study should be made of each individual case to determine what amount of net should be fixed by the Government, for especially in the case of the smaller bodies of water so much harm could be effected by excessive fishing in the short space of even one season that the fishing might remain hopelessly depleted for many seasons thereafter.

As a general rule it would seem inadvisable to issue any commercial net licenses whatsoever where there is not a clear water area of at least ten miles square, for the normal production of lesser areas must be too small to permit of profitable commercial fishing operations, except at the expense of the future supply of fish. It would seem also that in waters of even greater area than ten miles square, where sporting fish, such as the black bass, the mascalonge and trout, are to be found, it would be far better to issue no commercial licenses at all, for the value of the traffic attracted by the sporting fishes will ultimately, if it does not actually at present, far exceed the small profits to be made out of the commercial fishing of such waters, and it must, therefore, be the part of wisdom to safeguard the perpetuation of these sporting fishes. The only condition under which licenses for commercial fishing might possibly be issued in such cases with advantage would be where a local market was sufficiently great to take the total catch of the number of licenses issued. In such instances the waters would be but fulfilling their proper functions, but the licenses issued for the purpose of supplying this local demand should be endorsed to that effect, and the inspection should be sufficiently potent to ensure this provision being enforced.

As with the great lake fisheries, so it would seem to be the case with the fisheries of the minor lakes, namely, that the value of the licenses to the licensees must vary considerably in the different bodies of water. Consequently it would appear that the system of licensing should not be as at present a fixed sum applicable equally to any lake or part of a lake, but should be an indeterminate sum to be fixed on the basis of the previous or last year's catch, and adjustable subsequently on the results of the returns of their catch sent in by the licensees; in fact, that the system of licensing should be similar to that suggested for the great lakes. It is also to be noted that the risks and difficulties attendant on commercial fishing are, as a rule, very much lightened in the case of smaller bodies of water, and that, consequently, a greater catch can be secured for a considerably less effort than in the deep waters of the great lakes. It would appear, therefore, reasonable to suppose that in many instances there should arise competition for the privilege of fishing these easy and profitable waters, and, consequently, that were the licenses put up to public tender, a considerable profit would accrue to the public. In regard to these waters, however, it must be confessed that, especially in the less settled districts, it is more advantageous to the Province to have the profits accruing from the commercial fishing of these waters go into the pockets of some needy local settler or resident than merely swell the banking account of some individual or company engaged in other matters, who undertake the enterprise purely as a speculation, have no interest in the matter other than the quick returns to be derived therefrom, and who are neither acquainted with the process of commercial fishing or with the areas over which they are allowed to fish by virtue of the license they have obtained. In all cases in this class of water trafficing in licenses should be most rigidly suppressed and the applicant or tenderer for a license should be required explicitly to state whether or not he purposes himself to undertake the actual fishing, and whether or not he is a local resident.

The same objections noted in regard to the introduction of this system to the great lake fisheries undoubtedly exist, although in a somewhat modified form. The comparative ease, for instance, with which fishing can be conducted largely discounts the necessity for the development of a distinct class of fishermen for these waters, and in the majority of cases the equipment to carry on fishing operations would neither be large nor expensive. The fact, also, that it might be necessary to close down the fisheries in the event of a material diminution in catch being

disclosed would raise a new difficulty should the tender be, as recommended in regard to the great lakes, for a term of years. Under reasonable fishing and good supervision this, however, should not frequently
occur, and in the event of it doing so there would be no difficulty in
arranging a proportionate rebate to the licensee, or even, perhaps, of
changing the location of his license to suitable adjacent waters for the
balance of the term. Moreover, where a licensee in restricted waters had
conducted his business on lines best calculated to ensure a continued
product from the waters and had, in all probability, some considerable
capital, in proportion at least to his means, invested in nets, boats, storehouse and other equipment, not only would a distinct hardship occur
should he fail to secure a renewal of his license at the expiration of its
term, but it is doubtful whether it would be to the advantage of the Province to risk obtaining a less satisfactory licensee for the sake of a few
dollars. This, however, might be adjusted by providing that where a
licensee conscientiously fulfilled all the requirements of the law throughout the term of his license, he should be entitled to a renewal of it on
the same terms on which he originally acquired it, or on payment of such
additional fee as might be deemed just by the Government.

Your Commissioner would, therefore, most strongly recommend:

(1) That no licenses be issued for commercial fishing in inland
lakes which have not a clear water area of at least ten miles square.

(2) That no licenses whatsoever be issued for commercial fishing
in inland lakes over which rigid inspection cannot be provided.

(3) That no licenses be issued for commercial fishing in inland
lakes other than the very large ones, which are the habitat of the black
bass, speckled trout or maskinonge, except where a local market needs
to be supplied, and then only and exclusively for the requirements of
that market.

(4) That the value of a license be determined in the same way as
recommended for the licenses of the great lake fisheries.

(5) That subsequent to the establishment of Provincial fish agencies
and the introduction of a more effective system of administration of the
fisheries, the experiment be made of placing the license issued for certain inland waters of the Province up to public tender, care, however,
being taken to prevent the licenses from falling into the hands of specu-
lators and to place them as far as possible with local residents or settlers.

(6) That all licensees be required to render monthly sworn returns
of their catch on forms provided them for the purpose, and that such
returns must be countersigned on oath by the responsible fishery overseer.

(7) That careful study be made of each lake in which commercial
fishing is to be allowed in order to determine the extent or amount of
nets which it is expedient to allow to be operated, and the periods and
localities in which spawning of the commercial fishes takes place in
order that these may be rigidly protected.

(8) That careful returns be compiled of the annual yield of each lake in order that as soon as a marked decrease becomes apparent in any one lake, no further licenses may be issued for it during a term of years, so as to allow of restocking by natural processes.

LAKE OF THE WOODS.

The location and peculiar configuration of the area known as Lake of the Woods have given rise to problems in connection with its fisheries which require individual investigation.

A glance at the map will show that, broadly speaking, the area is divided into two portions by the great neck of land called the Big Peninsula, the body of water to the south of it being for the most part open, while that to the north of it is merely a network of channels between innumerable islands of all sizes and descriptions. The international boundary, which runs almost north for some thirty odd miles from the point where the Rainy River enters the lake, places more than half of the open water area of the southern portion under the control of the United States, but turning then to the west leaves the northern portion entirely in Canada, while the Manitoba boundary line touches both the northern and southern portions on their western extremities. For the most part the lake, which lies, of course, in the Hudson Bay watershed, is comparatively shallow, and with the exception of a small passenger steamer plying between the towns of Rainy River and Kenora is not used for commercial transportation purposes at present, nor would it appear likely that its waters will ever serve to any great extent as a highway of commerce.

The waters themselves, however, were originally teeming with fish, of which the most valuable commercial species were the sturgeon, the whitefish, the pickerel and the lake trout, and as the country opened up great quantities of fish were removed from them on both sides of the boundary line, with the result that to-day the sturgeon has practically ceased to exist all over the lake, and the quantities of whitefish and trout have very considerably diminished, especially in the American waters, which have been fished far more strenuously than the Canadian waters of recent years. The International Fisheries Commission, indeed, have given weighty consideration to the state of the fisheries in these waters, and in the proposed international code most excellent regulations have been devised to be applicable to Lake of the Woods and Rainy River, dealing with such questions as the mesh, class and disposition of nets, classes of fish that may be fished for, methods of fishing and size limits. These regulations, however, do not altogether dispose of all the difficulties peculiar to the Ontario fishery situation.

The bulk of the commercial fishing in Canadian waters is carried on in the northern of the two zones already referred to, the headquarters of the industry being located at Kenora at the northern extremity of the lake, and the industry itself being vested in the hands of one company.

known as the Armstrong Trading Company. It is evident that in the narrow channels and waterways of this area, once the general movements of the fish have been ascertained, the operation of any commercial nets is liable to prove peculiarly deadly. On the other hand the number of licenses issued for pound nets in these waters is limited by the Department of Game and Fisheries to 14, and this fact, together with the innumerable diverse routes open to the fish as they move about on their feeding grounds, has undoubtedly tended towards the maintenance of the supply in Canadian waters. Indeed, in regard to whitefish, which are to-day the most valuable commercial fish of the lake, it must be noted that under the direction of the Armstrong Trading Company the fishermen use a mesh of net for the gill net fishing considerably greater than the minimum at present allowed by law, thus confining their catch voluntarily to the larger fish, so that, although there has, in all probability, been a marked decrease in the weight of fish caught as compared with the initial years of fishing, when the waters were practically virgin, the Northern Zone at least cannot be held to be in any danger of immediate exhaustion under the existing measure of fishing.

The town of Kenora and surrounding country do not as yet afford a market sufficiently great to consume the present commercial catch of the Canadian waters of Lake of the Woods, so that if commercial fishing is prosecuted on its present scale the fish obviously have to be shipped to other markets. To the East the markets of Port Arthur and Fort William should not, apparently, be in need of any outside shipments, seeing that they should be able to avail themselves of the fisheries of Lake Superior, so that the natural and logical market for the product of these waters would appear to be Winnipeg, and it is, in fact, to Winnipeg that the bulk of the fish is at present despatched. Whether or not Winnipeg is the ultimate market of these fish is more than questionable, the probabilities appearing to be that the major portion finds its way to the south of the international boundary line.

In view, then, of the general measures for the conservation of the commercial fisheries, and of whitefish and lake trout in particular, discussed in previous sections of this report, and especially in regard to the recommendation in favor of the prohibition of export of these two varieties, it remains to be examined what effect these measures would have on the waters under discussion.

Under the proposed international regulations the capture of sturgeon is strictly forbidden for a term of four years, so that in expectation of their speedy promulgation this fish need not further be considered.

The species of lake trout inhabiting these waters would appear from the testimony of the manager of the Armstrong Trading Company not to be of great value for export commercial purposes, as the fish, apparently, softens rapidly on ice and loses its color, thus considerably depreciating its market value. The variety of whitefish, on the other hand, is commercially second to none, and, consequently, the whitefish fisheries must be considered a valuable Provincial asset.

In dealing with the question of the prohibition of export of white-fish and lake trout, the matter was discussed from its purely international aspect, and it is evident that if such prohibition were effected by Dominion regulation and made applicable to all Canadian waters in which whitefish at least are found, there would be no need for any special precautions in regard to the whitefish of Lake of the Woods, for it would be only to the advantage of Ontario to have a market for its superfluous fish in the Provinces bounding it on either side. If, on the contrary, the measure had to be effected by the Province through the endorsation of licenses and other means already indicated, it is plain that an avenue would still be open to the foreign monopolies at the Eastern and Western extremities of the Province, for obtaining the bulk of the Ontario fish whose international export the Province was attempting to prohibit, by causing the fish to be shipped to the nearest suitable points in Canada outside the Provincial boundaries and thence trans-shipping them across the border, thus defeating the objects of the Provincial measure, for no Provincial legislation could be framed to embrace the destination of the fish after it had legitimately left the Provincial boundaries. It would seem, therefore, that under these circumstances special steps would have to be taken to guard against this eventuality. The establishment of Provincial fish agencies would, in all probability, tend to achieve this object satisfactorily, but as far as Lake of the Woods is concerned, the fisheries of which are so distant from the more densely populated areas of the Province and where there is only one company in operation and that a Canadian company, chiefly owned by Winnipeg interests, it would at first sight appear that the establishment of a branch agency might entail a hardship on a legitimate Canadian enterprise, for, although one of the chief purchasers of the Armstrong Trading Company is, in all probability, the American fish trust, it would seem that the concern itself is operated on Canadian capital by Canadians. Undoubtedly the surrounding territory will eventually maintain a very much greater population than at present, for both the agricultural and mineral possibilities appear to be considerable, and it is, in consequence, essential to conserve these valuable fisheries. It is also beyond dispute that the possible fish markets along both the Canadian Pacific and Canadian Northern Railways are at present entirely unexploited, so that there is a considerable field for commercial enterprise in this direction. Possibly some arrangement might be entered into with the Company in regard to the disposal of its fish with a view to securing its co-operation in fostering the market in Kenora and in the lesser towns on both railways, and also in regard to the non-export of the fish from Winnipeg. The existence of a Provincial fish agency might, indeed, render this all the easier to bring about, for the company would be able to ship to the agency, for ultimate disposal in the Province, all fish in excess of the requirements of its own markets and be assured of obtaining a fair average return. In the event, however, of the company being unwilling to enter into any such arrangement, the most obvious means of achieving the desired end would appear to lie in the limitation of the licenses issued, so that the total catch from these waters could not be in excess of the actual present requirements of the surrounding territory, and in endorsing such licenses as were issued with a provision to the effect that the catch was to be disposed of for local consumption only, or to the nearest branch Provincial fish agency, leaving it to the superintendent of this latter institution to develop the fish markets in the Kenora and Rainy River districts.

In regard to the fact that the majority of the Canadian licenses issued for commercial fishing in Lake of the Woods are under the control of one company, it is to be noted that in view of the location of the waters the present development of the surrounding territory and the fact that it is a Canadian company, presumably catering to Canadian people, so long as the fisheries are conducted on their present scale this is probably the best method of operating these fisheries, in spite of the fact that it might be held to constitute a monopoly, for it concentrates under one Canadian control the disposal of the fish when caught and thus should simplify the enterprise of creating and developing a good local market throughout the surrounding territory, and, where necessary, the problem of bulk shipments. It would seem, however, that the Government might reasonably expect a somewhat higher revenue from these fisheries than that at present derived from the sale of licenses at fixed prices, as also that the introduction of a certain amount of competition might result in placing those who engage in the actual business of fishing in an independent, instead of practically a subordinate, position without materially affecting the position of the Armstrong Trading Company. Consequently it might be advantageous to place at least the pound nets up to public tender, the district for which the license was issued being specifically stated on the same. Should a branch Provincial fish agency be established at Port Arthur or Fort William it is plain that the competition thus created would at once become effective, although without such an institution it would, in all probability, remain nominal. As the surrounding country becomes populated, however, and the local fish markets develop, the value of these licenses should increase considerably, so that by the adoption of such a measure the Government would be placing itself in a position to take a proper advantage of such increase as it occurred.

In connection with the commercial fisheries of Lake of the Woods a problem has developed which has given rise to considerable local argument and discussion. Formerly there existed in these waters considerable quantities of pickerel and mascalonge, both of which fish are acknowledged to afford good sport to the rod angler and consequently to constitute a material attraction to visitors and sportsmen. The prosecution of commercial fishing on a considerable scale has had, however, the result already noted in the section on the lesser lakes of the Province.

namely, the rapid disappearance of both these varieties. The peculiar beauty of the northern portion of Lake of the Woods, with its innumerable woody islets, enchanting scenery and practical immunity from very high seas, renders it eminently suitable for a great summer playground, and its accessibility has already resulted in attracting to it numbers of persons from Winnipeg and vicinity, as well as a goodly proportion of Americans, to pass the summer months in this neighborhood. The citizens of Kenora have become alive to the great importance of this annual influx of visitors, many of whom have built for themselves beautiful homes on the mainland or on the islands, and, as must always be the case, leave behind them each year tribute in the shape of cash for all the necessaries and luxuries of life, and, by their very coming, create enhanced values of real estate both in the town and surrounding country. Although this traffic has already attained very considerable proportions they are bent on further exploiting its possibilities by every means within their power. Municipal enterprise is being directed towards this end in the erection of a fine modern hotel and other measures for the comfort and convenience of the visitors, and there can be little doubt that under their energetic direction each succeeding year should disclose a material increase in the numbers of persons attracted to the locality. The value of the tourist traffic is held already to have greatly surpassed the total possible value to be derived from the commercial fisheries, and it is, therefore, with considerable indignation that the rapid disappearance of the pickerel and mascalonge and the diminution in the numbers of lake trout have been observed.

It is claimed that in the vicinity of Kenora it is now practically impossible to catch a pickerel or a trout, where both used to be plentiful, and that an angler can now fish for a week over mascalonge grounds without once getting a strike where formerly a good catch was assured any and every day of the week, and that as a result of this the male section of those visitors who have built their summer homes in the locality spend yearly less time in them, and that others will not come for more than a day or two at a time. This diminution is naturally attributed to the baneful effect of commercial netting now carried on by legal and illegal means, and, as a consequence, a strong movement is on foot to abolish all commercial fishing practically throughout the northern zone—that is, over the whole of that area which affords such picturesque and attractive cruising and camping grounds to the summer visitors, and farther, to secure the erection of Provincial hatchery plants for the purpose of restocking these waters with mascalonge, pickerel and trout and introducing into them the black bass.

Undoubtedly the matter is worthy of the most serious consideration. The value of the tourist and annual summer visitor traffic has been strongly called to attention in the Interim Report of this Commission, as also the potentialities existing in sporting fish as an attraction to the same, and perhaps no better instance of this could have arisen than the case under review.

The trout in these waters is, as before mentioned, not particularly valuable as a commercial fish, but it is, nevertheless, held in local esteem as a sporting fish, especially in the spring and fall when the waters are cool. The mascalonge is not a commercial fish under present regulations, and its disappearance is to be deplored alike from its attractive qualities to the angler as from the evidence thus adduced of inefficient supervision of the fisheries. The pickerel, which is a commercial fish of considerable value, is also highly attractive to many anglers, and its presence throughout the waters of this region is, therefore, much to be desired. These fish are all indigenous to these waters and formerly abounded in them, and if the ambition of the citizens of Kenora to make Lake of the Woods the great summer gathering place for the middle west of America is to be achieved, something will have to be done to replenish and maintain the supply of all these varieties, not only in the immediate vicinity of Kenora, but also over a goodly portion, at least, of the Northern zone. To prohibit commercial fishing, however, throughout the Northern zone, as desired by many of the citizens of Kenora, would be a serious blow to the Canadian commercial fishing industry of this lake, for it would remove more than half the available area from the operations of the net fishermen, and, moreover, that area which is probably the most prolific at the present time, the most easily fished, and the nearest to the logical and actual headquarters of the commercial fishing industry of these waters at Kenora. Such a result would not appear to be at all desirable or in the best interests of the surrounding district, for the commercial fisheries, properly conducted, are an obvious and tangible asset of no small value, and with the local and adjacent fish markets fostered and developed should prove of economic and material benefit alike to the citizens of the region and to the summer visitors who might be attracted thereto.

Compromises are proverbially unsatisfactory to all parties, but in this case it would seem that some middle course is unavoidable if the greatest value to the Province is to be extracted from the possession of this uniquely beautiful, attractive and, at the same time, commercially productive area of water and countless islands.

The key to the situation would appear to lie in control. At the present time there is an overseer at Kenora burdened with a vast district extending from the Manitoba boundary to Port Arthur, and including the commercial and angling fisheries of Lake of the Woods, who, be it noted, is not even provided with a boat of his own wherewith to inspect the fishermen at work or supervise the collection of non-resident angler's tax, but has to depend on what craft he may be able to hire for the purpose of the occasional tours of inspection which the care of so great a district alone enables him to undertake. Obviously during the fishing season there is ample work for at least one man patrolling the lake to see that the licensed nets are properly set, that no illegal nets are being used, and that poachers from across the line are not fishing in

Ontario waters through the southern portion of the lake; and to ensure also that campers and canoeing parties are conforming generally to the regulations and laws of the Province and of the Dominion. To enable this work to be properly performed adequate equipment would plainly have to be provided. In addition to this no commercial shipment of fish should leave Kenora or vicinity without rigid inspection, which would entail the presence of an inspector practically continuously in Kenora, and it would appear that this official should also be charged with the collection of the non-resident anglers tax and the enforcement of the angling laws in the vicinity of Kenora, for which duties he would have to be furnished with a suitable launch. Having once provided for the adequate patrolment and protection of the fisheries generally, other measures could be then introduced for the protection of the sporting fishes as deemed necessary, with the certainty of their being carried into actual effect.

It would appear advisable, as already stated earlier in this section, to indicate clearly on each commercial license issued the exact area for which it was valid. By this means an effective protection could be afforded to the mascalonge grounds and localities particularly adapted for pickerel or lake trout trolling, as such could be excluded from commercial fishing by the provisions of the license. An area within a given radius of Kenora could be closed altogether to commercial fishing, and an adequate hatchery plant could be installed within the closed district to ensure the maintenance of the supply of the sporting fish therein, and further, if it were deemed necessary, commercial fishing for the pickerel, trout or any other variety of fish might be stopped for a term of years.

If such measures were put into active effect there can be little doubt but that they would meet the needs of the situation as felt by those interested in the development and exploitation of a great tourist traffic. while at the same time they would not bear too hardly on the established commercial fishery interests. It is evident, however, that as the value of the tourist traffic will be eventually, if it is not actually at present, immeasurably greater to the Province and to the vicinity than the direct and indirect revenue to be derived from the commercial fisheries, if an adequate staff, properly equipped to enforce these measures, is not provided, by which means alone such measures could be rendered effective, it would be better to sacrific the commercial fisheries to the extent of excluding them altogether from the northern zone, for although illegal netting would, in all probability, still flourish under inadequate supervision, at least the legitimate nets would be eliminated, and with an inspector even occasionally at Kenora open shipments should become impossible.

In regard to the question of the introduction of black bass into these waters, if it were possible to achieve it, it would undoubtedly add greatly to the attractiveness of the district from the point of view of the visiting sportsmen tourists. An experiment in this direction was made some years ago, through the enterprise of local citizens, who caused a small and isolated lake in the vicinity of Kenora to be stocked with some small-mouthed black bass. The results of the plantation have been most satisfactory, and the waters of this little lake are to-day said to be teeming with bass. This, however, unfortunately constitutes no proof that the waters of the Lake of the Woods are suitable for bass life, and, indeed, it is questionable if such will prove to be the case. Except in a few cases near the height of land the black bass does not seem to be indigenous to the waters of the Hudson Bay watershed, although its occurrence in some of the main waterways near the height of land has obviously afforded it opportunity to spread over the whole of this water system. Consequently before undertaking plantations of fry or parent fish, or the institution of bass breeding ponds, it would be advisable to have a careful scientific investigation made of the waters and food supply in them, to ascertain if the introduction of this sporting fish into these waters is feasible. Even were it deemed impossible in regard to the waters of Lake of the Woods, the successful experiment above noted would seem to point to the fact that many of the numerous smaller lakes of the district could be advantageously made use of for this purpose, but even in regard to these it would be wiser to conduct scientific investigations before incurring the expense of further experimental plantations.

RECOMMENDATIONS.

Your Commissioner would, therefore, recommend:

(1) That the warden staff of the Lake of the Woods district be increased by at least two men during the fishing season, and that two launches of the class C type, as recommended in the Interim Report of this Commission, be provided for these waters.

(2) That the provisions recommended in regard to commercial net and other licenses in connection with the great lake fisheries be applied also to those issued for Lake of the Woods.

(3) That the co-operation of the Armstrong Trading Company be invited in the matter of developing an active fish market in Kenora and throughout the Rainy River District, and that if possible some arrangement be come to with that company in regard to the export of whitefish and lake trout.

(4) That commercial fishing for pickerel in this district be prohibited for a term of three years.

(5) That within a radius of fifteen miles of the town of Kenora no commercial fishing whatever be permitted.

(6) That areas of water which are or have been the favorite habitat of the mascalonge be carefully ascertained, and closed altogether to net fishing of every description.

(7) That in connection with the system of fish hatcheries, already recommended in this report, a fish hatchery plant be installed in this region to handle whitefish, trout, pickerel and mascalonge.   .

(8) That steps be taken to ascertain scientifically whether or not the waters of Lake of the Woods and surrounding lakes are adapted to the maintenance of black bass life, and in the event of this being found to be the case, for the establishment of a series of bass breeding ponds in the district.

(9) That the commercial net licenses issued for Lake of the Woods be endorsed with a clear statement of the district for which they are valid, and that subsequent to the establishment of Provincial fish agencies and the introduction of a more effective system of administration of the fisheries, as recommended in the above and other sections of this Report, the experiment be made of placing at least the pound net licenses up to public tender.

LAKE NIPIGON.

At the present time very little is known as to the possibilities óf the commercial fisheries in this beautiful sheet of water. Some years ago a company was formed for the purpose of exploiting these fisheries, but, although the necessary licenses were obtained, no great efforts were made to take advantage of them, owing chiefly to the difficulties of transportation which at that time precluded the possibility of getting the fish to the markets excepting during the winter months, and, in consequence, after a short season of apathetic operation and indifferent financial success, the company relinquished its undertaking. Since then no further experiments have been made in the direction of testing these fisheries. From these restricted operations, however, taken in conjunction with the experience and observations of local inhabitants and Indians, there is sufficient evidence to warrant the assumption that the lake contains goodly quantities of the better classes of the commercial fishes, such as the lake trout, whitefish, sturgeon and pickerel.

At the present time a light steam railway, running in connection with a steamboat service on the lower reaches of the Nipigon River, connects South Bay on the lake with Nipigon Station on the Canadian Pacific Railway on Lake Superior. A mile or so to the north of the lake the roadbed of the Grand Trunk Pacific Railway is already in process of construction, and a deviation has been built to Ombabika Bay on the lake, while the proposed route of the Canadian Northern Railway will bring it within touch of the lake's eastern shores. It would seem, therefore, that the time is fast approaching, if, indeed, it has not actually arrived, when serious efforts will be made to exploit the commercial fisheries of Lake Nipigon, and it remains, then, to be examined how far it would be advisable to encourage such an enterprise.

The lake itself lies within the boundaries of the Nipigon Forest Reserve and drains into Lake Superior through the channels of one of the most beautiful and extraordinary rivers in the world, the River Nipigon. This river, with its cold, clear-green waters, with its wonderful pan-

6 F.C.

orama of exquisite forest scenery, its splendid waterfalls and series of unnavigable, white-crested rapids, has long been celebrated as one of the outstanding beauty spots of the continent, and has been the Mecca of many a tourist from all parts of America and Europe, not the least of its attractions being, however, the fact that amidst all the charm of its unique and entrancing scenery sport is to be enjoyed in the shape of angling for speckled trout of such size and gameness as are to be found in but few districts of the world. Naturally the difficulties of transportation and navigation in the past, combined with the excellence of the sport on the river itself, have tended to keep the great majority of the visitors on the river, and to prevent all but the most venturesome, with considerable time at their disposal, from ascending northwards into the lake, exploring its archipelagoes and shores, and testing the angling possibilities of its waters and those of the numerous rivers and streams flowing into it. It is known, however, that speckled trout of great size abound in certain parts of the lake, and in most of the rivers which feed the lake, and it is indisputable, also, that the beauty of the scenery over a great portion of the lake and throughout the bulk of the surrounding territory is such that the construction of easy transportation thereto cannot but result in the advent of many visitors, anxious to see it for themselves and to enjoy the magnificent sport of almost virgin waters. It would seem, therefore, of the greatest importance to safeguard the perpetuation of the speckled trout in Lake Nipigon in the event of commercial fishing operations ever being permitted in its waters.

There can be no doubt but that the coming of the Grank Trunk Pacific and Canadian Northern Railways into this region will be followed by a considerable opening up of the country in the vicinity of Lake Nipigon, owing to the latent mineral, timber and agricultural potentialities of the area. To the south, the fisheries of Lake Superior should well be able to supply all the needs of an increasing population along its shores and it would appear, therefore, that the ultimate destiny of the commercial fisheries of Lake Nipigon should be to supply wholesome and cheap fish to the future population of the country to the north, east and west of it. There can be no great material benefit to the Province at large from the speedy exploitation of these fisheries, for the revenue to be derived therefrom would be but trifling and, under the existing system of administration and condition of the commercial fisheries situation, as disclosed in previous sections of this report, there would be considerable danger of these comparatively shallow waters being rapidly depleted should they be given over to the greedy operations of the monopolies or their myrmidons. On the other hand, there should be a material benefit to the Province to be derived from these fisheries in the future in supplying a cheap fish food to a growing population in the surrounding region.

It has been claimed that the lake is at present overstocked with fish and that as a result there is a paucity of food which is reflected in the size and quality of the fish, and in consequence that commercial fishing would be advantageous to the fisheries. It would seem, however, that it will be ample time to test the correctness of this theory when there shall have been established in the region a Canadian population sufficiently large to consume the fish produced by these waters. At the present time it would appear that all the fish that is required by residents along the shores of the lake can easily be obtained by trolling and angling. No impediment, however, should be placed in the way of local residents taking advantage of the fish products of the lake, so that if the numbers of persons locating in any of the existing settlements or surrounding territory should warrant it, some form of license might well be issued as occasion demanded to supply their wants. Licenses have, indeed, already been issued for the benefit of the construction gangs along the line of the Grand Trunk Pacific Railway, and the extension of this system of practically domestic licenses would seem admirably adapted to the gradual exploitation of these fisheries as, in due course, settlement occurs. It would appear, however, inadvisable to issue very many such licenses without making provision for the inspection of the fish, as on no account should the netting of speckled trout be tolerated.

Your Commissioner would, therefore, recommend:

(1) That no commercial net fishing be allowed in Lake Nipigon for the present.

(2) That as occasion arises a modified license be issued to meet purely local needs, but that in general the domestic license, strictly for family purposes, be the only license issued for these waters.

(3) That steps be taken to ascertain scientifically what classes of fish inhabit these waters, as also their main feeding grounds and spawning beds, in order that accurate knowledge may be available to guide the subsequent development of these fisheries.

(4) That special care be taken to issue no domestic or other license for areas which are the habitual feeding or spawning grounds of the speckled trout.

THE DOMESTIC LICENSE.

This license, for a very limited amount of net, is issued for the purpose of enabling residents along the banks of rivers or on the shores of lakes to catch sufficient fish for the needs of their families, the understanding being that the catch is solely for home consumption and not for trade purposes at all. Undoubtedly local inhabitants should be enabled to take advantage of the products of the waters in their vicinity. The ordinary methods of angling are, of course, open to them, but there are classes of fish, most excellent for food purposes, which cannot be caught by hook and line, as also certain seasons of the year when all the male members, at least, of a family are busily employed throughout the day on the farm or in other directions. It was to meet these conditions that the domestic license was devised. It is to be noted, however, that local residents have no more right to the fish in waters near to their homes than has any other citizen of the Province, for the fish belong to the community, so that the dispensation accorded them in the form of a domestic license is a privilege which should not be abused to the detriment of the general population. Unfortunately, however, it would seem that this fact is often unappreciated by the holders of these licenses, and that the license is abused in certain localities, both in the capture of sporting fishes and in trading, or peddling the catch in the surrounding district.

The value of the sporting fish in the rivers and lakes is so great to the Province that to kill them off by persistent netting is nothing short of an economic crime. If the residents of any locality desire to catch these particular classes of fish, the legal means are open to them as to other citizens of the Province under the limitations imposed by law. It is evident, however, that the placing of nets in localities which are largely inhabited by sporting fishes cannot but result in the capture of some of them, even though the intent of the owner of the net might be only to catch other varieties. Where domestic licenses are deemed to be necessary in such localities, it is difficult to determine a means of remedying this evil, but one solution, at least, is to be found in the education of the residents in these country districts to the value of the sporting fishes to themselves as a means of attracting to their vicinity the sportsman-tourist who must inevitably enrich them to the extent of the money he is bound to spend in the district. Once the residents fully appreciated the economic benefits of a regular summer tourist traffic, care would assuredly be taken by them to place their nets in such places where the least possible harm would be done to the sporting fish. In any case, if deliberate netting of sporting fish can be proved against the holders of a domestic license, the punishment should plainly be severe.

In regard to the trading of fish caught under this license, even though they are not sporting fish, it may be argued that citizens living at some little distance from the waters should be equally entitled to share in their products as those who live on the shores or banks. This, however, while correct in theory, does not affect the scope of the license under discussion, which is issued for domestic purposes only, but does not debar the licensees from giving away any surplus fish to their neighbors in the vicinity, but, on the contrary, the fact that in certain localities there may be a demand for fish, which as a matter of fact is already the case in several country districts, is merely an indication that there will arise a market for fish throughout the whole Province, if the matter is properly taken in hand, which should and could be satisfied by legitimate means.

The main evil of the domestic license lies in the impossibility of supervision, for however energetic an overseer may be, he could not personally view the catch at each lifting of the domestic nets, nor even keep close tabs on what is being caught, and thus, not only might sporting fish be steadily destroyed, but the small and immature of other varieties might be taken in quantities and the mature fish in considerable numbers at seasons of spawning when they run into the shoals, thus tending to the rapid depletion of the waters, for the sake of a comparatively trifling gain to one or two individuals, or owing to the negligence or wilful disregard of the laws on the part of certain licensees.

The cases where there is an actual need for fish food to maintain existence are, fortunately, comparatively rare, and though, as before noted, there are seasons of the year when it may be impossible for the average farmer or his family to devote sufficient time to catch enough fish to live upon, such seasons are not, as a rule, prolonged, and there is, therefore, in the average case no apparent reason why any dispensation whatever should be granted the farmer over the average citizen, but most especially so where even the limited amount of net accorded by the domestic licenses can result in serious injury to the sporting fish. It must be remembered, also, that even in the case of those fish, such as the herring, which can only be caught by means of nets, such fish constitute no small portion of the food of such sporting fish as, for instance, the lake trout, and consequently the sporting fisheries may easily be injured by ruthlessly destroying them. It would seem, therefore, that the greatest care should be taken in the issuance of domestic licenses; that as far as possible they should be restricted to localities where the necessity for them as a means of procuring sustenance actually exists, and that it would be advisable not to issue such licenses at all for small bodies of water in which sporting fish exist.

Where there is a demand for fish inland from waters for which domestic licenses are issued, and the waters themselves are of sufficient size to warrant commercial fishing, plainly this demand should be satisfied by a modified commercial license, issued for local needs only, but where the waters are too restricted to allow of commercial fishing by the importation of fish from other sources, but under no circumstance should the domestic license, even in a small way, be allowed to usurp the functions of a commercial license. To the fact that in some districts it has done so may be largely attributed the rapid decrease of all classes of fish in these waters, so that it is evident that measures should at once be taken, where this has occurred, to prevent any further damage being wrought. The local overseers are, of course, the officials in whose hands the enforcement of the laws in this regard rest, and the necessity for loyal, active and energetic officers, unbiassed by considerations of personal friendship or party politics, is all too obvious. Each net should be visited by them as frequently as possible, and lifted in order to ascertain the nature and extent of the catch, and whether the licensee is himself lifting the net sufficiently often to ensure there being no waste, and under no circumstances should the nets ever be allowed to be placed on or near the spawning beds during the periods of spawning of any class of fish fit for food. Reports, also, of illegalities in regard to trading should be promptly investigated, and when the charge is found to be correct, the penalty should not alone be confined to the cancellation of the license of the offending party, but should be supported by a fine sufficiently large to impress on the minds of all holders of these licenses the inadvisability of infringing their provisions even in the least degree.

Your Commissioner would, therefore, recommend:

(1) That a pamphlet be drawn up setting forth the economic value of the sporting fishes to the community, and that the same be issued with each domestic license, together with a separate printed extract from the fishing laws and regulations in regard to the capture of sporting fishes, and a clearly worded notice as to the prohibition of trading from the licenses.

(2) That any infringement of the trading provision be punished unconditionally by the cancellation of the license of the offender, and the imposition of a fine of not less than $50 or more than $100, and that the offender or any member of his family resident with him be ineligible for such a license for a period of five years.

(3) That the setting of greater lengths of net than provided for by the license be taken as evidence of trading, and that no further proof be necessary for the infliction of the full penalities for trading as above recommended.

(4) That the penalty for the deliberate netting of sporting fish be $20 for the first offence, $50 for the second, and for the third offence cancellation of the license together with a fine of $100, and that in this latter case neither the offender, nor any member of his family resident with him, be entitled to a license for a period of five years.

(5) That no nets under this license be allowed to be placed on or near the spawning beds of any class of fish fit for food during the season when such fish are engaged in spawning.

(6) That the issuance of domestic licenses be as far as possible restricted to localities in which fish food may be considered a necessity of existence, and that, except in such instances, no domestic license be issued for rivers, or for lakes with a clear water area of less than five miles square.

(7) That where a local demand for fish is sufficiently large and the extent of water warrants it, a modified commercial license for 100 to 500 yards of net be issued for such waters, but that no such license be issued where adequate supervision cannot be exercised, and that no trading in the fish caught under the license be permitted outside of the immediate locality.

WINTER FISHING.

Under the provisions of the proposed international fishery regulations netting under the ice in international waters is prohibited, together with the use of spears, grappling hooks or naked hooks, torches, flam·

Winter Fishing Shack, Sarnia Bay.

Some of the Winter Fishing Shacks on Hamilton Bay.

beaux or other artificial lights, and it would appear most desirable that these restrictions should be extended to the inland waters of the Province. When a hole is broken in the ice fish are readily attracted to the light thus let into the water, and in consequence fishing carried on under these conditions is liable to prove particularly deadly, for as the effect is apparently the same on all classes of fish, it is impossible for the fishermen to regulate the varieties of fish that his net or hooks will secure for him, or to distinguish the species should he be using the spear. Moreover, when the spear is being used, a considerable number of fish will inevitably escape with a more or less serious wound, and it is safe to assume that there must ensue a considerable waste wherever this method of fishing is adopted. As has been pointed out in a previous section of this report, the more restricted the area of a body of water the more easy is it to accomplish its depletion of fish, and since it is evident that fish are particularly defenceless against these methods of winter fishing almost as much, indeed, as against nets when they are congregating on their spawning beds, it follows that it must be even more dangerous to countenance them in the lesser lakes or rivers of the Province than in the waters of the great lakes, especially so when these lakes or rivers are the habitat of any of the sporting fishes, for these will not fail to suffer in like proportion to the other varieties. Evidence has been secured sufficiently convincing to show that in the case of Hamilton Bay the rapid disappearance of the bass was in no small measure due to winter spearing, for which many licenses have been issued in the past, and this in spite of the fact that the bass probably does not commence to move until a few weeks prior to the breaking up of the ice. Hamilton Bay, moreover, is by no means an isolated instance. There can, of course, be no objection to any citizen of the Province breaking a small hole in the ice and angling with hook and line in order to secure for himself and family what fish may be required. In fact, such would appear to be the rational means of winter fishing throughout the bulk of the Province, and the only method that should, in general, be encouraged, or even allowed, by the Government. It might, however, occur that in certain of the remoter and unsettled portions of the Province it was essential for some settler to secure a quantity of fish. In the winter the fish are easily kept frozen, and by the use of a net it would be possible to lay in a store sufficient for the winter months with comparatively little effort and within a short space of time, thus freeing the settler from the necessity of giving further thought to this source of food supply, and enabling him, perhaps, to busy himself in profitable trapping and lumbering operations at some distance from his home. In such cases, no doubt, the issuance of a domestic license for a limited amount of net would seem desirable, but on no account should trading under the license be tolerated. Again, it might possibly occur that to some community in the wilder regions of the Province fish food in the winter months was a necessity of existence. In such cases it might be found advisable to issue to one individual a commercial license for a sufficient amount of net to meet this local requirement, but trading from such a license outside of the immediate locality should not be permitted. In all instances, however, where either a domestic or commercial license was applied for, each case should be considered on its merits and individually investigated by a competent official, for it could under no circumstances be expedient or desirable to issue such privileges except and only where actual necessity was established.

Your Commissioner would, therefore, recommend:—

(1) That the provisions contained in the proposed international fishery regulations in regard to netting under the ice, and the use of spears, grappling hooks, naked hooks, torches, flambeaux, or other artificial lights, be made generally applicable to all the waters of the Province.

(2) That in the wilder and remoter portions of the Province an exception be made to the above recommendation in so far that where the necessity for a supply of fish as a food, either for a small community or for an individual settler, is found to exist after due investigation by a competent official of the Government, a commercial license for an amount of net sufficient to supply the purely local need may be issued in the case of the small community, and in the case of the settler, a domestic license for a limited amount of net, but that under no circumstances should trading under such domestic license be tolerated, or trading under such commercial license outside of the immediate locality for which the license was issued.

THE STURGEON.

Of all fishes to be found in the Provincial waters the sturgeon is individually by far the most valuable at the present time, chiefly owing to the extraordinary commercial value of caviar, which is made from the roe of this fish. The sturgeon formerly abounded throughout the great lakes, running frequently to an enormous size, and was found also in great quantities in Lake of the Woods and many of the lesser lakes and rivers of the Province, but the rapidly increasing demand led to such a vigorous pursuit of it that in those accessible waters of the Province which have been fished commercially its numbers have dwindled almost to vanishing point. In the proposed code of regulations for the international fisheries of the great lakes and Lake of the Woods attention is strikingly called to this fact by a provision to the effect that no sturgeon shall be fished for in any of the international waters for a period of four years from the date of promulgation of the regulations, and it would seem more than probable that once these provisions are in force it will be found desirable to extend this term in order to give the fish a reasonable chance of extensive reproduction.

The sturgeon was not always held in high esteem on this continent,

Winter Fishing for Pickerel with Bob Lines.

but on the contrary for a long time was viewed as a nuisance by the fishermen on account of the damage it would do their nets and because, also, white people were prejudiced against its use for food. More often than not the fish, when taken, were knocked on the head and thrown back into the water, or left in heaps on the beach to rot or to be carried off by the farmers and used as fertilizer, while during this period, if the fish could be sold at all, they would not bring the fishermen more than ten cents apiece. In striking contrast to this figure is the record of a sale of 96 sturgeon in 1899 for $3,923, or a little over $40 apiece. About 1860 the first efforts were made in the great lake region in the direction of smoking the flesh of the sturgeon, and between that date and 1880 the trade in the fish developed in a marvellous fashion, owing to the demand for the smoked flesh and for the bladders, which were manufactured into isinglass, but chiefly on account of the great European demand for caviar, reaching in 1880 for the continent a total of nearly 12,000,000 pounds of sturgeon products. The following figures show the approximate condition of the trade in sturgeon products of the great lakes from that year onwards:—

STURGEON PRODUCTS OF THE GREAT LAKE FISHERIES.

Year.	Pounds.	Value.
1880	7,557,383	unknown
1890	4,289,759	$148,360
1899	1,176,818	111,389
1903	638,898	53,017

It may be noted also that Lake St. Clair, which in 1880 produced in the neighborhood of 500,000 pounds, of recent years has furnished never more than 10,000 pounds, while the catch of Lake Erie has fallen to about one sixtieth of its former proportions. That the demand for caviar was mainly responsible for the increased value of the sturgeon is clearly established by an examination of the comparative price of that material at the various periods. In 1885 caviar brought from $9 to $12 per keg of 135 pounds; in 1890 the value had increased to $20; in 1894 to $40, and by the end of that decade to $100, while since that year the price has soared considerably over $1 per pound. So great, indeed, has been the demand that in certain instances the eggs of whitefish have been made use of in an attempt to meet it.

These figures will be sufficient to show both the present-day commercial potentialities of sturgeon fisheries and the lamentable diminution that has occurred in the output in this respect of the great lakes, and to prove also that under economic management these fisheries could have been made a permanent asset of enormous value to their owners. In this connection it is interesting to note that in Russia the sturgeon fisheries are most rigourously protected and afforded a source of considerable revenue to the Government. The leases of the different locations in the Caspian Sea fisheries, which are the greatest sturgeon fisheries of that country, are auctioned off every three years, being let to the highest bidder, who is compelled to pay in cash the exact value of the fishing plant to the former lessee vacating it. The value of the caviar production of the Caspian Sea alone is worth from ten to fifteen million dollars per annum.

According to Mr. C. W. Nash, the well-known icthyologist, there is but one species of sturgeon in the waters of the Province, although this scientific view is disregarded by the bulk of the commercial net fishermen, who have named the smaller specimens of the fish which are caught in their nets the rock sturgeon, and claim that it is a distinct variety. While, as before noted, the great lakes, Lake of the Woods and the more accessible waters of the Province generally have been largely depleted of sturgeon, there are nevertheless many localities in Ontario into which the commercial net fishermen have not yet penetrated, where the sturgeon still exists in comparative abundance, more particularly in the northern and western portions of the Province. In these areas the chief enemy of the fish would seem to be the Indian, who appears to be particularly partial to its flesh, and places his nets across the channels it must pass in its spawning movements, drying and smoking the flesh for future consumption and making use of the tough skin for diverse purposes. The value of the sturgeon is by no means likely to decrease in the future, more especially in view of the fact that the demand for caviar continues to increase and altogether to outstrip the supply, and it would seem, therefore, that some measures should be taken to safeguard such sturgeon fisheries in the Province as are still unimpaired. The difficulty of perpetuating a fish which is pursued chiefly for its roe must in any event be great, but in the case of the sturgeon this difficulty is enhanced by the facts that the fish is a bottom feeder and peculiarly easy to catch in confined water areas, and also that experience has demonstrated the great difficulty of securing ripe spawn and ripe milt at the same time, where hatchery operations are contemplated or attempted. The value of the sturgeon fisheries, however, is so great that their presence in the Province constitutes an asset which should not remain unexploited, so that it would appear that no efforts should be spared to restock waters already depleted of this fish, and that in the case of unimpaired fisheries and subsequently in that of waters in which restocking is successfully accomplished, some means should be sought whereby exploitation of the fisheries may be effected to the greatest advantage of the public without endangering the perpetuation of the fish in the Province.

Past experience has clearly demonstrated that in the hands of the ordinary commercial net fishermen, no matter in what class of water, the pursuit of the fish results in its rapid disappearance, and it would, therefore, seem advisable to debar the net fishermen, totally or in part, from profiting by the capture of this fish, for where there was little or no profit to themselves to be derived from its capture, they could at least be counted on not deliberately to pursue it. Then, in order to obtain for

A Sturgeon in the Rainv River District.

Hauling in a Six-foot Sturgeon, Lake Huron.

the public the greatest benefit from the occurrence of these fisheries in the Province, two means suggest themselves as available, namely to adopt the Russian system of subdividing the available fishery areas into locations and auction the sturgeon fishing privileges in the same at fairly frequent intervals of time, making provision for a limited open season, restrictions as to size, and for the very strict supervision of the fisheries, or else, after the Provincial Fish Agencies should have been established, to enact that all sturgeon captured under the ordinary commercial fishing licenses issued by the Province, which could not be returned uninjured to the waters, should be shipped to the nearest government fish agency at the expense of the Government, the fisherman being paid a small fixed sum for each fish thus shipped, and to operate the sturgeon fisheries by or under the immediate direction of an efficient staff of overseers, the expenses being born by the government and the products disposed of for the benefit of the public treasury. Under either system the sturgeon fisheries would thus be made to produce a considerable yearly revenue to the Province, increasing as new waters in which the fish exists are opened up under the development of transportation facilities, but the latter would have the great additional advantage that under it a sufficiency of eggs should always be obtainable for hatchery purposes, which in view of the depleted condition of the bulk of the Provincial waters is no slight consideration. Under this system, the sturgeon would become for all practical purposes a perquisite of the Crown, but it would be necessary to make allowance for the necessities of the Indians who in certain localities are largely dependent on the flesh of this fish for their supply of food. In doing so, however, it should be made a specific and punishable offence for an Indian to trade or barter with this fish outside the limits of an Indian reservation.

Your Commissioner would, therefore, recommend:

(1) That the sturgeon be declared a perquisite of the Crown, and that commercial fishing for the sturgeon be prosecuted, in such waters as may be deemed desirable, by or under the immediate direction of Government officials, the expenses being born by the Government, and the fish sold for the benefit of the public Treasury.

(2) That where under the ordinary commercial fishing license a sturgeon is inadvertently captured, and cannot be returned uninjured to the waters, it be required of the licensee to ship forthwith to the nearest government fish agency at the expense of the government.

(3) That illegal trading in sturgeon be punished by a fine of $100 for the first offence on each of the parties concerned, and for the second offence by a fine of $200 on each of the parties concerned, together with the cancellation of the licenses, if any, under which either or both parties are conducting their business.

(4) That in certain localities where the sturgeon is one of the principal foods of the Indians, the above provisions be relaxed so as to allow of the Indian taking this fish for their own use in the vicinity of their

7 F.C.

reservations or habitations, but that under no circumstances shall Indians so privileged be allowed to trade or barter the fish outside of their reservations.

(5) That special attention be paid to restocking the Canadian waters of the great lakes and of Lake of the Woods with sturgeon.

(6) That all trading, trafficking in, or shipping of the roes of the sturgeon or whitefish, or of black caviar composed of or secured from the roes of the sturgeon or any other fishes of the Province whatsoever, be prohibited throughout the Province, excepting when such roes or caviar shall have first been secured from a duly authorized Government official and a certificate for the same issued; and that any infringement of this regulation be punishable by a fine of not less than $100 on each of the parties concerned, together with a cancellation of the license, if any, under which either or each of the parties concerned are conducting their business.

The Carp.

Some thirty years ago the German carp was imported to this continent, mainly for the purpose of stocking small ponds and lakes, its vaunted edible qualities being lauded by the press generally, and its peculiar tameness and adaptability to life in show ponds and other restricted waters arousing a veritable storm of enthusiasm for the experiment. The fish, however, fell far short of what had been expected of it in almost every respect, for not only did it fail to find favour as a food in comparison with the more delicately flavoured local varieties of fish, but also chiefly owing to ignorance of the proper methods of handling it on the part of the majority of those into whose ponds it was introduced, it appeared at first even to flourish none too well. As a result the enthusiasm for the carp very soon subsided, but little attention was paid to it even where it had been introduced, and its introduction into public waters, either by deliberate plantation or through its escape into them from the ponds in which it was confined at times of flood or freshet, created but little stir or comment. To-day there is, in the fresh waters of this continent at least, no fish against which more scathing or widely divergent indictments have been hurled.

In the thirty years which have elapsed since its importation the carp has thriven and spread in a most remarkable manner, equally astonishing, in fact, as the extraordinary increase and dispersion of the imported English sparrow, until, as in the case of the sparrow, it has become perfectly apparent that the day has passed when it could be exterminated, and that for better or worse it has come to stay.

The carp has been dubbed the hog of the waters and the simile would not appear to be inapt, for, living as it does in comparatively shallow waters and feeding chiefly on the bottom, almost anything in the shape of vegetable or animal life that will pass into its small mouth appears good to it as food, and it will grub and burrow in the mud, digging up the vegetation in search of roots or, perhaps, various forms of animal life. It is a hardy fish, as evidenced by the varying conditions and temperatures to which it will adapt itself. Indeed, instances have been known where the fish has been frozen stiff for considerable periods and resuscitated when thawed out, while in Germany, where the fish is much appreciated and its consumption is general, it is frequently packed for the market in wet moss and under these conditions remains alive for no little time. It is recorded also that the top layers of these fish, when packed on ice and shipped by freight from Ohio to New York, are frequently found to be alive on reaching the market.

It is held by some that the carp will live to an extraordinary age, 100 to 150 years, and attain a weight of from 80 to 90 lbs., and although there appears to be little reliable evidence as to the correctness of these statements, at least it is certain that under favourable conditions the fish will live a great many years and attain a very considerable weight, specimens well over 20 lbs. having already been caught on this continent.

The carp, which commences to breed, apparently, in its third year, is remarkably prolific, as evidenced by the fact that one reliable authority has placed the average number of eggs of a 4 to 5 lb. fish at 400,000 to 500,000, while other instances are recorded of larger fish containing eggs to a number exceeding two millions. It is a school breeder, however, and particularly careless in the matter of its eggs, which are scattered over the vegetation in the shallow waters and left to take care of themselves without any further precaution on the part of the fish. To this fact may, perhaps, be attributed in part the abnormal increase in the carp in the waters of this continent, for the habitual enemies of spawn would not have been seeking for it in the open places in which it is left by this imported fish, and thus an abnormal percentage of eggs would have been successfully hatched. This, however, would in the course of time adjust itself, as sooner or later the spawn eaters will become aware of the new location of desirable food, and doubtless this will act as a check to a further proportionate increase as compared with that of the past thirty years.

In regard to Provincial waters it may, generally speaking, be said that the carp prefers the warmer waters to the colder, and, as it is a fish that habitually lives in shallow water, the great lakes, with the exception of Lake Erie, are not particularly adapted to its life. Consequently it is unlikely that it will appear in other waters of the great lakes in such quantities as in Lake Erie, although it may be expected to work its way up many of the rivers, in fact it has already done so, and, finding lakes or localities favourable to its existence, rapidly multiply therein. A well-known instance of this is furnished by Lake Simcoe, where the carp have firmly established themselves and appear to be very rapidly increasing.

The carp has been accused of many villanies, chief amongst which are that it drives the black bass from its nest, that it is a spawn eater, that it devours the young of other fishes, that by rooting in the mud it renders the water so roily that the breeding grounds of other fishes are spoiled and the fishes themselves forced to abandon the locality, and lastly, but by no means least, that it destroys the beds of wild rice and celery which in the past have been the favorite feeding grounds of the wild ducks. To this latter charge, at least, it would appear that the carp must be held guilty, although, perhaps, not quite to the extent to which it is accused, for there are well-known instances, such as certain portions of the St. Clair Flats and Lake Simcoe, where since the appearance of this fish in numbers the wild rice and celery beds have rapidly disappeared. The rooting habits of the fish, previously referred to, would account for this, especially as it is particularly fond of weedy and marshy places such as are afforded by beds of these descriptions. The other charges, however, are not so easily established. The male black bass on its nest is no despicable warrior, and it is more than doubtful whether the sluggish and cowardly carp would not prefer to retreat than to give battle to such an antagonist. Possibly schools of this fish passing over the district in which the black bass were nesting might dislodge the guardians of the nests, but there is no authentic proof of this as yet, while specific instances have, on the other hand, been adduced of an improvement in the bass fishing coincident with the arrival of the carp. Doubtless if the male bass were absent for any reason from the nest, the carp would eat the spawn if it chanced that way, as it would other spawn that it might come across in the course of its painstaking search for food, for, as before stated, to the carp all food is desirable which will pass into its mouth, but the carp has yet to be proved guilty of being a regular and persistent spawn seeker and eater, investigations of the stomachs of many of them having failed to establish any such proclivities. The feeding methods of the carp cannot fail to render the water roily, and it is, therefore, well possible that when the carp takes possession of more or less restricted areas of water, such a clean water loving fish as the black bass will depart, but other deep water sporting fishes, such as the pickerel and lake trout, would not be affected, nor does it seem probable that the spawning beds of those fishes which seek the sandy or rocky reefs could be materially injured by the carp. As to the charge of voraciousness in regard to the young of other fishes, the small, sucker-like mouth and general sluggish disposition of the carp are against the supposition that it can be a persistent hunter of swimming fishes, although undoubtedly it would gladly devour any small fishes that it could easily secure, so that its depredations under this head are assuredly insignificant. On the other hand it has been established that young carp are very acceptable food to the black bass and other sporting and predaceous fishes.

The main objections to the carp would thus appear to be that it renders waters roily and destroys much aquatic vegetation suitable as food for ducks, and that in so doing it may be disturbing aquatic conditions generally to a degree sufficient to materially affect the existence of other forms of fish and animal life.

In favour of the carp the most salient feature is undoubtedly its commercial value. Already a considerable market for it has been developed in the larger American cities, the average price to the fishermen being from 1½ to 2½ cents per pound, and the chief consumers, Germans and Jews. Trade in this fish from the waters of Lake Erie has already reached no small proportions. Special seine licenses are issued for its capture, the carp being such an active and wary fish that it can but rarely be caught in gill or pound nets, and by means of these seines many tons are now annually removed averaging from 5 to 8 lbs. in weight. It is plain, therefore, that the carp will afford a cheap food, not only to the Germans and to the Jews, whose fore-parents better understood how to prepare the fish for the table, but also to the poorer classes of the community in this Province as the population increases. Moreover, a red caviar, much esteemed by the Jews, can be manufactured from the roe of carp, and since no means as yet has been discovered of rendering this caviar the blue-black colour of sturgeon caviar, it is always easily recognisable, so that there could be no objection to the development of this enterprise. The palate, sometimes called tongue, is in some portions of the world considered also a great delicacy. Further, if no other use could be found for carp, at least a profitable industry could be founded by turning them into valuable fish fertilizer.

Two other points in favour of the carp have been claimed by its champions, namely that it is a powerful factor in the destruction of the fluke worm, so injurious to cattle and sheep, supposedly consuming the parasite which causes the disease while in its systic state, attached to the leaves of grass, or while in its intermediate host, the common fresh water snail Limnaea, and also that it will consume the larvæ of noxious insects, notably those of the mosquito. Moreover, the carp may, to some degree, in rivers below cities do important service as a scavenger, destroying the germs of certain human diseases.

It will be seen, therefore, that there is something to be said for the carp as well as against it, and as it has come to stay, it will obviously be best to seek the greatest possible profit from it. The majority of the citizens of the Province claim that the carp is not palatable, owing to its muddy flavour, but this would appear to be due largely to faulty methods of preparation. The Germans have many various ways of preparing the fish into most excellent dishes. Dr. S. P. Bartlett, a champion of the carp, makes the following suggestions on this score:—

" Kill as soon as caught by bleeding, taking out all the blood. Skin, soak in salt water for several hours, then parboil and bake, basting frequently."

Some dressing is also suggested. In any case it would appear that popular dislike of carp as a food is in part, at least, due to prejudice, for there are instances on record of this fish having been served in hotels and restaurants under other designations, such as bluefish, without apparently being detected by the majority of the guests, while on one occasion, under the title of Red Snapper, it was served at a dinner of a well-known American Fish and Game Club and was acknowledged to be a most palatable dish. Moreover, Germans will frequently select this fish by choice in preference to the finer American varieties, while, as already noted, the Jews are particularly partial to it. Experiments have been made in smoking the flesh of the larger fish and preparing them after the manner of sturgeon meat, and in this form it is claimed that they are also exceedingly palatable.

Finally, as sport for anglers, the carp can, it would seem, lay some claims to distinction, although it is doubtful whether such will be admitted in this Province to any large extent so long as the black bass, the speckled and lake trouts and other sporting fishes are to be found in abundance. In Germany carp fishing is a popular sport and the Father of Fishing, the redoubtable Isaac Walton, devotes a whole chapter to this fish. That in certain localities of this continent its merits in this respect are already winning recognition, the following extracts from remarks by Dr. S. P. Bartlett, of Illinois, will sufficiently prove:—

"The carp when hooked is a vigorous fighter and care must be taken that he does not break the hook, or break out the hook from his mouth. I would advise the use of a landing net. I have found the best bait to be a dough ball, made by boiling cornmeal to a good stiff mush and then working the ordinary cotten batten into it until it becomes hard and stiff, rolling it into little round pellets about the size of a marble. Fried potatoes, sliced raw and fried until they become stiff, not brittle, is also a good bait. I have seen as many as 200 people fishing along the shores and nearly all of them get fair strings. One day, within a distance of three miles on the Illinois River, I counted 1,103 people fishing with hook and line, and on investigation it developed that a large per cent. of them were taking carp. The majority of those caught weighed a pound, and as heavy as five pounds, all of them probably used as food."

Dr. Bartlett also quoted from the letter of a prominent sportsman of the State, Mr. D. M. Hurley, of Peoria, Ill.

"Carp fishing with hook and line has now taken its place with bass and other kinds of fishing. All along the river in this locality carp are being caught freely with hook and line this year, and to say that they are gamey is not half expressing it. I have talked with no less than 25 persons who were busy catching carp and in every instance I was told that it was rare sport to hook a carp, as it was quite as much a trick to land one as it was to land a bass. Dip nets were used generally to land the carp, as the activity of the fish when jerked out of the water would tear the gills and free the fish quite often. The bait used when fishing for carp is dough balls and partly boiled potatoes, the latter being the best in the opinion of the majority. The carp will bite on worms also quite freely. An old German, who lives here, goes daily to the rivers with a regular fly-casting pole and reel to fish for carp. Of course he exchanges the fly for the regulation hook, but he uses his reel in landing the carp and says that there is no finer sport than fishing for carp. As for the sport of catching carp with hook and line I consider it equal to anything in the way of pleasure fishing, as the fish is gamey and will fight as hard against being landed as bass or other game fish, and is to be handled with precaution on account of the tender gills, which will often tear when hooked by an inexperienced angler. In the past two years carp have become popular where they were unpopular, because of the wearing away of the prejudice that they were of no benefit to the angler on account of the belief that they would not take the hook. Now it is different, as the very ones who were so loud in their protest against the carp have found great sport in taking them with the hook and line, and it is wonderful to hear the change of sentiment as to the carp for food purposes. They are a good fish now and fit for a king in comparison to what was said of them while the prejudice still existed. To my mind the carp is a good fish for food purposes and is fast finding favour in the West in every way, now that the angler has found that it is the coming fish for sport."

Thus it will be seen that even on this continent the carp has its champions as a sporting fish, and that already many are profiting through the pleasure of its pursuit. It must also be remembered that the class of angling which alone will satisfy the fastidious and expert angler is not demanded in general by the masses, who as a rule are entirely content so be their efforts are rewarded by a little sport and the capture of some edible fish.

In conclusion, then, it would seem that where the carp is found to be working damage, steps could advantageously be taken to reduce its numbers to a minimum, although in allowing seining for this fish the greatest possible precautions should be taken to prevent the destruction of other, and especially the sporting, varieties of fish, but that, in view of the fact that it is impossible now to exclude the fish from much of the Provincial waters, it would be the part of wisdom to educate the people in some measure to its edible, sporting and other qualities. Your Commissioner would, therefore, recommend:—

(1) That the present policy of issuing seining licenses for the capture of carp only, in districts where this fish is found to be abundant and working harm, be continued provided that proper government supervision can be and is arranged for, but that if possible this work be undertaken in inland waters by officers of the government.

(2) That a pamphlet be drawn up for circulation among the citizens of the Province with a view to educating them to such advantages as are possessed by the carp, especially as a food and sporting fish.

THE PROPOSED INTERNATIONAL FISHERY REGULATIONS.

The proposed code of international regulations for the protection and preservation of the food fishes in international boundary waters of the United States and Canada deals comprehensively with many questions in connection with the commercial fisheries of the Province, and the presumption that the day cannot now be far distant when this code will be promulgated has deterred your Commissioner from entering upon a discussion of them in this report. There has, however, already been a considerable delay in the promulgation of these regulations and it cannot be denied that the same causes which have operated to this end in the past may conceivably continue to do so in the immediate future. There is an urgent necessity at the present time for a revision of the regulations in regard to such matters as the construction and location of pound nets, the mesh of nets, the amount of netting, the prohibition of netting in certain localities, the closing of the sturgeon fisheries in the great lakes and the prohibition in these waters of netting under the ice and the use of naked hooks and spears, flambeaux, torches and other artificial lights, besides various other matters disposed of by the proposed regulations. It would, therefore, seem advisable to take steps to ascertain from the Dominion Government the probability of the near promulgation of the international regulations and in the event of no satisfactory assurances being received that promulgation will shortly take place, to attempt to introduce or to have introduced measures affecting these questions on the lines indicated in the proposed international regulations. By so doing the situation would in no way be complicated, but on the contrary prepared and simplified for the introduction at a subsequent date of international regulations which have seemed wisest to the joint Commissioners of the United States and Canada.

It is proverbially unwise to attempt to cross bridges before they are reached, and in consequence criticism of the proposed international regulations as a whole is not attempted in this report, but attention is called to the following point as it would appear to open the way to various misunderstandings and difficulties.

At the commencement of the regulations are set forth various definitions of terms subsequently made use of in the code, and therein the expression " Coarse Fish " is defined as " suckers and other fish of little value as food for man." In the body of the regulations as affecting the fisheries of the great lakes are various clauses prohibiting the placing of nets in certain localities such as St. Mary's River, St. Clair River, Detroit River, Niagara River, St. Lawrence River, where such constitute the international boundary, or in Lake Erie within one-half mile of the international boundary, and prohibiting also the use of trap nets, but a succeeding clause dealing with the fishing for coarse fish would appear to nullify much of the value of these wise provisions. The clause in question reads as follows:—

" Nothing in these regulations shall prohibit the use of the seines, fyke nets or other nets exclusively for the capture of the carp, eels and coarse fish. When fyke nets are used for such a purpose the wings and leaders shall not extend more than 10 feet from the entrance."

Consequently, in all the waters of the great lakes there would appear to be no obstruction to the use of the trap or any other class of net, so be that the intention was avowed of catching only coarse fish. Some such clause had plainly to be inserted to meet the eventuality of either country finding it necessary to remove quantities of certain classes of fish, such as the carp or pike, but the omission of the stipulation that such nets should be employed by government officials only, obviously throws this privilege open to the public. Unfortunately, the very waters in which fishing, except for coarse fish, is prohibited distinctly by the regulations, as well as much of the shallower water throughout the great lake system, in addition to supporting such varieties of fish as the pike, perch, bullhead, carp, mullet and sucker, contain also in many instances such valuable sporting fishes as the black bass, the pickerel and mascalonge, and, as has already been shown in previous sections of this report, where netting occurs in such waters, but especially trap, hoop, or pound netting, it has up to the present at least been found impossible to check the rapid decrease, in many cases, indeed, the total extinction, of these sporting varieties of fish.

The definition of coarse fish as above quoted may, of course, not be intended to include the catfish, mullet, perch, or pike, as it would plainly be a valid contention that such fish have an appreciable value as food for man, both from the point of view of physical and material economy, but on the other hand, those interested in securing such licenses would have apparently an almost equally powerful argument in comparing either the food or economic value of these fishes to that of the whitefish, the herring, the lake trout, or the pickerel. That sportsmen in many localities would most assuredly protest against any such netting being allowed, is certain, and seeing that the definition of coarse fish, as enunciated in the proposed international regulations, is so vague, the whole matter might easily give rise to intricate and prolonged legal proceedings to determine its exact interpretation according to law. The issuance of the licenses, however, would of course rest with the Province, so that, although under the provisions and definitions of the proposed international regulations, should these come into force, there would appear to be the possibility of considerable divergence of opinion and friction, the means of avoiding it would still remain in the hands of those in charge of the administration of the Provincial fisheries.

How far in such large water areas as those of the great lakes, or in the narrow channels of the international rivers, it is to the benefit of the commercial and sporting fisheries to remove such fish as the pike, the carp, suckers, eels, bullheads, is a most difficult matter to determine, for each undoubtedly has its function to perform in the general scheme of nature. Occasionally a situation will arise, such as those of the abundance of carp in Lake Erie and of suckers in the Georgian Bay region, where it would plainly be advisable to take measures to decrease the quantities of these fish, and doubtless, also, where other more valuable fishes are being removed from the waters, it is expedient also to remove a proportionate amount of less valuable varieties. In all cases, however, but especially in rivers, channels, bays and restricted or shallow water areas generally, the granting of ordinary commercial licenses for this purpose cannot but be accompanied by grave danger to other classes of fish, and particularly so when very strict and efficient supervision cannot be guaranteed. Indeed, it would appear to be more than probable that the harm done by such means very frequently would be immeasurably in excess of any benefits derived from the removal of predaceous or coarse fishes.

Thus, unless the strictest supervision could be ensured, it would appear on the whole to be inexpedient to issue ordinary commercial licenses for the taking of coarse fish only in rivers, channels, bays, restricted and shallow waters generally, especially so in those known to be the haunts of valuable sporting fishes, but rather, where the removal of such fishes has become desirable, to undertake the work with Provincial officials, as has already been done in regard to the ling and other too abundant predaceous and coarse fishes in the waters of the Rideau Lake system.

Your Commissioner would, therefore, recommend:—

(1) That steps be taken to ascertain, if possible, from the Dominion Government the probable date of promulgation of the international fishery regulations.

(2) That in the event of the promulgation of these regulations being indefinitely postponed, efforts be made to secure the introduction of measures in regard to the construction and location of pound nets, the mesh of nets, the amount of netting, the prohibition of netting in certain localities, the closing of the sturgeon fisheries in the great lakes and Lake of the Woods, and the prohibition in these waters of netting under the ice and the use of naked hooks, grappling hooks and spears, torches, flambeaux or other artificial lights, on the lines indicated in the proposed international fishery regulations.

(3) That in the event of licenses being issued for the capture of coarse fish only, the specific fish that may be caught be mentioned clearly on the license.

(4) That in rivers, bays, channels, shallow and restricted waters, the general policy be adopted of undertaking the removal of undesirable fish when necessary, as a Provincial enterprise, but where this is not feasible, that licenses for this purpose be only issued where absolutely strict supervision can be assured, and that in such cases any infringe-

Mid-day on the Lower Steel River, Thunder Bay District.

ment of the license in the matter of the deliberate destruction or sale of sporting fishes be punished by a fine of not less than $100 on each of the parties concerned, together with the cancellation of the licenses, if any, under which the business of either is being conducted, and that the offenders be debarred from securing any commercial fish license whatsoever for a period of five years.

THE SPORTING FISHERIES.

THE ECONOMIC FUNCTION OF THE SPORTING FISHERIES.

The truth of the old saying, "All work and no play makes Jack a dull boy," has long been recognized by those connected with or interested in the moral, physical and educational development of the child and youth, and under the advance of modern civilization greater efforts are continually being put forth to ensure for all young people throughout the early years of their business careers an abundance of wholesome diversions. Moreover, in view of the fact that fresh air is one of the prime necessities of a healthy body, especial attention is paid to sports, games and other means of inducing them to spend a considerable portion of their leisure hours out in the open. The importance, however, of drawing the older citizens, most of whose time is spent in the office or factory, out into the country or on to the waters of the lakes and rivers, where they also may breathe for a space pure and invigorating air, is more generally overlooked, and yet it is more than doubtful whether from the point of view of the well-being and prosperity of the nation this is not an equally important problem. Much of the physical deterioration prevailing in the more congested areas of great cities, and the vices and evils existing in cities and towns alike, are to be attributed in great part to lack of sufficient inducement to the people to seek health and wholesome exercise elsewhere than on the streets, and it must, therefore, be apparent that where an attraction does exist which is capable of drawing thousands daily, or at least weekly, out into the open air and providing them with both exercise and amusement, it must be morally and economically advantageous to foster and develop that attraction by every possible means. The potentialities of angling rank high in this regard. The sport is suitable to both sexes and to all ages, from the young child to the old man and woman. It is within the means of the poor as of the wealthy, for the most expensive equipment is but little guarantee of greater success than that which will be attained with the humblest tools, as is well evidenced by the fact that in 1909 the largest recorded small-mouthed black bass of the year caught in Provincial waters was captured by an eleven-year-old child by means of an ordinary pole with a hook and line attached thereto, while also it must be remembered that with the masses, at least, the extent of the catch will always remain the most important factor.

The Province of Ontario is particularly fortunate in the possession of innumerable rivers, streams and lakes, many of which in the present, and practically all of which in the past, abounded in fish of many varieties, a goodly proportion of which were amenable to the allurements of the baited hook. Consequently if properly appreciated and administered the sporting fisheries of Ontario should play a role in the creation of moral and physical prosperity, growing in importance yearly as cities and towns continue to develop and the population to increase.

That the ordinary working man will only too gladly avail himself of the opportunity of angling is evidenced by the numbers who either singly or with their families engage in this pastime in those localities where even moderately good fishing is to be had, but, as the majority of human beings are prone to be somewhat impatient of negative results to their efforts, that number very rapidly decreases in proportion as the fishing deteriorates. It would seem, then, of particular importance to maintain the sporting fisheries in the neighborhood of cities and towns to the highest possible level of abundance, and the larger the city the greater will be the importance of so doing, owing to the proportionate difficulty that is coincident with the growth of cities of providing suitable open-air distractions and amusements for the masses. Hook and line fishing within reasonable limits, and especially in the case of large water areas, will never impair the fisheries to the degree that is effected by means of even a limited amount of nets in the waters, and it would seem, therefore, that no matter where situated, it is extremely inadvisable to permit any commercial net fishing whatsoever in the immediate vicinity of cities and towns where any fishes to be caught by hook and line are at present to be found, or have previously been known to exist. The total commercial fishing area of the Province is so great that those engaged in the commercial fishing industry could not claim that any injustice was being done them by prohibiting the use of nets in such waters, and if the policy were adopted of barring all commercial fishing whatsoever within at least a five mile radius of cities and towns, even to the extent of prohibiting commercial hook and line angling, not only would the fishing interests on the whole be unaffected, but a wise and proper provision would be thereby made for the wholesome and healthy recreation of their inhabitants to-day, and for the needs in this direction of an infinitely greater population in the future. It is plain also that such a measure would greatly simplify the maintenance of the supply of sporting fishes in these areas by artificial means, where such was found to be necessary.

In addition to supplying an incentive for healthy outdoor amusement to the citizens of the Province, the sporting fisheries fill another role of probably equal economic importance, referred to at length in the Interim Report of this Commission, in that they afford a most potent

F. C. Armstrong's Home Camp, for Tourists Visiting the Steel River, on Clear Water
Lake, Near Jackfish.

attraction to the sportsman-tourist from other Provinces and countries
to visit and pass some time in the Province. An annual influx of visitors
is bound to bring immediate pecuniary benefit, for they must pay for the
necessities of life, and in addition can confidently be expected to spend
money in other directions than those of plain living expenses. Perhaps
no better illustration of this could be adduced than the importance
attached locally to the annual exhibition held in this city. It is impossible, in fact, to conceive of the outcry there would be amongst the merchants of Toronto were it proposed to abandon this feature, and yet,
while equally great or even greater benefit to the Province at large is
to be derived from the angler tourist who passes a week or more in some
remote village, or even in the wilds, in pursuit of his favorite pastime as
from the visitor to Toronto's Exhibition, this fact has not at yet come to
be generally, or in many instances even locally, recognized. Consequently
lakes, rivers and other waters in which sporting fish formerly existed in
abundance and whither there journeyed yearly a proportion of ardent
anglers both from Provincial towns and also from abroad, have in many
instances not only been depleted of their sporting fish, but the local residents have themselves been the chief means of effecting this depletion
through illegal or excessive netting, or disregard of the fishery regulations, remaining the while oblivious to the material harm they were
working to their district and to the Province through the reckless destruction of the valuable sporting fishes. Naturally enough the visiting
angler-tourist requires good sport for the money he expends to secure it,
and if he cannot obtain it in one locality he will inevitably move to another. In most of the States and Provinces of the central and northern
portions of this continent angling of some description is to be had, so
that it is evident that unless the sporting attractions of Ontario's fisheries are maintained to a higher level than the average, the Province
cannot hope to attract an increasing number of annual visitors bent on
angling, but rather that the number will steadily decrease. The accessibility of Ontario and the excellence of her sporting fisheries in the past
have already built up for her no inconsiderable angler-tourist traffic, but
so many of her water areas have already become more or less depleted
that the complaints of visitors are to be heard on all sides, and had she
not possessed such a vast number of waters to draw on doubtless a
diminution in the yearly traffic would already have occurred. In any
case every dissatisfied visitor is a misfortune to the Province, and if the
percentage of waters, depleted or comparatively depleted of sporting fishes,
continues to increase as it has in the past few years the effect on the angler-tourist traffic cannot but be most serious. It is to be noted also that
the waters which have suffered the most in this respect are, in many instances, those most accessible; the very waters, in fact, which, if well
stocked with game fish, should be drawing to them yearly the greater
number of visitors from outside, and the fact that this is the case must
militate against the popularity of the Province as a general tourist re-

8 F.C.

sort, for many who would be willing to undertake a short journey either alone or with their families for the sake of securing good sport during the summer vacation would be deterred from coming in proportion as the distance to be traversed and the difficulties of access become increased. Plainly, therefore, it is of the utmost importance from the viewpoint of encouraging the angler-tourist traffic that the sporting fisheries in the more accessible waters of the Province should be rendered as prolific as it is possible to make them, and especially so in cases such as the Muskoka district, where the natural beauty of the scenery and formation of the region generally render it eminently suitable for the purposes of a great summer playground, while, were it not for this factor, the locality would be comparatively useless and unprofitable to the Province.

From the returns of the $2.00 non-resident angler's tax it is certain that at least 20,000 anglers visited the Province from outside during the past season, but it is acknowledged that as yet the collection of this tax has by no means been perfected, and consequently the actual numbers of tourists who angled in Provincial waters was assuredly very much greater than this figure. Unfortunately no means other than the non-resident angler's tax of ascertaining the number of summer visitors from outside the Province are available, but it is obvious that a great proportion of those who purchased the licenses would have been accompanied by their families or friends, some of whom did not care to do so, which again would very materially swell the total count. That each of these persons was directly responsible for some cash being left in the Province is evident, for board and lodging, for transportation, recreation of all descriptions, and perhaps for luxuries, as likewise that the total amount thus accruing to the Province must have been a very considerable sum. Its exact proportions could, of course, never accurately be determined, but if some method of approximating the number of annual visitors attracted by the angling and scenery could be devised, it would at least form a basis on which an estimate could be formed, and thus constitute a direct education to the citizens of the Province at large as to the immense value to themselves of the sporting fisheries which, in all probability, are directly or indirectly responsible for at least 50 per cent. of the summer tourist traffic. A rough approximation of the number could at least be arrived at by requesting the keepers of hotels and boarding houses to furnish returns of all visitors from inside and outside the Province, other than those whose stay was in connection with business only, and in the country districts, at least, the overseers might well be utilized to check such returns or even themselves to compile them.

The number of points along the great extent of the boundaries of the Province which afford easy ingress to visitors from the east and west and south naturally result in a considerable dispersion of the visiting tourists, and as the country opens up and transportation facilities increase the range of the summer visitors will inevitably expand, especially so if, as is to be hoped, their numbers considerably augment. The importance, therefore, of maintaining the sporting fisheries generally throughout the Province to a high level of excellence is apparent, as likewise of safe-guarding even those waters which are at present practically beyond the reach of even the most adventurous tourist. The greater the dispersion of the visitors the greater will be the benefit to the Province at large, for it is prceisely in the more sparsely-settled regions that their cash will be productive of the most immediate good, seeing that it is the poor settler or farmer, with whom ready money is almost invariably scarce, who will first secure it and benefit by it as it passes on its way into the ordinary channels of trade in the Province.

The summer visitor, however, is not merely advantageous to the Province from the ready cash which he leaves behind him. In Ontario there are abundant opportunities for the investment of capital, and there is no better method of attracting capital to a locality than giving ocular proof of its potentialities to those who possess or control it. Men may read at a distance of great chances and great developments, and remain apathetic or unimpressed, but if those great chances or developments come under their own immediate notice they will, as a rule, commence to take a lively interest in them. In addition to the capital launched into the Province for the purchase of real estate or timber limits, many an instance could be adduced to-day of a thriving industry or concern in this Province which owed its initiation to the fortuitous chance of a summer visit, and in the majority of cases the prime cause of the visit would be found and acknowledged to be the quest of some variety of sport. Each successful investment, as also each satisfactory enlighten-ment of a responsible business man from abroad as to the favorable con-ditions for the investment of capital in the Province cannot but act as an advertisement for Ontario and result, in some measure at least, in turning the eyes of those with capital to invest towards her. It is evi-dent, therefore, that nothing that will in any way assist in bringing into the Province the more wealthy class of visitors and sportsmen-tourists should be ignored, especially not such a prime factor in this regard as the sporting fishes.

There are, of course, in the Province certain localities, such as the Rideau Lake System, the Kiawartha Lakes and Muskoka district, where the value of the tourist traffic is recognized, and where also the sporting fishes are accorded at least a measure of their true worth as a factor in the attraction of tourists, but it is, perhaps, in the extreme west of the Province that the beneficial attributes of the sportsman-tourist and the attractive power of the sporting fishes are most appreciated and under-stood. At Kenora, with all the advantages of its location on the shores of beautiful Lake of the Woods, already a great summer tourist traffic has been developed by the energy of its citizens. At Port Arthur and Fort William, the rivers flowing into Lake Superior, notably the noble Nipigon River, have played no small part in attracting tourists to the district, eager to land the sporting speckled trout. But at Kenora, as at

Port Arthur and Fort William, the citizens believe in the future of their cities; they believe, also, in the timber, mineral, agricultural and other potentialities of their districts; and they realize not only that to expand their cities and exploit these inherent advantages it is necessary to attract capital, but that one of the surest means of inducing the more wealthy classes to visit the districts is to offer them prospects of really good angling. At Kenora, as before noted in this report, a strong movement is on foot to bar all commercial fishing in Lake of the Woods and other waters within a radius of 50 miles of the town, and to stock these waters with black bass and other sporting fishes, while at Fort William and Port Arthur the keenest interest is evinced in the question of re-stocking the rivers and lakes of the surrounding country which have unfortunately become depleted.

It would seem, therefore, that in the Province to-day a realization of the economic role of the sporting fishes in regard to the development of a tourist traffic has not only taken root, but commenced to spread its shoots, and that it would require but steady effort in the direction of popular education over a comparatively short period of years to effect a general recognition of its vast importance. For the Government to undertake such education would plainly be advantageous to the whole Province.

THE SPORTING FISHES.

Angling as a sport or pastime has for many generations claimed thousands as its devotees throughout the world, and many and various are the classes of fish which are enshrined in the beautiful literature to which this subject has given birth, in almost every tongue of the civilized world. The pleasure of being out in the open air; the natural beauty and fascination of the scenery or the peacefulness and solitude of the surroundings, and, in some cases, the hardships and difficulties to be encountered, together with the skill required for success, the excitement of the struggle and the joy of victory, have all contributed their quota to the popularity of this sport, and it is not too much to say that there is no land in the world where it is more generally appreciated than on this continent.

There are those who, armed with delicate and expensive equipment, have brought their skill to the point of a veritable art, and will only pursue such fishes as will give them a prolonged and vigorous struggle under conditions which will afford their art full play. Those there are, again, who prefer to have their angling under the easiest possible conditions, and still others who, whether their tackle be inexpensive or costly, care rather for the amount of the catch than for the skill required to effect it, setting more store on some measure, at least, of success than on either the gameness or variety of the fishes captured. Strictly speaking, in so far at least as this continent is concerned, it is doubtful whether the title of "sporting" would be accorded to any fish by the majority of expert anglers which was not alike possessed of good fighting and edible qualities, but the expert anglers are in a great minority as compared with the masses who often or occasionally indulge in angling, and it must, therefore, be conceded that under the term sporting fishes there might well be included all such fish as afford sport to a fair proportion of the population, the more so as even amongst the expert rod anglers themselves there are to be found cases of considerable divergence of opinion. The yellow pike or pickerel, for instance, has only recently come to be looked upon as a sporting fish in this Province, and even so only in certain localities, whereas in the United States it has long been accorded high rank; while, again, trolling the deeper waters for lake trout with powerful rod and heavy copper line, is by some despised, but by many regarded as a most delightful and exhilarating sport.

The sporting fisheries of the Province should, therefore, not be considered as confined only to those classes of fish whose game and edible qualities have resulted in their universal classification as " sporting," but should be viewed as embracing other classes of fish whose pursuit affords recreation and sport to thousands. Thus under this heading there must be included, besides the bass, the speckled trout, the mascalonge, lake trout and pickerel, such coarser varieties as the pike, perch and rock bass, and perhaps even the more despised bullheads, carp and mullet, for while the term "sporting fish" in regard to them may, in its strictest sense, be a misnomer, their pursuit and capture, while despised and neglected by the expert rod angler, is none the less esteemed a most excellent sport either by the young or by the masses.

For many of the coarser fish there is, of course, a steady demand on the fish markets of the greater cities as a cheap food, and again both lake trout and pickerel, while undoubtedly in a sense sporting fishes of considerable importance, are none the less commercial fishes of the highest rank, and as such of great economic worth to the Province both as a food and as a commercial commodity. The commercial use of the black bass, mascalonge and speckled trout is forbidden by law, but it would plainly be inexpedient and impossible to prohibit the commercial exploitation of all those fishes embraced by the widest definition of the term "sporting" throughout the waters of the great lake system. There are, however, localities, both in the great lakes and in other portions of the Province, where the economic value of such fishes as a means of providing sport is already far in excess of the actual commercial value, such, for instance, as the vicinity of cities and towns, and those regions most particularly adapted for the entertainment of a large number of summer visitors. This latter fact was well emphasized by the Dominion Royal Commission of the Georgian Bay Fisheries, which included among its recommendations the setting aside of a very considerable area in that region to be treated as an exclusive sporting fish preserve. There can be no doubt but that it would be to the advantage of the Province were all such waters to be similarly treated.

In previous sections of this report dealing with the commercial fisheries various recommendations have been made which have also a direct bearing on the sporting fisheries, notably as to the prevention of commercial fishing in rivers and lakes with less than a clear water area of ten miles square, the limitation of domestic licenses, the prohibition of spearing or netting in the winter, and the removal of predaceous or coarse fishes from those areas in which commercial fishing is deemed inadvisable by Government officials, or at least under direct governmental supervision, so that it is needless again to discuss these matters under the present heading. There is, however, one other question closely allied with these problems which remains to be examined, namely, the fishing for lake trout and pickerel in those inland waters for which commercial licenses are, or will be in the future, issued. Both varieties of fish are, as a rule, to be found in such waters and naturally constitute no inconsiderable portion of the catch of the commercial net fishermen, while, in addition, the commercial value of their flesh is high. Consequently, were the net fishermen to be debarred from fishing for or selling these fish it would appear that it might materially affect the possibility of their making a success of the enterprise. On the other hand, as already pointed out, the great lake commercial fisheries should be amply sufficient to supply the general market of the Province and the function of these lesser water areas, stocked with commercial fishes and of sufficient size to render commercial fishing permissible, is undoubtedly to fill the needs of a purely local market, and should be confined to this purpose. If this latter fact should come to be recognized and adopted as a general policy, as recommended in this report, it is evident that only a local resident would engage in the business of commercially fishing such waters, or, in fact, that the business would, as a rule, be undertaken by some individual as a means of augmenting an income derived from other sources. The hardship to the fishermen, therefore, in prohibiting the commercial fishing of lake trout or pickerel in confined water areas would be very appreciably diminished under such conditions. The value of both these fishes is undoubtedly great as an attraction to tourists, and in addition to this, if the fishing for either or both varieties was good, even though there might be a possible local market sufficient to consume all that might reasonably be caught under a commercial license, the residents of the surrounding district could be counted on to take full advantage of the excellence of the fishing in their vicinity, and thus the distribution of the fish as food through the neighborhood would be almost equally well effected as could be accomplished through commercial trading. It would appear, then, that in the lesser inland waters throughout the Province it would, on the whole, be advantageous to prevent, as far as possible, the commercial exploitation of either the lake trout or pickerel. The supervision of fish shipments, which are the products of small lake commercial fisheries, should be easily effected so that even though general trading in the fishes could not be prohibited in the Province so long as they remain legal commercial fishes when caught in the great lakes, at least what lake trout and pickerel where netted in such instances would have to be disposed of locally, and it should be comparatively easy, therefore, to bring home the offence to the offender. The endorsation of the commercial licenses issued for the lesser lakes in which it was desired to stop commercial lake trout and pickerel fishing, with the prohibition of netting or selling either fish under the license, would appear to meet the requirements of the case, provided a reasonable penalty was imposed for any infraction of the provision. Such a step would, of course, be within the jurisdiction of the Provincial Government. It is apparent that the value of the commercial license would by this means be somewhat diminished, for the trout and pickerel command an especially high price, but, on the other hand, there can be no urgent reason advanced for the commercial exploitation of the fisheries of the lesser lakes under the ordinary commercial license, at least not at the present time, so that, even if the measure did result in the sale of a less number of such licenses, there would be no occasion for great regret on that score.

THE DISTRIBUTION AND CHIEF CHARACTERISTICS OF THE RECOGNIZED GAME FISHES OF THE PROVINCE.

THE SMALL-MOUTHED BLACK BASS.

It is generally acknowledged that at the present time the black bass is the most important of all the sporting fishes to be found in the Province. Its fighting qualities are second to none; as a table fish it is the peer of any, and consequently it is not only most highly esteemed by the anglers of the Province, but affords also an immense attraction to those who live without the Provincial borders. The range of the black bass is considerable, and it is found in more or less abundance throughout most of the waters of the eastern and central portions of the Province, as well as in certain portions of all the great lakes, with the exception of Lake Superior. To the north it does not appear to any great extent in the waters of the Hudson Bay watershed, excepting, perhaps, near the height of land, while to the west it does not occur much beyond the eastern limits of the Algoma district with the exception of a few rivers and lakes in the Rainy River district, which, although themselves a part of the Hudson Bay watershed, are close to the height of land in Wisconsin territory, south of which this fish again appears in abundance. Although the range of the black bass is thus seen to be very extensive, it does not occur naturally in all the waters of the area indicated. The Algonquin National Park, for instance, in which lie a network of lakes, and where also are the headwaters of several important rivers in the lower reaches of which the black bass does occur, possessed no fish of this description until the experiment was made of introducing them. It is to be noted also that, generally speaking, to the north of the latitude of Georgian Bay, even where the fish does occur, it is, as a rule, not in such great abundance as in the more southern waters, and it is evident, therefore, that those waters, such as the Bay of Quinte, the Ducks near Kingston, the Rideau Lakes and Kiawartha Lakes, which have become famous in angling circles as particularly prolific in black bass, even though of recent years their reputation may have waned owing to the depletion which has occurred, should be most highly esteemed, cared for and preserved by the Province, for it is a practical certainty that no such magnificent fishing grounds for black bass in Ontario remain to be discovered in the future.

In general the black bass seems to prefer cool, clear waters, having a rocky or gravelly bottom. It is a voracious and cannibalistic fish, its food consisting chiefly of insects, crustaceans and small fish, but when it is hungry it will, apparently, consume almost anything which it can overpower. At the approach of winter it ceases to feed and lies dormant under logs, weeds or rocks, until shortly before the ice commences to move, when, as the warmth of the water increases, it rapidly regains both its energy and appetite. The spawning season commences in May and is over early in July, the actual date of commencement appearing largely to depend on the temperature of the water. The male fish prepares a nest by scooping out a shallow hole in sand or gravel, and when this has been accomplished to his satisfaction he proceeds in search of a mate. At this period the males are most pugnacious and desperate encounters frequently take place between them. Having found a mate and successfully conducted her to his nest, the male fish has to court the female in order to induce her to void her eggs, which he does by rubbing himself gently against her sides. When the spawning process is complete, the female fish departs and the male mounts guard over the nest. Incubation lasts approximately from seven to fifteen days, but the male fish does not leave his charge until the small fishes are able to swim and thus more or less look after themselves, and while engaged in this duty he will attack and drive away anything which approaches the nest. Consequently it is of the utmost importance that the fish should be protected at this period, for he will rush at almost any lure for the purpose of chasing it away, deeming it a dangerous intruder, and thus lends himself to easy capture. In such cases the destruction is not limited to the parent fish alone, but will almost inevitably result in that of the progeny also, for in the neighborhood of the nests there are invariably a host of enemies of spawn and very young fry, such as chub, minnows and other creatures, which alone are kept at a distance by the presence of the guardian over the nest.

The bass will on occasions take the fly, more frequently so in some

Black Bass.

localities than in others. It can also be captured still fishing or trolling with a variety of baits, such as the angle-worm, trolling spoon, frog and natural or artificial minnow. It is, however, not always an easy matter to induce it to bite, especially so where food is plentiful. Frequently it will approach the bait, sometimes taking it into its mouth and playing with, without swallowing, it. On the other hand, there are times when the fish bite greedily and without hesitation at almost any bait that may be offered, and on such occasions it is possible on good bass grounds to land considerable numbers of the fish. In any case, once the bass is hooked, it rushes away at great speed and commences to fight most vigorously. In the course of the struggle it will, as a rule, break water two or three times, and the battle can never be considered as won until the fish has actually been landed, for up to the very last moment it will resist capture with all the strength and energy it possesses. In fact it is not too much to claim for the small-mouthed black bass that there is no fish in the world which weight for weight will fight with more persistent determination, and it is incontestable that it must be accorded premier rank among the game fishes of the Province, alike for the sport which it provides throughout the wide area of its distribution to the citizens, and for the attractive power which it possesses, to draw enthusiastic anglers to Ontario from all parts. In weight the small-mouthed black bass ranges up to 6½ to 7 lbs., though fish of this size are but infrequently caught. A 2 to 4-lb. specimen, however, can be counted on to give the angler all that he requires in the way of magnificent sport.

THE LARGE-MOUTHED BLACK BASS.

The large-mouthed black bass, sometimes known as the yellow or green bass, is not infrequently confounded with the small-mouthed variety. Its distribution is almost coincident with that of the latter, namely, the eastern, southern and central waters of the Province, but it does not range quite so far to the north. As a rule this fish prefers those waters which have a mud bottom and in which, consequently, there is an abundance of aquatic vegetation, so that it occurs in greatest abundance in quiet lakes and bays, but it appears to be capable also of adapting itself to running waters and even to thrive therein. As in the case of its small-mouthed relative, the spawning season commences in May and is completed early in July, being determined largely by the temperature of the water, and it also constructs a nest which it scoops out of the sand or mud for the reception of the eggs. Incubation lasts from one to two weeks, varying with the temperature of the water, the young bass remaining in the nest for about a week after emerging from the eggs, and until these latter are ready to move away the parent fish remains on guard. The principal foods are fish, frogs and crustaceans, and in the summer months it is most usually to be found under overhanging banks, in the shelter of sunken stumps or logs, or in holes among the weeds. As the weather becomes cold, the fish, as a rule, seeks deep waters and hibernates either in the mud or under sunken logs or rocks.

As a sporting fish the large-mouthed black bass ranks high, even though it is not, as a rule, quite so vigorous a fighter as the small-mouthed bass. The introduction of bait-casting as a means of angling has greatly enhanced its value in this regard, for the very places in which it is most usually to be found are those which it would be most difficult, or even impossible, to fish by ordinary still fishing or trolling methods. It cannot be denied that this class of angling is most fascinating, the skill required to cast the bait from 30 to 100 feet exactly into the desired spot over a hole in the weeds or alongside some sunken tree-stump or log being equally high as that exacted in the art of fly fishing, while the nature of the surroundings very frequently adds greatly to the difficulties of landing the fish after it has been hooked. Perhaps the best fishing grounds for this purpose in the Province occur in the drowned lands to be found along the Rideau Lake system, and it would be hard, indeed, to discover waters more admirably adapted to the requirements alike of the fish and the bait-caster.

The large-mouthed bass is, of course, to be caught by other means than bait-casting. It will at times rise freely to a fly, and in many localities, where the surroundings permit of it, still fishing with the angle-worm, frog or minnow is productive of good results, while it is also to be captured on occasions by trolling, either in those running waters in which it occurs or in the vicinity of its habitual retreat among the tree-stumps or weeds. It is a powerful fish and when hooked fights much in the same way as the small-mouthed bass, making a series of desperate rushes and occasionally, but not so frequently, breaking water, but, as before noted, it is apt to be a trifle faint-hearted and to give up the struggle more readily than would ever its small-mouthed relative. It is an excellent table fish and in this Province runs in weight up to 6 or 7 lbs., though such large fish are not often to be secured.

THE BROOK TROUT.

In the days prior to the advent of civilization the brook, or as it is frequently styled the speckled, trout, abounded in most of the streams and rivers of the Province flowing into the great lakes and St. Lawrence River, and occurred also in the waters of many of the lesser lakes. The fish, however, which is not, strictly speaking, a brook trout, but a close relative of, if not identical with, the celebrated char of North Britain and the European continent, requires both cool, clear waters and an abundance of shade in order to thrive, and the opening up of the country has, in consequence, very considerably affected its distribution. It is a well-known fact that the removal of the forest will inevitably effect material changes in the nature of the waters of a district, and this fact is well illustrated by the streams of southern Ontario, for many of those which formerly might have aspired to be styled rivers have fallen to the level of brooks, swept by freshets in the spring and with but a trickle of water in the summer months where formerly there was an abundant and steady flow. It is to be noted also that the temperature of the rivers and streams is raised by the removal of the forest, and especially so in such cases where no shade trees are left to line the banks. The brook trout will not thrive in warm waters, nor in waters absolutely destitute of shade, and consequently has disappeared from many waters which it formerly inhabited. Naturally enough this has occurred most noticeably in the more settled portions of the Province, for it is these which have been the most thoroughly shorn of their timber. Pollution of the waters, through the dumping of poisonous or deleterious matter therein by towns and factories, has also in certain localities played no inconsiderable part in the extinction of the fish, and a like charge, it is to be feared, must be levelled against the ruthless overfishing, both angling and netting, which has but all too frequently taken place and which, although due in part, no doubt, to the excellence of the sport afforded by the fish, cannot but chiefly be attributed to the high estimation in which it is held for table purposes and the consequent good price that can be obtained for it. The sale of the fish is prohibited by law, but unfortunately this has as yet far from checked illegal trafficing in it. In many of the Provincial cities and towns, including even Toronto, it continues to be peddled, and some even of the regular fish dealers are not entirely innocent on the score of handling it surreptitiously.

While, then, the natural range of the brook trout may be considered as including much of the eastern and southern portions of the Province, it is unfortunately the case that it has largely disappeared from this area through the causes above enumerated, although in a few of the wilder regions, where timber is still standing and civilization, generally speaking, has not as yet intruded to any great extent, it may still be found in comparative abundance. In the Algonquin National Park, for instance, many of the little lakes and streams of that wild and beautiful district are well stocked with the fish, and the same may be said of other portions of the Ottawa River basin and of more or less isolated localities to be found in Haliburton, Hastings and other counties. Those waters, also, which drain into Lake Huron and Georgian Bay may, for practical purposes, be said not to be brook trout grounds at the present time, although in the Parry Sound district and other localities there are places where good fishing is still to be secured, for it is not until the streams of the Algoma District are reached, which flow into the North Channel, that the fish commences to appear in appreciable quantities. Thence, however, westward it is to be found in most of the rivers and lakes flowing into Lake Superior, reaching its zenith of abundance and size in the Thunder Bay District. In this region are situated the Nipigon River, already world-famous for its magnificent trout fishing, and many other fine streams, such as the Steel, and it is to be noted also that the fish is abundant in portions of Lake Nipigon and in most of the rivers and streams which flow into it. To the west of this, again, in the Rainy River District, the fish does not appear to exist at all in the waters of the Quetico Forest Reserve, the Rainy River, Lake of the Woods or surrounding territory, and in the northern and western portions of this district it is doubtful whether it occurs anywhere in very great abundance. Its distribution, in fact, in those waters of the Province which drain into James or Hudson Bay. would seem to be more or less confined to the regions north of Lake Superior, and it is, apparently, most abundant in the neighborhood of the height of land. There is, indeed, no doubt that many of the rivers and lakes of this watershed in both the Thunder Bay and Algoma districts are as well stocked with brook trout as almost any of the waters flowing into Lake Superior. It is an unfortunate fact that already many of these latter waters are beginning to show the effects of illegal netting, and if the brook trout is to be perpetuated in them steps should be taken at once to check this nefarious traffic. It is certain also that the building of the Grand Trunk Pacific and the Canadian Northern Railways will throw open a great new territory north of Lake Superior in which excellent brook trout fishing will be readily secured. In view of the importance, therefore, of this fish as an attraction to anglers, both from at home and abroad, it would seem that the greatest precautions should be taken both in the Superior basin and in the virgin territory to the north of the height of land not to repeat the mistakes made in the older portions of the Province, but to ensure that a sufficiency of forest shall be left standing to maintain the steady flow and normal temperature of the waters, and that the shade along the banks of the rivers and lakes shall be jealously preserved.

The brook trout is a voracious feeder, living chiefly on small fishes, insects and crustaceans. The size which it attains depends largely on the nature of the waters in which it lives and the food to be obtained therein. In small streams it may mature at a length of six or eight inches and a weight of only a few ounces, while in larger bodies of water, with an abundant supply of food, it will reach a length of eighteen inches or more and a weight of from 6 to 8 pounds. Large fish such as this are still to be taken in the Nipigon River and Lake Nipigon, and in that region fish of from three to five pounds are by no means uncommon.

The spawning season of the fish extends from August in the north to December in the south, the trout running up towards the headwaters of streams and depositing their ova on the gravelly shallows. The number of eggs produced by the female depends largely on the size and age of the fish, those in their second year voiding from 50 to 250 eggs, while larger fish may lay as many as 1,500. The period of hatching depends in great measure on the temperature of the water, varying from thirty-two days in warm weather to one hundred and sixty-five in cold. In the early part of the summer the trout prefers the ripples and shoaler parts of the stream, but, as the temperature rises with the approach of hot weather, it returns to the deeper pools or the vicinity of cold springs, where it remains until the return of autumn urges it once more up stream to spawn. The close season for brook trout commences at present on September 15 and extends to April 30 of the following year, so that over the best brook trout fishing grounds of the Province, namely, in the North land, some of the fish are already ripe, or even commencing to spawn, some weeks prior to protection being afforded them. In this region, however, the latter part of August and the two first weeks of September are undoubtedly, with the possible exception of early May, the most pleasant period for angling, as the fly and mosquito, so prevalent through the summer, have by that time practically disappeared, and, moreover, this is also the time of year most convenient for vacation purposes to a great number of sportsmen. It would seem, therefore, on the whole, to be inexpedient to shorten the close season, but the fact that spawning commences so early in this region renders it all the more important to lose no time in the institution of hatchery plants in order to ensure the continued abundance of the fish.

The fame of the speckled or brook trout as a sporting fish is so universally known that there is no need to insist on its merits in that respect, excepting, perhaps, to note that the brook trout of the Province is the equal in this respect of any to be found throughout the world. In the northern waters the fish will, as a rule, rise readily to the fly in the early morning, in the evening and for some hours after nightfall, but often decline to do so during the heat of the day. This, however, would not appear to apply to the almost virgin waters entering Lake Nipigon from the north, east and west, nor to those waters to the north of the height of land, where the fish appear to be so numerous and greedy that catches have been made with the fly when the day was already warm and the sun high in the heavens, doubtless owing to the fact that the very abundance of the fish entails a comparative scarcity of food. In general, however, the trout can be induced to strike at a worm, a frog or minnow at almost any period of the day, and although the historic traditions of speckled trout angling condemn such methods and place those employing them without the pale in the opinion of exclusive fly fishermen, there can be no doubt but that both the very early morning and after dark in the evening are not times of the day which appeal to the vast majority of those who indulge in this sport either in Canada or in the States, and that by far the greater number prefer to start their angling after breakfast and put up their rods at sundown. Moreover, it is only comparatively few who have the opportunity of becoming expert fly-casters, so that it would seem that much of the brook trout angling of this Province is destined to continue to be effected in total disregard of the ethics of the present day fly fisherman and of the ancient traditions woven around the pursuit of this splendid sporting fish. While this to a certain extent may seem a pity, and must inevitably act in the direction of accelerating the diminution of the supply unless

special measures for artificially maintaining it are introduced, it cannot be denied that the prime benefit to be derived from the possession of
fisheries, in a land where those fisheries belong to the public, lies in
affording the greatest pleasure and satisfaction to the greatest number,
both of residents and visitors, so that, although it might be advisable
in certain instances to set aside brook trout rivers for fly fishing only,
in general it would be inadvisable to introduce any such restrictions.
The paramount necessities are to prevent netting, to stamp out commercial trading in the fish and to safeguard the waterflow and shade.
If these matters are attended to the fame of the brook trout fisheries of
the Province, in the north land at least, will continue to grow, to the
material benefit not only of the residents in the localities which furnish
the sport, but of the citizens of the Province at large.

THE MASCALONGE.

The mascalonge, sometimes called the maskinonge, or muskellunge,
longe or lunge, is the largest and most formidable member of the pike
family to be found in the waters of the Province. The markings of this
fish are so many and various, even in the same locality, that it is not
always easily distinguished from the pike by those not well acquainted
with its general appearance and general characteristics. In the young
the upper half of the body is, as a rule, covered with small, round black
spots, but these usually change their shape or disappear as the fish
increases in size. In mature fish the spots are more diffuse, sometimes
enlarging to an inch and more in diameter, or else, by coalescing, form
broad vertical bands, while in others again there are no distinct dark
markings at all. The majority of mascalonge in provincial waters
appear either to be unmarked or to show only faint bars, the spotted
form being the most uncommon.

The distribution of the longe is somewhat irregular. It occurs in
the St. Lawrence River, chiefly about the Thousand Islands, in the
waters of the Trent Valley, Lake Scugog, Lake Simcoe and many of the
lesser inland lakes. Again in Lake Erie and the Georgian Bay it is
comparatively common, the most famous district for it, perhaps, in the
whole Province occurring in these latter waters, in and in the vicinity
of French River. Further west it is still to be met with in certain portions of Lake of the Woods, in spite of the fact that netting would appear
greatly to have reduced its numbers in those waters, and there would
seem to be little doubt but that as the range of the angler extends over
the country in the Lake of the Woods region, it will be found to exist in
various of the waters of its lesser lakes. How far the range of the fish
extends to the north has not yet been accurately determined, but it
does not appear to occur north of the height of land. It is evident,
however, that the very localized distribution of this fish must endanger
its perpetuation unless the most stringent measures are taken to suppress illegal netting and to ensure that the bag limit is enforced.

Mascalonge.

9 F.C.

Like all pike, the mascalonge is a voracious and cannibalistic fish, and is possessed of a very large mouth armed with teeth of considerable size which give the fish extraordinary power in holding its prey. In habits it is a solitary fish, lying concealed among aquatic plants at the sides of the channels or beneath shelving rocks in open waters, and from its place of hiding will dart forth upon any living thing which is unfortunate enough to come within its reach and small enough to become its prey. At spawning, which occurs soon after the ice goes out in the spring in the shallow waters about the reed beds, the fish pairs, the female depositing a large number of eggs which hatch out in from fifteen to thirty days according to the temperature of the water. The mascalonge has been known to attain a gigantic size, running up to 80 or 100 lbs., but it is rare to-day to hear of specimens over 50 lbs. being caught. Fish up to 40 lbs. are, however, still caught each year.

As a fighter the longe is justly celebrated and the great weight sometimes attained by the fish renders the pursuit of it all the more exciting. As a rule, the moment it is struck, it will break water and tear away in a tremendous rush, subsequently during the struggle repeating these manoeuvres time and again until it becomes exhausted. Fishing with a stout trolling rod it is rarely that specimens of greater weight than 10 lbs. can be brought to the gaff in less than 20 minutes and as the size of the fish increases so in proportion does the time required to land it, until in the case of very large fish, to weary one out taxes the strength and endurance of a strong and practised angler. So powerful are the jaws of the longe and so wicked its disposition that even in the case of the smaller fish it is usually found advisable to stun it before taking it into the boat, while in the case of larger fish, which are so strong that they will frequently tow a boat considerable distances, it is as a rule not attempted to take them into the boat, but a landing is effected at some shallow or convenient spot and the fish brought in to shore.

The method of angling for mascalonge is trolling from a boat with a spoon or other artificial bait, but the very largest fish would appear to be most readily lured with a live fish carefully attached to the hook so that it will not drown, but swim in natural fashion after the boat as it slowly moves along. Trolling is, of course, equally effective when either the rod and line or the hand line are employed. The latter, however, can hardly be considered a sporting method for so noble a game, and in view of the fact that the distribution of the mascalonge is comparatively limited, that to those sportsmen who desire a prolonged and desperate struggle it is above all fish to be found in Provincial waters the most attractive, and that consequently not only many anglers of the Province but also an equally great or greater number from abroad can be counted on to spend some time yearly in its pursuit, it would seem that angling for this fish might well be restricted to the rod and line. The mascalonge grounds are as a rule so well defined that this would be by no means difficult to arrange. Other sporting fishes are of course to be found in the waters inhabited by the longe, and it might obviously occur that in hand trolling for such fish a longe might be hooked, but the nature of the bait used would in general preclude the hooking under such circumstances of all but the smaller specimens and so hardy is the fish that some, at least, of the fish thus hooked could be returned to the water with a fair prospect of remaining alive. If, therefore, a regulation to this effect were included in the regulation prohibiting hand trolling for mascalonge, it should result in the saving of a proportion of the fish thus caught. It might, perhaps, be argued that to prohibit hand trolling for the longe would debar a number of people from this class of fishing who would otherwise enjoy it, especially those of the weaker sex, but it must be conceded that it is essentially a man's and a sportsman's fish, and it would appear, therefore, that it might well be considered and treated as such.

The best season of the year for longe fishing is the autumn, for then the fish is hard and in prime condition and its fighting qualities at their very best. At this period of the year also its flesh is firm, flaky and of excellent flavour, whereas in the summer months it is apt to taste rather weedy.

THE LAKE TROUT.

The lake trout, which is variously known also as the salmon trout, grey trout, togue or tuladi, is the largest representative of the coarse charrs existing in fresh waters, attaining a length of several feet and a weight up to 60 lbs. and more, though it is infrequently at the present time that fish over thirty pounds in weight are secured in this Province. The coloration is extremely variable, being sometimes grayish, sometimes pale, and sometimes almost black, but in all cases with rounded pale spots which are often tinged with red, while on the back and the top of the head there are fine vermiculations resembling those of the brook trout. This variety in colouring has given rise to the belief that there are several distinct species of this fish, but it would appear to be doubtful whether there are more than at most two scientifically distinguishable species. The local peculiarities in the markings, therefore, which are to be observed in the fish of certain lakes may perhaps be attributed to the characteristics of the particular waters.

The lake trout is to be found throughout the great lakes and in most of the larger and many of the smaller inland lakes of the Province. It is a highly predaceous and voracious fish, and will devour almost anything, its principal food consisting of herrings, young whitefish and other soft-finned fishes. In the general it frequents the deeper waters, but is to be captured in waters of almost any depth, being taken usually near the bottom. The spawning season varies greatly according to the locality, commencing in the northern waters early in October and in more southerly regions not until November. The close season for this

A Fine Spot for Pickerel near Lake La Croix, Rainy River District.

fish, however, has been fixed from November 1-30, so that in many localities the fish is afforded no protection whatsoever during the period of reproduction. Whatever may be the merits of the contention, as applied to the commercial fisheries of the great lakes, that the fish is of such a hardy and rapacious nature that it is well able to look after itself even under such conditions, this would obviously not apply in the case of smaller bodies of water where the numbers of the fish are comparatively few, and in consequence, in those lesser lakes in which the lake trout affords sport to residents or visitors some measures should at once be taken to protect the fish at the local time of spawning against both netting and angling. The fish spawns in water from 10 to 100 feet deep, the eggs being deposited on the reefs of honeycombed and similar rocks. The flesh of the lake trout is highly esteemed for food purposes, and it ranks very high amongst the table fishes of the Province.

As a sporting fish the lake trout is esteemed by many, and it is to be noted that in certain of the lakes of the eastern portions of the Province, such, for instance, as some of those in the Rideau Lake system, Haliburton and adjacent counties, it is claimed that the local variety excels in fighting qualities. Should this be established beyond dispute, it would plainly be possible, under a system of adequate hatcheries, to pay especial attention to these particular breeds and.experiment in the direction of introducing them into other waters. The depth at which the fish is most commonly to be found during the angling season necessitates the use of a heavy copper line or else very heavy sinkers, while the bait used is some form of spinner or spoon. As a general rule the slower the trolling the better will be the results, provided only that the bait continues spinning, but even in the best waters success is a matter of considerable hazard. The early morning, late afternoon and evening would appear in general to afford the best opportunities. The fish when hooked offers considerable resistance, making several rushes and using its weight to the fullest advantage, so that, in the case of large trout, the struggle is often prolonged. The weight of the sinkers or of the copper line, as the case may be, naturally militates against the liveliness of its resistance, and by many anglers the fish is, in consequence, dubbed sluggish. Where, however, in fairly shallow waters an ordinary line and heavy trolling spoon will attain a sufficient depth once hooked it will display such vigour and persistence as will satisfy the most exacting angler. In any case there are always to be found a great many people who are intensely desirous of capturing a large fish, and to these, in spite of the uncertainty of the fishing, and in spite of a possible deadness in the struggle, the lake trout will always remain a most attractive game fish.

YELLOW PICKEREL.

The yellow pickerel or pickerel possesses the distinction of laying claim to three other names which are in common use, namely wall-eyed pike, pike-perch and dore, and in addition to these, the young, when pale in color, are sometimes, but especially in the Lake Erie district, styled blue pickerel, although an allied species of less commercial value and smaller size, the sand pickerel or sauger, is also commonly known under this designation. The range of the pickerel appears to extend practically all over the Province, but it occurs, perhaps, most abundantly in the great lakes and rivers falling into them. In the warm weather the fish seeks the deeper waters and is to be met with at those times by anglers in places where the cliffs descend abruptly into the depths. In the spawning season, however, which occurs early in the spring, it runs on to the gravelly or sandy bars in shoaler water, or up the rivers, for the purpose of depositing its eggs. The fish has been known to attain a great size, specimens of 25 lbs. weight having been recorded, but at the present time 10 lbs. is considered an exceptional fish and it is but rarely that an angler will be fortunate enough to secure one of such weight. The pickerel is voracious, feeding chiefly on such other fishes as it can overpower, and on those insects, frogs and crustaceans which occur in its particular locality. As a food fish it ranks particularly high, its flesh being exceptionally well flavoured, firm, white and flaky, and consequently it is not only in great demand, but most energetically pursued by the commercial net fishermen on account of its high market value, for at the present time it is rated as a commercial fish.

As a sporting fish the yellow pickerel is by no means to be despised, for not only will it offer a vigorous even though somewhat brief resistance after it is hooked, but its distribution is wide and it occurs in many waters which would otherwise be destitute of sporting fish, except perhaps a few lake trout. The pickerel will as a rule strike greedily at almost any trolling spoon or imitation minnow, and the most usual method, therefore, of angling for this fish is trolling from a boat, although in certain localities where the shore line is favourable it can frequently be captured from land. At the present time the game qualities of the pickerel are not generally appreciated by the citizens of the Province, chiefly owing to the superior merits in this respect of the black bass and speckled trout, but visitors from across the border accord it high rank among the sporting fishes, and would often as lief fish for pickerel as for any other class of fish. Consequently it would appear that the yellow pickerel should be accorded its due, and that in the lesser waters, but especially in those not inhabited by black bass or speckled trout, steps should be taken to protect it both against the commercial and domestic net fishermen. In some localities, indeed, it will undoubtedly become necessary to increase and maintain the supply of this fish by artificial means. Already a small hatchery for this purpose has been established by some enterprising citizens at Sparrow Lake. Under a system of Provincial fish hatcheries, however, to deal with the commercial fisheries, as recommended in this report, great attention would naturally be paid to the valuable pickerel, and consequently there.

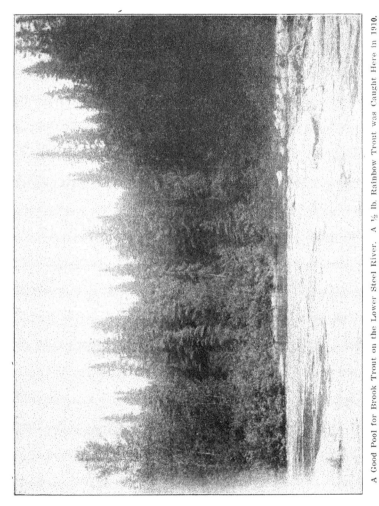

A Good Pool for Brook Trout on the Lower Steel River. A ½ lb. Rainbow Trout was Caught Here in 1910.

should be no difficulty at all under such circumstances in obtaining sufficient fry to stock any waters for sporting purposes that might be deemed desirable.

THE RAINBOW TROUT.

The Rainbow Trout, although not indigenous to Provincial waters, must be accorded a place among the game fishes at present to be found in the Province. The fish, (salmo Irrideus), is a native of the waters of some of the western states of the Union and was first introduced experimentally into the St. Mary's River by the Michigan authorities some thirty years ago, as well as into various other rivers and streams of that State. In the intervening time it has thriven exceedingly and in the St. Mary's River has been known to attain a very great size, a specimen of 14 lbs. weight having been caught by angling in the Canadian waters of the Soo Rapids in 1909, while in the press of 1910 the capture in a net of a monster weighing 35 lbs. was recorded as a fact. A few of the Provincial streams in the neighborhood of Sault Ste Marie were planted with the fry of this fish, obtained by citizens of that town from the Michigan hatchery, but it is impossible to determine exactly the area in Ontario over which it is now distributed. Doubtless in the course of time it may be expected to spread west into all the streams entering Lake Superior and indeed a small specimen of about ½ lb. weight was caught as far west as the Steel River in 1910. Possibly, also, it may eventually occur in the rivers and streams flowing into the Georgian Bay or North Channel.

The Rainbow Trout feeds chiefly on shrimp, insects and larvæ of insects, while the larger specimens in the St. Mary's River are known to be fond of the cockedoosh, (a species of minnow), and of small herring. In general, however, the fish, unlike the speckled trout, is not cannibalistic, and this fact greatly facilitates the raising of young fry to the fingerling stage in hatcheries. It prefers waters as a rule of somewhat higher temperature than those most favorable to brook trout, and can be expected to spawn in Canada from about the middle of May to the middle of June, while the period of incubation should be approximately 50 days. The rainbow prefers a gravel or mixed gravel and stony bottom for spawning purposes, though if these are not available they will spawn on clean sand.

In game qualities the rainbow trout ranks very high, being held by many to excel even the brook trout in this respect. It is to be captured with a live minnow or cockedoosh, or by means of various artificial baits, such as a small trolling spoon or artificial minnow. Strips of fat pork are said also to be effective with the larger specimens, while the trout will also rise to a fly, the best for the purpose being light or bright ones, such as the Parmachine Belle and Junglecock. No more exciting sport could be desired than to tackle a large rainbow in the turbulent waters of the Soo Rapids, where the fish is now to be found in considerable quantities and already the fame of the fish in this particular locality is becoming widely known. It is to be noted also that as a table food the rainbow trout ranks second to none among the sporting fishes.

DISTRIBUTION AND CHIEF CHARACTERISTICS OF OTHER FISHES WHICH PROVIDE SPORT AND AMUSEMENT TO MANY ANGLERS.

THE PIKE.

The common or northern pike, sometimes known as the Jackfish, is distributed throughout the Province wherever there are sufficient weeds to afford it shelter, from the extreme north in the Hudson Bay watershed to the great lakes in the south, and from eastern portions of the Province to the Rainy River District. It is a most voracious fish, feeding upon any form of animal life which it is able to overpower. It has been known to attain a very great size under favourable circumstances, but in those waters which are the more generally fished to-day it has been pursued to such an extent that specimens much in excess of 10 lbs. are now comparatively rare. The fish spawns in the early spring, as soon as the ice moves out, running up on to the rush beds or shallow, grassy places for that purpose. The females are most prolific. In general the pike is to be found in amongst the weeds, or in close vicinity thereto, lying as a rule concealed in them and darting out from its hiding place on any smaller form of animal life that passes within its range. The voracity of the pike renders its presence somewhat undesirable in those waters in which the finer classes of sporting fishes are to be found, but even in these instances, its size in particular renders it attractive to many anglers, while in other localities, more especially in some of the waters of the Hudson Bay watershed, it is frequently the only fish capable of affording sport to would-be anglers.

The pike is not as a rule accorded the rank of a sporting fish, but this is to be attributed largely to the fact that most of the angling for it occurs in the summer months when it is lying inactive amongst the weeds and, in consequence, is comparatively weak and flabby. In the autumn when the weeds have died down and this wolf of the waters is compelled to hunt for its prey in the open, it becomes a different fish, lean, active and muscular, and it is no exaggeration to say that at such times a large specimen will tax the skill and endurance of an expert angler to their uttermost and provide him with most excellent sport. Even, however, in the summer months, when it becomes quickly exhausted, the first rush and savage tugging of the fish at the line will stir the pulses of those who enjoy the sport of angling. It is most

Male and Female Rainbow Trout Caught on a Cockadoosh in the Canadian Soo Rapids, 1910.

14 lbs. Female Rainbow Trout Caught in the Canadian Soo Rapids, 1910.

usually caught by trolling with live bait, or with some form of spoon or imitation minnow.

The flesh of the pike in the spring and summer is as a rule not much esteemed, being soft and weedy in flavour, but in the autumn, when the fish has become muscular, the flesh is firm and pleasant to the taste. It is to be noted also that the Indians are at all times particularly partial to this fish and would, in many localities, eat it in preference to other, more generally deemed finer, classes of fish. In the greater fish markets there is a steady demand for pike and the fish, in consequence, is dealt with in large quantities commercially, but so prolific is it and so general its distribution that, even though it is capable of and does afford amusement and sport to thousands every year, there would appear to be no necessity for its protection excepting in the vicinity of cities and towns, and in those other localities, perhaps, where no other good angling is to be secured.

THE WHITE BASS.

The white bass should, perhaps, together with the pike, be accorded a place amongst the recognized sporting fishes. It occurs in all the great lakes, rarely, however, ascending the streams, although at times it is abundant in the mouths of the larger rivers. It rarely attains a weight in excess of 1½ lbs., and is a gregarious fish, usually swimming in shoals in considerable numbers. Its spawning season occurs in May or June. It will take the minnow bait readily and in addition in the summer months rises well to the fly, while its fighting powers are by no means to be despised. The flesh is most excellent when freshly caught.

THE SPECKLED BASS.

The speckled bass is to be found in most of the Provincial waters from Quebec to Lake Huron, its most general habitat being ponds, lagoons, and sluggish streams where there is an abundance of aquatic vegetation, under which it will lie in wait for the insects, crustaceans and small fish which constitute the bulk of its food. It spawns in the early summer and is said to scoop out a nest in the sand much after the fashion of the black bass. The weight which it attains is not frequently much in excess of 1 lb. The fighting powers of the speckled bass, when hooked with light tackle, are by no means inconsiderable, and even though its efforts may not be very persistent, the fact that it is gregarious and that, in consequence, considerable numbers are often to be caught when a favourite haunt is discovered, renders it attractive to many anglers. As a table fish it is excellent when taken from clean waters.

THE ROCK BASS.

From east to west the rock bass occurs generally throughout the waters of the Province, although its northern range has not as yet been accurately determined. It is most usually to be found in dark holes in streams and lakes, where acquatic vegetation flourishes, or in the neighborhood of docks and timber which afford shade, and it emerges towards nightfall from its retreat and roams the waters in search of the insects, crustaceans and small fish which constitute its food. Spawning in May or June, it scoops out a nest for the eggs on some gravelly or sandy bar and over this nest the parent fish mount guard until in due course the eggs are hatched and the young fry able to look after themselves.

The rock bass will afford fair sport to the angler when taken on light tackle, its chief value, however, lying in the fact that it will take almost any bait, even on the coarsest tackle, and in consequence is eagerly sought by the younger members of the population who can easily secure a good string of the fish when they are fortunate enough to discover a good place. When taken from clear, cold water, its flesh is distinctly pleasant to the taste and it is generally adjudged a very fair eating fish throughout the Province.

PERCH.

The yellow perch is to be found in most of the streams and lakes throughout the Province, and is, perhaps, one of the most abundant fishes. In size it will run from ten to twelve inches, rarely, however, attaining a weight of more than 1 lb. It is a spring spawner and its flesh is so delicate in flavour that it is held in high esteem as a table fish. There are in fact few fish which excel it in this respect. The perch is not possessed of very considerable fighting qualities or determination, its chief attractiveness in regard to sport being that it is to be caught by anyone at almost any season of the year with almost any description of tackle. There can be no doubt that in the matter of drawing the residents of cities and towns out into the fresh air the perch plays no inconsiderable role, and should, therefore, be esteemed accordingly.

THE SUNFISH.

The yellow or common sunfish occurs in most of the waters of central and southern Ontario up to Lake Huron, beyond which it has not as yet been recorded. In size it will grow to 8 inches in length and the weight of half a pound. Spawning in May and June, the fish seeks shallow water, scooping out a nest in the sand or mud, the males guarding the nests with the greatest jealousy until the young have been hatched. This little fish affords excellent sport to many a youngster throughout the districts in which it is found, and is not to be despised as a table food.

Another variety, the blue sunfish, is to be found in certain localities, notably in some of the Rideau Lakes and in Lake Erie and its tributaries, which in habits closely resembles the yellow sunfish, but which will reach a greater size, running sometimes in weight up to a pound. In proportion to its size it will afford the angler most excellent sport, being possessed of fighting qualities little, if any, inferior to those of any fish to be found in the Province, while as a table fish it is held in high esteem.

THE COMMON MULLET.

The common mullet, which is the handsomest and best representative of the sucker family in Provincial waters, abounded in the great lakes from the St. Lawrence River to Lake Superior, but owing to persistent netting in the spawning season it has now become comparatively scarce. The fish passes most of its time in deep waters, but in the early spring, as soon as the ice breaks up, it runs up the rivers and streams to spawn, forcing its way through the swiftest torrents in order to reach the gravelly beds upon which it deposits its eggs. While in the streams the mullet will readily take a worm bait, and though it is by no means a vigorous fighter, owing to its weight, which frequently runs as high as 4 or 5 lbs., it will afford fair sport to the angler, especially if it be taken in the swifter waters.

THE COMMON CATFISH.

The common catfish, sometimes known as the bullhead, occurs practically throughout the Province in quiet streams, ponds or bays, especially in those having a muddy bottom. It is an omnivorous feeder, not despising anything in the shape of animal food, and will feed in all depths of water from the top to the bottom, although its most usual method is to grub about in the mud seeking for what it may devour. The catfish spawns in June, in quiet shallow waters in the vicinity of aquatic weeds, clearing out a slight depression in the sand or mud to act as a nest, over which the parent fish, but especially the male, watches with jealous care. The eggs hatch in about a week and subsequently the young, which at this stage much resemble small black tadpoles, follow the parent fish along the shores until about the middle of July, after which they scatter and shift for themselves in deep, weedy water.

As a food the catfish does not rank high in popular estimation, but this may to a large extent be attributed to its appearance, which is far from prepossessing. There are, however, many persons who prefer it to any of the coarser fishes. It can lay no claims to fighting powers, but to the small boy, and even to many older persons in the Province, the catching of a catfish with a hook and line affords a constant and healthy amusement, and in a modest form, at least a measure of true sport in its widest sense, for amongst all classes of the population there are always to be found a fair percentage of those who, like a certain squire, would rather hunt rats in a barn with a pug or fish for sticklebacks in the village stream with a piece of cotton and a bent pin than take part in the finest game yet devised by man.

10 F.C.

THE RESTOCKING OF DEPLETED WATERS AND THE INTRO-
DUCTION OF NEW VARIETIES OF SPORTING FISHES.

When waters have become depleted of any given variety of fish and it is desired to restock them with the same, two main considerations at once present themselves; firstly, the securing of a sufficiency of eggs, fry, fingerlings or parent fish to effect the purpose, and, secondly, that of ascertaining whether for any reason since the depletion occurred the waters have become unsuited to the life of the particular fish. It is apparent, moreover, that even in those waters which have not become depleted, but which are annually the fishing grounds of many anglers, there is liable to occur a diminution in the quantities of the sporting varieties of fish, especially so in the more restricted areas, so that if it be desired to maintain a goodly supply in them, restocking operations in these cases also become a necessity.

In order to undertake restocking operations, it is necessary to make provision for obtaining a supply of the varieties of fish which it is desired to utilize. To this end transferring mature fish from one locality to another might be effective under favourable circumstances, but as a general rule it is a matter of considerable difficulty to find localities in which the better class of sporting fishes are so abundant that a number of any one variety could be advantageously or even safely removed from them. The modern scientific hatchery, however, affords a means of attaining the desired end without materially robbing one area in order to stock or restock another. In another section of this report it has been pointed out that in order to maintain the commercial fisheries to their present yield it is practically indispensable that the Province should embark on considerable hatchery operations. Should this be done, it would obviously very much simplify the maintenance of the sporting fisheries also, for in the commercial hatcheries there would in any case be dealt with such valuable sporting fishes as the lake trout and pickerel, besides many of the coarser fishes which pro- vide sport, and it would plainly be a simple matter to arrange for the distribution of such of these as might be required for sporting purposes. It would, moreover, entail but little additional expense or trouble to handle the eggs of the mascalonge in these commercial hatcheries. It would seem, then, that in so far as the needs of the sporting fisheries are concerned there are but two varieties of fish, indigenous to the Province, for which hatcheries, separate from the general commercial hatcheries, would have to be provided, namely the speckled trout and the black bass.

There are in existence on this continent no small number of hatch- eries conducted as private enterprises from which the fry, eggs, finger- lings or mature fish of certain sporting varieties, but chiefly of the speckled trout, can be obtained. The main reason for the appearance of the private commercial hatcheries in the States has apparently been,

Long Island, N.Y.,
Fish Hatchery.

Long Island, N.Y.,
Fish Hatchery,
showing system of
separated tanks for
Fingerling and
Young Trout.

Long Island, N.Y.,
Fish Hatchery,
showing Young
Brook Trout in
Tank.

not the demand for fry by anglers, but the steady demand and great price to be obtained for speckled trout on the markets of New York and other great American cities. In this Province, however, the majority of citizens would be unwilling to pay the fancy prices for this fish which prevail in the markets across the border, more especially so as it entails purchasing little more than a name, the liver-fed brook trout being devoid of nearly all the delicacy and flavour which have rendered the wild fish famous as a table dish. The great quantities of fish which have to be raised for market purposes in order to make the enterprise financially successful have resulted in the hatcheries in certain ins- tances being able to dispose of large quantities of eggs or fry at a less cost than it would have taken the State hatcheries to produce them. In spite of this fact, however, both the uncertainty of this source of supply in the present and in the future end the constant and steadily increasing demand for brook trout eggs wherewith to restock public or private waters have led the Federal Government of the United States, as well as many of the individual States also, to interest them- selves on an increasing scale in the enterprise of raising trout as a measure of profitable and sound economy. In this Province, where the sale of brook trout is forbidden, and the only market for fish artificially raised would, apparently, in any case be Toronto, and at that a most limited one, it would appear impossible that for many years to come the private commercial brook trout hatchery should be a profitable enterprise, or that eggs or fry could be obtained in sufficient quantities from private Canadian sources to meet the needs of the Province at lower prices than those at which they could be produced by Provincial hatcheries, while to rely on the private firms of a foreign nation for a future supply would seem far from desirable or wise. It would appear, therefore, that in regard to brook trout where restocking measures have to be instituted as a permanent undertaking, as should undoubtedly be the case in this Province, the Government might well embark on the undertaking, and insure through the institution of special provincial brook trout hatcheries an adequate supply of fry or fingerlings being always obtainable.

One of the main factors, if not the main factor, in a successful brook trout hatchery is an abundant supply of cold, clear water, such as is not to be found in every locality, but in the region of the north shore of Lake Superior conditions in this respect are peculiarly favorable. The speckled trout in these waters, moreover, are of the first quality, and this fact together with the actual and potential value of the whole region, but of the Nipigon district in particular, as a resort for speckled trout anglers, not only most undoubtedly singles it out as the logical site for an exten- sive provincial brook trout hatchery, but renders certain also that the initial outlay and running expenses would be more than counterbal- anced by the benefits to be derived from it. There can be no question, in fact, that the first brook trout hatchery of the Province should be established on or in the vicinity of the Nipigon River. Subsequently, additional brook trout hatcheries could be established with advantage in such localities as, for instance, the Algonquin National Park, and cases might also occur in the interior portions of the Province where this fish might be advantageously handled by small branch commercial fish hatcheries in conjunction with lake trout, pickerel or other local fishes; when it was found, in fact, more economical to do so than to transport the ova or fry considerable distances to and from the larger hatcheries, but when the system of hatcheries had once been established in the Province, the cost of the institution and running of these small branch hatcheries would be so inconsiderable that it would impose no appreciable burden on the Provincial Treasury.

In the case of the black bass, which will not allow itself to be stripped of its spawn or milt and consequently cannot be handled by the ordinary means employed in the ordinary commercial fish hatcheries, it would be necessary to establish bass breeding ponds at various points throughout the bass region, for as compared with many other fishes the bass produces but a small number of eggs and the difficulty of obtaining a sufficient supply of fry or fingerlings is, therefore, proportionately increased. Of all the sporting fishes of the Province, however, the black bass is undoubtedly at the present time the most important, not only for the magnificent sport which it affords alike to citizens and visitors, but from the fact that it is unaffected by the onward march of civilization and will continue to thrive in waters surrounded by cleared and cultivated lands in consequence of which, as the more cleared areas are likewise the most densely populated and the most easily accessible, it fills the angling needs of a greater percentage of the provincial population and the visitors from abroad than does any other sporting fish. It is evident, therefore, that the comparatively small expense involved in the establishment and maintenance of a few series of bass breeding ponds through the bass regions of the Province would be more than justified by the importance of the results to be obtained from them. Already in the neighborhood of Brantford one such series of breeding ponds has been established by the Province and the extension of this undertaking to other localities would appear to be most desirable. It is to be noted, however, that as in the case of the commercial fish hatcheries it would in all cases be expedient to determine scientifically the suitability of the site for the hatchery before attempting its establishment.

In regard to the question as to whether the conditions prevailing in waters which have once become depleted will allow of effective restocking, this is plainly a matter for scientific determination. Measures may have to be undertaken, such as the removal of coarse or predaceous fishes, before the plantation of fry or fingerlings would be productive of results, while, again, as in the case of the brook trout, provision might have to be made for shade and a steady flow of the waters before the fish could be expected to thrive, and, further, such matters as the present condition of the aquatic vegetation and the continued prevalence of a sufficient supply of food would have to be taken into consideration, for it is always possible that the local conditions may have altered in these respects, or that gradual changes occurring in regard to them may have played no inconsiderable part in the disappearance of the fish from the waters. It may, perhaps, be interesting to note that in the Adirondacks, since the cultivation of the forest has been seriously undertaken,. resulting not only in the provision of shade but also in a more steady flow of the waters in that region, it has been found possible successfully to reintroduce speckled trout into the headwaters of streams from which this fish had long since disappeared, so that it might, apparently, still be feasible to restock some of the streams and rivers of the less settled portions of central Ontario with this popular sporting fish under careful and adequate direction. Where it is desired to introduce fish, indigenous to the Province, into provincial waters in which they have not previously occurred, the same necessity would exist for a careful scientific investigation, for it is plainly but waste of time, effort and money to plant fish in waters which do not contain suitable food or in which the general environment is unadapted to their life.

The introduction into a country of any new form of wild animal life is fraught with considerable risk and uncertainty, not only in regard to whether the creature will itself thrive under the new conditions, but also in respect of the effect its appearance will have on indigenous species. There are, however, to be found in almost every community those who, in the course of their travels abroad, become enthused with the sporting or edible qualities of some beast, bird or fish, which is not indigenous to their native soil or to the locality in which they live, and without consideration of the results that may ensue or of the feasibility of the experiment, clamor for its introduction into their own district. Undoubtedly even in Ontario, with all its advantages in magnificent fisheries and extensive hunting grounds for wild fowl and larger game, there are localities into which new varieties of sporting creatures could with advantage be introduced, but it would appear safe to say that in general expert opinion should first be obtained as to the advisability of such a measure, particularly so in the case of fish, where the existence of suitable food for all stages of its life can only be ascertained by scientific research.

Two new varieties of fish, at least, have been introduced into provincial waters within the last thirty years, the carp and the rainbow trout, chiefly through the agency of American enterprise. To the former of these a separate section of this report has been devoted, so that it will suffice here to note that not only have such sporting qualifications as it possesses so far been ignored by the citizens of Ontario, but that its excessive and totally unexpected increase in certain localities is held by the majority of sportsmen to have worked considerable havoc both in regard to the sporting fisheries and the wild duck shooting. However this may be, it must at least be acknowledged that there is a substratum of truth to their accusations, and that, consequently, the instance of the carp well emphasizes the dangers which attend the introduction of new varieties of fish into waters already well stocked with fine species and from which no human agency as yet devised can ever entirely remove them. The rainbow trout is a native of the Pacific coast region, and as noted in a previous section is already comparatively abundant in the Canadian waters of the Soo and vicinity, and further, is apparently spreading into other waters which are the habitat of the speckled trout. The comparative sporting qualities of this fish with those of the speckled trout afford material for a divergence of opinion amongst sportsmen, but it would appear in general that the two varieties do not, as a rule, harmonize well, and that, therefore, as the rainbow will usually attain the greater size, it is the speckled trout which is the most likely to suffer. The region of the north shore of Lake Superior is so well furnished with and adapted to speckled trout that no improvement from the point of sport could have been desired other than that these fisheries should have been jealously conserved and maintained to the highest point of abundance. The advent of the rainbow trout, however, will almost certainly have some effect on the speckled trout in this area in the future, particularly in the lower reaches of the rivers which are, as a rule, the warmest and, therefore, the most favorable to its growth, and this fact is to be deplored, for not only is there doubt as to the sporting merits of the rainbow as compared with the speckled trout, but unquestionably the historic sporting qualities of the latter fish render its attractive power in regard to angler visitors vastly greater than those of the less famous rainbow. While plainly nothing can now be done to check its natural encroachment on this region, at least it would appear the part of wisdom not to assist it by permitting any further plantations in Canadian waters throughout this district.

There are cases in the Province of more or less isolated waters destitute of sporting fishes, and other cases, such as the Rainy River District, where the pickerel and lake trout, in none too great abundance, are practically the only high class sporting fishes to be found throughout a considerable area, where the introduction of some sporting variety of fish would be of material advantage to the neighborhood. Undoubtedly in many of such instances scientific research would disclose the possibility of successfully introducing one or other species of game fish to be found either in the Province or without its borders. The ouinaniche of the eastern Provinces, the goldeye of Manitoba, and the cutthroat trout of Alberta are, for instance, game fishes of the highest class and might be used for this purpose where favorable conditions were found to exist in addition to or in preference to provincial varieties.

Indeed, it would appear that a system of interprovincial co-operation might easily be developed whereby supplies of such fish or their spawn, occurring in one Province and desired by another, might be obtained in exchange for other fishes or their spawn produced in that Province. Such a system would plainly be to the benefit of the Dominion and, at the same time, in the best interests not only of economy, but also of sport in the various Provinces. In all cases, however, the material benefits to be derived from the introduction of a foreign species should be clearly established, and its relation to other sporting fishes most fully weighed in the balance before such experiments are attempted.

THE POLLUTION OF WATERS.

}any varieties of fish, but more especially the finer forms, such as the speckled trout and the black bass, will only thrive in such waters as are clean and clear. All varieties of fish are affected in comparatively restricted waters by the introduction into them of noxious chemical matter. The progress of civilization is attended by the appearance of towns and villages on the shores of lakes and on the banks of rivers, from which there will find its way into the waters a greater or less amount of sewage. Fortunately, however, the baneful effects of the dumping of sewage into such restricted waters has become generally recognized, and various methods have been devised for treating it, so that in the case of the larger towns, at least, the waters of the Province should cease to be materially polluted from this source. It is to be noted, however, that in certain localities the presence of quantities of sewage in the water has undoubtedly in the past contributed materially to the disappearance of both the brook trout and black bass, and that even if the weightier considerations of the health of the residents who live below the spot at which the sewage enters did not exist, it would still be of the utmost importance from the point of view alone of the maintenance of the sporting fisheries to check this evil to the uttermost possible extent.

In so far as the fisheries are concerned the most destructive pollution is not, however, as a rule, effected by deposits of sewage, but by waste products of certain factories, highly charged with chemicals and deadly alike to animal and vegetable life, or else, as in the case of sawdust, particularly dangerous to fishes, especially those of the finer and more delicate varieties. There are on the statute book regulations which prohibit the depositing of such matter in the waters of the Province, but unfortunately it has to be recorded that in general these excellent regulations are not strictly enforced; in some cases, even, not enforced at all; with the consequence that material damage continues to be wrought by this means to the sporting fisheries. It would seem, therefore, of the greatest importance that steps should at once be taken to secure the rigid enforcement of the laws in regard to water pollution throughout the Province, and that, as the fault in general lies with companies or individuals in a more or less prosperous condition financially, the penalties for any infringements of these laws should be made proportionately high.

The great resources of Ontario in timber would appear to indicate that in the by no means distant future there will become established in the various sections of the Province large and important paper mills. The localities in which this is the most likely to occur are, as a rule, those in which the rivers that would be largely utilized for driving the logs to the mills contain in abundance some of the finest classes of sporting fishes, and it is to be noted that the waste products of sulphide mills are particularly injurious to fish life. There has, however, been discovered a process of utilizing these waste products, and already in the Adirondacks it has been put into operation in connection with sulphide mills there established. By this process a material is manufactured to which the trade name of glutrin has been given, and which is used for briquetting, moulding and various other purposes. It has, moreover, been successfully demonstrated that, run in connection with a sulphide mill as a by-product, the operating expenses of producing glutrin will be more than covered by the profits, so that it would seem advantageous to give this fact the widest possible publicity amongst those who are at present, or will be in the future, interested in the establishment and operation of paper mills. There can under no circumstances ever be the slightest excuse for permitting the pollution of waters and the consequent destruction of fish by factories which make use of chemicals, for there are in every instance well known methods of destroying and rendering innocuous the waste products which it is a matter of but slight expense to provide for, but especially so is this the case when means are available for converting the waste products into even a slight profit. The harm wrought to the sporting fisheries by the chemical pollution of rivers and streams in the past has been so great and so apparent that it plainly behooves the authorities to see to it that no further damage is effected in this direction, especially in those regions which have hitherto escaped this great evil.

LIMITATION OF CATCH.

In the case of five of the most important sporting fishes of the Province regulations have been enacted by the Dominion Government limiting the numbers of such fishes which may be killed and carried away by any one angler in any one day, and forbidding the killing of fish of less than stated dimensions, the actual measurements varying in each particular case. The fish in question are: The small-mouthed black bass, large-mouthed black bass, mascalonge, speckled trout and pickerel.

It cannot be gainsaid that the limitation of catch is a most wise and necessary precaution to provide against an excessive drain being placed on the sporting fisheries of the Province, for not only are the numbers of the sporting fishes strictly limited in the localities in which angling for them can be enjoyed, but also, although credit must be given to the average sportsman of voluntarily limiting his catch to what he knows can be used, for the sale of these fishes, with the exception of the pickerel, is forbidden, there are always to be found a minority of anglers whose chief aim and ambition is to secure a bag of inordinate size, to the extent, if possible, of establishing a record, quite regardless of whether the fish killed can be used for food or whether they will have to be wasted. In the past, before the enactment of restrictions, great strings of fish of all these varieties were secured by individual anglers within the space of a few hours in various sections of the Province, and the publication of photographs of these hauls and accounts of these exploits in the daily and sporting press undoubtedly fired the imagination and desire of many a would-be record breaker to go and do better if he could. In all probability the Province thus secured a considerable advertisement in the angling circles of the continent, but the price in certain instances was high, for as the population grew and the stream of visitors from outside increased, the finest fisheries gradually showed signs of becoming exhausted, and even the introduction of the limitation of catch has not yet succeeded in effecting their rehabilitation. The practical impossibility of supervising the catch of each individual angler where thousands throughout the Province are out on the waters at the same time is apparent, and it would seem, therefore, that the time has arrived when some steps should be taken officially to put a stop to the publication or display of pictures which represent individual catches of game fishes in excess of the numbers fixed by law, for as before noted some persons will inevitably be incited thereby to seek to emulate or surpass the feat recorded. This cannot but result in material harm to the sporting fisheries which, through the Province at large, are not in such a flourishing condition as to warrant any unnecessary strain being placed upon them. Undoubtedly both the pictorial press and the railways, who have been the chief offenders in this respect, would be only too willing to co-operate with the Government if the matter were properly placed before them, and it would, therefore, seem that steps should at once be taken to this end.

A point has arisen in connection with the clauses dealing with the limitation of catch which has already given rise to considerable discussion and some ill-feeling, and which, although the matter has been referred to the authorities at Ottawa, has not as yet been officially ruled upon. Inasmuch as this question is likely to have a considerable effect on the annual influx of visiting anglers, it is without doubt of great importance to the Province.

The clauses dealing with the limitation of catch of black bass read as follows:

BASS.

(c) No one shall fish for, catch or kill in any of the waters of the Province in one day by angling, or shall carry away a greater number than eight small or large mouthed black bass.

(d) No small or large mouthed black bass less than ten inches in length shall be retained or kept out of the water, sold, offered or exposed for sale or had in possession, but anyone who takes or catches such fish of less than the minimum measurement named, which measurement shall be from the point of the nose to the centre of the tail, shall immediately return such fish to the water from which it was taken, alive and uninjured.

The point at issue is whether the angler must of necessity cease angling when he shall have successfully landed eight fish of legal size, or whether it is legal and within the spirit of the law for him to return such uninjured fish of legal size as he chooses alive to the waters and continue fishing so long as he desires, or until he has actually killed eight fish.

In nearly all good bass waters there are times and occasions when the angler will be fortunate enough not only to find the fish striking greedily at his bait, but also some particular spot in which the fish are congregated thickly. In those waters in which the fish are the most abundant this will occur the more frequently, and these localities are, as a rule, the principal resorts of visiting anglers. To the majority of sportsmen much of the pleasure of angling for black bass lies in the struggle with the fish after it has been hooked. Frequently it will occur that the bass cannot be induced to take the lure through long hours of monotonous angling, so that when patience and persistence are rewarded by the discovery of some spot in which the fish are both abundant and eager to bite, the angler for the nonce is in an earthly paradise and naturally desirous of making the uttermost of his opportunities. On such occasions, however, it is plain that to those who wished to abide by the spirit of the law the period of enjoyment would be most brief if the law is to be interpreted in its apparently literal sense, namely, that it is illegal to " fish for " more than eight fish of the legal size, regardless of whether or not those landed in an uninjured condition have been returned to the waters. When it is considered that the visiting angler, and, in many cases, also the resident of the Province, is put to considerable expense to secure his sport, and, moreover, that the non-resident is charged a fee of $2.00 for angling in provincial waters, it is apparent that visitors and citizens alike will be apt to protest at having their sport for the day curtailed, perhaps, to the short space of one-half hour, more especially when they have not even killed their limit of fish as allowed by law in order to avoid waste. This fact has been well illustrated, indeed, by letters, from non-residents especially, which have appeared in the public press, asking for an interpretation of the law, and declaring that if no more than eight bass of legal size could be angled for, even though the uninjured fish were carefully returned to the waters to furnish sport for themselves or brother anglers on some future occasion, not only would they and their immediate friends, who desired to abide by the spirit of the angling regulations, refrain from angling in the future, or discontinue their annual visits to the Province, as the case might be, but that thousands of others would be similarly affected, thus clearly indicating the great economic factor at stake in the decision of this problem.

The black bass can be captured on a variety of baits, those in most ordinary use being the common trolling spoon with a three hook gang at the rear end, the single hook or, possibly, two small hooks with an angle-worm, minnow or frog attached thereto, and the fly, which is, of course, a single hook. In a great many cases, but more especially when the single hook is being used, the fish will be hooked in the tough membrane of the lip or mouth, and in such instances the hook can be removed without in any way injuring the fish if care is taken first to wet the hand before handling it, the rubbing of a dry hand being liable to cause fungus to appear on the fish if it is subsequently returned to the water. The bass, indeed, is such a hardy fish generally that unless it is hooked in the gills or swallows the bait so that the hook or hooks cannot be removed without injuring the gills, it will suffer no evil effects either from its struggles or from the slight handling that is necessary to release it, and, in fact, has been known beyond dispute to take the bait again within a short period of its return to the water. Hence it will be seen that there would be reasonable grounds for complaint in a regulation which forbade the " fishing for " more than eight fish of legal size where the uninjured fish were carefully returned to the water by the angler.

Undoubtedly it may be argued that there is a danger, if it is deemed lawful for an angler to catch as many bass as he chooses, provided that he does not kill or injure more than the legal limit, thus leaving it to his discretion to decide as to which fish are uninjured, that instances might occur where seriously wounded fish would be thrown back into the water, but it is to be noted that the same danger exists if the angler is restricted to " fishing for " eight fish of legal size, so that it does not materially affect the question. Moreover, in most localities where it would be possible comparatively often to exceed the limit if so desired, which ever way it might be construed, a great proportion of the angling, especially that done by visitors, is carried on under the eyes of licensed guides, who not only by virtue of their licenses are bound to see that the angling laws are obeyed, but have also, as a rule, the additional incentive or personal profit to urge them to do so, seeing that if the fisheries wane, so in proportion will the number of tourists who provide them with such profitable employment. These men, therefore, could in the majority of cases, at least, be counted on to see that injured fish were killed, even if by so doing sport had to be abandoned for the day. It cannot be denied, however, that when angling is carried on with gangs of hooks, the probability of seriously injuring the fish is very much greater than when single hooks are used, and it would seem, there-fore, that while in general there is no likelihood of material injury to the black bass fisheries occurring through the capture of numbers of fish by individual anglers, so be that the uninjured fish are carefully returned to the water and the total kill is not in excess of the legal number, it might be advisable to continue the present presumptive re-striction against " fishing for " more than the legal limit that may be killed when this class of bait is used.

An interesting feature of the present regulations is that while " fishing for " more than eight bass of legal size can be construed as illegal, this provision cannot apparently apply to fish of less than legal size, for, as shown by the clauses previously quoted, special provision is made in regard to these, not only that they are to be returned to the water alive and uninjured, but also that it is illegal to keep or retain them out of the water or to have them in possession. Consequently, it would seem that no matter how many undersized fish an angler might take, nor how many of them he might seriously or mortally injure, he could not under the law retain them out of the water, much less count them as part of his legal kill. This, it must be allowed, is somewhat of an anomaly, for the young fish are, potentially at least, as valuable as the older, and, moreover, the young fish are also likely to be the most delicate and, therefore, the most easily injured. So voracious is the bass that the size of the bait in general use for the larger fish will not deter the smaller fish from taking it, provided that it can get it into its mouth, or in many cases of striking at it even if it cannot, so that espe-cially in trolling with a spoon in localities where bass abound, it is evident what destruction of young bass may easily occur. It is, of course, a wise precaution to limit the size at which fish may be legally taken, but it is obviously of little avail to return fishes of less than legal dimensions to the water only to suffer and die. Rather would it appear that where little bass are injured the law should compel their retention as part of the legal count. Objection might be taken to such a regula-tion as opening the way to the destruction of uninjured, undersized fish by anglers who were unable to secure larger ones, and unquestionably the present regulations were devised to meet this contingency. Doubt-less under the present regulations some undersized fish are illegally killed and retained, and doubtless, also, this would be the case if the regulations were amended as suggested. but the majority of anglers are sportsmen, anxious to abide by the law, and this fact, together with the prevalence of the licensed guide in the districts in which the best fish-ing is to be secured, would seem to afford a guarantee against any such eventuality on a large scale. It might again be argued that it would be a hardship to the angler to compel him to count in his day's limit such small fish as he was unfortunate enough to injure, but the majority of such cases would occur when trolling with a spoon and gang of hooks, and, if it were ruled legal to "fish for" more than the legal number provided the uninjured fish were returned to the water, plainly it would be within the discretion of the angler to change his bait to a single hook and thus greatly minimize the chances of having his sport brought to a premature conclusion owing to the capture and injury of small fishes. In this regard, also, it may be noted that there is on the market to-day a barbless hook which, while possibly not quite so effective as the barbed variety, is none the less highly efficacious. Most of the injuries that fish receive can be directly attributed to the agency of the barb, so that the possession of a few barbless hooks should still further tend to prolong the period of sport open to the angler whose catch is nearing its legal limit.

In regard to brook trout, the restrictions imposed vary from those affecting the black bass in that a weight of fish that may be caught, namely, 10 lbs., is mentioned, while the number of fish that may be killed is placed at thirty and the legal limit of size at six inches, the double restriction as to weight and size having been devised to meet the great difference in dimensions at which the trout will mature under varying conditions. With these exceptions the wording of the regulation is in general precisely similar, and much of what has been written in regard to the black bass applies equally in this case.

The trout can be caught on the fly by trolling with a spoon or other artificial bait, or with the angle-worm or live minnow, and it is plain that some fish will be injured and some uninjured when landed. More-over, there is the same question as to the interpretation of the law in regard to what number of fish may be fished for and whether it is within the spirit of the law to return uninjured fish to the water and to continue angling, although the actual weight or number of fish landed may be in excess of that allowed by law.

The brook trout, however, is in the majority of cases less rugged a fish than the black bass and, in consequence, is more likely to be injured in the process of handling, even though the hand be carefully wetted and every precaution taken. It is not intended in the least to imply that the fish cannot be returned to the waters to live and thrive, for undoubtedly many instances could be adduced to the contrary, but the comparative delicacy of the fish would at all events appear to be an argument in favor of restricting the number of trout which may be " fished for " to the number which may be caught. Another point, also, to be noted in this regard is that in the more populated and accessible portions of the Province where the brook trout does occur, it does not, as a rule, run to a very great size, so that neither from the point of view of the weight or of the numbers which he might legally catch could the angler claim that any undue hardship was being inflicted on him. In fact, only in one section of the Province, the region to the north of Lake

Superior, where the trout sometimes run to a weight of several pounds
and where, consequently, ten pounds of trout might under favorable
conditions be quickly secured, would there appear to be any possible
argument in favor of interpreting the present law other than in its apparently literal sense, or of amending it, and even there the bulk of
the country is so wild that the numbers of anglers who penetrate into
it are comparatively limited, so that there is but a limited capacity for
the consumption of the fish, while, on the other hand, where trout is
required for food purposes, it would be, and actually is, taken without
consideration of the restrictions imposed by law. In certain portions
of this region, where there was adequate supervision, it might perhaps
be advantageous to amend the law as suggested for black bass, but
where adequate supervision in this region cannot be provided and
throughout the remaining portions of the Province it would appear best
in regard to brook trout fishing that the present regulations as to the
weight and numbers of fish that may be caught should remain in force
and be construed in their most literal sense.

In the matter of returning all brook trout of less than six inches
in length to the water, much the same arguments could obviously be
advanced as in the case of the black bass. The problem is not, however,
entirely analogous. While undoubtedly in some little streams where
brook trout exist the fish will mature at six inches, in the bulk of the
brook trout waters of the Province it will attain a considerably larger
size. In those streams where it runs smallest the very size of the fish
will preclude offering it bait other than on a very small hook, while in
other waters where larger trout exist, although it may fall a victim to
the fly in ordinary local use, a trout of less than six inches will, as a
rule, refrain from attempting to swallow such bait as spoons and imitation minnows, the coarse hooks of which frequently cause such serious
injury to the fish, for the very appearance and size of the lure, resembling, in fact, that of some swimming fish, would be calculated to
drive the young trout into shelter, seeing that the larger specimens of
even its own tribe would most gladly devour it, with which fact it is
instinctively well acquainted. Consequently, the bulk of the fish below
legal limit that would be caught would be landed by a small hook lodged
in the tough membrane of the mouth in all probability, and not, as in
the case of the young bass, by impaling themselves more or less severely
on the barbs of larger hooks, for the bass of between eight and ten
inches can plainly, and will, tackle a very much larger bait than ever
could a little trout of between four to six inches. It would seem, therefore, that a higher percentage of the young trout caught than of young
bass should be landed uninjured, and taking all things into consideration, in the case where all the undersized of both varieties had to be
returned to the water regardless of whether they were injured or not, a
higher percentage should, also, live. In addition to this the very nature
of the waters in which young trout are usually most abundant render

them peculiarly easy to fish, much more so than in the case of young bass, so that it is unadvisable to give the slightest loophole for the taking of young fish in quantities, more especially so when it is remembered that even the very little trout are highly prized for the table, and, although the traffic is illegal, command a high price in many localities, a thing which cannot be said of the very small bass. It would, then, on the whole, in the case of brook trout appear to be inexpedient to effect any change in the present law which requires all fish of a less length than six inches to be returned to the water.

But four mascalonge may be killed by an angler in one day, but in regard to this fish it is to be noted that the size of the hook in common use for its capture, as well as the method of taking the bait which is typical of the fish, practically exclude the possibility of returning the larger specimens, at least, uninjured to the water.   In view of these facts, as also that longe grounds are none too plentiful, that in them longe of 10 lbs. are quite frequently to be caught, and that the fish will run to such a size as 40 or 50 lbs., it must be admitted that four fish is an ample bag for one angler in one day.   The angler, therefore, should be satisfied to rest content with the fortune of war in the matter of what sized fish he may succeed in landing, and should not be allowed to " fish for " more than the number of legal sized fish that he is allowed by law to kill.

Mascalonge of less than 24 inches may not be retained, but must be returned alive and uninjured to the water.   A fish of even twenty inches is already of a good size, with a large enough mouth to swallow any ordinary bait, so that it is apparent that so far as injuring the undersized fish is concerned, it is practically without the power of the angler to prevent it.   In fact, in the great majority of cases the small longe will be more or less seriously injured before it can be released from the hook.   Moreover, so vigorous and vicious are even comparatively small specimens of this fish, and so sharp their teeth, that but few anglers would care to attempt to remove the bait from the mouths of any of them without taking the wise precaution of stunning it.   The effect of the blow necessary to accomplish this, added to the almost inevitable wounds accompanying the removal of the bait, render it doubtful whether in the majority of cases the young fish will recover, even though returned to the water, more especially seeing that, while helpless and wounded, it is an easy prey for its enemies, the larger specimens of its own kind and the common pike.   To fulfil the requirements of the law in this respect would appear, then, in general to be impossible.

Trolling for longe over the grounds which it inhabits it is impossible to foretell what sized fish will take the bait.   It would plainly be a hardship to the angler to require him to give over angling when he had secured four small longe under the legal limit, but, on the other hand, it might be urged that some effort should be made to check the waste of young fish and that, after an angler had landed six or eight

11 F.C.

undersized fish, he should be required to cease angling. The majority of longe anglers are, however, out after the large fish, and regard the small fish as a nuisance which they would gladly avoid, and seeing that angling for longe is apt to be a strenuous pleasure if a large fish is hooked and that the spirit of the sport itself is a hard tussle with a strong and vigorous fish, only those who enjoy the exercise of a prolonged and exhausting fight will in general indulge in it to any extent. To obtain this sport many of them will have come from afar and will have but a limited time at their disposal to enjoy it, so that in as much as the majority of them can be counted on not to cause any undue waste by deliberately angling for undersized fish, it would appear inexpedient to penalize them to the extent of forcing them to abandon angling for the day should they be unfortunate enough to hook and land a few undersized fishes which, after all, would afford them but poor sport for the money they were expending. It would seem, therefore, best in the case of the undersized mascalonge to allow the present law to stand unaltered in its literal sense.

Finally in regard to pickerel, the catch of which is limited to twelve, and the legal size placed at fifteen inches, it is to be noted that in the majority of waters in which pickerel are to be found it will not often occur that more than twelve of the fish of legal size will be taken in a reasonable day's angling, for it lives, as a rule, in the deeper waters and trolling for it over a considerable area is the only and somewhat uncertain means of securing it. There are, of course, exceptional instances of localities in which it is particularly abundant, where angling for it can be carried on successfully from the shore, or catches in excess of the legal number made within a short space of time, but even in such cases the bait most frequently in use would be the trolling spoon or imitation minnow, with its gangs of hooks, and consequently, although a very hardy and robust fish, it would be liable very often to suffer material injury when the bait was being removed, even had it escaped serious damage while in the water. In view of these facts, and seeing that the capture of twelve of as sporting a fish as the pickerel, of a greater length than fifteen inches, should under any circumstances be considered a good day's sport by anyone, it would seem advisable that angling operations should be brought to a close when the legal limit has been landed, even though, perchance, some specimens may have been returned uninjured to the water.

In regard to the question of returning the undersized fish to the water, it is plain that where they swallow a bait intended for a larger fish they will be all the more likely to be seriously injured. On the other hand, the danger of catching great quantities of such undersized fishes would not appear to be great, except, perhaps, in isolated instances, so that as the loss to the fisheries would not be very serious even in the event of a large percentage of those returned to the water subsequently dying, it would, perhaps, be more advantageous to allow the present law to stand than to attempt to amend it.

A feature peculiar to the pickerel fisheries is that the pickerel is the only fish in the Province, recognized alike as a commercial and sporting variety, on which a limitation of catch is imposed in regard to anglers. It is evident that in those localities where commercial netting and angling are carried on side by side, the angler has just cause to complain of any restriction being imposed on his catch when no such restriction affects the commercial net fisherman, whose operations are, as a rule, by far the most deadly. As pointed out previously, however, the pickerel has only of recent years come to be recognized as a sporting fish of high class in this Province, and doubtless the limitation of catch imposed by law was introduced to meet the needs of certain restricted waters where the pickerel was the leading sporting fish, and where, as a rule, no commercial netting was being conducted. In such cases it is plainly necessary to limit the number of fish which may daily be removed by any one angler. The pickerel is, of course, a fish of the highest commercial value, and in view of this fact, as also that it is largely a deep water fish, it would evidently be inexpedient generally to bar its commercial exploitation in the waters of the great lakes, but having regard to the rapid advance in popularity of the fish amongst citizen anglers and the indisputable attraction it possesses for American visitors, it would seem that, as pointed out in a previous section, the time has perhaps arrived when commercial netting for it should not be permitted outside of the waters of the great lakes, or at least in those localities where it affords sport to a large number of either citizens or visitors.

MINNOW SEINES.

One of the best baits for small or large mouthed black bass, pickerel and speckled trout is the minnow, which is one of the natural foods of the fishes. There is, in consequence, a great demand for minnows in most parts of the Province in which anglers from within and without congregate during the summer months. At the present time the law forbids the seining of minnows other than under license, and the angler who desires to make use of the little fishes as bait must either secure them from some person who possesses a seining license, or else capture them himself by some other means, such as a small dip net. The minnow seine license costs $5.00, entitling the licensee to 30 feet of seine net and, as for bait purposes the live minnow is greatly superior to the dead, it is usual for those holding these licenses to possess some form of minnow pail in which they store the minnows pending a demand for them, eventually retailing them to the angler at prices varying from one to three cents per fish.

There are in this Province a great variety of small fishes which never attain a length of more than two or three inches and which are commonly styled minnows, but, broadly speaking, it may be said that the minnow when free in the water is lively, active and wary, only abounding in such shallow places where food is plentiful, so that for practical purposes it is impossible for the majority of anglers to secure a sufficiency of them without having recourse to some holder of a minnow seine license, for not only are their favorite haunts frequently at some distance from the town or village, but even when these have been reached, the dip net will prove too cumbersome a weapon to effect the capture of more than a stray specimen or two sufficiently large to be suitable for angling purposes.

Thus it will be seen that the possession of a minnow seine license is of considerable pecuniary value to the holder, for a species of local monopoly is created and, as the demand increases, so can the charge in proportion if the licensee so desires, for there is no restriction placed on the price at which the little fishes may be retailed. Moreover, the supply available will depend largely on the energy of the licensee. In various instances it has occurred that the local supply of minnows was greatly below the demand, which appeared to be due either to the laziness of the licensee or to his unwillingness to pay for adequate help, and in such cases not only are the complaints of the anglers most vigorous, but also those of hotel keepers and merchants generally who are interested in the summer tourist traffic, for it is apparent to them that such conditions are not favorable even to a maintenance of the trade, but, on the contrary, are calculated to damage it materially. The price, also, in such cases will almost invariably soar, for there will, as a rule, be found one or two individuals prepared to pay without after-thought any sum, provided only they get what they require, and this entails a hardship on the generality of anglers whose funds are not unlimited, and cannot but be prejudicial in its effect on the tourist traffic in the district. It is plain that where during three or four months of the year there are a number of anglers anxious to purchase one or two dozen minnows six days in the week, the possession of a license should net the licensee from $2.00 to $4.00 or more per diem, and, moreover, unlike the guide whose license costs $2.00 and whose wages average from $2.00 to $3.00 per diem, so long as there are anglers, so long will his trade be steady and continuous, for it is independent of the personal caprice of the individual angler or of popular reputation. If, therefore, the licensee discovers that by raising the price of his minnows he can continue to make an undiminished income with considerably less effort to himself, or at less expense if he engages help, it is quite likely that he will be tempted to do so without regard to those whom he is injuring by so doing. It would, of course, be possible by issuing more than one license to a locality to create competition, and thus not only keep prices down but at the same time ensure a sufficient supply to meet the local demand. The main objections to such a course are, however, that in by far the greater number of cases there is only enough work in this line adequately to compensate one man who makes a genuine business of it, taking into consideration the help that he might have to hire and the time that he would have to devote to it, and, secondly, that it would tend to an undue destruction of small fishes, which are one of the main foods of many of the best sporting fishes, for each licensee would be careful always to have an abundant supply in order not to lose his proportion of the trade, and the minnows cannot be retained alive in captivity for very long periods.

It would seem, therefore, that so long as the seining of minnows can only be legally conducted under license special care should be taken to ascertain that the licensees are supplying the needs of the public to the best of their ability, and not to re-issue a license to any man who through lack of energy or for other reasons within his control fails to produce a supply equal to the demand or abuses his privilege by the imposition of exorbitant charges.

Already the expenses of the angler visitors are by no means inconsiderable, including as they often do not only board, but the hire of one or more guides, oarsmen, canoes, boats, launches, etc., and it becomes, therefore, a question whether it is really advisable to place the additional burden upon them of forcing them to purchase their minnows. In any event there would always be those who preferred to do so rather than take the trouble themselves, so that there would always be likely to be some trade in this direction. It would, as a rule, seem impracticable for the guides, the major part of whose day is spent on the waters with the anglers, to undertake to provide minnows, and, consequently, an independent individual would apparently be enabled to carry on the business at a profit. There are, however, many anglers to whom expense is a great consideration, who would much prefer to take the trouble of securing their own bait, seeing that by so doing they would save several dollars a week, and as these constitute as high a percentage as, perhaps, a half of the total number of anglers, their interests should plainly be considered.

The main reason for the introduction of the minnow seine license was to prevent, in so far as possible, the destruction of fish of immature varieties, it being held that the average angler was not sufficiently expert to distinguish between such and the true minnows. Undoubtedly this is the case, but, on the other hand, it is questionable whether the average licensee under the present system is any more competent. The centralizing of the capture of minnows, however, renders supervision by government officials comparatively easy, or at least is calculated to do so, so that the present system is plainly advantageous in that respect, but it is to be noted that no real effort has ever as yet been made to determine what proportion of young fishes of valuable species are likely to be caught among minnows where small lengths of seine net are employed. It cannot be denied that the present system entails hardship on many anglers, and, moreover, it is to be remembered that in many of the wilder districts, where it will not pay an individual to purchase a minnow seine license, there are none the less often a proportion of anglers who, if they desire minnows, will practically be forced to break the law. It would appear, therefore, expedient to make some effort to ascertain what the extent of the danger to the young of valuable sporting and other fishes may be from the use of limited lengths of seine net for the purpose of catching bait; whether, in fact, that danger which was mainly responsible for the introduction of the present law is not more imaginary than real. To establish this beyond dispute it would be necessary to make extensive investigations throughout the Province. The fact that the majority of licensees maintain minnow pails would afford a means of determining the extent of the damage now being wrought, if the pails were to be examined by an expert icthyologist, and, as the number of licenses is comparatively limited, it would plainly be possible for an expert not only to inspect a high proportion of them in the course of a few months, but at the same time to attend the actual seining operations and form a reliable opinion on the number of young and valuable fishes that are on the average liable to be thus secured. The Province is fortunate in numbering among its citizens an icthyologist of the highest rank, Mr. C. W. Nash, and it would seem that the importance of the issue at stake would more than warrant the expense that would be incurred by securing his services to make a report on this question, which only an expert could ever properly decide. Should such an investigation be carried out and the danger to the immature of valuable species was found to be but slight, it is beyond dispute that it would be most advisable to amend the present law to the extent of permitting the individual angler the use of some feet of minnow seine net for the purpose of securing his own bait, and under such circumstances it would probably be found necessary to reduce the cost of the minnow seine license, used for commercial purposes, very considerably.

THE NON-RESIDENT ANGLER'S LICENSE.

The non-resident angler's tax has proved of value from two points of view, firstly in producing a considerable direct revenue to the Province, and secondly as affording some index of the numbers of visitors to the Province from without who engage in angling and who may, therefore, be deemed to have been influenced in their decision to visit the Province on account of the sport to be obtained there. There would seem to be almost unanimity of opinion among the angler tourists that the tax is both just and reasonable provided only that the money thus collected is devoted to the purpose of conserving the sporting fisheries and thus providing them with good sport. The collection of the tax, however, still leaves much to be desired, for as noted in the Interim Report of this Commission there is no question that a number of non-residents do not at present pay, either because they are not approached by the official empowered to collect it, or because they remain in ignorance of the existence of the tax. The great majority of the visiting anglers enter the Province by rail, and board at some hotel or lodging house for at least a portion of their time. A percentage of the $2.00 tax is at present paid to the official who collects it and in some districts forms no inconsiderable part of his income. If, however, the government officials received adequate remuneration, there could be no hardship in enlarging the numbers of those entitled to issue the licenses and collect the percentage, and, as the railways, hotels and boarding houses handle the bulk of the traffic, there would seem to be no possible objection to throwing open the issuance of the non-resident anglers licenses to them. In fact, it would appear highly advantageous to do so, for by this means undoubtedly a far higher percentage of visitors would pay the fee than at present, seeing that a far greater number of persons would be directly interested in its collection. Moreover, the railways, and the majority of hotel and boarding house proprietors, are financially trustworthy, and could be relied on to carry on the work under whatever system was adopted.

GANGS OF HOOKS.

In the proposed regulations affecting the international fisheries of the great lakes provision is made against the use of artificial baits with more than three hooks, or more than one burr of three hooks, attached thereto. At the present time the variety of artificial baits on the market is very great, and unfortunately there has developed a tendency in certain instances to furnish the lure with a great quantity of hooks or gangs of hooks. Lures thus equipped are plainly most destructive, for if the fish but approaches it is liable to be hooked in some portion of the body and in its struggles other hooks will almost certainly gain a hold. Such methods of angling cannot be deemed sporting, for not only do they almost annihilate the chances of the fish to escape once it has been hooked, but also tend to minimize the play which the fish can afford the angler. More especially is this the case with the smaller sporting fishes, such as the black bass and speckled trout, and even in angling for larger fishes such as the lake trout and mascalonge there can be no necessity for the employment of such deadly engines, for one large hook firmly embedded is, as a general rule, sufficient to land a fish, and in any event one gang of three hooks should be ample to accomplish this end even with fishes of the greatest weight and activity. It would seem, therefore, that throughout the waters of the Province no artificial bait should be permitted to be used which has more than three hooks, or to which is attached more than one gang of three hooks.

RECOMMENDATIONS.

Your Commissioner would, therefore, recommend:—

(1) That no commercial net fishing, or net fishing of any description other than minnow seining for bait purposes, be permitted in the

waters of the Province within five miles of any city or town, this provision, however, not to apply to the use of dip nets by anglers or to the
removal of undesirable fishes by government officials.

(2) That the following areas be considered sporting fish reserves
and that no commercial net fishing or net fishing other than minnow
seining for bait purposes be permitted in them, this provision not to
apply to the use of dip nets by anglers or to the removal of carp, suckers
or other too prevalent coarse or predaceous fishes by Government officials or under direct governmental supervision:

The Rideau Lake System, the Bay of Quinte west of the bridge at
Belleville and including Wellers Bay and Hay Bay; an area at the
entrance to the St. Lawrence River bounded on the west by a line drawn
from the south westerly extremity of Wolfe Island to the easterly
extremity of Amherst Island and thence northerly to the western end
of Collins Bay, and on the east by a line drawn from the eastern
extremity of Amherst Island to the town of Gananoque; the Kawartha
Lakes; Rondeau Bay and Long Point Bay in Lake Erie; Lake Simcoe;
Muskoka Lakes; Lake Nipissing and French River; River Thames;
Lake of the Woods within fifteen miles radius of Kenora; and the district in the Georgian Bay defined by the Dominion Government Georgian Bay Fisheries Commission and recommended by it for the purpose
of a sporting fish reserve.

(3) That the artificial propagation of all classes of sporting fishes
be undertaken by the Government; that of lake trout, pickerel, mascalonge and coarser fishes in conjunction with the commercial hatcheries
already recommended; that of brook trout by the erection of a special
hatchery on or in the vicinity of the Nipigon River and subsequently,
if necessary, in other districts; and that of black bass by the institution
of a system of bass breeding ponds at various points throughout the
bass region.

(4) That the exact location for a brook trout hatchery or for a
system of bass breeding ponds be determined by a duly qualified scientific icthyologist.

(5) That special attention be paid to the waters of the sporting
fish reserves, above recommended, and of provincial forest reserves, in
regard to assuring and maintaining an abundance of the best class of
sporting fishes in them.

(6) That where a demand arises for the introduction into any of
the Provincial waters of a fish, either indigenous to other portions of
the Province or from without the Provincial borders, which has not
hitherto inhabited the same, scientific examination of such waters be
made to ascertain their suitability before any experimental plantations of the particular variety of fish is made; and that it be part of
the duties of the Scientific Research Department, previously recommended to be established, to conduct such examinations, to supervise,
where necessary, the experimental plantations, and to endeavour to

stock with suitable varieties of sporting fishes such waters in the access-ible portions of the Province as are at present devoid of them.

(7) That steps be taken to secure the co-operation of the public press and of the railways in regard to the suppression of illustrations, photographs or narratives depicting the capture by individuals of more than the legal limit of any variety of fish.

(8) That steps be taken to secure an amendment to the present laws in relation to the numbers of black bass that may be caught in one day by one angler, and as to the disposal of black bass of less than legal size, to the end that it be declared legal when fishing with a fly or single hook to return uninjured fish to the water and to continue fish-ing until the legal limit has been killed; that bass less than legal size which have been injured in the process of catching or landing or subse-quently by handling be retained by the angler and counted as fish in the total of his legal catch; and that the legal limit of catch for black bass be raised to ten fish.

(9) That especial care be taken in the speckled trout region to the north of Lake Superior, when timber limits are being leased, to maintain at least a fringe of trees along the banks of trout streams and rivers, sufficient to afford the shade necessary to the fish's existence and to prevent any undue raising of the temperature of the waters in sum-mer months; and that, if possible, the regular waterflow of such streams and rivers be conserved by maintaining around their headwaters an adequate belt of forest.

(10) That a special patrol officer be appointed in the spring of 1911 whose sole duty shall consist of watching and inspecting the mouths and lower reaches of the rivers and streams entering the northern borders of Lake Superior with a view to checking the illegal netting at present being conducted in these waters, and that the said officer be provided with sufficient funds to enable him to hire what trans-portation he requires wheresoever he needs it in order efficiently to dis-charge his duties.

(11) That for the present no further plantations of rainbow trout or other imported trout be allowed to be made in the Canadian waters of Lake Superior or Georgian Bay or in the rivers and streams draining into them.

(12) That steps be taken to secure an amendment to the present regulations in regard to mascalonge fishing to the effect that hand trolling for this fish be prohibited and rod and line angling be enacted the only legal method of capture.

(13) That in all lakes of less area than 20 miles square the com-mercial exploitation of pickerel and lake trout be prevented in the future.

(14) That throughout the waters of the Province the use of any bait furnished with more than three hooks or one gang of three hooks be declared illegal.

(15) That the services of a competent scientific icthyologist be secured to make an investigation during the angling season of 1911 as to the extent of damage, if any, wrought to the fisheries of the Province under the present system of minnow seine licenses by the capture of the immature of sporting or other valuable fishes, and as to the probable effect in this direction of permitting individual anglers the use of a few feet of minnow seine, and to render a report to the Government on these subjects.

(16) That the law in relation to the pollution of waters by factories and mills be most rigidly enforced throughout the Province and that steps be taken to have the penalty for deliberate violation of this provision raised to a sum of not less than $500.

(17) That the issuance of non-resident anglers' licenses be placed in the hands of transportation companies and reputable hotel and boarding house proprietors, in addition to the government overseers, and that the present percentage as paid to the government overseer be paid for each license to the issuer of the same.

(18) That steps be taken to secure from hotel and boarding house proprietors lists of non-resident and resident tourists visiting their houses each year, in order that reasonably accurate statistics of the extent of the tourist traffic may be secured.

THE PROVINCIAL FOREST RESERVES, GA 1 E AND FUR-BEARING ANI 1 ALS.

THE FORESTS.

In discussing the problems connected with the Provincial Forest Reserves, the game and fur-bearing animals it is clearly impossible to avoid touching generally on the forests of the Province, for not only do these afford shelter to the bulk of the big game and much of the small game and fur-bearing animals, but also, as they are conterminous in many instances with the Provincial Parks, matters affecting them as a whole must exercise an equal influence over the adjoining Parks.

The great value of the forests is gaining yearly in recognition. The marked rise in the price of timber, the enormous and increasing demand for pulpwood to be manufactured into paper, and the threatened shortage of supplies in this direction in the United States, have all combined to call attention to the wonderful resources of Ontario, and to their actual intrinsic worth. The diminution in the waterflow of rivers and streams in those sections of the Province denuded of their forests has but helped to accentuate the lessons to be learned from the unfortunate experiences of Spain, France and China, that the even flow of rivers and streams is dependent to a very large extent on the existence of forests about their headwaters; that the rainfall and climate are both materially affected by the removal of the forests; and that, as agriculture depends on the water supply, and agricultural exploitation of the land is the backbone of national prosperity, the conservation of the forests is of the most vital importance to the population at large. The rapid developments also in the utilization of waterpowers and the certainty that as fuel becomes scarcer waterpower will have to take its place for many purposes have undoubtedly very materially added to the importance of the forests which are, as it were, the custodians of the springs from which these waterpowers draw their sources.

While the wise general policy of the present administration of the Province in regard to the forests indicates clearly that these matters have received and are still receiving the careful and weighty consideration they deserve, it is none the less doubtful whether the general public has as yet become alive to their vast significance, both in the present and in regard to the near and distant future. It would seem, indeed, that the efforts of the Canadian Commission of Conservation and Canadian Forestry Association to this end might well be augmented by the publication and distribution of literature and general dissemination of knowledge on this subject broadcast throughout the Province at provincial expense, for so long as the general public remains ignorant of the vast values at stake, so long will it remain doubtful whether a sufficiency of funds will ever be provided to safeguard and ensure the perpetuation of the forests, whereas, when once the public had become fully seized of the economic functions of the forests in addition to their actual intrinsic value, it cannot be doubted that public demand would ensure the provision of ample funds for their proper conservation, exploitation and general management.

Forestry is an art of the highest order, and in view of the causes before mentioned, an art that is becoming yearly of greater importance. The fundamental basis of its teaching is that the forests, if properly administered, are not a fleeting but a permanent asset to the nation, and that to regard or treat them as anything else than permanent is the rankest of folly. Naturally, on a continent so abundantly furnished with magnificent forests as America, it took a considerable number of years for these basic truths to be preceived and acknowledged even by the administrations, but the laws of nature operate the same the world over, and that which wanton and extravagant wastefulness had taught the older nations of Europe years before came at last to be impressed on thinking people in America also. Fortunately the havoc wrought by improper methods of cutting and of administration of the timber resources has not as yet affected the vast bulk of the provincial timber areas. Of the 140,000,000 of acres comprising the total area of the Province there is still unsurveyed approximately 94,000,000 acres, and while 24,000,000 acres have been alienated by sales, locations, etc., there still remains vested in the Crown 116,000,000 acres, much of which is covered with valuable timber. Under the wise policy of the present administration no township is thrown open to settlement without careful inspection by a competent official, and if such township is found to contain less than 40 per cent. of good land, it is withheld from settlement for the growing of timber, thus largely checking the evil, so prevalent at one time, of allowing people to take up rough land, ostensibly for farming purposes but actually for the value of the timber on it, the land being thus withdrawn from the operation of the timber license for all timber excepting pine, and consequently depreciating the value of a timber license in the district without compensatory benefit to the public, for, when the supposititious settler had removed the timber, he departed, leaving the land shorn of its trees and unimproved in other respects.

At the present time it is estimated that the timber resources of the Province attain a value of three or four hundred million dollars. This, of course, is merely a rough approximation, based on the material value of the woods on the market, and takes no account of the indirect value of the standing forests. Were these to be taken into consideration also, including the natural or economic irrigation of opened lands or of lands unopened, the actual or potential value of all waterpowers in the Province, the rainfall and the climate, it will be seen that the intrinsic worth of the forests to the Province would be a sum so gigantic as to be almost incalculable. So vital, indeed, is this asset that almost any expenditure would be warranted in order to perpetuate and preserve it.

Unfortunately the forests are not immune from dangers. Fires, disease and other scourges are liable to attack them. In addition to this, the growth to maturity of a tree is always a lengthy process; in the case, indeed, of many of the more valuable species occupying a period of time in excess of the average human span of life; so that if fire or disease is allowed to run unchecked, or if the cutting is carried to such excess that natural reseeding becomes impracticable, it is apparent not only how greatly the forest asset may be quickly impaired, but also that many years will be required to make good the damage effected even under the most favourable circumstances. It is apparent, therefore, that it cannot but be the part of wisdom to take sufficient precautions to reduce the risks of fire or other scourges to a minimum and to adopt such measures as will prevent excessive cutting.

The temptation to a licensee or owner of a timber limit to take the utmost profit in the shortest possible time without regard to the future is plainly great, and, indeed, in some countries such as Germany and Sweden it has in consequence been held better in the public interests that the State should administer and exploit the forests rather than risk their destruction or depletion through individual greed or incapacity. In a forest there will be found trees of all ages, and it is obvious that, no matter how long it may take trees to mature, if the percentage of cut is adjusted to the normal growth, an area of forest will continue to yield at least an even production of timber, the value only varying as the market price rises or falls. Under scientific management, however, it has actually been proved feasible very materially to increase the annual production of a forest. In 1865 the average yield of 7,000,000 acres of Prussian forests was approximately 24 cubic feet, affording an average revenue of 72 cents per acre; in 1904 the average yield had been increased to 65 cubic feet, affording an average revenue of $2.50 per acre. Indeed, not only does the rate of production in Prussian forests appear to have been almost trebled in 75 years, but the quality, also, to have been improved, seeing that the proportion of saw lumber has increased from 19 per cent. to 54 per cent., while the yearly revenue from this source is now upwards of $17,000,000. Whether under any system by which timber limits are thrown open to public tender it will ever be possible to regulate the cut to achieve the result of taking only the normal increase, is doubtful, for naturally the licensee looks only to the profits to be derived from his venture and has no further personal interest in the forests after the expiration of his license. Indeed, so systematic and methodical must the cutting be to ensure only the proper amount being taken that it cannot be doubted but that, except in exceptional instances, the State, unaffected and unbiassed by considerations of personal gain, is alone capable of carrying such policy into effect. Moreover, it must be remembered that the adequate protection of the forests from fire and other scourges, and the proper regulation of the amounts to be cut, will under any system entail a considerable expenditure. The necessity for these precautions is now widely acknowledged, the only obstacle, in fact, being in most cases the wherewithal to put them into effect on a sufficiently great scale. Such expenditures are obviously but a reasonable insurance premium on a vast but destructible asset, and yet so long as the public is not fully seized of the national significance of the forests, so long will there be hesitation and diffidence in embarking on increased investments in this direction. At present the actual amount spent annually in the Province on this form of insurance is but a fraction of a mill of the material worth of the forests as wood, but a small fraction, indeed, of the yearly revenue derived from the forests, and it cannot be doubted that a far greater sum could with reason be allocated yearly for the study, care, management and protection of the provincial forests if they are to continue to exist and to afford a steady, indeed a constantly increasing, revenue to the Province.

Perhaps the solution of the difficulty is to be found in the principle of state exploitation of these resources on an increasing scale. The timber area of the Province is so vast that at present, at least, there would be no necessity to put an end to the existing policy of placing some of the timber limits under license to private individuals, but were the Government itself to undertake the exploitation of a proportion of its limits and gradually expand its enterprise in this direction, it cannot be questioned that an annually materially increasing revenue would result, more than sufficient amply to provide for a forestry service adequate to the needs and worthy of the Province. That such a service is needed is beyond dispute. A vast field is open to scientific research and management throughout the forests, to the reforestration of burnt areas and to seeding or planting in sections barren of trees, and an equally vast field to the organization of a staff, not only capable of enforcing such laws and regulations as may be in force, but able, also, to cope successfully with disease and fire wheresoever they may occur.

FOREST FIRES.

Almost every year there has, unfortunately, to be recorded some material damage to the forests of the Province through the destructive agency of fires, and all too frequently there is chronicled in accompaniment the loss of other valuable property, occasionally, even, of human lives. The terrible forest fires which occurred in several of the western States of the Union during the summer of 1910 would alone have been sufficient to mark the year as disastrous in this respect and to have called widespread attention to the danger of allowing conflagrations of this nature to outstrip the possibilities of human control, but, as though this was not sufficient, the fires which had raged in the western portions of the Province and across the border in that vicinity intermittently throughout the summer months, suddenly sprang into renewed life in Minnesota in the early fall and, swept forward by a powerful wind, carried death and destruction before them right to the provincial borders, where in spite of the protection of the broad Rainy River men had to labour both day and night to save provincial habitations and enterprises from utter annihilation. The appalling suddenness of this holocaust and its proximity to the Province brought the disastrous nature of it closely home to the citizens of Ontario, and it cannot be doubted afforded an excellent object lesson of the inexpediency of penurious provision for the protection of the forests against fire.

To the average man, no doubt, the reading of the destruction of miles of standing forests conveys but little of its true significance. He can hardly appreciate the gigantic figures arrayed before him as to the square feet of timber burnt or the estimated value of the same in millions of dollars. He may, perhaps, be aghast at the loss of life or suffering and hardships endured by those who were fortunate enough to escape the flames. He may even dimly realize that these people have lost their homes, their possessions, their all. But the effects on nature are as a closed book to him. He has not seen; he cannot understand.

The stately forest, stretching unbroken for miles, harbours countless wild animals, birds and insects. Life, indeed, is seething in it. The soil on which it stands is nursed and enriched by its fallen foliage and trees, which in many instances cover even the bare rocks sufficiently to allow of the seeds taking root right over them and which form always a natural basin where the rain drops may fall and accumulate, to percolate subsequently into the crevices of the rocks, from which again they will appear in the form of a gushing spring. Just as on the even outpouring of the spring will depend the flow of the brook, the stream and the river, so does the spring itself depend on the existence of its damp and mossy forest reservoir for its waters. The forest fire is capable of destroying all; animals, birds, insects, vegetation and soil. The voice of the forest is hushed, and the death of the trees is not only accompanied by the annihilation of one of nature's great water storages, so vital to the prosperity of some, perhaps far-distant, agricultural community, but by the disappearance of an important factor in the regulation of both climate and rainfall over a considerable region.

The picture of a forest destroyed by fire almost baffles description in its appalling horror. Unrelieved by the accustomed sounds, the cheerful note of songbirds, the chirruping of squirrels or chipmunks, the calls of animals or the humming of insects, deathly silence reigns oppressive and supreme. Great trees and small trees alike, black, bare and gaunt, stand shivering as the breeze soughs a mournful dirge through their ranks, ghastly skeletons of nature's once beautiful handiwork, or else lie prostrate on the ground, charred, burnt and shrivelled, grim spectres of a useful past, proclaiming the passage of ruthless death, the advent of desolation and decay. No butterfly or moth flutters over the withered and blackened leaves; no little creature or insect crawls from among them, startled by the approaching footfalls. Far down into the accumulation of twigs and decaying vegetation which has formed the forest bed, into the mossy and spongy soil which in the past has held water to furnish life to the trees growing on it, the relentless fire has eaten its way and left in its train a mass of useless cinder from which all nutriment has been utterly scorched. The human visitor to this tragic scene will have himself alone for company; will hear his own breathing; will be conscious of his own heartbeats; will be almost terrified at the sounds of his own footsteps; for life has been extinguished, the silence of the grave will surround him, and it will seem almost sacrilege to break the all-pervading quiet of the dead. In due course the action of the winds will blow away the cinders, and the bare rocks, over which once grew the forest, will be exposed to view in all their unbeautiful and grim nakedness, and the region will remain barren and in all probability useless to man's welfare until, perhaps, after the lapse of centuries nature once again shall have succeeded with indomitable patience in recovering the rocks with a fresh soil.

The extent of the havoc wrought by a forest fire depends in great measure, of course, on the conditions prevailing at the time of its occurrence, but generally speaking the greatest harm is effected during periods of prolonged drought, for then, not only are the trees and shrubs parched and their foliage likely to be withered and dry, but the debris of the forest on the ground, the grass, the moss and the very soil are like so much tinder to the flames. So long as the soil is damp and full of moisture the damage done by fire will be confined to the standing trees and a certain amount of animal and insect life. Indeed, it is possible under such conditions for an area to be burnt over more than once and yet not suffer irreparable injury, for unless a high wind prevails at the time some trees will almost always escape with little or no damage, and if the withered trees are removed, which can be done to commercial advantage if undertaken promptly before decay sets in, reseeding will be accomplished naturally, for the soil will not have been seriously affected. Where, however, the soil is once destroyed, human agencies are powerless to replace it and the harm is in consequence irreparable. It is impossible to foretell the extent of the damage that a fire in any particular region will cause, for it depends so greatly on the condition of the forest at the time when the fire occurs, and similarly it is impossible to foresee the extent of a forest conflagration which has once got well under way, for it will depend chiefly on such matters as wind and rain which are altogether beyond human control.

The causes of fire are many and various, natural and human agencies both playing their parts in initiating them, but it is at least evident that, since the smallest beginning may result in untold damage over enormous areas if not promptly checked, the time has come when provision should be made to stamp out the fires wheresoever they occur in accessible portions of the Province before they shall have had time to gain leeway and spread, for once the fire has succeeded in covering a wide stretch of country and is being fanned by a wind, or has a hold of the soil, even with abundant help and ample appliances it is a matter of practical impossibility for man to check it. The sparks from the tree tops will fly through the air to the front and to the sides, igniting whatever they may chance to light upon; the flame in the soil will eat its way unperceived and underground for considerable distances, smoldering slowly so that perchance men may imagine that it has been extinguished, only to break out again at some fresh spot where a dry or withered root affords it an opportunity of bursting into flame. The only way, indeed, to deal satisfactorily with forest fires is to extinguish them at their birth, but to make arrangements to do so over so vast an area as that covered by the provincial forests cannot but be a great and expensive undertaking. There can, however, be no doubt that the value of the forests will warrant every effort that may be made in this direction.

As before noted the forest fires may be originated by human or natural agencies. The latter, however, is in all probability a comparatively rare occurrence. In the majority of cases man is directly responsible. Right through the heart of the forests he has carried roads, along which speed great engines of steel and iron, driven by steam, belching out sparks as they fly along. Other railroads are in course of construction and great gangs of men, a large percentage of whom are foreigners barely able to speak the language of the country and with little or no personal stake in it, are employed throughout the summer months, building them. All around them is forest. Fires are built for this purpose or that; tobacco in all its various forms is smoked; matches are continually being struck and carelessly thrown away; while the incipient fire resulting from any of these causes may easily pass unobserved or unchecked by those in authority who cannot be everywhere at once and have other important matters to attend to. On these construction lines, however, perhaps the most dangerous of all agents in the matter of fire is the "jumper," the man who not being over fond of work joins a camp for a few days and then betakes himself leisurely to the next along the right of way. These individuals are as a rule not only shiftless but careless. Walking along the right of way they smoke their cigarettes in enjoyment of the beautiful surroundings, tossing the ends aside into bracken with the utmost unconcern of possible eventualities, or else, wearying, perhaps, of the monotony of solitude, they build themselves a little smudge to keep off the flies while they sleep or to boil a pan of tea, and after thus refreshing themselves move on again, not thinking to stamp out the smudge, but leaving it to take care of itself. Then again prospectors are here, there and everywhere throughout the forests, lighting their camp fires and smudges, smoking their pipes, practically beyond supervision of government officials; the Indian is on the trail for one purpose or another, unconcerned and somewhat fatalistic as to consequences from fires left burning; the tourist and pleasure seeker, both citizen and visitor, all too frequently thoughtless in action, are in the woods in considerable numbers precisely at those periods of the year when conditions are most favourable for a forest conflagration; and finally, the dwellers in the forest, the settlers who have built their little homes therein, are not altogether beyond reproach in the matter of maintaining precautions against fire either when clearing land or when burning waste material. In addition it must also be recorded that, if dame rumor is not altogether at sea, there are certain individuals so debased and shameless that they will deliberately set fire to certain forest areas in order to force the hands of the government in the matter of throwing the limits open to the lumberman. Small wonder, then, when all these things are considered, that forest fires should occur yearly. Indeed, the only marvel would appear to be that they are not more frequent or more serious.

So great is the potential harm that may arise out of an inadvertent act or temporary carelessness in the woods that it would seem only just that wherever the origin of a forest fire can be traced to an individual, that individual should be made to suffer punishments and penalties commensurate at least with the damage wrought. There can seldom be any excuse for allowing a fire to start. If a man were to set fire to a government building or even to a building owned by some private

12 F.C.

individual or corporation and his guilt were brought home to him, the offender would meet with but little leniency in the courts or sympathy from the public, and there is no apparent reason why any individual should be held guiltless or escape punishment who either maliciously or through wilful carelessness is the direct cause of the loss of thousands, perhaps millions, of dollars' worth of property to the public of the Province through setting fire to the forests. Indeed, it can hardly be doubted that a few instances of rigorous investigation and prompt, drastic punishment would tend to awaken those who go into the forests for one reason or another to the importance of and necessity for exercising the most unremitting vigilance and caution.

If the above conclusions are just in regard to individuals, plainly they must apply equally, if not with added force, to corporations such as the railways, to whom the public has granted most valuable privileges from which they derive very considerable profits. Unfortunately, it is only too certainly the case that by far the greater number of forest fires which have occurred in the Province of recent years must be attributed to the direct agency of the steam engine, and yet no effort is or has been made to obtain from the corporations adequate compensation for the damage effected through their operations. Along certain sections of the Canadian Pacific Railway between Sudbury and the provincial boundary the stumps of trees, black or grey as the fire was recent or remote, bear mute witness to the fiery devastation of the steam locomotive, and from Port Arthur to Rainy River, along the line of the Canadian Northern Railway, it is the same story repeated, great stretches of black and desolate burn. How far this destruction has been carried on either side of the rights of way will depend on the conditions prevailing at the times of the various and constantly occurring fires. In some localities it will be deeper; in some not penetrate so far into the interior; but in all cases the most casual observer cannot fail to note that considerable tracts of country on either side of the lines have been laid waste and rendered desert, unhabitable and unproductive. Through the heart of the forest country lying between Lake Superior and Hudson's Bay the Grand Trunk Pacific is now penetrating, while the Canadian Northern Railway is preparing to do so, and it is to be feared that unless most stringent and special precautions are taken a similar fate awaits these regions, and that the Province will suffer losses at the hands of these railways which could hardly be estimated in currency.

It has been estimated that in the region traversed by the Grand Trunk Pacific Railway alone there are 300,000,000 cords of wood suitable for making pulp and paper. The rivers of the region are numerous and large and the wood can be easily floated down to the vicinity of the railway, where, doubtless, under the wise provincial provision which enacts that all pine saw logs, spruce pulpwood and hemlock must be manufactured into lumber, pulp or paper in the Province, it will be so treated, thus opening up an enormous new area to settlement and profitable commercial enterprise. It can be appreciated, then, what a calamity it will be to the Province if this magnificently wooded area is burnt and destroyed as have been other territories through which railways pass, by the very agency, in fact, employed to throw open their resources. Even though the cost be high, measures should plainly be taken to prevent any such eventuality, and it would seem but reasonable that in all cases the railways themselves should bear the main share of the burden, no matter what measures it may be deemed necessary to enact.

It is impossible to determine the value of the game inhabiting the forests of the Province, and it is impracticable, also, to determine accurately the loss in game sustained through any particular forest fire. Such evidence as there is to be had on the subject, however, would seem to point to the fact that it is considerable, doubtless, indeed, increasing in proportion to the extent of the fire and the velocity of its spread. All living creatures become alarmed at the approach of fire, and although the natural tendency is to escape from it by running or flying away in the opposite direction to which it is approaching, fear and smoke would appear to combine to confuse the wild creatures very much as they frequently do mankind under similar conditions, with the result that sooner or later, still fresh and untired, or else exhausted in their efforts to flee, they turn and rush into the very peril they are seeking to avoid and are destroyed. Birds and small animals, which have more or less fixed locations, probably suffer to greater extent than the larger animals such as the moose, caribou and deer, whose ranges are usually more considerable, but there would seem to be little doubt but that even these perish in numbers when the fire covers a considerable extent of territory and sweeps forward with inconceivable rapidity under the fanning of a high wind.

Great areas of forest land have been set aside by the administrations of the Province as public reserves or parks, to act amongst other considerations as a haven for wild creatures where they may breed and multiply in security, but the forest fire disregards imaginary boundaries in its advance and will as greedily devour a provincial forest or game reserve as any other section of the forest area, whether it starts from outside the reserve or within its borders. Small avail is it to afford the wild creatures security against man's depredations if they are to be driven from their haven by a forest fire or to perish in its flames. Indeed, all the main objectives sought to be obtained through the setting aside of these forest areas as reserves must fail to materialize where the forest fire has passed or raged unchecked. It is evident, therefore, that if it be wise to maintain these parks, and on this score there can be no two opinions, it must not only be the part of wisdom, but actually, indeed, imperative, to furnish them with a staff sufficiently well equipped to be able successfully to cope with any fires that may approach from outside or originate within them.

ᴹETHODS OF CHECKING FOREST FIRES.

The difficulty of checking a forest fire once it has obtained a good start and other conditions are favourable to its spread were well illustrated in the Rainy River District during the past year. The heat generated by a blaze of this nature is stupendous; the sparks, blown from the crowns of trees, will fly great distances on the wings of the wind and thus carry the fire forward with astonishing rapidity, and when the soil is sufficiently dry, the flames will eat their way into it and travel underground, to break out in some fresh spot and thus baffle the efforts of those attempting to extinguish them. In fact, the fire will sometimes smoulder for days in the ground, only very occasionally, if at all, bursting into flame, and though under these conditions it is not so alarming or so difficult to tackle, perhaps, as when the trees are blazing from trunks to crowns, it is none the less necessary to take measures to check its spread, for it will need but the rising of the wind to restore it to life and renewed activity. Indeed, as has been pointed out in a previous section, the desideratum on all occasions is to extinguish the fire as soon as it is discovered, no matter how insignificant or comparatively dormant it may appear, for the little incipient fire started by a cigarette end, a match, a smudge or a spark may easily develop into a conflagration entailing thousands of dollars' worth of damage. It is evident, therefore, that wherever a great number of catches of fire are to be expected in a forest area, the greatest efforts should be put forth to ensure these catches being extinguished before they have time or opportunity to spread.

There can be no question that the most fruitful of all sources of fire catches is the steam engine, for sparks and cinders are continually being emitted from the funnel to fall on either side of the right of way, and it is only too obvious how easily, when the vegetation and ground are dry, a blaze may result. There are in force certain regulations enjoining the railways to keep their rights of way clear of inflammable material and enforcing also the use of spark-arrestors, but even were these regulations carried out to the letter, which unfortunately would appear far from being the case in many instances, it is doubtful whether, as long as coal supplies the motive force of the engine, immunity from fire catches can either be expected or attained. This question has, indeed, come markedly to the fore of recent years in various of the States of the Union, and it would seem more than probable that the day is not far distant when many of the railways on this continent will be required to make use of some other material than coal when traversing forest belts. It would, in fact, appear that any additional expense incurred in fitting or building engines to consume some form of oil, and in the cost of the oil itself as fuel, could never even approach the sum total of the damage which is almost inevitably caused by the coal cinders and sparks, and for which compensation might reasonably be claimed from the railways.)ost especially would this apply where new lines are being cut through a virgin or almost untouched forest area, for there, with the forests still standing and unburnt, the conditions about the rights of way will be most favourable for the destructive agency of fire. The great bulk of the present forest resources of the Province are only now being pierced by railways and doubtless in the near future still other roads will be planned and constructed in these regions, so that it would appear that this question of fuel consumption by the railways might well receive the most earnest consideration of the provincial administration.

Even, however, where the engines consume coal a great deal can be done to lessen the risks of fire. There can plainly be no excuse for the railways failing to keep their rights of way clear of inflammable material or debris, or not complying with the regulations in regard to the use of spark-arrestors, and in view of the fact that these are wealthy corporations the penalty for any laxity or remissness in these directions should be punished with a fine sufficiently severe as to render any repetition of the offence unlikely. Government inspectors should be along and about the roads continually, and when any clearing is obviously needed and it is not promptly executed by the railway officials, it should be carried out under the direction of the government inspector and the expense charged to the railway company in addition to a commensurate fine. The question, indeed, of efficient patrolment of railways in operation is of no less, if not actually of greater, importance than that of railways under construction, for although undoubtedly the construction gangs on the latter require constant watching, the chances of fires being started by them and not extinguished promptly are not to be compared with those of a series of engines passing to and fro, by day and by night, vomiting forth a stream of cinders and sparks. The construction gangs in the forest areas receive close attention from the provincial authorities, but unfortunately the arrangements for the protection of the forests along rights of way of railways already in operation are far from effective, which fact is only too well evidenced by the scenes of desolation extending far and wide on either side of the Canadian Pacific and Canadian Northern railways in western Ontario.

All railways maintain section gangs at fixed intervals along their lines whose duty it is to patrol and inspect the line daily to insure its being in good repair. These parties as a rule travel on handcars of some description which can be halted and removed from the tracks wherever necessary. If some such system of patrolment for the purpose of extinguishing incipient fires could be inaugurated throughout the forest regions of the Province, there can be no doubt but that there would immediately ensue a great diminution in the number of forest fires. Nor would such a scheme appear to be impracticable. The lines through these forest areas are in the majority of instances single track and there is not an enormous press of traffic upon them. It would, of

course, be advisable that every train should be followed at a reasonable
distance, but with gangs stationed at suitable distances and properly
organized and instructed, this should not present an insuperable difficulty. The men would have to be furnished with a suitable equipment
of spades, axes and buckets and these could be conveniently carried
on the handcars, for no great amount of equipment is needed successfully to cope with fire catches in their initial stages.

An excellent illustration of the effectiveness of this plan is afforded
by the De Lotbiniere limits in the Province of Quebec. Through many
years the owners have caused every train during the dangerous
season to be followed at an interval of about half an hour
by a gang of men on a handcar provided with suitable equipment, and the result has been that while innumerable catches have
been extinguished, the limit is still unburnt and under the careful
and scientific direction of its proprietors is yielding as great a cut of
timber to-day, with the exception of pine, as it was fifty years ago. It
was recorded, indeed, by Mr. de Lotbiniere himself on one occasion as
an illustration of the advantages of the system that in following one
train through the comparatively short width of the limit, some 12 miles,
one gang extinguished no less than 9 catches and incipient fires caused
by its locomotive. When it is realized that each and every catch might
have developed into a conflagration which would have destroyed the
limit, it becomes apparent how intense is the danger to the forests from
railway cinders and sparks and how vital and urgent is the necessity
for devising some means of coping with this evil.

The expense of instituting fire patrols of this description along
the railways throughout the forest area of the Province would undoubtedly be great, but it cannot be questioned that if even one great forest
fire were thereby averted, it would not only be justified, but have paid
for itself many times over. It is plainly wrong that the railways should
be suffered to wreck and destroy millions of dollars' worth of public
property. The forests belong, indeed, to the Crown and are, therefore,
administered and cared for at the expense of the Province, but it would
be without the bounds of reason to expect the Province to undertake
expenditures to guard against the special risks to its property ensuant
on railway operations, seeing that these corporations, no more than
private individuals, have no right to cause injury to property which
does not belong to them. An Act of the Ontario Legislature authorizes
the placing of fire rangers along the railway lines and charging the expense of their maintenance to the companies concerned, and in 1909
the railways paid $66,712 on this account, chiefly, however, in connec-
tion with railways under construction, but it would seem that in so far
as the railways in operation are concerned a more effective system, on
the lines above indicated, is much to be desired, and although the operation of such a system would inevitably entail increased expenditures
when the gigantic sums involved in railway construction and operation

are concerned, it is not to be credited that such comparatively trifling additional expenditure would materially affect the enterprises or act in any way as a deterrent to their initiation. As, however, these expenditures have not been demanded in the past, there would naturally enough be some protest from the lines at present in operation, but it must be remembered that the railroad development through the great bulk of the provincial forest area is only now commencing to emerge from its infancy, and that the issues at stake are truly vast. If some opposition will have to be encountered now to effect the introduction of such a measure, in twenty years time that opposition will have immeasurably increased, and if the opposition of to-day is allowed to prevail, the probabilities are that, meanwhile, great stretches of Ontario's fair and valuable forests will have been withered, shrivelled and destroyed, owing to the very largely preventible incendiarism of the steam engine.

It has been pointed out in another section that one of the chief causes of forest fires is the carelessness of prospectors, trappers, hunters, Indians and other individuals in the woods. Notices and warnings as to the regulations may be and are posted up in the forests; efforts may be and are made to hand personally to each individual entering or in the woods copies of the regulations, and to administer to each a verbal warning; but even the most careful man may make a slip, and it may safely be said that the bulk of those whose occupations lead them into the woods at some time or another will be careless in the matter of a match, lighted tobacco, or even, perhaps, the cooking fire. Evidently it is not possible closely to patrol the whole of the great forest areas of the Province, or even those sections into which some numbers of men penetrate, and consequently the individual himself has to be relied upon, but, nevertheless, there remains the great necessity of getting organized and intelligent effort to work on a fire before it has time to make much headway, if the forests are to be saved from burning.

In almost every region there are points from which a considerable view of the surrounding country can be obtained. In New York and other States it has been found highly effective to take advantage of such sites for the erection of fire lookouts. Where, perhaps, tree-tops impede the view, a rough tower of timber is constructed, and in any case a detail of men is kept on watch, furnished with a large scale and reliable map and with a good pair of field-glasses, and the station itself is connected by telephone with other stations and with the fire superintendent of the district, the men thus employed, from the superintendents down to the rangers, having no other duties or occupations than those of protecting the forests against fire. The advantages of such a system are apparent. Great tracts of territory can be observed, and after but little practice, with the aid of a good map and field-glasses, the lookout men can fairly accurately determine the location of any fire which breaks out. The whole system being in direct speaking connection with the superintendents, he can issue his orders, make his dispositions and arrangements, receive reports and, where necessary, enroll additional assistance and despatch it to the scene of the fire. Two of the greatest difficulties encountered in dealing with forest areas are thus largely eliminated, observation and communication, and it goes without saying that an organization, numerically inferior, but equipped with means of observation and in constant communication with its chief, will be vastly more effective than one which, although greater in numbers, lacks cohesion and convenient direction. While some additional expense would be entailed in the adoption of such a scheme throughout the forest area of the Province, especially in the initial installation of the field telephones, it would not appear likely to be very considerable, for undoubtedly under such conditions a staff numerically less in proportion to the area patrolled than at present employed would be found sufficient efficiently to discharge the duties. It must be remembered that while already the Province is expending great sums annually on ranging the forests, these sums will be bound to increase very rapidly as further tracts of forest area are rendered accessible through the advent of new railroads, and, consequently, that an additional present expenditure which will tend to reduce the charges under this head in the future cannot but be fully justified. There can be no doubt but that in the Province the difficulties of observation and communication have played a large part in enhancing the destruction wrought by fire in the past. Rangers, by long days' journeys out of touch with their chief, have remained unconscious of fires starting and gathering leeway at, perhaps, no great distance from their camps, because, surrounded by forests and with no facilities for observation provided for them, they were unable to see, and then, when they became aware of the conflagration, it was already long past the power of two men to cope with, while the very distance to be travelled precluded the possibility of obtaining sufficient help in time. Although a pair of energetic men reaching a fire before it has attained great proportions can often extinguish it, or, at least, confine the extent of its spread, it would seem that, in many cases, where facilities for observation are not provided, and where the men are separated by long distances from their chief, as also from assistance, their presence in the woods as fire rangers, pure and simple, is almost, if not quite, useless. Means of observation and rapid communication are and ever will remain prime factors in the protection of the forests from fire, and it would indeed appear that the time has come when at whatever expense Ontario's fire ranging service should be equipped and organized in such a way as to facilitate the efficient discharge of its duties at all times and in all places under adequate direction and control.

Having regard to security of the forests from fires various States of the Union have enacted a measure requiring the lopping of branches from all timber felled. Except in seasons of prolonged drought the bed of the forest will contain a considerable amount of moisture, which will tend to impede the progress of fire. Trees, branches and shrubs falling on to the moist bed soon become sodden and rapidly decay, whereas such timber as for one reason or another perishes but cannot reach the ground becomes hard, dry and brittle, in fact an easily inflammable material and excellent fuel to add strength to the flames. The less of this dried-up timber there is in a forest, the less will be the danger of fire gaining a firm hold, and there can be no question that the lopping of tops and branches not only accelerates the decay of the waste brush and timber, but inasmuch as this debris is laid out on the ground instead of being propped up, intertwined and entangled in an inextricable jumble, the fire, if it comes before decay has set in, will be less likely to flare up high, shoot sparks into the air and thus start crown fire, so that not only will it be easier to approach it but also to extinguish it, and in addition to this, the course of the rangers through the forests is not impeded by the continual encountering of great obstructions formed of the brush and debris remaining from timber which has been felled by the lumbermen. Most particularly would the lopping of tops and branches appear desirable in the lumbering of soft woods, for the waste of these decays more slowly than that of hardwoods, and, as a rule, more of it in proportion is left behind. The objection to the enactment of such a measure for general application throughout the forests of the Province would be the cost involved, but it would appear that in some forests experience has proved it to be actually inconsiderable, three cents per standard and ten cents per cord of pulpwood having been found in New York State, for instance, to be representative figures under normal circumstances. Against this increased cost it is claimed that a saving of wood is effected, and a saving, also, in guttering and skidding, and in illustration of these claims the following passage from the 15th Annual Report of the New York State Forest, Fish and Game Commission is quoted:—

" One operator, estimating the cost of lopping at 2½ cents, remarks that to offset this he was able to run a skidding crew about one man less to each team, and also occasionally got a log that otherwise would be left. The actual additional cost he did not think would be over 5 cents per thousand feet board measure. He believed that when four foot pulpwood was taken the cost of lopping would be entirely made up in the extra amount of wood he would get. In addition his forest was left in better condition than under the old plan, and he believes it decreases materially the danger of forest fires. A remarkable saving in connection with lopping was made by another operator who has been getting spruce for sawlogs, taking the timber out with what was considered good economy. He left the lopping until after the timber was removed and then went through, lopping the branches and taking the timber out of the tops for pulpwood. In this operation, with a force of eight men and a horse employed six days, ninety-seven cords of pulpwood were obtained that would bring him $7.00 per cord delivered at the mill. This is an average of two cords per man, making a very profitable operation."

Finally, in favor of this measure it is further held that as the timber cut has to be lopped, greater care is taken not to fell trees which cannot be used, thus effecting a saving of small trees, and also that the brush spread out on the ground tends to retain the moisture during the process of decay and thus facilitate the germination of seeds which may fall upon it. It is to be noted, also, that in particularly dry or dangerous localities it would be feasible under such a regulation to require the lumbermen to pile and burn the brush without imposing on them any undue hardship, for in any case where heavy cutting is done it is necessary to clear the roadways of debris to draw the logs to the skidway, and where the lopping has been properly done, the material will be in good shape for handling and can be as easily piled as spread. The density of the undergrowth, however, and in fact the general nature of the forests, must materially affect the practicability of introducing such a measure, and while, therefore, the principle is undoubtedly well worthy of most earnest consideration, it must remain with the forestry experts to decide whether it is feasible to enact such a regulation to affect, at least, all future timber licenses in Ontario. There can be little doubt that if such a measure could be enforced, it would prove no small factor in checking the ravages of forest fires in the Province.

So rapid can be the development and so disastrous the effect of a forest fire on the public timber resources of the Province that some system should plainly be devised whereby not only should every male citizen, resident or visitor of mature years in the forest area, no matter what his occupation so be he is physically capable, be available at a moment's notice to proceed to the scene of a fire to assist in fighting it, but also responsible officials should be stationed at convenient and strategic points, able and fully empowered to call out such assistance as they may deem necessary. Where a settlement, village or even town is threatened, all its male inhabitants will naturally be perfectly willing to use their best endeavors to save it, but where the danger affects a community or locality at some little distance, their services are not so easily secured. To call for volunteers is almost invariably to court delay, and almost equally invariably to insure shortage of help, and the results of both these evils cannot but be a considerable augmentation of the damage effected. Where it was understood that each male citizen or resident was liable to this service, there could be no question of equivocation, and there can be little doubt but that the placing of the power to call on them to fulfil this obligation with responsibility and trustworthy citizens or officials throughout the forest regions would tend to the rapid extinguishment of many a fire that would otherwise be left to run its own course, provided only that it did not endanger a town or village. A small sum in the nature of a retaining fee might, perhaps, be paid to private citizens undertaking this duty, and it would, of course, be understood that they themselves would accompany any parties which they deemed it necessity to send out. When, however, the occasion arose for action, each man of the party should receive a reasonable wage from the Province for each day of absence from his home, which expenditure would plainly be more than compensated by the saving of the public timber that would be effected by this means. It would obviously be necessary to select thoroughly reliable persons to exercise this authority, but it is not to be doubted that throughout the forest regions plenty of such are to be found. In addition to this, moreover, it would seem advisable that some equipment should be maintained at strategic points, ready for use in an emergency, for numbers of men are of little avail if the wherewithal with which to fight the fire is not in their possession. Such equipment, comprising spades, buckets, axes and, perhaps, dynamite, would entail but little cost to provide, but its presence at the required time and at the right place might easily be the means of averting a terrible disaster.

THE FIRE RANGING SERVICE.

It has already been pointed out that there remains vested in the Crown an enormous acreage of forest lands in this Province, and that to protect this great asset the Province annually expends considerable sums of money. Some 20,000 odd miles are at present subject to license, and the custom arose of placing rangers on the land licensed, half the cost of whose maintenance was borne by the Crown and half by the licensee. In 1910, however, it was decided by the administration that in view of the increased value of stumpage and the small proportion that accrued to the Crown, the licensees might properly be assessed for the full cost of the maintenance of the fire rangers placed on their land, and a measure to this effect was introduced, and is still in force. In general the licensee is accorded the privilege of selecting his own ranger, it being deemed that, as a rule, he will be in position and sufficiently interested to select a properly qualified man for the purpose, but the right is maintained by the Crown of removing such appointees for incompetency or improper conduct and replacing them with others nominated directly by the Crown. Where the licensees do not apply to have rangers placed on their limits, a suitable man is selected by the Department for that purpose, placed on the limit, and the expense is duly charged to the licensee. In each district there is a supervising ranger whose duty it is to see that the rangers are on their proper beats and that the work is being properly carried out. Some 450 rangers are thus employed. In addition to this rangers to the number of some 200 are maintained to take care of the forest reserves, at a cost to the Crown of approximately $76,000, and further, along lines of railways in the forest areas, along rivers that are used as highways and in other ex-

posed regions some 200 rangers are placed on duty at a cost of approximately $80,000. The men are in general employed for five months, from
the commencement of May until the end of September, only a very
small number indeed being kept permanently on the staff, and these
chiefly in connection with the public parks. Undoubtedly during the
winter months the forests are immune from fire and the moisture in the
early spring eliminates, as a rule, any very serious danger in this direction, but it is to be observed that under the present arrangements the
forests are left practically without protection during October, during
which month in many years the danger of forest fires on a considerable
scale will have by no means disappeared, so that it would seem that at
least a fair percentage of the men should be employed for some weeks
longer than at present, so long, at least, as the present system continues
in force, for the money spent during the five preceding months in forest protection will have practically been spent in vain if large areas
of valuable timber are destroyed after the rangers have left their beats.

It cannot be doubted that with so vast an acreage of public forests
it would be economically sound to maintain a considerable permanent
staff of foresters, sufficiently well educated and seized of forest lore to
be able under scientific direction to look after the well-being of the forests throughout the year, in addition to undertaking fire ranging duties
during the summer months. Such a corps could be augmented to the
required extent during the dangerous seasons, but by this means there
would, at least, always be on the ground a fair percentage of rangers
not only thoroughly acquainted with their beats, the most dangerous
localities and the quickest and easiest routes to any given point, but
versed and efficient in their duties of proved energy and discretion and
with a more or less personal interest in the particular tract of forest
over which they ranged. The presence, also, of such a corps in the event
of fire could not but be most advantageous, for the measures necessary
to extinguish it require to be co-ordinate and discharged under disciplined direction. Under the present system co-ordination is sadly
lacking; co-operation, as has been pointed out before, frequently impossible; and discipline and direction, in the past at least, but all too frequently non-existent. There would undoubtedly be no difficulty in filling the ranks of a permanent provincial forestry corps with suitable
men, for not only is the life attractive and interesting to many, but unquestionably the creation of such a service would result in the broadening of the present educational facilities in the Province to fit men for
these posts, and in view of the experience of other and older countries
in the economic administration and exploitation of forests, the sooner
such a service is inaugurated in Ontario, the better it will be in regard
to the permanent interests of the public demesne.

Perhaps the chief failing of the provincial fire ranging service in the
past has been its inability to place trustworthy physically and mentally
capable men on the various beats. Unfortunately the duties in many

cases were not regarded seriously by either the incumbents of the office or their immediate superiors, and this position of moral responsibility degenerated into a holiday vacation or pleasant and comparatively profitable period of leisure at the expense of the public treasury. Applications for the posts were numerous by various classes of men desirous of passing some months in the woods with the incidental opportunity of making a little money, and personal or party influence was all too frequently paramount in securing the nominations, with the results that attendance on the beats was often irregular, appointees entered on or abandoned their duties late or early by several weeks as the case might be, and men were styled and drew pay as fire rangers who were both mentally incapable of appreciating their responsibilities and physically of discharging them, or else, by fault of their youth or inexperience in woodcraft, canoe handling and fire fighting, absolutely inefficient and useless. Days and weeks were passed in angling, canoeing, bathing and other pleasant pursuits; firearms were carried and discharged indiscriminately to the destruction of small birds, animals and, it is to be feared, of game generally; and, like Nero in his palace, the ranger would sit making music in his tent while some portion of his charge blazed merrily and was consumed and destroyed by fire. Fortunately these matters have come to be fully appreciated by the present Minister in charge of the Department, and under his wise direction most stringent measures have been and are still being devised and enacted to remedy this unsatisfactory state of affairs. Only recently fresh endeavors in this direction were announced in the public press, and it is satisfactory to note that in the approaching fire ranging season the carrying of firearms by rangers will be absolutely forbidden, and the men not only compelled to be on their beats for the periods for which they are engaged, but have work allotted to them sufficient to keep them busily employed. That the ranger drawing good pay from the Government should be allowed to rest at ease so long as there is no fire is plainly an absurdity, for in the forest there will always be more work than can be done in clearing pathways and portages, lopping and burning debris, improving the portage landings, making channels for canoes in shallow rapids and an infinity of other occupations tending not only to facilitate easy and rapid progress through the woods, but inasmuch as they do this and also remove a considerable amount of inflammable material, to the lessening of fire risks also. In fact such duties are the obvious routine work of an efficient ranger, for unless they have been conscientiously discharged, his most energetic efforts in the case of fire breaking out will, in all probability, be of but little avail. There will, however, under the present system always remain the difficulty of ascertaining how far a man applying for the post of ranger possesses the necessary qualifications.

A good proportion of the posts have in the past been filled by students and other young men from the towns; and while this no doubt will continue to be the case, it is not to be expected that a high percentage of them will have much knowledge of fire fighting, woodcraft or canoe handling, so that, although if the regulations are stringent, the system of supervision improved and better organized and their duties thoroughly explained to them, doubtless the majority of these men could be counted on to use their best endeavors faithfully to discharge their responsibilities, there would still remain great areas of forest under the care of men so inexperienced as to render their work of but small value. The fires, as a rule, are not to be expected during the early weeks of the fire ranging season, so that these inexperienced men have some opportunity of becoming used to their surroundings, but it is none the less an indisputable fact that it takes more than a few weeks, even than a few months, to initiate a novice into the mysteries of woodcraft and canoe handling and to transform him into an efficient ranger. If a permanent forestry corps was established, as previously suggested, the breaking in of novices to the work would be greatly facilitated and much of the dangers from incompetency and inexperience largely eliminated, but even under the present system it should be possible to take some measures to bring about these results.

The rangers, as a rule, work in pairs and there are, in all probability, always available a sufficiency of applicants for the posts to furnish fifty per cent. of the required number who not only have had considerable experience in the woods, but have actually discharged the duties of fire ranger on some previous occasion. If a register were kept of the names of men who have filled these positions, with a record of their qualifications and of the way their duties had been discharged, it would seem that in all cases it should be possible to have one, at least, of a pair of rangers experienced and efficient, and if it were so ordered that this man was given authority to arrange for the discharge of the duties of the post by the pair and made responsible for it, there can be little doubt that material benefit would accrue. It might, perhaps, be necessary to distinguish between experienced and inexperienced men in the matter of pay, and, in fact, some such steps would appear not only reasonable but fair, but at all events the inauguration of such a system would at least have the merits of preventing two young and inexperienced students being placed together on a beat to while away the time in unprofitable idleness, and of more or less preventing the chumming of two experienced but lazy lumber-jacks on some beat as a means of passing the summer months. The responsibilities of the posts are serious, and, although undoubtedly the pleasure of the outing would be spoiled to many if they were unable to select their partner or be assured that he would, at least, be of the same station in life as themselves, the matter is altogether too grave to allow of such trifling considerations carrying any weight. Indeed, fire ranging is and should be regarded as a business undertaking, and the fact that this is the view of the Department on the subject should be most clearly impressed not only on the superinten-

The Mosquito Bar, in Common Use by Rangers and Others in the Woods.

dents and chief rangers, but also on all applicants for and appointees to the position of ranger.

Practically all the big game and no small proportion of the small game of the Province is to be found in the forest regions, and in addition to this the angling in these districts is often first class. There can be no question that at the present time neither the game nor the fishery laws of the Province are very well observed in the wilder regions, and the difficulties attendant on their proper enforcement in these districts are too obvious to need recapitulation. The inland fisheries, both sporting and commercial, the game of all descriptions, and the fur-bearing animals to be found in the forest areas unquestionably constitute a very great asset which it is of the utmost importance to conserve, and it is plainly expedient that to this end every government official, whose duties lie in the woods, should be an active agent in their protection. At the present time the fire rangers are, indeed, supposed to enforce the game laws and fishery regulations, but it is to be noted that these laws and regulations are numerous and complex, that it is not to be expected that a novice in the woods shall have leisure and time to master them thoroughly, and that in all too many instances, even though the ranger detects an infraction of the law, he has little or no facility for bringing home the offence to the offender. Trapping and shooting through the close seasons and the netting or dynamiting of streams are all calculated materially to impair the resources of the Province in fish, game and fur-bearing animals, and yet all these operations occur and recur throughout the forests, if, perhaps, not quite so much during the fire ranging season, at least with considerable frequency both prior to it and after its close. Such a state of affairs is plainly to be deplored, for in addition to the obvious evil of allowing the laws to be set at naught and treated with contempt, these resources are far from being inexhaustible, and it is lamentable that the greed or slaughter lust of a few individuals should be allowed to perhaps ruin them irretrievably. In the interests, therefore, of economy in the protection of game it must be apparent how great a factor would be a permanent forestry corps, thoroughly acquainted with the forests, equipped with the means of observation and communication, and versed not only in the forestry regulations, but in those appertaining to the fisheries and game also. In fact, the institution of such a corps, when inter-departmental co-operation had been thoroughly attained, would in large measure obviate the necessity of maintaining great numbers of game and fishery overseers in these districts, and seeing that if the game, fisheries and fur-bearing animals of these regions are to be conserved greater expenditures on the service to protect them are quite inevitable, it is plain that a saving would be effected if this additional expenditure could, in part at least, be merged in that necessary to secure the adequate protection of the forests. Under the present system a copy of the game laws should be in the possession of every ranger, and it should be explained to him that the enforcement

13 F.C.

of these laws is one of his duties, and that it behooves him, therefore, to become intimately acquainted with them. Parsimony in the matter of literature of this nature is obviously ridiculous, for it is evidently absurd to inform a man that he is supposed to enforce regulations when, as at present all too frequently, he has no means of ascertaining what those regulations are. It would, indeed, seem preferable that every ranger should be supplied with a number of copies of the game laws and fishery regulations on the chance of being able to distribute them to prospecting and other parties in the woods, together with the fire and forestry regulations with which he is now supplied for that purpose, rather than that he should find himself in the position of not even possessing one copy for his own education and guidance.

RECO1 1ENDATIONS.

Your Commissioner would, therefore, recommend:

(1) That for the purpose of scientific regulation and care, and for the better protection of the forests, a provincial forestry corps be established without delay.

(2) That steps be taken to ascertain whether it is practicable for railways operating through forest regions to burn some other material than coal which will be less dangerous in the direction of causing forest fires, and, if feasible, to compel the railway companies operating through the forest regions of the Province to do so.

(3) That stricter attention be paid to the enforcement of the regulations in regard to the use of spark-arrestors and to the keeping clear of the rights of way by railways, and that the penalties for non-compliance with these regulations in the Province be raised sufficiently to render them of material importance to these corporations.

(4) That where the origin of a fire can be traced to the operations of a railway company, the company responsible be assessed for the full estimated value of the damage to public timber lands effected.

(5) That during the dangerous seasons for fire the railways be required to maintain fire patrols throughout such sections of forest belts as they traverse, furnished with handcars and adequate equipment, to follow up the various trains passing over their lines for the purpose of extinguishing catches and incipient fires.

(6) That steps be taken to secure the better patrolment of the rights of way of railways in operation in forest areas by government officers.

(7) That wilful carelessness in regard to the starting of forest fires in the public forests of the Province by any individual whatsoever be made an indictable offence, punishable with severe penalties, and that where the origin of a fire can be traced to the wilful carelessness or neglect of any individual, such person be punished by fine and imprisonment commensurate with the extent of the damage done to public property through his instrumentality.

An Alligator in the Rainy River District.

A Log Boom, Rainy River.

(8) That a system of lookout stations be gradually introduced throughout the public forests of the Province; that each such station be supplied with a large scale map of the surrounding region, a pair of field-glasses and, if necessary, an instrument for determining distances; that use be made of field telephones for inter-communication between such stations, and between such stations and the chief fire or forest officer of the district, in order to facilitate rapid concentration and control; and that a system of lookout stations and field telephones be instituted in the Provincial Forest Reserves without delay.

(9) That Crown timber agents, magistrates and other responsible officials or private citizens throughout the forest areas of the Province in towns, villages or settlements, be made Fire Officers; and that power be vested in them to call on each and every male citizen of the Province, or resident or visitor in their locality of mature years to proceed to any point designated by them for the purpose of fighting forest fire, and that such officers be paid a small annual retaining fee.

(10) That where a fire officer calls on citizens or others to perform this duty he be required to accompany and control the force, and that reasonable compensation for each day of absence from home, or while such services are being rendered be paid at the public expense to each and every individual so employed, including the fire officer.

(11) That in each town, village or settlement, or locality where a fire officer is appointed, a reasonable amount of equipment, suitable for fighting fire, be maintained by the government under the care of the fire officer.

(12) That a system be introduced whereby not only shall a record of the services of each fire ranger employed by the government be kept, but in so far as possible the placing of two inexperienced or untried men together on one beat shall be prevented, and whereby the experienced man of satisfactory previous service shall be placed in charge of the party of two, where the rangers work in pairs, and receive some slight additional remuneration.

(13) That each fire ranger employed by the government be instructed that part of his duties is to keep portages and channels clear, improve access to portages, lop branches, remove inflammable wood, and such other matters as will tend to improve communications and fire fighting facilities throughout his beat, and that steps be taken to see that such duties are adequately performed.

(14) That each fire ranger employed by the government be supplied with copies of the game laws and fishery regulations for distribution to those whom he may encounter on his beat; be required to make himself acquainted with these laws and regulations and be instructed as to his duties in regard to their enforcement.

THE PROVINCIAL FOREST RESERVES.

So well has the advisability of conserving the valuable pine resources of the Province been appreciated in Ontario that at the present

time some 20,000 square miles on which considerable belts of pine, estimated at about nine billion feet and valued at some $90,000,000, exist,
have been removed from settlement and declared forest reserves, and by
this means, also, not only has it been in certain instances possible to provide a haven for wild creatures and birds from the hunter, but also to
safeguard the headwaters of many important rivers and streams. The
areas of the principal reserves and the headwaters of the chief rivers
occurring in them are approximately as follows:

Reserve.	Area.	Rivers.
Temagami Forest Reserve	5,900	Montreal, Malabitchuan, Sturgeon, Vermilion, Wanapitei, Onaping, Frederick House and Mattagami.
Mississagi Forest Reserve	3,000	Mississagi, Wenebegon, White, Sauble, and branches of the Spanish.
Nipigon Forest Reserve	7,300	Nipigon, Black Sturgeon, Gull, Poshkokagan, Pikitigushi, Onaman, Mamewaminikan, Sturgeon and Wabinosh.
Quetico Forest Reserve	1,560	Rainy River and tributaries, Maligne, Sturgeon and Quetico.
Algonquin National Park	1,930	Petawawa, Madawaska, Muskoka, Amable du Fond, South, and Maganetawan.

In the Interim Report of this Commission attention was called to
the great potential value of these reserves in regard to the game resources of the Province, and it is not to be doubted that as the years roll
on and the wilder and remoter portions of the Province are opened up
this fact will become more widely recognized and appreciated. At the
present time the Algonquin National Park is the only actual game reserve of the Province, being, in fact, a game reserve and not a forest
reserve, but in the past at least a measure of protection would seem to
have been afforded the game in most of the reserves owing to the fact
that the carrying of firearms therein has been discouraged, and it would
appear to require but the passing of an Order-in-Council to render the
carrying of firearms in all reserves illegal. It is sincerely to be hoped
not only that such action will be taken without delay, but also that all
the provincial forest reserves will be declared game reserves in the strictest sense, to include all varieties of game and fur-bearing animals, and,
further, that this feature will be introduced at the time of the creation
of any new forest reserves in the future. The importance to the Province, indeed, of the policy of forest reserves is so vast and far-reaching
in its effects from so many points of view besides that of game that it is
to be hoped that further additions to the provincial reserves will be made
in the north country into which the railways are now penetrating.

In a previous section it has been noted that the placing of a forest
area under reserve does not remove from it the danger of fire, and that
where fire succeeds in penetrating into a reserve much of the material
and potential value of it is destroyed. Valuable timber will be consumed

Ranger's Hut in the Algonquin National Park.

and the headwaters of rivers and streams deprived of their protection; the beauty of the scenery will be ruined and the attraction to citizens and visitors to take advantage of the reserve will by so much be diminished; game, both big and small, birds, fur-bearing animals and other creatures will be driven from the locality even if not actually perishing in large numbers; and the damage done in these directions is in large measure irreparable for many and many generations. It is plain, therefore, that too great precautions can hardly be taken to prevent such a calamity. The safety of the reserves against fire, however, cannot be secured without considerable expenditure and enterprise. At present permanent staffs are maintained in some of the reserves, while in others rangers are only sent in during the dangerous seasons for fire, but in no case has any provision been made for rapid communication or concentration, and in almost every case, even were these indispensable adjuncts of efficient fire ranging present, the staffs would still be undermanned. In addition, also, to the problem of fire protection it must be observed that where no rangers are in a reserve for seven months of the year, it is not to be disputed that advantage will be taken of the circumstance to the detriment of the game and fur-bearing animals in it. There can be no question but that it is most desirable that all provincial forest reserves should be game reserves also, and, if it is worth while setting aside reserves for the purpose of fulfilling certain definite functions, it must be equally worth while to insure in so far as possible that neither fire nor man shall interfere with their so doing. If, then, the solution of the problem of adequate protection and ranging of all the provincial forest reserves and game reserves, and equipping them generally to meet all probable contingencies, is dependent on the provision of funds, which in all probability it is, seeing that the present chief of the Department is so well seized of the importance of this question, the matter would appear to resolve itself into determining some method or means whereby the work performed by the rangers can be made to produce an income sufficient to cover at least a considerable proportion of their wages, or, in other words, to render the reserves a producing asset in regard to revenue, in addition to being an efficacious but silent and non-producing factor in the general policy of conservation.

One method of so doing was suggested in the Interim Report of this Commission, and has already been adopted in the Algonquin National Park, namely, the taking of beaver by the ranging staff under the dircetion of the superintendent and selling the pelts for the benefit of the public treasury. It would seem that the basic idea contained in this scheme might well be extended. The forest reserves are maintained for the benefit of the community of the Province and at public expense, so that the fullest value of any possible products of these reserves should plainly be secured to the public. It cannot be doubted that in all the large forest reserves of the Province there are a great number of valuable fur-bearing animals of various descriptions, and under an efficient system of protection all the year round it would appear morally certain that these creatures would increase and multiply very rapidly, to the extent, even, of becoming too numerous. In the natural course of events they would spread over the surrounding country to add grist to the mill of the individual trappers in those localities, and it would seem that the additional profit which would thus accrue to private individuals through the existence of the reserves might well, in part at least, be diverted into the public treasury which is bearing the burden of the protection of the reserves. The price of fur of almost every description continues to rise, and if competent men were placed in the reserves to supervise the work and determine the numbers of each variety of animal that could be caught and removed without detriment to, if not actually to the advantage of, the reserves, there can be little question that with so great an area as 20,000 square miles at its disposal, which area, be it noted, may reasonably be expected to become augmented in the future, the government would experience little difficulty in securing a sufficiency of pelts annually to provide through their sale funds sufficient at least to cover a high percentage of the cost of adequately ranging and equipping the reserves, if not actually to produce a surplus income.

At the present time it would seem to be the case that considerable quantities of fur are secured by Indians and other individuals in some of the reserves, particularly so in the case of the Quetico Forest Reserve where the fur-bearing animals are comparatively abundant in certain localities and no rangers are provided during seven months of the year, while the reserve itself has not been declared a game reserve, and it is apparent that the sums of money now acquired by the individuals who now engage in this occupation not only could be far more profitably and serviceably utilized in perfecting the arrangements for the protection of the reserves, and in the maintenance of adequate staffs in them, but would go a long way in rendering these matters feasible of accomplishment without adding to the burden of the public treasury.

Attention has been called to the fact that there is ample work for the fire rangers in the forests at all times, irrespective of whether there is immediate danger of fire. Particularly so is this the case in the forest reserves, for as these can reasonably be expected to be visited by at least some citizens and visitors from outside, an additional cause is provided for keeping the portages clear, rendering access to them easy, and generally making conditions as pleasant as possible. There can be little doubt but that as the country opens up the reserves will attract increasing numbers of visitors to them, for forest scenery is always fascinating to the townsman and a vacation to the wilds an attractive proposition to many. In the Interim Report of this Commission the question of establishing a registration fee for visitors to the reserve was discussed, and it would seem that such a measure would be useful both in providing an increasing revenue and in affording statistics of the extent of the tourist traffic in the reserves, but in any case it is plain that as the reserves are the property of the public, citizens of the Province visiting them may justly expect to find conditions in them reasonably comfortable for travelling. The work already indicated, if properly carried out, would go a long way towards effecting this, and at the same time would be acting in the direction of preventing the risks of fire and facilitating the means of coping with it should it occur. In addition to such work it would seem that the rangers in a provincial forest reserve might also be required to clear and prepare a number of camping places at suitable points and maintain the same in good order, ready for use by whomsoever chances to pass, for there is nothing that the casual visitor to the forest, tired and weary after the unaccustomed exercise of a long day's canoeing and portaging, will appreciate more than to find a well-chosen and clean camping ground awaiting his occupation, with the tent poles all ready to hand and other facilities and conveniences perhaps also provided. Springs occurring along the portages and other paths likely to be frequented should be cleaned, built around with some form of rough guard, and furnished with a drinking vessel, and notices might well, also, be put in conspicuous places, as is done in some of the reserves in the United States, indicating the direction and distances of prepared camping grounds. In carrying out all these various tasks, not only would the ranger be kept busily employed and in hard enough condition to cope with any emergency that might arise, but in so doing he would, also, inevitably become more intimately acquainted with his beat, all of which could not but tend to his increased efficiency.

In all reserves it would seem that, whatever the dimensions of the permanent staff, there should always at least be a superintendent living on it all the year round, so that he may become well acquainted with the whole of the district and the conditions prevailing in it and in the surrounding country, and thus be in a position intelligently to direct the work of his rangers, to take advantage of the natural features of the locality in preventing the incursion of fire from outside or in dealing with it should it occur inside, and to take measures to prevent trespasses of every nature at all times of the year. All these matters plainly require study, preparation and knowledge of the district, and it is not to be expected that men appointed for a few months of, perhaps, one year only, should either have the inclination or the interest to delve deeply into them.

It would seem, also, that in those reserves where the tourist or other traffic has already reached goodly proportions and where, in consequence, the presence of the superintendent at headquarters is necessary for prolonged periods, a chief ranger should be provided to act under the orders of the superintendent, and to be continuously on the move to see that the rangers are on their beats and conscientiously discharging their duties. The need for supervision of the rangers is quite apparent, and it is equally plain that over the great stretches of forest country which constitute the reserves the time of one man would be fully occupied in each

reserve visiting the various beats and inspecting the work done. A superintendent chained to his headquarters for days at a time could never
satisfactorily discharge this most important duty.

Further, it would appear that in the interests of systematic administration and co-ordination of the arrangements in the different reserves
the time is approaching, if indeed it has not come, when an official should
be appointed exclusively to supervise the provincial forest reserves. A
great many improvements will most certainly have to be carried out in
these reserves; a great deal of work will always be on hand in them;
and just as there will always be the necessity of supervising the rangers
on their respective beats, so also would it appear indispensable that each
reserve should be more or less frequently visited by a responsible official
to insure that the instructions and wishes of the Department are being
carried into actual effect. It is impossible to reduce to writing in a few
brief orders the perfection of organization and arrangement in all its
detail which it may be desired to produce, and the interpretation of such
orders on the subject as are issued will almost invariably be construed
in different ways by different persons. It is plainly impossible for the
)ﬁnister of Lands, Forests and)ﬁnes to devote sufficient of his time to
attend personally to the carrying out of the full detail of his plans in
regard to all the provincial reserves, and it must appear, therefore, that
he should have to his hand an instrument for insuring that his instructions in this regard are being carried out in the manner he intends. That
there is ample work to keep such an official busy throughout the year is
evident, and it can hardly be doubted that the provincial reserves would
benefit greatly were such an appointment made, for not only would it
tend to prevent the lack of interest or control on the part of the superintendents and their staffs, but it would mean, also, that sound and
effective organization would be introduced into one and all of them, and
such improvements and devices as were found to be effective in one reserve could promptly be introduced into the others also. If the sugges-
tion, previously made in this section, of utilizing the fur resources of the
reserves as a means of obtaining revenue were carried into effect, it
would afford an additional reason for the creation of such a post and
enhance its importance, for undoubtedly the sums involved would soon
attain considerable proportions and the necessity for close supervision
of the catch and the collection and disposal of the pelts would become
imperative. It is, moreover, beyond doubt that at the present time not
only are the public, to a great extent, ignorant of the attractions of the
various provincial reserves and the facilities afforded in them, but that
in several of them there yet remains much to be learned by the authorities. A permanent official, occupied exclusively with the care of the
reserves, could be expected to collect and collate all useful information on the subject, so that the same might be published by the
government in handy form for public information. There can be little
question that if the scenic, canoeing, angling and camping facilities of

the reserves were better known, a considerably greater number of citizens and visitors would visit them annually, and as these reserves are in one sense public parks, retained for that purpose, it would seem advisable that full information concerning them should be available to the public. The work, therefore, in this direction of such an official as suggested would be most useful.

As the number of visitors to the reserves increases there will almost inevitably arise a demand for guides to conduct parties through them, and, as in the case of the Algonquin National Park, a supply of guides will appear to meet the demand. The fire rangers in a reserve and for the matter of that the fire rangers throughout the forests can be expected to be particularly careful in the matter of starting forest fires, and, indeed, the penalties for the slightest carelessness on their part in this direction should be most severe, but in the reserves, at least, it should be enacted not only that the licensed guide is responsible for every precaution being taken by his party, but also that any carelessness on his part in this respect, which is detected, will be visited by the immediate cancellation of his license, no matter where he may be or how inconvenient the same may prove to his party, and that the cancellation of a license on these grounds will bar the licensee from ever obtaining another one. Camp fires left unextinguished are a most fruitful source of danger, and yet, although this is a well-known fact and the offence is altogether inexcusable, it all too frequently happens that fires are not properly put out before a camping ground is abandoned. The tourist, also, is prone to be light-hearted in the woods and inconsiderate of the dangers of fire, and this spirit of levity is apt on occasions to communicate itself to the guides. It should, therefore, in all cases be most clearly impressed on the guides that any remissness on their part will not be tolerated, but will be punished by the full penalties, and that it is a chief feature of their duties to warn the persons by whom they are engaged against recklessness in this matter and rigidly to check any tendency to, or display of, carelessness in this respect.

The general carrying of firearms in the reserves may, it appears, shortly be forbidden, and from the reports recently published in the public press it would appear that in the future this same wise provision will be made applicable to rangers also. An idea would seem to be prevalent amongst the public that a firearm is an indispensable part of the equipment necessary for a stay in the wilds as a protection against the wolf. In most of the provincial reserves no doubt wolves do exist, and this is naturally to be expected, for all wild creatures, such as the deer, will quickly discover regions where they are afforded even comparative immunity against the hunter, and where the deer congregate, there also, will appear the wolf. The presence of wolves in the reserves is to be regretted on account of the numbers of deer which they destroy, but, although their voracity and destructiveness in regard to deer is stupendous, it cannot be claimed for the Ontario wolves either that they are partial to human flesh or that they are prone to attack human beings. In fact, the most careful investigation tends only to accentuate what an arrant coward is the wolf of the Province in the neighborhood of a human being. The howling of wolves, or a glimpse of one or two of them, is apt occasionally to frighten the nervous, with the result that wild stories have been circulated of men having been treed for hours by wolves, and having only escaped after prolonged periods of suspense and terror, but as a matter of fact no single instance has as yet, it would appear, been authenticated of a grown man or woman being attacked, much less killed, by wolves in the woods of Ontario. Thousands of instances on the contrary can readily be adduced proving the absolute security of human beings in this regard, and it would seem, therefore, that this erroneous plea for the carrying of firearms in the reserves has been rightly disregarded.

There are, however, timber prospecting and other concessions issued in certain of the reserves which involve the presence in the reserves of parties or gangs of men, and there are, also, in certain instances indi-- viduals desirous of crossing the reserves for the purpose of reaching the country beyond them, while outside of the reserves the carrying of fire- arms is not, of course, illegal at the present time. The possession of firearms in lumber and other camps is always to be deplored, for the illegitimate destruction of game that is effected by lumber-jacks and others from such camps is, in many cases, great and yet at all times most difficult to prove. In the case of the reserves, at least, some measures should plainly be taken to prevent the possibility of this evil occurring from this source, as well as from prospectors and other par- ties. In many instances, however, the lumber jack and prospector carries most of his worldly possessions about with him, and should he chance to be the owner of a gun, it might be hard on him to compel him to dispose of it or leave it behind when entering a reserve, for these per- sons are frequently of a more or less nomadic disposition and conse- quently unlikely to come out of the reserves at the point at which they enter them. Again, in the case of the traveller who might find it neces- sary to cross the reserves on his road elsewhere, it would be an obvious injustice to force him to abandon his firearms or to penalize him for carrying them across the reserves. It would seem, therefore, that some system might well be devised and enacted to meet special contingencies of the nature indicated. In some reserves, outside of the Province, it has been found both simple and effective for the superintendent or rangers, as the case might be, to seal all firearms which for one reason or another have to be taken into the reserves, the breaking of the seal by the owner of the weapon while in the reserve being deemed proof of an infringement of the game laws. There might, of course, be some little difficulty experi- enced by those entering the reserves by unfrequented routes in getting their firearms sealed, but if due discretion were used in this regard, it would seem that the introduction of such a system into the reserves of this Province would be beneficial, for it would eliminate to a great degree the trespasses perpetrated by means of the firearms which on one excuse or another are now taken into the reserves, and would, moreover, greatly facilitate the detection of such offences. It is not, of course, intended to imply that firearms, even though sealed, should be allowed generally to be carried in the reserves, for unquestionably the prohibition of the carrying of firearms altogether is the surest means of affording protection to the game, but that in those cases where the law cannot be enforced without undue hardship the system indicated should be available to guard against the weapons being made use of while the owner was staying in or traversing the reserves.

As before noted, the forest reserves of the Province contain a great quantity of valuable pine, and there is, of course, to be found in them also an abundance of timber suitable for pulpwood and other purposes. In some of the reserves lumbering concessions, granted many years ago, are still in force, but it is to be noted with satisfaction that the Government has had this matter under its consideration with the result that arrangements have recently been made to buy out the lessees in the Algonquin National Park. There can, indeed, be little question that ordinary lumbering for commercial purposes is neither calculated to improve the scenery nor to add to the pleasure of tourists visiting the reserves, and is, moreover, a source of considerable danger to wild life, so that it would appear that the efforts of the present administration to abolish lumbering in the reserves cannot be too highly commended. There are, indeed, such vast areas of forest lands available for pulpwood and other timber in the Province that there would appear to be no excuse for throwing open any further concessions in any of the reserves in the future, more especially so as the Grand Trunk Pacific Railway will render accessible a new area capable of meeting the demands for pulpwood, at least, for many years to come. The pine on the reserves is undoubtedly very valuable and in regard to the belts of these trees, as of other varieties of timber, it is to be noted that in the best interests of the forests it is often advisable to remove yearly a percentage of trees, which having attained old age will otherwise fall and decay, or for other reasons connected with the attainment of full growth by the bulk of the timber, as also, of course, in the event of an area having been burnt over. It has been proved in other countries that under scientific direction and management forests can be made to produce an annual crop, as do other products of the soil, without impairing the available quantity of timber and without in any way injuring the scenic effects. It would seem, therefore, that if a permanent forestry corps were established, one of its duties might well be to care for the reserves after this fashion, but in any case it may be observed that, were it deemed advisable for one reason or another to remove timber from the reserves, it would appear that the operation might with advantage be undertaken by the Government for the benefit of the public treasury, for after all, under the license system, the bulk of the profits is diverted into private pockets.

THE NIPIGON FOREST RESERVE.

The Nipigon Forest Reserve stands unique among the provincial parks in that it contains one of the finest and most beautiful sheets of water in the Province, Lake Nipigon, and a river, the River Nipigon, already world-famous for the grandeur of its waters, the magnificence of its scenery, and the splendid trout angling that it affords. It is hardly open to doubt that the advent of the Grand Trunk Pacific and Canadian Northern railways into this region will result in an ever increasing number of tourists visiting this reserve and taking advantage of its splendid angling. So important, indeed, from the point of view of the tourist traffic are, and will continue to be, the trout fisheries of the River Nipigon, and also, in fact, those of the rivers and streams flowing into Lake Nipigon, that too great attention cannot well be paid to conserving and maintaining them.

There has unfortunately in the past been a considerable traffic in the skins of large speckled trout taken from these waters. Both in certain portions of Lake Nipigon and in the shoaler waters of the River Nipigon the fish congregate thickly during the spawning season, and advantage has been taken of this fact by Indians and others unlawfully to secure quantities of large fish by placing nets on the spawning beds or by spearing. The skin of a six to eight pound trout has commanded a comparatively high figure and the firms trading in the district have apparently all of them been only too willing to purchase as many as they could get, retailing them subsequently to the railways and others interested, or even using them themselves, for advertising purposes, and also, it must be confessed, selling them to certain of the visiting anglers whose prowess or good fortune has been insufficient to gain for them the anticipated trophy in the shape of a large trout, and who purchase the skin they had hoped but failed themselves to secure. The number of fish which attain the maximum size must obviously be limited and it is apparent, therefore, what an enormous number of trout of lesser size will be slaughtered in the process of securing several hundred skins of specimens of the largest dimensions, and it cannot be doubted that this traffic has in some considerable measure been responsible for the diminishing numbers of trout in these waters. In any case it is illegal to take the fish by netting, and it is hardly to be doubted that the traffic in skins is illegal also under the Order-in-Council forbidding the sale of speckled trout in the Province of Ontario. However this may be, the traffic should plainly be suppressed at once, for unfortunately it still continued to some extent during the past season.

A special license has to be obtained in order to angle in Lake Nipigon, Nipigon River and adjacent waters, the charge for permanent residents of Canada being $5.00 for two weeks and $10.00 for four weeks, and for non-residents of Canada, $15.00 for two weeks or less, $20.00 for three weeks and $25.00 for four weeks. Seeing that the

Nipigon River from
Centre Camp, Pine
Portage.
Many fine speckled
trout have been
caught between the
two islands.

Ranger's Hut on
the Nipigon, and the
Mosquito Proof and
Fly Proof Tent of
the Commission.

View from the North
End of Pine Port-
age, Nipigon River.

14 F.C.

angling to be secured in these waters is altogether exceptional, there can
be no doubt as to the wisdom of imposing a special charge for the privilege of enjoying it on visitors and citizens alike, both with a view to
conserving the fisheries and of obtaining the maximum benefit from their
existence to the general public. It is, however, to be noted that near the
mouth of the River Nipigon is situated the village of Nipigon, and that
the river itself is only two hours by rail from Port Arthur and Fort
William, so that there are, in consequence, quite a number of anglers
resident in the district generally anxious to enjoy the sport during the
weekends, or for two or three days when opportunity offers, and there
is a distinct feeling in these quarters that a hardship is being inflicted
by compelling residents in the vicinity to pay $5.00 for their angling for
each period of a day or two only when a fortnight or more intervenes
between the visits. Indeed, it would appear that, during the last year or
two at least, the collection of the license from residents in the vicinity
has been very lax on this account, and that quite a number of such persons have more or less frequently fished some of the lower pools of the
river, particularly in the neighborhood of Camp Alexander, without
paying any license at all. It is evident that whatever a law may be,
it should be enforced, for failure to do so is morally evil in its effect.
Moreover, in a matter such as this, where exceptional expenditures are
being borne by the public to conserve and maintain exceptional fisheries,
there is no apparent reason why the resident in the vicinity should be
allowed special privileges over other residents of the Province. On the
contrary it would seem but just that the law applying to one should
apply equally to all, and this undoubtedly is the intention of the authorities. There may, however, be reasonable grounds for the contention that
an undue hardship is inflicted on residents in the vicinity through the
minimum cost to fish these waters being fixed as high as $5.00. Undoubt-
edly those who reside in the neighborhood will be in a position more
frequently to visit the reserve than those who live at a distance, and,
also, these visits, while more frequent, will be less likely to be prolonged
for even fourteen days. Moreover, there are and will be cases when residents of other portions of the Dominion, travelling by, would avail themselves of the opportunity of a day or two's fishing, but are deterred by
the present cost of the license taken in conjunction with other unavoidable expenditures. Consequently it would seem that some steps might
be taken to meet these conditions. A charge of $1.00 per diem should be
quite satisfactory to those who in passing wish to fish for a day or two
only, or to those who from neighboring towns or villages visit the reserve
for the purpose on one or two occasions only during the year for periods
of a very limited number of days, and at the same time would be a fair
recompense to the public. To accommodate those whose opportunities
of indulging in the sport afforded by these waters are frequent, but of
brief duration, a season pass might be instituted, to cost $10.00 and to
cover thirty days in the reserve no matter when taken during the open

season for speckled trout, it being required of such pass holder to have
his license endorsed with the periods of his stay on the occasion of each
visit. The cost of the license to cover four successive weeks of angling
in the reserve is at present $10.00, so that by instituting a season pass as
suggested the percentage of charge to the number of days of presumptive angling as at present existing would not be materially affected.
It would seem certain, in fact, that if the suggested amendments in
regard to the scale of licenses for residents of Canada are carried into
effect, not only will they prove a great convenience to many, but also
should act in the direction of increasing the revenue from this source,
seeing that there would no longer be any possible excuse for laxity in
the collection of the monies due to the Government. It is to be noted in
this regard that there is vested in the proper quarters authority to grant
a limited number of complimentary licenses, and doubtless this power
is wisely administered, so that if such licenses are not obtainable by
certain gentlemen of local or political prominence, they should be
required to take out the regular license like any ordinary citizen, and
not be allowed, as has too frequently been the case of late, to angle in
these waters without a license of any description whatsoever. In regard
to the non-resident licenses as at present existing, it would appear that
it is deemed both reasonable and just by the majority of visitors that
additional fees should be charged them and that the present scale is
equitable.

There can be little doubt but that one of the main causes which led
to the introduction of a special angling license for the Nipigon Reserve
was the desire to conserve the brook trout fisheries of this region. There
are naturally many other varieties of fish in these waters which are capable of affording sport to anglers, such as the lake trout, pickerel and
pike in Lake Nipigon and River Nipigon, and the latter two in all probability in most of the other streams of the district also, while there is
at least one instance in the reserve of a comparatively isolated lake well
stocked with black bass. As the regulation reads at present the license
fee is charged for " fishing in Nipigon River, Nipigon Lake and adjacent
waters," so that it is apparent under the law as it stands there is no distinction in regard to the class of fish angled for. There can be little
doubt that this is a reasonable precaution, for over a great deal of these
waters, most particularly in the River Nipigon and other streams, it is
without the power of the angler when trolling or bait casting to decide
on what fish he will catch, and though his intention might be to secure
a pike or pickerel, a speckled trout might become attached to the hook.
In general, also, it is to be noted that visitors would hardly go to the
expense of visiting the reserve for the purpose of angling for pike, pickerel or lake trout, which they could find in equal or greater abundance
at far less expense to themselves in more accessible portions of the
Province, and in the case of the lake containing bass, already referred to,
it would seem altogether improbable that visitors would journey so **far**

to angle in this lake when excellent bass fishing can be secured over so wide an area on this continent. The occurrence, moreover, of a bass lake in the midst of this trout region undoubtedly enhances its value in the variety of sport which it affords to the visiting anglers. On Lake Nipigon there are a number of small settlements and undoubtedly the number of persons living permanently in this vicinity will rapidly increase when the Grand Trunk and Canadian Northern railways are completed. At the present time unquestionably a considerable propor- tion of the persons resident on the shores of the lake indulge in angling, chiefly for lake trout and pickerel, without paying the license fee which would appear to be called for under the law. It would be impossible to begrudge persons living in so wild a region the privilege of taking a few fish from the waters of so great a lake as Lake Nipigon without pay- ing a license, and, indeed, the matter is only called to attention for the reason that there are undoubtedly great numbers of magnificent speckled trout in the lake, as well as of other sporting fishes such as the pickerel and lake trout, and when the opening of the railways brings not only an increased number of permanent residents to the neighborhood but some visitors, at least, from outside, all anxious to fish these waters, it will have to be decided in how far the special license is to be enforced on the lake, for it would plainly be inexpedient to apply the license to some and not to others. Probably when the fisheries of the lake become better known, it will be possible to locate the areas inhabited chiefly by the speckled trout, and it would seem that if all such areas, together with all streams and rivers in the reserve, were declared subject to license, both to residents and visitors, it would sufficiently well meet the case, for undoubtedly great stretches of water would remain available to those who did not wish to angle for speckled trout in particular, but were con- tent to confine their efforts to other varieties.

The expense of fishing the Nipigon River is at present very consid- erable to the average individual. The waters of the river are rapid and dangerous in many places; in others altogether unnavigable; so that the angler visitor is practically compelled to take with him one or more guides. The exploitation of the tourist traffic has fallen into the hands of three firms trading at Nipigon Village, each of whom undertakes the complete outfitting of parties, including the furnishing of tents, canoes, guides and provisions, and it is not overstating the case to say that both arrangements and charges are in general excessive. This is naturally to be deplored, for it must obviously tend to keep would-be visitors away, but on the other hand there is no apparent remedy other than that the authorities controlling the reserve should institute and operate a gov- ernment outfitting agency, and thus reduce expenses to visitors to a minimum. Such a step, however, will probably be adjudged impracticable, although it would have one great advantage, in addition to saving the visitor considerable sums, which is worthy of consideration, namely that by employing only trustworthy guides, if necessary, indeed, importing

French-Canadians or others from other portions of the Province for the purpose, the tourist would not be left to run the risk of being paddled through dangerous waters by Indians or half-breeds under the influence of liquor for a period of time after leaving the starting point, or else unversed in the locality and unskilled in the management of a canoe; unpleasant and dangerous experiences, in fact, such as were actually encountered by this Commission when visiting this reserve. Possibly the opening up of the country through the advent of new railways into the region will tend of itself to improve this state of affairs, for it cannot be doubted that many of the rivers flowing into Lake Nipigon will in due course furnish sport to many anglers and thus not only should fresh competition arise in the matter of outfitting visitors, but the expense, also, to the visitors should diminish, seeing that many other of the rivers of the district will in all probability afford sport equal, or nearly so, to that obtainable on the Nipigon River itself, and will be more accessible and more easily fished, so that visiting anglers will select these to go to rather than the Nipigon River unless the outfitting charges for the latter materially decrease.

The comparatively high license charged for the privilege of fishing the River Nipigon would appear to warrant the expectation on the part of visitors that everything will have been arranged for their comfort. The conditions on the river, however, fall far short of what could reasonably be anticipated in this direction, although it is to be noted that the visit of the Minister of Lands, Forests and Mines, who appreciated this fact to the full, resulted in the immediate institution of measures which will to a great extent remedy this state of affairs, if properly carried into effect. There can be no question that in so valuable a tourist centre as this portages should be kept clear and in good order, landing places provided and made easy and convenient for ladies as for men, numerous camping sites prepared in convenient localities and kept clean, and in general everything made as pleasant to the visitor as possible. A considerable staff of rangers is maintained on the river and would be more suitably employed in attending to these matters under the direction of the superintendent than in lounging in the log huts provided for their use more than half the day, and spending the balance in angling, gossiping with the Indian guides, and other similarly useless occupations, as appears to have been the custom prior, at least, to the visit of the Minister, last summer. In addition to these improvements undoubtedly a great deal could be accomplished in the matter of improving angling facilities along the banks. Too frequently it is the case that only one side of the river for long stretches is fished at all for the reason that only on one side is there a convenient pathway, and further, even where paths are available, for long distances it is impossible to fish in any manner whatsoever owing to the density of the overhanging vegetation, although in numerous instances pools, channels, rapids and other inviting and likely spots for sport have to be missed on this account. Under

Rapids on the Nipigon River.

View of Nipigon River from Pine Portage.

present conditions a very small fraction of the available water area can be fished at all, and this, no doubt, may in some measure account for the diminishing success of anglers in recent years, for where certain localities are thrashed day after day throughout the season by a variety of anglers, and no other places are open to the trout, it is but natural that the fish should avoid these spots and seek quieter retreats. It would seem, therefore, most advantageous that some effort should be made to clear places here and there along both banks of the river at reasonable distances apart in order to open up the extent of river which can be fished.

A limit of catch of 30 speckled trout of 10 lbs. weight of this fish to one angler in one day is in force in the reserve as throughout the Province. It would seem that the guides, some of whom are indisposed to work to such a degree that they willingly take advantage of any excuse to avoid it, in certain instances impose on the visitors to the extent of forcing them to abandon sport for the day when 10 lbs. weight of fish of any variety has been caught. No regulation to this effect is in force, or in the least necessary, so that it would appear that steps should be taken to apprise each visitor of the true facts of the case. In regard to the limitation as to speckled trout it may be observed that the fish landed at the present time in the Nipigon River run probably on an average about two pounds, while much larger fish are to be taken and are still caught comparatively frequently each year. It is apparent, therefore, that if the angler is fortunate the period of his sport is likely to be very brief, and in view of the charge made to the angler for the privilege of angling, this would appear, perhaps, to constitute a hardship. In another section of this report the question of returning uninjured fish to the water has been discussed, and it has been shown that it is feasible to do so in the case of fish lightly hooked in the membrane of the mouth, provided due precautions are taken in the matter of handling. No angler could desire, or should be allowed to kill, more than ten pounds weight of trout in one day, but it would seem that in view of the exceptional size of the trout in the Nipigon River the angler might be allowed some measure of privilege in the matter of returning uninjured speckled trout to the water and so prolonging his legal period of sport. Fly fishing is the method of angling least likely to injure the trout which are hooked, and if the privilege were granted to those employing this method, doubtless it would prove generally satisfactory to the visitors and at the same time would be calculated not to materially injure the fisheries.

An interesting point arises in the question as to whether rangers in this reserve are entitled to angle for speckled trout. The public is charged a comparatively high fee for the privilege and the rangers themselves are paid an excellent wage at the expense of the public. Under the circumstances previously noted, where the ranger had, apparently, nothing much else to do than angle in order to pass away the time, it is plain that, if he were any sort of a fisherman, he would soon become aware of the most likely spots on his beat and thus be likely to secure quite a number of fish during the course of the season. Further, it could hardly be but galling to the visitor, under license and other expenditures, to find the rangers fishing the same waters as himself and if not actually securing the greater share of the sport, at least by their operations tending to lessen his chances of success. Indeed, more than one complaint on this score was to be heard during the past season. It would seem, however, that care will be taken in the future to keep the rangers fairly busily employed so that their leisure hours for angling will in any case be materially diminished and there will be, in consequence, considerably less likelihood of their interfering with the sport of visiting anglers, but there appears none the less to be little, if any, reason for exempting the rangers from the normal fee should they desire to angle, other than that they may be able to secure fresh fish for their consumption. There are practically throughout the length of the river localities where the coarser fish, such as the pike, abound, and it is to be noted that in these cold waters the flesh of the pike is firm, flaky and not at all unpleasant to the taste. In such localities, also, the pickerel is often to be found, and is, of course, a splendid table fish. Eight or more rangers removing speckled trout from the river almost every day for five months would obviously be a considerable drain on the resources of the river, and as one of the principal objects of this reserve is to secure the perpetuation of the River Nipigon's magnificent speckled trout fisheries to the public, it would seem that if the rangers require fish for food, they might reasonably be required to angle for and take only the coarser varieties, and that in the event of their being desirous of angling for speckled trout they should be treated in the same manner as the general public and compelled to take out the ordinary license.

Although no small portion of the duties of the rangers on the River Nipigon must plainly occur in the vicinity of the river itself, it should also be made clear to them that the forests of the reserve on either side of the river are under their charge and some system should be devised whereby these tracts may be frequently patrolled. At the present time a light railway is in operation a short distance to the west of the river from Camp Alexander to South Bay, and already the apparently inevitable results of a steam engine are in evidence on both sides of portions of its right of way in the gruesome spectacle of burnt and ruined timber. Apparently but little attention has in the past been devoted either to this railway or to the forests on either side of the river in general in the matter of fire ranging, and it would seem most expedient that greater efforts should be made in this direction in the future.

The extent of the reserve is very great and the superintendence of its rangers is complicated by the necessity of supervising the tourist traffic and the collection of the license fees from anglers on the river itself and by the construction of the Grand Trunk Pacific Railway. Lake Nipigon, moreover, is a body of water easily disturbed by wind

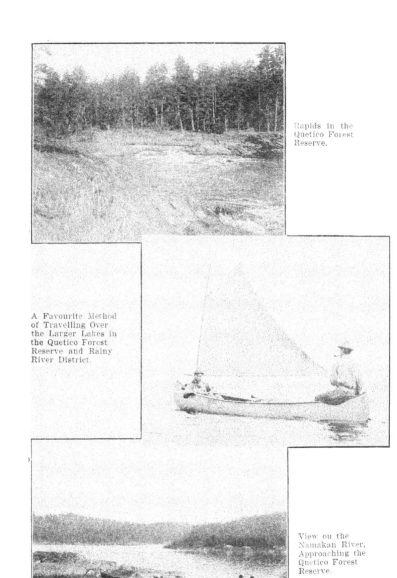

Rapids in the
Quetico Forest
Reserve.

A Favourite Method
of Travelling Over
the Larger Lakes in
the Quetico Forest
Reserve and Rainy
River District.

View on the
Namakan River,
Approaching the
Quetico Forest
Reserve.

and very frequently unsafe, in consequence, to all but comparatively large boats. At the present time the superintendent has his headquarters at Nipigon village at the extreme southerly end of the reserve, and is provided with no boat with which to move about the lake or cross it, but is forced to depend on the steamer plying between certain points on it in the interests of the firm of Revillon Brothers. His charge includes the river and lake with the forests on either side of them, although at the present time the right of way of the Grand Trunk Pacific Railway is under a separate fire ranging service. The construction of the Canadian Northern Railway as projected would appear likely to still further enhance the difficulties of ranging and of supervision of the same. Even though the same policy were pursued for the protection of the forests during the construction of this railway as has been followed in the case of the Grand Trunk Pacific Railway, namely of allocating a separate body of rangers under separate control to the work, it is plain that when the railways are in operation there will remain at least an equally great necessity for strict precautions against fire, and, therefore, it is only reasonable to presume that ultimately those sections of railway which pass through the reserve will be included in the charge of the superintendent of the reserve. It would seem, then, that some little reorganization of the present system might be advisable in the near future, in order that it may be capable of expansion as necessity arises without impairing or upsetting its arrangements.

The superintendent must in any case be a very busy man, with so vast a district under his charge, and he should obviously be provided with a boat of sufficient size to enable him to move about the lake in all weathers and in all directions. A boat of the Class B type, as recommended in the Interim Report of this Commission, would appear most suitable for the purpose. The logical headquarters of the superintendent should apparently be at some point on the south shore of the lake, whence he can readily move to any point of the reserve, and as the terminus of the light railway, previously referred to, is located at South Bay, where there is convenient shelter for a boat, doubtless this would be found to be the best location. It would obviously be impossible for the superintendent to devote very much of his time to the protection of the forests against fire if his presence is required more or less continuously on the river for the issuance of angling licenses and the collection of the fees, so that it would be indispensable that he should be furnished with some form of deputy to attend principally to this duty. The configuration of the territory breaks the reserve into two distinct portions, the northern including Lake Nipigon and the forests bounding it to the north, east and west; the southern, the River Nipigon with the forests on either side of it. The Canadian Pacific Railway is at present the chief means of access to the River Nipigon for visitors and must continue to be so until the other railways are in operation, but eventually this monopoly will disappear and stations or getting-off places on the other railways become available to the tourist. Perhaps, therefore, the best arrangement for the supervision of the ranging in the reserve would be to furnish the superintendent with two permanent chief rangers; one to be located in the northern section, with headquarters at Ombabika Bay or some other suitable point; the other in the southern section, with headquarters at Nipigon station. By this arrangement the superintendent would no longer be more or less tied to the vicinity of the Canadian Pacific Railway station at Nipigon village during the dangerous months for fire, but would be enabled to move freely about the reserve at all times and see that the work of every description was being properly carried out. Moreover, provision would thus be made for treating the reserve as a whole under the conditions which at no very distant date will prevail in it.

It is to be noted that at the present time very little is known of the angling potentialities of Lake Nipigon and the rivers and streams entering it, beyond the general fact that speckled trout are abundant in some parts of the lake and in most, at least, of the rivers and streams flowing into it. It would seem that under an active superintendent, relieved of duties which keep him practically continuously in the vicinity of the river, investigations might well be instituted in the direction of ascertaining the extent of these sporting resources, for undoubtedly a good many anglers will avail themselves in due course of the new railways to visit this region and it cannot but be the part of wisdom to have acquired some information as to them prior to their arrival. In fact, even outside of the reserve in this region it would seem highly advantageous that some authentic information should be gathered as to the available fisheries and game, and as to the best methods of protecting the same, for at the present time information on this subject is practically non-existent, and yet both the fisheries and game should prove a considerable asset to the Province if properly viewed and treated. The appointment of a special officer for this purpose would appear to be the most suitable method of acquiring accurate information.

Various rumors were afloat during the past year as to the intentions of the Government in regard to pulpwood concessions in the reserve. Whatever the truth of these may have been, or whatever the future intentions of the Government may be in this regard, it is to be hoped that under all circumstances the beauty of the scenery around the river and lake will be most rigidly safeguarded by the maintenance in its wild form of a wide belt of trees, and further, that under no circumstances will the noble River Nipigon ever again be subjected to the log driving operations of some lumber concessionaire, for it is not to be doubted that the scenery of both river and lake constitute one of their principal attractions, or that log driving down the river would immeasurably depreciate, even irretrievably ruin, the trout fisheries.

A Portage in the
Quetico Forest
Reserve.

A Rough Portage
in the Quetico
Forest Reserve.

Tracking in the
Quetico Forest
Reserve.

THE QUETICO FOREST RESERVE.

The most recent addition to the provincial parks of Ontario is the great Quetico Forest Reserve, situated in the extreme west of the Province in the Rainy River District. One of the most interesting features of the reserve is the fact that its creation has afforded an opportunity for international co-operation in the matter of the conservation of wild life, for its southern borders touch for some distance the International boundary and are conterminous with an extensive reserve on the southern side. At the present time the reserve is well out of the path of civilization and is, in fact, somewhat difficult of access, but the citizen or foreign tourist, who takes occasion to visit it, is well repaid for his trouble in the general beauty of the scenery that meets his eye and in the abundance of wild life that is to be seen almost everywhere, and there can be little question that as the attractions of the reserve in these directions become better known, greater numbers of both citizens of the Province and visitors from outside will yearly take advantage of them. The peculiar appellation of the region in which it is situated, the Rainy River District, is perhaps somewhat calculated to keep visitors away, but as a matter of fact this name, which was derived from that bestowed on the great river flowing through it by the old-time French-Canadian pioneers, is but a mistranslation of the French word " Reine," and the district itself enjoys a climate as pleasant, bracing and dry as that of any other portion of the Province.

But little accurate information of the geography of the reserve is available. Ten rangers, working in pairs, are placed in it for five months of the year which constitute the fire ranging season. This force is collected at and despatched from Fort Frances and gains access to the reserve either by the Namakan River or through Lake La Croix, and is under the superintendence of a chief ranger, but as under favourable circumstances it will take three days for the men to reach the nearest and most accessible beat and as also there is not one permanent member of the corps, it is only too evident that not only will there be a temptation in so wild and distant a region for the men to neglect their duties, but also there will be but little probability of accurate information as to the geography, or timber, game, mineral and other resources of the reserve being obtained by this means. Indeed, a trip through the heart of the reserve disclosed the fact that in the majority of cases the rangers keep to the larger rivers and lakes, remain in blissful ignorance of the geography of their beats, and undertake or attempt but very little work. Consequently, not only is the great bulk of the reserve left practically uncared for, but routes of access to the inner portions remain unexplored and throughout the reserve portages have become overgrown or concealed and their landings, in this wild country in almost every instance difficult, have remained unimproved, so that the difficulties of successful ranging have in no way been removed for the ranging service of future

15 F.C.

years. There can be no doubt that in this region, so far distant from civilization and from assistance, if ranging with a small staff of men is to be of any avail, no means of facilitating it can safely be neglected. In fact, the very inaccessibility of the reserve at present would seem to render it all the more imperative that not only should it be thoroughly explored and trails to every part of it be opened up and kept clear, but that steps should be taken to insure that the rangers become intimately acquainted with their beats and that a system be devised and introduced whereby the utmost advantage may be taken of the small staff available in the event of fire breaking out in any section of it, by rapid concentration of the whole force, if need be, at the point of danger. It has unfortunately to be recorded that a brief visit to the reserve disclosed the fact that considerable areas of it have already been burnt over, and in fact it would appear that perhaps the finest pine belt of the reserve, that occurring on Eden Island in Lake Quetico, estimated at 20,000,000 feet, was only with the greatest difficulty, and at that only owing to a change of wind, saved from destruction by fire, so that it is apparent that if the reserve is to fulfil its functions and to be conserved to posterity, greater expenditures will have to be devoted to the maintenance of a more adequate staff to protect it.

Moose, deer, fur-bearing animals and wild life in general abound in the reserve. On one occasion, within the short space of an hour or two, no less than 14 moose were counted, and so fearless are these creatures in this locality that it was almost invariably possible to approach to within a few yards of them in canoes. So inquisitive, indeed, was one specimen that while the party was lunching on one bank of a stream, it entered the water from the other bank and swam across towards it, and when canoes were launched and started to meet it, it was not until the prow of one canoe actually touched its head that it could be diverted from its purpose. Tracks of moose and deer were everywhere to be seen in abundance, and those of bear and wolves were not infrequently observed, while it was of rare occurrence that the morning would not reveal the inquisitiveness of the smaller creatures by the tracks or marks of numerous varieties around the vicinity of the camp. At the present time no protection is afforded the reserve from October to May, and the very abundance of the big game and fur-bearing animals undoubtedly offers very great temptation to the hunter and trapper who is aware of this fact. Indeed, investigation of such evidence as was obtainable and the examination of numerous witnesses all tended to indicate that advantage is taken of the unguarded condition of the reserve and that considerable depredations in these directions are annually effected. In the winter, when the lakes are frozen over and the forests bare, travelling is very considerably facilitated, and it would appear that hunters and trappers alike enter the reserve, chiefly, perhaps, from the States, and shoot the moose and other game and capture the fur-bearing animals to their heart's content, removing their trophies across the border

Bear Lake Portage,
on the way to the
Quetico Forest
Reserve.

Camp Eden Island,
Lake Quetico.
It is estimated that
there is 20,000,000
ft. of pine on this
island.

A Corner of Lake
Seiggilagan.

before the snow melts and before the appearance of the provincial rangers. In addition to this it would seem that various families of Indians, located in the vicinity, establish their winter hunting and trapping grounds within the confines of the reserve. It is, of course, not to be expected that over so great an area, which has been placed in reserve only comparatively recently and which is so difficult of access, the ranging service and general arrangements should have been sufficiently perfected, within the short space of time available, to prevent all illegal depredations on the wild life in the reserve, but it would appear from the evidence obtained in the locality that the extent of these depredations is in all probability very considerable and consequently that, unless something is done to check them in the near future, the game and fur-bearing resources of the reserve will be materially impaired. In fact, the reserve should be declared a game reserve without delay, and there is little question but that some proportion of permanent staff is much to be desired, and it would hardly appear to be erring on the side of extravagance to suggest that four permanent posts of two rangers each should be established in this great reserve under the direction of a permanent superintendent. If even so small a staff as this were maintained and the posts placed at strategic points, although in the winter it would be impossible to watch every means of ingress into the park, at least the principal and most frequented winter routes could be watched and patrolled, and undoubtedly a great deal of good would be effected. Perhaps the best location for such posts would be:—

(1) Lake La Croix, near the mouth of the Namakan River, thus controlling three main routes into the reserve, Namakan River, Maligne River and Crooked Lake.

(2) Quetico Lake on Eden Island, thus controlling the district about and routes over Quetico Lake, Quetico River, Jean Lake and Long Lake.

(3) Pickerel Lake in the vicinity of Pine portage, thus controlling routes by Pickerel Lake, French River and Batchewang Lake.

(4) Basswood Lake at its eastern end, thus controlling the waterways of Agnes Lake, Birch Lake and Basswood River.

By this means the international boundary would be watched at two points and provision would be made for the interior portions of the reserve.

In regard to the angling facilities afforded by the reserve it is to be observed that in Basswood Lake and Basswood River black bass of good size are alleged to have been caught, but that in so far as is known this fish does not occur in other portions of this region in Canadian territory. There is in general no difficulty for the angler to secure all the fish he requires for food. In most of the lakes there would appear to be an excellent variety of lake trout which can be secured by trolling. Quetico and Jean Lakes, two of the most beautiful lakes of the district and possessing waters of a wonderful clearness and light green colour, are particularly noteworthy in this respect. In almost all the lakes pickerel are to be caught and there is, also, throughout the region an abundance of pike which in these waters appear to be somewhat more vigorous and gamey than the average of their kind, and fairly pleasant to the taste. The existence of the mascalonge in the reserve has not as yet been determined, although rumours of its capture in certain of the lakes are occasionally to be heard, but the occurrence of this fish in the waters of Lake of the Woods would appear to indicate that there is a reasonable possibility of such being the case. The question of whether it is feasible to introduce other varieties of sporting fishes into these waters and whether it would not be expedient to make some attempts in this direction is worthy of consideration, for the general scenery of the park is so beautiful, its facilities for pleasant camping, bathing and canoeing so peculiarly attractive, and its opportunities for the observation of wild life so great, that there can be but little question that in the natural course of events it will ultimately become one of the most popular tourist resorts of that region, and the additional feature of really first-class angling would but tend to hasten the march of events in that direction. The Quetico Forest Reserve is indeed a most valuable acquisition to the public parks of the Province and the Government is to be warmly congratulated on its creation. It remains only to be hoped that in the course of a few years means of access to it will become improved, its numerous attractions and advantages more widely known, and that in the meantime it will be found possible to perfect the arrangements for safeguarding its many valuable resources throughout the year.

RECOMMENDATIONS.

Your Commissioner would, therefore, recommend:—

(1) That all existing provincial forest reserves be declared game reserves without delay; that in the creation of any new reserves in the future this provision always be included; and that the general carrying of firearms in the reserves be forbidden.

(2) That a sufficient staff be maintained in each of the provincial forest reserves throughout the year to insure the protection of the game and fur-bearing animals in them.

(3) That a permanent superintendent be appointed for each provincial forest reserve.

(4) That an inspector of provincial forest reserves be appointed.

(5) That the exploitation of the fur resources of the provincial forest reserves be undertaken by the Government for the benefit of the public treasury; that the necessary trapping be conducted by the permanent staff under the direction of the superintendent; and that the pelts thus obtained be branded with a government mark and sold by public tender.

(6) That visitors to provincial forest reserves be required to pay a registration fee of 50 cents for residents of Canada and $1.00 for non-

John Ottertail, Lake La Croix, who acted as Guide to the Commission in the Quetico Forest Reserve.

residents, provided only that residents and non-residents taking out any special game or angling license as required in any of the provincial parks or reserves be not required to pay this fee in addition to that of such license.

(7) That special attention be paid in the provincial forest reserves to the comfort of visitors in the matters of keeping portages clear, preparing camps and landing places and posting up suitable information as to these and other matters at convenient points.

(8) That the license of any guide employed in any of the provincial forest reserves be forthwith cancelled on the detection of any carelessness on his part in regard to due precautions against fire, no matter where or when such detection may take place, and that this regulation be explained to tourists employing guides in the reserves.

(9) That a system be instituted whereby all such firearms as for one reason or another have to be carried through provincial forest reserves may be sealed with a government seal.

(10) That where for any reason it may be deemed expedient to cut timber in a reserve the work be undertaken by the Government and the timber sold for the benefit of the public treasury.

(11) That trafficking in the skins of speckled trout be rigidly suppressed, particularly in and in the vicinity of the Nipigon Forest Reserve, and that special measures be taken to prevent Indians spearing or netting speckled trout in Nipigon River, Lake Nipigon and adjacent waters during the spawning season of that fish.

(12) That steps be taken to provide better angling facilities along both banks of the Nipigon River by making small clearings at suitable distances apart in the neighborhood of pools, channels and rapids.

(13) That the scale of angling licenses for permanent residents of Canada to fish in the waters of the Nipigon Reserve be arranged as follows:—

(1) A charge of $1.00 per diem, or

(2) A charge of $5.00 for 14 consecutive days, or

(3) A charge of $10.00 for 30 consecutive days, or

(4) A charge of $10.00 for 30 days angling in the reserve during the angling season,

it being provided that in the latter case on each successive visit the holder of such a license be required to have the periods of his stay endorsed thereon by the competent authority, failing which the license to be deemed cancelled.

(14) That the collection of the special license for angling in the Nipigon Forest Reserve be rigidly enforced in the future.

(15) That it be declared legal when fly-fishing in the Nipigon Forest Reserve to return uninjured speckled trout to the water and to continue angling for this fish even though the weight or number of fish actually landed is in excess of the legal number imposed by law, provided only that in no case shall more than the legal number or weight of speckled

trout be killed and that all such fish as are in any way injured must be retained or counted as retained.

(16) That rangers on the Nipigon River be debarred from angling for speckled trout unless purchasing a license to do so.

(17) That special precautions against fire be taken in regard to the light railway operating through the Nipigon Forest Reserve between Camp Alexander and South Bay.

(18) That the permanent staff of the Nipigon Forest Reserve be increased by two chief rangers; one to be stationed in the lake section and one in the river section; that the headquarters of the superintendent be situated in the centre of the reserve; and that a boat of the Class B type, as recommended in the Interim Report of this Commission, be placed on Lake Nipigon; and that greater attention be paid to the patrolment of the forests in this reserve.

(19) That under no circumstances timber be allowed to be cut in the Nipigon Forest Reserve in such a way as to impair the beauty of the river bank or lake shore scenery.

(20) That an official be appointed to examine into and report upon the fishery and game resources of the territory surrounding Lake Nipigon and to the northward of the Grand Trunk Pacific right of way.

(21) That a permanent staff of at least one superintendent and eight men be maintained in the Quetico Forest Reserve and that permanent posts be established on Lake La Croix, near the mouth of the Namakan River; on Eden Island in Quetico Lake; on Pickerel Lake in the vicinity of Pine portage; and at the eastern end of Basswood Lake, for the use of rangers in the winter months.

(22) That steps be taken to insure the patrolment of the interior portions of the Quetico Forest Reserve; to open and improve communications throughout it; and to secure accurate information as to its geographical features and other resources.

THE GAME RESOURCES OF ONTARIO.

In the variety of its game the Province of Ontario is peculiarly fortunate, but it is unfortunately the case that of recent years there has in almost every species been a marked decrease in numbers. To a certain extent this was, of course, to be expected, for as the natural habitat of the greater portion of the game of any country is the forest or wild lands, the advance of civilization and the increase of population inevitably tend to limit the areas available to the game. In Ontario, however, the general decrease has not only been noticeable in the more settled districts but almost equally in those more wild and remote but into which the hunter can and does succeed in penetrating.

The diminution in the quantities of game is almost invariably accompanied by an increase in the number and severity of the restrictions placed upon its pursuit, but it must be apparent to every thinking

A Log Slide, Grassy Lake.

person that no matter how wise or necessary the enactment of such restrictions may be, the regulations themselves are worse than useless and bound altogether to fail in providing the desired remedy, if the means of enforcing them are not available   There is little doubt, indeed, but that at the present time far less rigorous laws and regulations in regard to the open seasons for the taking of game of many varieties would be found to be amply sufficient to insure the maintenance of an abundant supply if only they were obeyed to the letter by all and sundry, but in this Province, at least, it would appear to be all too often the case that otherwise law-abiding citizens disregard the game laws and break them with impunity, or else deem it no dishonesty or shame to abet or connive at their infraction by taking advantage of the misdeeds of others to satisfy the greed of their own appetites.   That this state of affairs is in large measure due to the inefficiency of the officers appointed to act as game wardens and overseers cannot be doubted, for where the officer charged with enforcement of the law is careless or lax in the discharge of his duties, willing to shut his eyes to flagrant offences or even himself to commit them, the public plainly will not be impressed with the necessity for obeying the laws, but rather will be educated to treat them with contempt.

Ideal legislation in this line is that which will allow the greatest amount of sport for the longest possible time, but in Ontario long open seasons cannot as yet safely be attempted in the majority of cases, especially in regard to the larger forms of game, for game is fast diminishing, and until the system for enforcing the observance of the game laws is vastly improved, the standard of its officers raised and the public itself taught to respect and obey the laws, the prime necessity must remain to endeavour to save the game at all costs while these matters are being contemplated and effected.   Doubtless some hardship will be wrought on hunters in the process; some dissatisfaction be voiced among them and by those who appreciate game for table purposes and consequently protest at being deprived of their sources of supply or having the same very much curtailed; but these are trifling considerations when weighed in the balance against the importance of perpetuating the game, and the selfish interests of the few must be sacrificed for the present and ultimate benefit of the majority.   Even under an adequate system of control some offences will be detected and punished, some persons will be deterred from breaking the law; so that it is apparent that while the outstanding necessity of the case in this Province is to remedy the system of administration and improve the staff, the imposition of additional difficulties in the way of the hunter or additional restrictions upon him can be counted on to achieve some measure of good in connection with the number of creatures slaughtered.

Some complaints have been made against the reduction to one deer only of the number of deer that may legally be killed under one license and to the suggestions, also made in the Interim Report of this Commission but not as yet adopted, that the open season for deer be made a fortnight later than at present and that the killing of bucks only be permitted, but these and kindred measures and recommendations are enacted and made to meet the necessities of the case as they exist; as a temporary but indispensable means of saving the game resources of the Province from extravagant depletion, if not absolute annihilation. Once some method of increasing or maintaining the supply of game had been discovered or devised, or once some means were available for rigidly enforcing such laws and regulations as might be in force, it would at once become possible in a great many instances to relax the restrictions in regard to numbers, and also, in all probability, to greatly extend the open seasons for many varieties so as to meet practically all the various opinions and wishes on the subject. This is, indeed, the objective which it should be sought to attain, and its achievement rests equally in the hands of the administration and the general public.

One of the principal causes of the destruction of game and wild life generally is the indiscriminate carrying of firearms in the wilder portions of the country. Indeed, in some regions it is quite the exception to meet a man not armed with at least one weapon, and for the convenience of those who chance not to be so supplied, as a rule the young boys and youths of the district only, there is in such cases but small difficulty in renting a firearm for a small sum. All the hardware stores and most of the general stores also in these regions carry a large stock of weapons of many varieties in addition to making a practice of renting second-hand weapons as occasion offers, and it would seem inevitable that so long as this condition prevails the greatest difficulty will be experienced in safeguarding, even perhaps perpetuating, the game in these localities. In no case is the necessity for the habitual carrying of firearms apparent, and in fact it is a menace to peaceful citizens traversing these regions, but while the promiscuous exposing for sale and selling of firearms is permitted doubtless the practice will remain in force. In so far as the protection of game and wild life is concerned there can be little question that it would be most highly advantageous were a gun tax put into force and some control over the exposure for sale and the sale of firearms exercised, more partienlarly in the direction of preventing the sale or renting of any variety of them to any but *bona fide* citizens or to those who had not as yet attained the legal age of maturity, but to recommend such a measure, affecting so great a diversity of interests and occupations, would, perhaps, be trespassing beyond the limitations of this Commission's range. At least, the resident hunting license, recommended in the Interim Report of this Commission, could be expected to effect some good in this direction, more especially so if it were enacted that to be in the public forests or on the public wild lands in the possession of firearms without such license during the open season for any species of game whatsoever was an indictable and punishable offence.

Logging.

Lumber Camp near Fort Frances.

As before noted, it is quite beyond dispute that at the present time there are innumerable illegalities continually being committed, and it is equally certain that a great deal of the game of many species is unlawfully used for commercial purposes. Most especially so would this appear to be the case in regard to moose meat, venison and partridge in the smaller towns and villages of certain sections of the Province. In general it should not prove a very difficult undertaking to ascertain that such conditions are prevalent, for the matter is usually one of common local knowledge and there are in almost every community to be found persons law-abiding themselves and willing to supply the necessary information provided that they shall not be required to become involved in any prosecution that may ensue. Naturally in small communities it is an unpleasant task to bear open testimony against a neighbour for an infraction of some minor law, and in some sections of the Province, moreover, action of this nature would be far from tacitly resented by the person who committed the offence. Similarly, where local overseers are paid such trifling sums for their services that they are forced to busy themselves in other occupations in order to earn a living and consequently have but little incentive to respect the dignity of their position or to discharge their duties energetically, the temptation is plainly great to overlook the shortcomings of neighbors or friends, with whom, may be, they are associated in business or other occupations every day of the week, in the matter of transgressions of the game laws, or, again, to fear reprisals in the event of indicting the offender. No excuse can be advanced for this attitude of mind on the part of those who take monies to perform certain services in the interests of the public which they will not or cannot discharge, but it is evident that so long as the present system remains in force, so long will a percentage, at least, of the overseers continue deliberately, even though, perhaps, against their wills, to be inefficient. From this fact it would seem that two deductions may safely be made; firstly, that it would be infinitely better to have fewer officials engaged exclusively all the year around in the discharge of their duties, paid sufficiently to raise the dignity of their office at least to that of an average constable and with sufficiently wide territories to remove from them the fear of reprisals in carrying out their duties; and secondly, that until, at least, such a system has been established, information obtained from no matter what source should be followed up and investigated. If, indeed, it once became generally known that the Department was not only willing, but had some means at its disposal for the investigation of complaints and reports of illegalities, it cannot be doubted that information would pour in from all sides and that this would act directly to the checking of, at least open, violations of the law in regard to the exposure and sale of game, for when every member of a small community would be aware of it, and anyone of it might decide to send in a report, which report it was known would be investigated and not pigeon-holed, he would have, perforce, to be a hardened and reckless malefactor who would care to run the risks.

16 F.C.

It would seem, therefore, that in the reorganization of the service for the protection of game the objective to be attained is a force, numerically less than at present supported, but carefully selected for energy, discretion and capability, well disciplined and organized, and with each and every member independent of other avocations or business affilia·tions for a livelihood, and that, also, pending such reorganization and during the process of its institution some special officers should be maintained at the disposal of the Department to act in the capacity of secret investigators of information that may be received, no matter from what locality, and, if necessity arises, as competent representatives of the Government to arrest and indict violators of the law.

BIG GAME.

The largest existing species of the deer family is the moose which is still to be found in the wilder portions of the Province. The head of a moose forms a magnificent trophy, and for this reason, if for no other, the moose would be eagerly sought after by the big game hunter, but in addition to this the flesh of the moose is most palatable and the carcass has, in consequence, a very considerable value. While it has been found that in captivity the moose is the most sensible of all deer, the least timid and the least easily upset, it is none the less, when running wild, of a shy and retiring disposition in so far as man is concerned. It would seem, indeed, that for its perpetuation in a wild state, at least, it requires a considerable range of wild and wooded territory where it will not be affected to any appreciable extent by the presence of man during the greater portion of the year, and that it will rapidly disappear from a district before the encroachments of civilization. Consequently, it is only to be expected that as the Province opens up the available moose areas will gradually diminish. There are, however, many sections of the Province which never will be suitable for agriculture or in all probability adapted to the requirements of any considerable population, so that with due care and management it should be possible to perpetuate the moose in Ontario for a very long time to come.

At the present time there are undoubtedly considerable areas inhabited by moose, and undoubtedly, also, considerable quantities of moose still remaining in certain of them, but every year the retreats of the creature are diligently searched by an increasing number of hunters during the open season, and as transportation and other facilities render their retreats more and more accessible, it is only too apparent that the drain on the supply is likely to be very much in excess of the normal increase. More particularly so will this be acknowledged to be the case when it is remembered that the settlers in these regions, as well as the Indians, rely in large measure on the moose for at least their winter supply of meat, and that in the villages and settlements of the remoter regions moose meat is still, unfortunately, a fairly common commercial commodity. The size of the animal, also, militates against its chances of escape if once it is preceived by the hunter, and the largeness of its tracks renders it comparatively easy to follow up.

The bull moose is polygamous and a vicious fighter during the rutting season, which commences, as a rule, in November, though apparently not so disposed at other periods of the year, for in the summer months in localities where moose are abundant, grown bulls are to be seen grazing and drinking together in complete amity. The cows herd shortly before the rutting season commences and remain with the bulls during the winter months, but separate before the calf is born and remain alone with the calf until the following rutting season approaches. It would appear that in the majority of cases but one calf is born to a cow. A curious feature is the apparent nomadic propensity of the moose. Some areas, which once contained moose in abundance, and where there is no apparent reason for their disappearance, are now almost destitute of them, while others, which some few years ago the moose was not known to inhabit, harbor at the present time considerable numbers. How far the presence of the caribou and deer affect the moose it has been impossible to determine, but it would seem that in certain instances, at least, the appearance of the moose in numbers has been coincident with the disappearance of the caribou from the locality, and that the appearance of deer in numbers has been followed by a marked diminution in the numbers of moose, although, of course, there are instances of localities in which two, or even all three, varieties are to be found.

As pointed out in the Interim Report of this Commission, one of the principal difficulties in connection with the perpetuation of big game is removed by the prohibition of the slaughter of the female. Most particularly so is this the case when the males are polygamous. The destruction of a cow or doe entails a loss of reproductive capacity far in excess of that caused through the death of a bull, for the duties of the bull will be performed by another of his sex, even though such other be required to attend to several cows or does, whereas the function of the cow or doe can be replaced by no other of its sex. As an illustration of the effectiveness of saving the females from the hunter, where this law is rigidly enforced in common with other laws and restrictions in regard to seasons and numbers, it is interesting to note that in New Brunswick it is an established fact that there are actually more moose to-day in spite of the increased population and in spite of the inevitable encroachments of civilization than there were two centuries ago. The restriction against the killing of cows or does is objected to by some persons on the grounds that it interferes with nature's arrangements for the maintenance of good stock. It is claimed that the majority of hunters go after the head; that the proportion of the finest bulls—that is, those presumably best for breeding purposes—killed is therefore high; and that the percentage of bulls slaughtered is in any event greater than that of cows. This argument would not appear to be valid in so far, at least, as this Province is concerned, for the meat of the cow moose is usually more tender than that of the bull, and consequently more highly esteemed for food purposes by those who are more concerned with the meat than with the head, such as the settlers and Indians, and it is an indisputable fact that a very large proportion of the total numbers of this animal killed during the year meet death at the hands of settlers and Indians, while in the case of the deer, even though the distinction be- tween the flesh of the male and female is, perhaps, not quite so clearly marked, the doe is, nevertheless, as a rule, found to be more tender than the average buck. . It is further claimed that by forbidding the killing of females the percentage of bulls to cows will be so dangerously de- creased that the young, weak or decrepit bulls, which are the least likely to attract the hunter, and consequently the least likely to be shot, will play a far greater part in the perpetuation of their species than they would under nature's ordering, for where the spoils are to the victor in a fight, the young, weak or decrepit bulls are likely to go lacking. Ex- perience, however, would not appear to substantiate this contention, for no one could accuse the moose of New Brunswick of having deteriorated to any marked degree. It would seem, therefore, that this wise pro- vision has been rightly applied to Ontario, for the decrease in the num- bers of moose in recent years is indisputable, its securest retreats are gradually but incessantly being rendered accessible, and there can be little question that unless the measure is maintained and strictly en- forced the day would soon arrive when the diminution of the moose would become so plainly marked and generally recognized that far more drastic measures would have to be enacted if it was to be perpetuated in the Province. If the measure is vital to the perpetuation of the moose and caribou, it would appear in no less degree to be equally so in the case of deer, and it is, therefore, to be earnestly hoped that the provision will be extended to cover this animal also.

The restriction of one moose to a hunter is reasonable, and no com- plaints have been recorded on that score, although through many por- tions of the moose area rumors are afloat of head hunters and others tak- ing far greater numbers when opportunity offered. Particularly so was this the case in the Rainy River District, in the neighborhood of the in- ternational boundary, but seeing that, if, as seems probable, some offences of this nature were committed, the offender, in all probability, had no license at all, it does not affect the question of a reasonable bag limit, but serves only to enhance the necessity for better protection.

In regard to the open season, as at present existing, it is to be hoped that a distinction is made between the country to the north and south of the main line of the Canadian Pacific Railway, from Mattawa to the Manitoba boundary; the open season for the northern area extending from October 16th to November 15th, inclusive, and that for the south- ern area from November 1st to November 15th, inclusive. The great bulk of the territory in which moose is now to be found naturally lies in

Moose Leaving the Water.

Moose in the Water.

the northern section, the only very considerable exception being that portion of the Rainy River District lying to the south of the Canadian Pacific Railway. The growing scarcity of moose in the southerly regions generally and the earlier advent of snow in the northern doubtless both played their parts in the selection of these dates. It is to be observed, however, that the Temiskaming and Northern Ontario Railway has already pushed up into the northerly regions, while the right of way of the Grand Trunk Pacific Railway has already been cut, all of which is tending to render this area more accessible, and will continue to do so in increasing measure in the future. It becomes, then, a question whether it would not be advisable to reduce the open season for moose in the north lands to the period of time now prevailing in the southerly regions. The provincial resources in moose are mainly located in it; the more southerly regions have been largely depleted; the total numbers of moose throughout the Province are known generally to be decreasing; and supervision in these regions of the settlers and Indians is at all times difficult in regard to game. For these reasons it would appear that such a step would be in the best interests of the perpetuation of this noble animal in the Province. It is to be noted, also, that in those sections of the Rainy River District where the moose is now hunted, there is practically no difference in climate between the northern and southern sections as now differentiated between in the matter of open seasons for moose, while moose are apparently as proportionately numerous to the south of the Canadian Pacific Railway as they are to the north of it in this region, so that the differentiation now in force is a manifest absurdity when applied to this district.

The question of the best dates for a general open season of two weeks throughout the Province is somewhat difficult to decide upon. There can be but little doubt but that the open season for all species of deer found in Ontario should be the same, where all are liable to be found in approximately the same areas, and that the presence of the hunter in the woods in legitimate pursuit of one variety cannot but endanger the others. In the Interim Report of this Commission a recommendation was made that the open season for deer be declared from November 15th to 30th, and the reasons for the making of this recommendation were fully set forth therein. Objection to it has been taken by some hunters on the grounds that snow is to be expected by that time throughout the bulk of the deer country, and tracking will thus be rendered easier. Granting that this is the case, it would seem that the objection is fully compensated by the advantage, also incidentally deemed an objection by some, that the general conditions will be less pleasant for the hunter, and that consequently less persons can be expected to go into the woods after the deer. Pending the introduction of an effective game warden service it is, as before observed, necessary to make hunting a little difficult. A more forcible objection has been advanced, namely, that the rutting season is in full swing and that the flesh of bucks is unsavoury during this period. Undoubtedly both these contentions are facts. The presence of hunters in the woods will tend to scatter the deer, which is to be regretted in the rutting season, but it is to be noted that the same effect is produced more or less under the dates of the open season as at present existing, while none the less the bulk of the deer appear to succeed in performing the functions necessary for reproduction. The meat of the males is certainly strong in flavour during this period, but, although some meat in consequence might be wasted, it would appear that the obvious results can only be a diminished demand for it and in consequence a diminished slaughter, which after all are the principal objectives now to be sought. Were these dates applied to the moose, the above remarks would be applicable to its case also, in the main, but it must be acknowledged that as the bull moose is so strong and so vicious during the rutting season, this might be held to constitute a sufficient reason for not sending hunters into the woods when the rutting season is in full swing, and also that a hardship may be wrought on the settlers, who depend on the moose in many instances for their winter's supply of meat, if they were compelled to take bulls whose flesh was more or less rank. The rutting season of moose, however, would appear to extend over the latter portion of October, the whole of November, and on into the early portions of December, so that if the open season is to be declared during this general period of the year at all, which from most points of view is undoubtedly the proper one, it would not appear that the considerations above referred to would be more applicable or carry more force in regard to the latter two weeks of November than in regard to the earlier portions of that month. There would be, moreover, one great advantage in having the open season during the latter two weeks of November, namely, that the weather by that time throughout the moose and deer country will almost invariably be sufficiently cold to allow of the preservation of the meat by freezing, whereas earlier in November or in October this might not always be the case. Most particularly is this point of importance to the settler and others who shoot to obtain food for themselves and families, for it is of small avail to grant them privileges in regard to the taking of big game if the weather conditions during the periods of privilege will prevent their being able to preserve the meat.

The woodland caribou, or American reindeer, is, in all probability, still more or less abundant in the extreme northerly portions of Ontario, but it would seem to have diminished considerably in numbers in the more accessible localities. The caribou, like the moose, appears to avoid the proximity of civilization, to require considerable areas of wild land over which to roam, and to move from one district to another without any very apparent reason. Large tracts of forest and wild land in this Province are undoubtedly adapted to sustaining the caribou, and contain plenty of suitable food, but from many of them it seems to have departed. As a rule the caribou can be more easily approached than the moose, being neither so alert nor so cunning, but it is unquestionably a magnificent animal and a valuable asset to the provincial game resources. Its comparative scarcity in the accessible portions of the Province, therefore, renders it most imperative that every precaution should be taken to preserve it. The same remarks, therefore, in regard to the length and period of the open season for moose would apply equally to the caribou. In fact, the principal necessities in regard to the moose, caribou and deer are to have one open season for all three of them, applying equally to all parts of the Province; to restrict the killing to the males of the various species; and for the present, at least, to reduce the period of the open season for all three varieties to a maximum of fourteen days.

A matter of no little interest to the public would be the publication from time to time of statistics showing the numbers of big game taken in the course of an open season. The possession, in fact, of information on this subject by the Department would appear to be most desirable, for it would seem to afford the only reliable basis on which to found restrictive legislation dealing with this subject. Licenses to hunt big game have to be taken out by both residents and non-residents, the charge for the latter being considerably in excess of the former, and it would seem that no undue hardship would be placed on any licensee by requiring him to furnish the Department from which the license emanates with full detail of his kill. If a coupon for the purpose were attached to the license, no doubt the great majority of hunters would willingly comply with the condition, and there can be little question that the approximate statistics obtained by this means would be both useful and interesting.

Unfortunately it must be recorded that in certain portions of the Province the weight of evidence obtainable points unmistakably to the fact that considerable destruction of big game must still be attributed to the presence in the woods of lumber camps and other enterprises involving the feeding of gangs of men by private companies and individuals. As a rule it would seem that the larger concerns are not guilty in this respect, but in addition to making ample provision for food supplies for their men, issue also strict instructions to their foremen against the illegal taking of game, and that it is, in fact, the smaller concerns who are the most persistent offenders. It is perfectly apparent that in a district where big game is comparatively abundant a great saving will be effected to the timber licensee or contractor if the butcher bill can be reduced by some thousands of pounds of meat secured at little or no expense in the forest, and, indeed, there is little doubt that in some cases men are employed solely for the purpose of hunting for certain of the camps, regulations on the subject notwithstanding. The difficulty of obtaining accurate information as to such infractions of the law is considerable, for, as a rule, the camp is situated at some considerable distance from a railway, and even if the visits of the overseer could occur

with reasonable frequency, which in general they do not, and come in
the nature of a surprise, the object of the visits would be known to one
and all, steps would be taken to conceal all traces of malefactions, and
only food of an unimpeachable character would appear on the tables during the overseer's stay. In fact it would seem that where such infractions of the law occur some steps are, as a rule, taken to guard against
surprise or detection, such as keeping a supply of beef on hand and con-
cealing the deer or moose meat at some little distance from the camp.
There can be no question that it is imperative to put a stop to these
practices, and the most feasible means would appear to be to employ a
certain number of specially selected men, who would habitually seek employment in the woods, to engage in suspected camps; work there and
acquire the necessary information; leave, having done so, on some such
pretext as would actuate the ordinary lumber-jack; and, returning to
civilization, place the information in the hands of the nearest overseer
or magistrate, so that it could be acted upon and the offenders indicted
without, as a rule, connecting the informant with the detection of the
crime. It would seem, also, that where these practices could be brought
home to the offending parties a very heavy fine should be inflicted on
them, in addition to the ordinary fine for the illegal destruction of each
separate animal. Undoubtedly if such measures were put into force a
great saving of game would be effected annually to the advantage of the
Province.

THE SETTLER IN RELATION TO GA) E.

A most difficult and vexed question is that of the rights and privileges of the settler in regard to game. There can be no question that the
primary function of game in all wild countries is to supply food to the
natives inhabiting it or to the pioneers opening it up. As a rule during
the latter process there is a tendency to reckless waste, and it cannot
be said that the experiences of Ontario have furnished any exception to
the general rule. In consequence the inevitable result has ensued, even
in those districts which are as yet still but very sparsely populated,
namely, that the quantity of game of all descriptions has materially
diminished. It would, however, be impossible to blame the early settlers
in a new land for their prodigality, for theirs is an unusual and, in many
instances, a hard life, game a necessity of existence and hunting the
habitual form of recreation, while the very abundance of the game tends
to obliterate their faculty for perceiving that the day of reckoning in
depleted quantities of game must eventually arrive, or even of themselves
acknowledging that the diminution is taking place after it has already
become only too apparent.

In a country developing in civilization and increasing in population the pioneer settler still performs a service to the public which it
is hard to estimate at its intrinsic value. New country is broken up,

prepared and improved, to the increase of the public wealth and to the ultimate benefit of posterity, at the cost to the settler and his family of an existence below the general standard of comfort and prosperity of the community. It would seem unreasonable, therefore, to begrudge some little advantage to these pioneers over the rest of the community in the matter of game privileges. On the other hand game is undoubtedly a public asset, which, after its primary function has in large measure disappeared, none the less continues to be of equal, if not increasing, value in its general effect on the moral and material welfare of the population, and it is evident that as the game areas and game diminish before the advance of civilization, those living on the land under conditions of average comfort, or with reasonable facilities to do so if they choose at their disposal, can no longer expect to be privileged above the general community in the matter of game, but must rest content to submit to the regulations and restrictions which are imposed on the public in the interests of the common weal. The game constitutes a public asset, and the fact that a man lives in the country instead of in a town cannot alone be held sufficient cause to warrant any exceptional claim or privilege on his behalf on the game in the vicinity. If, therefore, it may be deemed advisable to privilege a few under exceptional circumstances and for exceptional services rendered, this can in no sense be held to justify the extension of the privilege to those not so circumstanced. These matters have long been within the knowledge and consideration of the administrations of this Province, and serious efforts have been made to solve the problem in a manner which would be both equitable and advantageous. Unfortunately, however, the solution appears not as yet to have been found.

At the present time a resident of the Province is required to take out a license to hunt deer, moose or caribou, the cost of a deer license being $2.00, and that for moose or caribou $5.00. Under the former license but one deer may be killed, and under the latter but one bull moose or one bull caribou. In proportion, therefore, to the amount of flesh on these animals and the value of their hides and heads, it will be seen that the charges are by no means excessive. In the case, however, of the settler living in unorganized districts, the license fee in regard to deer is relaxed, and he is given the privilege of taking one deer for home consumption free of all charge. In 1907 this privilege was extended to settlers in certain of the organized but wild regions, but was cancelled during the course of the year 1910. The right of the settler in the unorganized districts to take one deer is not held to cover either moose or caribou, nor is it legal for him to take the deer except in the legal open season.

In regard to the system of distinguishing between organized and unorganized districts, it may be observed that in very many instances conditions of life in the former are equally, if not more, severe than in the latter and, consequently, that residents in such areas have some grounds for complaint that they are unjustly penalized for the slight privilege of organization. The organized districts, however, even though the con- ditions under which the settlers live may be equally hard as those pre- vailing in adjacent unorganized districts, are in the main the most acces- sible, and naturally, therefore, the more liable to be visited by hunters during the open season. It was proved that the privilege accorded the settlers was in no small measure being abused to the undue destruction of the game and to the evasion of the bag limits imposed on hunters by law, and it would seem, in consequence, to have been deemed wise to re- strict the privilege to the greatest possible extent. Unfortunately it is the case that in the wild portions of the Province it is so easy and com- paratively safe for persons resident in them to break the game laws that the temptation to do so is great, and there can be little question that in these regions, whether they be organized or unorganized, if the settler makes up his mind that he requires a moose, a caribou or a deer, he will take it, whether or no he is privileged to do so by law. No means, ap- parently, are available to alter this condition, and it would, therefore, seem wise to face the facts as they exist and to seek some means whereby the settler in all truly wild regions may be enabled to take a sufficiency of game to meet his actual necessities, as he does at present all too often illegally, under the provisions and protection of the law. In considering a scheme whereby this may be effected the most obvious difficulties are to determine to what areas the privilege should be applied; whether or no some compensation should be exacted for the privilege; the amount of game that should be allowed to be taken; and the extent of territory the privilege should be held to embrace in each individual case.

It has already been noted that discrimination between organized and unorganized districts has been found unsatisfactory in regard to game privileges in that organization does not of necessity imply immediate or rapid amelioration of circumstances. In both cases there are to be found settlers performing the service of opening up the land and having a hard struggle for existence; while in both cases, also, there will be found a percentage who have settled in the area as a means of exploiting its tim- ber resources and make no effort to open up or improve the land. The true pioneer class are obviously earning some special privileges in regard to game, but it would seem that the latter class can in no sense be deemed worthy of especial consideration. Similarly, under the provisions of the law, holdings in wild regions may be acquired by persons engaged dur- ing a great portion of the year in other localities and in other occupa- tions, provided only that certain clearings and improvements shall be effected over a stated period. In the bulk of such cases the holding is acquired as a speculation, and although some small improvements have to be carried out, there is no intention on the part of the owner to reside permanently upon it. In the majority of such cases, also, the quasi set- tler will be in a financial position equally favorable to that of the aver- age citizen, so that from no point of view can he rightly claim exemption from licenses of general application. It would seem, therefore, that a *sine qua non* for privilege in the matter of game licenses should be permanent residence on a holding in a wild region, together with cultivation of the soil or the effecting of considerable improvements.

Another point in this regard that has to be considered is the question of the location of the holding. There are many instances in the Province of truly wild regions within close proximity to thriving towns or villages, and where in general, if the settler's lot is a hard one, it is more due to himself than to circumstances connected with his surroundings. One, if not the only, object in granting exemption is to allow of the settler and his family obtaining the food necessary for existence, which could be obtained practically in no other way owing to the location of the holding, or else, which the settler could not afford to purchase owing to his straightened circumstances. In the case of settlers in wild regions living in the vicinity of towns and villages, food supplies can often be obtained with comparative ease, and the wherewithal to purchase them should usually be forthcoming if the settler exploits his land to advantage and avails himself of local facilities to work and earn money like the average individual. There can be no advantage in allowing the privilege in any sense to degenerate into an incentive to laziness, and it would seem, therefore, that in instances of this nature these matters should be taken into consideration in determining whether or no the settlers in the locality should be granted the privilege.

Beyond the general principles as above enunciated there would seem to be no means of devising any cast-iron rule for general application by which it could be determined to what areas the privilege should apply. In fact, arbitrary delimitation has, as already noted, proved highly unsatisfactory. Consequently, the case of each district should receive individual attention, and decision in the matter must plainly rest with the Department concerned. It is to be observed, however, that various Departments maintain officers at different points throughout the Province in addition to that of Fish and Game, and under a proper system of interdepartmental co-operation no difficulty should be encountered by the Department of Fish and Game in securing fairly accurate information as to the conditions prevailing in any particular district by this means, and further, there are in almost every case to be found responsible citizens living in the general district both able and willing to furnish reliable information as to the conditions existing in the remoter and wilder sections of the locality.

In regard to the question as to what compensation might justly be expected from the settler in return for the privileges granted him in the matter of game, it is to be noted that under the present system nothing at all is required of him. It cannot be claimed, however, that the system has worked well or that the settler has been educated to esteem the privilege at its true worth. One of the chief difficulties in the perpetuation of big game over a wide extent of territory is to form an accurate

idea of the numbers which annually are being slaughtered, and yet without such information suitable legislation can only by hazard be enacted.
When a license is in force, it is plainly feasible and advantageous that
the licensee should be required to furnish information as to his kill to
the Department concerned, so that the authorities may be advised as to
the numbers of any particular variety of animal killed during any one
open season. It can scarcely be denied that such information should be
in the hands of the authorities, and seeing, therefore, that no small percentage of the big game annually slaughtered in this Province meets
death at the hands of some settler, provision should be made to obtain
figures of the kill effected by settlers as well as of that effected by the
ordinary hunter. It is, moreover, to be observed that the possession of
a permit, even though that permit costs little or nothing, is calculated
in some degree to impress the holder with the extent of the privilege
accorded him, and the trouble to the settler in obtaining such a permit
is more than offset by this advantage. Pecuniary considerations, however, will often largely influence the value attached to any particular
article. It would seem, therefore, that where the settler is to be granted
a privilege, not only should he be required to have in his possession a
permit granting him the privilege, but that he should be required to furnish statistics of his kill to the Department before such permit is renewed each succeeding year, and further, that to enhance the value of
the privilege in his eyes and to educate him to its responsibilities, as well
as to cover the cost of the issuance of the permit, some small registration
fee might also well be required of him. The actual amount of such fee
would not appear to be of material importance, provided only that it was
small, and 25 to 50 cents should be amply sufficient for the purpose. In
addition to these things it might, perhaps, also be required of the settler
that he check, as far as possible, all illegalities and report all infractions
of the law that come under his notice to the proper authorities at the
first opportunity, but in any case he should be given to understand that
any infraction of the game law on his part, or should he connive at or
abet such infraction on the part of others, not only will disqualify him
or any member of his family resident with him from obtaining the renewal of such permit, but will be likely to influence the authorities in
the matter of renewing the permits of his neighbors in the district, or, in
other words, that the exemption accorded him is a privilege and in no
sense a right appertaining to his mode of life or to the locality in which
he happens to live. Where, indeed, in any district offences against the
game laws or abuse of the settlers' privilege were found to be at all common or numerous, it would seem that all settlers' permits should at once
be cancelled, regardless of the hardship entailed on, perhaps, one or two
law-abiding citizens therein.

In the matter of the issuance of permits to settlers, the authority
should plainly be made as broad as possible consistent with due caution,
and be vested in such officials as magistrates, overseers, provincial con-

stables and the clerks of the organized districts nearest to the areas which have been selected for privileged treatment by the Department, but it should be clearly impressed on each such official that not more than one such permit was to be issued to a family residing together, and that no permit was to be renewed until such conditions as might be required of the settler had been discharged.

The question next arises as to what amount of game the settler should be entitled to kill under his permit. Attention has been called to the fact that while undoubtedly moose, caribou and deer may occur together or in adjacent localities, this is not the rule, but rather that where one is abundant the others will be comparatively scarce. In regard to moose and caribou, to the taking of which the settlers' permit does not at present extend, it is plain that if either of these is the animal chiefly to be found in the district, the privilege extended to the bona fide settler should include these animals. The great size of the creatures should preclude any necessity of the settler requiring more than one in the course of a winter, if care is taken not to waste the meat, for it may here be observed that whatever the privilege extended to the settler he must in no way be allowed to take game other than in the legal open season. The moose or caribou will produce an enormous amount of meat, and if shot in the open season, when the weather is cold, the meat can easily be maintained in good condition throughout the winter. To shoot these large animals in the summer is bound almost to entail the waste of an enormous amount of meat, so that for this reason, if for no other, the taking of deer in the summer months must be most rigidly suppressed. Moreover, it is in the winter especially that the settler can be expected to feel the pinch of necessity, and it is to meet this condition that the privilege is accorded him. In the summer months the fruits of his own labor should produce him sufficient upon which to live, and in any case the practically free gift of so great and valuable a creature as either a moose or caribou cannot but be considered an ample discharge of its duties in this direction in regard to the settler on the part of the general public. While, therefore, the privilege extended to the settler might well include moose and caribou, one specimen of either one or the other variety, but not of both, must be deemed ample for his needs.

In regard to deer the recent reduction of the legal limit to one, instead of as formerly two, will undoubtedly have effected a hardship in the case of some settlers should they have abided by the law. Two deer will afford a reasonable amount of meat for a settler's family during the winter months, but one deer, in the case of fair-sized families, at least, is bound to reduce the daily ration to very small proportions. Undoubtedly even this meagre allowance will be considered a great help, but it would seem that if there is a real necessity for granting a privilege to the settler at all, that privilege might well be enlarged to meet the necessities of his case to the full. Where, therefore, the settler kills only deer under his permit, it would appear that he should be allowed to take two, and further, also, that he might well be allowed to take one deer in addition to either one moose or one caribou.

There can be no necessity to legalize the taking of small game by the settlers, for the settlers, who live in the wild regions, know more or less the location of such small game as there is in their vicinity and are in a position to take the utmost advantage of the legal open seasons. Consequently, those restrictions which are placed from time to time on certain species of small game should be observed by the settler, and he should be made to realize that offences in regard to small game will disqualify him from any privileges in regard to big game.

Finally as to the extent of territory over which the settler should be entitled to shoot the game allowed him by privilege, it is evident that some limitation should be imposed in the interests of the public, for inasmuch as there will only be certain localities in which it is deemed desirable to grant settlers' permits, if no limitations were made the settler would on occasions be found hunting in areas for which no such permits were granted, and the residents therein would have just cause to complain. In almost every case where it is at all desirable to grant the settler special privileges in regard to game one variety or another will occur in comparatively close proximity to his holdings. It remains, then, but to determine an area wide enough to suit all cases, and there can be little question that a radius of ten miles from the habitation of the settler should be amply sufficient. It is not to be expected, of course, that this restriction could be very rigidly enforced, but it would serve to call the attention of the settler to the importance attached by the authorities to the privilege accorded him, and at the same time would facilitate the work of the game wardens in dealing with patent infractions of the privilege, such as where the settler shoots for other persons and for their benefit in regard to meat at some considerable distance from his home. In this connection, also, it may be observed that the settler when hunting should be required to carry his permit on his person.

THE INDIAN IN RELATION TO GA) E.

One of the principal factors in the destruction of game is the Indian living in the wilder regions. Considerable reservations have been set aside for the Indians in various portions of the Province, and there is no doubt that within the limits of such reservations the Indians are entitled to hunt game of all descriptions when and how they please. These reservations, however, in some cases are not sufficiently wide to provide for all the requirements of the Indians in the matter of game, or else have been more or less depleted of the game in them by the Indians themselves, and the result has been that in various portions of the Province the Indians have hunted, fished and trapped at all seasons of the year on Crown lands or water without the limits of their reservations. The rights of the Indians in this connection would appear as yet

Indian Encampment, Showing Wigwams, Rainy River District.

Indian Graves, Rainy River District.

17 F.C.

not to have been definitely settled by the authorities. It is not the purpose of this Commission to enter upon a discussion as to the treaty rights and privileges of Indians, but merely to call attention to certain features of this problem which are of no little importance to the Province.

In the wilder regions of Ontario the Indians are not, as a rule, addicted to agricultural pursuits and depend for their food very largely on what they can succeed in securing in the way of fish and game. In the main, also, it may be said that the Indian is not an energetic person, excepting when actually engaged in the pursuit of some wild creature, nor as a rule one possessed of great perspicacity in financial matters. Consequently, although many indians in these regions will at times undertake some form of labour, such as guiding or the moving of merchandise, for which they receive good pay, and will, also, sell the results of their trapping operations which not infrequently net them considerable sums, in general they are loath to undertake prolonged or steady work, and what money they make disappears with astonishing rapidity, so that during a great portion of the year food is with them a question of no little moment. Although doubtless there could be adduced many instances to the contrary, as a rule the Indian would not appear to be of a wasteful disposition in the matter of food, especially in regard to that secured by hunting, so that on the whole it may be assumed that what game the Indian does take for his own purposes is at least made use of. If, therefore, the depredations of Indians were confined to their own requirements, there would, perhaps, not be much cause for complaint. Unfortunately, however, this is far from being the case. In the wilder portions of the country there are in many localities to be found individuals only too willing to purchase from Indians such game as the law forbids their taking themselves, and so long as the Indian can take game with impunity during the close seasons on public lands, so long would it seem inevitable that there should be a market open to him; in fact, a direct incentive to him to break the laws which apply to the white man.

Fish, game and fur-bearing animals are obviously an exhaustible asset, and restrictions in regard to their taking have been necessitated owing to their diminishing numbers. If the Indian is enabled to enter any area and take what game he chooses to any extent he desires, not only is it apparent that the effect of the restrictions will be largely discounted in that area, but that the white inhabitants of the area will have reasonable cause for complaint and indignation. Various instances of this unsatisfactory state of affairs are readily to be found in the Province. The beaver, which had become very scarce throughout Ontario, was placed under protection for a period of years, which protection is still in force. The Indian, who can take the beaver if such exists on his reservation and, moreover, is somewhat partial to its flesh, will not and has not been deterred in many instances from so doing on public lands, mainly for the reason that he seldom encounters any difficulty in disposing of the skins at a remunerative figure. In fact, the value of the pelt is a direct incentive to him to take all that he can secure, with the consequence that where under normal conditions he would have taken but one or two of a family, his greed now leads him to exterminate it, for he is naturally improvident in regard to the future. Speckled trout may not be netted and are jealously preserved for sporting purposes. The Indian appears on some of the finest waters and proceeds to place his nets in the channels or on the spawning beds, removing as many fish as he deems necessary and undoing in a very short time all the good which has been effected by protection and a close season. The moose and deer may be fairly scarce in a locality, and the local resident may be eagerly awaiting the approach of the open season in anticipation of hunting some specimen which has taken up its quarters in the vicinity of his habitation. An Indian passing by while the creature's horns are still in velvet or it itself is fat and unsuspicious, shoots it with supreme unconcern of laws and regulations before the eyes, perhaps, of the resident, and proceeds to regale himself upon it and remove such portions of the carcass as he requires. The partridge, owing to its growing scarcity, was until the last season on the protected list throughout the year, and even now is in no such abundance that anywhere there can be said to be too great a supply in comparison with the local demands or needs of sportsmen. The appearance of a family or more of Indians in a neighborhood will as a rule be coincident with the disappearance of the coveys. Wild duck and other birds are afforded protection during the season of the year when they are nesting or caring for their young. The Indian is no ultra-sentimentalist, and should he feel so disposed will as lief shoot a mother bird on the nest or with chicks as any other. The list could be indefinitely prolonged, but enough has been said to show that the present situation is, to say the least of it, unsatisfactory, and that some effort should be made without delay to come to an agreement or arrangement on the matter which will be both equitable to the Indians, fair to the public of the Province, and as far as possible in harmony with the general principles of conservation. In any case it must be apparent that the present situation demands that the whole question of the rights of Indians should be cleared up once and for all in regard to game on public lands, for the matter will plainly have to be faced some time, and it would certainly seem that the sooner this is done the better will it be in the interests of law, order and administration.

Whatever the decision may be in regard to the rights of Indians in the matter of game on public lands, it must be evident that it should be made a most serious offence, punishable with severe penalties, for any white man to pay or incite an Indian to violate the white man's game law in any respect, or to take advantage of such violation in the slightest degree. In fact, imprisonment together with a heavy fine would appear none too severe a punishment for the offence. It is evident, also, that no injustice would be done to the Indian by making him liable to

An Indian Dog.

A Group of Indians, Rainy River District.

imprisonment or fine where he barters or attempts to barter any form of game proscribed by the white man's law or during the period when such game is out of the legal season, except and only within the limits of his reservation and there only among his own kind. The principle of allowing Indians to do so in respect to game, fur or fish would not only be a manifest injustice to the general public and an incentive to general disregard of the laws, but a palpable absurdity into the bargain. At the present time the Indian's chief depredations are undoubtedly due to cupidity born of the knowledge that he can dispose of his spoils to the white man. A few instances of really rigorous punishment applied to both white man and Indian concerned in such a deal would undoubtedly go a long way to check the present extent of this evil. A method of dealing with the question of trapping will be discussed in a succeeding section, but in regard to game and fish it may be observed that the most satisfactory manner of disposing of this problem, from the point of view, at least, of economy in natural resources, would be to have one law applicable to white man and Indian alike in regard to open seasons and bag limits on public lands, with the privilege to the Indian of securing a permit to take all such game as the law allowed free of charge. There can be little doubt that the special privileges in regard to big game mentioned in a previous section of this report in regard to the poor settler in wild regions should be amply sufficient to provide for the wants of any Indian family also during the winter months, and in the summer the Indian family, like the family of the settler, should be able to subsist comfortably on the proceeds of the winter's trapping or other work, on such products of the soil as their energy causes to be produced or which are to be found growing wild in the neighborhood, and on the fish which they are so adept in catching.

Another point to which attention has to be called in regard to Indians in relation to game is that within or in the immediate vicinity of certain of the provincial forest reserves there are Indian reservations and in one instance, at least, that of the Quetico Forest Reserve, it would appear that the Indians habitually hunt and trap therein. It is to be observed that if the game in a reserve is to be hunted, one of the principal values of such reserve will disappear, and further, that if trapping is to be conducted in a reserve, it would appear that, as previously noted in this report, the profits should accrue to the public to offset the charges for the protection of the reserve. Whether or no it is any more feasible to prevent Indians hunting and trapping in a provincial forest reserve than on any other public lands is a question which will have to be decided upon by the proper authorities, but at least it must be apparent that if the provincial reserves are to fulfil their proper functions in regard to game of all descriptions, the greatest efforts should be made to keep the hunting Indian out of them, or at least to limit his operations to the removal of such fur-bearing animals as may be deemed advisable by the authorities under the supervision of government officials and for

the benefit of the public treasury. It would seem, therefore, that were
it possible to do so, it would be most advisable to make fresh treaties
with the Indians in these localities and transfer them to other reservations at a distance from the reserves.

One, point, however, strongly in favour of the Indian and half-breed
must be mentioned, namely that when out of reach of the illicit purveyor
of strong liquors he is not only in most instances simple and trustworthy,
but from his very methods of existence a most proficient woodsman, in
the sense that paths and tracks of the forest stretch out before him like
an open map should he only once have traversed them, and that the ways
and secrets of wild life are known to him from his early childhood.
Perhaps, therefore, it might be possible to take advantage of these traits
in the Indian character, alike to the benefit of the Indian and of the
general public. In the less accessible reserves, and, in fact, in the
remoter sections of the forest area which are now or will be shortly
patrolled by government rangers, there would seem to be an opportunity
of turning the Indian to good account. Under adequate supervision
there is no apparent reason why he should not become an efficient
ranger. Starting with a great initial advantage over the average white
man in the matter of woodcraft, he is equally, if not more, expert than
the average white man as a canoeist also. He is not afraid of being
alone in the woods and can travel from point to point rapidly, dispensing with much of the impedimenta which would be considered indispensable by the ordinary white ranger. It would, indeed, but be necessary to explain to him the nature of the duties he was expected to perform and to make arrangements for insuring the supervision that in
any case would be indispensable. Well supplied with food the necessity
or temptation to hunt would disappear, for as before observed the
Indian is not as a rule wasteful in regard to provisions. Perhaps the
main objection to employing the Indian in this fashion would be held
to rest in confiding into his hands the authority of ranger and warden
in regard to white men working in the woods. In as much, however, as
he is no great linguist, and uneducated to distinguish between the various classes of white men, it would seem that he could be counted on to
discharge his duties without fear, favour or affection. Two instances,
at least, in this Province of the employment of Indians for this purpose
have proved thoroughly successful, and it would appear that in the more
general application of the principle might be found a solution to the
many difficulties and problems connected with the Indians in the wilder
regions.

RECO X X ENDATIONS.

Your Commissioner would, therefore, recommend:—

(1) That a resident hunting license of $1.10, as recommended in
the Interim Report of this Commission, be imposed without delay for the
privilege of hunting any species of game in the Province for which no

license is at present in force; that those persons recommended to be exempt from the operation of such license be required to obtain a permit in lieu of the license; and that it be declared illegal to be in the possession of firearms in the forests or on the wild lands belonging to the Crown during the open seasons for any game whatsoever without such license or permit, unless such firearms shall have been sealed with a government seal.

(2) That all holders of hunting licenses or permits whatsoever be required as a condition of obtaining the same to furnish the Department, on a form provided with the license or permit for that purpose, with statistics as to the game shot or killed under such license or permit, and that information based on these returns be given to the public yearly as to the amount of game of each species killed in the Province.

(3) That the open season for moose and caribou throughout the Province be limited to two weeks and be made coincident with the open season for deer.

(4) That the shooting of does be prohibited in the future.

(5) That *bona fide* settlers in the more newly settled regions of the Province, whether in organized or unorganized districts, domiciled on their holdings generally throughout the year and effecting actual improvements in the same or subsisting chiefly on the agricultural products of such holding produced through their own efforts, be, at the discretion of the responsible Department, granted permits to the extent of one only to each family resident together authorizing them to take, during the open season for such game, one moose or one caribou and one deer, or else two deer, for the use of themselves and family, provided only that the said permit be valid only over a radius of ten miles from the habitation of the settler; that no trading in the game secured under the permit be tolerated; and that in consideration of receiving a permit the settler be required to pay a registration fee of 25 cents, and to furnish the Department, on a form provided him with his permit for that purpose, with statistics of the game taken by him under such permit.

(6) That a settler's permit as above recommended be renewed only after the required conditions shall have been properly executed; that any infraction of the game laws on the part of the settler or connivance by him at the same on the part of others be deemed sufficient cause for the immediate cancellation of his permit and for his disqualification from obtaining such a permit for a period of five years; that such disqualification shall be held to apply to all members of his family or other persons resident with him; and that where infractions of the game laws become at all numerous in any district for which such permits are issued, all such permits issued for the district be cancelled and not renewed for a period of five years.

(7) That the settler be required to have his permit on his person when engaged in hunting.

(8) That special steps be taken to prevent the use of deer or moose meat, illegally taken, in lumber or other camps located in the woods, by engaging the services of reliable men to work in suspected camps and report infractions of the law to the proper authorities, and that a fine of $250.00, in addition to the present legal fine for each animal illegally taken, be imposed on the licensee or contractor responsible wherever it can be proved that moose, caribou or deer meat or other game has been illegally supplied to the gangs or working parties employed by him.

(9) That any white man inciting, abetting, paying or causing an Indian to violate the game laws in any respect or taking advantage of any such (presumptive) violation on the part of the Indian be made liable to a fine of not less than $100 in addition to such other fines or penalties as would be imposed by law on account of the game or pelts thus secured.

(10) That, if possible, it be declared a crime, punishable by imprisonment or fine, for an Indian to barter or attempt to barter any game whatsoever, including the pelts of fur-bearing animals, taken during the legal close season for such game as may be in force in the Province, except and only among his own kind within the limits of an Indian Reservation.

(11) That, if possible, steps be taken to have the game laws made applicable to Indians in so far as all public lands and waters are concerned; that under such conditions the Indians be accorded the same privileges as recommended for the *bona fide* settler; free of all charge and conditions other than that they be required to secure a permit to hunt on public lands, to have such permits on their persons while hunting and report to the Indian Agent what game is taken under such permits; and that steps be taken to secure from the Indian Agents statistics of the game slaughtered by the Indians under such permits.

(12) That steps be taken to prevent the Indians hunting in any of the Provincial Forest Reserves.

(13) That where Indian reservations are located in or in the vicinity of provincial forest reserve steps be taken, if possible, to come to some arrangement with the Indians inhabiting them whereby they shall surrender such reservations in return for lands at a distance from such reserves.

(14) That the experiment be made of still further developing the existing policy of employing a few Indians as fire rangers in the provincial forest reserves.

FUR-BEARING ANIMALS.

In its fur-bearing animals the Province of Ontario possesses an asset of enormous value, but the ever rising market worth of the pelts of practically every species, the growth of population and the increasing accessibility of many of its wilder regions have tended to and resulted in a great diminution in the numbers of nearly all varieties. So much

A Scene in the Quetico Forest Reserve.

so was this the case in regard to the beaver and the otter that it was found necessary to prohibit altogether the taking of these animals for a period of years in order to save them from extinction, which restriction is still in force, and it can hardly be doubted that some method of exploiting these resources generally on more economic principles than those at present prevailing should be sought and put into effect if similar drastic measures are not to become necessary to ensure the perpetuation of most of the other species. The variety of valuable fur-bearing animals in the Province is great, including beaver, otter, mink, skunk, racoon, ermine, marten, fisher, lynx, fox, and muskrat, and if due precautions are taken it should be possible to perpetuate all these valuable animals, in spite of the opening up of the country, for a great many generations to come. Most species are comparatively prolific and this fact is alone sufficient to prove that only most extravagant methods of exploitation will result in their depletion. The effects of protection are almost invariably rapid and wonderful in regard to them as is well instanced by the case of the beaver, which a few years ago was almost extinct in the accessible portions of the Province, but which since the prohibition of taking has reappeared in considerable numbers in certain localities; to such an extent, indeed, that from some quarters complaints have been received that they are becoming too numerous and effecting damage owing to their propensity for damming creeks and other waterways. Instances of such complaints are, however, rare and there can be little question that it will be the part of wisdom to afford protection to the beaver against the operations of the ordinary trapper for many years to come, for the houses constructed by these creatures render them peculiarly easy to locate, and once located it is a simple matter to exterminate a whole family. Indeed, it would not seem unreasonable to suggest that where in any locality the beaver are found to be too numerous, the work of thinning out their numbers should be undertaken by the Provincial authorities for the benefit of the public treasury, and that, in fact, the beaver should be regarded throughout the future as a perquisite of the Crown, and protected and exploited accordingly. The beauty of the beaver's fur, its durable qualities and the difficulty of securing a supply at all proportionate to the demand ensure that, at least, little if any diminution will occur in the value of its pelt for many years, and if the government undertook its exploitation, stamped all pelts with a government mark and took only pelts of mature beaver that were in prime condition, it is not to be doubted that Ontario beaver skins would become famous throughout the world, or that a very great revenue would accrue to the Province through this means. The danger of the extermination of the beaver, where they may be taken by one and all, has been clearly demonstrated and established by disastrous experience. The varieties of fur-bearing animals in the Province are numerous. It would seem, therefore, that not only would no hardship be done to the average trapper should the Government undertake such an enterprise, but that it would be the best means of ensuring the perpetuation of the beaver and of deriving the greatest possible benefit from its existence for the public.

The value of fur rests not only on the beauty and durability of the pelt, but in a large measure, also, on its comparative abundance. Some pelts, indeed, which are very scarce, fetch almost incredible sums on the open market. Nevertheless there can be little question that the sum total of the trade occurring in the pelt of the least individual value, that of the muskrat, is going, or has come, to outstrip in value that of any other fur-bearing creature found in the Province. The muskrat therefore is worthy of especial consideration. Like many other fur-bearing animals it is afforded some measure of protection, the taking of it between May 1 and December 1 being prohibited, as likewise the shooting of it during the month of April and the spearing of it at any time, while it is also enacted that the muskrat house may not be cut, speared, broken, or destroyed at any time. The creature itself is about four times the size of an ordinary brown rat, with a tail, compressed, thickest about the middle line and tapering to a rather acute point, about two-thirds as long as the head and body. Except the beaver no other fur-bearing animal of the Province leads a more aquatic life. Its feet are specialized for swimming; its fur waterproof; and its tail serves as an efficient rudder. The muskrat derives its name from the peculiar musky odour given off chiefly by its large perineal glands, which odour to some extent pervades the whole skin, particularly in the summertime. While chiefly nocturnal in habits the little creature, where seldom disturbed, may be seen at work in bright sunlight, especially when constructing winter houses. These houses are for the most part constructed of rushes, grasses, roots and stems of aquatic plants, heaped up without orderly arrangement until the dome-like top rises from 18 inches to 2 or 3 feet above the water. The mud often seen on the outside of the houses seems to be collected accidentally with the roots. In the portion of the house above water an interior chamber is constructed from which two or three passages lead downwards to points below the frost line in the water. These houses are mainly for winter shelter and the storage of food, and as a rule are inhabited by one family only, though sometimes, when ice or frozen ground prevents the use of burrows, a larger number will temporarily find accommodation in them. In banks of streams and ponds the muskrats will construct burrows, the entrance usually being under water at a sufficient depth to prevent their being closed by ice, the burrows extending from 10 to 50 feet into the bank, and terminating in a rough chamber in which sometimes is to be found a nest composed of dried vegetation. When burrows are available the muskrat occupies them in winter and summer, but where water is shallow in ponds and marshes the entrances will often be closed by ice and the creatures forced to make use of the houses. As cold weather approaches they become very active, building, adding to their houses, deepening the channels leading to the burrows, and they do not hibernate during the winter.

There would appear to be considerable diversity of opinion in regard to the breeding habits of the muskrat, but the bulk of evidence would tend to show that normally there are three or more litters in the course of a year of an average of from three to eight, and that the young of the first litter of the year, which arrive early in the spring, themselves breed in the fall of the same year, for the creature must be unusually prolific to account for the wonderful replenishment of marshes during the close season which have been depleted by vigorous trapping.

The muskrat is principally herbivorous, devouring the roots, stems, leaves and fruit of aquatic plants and being partial to nearly all garden vegetables. It will, however, on occasions take animal food, and in some localities during the winter months feeds largely on mussels and such slow-moving fish as the carp, which bury themselves in the mud at this season of the year. Cases, also, have occurred where they have been known to attack trapped or wounded members of their own kind and are said, when hard pressed for food, to devour the weaker members of their own community.

In the raw state the fur of the muskrat is dense and soft, not unlike that of the beaver though the pelage is shorter and less close and somewhat inferior in durability. The colour varies with the season and locality and the fur is in primest condition in the early spring. The earliest demand for muskrat skins was for the manufacture of so-called beaver hats, and when replaced by silk in the manufacture of hats, they next became popular as imitation of sealskin. The modern fur dresser and dyer has, however, found means of imitating nearly all the most costly furs with that of this animal and a continuous and great demand for these pelts on this account alone has been created. The London market affords a good idea of the growth of this demand. From 1763 to 1800 the total number of skins imported and sold in that market was 2,831,- 453, an average of less than 75,000 yearly. From 1851 to 1890 inclusive the importations were approximately 99,893,591, or a yearly average of about 2,500,000, while the average sales of recent years have been over 4,000,000 per annum. Prices are largely based on returns from the London auctions. although the number of pelts retained for home use is increasing rapidly, and it is unquestionable that the prices show a tendency to rise steadily. In Baltimore, for instance, the buyers paid 35 cents apiece in 1909 for brown skins ungraded, whereas in 1910 they were paying 65 cents for the same class skin, while in Toronto in the spring of 1909 a prominent firm of furriers was paying 45 cents a skin and in the the spring of 1910, 75 to 80 cents a skin.

The muskrat is peculiarly defenceless in the wintertime when it is congregated in its burrows and houses, and although the law explicitly forbids the breaking into houses, it is unfortunately the case that this regulation is all too frequently disregarded in a great many portions of the Province with the result that not only are quantities of the little animals left without food and shelter to perish without profit to mankind, but in many instances whole families are wiped out to the detriment of natural reproduction. It would seem, indeed, that the present open season is altogether too long, and occurring as it does just when the greatest harm can be done, is productive of an undue and economically wasteful slaughter. It has been noted that the skin is primest towards spring and that the value of the trade in this fur is steadily increasing. The creature itself will thrive in ponds, marshes, canals and streams, surrounded more or less by civilization and from which other fur-bearing creatures will have largely disappeared. It is apparent, therefore, that with an eye alike to the present as to the future the utmost precautions should be taken to insure the perpetuation of an abundant supply of this valuable animal. There can be little doubt but that vigorous and systematic trapping over a far shorter period than that now allowed by law would be sufficient to produce all the rats that should be taken, having regard to the maintenance of the supply, and it would seem, therefore, not only that the season should, in the interests of the trappers themselves, be considerably curtailed, but that it should occur at that season of the year when skins are primest and the least irreparable damage is likely to occur. So long, indeed, as trapping muskrats is permitted throughout the winter months, so long will it be exceedingly difficult to enforce the regulations in regard to the breaking open of the houses, while if trapping is prohibited during the major portion of the winter there will be no excuse, or at least very little, for the hunter to be visiting the grounds with his traps. Consequently it would appear that the open season for muskrats could, without undue hardship to the trappers, without materially diminishing the annual catch, and at the same time in the best interests of economical conservation, be fixed from Ｊ arch 16 to April 30, both days inclusive.

One objection that would in all probability be made to the suggested alteration in the dates of the open season for muskrats is that the mink is often to be caught in approximately the same localities. Undoubtedly this is the case. The mink, whose beautiful fur causes it to be much more highly esteemed than the muskrat, is widely distributed throughout Ontario, but it is to be observed that in the more densely populated sections of the Province, in those areas, in fact, where the muskrat will be the most vigorously and persistently hunted, and where in consequence the greatest danger of extermination will occur, the mink has become comparatively scarce. Trapping operations, therefore, for mink in such localities would not in all probability be very extensive even were the present open season for mink, December 1 to May 1, left unaltered, for to trap for this creature alone would not be a very profitable undertaking and it is more than probable that a few instances of rigorous punishment in regard to the illegal taking of muskrats under such circumstances would result more or less in the abandonment of such operations where muskrats were plentiful. That this should tend to an increase of the mink in these areas cannot be doubted, and the fur of this creature is so valuable that this could not but be considered a distinct advantage. The muskrat and the mink are at the present time classed together in the matter of an open season and it might appear that the curtailment of the season sugested for muskrat could with advantage be applied to mink also, but the cases are not analogous. Undoubtedly the numbers of the mink are decreasing and shortening of the season might be advantageous, but the fur of the mink is primest during the early winter and the question in regard to mink is rather whether it would not be more advantageous to advance the season for mink to include the two latter weeks of November than to prohibit its taking during the early winter months. In any case, however, it is apparent that even if some objections to the suggested dates for the muskrat season were made on account of the trapping of mink, they should not be allowed to carry weight for the reasons that the change would be of the very greatest benefit in regard to the maintenance of the supply of muskrats; that in proportion to the amount of damage now effected in the ranks of the muskrats by the prolonged open season the value of the mink fur secured in such localities is but a trifling consideration; and finally that the proposed change should tend to increase the numbers of mink, at least in the more populated sections of the Province.

TRAPPING.

In the previous section attention has been called to the general diminution in the numbers of fur-bearing animals, and it would seem that this diminution cannot but in large measure be attributed to the system of trapping prevailing in the Province. Many years ago, when the Hudson Bay Trading Company was practically the only firm trading in furs on a large scale, the maintenance of the supply of animals was more or less assured owing to the fact that the individual agent or factor in charge of a station or district viewed with concern anything that would tend to a lessening of his receipts, and consequently, if the fur of any particular variety of animal showed signs of becoming scarce in any district, measures were as a rule taken to discourage its capture and thus afford the species an opportunity to recuperate. The opening up of the country, however, brought in its train the inevitable competition, and numerous firms started in to exploit the fur in opposition to the Hudson Bay Trading Company with the result that a ready market was at all times open for almost any variety of fur, individual interest in the maintenance of the supply gave way to rapacity and greed, and precautionary or conservation measures passed from the thoughts of one and all engaged in the business, becoming, in fact, only feasible of application through the agency of the crown. Far and wide has the competition forced its way until even in the most northerly extremes of provincial

18 F.C.

territory it is now in full swing, and in consequence, throughout the length and breadth of the Province fur-bearing creatures are relentlessly pursued without much regard to age and without consideration of dwindling numbers or the laws of reproduction, except and only in such cases as those of the beaver and otter, where the state has intervened to save the animal from extermination. In regard even to these protected animals the rights of the Indians, who in the north lands at least are in the majority among trappers, to take these animals at their pleasure and even to dispose of their pelts to the white man, have not as yet been definitely disposed of. In view of such a situation it is small wonder that the number of fur-bearing animals is steadily diminishing.

Another noteworthy feature is that this great natural resource, this vast and valuable public asset, has been allowed to be exploited to the huge benefit of private individuals and firms without contributing more than an insignificant pittance to the public revenue. At the present time a fee of $10 is charged to non-residents for the privilege of trapping, but no charge whatsoever is made in the case of trappers, buyers or dealers, resident in the Province. It would, indeed, seem that in this state of affairs there lies a distinct injustice to the public, for the great profits that are made in the taking and disposing of furs are only accumulated at the expense of the property of the public.

In seeking for a remedy to the general situation the first consideration must plainly be the conditions under which the actual trapping is carried out. In this regard it is to be observed that trapping affords a means of securing an income sufficient for the year in a comparatively short space of time and with comparatively little effort. On the other hand the extent of territory that must as a rule be covered to secure numbers of the animals living in the forests precludes the probability of one man earning in average years very great sums by this means, while the uncertainty of the measure of success and the conditions of life under which the operations are prosecuted tend to lessen its attraction to the majority. Consequently, it has come about that the white men engaged in the ordinary trapping business in the forest areas are either the settlers in those localities, who avail themselves of this opportunity for obtaining cash either in preference to engaging in lumbering operations or because no opportunities to do so are open to them, or else those from the villages, settlements and towns who by preference select the life rather than engage in other more steady occupations. Of this latter class it may safely be said that in general their moral calibre is not high or their value to the community of much account, and that, as a class, they are by no means deserving of the privilege of exploiting public property free, gratis and for nothing. It is to be noted, also, that the average moral standard of these men is not sufficiently high to encourage the belief that the majority could ever be relied on to obey the laws in regard to the taking of animals so long as any possible channels for the disposal of illegally taken pelts remained open to them. In such cases, therefore, at any rate a license fee should be exacted for the privilege of trapping.

In regard to the settler, it may be observed that it requires but small labour and but little good fortune for such of them as engage in trapping throughout the winter to catch fur sufficient to net them sums considerably in excess of $300, and, therefore, it could not be accounted a hardship if a small percentage of this sum had to be paid to the government for the privilege of undertaking trapping operations.

In the case also of the trapper, operating from towns or villages and chiefly interested in the capture of muskrats, plainly it would only be reasonable to expect from him some compensation for the profits accruing to him through the destruction of wild animals. No little trapping of muskrats is, of course, carried on by lads from farms and villages, but the value of the skins, as quoted in a previous section, is sufficient proof that those who wished to trap muskrats could well afford to pay a reasonable fee for the privilege of doing so on public lands.

There remains, then, but the Indian to be considered. The nature and habits of the Indian throughout the great bulk of the Province tend to prevent his entering upon the generality of those occupations which afford a livelihood to the white man. His domain is pre-eminently the woods; his craft, that of hunter, trapper, and woodsman. In general but small advantage accrues to the community through the existence of an Indian, other than through those functions which he can discharge in his native element, the woods, while, as before observed, the pursuit of trapping is not in general calculated to attract the better class of white man in the wilder regions to undertake it, but on the contrary rather to serve as a means of gaining a competency for the shiftless and lazy. It would, therefore, appear that while there can be no great advantage in encouraging the white man to undertake trapping as a sole or chief means of livelihood, such advantage would exist in the case of the Indian, for not only would he thus be made to contribute materially to the public welfare, but his energies would be applied in the direction most suited to them. Consequently, even though a license fee might with advantage be imposed on all other residents of the Province for the privilege of trapping, the Indian should remain exempt from such license fee, and be given a permit to trap free of charge.

A great many of the illegalities perpetrated in connection with the fur-bearing animals are directly to be attributed to the presence throughout the country of numbers of pedlars and small traders only too willing to purchase all that they can secure in the way of fur no matter where, when or how it may have been secured. It cannot be claimed that the presence of these men in the wild lands is of material advantage to the community, for by their methods of trading not only do they encourage lawlessness, but add, also, materially to the difficulties of the reputable dealers in obtaining furs. It is plain, moreover, that but slight control can ever be exercised over them, for they have no stationary place of business and can readily slip unobserved across the provincial borders, should they so desire, with an accumulation of illegally taken pelts. If, therefore, a license fee were placed on fur buyers sufficiently high to deter the majority of these persons from purchasing a license, it would apparently not only be in the best interests of the public, but of the legitimate fur trade also. There can be no question that if the trapper is licensed, so also should be the buyer of raw or undressed furs, for the latter, in the main dealing with furs on a much larger scale than can ever the individual trapper, will make correspondingly greater profits. In the case of the buyer, also, it is to be remembered that dealing in raw and undressed furs he takes his profit for no other service than that of passing them on to those who will improve them, and that the profits thus accruing to him are at the expense of a natural resource which is the property of the public. It would seem, therefore, that not only should the buyer of raw or undressed furs be licensed, but that the license fee charged him should be sufficiently high to prevent the great majority of the lower class pedlars from purchasing such a license. It could not, of course, be expected that non-possession of such a license would either altogether or at once put a stop to the practices of these gentry in dealing with furs, but at least the imposition of such a license should materially facilitate the detection of offences.

In the case of fur-bearing animals, as in the case of game and fish, it is a matter of no little importance to have comparatively accurate statistics of the annual yield, for by this means alone can either an increase or decrease be definitely ascertained, and the proper measures taken accordingly to impose or remove restrictions. If trappers and buyers were licensed as suggested there would be no great difficulties in the way of obtaining such statistics, for the licensee in either case could reasonably be required to furnish figures on a form provided him for that purpose with his license. Moreover, the furnishing of returns of this nature would go a long way towards checking illegalities. If the trapper was required to send in a return of the numbers of the various species of animals caught and of the persons to whom the pelts were sold together with the license numbers of such persons and the dates of the sales, and the buyer to make out a return in duplicate, one to be sent in to the Department and one to be retained by himself, showing all purchases of raw or undressed furs and the persons from whom such pelts were obtained, together with the license numbers of such persons and the dates of the purchases, it would plainly be a simple matter to exercise close supervision on the buyers and exceedingly difficult for them to have furs in possession unaccounted for, while, where any illegalities were suspected, it would materially facilitate their investigation. In addition to this, as it is possible for an expert to determine more or less accurately the season in which a skin has been taken, not only would it be inexpedient for a dealer to have a pelt taken out of the proper season in his possession, but it would immediately be possible to trace the offence home to the person who had actually taken the animal, so that all parties to the offence could be punished.

The economic value of the fur trade is so great that infractions of the law in regard to it should be treated with the utmost severity and the penalties made correspondingly high. In fact, in addition to a heavy fine on account of each animal taken or each pelt bought or traded, any irregularity should be punished by cancellation of the license of the offending persons, and the disqualification of such persons from obtaining another such license for a period of at least five years.

In the case of Indians it is plainly to be desired that they should conform to the laws and regulations in force in regard to the fur-bearing animals, and it is not to be doubted that in the main they would do so were it once made apparent to them that not only would it be almost impossible for them to dispose of skins illegally taken, but that infractions of the law would be visited by a cancellation of their permits to trap and trade in furs with white men. In regard to the returns as suggested to be furnished by the trapper, the buyer from an Indian should be required to fill them in and forward them to the Department where the Indian was insufficiently educated to attend to this work himself.

As before noted the lack of any incentive to the trappers to conserve the supply of animals has been one of the main factors in their depletion. At the present time on public lands it is open to any resident to trap wheresoever he chooses, and the trapper is, in consequence, urged on to catch all that he can, regardless of the ultimate consequences, by the knowledge that if he spares, someone else will likely happen along and destroy. To remedy this evil and to encourage conservation it would seem that a license or permit to trap should be endorsed with the approximate area for which it is valid, and that it should be made an indictable and punishable offence to trap on Crown lands outside the limitations designated on the license or permit, or at least on any area which may have allocated to another trapper. The licensee, also, so long as he obeyed the laws, should be entitled to a renewal of his license on demand. By these means an individual interest in his territory should be developed in the trapper, for not only would he have the sense of proprietorship and the security afforded by the knowledge that others could not legally impair his grounds, but also, there would be the incentive of personal profit in future years to urge him to take only a proper proportion of animals of each species and to encourage their increase, for as in many cases the land about him for miles would have been allocated to others, the depletion of his territory below the point where it was profitable to trap over it would necessitate a move to some considerable distance, should he desire to continue in the business, a thing which in many cases, particularly that of the settler, would be most inconvenient, if not well nigh impossible.

It is to be observed that if a license of $5.00 on trappers and a

license of $50 on buyers of raw or undressed furs were imposed, a consid-
erable revenue would accrue to the government. In previous sections
of the report attention has been called to the necessity for improvements
both in the service of protection against fire and that of fish and game
wardenship, which would involve considerable expenditures of money.
It would seem, then, that as the fur-bearing animals are the creatures
of the forests and a natural resource of a kindred nature to game, the
revenue derived from this source might well be devoted to the improvement of these two services. It is to be noted, also, that it might well be
questioned whether, even with the imposition of the suggested licenses,
the public would be receiving adequate compensation for the exploitation of the fur-bearing animals. By the introduction of the license
system, however, the way would at least be prepared for raising a greater
revenue from this source should such be desired in the future, for statistics would be available on which to form an estimate of the average
profit to the trappers and dealers, and the system of recording catches
and sales would be in force which would greatly simplify the collection
of a tax on pelts should such ever come to be imposed.

In connection with the law as it stands at present one point
merits consideration. A permit, for which no charge is made, has to
be obtained, not later than within ten days of the close of an open
season, to entitle the trapper to be in legal possession of furs. In the
case of mink and muskrat the open season extends from December 1 to
April 30, inclusive, and men are engaged in the capture of these animals
until the last day of the legal open season. In some portions of the
Province trapping is carried on at a distance from civilization and it is
a practical impossibility for the trapper to get out from his grounds
with his furs within the specified time for securing a permit owing to
the fact that while the ice at this period is dangerous for travelling, it
frequently does not disappear from inland waters until nearly June
sufficiently to allow of canoeing. Consequently, either the trapper must
abandon his occupation some weeks prior to the close of the open season
in order to get his permit in sufficient time, or else he becomes liable to
fine and the confiscation of his pelts. While no general relaxation of the
law is in the least desirable, it would seem that in certain regions magistrates might be empowered to use their discretion in the matter, provided the trapper could show that he had left his grounds at the earliest
possible date after the close of the open season. In this connection it
may be observed that under the license system previously suggested the
returns from the buyers should be required to be posted to the Department within ten days of the close of the open seasons, and that it should
only be possible for them to purchase the furs of trappers who could
not get in from their grounds within this period by obtaining a permit
to do so from the proper authority, and that the trapper, so situated,
should be required to make affidavit that his furs had been taken within
the legal open season and to secure a permit to authorize him to keep his

furs in possession should he for any reason be desirous of so doing. It would seem that the local magistrates might well be constituted the authority to deal with such cases at their discretion under the general instructions of the Department of Fish and Game.

WOLVES.

Attention has been called in previous sections of the report to the diminution of game in the Province and to various causes therefor, but it must be acknowledged that as a destructive agency in so far as four-footed creatures are concerned the wolf must be accorded no small distinction. Unfortunately, almost throughout the forest areas the timber wolf is to be found in greater or less abundance and the depredations of this animal on the ranks of the deer are annually enormous. It is a natural and inveterate hunter, and not satisfied with killing that which it requires for food, will hunt and slay for the mere pleasure of so doing. In general it operates in pairs or small bands, following up its quarry at a leisurely trot by the sense of smell with a persistency that but seldom is thwarted, but the greatest of its opportunities to work damage and destruction occur in the winter months when the snow drifts are deep and the deer yarded. Then, with its prey helpless and at its mercy the wolf approaches and kills to its heart's content. Wherever the deer are to be found in the Province, there will the wolf also be found, and if for one reason or another the deer migrates from any area into another, the wolf will follow suit, as was well instanced in the Rainy River district, where the deer were practically unknown until recent years and the wolf comparatively scarce, but where no sooner did the deer commence to appear in numbers, driven northward in all probability from Minnesota by the forest fires raging in that State, than the wolf arrived also, and its numbers are now, apparently, steadily increasing. When each adult wolf will kill in all probability one or two deer each week of the year, it becomes at once apparent what an enormous drain on the deer supply there must be from this cause where wolves become at all numerous. The extent of the damage wrought to moose and caribou is less certain, but at least it would appear more than probable that some destruction of these animals is effected by wolves, more particularly in regard to the calves. In the western portions of the Province there is also to be found the brush-wolf, which prey largely on the smaller fur-bearing animals, such as the fisher and marten, in addition to other game, and is consequently the cause of no small loss to the Province.

The wolf is by nature one of the most cunning of animals, and it is but rarely that he will afford the hunter an opportunity of shooting him or will suffer himself to be caught in an ordinary form of trap. The most usual and effective method for the destruction of this harmful creature would appear to be poisoning.

The necessity for reducing the number of wolves to a minimum cannot be gainsaid, but none the less many objections have been advanced against the lavish use of poison for the purpose, and in fact in this Province at the present time it is illegal to place poison for wolves where any other game is liable to find and take it. It is claimed that where poisoned meat is placed on the ground, other smaller creatures, such as the mink and fisher and various birds, will almost invariably be the first to discover it, and that in consequence not only will there be a considerable destruction of wild life for the sake of a problematical chance of destroying a wolf, but that there will be likely to occur, also, a loss of valuable fur, inasmuch as the smaller fur-bearing animals will more frequently than not succeed in crawling to some little distance before they die and thus escape the notice of the trapper or hunter laying the poison. Even more extravagant assertions in regard to the extent of damage done by poison have been advanced in the case where poisoned meat is placed on the ice towards spring and left there to fall into the water, together with such creatures or their carcasses as may be poisoned thereby, but it would seem that where due precautions are taken in the matter of placing the poison in the meat and in the location of the bait itself, not only should the destruction of other forms of wild life be comparatively trifling, but waste of fur also should be rendered most unlikely, for the poison can be placed in sufficiently large pieces or quantities as to ensure the almost immediate death of any creature devouring it.

There can be no question as to the necessity for destroying a greater number of wolves annually than is at present effected, for it would appear that in several sections of the Province, at least, wolves are increasing. Poisoning is acknowledged to be the only effective method of destroying wolves, but in this Province poisoning must be held to be practically illegal, although the wolf is not protected against it, for under the Act all such fur-bearing animals as are afforded any form of protection are deemed to be game; the poisoning of all fur-bearing and other animals classed as game is forbidden; and it is plainly impossible to place poison for wolves where it can by no possible means endanger any of these creatures, and at the same time be effective. At the present time the law is more or less winked at. If it is necessary to encourage the killing of wolves, the placing of poison should plainly be rendered legally feasible for this purpose, within reasonable bounds. The licensing of trappers would appear to afford a means of doing so without encouraging the too general use of poison, which cannot but be more or less dangerous to other forms of wild life. If only licensed trappers or Indians holding a permit to trap were entitled to use poison for the purpose of killing wolves, and then only in localities where but small harm to other creatures was to be anticipated, there would not only appear to be but little risk of much damage to wild life being effected, but if in addition the claimant to government bounty were required to send in with his claim the number of his license, the possibility of fraud in this connection would be very greatly diminished, for it would be practically impossible for anyone not so licensed to kill any number of wolves, for poisoning, the only effective method, would be illegal for such person, while, again, the license number would indicate the exact area in which a wolf or wolves had been taken by poison by the trapper and any excessive number of claims under such circumstances would be easily detected. It might, however, be advisable to require of all trappers making use of poison to burn the carcasses of all creatures destroyed thereby, in order to reduce the chances of death to other animals through devouring them to a minimum.

At the present time a bounty of $15 is offered by the government for the destruction of a wolf; the claimant to the bounty being required to furnish the ears of the animal in proof of its destruction. Unfortunately, cases have occurred of late where extensive frauds have been perpetrated on the government in this connection, large quantities of wolf ears having been imported from without the Province and bounties claimed and paid for animals which had never been within miles of the provincial borders. The detection and severe punishment of offences of this nature in the western portions of the Province will undoubtedly have had a beneficial effect in the direction of preventing their recurrence, but it is to be observed that so long as the ears only are required by the Government in substantiation of a claim, so long will it be comparatively easy to perpetrate the fraud. The time, patience and good fortune necessary to secure a wolf militate largely against very active prosecution of its pursuit by those engaged in ordinary trapping operations. The skin of the wolf, undamaged, is worth in the neighborhood of $5.00. It would seem, therefore, in the best interests of the Province that a more substantial bounty should be offered the trapper for the destruction of wolves, and that if the bounty were raised to, say, $25 and the whole skin required by the Government in support of a claim, not only would a considerably greater number of wolves annually be taken, but that the chances of fraud in this connection would be materially diminished. Moreover, the skins would retain their full value, instead of being mutilated and thus depreciated, and consequently not only would less of these pelts be wasted, but by selling them the Government would in some measure, at least, be recouped for the additional bounty. Undoubtedly special steps should be taken to reduce the numbers of wolves in the Provincial Forest Reserves to a minimum, and where a permanent staff of rangers is maintained, it would appear that there should be no difficulty in so doing, if the matter is taken energetically in hand.

RECOMMENDATIONS.

Your Commissioner would, therefore, recommend:—

(1) That the beaver be declared a perquisite of the Crown through-

out the Province; that where or when in any district beaver are sufficiently numerous that trapping can be advantageously conducted without endangering the perpetuation of the creature in such district, trapping operations be undertaken by officers of the Government; the pelts
thus secured branded with a government mark and sold by public tender
for the benefit of the public treasury; and that it be declared illegal for
any private person whatsoever to have in possession, barter or trade in
raw or undressed beaver pelts in the Province of Ontario which are not
so branded, no matter where such pelts may have been obtained, other
than when a permit for this purpose shall have been obtained from the
Government.

(2) That the dates for the open season for muskrat be amended to
) arch 16 to April 30, both days inclusive.

(3) That a license fee of $5.00 be charged to citizens and *bona fide*
residents of the Province for the privilege of trapping on public lands;
that Indians only be exempt from this charge, but be required to obtain
a permit in lieu of such license; and that each person while engaged in
trapping be required to carry his license or permit on his person.

(4) That the approximate area which may be trapped over be
designated on the license or permit issued to each trapper; that it be
declared an indictable and punishable offence to trap on Crown lands
outside the limits designated on the license or permit; and that a trapper be entitled to a renewal of his license or permit over the same area
provided only that he shall have in no way disobeyed the game laws, and
shall have complied with the provisions of his license or permit.

(5) That all fur-buyers and dealers in raw or undressed furs,
engaged in this business in Ontario, be required to take out a license;
that the charge for such license be $50; and that in the case where more
than six collecting stations are maintained by one firm, or more than
six buyers or agents employed by one firm at various points throughout
the Province for the purpose of collecting furs, an additional license fee
of $10 for every such station or agent be charged.

(6) That all trappers or fur-buyers as a condition of license or
permit be required to furnish the Department, on a form provided with
the license or permit for that purpose, with statistics of the numbers
and species of each animal killed, sold, bought or otherwise disposed of;
that in the case of Indians or other trappers being unable to write, it be
required of the buyers purchasing from them to fill in their forms for
them and forward the same to the Department; and that such returns
be required to be posted to the Department within ten days of the close
of the legal open season.

(7) That provision be made on such forms for distinction between
each sale, gift, trade or purchase effected, of the various dates thereof,
and the license numbers of the persons with whom each transaction was
effected; and that it be made an indictable offence, punishable by fine
and cancellation of the license, to render false or incomplete returns

on these matters, provided only that where the figures for Indians or other trappers shall have been filled in by the buyer, such buyer shall be held responsible for the figures.

(8) That any illegalities in connection with the trapping of fur-bearing animals or the bartering, purchasing, holding or trading in the pelts of the same, be made punishable by a fine of not less than $5.00 for every such creature trapped or pelt bartered, purchased, held or traded, together with the cancellation of the license of the trapper, buyer or dealer so offending and disqualification of such person from obtaining a license for a period of five years; provided only that in the case of firms maintaining a number of agents for the purpose of trapping, or purchasing pelts of fur-bearing animals, if it could be proved that a firm had taken reasonable precautions to guard against such infractions of the law and had no knowledge of the same, the license of such firm be not cancelled, except when two offences in its behalf occur in one year, but in such cases the trapper or buyer of the firm be treated as a private individual.

(9) That, if possible, steps be taken to have the close seasons for fur-bearing animals observed by Indians on public lands under pain of equal penalties as applicable to white men, and that in any case it be made an indictable offence, punishable by fine and imprisonment for any Indian to barter, trade or attempt to barter or trade the pelts of fur-bearing animals protected by law or taken during the legal close seasons for such animals, except and only among his own kind within the limits of an Indian Reservation.

(10) That, as at present, a trapper or buyer be required to obtain a permit within 10 days of the close of the open season for any fur-bearing animal to have the pelts of the same in possession; but that where, owing to natural cases, it is impracticable for the trapper to obtain such permit within the legal period, steps be taken to constitute an authority in each such district to grant such permits at its discretion after due investigation; and that in such cases any subsequent sale or trade of the pelts thus held be only effected under permit granted by the same authority, and provided that a record of such transaction is forwarded to the Department.

(11) That the bounty on wolves be raised to $25.00; that it be required of each applicant for such bounty to forward the entire skin of each wolf, unmutilated, together with each claim made; and that where such applicant is trapping under license or permit, the number of such license or permit be clearly marked on each claim.

(12) That the present regulation in regard to the use of poison be amended in so far as to legalize and render feasible the use of such material for the taking of wolves only by trappers operating under license or permit of the Province, provided only that due precautions be taken to select such localities for the purpose where the minimum amount of harm is likely to be done to other wild creatures or domestic

animals, and that the trapper be required to burn the carcasses of all such creatures whatsoever that may be killed by such poison.

FEATHERED GA)E.

It has, unfortunately, to be recorded that the quantities of the various species of feathered game to be found in Ontario have in almost every case and in almost every district considerably diminished, and there can be little question that the main cause of this regrettable state of affairs is overshooting. One of the chief difficulties coincident with the enactment of restrictive legislation in regard to the shooting of several species of feathered game in such a country as this is that, while the most logical dates for the open seasons for the various species are not always identical, the birds themselves are to be encountered largely over the same areas. It has, indeed, been demonstratd to be almost impossible to protect one variety by a close season during a period when other varieties might be legally shot. Another obvious difficulty is the matter of meeting the local conditions prevailing over such a wide area by general legislation. It may, in fact, be confessed that to do so would appear a practical impossibility; at least, to the extent of completely satisfying the wishes of all the sportsmen living in the various districts. Further, the fact that certain varieties of game birds are migratory enhances the difficulty of affording them adequate protection, for there will inevitably be some considerable protest at depriving citizens of game for the benefit of a neighboring nation. To further complicate the situation, feathered game is so small and so comparatively quickly and easily disposed of, that the detection of offences against such restrictions as may be imposed is exceedingly difficult over such a wide region as the area of Ontario, and consequently the laws in all too many instances are broken with impunity. In addition to this, also, feathered game is so highly esteemed for table purposes that reputable citizens, who themselves would not break the law, in certain cases abet its infraction by others through the repeated purchase of illegally taken game. In view, then, of the general situation as it exists in regard to feathered game, it is necessary briefly to examine into the laws and conditions affecting the various species.

At the present time a close season is afforded to the woodcock, the partridge and the quail, the dates for each bird being:—

Woodcock .... October 15—November 15
Partridge (grouse) .... " 15— " 15
Quail.......................................November 15— " 30

The woodcock is a migratory bird, and there can be but little question that in certain of the southern portions of the Province it arrives frequently before the open season commences and is flighting after the season has closed, although the main flight seems usually to occur during the course of the open season. Naturally enough sportsmen, with

whom the bird is a favorite, feel it a hardship not to be able to shoulder
a gun during the periods of the woodcock's stay in their vicinity on its
way to southern climes and demands are made that the open season be
extended to include the whole of October and November. The partridge,
or ruffed grouse, which had become so scarce that a close period of two
years had to be afforded it to recuperate its numbers, is in many sections
of the Province in condition to be shot by the middle of September, while
in other localities the opening of the season so early, when the young
may perhaps not have matured, or in any case the birds are packed and
disinclined to break coveys, would result in inordinate destruction.
Again, in certain areas the partridge would afford good sport well into
December, whereas in the northerly regions, the snow drives it into the
trees and it becomes a simple matter to slaughter it, although shooting
under such conditions cannot be deemed a sport. The quail breeds somewhat later than the partridge, and occasionally raises a second clutch,
so that it would not be safe or advisable, as a general rule, to open the
season early in the fall for this bird. Under the present arrangement
whereby the opening of the season for quail coincides with the closing
of the season for partridge and woodcock, none of the birds, as before
observed, derive the full benefit from the protection afforded them, and
it is to be noted, also, that there is reasonable force in the contention
that so short a season as a fortnight tends in the direction of excessive
slaughter, for where the sportsman has but so brief a period for his
sport open to him, he will be encouraged to make the most of his opportunities. In this regard it should be remembered that a great number
of sportsmen have businesses or other occupations which necessitate
their close attention, and in consequence cannot spare more than a day
or two at most each week to hunt or shoot, and that, therefore, a very
short season is a distinct hardship to them.

There can be no question that in the general interests of the community it is better in so far as possible to make the open seasons for
birds or creatures inhabiting more or less the same regions or localities similar throughout the Province, for differentiation between adjacent localities tends not only to difficulties in administration and in
the enforcement of the laws, in addition to excessive legislation, but also
to considerable local friction. Consequently, even though admittedly it
is impossible to satisfy every one or to meet each and every local condition or requirement, this broad principle should, in so far as possible,
govern the fixing of the dates for open seasons. Undoubtedly the
desideratum would be an open season of considerable duration, to include both large and small game, so that for the greatest possible time
sport should be available to the sportsman and game food to the general
public, but to arrive at such a situation it is necessary, first, to have
produced an abundance of game, a sentiment among the public at large
which will put an end to widespread malpractices or connivance at the
same, and a staff of wardens capable of and able to enforce such restric-

tions as have to be made. No one, unfortunately, could claim that such a situation exists in Ontario to-day, and consequently the best that can be done is to have comparatively short open seasons, in so far as possible, coincident with each other. Too short a season is, as already been noted, objectionable on certain grounds, while a very protracted season has already proven itself too dangerous for certain birds under existing conditions. A six weeks' season for partridge and woodcock, from October 15th to November 30th, and a four weeks' season for quail, from November 1st to 30th, would, therefore, appear to be the nearest approach to the ideal which can at present safely be ventured.

In regard to wild ducks, the open season for which extends from September 15th to December 15th, it is to be noted that all of these birds are more or less migratory, and that almost throughout the Province their numbers have greatly diminished of recent years. Various causes have been assigned for this; various remedies tried and suggested; but no effort has as yet been made to strike at what is apparently the root of the evil, namely, excessive destruction. The popularity of the duck as a table dish and its former exceeding abundance resulted in the development of an enormous market for the bird, and the demands of this market show no signs of diminishing in proportion to the dwindling numbers of ducks, but on the contrary to be steadily increasing. In fact, it would not be too much to say that in general it is the market hunter who is chiefly to blame for the diminishing quantities of ducks in the Province and not the sportsmen of the Province, the carp or other extraneous circumstances. It is apparent that no matter what size a marsh may be, the continued and energetic operations of the market hunter, resulting in the slaughter of great quantities of ducks practically every day, not only must effect a terrible drain on the ranks of the ducks, but must also tend to drive them away, for like other creatures ducks require a modicum of rest and peace in order to remain in a given locality. There can be little doubt but that the prohibition of the sale of ducks would result in a very rapid augmentation of their numbers, but it is unquestionable that such a measure would encounter a storm of protest and abuse. Moreover, the object of conservation is not to deprive the public of game, but rather to insure that the public shall be able to take advantage of it. In certain cases where a variety of game becomes very scarce it becomes imperative to place restrictions on its sale in order to eliminate the market hunter, but such a measure is, in a sense, but a final recourse, for though under it the public are still afforded opportunities to obtain game, if they will, by shooting, or if they can, as a gift from friends who have done so, the majority of the public is, in all probability, not in a position to secure the game, and in consequence is deprived of it altogether. This situation has, indeed, given rise to a more or less widespread feeling that sport is the rich man's pastime, and game the rich man's perquisite, and that the game laws are devised in the interests of the wealthier classes of the community. Such a belief is plainly erroneous and much to be deplored, but it serves at least to exemplify the necessity for not lessening, unless absolutely imperative to do so, the varieties of game purchaseable by the public, but rather, where feasible, to augment them. On the other hand the sportsmen of the Province undoubtedly merit some consideration, for they are a very numerous body, comprising all classes and occupations, and if for no other reason than that it is an injustice to them, the depletion of the numbers of ducks through the operations of market hunters cannot but be deemed highly regrettable. Moreover, it is perfectly apparent that if the diminution of recent years continues in like proportion in the future, not only will the sport of the sportsmen have been ruined, but there will be but few ducks remaining for the public market.

Practically all varieties of ducks are migratory and objection will inevitably be made to any further restrictions on their slaughter on the grounds already mentioned in regard to the woodcock, but although there is some foundation for this argument, it is most sincerely to be hoped that the day is not far distant when the open seasons for all migratory birds throughout the continent will be fixed by an international commission, for in the creation of such a body would appear to lie the chief hope, not only of satisfactorily disposing of this problem, but even of perpetuating in any numbers the migratory game birds. Indeed, every effort should be made by each administration, by each sporting association or club, and by each individual sportsman or lover of wild life to hasten the day when such an international body shall be appointed to regulate such matters. Meanwhile, it may be observed that, after all, the perpetuation of the birds is the chiefest consideration, and that it cannot be the part of wisdom in any way to assist or connive at their extermination. It is better, indeed, to fight a good fight for a losing cause which is just, than ignobly to abet an evil, mainly because it is being perpetrated by others.

In view, then, of these considerations it would seem that at the present time the most reasonable course to pursue is to limit the individual daily bag of ducks, taken on public lands, marshes or waters, to some reasonable number. Plainly this will not result in the disappearance of the market hunter, but at least it will serve as a check on his depredations. It may be argued that it will be difficult to enforce such a law, or, again, that it will entail a hardship on sportsmen, but it is to be observed that a bag limit is imposed in regard to certain of the sporting fishes, and the law is fairly well enforced and obeyed, to the advantage of the fisheries, and that, also, say thirty ducks is a reasonable bag for any individual sportsman in one day.

At the present time the ducks get but one day's rest a week from the hunter, namely, Sunday, and it is widely held that if a greater period of immunity were granted the birds in which they could rest and feed in peace, not only would it, by shortening the period of time available to the hunter, result in a decreased slaughter, but would tend, also, to keep the ducks for longer periods on the feeding grounds on which they settle. There would appear to be much force in the contention, and it is not to be doubted that a considerable effect would be produced on the numbers of ducks by limiting the number of days on which they might legally be shot. It is by no means easy, however, to determine what would constitute a reasonable period of time for this purpose or which days would best suit the convenience of the majority of sportsmen. It would seem, perhaps, best on the whole that the close period should be integral, for alternating close and open days would be apt to lead to confusion and, in any case, would enhance the difficulties of enforcement of the law over so wide an area as the Province. Sunday is a close day already, and Saturday, in many parts of the Province, affords numerous hunters their only chance in the week of enjoying this sport, while Wednesday is also in some localities and in some businesses made use of for the purpose of a weekly half-holiday. It would seem, therefore, that Monday of each week might in any case reasonably be added to the list of close days for ducks on public lands, waters or marshes, nor is it to be doubted that it would be of material advantage if Tuesday of each week were included also.

The shortening of the open season for wild duck by the elimination of the first two weeks in September was undoubtedly a wise and beneficial measure in regard to the great bulk of the Province. It has, however, given rise to a situation somewhat akin to that already referred to in the case of the woodcock, partridge and quail in that, as it remains legal for the hunter to shoot plover, rail and snipe from September 1st, many of them will be found in the marshes during the first fortnight of September and, consequently, not only is it most difficult for the wardens to enforce the close season for ducks during this period, but undoubtedly also the ducks will not derive the full benefit of the additional protection afforded them through the postponement of the opening of the duck season to September 15th. There is no apparent advantage in or necessity for making the open season for the waders different from that for ducks sufficient to compensate for this great disadvantage, and it would, therefore, seem most desirable that the open season for ducks, plover, rail and snipe should be made coincident.

Another migratory bird, the numbers of which annually visiting the Province have materially decreased, is the Canada goose. Probably no bird is more wild or more wary than the goose, and yet it is not to be doubted that the main cause of the decreasing numbers of the bird in the Province has been the reckless overshooting and slaughter that has taken place whenever opportunity offered. As remarkable an illustration, as perhaps could be found anywhere, of how wild fowl appreciate a measure of security and of the instinct that will guide them in increasing numbers to localities where it is accorded to them, is furnished by the experience of that genuine sportsman, Mr. Jack Miner, of Kingsville,

Wild Geese on Mr. Jack Miner's Pond, April 9, 1909.

Ontario. Mr. Miner is no game-hog, and when in the spring of 1908 eleven wild geese settled on a little pond in the vicinity of his house and joined the flock of 16 tame birds that lived on it and on another little pond immediately in front of his house, he refrained from disturbing them and prevented others from doing so also. The birds soon became accustomed to their surroundings, and even though Mr. Miner subsequently shot five of the eleven wild birds, the remainder came back and joined the tame flock on the pond in front of the house, where they stayed until May 15th, when they migrated north. On March 20th, 1909, 32 wild geese arrived and settled on these little exposed ponds, where they were accorded the same treatment as in the previous year, and though on this occasion Mr. Miner shot 12 of them on April 10th, the remaining 20 stayed on until they took to wing on their way to the north lands on May 1st. On March 4th, 1910, 30 wild geese arrived, and from that date on the flock continued increasing until some 250 or 300 wild geese were assembled on the two ponds. Mr. Miner allowed 36 to be shot, but the balance as before did not abandon the ponds on that account, but remained on until the time arrived for the northward migration. The accompanying illustrations well indicate the exposed nature of the pond immediately in front of the house, and it is exceedingly doubtful whether such photographs of this exceedingly wild bird have ever before been taken. The facts, however, that the birds were willing to live in such a public and exposed place for several weeks on end and to become so used to the presence of human beings, as the photographs prove them to have been, clearly indicate what the result would be, not only to the numbers of wild geese, but to those of other waterfowl and game birds, if the great bulk of the shootists were as good sportsmen as Mr. Jack Miner, of Kingsville, and confined their annual slaughter to the bounds of reason.

The open season for pheasants, which was declared during the past year, resulted apparently in the satisfactory discovery that the birds were more plentiful than had been supposed, and most excellent sport would appear to have been enjoyed. Sufficient time, however, has not yet elapsed to enable a determination to be arrived at in regard to the advisability of repeating the experiment of an open season during 1911. Careful investigations should be made on this point by the proper authorities, for the pheasants in some localities have become so well acclimatized and are thriving to such an extent that it would be a grievous mistake to allow their numbers to become unduly diminished. The question, also, as to the shooting of hen birds merits consideration. The past season was very properly only open to cock birds, and this restriction would, on the whole, seem to have been fairly well observed. Moreover, it would appear to have won the approbation of many sportsmen, as the hens were apparently so easy to find that it would have been a simple matter to have killed great numbers of them. It is to be noted, however, that to maintain good stock, the percentage of cocks to hens should not in general be allowed to fall below one to four or five, and also that it is at all times expedient to kill off old hens, as these will frequently interfere with the breeding of younger hens. Consequently the percentage of cock birds available for breeding in the spring should be roughly ascertained, and, if it is found to be unduly small, provision might be made for this contingency when next an open season is declared, either by throwing open one or two weeks of the season to the shooting of both cocks and hens, reserving the remainder of the season for the shooting of cocks only, or else by allowing the shooting of hen birds, in addition to cocks, on certain days of the week throughout the season. The pheasant is such a handsome bird and provides such fine sport, in addition to being so highly esteemed a table delicacy, that it is a matter for congratulation that it is catching on so well in certain portions of the Province, and it is well worth while taking some little pains to insure its perpetuation.

The prairie chicken, which formerly was comparatively plentiful throughout a great portion of the Rainy River District, has now practically become extinct in that region. Various causes have been assigned for this, but it would seem as usual to have been mainly the fault of indiscriminate and excessive slaughter. The prairie chicken is a magnificent game bird, and equally popular for table purposes, and in addition to the areas in the Rainy River District there are other portions of the Province where it would, in all probability, thrive. It is not so nervous a bird as the ruffed grouse, and far more easily domesticated. Moreover, as it prefers the open to the woods it would be unlikely to materially affect the grouse or partridge, and in addition is a most valuable bird to the agriculturist. It would seem, therefore, that it might well be worth while to try and reintroduce this bird into Ontario.

The question of private game preserves is one that merits some little attention. In this Province the principle has been adopted of keeping the shooting on Crown lands open to the public, and of not alienating the sporting rights over them to private individuals or clubs. There can be no question that this policy is both the wisest and the fairest in the interests of the general public. As, however, sections of the country become populated and taken up by the agriculturist, the areas of Crown lands in them inevitably become diminished or disappear, and the question of game in such areas is on an altogether different footing to that prevailing over the great bulk of the Crown wild lands. The farmer has the right to post his lands, and if he is fond of shooting will probably do so if there is any game to shoot, more especially so should he have taken any measures to produce or maintain that game. Moreover, such stretches of public lands as there are in these districts are peculiarly accessible to the hunter, and the difficulty, therefore, of maintaining a supply of game in them is materially enhanced. In fact, in the settled portions of the Province it would seem that the only practical means of perpetuating the game lies in a measure of individual, in addi-

Wild Geese on Mr. Jack Miner's Pond, Kingsville, Ont., April 15, 1910.

tion to governmental, conservation. The shooting of the farmer has a distinct value; that of his neighbors also. By posting their lands and thus conserving the game on it, and by combining to any desired extent, they have in their possession a shooting which can be annually leased for a fair sum at least. Where the farmer does not post his land or take interest in game, all and sundry will shoot the game over it until all game has disappeared, and with it a legitimate source of income to the farmer. Plainly it is better to have the game on the farm, and that the farmer should profit from it, than that there should be no game, and consequently no profit from it to the farmer or anyone else. Indeed, there can be little doubt that as the population increases and shooting becomes more difficult to obtain, there will be an ever-increasing field for profit in game of which the farmer should take advantage, and that when this fact becomes more generally recognized by the farmers, game will increase through the efforts of the farmers in raising and protecting it.

A very similar situation arises in connection with duck preserves over duck marshes in populous neighborhoods. The indiscriminate shooting that will occur throughout the length and breadth of public marshes in such localities day after day during the open season, is calculated to insure that the ducks will be slaughtered and, to a great extent, driven away. Moreover, should ducks breed in these marshes, frog hunters and others will be here, there and everywhere disturbing them and working considerable damage. On the other hand, the existence of a private preserve in such a locality tends to remedy many of these evils. In the majority of cases the preserve is well looked after and the breeding ducks are not disturbed, while, also, precautions are, as a rule, taken to prevent shooting on warm or still days when ten shots fired will be likely to drive away more birds than 1,000 shots on a windy day, and to limit the extent of the shooting, as likewise the hours between which it may take place. As a result of these precautions the ducks are enabled to feed and secure a measure of rest, and, in most cases, not only do they become plentiful on the preserve itself, but the shooting over adjacent territory is also considerably improved. The general sentiment of the population of this Province is undoubtedly against the private duck preserve, especially when it is instituted over marshes which long have been open to the public, but it is a question whether in the more densely populated and most accessible areas a greater measure of preserves will not become actually necessary in the future, if the shooting is to be maintained to any degree of excellence. In the wilder and remoter regions there can be no advantage in or necessity for such preserves. In fact, in such regions the public rights to the shooting should be most jealously safeguarded; and, indeed, in the older portions of the Province, even though a preserve is apparently in many ways advantageous, especially when situated in some portion of an extensive marsh, every effort should be made to insure that in all cases the bulk of the marsh remains open to the public, and that small isolated marshes, which afford even limited sport to the many, shall not be alienated from the public for the benefit and the privilege of the few.

RECO))ENDATIONS.

Your Commissioner would, therefore, recommend:—

(1) That the dates of the open seasons for partridge (ruffed grouse) and woodcock throughout the Province be made: October 16th to November 30th, inclusive; for quail, November 1st to 30th, inclusive; and for plover, rail and snipe, September 15th to December 15th.

(2) That on all public lands, marshes or waters it be declared illegal for any person to shoot, kill or take more than 30 wild ducks, all species and varieties of wild ducks and teal included, in any one day, provided only that such restriction shall not be held to apply to such areas as are posted and maintained as duck preserves.

(3) That 'Monday of each week during the open season for ducks be declared closed to duck shooting on public lands, marshes or waters.

(4) That adequate steps be taken to ascertain the desirability of declaring an open season for cock pheasants during the year 1911, and in the event of an open season being decided upon, of legalizing the taking of a proportion of hen birds.

(5) That all possible efforts be made by the administration in the direction of encouraging the introduction of international regulations in regard to the killing or taking of migratory game and other birds.

(6) That the principle be maintained of not alienating the shooting privileges over Crown lands, marshes or waters in the wilder portions of the Province to private individuals, clubs or corporations; that in the more populous and opened sections of the Province, should it be deemed desirable to grant such privileges in the interests of propagation and conservation, the extent of public land, marsh or water over which shooting rights are thus alienated from the public be strictly limited; and that in no case an entire marsh or water area suitable for wild ducks be thus alienated.

THE COLLECTION OF NON-RESIDENT LICENSES AND COLD STORAGE.

In some sections of the Province there is little doubt but that a considerable number of non-residents hunt, shoot and fish without paying the legal license fees. Most particularly so would this appear to be the case in the vicinity of border towns. The great majority of sportsmen who visit Ontario from outside undoubtedly enter the Province through the border towns, and it has been suggested that, as a means of counteracting as far as possible the evasion of the shooting and angling licenses by such persons, where they have in their possession on entering the Province hunting dogs, guns or angling equipment, they

A Misty Day on the Steel River, Thunder Bay District.

A Corner of Rainy Lake.

should be compelled to take out the corresponding license as a condition of their property being passed through the Customs, irrespective of any declared intention to hunt, angle or otherwise. There is but little question that considerable amounts of money would be collected by this means which otherwise would be lost to the treasury, but it is to be observed that this would be a somewhat arbitrary measure and likely, in many cases, to be resented by the visitor as an imputation of dishonest purpose. Further, the Customs' officials are not under Provincial control, and consequently the measure would thereby be somewhat complicated, and in addition to this, the Province maintains a warden force to enforce the regulations, and if that warden force is inefficient, it is the Province and not the visitor which is to blame. Undoubtedly there will always be some strangers anxious to escape the payment of the non-resident hunting, shooting or angling license fees, and sufficiently ignoble to resort to such means as false registering to accomplish their purpose, but under an efficient system of administration the chances of detection should be so great as to reduce the numbers of such would-be evaders of the license fees to a minimum.

Some objection has been raised to the regulations whereby game may not be kept in cold storage by firms engaged in that business longer than the 16th day of January following after the close of the open seasons. A license fee of $25 is charged for the privilege of storing game. It is claimed that the fee is so high that in many cases the amount of game dealt in by the firm does not cover the cost, and that a longer period should be open to the firms in which to dispose of the game. The main reason for the enactment of the regulation was plainly to afford a safeguard against the illegal slaughter of game during the close season, and it is not to be doubted that as a means of protection the law, as it stands, is generally effective. To prolong the period in which indigenous game might legally be dealt in from cold storage would, therefore, not appear advisable, and if an injustice is being done the cold storage firms, the best means of remedying it would evidently be to reduce the license charge. The cold storage firms, however, can be relied on to take this matter up themselves when the majority feel the necessity of so doing, and it may be observed that a high license is beneficial in that it tends to centralize the storage of game and thus renders supervision comparatively easy. In regard to game that is not indigenous, or, in other words, which is imported from outside the Province, seeing that such game could be shipped in bond to the importer and the shipment only released under authority of a government inspector, it would seem reasonable that cold storage of such game could safely be permitted for longer periods than at present allowed by law. The laws in relation to public carriers afford considerable protection to indigenous game, so that even though in such a case as that of the English pheasant which is now to be found in certain restricted portions of the Province, the imported bird could not be distinguished from the local variety, no great harm would be likely to accrue; in fact, not more so than under the present system; for the majority of purchasers would buy from a reputable dealer whose importations would have been franked by a government inspector, and there should be little, if any, additional difficulty to that experienced at the present time in detecting illegal trafficking in local or indigenous game. It would seem, therefore, that under the present graduated license for the privilege of importing and storing game the cold storage firms might be allowed to import game from abroad and deal in the same until March 31st, provided that due arrangements were made to inspect and check the shipments, in addition to the cold storage houses during the extended period. There is little doubt but that in the future various enterprises will develop in the Province in the direction of game farming chiefly for market purposes, which will necessitate some modifications of the present laws in regard to the sale and cold storage of game, for it is plainly in the interests of the public that such enterprises should be afforded reasonable opportunities of marketing their products, seeing that an increase in the diversity of wholesome foods available to the public cannot but be of general advantage. It will, however, be time enough to deal with such a situation when the enterprises have been or are in the process of being established.

RECO)) ENDATIONS.

Your Commissioner would, therefore, recommend:—

That under the present scale of license cold storage firms be allowed to import, hold in cold storage and deal in game thus imported up to and including March 31st of each year, provided only that all such importations shall only be released from bond on a certificate being obtained from the proper authority; that such certificates must be held on the premises so long as any proportion of the game is held in cold storage; that no game whatsoever be held in cold storage without such certificate after January 16th of each year; and that adequate steps be taken to arrange for the inspection of cold storage premises throughout the period indicated.

GA) E FAR) S.

In a previous section it has been pointed out that in the raising of game for market purposes there exists an opportunity for profitable commercial enterprise, and that any addition to the permanent food resources of the community cannot but be advantageous. It has been noted, also, that in the more cultivated sections of the Province a great deal can be accomplished in the direction of increasing the supply, or even the varieties, of game through the efforts of those cultivating the soil, and that not only is such an eventuality much to be desired, but worthy, also, of every encouragement in the interests of the farmers, the sportsmen and the public at large. In the United States these questions are receiving ever increasing attention, many individual states as well as private individuals or firms having become interested in the production of game on a large scale, and it may here be noted that a movement of no little dimensions has arisen in the direction of still further augmenting state and individual efforts in regard to the production of game, it being claimed that the principle involved affords the soundest, if not actually the only satisfactory, solution to the problem of perpetuating the game of the country, placing game food within the reach of the bulk of the population, and at the same time of securing such an abundance of wild creatures that there will be an abundance of sport for everyone without the necessity for irksome restrictions. It cannot be denied that there is very considerable truth in this contention as a whole, but it is apparent that until the game farm shall have made its appearance in this Province and be producing considerable quantities of game, there must remain the most urgent necessity for safeguarding the wild creatures, and that under any conceivable conditions some measure, at least, of protection to them will be found not only advisable but indispensable. There is, moreover, an under-current of thought connected with the widespread cultivation of game in which may ultimately be found a menace to public rights and privileges in regard to hunting and shooting. Some varieties of game can be more advantageously or easily raised under semi-wild conditions, while under completely natural conditions most indigenous game will thrive and multiply to an astonishing extent if afforded more or less complete protection. Hence, under the cloak of the production of game there will almost inevitably appear the lean head of purely selfish interests, clamouring to be apportioned the shooting rights over large areas of public lands and claiming to be a public benefactor in the direction of game protection and propagation, while the public are excluded from participating in the sport to be found over the territory allotted or leased to it. The legitimate game farm, even though it be of some considerable size, and the small preserve in a country thoroughly opened up and under cultivation are one matter; the alienation of public shooting rights over large areas of public lands is altogether another. Consequently, while encouraging the game farm and bowing to necessity in the case of the small preserve in populous sections of the Province, no consideration or argument should be allowed to affect the principle, fortunately so firmly rooted in Ontario, that sport on public lands is the heritage of the people at large, or to countenance any departure therefrom in regard to the vast areas of Crown lands in the wilder sections of the Province.

There are in various portions of Ontario areas of wild and rough land from which the timber has been largely removed, but which will never prove of much service to the community in the matter of agriculture. Such areas will in many cases be found to be suitable to the purposes of deer farming. Deer are comparatively prolific. The rutting season occurs in the fall or early winter and the period of gestation is about seven months, the fawns being usually born about May or June. The young does breed when about seventeen months old and have usually but one fawn the first time, but subsequently two fawns are produced in the majority of cases. As instancing the rapid increase of deer may be noted the case of the Otzmachon Rod and Gun Club, Clinton County, Pa., which placed about 90 deer in its 4,000 acre park and in six years had 2,000 head and were expecting an additional 1,000 fawns in the early summer. Deer are easily and cheaply raised, and comparatively hardy, living approximately twenty to twenty-seven years. They will eat wild rye and other soft grasses, buds and leaves of trees, growing wheat, clover, peas, barley, oats, vegetables, corn, bran, chops or fruits, in fact, almost anything except dry hay. The cost of feeding them in suitable localities has been estimated at one-half a cent each per day. They are easily confined by a woven wire or barbed wire fence 6½ feet in height. In addition to the fact that were deer more readily obtainable doubtless quite a number would be purchased for small parks and enclosures; the creature is commercially valuable in that its flesh is an excellent meat for human consumption, and the horns, hides and even hair are articles of commerce. The dietetic value of venison is enhanced by the fact that it is especially adapted to invalids who require a nourishing yet easily digestible food. In a recently published table showing the time required to digest foods, grilled vension is given front rank with boiled tripe and boiled rice, as requiring but one hour for complete digestion, whipped raw eggs, boiled barley and boiled trout, as well as asparagus and a few other vegetables are shown to require an hour and a half; while grilled beefsteak and mutton require three hours for digestion and grilled or roasted veal or pork five hours or more.

Deer horns, although deciduous, are solid processes, produced from the frontal bone, and have the physical as well as the chemical properties of true bone. The material produces much gelatin by decoction and the waste pieces of the horns used in the manufacture of knife handles are either made into gelatin or boiled down into size used in cloth manufacture. At one time deer horn was a prominent source of ammonia. Some thirty years ago in Sheffield, England, some 500 tons of deer horn, representing the antlers of fully 350,000 deer, were used annually in the manufacture of handles of knives and other instruments. Deer skins, as tanned and dressed by the Indians, are manufactured into moccasins, racquets, toboggans and other articles for sale, while deer hide also makes an excellent leather. Deer hair has a peculiar cellular structure and is used in some parts of the world for stuffing saddles, to which purpose it is especially adapted.

It will be conceded, therefore, that under suitable conditions deer farming should indeed prove a profitable industry. In this connection it may be observed that it will, in all probability, be found feasible to exploit both moose and caribou by similar methods, and doubtless also to introduce other varieties of deer, should such be deemed desirable.

The moose, which is closely allied to the European elk, is held to be naturally adapted to domestication. Instances have occurred where the animals have been trained to draw a sleigh, and at one time it would appear that the elk was fully domesticated in northern Scandinavia, and in general use to carry couriers from one place to another. The elk, it is stated, was swifter than the reindeer, and in certain instances covered over 230 miles in a single day, and it is further alleged that the use of the elk was finally forbidden in this region owing to the facilities it afforded to prisoners and criminals to escape, and its domestication consequently abandoned. Moose-hide is so thick and hard that the leather is said to have been known to have resisted musket balls.

No attempts have as yet been made to domesticate the caribou or Canadian reindeer, although these animals differ but little from the Old World species. Some authorities are of the opinion that both the woodland and barren ground caribou are capable of domestication, and it is evident that such a step would be of material benefit in the extreme northerly sections of the Province. In any case, even where reindeer are imported, as has occurred in some instances on this continent, crossing the European species with the indigenous and wild variety would doubtless be found to produce animals of greater strength and size, and the native caribou could be constantly drawn on for new blood as has often been done in the case of wild reindeer in northern Europe and Siberia.

The game farm affords a means of producing annually and comparatively cheaply a quantity of birds and eggs of indigenous or imported varieties. Undoubtedly the indigenous varieties, as a rule, will be found to be the best adapted to the purposes of farming, for already they will be acclimatized and the food most suited to them will be found existing naturally to some extent on the farm, while in addition to these advantages there will be a readier market for the sale of the eggs and birds for sporting purposes, for there will be less risk attending their plantation. In the United States considerable attention has been paid of late to the farming of game birds, the greatest efforts having apparently been put forth in the direction of imported varieties, such as the pheasant and the Hungarian partridge. While these experiments have not in many instances been an unqualified success, the fact that many states and individuals are still conducting them on an increasing scale would serve to indicate that the enterprise has taken firm root and can be expected materially to develop in the future. In New York State, for instance, a sum of $12,000 was recently devoted to the purchase of a game farm, the erection of a suitable plant and the acquisition of a suitable number of birds for stock purposes. Seventy-five acres of this farm have been fenced with woven wire eight feet high and pens built therein. The birds principally dealt with are the pheasant and Hungarian partridge, and it is estimated that the state should be able to supply six thousand or more birds and a thousand eggs each year for propagating and stocking purposes.

The actual cost of running a game farm will depend very largely on the variety of birds raised and the initial expense, of course, of acquiring land suitable to the purpose, as well as the cost of stock birds, but in this Province, at least, it is evident that the value placed on game birds, both alive and dead, is such that there cannot but be a great margin of profit to the farmer. The ringneck pheasant is not, in all probability, adapted to the bleaker portions of the Province, but it has already been demonstrated a success in certain of the southern districts, and there can be little doubt that not only would a game farm dealing in this bird be a profitable investment, but that its cultivation affords a means to the ordinary farmer in those areas of considerably augmenting his income at but little trouble or expense.

A pheasantry may be started with mature birds or eggs, although, as a rule, it has been found more economical in the long run to acquire the parent birds. The price of pheasants varies considerably according to the season, being cheapest at the close of the breeding season, an average cost for ringnecked or English pheasants being, perhaps, $5.00 a pair. Any well drained ground is suitable for pens, but a gentle slope of sandy loam, comparatively cool in midsummer, furnishes ideal conditions. Clay is the poorest soil for the purpose, as it is likely to foster disease. The pens should be provided with plenty of both sunshine and shade and constructed like ordinary poultry runs. Each pen should cover at least 100 square feet, for contracted quarters are apt to induce disease. A small open shed or enclosure at one end of the pen is advantageous in that it provides shelter and a dry dusting place. The floor of this shed should be natural earth, to furnish dust baths for the birds, for dust baths are as essential to pheasants as to poultry, freeing them from lice and keeping their plumage in good condition. Mortar, cinders and plenty of grit should be kept in the shed. Extra communicating pens, alongside those in use, have been found advantageous as, in many instances, a hen, stopping laying in the one, will be induced to resume laying by removal to another, and opportunity is afforded, also, of freshening the ground. The pens and sheds should be kept scrupulously clean. The pheasant is polygamous and the male pugnacious during the breeding season, so that each pen should contain one cock to three to five hens. Eggs should be hatched under barnyard hens or turkeys, for though broody, the pheasant hens are wild, and it has proved difficult to obtain good results by leaving them to hatch the eggs. In selecting a hen for the purpose it is essential that she be free from scaly leg, roup or lice. The young should go without food for the first twenty-four hours after hatching, and at the end of that period, or at least within a day or two of hatching, the hatching box should be removed to the rearing field which may be meadowland, a clover field or an orchard, in which coops are provided. These coops should be at least 30 yards apart so as to allow plenty of territory to the various broods. Suitable food is held to be of the utmost importance, and there are a variety of opinions on the subject, but in general it may be noted that not only does variety tempt the appetite, but with the chicks the transition from soft to hard food must be gradual. Ant eggs are a most suitable food, but if a sufficient supply cannot be obtained throughout the season, it is better to avoid their use altogether, as chicks are liable to reject other food after being fed on them. Maggots, mealworms, finely ground meat and almost any soft bodied insects are excellent substitutes for ant eggs. For the first three or four days the chicks are usually fed on a stiff custard of eggs and milk, but subsequently more substantial food is added. A good general rule appears to be to vary the food as much as possible and to be liberal in the matter of green foods. After two or three weeks coarser ground food may be supplied safely, and grain gradually increased until the fifth week when whole wheat, barley, cracked corn, oats and buckwheat may be added. Sunflower seeds, boiled potatoes, chopped onion and baked bread crumbs are also useful to vary the diet as the chicks approach maturity.

With other game birds generally similar requirements will be found necessary, varying only in regard to the temperament of the bird and somewhat, also, in regard to the most suitable foods. Both the ruffed grouse and quail have been successfully raised on farms, in some instances on the same land, and other varieties of grouse, such as the prairie chicken, have also been successfully cultivated. It should, indeed, be both feasible and profitable to raise both indigenous and imported varieties of these birds almost throughout Ontario, and it cannot be doubted that more enterprise on the part of the farmers in this direction is much to be desired.

A further field is open to the game farmer and owner of suitable land in the raising of fur-bearing animals. The beaver, otter, marten, mink and silver and blue fox are amongst the animals whose partial domestication would be profitable and doubtless will be undertaken on a considerable scale in the future, but of all fur-bearing animals occurring in this Province the muskrat affords the easiest opportunity for successful exploitation in this direction. The celerity with which the creature multiplies has been indicated in another section of this report, and the rapidly increasing price of its fur renders it almost a certainty that advantage will be taken of suitable localities by individuals and firms to augment the income derivable from such property through its cultivation, as has already been done in certain instances in the United States. The Cedar Point Hunting Club, of Toledo, Ohio, controls 5,000 acres of marsh at the mouth of the Maumee River near Lake Erie. In the winter 1903-4, after the muskrats had been left undisturbed for two years, they were trapped for the benefit of the club. In a single month 5,000 were taken, the skins being sold at 25 cents a piece and the carcasses at $1.00 per dozen. The extensive marshes of Dorchester County, Maryland, are a centre of muskrat production. Formerly the owners of marshes in this vicinity paid little attention to them. Trappers were

20 F.C.

allowed to take muskrats wherever they chose and the marsh land could have been bought for less than 50 cents an acre. At the present time some of the marshes are worth more, on a basis of the income derived from them, than cultivated farms of like acreage in the same vicinity, owing to the muskrat. As a rule trapping privileges are leased, and both trapper and owner protect the marshes from poaching. As instancing the values thus attained the following quotation is made from a Bulletin issued on the subject by the United States Department of Agriculture:

" The owner of one tract of marsh informed the writer that he bought it three or four years ago for $2,700. It is leased for half the fur and yielded him in 1909, $890, or about 33 per cent. on the investment. The owner of a small piece of marsh—about 40 acres—bought it in 1905 for $150. Leased for half the fur it has yielded the owner $30, $60, $70 and $100 for each of the four years 1906-1909. . . . The owner of a 1,300 acre tract of marsh trapped it this season with the aid of his sons and secured over 5,000 muskrats, which were sold for $2,300."

It is interesting to note, also, that as a food the muskrat has a place in certain markets, such as Philadelphia, Baltimore and Wilmington, where it is sold as " marsh-rabbit," although no effort is made to conceal its identity, and not only do well-to-do people buy and eat it, but that since the animal is caught principally for its fur and the additional labor of preparing the meat for market is but trifling, it can be sold very cheaply. In Baltimore in 1908 the retail price was about 10 cents each, and the wholesale price about 7 cents each, and the demand at these prices appeared to be considerably in excess of the supply. The flesh of the muskrat was generally esteemed by the aborigines of North America and the early colonists soon learned to eat the animal also. At the present time opinions appear to differ as to its edible qualities, some maintaining that its musky flavor is so strong as to prevent all but the starving from eating it, while others aver that it is game worthy of an epicure with a flavor somewhat akin to wild duck that has been shot in the same marshes where it has fed, or have even compared its flavor to that of the famous terrapin. Indeed, annual muskrat banquets are by no means uncommon with gun clubs in certain of the western states of the Union. The flesh of the muskrat is dark red in color, but fine grained and tender. Care should be taken in skinning it that the fur does not touch the flesh, to avoid cutting into the musk glands and to trim off any subcutaneous glands that may adhere to the meat. Various recipes for either stewing, frying or roasting muskrat can be readily obtained. It is doubtful whether many of these creatures are consumed by white people in Ontario at the present time, but there would appear to be no reason why the carcass of the muskrat should not become an article of considerable commercial value in the Province, and thus tend to increase the profits of those who become interested in its cultivation.

An attempt has been made in this section to indicate the feasibility of raising and propagating game of many species and varieties, and the great economic possibilities that exist in such enterprises, and it remains, therefore, but to note that the whole matter is of such importance from the points of view of sport, of the perpetuation of game, of the available food supply of the population and of the creation of new and prosperous industries, that it is well deserving of the special consideration of any administration. It would seem, then, that the government might well give the citizens of the Province a lead in the introduction of the system into Ontario, for in no matter which direction applied the undertaking would almost certainly prove highly profitable financially, if due economy were exercised and due precautions taken, and it cannot be doubted that the success of the governmental experiments would be followed by the institution of many similar enterprises throughout the Province.

RECOMMENDATIONS.

Your Commissioner would, therefore, recommend:

(1) That a Provincial Game Farm be established in a suitable locality for the purpose of raising deer; demonstrating the practicability of such an enterprise as a profitable commercial undertaking; and encouraging the establishment of such enterprises by private firms or individuals throughout the Province.

(2) That a Provincial Game Farm be established in a suitable locality to raise, propagate and distribute the indigenous game birds of the Province, and to obtain and distribute the eggs of the same; to deal in a similar manner with such varieties of non-indigenous game birds or game birds which have become extinct in the Province as may be deemed desirable; to demonstrate the practicability of such an enterprise as a profitable commercial undertaking; and to encourage the establishment of such enterprises by farmers, private firms and individuals throughout the Province.

(3) That a suitable area of marsh or other territory, the property of the Crown, be set aside by the government for the purpose of muskrat cultivation, in order to demonstrate the practicability of such an enterprise as a profitable commercial undertaking and to encourage the exploitation of lands for this purpose which otherwise are or would be more or less unprofitable.

FROGS.

A creature of no small economic value is the bull frog which, in various sections of the Province, was once exceedingly abundant. It constitutes one of the favorite foods of certain of the wild ducks and, moreover, is a valuable contribution to the available fare of such highly esteemed sporting fishes as the black bass and mascalonge, while frog legs are generally considered a delicacy on account of their tender flesh and pleasant flavor, and, in consequence, command a good price in the markets of the Province. Too little attention, however, has been paid to the frog in the past and very rapid depletion of its numbers has been and continues to be effected. In two counties only at the present time is the frog afforded any protection at all.

The main habitat of the frogs is, of course, the marsh. In the breeding season, which commences as a rule as soon as the weather begins to turn warm, and continues apparently until July, the frogs band, and it is during this period that they are most usually pursued, it being claimed by the frog hunters that hunting at other periods of the year would not be a profitable enterprise. The usual time of hunting is the night when the frogs, busily engaged in reproductive functions, are peculiarly insensible to danger, and when, in consequence, considerable numbers of them can easily be secured with the aid of a lantern. The tadpole takes, apparently, two years to mature, and this fact alone would seem to indicate the necessity for affording the frogs at least some measure of protection during the breeding season, for the longer the period of time required by any creature to mature, the more easily will it become exterminated.

The hunting of frogs during the breeding season is harmful in other directions, however, of no little importance. Precisely at this period of the year the wild ducks are breeding in the marshes, and whether on the nest or with the young require seclusion and peace. The advent of the frog hunters in numbers into the marshes can only be calculated to scare and frighten the ducks at this important season, with the result that nests will be abandoned, eggs trodden on and crushed, and some percentage, at least, of young ducks perish or be destroyed, all of which in view of the general diminution in the quantities of ducks throughout the Province is much to be deplored.

It would seem, then, that not only should protection be afforded to the bull frog on account of its extensive economic value and for the reason that it takes so long to mature, but that for the better conservation of the ducks and to permit of their breeding operations being as successful as possible, it is imperative that the frog hunters should be kept out of the marshes for a portion, at least, of the banding season. The exact period of the banding season depends in all probability on the weather conditions to a considerable extent. In many instances it will undoubtedly be in progress throughout the month of April and in many instances, also, continue on into the month of July. It is plain, however, that the market interests and many citizens could be expected to complain if the whole of this period were declared closed to frog hunting, more especially if it be true, as asserted, that the frogs can only be hunted profitably while banding. It becomes, then, a matter of determining reasonable dates for a close season. In view of the fact that the greatest harm will be done to the ducks by the frog hunters during the months of May and June it would seem, perhaps, advisable to select this period for the purpose, and it cannot be doubted that even such partial protection during the important season of reproductive activity would tend materially to increase the numbers of frogs to the advantage of the frog hunters themselves and of those sections of the community who like to eat them, to the better propagation of the ducks breeding in the marshes, and to the improvement of the food supply of ducks, black bass and mascalonge.

RECOMMENDATIONS.

Your Commissioner would, therefore, recommend:—

That a close season for frogs be declared throughout the Province extending from May 1 to June 30, both days inclusive.

PUBLICITY.

In the Interim Report of this Commission and in various sections of this report attention has been called to the value of the tourist traffic. It has been established that the benefit derived from this traffic affects all classes of the community in that the greater portion of the monies expended by the tourists will remain to circulate in the Province, and it has been shown that the presence of the tourist is calculated to lead to the investment of capital and to the initiation of new and prosperous enterprises in the Province. Undoubtedly the Province of Ontario is exceptionally fortunate in the variety of attractions which it possesses for tourists. In addition to splendid cities and towns, there is an almost unrivalled variety of beautiful scenery. In the winter ice-boating, sleighing, skating, snowshoeing and other outdoor sports and amusements are well calculated to allure the inhabitants of warmer climes; in summer, facilities for canoeing, bathing, camping and a sojourn in the woods in a bracing and healthy climate should afford a sufficient inducement to the dwellers in cities and towns without the Provincial borders to take advantage of them; while in addition to all these things there is still to be secured angling for a number of popular fishes and hunting of many species of feathered and larger game. Moreover, the location of Ontario renders the Province peculiarly accessible to the most populous area of the entire continent. With all these natural advantages for the development of a great tourist traffic it would indeed seem most improvident for Ontario to refrain from attempting their adequate exploitation.

Other provinces and states have grasped the importance of this matter. Maine, for instance, derives an enormous annual income from the tourist, more particularly from the sporting tourist, traffic which has been carefully sought and cultivated for a considerable period of years. British Columbia, proud of her magnificent trout streams and salmon waters, conscious of the attractions afforded by her mountains, her lakes and her forests, by her big and feathered game, has spared no effort to attract visitors from outside, realizing that the monies expended by the state in compiling useful information and circulating it in illustrated book form by the thousand on this continent and abroad, alike in English and foreign languages, is not a waste of money, but an investment which most assuredly will repay itself many times over not only in the sums actually paid out by the tourists who have been attracted thereby, in the incidental costs of their visits, but in the widespread advertisement it will give to the wonderful opportunities awaiting the sportsman, the settler and the capitalist.

In the yearly report of one of the principal banks operating in Canada, Ontario was stigmatized as the Province of neglected opportunities, in that there lay to hand agricultural and other possibilities, equally, if not more, attractive than those existing in other Provinces, but that this fact was so little appreciated that young people generally left their homes and went west in search of that fortune which was more surely awaiting their energies in their native Province. If the criticism is well founded, as there can be little doubt that it is, the necessity is plainly great that the community should receive enlightenment as to the resources of its own possessions, for so long as the general public remains ignorant of or apathetic in regard to them, so long will their due exploitation remain unaccomplished, their potentialities lie hidden from the world, and knowledge of them abroad be difficult if not impossible to obtain.

From every point of view, then, it would appear that a great need exists at the present time for greater publicity in regard to the resources, possibilities and attractions afforded by the Province. In no one direction, however, would this seem to be more desirable than in the matter of a wider dissemination of knowledge in regard to the climatic, scenic, sporting and other facilities calculated to draw visitors to Ontario.

At the present time little or no effort is made by the Province in this direction, and such information as is to be had on this subject is collected and supplied by railways and other transportation companies directly interested in the tourist traffic. Consequently, in many instances the scenic attractions are unduly magnified, accommodation and comforts somewhat misrepresented and the sporting facilities overstated beyond all reason, with the result that encountering the real, where he had anticipated the imaginary, the tourist is all too often dissatisfied merely because his expectations are not realized. Wardens, rangers, overseers, constables and, in fact, innumerable governmental officials are scattered all over the Province, and it should be a simple matter for the Government to collect and collate all such information as will be desired by, or would be useful to, the tourist. It cannot be doubted, moreover, that the issuance of accurate information on these points in attractive form would very materially swell the numbers of annual visitors from all parts, if adequate provision were made for free distribution both at home in the Province and abroad.

Of all natural resources, for it should be esteemed as such, scenery s in all probability the most economically profitable, for no material portion of it is lost to the community in return for the cash which it tends to attract. Fish and game, also, constitute a natural resource which should be permanent if properly conserved, and should, therefore, be more highly esteemed than those resources whose exploitation is synonymous for their disappearance. Mineral, once taken from the ground, ceases to be an asset. Much of its worth finds its way abroad in the shape of dividends. Fish and game, however, have recuperative powers, sufficient within certain limits to meet an annual drain without impairing their value. Their greatest economic worth lies undoubtedly in the attraction they possess for the tourist, for the intrinsic value of a few fish, a few birds or some larger animal, as well as the proportionate expense of protecting, or even producing, them, caught or killed by the visitor, is offset many times over by the cash paid by the visitor to secure the sport. No effort, therefore, should be spared to obtain the greatest possible income from these natural resources of scenery, fish and game, which they can be made to produce, and it would seem beyond doubt that the first step towards their adequate exploitation must and should be the collection, publication and free distribution of all possible information concerning them by the Government of the Province.

RECOMMENDATIONS.

Your Commissioner would, therefore, recommend:—

That steps be taken by the Government to secure and collate accurate information concerning the scenic, touring, sporting and other attractions of the Province likely to prove of use to those visiting Ontario and to the citizens of the Province, or to draw visitors to Ontario, and to publish such information in such form and cause its free distribution to be effected in such a manner that the facilities afforded by the Province in these directions will become more widely advertised and known.

A SCHEME FOR THE IMPROVEMENT OF THE FISHERIES AND GAME PROTECTIVE SERVICES.

It has been the unpleasant duty of this Commission to report most adversely on the system, the equipment and the efficiency of the Fisheries and Game Protective Services. Attention has been called to the fact that both commercial and sporting fisheries, as well as four-legged and feathered game of the Province are becoming rapidly depleted. The necessity for complete reorganization has been insisted upon. While it has been recognized that undoubtedly the reorganization of the present system will take time to complete and that efficiency can only be attained in all departments of the services through greater expenditures of money, the urgency of initiating reforms while there is yet something to conserve has been clearly demonstrated. It remains, then, but to outline a general scheme by which the reorganization and improvement of the protective services can be effected.

The main consideration is undoubtedly the creation of an authority with sufficient leisure to master the intricacies of the many problems involved and with sufficient power to initiate and carry through a scheme of reorganization. This matter has, however, already been dealt with and recommendations on the subject made.

In regard to the *personnel* of the outside service, the baneful effects of political patronage and underpayment have been brought to attention and certain recommendations made in regard to them. It has been pointed out that men who are not fitted for their positions or who have to engage in other pursuits to earn a living cannot be expected to make really efficient officers, and that one of the main evils of the present system is that the underpaid overseer or warden is liable to be influenced in the discharge of his duties by business affiliations or personal friendship, or again overawed by considerations of possible harm to himself or property. It has been shown, in fact, that a permanent force of well paid officials is an imperative necessity at the present time.

The Province covers such a wide area that the situation both in regard to the fisheries and game differs widely in the various regions. Two inspectors are at present maintained by the Department of Game and Fisheries, but it can hardly be expected of even such capable and efficient officers as those now occupying these positions that they should be able to fully comprehend the peculiar difficulties occurring in each locality or its individual requirements in complete detail, or that they should be able to see to it that their duties are being properly performed by the various wardens and overseers. In fact, this would be an impossibility for any two men to accomplish. Having such immense areas to cover they can become intimately acquainted with none in the course of their professional duties, and if they succeed in doing so, it cannot but be by hazard of birth or previous dwelling in them, or else at the expense of other districts. It is nevertheless essential to efficient and economic administration that the organization in each area should be perfected and the supervision continuous. To attain this objective, therefore, it would seem indispensable that the Province should be subdivided into convenient areas, and that in each of them there should be stationed an official who should become intimately conversant with the conditions prevailing in it, and under directions from the controlling executive, both organize and supervise the protective services apportioned to it.

The creation of such officials would imply that in each region there would be an officer of superior intelligence and rank, devoting his energies to its particular necessities and directly interested in solving its individual problems. Not only, indeed, would organization be more easily perfected by this means and supervision afforded, but the con-rolling executive would be kept reasonably well advised of the actual conditions prevailing throughout the Province, which at the present time would appear to be far from being the case, judging from the almost unanimously favourable reports as to conditions furnished by the various wardens and overseers and published yearly by the Department of Game and Fisheries. It would, of course, be essential to select only men of high attainments and adequate qualifications for these responsible positions, and to secure the services of such men good salaries would have to be paid.

Coincident with the appointment of such an officer to a district it would be necessary to furnish him with some measure of reliable, permanent staff, most carefully selected and comprising only men physically, mentally and morally suited to the posts, and with sufficient qualifications of the special nature required to enable them adequately to discharge their duties. Even a numerically small staff of this nature would insure an immediate improvement in the local situation during the period in which the chief officer of the district was studying its problems and planning reorganization. Doubtless the ranks of such staff could be filled to some extent from the men at present employed in this class of work, for that there are many good and efficient officers in the service at present goes without saying, and it is to be noted, also, that not only should these officers be paid a sufficient salary as to ensure the right class of men being obtained, but also that, as their exclusive services would be required and paid for, they could be expected to cover considerable areas of territory which would at once remove them from those local influences which under the present system militate so strongly against the proper discharge of their duties.

A scheme of reorganization as above indicated would have several advantages in addition to those already enumerated. The presence in each area of an officer of superior rank and mentality should materially facilitate inter-departmental co-operation, for such officer would naturally be expected to study the numbers and distribution of provincial constables and fire rangers in his district and to take such matters into consideration when planning local organization. In other words, it should lead to economy in administration. Again, reorganization could be effected without any undue upheaval or disturbance, and over a period of time, for, if it were deemed advisable, the provision of a staff and adequate equipment could be undertaken by districts as funds became available. Moreover, the process of replacing the present officials, where it was decided to dispense with their services, would in any case be but gradually effected. Further, fewer positions with adequate salaries attached thereto would be calculated to attract the right class of men; the wider districts to be covered by each officer would render incompetency more noticeable; and at the same time both the increased area to be covered by the individual officers and the direct personal interest of a chief district officer in the efficiency of his staff would tend

materially to diminish the risks of petty or local favouritism in appointment, or the retention of incompetent or lazy officials. Moreover, once
a district had been staffed, organized and equipped, it should be possible
to more or less satisfactorily meet the difficulty of fixing open seasons
for game to accord with the climatic and other conditions prevailing
therein.

If it were possible to separate the protective service of the commercial fisheries from that of the sporting fisheries, and that of the sporting fisheries from that of game, doubtless many of the obstacles to
efficient administration would materially diminish, but plainly the maintenance of three separate services would be impracticable on the score
of expense, and in addition to this, the areas in which the various pursuits are conducted and the characteristics of the operations themselves are so intimately connected in many instances that it would be
almost impossible to apportion the duties to the various officers of each
service. Consequently, the three services have to be more or less combined in one. It is apparent, therefore, not only that the district officers or inspectors should be as at home on water as on land and that a
proportion of their permanent staffs should be especially qualified in
either one or the other direction, but also that it would be necessary in
determining the districts to apportion a reasonable and fair proportion
of the vast fishing areas of the Province to each. In this regard both the
great lake and inland fisheries would have to be considered. It would,
of course, be possible to subdivide the provincial fishing and land areas
in a multitude of different ways for each of which some advantages could
be claimed, but in view of the fact that although some measure of decen-
tralization in regard to the protective services appears to be necessary,
this should not be carried to an extreme for reasons, amongst others, of
economy. The following allocation of districts is suggested in the belief
that it fulfills the main requirements of the present situation:—

(1) The eastern counties of the Province up to and including the
counties of Renfrew, Hastings and Prince Edward.

Main Fisheries: St. Lawrence River, Bay of Quinte, and eastern
portions of Lake Ontario from Prince Edward County east to the St.
Lawrence River, the Rideau Lake system and the Ottawa River.

(2) The counties of Haliburton, Muskoka District, Simcoe, York,
Ontario, Durham, Victoria, Peterborough and Northumberland.

Main Fisheries: Lake Ontario westward from Prince Edward
County, Kawartha Lakes, Lake Scugog, Muskoka Lakes and Lake
Simcoe.

(3) The western peninsula south of and including the counties of
Halton, Wentworth, Brant, Oxford, Middlesex and Lambton.

Main Fisheries: Niagara River, Lake Erie, Detroit River, Lake
St. Clair, St. Clair River and Thames River.

(4) Counties of Peel, Waterloo, Perth, Huron, Bruce, Wellington
and Dufferin.

Main Fisheries: Lake Huron.

(5) Districts of Parry Sound, Nipissing and Algoma and Manitoulin Island.

Main Fisheries: Georgian Bay, North Channel, Lake Nipissing, French River and St. Mary's River.

(6) Districts of Thunder Bay and Rainy River.

Main Fisheries: Lake Superior, Lake of the Woods and Rainy River.

It would of course be necessary for the controlling executive to have at its disposal one or two inspectors of superior rank to the district inspectors and in addition, as pointed out in another section, to have available the means of investigating promptly complaints as to irregularities occurring in any portion of the Province. For this latter purpose a few specially qualified men would have to be selected as secret service agents, for there is unquestionably plenty of work to keep such men busy throughout the year and it would be more economical to maintain them on salary and more satisfactory, than to engage detectives from private firms for the purpose and run the risks of careless, incompetent or unreliable persons undertaking the work.

In regard to the equipment, types of the most suitable craft for provincial purposes were furnished in the Interim Report of this Commission, the approximate cost of the same indicated and the necessity demonstrated for the Province to build and acquire a fleet especially adapted to the work to be performed instead of continuing to lease more or less unsuitable boats or purchasing second-hand craft of inferior qualifications. The expense of so doing would obviously be considerable, but if the expenditure was spread over a period of years this should prove no insuperable obstacle. The system of districts, as above recommended, should, moreover, facilitate the process of determining the actual requirements in this direction, for to insure economy and at the same time efficiency, very intimate knowledge of the waters and conditions prevailing in each locality and district are obviously necessary, while in addition the system itself would afford a simple means of gradually and effectively instituting the improvements necessary in this direction.

Summarizing, then, the scheme as above outlined, there would be a controlling executive with two inspectors and a small number of secret service agents at its disposal, six district inspectors and a permanent staff of indeterminate numbers in each district. If the scheme were adopted simultaneously throughout the Province and reasonably good salaries paid, the additional cost of the personnel over that at present borne would at the outset be approximately as follows:

Two Chief Inspectors, increase in pay from $1,600 and $1,500 per annum, as at
    present paid, to $1,800 per annum each.............................. $ 500
Four Secret Service Agents, at $1,200 p. a. each........................... 4,800
Six District Inspectors, at $1,500 p· a. each.............................. 9,000
A staff of six permanent men in each district, or 36 men in all, at $900
    p. a. each.. 32,400

        Total.. $46,700

As pointed out already some portion at least of the permanent staff would in all probability be selected from those already holding office, so that a saving would be effected in this direction, and as an increase in the permanent staffs was gradually effected, the salaries of those officers whose services were dispensed with would offset to no little extent this expense, for the higher paid officer would be required to cover considerably greater extents of territory than those now assigned to the numerous and underpaid officials.

The American representative of the International Fisheries Commission submitted to his Government a schedule of the equipment in his opinion necessary for the purpose of adequately enforcing the international fishery regulations in American waters of the great lakes, involving an expenditure of $46,000. An examination of the detail would tend to the conviction that the cost of the boats recommended has been somewhat underestimated by the Commissioner, but assuming that Ontario, which is concerned with practically the whole of these fisheries, should decide to acquire an equipment of equal proportions, thus materially lessening the necessity for the Dominion Government to do so, and assuming, also, that an effective equipment was to be supplied to each overseer where required on the inland fisheries, it would not seem that the total expenditure of building new boats for the purpose could by any possibility exceed $150,000.

In regard to provincial fish hatcheries $60,000 would prove in all probability more than amply sufficient to meet the immediate requirements of the Province in this direction, while, when once the full equipment of the hatcheries on this appropriation had been established, the annual salary bill in connection with such hatcheries could not apparently exceed $15,000, if, indeed, it would even approach that figure.

It would seem that an extensive and entirely adequate plant for a provincial fish agency could be constructed at the various points deemed necessary at an expenditure not exceeding $15,000, and that $5,000 should be fully sufficient to pay the salaries of the necessary officials, while in connection with game farms $30,000 should be ample to cover enterprises in this direction in connection with deer, game birds and fur-bearing animals, and $5,000 amply sufficient to meet the salary bill in connection with them once they should have been fully established; no account being taken of the almost certain profits to be derived from these two enterprises.

Assuming, then, that the reorganization of the personnel was effected as suggested, and, moreover, simultaneously throughout the Province; assuming that the expenditures on equipment, hatcheries, fish agencies and game farms were spread over six years; and including the full running expenses of hatcheries, fish agencies and game farms from the start as though such had already been fully established, the additional cost to the Province during the installation period of six years would be:

Personnel	$ 46,700
Construction of hatcheries (60,000)	10,000
Operating expenses of hatcheries	15,000
Construction of plant for fish agencies (15,000)	2,500
Operating expenses of fish agencies	5,000
Establishment of game farms (30,000)	5,000
Operating expenses of game farms	5,000
Equipment of fisheries protective service (150,000)	25,000
Total	$114,200

At the end of this period, the capital outlay being completed, the approximate increased expenditure over that at present born would, therefore, be:

Personnel	$46,700
Operating expenses of hatcheries	15,000
Operating expenses of fish agencies	5,000
Operating expenses of game farms	5,000
Total	$71,700

To meet this additional charge, if the recommendations contained in this report were adopted, there would be the income derived from a resident hunting license of $1.10, alone estimated at $100,000; increased income from the fisheries owing to the cost of the license being determined by the amount of fish caught, the bonus derived from tenders for fishing licenses, and the licensing of fish buyers; the value of the sturgeon and beaver, recommended to be treated and exploited as perquisites of the Crown; the revenue derived from the licensing of trappers and fur buyers; increased fees from non-residents for angling and hunting privileges owing to a wider system of collection under more efficient supervision; registration fees from visitors to provincial forest and game reserves; and finally that portion of the income derivable from the exploitation of timber or fur-bearing animals in the provincial parks not required for the improvement of their staffs or equipment, for as these parks are maintained in the interests of conservation generally, some portion, at least, of any income derived from them might legitimately be applied to general conservation measures throughout the Province. It cannot be doubted that from all these sources an income would be derived, not only ample to meet all the requirements in the directions indicated, but capable, also, at least when the necessary improvements should have been carried into effect, of furnishing a very substantial surplus revenue to the Province.

RECOMMENDATIONS.

Your Commissioner would, therefore, recommend:

(1) That the general reorganization of the fisheries and game protective services be undertaken without delay.

(2) That an executive, as already recommended by this Commission, be created to have charge of these matters, and that such executive have at its disposal:

Two Chief Inspectors at a salary of $1,800 per annum each, and

Four Secret Service Agents at a salary of $1,200 per annum each.

(3) That for the purposes of the organization and administration of the fisheries and game protective services the Province be subdivided into six districts, approximately as designated in this report; and that an Inspector be placed in each such district, at a salary of $1,500 per annum, whose duty it shall be to study the requirements of the district, plan the organization of the protective services therein on the most economical lines, carry the same into effect under the direction of the chief executive, and be responsible for the adequate supervision of the wardens and overseers in such district and that their duties are properly performed.

(4) That as each of the above administrative districts is created, a staff of not less than six men, at a salary of $900 per annum each, be assigned to the District Inspector placed in control of it, and that an increase of the permanent staff of each district to the numerical strength deemed necessary be carried subsequently into effect by the gradual elimination of the underpaid or inefficient officers and the substitution in their place of others, specially selected and duly qualified to discharge the duties they will be expected to perform; and that such officers receive remuneration at the rate of $900 per annum, be assigned considerably greater territories than those now generally covered by overseers, and be required to devote their whole time and energies to the government service.

ACKNOWLEDGMENTS.

Your Commissioner is indebted to all those gentlemen and corporations mentioned in his Interim Report for continued favors and courtesies:

To)r. Paul Reighard, of the University of)ichigan, for valuable information and the privilege of making use of his maps in this report;

To Hon. W. E.)eehan,)agistrate W. W. O'Brien,)essrs. J. J. Carrick, M.L.A., W. A. Preston, M.L.A., Dr. Smeddie, M.L.A., H. H. Collier, K.C., George Drewry, John)iner and many other gentlemen for encouragement and advice;

To Superintendent Joseph Rogers and many of the provincial constables for courtesies, valuable information and assistance;

To Crown Timber Agents L. E. Bliss and A. O. Watts for assistance and useful information;

To)r. H. J. Bury for services in the Quetico Forest Reserve, for much valuable information and for courteous permission to make use of various photographs in this report;

To Captain R.)anley Sims, D.S.O., for consistent and conspicuous ability in the discharge of the arduous duties of secretary to this Commission.

CONCLUSION.

An attempt has been made to delineate in the pages of this report the situation as it has been found to exist in regard to the commercial and sporting fisheries, the game, the fur-bearing animals and the provincial forest reserves. No claim is made that the recommendations submitted would, even if adopted, finally dispose of the many difficulties inherent to the problems connected with these matters, or even that the range of subjects embraced by the report is in any way complete or comprehensive. Undoubtedly, there remains a very extensive field for careful investigation in many directions affecting these questions; undoubtedly, also, many of the matters investigated and reported upon are of so complex and difficult a character that a variety of opinions as to the best methods of treating them satisfactorily must inevitably exist. Within the limits of the available time, however, an effort has been made to deal with as many of the important problems as possible, while in approaching each individual problem and considering its best solution the main objective has been kept steadily in view of ascertaining the fundamental causes of the difficulties or of the conditions and of applying to them the fundamental principles of economy and conservation. An increased expenditure is inevitable if the conservation, even the perpetuation, of the fisheries, fur-bearing animals and game is to be achieved, but the economic importance of these resources is so infinitely great that to permit of their annihilation for the sake of effecting a paltry saving in the annual disbursements for their protection cannot but be adjudged the height of economic improvidence. The situation is bad to-day; in a few years, if matters are not, meanwhile, improved, it must inevitably be worse, if not altogether irreparable. Surely, then, it must be the part of wisdom to take time by the forelock and introduce the reforms which are so vital to the conservation of these resources before it shall have become already too late, more especially so when the means are available for raising the revenue necessary to meet the increased expenditure out of income without unduly or unfairly burdening any one class or profession of the community.

KELLY EVANS,
Commissioner.

March 7th, 1911.

INTERIM REPORT

OF THE

Ontario Game and Fisheries Commission 1909-10.

To the HONOURABLE JOHN MORISON GIBSON,

Lieutenant-Governor of the Province of Ontario.

MAY IT PLEASE YOUR HONOUR,—The undersigned, appointed by commission under the Great Seal of the Province, bearing date the seventeenth day of July, A.D. 1909, to makes enquiries, take evidence, and report generally upon all matters appertaining to the game fish, the fisheries and the game of the Province of Ontario, which may injuriously affect the same, and any methods possible to increase their economic and other value to the masses of the people, begs leave herewith to submit an interim report.

The instructions accompanying the Commission direct that the investigation shall include the following particulars:

1. The condition of the fisheries and game within the Province of Ontario and the adjacent waters, including:

2. The advisability of establishing provincial fish hatcheries, including the estimated cost of maintenance and construction, the best methods of operation, and other matters relating thereto;

3. The alleged existence of contracts between fishermen within the Province of Ontario and foreign fish companies and individuals, together with the effect of such contracts (if any) upon the fisheries of Ontario;

4. The matter of foreign fish companies and individuals encouraging breaches of the law on the part of fishermen and others resident in Ontario;

5. The qualifications, conditions of service, skill, efficiency (physical and otherwise), desirable for fisheries and game officials;

6. The condition of the present equipment of the Department, together with the additional requirements (if any) in this regard in the matter of launches, boats, etc.;

7. The advisability of the co-operation by the officers of other departments of the Government, and of other corporations, with the officers of the Department of Game and Fisheries, in assisting in the practical enforcement of the game laws and fishery regulations;

8. Questions relating to the management of the public parks and forest reserves, especially in so far as the tourist sportsman traffic is concerned;

9. All matters and things relating to fish and game which may assist in the efficient management of the Game and Fisheries Branch of the public service in Ontario, or be of economic advantage to the Province.

In entering upon the duties assigned to him, your Commissioner confidently anticipated bringing his labours to a conclusion within the space of a few months, counting upon the proposed International Fisheries Treaty (dealing with the international waters of the Great Lakes, and promulgation of which was promised originally for about December 1st) to remove many of the most difficult and vexed problems connected with the fisheries, and, also, be it admitted, not fully realizing the immensity of the work entrusted to him.   Owing mainly to the unexpected delay in the promulgation of the International Fisheries Treaty, and also in a measure to the great range and intricacy of the questions to be dealt with, the necessity of collating evidence and data only obtainable by personal investigation and enquiry in widely-scattered localities, and the desirability of studying various aspects of certain of the questions involved during the different seasons of the year to which they are peculiarly pertinent, your Commissioner has been unable to complete a report on all the questions called for by the Commission.   In view, however, of the fact that a close study of the main factors in the present-day situation has decided your Commissioner to urge strongly upon Your Honour the adoption of certain broad principles, involving changes in the Government administrative service and expenditure of public moneys, your Commissioner has embodied the same in this interim report, in order that the principles may receive Your Honour's consideration while the details are being prepared for inclusion in his final report; and, in addition, he deals with such other questions as he considers it expedient to bring promptly to Your Honour's attention.

WARDENS AND OVERSEERS.

Under the stress of modern civilization the jack-of-all-trades is rapidly being replaced by the specialist in every branch of business and commercial life.   It is not sufficient for a man to be a respectable citizen, with just enough knowledge of his profession to enable him to disguise his own incapacity beneath a veneer of self-assurance.   To get on in the world, to make good, a man must know his gun—lock, stock, and barrel; his business from top to bottom and inside out.   The professional man grasps this, and attunes himself to the situation; the business man realizes it, and, as employer, demands it of his employees. Unfortunately, however, in the machinery for the enforcement of the regulations, designed to conserve for the people some of the natural food resources of the Province, this most important fact seems to have been neglected, or, at least, overlooked.

The organization of the outside service of the Department of Game and Fisheries is not the creation of one man or of one political party. It is, on the contrary, the child of circumstance, nurtured by the partizan spirit of political patronage, and handed down from one Administration to another. Though of late years a very distinct improvement has taken place, the briefest study of the system will disclose the necessity for radical reform.

That the men entrusted by the Government with the enforcement of the law on the waters of the Province or in its woods should be expert sailors or woodsmen, as the case may be, and physically capable of discharging their duties, none will be found to deny; as likewise the fact that to employ those who are not, is, in the efficacy of its pecuniary investment, closely akin to casting gold into a bottomless pit. And yet, owing to the exigencies of political life in this Province, these elementary considerations have been in the past all too frequently disregarded in the selection of officers for the warden services.

That a subordinate officer, entrusted with the enforcement of the game and fishery regulations over a district comprising many miles of lake and woodland, should be 90 years of age; that an officer of the outside service, occupying a position of some importance, should generally have the reputation among persons in his district of being unused to the handling of a boat, and timid of venturing his person on the water; that another fishery officer should be very intimate with the agent of a foreign company, trading as a Shylock among the simple fisherfolk of his district; that a game warden should have no woodcraft, and be afraid to venture alone into the woods; that another should attach himself to a shooting party and indulge with them in the illegal destruction of game during the closed season—these are, to say the least of it, absurdities; and yet they are but a few of the instances brought to the attention of your Commissioner, and are the inevitable and direct outcome of a system in which the most obvious and indispensable qualifications have been brushed aside in favor of a party rosette.

That any man will work, or even devote much time or energy, on that for which he is not paid at least a living wage, is open to the gravest doubt; but where something is offered for nothing, even though that something be the most paltry pittance, the applicants will undoubtedly be numerous, and but rarely of a truly desirable class. The paying of stipends, ranging from $25.00 to $200.00 (stipends such as those with which the pay sheet of the Game and Fisheries Department abounds), appears so closely akin to paying something for nothing that the difference is almost indistinguishable.

In the selection of officers for the outside service of the Department of Game and Fisheries it would seem that the principal general requirements to be looked for are good character and sobriety, health, energy, strength, fearlessness, tact, thorough knowledge of the game laws and fishery regulations, and education sufficient to read and write; and that, in particular, for the Fishery Protective Service, knowledge of the different fishes, experience in the handling of boats, knowledge of the waters to be patrolled; and, in particular, for the Inland Service, knowledge of the denizens of the woods, their characteristics and habits, thorough expertness in the handling of a canoe, and experience in life in the woods and woodcraft, should be considered indispensable attainments.

Your Commissioner is of the opinion that most of the harm done to the fish, game, and fur-bearing animals of the Province is the work of a comparatively small number of utterly unscrupulous and lawless individuals, for the most part well known in the districts in which they operate, and especially so in the more sparsely settled regions. These persons often terrorize the community to such an extent that information as to their depredations is difficult to obtain; and to expect officers, paid the paltry sums at present given as wages to a large number of the officials of the outside service, to run the risk of bodily injury at the hands of these persons, is ridiculous. That open threats have been made, and are being made, by individuals in regard to what they will do if any attempt is made to interfere with their actions is well known; and your Commissioner would recall the fact that, even within the sound of the bells of the City Hall of Toronto, and but three or four years ago, shots were fired at an officer who was attempting to carry out his duty in stopping illegal fishing in Toronto Bay.

J r. Oliver Adams, Vice-President of the Headquarters of the Ontario Forest, Fish and Game Protective Association, who has done so much in awakening public interest in fish and game protection throughout the Province, and who took an active part in arousing the citizens of Gananoque and vicinity to the importance of the protection of game fish in the St. Lawrence River, became a martyr to the cause he espoused. When he commenced building operations on a fine residence on an island near Gananoque he was warned by many citizens that he would probably have his house burned by the lawless element. This warning proved to be no vain one, as shortly after he vacated his summer home last year it was burned to the ground, clearly by incendiaries; and, so far, the perpetrators of this outrage have not been brought to justice. The late Colonel Cantley, who expended a large sum of money in erecting buildings, etc., for a summer resort on J innicoganashene Island, in Georgian Bay, in conversation with your Commissioner, stated that he had often seen illegal nets placed right across the channel near his island as soon as the Government patrol boat had passed, but that he dared not give any information, as he felt that, if he did so, his property would be burned down in the winter.

J any other instances, bearing out the same contention, have been brought to your Commissioner's attention during the tenure of his Commission; but in each instance the information so given was on the condition that the informant's name should not be published, for fear of what would happen to himself or property at the hands of certain lawless persons in his district.

Your Commissioner believes that the number of persons capable of such outrages is very small, and that the general mass of the public is in no way in sympathy with them and would support the authorities acting with energy and determination in enforcing the law and establishing security of life and property.

The present fishery regulations provide that a licensed net fisherman who is convicted of a violation of the law shall have his license cancelled, and that he cannot receive another for two years. The extension of this principle in cases of glaring offences against the fishery regulations or game laws would seem most excellent and advisable.

In regard to the present system, whereby wardens are paid a percentage of the angling licenses which they collect, the inducement of personal gain, in certain cases, would appear to influence the officer to devote most of his time to this work, to the detriment of other, at least equally, important duties. At the same time, without some such inducement, the collection of the angling tax would, in all probability, not be effectively carried out. As it is, chiefly owing to the fact that the license system is of comparative recent institution, and the machinery of collection, therefore, not yet in thorough working order, many persons escape the payment of the fee. The advantages and disadvantages of the present system are so nearly equal that the only solution would appear to lie in the broadening of the authority entitled to issue licenses and collect the percentage.

In his full report your Commissioner will submit a comprehensive scheme, dealing with the numbers of the wardens that he will recommend, the districts they should cover, and the duties they should perform in the summer and in the winter.

Meanwhile he would most strongly urge upon Your Honour that:

1. No officer of the outside service of the Department of Game and Fisheries be employed on a salary less than sufficient to maintain himself upon it.

2. No officer, employed by the Department of Game and Fisheries on its outside service, be allowed to carry on other work, or engage in any other commercial or business enterprise while so employed, except in cases where such officer is in the employ of, and paid by, some corporation or association, and only commissioned by the Government.

3. The commissions of all officers of the outside service of the Department of Game and Fisheries who are receiving less than $500.00 per annum, or a pro rata amount for temporary services, be cancelled as rapidly as it is possible to reorganize the Outside Survey, in accordance with the principle of fewer and better paid officials.

4. No officer be in future engaged or employed by the Department of Game and Fisheries on its outside service who cannot furnish satisfactory proof of such knowledge and experience, and be of such

physique and good character, as to render him likely to prove of value to the particular branch of the service into which he is placed.

5. The number of persons authorized to sell non-resident anglers licenses or hunting permits be increased sufficiently to ensure these licenses and permits being very easily procurable.

ADMINISTRATION.

While it is possible to improve in detail the present game laws and fishery regulations, they are in the main fairly satisfactory, but it is in the machinery of enforcement that the principal fault lies. The general system of the organization of the Department has been passed down by the previous to the present administration. Improvements have been made, and very much greater energy shown by the officers, within the last few years, but the existing method of appointment of officers of the outside service, as has already been set forth, is radically wrong. Until this system is swept away the Department, in the opinion of your Commissioner, will never reach the point of efficiency desirable for the general welfare of the Province.

The necessity for the protection of fish and game was, of course, felt in the much more thickly populated Republic to the south of us long before it was felt here. In seeking for a solution to the problem of efficient administration your Commissioner has given close study to the evolution of fish and game protection in the United States, and to the results that have followed upon the various experiments which have been made in this direction by the different states. It would be out of place to attempt anything approaching a history of this evolution in a report of this nature, but, seeing that the majority of the states starting on different lines, and working under different conditions, both climatic and temperamental, have converged to and arrived at a fundamentally identical system of administration for the conservation and development of their resources in fish and game, a short account of the Commission and Warden system is herewith submitted.

The offices of game commissioner and state game warden of the present day are not the outcome of spontaneous growth, but the outcome of numerous experiments and modifications necessitated by the growing importance of the subject of preserving game. Originally game protection was left to sheriffs and other local officers, and later, after the appointment of fish wardens, was included incidentally among the duties of that office. The development of the office of state game warden from that of fish warden occupied nearly half a century, and was marked by various experimental steps. Maine was the first state to appoint an officer to protect fish, doing so in 1843, and in 1852 Maine again led the way by appointing special officers to act as moose war-

dens in a number of the counties of the state. In 1858 the example of
Maine was followed by New Hampshire, and in 1865 the first fish commission came into existence in that state, Massachusetts following its
example the same year, and Connecticut and Vermont two years later.

In Maine the game laws were gradually extended to include game
birds as well as big game, and in 1878 the duties of the warden were
extended under the new title of County Moose and Game Warden. In
this same year the Fish Commission of New Hampshire was reorgan-
ized as a Board of Fish and Game Commissioners.

In 1887 Minnesota established the office of State Game Warden, and
in 1888 New York that of Chief Game and Fish Protector.

It is not proposed to trace in detail the evolution of the powers or
duties of fish and game commissions and wardens, but it is evidence
of the superiority of this plan that to-day no less than forty states have
adopted it.

There has been, and still is, much diversity of opinion as to the
advantage of a single officer over a board. Minnesota at one time
entrusted the work to a single officer, the State Game Warden, under
the Act of 1887, but four years later established the present system of
a Board of Game and Fish Commissioners. Montana, on the other
hand, in 1895 established a Board of Game and Fish Commissioners,
but three years later replaced it by a State Game and Fish Warden.
New York has tried both plans, but has now placed the work in the
hands of a single commissioner. This gentleman, Commissioner James
S. Whipple, discussing this question at the convention of the New York
State Forest, Fish and Game League, made use of the following words:

" In my opinion no commission of five could succeed. No member
of it is vitally concerned with success. Each anxiously tries to shift
the burden of difficult or intricate questions to the other, and so each
seeks to escape responsibility. What we need is one man, one commissioner, as is now the case. That man cannot escape responsibility. He
must face each and every question. He knows that he must make good
or go under."

 ⋅ At the present time one territory and fourteen states commit the
administration of their game laws to commissions, whose membership
ranges from three to six. As evidence of the desire to keep these commissions non-political it may be mentioned that in Ohio not more than
three of the five members, and in New Jersey not more than
two of the four members may belong to the same political party, and
Pennsylvania prohibits the appointment of any two of the six commissioners from the same senatorial district. As a precaution against the
retirement of all the members at the same time, Ohio, in the Act creating the commission, provided that one should be appointed for one
year, another for two years, another for three, and so on, and that at
the expiration of their respective terms the successor should be appointed for five years. By this means there is always a quorum familiar
with the duties of the Board, and the greatest efficiency is assured.

Pennsylvania has adopted a similar plan. The terms of service of the commissioners vary from two years in Arizona and Connecticut to five years in Massachusetts, New Hampshire, New Jersey and Ohio.

Twenty-three states and territories provide for a single official to direct the affairs of their game department, the title of the office varying somewhat with each state. In Tennessee the office of State Warden is a cabinet position, the Department of Game, Fish and Forestry having been made one of the departments of state government; and the same applies to the office of Fish Commissioner in Pennsylvania. In every state, with the exception of Alabama, where the warden is elected by the people, the officer is appointed by the Governor, and with few exceptions confirmed by the Senate. The term of office varies from two to eight years.

It will be seen, therefore, that the result of experience in the United States is in the direction of creating an office for the control of the fisheries and game removed as far as possible from the influence of party political considerations.

It may be argued that the creation of some such independent authority in connection with this branch of the public service has already been tried in Ontario, as, following the recommendations of the Royal Commission of 1892, a permanent Game Commission was appointed, and remained in force until it was disbanded by the new Game Act. This permanent commission was designed to act principally in an advisory capacity. Its membership was large, its members scattered throughout the Province, and its chairman deeply immersed in other occupations, so that its usefulness was much impaired, and it did not constitute a fair test of the commission system.

The several principal recommendations to follow in this interim report contain in themselves powerful and additional reasons for the adoption of such a course, and your Commissioner would, therefore, strongly urge upon Your Honour the advisability of placing the Department of Game and Fisheries under the control of a small, working commission, somewhat after the model of the Temiskaming and Northern Ontario Railway Commission, but with its membership reduced to the smallest possible number, and, while this interim report will be found to contain recommendations for an increased expenditure of public moneys by the Department of Game and Fisheries, especially in the establishment of provincial fish hatcheries, an adequate equipment for the patrol service, and higher salaries for wardens, your Commissioner would not recommend these expenditures or improvements unless his recommendation of placing the Department of Game and Fisheries under a commission is acted upon by your Government, for the reason that the present system has not produced the most efficient subordinate officers, nor is it calculated to do so in the future, and, failing a supply of thoroughly efficient subordinate officers being assured, he considers the moneys involved in the proposed recommendations would be, in all probability, spent in vain.

THE COMMERCIAL FISHERIES.

Until the promulgation of the uniform Fishery Regulations, under the treaty between Great Britain and the United States, for the control of international waters, it would be futile for your Commissioner to report on this section of the enquiry entrusted to him under the instructions accompanying his commission, but in view of misleading statements which have appeared from time to time in the public press as to the depletion of our Great Lake fisheries not being as serious as alleged, he desires to draw to Your Honour's attention the following facts in regard to the decrease in the numbers of our finest commercial fish, namely, the whitefish. The documents consulted include:

The Federal Government Royal Commission's Report on the Fisheries of Ontario of 1893-4; The Ontario Government Royal Commission's Report on Game and Fish of 1892; The Reports of the Department of Marine and Fisheries of the Dominion Government; The Reports of the Department of Game and Fisheries of the Ontario Government.

In examining the tabulated returns of the fisheries of the Province of Ontario it will be noted that the methods of compilation observed have been somewhat changed from time to time. The earlier reports were so arranged as to render a comparison of the weight of fishes, caught in different years, more easy than the present system, which, while making a comparison of the values in money simple, renders it impossible to get the difference in the weights of the catch of the different fishes without some considerable labour.

Below is given a comparative table, calculated from the Blue Book of the Department of Marine and Fisheries at Ottawa, of 1873, and the report of the Department of Game and Fisheries for Ontario, of 1907:

TOTAL CATCH OF WHITEFISH IN THE GREAT LAKE SYSTEM ALONE.

Year 1873.	Year 1907.	Decrease.	Per cent of decrease.
4.851.872 lbs.	2,499,870 lbs.	2.352,002 lbs.	48

The quantities of whitefish, however, in Lakes Erie and Ontario especially, and also in the upper lakes, were vastly greater some years previous to 1873 than in that year, according to the sworn testimony of many commercial fishermen, given before the Dominion Fisheries Commission of 1893, as the following quotations prove beyond shadow of doubt.

Mr. Albert Hutchins, commercial fisherman since 1850, under oath stated:

"I have fished in Lake Ontario about thirty years for whitefish and trout; the great majority were whitefish, and were caught at Wellington Beach. They were caught very numerously with seines, as many as 5,000 to 10,000 in one haul during the night; this was in the summer time, in July and June. These were salted or sold on the ground to dealers. I have caught as many in a season as would allow the owners of the seine for their share about $2,000, the other $2,000 would go to the fishermen. Even more than this number were caught sometimes. Fishing was carried on in the fall of the year also. White-fish were thick also everywhere in Lake Ontario at that time. I have known as many as 90,000 to be taken in one haul in one night. I was present and saw them counted. I have often known from 5,000 to 10,000 being taken, and have taken 40,000 myself in a seine several times. This was in July, at Wellington Beach. Those that were saved of the 90,000 hauled were salted; many of these were lost because they could not be taken care of. There was another haul as large as this taken at West Lake Beach. The net was a 175-rod seine. The fish were wonderfully numerous. But when I left Lake Ontario fourteen years ago there was no whitefish to be had by the fishermen where these great hauls had been made before; in fact, the whitefish fishery had ceased to exist. There was no more of it. I left Lake Ontario to fish here, and a number of other fishermen left there for the same cause."

Mr. John Lang, fisherman and fishdealer, testifying as to the fisheries in Lake Huron about Kettle Point, stated:

"Whitefish were very plentiful in former years; as many as forty or fifty barrels in one haul, say five thousand fish, was an ordinary catch. These fish have fallen off very greatly."

Noah Jolie, a fisherman of forty years' experience, stated that about eighteen years before (1874) he had had two fishing grounds on the Detroit River, and that both grounds produced about 70,000 fish, or an average of about 20,000 per net. At that time, as far as he could remember, there were some fifteen or twenty grounds on the Canadian side of the river, of which some were better and some worse than his. He gave up fishing about thirteen years before (1879) because fish became so scarce that it no longer paid him to continue in the business.

James A. Smith, shipwright and boatbuilder, but formerly for thirty-five years a fisherman and fishdealer, stated:

"Whitefish were so plentiful in Lake Ontario that with one seine— I owned half of it and it was a fifty-rod seine, too—we put up in one month 180 barrels for our net's share. The other men, eight in number, would get the equivalent to 180 barrels amongst them; this was in the month of June, in 1869 or 1870, and was on Consecon Beach. There were other seines fishing also, but probably not so large in extent as ours. The same year, in November, the fish were very numerous, and all larger fish than usual, weighing about two and three-quarters pounds; as many as we could barrel we caught and salted, but a great many besides were lost. Whitefish were so numerous that they were hauled away for manure for use upon farms. The whitefish were so plentiful that in hauling the seines they could not pull them in on shore; they had simply to dip out what they wanted of the fish with small nets, and let the rest go. The fish were miraculously numerous, but when I left Lake Ontario some fifteen years ago (1878) whitefish were almost exterminated. Four thousand whitefish were many times taken in a haul in one night; salmon trout and whitefish in Lake Ontario were vastly more numerous than they ever have been in the Georgian Bay."

The Royal Commission appointed by Your Honour's predecessor in office in 1892, reported in no uncertain terms on the depletion of the fisheries, as the following quotation will show:

P. 194. "The extent to which netting is carried on is also inconceivable, and the spawning grounds are stripped year after year, until in many places where fish abounded formerly in large numbers there is no yield now at all."

With these figures and evidence it is unnecessary to seek further for proof that the whitefish in Lakes Erie and Ontario existed, within the memory of men still living, in numbers so immense as to be hardly credible to the younger generations of to-day, and that the present deplorable condition, as compared with the past, of the fisheries of the Great Lakes has not been brought about by the unpreventable causes. What these causes were, how it would be possible to change or ameliorate them, and what steps should be taken to make the fisheries of the Great Lakes once again produce a splendid cheap food for the masses of the people, will be taken up in your Commissioner's final report, after the promulgation of the regulations governing international waters, under the treaty between Great Britain and the United States.

Besides the quotation already mentioned, from the Royal Commission's Report of 1892 (Ontario), calling attention to the depletion of the waters, your Commissioner would also draw to Your Honour's attention a recommendation of that Commission as to restrictions in the use of nets, which reads as follows:

"Your Commissioners are of the opinion that pound nets should be entirely abolished in the waters of the Province, and that no gill netting should be allowed except by special permission from the Game and Fish Commissioners."

The quantities of fish can hardly be said to have increased since 1892, and your Commissioner is of the opinion that greater need of restriction exists now than when the recommendations of the Royal Commission referred to were made and ignored.

The action of your Government in not allowing netting in Lake Nipissing and the Thames River has resulted in much good, and your Commissioner would strongly urge the policy being continued, and that netting in inland waters be still further restricted.

EQUIPMENT FOR THE FISHERY PROTECTIVE SERVICE.

Your Commissioner has had the opportunity of inspecting a number of the boats employed by the Department of Game and Fisheries on protective duties, and found that none of them met all the requirements of the work they were expected to perform. They are of widely different speeds and builds. One of them, indeed, the Edna Ivan, employed under charter by the Government, is so utterly unsuited to protective service work that she should on no account be further chartered by the Government for this purpose. Among the smaller patrol craft a very wide divergence exists in regard to size, speed and other qualifications, some of them, in fact, having been constructed by amateurs possessing little or no previous experience in boatbuilding. The fishery regulations on the Statute Books bear witness to the recognition by the authorities of the importance of the fisheries, both on the Great Lakes and the inland waters, to the general welfare of the community, and it is therefore manifestly the duty of the authorities to provide an adequate equipment to ensure the proper enforcement of the regulations governing the fisheries.

It is an accepted axiom, applicable to all great enterprises, that the truest economy lies in the perfection of machinery. Makeshifts, while providing a convenient subterfuge for escaping present expense, but add to the weight of the ultimate inevitable bill, while at the same time striking dangerously close to the roots of present efficiency.

That which applies to the daily life of all commercial enterprises is equally true of great governmental undertakings, and, as the fishery regulations have been framed for the purpose of conserving a great source of public wealth, the more perfect the machinery which has to enforce those regulations, the more true will be the economy of the government policy, and the more profitable and stable its results. One of the most important factors in the machinery of enforcement is equipment, for without adequate equipment the most perfect officers find themselves at a hopeless disadvantage, and their most strenuous efforts are likely to be nullified.

In examining into the question of a suitable equipment for the enforcement of the fishery regulations, it becomes at once apparent that the natural conditions prevailing must exercise a predominant influence on the selection of the same, and a brief study of these will reveal the fact that they can be classified under three main headings:

A. The outer and most exposed portions of the Great Lakes, and places where large tugs and fishing boats operate.

B. The inner, shallower and partially sheltered waters of the Great Lakes and Georgian Bay.

C. The waters of the lesser inland lakes and rivers.

Undoubtedly an adequate protection of our commercial fisheries demands protective cruisers of some size on Lakes Huron and Superior, as well as the Vigilant on Lake Erie. This tacitly seems to be the admitted duty of the Dominion Government, and should cause no difficulty if operated in conjunction with the new naval policy as a training school for seamen, but, as this Class A type of boat would seem to be outside the scope of the provincial equipment, your Commissioner will not further refer to it.

As regards the classes of boats to meet the conditions of B and C, it is plain that the type of boat that could live, if caught out in the storms of Lake Superior or the Georgian Bay, would not be the most suitable craft for the intricate channels of the Rideau Lake system, while the boat that could fearlessly navigate these same channels would be unable to face the rough seas of the Great Lakes. To be efficient, the Government officers must be able to be out in all weathers when other craft are on the waters, and likewise able to penetrate the shallowest bays and channels where illegal operations can be carried on. Hence the main factor for the boats of Class B is seaworthiness (with as light draught as consistent therewith), for those of Class C, draught.

The next main consideration in the selection of a suitable equipment is the nature of the duties to be performed by the officers. To one may be assigned as his principal duty the supervision of the licenses, nets and operations of commercial fishermen scattered over a great extent of sparsely settled territory, and involving, more or less frequently, the passage of rough or dangerous waters; to the next may fall the task of collecting the license fee from foreign angler-tourists throughout a popular lake and river district, supervising the anglers' catch of fish, while keeping an eye on the narrow channels and creeks of his territory to see that no illegal netting is carried on therein. In cases such as the first, owing to the size of the craft necessary to carry on the work, to secure his safety in storms and rough weather, and to more efficiently discharge his duties, the officer will have to be given assistance. In cases such as the second the officer can, as a general rule, handle the work alone. Hence it will be seen that the boats of Class B would be required to carry a regular crew of two or more, and those of Class C only one.

The third main consideration is speed. The officers should be able not only to move freely about in the district, but also to cover a considerable extent of territory daily. Where the appearance of an officer in any particular locality occurs at regular and well-known intervals, or where, on his appearance, those engaged in illegal operations can upsail and make good their escape without trouble, the usefulness of the officer cannot but be grievously impaired. At the same time it would be impossible for the Government to provide boats for its general service from which the speed freaks of an occasional illegally engaged tourist-angler could not escape if so desired. It would appear, therefore, that the speed should be so adjusted as to enable the officers to cover their territory with reasonable frequency, to give them sufficient freedom of movement to prevent their comings and goings being anticipated and discounted by malefactors, and to enable them to manœuvre, on at least an equality of speed, with the average craft with which they have to deal, while at the same time reducing the fuel consumption to an economic minimum.

Great strides have been made of recent years in the construction of all manner of craft, but in no type has the advance been more marked than in that suitable for the waters of this Province. The introduction of gasoline has revolutionized the relation of size to speed, while decreasing the cost both of construction and maintenance. Some prejudice exists in certain quarters against the use of gasoline as a motive power for boats, but this prejudice is not well founded on fact. There are now in existence thousands of gasoline boats of all classes and descriptions, from the sea-going cruisers, which have voyaged to Bermuda and back, to the commercial fisherman's smack with its auxiliary gasoline engine. On the waters of the south, about Florida, there are a multitude of houseboat cruisers and yachts driven by gasoline on the inland waters of this continent, and in fact on inland waters throughout the civilized world their name is legion, so that, in spite of a few serious accidents, it is correct and safe to declare that the ratio of accidents occurring with gasoline engines to-day is no higher than with steam engines. Where the engines are handled by competent men investigation proves them to be efficient, serviceable and economical, and the prejudice against them, as likewise the troubles experienced by some persons with them, are directly attributable to men without sufficient training being placed in charge of the engine. To confide any engine to an inexperienced man is to invite trouble, if not actual disaster, and this is equally true of those whose motive power is steam or gasoline, though not so often attempted with the former as with the latter. In regard to cleanliness and comfort there can be no comparison between the steam and gasoline engine for use on comparatively small boats, as with the latter not only are coal dust and ashes avoided, but, properly handled, there is little or no smell attached to them, while in the matter of available space, the saving secured by the installation of the small gasoline engine instead of the more cumbersome steam engine must be obvious to the veriest tyro.

After mature consideration of the whole situation, your Commissioner has come to the conclusion that, in the interests of both ultimate economy and present and permanent efficiency, the time has come to discard the present haphazard and unsatisfactory system of chartering or acquiring boats for the Fishery Protective Service, possessed of only a few of the essential requirements, and for the establishment by the Province of a fleet of boats designed especially for the work they are required to perform. With this in view, and taking advantage of the experience and knowledge of some of the officers of the outside service of the Department, he has drawn up a schedule of requirements for the

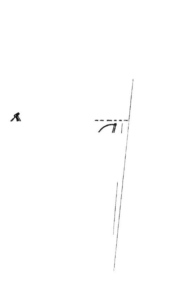

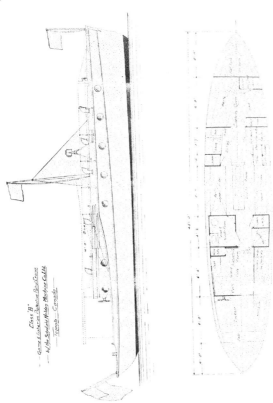

Class "B"

Great Lakes or Seaboard Power Crane

by the Standard Heavy Machine Co Ltd

Toronto — Canada

types of craft that appear to him to be indispensable for the efficient execution of the Government service, and has had the same submitted to a leading marine architect, through a prominent Toronto boat-building and engineering firm, with the result that, attached to this report will be found designs of such craft. As the schedule of requirements submitted to the designer contains concisely your Commissioner's views on this subject, he has embodied it in the report, and in so doing would call attention to the fact that the greatest possible economy, consistent with efficiency, was his chiefest consideration, that ventilation and sanitation have been provided for, and that the comfort of the crew, who in the larger boats will be expected to live on board continuously, and in the smaller boats may have to do so occasionally, as well as that of the inspectors and other Government officials who have to make use of these boats on their various duties, has been most carefully borne in mind.

SCHEDULE OF REQUIREMENTS FOR FLEET OF SMALL CRUISERS FOR THE FISHERY PROTECTIVE SERVICE OF THE PROVINCE OF ONTARIO, PREPARED BY YOUR COMMISSIONER, AND ON WHICH THE DESIGNS HEREWITH SUBMITTED ARE BASED.

There are two classes of boats necessary for the patrol of certain inland waters of the Province of Ontario, and of portions of the Great Lakes.

Class B. Boats suitable for portions of the Great Lakes, and for inspectional purposes elsewhere.

Class C. Boats suitable for the inland waters of the Province, such as Lake Simcoe, the Kawartha Lakes, the Rideau Lake System, Lake Nipissing, etc., and possibly certain portions of the intricate inner channels and bays of the Georgian Bay.

In the construction of both types of boat the greatest economy must be observed as far as the interior fittings and appearance are concerned.

Class B. Six of these boats at least may be required for the waters of the Georgian Bay and portions of Lakes Superior and Huron with the following requirements:

1. *Speed.* Eleven miles an hour under ordinary service conditions.

2. *Seaworthiness.* The lines must be easy, and designed to produce an unusually good sea boat, as, while it is not aimed that they will be patrolling for the most part in the outer waters, but rather that they will be cruising among the islands and in the inner waters, at the same time going from place to place, crossing gaps, etc., they may be called upon to encounter heavy seas.

3. *Crew and Accommodation.* A permanent crew of three men, all protective officers, but taking the duties of captain, gasoline engineer and cook. It is desired to give the gasoline engineer and cook comfortable berths, and to have the captain, if possible, in a stateroom, either

separated by curtains or preferably by a light partition. It is necessary that there should also be a small stateroom, containing a berth, to be used occasionally by the inspectors, the Deputy Head of the Department or other Government officials, and this room to be used by the captain for his charts, office, etc., and also as a mess room. As these boats will be in commission from the opening of navigation until the close of the same, and it is designed that they be kept away from their home ports as much as possible, simple, plain comfort for the crew is required. A gasoline stove should be large enough to have a small oven; locker room should be reasonable; w. c. and a good large wash basin provided; the cockpit accommodation cut down to the very smallest point, as the boat is in no sense a pleasure boat, and besides this, the smaller the better in case of shipping heavy seas, and should be, of course, self-bailing; the cabinhouse above the deck should be strong and capable of standing heavy seas, the same applying to any deadlights or glass windows, for which emergency storm coverings should be provided; the icebox should be part of the refrigerator and should be filled from outside, and it would be well to provide for some form of ice-water filter near the refrigerator; good ventilation must be provided, especially for the galley and washroom, and the designer should bear in mind that in some of the inner channels the heat in summer may be excessive. The bow should not be straight stem, but with an easy curve under the forefoot. It must be borne in mind that these boats will occasionally have their bows pulled up on flat rocks.

4. *Draught.* The draught should be as light as possible consistent with sea-going qualities, but should not exceed three feet.

5. *Dinghy.* The vessel should be planned to take on board a small boat or dinghy, when necessary on account of heavy weather, but as a rule the same would be towed. Davits not desirable, and it would be better, if possible, to provide some form of cradle on top of the cabinhouse. The dinghy should be light, but capable of holding three persons, and will be used to lift illegally placed nets, etc. The designer should therefore furnish lines for these dinghies, taking especial care to provide a good towing boat, which at the same time will fill the other requirements mentioned.

6. *Measurements.* The designer should bear in mind that these small protective vessels are in no sense pleasure craft, and that, while he is not bound down to length or beam, it is desirable that the vessel should be as small as possible commensurate with the requirements outlined, with no eye to show or display, but with the principal considerations, plain comfort for the class of men indicated, seaworthiness and efficiency. From the inspection of other designs it appears to me that 45 feet should be amply sufficient, and I hope the designer may get under this length.

Class C. The type of boat required for this class is more of the hunting launch variety. It is not intended that the men running these boats should be out over night, but at the same time occasionally it may be necessary for them to be so.

1. *Speed.* The speed of these boats under ordinary service conditions should be ten miles an hour.

2. *Crew.* The crew would consist of one, or possibly two on occasions. The steering gear, therefore, and engine control should be beside each other.

3. *Accommodation.* As these boats will be in commission from the early spring to the late fall, and as occasionally the officers must sleep on board, enough covering should be provided to give two bunks, a very small gasoline stove, a very small refrigerator, and some form of hatch or doorway.

4. *Draught.* The lighter the draught the better for this class of boat.

As in Class B, these boats are in no sense pleasure craft. They should be strong and serviceable, and built with an eye to the greatest economy. They will not tow a dinghy, and must be small enough to manœuvre for the picking up of nets, etc. The forefoot should be cut away and well shod, as they will be pulled up on the shore from time to time.

The views of your Commissioner have been most successfully grasped by the designer and are cleverly set forth in the accompanying blue prints.

The estimated cost of the Class A type of boat is about $4,300.00, and that of the Class C type, $1,850.00, which includes furnishings of all descriptions, sanitary mattresses, ventilators, engines and installation of same, cooking utensils, bedding, cutlery, etc. As regards the type of engine for the Class B boat the following is an extract from the letter of the expert who made the designs for the boats:

"As to the engine power necessary for the Class B boat, it would take about a 4-cylinder, 4-cycle engine of at least 30-horsepower to get the speed, and a 40-horsepower would be preferred. I would hesitate to guarantee eleven miles with any lesser power than the above with so heavy a boat, as, by my figures, a boat of this size and displacement, about 16,000 pounds, would go at the most 11.05 miles statute with a 24-horsepower engine, but this is too small a margin to give any guarantee on. I would prefer to place a 30-horsepower, which would give ample power and would last longer, because it could be run slower. Using this engine, a speed of 12.20 miles would be realized."

With regard to Class C boats, a Toronto firm of boat and engine builders writes:

" With regard to the 25-foot boat, we believe a 2-cylinder, 15-horsepower of our own make would give the full ten miles an hour, and we will guarantee this engine to stand up under the most exacting strain and under all conditions. Perhaps it would be well to mention the fact

22 F.G.

that with our muffler, and under water exhaust, this out&t will be absolutely noiseless, and, if used at night, the protective officers can
approach to within a very few yards of poachers, etc., without being
heard. It appears to us that this ought to be quite a feature for this
particular service."

In recommending these types of boats for the Fisheries Protective
Service your Commissioner only does so with the proviso that the engi-
neers of the larger class, and the officers in charge of the smaller craft,
shall hold certificates of proficiency from a reliable firm of gasoline
engine manufacturers, and that no inexperienced or untrained man
shall be allowed to handle them. This would, of course, entail some of
the men having to pass some weeks in the shops, but the advantages
accruing in immunity from breakdowns and general care of the engines,
would more than compensate in the long run for any slight expense or
inconvenience incurred, and the adoption of such regulation would be
in the interests of true economy.

In this interim report your Commissioner does not deal with what,
in his opinion, should be the full equipment for the Province of boats
of the types indicated. He has, however, selected an area, Georgian Bay
and portions of Lake Superior and Lake Huron, as one which he considers to be urgently in need of an improved Fishery Protective Service.

He would recommend to Your Honour that six (6) boats of the
Class B type be acquired by the Province and be stationed on the area
above mentioned, with the following apportionment of patrol districts:

1. The easterly portions of Lake Superior to St. Joseph's Island.

2. From St. Joseph's Island to the west end of Georgian Bay about
Killarney, taking both sides of) anitoulin and the Ducks.

3. Killarney to Point au Baril.

4. Point au Baril, taking in the rest of Georgian Bay, down to
Penetanguishene.

5. Penetanguishene to Tobermory, including Cove Island and surrounding islands.

6. Tobermory down to Goderich.

For these boats he recommends a crew of three, all of whom should
be appointed deputy overseers, to consist of:

A captain, who should have a thorough knowledge of the waters in
which he is to cruise, previous experience as a professional mariner and,
if possible, in the handling of small boats, and be used to taking command.

An engineer, who shall have a certificate of proficiency from a reliable firm of gasoline engine manufacturers.

A cook who shall have had reasonable experience as such, be prepared to act as general utility man, and at the same time be experienced
in the handling of oars, and of sufficient intelligence to undertake, when
necessary, the duties of his office as deputy overseer.

All three men must possess the attribute of personal fearlessness,

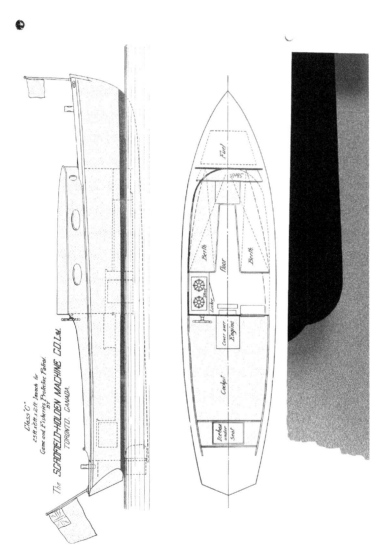

Class "C"
23 ft. x 6 ft. x 2 ft. launch for
Game and Fisheries Protective Patrol.
BY
The SCHOFIELD-HOLDEN MACHINE CO. Ltd.
TORONTO, CANADA.

Fuel

Berth

Floor

Berth

Locker

Cover over Engine

Cockpit

Icebox under Seat

and be prepared to discharge their duties conscientiously in the face of inclement weather or other personal risk, besides such qualifications as the dignity and exigencies of their office demands, such as physical fitness, tact, and a certain amount of education.

In regard to salaries, your Commissioner would recommend that the captain be paid $60.00, the engineer $55.00, and the cook $45.00 per mensem, in addition to receiving board whilst the boat is on actual service and away from the home port, and at these figures he is confident that no difficulty would be experienced in obtaining the services of really competent and suitable men.

The initial cost, therefore, to the Government of this recommendation will be approximately $27,000.00.

The cost of maintenance, assuming that the captain is a permanent official, and employed during the close of navigation on other protective duties inland, and that the engineer and cook are employed only during the seven months that the boats are in commission, will be approximately:

Salary of Captain..............................	$720 00	$4,320 00
Salaries, Engineer and Cook (7 months)............	700 00	4,200 00
Board, 3 men for 30 weeks $10.50 per week........	315 00	1,890 00
Gasoline, oil and accessories, allowing 5 hours' run per diem, 6 days per week, for 30 weeks	500 00	3,000 00
Minor repairs, say...............................	100 00	600 00
Totals	$2,335 00	$14,010 00

It must be understood, however, that this sum is not an increase over and above existing expenditures, for the salaries of all the fishery overseers for this district, the wages of the help assigned to them in certain instances, their board while absent on patrol, their mileage allowance, the hire and repairs to their craft, etc., must all be set against it. Disbursements of this nature for the districts in question, according to returns already presented to the House, would appear to amount approximately to $13,000.00.

As regards the class C type of boat, your Commissioner's full report will contain a recommendation as to the numbers of these boats required by the Province and the districts that should be assigned to them. Pending the submission of this report, he would recommend that no other type of boat should be acquired by the Government for use on the inland waters of the Province, and that a few of them should be at once ordered and put in commission as soon as possible for service on the waters of the Rideau Lake System, the Kawartha Lakes, Lake Nipissing, Lake Simcoe, etc. He would, however reiterate that no boat of this type should be handed over to a warden or overseer until such warden or overseer has procured a certificate of proficiency in the working of the engine, preferably from the firm installing and guaranteeing same.

FISH HATCHERIES.

In dealing with this question it is taken as an axiom that it is the duty of the state to conserve for the people, and if possible improve sources of food supply, and that the importance of an abundant supply of fish food ranks second to none.

Ontario has been endowed with exceptional advantages for obtain ing a liberal supply of fish food, owing to its position on the Great Lakes. the magnificent lakes scattered throughout its interior, and its numer ous rivers and streams; but, owing to many causes, chief of which may be said to be forest destruction, pollution, and over-fishing, and the fact that the commercial fishing is practically controlled by a foreign cor poration, not only are the people of Ontario deprived to-day of an abun dant supply of cheap fish food, but what is far more serious, the fish food supply of the future is seriously threatened, unless immediate steps are taken to counteract existing conditions. When the rapidly-increas ing population is taken into consideration, and the fact that most of these people come from countries where they have been accustomed to rely on cheap fish as one of their principal foods, the importance of the question to the future welfare of the community can be realized.

In this regard it will not be out of place to quote a passage from the report of the Commissioners of Fisheries and Game of Massachusetts. which very clearly sets forth the reasons for the artificial hatching and rearing of fish:

"The practice of maintaining and protecting the fisheries of publi waters at public expense is of long standing, and is firmly establishe in well nigh all densely-populated states and countries as both expedien and profitable Two definite methods are in vogue:

"1. The regulation of fishing for the purpose of protecting th adults, either (a) during the breeding season, or (b) in cases where th demand exceeds the natural supply; either by reducing the number o fish taken during the year, by limiting the catch, or by limiting th number of days upon which fish may be legally taken—i. e., a clos season—or, again, by prescribing how and by what apparatus fish ma, or may not be taken.

"2. The artificial hatching and rearing of young fish, and subse quent stocking of the water by the liberation of fry just hatched or o one- or two-year-old fish.

"The purpose for which such laws are instituted is absolutely cor rect. If the adults of both sexes are not protected, the number of fertil eggs laid is immediately reduced. Then necessarily follows a decreas in the number of the young hatched and a proportionately smaller num ber of immature fish. Observations indicate that in a natural trou brook, undisturbed by man, an optimum population of all classes of lif is established; enough insect larvæ, adult insects, worms, crustacea, an small fish of various species are present to furnish food for a rather con stant number of young trout. Further, practically enough large adult trout are present to eat at least 90 per cent. of the trout fry before these young reach the breeding stage, and to furnish a number of offspring practically just sufficient to furnish food for themselves and similar large fish. Thus a surplus of not more than a pair or two comes to maturity out of the hundreds of annual progeny of each pair of breeding fish, to replace the old trout which pass on through accident or senile decay.

" When, however, man appears, and a considerable number of the breeding fish are removed by him, the most important consequence is a sudden diminution in the number of eggs laid and a corresponding diminution in the number of fry hatched; consequently, a relatively larger proportion of young fish, which are destined to go as food for the ' big fellows.' A two-pound trout, for example, requires a certain weight of animal food per day. He will persistently hunt until this amount is secured and his voracious appetite is satisfied. If, then, only a relatively small number of small trout are present, it is possible that every one of these may thus fall victims; and not alone an actually smaller number, but even no surplus fry, may remain to grow to become breeding adults. When this occurs the trout fishery in that brook declines, and the waters soon become occupied by less valuable fish, or else the stream remains unproductive, yielding either nothing to man, or, at least, less than its normal productive capacity. * * * The necessity of meeting these conditions has led to biological studies which prove the following facts of economic importance:

" 1. More trout fry can be secured by artificial impregnation of the egg than are ordinarily hatched under natural conditions.

" 2. The trout fry can be reared artificially in immense numbers, with less mortality, than in nature.

" 3. By an increased quantity of food the rapidity of growth may be accelerated, and by substitution of an artificial food in place of young fish a greater weight of trout may be secured at less expense."

In the United States, not only the Federal Government, but almost all the individual states, are increasing the yearly production of fish by means of enlarged or additional hatcheries. An idea of what is being done in this direction may be gained from the following figures, taken from the thirteenth annual report of the Forest, Fish and Game Commission of the State of New York:

SUMMARY OF FISH DISTRIBUTION FOR THE YEAR ENDING DECEMBER 31ST, 1907.
IN THE STATE OF NEW YORK.

Brook Trout	1.815,950	Frostfish	3,100,500
Brown Trout	1,051,750	Maskalonge	5,000,000
Lake Trout	8,758,900	Pike Perch	36,855,000
Rainbow Trout	822,100	Shad	566,100
Small Mouth Black Bass	11,000	Smelt	100,000,000
		Tomcod	65,600,000
		Whitefish	15,510,300
Total Game Fish	12,459,700	Total other fish	226,631,900

In regard to fish, protection means both preservation and propagation. The remarkable fecundity of the fish is an ever-growing amazement to the student of ichthyology. The ova are smaller than in any other class of animal, yet the ovaries in many fish are larger than the rest of the body. Taking advantage of this fecundity, with the aid of modern science and appliances, it should be possible to maintain in our Great Lakes and other waters the approximate balance of fish that nature intended, which, as before pointed out, is in all probability the optimum—that is, always provided that the system of artificial propagation works hand in hand with reasonable protection of the adults of the various species during the periods that they are engaged in the reproduction of their species, for to rely on artificial means alone to accomplish the work of nature is to court disaster.

In this Province a close study should be given to the selection of the most suitable varieties of fish for the different inland waters. As an illustration of this may be quoted the salmon trout of the Great Lakes. This most excellent food fish, when planted in the confined areas of our lesser lakes, never seems to attain the same game qualities as the species indigenous to the particular lake; neither is their flesh, as a rule, so palatable. Many of our inland lakes have salmon trout peculiar to themselves, and it would seem well, under any system of provincial hatcheries, to make provision for maintaining these varieties and testing their suitability for surrounding waters.

It has been impossible, in view of the many questions that have presented themselves to be dealt with by this Commission, to accumulate sufficient detailed information on the establishment and working of hatcheries on the most modern, practical, and economical basis, to draw up a scheme for provincial hatcheries to be presented with this interim report, but such a scheme will be prepared and presented with the full report at a later date.

Meanwhile, your Commissioner would most strongly urge upon Your Honour the adoption of the principle of provincial hatcheries, to be scattered throughout the Province, in locations selected with a view to the easy gathering of the spawn, and general facilities for distribution over the area to be fed by each, the whole system being so devised as to deal with all classes of food and game fish, and fish known to be the natural food of same, as it is only by maintaining the balance of nature that the best results can be obtained.

Possibly no enterprise in the world is so dependent upon the skill, faithfulness, and enthusiasm of those in charge as that of fish hatcheries. The work of a whole season may be ruined and the expenditure of considerable sums of money wasted, by a few hours' negligence. Ontario is placed in the happy position of being able to take advantage of the experience of, and expensive investigations undertaken by, not only practical hatchery men and state fish culturists, but also by scientific university professors and experts, in the United States and other countries.

It must, however, be realized that in starting hatcheries of her own, the Province has not at present the necessary *personnel,* and should most certainly not commence experimenting with amateurs; but, rather, should take up the art at the point it has now reached. In due time Ontario citizens will be trained, and will acquire the necessary skill; but for the first hatcheries it is obviously essential to obtain the services of non-residents who have had long, practical experience in the erection, maintenance, and general operation of the different forms of hatcheries.

BASS BROODERIES.

That Ontario already has a large tourist traffic, coming in from outside and attracted by the angling, it is only necessary to look at the returns of the non-resident anglers' tax to realize; and that this tourist traffic can be developed into one of the largest economic factors in the prosperity of the Province, provided good angling facilities are forthcoming, few who have knowledge of the geography of the Province, with its vast areas of forest lands and streams, unsuited to agriculture; its magnificent lakes and waters, offering alike beautiful scenery and a splendid climate, and its ever-growing transportation facilities, or who have studied the development of the State of Maine, where it is estimated that the tourist traffic brings into the state yearly a revenue of twenty-five million dollars, would be prepared to deny. A study of this question will reveal the fact that in this Province, as an attraction to anglers of all classes, our own citizens, as well as those from other provinces and states, the black bass stands in a class by itself. Its importance, therefore, from the point of view of developing the tourist traffic of the Province, as well as of affording a healthful recreation to our own people, cannot be overestimated.

The black bass, however, differs from the majority of fish, in that it cannot be forced to yield its eggs, or fertilize the same; and hence ordinary methods of artificial propagation, as used in hatcheries for other varieties of fish, are unavailing. Moreover, compared with other fishes, the black bass produces a small number of eggs, the number varying from about 2,000 to 9,000. A system has been devised by which use is made of small ponds, cleared of other fishes and injurious matter, for the purpose of inducing the bass to breed under normal conditions; and the young, resulting, are then carefully nurtured and reared, until in a suitable condition for transplantation.

In view of the vast numbers of bass that are taken out of the waters of this Province yearly, the comparatively small number of eggs produced by the female and the improbability, to say the least of it, that, in the small lakes and rivers at least, the present supply will be maintained unless special measures are taken to increase the propagation, your Commissioner would strongly recommend the adoption of the principle of bass control ponds, to be scattered throughout the Province in suitable locations; and though time and opportunity have been insufficient to enable him to draw up a scheme for presentation with this interim report, such a scheme will be drawn up and be presented with the full report of this Commission at a later date.

CO-OPERATION.

In the enforcement of laws the good-will and support of the people is a most important factor, for no government can afford to maintain indefinitely a sufficient force of officials to ensure the obeying of laws of which the general public does not approve. Most particularly does this apply to the enforcement of the game laws and fishery regulations of this Province on the public waters and wild lands. To patrol these vast areas closely would entail an army corps of officials and an expense far in excess of the funds at the disposal of the treasury; while to patrol them with a limited number of officers implies wide districts for the officers to cover, and consequently a greater dependency on the people themselves, not only to obey the laws, but to demand their observance by others, resident in or visiting the localities in which they live.

There is no more misguided policy for a government than to have laws on the statute book which it cannot, or does not, enforce, for connivance at infractions of the law is synonymous with connivance at public moral deterioration.

Hence, in reviewing the question of possible co-operation by officers of other departments of the Government, and other corporations, as called for in the instructions of his commission, your Commissioner deems it his first duty to call the attention of Your Honour to the urgency of enlisting the co-operation of that greatest of all provincial corporations, the public of Ontario.

That the laws and regulations in regard to fish and game of the Province are sound in principle your Commissioner is convinced; as likewise that the great mass of the people are law-abiding, and prepared to support the enforcement of the laws once they understand what they are and the purposes for which they have been made. Unfortunately, however, investigation has disclosed to him the fact that not only is there considerable vagueness in the public mind as to the provisions of the laws and regulations, both in their requirements and in their admin-istration, but also a very widespread misapprehension of the purposes for which these laws and regulations have been framed. Unconscious violations of the law are of common occurrence; magistrates all to fre-quently display their ignorance of its provisions in unauthorized total or partial remissions of its penalties, and the commercial fisherman, the settler, and the pothunter appear more often than not to view those resources of nature in which they are interested as their own peculiar birthright and possession, to be squandered at their pleasure, without regard to vested public rights or to their future economic value, holding, indeed, in many instances that all restrictive laws and regulations are but the device of an unrighteous and selfish band of individuals, known to them as sportsmen, to steal their birthright for themselves. The general public, meanwhile, remains dull and apathetic, merely because it does not appreciate the greatness of the issues at stake.

The awakening of the public to the importance of these issues not only would ensure public co-operation, but would carry with it comprehension of the value of the natural resources of the Province on the part of its greater corporations, and a desire to assist in developing and exploiting their almost boundless possibilities. Specific education is an important means of awakening the public sentiment, and such education must comprise a lucid exposition of the economics of the questions involved. The public must be taught to understand that the fishery regulations and game laws have been devised in their own interest, and must be encouraged to take pleasure in conforming to the same; magistrates must be instructed to learn and enforce the provisions of the laws; but, above all, it is important that the general public, together with the settler, should realize that the living deer is many times more valuable to them than the same deer dead; together with the agriculturist, that the birds of the air are the farmer's best friends; together with the commercial fisherman, that the capture of fish in the season devoted by nature to reproduction but spells ultimate and utter depletion.

The blue books of the country contain carefully-prepared statistics, giving full information as to the amount of coal and other minerals mined, of cereals raised, of butter and cheese manufactured for export, etc., but one source of wealth possessed by the Province of Ontario—as well, in fact, as by most of the other provinces of the Dominion—is not included in these returns. The tourist traffic is the source of wealth referred to.

In several countries the value of this traffic is recognized and understood, not only by the authorities, but by the general public also. Possibly the best example of this is the Republic of Switzerland, where attractions of mountain scenery, an invigorating climate, and winter and summer sports draw thousands of tourists annually, who leave vast sums of money behind them, to enrich not only the hotels, which may be numbered by the thousand, but to circulate freely among all classes of the population.

The tourist traffic of Italy, attracted by its wonderful climate and by the historic associations and art collections of its many beautiful cities, is enormous, and its importance is realized by the authorities and people alike.

As an example of the value of fish and game as an attraction to the tourist no better case can be quoted than that of the State of Maine.

In 1867 a commission, appointed by the State Legislature, made an exhaustive enquiry into the conditions prevailing then, and the report submitted stated that the inland fisheries were practically valueless, there was no moose in the state, and deer in only one small district. This condition had been brought about, not by the visiting sportsmen, but by the residents themselves, the game having been shipped for commercial purposes to the larger Eastern cities. After this report was received, the Legislature passed very strict laws, which were at first enforced with great difficulty, but which in the end won public support. In the year 1902, in order that the Legislature might be well advised as to what the tourist traffic amounted to, the state authorities carried out a summer census of all the visitors in the interior portions of the state. These figures showed that 133,885 persons came into the interior portions of the state, the principal attraction being the excellent fishing and shooting provided.

Two years ago your Commissioner enquired from Hon. L. T. Carleton, State Commissioner of Fisheries and Game, whether this traffic had increased, and Jr. Carleton was good enough to take the question up with Colonel Boothby, General Passenger Agent of the Jaine Central Railway, and this official stated that, from statistics in his possession and from other sources of information, he was of the opinion that quite 250,000 people came into the interior portions of the state during 1907, attracted principally by the fishing and shooting.

Senator Frye, a well-known statesman, has stated that in all times of financial depression the State of Jaine feels the conditions less than any other state in the Union, owing to the fact of this sportsman-tourist traffic, which at these periods does not seem to shrink as might have been expected.

Officially, the authorities of the State of Jaine estimate the amount of money left behind by each individual who comes into the interior portion of the state at an average of $100.00. Those who have studied the question are of the opinion that this is a very conservative estimate; and, if it be accepted as a basis, it will be found that, taking the Government statistics for 1902, there would have been left in the state that year over thirteen million dollars; and, if the figures of the railroad official are accepted for 1907, the gigantic sum of twenty-five million dollars would be the result of the tourist traffic for one year.

The Province of Ontario is very happily situated, geographically, to take the fullest advantage of the possibilities inherent in its game fish and game as an attraction to the tourist. It lies within easy distance of the populous and ever-growing cities of the State of New York, and is as easy of access to the residents of the Jississippi Valley as is the State of Jaine.

Some little prejudice exists among a portion of the population of the Province in regard to the influx of visiting sportsmen, the idea being that, should great numbers come in, the sport will be ruined. On reflection, however, it will be seen from the history of the evolution of this class of traffic in the State of Jaine that this belief is not founded on fact, for, as has already been pointed out, in 1867 the game and fish of the state had practically disappeared, not through the action of visiting sportsmen, but through the slaughter carried on by the residents themselves; but, once the public became advised of the value of this attraction in the development of the tourist business, such splendid protection was furnished that to-day not only is twenty-five million dollars attracted annually to the state, but the residents themselves obtain much better fishing and shooting than ever existed in the state before.

The returns of the Department of Game and Fisheries of the Province of Ontario show that from the non-resident anglers' tax of $2.00 per head approximately $17,000 has been collected during the year. It must be borne in mind, however, that this license fee has only been collected for three years, and that the machinery for its collection is not yet perfected; and, indeed, at the present time it may fairly be assumed that only about one-half of the possible amount is actually collected. Then, also, it should be realized that this $17,000 direct revenue means an indirect revenue to the Province of something approaching $850,-000.00, taking the average used by the Maine officials as a basis of calculation, namely, $100.00 per capita. It must also be borne in mind that for one person who pays this fee there are, on an average, one or two members of the family who do not care to angle, and who, therefore do not take out any license to do so, but who will none the less be spending their pro rata amount in the Province.

From information in the possession of your Commissioner, obtained from railroad officials, hotel proprietors, etc., he estimates that quite three million dollars comes into the Province annually, which would not be brought in if there were no angling or shooting; and, further, your Commissioner is of the opinion that were the fish and game of the Province to be seriously considered from their economic aspect by your Government, the public, and the great financial institutions, such an improvement would take place in the sport, through the establishment of hatcheries and adequate general protection that the sum referred to would be immensely increased. The State of Maine is only about one-eighth the size of the Province of Ontario, and there is no reason why the immense sums derived from its tourist traffic and now enjoyed by that state should not in the course of time, and by intelligent effort, be equalled, or even surpassed, in the Province of Ontario, the free circulation of which would mean the building of numerous hotels, improved railway and steamboat transportation, increased value of real estate, employment for thousands of registered guides, and the development generally of the machinery to handle a quarter to half a million annual summer visitors.

The scarcity of ready money among the poorer settlers in the back townships is admitted, and no manual labour is better paid that that of guide or oarsman, employed by visiting sportsmen; and, were the settlers more alive to the opportunities of obtaining considerable sums of money by taking up this work, your Commissioner believes such settlers would become interested in the protection of fish and game in their neighbourhood, and realize that its greatest value to themselves is as an attraction to the visiting sportsmen. It may be of interest to note that no less an authority than Hon. L. T. Carleton has estimated that the value of a moose running in the woods is quite $500.00, whereas the same moose dead, and looked upon from its food value alone, is worth only a fraction of this sum.

The value of fish and game from a sentimental point of view is of doubtful importance in this commercial age, but your Commissioner would point out that, in addition to the arguments above set forth, the health of the citizens of the more crowded centres is admittedly much improved by a holiday spent in the woods and on the water, and that the attraction of fish and game to draw city folk countrywards is of importance to the body politic from this point of view.

He believes that were the facts and figures above given more thoroughly understood by the masses of the people of the Province, a strong vigorous, and healthy sentiment would readily develop in all classes of the community, as it has in the State of Maine, and especially among the settlers in the regions where sport is chiefly found, or can best be improved.

In the United States the importance of educating the people in this direction is recognized. The Department of Agriculture at Washington has been, and is to-day, carrying on this work energetically. Bulletins are issued by it on various subjects, such, for instance, as the value of the quail to the farmer as an insect destroyer, and of the usefulness of other birds in assisting the farmer in destroying noxious weed seeds, insects, and harmful vermin, and are freely circulated. Commissioner Whipple, of the New York State Forest, Fish and Game Commission, stated recently, at a convention of the New York State Forest, Fish and Game Leagues, that at least 100 nights of the year be devoted to giving lectures throughout the state, with the view of advising the public of the objects of his commission and as to the advisability of supporting its efforts.

The following extract from the 1908 report of the Game and Fish Commissioner of the State of Alabama exemplifies very clearly the necessity of some such action on the part of the authorities:

"As a result of scientific research of the most extended nature it has been ascertained that the cause of the prevalence of many maladies, and the problem of weed control, is largely attributable to the slaughter of our insectivorous birds, which in the past have been wantonly murdered by the million. Birds annually destroy thousands of tons of noxious weed seeds, and billions of harmful insects; they were designed to hold in check certain forces that are antagonistic to the vegetable kingdom. A noted French scientist has asserted that without birds to check the ravages of insects, human life would vanish from this planet in the short space of nine years. He insists that insects would first destroy the growing cereals, next would fall upon the grass and foliage, which would leave nothing upon which cattle and stock could subsist.

The possibilities of agriculture having been destroyed, domestic animals having perished for want of provender, man, in his extremity, in a barren and desolate land, would be driven to the necessity of becoming cannibalized, or subsisting exclusively on a diet of fish. Even granting that only a portion of what the eminent Frenchman asserts is true, it is easy to glean from his theory that birds are man's best allies, and should be protected, not only on account of their innocence, bright plumage and inspiring songs, but because they render to the farmer valuable assistance every day."

It would seem, therefore, that not only is the education of the people to an appreciation of the value of the fish, game and birds of the Province a necessity, but that in its undertaking there is ample scope for cordial co-operation between the Departments of Agriculture and Game and Fisheries. Mr. C. W. Nash, the eminent ornithologist and ichthyologist, by means of a series of lectures to farmers, has done excellent work in this direction, and your Commissioner believes that the broadening and extending of such a system, together with the free distribution of educative bulletins on all matters appertaining to the subject, would produce most far-reaching and satisfactory results.

Your Commissioner would also point out that the duties of certain of the officials of the Department of Lands, Forests and Mines, such as the fire rangers, as well as those of the newly organized provincial constabulary, bring them into close touch with matters intimately connected with fish and game protection, and that the loyal co-operation of these officers in the enforcement of the game laws and fishery regulations is most earnestly to be desired. The provincial constabulary force, under its new chief, may well prove an invaluable aid to the officers of the Department of Game and Fisheries, for it is, to a certain extent, a secret service; and will, therefore, at times have in its possession information not otherwise procurable by the Department of Game and Fisheries.

As regards corporations, who are in a position to co-operate with the Department of Game and Fisheries, and whose co-operation it would seem most advisable to secure, your Commissioner would draw Your Honour's attention to the fact that the great railways have a definite and acknowledged financial interest in the maintenance of the fish and game in the Province, as an attraction to tourists, and thereby as a means of swelling their passenger receipts, while at the same time, owing to the nature of their organization, they are most advantageously situated, especially in the more sparsely settled regions through which their lines run, to render this co-operation effective. Your Commissioner is happy to be able to report that he has had the opportunity of pressing upon certain of the companies the desirability of their assistance in the matter of fish and game protection, and has met with a most courteous and sympathetic hearing. Your Minister of Public Works has been pleased to agree to commission as deputy overseers any officials appointed and paid by the railroads t take an active part in the protection of fish and game, and already th Algoma and Hudson Bay Railway Company, after consultation wit your Commissioner, has taken advantage of this offer to appoint suc an officer. At the present time, also, the managements of some of th greatest railroads, operating in this Province, have under consideratio plans for assisting the authorities in a parallel direction, and your Con missioner hopes that before the presentation of his full report thes plans will have matured, and taken definite shape, so that he will b enabled to present them therein.

Your Commissioner would reiterate once more that, to develop an exploit the natural advantages of the Province in fish and game, cl mate and scenery, to make barren and wild lands productive of a grea income to the Province, and to build on solid foundations, which wil secure the fruits of these efforts to all future generations, it is necessar that, not only should the officers of the various Government Depar ments, nearly or remotely interested, most cordially co-operate, but tha the interest of the public must be awakened, and its co-operation so licited and won, which can only be effected by educating the public to realization of the issues at stake.

The storehouse of nature, filled with treasures of incalculabl value, are none the less exhaustible. The history of this continen has proved that the wanton destruction of to-day but spells the extin tion of a whole species to-morrow. To bring the people to a realiza tion of these matters should be the ambition and care of a governmen and hand-in-hand with an aggressive educative policy for this purpo there should be adopted a policy of conservation, framed on broad line such as those pictured by President Roosevelt in his instructions to t National Conservation Commission, on its creation in 1908, when wrote:

" Our object is to conserve the foundations of our prosperity. W intend to use these resources, but to use them so as to conserve ther No effort should be made to limit the wise and proper development an application of these resources; every effort should be made to prever destruction, to reduce waste, and to distribute the enjoyment of ou natural wealth in such a way as to promote the greatest good to t greatest number for the longest time."

Your Commissioner would, therefore, most strongly recommen that:

1. The officials of all Government departments, nearly or remote connected with matters appertaining to the protection of fish, gan and birds, be instructed to co-operate, cordially and loyally, with tl officials of the Department of Game and Fisheries.

2. The Department of Agriculture, together with the Department Game and Fisheries, undertake the education of the people to the ec nomic value of the birds, as the safeguards of agriculture, and of fi.

and game, both as sources of food supply and as an attraction to the
tourist, by means of bulletins, such as published and circulated by the
Department of Agriculture at Washington, and by an amplification of
the lecture system, such as already conducted by \ r. C. W. Nash.

3. Every encouragement be given to any corporation desirous of
assisting the Government in the enforcement of the game laws and fishery regulations.

PROVINCIAL PARK PRESERVES.

The Province of Ontario contains many thousands of acres of wild
and wooded lands, whose geological formation discloses no valuable
mineral resources, and forbids the possibilities of agriculture, but whose
natural beauty is a constant joy to those fortunate enough to visit
them, and whose peaceful sylvan recesses and rugged fastnesses
afford a luxurious home for the song, insectivorous, and game bird, as
well as for the moose, the deer, and the many smaller but valuable fur-
bearing animals. It has been said that nothing in nature exists without
a cause, and if a reason be sought for the existence of these wild and
beautiful lands, what nobler or grander one can be conceived than that
they are designed to be the perpetual and unspoiled playground of a
great and populous nation, wherein its sons and daughters may seek
both health and recreation, and where bird and beast alike may exist
under adequate protection?

The progress of modern civilization has entailed extravagant demands on nature, and the blatant call of demand drowned the feeble
plaint of an ever-diminishing supply. Fortunately, however, a powerful
voice was raised in time, and the nations of the continent were made to
understand that it is easier to fell than to grow, easier to exterminate
than to create. It had long been realized that all wild life reproduces
itself more prolificly and healthfully under natural conditions, and it
required but the launching of the idea of Government-owned park preserves for the principle to be cordially welcomed and accepted by all
classes of the community. Throughout this continent the adoption of
the principle has been remarkable both for its rapidity and for the variety
of its application. Sea-girt islands have been selected as breeding places
for the gulls, where no man may venture to shoot; ranges of wild land
and hills have been assigned to the elk to make his home in, and others
to the moose or smaller forms of deer life and birds; hills and mountains have been declared the sanctuary of the mountain sheep and goat,
and vast tracts of devastated timber lands have been set aside, to be
sown with the seed that will produce the lumber for generations yet to
come.

Already the success that has attended the movement has been most
marked, and not only are certain species of birds and beasts, formerly
in danger of extinction, once again beginning to multiply in the pre-

served regions, but, in common with other four-footed and winged creatures, are spreading in increasing numbers over contiguous districts. In fact, it may be said that in the national park preserve has been discovered the secret of perpetuating our big and other game.

Ontario has not been behind in grasping the wisdom of this policy, and in the Temagami, Algonquin, and other provincial parks the helmsmen of her destiny have set aside, alike for the people of to-day as of to-morrow, great tracts of land, where nature may continue to hold undisputed sway, where the birds and beasts may thrive and breed, to spread in plentiful numbers over the surrounding territory, and where men and women may seek simple and healthy repose from the cares and worries of strenuous modern life.

The area of the Province, however, is so vast that there would still seem to be scope for the extension of this most excellent principle.

At the time the pine timber was being taken out from the territories where very little land suitable for agriculture existed, men went in on the wave of the lumber industry, and, picking out a spot where there chanced to be a little arable soil, fit to produce oats, hay and potatoes, etc., proceeded to erect a small home, finding employment during the winter in the shanties, and in the spring on the drive, after which they devoted themselves to raising the crops indicated, and for which they obtained high prices among the lumbermen. After the pine was taken out and the wave of lumber operations receded, these men were in many cases left high and dry, with wives and families to support. The land they owned not being really suitable for agriculture, they eked out a very poor livelihood. Their homes are often far removed from schools, and consequently their children do not have the same opportunities for education as exist generally throughout the Province. These men have, to a certain extent, become dependent on the game and fish of their neighborhood to furnish no small proportion of their daily food. It would seem that the welfare of the Province would be advanced were their condition ameliorated. The purchase of holdings of this nature would give cash to these poor settlers, with which, if homesteads were allocated to them in more fertile regions, and free transportation to the same provided for them, they would be enabled to start life afresh under more advantageous circumstances, whilst these same lands, so barren and useless to the settler agriculturist, would be a suitable and profitable addition to the park preserves of the Province and for reforestation.

Since undertaking his present duties your Commissioner has had the opportunity of visiting only one of the provincial park preserves— the Algonquin National Park. The extent of this park is some 45 by 45 miles, comprising, approximately, 24 townships; and, though the objects of the park are being in many respects fulfilled, and bird and animal life increasing, after consultation with the Park Superintendent, and from other sources of information, your Commissioner has been forced o the conclusion that the staff of rangers for the efficient wardenship of he park is totally inadequate.

At the present time there are but fifteen rangers, and in a broken und woody country of this description it is vain to expect such a small staff to provide proper and sufficient protection. M r. Shier, a lumberman of twenty-five years' experience in the woods of Northern Ontario, in giving evidence to your Commissioner on this point, remarked:

" In my opinion, you ought to have two men to one township."

Although a staff of such a size as indicated by this gentleman would be beyond the funds at present available, nevertheless some addition to the permanent staff of the park is most urgently needed. The Superintendent of the park is in the anomalous position of being responsible for the efficient discharge of their duties by the wardens, while, at the same time, being required to be practically continuously at his headquarters, in order to deal immediately with any malefactors the rangers may bring before him. That some supervision of the rangers is necessary would seem to be obvious, as likewise that to supervise their work effectively would entail an inspector being almost continuously in the woods the year through; but, on the other hand, it is equally plain that someone is required at headquarters to discharge the magisterial functions of superintendent and to attend to administrative details. It would appear, therefore, that a chief ranger is a necessity, to work directly under the Park Superintendent; and, though an experiment in this direction proved unsuccessful, the falling of one into evil way does not imply that another would, of necessity, do likewise. In fact, your Commissioner believes that in the Province of Ontario many a suitable man, both able and willing to discharge the duties of such a post, is to be found, if only they be sought amongst the ranks of those whose life records and experiences prove their suitability.

One of the main difficulties which seem to attend the efficient wardenship of the park is that, at the present time, the rangers cannot arrest or pursue further than one mile outside the park boundaries. Such a state of affairs is subversive of good results, and weakens the authority of the wardens, for to chase an offender out of the park and then be obliged to let him escape, is but to encourage the offender in the belief that he can return to his malefactions with impunity, and to discourage the wardens in attempting to arrest. The laws and regula- tions have been designed to check these classes of offences. Placing obstacles in the way of the enforcement of the law is the surest way of encouraging the commission of these offences.

Another difficulty encountered in the wardenship of the Algonquin National Park is that the boundaries of the park admit of entrance being gained thereto by numerous waterways from outside. M any a man, therefore, can easily slip into the park unobserved, making use of these waterways, and starting from the lakes outside. In fact, the pres- ence of a chain of lakes immediately outside the boundaries of the park

23 F.G.

would appear not only to be a source of strategical weakness from the point of view of efficient administration, but, judging from the evidence of the park superintendent, the actual cause of a very great portion of the troubles experienced by himself and staff.

In dealing with the subject of provincial park preserves, your Commissioner desires to call to Your Honour's attention the great increase of beaver within them. From the evidence collected by him on this point he feels assured that these animals have now attained to such numbers that to remove the normal increase would be proper and advantageous to the parks. Such a system, in the matter of game, is worked by the authorities in Germany; and, were it adopted in Ontario, would provide a very considerable revenue, sufficient, in all probability, to at least bear all the expense of the maintenance of the parks. As accurate as possible a census of the beaver should be taken annually, the numbers to be taken decided upon, and the localities for the taking carefully selected by the responsible authority, arrangements made for the proper treating and preparing of the pelts; on each pelt should be branded a Government mark, and when the pelts are ready for the market they should be advertised for tender or sold by auction. The killing of beaver should only be entrusted to thoroughly competent and reliable officials, as it would, in the opinion of your Commissioner, be dangerous and unprofitable to undertake it with officials whose probity, at all events, was not absolutely beyond question. In fact, it would seem that the supervision of this work should be one of the duties of the Chief Ranger referred to in a preceding paragraph.

As the population in Ontario grows and its tourist traffic develops, the number of visitors to the public parks will inevitably be greater, and the demand for guides will steadily increase. The science of forestry has made rapid progress, and undoubtedly will play an important part in the future economics of the Province. Already, indeed, much attention is being paid to the prevention and extinction of forest fires, and the Department of Lands, Forests and Mines employs quite a considerable number of fire rangers at certain periods of the year. In the University of Toronto a special forestry class is held, under the supervision of Professor B. E. Fernow, and it has been brought to the attention of your Commissioner that anything that can be done to assist these young men to a practical knowledge of the woods is a step in the direction of the future prosperity of the Province. Practical knowledge of the woods can only be obtained by personally visiting and living in them. The expenses of education bear pretty hardly on the pockets of many of the ambitious young men of to-day. Employment as guide or forest fire ranger would appear to offer these young men not only a practical road to knowledge of the woods, but also an opportunity of making a little money with which to carry on their education. Young men, attested by Dr. Fernow to be proficient canoemen and swimmers, to have a reasonable knowledge of cookery and the theoretical side of woodcraft, and to be of good character and physique, should make ideal guides for the average tourist, for they would be cleanly in habits and polite in manners; and, in a very short space of time, would be equally at home as the woodsman in the particular districts in which they were employed. Other young men, without the particular qualifications necessary for guiding, would, at least as fire rangers, be obtaining practical knowledge of the woods, of life in the same, and of the practical side of fire protection for the forests, as also, probably, of fire extinguishing.

The people of Ontario, as a whole, maintain the park preserves, but only a proportion of the people are able or desirous of making use of them; and, therefore, it would seem not to be unreasonable to attempt to lighten the burden on those who do not by imposing a small fee for the privilege on those who do. A registration fee of 50 or 75 cents would deter none from coming, but would furnish an additional source of income to provide for the cost of maintenance and, equally important, provide statistics as to the numbers making use of the parks.

Your Commissioner would, therefore, recommend that:

1. Power be taken to expropriate gradually the holdings of settlers in barren and unprofitable lands, adjudged unsuited to agriculture, the said settlers being offered free lands in districts more suited to agriculture, and, with their wives, families and belongings, free transportation to same.

2. The following townships be added to the Algonquin National Park: To the south—Livingstone, Laurence, and Nightingale. To the east—White River, Clancy (east half), Guthrie, Barron, and Edgar.

3. A chief ranger be appointed for the Algonquin Park.

4. The number of rangers in the Algonquin National Park be increased to 24.

5. A system of taking the normal increase of beaver be adopted for the provincial park preserves, pelts to be taken by Government officials, branded with the Government brand, and sold by tender or auction, the proceeds of such sales being devoted to the maintenance of the provincial park preserves.

6. The students of Dr. Fernow's forestry class be encouraged to go into the woods and act as guides in the provincial park preserves when it is attested by Dr. Fernow that they have the proper qualifications, and be employed, as far as possible, as forest fire rangers, or rangers' assistants, by the Department of Lands, Forests and Mines, free transportation to their destination and back being provided at the public expense.

DEER.

One of the penalties of advancing civilization in all countries has been the comparatively rapid disappearance of the larger forms of wild animal life indigenous to them. The axe of the woodman, the opening of a country to agriculture, the creation of trade and transportation routes, with the consequent increase of population and the facilities thereby afforded for the exploitation of newly-opened lands to supply the demands for game from established towns and cities, have all played their part; but on this continent an additional factor must be credited with a large share of the responsibility. Each man child born to the country seems to have inherited in most pronounced form the hunting instinct and, in the past at least, something of the lust of slaughter. The truth of this, and its full meaning, was probably first realized when the two nations of North America awoke to the fact that the buffalo were no more. Certain it is, however, that efforts to counteract these combined influences are of comparatively recent date.

In the United States, where civilization made the more rapid progress and population the more rapid increase, the effects of wanton destruction were first noticed and felt, and consequently game protection advanced there by rapid strides, whilst in Canada it still remained in its infancy. Now that Canada, in her turn, has entered upon her era of increase and development, it would seem but wise for her provinces to take advantage of the experience of those who, in these respects, have already passed through the stages of evolution in which they to-day find themselves.

That the economic value of deer can ever even approximate to that of the fish is not to be contended, either as a source of food supply or as an inducement to the tourist, for in the scheme of nature there is no provision made for abnormal reproduction of game animals, such as exists in the fishes, and also almost every man, and a great many women, are expert anglers, and in the course of the year find some opportunity of displaying their skill, while in these days only a proportion of the male population have either the means or opportunity to venture into the woods in search of deer. The economic value of deer, however, though less than that of fish, is none the less very high, and should by no means be overlooked or underestimated; for, outside of the money brought into the Province thereby, there is still the consideration so ably set forth in the 1908 report of the Game Commissioners of Pennsylvania:

"Through the increase of game we feel that an incentive to outdoor exercise and recreation is supplied that cannot be secured through any other process. An experience in camp life and in handling and caring for firearms is secured that is of great worth to our citizens who indulge in hunting, through which they, as individuals, secure better health, and are, therefore, better fitted to fill the place allotted to each in his respective community. These things together—better health and, therefore, better citizenship—joined to experience in camp life and in the handling of firearms, appear to us of great value to the state and the nation, as they surely raise our standard of defence in time of trouble, in the shape of war, either from within or from without, far above that of any people who do not hunt. We feel that the presence of game is of great value to the state, and that hunting is a necessary adjunct to our national success; and that, therefore, the state owes it to itself to provide some method whereby game can be increased." ˎ

The Province of Ontario has been abundantly endowed by nature with forests and wild lands well suited to the maintenance of large herds of deer, and her ranges were originally stocked to their utmost capacity. Owing, however, to the advance of civilization, with its train of consequences before enumerated, as likewise to the fact that for many years the slaughter of deer was practically unchecked, great ravages have been made on the numbers of the deer, with the result that to-day in many localities their ranks are sadly thinned; and it would appear to be the almost unanimous opinion of those who have studied the subject, or take a personal interest in it, that some steps should be taken, and that immediately, if the deer are to be conserved to the Province. In any case, without taking a pessimistic view of the situation, it can be safely said that further conservation measures on the part of the authorities are a necessity, for the diminution in the numbers of deer almost throughout the entire Province is well marked and admitted, and that the time for these measures is now, when the material available is still ample for the upbuilding of a great and permanent supply.

Fortunately the experience of our neighbours has proven that, as expressed by the Game and Fish Commissioners of Minnesota in their 1908 report:

"Deer respond readily to protection, thrive and multiply in the vicinity of settlements, when not molested in close seasons, domesticate easily, and may be retained in abundance under ordinary restrictive laws."

So that, by studying the laws of our neighbours, and selecting those which have been most efficacious and beneficial, it should be possible for the authorities to ensure the conservation of at least an equal supply of deer to posterity as exists at present, without laying any undue hardships on the sportsman-citizen of to-day.

Advocates of reforms in the deer laws are as numerous as the remedies they suggest, but, in the opinion of your Commissioner, Dr. Hornaday, the eminent naturalist and head of the Bronx Zoological Society, placed his finger on the vital issue when, in an interview accorded to your Commissioner, he stated:

"There is no surer method of exterminating any variety of big game than to allow the destruction of the females."

In enlarging upon this subject, he pointed out that the adoption by hunters of a motto,

" Never shoot until you see the horns."

not only means the preservation of many does to produce one or two fawns in the ensuing spring, but in itself is the most powerful safeguard that can be devised by the state for the protection of human life in the woods, for almost all the hunting accidents, which on this continent are so lamentably numerous as to be almost a public scandal, occur through snapshooting at a moving object whose nature, even, cannot be discerned.

That such a law would be viewed by many in this Province as a disagreeable innovation is probable; but it must be remembered that all innovations, from the umbrella to the telegraph, have met with opposition at the hands of a prejudiced populace, and time and again has it been proved that the popular prejudice will disappear with extraordinary rapidity if the innovation or measure is intrinsically good and worthy of popular approbation.

Considering this question to be of great importance, your Commissioner feels no hesitation in quoting at some length from the reports of the various fish and game commissions and wardens in the United States, where conditions are, perhaps, even more critical in respect to deer than they are in this Province, and where the men in touch with the conditions can speak from experience of an actual application of such a law.

The Chief Game Protector to the Game Commissioners of the State of Pennsylvania writes in his report of 1908:

"When the bill proposing to limit the killing of deer to a male deer with horns, and which afterwards became law, was first introduced, I was opposed to the measure. * * * I thought that if a measure of this kind became law it would be very apt to result in trouble to many men who otherwise intended to be honest; that because of the thick underbrush found in the deer territory, the high bracken and rough country, it would be almost impossible to determine the sex of a deer until the deer had been killed. I preferred the making of an absolutely closed season for deer, if protection to that extent was found to be necessary, and I at once began a canvass of the Senate and the House of Representatives relative to these matters. I also consulted sportsmen and other men who were in the habit of going into the woods during the deer season regarding their thought on the subject, and found that, almost without exception, the bird hunters, the rabbit hunters, the lumbermen. the land-owners, and the people generally who desired to go into the woods during the last two weeks of November, including many deer hunters, favoured the passage of this measure. They argued that they, as citizens of this commonwealth, had just as much right to be in the woods at that time as had the deer hunter, and that, under the then existing law, there was not one moment of all that time that the life of any one of them was safe. They claimed that they, as human beings, were just as much entitled to protection as were the deer. I found from statistics gathered by the Biological Survey at Washington, D.C., that forty-eight men had been killed and one hundred and four wounded within the United States by deer hunters during the pen season of 1906. I, therefore, refrained from opposing this bill efore the Legislature, and urged the Governor to sign it when it came efore him. I am now satisfied this is one of the best measures ever placed upon the bucks of Pennsylvania. * * I am certain that no more deer have lost their lives, in violation of law, since the passage of this act than would have been killed illegally during the same period had there been an absolutely closed season. * * * I am confident the great majority of hunters respect this law. * * * It is, of course, a new idea, and very trying to deer hunters in this state to hold their fire when a fine doe or deer of any description stands in front of them. Yet this was almost invariably done. * * * From data collected I am satisfied that the number of bucks killed last year did not exceed one-fourth of the number of deer killed during the fall of 1906, and would not exceed two-thirds of the number of bucks killed during that season. * * * The great majority of the deer hunters I have met last fall, both during the season and since that time, although frequently disappointed in not securing a deer, expressed themselves as satisfied with the law. The feeling of personal security surrounding each one apparently far outweighed any pleasure they might have derived through the killing of deer. * * * I noticed that, almost without exception, the opponents of this law were men who did not realize the value of this act as a preserver of human life, or a man whose sole desire was to kill, no matter what the result might be to others. * * * The number of deer killed in this Commonwealth during 1906 was in the neighbour-hood of 800. Of this number, perhaps 350 were bucks and the remaining 450 were does. From positive reports received from several counties not more than 200 bucks were killed last year, or at least during the past season, throughout the entire state, and I believe I am within bounds when I say that not more than thirty does will be found to have lost their lives. * * * If these figures are correct, and the same ratio of killing was followed as last year, we have spared to us about 150 bucks and about 420 does, or 570 deer in all. The majority of does give birth to two fawns, so that I think an estimate of one and one-half fawns to a doe for this year would be fair and reasonable. Six hundred and thirty fawns, added to 420 does and 150 bucks, will give us 1,200 deer to start with this fall that we would not have had under the old law. This seems to be a good showing, and one that would justify a continuance of this law, were its sole and only object to preserve and increase our deer; but as the chief purpose of this act was the preservation of human life and limb, this addition to deer life in the state is only incidental. Still it means much."

The State Fish and Game Commissioner of Vermont, in his 1908 report, writes:

" The prime reason for the rapid increase undoubtedly has been in the protection of does, allowing deer with horns to be taken only.

It is also known to the Commissioner in several instances where the hunter's life has been in jeopardy, but saved through the caution of other hunters waiting to see if what they supposed to be a deer had antlers, when, to their surprise, another hunter came into view. For this one reason the law is a protection to human life. Eight out of ten illegally shot, or killed by dogs, are does."

The State Game and Fish Commissioner of Alabama, in his First Biennial Report of 1907-8, writes:

" The provision of the game law limiting the killing of deer to bucks only has had a most salutary effect on the efforts of the state to save these beautiful and valuable animals from extermination."

The State Game and Fish Commissioner of Colorado, in his Biennial Report for 1907-8, writes:

" The law existing immediately prior to the passage of our pres-ent law forbade the killing of any deer, except that each person could kill one deer with horns. That excluded the killing of fawns of either sex, and the killing of does. This afforded the deer an opportunity to increase in their natural way, and during the years that law was in existence a marked increase was noticed, practically all over the state, where deer are found; but under our present law, taking into consid-eration the loss of fawns, because of the killing and crippling of the mother, and the separating of the fawns from the does, leaving the former in the deep snows of the mountains, and the consequent exposure to all the natural enemies of its kind, I believe I am safe in saying that by far a larger per cent. of the does and fawns were lost to the state than of bucks. This tends more than anything else to the extermination of the deer. In order to increase the deer, the does must be protected first, in order that they may bear increase, and the increase must likewise be protected until it can be given a chance to mature and produce more of its kind."

The above quotations, in the opinion of your Commissioner, con-stitute succinct and convincing testimony to the efficacy of such a mea-sure, both from the point of view of conserving the deer, if not of obtaining an actual increase in their numbers, and as a protection to human life and limb, and render it unnecessary for him to make any further remarks on this subject.

Attention has been called to the demand from cities and towns, whose inhabitants often cannot spare the time to go into the woods themselves to kill a deer, for game food, and in Ontario the demand for deer meat is so great that in many of the smaller towns and vil-lages the butchers handle very little other meat at all during the sea-son in which deer meat can be legitimately sold. This demand obvi-ously produces the market hunter and, in addition, also encourages many a man to go into the woods after deer who would not do so unless he were assured of recouping himself for his time and trouble. It is plain, therefore, that the prohibition of the sale of venison constitutes almost as powerful a protective weapon in the hands of the Government as would the enforcement of a close season all the year round, and at the same time bears less hardly, not only on the hunters, but also on the general public who enjoy their venison steak and chop, though, of course, even such a measure as this should not be enforced longer than absolutely necessary, as the policy of the Government should always be to give to the general mass of the public every opportunity of enjoying the natural food resources of the Province.

In regard to the period of the open season, there would seem to be a pretty general opinion abroad that the dates have been fixed too early, and that throughout a very considerable portion of the Province the meat of the deer is in consequence often wasted, owing to putrefaction before it can be removed. The climatic conditions of the accessible portions of the Province are, broadly speaking, such that no considerable quantity of snow need be anticipated in an average November or weather sufficiently and continuously cold as to prevent the melting of the snow, should it fall, under the rays of the sun. The temperature, however, is, as a rule, markedly lower at the end of the month of November than at the beginning. Consequently it would seem that if the season fell fifteen days later in the year there would not be much risk of snow tracks assisting the hunter, whilst, not only would the deer meat be less likely to spoil before being removed from the woods, but also the later season will make, or at least threaten to make, things harder for the sportsman, and, as Dr. Hornaday remarked to your Commissioner when discussing this point:

"Anything which accomplishes this, tends towards the preservation of the species."

Your Commissioner would, therefore, most strongly recommend that:

1. The open season for deer be fixed from November 15th to November 30th in each year, both days inclusive.

2. The bag limit for each hunter during each open season be fixed at "one horned deer."

3. The penalty for exceeding the bag limit, or for killing a doe or fawn, be not less than $25.00 or more than $100.00.

S M ALL GA M E.

The object of protection is primarily to perpetuate existing and indigenous species of game, for the extinction of any species is recognized to be a direct economic loss to the community. In particular cases, also, protection may occasionally be used to allow the firm establishment and acclimatization of a newly introduced species. In no case is the object of protection to deprive the public of the advantages of its natural resources in fish and game as a source of food supply.

Restrictions on the sale of game, though frequently necessary for the preservation of a species, are almost invariably unpopular with the majority of the public, for game is a highly esteemed table delicacy, for which no satisfactory substitute has ever been discovered, pleasing, indeed, to the palate of rich and poor alike, and, while everyone eats, it is the minority only who can be expected to appreciate and view the diminishing numbers of any particular variety with alarm, and with sufficient unselfishness to be willing to sacrifice their epicurean or sporting proclivities for the good of future generations.

ꓭany varieties of game retain to a great extent their characteristics of hide, fur, or plumage under varying climatic conditions, so that in legislating for the protection of any individual species, it was found neecssary to forbid trade in that species in any shape or form during the closed season, in order to make that closed season really effective, for there was usually no practical means of distinguishing the imported from the native variety, and, if the former were on the market, no amount of legislation could prevent the latter appearing there also.

The principle is most undoubtedly sound, and not only for the above reason, but because, also, the onward march of conditions leading to the necessity for protection is very similar always in contiguous provinces and states, and the closing of the markets in all is a surer guarantee of protection than any measure each, individually and alone, could ever have devised, for it removes the possibility of trade on a large scale at a profit.

Where, however, no inter-provincial or inter-state affiliation of interests need be considered, and where the importation for sale of a species from a foreign country, to which no harm will be done by such importation, will mean the placing of a certain variety on the market at such a price as not to tempt the local market hunter to slaughter the indigenous species in competition, or where there is convincing evidence that such importation will not affect the demand for the indigenous animal, it would seem that the principle of the prohibition of the sale of that particular species during the closed season could be safely and advantageously departed from. Certain classes of game lend themselves readily to domestic raising and in some of the states of the Union the raising of game in captivity has already been placed on a profitable commercial basis, thus creating a new industry, and affording a variety in food to the people at a reasonable price, both highly desirable objectives from an economic point of view. Legislation to allow for the sale all the year round of game thus raised has not as yet been perfected, and requires considerable elaboration of machinery, in order to be feasible under existing protective laws, so that. outside of drawing to Your Honour's attention this new industry, and its economic value, and the advisability of preparing for its introduction into this Province, your Commissioner will not in this interim report deal with the question of game farms, but will confine himself to a discussion as to the advisability of allowing the importation and sale of two particular species, the pheasant and the rabbit.

The pheasant, which has been introduced into portions of Southern Ontario, is undoubtedly a very fine game bird, and, in addition, though perhaps not quite so toothsome a delicacy as the native partridge, none the less much prized for its edible qualities. Under protection it may be said to have thrived in the districts in which it has been introduced, but, owing to the severity of the winter, and its constitutional and physical peculiarities, it can never be expected to adapt itself to the greater portion of the Province, or to live and multiply therein in a wild state.

In England thousands of these birds are raised under domestic conditions, and on attaining maturity, are released in the woods to furnish sport, and, subsequently, a market commodity, which, though comparatively expensive, is, nevertheless, within the means of a great portion of the public, largely, indeed, filling the general demands for game above referred to.

To take advantage of the English market, during the English open season, would seem to afford a means of satisfying the demand for game at a reasonable price in this Province, without in the least hurting the interests of those residents of Ontario on whose properties pheasants are to be found, and without offence to the principle of inter-state co-operation, for the price at which they could be placed on the market would hardly allure the poacher to devote time and trouble to securing the local bird at the risk of incurring the penalties of the law, but, none the less, would, if an open season were allowed, permit those on whose properties pheasants were to lease their shooting to advantage, or if they preferred to shoot themselves, afford them a ready market for their birds, sufficiently remunerative to arouse their continued interest in the maintenance of the birds on their properties, and yet not sufficiently profitable to incite avaricious cupidity to slaughter every possible specimen for the sake of immediate gain.

The cotton-tail rabbit, indigenous to the Province, is, your Commissioner presumes, protected under that section of the Game Act dealing with hares, and consequently the sale of rabbits is debarred in Ontario during the greater portion of the year. In England the rabbit is practically a staple food, exceedingly cheap and much relished by the masses, affording, as it does, a tasty and wholesome dish, and it is safe to assume that very many old country men, now residents in Ontario, would gladly welcome and support a market of reasonably priced rabbits all the year round, and that their example would be followed by other sections of the community.

In Australia, as is well known, the rabbit is a pest, and consequently cheap, and your Commissioner has learned that it is possible to import these animals, frozen and in their skins, and place them on the market here at a figure not greatly in excess of that of the indigenous cotton-tail. The Wm. Davies Company of Toronto have already placed a shipment of these rabbits on the market with considerable success, selling them at 75 cents per pair, dressed, as compared with the average price of the cotton-tail, 50 cents per pair.

In this Province the indigenous cotton-tail is apparently not much relished as a food, and, judging by its price on the New York and Chicago markets, some 22 cents per pair, it is not very much esteemed by our neighbours to the south. The chief reason for this would appear to lie in the fact that its flesh is somewhat hard and bitter to the taste. The English or Australian rabbit, however, possesses a flesh more akin to that of veal in appearance, and is, in addition, sweet and slightly gamey to the taste. While this rabbit is a grazer, the cotton-tail is a browser, and, moreover, owing to its habits of retiring into the swamps and rough lands in the summer months, comparatively safe from the pot-hunter, during a great portion of the year. In appearance the two varieties are comparatively easy of distinction, and it may also be noted that, while the skin of the Australian rabbit is tough and can easily be removed whole, this is not the case with the indigenous cotton-tail, whose hide is much more brittle.

The rabbit is a prolific breeder, whose only known use in nature is to serve as a food for certain carnivorous animals and birds. It is, however, accepted by the best authorities to be unwise on general grounds to run the risk of upsetting the balance of nature by the extermination of any particular species, even though its uses to man may not be apparent, for the reason that no one can foresee the result of such extermination. The habits of the cotton-tail, however, as has been pointed out, are such as to largely eliminate this risk, and so, although the imported Australian rabbit would actually be fetching on the market a higher price than the indigenous rabbit, it would seem that the advantage of securing a reasonably cheap, wholesome and constant game food for the people outweighs the consideration of any problematical risk to the existence of the local variety, especially in view of the facts that the importation of the Australian rabbit would in no way be violating the principle of inter-state co-operation, and that the marked difference in flavour would in itself be a potent factor in the prevention of the substitution of the local variety.

As a game food, the price of 75 cents per pair, dressed, averaging 5 to 6 lbs., is not excessive, but it may be noted that, if the trade in rabbits grew to large enough proportions to warrant the purchasing of great quantities in Australia, and their importation via British Columbia, instead of as at present purchasing from the wholesale market in London, England, the price would, in all probability, be considerably reduced.

Your Commissioner is pleased to report that on all sides there is evidence that the close season of two years has had its beneficial effect, and that the finest native game bird of the Province, the

Canadian partridge (ruffed grouse), is distinctly on the increase, so much so, indeed, as to justify the proclaiming of an open season in the fall of the present year. This bird, prized alike for its sporting and edible qualities, is fortunately distributed over almost every section of the Province. Unlike the pheasant, it does not lend itself readily to domestic rearing, and consequently its price remains high in all countries, so that there exists no reason or inducement to encourage its importation for market purposes, or to sanction the sale of the imported bird during the close season.

In the past the open season for this bird has been from September 15th to December 15th. It would appear that the opening of the season, however, fell too early, for the reason that, as a rule, the coveys remain packed until the weather begins to turn cold, and are disinclined to take to wing, and in consequence the destruction of an entire covey is frequently an easy matter. That, if there be an open season for partridge, the deer hunter should be entitled to profit by it, would seem to be reasonable, for his bag of deer is limited, and the partridge would provide him an alternative sport to compensate for his outlay, besides being a most welcome addition to the camp menu. Many persons, however, who like to hunt the partridge, from motives of personal security, prefer not to venture into the woods when the deer hunters are afoot, and the convenience of these sportsmen also must be considered in deciding on suitable dates for an open season, although in framing dates for an open season on different classes of game the broad principle of making them as far as possible coincident should never be lost sight of, for, when the hunter is in the woods after one class of game within the provisions of the law, the lives of other classes cannot but be in jeopardy, for the temptation is obviously great, and frail human nature is but all too likely to succumb to its allurements. Hence, in considering the question of a suitable open season for partridge, a reasonable medium would apear to be attained by fixing the dates from October 15th to November 30th.

Your Commissioner would, therefore, recommend that:

1. An experimental open season be declared for cock pheasants in Ontario from October 15th to November 15th for the current year, both days inclusive, and that their sale be permitted during this open season, and for one month thereafter.

2. The importation of English or European pheasants, in bond through Atlantic seaports, be permitted during the open season in England, and that the sale of same be declared legal during the English open season, and for one month thereafter.

3. It be declared lawful to import Australian rabbits, frozen and in their skins, in bond through Atlantic and Pacific ports, and to sell them in the Province of Ontario throughout the year.

4. An open season for partridge be declared for the current year from October 15th to November 30th, both days inclusive.

RESIDENT HUNTING LICENSE.

Among the many causes which have worked for the protection of game and birds on this continent one of the most powerful has been the gradual arousing of the people to the value of human life. The opening up of its vast areas was only accomplished by the adoption of a policy which courted immigration, and which resulted in the arrival of thousands upon thousands of aliens, of all nationalities and classes, to spread over the land. Vast numbers of these immigrants belonged to the fiery-tempered peoples of Southern and Eastern Europe, accustomed in their own countries to the vendetta, the secret societies, and the family feud, and consequently bred and reared in the belief that each male, at least, should carry with him always the wherewithal to slay. The settler inhabitants of the land, living in the more or less secluded loneliness of the great wilds, dependent to a certain extent on the game resources of the district for their food, and with the recollections and traditions of Indian forays still fresh in their minds, naturally enough were practically all provided with firearms, and the wave of alien immigration unfortunately but confirmed them in the advisability of such precaution. Consequently at one time, outside of the big cities, every man was armed. The possession of a firearm is a direct incentive to shoot, if only for practice, so that, with the incoming of the immigration wave, there swept over the continent also a tempest of ruthless slaughter, not only of the big game and game birds, but of every living creature that could run or fly.

Demand will always create supply, so that, naturally enough, a great interest developed in the manufacture and sale of firearms, spreading its ramifications over the whole country, gathering into its net every hardware merchant on the continent, ready to resist tooth and nail attempts at legislation detrimental in the slightest degree to its trade interests.

The universal possession of firearms, however, led not only to the indiscriminate slaughter of bird and beast, but, as was to be expected, to a terrible waste of human life, with the result that, as the population gradually increased, and news facilities grew greater, the folly of the sanctioning of the universal carrying of firearms dawned on a people just awakening to the value of human life. In spite of the efforts of the firearms interests, legislation was passed, restricting the carrying and possession of firearms, and thus one great step towards the protection of game and birds was taken, for there is no greater menace to the game and bird life of a district than the Italian or other Southern European, wandering over it armed with a gun, and no legislation more difficult to introduce than that which antagonizes an interest whose representatives are to be found in every town and village.

The evolution of game protection has been traced in another section of this report, so that here it will suffice to note that accompanying an appreciation of the value of fish, game and birds, and of the fact of their rapid diminution in numbers, they developed an understanding by the people of the loss they themselves were sustaining through the slaughtering and depredations carried on by aliens and foreigners, and from this understanding grew the desire to protect the public property, and to exact some monetary compensation, at least, for that which was destroyed for the amusement or benefit of the alien or nonresident. The desire bore fruit in the imposition of alien and non-resident hunting licenses. The advantages of such taxes, both as revenue producers and indirect protectors of game and birds, were so obvious that the principle spread rapidly over the whole continent. The collection, however, of these taxes was no easy matter, for no game warden can be expected to know every resident of a state or province, and men cannot be obliged to produce certificates of identification and residence, except when called on by law to produce such identification in the form of a license.

Consequently, the imposition of the alien and non-resident licenses was directly responsible for the birth of the idea of a resident license, and this idea matured rapidly and assumed concrete shape, not only for the sake of assisting the administration of the non-resident and alien laws, but because of a growing conviction in the public mind that those who gain recreation and amusement from the protection of fish and game cannot fairly claim that an injustice is being done in asking them to pay for at least a portion of the protection afforded by the state to their favourite sport, an argument, indeed, which has been constantly advanced by persons of all classes to your Commissioner in the pursuit of his present inquiries.

In the United States the policy of a resident hunting license has been adopted by one state after another, until to-day it is in force, in some shape or form, in over thirty of the states of the Union, and it may also be noted that in the recent session of the Legislature of the Province of Saskatchewan the new schedule of licenses enacted includes a $1.00 Bird License for residents of cities, towns and villages.

In Ontario there exists to-day a resident license of $2.00 for the hunting of deer, but further than this the idea has not been carried.

The danger to human life through the promiscuous carrying of firearms has already been referred to, and, although the enactment of a resident hunting license would not be so great a preventative of this evil as the imposition of a gun license, nevertheless it would undoubtedly prove a powerful factor in that direction, while at the same time be less likely to arouse the active antagonism of the gun manufacturers and hardware merchants. The value of such measure in the protection of game and birds, the economic worth of which, as an attraction to tourists and as farmers' best friends, has already been pointed out in a previous section of this report, would also plainly be enormous.

The third great advantage of a resident hunting license is its revenue-producing qualities, which would enable the administrative and protective services of the Department of Game and Fisheries to be placed on a splendid footing, provided with an adequate equipment and with sufficiently paid and efficient subordinate officers, and able financially to undertake all necessary measures of conservation and propagation. An estimate of what such a license will produce can be formed from the information, based on the United States statistics, given to your Commissioner by Dr. T. S. Palmer, of the United States Biological Survey at Washington, who deals particularly with returns of this nature, and who stated that the numbers paying the resident hunting license, in the different states in which it is in force, ranged from 4 to 10 per cent. of the population, running highest in those districts in which population was most evenly distributed, and least in the territories where the bulk of the population was confined in great cities.

This same authority, as an estimate of the possibilities in Ontario, gave as his opinion that from 3 per cent. to 5 per cent. of the population could be expected to pay the fee, if such a license were imposed. This, on a basis of 2,000,000 souls in the Province, would mean a revenue of from $60,000.00 to $100,000.00. Your Commissioner realizes that to decide whether the bulk of the people is ready to favour such a tax, even though its advantages are so apparent, is a most difficult matter, but unhesitatingly states it as his opinion that any license, whether it were a Nipigon fishing license, a non-resident angler's tax, or even a hunting license, would be cheerfully paid by the majority of sportsmen, if the Government adopted a policy of devoting all the moneys so received entirely and directly to the protection of the fisheries, game and birds.

Many of the states of the Union who have adopted such a license, following the French system, exempt landowners from its operation, and your Commissioner is decidedly of the opinion that, in the enactment of such a measure in this Province, it would be advisable to exempt both the farmer and the settler on their own lands and adjacent waters, for to afford them this privilege over the rest of the community is to take the first step in their education as to the economic possibilities of game and birds, and these are most essentially the classes whom it is imperative to educate in this direction. Naturally, also, as such a license would be a hunting and not a gun license, it would in no way be operative against those who engaged solely in trap or target shooting.

That the state has sovereign right over the game within its borders has been established in law, and it would therefore seem not to be unreasonable for the state to impose a charge on those of its community who profit at the public expense, whether it be by big game or small, by four-footed creatures or by those that fly, even though by reason of their scarcity the charge for hunting certain species might have to be placed at a higher figure than others, providing always that the purchase of the more expensive license, even though for a limited period.

would carry with it all the privileges obtained by the purchase of the less expensive license. That such a license is beneficial as a deterrent to the promiscuous carrying of firearms, and as a protection to fish and game, your Commissioner has tried to show; that it would be a great revenue producer is undeniable, and, in conclusion, your Commissioner would point out that, though considerable opposition should be expected from the firearms interests, and from certain sections of the community, who, humanlike, desire to continue getting for nothing that for which they are not called to pay to-day, this revenue, if applied to conservation and propagation measures, would act directly in the best interests of both classes, for the increased protection would mean more plentiful game, to gladden the heart and provide sport for the genuine sportsman, and to attract in ever-increasing numbers the sportsman tourist, whose purchase of guns, ammunition and other similar supplies would swell the receipts of the hardware merchants.

Your Commissioner would, therefore, recommend that:

A resident hunting license of $1.10 (the 10 cents going to the officials or persons entrusted with the issuance of the licenses) be enacted for the privilege of hunting game or game birds of all descriptions not specifically provided for under the present Game Act, but that *bona fide* farmers and settlers be exempt from the operation of such a license, in so far as their own lands, or waters contiguous to same, are concerned; and that the purchase of a hunting license for any special animal or animals, if such license be of greater value than $1.10, carry with it all the privileges extended through the $1.10 license.

LING.

Attention has recently been called in the newspapers to the high cost of food, and without entering into a discussion of this most vexed problem it can be stated broadly that in adopting measures that will provide cheap food for the masses a Government is acting in the best interests of the community.

Owing to the non-promulgation of the International Fisheries Treaty your Commissioner has decided not to include in this interim report the result of his enquiries under this head as regards fish in general, for the reason that the terms of the treaty may fairly be expected to materially alter existing conditions. He is pleased, however, to be able to report that, through his instrumentality, an experiment is now being made to provide a really cheap and palatable fish food in the shape of ling. The burbot, or ling, is our only fresh-water representative of the cod family. It is a highly predaceous fish, very destructive to other fish life, and, as will be seen from the Report of the Department of Game and Fisheries for 1908, increasing rapidly in the waters of the Rideau Lake System.

On investigation your Commissioner discovered that the flesh of

24 F.G.

this fish is eaten in many localities, and in some, indeed, is esteemed a delicacy, and in view, therefore, of the fact that the catch of ling by the Government officers on the Rideau Lake System was being given to the farmers to feed to their pigs, your Commissioner entered into negotiations with the Department of Game and Fisheries, and the William Davies Co., with the result that the Company undertook to purchase a certain quantity of this fish from the Government at one and a half cents per pound, and to place them on the market at a price not exceeding six cents per pound. The first consignment is already on the market at a price of five cents per pound, and the William Davies Company reports that the experiment is succeeding as well as could be expected, and that already some second orders for this fish have been received from those who have tried it. In this way your Commissioner hopes that he has succeeded in opening a new channel of cheap food, but he would point out that in the lakes where the ling abound there are also to be found the bass, the pickerel and other sporting fish, which attract the angler, and that the removal of the ling was undertaken by the Department of Game and Fisheries entirely on its own initiative, as a measure calculated to increase the numbers of the sporting fish in these waters.

To allow the Government officers to remove these harmful fish during the winter months when their duties are light seems eminently desirable, and even profitable, if a reasonable market can be established for the ling, but to lease such fishing to commercial fishermen, or to allow others to engage in it, would, in the opinion of your Commissioner, be a very grave mistake, as it would be admitting to these confined waters the thin end of the wedge of general commercial fishing.

REVENUE AND EXPENDITURE.

The question of conservation of the natural resources of the Province is vital to the present, but more especially to the future, prosperity of the community, and in consequence legislation dealing with it should be framed on the broadest possible lines, comprehending alike the conditions of to-day and the economic possibilities of years to come. If the conception of a policy is correct, and its broad general lines be adhered to, the details can be filled in, amplified and perfected as opportunity permits, and, even if a mistake in one of them should be made, it will in no wise endanger the whole fabric. In pursuing his enquiry and framing his recommendations, your Commissioner has had these principles ever before him.

In this interim report he has endeavoured to show the magnitude of the issues at stake in the conservation of game, game fish, and fisheries, alike as a source of wealth to the community, through the upbuilding of a great sportsman-tourist traffic, as for their intrinsic value as a source of food supply, not only in support of the measures he recommends, but because he felt that in the past comprehension of the vast scope of this problem has been somewhat limited in perspective and vague. In approaching each question, however, not only has he had in mind the necessity for a wide range of view, but also the fact that the public welfare demands expenditures in many directions, and that the public purse is limited.

The base, therefore, on which his plan has been built is that in view of the present and future economic possibilities inherent in the fisheries, the game fish and the game of the Province, the full income derived from these sources to-day should be expended upon their conservation and development for at least a few years to come.

All moneys accruing to the public must of course be paid into the general treasury, but the Department of Game and Fisheries should be entitled to frame its budget for the ensuing year on the basis, at least, of its earnings for the current year, or better still, on a basis which will embrace the automatic and anticipated increase to its revenues for the ensuing year. A comparison of the revenue of the Department of Game and Fisheries with its expenditures for the years 1908-9 will disclose the fact that each year there has been a surplus of between $30,000 and $40,000. In these figures the cost of the inside service of the Department, which is charged under another head, is not taken into account. Assuming that this would amount to $15,000, there still remains a considerable sum in surplus revenue. Your Commissioner, however, realizes that this sum would not be sufficient to meet the additional maintenance charges which would occur in the adoption of the various recommendations contained in this interim report, but on the other hand he is convinced that an outside service, much more efficient in personnel and equipment, would ensure a very material increase in the revenue derived from the license fees, for at the present time it would seem probable that, in the non-resident anglers' tax at least, not more than 60 per cent. of the sums due to the Government are being collected; so that it would not be unreasonable to anticipate that a considerable proportion of the increased expenditure can be met out of the increased revenue.

Your Commissioner has further pointed out in this report that by the adoption of a resident hunting license of $1.10, an additional revenue of between $60,000 and $100,000 can be obtained. This, in conjunction with the utilization of the present annual surplus, and the anticipated gain in revenue from the more rigid collection of existing license fees, would give a sum amply sufficient to meet out of income, not only increased charges of maintenance, but also the initial cost of added equipment.

Your Commissioner, in this interim report, has not elaborated in detail to cover the Province his scheme for wardens, equipment or hatcheries, but, inasmuch as he realizes that the present time may be deemed inopportune by your Government to impose a hunting license, he desires to point out that, failing the adoption of that source of revenue, his scheme, as herein presented, would still make no extravagant demands on the public purse.

The increased pay to efficient wardens would be largely met out of the salaries of the many underpaid men whose commissions would be allowed to lapse, for a man whose whole time is paid for can reasonably be expected to cover more ground than a number of men given a salary insufficient to warrant them devoting their whole time to the work.

The maintenance, also, of the boat equipment suggested would largely be counterbalanced by relinquishing the leases on other craft. In this regard it may be noted that for the region of the Georgian Bay and portions of Lake Superior and Lake Huron, for which six Class B boats, each with a crew of three men, have been recommended, the Department of Game and Fisheries estimates the present expenditure at roughly $13,000, as against the $14,000 estimated under the scheme which, considering the greatly improved service and the considerable area covered, does not appear to be a very serious increase.

That the equipment recommended, and the employment of competent men only, would give a better service, and consequently ensure a higher revenue from licenses than that at present secured, has already been pointed out, so that, in voting a special grant to cover the initial purchase of the boats of Classes B and C, the Government would be making an investment whose returns should be sufficient to cover the outlay within the period of a few years. In the establishment of hatcheries, even if funds were available, your Commissioner would not recommend for the first year the erection of more than two or three, and for this purpose a sum of $10,000 would be amply sufficient. The maintenance charges for each hatchery should not exceed $2,000. The establishment of a series of bass control ponds in a suitable district would cost but a small sum, say $1,000 to $1,500 at the outside, whilst the maintenance charge would be approximately the same.

The revenue for 1910 may fairly be assumed at $110,000, although your Commissioner understands this is $10,000 in excess of the estimate prepared by the Department of Game and Fisheries. Its officials admit, however, that their figures are most conservative.

While not attempting to furnish an elaborate budget, your Commissioner submits the following figures in support of his contention that the gradual adoption of the recommendations contained in the report are feasible, even within the bounds of an income unassisted by a hunting license.

Special Grant for 6 Class B Boats	$25,800 00
Special Grant for 6 Class C Boats	11,200 00
Special Grant for 3 Hatcheries and 1 series of Bass Control Ponds	10,000 00
Total	$47,000 00

Your Commissioner does not assert that this sum could be met out of the present annual income of the Department, but he points out that placing the life of a boat at 15 years, that of the engine at 10 years, with probably a further life after scraping and refitting, and the life of the hatcheries at 30 years, assuming the price of money at 5 per cent. and looking at the equipment as capital expenditure the following would give the amount fairly chargeable to income, including a sinking fund to amply cover the capital expenditure:

Sinking Fund, annual charge	$ 3,500 00
Interest charges, 5% over the whole period on $50,000 00	2,500 00
Maintenance of Hatcheries and Bass Control Ponds	7,000 00
Annual Charges. Total	$13,000 00

Taking the 1908 expenditure at $70,000, and the estimated revenue for 1910 at $110,000, there remains a surplus of $40,000. Deducting amount chargeable annually to the added equipment, from this surplus, there remains a balance of $27,000 available to meet other recommended increased expenditures.

ACKNOWLEDGMENTS.

In pursuit of his investigations your Commissioner has been accorded, on all hands, most courteous and invaluable assistance.

To the Commissioners and Game Wardens of the states of the Union he is indebted for the gift of their latest reports, game laws, and other official documents.

To the first President of the Ontario Forest, Fish and Game Protective Association, Honourable Chief Justice Sir Glenholme Falconbridge; to Mr. Oliver Adams, Vice-President of the same organization, and to many members of the same, to Hon. L. T. Carleton, Hon. W. E. Meehan, Dr. Wm. T. Hornaday, Dr. T. S. Palmer, Commissioner Whipple, Professor E. E. Prince, Dr. B. E. Fernow, Mr. John Pease Babcock, and many other distinguished gentlemen for kind advice and assistance; to the officials of the Department of Game and Fisheries for cordial cooperation;

To the Grand Trunk Railway Company, the Canadian Pacific Railway Company, the Canadian Northern Railway Company, and the Toronto, Hamilton and Buffalo Railway Company for their generous assistance in furnishing him with free transportation over their lines.

He also wishes to bear testimony to the capable services rendered by Captain R. Manley Sims, D.S.O., whom he was fortunate enough to secure as secretary for the work of the Commission.

CONCLUSION.

In presenting this interim report on those matters which he deemed it expedient to bring promptly to Your Honour's attention your Commissioner would crave leave to make the following remarks:

In the pursuance of his enquiries he has had constantly before him that you were expecting and relying on him to report to you truthfully, honestly and to the best of his ability, and according to the knowledge he acquired in the course of his investigations, upon those matters mentioned in the terms of his commission, and consequently he has spared neither time nor energy in endeavouring to gather all such information as he thought would be of assistance to you in coming to a just and true conclusion upon the matters herein reported upon.

He realizes that his recommendations, if adopted, will entail somewhat drastic changes and innovations; he understands that the Government of the Province is conducted upon well established party lines, and that in dealing with most matters of regulation and administration political exigencies must, in the nature of things, be expected to influence the action of the Executive, but his enquiry has so convinced him of the vast economic potentialities inherent in the fish and game resources of the Province that he has felt impelled not to shirk the task, but without fear, favour or affection to point out to Your Honour that, in his opinion, the public welfare can only best be served by the elimination of party interests in these matters, by placing of their conduct in the hands of a non-political commission, and by devoting greater sums to conservation and exploitation of these resources than the present policy contemplates or allows.

KELLY EVANS,
Commissioner.

Toronto, Feb. 5 1910.